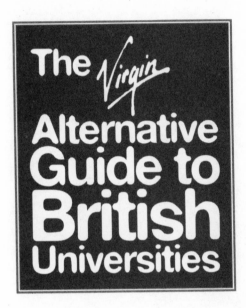

The Virgin
Alternative
Guide to
British
Universities

D1513595

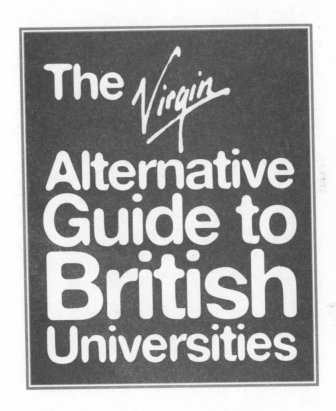

The Virgin Alternative Guide to British Universities

Piers Dudgeon

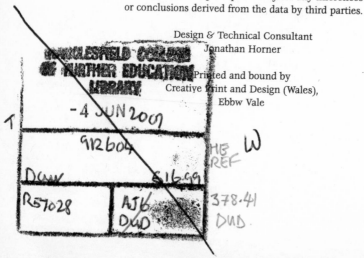

THE VIRGIN ALTERNATIVE GUIDE

'The best bar none... Most university guides tell you what grades are needed for entry, but fail to give any impression of what it's really like... *The Virgin Alternative Guide* bridges this gap. Amusing contributions from students already on their way to degrees detail the nitty gritty of student life at each institution, including accommodation, health, living on a shoestring, low- and high- workload courses, union life, societies, sports and – last but not least – watering holes and where to get a decent curry... The guide is based on thorough research [and] includes an official facts section, covering acceptance requirements to employment expectations.'
Times Educational Supplement

'Glistening with success – a worthy contender for the best all-purpose buy for the aspiring undergraduate.'
Yorkshire Post

'This is a very impressive piece of work... a serious and honest picture of student life at each major higher education establishment in the UK... VAG looks set to take over as the nation's favourite antidote to the occasional excesses of the higher education marketing professionals.'
Careers Adviser

'The guide offers racy but reliable profiles that focus as much on the way of life as academic considerations.'
Daily Telegraph

'The value of this book lies in the info-crammed pages on universities, starting with Aberdeen and ending with York.'
The London Evening Standard

'Lesson learned... Get studying this guide!'
Sun

'Welcome to VAG, an invaluable assessment... raw, earthy and direct.'
Wolverhampton Express & Star

'It's the warts and all approach to help students make their choices.'
Leicester Mercury

'Serious and honest'
Times Higher Educational Supplement

'Where you can believe what you read'
Cardiff Western Mail

'Just the thing to make a truly informed choice'
Dundee Sunday Post

CONTENTS

University Location Map   8
Introduction   11
Alternative University Rankings   17
Entry Requirements & Subject Ratings   20

A

Aberdeen University   37
Abertay Dundee University   41
Aberystwyth University   43
Anglia Ruskin University   47
Aston University   50

B

Bangor University   54
Bath University   58
Bath Spa University   63
Bedfordshire University   66
Birkbeck College   70
STUDENT BIRMINHAM - THE CITY   70
Birmingham University   71
Bolton University   76
Bournemouth University   79
Bradford University   83
STUDENT BRIGHTON - THE CITY   87
Brighton University   89
STUDENT BRISTOL - THE CITY   93
Bristol University   94
Bristol West of England University   98
Brunel University   103
Buckingham University   107
Buckinghamshire Chilterns Uni College   110

C

Cambridge University   112
Canterbury Christ Church University   123
STUDENT CARDIFF - THE CITY   126
Cardiff University   128
Uni Wales Institute, Cardiff (UWIC)   132
Central England University   135
Central Lancashire University   139
Chester University   143
Chichester University   146
City University   149
Coventry University   153
Cumbria University   156

D

De Montfort University   158
Derby University   162

Dundee University   165
Durham University   170

E

East Anglia University   175
East London University   179
Edge Hill University   183
STUDENT EDINBURGH - THE CITY   185
Edinburgh University   187
Edinburgh College of Art   191
Essex University   192
Exeter University   196

F

Falmouth University College   201

G

Glamorgan University   202
STUDENT GLASGOW - THE CITY   205
Glasgow University   206
Glasgow Caledonian University   211
Glasgow School of Art   214
Gloucestershire University   214
Goldsmiths College   217
Greenwich University   221

H

Harper Adams University College   224
Heriot-Watt University   225
Hertfordshire University   229
Heythrop College   233
Highlands and Islands (UHI)
   Millennium Institute   233
Huddersfield University   234
Hull University   238

I

Imperial College, London   242

K

Keele University   247
Kent at Canterbury University   250
King's College London   255
Kingston University   258

L

Lampeter University   262
Lancaster University   265
STUDENT LEEDS - THE CITY   270
Leeds University   271

Leeds Metropolitan University 276
STUDENT LEICESTER – THE CITY 280
Leicester University 281
Lincoln University 284
STUDENT LIVERPOOL – THE CITY 288
Liverpool University 290
Liverpool Hope University 293
Liverpool John Moores University 297
STUDENT LONDON – THE CITY 302
London Metropolitan University 303
London School of Economics
& Political Science (LSE) 307
London South Bank 311
Loughborough University 315

M
STUDENT MANCHESTER – THE CITY 320
Manchester University 322
Manchester Metropolitan University 327
Middlesex University 331

N
Napier University 334
STUDENT NEWCASTLE – THE CITY 337
Newcastle University 339
Newport University 344
Northampton University 347
Northumbria University 349
STUDENT NOTTINGHAM – THE CITY 353
Nottingham University 354
Nottingham Trent University 359

O
Oxford University 364
Oxford Brookes University 374

P
Paisley University 378
Plymouth University 381
Portsmouth University 386

Q
Queen Margaret University College 390
Queen Mary, University of London 391
Queen's University, Belfast 394
STUDENT BELFAST – THE CITY 399

R
Reading University 400
Robert Gordon University 404

Roehampton University 407
Royal Academy of Music 409
Royal Agricultural College 410
Royal College of Music 410
Royal Holloway, London University 410
Royal Scottish Academy 414
Royal Welsh College of Music & Drama 414
Royal Veterinary College 415

S
St Andrews University 415
St George's, University of London 419
St Mary's University College 420
Salford University 420
School of Oriental &
African Studies (SOAS) 424
School of Pharmacy 425
Scottish Agricultural College 425
STUDENT SHEFFIELD – THE CITY 426
Sheffield University 427
Sheffield Hallam University 432
Southampton University 436
Southampton Solent University 441
Staffordshire University 444
Stirling University 447
Strathclyde University 451
Sunderland University 455
Surrey University 459
Sussex University 463
Swansea University 467

T
Teesside University 471
Thames Valley University 475

U
Ulster University 478
University College London 481
University of the Arts, London 486

W
Warwick University 488
Westminster University 492
Winchester University 496
Wolverhampton University 499
Worcester University 503

Y
York University 506
York St John University 510

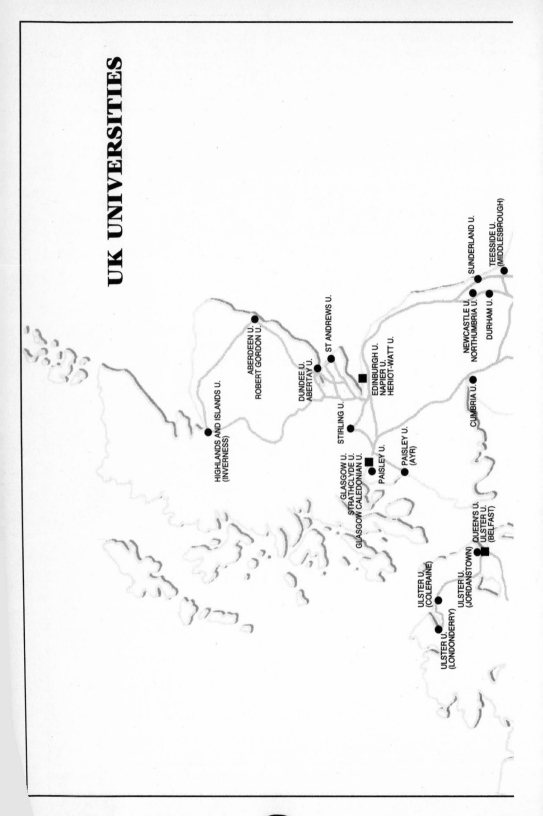

UK UNIVERSITIES

HIGHLANDS AND ISLANDS U.
(INVERNESS)

ABERDEEN U.
ROBERT GORDON U.

DUNDEE U.
ABERTAY U.

ST ANDREWS U.

STIRLING U.

EDINBURGH U.
NAPIER U.
HERIOT-WATT U.

GLASGOW U.
STRATHCLYDE U.
GLASGOW CALEDONIAN U.

PAISLEY U.

PAISLEY U.
(AYR)

CUMBRIA U.

NEWCASTLE U.
NORTHUMBRIA U.

SUNDERLAND U.

DURHAM U.

TEESSIDE U.
(MIDDLESBROUGH)

ULSTER U.
(COLERAINE)

ULSTER U.
(LONDONDERRY)

ULSTER U.
(JORDANSTOWN)

QUEEN'S U.
ULSTER U.
(BELFAST)

INTRODUCTION

WHAT IS IT ALL ABOUT?

It is fascinating to sit in on the deliberations of careers teachers during this uncertain time, when Government, 'of economic necessity', is hell bent on getting 50% of all 18-year-olds into University by 2010, and university lecturers are shaking their heads at the low standards of some of those they are now having to teach.

Lecturers' complaints, gathered together recently in *The Times Higher Educational Supplement,* range from immaturity to an inability to think clearly and develop arguments, and even to spell and punctuate correctly.

There are signs that the university machine, grinding its way through less than high calibre material, is beginning to suffer. Last week, a Professor walked out of Bournemouth University because he wasn't allowed to fail 13 students who were not up to the course he ran. They had been failed by him and by a second marker, and their markings had been endorsed by the examination board. But they were overruled, and the Professor resigned.

The implication of the report was that the Government's open access policy is introducing students to university who are simply not equipped to take advantage of it. Further, that there is a danger of dumbing down - passing students who have been failed - in order to control the drop-out and non-completion rates that result.

But that isn't all. There is a peculiar double movement. While at one end, university admissions are leaning over backwards to meet their Government benchmarks to get the 'new undergraduates' in, at the other end they are actually becoming more selective, inventing new ways of creaming off the intellectual elite.

With more and more universities asking the maximum three As at A level or 360 points for their courses, there is nowhere else to go in the matter of finding the best sixth-form minds.

While Bournemouth staff are scrapping over where the failure line should be drawn for the 'new undergraduate', there is a parallel scrap going on to invent ways to discriminate more finely between 'traditional applicants' for the most popular and demanding courses - not only Medicine and Dentistry, but also History, Law, Mathematics, Computer Science, Modern and Mediaeval Languages, Natural Sciences, Engineering and Economics.

With everything being turned on its head, I found myself talking to one of our most experienced public school sixth-form careers teachers to find out what was going on at his end of things.

Chris Conway is a seasoned careers teacher at Shrewsbury, a major 'boys-only' public school. He takes his job seriously enough to have been 'an observer' on an undergraduate selection panel for UCL medical school in order better to advise those of his pupils who want to study Medicine.

When the boys enquire what they will be asked at interview, he can tell them. More than 10% of his 150-strong sixth form regularly gets into Oxford or Cambridge, and he sees it as his business to work out how to win where the competition is most fierce - at Oxbridge, at our medical schools, and in our most sought after Top Ten universities.

I discovered that while politicians are bringing class, applicants' postcodes and the educational history of their parents to bear on selection, Mr Conway, and others in his position, are playing an altogether different game.

> *'Impressive GCSEs, with a good number of A* grades, high performance in AS modules and the prediction, or actuality, of all A grades at A-level now get you only to the starting gate.'*

COMPETING FOR THE BEST

'A large part of my job is to teach the sixth-form how to play the game, to know the rules of the game. It is important to understand the criteria for selection and attempt to view the whole process from the perspective of the university admissions team.

'In our boys' and their parents' minds, Oxford and Cambridge still form the pinnacle of academic elitism. If the Oxbridge style of learning and the courses offered, the attractions of small group teaching (which can be as low as 1:1), being surrounded by able and ambitious fellow students, having excellent resources and financial support, and enjoying the status of an Oxbridge degree at the end, do appeal, then it is worth trying to understand what these universities are looking for in their prospective undergraduates.

'They have an application system, which while part of the UCAS system also demands a separate (and early) application peculiar to them. There is an interview and there may be a special paper to take. But this is true not only of Oxford and

Cambridge. In the UK there are thirty-one medical schools that interview a significant proportion of prospective candidates, and a handful of them are now using the special BMAT test to identify the high levels of scientific thinking they require of their students.

'However, now the majority of institutions are backing another discriminating test, UKCAT, which aims to test more general thinking skills. Interviews at non-Oxbridge universities are also conducted with candidates for other courses (such as music and art), and some universities now require prospective law candidates to take what is called the LNAT test.

'I went to a presentation about the LNAT. The stated reasons for doing it were 1. that it would test thinking skills that would be appropriate for a law degree (which A levels were not), and 2. that the test would identify people who had talent, who think naturally like lawyers need to think. In other words, it was a way of getting suitable people onto the course who were not able to get on it by the traditional A level route. One of the universities that had wanted to incorporate LNAT into their selection procedure last year decided to drop it because they didn't feel it gave them any more information about candidates than they were getting previously, but some law departments still do insist on candidates taking it.

'First and foremost it is important to understand that Oxford and Cambridge, and a number of our top universities, are unashamedly academic, elite institutions, and clearly the Government view that the A level system is the Gold Standard does not add up if the top end is not differentiating in the way the selective universities want it to and they are having to resort to tests of their own.

'Two years ago I did research into three subjects - English, History and Law - where competition for places is extreme at our best universities. I rang up Bristol, Durham and Birmingham and talked to them and also went up to Durham to see the three departments. I was presented with clear evidence that selection problems are not confined to Oxbridge and are not the result of discrimination against independent schools (which in our case many parents and boys believe it to be).

'If you consider universities such as Bristol and Durham, applicant-to-places ratios of about 10-15:1 are not uncommon, and grade inflation has meant that the academic standards have risen accordingly, so that it is now realistic to think in terms of 90% or even 95% of applicants being predicted all A grades at A-level for these subjects. We now know that competition is not just at Oxford and Cambridge and that the application procedure to our best universities is a game with clear rules of its own, which runs beyond A level examinations.

'Impressive GCSEs, with a good number of A* grades, high performance in AS modules and the prediction, or actuality, of all A grades at A-level now get you only to the starting gate. In simple terms, at the highest level, far too many students achieve these for that filter to be sufficiently discriminating. Thus the universities have felt the need to look beyond A level grades. Cambridge now requires the UMS scores of AS modules, for example, and in reality are looking for levels around 90%, rather than simply 80%, which earns an A grade at AS. The top universities are also looking for other information which can help them in the selection process.

'Besides the growth in national aptitude tests - BMAT, LNAT, UKCAT - any information that a candidate can provide which can offer objective evidence of their ability above that provided by the standard exams will be useful, and in this regard, success in national or international competitions such as the maths, physics or chemistry Olympiads can be extremely valuable.

'The key point is that it is not good enough to be able compared to your fellows at school; you have to demonstrate your ability at a national level.

'To get on the best courses at the best universities, you must be a good candidate. First, prove yourself to be academically able at a national level, and second, show clear evidence of a real interest in your chosen subject.

'If the final point of the selection process is an interview, it has to be earned. Cambridge do not interview every candidate, and Oxford only aim to interview about 85%. As for the aspiring medic, the first hurdle is to impress enough with your UCAS form in order to be called for interview. If you are applying to study other subjects at our top universities where competition is extreme and which do not run competitive interviews, the UCAS form is the only evidence other than exam results and predictions on which they make their selection. The written application must therefore be impressive. As with Oxbridge, think in terms of having to demonstrate both ability and interest in order to become a good candidate.

'On the UCAS form, ability is addressed by your exam results so far, and the school reference with its embedded A-level predicted grades. But showing real interest in your chosen subject is vital, and must be part of your Personal Statement. Very often when people who are clever are rejected by Oxbridge, you can trace it back to the fact that they are not really interested. If you are truly passionate about a subject, you do not choose it, it chooses you. You will be reading books beyond set texts, attending lectures, undertaking work experience (if that is relevant), because you want to.

'Remember that the focus of the UCAS form does need to point towards the academic nature of the course applied for. The top universities are staffed by men and women who are at the forefront of their subject, and who are primarily driven by the love of it. Masses of work experience which provides interest in the vocational aspect of a course may not be so helpful in promoting your academic cause.

'Work experience has long been ingrained in the process of medical applications. Traditionally this has been linked to acquiring some medical knowledge and gaining practical experience of the work that doctors do. Nowadays, however, medical schools are unlikely to be "wowed" by a list of work experience placements, however exotic the medical procedure. What they want to know is, "What have you learned from your work experience?"

'The impressions you have gained from talking to doctors, nurses and patients in any walk of medicine - however humble - can be valid. They want to know that your experiences have made an impression on you, so make sure your Personal Statement goes beyond the superficial - *make it personal*.

'This aspect of the UCAS form is your opportunity to register your enthusiasm for your chosen subject (and in this vocational case, also the career). In the competitive arena of medicine, it is massively significant.

'The "caring" factor is an aspect of the application to read Medicine which was unnecessary a few years ago, but is now seen to be crucial. Evidence of long-term commitment to people and caring for them is a great help, not only because it does tick the right box, and give you a very valuable insight into the less glamorous side of medicine, but also because it can provide the sort of case studies which enable you to show that you have delved below the surface of the subject.

'I know they will take a range of people into medical school, but I do think they want people who genuinely do care. It's not just caring, it's more, were you really, genuinely excited by it? It's a real feeling…it comes down to *passion*.

'My experience of my own pupils talking about their work experience is sometimes that they could be talking about a tractor engine, when what you want to hear is that they were fantastically impressed by this doctor and they wanted to be like

> '*Very often when people who are clever are rejected by Oxbridge, you can trace it back to the fact that they are not really interested. If you are truly passionate about a subject, you do not choose it, it chooses you.*'

them, or they really understood why this patient was in such distress, or the family of the patient was so worried.

'Again, a knowledge and understanding of the world of medicine that you are about to enter is essential. Medical Schools in the UK are now explicitly designed to fulfil the needs of the National Health Service. You will have to understand the NHS and where the problems lie with it.

'So to the interview itself. Be it at medical school, Oxbridge or elsewhere, it has been said, and research has shown, that interviews do not select the best candidates for a post, but are very good at selecting people with whom the selectors could work successfully.

'This is the key point to understand. To get the most out of Oxford or Cambridge you must be happy with the teaching style they offer, but also understand that the personal nature of it means that you will be working with the dons. There is personal interaction and you need to convey to the interviewers the feeling that you are someone who is not only enthusiastic and passionate about their subject, but who is eminently teachable within the Oxbridge framework. Because our top universities are staffed by men and women who are primarily driven by the love of their subject, to some extent teaching hinders their aims. The notion of wasting time trying to teach students with whom they cannot connect is clearly abhorrent to an Oxbridge don.

'Most medical schools offer a great deal of advice about their interview process, and candidates would be foolish not to read the relevant website, particularly when Manchester, for example, publishes some of the questions they will ask!

'Interviewers will be looking to probe the candidate's suitability in the broad areas of academic ability, medical knowledge and interest and caring attitude mentioned above, as well as assessing evidence of communication skills. That you have such knowledge and caring interest, and can express that well in interview, will of course facilitate their assessment of your communication skills. It is all about an ability to interact with people. Do not settle for monosyllabic answers!

'Questions are likely to be general at the start, so expect something of the "Why do you want to study medicine?" or "Why do you want to study medicine here?" variety. These are difficult to answer without sounding trite, but be ready for them. They are likely to follow up what has been gained from the work experience undertaken, and it is crucial that any medical process observed and described in the personal statement is followed up with some research - otherwise it does make a claim to be interested in medicine somewhat lame. My experience is that the key point is to be able to convey true enthusiasm and a burning desire to become a doctor.

'Two final points. Most candidates seal their fate within a very short period. Make sure that the first impressions you give are positive, they are so important. Second, what should you wear? It is important to be comfortable. However, comfort is not just physical, it also reflects a state of mind. If you are dressed in very casual clothes, but all the other candidates and interviewers are in suits, you may feel physically at ease, but extremely worried. Once again, think of it from the interviewer's viewpoint. If you are going for a medical interview, remember you are hoping to gain admission not just onto a course, but into a profession - so, although you don't need to have a stethoscope around your neck and carry a skeleton, dress professionally. On the other hand, if you go for an interview for an Art course in a suit, it will look more than a little out of place.

'Ultimately, in any competitive situation, the only way to succeed is to be better than the competition. In this context it is important to realise that this does not just mean in terms of ability, but also that you have to "want it more".

'Overall, if applying to oversubscribed popular courses, then do your homework: try to work out what is being looked for; prepare your application thoroughly; take every opportunity to show interest and enthusiasm - and, finally, hope for a slice of good luck!'

THE NEW ADMISSIONS TESTS

It is worth knowing about all these tests, as it is fair to assume that they are going to become increasingly important to getting into university. At time of writing, they are as follows:

UKCAT - UK Clinical Aptitude Test - is required by medical and dental schools at Aberdeen, Brighton and Sussex universities, Cardiff, Dundee, Durham, East Anglia (UEA), Edinburgh, Glasgow, Hull York, Keele, King's College London, Leeds, Leicester, Manchester, Newcastle, Nottingham, Oxford, Peninsula (Plymouth & Exeter), Queen Mary, Sheffield, Southampton, St Andrews, St George's University of London. See www.ukcat.ac.uk

BMAT - the BioMedical Admissions Test - is required by the following medical and veterinary schools: Bristol Veterinary School, Cambridge, Oxford, Royal Veterinary College, UCL, and Imperial. See www.bmat.org.uk

GAMSAT - the Graduate Medical School Admission Test - is required by St George's London, Nottingham, Peninsula Medical School (Plymouth & Exeter), and Swansea. See www.gamsatuk.org

MSAT - Medical School Admissions Test - is required by King's College London, Queen Mary, and Warwick. See msat@acer.edu.au

LNAT - The National Admissions Test for Law - is required by Birmingham, Bristol, Cambridge, Durham, Exeter, Glasgow, King's College London, Manchester Met, Nottingham, Oxford, and UCL. All candidates will sit the test at a computer terminal monitored at a test centre. See www.lnat.ac.uk/ and www.kaptest.co.uk for an online practice test.

HAT - History Aptitude Test - is required by Oxford. See www.history.ox.ac.uk/prosunder-grad/applying/hat_introduction.htm

MML - Modern and Mediaeval Languages Test - is required by Cambridge. See www.mml.cam.ac.uk/prospectus/undergrad/applying/test.html. Also, www.cam.ac.uk/admissions/undergraduate/courses/mml/tests.html

STEP - Sixth Term Examination Papers - are required to read Mathematics at Cambridge. See www.maths.cam

TSA - Thinking Skills Assessment - is required mainly to read Computer Science, Natural Sciences, Engineering and Economics at some 20 Cambridge colleges. See tsa.ucles.org.uk/index.html

LOOKING FOR REAL VALUE

The danger, of course, is that the horrendously competitive spirit, which the dumbing down of our education system is encouraging, may distort the picture of what going to university is truly about. Indeed, one good thing about Government policy is that it is forcing us to look closely at what we really want out of a university education.

Employers tell us that they want well-trained minds, but that they are going to need more than a piece of paper certifying that candidates have a 2:1 or first-class degree. They are on record that there are two things even more important to the graduate recruiter than that piece of paper - enthusiasm and an ability to communicate, and that pretty soon after these comes an ability to solve problems, to communicate on paper and to work well in a team.

A doctor with a sense of humour can transform a geriatric ward in seconds. I recently watched it happen. It is easy to see how important communication skills are to many professions. And if we are also good at solving problems and our enthusiasm comes from a commitment to what we are doing, clearly we will be more useful, more employable.

So, value in a university education to a graduate

employer is 'training plus'. And since, according to a recent report by the Association of Graduate Recruiters, half of major employers are unable to fill their graduate vacancies because the graduates that come to them lack this 'training plus', this X-factor of Higher Education, it is as well to consider which universities have it on offer.

You will notice that in the Guide we talk a lot about the extra-curricular scene at University, because that is where this 'training plus' can occur, but you need to get into a frame of mind that will encourage it from the very start, from the moment you decide what subject to study.

Time and again the undergraduates we speak to regret their choice of subject.

Misham Bhana, Edinburgh, reading Medicine: 'Don't do Medicine unless you're sure you definitely want to be a doctor. Sounds obvious, but there's a lot of clinical work in the course and if you don't enjoy talking to patients you'll probably hate it.'

Garry Beardsworth, Leeds Met: 'Make sure you are completely certain about your university choice. I made the mistake of rushing into a degree in Architecture, and I didn't enjoy it at all. It's one of the most difficult and embarrassing things to admit to your parents, when they have ploughed vast amounts of money into it.'

Aneesa Patel, Aberdeen: 'Make sure your course is the one you want to do. You would be amazed how many unhappy students are doing courses because their friends were, or their parents wanted them to.'

So, opt for something that *you* really want to do. This is absolutely fundamental. You are about to study this subject for three or four years at a far higher level than you studied at A level. Think about this very carefully.

Then look for a course that brings the subject alive for you. There will be other considerations. Is the points requirement realistic? Is the course accredited by the right professional body? Does it have any other vocational advantages? But most important, when you read about the course on the university web site, how does it make you feel? Does it make you want to get involved?

We are used to talking about the difference between vocational degrees (like medicine or engineering) and academic ones (like philosophy or classics), but this actually conceals a more significant difference between receiving a training (be it a vocational or an academic training) and receiving an *education*.

The difference between being trained and

being educated at the highest level lies at the heart of what 'value plus', this X-factor, is all about. In this sense, to be an *educated* architect or nurse or civil servant is to bring more to the occupation than mere training.

Some universities seem to be more aware of this than others. There may be several courses that catch your eye, so look very carefully at the university behind each one of them.

Alastair Atkinson, Trinity Hall Cambridge: 'When choosing a university, think carefully about the course, but equally carefully about whether you'd like to live in a given place for 3-4 years.'

James Scholes, St Andrews: 'Visit your choices. Really look at the university, town, accommodation, things to do. The next time you're there, it'll be for 3 years.'

Deanne Armitage, Durham: 'Speak to people already at your chosen university doing your course. Visit your choices. Turns out Durham is the most boring town on earth. Also, weather...itís freezing up here.'

But it isn't just the practical issues of climate, social life, and so on. Although these, and cost of living and accommodation, are significant, look at what extra, beyond the lecture hall, your short-listed universities promise you. Consider them in the light of this 'value plus'.

Murray James, Newcastle: 'My social life revolves around two student societies I joined: Rugby League and Theatre Society. You get to know people in the team or cast, you get to know them very well. But then socialising becomes independent from the societies - you find your friends and you stick with them. My best friends at Uni are members of my societies.'

The value of belonging to these societies is not simply in the friends he has made, however:

'In Rugby League I am club secretary and play for the university 1st XIII. In Theatre I have written and directed a pantomime, numerous sketch shows and performed in plays. These are my hobbies, so I take great enjoyment in supplementing my studies with FUN. And beer.'

In his review of Newcastle, Murray rails at the Student Union for the charges they levy on his shows - they charge him £200 a night to put them on. But what is hidden from view is that he is learning how to originate, produce and make money out of a project all of his own, how to communicate and negotiate with the Union, how to enthuse others and how to solve problems that crop up along the way.

That is what a university education should be about, as much as the subject he is studying and in which he is being trained. Perhaps more so, for one day Murray's 'hobby' may become his life.

STATS AND MORE STATS

You will notice a lot in the Guide about where particular courses actually lead in terms of employment. Our info on graduate employability is no longer limited to how many graduates each university manages to get into employment six months after graduation.

Today, we tap in to the Government's Higher Statistics Agency database in Cheltenham, which records where almost everybody ends up and from which uni/subject/department they come. We now know, for example, that City University or Heriot-Watt are more focused on getting graduates jobs in the financial sector than Oxford, and which departments they come from. So, if you want a job in the financial sector, it should interest you to look at all these and, indeed, at London Metropolitan, York, Essex, Bournemouth, East Anglia and Imperial College. This year we have an interesting new line of information sourced in the statistics agency, HESA, and developed in the pages of the Times Higher Education Supplement. It pinpoints which unis get their student real 'graduate track' jobs, real jobs that students might expect to get only by going to university.

Again, the Joint Funding Council's Research Assessment gives an idea of a university's academic strength in depth. They rate subjects on an ascending points system of quality: 1, 2, 3a, 3b, 4, 5 and 5*. We have included those given 5, 5* and 6*, ignoring the lower levels. Grade 5 indicates International Excellence in some sub-areas and National Excellence in virtually all others; 5* indicates International Excellence in a majority of sub-areas and attainable levels of National Excellence in all others. Later, a number of university departments were awarded top-flight 6* status, the best you can get. As you read through the book, you will begin to notice the Academic Excellence box for each entry, which carries this important information. Heed it.

Throughout, we refer to teaching assessments and teaching inspections, and each uni carries an Academic Excellence box, which makes use of them. The ratings and scores are the result of inspections by the QAA (www.qaa.ac.uk) and Higher Education Funding Councils for Scotland and Wales. Only Government-funded institutions are subject to inspection (Buckingham University is not). England and Wales began their programme of inspections with three ratings, Excellent, Satisfactory, Unsatisfactory, while Scotland marked their assessments Excellent, Highly Satisfactory, Satisfactory, Unsatisfactory. Later England and Scotland scored universities with points (maximum 4) on each of six criteria:

4 points each: maximum score = 24 points

1. Curriculum Design, Content, Organisation
2. Teaching Learning and Assessment
3. Student Progression and Achievement
4. Student Support and Guidance
5. Learning Resources
6. Quality Assurance and Enhancement

So, when you come across these assessments, bear in mind that the top mark is 24 (or Excellent) and we don't regard a course worth recommending if it is not rated better than 17 (or Satisfactory).

Just to confuse us further, the QAA has in recent years adopted yet another way of assessing course teaching. Assessments are in two parts: Academic Standards and Quality of Learning Opportunities. Academic Standards (curriculum, student achievement, etc) are marked with a C for Confidence, or NC for No Confidence. Often there is then more detail. Quality of Learning Opportunities is defined under three headings: Teaching & Learning, Student Progression, and Learning Resources. Each section is marked C (Commendable) or A (Approved) or F (Failing). So, in the Subject Entry Table, which follows, if you read C, it means that there is Confidence in the provision; if C/CAC, that there is a mixed assessment of the teaching – two aspects are Commendable, but one (in this case, the second, Student Progression) is merely approved. The best a course can do is C/CCC; the worst is NC/FFF. The latter never shows. Today, the assessments are softer in the marking than they were, but if there is a recent assessment of a course you are considering, read the assessment in depth on www.qaa.ac.uk.

Piers Dudgeon, April 2007

ALTERNATIVE UNIVERSITY RANKINGS

As this Guide makes plain, there's more to University than academia, even though league tables traditionally concentrate on that aspect alone. Our categories concern teaching, but focus too on student culture, on extra-curricular involvements, societies, club activities, media and arts awards, and on employment prospects. One or two facts for some of the newest universities were unavailable. Those institutions have been omitted

There are five categories, each worth 20% of the total figure, which determines ranking.

SCENE refers to campus/city/town entertainment and social scene, and is a percentage computation of the star system included in the *What It's Really Like* box with each university entry.

UNION includes the number of societies on offer,

national team sporting success and national awards for drama and media. Small universities, those with less than 8,000 full-time undergraduates, are weighted (+25 points).

TEACH computes the Excellence percentages included in the *At A Glance* box with each university entry, the number of students that graduate with a first or upper second, and most important, the student-to-staff ratio at each institution.

JOBS computes graduate track employment prospects, referred to in the introduction and in the *Where Graduates End Up* boxes with each entry.

APPEAL Drop-out rates, the percentage by which applications rise or fall, and each university's acceptance rate indicates appeal.

UNIVERSITY	SCENE	UNION	TEACH	JOBS	APPEAL	TOTAL
1. Bristol	20	13.4	16.6	16	16.8	82.8
2. LSE	20	12.6	16.4	16.4	16.8	82.2
3. Nottingham	20	16.8	16	14.2	14.6	81.6
4. Edinburgh	20	14.6	16.8	14.2	15	80.6
5= Leeds	20	15.8	15	14	15	79.8
5= Imperial	18	14.4	17.2	16.8	13.4	79.8
7. Warwick	16	17.6	16.2	14	15.8	79.6
8. University College	20	11.2	17	15.6	15.2	79
9. Manchester	20	13.8	16.2	13.4	14.2	77.6
10. Birmingham	20	14.2	14.8	13.6	14.2	76.8
11. Bath	14	14.6	15.6	16.0	15.9	76.1
12. Cardiff	20	14.6	12.8	14.8	13.8	76
13.Cambridge	14	14.2	17.8	17.4	12.2	75.6
14. King's London	18	10.6	15.6	16.2	15	75.4
15. Newcastle	20	13.2	14	15	13	75.2
16. Liverpool	20	11	14.4	14.6	14.8	74.8
17. Sheffield	20	13.8	13	13.8	13.6	74.2
18. Oxford	14	14.2	18	15	12.8	74
19= Glasgow	20	12.4	15.8	13.2	12.2	73.6
19= Leicester	20	11.4	14.2	13.2	14.8	73.6
21. Exeter	16	14	14.2	12	16.6	72.8
22. Royal Holloway	16	12.4	15.8	13.4	15	72.6
23. York	14	14.6	16	13.2	14.2	72
24. Southampton	14	13.6	15.4	14	14.6	71.6
25. Durham	14	14	14.6	14.4	14.4	71.4
26. Brunel	18	12.6	13	12.8	13.6	70
27. Strathclyde	20	8.4	15.2	13.8	12.2	69.6
28. St Andrews	10	14	17	13.2	15.2	69.4
29. Surrey	12	11.2	14	16	15.8	69
30. Sussex	18	11.6	14.2	11.8	13	68.6
31= Aberdeen	16	10.8	15.4	14	12	68.2

UNIVERSITY	SCENE	UNION	TEACH	JOBS	APPEAL	TOTAL
31 = Loughborough	14	11.4	14.2	14.2	14.4	68.2
33 = Aston	18	5.4	14	15.2	14.2	66.8
33 = Queen Mary	18	7.2	13.6	14.4	13.6	66.8
35. Nottingham Trent	18	10.8	11.6	12.6	12.8	65.8
36. East Anglia (UEA)	16	10.8	14.4	11.8	12.6	65.6
37. Queen's Belfast	14	10	14.2	14.4	12.8	65.4
38. Sheffield Hallam	18	10.8	11.6	12.2	12.6	65.2
39 = Leeds Met	20	8.2	9.8	12.6	14	64.6
39 = Northumbria	18	11.2	12.2	12.6	10.6	64.6
39 = Essex	14	11.8	13.4	12.6	12.8	64.6
42 = Lancaster	14	10	14.6	10.8	15	64.4
42 = Dundee	16	8.8	13.2	14.4	12	64.4
44. Kent	14	10.2	13.4	13.4	12.6	63.6
45. Liverpool J M	18	9.6	11.4	12.2	11.6	62.8
46 = Plymouth	16	10.8	12.8	11.2	11.8	62.6
46 = Reading	14	9.2	14.2	11.8	13.4	62.6
48. Brighton	14	9.4	12.8	13	13.2	62.4
49. Bournemouth	16	9.6	12.8	11.4	12.4	62.2
50. Oxford Brookes	14	8.8	13	13.6	12.4	61.8
51. Bradford	14	9.6	12.2	14.6	11	61.4
52. Heriot-Watt	16	9	13.2	11.4	11.4	61
53 = City	14	4.8	13.2	15	13.6	60.6
53 = Hull	16	6.6	13	12.8	12.2	60.6
55. Stirling	10	10.4	15.8	11.2	12.6	60
56. Manchester Met	18	8	10.2	11.4	11.4	59
57. Bristol UWE	16	6.4	12.4	12	11.6	58.4
58. Goldsmiths	16	3.8	12.2	11.8	14	57.8
59 = Ulster	12	9.2	12.2	12.6	11.4	57.4
59 = Keele	10	10.8	12	13	11.6	57.4
59 = Kingston	16	5.2	11.2	13.2	11.8	57.4
59. London S. Bank	16	5.4	12.2	13.2	10.6	57.4
63. Swansea	14	9	10.6	12.2	11.4	57.2
64. Cardiff UWIC	16	9.8	8.8	11.4	11	57
65 = Central England	16	2.8	13.2	12.4	12.2	56.6
65 = Robert Gordon	14	6	11	15.2	10.4	56.6
67. Portsmouth	14	7	11.4	11.4	12	55.8
68. Sunderland	14	8.4	11.2	12.4	9.4	55.4
69 = Gloucestershire	12	10.8	10	11	11	54.8
69 = Chichester	10	6.8	11	13	14	54.8
71 = Salford	16	3.6	12	11.2	11.4	54.2
71 = Canterbury	12	5.2	11.4	12.6	13	54.2
73 = De Montfort	18	4.4	10.4	11.6	9	53.4
73 = Abertay Dundee	14	6	10	14.8	8.6	53.4
73 = Coventry	12	5.8	12.4	12.2	11	53.4
76. Middlesex	14	6.4	10.4	11.2	11.2	53.2
77. Hertfordshire	12	5.6	10.6	13	11.4	52.6
78 = Westminster	16	2.2	12.6	10.2	11.4	52.4
78 = Central Lancashire	14	5.8	10.6	12	10	52.4
80. Bath Spa	12	3.4	12	9.4	15.4	52.2
81. Glasgow Cal	14	2.8	12	11.6	11.4	51.8
82. Northampton	12	6.2	9.6	10.4	13.4	51.6
83. Anglia Ruskin	12	2.8	11.2	12.4	12.6	51

UNIVERSITY	SCENE	UNION	TEACH	JOBS	APPEAL	TOTAL
84. Greenwich	14	2	10	12.6	12.2	50.8
85 = Wolverhampton	12	6.8	11	10.2	10.4	50.4
85 = So'ton Solent	12	7	9.8	9.6	12	50.4
87. Bangor	10	5	10.2	12.8	11.6	49.6
88 = Napier	14	3.2	11	11.6	9.4	49.2
88 = Paisley	16	3	10.8	10.4	9	49.2
90 = Bedfordshire	12	4.2	9.6	8.4	14.8	49
90 = East London	16	2	9.8	11.2	10	49
90 = Teesside	16	2.8	9.4	12.4	8.4	49
93. Glamorgan	12	7	9.2	11.6	9	48.8
94 = Aberystwyth	10	7.8	9.8	10	10.8	48.4
94 = Winchester	10	4.2	12.2	9.6	12.4	48.4
96. Derby	12	3	10	12	10.8	47.8
97. Huddersfield	12	3.8	10.2	10.2	10.8	47
98. Staffordshire	12	3.4	9.8	10.8	10.2	46.2
98. Lincoln	10	7	8.4	9.6	11	46
100. Thames Valley	14	0.2	8.4	12	9.2	43.8
101. Lampeter	10	3.4	8.6	10.4	7.2	39.6

ENTRY REQUIREMENTS
& SUBJECT RATINGS

Browse our Subject table on the following pages, and use the UCAS course finder (www.ucas.com).

Column 1 shows the ball-park official offer level, based on the UCAS points tariff.

Column 3 shows the teaching ratings by outside inspectors under the aegis of the Quality Assurance Agency. See www.qaa.ac.uk for their latest judgement in full on the university departments you are considering, and see our Introduction (page 16) for an explanation of how the QAA's muddling ratings work. Basically, what you want to see is a score close to 24, Excellent, Highly Satisfactory, or C/CCC, which shows complete confidence in the course. Look with an interested eye at those top-value universities which score well at inspection but ask less points. Equally, look with suspicion at the high-demanding unis which performed less well on inspection.

A full account of the new UCAS points tarrif is given on the UCAS website.

A LEVEL POINTS TARIFF
INTERNATIONAL BACCALAUREATE

A Level Grades	UCAS Points
A	120
B	100
C	80
D	60
E	40

AS Level Grades	AS Level Points
A	60
B	50
C	40
D	30
E	20

Last year, for the first time, UCAS pulled the International Baccalaureate into the tariff, and many felt that it gave it a very soft ride.

Basically, you have to study six subjects for the IB, three to a high level, three to a standard level. A pass earns you 4 marks. So, if you pass all six subjects you amass 24 marks, which UCAS have made equivalent to 280 points in the their tariff. As this is almost three B grades at A level, and many IB students expect to do much better than pass, you can begin to see why A-level diehards raised something of a stink.

IB POINTS TARIFF

IB Diploma Marks	UCAS Points
24	280
25	303
26	326
27	350
28	373
29	396
30	419
31	442
32	466
33	489
34	512
35	535
36	559
37	582
38	605
39	628
40	652
41	675
42	698
43	722
44	744
45	768

ACCOUNTANCY/FINANCE

Specific Accounting teaching assessments undertaken: De Montfort, East London, Edinburgh, Leeds MetLondon South Bank, Napier, Paisley, Strathclyde. See www.qaa.ac.uk/reviews/reports/subjIndex.asp

ENTRY	UNIVERSITY	RATING
		Economics/Maths
High		
340 points +		
	Warwick	24/22
	Queen's Belfast	24/22
	Manchester	24/22
	Exeter	22/22
	Southampton	24/20
	Newcastle	23/23
Medium-High		
280-320 points		
	Bath	24/24
	Queen's Belfast	24/22
	Glasgow	Highly Satis
	Cardiff	Excellent
	City	22/23
	UEA	23/23
	Lancaster	-/22
	Bristol	23/23
	Reading	22/21
	Aberystwyth	Excellent
	Aston	-/19
	Birmingham	23/24
	Sheffield	21/21
	Leeds	22/22
	Edinburgh	C/CCC
	Newcastle	23/23
	LSE	23/22
	Nottingham	24/23
	Kent	23/21
	Hull	22/22
	Liverpool	22/23
	Royal Holloway	-/22
	Manchester	24/22
	Loughborough	23/22
	Strathclyde	C/CCC
	Northumbria	22/21
	Brunel	22/22
	Swansea	
	Ulster	22/22
	Westminster	-/20
	Essex	24/20
	Durham (Stockton)	
	Queen's Belfast	24/22
Medium		
220-260 points		
	Bradford	21/
	Abertay Dundee	Satisfactory
	Bangor	
	Portsmouth	21/22
	Gloucestershire	
	Keele	23/22
	Aberdeen	Highly Satis

ENTRY	UNIVERSITY	RATING
Medium	Kingston	21/23
220-260 points	Robert Gordon	Highly Satis
	Bournemouth	22/-
	Queen Mary	-/21
	Stirling	Highly Satis
	Oxford Brookes	24/22
	Westminster	20/20
	Kent	23/21
	Brighton	-/22
	Nottingham Trent	22/21
	Manchester Met	20/20
	Buckingham	
	Leeds Met	24/-
	Sunderland	
	De Montfort	C/CAC
	Dundee	Excellent
	Liverpool JM	22/21
	Central England	21/-
	Sheffield Hallam	22/23
	Heriot-Watt	Highly Satis
	Salford	20/21
	Glamorgan	Excellent
	Bristol UWE	23/21
	Hertfordshire	23/21
	Huddersfield	-/21
	Plymouth	-/20
	Staffordshire	24/-
	Lincoln	
	Napier	C/CCC
	Coventry	23/23
Low-Medium		
80-200 points		
	Glasgow Cal	Highly Satis
	Paisley	C/CCC
	London Met	24/21
	Wolverhampton	22/20
	Portsmouth	21/22
	Sunderland	
	East London	C/CAC
	London South Bank	C/ACC
	Teesside	
	Luton	
	Northampton	
	Anglia Ruskin	20/-
	Middlesex	21/20
	Southampton Solent	22/-
	Bolton	-/20
	Greenwich	20/19
	Gloucestershire	
	Bucks Chilterns	
	Thames Valley	19/-
	Newport	
	Central Lancs	22/19
	Northumbria	22/21
	Central England	21/
	Leeds Met	C/CAC
	Canterbury	-/22
	Hertfordshire	23/21
	Derby	-/21
	Plymouth	-/20
	Worcester	

AGRICULTURE, FORESTRY, AGRICULTURAL SCIENCES

Go to www.qaa.ac.uk/reviews/reports/subjIndex.asp for recent teaching inspections; www.qaa.ac.uk/reviews/reports/archive/oldSubjIndex.asp for reports prior to 2000.

ENTRY	UNIVERSITY	RATING
Medium-High		
280-320 points		
	Edinburgh	
	Newcastle	22
	Stirling	
	Queen's Belfast	21
Low-Medium		
220-260 points		
	Stirling	
	Aberdeen	
	Newcastle	22
	Bangor	Excellent
	Nottingham	23

ENTRY	UNIVERSITY	RATING
	Reading	21
Low		
100-200 points		
	Nottingham Trent	C/CCC
	Aberystwyth .	Satisfactory
	Plymouth	22
	Scot Agric Coll	C/CCC
	Sparsholt	20.C/CCC
	Harper Adams	23
	Bristol West England	20
	Derby	
	Central Lancs	18
	Salford	
	Queen's Blfast	21
	Greenwich	20
	Highlands & Islands	C/C-A/C
	Liverpool JM	
	Writtle	19
	Bishop Burton	C/CCA
	Royal College Agric	

BIOSCIENCES

Assessments have been made for both organismal and molecular biosciences; where the outcome was different, the first of the two scores in column 3 relates to organismal biosciences.

ENTRY	UNIVERSITY	RATING
Very high		
360 points +		
	Cambridge	24
	Imperial College	22
	Oxford	24
	Warwick	23
High		
340 points		
	Cardiff	Excellent
	Durham	24
	East Anglia	22
	Exeter	22
	Leicester	22
	Sheffield	24
	Manchester	23
	Lancaster	21
	Royal Holloway	24, 21
	Nottingham	23
	St Andrews	Excellent
	Sussex	22
	University College	24, 22
	Birmingham	24, 23
	York	24
Medium-High		
280-300 points		
	Anglia Ruskin	21
	Aberdeen	Excellent
	Queen's Belfast	21
	Aston	23
	Bristol	22, 24
	Bradford	20
	Brunel	22
	Cardiff	Excellent
	Durham	24
	Exeter	22
	Dundee	Excellent
Medium-High	St George's London	
280-300 points	Leicester	22

ENTRY	UNIVERSITY	RATING
Medium-High	Essex	23
280-300 points	Aberystwyth	Excellent
	East Anglia	22
	Edinburgh	Excellent
	Bournemouth	
	King's College (KCL)	22
	Leeds	22, 23
	Liverpool	19
	Manchester	23
	University College	24, 22
	Queen Mary	22
	Manchester Met	22
	Southampton	23
	Swansea	Excellent
	Lancaster	21
	Newcastle	22, 24
	Reading	21
	Royal Holloway	24, 21
	St Andrews	Excellent
	Sheffield	24
	Stirling	Higly satis
	Strathclyde	Highly satis
	Surrey	21, 22
Medium		
200-260 points		
	Hull	23
	Anglia Ruskin	21
	Kent	24
	Leeds	22, 23
	Brighton	22
	Bradford	20
	Bristol UWE	24
	Napier	Highly satis
	Central Lancashire	22
	Bangor	Excellent
	Abertay Dundee	Highly satis
	Chester	21
	Glamorgan	Satisfactory
	Coventry	16, 19
	Gloucestershire	
	Keele	22, 21
	Glasgow	Excellent
	Plymouth	22
	St Andrews	Excellent
	Stirling	Higly satis

ENTRY	UNIVERSITY	RATING
Medium		
200-260 points		
	Salford	24
	Queen's Belfast	21
	Ulster	21, 22
	Glasgow Caledonian	Highly satis
	Heriot-Watt	Highly satis
	Leicester	22
	Northumbria	21
	Nottingham Trent	24
	Oxford Brookes	23
	Sunderland	24
	Sheffield Hallam	22
	Manchester Met	22
	Wolverhampton	23
Low		
80-180 points		
	Nottingham Trent	24
	De Montfort	21
	Roehampton	23
	Bristol West England	24
	Portsmouth	22
	Central Lancashire	22

ENTRY	UNIVERSITY	RATING
Low	Staffordshire	22
80-180 points	Kingston	24
	London South Bank	20
	Canterbury	21
	Cardiff (UWIC)	Excellent
	Essex	23
	Glasgow Caledonian	Highly satis
	Heriot-Watt	Highly satis
	Derby	22
	East London	19
	Greenwich	20
	Nottingham Trent	24
	Liverpool	19
	Liverpool J Moores	23, 22
	Bedfordshire	22
	Middlesex	
	London Met	18
	Paisley	Highly satis
	Robert Gordon	
	London South Bank	20
	Westminster	21
	Worcester	20
	Wolverhampton	23

BUSINESS/MANAGEMENT

Go to www.qaa.ac.uk/reviews/reports/subjIndex.asp for recent teaching inspections; www.qaa.ac.uk/reviews/reports/archive/oldSubjIndex.asp for reports prior to 2000.

ENTRY	UNIVERSITY	RATING
Very high		
360 points		
	Bath	Excellent
	Warwick	Excellent
	Cambridge	
	Lancaster	Excellent
	Northumbria	22. C
High 300-340 points		
	Surrey	Excellent
	Aston	24
	Birmingham	21
	City	23
	Exeter	22
	Royal Holloway	21
	Loughborough	22
	Durham	
	Northumbria	22. C
	Imperial	
	Glasgow	
	Manchester	24
	King's London	
	Cardiff	
	Leeds	22
	LSE	24
	Newcastle	
	Nottingham	Excellent
	Nottingham Trent	Excellent
	Queen Mary	
	St Andrews	C/CCC
	Sheffield	
	Southampton	23
	Sussex	
	York	22
Medium-High		
260-300 points	Bournemouth	22

ENTRY	UNIVERSITY	RATING
Medium-High	Edinburgh	C/CCC
260-300 points	Coventry	22
	Aberystwyth	
	Bradford	
	Aberdeen	
	Brunel	
	Chester	21
	Aston	24
	De Montfort	
	East Anglia	23
	Essex	
	Exeter	22
	Imperial	
	Reading	21
	SOAS	
	Keele	21
	Gloucestershire	
	Kent	21
	Heriot-Watt	
	Hull	23
	Keele	21
	Leicester	
	Kingston	
	Loughborough	22
	Liverpool	23
	Leeds	22
	LSE	24
	Manchester	24
	Oxford Brookes	24
	Queen's Belfast	23
	Salford	
	Stirling	
	Swansea	
	Strathclyde	
	Ulster	24
	Westminster	20
Medium		
200-240 points		
	Abertay	C/AAA
	De Montfort	
	Northumbria	22.C

ENTRY	UNIVERSITY	RATING		ENTRY	UNIVERSITY	RATING
Medium	Glamorgan			Low		
200-240 points	Bath Spa	20		60-180 points		
	Chester	21			Anglia Ruskin	20. C
	Lincoln				Bolton	
	Liverpool Hope	24			Canterbury	21
	Heriot-Watt				Cardiff UWIC	
	Bangor				Central Lancashire	22
	Edge Hill				Chichester	19
	Bradford				Derby	22
	Bristol West England	23			East London	
	Sunderland	C/CCC			Glasgow Caledonian	
	Central England	21			Greenwich	20
	Gloucestershire				Highlands & Islands	C/CCA
	Huddersfield				Leeds Metropolitan	24
	Kent	21			Liverpool J Moores	22
	Kingston				Bedfordshire	
	Lampeter				Middlesex	22
	Liverpool J Moores	22			London Met	24
	Manchester Met	23			Newport	
	Napier				Northampton	
	Nottingham Trent				Paisley	
	Plymouth				Queen Margaret	
	Aberdeen				St Mary's College	17
	Hertfordshire	23			Salford	
	Hull	23			Scottish Agricultural	
	Salford				Sheffield Hallam	21
	Sheffield Hallam	21			Southampton Solent	22
	Staffordshire				London South Bank	20
	Roehampton				Teesside	
	Brighton				Thames Valley	19. C
	Buckingham				Wolverhampton	23
	Portsmouth				Worcester	21
	Robert Gordon				York St John UC	21
	Westminster	20				
	Winchester	22				

● ●

COMPUTER

Go to www.qaa.ac.uk/reviews/reports/subjIndex.asp for recent teaching inspections; www.qaa.ac.uk/reviews/reports/archive/oldSubjIndex.asp for reports prior to 2000.

ENTRY	UNIVERSITY	RATING
Very high		
360 points		
	Imperial	Excellent
	Oxford	Excellent
	Cambridge	Excellent
	Manchester	Excellent
	Southampton	Excellent
	Durham	Satisfactory
	Nottingham	Satisfactory
	Strathclyde	Highly Satis
	Warwick	Excellent
High 320-		
340 points		
	Imperial	Excellent
	Kent	Excellent
	Bristol	Satisfactory
	York	Excellent
	UCL	Satisfactory
	Birmingham	Satisfactory
	St Andrews	C/CCC
	Glasgow	Excellent
	Reading	Satisfactory
	Liverpool	Satisfactory
	Lancaster	Satisfactory
	Cardiff	Satisfactory

ENTRY	UNIVERSITY	RATING
High 320-	Sheffield	Satisfactory
340 points	Sussex	Satisfactory
	King's London	Satisfactory
	Leeds	Satisfactory
	Bath	Satisfactory
	UEA	Satisfactory
	Aston	Satisfactory
Medium-High		
280-300 points		
	King's Coll	Satisfactory
	Heriot-Watt	Highly Satis
	Queen Mary	Satisfactory
	Manchester	Excellent
	Nottingham Trent	Satisfactory
	Royal Holloway	Satisfactory
	Sussex	Satisfactory
	Greenwich	Satisfactory
	Essex	Satis. C
	Kent	Excellent
	Liverpool	Satisfactory
	Abertay Dundee	Satisfactory
	Lancaster	Satisfactory
	Loughborough	Satisfactory
	Northumbria	Satisfactory
	Reading	Satisfactory
	Surrey	Satis. C
	Durham	Satisfactory
	City	Satisfactory
	Sheffield	Satisfactory
	Lincoln	Satisfactory
	Dundee	Satisfactory

ENTRY	UNIVERSITY	RATING		ENTRY	UNIVERSITY	RATING
Medium-High					Buckingham	
280-300 points					Chester	Satisfactory
	Bournemouth	Satisfactory			Glamorgan	Satisfactory
	Exeter	Excellent			Staffordshire	Satisfactory
	UEA	Satisfactory		*Low*		
	Edinburgh	Excellent		*80-200 points*		
	Aberystwyth	Satisfactory			Edge Hill	
	St Andrews	Highly Satis			Chichester	
	Strathclyde	Highly Satis			Cumbria	
	Swansea	Excellent			York St John	
	Newcastle	Satisfactory			Manchester Met	
	Brunel	Satisfactory			Bristol UWE	Satisfactory
	Leicester	Satisfactory			Nottingham Trent	Satisfactory
	Aston	Satisfactory			Manchester Met	Satisfactory
	Central England	Satisfactory			Hertfordshire	Satisfactory
	Ulster	Satisfactory			Abertay Dundee	Satisfactory
	Goldsmiths				Bradford	Satisfactory
	Westminster	Satisfactory			Glasgow Cal	Satis. C/CAC
Low-Medium					Brunel	Satisfactory
220-260 points					Coventry	Satisfactory
	Aston	Satisfactory			Roehampton	Satisfactory
	Abertay Dundee	Satisfactory			Westminster	Satisfactory
	Lincoln	Satisfactory			London South Bank	Satis. C/CAC
	Bradford	Satisfactory			Huddersfield	Satisfactory
	Brunel	Satisfactory			Leeds Met	Satis. C/CCC
	Paisley	Satisfactory			Liverpool JM	Satisfactory
	Sunderland	Satisfactory			Bedfordshire	Satisfactory
	Portsmouth	Satisfactory			Middlesex	Satisfactory
	Northumbria	Satisfactory			Central Lancs	Satisfactory
	Ulster	Satisfactory			Hull	Satisfactory
	Reading	Satisfactory			Kent	Excellent
	Swansea	Excellent			Dundee	Satisfactory
	Strathclyde	Highly Satis			Bournemouth	Satisfactory
	Teesside	Excellent			Plymouth	Satisfactory
	Glasgow	Excellent			Anglia Ruskin	Satis. C/CCC
	Hull	Satisfactory			Cardiff UWIC	Satisfactory
	Loughborough	Satisfactory			Sheffield Hallam	Satisfactory
	Lancaster	Satisfactory			Kingston	Satisfactory
	Essex	Satis. C			East London	Satisfactory
	Queen's Belfast	Satisfactory			Lampeter	
	Plymouth	Satisfactory			Bolton	Satisfactory
	Aberdeen	Satisfactory			Wolverhampton	Satisfactory
	Brighton	Satisfactory			Aberystwyth	Satisfactory
	Gloucestershire	Satisfactory			Canterbury	Satisfactory
	Stirling	Satisfactory			Worcester	
	Keele	Satisfactory			Napier	Satis. C/CCC
	Oxford Brookes	Satisfactory			Sunderland	Satisfactory
	Goldsmiths				Portsmouth	Satisfactory
	Greenwich	Satisfactory			De Montfort	Satisfactory
	Kent	Excellent			Derby	Satisfactory
	Kingston	Satisfactory			Greenwich	Satisfactory
	Salford	Satisfactory			Newport	Satisfactory
	Bangor				Liverpool	Satisfactory
	Ulster	Satisfactory			London Met	Satis. C/CAC
	Hertfordshire	Satisfactory			Southampton Solent	Satisfactory
	Liverpool	Satisfactory			Thames Valley	Satisfactory
	Heriot-Watt	Highly Satis			Robert Gordon	
	Bristol UWE	Satisfactory			Paisley	Satisfactory
	Nottingham Trent	Satisfactory			Highlands & Islands	
	Manchester Met	Satisfactory			Glamorgan	Satisfactory
	Coventry	Satisfactory				

● ●

DENTISTRY

ENTRY	UNIVERSITY	RATING		ENTRY	UNIVERSITY	RATING
					King's College	24
Very high	Queen's Belfast	24		*High 320-*	Birmingham	22
360 points	Liverpool	21		*340 points*	Bristol	19
	Dundee	Highly Satis			Glasgow	Highly Satis
					Newcastle	23

ENTRY	UNIVERSITY	RATING
High 320-340 **points**		
	Leeds	23
	Manchester	24
	Queen Mary	24
	Sheffield	23
	Cardiff	Excellent
	Peninsula	N/A

ENTRY	UNIVERSITY	RATING
Low-Medium	Dundee	Highly Satis
120-240 points	Manchester	24
	Cardiff UWIC	Excellent
	Manchester Met	21
	Portsmouth	23
	Bristol UWE	21 (Equine)

*These are Dental Technology or Oral Health degrees.

ECONOMICS

Go to www.qaa.ac.uk/reviews/reports/subjIndex.asp for recent teaching inspections; www.qaa.ac.uk/reviews/reports/archive/oldSubjIndex.asp for reports prior to 2000.

ENTRY	UNIVERSITY	RATING
Very high **360 points**		
	Oxford	23
	Cambridge	24
	Warwick	24
	LSE	23
	Nottingham	24
	UCL	24
	Bristol	23
	Lancaster	
	Durham	24
High 320-340 points		
	Exeter	23
	Brunel	22
	UEA	23
	Newcastle	23
	Cardiff	Satisfactory
	Queen's Belfast	24
	Aston	
	Bath	24
	Reading	21
	St Andrews	Exce. C/CCC
	Manchester	24
	Birmingham	23
	Leeds	22
	Southampton	24
	Lancaster	
	York	24
	Essex	24
	Kent	23
	Loughborough	23
	Nottingham	24
	Queen Mary	21
	Sheffield	21
	Glasgow	Satis. C/CCA
	Royal Holloway	22
Medium-High 280-300 points	Dundee	Satisfactory
	Edinburgh	Satisfactory
	Essex	24
	Cardiff	Satisfactory
	Leicester	24
	Surrey	23
	Sussex	21
	UEA	23
	Hull	22
	Leeds	22
	Queen Mary	21
	Queen's Belfast	24
	Swansea	Satisfactory
	UCL	24
	Newcastle	23
	Brunel	22

ENTRY	UNIVERSITY	RATING
	SOAS	21
	Kent	23
	Liverpool	22
	Exeter	23
	Strathclyde	Satis. C/CCC
	Aberystwyth	Excellent
	Westminster	
Medium 220-260 points	Aberdeen	Exc. C/CCC
	Bradford	21
	Brunel	22
	City	22
	Coventry	23
	Ulster	22
	Goldsmiths	22
	Keele	23
	Queen's Belfast	24
	Salford	20
	Swansea	Satisfactory
	Heriot-Watt	Satisfactory
	Stirling	Exc. C/CCC
	Aberystwyth	Excellent
	Nottingham Trent	22
	Buckingham	
	Dundee	Satisfactory
	Kingston	21
	Manchester Met	20
	Oxford Brookes	24
	Bangor	Satisfactory
	Robert Gordom	Ulster
	Glamorgan	Satisfactory
	Staffordshire	24
Low 80-200 points	Bolton	
	Abertay Dundee	Exc. C/CCC
	Bristol UWE	23
	Central England	21
	Central Lancs	
	Liverpool JMoores	
	Anglia Ruskin	
	Northumbria	22
	Leeds Met	24
	Napier	Satisfactory
	Glasgow Cal	
	Greenwich	20
	Cardiff UWIC	
	East London	20
	Hertfordshire	22
	Kingston	21
	Portsmouth	21
	Middlesex	21
	Northampton	
	London Met	23
	Paisley	Satis. C/CCC
	Sunderland	
	Plymouth	
	Worcester	

ENGINEERING
MECHANICAL, PRODUCTION

Go to www.qaa.ac.uk/reviews/reports/subjIndex.asp for recent teaching inspections; www.qaa.ac.uk/reviews/reports/archive/oldSubjIndex.asp for reports prior to 2000.

ENTRY	UNIVERSITY	RATING
Very high	Cambridge	23
360 points	Oxford	23
	Bristol	Excellent
High 320-	Bath	Excellent
340 points	City	Satisfactory, 19
	Glasgow	Highly Satis
	Imperial	Satisfactory, 22
	Queen's Belfast	Satisfactory, 21
	Durham	22
	Newcastle	Satisfactory
	Liverpool	Satisfactory, 20
	Birmingham	Satisfactory, 20
	Queen Mary	Satisfactory
	Strathclyde	Excellent
	Swansea	Satisfactory
	UCL	Satisfactory
	Brunel	Satisfactory, 20
	Southampton	Satisfactory, 21
	Cardiff	Excellent
	Nottingham	Excellent, 24
	Loughborough	Satisfactory, 23
	Manchester	Excellent
	Lancaster	Satisfactory
	Warwick	
	Sussex	Satisfactory
	Sheffield	Excellent, 24
Medium-High	Aberdeen	Highly Satis
280-300 points	Bradford	Satisfactory
	UCL	Satisfactory
	King's Coll	Satisfactory
	Liverpool	Satisfactory, 20
	Robert Gordon	Highly Satis
	Sheffield	Excellent, 24
	Strathclyde	Excellent
	Staffordshire	Satisfactory
	Sussex	Satisfactory
	Leeds	Satisfactory
	Hull	
	Salford	
	Portsmouth	Satis. C
	Lancaster	Satisfactory
	Newcastle	Satisfactory
	Birmingham	Satisfactory, 20
	Brighton	Satisfactory
	Edinburgh	Satis. C/CCC
	Harper Adams	Satisfactory
	City	Satisfactory, 19
	Heriot-Watt	Highly Satis. C/CCC
	Hertfordshire	22
	Kingston	Satisfactory, 24
	Manchester	Excellent
	Warwick	
	Exeter	
	Brunel	Satisfactory, 20
	Cardiff	Excellent
	Loughborough	Satisfactory, 23
	Aston	Satisfactory
	Dundee	
	Leicester	
	Surrey	Satisfactory
	Oxford Brookes	Satisfactory

ENTRY	UNIVERSITY	RATING
Low-Medium		
220-260 points		
	Plymouth	Satisfactory
	Queen's Belfast	Satisfactory, 21
	Edinburgh	Satis. C/CCC
	Leeds	Satisfactory
	Leicester	
	Aston	Satisfactory
	Bradford	Satisfactory
	Brighton	Satisfactory
	Coventry	Excellent, 18
	Hull	
	Glasgow	Highly Satis
	Exeter	
	Surrey	Satisfactory
	Sheffield	Excellent, 24
	Queen Mary	Satisfactory
	Central Lancs	Satisfactory
	Central England	Satisfactory, 19
	Hertfordshire	22
	Manchester Met	Excellent
	Northumbria	Satisfactory
	Brunel	Satisfactory, 20
	Aberdeen	Highly Satis
	Bristol West England	Satisfactory
	Heriot-Watt	Highly Satis
	Huddersfield	Satis. C/CCC
	Napier	Satisfactory
	Ulster	Satisfactory
	Kingston	Satisfactory, 24
	Greenwich	Satisfactory
	Derby	Satisfactory
	Glamorgan	Satisfactory
	Portsmouth	Satisfactory
	Robert Gordon	Highly Satis
	Sheffield Hallam	Satisfactory, 21
Low	Swansea	Satisfactory
80-200 points	Central Lancs	Satisfactory
	Harper Adams	Satisfactory
	De Montfort	
	Robert Gordon	Highly Satis
	Southampton Solent	19
	Salford	
	Ulster	Satisfactory
	Bradford	Satisfactory
	Liverpool	Satisfactory, 20
	London South Bank	18
	Glasgow Cal	Satis. C/CAC
	Hull	
	Sunderland	Satisfactory, 19
	Teesside	Satis. C/CAC
	Coventry	Excellent, 18
	Northumbria	Satisfactory
	Dundee	
	Aberdeen	Highly Satis
	Hertfordshire	22
	Paisley	Highly Satis C/CAC
	Portsmouth	Satisfactory
	Sheffield Hallam	Satisfactory, 21
	Glamorgan	Satisfactory
	Wolverhampton	Satisfactory
	Kingston	Satisfactory, 24
	Greenwich	Satisfactory
	Liverpool JM	Satisfactory
	Plymouth	Satisfactory
	Bolton	Satisfactory
	Highlands & Islands	
	Cardiff UWIC	Satisfactory

ENGLISH

Go to www.qaa.ac.uk/reviews/reports/subjIndex.asp for recent teaching inspections; www.qaa.ac.uk/reviews/reports/archive/oldSubjIndex.asp for reports prior to 2000.

ENTRY	UNIVERSITY	RATING
Very high 360 points		
	Oxford	Excellent
	Cambridge	Excellent
	UCL	Excellent
	Durham	Excellent
	Warwick	Excellent
	Exeter	Excellent
High 320-340 points		
	King's College	Satisfactory
	Birmingham	Excellent
	UEA	Satisfactory
	Manchester	Satisfactory
	St Andrews	Highly Satis
	Southampton	Excellent
	Sussex	Excellent
	Newcastle	Excellent
	Bristol	Excellent
	Leeds	Excellent
	Sheffield	Excellent
	Cardiff	Excellent
	Liverpool	Excellent
	York	Excellent
	Glasgow	Excellent
	Nottingham	Excellent
	Royal Holloway	Satisfactory
	Lancaster	Excellent
	Leicester	Excellent
	Keele	Satisfactory
	Reading	Satisfactory
	Loughborough	23
Medium-High 280-300 points		
	Birmingham	Excellent
	Bournemouth	
	Brighton	
	Brunel	Satisfactory
	Glasgow	Excellent
	York	Excellent
	Kingston	Satisfactory
	Lancaster	Excellent
	Kent	Satisfactory
	Oxford Brookes	Excellent
	Swansea	Satisfactory
	Kent	Satisfactory
	UEA	Satisfactory
	Edinburgh	Highly Satis C/CCC
	Queen Mary	Excellent
	Cardiff	Excellent
	Liverpool	Excellent
	King's College	Satisfactory
	Manchester	Satisfactory
	Newcastle	Excellent
	Nottingham	Excellent
	Durham	Excellent
	Exeter	Excellent
	Bristol	Excellent
Medium-High 280-300 points	Leeds	Excellent
	Portsmouth	Satisfactory
	Sheffield	Excellent
	Reading	Satisfactory

ENTRY	UNIVERSITY	RATING
	Loughborough	23
	Goldsmiths	Satisfactory
	Manchester Met	Satisfactory
	Queen's Belfast	Excellent
	Dundee	Exc. C/CCC
	Essex	Satisfactory
	Hull	Satisfactory
	Sheffield Hallam	Excellent
	Strathclyde	Highly Satis C/CCC
	Aberystwyth	Excellent
	Bristol UWE	Excellent
Medium 220-260 points		
	Birmingham	Excellent
	Bradford	
	Brighton	
	UEA	Satisfactory
	Strathclyde	Highly Satis C/CCC
	Lincoln	
	Oxford Brookes	Excellent
	Portsmouth	Satisfactory
	Sheffield Hallam	Excellent
	Manchester Met	Satisfactory
	Nottingham Trent	Satisfactory
	Huddersfield	Satisfactory
	Edge Hill	
	Liverpool Hope	
	Dundee	Exc. C/CCC
	Essex	Satisfactory
	Hull	Satisfactory
	Northumbria	Excellent
	Stirling	Excellent
	Bournemouth	
	Central Lancashie	
	Ulster	Satisfactory
	Roehampton	Satisfactory
	Aberdeen	Highly Satis
	Leicester	Excellent
	Keele	Satisfactory
	Bangor	Satisfactory
	Winchester	Satisfactory
	Bath Spa	Excellent
	Chester	Excellent
	Chichester	Satisfactory
	Kingston	Satisfactory
	Leeds	Excellent
	Liverpool	Excellent
	Liverpool JM	Satisfactory
	Plymouth	Satisfactory
	Gloucestershire	Satisfactory
	Glamorgan	
	Salford	Satisfactory
	Staffordshire	Satisfactory
	Swansea	Satisfactory
Low 80-220 points		
	Bolton	
	Leeds Met	C/CCC
	Lampeter	Satisfactory
	Wolverhampton	Satisfactory
	Teesside	Satisfactory
	York St John	Satisfactory
	Northampton	Satisfactory
	Westminster	Satisfactory
	Worcester	Satisfactory
	London Met	Excellent
	Central England	Satisfactory

ENTRY	UNIVERSITY	RATING
Low		
80-220 points		
	Kingston	Satisfactory
	London South Bank	C/CCA
	Bedfordshire	Satisfactory
	Middlesex	Satisfactory
	Roehampton	Satisfactory
	Hertfordshire	Satis. C/CCA
	Northumbria	Excellent

ENTRY	UNIVERSITY	RATING
	East London	Excellent
	Canterbury	Satisfactory
	Bristol UWE	Excellent
	De Montfort	Satisfactory
	Greenwich	Satisfactory
	Buckingham	
	Newport	
	Sunderland	Satisfactory
	Bucks Chilterns UC	C/CAC

HISTORY

HAT - History Aptitude Test - is required by Oxford.

ENTRY	UNIVERSITY	RATING
Very high		
360 points		
	Oxford	Excellent
	Cambridge	Excellent
	Durham	Excellent
	UCL	Excellent
	Exeter	Satisfactory
	Bristol	Satisfactory
High 320-	LSE	Excellent
340 points	Royal Holloway	Excellent
	York	Excellent
	St Andrews	Excellent
	Southampton	Satisfactory
	Warwick	Excellent
	Durham	Excellent
	Birmingham	Excellent
	UEA	Satisfactory
	Cardiff	Satisfactory
	Glasgow	Highly Satis C/CCC
	King's London	Excellent
	Lancaster	Excellent
	Leicester	Excellent
	Liverpool	Excellent
	Manchester	Satisfactory
	Newcastle	Satisfactory
	Nottingham	Satis. C/CCC
	Sheffield	Excellent
	SOAS	Satisfactory
	Leeds	Satisfactory
	Sussex	Satisfactory
Medium-High		
280-300 points		
	Edinburgh	Excellent
	Southampton	Satisfactory
	Birmingham	Excellent
	Manchester	Satisfactory
	Glasgow	Highly Satis C/CCC
	Leeds	Satisfactory
	Swansea	Excellent
	Kent	Satisfactory
	Nottingham	Satis. C/CCC
	Oxford Brookes	Satisfactory
	UEA	Satisfactory
	Lancaster	Excellent
	Liverpool	Excellent
	Cardiff	Satisfactory
	Hull	Excellent
	Reading	Satisfactory
	Dundee	Highly Satis
	Aberystwyth	Satisfactory
	Leicester	Excellent

ENTRY	UNIVERSITY	RATING
	Essex	Satisfactory
	Queen Mary	Satisfactory
	UCL	Excellent
	Goldsmiths	Satisfactory
	Queen's Belfast	Excellent
	Huddersfield	Satis. C/CCC
Medium	Aberystwyth	Satisfactory
220-260 points	Westminster	Satisfactory
	Bangor	Satisfactory
	Kent	Satisfactory
	Lincoln	
	Sheffield Hallam	Satisfactory
	Keele	Satisfactory
	Plymouth	Satisfactory
	Kingston	Satisfactory
	Brighton	
	Liverpool	Excellent
	Cardiff	Satisfactory
	Glasgow Caledonian	
	Strathclyde	Highly Satis
	Bristol UWE	Satisfactory
	Gloucestershire	Satisfactory
	Northumbria	Satisfactory
	Nottingham	Satisfactory
	Nottingham Trent	Satisfactory
	Portsmouth	Satisfactory
	Dundee	Highly Satis
	Leicester	Excellent
	Dundee	Highly Satis
	SOAS	Satisfactory
	Brunel	Satisfactory
	Liverpool Hope	Satisfactory
	Hull	Excellent
	Chester	Satisfactory
	Coventry	23
	Goldsmiths	Satisfactory
	Chichester	Satisfactory
	Bradford	Satisfactory
	Greenwich	Satisfactory
	Aberdeen	Highly Satis
	Glamorgan	Satisfactory
	Oxford Brookes	Satisfactory
	Cardiff UWIC	
	Stirling	Highly Satis C/CCC
	Winchester	Satisfactory
	Central Lancs	Satisfactory
	Liverpool Hope	
	Bradford	
	Edhe Hill	
	Anglia Ruskin	
	Ulster	Satisfactory
Low	Bournemouth	
80-200 points	Derby	Satisfactory
	East London	Satisfactory
	Glasgow Caledonian	
	London Met	Satisfactory

ENTRY	UNIVERSITY	RATING	ENTRY	UNIVERSITY	RATING
	Liverpool JMoores	Satisfactory		Cumbria	
Low	York St John	Satisfactory		Roehampton	Satisfactory
80-200 points	Teesside	Satis. C/CCC		Northampton	Satisfactory
	Middlesex	Satisfactory		Buckingham	
	Hertfordshire	Satis. C/CCC		Newport	Satis (Comb Sts)
	Huddersfield	Satis. C/CCC		Worcester	Satisfactory
	Leeds Met	Satis. C/CCC		Bolton	Satisfactory
	Lampeter	Satisfactory		Canterbury	Excellent
	Manchester Met	Satisfactory		De Montfort	Satis. C/CCC
	Wolverhampton	Satisfactory		Sunderland	Satis. C/CCC
	Staffordshire	Satisfactory		Bath Spa	Satisfactory

LANGUAGES

MML - Modern and Medieval Languages Test - is required by Cambridge.

Go to www.qaa.ac.uk/reviews/reports/subjIndex.asp for recent teaching inspections; www.qaa.ac.uk/reviews/reports/archive/oldSubjIndex.asp for reports prior to 2000.

ENTRY	UNIVERSITY	RATING
Very high		
320 points		
	Oxford	21
	Cambridge	22
	UCL	21, Fr.; 23, Ger.
High 320-		
340 points		
	Cardiff	Satisfactory
	Manchester	19, Fr.; 21, Ger.
	Newcastle	22
	St Andrews	22
	Glasgow	22
	Bristol	20, Fr.; 21, Ger.
	Durham	22
	Leeds	22, Fr.; 22, Ger.
	Surrey	18
	York	22
	Southampton	18
Medium-High		
280-300 points		
	UCL	21, Fr.; 23, Ger.
	Manchester	19, Fr.; 21, Ger.
	Birmingham	18, Fr.; 19, Ger.
	Durham	22
	Royal Holloway	21, Fr.; 19, Ger.
	Edinburgh	21
	King's Coll	21, Fr.; 20, Ger.
	Leeds	22, Fr.; 22, Ger.
	Sheffield	21, Fr.; 20, Ger.
	Leicester	19, Fr.; 21, Ger.
	Heriot-Watt	21
	Essex	
	SOAS	23
	York	22
	Nottingham	16, Fr.; 22, Ger.
	Liverpool	22, Fr.; 19, Ger.
	Swansea	Satis, Fr.; Ex,Ger.
	Bradford	18
	Sussex	22, Fr.; 17, Ger.
	Bath	19
	Exeter	22, Fr.; 24, Ger.
	Surrey	18

ENTRY	UNIVERSITY	RATING
	UEA	19
	Hull	21
Medium-High	Lancaster	20, Fr.; 19, Ger.
280-300 points	Kent	19
	Aberdeen	22
	Strathclyde	22
	Aston	22
Low-Medium		
220-260 points		
	Aberdeen	22
	Keele	20, Fr.; 19, Ger.
	UEA	19
	Hull	21
	Bangor	Satisfactory
	Salford	20
	Ulster	20, Fr.; 19, Ger.
	Stirling	20
(Fr. only)	Brighton	20
	Queen Mary	23
	Aberystwyth	
	Chester	19
	Swansea	Satis, Fr.; Ex,Ger.
	London South Bank	22
	Nottingham Trent	17
	Glamorgan	
Low		
160-200 points		
(Fr. only)	Roehampton	19
	Strathclyde	22
	Anglia Ruskin	21
	Bristol West England	21
	London Met	19
	Liverpool JM	19
	East London	18
	Portsmouth	23, Fr.; 21, Ger.
	Manchester Met	21
	Wolverhampton	19, Fr.; 17, Ger.
	Westminster	23, Fr.; 20, Ger.
	Coventry	21
	Northumbria	23
	Hertfordshire	
	Napier	19
	Sheffield Hallam	19
	Cardiff UWIC	
	Middlesex	19
	Cumbria	
	Paisley	19
	Southampton Solent	
	Central Lancs	21
	Newport	
	Leeds Met	19

LAW

LNAT - The National Admissions Test for Law - is required by Birmingham, Bristol, Cambridge, Durham, Exeter, Glasgow, King's London, Manchester Met, Nottingham, Oxford, and UCL.

Go to www.qaa.ac.uk/reviews/reports/subjIndex.asp for recent teaching inspections.

ENTRY	UNI/COLLEGE	RATING
Very high *360 points*		
	Bristol	Excellent
	Cambridge	Excellent
	Birmingham	Satisfactory
	Leeds	Satisfactory
	Oxford	Excellent
	UCL	Excellent
	Newcastle	Satisfactory
	Exeter	Satisfactory
	Durham	Excellent
	King's London	Excellent
	Manchester	Excellent
	Nottingham	Excellent
	Lancaster	Satisfactory
	Cardiff	Satisfactory
	Queen's Belfast	Excellent
	Sheffield	Excellent
	SOAS	Excellent
	Warwick	Excellent
	LSE	Excellent
	Southampton	Satisfactory
High 320-340 points	Reading	Satisfactory
	Glasgow	Highly Satis C/CCC
	King's London	Excellent
	Leeds	Satisfactory
	Manchester	Excellent
	Queen's Belfast	Excellent
	Sheffield	Excellent
	Cardiff	Satisfactory
	Essex	Excellent
	Leicester	Excellent
	Exeter	Satisfactory
	Lancaster	Satisfactory
	Oxford Brookes	Excellent
	Queen Mary	Satisfactory
	City	Satisfactory
	UEA	Excellent
	Sussex	Satisfactory
	Liverpool	Excellent
	Kingston	Satisfactory
	Kent	Satisfactory
	Brunel	Satisfactory
	Surrey	
	Westminster	Satisfactory
	Aberystwyth	Satisfactory
	Strathclyde	Highly Satis C/CCC
Medium-High 260-300 points	Kent	Satisfactory
	Dundee	Highly Satis C/CCC
	Liverpool	Excellent
	Surrey	
	Swansea	Satisfactory
	Cardiff	Satisfactory
	Derby	Satisfactory
	Oxford Brookes	Excellent
	Kingston	Satisfactory

ENTRY	UNIVERSITY	RATING
	Edinburgh	Highly Satis
	Glamorgan	Satisfactory
	LSE	Excellent
	Central England	Satisfactory
	De Montfort	Satisfactory
	Manchester Met	Satisfactory
	Nottingham Trent	Satisfactory
	Strathclyde	Highly Satis C/CCC
	Ulster	Satisfactory
	Hull	Satisfactory
	Keele	Satisfactory
	Bangor	
	Stirling	
	Staffordshire	Satis. C/CCC
	Westminster	Satisfactory
	Coventry	Satisfactory
	Central Lancs	Satisfactory
	Aberdeen	Highly Satis
Medium *220-260 points*		
	Liverpool JM	Satis. C
	Huddersfield	Satis. C/CAC
	Gloucestershire	
	Heriot-Watt	
	Lincoln	Satisfactory
	De Montfort	Satisfactory
	Plymouth	Satis. C
	Portsmouth	
	Buckingham	
	London South Bank	Satisfactory
	Manchestere Met	Satisfactory
	Staffordshire	Satis. C/CCC
	Robert Gordon	
	Bournemouth	Satisfactory
	Hertfordshire	Satisfactory
	Aberdeen	Highly Satis
	Bristol UWE	Excellent
	Brighton	
	Northumbria	Excellent
	Sheffield Hallam	Satisfactory
	Kingston	Satisfactory
	Napier	C/CCA
	Abertay Dundee	Satisfactory
	Glamorgan	Satisfactory
	Stirling	
	Sunderland	
	Thames Valley	Satisfactory
	Chester	
Low *80-200 points*	Central England	
	Central Lancashire	
	Bedfordshire	Satisfactory
	Bolton	
	Derby	Satisfactory
	London Met	Satis. C/CAC
	Plymouth	Satisfactory
	Wolverhampton	Satisfactory
	Northampton	Satisfactory
	Glasgow Cal	Satisfactory
	Bucks Chilterns	C/CAA
	Middlesex	Satisfactory
	Paisley	
	Southampton Solent	Satisfactory
	Teesside	Satis. C/CAA
	Leeds Met	C/CCA
	Salford	
	Canterbury	
	Newport	

MEDIA

Go to www.qaa.ac.uk/reviews/reports/subjIndex.asp for recent teaching inspections.

ENTRY	UNIVERSITY	RATING
High 320-340 points		
	York	
	Sussex	21
	Goldsmiths	22
	Glasgow	
	UEA	23
	Cardiff	Satisfactory
	Royal Holloway	
	Nottingham Trent	21
	Lancaster	
Medium-High 260-300 points		
	Manchester	
	Bournemouth	22
	Sheffield	
	Leicester	21
	Bristol UWE	22
	Chester	
	Queen's Belfast	
	Edge Hill	20
	Birmingham	
	Newcastle	
	Southampton Solent	18
	Goldsmiths	22
	Stirling	Highly Satis
	UEA	23
	Essex	
	City	19
	Lancaster	
	Lincoln	17
	Southampton Solent	18
	Liverpool JM	22
	Central Lancs	22
	Central England	21
	Leeds	22
	Sheffield Hallam	19
	Glasgow Cal	Highly Satis
	Sunderland	22
	Bradford	
	Strathclyde	
	Aston	
	Keele	
	Salford	
	Brunel	20
	Ulster	21
	Aberystwyth	
	Huddersfield	18
	Surrey	
	Loughborough	
	Brighton	
	Dundee	
	Swansea	
	Queen Mary	
	De Montfort	20
	Wolverhampton	19
	Staffordshire	20
Low-Medium 200-240 points		
	Nottingham Trent	21
	Bristol UWE	22
	Falmouth UC	18
	Bradford	
	Cumbria	19
	Dundee	

ENTRY	UNIVERSITY	RATING
	Westminster	23
	Napier	Highly Satis
	Brighton	
	Cardiff UWIC	
	Staffordshire	20
	Salford	
	Kingston	
	Bath Spa	
	Chester	
Medium-High 200-240 points	City	19
	Bangor	
	Queen Margaret	
	Central Lancs	22
	Winchester	18
	Gloucestershire	20
	Glamorgan	
	Lampeter	
	Liverpool JM	22
	Edge Hill	20
	Robert Gordon	
	De Montfort	20
	Liverpool Hope	
	Huddersfield	18
	Lincoln	17
	Central England	21
	Middlesex	
	Plymouth	21
	Southampton Solent	18
	Ulster	21
	Oxford Brookes	
	Roehampton	
	Buckingham	
	Portsmouth	
	Coventry	18
Low 80-180 points	Hertfordshire	
	Manchester Met	
	Lampeter	
	Bolton	20
	De Montfort	20
	Abertay Dundee	
	Plymouth	21
	Central Lancashire	
	Derby	
	Glasgow Cal	Highly Satis
	Canterbury	20
	York St John	20
	Southampton Solent	18
	Bucks Chilterns UC	18
	Liverpool JM	22
	Portsmouth	
	Thames Valley	
	Staffordshire	20
	London South Bank	20
	Paisley	
	University of the Arts	20
	Central England	21
	Northumbria	
	Cumbria	19
	Wolverhampton	19
	Bedfordshire	22
	Leeds Met	19
	London Met	
	Worcester	
	Anglia Ruskin	18
	Middlesex	
	Teesside	
	East London	16
	Chichester	24

MEDICINE

UKCAT - UK Clinical Aptitude Test - is required by Aberdeen, Brighton & Sussex Medical School, Cardiff, Dundee, Durham, East Anglia (UEA), Edinburgh, Glasgow, Hull-York, Keele, King's London, Leeds, Leicester, Manchester, Newcastle, Nottingham, Oxford, Peninsula, Queen Mary, Sheffield, Southampton, St Andrews, St George's London. BMAT - the BioMedical Admissions Test - is required by Cambridge, Oxford, UCL, and Imperial. GAMSAT - the Graduate Medical School Admission Test - is required of graduate intake to St George's London, Nottingham, Peninsula, Swansea. MSAT - Medical School Admissions Test - is required of graduate/professional entry to King's London, Queen Mary, Warwick. Asterisks indicate foundation courses.

ENTRY	UNIVERSITY	RATING
Very high		
360 points +		
	Cambridge	21
	Oxford	21
	Queen's Belfast	22
	King's London	22
	Cardiff	Excellent
	UCL	21
	Imperial	21
	Dundee	Excellent
	St George's London	23

ENTRY	UNIVERSITY	RATING
	Edinburgh	Highly satis.
340 points		
	Peninsula	
	Birmingham	20
	Bristol	20
	Durham Newcastle	
	UEA	
	Keele	
	Hull-York	
340 points	Leicester Warwick	23
	Manchester	24
	Newcastle Durham	24
	Nottingham	
	Dundee	Excellent
	Liverpool	24
	Queen Mary	21
	Southampton	24
	St Andrews	Highly satis.
	Leeds	18
	Aberdeen	Excellent
	Glasgow	Excellent
	Sheffield	19
	Brighton & Sussex	
220 points		
	*Thames Valley	
	*Southampton	24
	*St George's London	23

PSYCHOLOGY

ENTRY	UNIVERSITY	RATING
Very high		
360 points		
	Cambridge	24
	Oxford	24
	Durham	23
	Bath	
	Warwick	21
	Exeter	23
	Cardiff	Excellent
High 320-		
340 points		
	UCL	22
	Lancaster	24
	Leeds	23
	Durham	23
	St Andrews	Excellent
	Loughborough	24
	Nottingham	24
	Sheffield	22
	Birmingham	23
	Oxford Brookes	23
	Liverpool	22
	York	24
	Bristol	23
	LSE	23
	Royal Holloway	24
	Sussex	21
	Kent	22
	Newcastle	24
	Manchester	22
	Reading	24
	Surrey	22
	Glasgow	Excellent
	Strathclyde	Highly Satis
	Leicester	24
	Southampton	21

ENTRY	UNIVERSITY	RATING
	Queen's Belfast	24
Medium-High		
260-300 points		
	Bristol	23
	UEA	
	Brighton	
	Bradford	
	Edinburgh	Highly Satis
	Durham (Stockton)	23
	Kent	22
	City	21
	Nottingham Trent	22
	Goldsmiths	22
	Brunel	22
	Oxford Brookes	23
	Kingston	
	Northumbria	22
	Dundee	Excellent
	Leeds	23
	Sheffield	22
	Surrey	22
	Bournemouth	
	Central Lancs	24
	Manchester Met	22
	Essex	22
	Hull	23
	Swansea	Excellent
	Keele	23
	Leicester	24
	Southampton	21
	Stirling	Excellent
	Portsmouth	23
	Exeter	23
	Aston	22
	Hertfordshire	23
	Bangor	Excellent
	Sheffield Hallam	24
	Coventry	21

PSYCHOLOGY

ENTRY	UNIVERSITY	RATING
	Ulster	23
	Hertfordshire	23
	Stirling	Excellent
	Lincoln	21
Medium *220-240 points*		
	Bristol UWE	22
	Aberdeen	Highly Satis
	Glasgow Cal	Highly Satis
	Wolverhampton	21
	Glamorgan	Satisfactory
	Greenwich	22
	Queen Margaret	
	Dundee	Excellent
	Huddersfield	20
	Plymouth	23
	Central Lancs	24
	Kingston	
	Winchester	21
	Manchester Met	22
	Westminster	24
	Liverpool JMoores	19
	Nottingham Trent	22
	Portsmouth	23
	Buckingham	
	Swansea	Excellent
	Sunderland	20
	Liverpool Hope	22
	London Met	22
	De Montfort	22
	Derby	20
	Gloucestershire	21
	Staffordshire	23
Heriot-Watt		
	Chester	20
	Southampton Solent	19
	Anglia Ruskin	22
	Salford	
	Edge Hill	22
	Keele	23

ENTRY	UNIVERSITY	RATING
	Lincoln	21
	Sheffield Hallam	24
	Bradford	
	Thames Valley	20
Low *100-200 points*		
	York St John	20
	Central Lancs	24
	Abertay Dundee	Highly Satis
	Bath Spa	21
	East London	23
	Cardiff UWIC	Excellent
	Bedfordshire	22
	Roehampton	23
	Northampton	20
	Nottingham Trent	22
	London Met	22
	Huddersfield	20
	London South Bank	20
	Teesside	20
	Central England	
	Greenwich	22
	Westminster	24
	Worcester	20
	Heriot-Watt	
	Manchester Met	22
	Bournemouth	
	Middlesex	21
	Canterbury	20
	Bolton	24
	Paisley	Highly Satis
	Bristol UWE	22
	Wolverhampton	21
	Glamorgan	Satisfactory
	Bucks Chilterns	21
	Napier	
	Newport	
	Cumbria	
	Leeds Met	20

SOCIOLOGY

ENTRY	UNIVERSITY	RATING
Very high *360 points*		
	Cambridge	
High 320- *340 points*	Durham	21
	Cardiff	Satisfactory
	Warwick	24
	Glasgow	Excellent
	Exeter	21
Medium-High *280-300 points*	Manchester	21
	Sussex	24
	Essex	22
	Durham	21
	Newcastle	
	UEA	16
	Nottingham	21
	Leeds	20
	Sheffield	Excellent
	Birmingham	24
	Edinburgh	Excellent
	Bristol	21
	Surrey	21
	Goldsmiths	21
	Royal Holloway	21
	Brighton	

ENTRY	UNIVERSITY	RATING
	Aston	
	LSE	20
	Salford	20
	Cardiff	Satisfactory
	Liverpool	21
	York	23
	Queen's Belfast	19
	Reading	22
	Bath	19
	Loughborough	23
	Lancaster	21
	Southampton	21
Medium *220-260 points*	Strathclyde	Highly Satis
	Keele	22
	Bradford	17
	Brighton	
	Bangor	Satisfactory
	Nottingham Trent	19
	Kent	21
Medium *220-260 points*	Hull	20
	Westminster	18
	City	19
	Leicester	19
	Goldsmiths	21
	Salford	20
	Aberdeen	Excellent

ENTRY	UNIVERSITY	RATING
Medium	Northumbria	20
220-260 points	Sheffield Hallam	22
	Oxford Brookes	21
	Queen Margaret UC	
	Kingston	21
	Coventry	21
	Central England	18
	Portsmouth	20
	Stirling	Excellent
	Swansea	Satisfactory
	Brunel	22
	Ulster	17
	Gloucestershire	20
	Chester	
	Cardiff UWIC	
	Liverpool Hope	22
Low	Manchester Met	21
100-200 points	Plymouth	20
	Bristol UWE	23
	Bangor	Satisfactory
	De Montfort	17
	Derby	18
	Liverpool JM	18
	Huddersfield	
	East London	19
	Greenwich	23

ENTRY	UNIVERSITY	RATING
Low	London South Bank	19
100-200 points	Roehampton	20
	Northumbria	20
	Staffordshire	17
	Central Lancs	18
	Middlesex	19
	Abertay Dundee	
	Northampton	20
	Teesside	19
	Worcester	21
	Bath Spa	22
	Sunderland	21
	Glamorgan	Satisfactory
	Bucks Chilterns	16
	Thames Valley	22
	London Met	17
	St Mary's	20
	Anglia Ruskin	20
	Edge Hill	Excellent
	Manchester Met	21
	Napier	
	Glasgow Caledonian	Highly Satis.
	Wolverhampton	20
	Paisley	Highly Satis.
	Leeds Metropolitan	

SPORT/SPORT SCIENCE

Go to www.qaa.ac.uk/reviews/reports/subjIndex.asp for recent teaching inspections; www.qaa.ac.uk/reviews/reports/archive/oldSubjIndex.asp for reports prior to 2000.

ENTRY	UNIVERSITY	RATING
Very high		
360 points +		
	Loughborough	23
High 320-	Bath	23
340 points	Birmingham	22
	Exeter	21
	Durham	23
	Glasgow	
	Hertfordshire	23
	Loughborough	23
	Queen Mary	
	Dundee	
	Sheffield	
	Salford	19
	Leeds	
Medium-High		
260-280 points		
	Liverpool JM	24
	Stirling	
	Ulster	23
	Swansea	
	Loughborough	23
	Sheffield Hallam	24
	Queen Mary	
	Edinburgh	
	Bangor	
	Liverpool JM	24
	Oxford Brookes	22
	Manchester Met	22
	Hull	20
	Brunel	23
	Durham	23
	Northumbria	21
	Brighton	22

ENTRY	UNIVERSITY	RATING
	Essex	
	Staffordshire	22
	Heriot-Watt	
	Southampton	
	Aberystwyth	
	Chichester	21
	Huddersfield	22
	Central Lancs	24
	Gloucestershire	21
	Middlesex	22
Low-Medium		
220-240 points		
	Coventry	21
	Sunderland	20
	Portsmouth	21
	Leeds	
	Dundee	
	Heriot-Watt	
	Wolverhampton	22
	Oxford Brookes	22
	Huddersfield	22
	Manchester Met	22
	De Montfort	23
	Edge Hill	20
	Hull	20
	Sheffield Hallam	24
	Abertay Dundee	
	Bournemouth	
	Salford	19
	Nottingham Trent	22
	Staffordshire	22
	Winchester	21
	Northumbria	21
	Hertfordshire	23
	Brighton	22
	Liverpool Hope	19
	York St John	21
	Kent	
	Robert Gordon	
	Napier	

ENTRY	UNIVERSITY	RATING	ENTRY	UNIVERSITY	RATING
	Gloucestershire	21		Thames Valley	22
	Chester	23		Cumbria	
Low	Manchester Met	22		Wolverhampton	22
80-200 points	Bradford			Strathclyde	
	Strathclyde			Northampton	19
	Kingston	22		East London	
	Bolton	21		Westminster	24
	Central Lancs	24		Gloucestershire	21
	Northumbria	21		London South Bank	22
	Hertfordshire	23		Greenwich	20
	Brighton	22		Chichester	21
	Cardiff UWIC			Huddersfield	22
	Salford	19		Luton	22
	Nottingham Trent	22		Middlesex	22
	Aberdeen			London Met	21
	Liverpool JM	24		Roehampton	21
	Leeds Met	22		Teesside	21
	Plymouth	23		Worcester	22
	Sheffield Hallam	24		Southampton Solent	21
	Newport			Lincoln	
	Canterbury	21		Derby	
	Glamorgan			Glasgow Caledonian	
	Bucks Chilterns	21		Bristol UWE	
	St Mary's	21			

VETERINARY SCIENCE

BMAT - the BioMedical Admissions Test - is required by Bristol and the Royal Veterinary College.

Those asterisked offer Veterinary Nursing degrees.

Go to www.qaa.ac.uk/reviews/reports/subjIndex.asp for recent teaching inspections; www.qaa.ac.uk/reviews/reports/archive/oldSubjIndex.asp for reports prior to 2000.

ENTRY	UNIVERSITY	RATING
Very high		
360 points +		
	Bristol	24
	Cambridge	23
	Royal Vet College	24
	Liverpool	24

ENTRY	UNIVERSITY	RATIN
340 points		
	Nottingham	
	Edinburgh	Excellent
	Glasgow	Excellent
300 points		
	Bristol	24
	Liverpool	24
	Royal Vet College	24
160-240 points		
	*Royal Vet College	24
	*Middlesex	
	*Central Lancashire	
	*Napier	
	*Anglia Ruskin	
	*Bristol UWE	
	*Bristol	24
	*Nottingham Trent	
	*Harper Adams	

UNIVERSITY OF ABERDEEN

The University of Aberdeen
Regent Walk
Aberdeen AB24 3FX

TEL   01224 272090/91
FAX   01224 272576
EMAIL sras@abdn.ac.uk
WEB www.abdn.ac.uk

Aberdeen University Students' Association
50-52 College Bounds
Aberdeen AB24 3TU

TEL 01224 272965
FAX 01224 272977
EMAIL [initial.name]@abdn.ac.uk
WEB www.ausa.org.uk

VAG VIEW

*A*berdeen is the oldest university outside Oxbridge, its Chair of Medicine was the first established in the English-speaking world, and King's College Aberdeen was founded in 1495.

As one of four ancient universities in Scotland, the teaching is traditional, seminars, tutorials, etc, and some of the lecture rooms full of traditional character (and draughts). They are adamant that the industrialisation of higher education will not deter their principal aims. 'When we debate higher education, we tend to talk about student employability and how institutions contribute to the economy,' says Principal C Duncan Rice. 'But there is not so much talk about traditional liberal learning and about the role the humanities and social sciences play in society.'

A university a seat of learning, what next? Consistent with this, they are creating a £54-million library, which is due to open in 2011, which they boast will do for Aberdeen what the Guggenheim Museum did for Bilbao. It is one part of a £198 million spend on academic resources in process.

Aberdeen University has a good

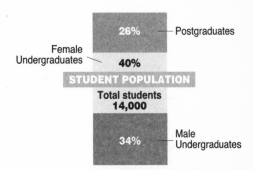

Female Undergraduates — 40%
Postgraduates — 26%
Male Undergraduates — 34%

STUDENT POPULATION
Total students 14,000

reputation without the stigma of being an Oxbridge wannabe, like St Andrews or Edinburgh. It, like the city, prides itself on a lack of pretension, and has had good showings in the university league tables. What that means is up for debate, but there are those who think that it augurs well.

FEES, BURSARIES

Non-Scottish-based UK residents pay £1,700 p.a. for all courses at Scottish universities, except Medicine, for which they will be charged £2,700 p.a. These will rise with inflation. 30 Merit Bursaries available for students resident in the UK with outstanding qualifications, worth £1000 p.a. Last year, there was a 1 in 4 chance of receiving an award. 10 + sports bursaries.

Several awards are made each year to especially talented musicians, including organ, choral and instrumental scholarships. The Elizabeth Wilson Scholarship is in place for Agriculture students resident in the North East of Scotland. The Charles Sutherland Scholarship is set aside for students of Agriculture, Engineering and Economics.

CAMPUS

Aberdeen is on the North East coast of Scotland, pretty much final step on the way to the Arctic (a couple of farms and the odd island notwithstanding). Easily reachable, if you've a bit

UNIVERSITY/STUDENT PROFILE	
University since	**1495**
Situation/style	**Civic**
Student population	**14000**
Undergraduates	**10350**
- mature	**10%**
- non EU undergraduates	**19%**
- male/female	**46:54**
- non-traditional intake	**26%**
- state school intake	**84%**
- drop-out rate	**12%**
- undergraduate applications	**Down1 %**

of time on your hands, Aberdeen provides a safe haven for those trying to get as far away as possible from parents, and the rest of civilisation.

The Granite City, as it is accurately called, harbours a bit of a cosmopolitan atmosphere (there's some docks) and a very long beach. The climate is raw, as are the people, but when the sun shines, everything warms up and it's actually a beautiful city.

The city itself is framed around Union Street, with the main university campus about a mile (and a lung-busting hill) north of the main centre. This is King's College campus, the oldest part of the university, located in the imaginatively entitled Old Aberdeen.

There are other campuses (or should that be campii?), one in town which is not used anymore, except to keep dead bodies for first year medics to play about with, the hospital, where they keep the live bodies for the rest of the medics to play about with, and the Hilton campus for Education, complete with its own halls of residence, established at the end of 2001 after the uni's merger with the Aberdeen arm of the Northern College of Education.

The university loves the fact that King's is around 500 years old and makes a point of telling you this at every opportunity. Look out for marketing-gone-mad photos of King's College all over the shop (the King's College Visitors' Centre Shop, to be precise) and on postcards, T-shirts, mugs, biros, novelty condoms (if only) and other useful items.

STUDENT PROFILE

They have a fair intake of non-traditional applicants. The successful completion of the Summer School for Access guarantees a place on most of the uni's degree courses. Success in this has been achieved without the usual flip side of a high drop-out rate.

Writes Rob Littlejohn, 'The students come in eight distinct groups: **Aberdonians,** who talk smugly about pubs in other parts of town and watch quietly as we get lost; **Country Teuchters** (pronounced '*choochters*' – there you know some

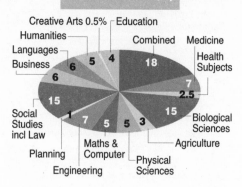

SUBJECT AREAS (%)

Creative Arts 0.5% — Education
Humanities
Languages
Business — 6 5 4 — 18 — Combined — Medicine — Health Subjects
6 — 7
15 — 2.5
Social Studies incl Law — 1 7 5 5 3 — 15 — Biological Sciences
Planning — Maths & Computer — Agriculture
Engineering — Physical Sciences

local dialect already), very similar to Aberdonians, but without the urban sophistication; **Edinburgh Public Schoolers,** a feature of most Scottish unis with better English accents than most of those south of the border and more money than sense; **Other Scots** – Scotland has a greater tradition of staying at home to study and we do get some Edinburghers keen to distance themselves from a public school education, Glaswegians pining for home, sectarianism and annoying accents, and Dundonians just happy to be somewhere else. There's also the **Huge Bands of Others** – Northern Irish, random English, foreign students and Greeks, the final lot warranting their own category for sheer number!'

ACADEMIA & JOBS

89% of Aberdeen's teaching is either Excellent or Highly Satisfactory, and they achieved a whole host of world-class Grade 5* and Grade 5s for research (see *Academic Excellence* box). The French department achieved the only 5* rating for the subject in the UK.

There are three 'Colleges': Arts and Social Sciences; Life Sciences & Medicine; and Physical Sciences.

The uni's reputation lies in its traditional founding disciplines – Medicine, Law, Divinity and Engineering, but they are strong across the board

---

WHERE ABERDEEN GRADUATES END UP

Health & Social Work: 24%; Education: 8%; Wholesale/Retail: 8%; Manufacturing: 4%; Financial Activities: 5%; Public Administration, Civil Service & Defence: 7%; Hotel/Restaurant: 6%; Transport & Communications (including Telecommunications): 2%; Construction:1%; Agriculture: 2%; Mining/Oil Extracting: 9%; Personnel: 0.5%; Computer: 1.5%; Business & Management: 1%; Accountancy: 3%; Media (including Film): 1%; Legal 1%; Architecture: 0.5%; Publishing: 1%; Advertising: 0.5%.

Approximate 'graduate track' employed **70%**

and reach out into the community as surely with their free, annual, 5-day literary event, *Word Festival,* which attracts 10,000 and injets £1.2 million into the local economy, as they do with their community-based clinical research.

Research-wise, there's innovation in the medical sciences in particular. Four Nobel prizes have been awarded for work carried out or begun at the University, including the invention of the life-saver insulin. A key role was played in the invention of Magnetic Resonance Imaging (MRI) and the discovery of enkephalins.

Elsewhere in the sciences, Marine & Coastal Resource Management and Tropical Environmental Science are unique to Aberdeen, while unique in Scotland are Cultural History, Rural Surveying, and Politics & International Relations.

Recently introduced programmes include BMus (Music), a combo of music and education. Chemical Engineering is introduced for the first time in 2007, as is a suite of new degree programmes concerning Global Challenges.

Every student gets their own personal Adviser of Studies to help shape the programme and offer support. The University library, spread over 5 sites, is one of the largest in Scotland, with over one million volumes in stock. They have 1,000+ computers (up-dated on a four-year cycle), many of which are available to students 24/7.

Many graduates go on to research in Medicine and Medical Sciences, Environmental and Life Sciences and Arts and Social Sciences. There are strong relationships with industry as well as with major research centres and international universities.

Other particular employment strengths include education (they major on Primary Teaching) and their wide-ranging cross-faculty combined honours courses yield a large number of jobs in areas such as accountancy-finance, property and agriculture.

Also, numbers of graduates find their way into the property industry through rural surveying and spatial planning degrees. Town & Country Planning earned a 19 point score at the teaching assessments and international Grade 5 for research.

Would-be solicitors should note Aberdeen's speciality in European, particularly Belgian Law. Quite a few graduates find employment in the police force.

Strong relationships with industry, major

ACADEMIC EXCELLENCE	
TEACHING:	
(Rated Excellent, Highly Satis. or 17+ out of 24)	
Economics, Geography, Sociology, Medicine, Cellular & Molecular Biology, Organismal Biology, French Studies.	**Excellent**
Chemistry, Geology, Maths & Statistics, Civil Engineering, Mechanical +Manufacturing Engineering, Theol., Finance & Accounting, History of Art, History, Law, Philosophy, Politics, English, Psychology.	**Highly Satis.**
Euro langs. other than French	**22**
Planning & Landscape	**19**
RESEARCH:	
Top grades 5/5*	
French	**Grade 5***
Community-based Clinical Subjects, Physiology, Biological Sciences, Plant & Soil Science, Pure Maths, Town and Country Planning, Law, Sociology, Theology	**Grade 5**

research centres and other leading international universities help ensure that courses are relevant to the requirements of the modern world and students are taught by lecturers who are leading the field in their area of expertise.

A traditional uni without the stigma of being an Oxbridge wannabe like St Andrews or Edinburgh. Excellent reputation in subjects for the professions - Law, Medicine, etc.

SOCIAL SCENE

September 2006 saw the completion of a huge-scale renovation project to develop and enhance catering and social facilities on campus. **The Hub** offers dining and retail, and drop-in centres, all under the one roof - they call it 'a one-stop shop for all your needs'.

The Students Association funds 100+ clubs and societies, counting sports ranging from football and karate to boxing and underwater hockey, and masses of cultural societies catering for the diversity of the international student body, plus a particularly busy University Music Programme - orchestra, choral society, chapel choir or concert band. The weekly student paper - free and run by students - is *Gaudie.*

Writes a student mole: 'The city boasts a huge variety of venues ranging from trendy clubs to old-

WHAT IT'S REALLY LIKE

UNIVERSITY:

Social Life	★★★★
Campus scene	**Small & friendly**
Student Union services	**Good**
Politics	**Internal**
Sport	**54 clubs**
National team position	**26th**
Sport facilities	**Improving**
Arts opportunities	**Drama, music exc.; film good; dance, art poor**
Student newspaper	**The Gaudie**
Student radio	**Aberdeen Student Radio**
Nightclub	**Chalkies, G-Spot**
Bars	**New student centre**
Union ents	**Guarded promise**
Union societies	**70+**
Most active society	**MedSoc**
Parking	**Adequate**

CITY:

Entertainment	★★★★
Scene	**Intoxicating**
Town/gown relations	**Good**
Risk of violence	**Low**
Cost of living	**Average**
Student concessions	**Average**
Survival + 2 nights out	**£60 pw**
Part-time work campus/town	**Good/excellent**

Union should be, a concoction of cheap drinks, ancient traditions, a cosy environment and right in the city centre. This cosy little bar, although situated off-campus, epitomises the history of the University. Offering all the standard things a union should, (pub quizzes, djís and entertainment) the Union will be the number one venue for the start of a night out.'

SPORT A new £23 million Regional Sports centre is constructed in partnership with the Local Council and Sportscotland and offers a wide range of sporting facilities, including a full size indoor

AT A GLANCE

ACADEMIC FILE:

Subjects assessed	**26**
Excellent/Highly Satisfactory	**89%**
Typical entry requirements	**349 points**
Application acceptance rate	**18%**
Acceptance rate for Medicine	**9%**
Students-staff ratio	**14:1**
First/2:1 degree pass rate	**66%**

ACCOMMODATION FILE:

Guarantee to freshers	**100%**
Style	**Halls, flats**
Catered	**41%**
En suite	**3%**
Approx price range pw	**£55-£108**
City rent pw	**£35-£100**

world pubs full of atmosphere and everything in between. There is an eclectic mix of music for gig-goers, which regularly attracts major tour gigs by the biggest names around; and for committed clubbers there is a whole host of dance floors in and around the city centre, serving up sounds of hip hop, dance, chart classics, indie, rock, latin beats, soul, cheesy pop and lots more.

'Check out these sites for current gig listings: www.gigs.co.uk, www.lemontree.org, www.thetunnels.co.uk

'For those who prefer a quiet drink and good conversation, there is a multitude of different settings, from hip wine bars and jazz clubs to cosy café bars and student hang-outs.

'And let's not forget our own Students' Union, the newest bar in town, which, although situated off-campus, epitomises the history and traditions of the University. Offering all the standard things a union should, (pub quizzes, dj's and endless entertainment) the Union is the number one venue for the start of a night out.

'The newest bar in Aberdeen is everything a

football pitch, indoor and outdoor athletics facilities, squash courts, full size hockey pitch and performance gym.

The new centre is the base for the Sports Union's 54 affiliated clubs and Intra Mural sports programme.

PILLOW TALK
Halls of Residence, either on-campus or nearby, offer traditional single study bedrooms or self-catering flats. These and university-administered property in the city have trained wardens in residence.

GETTING THERE
☞ By road: from south, A92 and ring road where you'll pick up signs; from north, A96 or the A92.
☞ By rail: Edinburgh, 2:30; Dundee, 1:15; Newcastle, 4:50; London King's Cross, 7:00.
☞ By air: Aberdeen International Airport.
☞ By coach: London, 11.30; Birmingham, 12.35.

UNIVERSITY OF ABERTAY DUNDEE

The University of Abertay Dundee
Bell Street
Dundee DD1 1HG

TEL 01382 308080
FAX 01382 308081
EMAIL sro@abertay.ac.uk
WEB www.abertay.ac.uk

Abertay Dundee Students' Association
158 Marketgait
Dundee DD1 1NJ

TEL 01382 308950
FAX 01382 206569
EMAIL enquiries@abertayunion.com
WEB www.abertayunion.com

VAG VIEW

*L*ocated on a modern campus in the city centre, Abertay has four academic schools: School of Computing, the Dundee Business School, School of Science & Engineering and the School of Social & Health Sciences. Formerly, it was the Dundee Institute of Technology.

Among its research centres is the International Centre for Computing and Virtual Entertainment (IC-CAVE). A defining mark is that it was the first university to offer Computer Games Technology as a degree. An Abertay student, David Jones, created Lemmings and Grand Theft Auto.

Now, too, it is a force in sport, and the graduate track employment record is very high. Also, it is beginning to redefine its localised self-image into a more rounded extra-curricular experience for students.

FEES, BURSARIES

Non-Scottish-based UK residents pay £1,700 p.a. Sporting Excellence Fund - £10,000. Centenary Scholarships: £1,000 - students must submit an essay of 1,500 words. Hardship Fund - £99,330, means tested. Mature Student Bursary Fund - £211,870 - targeted at childcare, accommodation and travel costs. The Nine Incorporated Trades of

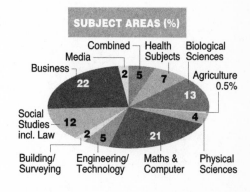

SUBJECT AREAS (%)

Combined Media	2
Business	22
Health Subjects	5
Biological Sciences	7
Agriculture	0.5%
	13
Social Studies incl. Law	12
	2
	4
Building/Surveying	5
Engineering/Technology	21
Maths & Computer	
Physical Sciences	

Dundee: £4,500 to fund 7 scholarships for students in financial need to follow part-time masters courses in business. The Robert Reid Trust: £1,000 for students from poor backgrounds.

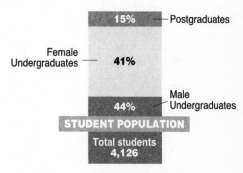

- Postgraduates 15%
- Female Undergraduates 41%
- Male Undergraduates 44%

STUDENT POPULATION
Total students 4,126

STUDENT PROFILE

Abertay accounts for a high local intake and sizeable mature and overseas student populations. The uni gets the largest access partnership grant from the Scottish Funding Council. There's a 37% take from the lowest four socio-economic groups and 25% from 'low-participation neighbourhoods'.

ACADEMIA & JOBS

Sports Trainers and Coaches flow strongest out of Abertay Dundee and Leeds Met. More than 7% of graduates of Abertay are so placed. There's a new sports science laboratory for their BSc Sport

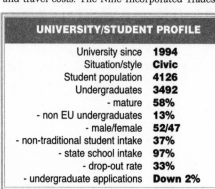

UNIVERSITY/STUDENT PROFILE	
University since	**1994**
Situation/style	**Civic**
Student population	**4126**
Undergraduates	**3492**
- mature	**58%**
- non EU undergraduates	**13%**
- male/female	**52/47**
- non-traditional student intake	**37%**
- state school intake	**97%**
- drop-out rate	**33%**
- undergraduate applications	**Down 2%**

WHERE ABERTAY GRADUATES END UP

Health & Social Work: 13%; Education: 8%; Wholesale/Retail: 15%; Manufacturing: 5%; Financial Activities: 9%; Public Administration, Civil Service & Defence: 12%; Hotel/Restaurant: 3%; Transport & Communications (incl. Telecommunications): 3%; Construction: 4%; Personnel: 1%; Computer: 5%; Business & Management: 1%; Accountancy: 2%; Media (including Film): 1%; Legal 1.5%; Architecture: 1%; Publishing: 0.5%; Sport: 7%.

Approximate 'graduate track' employed **74%**

Coaching & Development and Sport, Health & Exercise. And there's a canny nose for Management Science too.

Computer programmers are rife here. Ethical Hacking & Countermeasures is a world first, also Creative Sound Production, Mobile Entertainment, and Smart Systems - all new degrees. Their courses in computer arts and computer games technology were the first and they have 2 of only 4 in the UK to be formally accredited by the sector skills council for the creative industries, which supports 600,000 jobs across Britain and contributes more than £20 billion to the UK economy. There are good resources, including a computer arts design studio, an £8-million library, fully networked for the digital age, and over 1,200 personal computers available.

Nurses (SEN, SRN, RGN, etc) pour out of Abertay in similar quantity. New teaching and research facilities in the School of Social & Health Science were officially opened last year.

Consider, too, their BSc Forensic Sciences degree and BSc Forensic Psychobiology. Bestselling crime writer Ian Rankin opened a gruesome scene-of-the-crime-house here, and employment figures show that the department is highly productive.

Abertay is Scotland's top university for environmental research according to the national research assessment exercise. The Abertay Centre for the Environment, a £4 million research and knowledge transfer centre part-funded by the European Union, designed to provide small and medium-sized companies in Eastern Scotland with expert help in devising more environmentally-friendly products, services and processes.

There's a good reputation, too, for placing graduates from their BSc Civil Engineering and Dip HE Civil Engineering Studies, and although there's no dedicated BSc degrees in Quantity Surveying there's a strong current of graduates finding employment in this area, too. Also notable vis a vis graduate employment, Abertay founded Embreonix, Scotland's first graduate enterprise centre dedicated to helping students set up their own business

ACADEMIC EXCELLENCE

TEACHING:

Economics.	**Excellent**
Chemistry, Maths &	**Highly Satis.**
Statistics, Mechanical +	
Manufacturing Engineering,	
Civil Engineering, Cellular &	
Molecular Biology, Psychology.	

RESEARCH EXCELLENCE:
Top grades 5/5* **None**

AT A GLANCE

ACADEMIC FILE:

Subjects assessed	**14**
Excellent/Highly Satisfactory	**50%**
Typical entry requirements	**226 points**
Application acceptance rate	**23%**
Students-staff ratio	**21:1**
First/2:1 degree pass rate	**53%**

ACCOMMODATION GUARANTEE:

Freshers	**100%**
Style	**Halls, flats**
En-suite	**20%**
Price range pw	**£44.50-£74**
City rent pw	**£40-£80**

In the business sector, watch out for new BA (Hons) degrees scheduled for launch (subject to approval) September 2007: Management Studies (completely revised degree), Human Resource Management, International Management, Operations Management, Services Management, and Corporate Communications.

Finally, Abertay are European LLB Specialists.

SOCIAL SCENE

STUDENTS' ASSOCIATION As a result of the local intake, weekends didn't used to figure much in the Students' Association ents calendar, and the extra-curricular life was fairly lame. But now they have a £6 million Student Centre, which opened its doors to students for the first time in Spring 2005, and was opened again, officially, in October by

UNIVERSITY:	
Social Life	★★★
Campus scene	**Local, friendly**
Student Union services	**Developing**
Politics	**Activity low**
Sport	**25 clubs**
National teamposition	**94th**
Sport facilities	**Building fast**
Arts	**Dance, music, film average; art, drama poor**
Student magazine	**None**
Nightclub	**Basement**
Bars	**Lounge/Bistro, Sports Bar, Rooftop garden**
Union ents	**Wednesdays, Playground; Fridays, Slinky**
Union societies	**35**
Most popular society	**Role-Playing**
Parking	**Adequate**
CITY:	
Entertainment	★★★★
Scene	**Pubs, good live**
Town/gown relations	**Average**
Risk of violence	**Low**
Cost of living	**Average**
Student concessions	**Good**
Survival + 2 nights out	**£60 pw**
Part-time work campus/town	**Excellent/average**

Good variety of sports/pursuits available at the recreational level, with intra-mural activities, club sports and institutional competitions available to the progressively more serious competitor.. Besides their own gym facilities and £500,000 sports science laboratory (one of the best medicine facilities in the country), students must make do with free access to local facilities, walking distance or under 10 minutes by bus. These include Astroturf pitches and good swimming pools as well as the Caird Park Athletics Stadium, an International Sports Complex, and the Olympia, Lynch, Lochee and Douglas Sports Centres. Thera are also two premier league football clubs, the Scottish National Golf Centre, and championship courses at St Andrew and Carnoustie all within minutes of Dundee plus, in the nearby mountains, the Glenshee Ski Slopes.

With the success of their coaching degree and now the uni teams, there is an awareness of sport which will attract big investment in the future.

TOWN Pubs are the focus and the cost of living is low compared to Aberdeen, Glasgow and Edinburgh. See *Dundee Uni* entry.

PILLOW TALK

All freshers who return their accommodation application forms by September 1 in their year of entry are guaranteed places in self-catering halls/flats/houses, some of which are en suite.

Currently planning the construction of a 500-bed-space student village, provisionally scheduled for completion in time for the 2007/08 academic year.

GETTING THERE

☞ By road: M90, M85, A85, A972.
☞ By rail: Newcastle, 3:00; London Euston, 6:00.
☞ By air: Dundee Airport for internal flights; Edinburgh International Airport is an hour away.
☞ By coach: London, 10:05; Birmingham, 10:05; Newcastle, 6:05

Midge Ure. It includes bars, a bistro, shop, nightclub, theatre and exhibition space, as well as offices for the Students' Association and Welfare.

Daytime obsessions are satisfied this year by 35 clubs and societies, mainly sport.

SPORT Underway is an Elite Athletes Development Programme, which supports staff and students competing at national and international level.

UNIVERSITY OF WALES, ABERYSTWYTH

The University of Wales, Aberystwyth
Old College
King Street
Aberystwyth
Ceredigion SY23 2AX

TEL 01970 622021
FAX 01970 627410
EMAIL university-admissions@aber.ac.uk
WEB www.aber.ac.uk

Aberystwyth Guild of Students
The Union,
Penglais,
Aberystwyth
Ceredigion SY23 3DX

TEL 01970 621700
FAX 01970 621701
EMAIL sss@aber.ac.uk
WEB www.union.aber.ac.uk

VAG VIEW

*A*ber's location makes it a top choice for many applicants, while others might find this small seaside town limiting. Its academic strengths are in niche areas and will again appeal to some and not others: countryside management, tourism, international politics, Welsh/Celtic studies, Irish, geography and earth sciences, equine science, marine & freshwater biology, information & library studies, theatre, film and TV (there's a £3.5-million centre for these).

The uni certainly has its specialisms, its very Welshness can seem daunting to some, but it isn't long before you realise that what makes Aber a good bet is the way it delivers every aspect of student services right through academia and into the social side of the Students' Guild, whatever your expectations.

Yet applications are down, and there is no doubt that you are cut off from the main swell of things here. Also there is a poor staff-to-student ratio of almost 21:1, and a low 'graduate track' employment record of apparently only 50%.

> *The statistics speak for themselves – a high intake of students for whose families 'going to university' is not traditional, and a lowish drop-out rate, which indicates that once here, they want to stay. But applications are down again this year.*

FEES, BURSARIES

UK & EU Fees for 2007, £3,000. Welsh entrants are eligible for a grant of £1,800. Entrance scholarships worth up to £3,600 are available for all subjects, plus bursaries worth £2,000 for selected subjects. Also other awards are available for sporty, disabled, ethnic and musical applicants, and there are special bursaries of up to £2,000 for students from low income families.

CAMPUS

'Think Wales; think west; think coast,' write Pete Liggins and Kate Glanville. 'It is then slap bang in the middle, a lovely seaside town whose two main industries are tourists in the summer and students in the closed season.'

Most of the university, including the main Students' Guild building, is contained within the Penglais campus, set on a hill above beautiful Cardigan Bay. But there is another campus at Llanbadarn, less than a mile away and home to the Department of Information and Library Studies, the College of Further Education and the Institute of Rural Studies (a key element in Aber, they are, relative to size, the second largest graduate provider to land-based industries).

The sites are linked by a common telephone system, and there's a good bus service (if you're too lazy to walk).

STUDENT PROFILE

The student body is diverse. There are plenty of English here, though homage is paid to the Welsh hosts by their own countrymen, and the Students' Guild, or *Yr Undeb* as it translates in Welsh, plays a key role in supporting the native lingo: 'The unwritten rule is that you should accept anyone's right to speak in Welsh and not get paranoid that they are talking about you if you can't understand.'

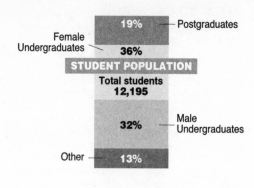

STUDENT POPULATION
Total students 12,195

- Postgraduates 19%
- Female Undergraduates 36%
- Male Undergraduates 32%
- Other 13%

UNIVERSITY/STUDENT PROFILE	
University College since	**1872**
Situation/style	**Campus-by-the-sea**
Student population	**12185**
Undergraduates	**8380**
- mature	**12%**
- non EU undergraduates	**4%**
- male/female	**53/47**
- non-traditional student intake	**28%**
- state school intake	**92%**
- drop-out rate	**11%**
- undergraduate applications	**Down 3%**

ACADEMIA & JOBS

Based at the Llanbadarn campus, less than a mile away from main Penglais, the Agriculture Institute offers the 4-year Agriculture with Animal Science cheap; there's also a 3-year option, Animal Science degree – health, nutrition, physiology, welfare of animals – but more searching at entry Animal degrees share Year One with other agric degrees.

You can also do Agriculture with Business, Marketing, or Equine Studies/Science (there's a fine Equine Centre and a new BSc Equine & Human Sport Science this year). Look, too, at the 4-year Organic Agriculture. Teaching Inspection Satisfactory, Forestry Excellent, but no Grades 5*/5 for research.

A core strength is Countryside Management (see also Agriculture & Countryside Conservation and Sustainable Rural Development). From the

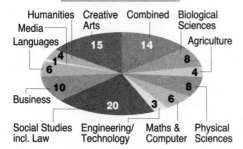

SUBJECT AREAS (%)

Humanities, Media, Languages — 4
Creative Arts — 15
Combined — 14
Biological Sciences
Agriculture — 8
— 4
— 8
— 6
— 3
Business — 6
Social Studies incl. Law — 10
Engineering/Technology — 20
Maths & Computer
Physical Sciences

Institute of Rural Studies come BSc Hons Countryside Conservation/ Management or Rural Resources Mgt (HNDs are also available).

In the Institute of Geography & Earth Sciences, there's Earth Planetary & Space Science, Environmental Earth Science (and with Education), Geography (there's a well-trod pathway for cartographers), and Water Sciences (see also the Marine Biology degrees). They took 'Excellent' in the assessments.

For years Aber has had a sound reputation for research in Politics (Grade 5*/world class), and there's something of a track record for vociferous politicking among the students, albeit quite far

back in the uni's history. There's a new £5 million HQ for the world-renowned Department of International Politics. For graduates today, all this opens up a sound route into the Defence industry. There is an Excellent teaching assessment and top grade for research.

Another strong research area is Drama/Dance/Performing Arts, and this strength also comes out in the uni's employment figures. Arts administrators, managers, and stage managers come out of here in number.

There is a good administrative reputation all round, it seems, with managers and administrators of one sort or another heading Aber's graduate employment list. Would-be museum archivists, curators, librarians should look with respect at their BA Museum & Gallery Studies and BA Information & Library Studies. There is a host of possible combinations. The latter, which asks only 180 points at entry, can be combined with American Studies, Art History, Drama, Fine Art, languages, Film & TV, etc, and their Museum & Gallery Studies joins the same joint honours scheme. The whole mind set in this area also favours research jobs in media and government.

But look, too, at the computer provision – software engineers dominate the employment figures. New courses include Artificial Intelligence and Robotics, Computer Graphics Vision and Games, Mobile and Wearable Computing.

Accountancy & Finance degrees are another strong employment niche. Finally, note, too,

WHERE ABERYSTWYTH GRADUATES END UP

Health & Social Work: 6%; Education: 8%; Wholesale/Retail: 15%; Manufacturing: 7%; Financial Activities: 6%; Public Administration, Civil Service & Defence: 13%; Hotel/Restaurant: 6%; Transport & Communications (including Telecommunications): 5%; Construction:1%; Agriculture: 2%; Personnel: 4%; Computer: 6%; Business & Management: 3%; Accountancy: 4%; Media (including Film): 2%; Legal 2%; Publishing: 2%; Sport: 2%.

Approximate 'graduate track' employed **50%**

WHAT IT'S REALLY LIKE

UNIVERSITY:

Social Life	★★★
Campus scene	**Contained, safe tight-knit & fun**
Student Union services	**Good**
Politics	**Top-up fees, Welsh education**
Sport	**44 clubs**
National team position	**68th**
Sport facilities	**Good**
Arts opportunities	**Good Arts Centre**
Student magazine	**The Courier Yr Utgom**
Student radio	**Bay Radio**
Nightclub	**The Joint**
Bars	**Bar 9, Cwrt Mawr, Outback**
Union ents	**Comedy, cheese, clubnights beach parties**
Union societies	**40**
Parking	**Good**

TOWN:

Entertainment	★★
Scene	**Scenic seaside**
Town/gown relations	**Good**
Risk of violence	**Low**
Cost of living	**Average**
Student concessions	**Poor**
Survival + 2 nights out	**£60 pw**
Part-time work campus/town	**Good**

Aberystwyth's specialist LLB Human Rights and specialist European Law and Business & Commercial Law degrees. In 2005 they introduced a new degree scheme in Criminology and new Legal Practice scheme. Law students can qualify now in Aber without need to proceed to Law College, and the fact that the Law Dept allows non-Law graduates to take a 2-year full-time or 3-year part-time Senior Status law degree.

The university's library has over 700,000 volumes and 4000 current periodicals in stock, as well as CD Roms, networked databases and other electronic sources, and a campus-wide, on-line teaching and learning initiative available to all students.

You will also have access to the National Library of Wales (over six million books, maps and prints).

SOCIAL SCENE

Aberystwyth is a small town but with students making up half the town's population if you are out for the night then you are bound to bump into someone you know or some one you would sooner forget. The best time in Aber is those sun shimmering days when there are half a dozen beach fire parties to chill out at.

STUDENTS' GUILD Llanbadarn has a shop and **Y Gwyllt - The Outback** (bar), entertainment facilities, discos and pool room. Back at base camp, in the Guild building (opened 2001), there's **Bar 9** and a nightclub, the **Joint**. **Cwrt Mawr Bar** is the halls pub on Penglais campus.

Unsurprisingly, this coastal resort is not a draw for big name bands, but 'live' is definitely part of the ents menu, which includes Monday comedy, karaoke; Wednesday night *Reload* and *Clasic hits*; Thursday night *Double Vision* and £1 *party*; Friday night *Flirt* and *Chart*; Saturday has a rolling program: *Beer Keller*, *School night*, and bands e.g. GLC. See www.aberguild.co.uk/ents/

Besides all this there are dance, art and drama workshop spaces, an art cinema, studio theatre and art gallery. Student media is pre-eminent with *The Courier* (*Yr Utgorn* - *www.thecourier.org.uk/*), *Ur Ytgorn* - Welsh language magazine, and Bay Radio. Oh, and the most active student society (one of about 50) is Indie Soc.

Political activity is high compared to many. Active Welsh Language Campaign. International Human rights and Peace and Justice issues are to the fore.

The Guild offers a range of NSLP skills courses, some to help develop skills through running clubs and societies, being a course-rep, getting involved in the student media or community projects. Others are straight 'key skills' courses of the kind that employers like to see developed alongside academic achievement. Doing these add credits and commands cash prizes.

SPORT It's a big thing at Aber, American Football being the current area of excellence. There are fifty acres of pitches and specialist facilities for water sports, including a boat house, an indoor swimming pool, two sports halls, an all-weather floodlit sports pitch, squash courts and indoor facilities for football, badminton, basketball, hockey and tennis. Cardigan Bay and nearby Snowdonia offer windsurfing and skiing opportunities, respectively, and there is orienteering, mountain-biking, rambling, sub-aqua and hang-gliding too.

TOWN On the entertainments front in town, there's a one-screen cinema, where films tend to be shown around two to three weeks after their actual release date. The flick makes up for this by being cheap, friendly and licensed – so you can have a

AT A GLANCE

ACADEMIC FILE:

Subjects assessed	**19**
Excellent	**42%**
Typical entry requirements	**299 points**
Application acceptance rate	**24%**
Student-staff ratio	**21:1**
First/2:1 degree pass rate	**59%**

ACCOMMODATION FILE:

Guarantee to freshers	**100%**
Style	**Halls, flats, houses**
Catered	**25%**
En-suite	**10%**
Price range pw	**£42-£86**
Town rent pw	**£50-£60**

pint while watching the film – and the programme sports some of the cheapest and best local advertising you will ever have the pleasure to view. The cinema's ethos seems to sum up the whole town; everything is more laid back here: the sun shines and things slow down; it's life without the big city stresses.

Aber is also blessed with a number of pubs –

'beyond definition; every taste should be catered for somewhere. There is something of a worrying trend, however, towards refitting and furbishing with an emphasis on American *tack*, for each of these is a true local – one in particular won't serve a pint of Guinness in less than five minutes.'

Safety is not an issue in Aberystwyth.

PILLOW TALK

Accommodation prices range from £42.20 for a twin room space (self-catering) to £86.48 for a single room in a catered residence, whereas in town, it's £50 to £60 per week energy exclusive for a single room (self-catering) with 50% retainer charged during the summer vacation. Plans are afoot for a new residence (self-catered) on the seafront in partnership with a private sector provider; the uni will manage the accommodation. All students' bedrooms are linked to the internet.

GETTING THERE

☞ By road: A484 from north or south; A44 from the east.

☞ By rail: London Euston, 5 hours. Chart your route carefully or you'll end up on a slow local line through the mid-Wales countryside.

☞ By coach: London, 7:00; Newcastle, 11:00

ANGLIA RUSKIN UNIVERSITY

Anglia Ruskin University
East Road
Cambridge CB1 1PT

TEL 0845 271 3333
FAX 01245 251789
EMAIL answers@anglia.ac.uk
WEB www.anglia.ac.uk

Anglia Students' Union
East Road
Cambridge CB1 1PT

TEL 01603 593272
EMAIL [initial.name]@angliastudent.ac.uk
WEB www.apsu.com

VAG VIEW

*T*he university comes out of Cambridgeshire College of Arts and Technology and the Essex Institute of Higher Education, which merged in 1989 to form Anglia Higher Education College. In 1991, this became Anglia Polytechnic, and Anglia Polytechnic University in 1992. Its recent re-naming as Anglia Ruskin University dispenses with its poly status for good.

It was a very swift rise. The student population increased from 7,000 in 1992 to the current level of 30,244, making it one of the fastest growing universities in the UK.

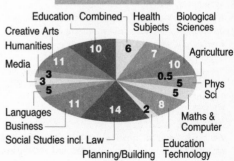

SUBJECT AREAS (%)

Education · Combined · Health Subjects · Biological Sciences · Creative Arts · Humanities · Media · Agriculture · Phys Sci · Maths & Computer · Education Technology · Planning/Building · Social Studies incl. Law · Business · Languages

10 · 6 · 7 · 10 · 11 · 3 · 3 · 5 · 0.5 · 5 · 5 · 11 · 14 · 2 · 8

14% — Postgraduates

Female Undergraduates — 60%

STUDENT POPULATION

Total students 30,244

26% — Male Undergraduates

UNIVERSITY/STUDENT PROFILE	
University since	**1992**
Situation/style	**City/town campuses**
Student population	**30244**
Undergraduates	**22713**
- mature	**74%**
- non EU undergraduates	**9%**
- male/female	**30/70**
- non-traditional student intake	**35%**
- state school intake	**97%**
- drop-out rate	**22%**
- undergraduate applications	**Up 23%**

This year undergraduate applications rose 22.7%. Perhaps this, together with its large non-traditional student intake (35%), very high mature student numbers (74%) and relatively under-developed student culture, accounts for the high drop-out rate with which we associate it.

There is a major policy move to tackle this. Student Support incorporates an email counselling service for students studying at distance from the uni (as many do) with a qualified and experienced counsellor. For others there is a Mentoring scheme for anyone in need of one-to-one support on a regular basis to help them plan their work and to talk about life as a student. For everyone there is a new 'Welcome to Anglia Ruskin' group helping new students to settle. Generally, a Student Adviser team provides a first point of contact, confidential counselling close to where students are studying.

CAMPUSES

Anglia Ruskin is based in Cambridge city centre and in Chelmsford, Essex, home since Spring 2000 to the School of Education and, since September 2002, to the Ashcroft International Business School, part-funded by the entrepreneur Lord Ashcroft KCMG, who was appointed chancellor of the university in November 2001. A new sports hall and student centre was also opened here in September 2004. This and further construction in process at Cambridge is part of a huge project to concentrate and enhance resources at the two campuses, and simplify and rationalise Anglia's once more scattered base.

FEES, BURSARIES

UK & EU Fees for 2007 entry: £3,070 p.a. For 2008 not yet known. Bursary for students in receipt of full HE Maintenance Grant £307 p.a. Full-time undergraduate home and EU students who pay

their fees and stay the course, £2,000 over three years. A similar scheme exists for some students undertaking certain part-time programmes of study. Twelve foundation scholarships up to £750 for students undertaking a study visit outside the UK. Sports scholarships and bursaries to students of high potential range from £500 to £1,000 p.a. in cricket, rowing, athletics and swimming.

STUDENT PROFILE

There's an eclectic mix of arty types, nurses, laddish engineers and teachers. This is a modern university. Many local and mature students come here more for Anglia's tickets into industry than anything else. Many are part-time, sponsored by employers.

Writes Jill Walker. 'We have lots of mature students, who make everyone work harder 'cos they are the only ones to do the reading. Lots of students are local. Cambridge is far more international than Chelmsford.'

ACADEMIA & JOBS

It is vocationally orientated, degrees translate into jobs. Programmes are designed in collaboration with employers in the health sector, in local government, in the legal sector, in engineering, in science-based industries, in the ICT sector, in media. There are work placements available with over 100 companies, and in-company award-bearing courses for such as Marconi, Ford, and Suffolk County Council.

There are eight Schools of study: Arts &Letters, Applied Sciences, Law, Languages and Social Sciences, Ashcroft International Business School, Education, Design and Communication Systems, Healthcare Practice and Community Health and Social Studies.

Training teachers was and is one of Anglia's core commitments, but health is now just as much a defining strength. Look closely at their Pharmacy,

WHERE ANGLIA GRADUATES END UP

Health & Social Work: 15%; Education: 15%; Wholesale/Retail: 16%; Manufacturing: 8%; Financial Activities: 6%; Public Administration, Civil Service & Defence: 7%; Hotel/Restaurant: 6%; Transport & Communications (including Telecommunications): 4%; Construction:1%; Personnel: 3%; Computer: 3%; Business & Management: 3%; Accountancy: 2%; Legal 2%; Architecture: 1%; Publishing: 2%; Artistic/Literary: 1%; Sport: 1%.

Approximate 'graduate track' employed **62%**

ACADEMIC EXCELLENCE

TEACHING:
(Rated Excellent or 17+ out of 24)

Social Work, Music, English.	**Excellent**
Philosophy	**24**
Nursing, Theology	**23**
Psychology	**22**
Modern Languages, Molecular & Organismal Biosciences, Art & Design	**21**
Sociology, Building & Civil Eng, Politics, Health, Management/ Business/Accounting	**20**
Land/Property Mgt, Town/ Country Planning, Electron & Electrical Eng, Mechanical/ Aeronautical & Manuf Eng, Education	**19**
Communication/Media Studies, Tourism/Hospitality Mgt, History of Art	**18**

RESEARCH:
Top grades 5/5*

English Language & Literature	**Grade 5**

nation's leaders in this area, and this years there is a new BSc (Hons) Information Security and Forensic Computing.

More traditional is their reputation for art and design. They offer Illustration as an integral part of the graphics course. A new Fine Art course was launched in 2004.

Look, also, at their large programme of drama degrees, which sets the scene at the **Mumford Theatre** on Cambridge Campus, and at a range of new degrees in the area of performing arts launched in 2004.

Would-be sound recordists should be aware of the HND and BSc Audio & Music Technology. There's also much activity in media, with a clutch of new degrees mooted, including Journalism.. Media production, and Publishing. Look too at the Music Technology degrees. This is a productive employment niche area for the uni.

Another significant graduate employment area is opened up by the Sports Science degree (a Coaching Science degree is also planned), which

AT A GLANCE

ACADEMIC FILE:

Subjects assessed	**33**
Excellent	**73%**
Typical entry requirements	**233 points**
Application acceptance rate	**23%**
Students-staff ratio	**20:1**
First/2:1 degree pass rate	**56%**

ACCOMMODATION FILE:

Placement of freshers	**Chelms. 100%, Camb. 95%**
Style	**Houses, flats, halls**
Catered	**None**
En-suite	**Chelms. 95% Camb. 50%**
Price range pw	**Chelms. £55-£90; Camb. £60-£95**
City rent pw	**Chelms. £55-£90; Camb. £60-£95**

Genetics, Health & Social Care degrees.

In nursing, Anglia offers Adult, Child, Learning Disabilities and Mental Health degrees, and BSc Midwifery, which dropped only one point at the assessments and has a low entry requirement

Again, Anglia is one of very few universities to offer optometry and ophthalmic .dispensing. They are also a big player in natural health therapy - acupuncture, reflexology and aromatherapy. Interesting, too, is Anglia's Vet Nursing degree at the College of West Anglia.

In business there's a new BA (Hons) Management and Leadership (work-based). In law, there are a number of new courses awaiting approval, including a solicitors exempting degree.

21% of graduates who go into the police force come via Social Studies departments (which include Criminology degrees as well as Law and Psychosocial Studies). Meanwhile there are four Forensic Science degrees. Anglia is one of the has links with the English Cricket Board's local Centre of Excellence. Anglia is among the Top 10 producers of physical training instructors in Education.

SOCIAL SCENE

STUDENTS' UNION Cambridge campus: new Helmore Building, complete with new Student Union office, music, arts and language laboratory facilities, new bar (**Kudos**) and nightclub/venue (**Academy**). Chelmsford: New Tindal building with Student Union office and new bar/venue (**Kudos**) and restaurant.

Ents - Cambridge: *'Touch'* club night on a Friday (cheesy tunes/disco); on Wednesday the union becomes pre-club venue for night out in the city's **Twenty Two - The Nightclub**; then there are open mic nights/comedy on a Tuesday. Sunday night has a quiz. They also showcase up and coming bands.

Chelmsford: *Spanked* on Tuesdays - fun and games; *Funkin' Marvellous* - Friday Night clubnight; *Rock It* - rock night on a Saturday.

SPORT There are tennis courts and a multigym on the Cambridge campus, and 100 metres away the Kelsey Kerridge Sports Centre with gym and nearby swimming pool. Half a mile north of the campus there are three football pitches, a rugby pitch and a cricket square. Ex-England Cricketers Mike Gatting and Peter Such helped to launch Anglia's new sports scholarships and bursaries. Rowing crews rack their eights at Cambridge Uni's Emmanuel College Boat House. At Chelmsford Campus, there's a new sports centre.

PILLOW TALK

No official guarantee, but in reality they can accommodate 100% freshers at Chelmsford and 95% at Cambridge. At Chelmsford there's a student village with en-suite rooms in flats of 3-6. At Cambridge there are en-suite and older style halls, along with uni-owned and leased houses. See *At A Glance* box for prices. New accommodation was opened at Sedley Court, in Cambridge, in September 2005 (150 en-suite rooms).

WHAT IT'S REALLY LIKE

UNIVERSITY:	
Social Life	★★★
Campus scene:	**Diverse**
Student Union services	**Improving**
Politics	**Cambridge: interest high; Chelmsford low**
Most popular societies	**Camb: RAG; Chelm: Mission Croatia**
Sport	**55 clubs**
National team position	**119th**
Sport facilities	**Adequate**
Arts opportunities	**Drama, music exc; dance good; film, art average**
Student newspaper	**The Apex**
Bars	**Kudos**
Union ents	**New nightclubs + tie-up with town**
Union societies	**32**
Parking	**Poor. Student issue at Chelmsford**

GETTING THERE - Cambridge

☛ By road (from London): M25/J27, M11/J11, A10. From west or east: A45. From northwest: A604. From Stansted Airport: M11.

☛ By train: London's Liverpool Street, under the hour; Nottingham, 2:30; Sheffield, Birmingham New Street, 3:00.

☛ By coach: London, 1:50; Birmingham, 2:45; Leeds, 5:00; Bristol, 5:30.

GETTING THERE - Chelmsford

☛ By road: A12, A130 or A414.

☛ By rail: London Liverpool Street, 35 mins.

☛ By air: 10 miles from the M25 and access to Stansted Airport and Heathrow.

☛ By coach: London, 1:40; Norwich, 5:00.

ASTON UNIVERSITY, BIRMINGHAM

Aston University, Birmingham
Aston Triangle
Birmingham B4 7ET

TEL 0121 359 6313
FAX 0121 333 6350
EMAIL j.r.seymour@aston.ac.uk
WEB www.aston.ac.uk

Aston Students' Guild
The Triangle
Birmingham B4 7ES

TEL 0121 204 4855
FAX 0121 333 4218
EMAIL president@aston.ac.uk
WEB www.astonguild.org.uk

VAG VIEW

*A*ston University, Birmingham, is a small
university, independent, and slap bang
in the eye of the urban vortex, yet sheltered
from any of the city's urban excesses in an
attractive, green-field campus bowl – a crisp
and tasty morsel in Birmingham's tangled
spaghetti junction. As a student said, looking
out, 'The dual carriageway acts as a kind of
natural barrier. You go under the flyover and
suddenly, wow! It's Birmingham.'

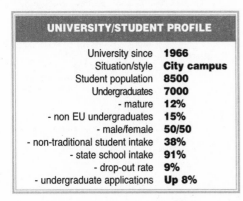

UNIVERSITY/STUDENT PROFILE	
University since	**1966**
Situation/style	**City campus**
Student population	**8500**
Undergraduates	**7000**
- mature	**12%**
- non EU undergraduates	**15%**
- male/female	**50/50**
- non-traditional student intake	**38%**
- state school intake	**91%**
- drop-out rate	**9%**
- undergraduate applications	**Up 8%**

Aston stands for science, engineering and
business, the strength of particular areas of
science highlighted by teaching assessments
– Pharmacy (full marks), Biological Sciences
and Optometry (23/24), and the teaching of
the BSc Human Psychology courses scored
22/24 ahead of the uni's traditionally strong
engineering departments (19, 20 and 21).
Then all its business and management
courses scored full marks – 24/24, and you
see why they say the Business School is one
of the best in Europe.

Aston is heavy on workload, extremely well
resourced and geared to top-class employment
by means of industry contact, study-abroad
programmes, language combinations (the QAA
rate German and French at 22/24) and
sandwich courses. Most Aston undergraduates
are on sandwich courses, and one advantage of
coming here is that your friends, like you, are
up for four years. Successful applicants score
around 320 points at A level. They take 38%
from families new to higher education, and
maintain a year-in-year-out, Top Ten record in
'graduate-track' employment.

FEES, BURSARIES

UK & EU Fees, 2007: £3,070 fee; for placement
year, £1,535. For 2008, + inflation rate. Bursary for
students in receipt of full HE Maintenance Grant is
£750 per year for students receiving full
maintenance grant, but on sliding scale - visit
www.aston.ac.uk/fees. Placement awards of £1,000
for all students on placement year. Additional £500
for all students on year abroad or unpaid
placements. 70% of students at Aston take
placement years, 10% abroad, and 95% paid,
average salary £14,000. Sports scholarships worth
£500 p.a. are available.

CAMPUS

Aston is very defined, very straightforward, very
scientific. You get what you see at The Triangle.
The clean lines of this modern, high-rise, plate-
glass, green-field Birmingham city campus
(complete with artificial lake) brook no idle intent.
And the no-nonsense efficiency far from cripples
any desire for after-work pleasure, either at the
Students' Guild or a walk away in the centre of
Brum itself. Do not, however, be over-sensitive to
the attentions that will be heaped upon you the
moment you walk through the doors, for this is a
determinedly close-knit community.

STUDENT PROFILE

You pick up serious suits in the business section,

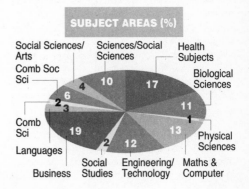

AT A GLANCE	
ACADEMIC FILE:	
Subjects assessed	**17**
Excellent	**71%**
Typical entry requirements	**328 points**
Application acceptance rate	**14%**
Students-staff ratio	**15:1**
First/2:1 degree pass rate	**69%**
ACCOMMODATION FILE:	
Guarantee to freshers	**100%**
Style	**Flats**
En-suite	**35%**
Price range pw	**£62-£96**
City rent pw	**£45-£90**

earnest, professional techies behind the superb lighting and sound systems in the **Guild Hall**, as they prepare for some serious Aston student live music evening (they know how to put a party together: Fusion – dance music – is the most popular society), and then there's the fresh-faced authenticity that binds it all together. Aston is the only university where someone like me will be met by union and university executives around the same table. There are no divides and there is an exuberance about their open, genuinely caring attitude, which some might find intrusive or a contra-current to the existential flow of undergraduate life, but it is in fact quite disarming. See what you think, sign up for Open Day.

Each year 150 volunteers elect to become Aston aunties and welcome freshers, on the basis that Auntie knows best. Every year they have different slogans, like 'We are family!' or 'The cream of Brum.'

For Fresher's Week they do city tours, campus tours, supermarket trips (?!), cultural crawls, canal cruises, fun things like go-karting and paintballing, an Alton Towers trip, and the departments all have other things organised, library visits and so on.

'We've all been out manning the car parks in the pouring rain, and the arrivals this year have been fantastic. I have been watching with admiration this year, as aunties go up to cars with a "Welcome, my name's so-and-so, I'm an auntie!" That's your first impression of Aston. We had a classic quote yesterday from a student whose parents had just left: "Oh, I haven't even been here for twelve hours yet and I feel at home already!"'

If any other union bod had said this I wouldn't have believed it. It's the sort of unlikely... but at Aston what you see really *is* what you get. You can thrust, you can parry, but 'you won't hear a thing against Aston from us,' admitted one of the Guild

sabbaticals. The attitude ensures one of the friendliest student environments in the UK.

ACADEMIA & JOBS

Broadly, Aston consists of three faculties: Life & Health Sciences; Engineering & Applied Science (Civil Engineering, Chemical Eng. and Applied Chemistry, Mechanical & Electrical Eng., Electronic and Applied Physics, Computer Science and Applied Maths); and Management Languages & European Studies. The latter includes the Aston Business School and School of Languages and European Studies. Note that Spanish is now offered in addition to French and German, and English Language is now also an option.

There are very good degrees dedicated to Optometry, the science of testing eyesight and prescribing corrective lenses. Nationally, more than 450 graduates become opticians each year. The leader in the field is Aston with around 27% of the graduate market. If you have your eyes tested in England there's a good chance that it will be an Aston graduate doing it. Teaching inspection 23. Grade 5 for research, that's international standing. See also the NHS-funded, 4-year professional health care degree in Audiology.

Aston also shines jobs-wise in the Pharmacy department, turning around 12% of its graduates into fully fledged pharmacists. The MPharm will take 5 not the usual 4 years if you elect to come in on a Foundation course rather than make the 300-point requirement at A level. They got full marks in the teaching assessments, one better than The School of Pharmacy in London.

Psychologists are another breed made by Aston better than by most. The programmes are various: BSc Human Psychology has a 4-year sandwich version and a Foundation course 'Year Zero' option. Look, too at Psychology with Management.

The Business School is one of the largest in Europe and one of only a handful in the world to have triple accreditation from the major European (EQUIS), American (AACSB) and MBA benchmarks of quality for business education. Related courses tackle the behavioural side of enterprise, such as Organisational Studies, Human Psychology and Psychology with Management. See also the new qualifying Law with Management Programme this year.

The Aston Business School is a vital part of what this uni is all about. There's a Grade 5 for research and full marks (24 points) at assessment. Note the 4-year sandwich BSc International Business & Economics (could add on French, Spanish or German), the International Business & Management degree, which offers the possibility of placement across the world. Look too at the 5-year

ACADEMIC EXCELLENCE

TEACHING:
(Rated Excellent or 17+ out of 24)

Pharmacy, Businesss & Management	**24**
Biological Biosciences, Optometry	**23**
German, French, Psychology	**22**
Electronic Engineering	**21**
Civil Engineering	**20**
Chemical Eng, Maths	**19**

RESEARCH:
Top grades 5/5*

Optometry, General Engineering, Business & Management, European Studies	**Grade 5**

WHAT IT'S REALLY LIKE

UNIVERSITY:

Social Life	★★★★
Campus scene	**Lively, caring suits & techies**
Student Union services	**Good**
Politics	**Interest low**
Sport	**35 clubs**
National team position	**99th**
Sport facilities	**40 clubs**
Arts opportunities	**Dance, music excellent; drama good**
Student newspaper	**The Aston Times**
Student magazine	**Wotsup?**
Nightclub	**Guild Hall**
Bars	**Einstein's, The Blue Room**
Union ents	**Twice weekly**
Union societies	**30**
Most popular societiy	**Fusion (dance music), Islamic**
Parking	**No**

CITY:

Entertainment	★★★★★
Scene	**Excellent**
Town/gown relations	**Average**
Risk of violence	**Average**
Cost of living	**High**
Student concessions	**Excellent**
Survival + 2 nights out	**£120 pw**
Part-time work campus/town	**Good/Excellent**

sandwich Int. Foundation in Business/Business BScs. There are also Business Computing options, and a whole raft of Business Administration combinations, with European Studies for instance.

Around 5% of Aston's graduates are among the 4,500-odd graduates going into Banking each year, and the uni figures impressively in management consultancy, too. Another 5% + go into the Transport business. Three BSc degrees are relevant here: Transport Management, Transport Planning, Transport & Environmental Planning.

Aston's Business School also dominate graduate employment in the areas of marketing and market research. The BSc Marketing (300 points), which comes also in a Joint Hons programme with Languages and Biochemistry – nice niche area).

And a word in favour of their electronic engineering and computer provision. For would-be software engineers on the smaller-uni ticket there are three key unis, Essex, UMIST/Manch., Aston.

Note that over 250 companies and organizations target Aston graduates each year, major companies making more than 100 annual visits to campus to promote themselves and recruit.

SOCIAL SCENE

STUDENTS' GUILD The Guild, which now has wireless internet throughout, offers the Loft and 3 venues. **The Loft** is a brand new social study area on the second floor. **Einstein's** is a community-style pub on the lower ground floor, featuring Karaoke and pub quizzes, and with big

> *Aston is mainly for science, engineering and business. It is very defined, very straightforward, very scientific. You get what you see at The Triangle, and students do seem to enjoy themselves.*

screen and two man-size pool tables. Then there's the recently refurbished **Blue Room** (a café by day), and the **Guild Hall**, which, together with the Blue Room, gives a max building capacity of 1150 for larger evening events

There are currently twice weekly events, featuring low priced drinks and national acts. They also feature fortnightly lunchtime acoustic sessions. And ents is not the only extra-curricular focus. There are masses of sports clubs and societies on offer. Media-wise there's the student magazine, *Wotsup?*, a newspaper called *Aston Times*, and there was a Radio Society which, for whatever reason, disbanded. 'We are a small uni and the same people are involved in putting on events and entertainments were doing the radio or TV. The Drama Club is very active.'

SPORT New University sports facilities include £300,000 all-weather floodlit pitch (off campus) and extension to Fitness Centre. On campus there are two sports centres – Woodcock (with swimming pool) and Gem Sports Hall (with a synthetic floodlit pitch), while out of the city the Recreation Centre spans 95 acres. There is slim evidence of national standards, it is sport for everyone; 'relaxed' is the word used, although the options are varied enough to include American Football, korfball and a variety of other alternative sports.

TOWN See, page 70, below: *Student Birmingham* .

PILLOW TALK
Self catering flats and houses, all on campus, all within 2 mins walk of each other and 5 mins walk from all other campus facilities. Flats vary in size from 4-12 students sharing. Freshers tend to be in larger flats. Convenient, friendly, safe. Internet access in all accommodation. All prices include bills. Telephones in all flats.

They guarantee to find all freshers flats who hold Aston as CF/UF choice and apply for accommodation before the end of July. No guarantee for clearing and Insurance students. Though none is officially catered, arrangements may be made to purchase meals on a termly basis (c. £280 per term for 2 meals a day). While weekly rent ranges from £62-£96, 70% of rooms cost £62. City rents are £45-£90, where the more expensive rooms tend to be private apartment developments with en-suite, 5 mins walk from campus or studios in the city centre. Plans are on the table for a multi-million pound, on-campus student village, to house 3,000 and be available from 2008.

GETTING THERE
☛ By road: M6/J6, A38M 3rd exit, then first exit at Lancaster Circus roundabout.
☛ By rail: Bristol Parkway, Sheffield, 1:30; London Euston, 1:40; Liverpool, Manchester, 2:00; Leeds, 3:00. New Street 12 mins' walk from campus.
☛ By air: Birmingham International Airport.
☛ By coach: London, 2:40; Bristol, 2:00.

UNIVERSITY OF WALES, BANGOR

University of Wales, Bangor
Gwynedd LL57 2DG

TEL 01248 382017
FAX 01248 370451
EMAIL admissions@bangor.ac.uk
WEB www.bangor.ac.uk

Bangor Students' Union
Gwynedd LL57 2TH

TEL 01248 388031
FAX 01248 388020
EMAIL undeb@undeb.bangor.ac.uk
WEB www.undeb.bangor.ac.uk

VAG VIEW

*B*angor started life on 18 October, 1884, in an old coaching inn – a promising beginning, particularly as half the student intake was female, which was swimming against the tide in 1884.

Today it is almost two-thirds female and, while not overly demanding at entry, has risen to be one of the best unis in the UK, with rigorous standards of teaching and applications up again (8%) this year.

FEES, BURSARIES
Welsh residents will pay up to up to £3,000 p.a. , but be entitled to a grant of £1,800, never to be repaid. Other UK residents will be charged deferred fees of £3,000 p.a. Bangor offer sport and academic

scholarships, most around £500 p.a. See www.bangor.ac.uk for more details. Over £2.5M worth of new bursaries and scholarships are available for those starting at Bangor in 2008.

CAMPUS

Setting the whole deal in context for the semi-final of University Challenge, Jeremy Paxman described the natural environs of Bangor – just across the Menai Strait from the Isle of Anglesey – as 'one of the most beautiful locations of any British university, between the beaches of Anglesey and the mountains of Snowdonia.'

North Wales is different from the rest of Wales: they're the real Welsh up here and Welsh is still the natural language over much of Gwynedd. It is a small, town-size 'city' community that manages not to protest at the regular incursion of a student population which more than doubles the local population at the start of each term. While not exactly a campus university, all the buildings, with the exception of the School of Ocean Sciences, which is a few miles from the Menai Bridge, are within walking distance of one another.

It is also cheap and safe.

STUDENT PROFILE

This is a large Welsh population, largely female, and a sizeable mature population. They have a vibrant volunteer community and one of the UK's longest established peer guide/'student mentoring' programme, ensuring a fine welcome and continuing student care.

Cutting-edge cool it is not. However, if you come to Bangor, you'll be sporty, interested in outward bound perhaps, maybe a classical music lover (there is an international reputation for music here). For, as one student put it, 'you'll probably find more night life in a tramp's vest.'

There's a healthy overseas contingent, too, and the uni goes out of its way to help them settle. The International Welfare Unit assists and advises, and orientation days are arranged to help international students get acclimatised to the country. The ELCOS (English Language Courses for Overseas Students) Unit provides instruction for those whose language skills need polishing. There's also an organisation (called 'Shekina') which offers help to wives and husbands of students and organises a range of activities, including English language courses.

For all freshers, Bangor has one of the largest welcoming schemes of any university, with second and third year students involved in a mentoring scheme to help new students settle in during their first weeks at University.

STUDENT POPULATION
Total students 12,397

- Postgraduates 17%
- Female Undergraduates 27%
- Male Undergraduates 40%
- Others 16%

ACADEMIA & JOBS

First, note the very high level of inspection results and research garlands in our *Academic Excellence* box, below It stands to reason that all those subjects are worth studying here.

A large number of graduates become primary school teachers (contributing, as the nursing degrees do, to the 64% female student population), a vital percentage of the overall graduate output destined for Education, which amount to about a quarter of total output and also includes secondary teachers and higher education lecturers.

Around 40% of undergraduates study Science, and many of these biological sciences. Biological Science courses range through Biology, Biomedical and Biomolecular Sciences, a series of Marine and Ocean Sciences (note the popular joint honours option of Marine Biology and Zoology, and unusual courses such as Marine Chemistry). New is a BSc Chemistry with Biomolecular Sciences.

There is a £3.5-million cancer research centre at the University, where The North West Cancer Research Fund Institute at the University's School of Biological Sciences conducts fundamental research into the causes of cancer.

Then come the Zoology degrees, one with Conservation; also Marine Zoology; and a BSc Marine Vertebrate Zoology is currently up for approval).

UNIVERSITY/STUDENT PROFILE	
University College since	**1884**
Situation/style	**Rural bliss**
Student population	**12397**
Undergraduates	**8370**
- mature	**28%**
- non EU undergraduates	**5%**
- male/female	**36/64**
- non-traditional student intake	**30%**
- state school intake	**95%**
- drop-out rate	**17%**
- undergraduate applications	**Up 8%**

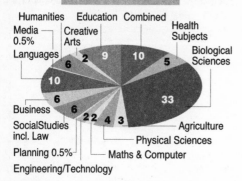

SUBJECT AREAS (%)

Humanities · Education · Combined
Media 0.5% · Creative Arts · Health Subjects
Languages · Biological Sciences
Business
SocialStudies incl. Law
Planning 0.5%
Engineering/Technology
Agriculture
Physical Sciences
Maths & Computer

German, Italian, Spanish and Welsh., and combinations with Media Studies and Entertainment Industries are mooted for 2008.

A new £10 million Business and Management Centre houses Bangor's School for Business and Regional Development, equipped with state-of-the-art facilities for over 500 students.

There's also a reputation for training museum archivists, curators, librarians. They come from across the board – humanities, languages, biological sciences and Law. There's also a preponderance of translators sufficient to put the Language Department among the Top 10 nationally. Note the new BA Music and modern language speciality.

Unique is the three languages degree (choose from combinations of French, German, Italian, and Spanish, which may be studied as 3 majors or 2 majors and a minor). Their Multi-Media Language Centre is a pioneer of digital language-laboratory technology. True to the uni's roots in North Wales,

And the BSc Psychology degrees (with such as Computing, Sport Science – rated 2nd in the UK, Neuropsychology, Clinical and Child Language elements). They have a world-class Grade 5* research rating for Psychology.

All of which produces a wide range of graduate employment, from lecturers to laboratory technicians, biologists to clinical and educational psychologists, chemists to animal health nurses and RSPCA inspectors, market research and business analysts to army officers, and physical training instructors to zoologists. Bangor are graduate employment leaders in zoology.

The uni is also successful in finding graduates employment in the areas of community and youth work and social work. Look at the BA Health and Social Care degrees, BA Psychology (also with Community Development) and Sociology. Also, Bangor is a big producer of hospital staff nurses (SEN) and, through the BSc Diagnostic Radiography and Imaging, medical radiographers.

Another defining element is the Agriculture & Forestry Department, rated international Grade 5 for research. Although forestry is fairly limited employment-wise, Bangor is the most productive nationally. They have some interesting specialities, including Conservation & Forest Ecosystems. There's an 'Excellent' for teaching and an international Grade 5 for research.

Environmental degrees (Chemistry, Conservation, Forensics, Science: the uni is ideally situated for the study of all things environmental, and there is a new £5 million building dedicated to that) draw the picture ever more clearly, and environmental officers are a definitive part of Bangor's graduate employment profile.

The development in 2004 of Law combination degrees - with Accounting & Finance, Business Studies, Criminal Justice, and Law with Social Policy and a unique Law with Environmental Conservation - continued recently with French,

ACADEMIC EXCELLENCE

TEACHING:
Chemistry, Welsh, Music, **Excellent**
Ocean Sciences, Theology,
Psychology, Forest
Sciences, Biological Sciences.

RESEARCH:
Top grades 5/5*
Psychology, Welsh **Grade 5***
Agric & Forest Sciences, **Grade 5**
Accountancy & Finance,
Sport/Health/Exercise Sciences,
Music

they offer degrees in a number of subjects through the medium of Welsh, as well as informal tuition in Welsh in various subjects. Naturally, too, they scored a Grade 5* for research into the mother tongue.

Up for approval for 2008 are language combinations with Journalism and Media Studies. Indeed, media is an area Bangor would like to expand into, and there are a number of joint honours degrees shortly to become available.

A notable feature of the provision is for students with disabilities – study support centres which house CCTVs, scanners and braille embossers. They also have induction loops and infra-red transmission equipment to help those with hearing difficulties, and ramps and lifts in the main buildings to help those with mobility problems. Their Dyslexia Unit is, they tell us, internationally renowned.

The academic structure delivers 6 'colleges', each a federation of schools. The College of Arts & Humanities schools are English, Welsh, History & Welsh History, Linguistics & English Language, Modern Languages, Music, Theology & Religious Studies, NIECI (The National Institute for Excellence in the Creative Industries), ELCOS (The English Language Centre for Overseas Students), and WISCA (Welsh Institute for Social and Cultural Affairs).

The College of Business, Social Sciences & Law has The Bangor Business School and schools of Law and Social Sciences.

The College of Education & Lifelong Learning has schools of Education and Lifelong Learning.

The College of Natural Sciences incorporates schools of The Environment & Natural Resources, encompassing Geography and Regional Studies, the schools of Biological Sciences and Ocean Sciences, the Welsh Institute of Natural Resources, encompassing the CAZS - The Natural Resources and the BioComposites Centre.

The College of Health & Behavioural Sciences has the schools of Healthcare Sciences, Psychology, Sport, and Health & Exercise Sciences, and The Institute of Medical & Social Care Research.

Finally, The College of Physical & Applied Sciences incorporates the schools of Chemistry, Electronics, and Computer Science.

SOCIAL SCENE

STUDENTS' UNION The uni has made a £1-million investment in the Students' Union. There's a 1,000-capacity, award-winning **Amser/Time** nightclub (open to the public and students at a discount) and two bars: the 390-capacity **Main** (**Prif Far**) and the 100-capacity basement bar, **Jock's**. Prices are very low.

> *It has risen to become one of the best universities academically... and, even if you accept a student's claim that you'd find more night life in a tramp's vest, Bangor, because of its geographical position, makes a plausible case.*

AT A GLANCE	
ACADEMIC FILE:	
Subjects assessed	**20**
Excellent	**45%**
Typical entry requirements	**286 points**
Application acceptance rate	**22%**
Student-staff ratio	**17:1**
First/2:1 degree pass rate	**54%**
ACCOMMODATION FILE:	
Guarantee to freshers	**100%**
Style	**Halls**
En-suite	**40%**
Price range pw	**£51-£75.25**
Town rent pw	**£40**

Wednesday is *Trash @* Main (rock, metal, indie), Friday is Racubah, Saturday Elevate (hard house & hard trance); Friday is *Sugar & Spice @* Amser/Time (chart hits). Otherwise, national tours – Cream, NME, orange, DJs: Rob Tissera, Mr Scruff, Scratch Perverts, Stanton Warriors, Norman J. Live music has brought Robert Plant, Toploader, Weetus, hundred Reasons, Funeral for a Friend, Lamarr, Dreamteam, etc.

There are twenty-five student societies – Community Action (student volunteers) is probably the most popular, mountain walking and football close behind. There's a Welsh-language student magazine called *Y ddraenen* and an English newspaper, *Seren*. In 2006 Rachael Ocsingberg was nominated for Best Photographer in the national student media awards.

Political activity is high, but centred on...Welsh language recognition. The drama soc, Rostra, is very popular. The uni has its own professional chamber ensemble and student symphony orchestra, chamber choir, opera group,

WHERE BANGOR GRADUATES END UP
Health & Social Work: 14%; Education: 23%; Wholesale/Retail: 9%; Manufacturing: 7%; Financial Activities: 6%; Public Administration, Civil Service & Defence: 10%; Hotel/Restaurant: 4%; Transport & Communications (including Telecommunications): 3%; Construction:1%; Agriculture: 2%; Personnel: 3%; Business & Management: 2%; Accountancy: 0.5%; Media (including Film): 1.5%; Legal 0.5%; Publishing: 1%; Sport: 2%.
Approximate 'graduate track' employed **64%**

chamber ensembles and concert band.

SPORT Rock climbing, paragliding, mountain biking, canoeing, sailing, and surfing are available as well as the usual team sports – rugby, hockey and football. Women's Rugby is traditionally strong. 1500+ participate weekly in sporting activities. You will benefit from a Lottery-sourced, £4.5 million extension to the sports hall. There's great emphasis on sport, thanks to the Sports Science and PE courses. Outward-bound activities, such as mountaineering, are especially popular, as are rowing, sailing and canoeing. This is a small uni and so makes a poor showing in national team competitions, but it does its own thing with flair. Sports scholarships are worth £1500 p.a.

TOWN 'As far as towns go, we ain't no Liverpool or Birmingham,' writes Becki Thurston, 'but that doesn't mean we're pants and boring. Although it's designated a city, it's diddy. The bonus is that we take over. There's nowhere doesn't feel like home. Wherever you go, wherever you are, you'll bump into someone you know. Trouble is, people know who you snogged last night, even before you've sobered up enough to realise!'

A positive advantage of Bangor's size is that competition between pubs etc. is strong. So prices are low. Besides pubs – Irish, Wetherspoons, **Fat Cat** and late-night pub/clubs **Joot** and **Joop**, you'll find café bars, restaurants (Spanish, Italian, Greek, Chinese, Indian), and two more nightclubs – **Octagon** and **Bliss**.

For arts lovers the city offers a varied mix of classical concerts; there are regular visits from such as the BBC National Orchestra for Wales and foreign orchestras, and the **Centre for Creative & Performing Arts**.

PILLOW TALK

A major redevelopment of accommodation site currently underway. Due to open in 2008. Nice, confident touch in offering summer-vacation halls accommodation to prospective undergraduates – with or without parents – to get a taste of the place.

WHAT IT'S REALLY LIKE	
UNIVERSITY:	
Social Life	★★★
Campus scene	**Outdoor, cheap, close-knit, Welsh, and full of life**
Student Union services	**Good**
Politics	**Internal**
Sport	**40 clubs**
National team position	**100th**
Sport facilities	**Good**
Arts opportunities	**OK**
Student newspaper	**Seren, Y ddraenen**
Student radio	**Storm FM**
Nightclub	**Amser/Time**
Bars	**Main/Prif Far, Jock's Bar**
Union ents	**Live acts, DJs, comedy**
Union societies	**25**
Most active societies	**Mountain walking, Football, Community Action**
Parking	**Good**
CITY:	
Entertainment	★★
Scene	**Scenic, fun**
Town/gown relations	**Average-poor**
Risk of violence	**Low**
Cost of living	**Low**
Student concessions	**OK**
Survival + 2 nights out	**£40-£50 pw**
Part-time work campus/town	**Good**

One hall exclusively for Welsh speakers.

GETTING THERE

☛ By road: A5, A55, A487; 90 minutes from M56.
☛ By rail: London Euston, 4:00; Birmingham New Street, 3:00; Manchester Oxford Road, 2:30; Liverpool Lime Street, 2:15.
☛ By coach: London, 8:00; Leeds, 6:15.

UNIVERSITY OF BATH

The University of Bath
Claverton Down
Bath BA2 7AY

TEL 01225 383019
FAX 01225 386366
EMAIL ask-admissions@bath.ac.uk
WEB www.bath.ac.uk

Bath Students' Union
Claverton Down
Bath BA2 7AY

TEL 01225 386612
EMAIL supresident@bath.co.uk
WEB www.bathstudent.com

STUDENT POPULATION

**Total students
16,608**

30% — Postgraduates

Female
Undergraduates — 21%

26% — Male
Undergraduate

Others — 23%

VAG VIEW

*B*ath is a small science and business-based university with a huge, world-wide reputation. There's no arts provision, yet it's first choice for many capable of Oxbridge, and as there are no arts undergraduates, the techies like it because they get to tread the boards rather than be banished backstage merely to fiddle with the wires.

Value is most obviously visible in the high teaching and research assessments, in its sports record, facilities and coaching expertise, and in its highly focused graduate employment record, bolstered by its language courses, IT facility and a very good sandwich-course provision.

CAMPUS

The self-contained campus is situated 2 miles south-east of the city. A central building houses the Library and Learning Centre (with 24-hour access), the Careers Office and Students' Union, all set around The Parade, a walkway not unlike a shopping precinct. The concrete and golden Bath stone buildings are unique, but, as I discovered, on a wet, wintry, foggy day they do not look their best.

Katie Mellors is in her first year, studying Business Administration. 'The City of Bath is in the South West of England, very close to Bristol. It is a beautiful city, lovely stone architecture, but after a while I craved to see good old fashioned red brick buildings. It is also very small, but if you take the time to look, there are little wonders around every corner. The train station is small but has good links with London and the rest of the country via Bristol, which is good for (besides other things) clubs and clothes shops cheaper than in Bath.

'The Uni itself is at the top of Bathwick Hill, away from main town. This is not a problem, as bright orange buses run regularly until 3am, and facilities on campus are great. The buses are also cheap (£1.50 return.) One thing the prospectus doesn't warn you about is the wind! It is very windy up here on the hill.'

FEES, BURSARIES

UK & EU Fees, 2007: £3,070 p.a. There might be a slight inflationary increase for 2008 entry. Bursaries of up to £1,500 are available for new students eligible for the full HE Maintenance Grant. For the past 26 years, Bath has offered sports scholarships. Also on offer are scholarships for students of chemistry, chemical engineering, modern languages and European studies.

STUDENT PROFILE

'In terms of social groups and finding friends, as a northerner,' writes Katie, 'I was a bit apprehensive about the amount of southerners and how they already new lots of people here. However, everyone is so accepting and friendly, and they all love my northern accent. Making friends here has been the easiest thing. Bath is an international university and caters for a wide range of cultures, hence they have an oriental shop and café, but they cater well beneath the surface too. Everybody mixes really well and you'll have lots of friends, no matter where you're from. The most noticeable social group is made up of sports types, but there is room for everyone. It is my experience that the sports socials are first class, Initiation and The Snowball being the most memorable.'

ACADEMIA & JOBS

Bath programmes are modular, consisting of self-contained units taught and assessed on a semester basis. The academic year is divided into two semesters.

'Lecturers are strict on the minor details like

UNIVERSITY/STUDENT PROFILE	
University since	**1966**
Situation/style	**City campus**
Student population	**16608**
Undergraduates	**7740**
- mature	**7%**
- non EU undergraduates	**9%**
- male/female	**54/46**
- non-traditional student intake	**16%**
- state school intake	**77%**
- drop-out rate	**4%**
- undergraduate applications	**Up 16%**

SUBJECT AREAS (%)

Combined Sciences — 19
Health Subjects — 7
Biological Sciences — 11
Physical Sciences — 7
Languages — 4
Business — 14
Social Studies — 6
Architecture/ Technology — 3
Engineering/ Technology — 16
Maths & Computer — 13

Policy Sciences is the signing of a £150,000 deal with the National Association of Funeral Directors, which may lead to a professional degree. And why not, they already have a Masters out of their unique Centre for Death and Society.

They lead the way, too, in guiding Electrical Engineering graduates into Telecommunications. Assessments again scored only 20 points out of 24, but the acid test is employment and employers love their graduates. Three new research laboratories costing over £1 million place the uni at the forefront of telecommunications, space and radio engineering research.

Defence, in particular the Royal Air Force, pick up graduates from this key area of Bath's academic programme. The Psychology & Communications Engineering tie-up holds intriguing possibilities.

Again, more than 4% of their graduates (engineering, science and computer science) become software engineers. They are strong, too, in placing computer programmers and systems analysts. Look at their BSc Computer Science, Computer Info Systems and Computer Software Theory – all 3/4 years depending on whether you opt for an industrial placement. Look, too, at the Physics with Computing 4-year sandwich.

Another key area is Architecture. Becoming an architect is a 6-year commitment, a 3-year BA Hons, a year practice placement followed by a 2-year BArch. See their 4-year sandwich BSc/Arch in the Faculty of Engineering & Design. There's an international Grade 5 award for research.

In science, Bath regularly find more physicists jobs than most other unis, and full marks at the teaching assessments give confidence. Entry for around ABC-AAB. They are among the top providers, too, for would-be biologists, and there's a Grade 5 for research here. Look also at the Chemistry degrees with Management or Drug Discovery ad-ons. For pharmaceutical manufacture and pharmacy, Bath also leads, this time with a world-class Grade 5* for research. Pharmacology comes as BSc in 3 years or as a MPharmacol in a 4-year sandwich.

Accountants and stockbrokers stream from the mathematical sciences and management areas. Finance, accountancy and business management are key strengths – around a quarter of the graduate employment picture. Meanwhile, the BSc Sociology with Human Resource Management gives them certain dominance in personnel.

Bath have among the best sports facilities in the country, and deliver around 25 graduates into the sector annually. I was told. 'The sports science course we now offer is really competitive; there are

punctuality,' writes Katie. 'But in seminars you really feel close contact with them, and that they care about your progress. My work is not as pressurised as my friends', but be prepared to work hard. Bath has a reputation to uphold. The internet is key to your time here. Most communication is by email, and such as lecture slides are to be found on the net. There is a connection in each room in halls, which makes it all very quick and efficient, and the library is central to the campus, with excellent resources and help on hand when you need it.'

Bath concentrate on seven areas – Sciences, Social Sciences (Economics, Politics, Psychology, Social Policy, Social Work, Sociology), Engineering, Pharmacy & Pharmacology, Business, Languages, and Sport.

Bath's impact on the employment market for engineers is impressive to say the least. Year on year they come high up in the Top 10, offering 4/5-year MEng Aerospace, Automotive, Mechanical, Manufacturing and Innovation/ Engineering Design degrees, with French and German, and useful sandwich possibilities. Teaching assessments range from 20 to Excellent in Engineering. Mechanical, Aeronautical and Manufacturing Engineering took world-class Grade 6* ratings at the research assessments. Now, they have won a £1 million grant to establish the Bath Institute for Complex Systems, which brings together scientists from maths, statistics, engineering, physics and biology to consider issues that will benefit areas such as aviation, communications technology and the oil industry.

Their language facility in the Humanities & Social Sciences faculty, which spills into other areas (Management included – see their excellent International management degrees), assures them a strong line in graduate translators and interpreters, even if it scored only 19 at assessment.

A new move in the Department of Social &

literally thousands of applicants.' Employment leaders are larger unis, Loughborough, Leeds Met...

Students with disabilities and learning difficulties now have free access to state-of-the-art laptops that cater specifically for their learning needs. The Assistive Technologies Initiative (ATI) will enable students at the University to borrow from a pool of 64 laptops containing software that can do everything from translating speech into written text, to helping people 'map' their thoughts and ideas. The University currently has 376 students who are registered as having a disability or learning difficulty - 224 with dyslexia - all of whom will be eligible for ATI support.

The proportion of employed Bath graduates in professional jobs is particularly impressive: 46% compared with the national average of 25%. Graduate employers target the uni, with 320 visiting in 2004-5 for recruitment purposes.

Many students do a work placement (either one year or two periods of six months) as part of their degree programme, and help getting good vacation experience is provided by the Careers Advisory Service.

Vectura, a company established by academics at the uni, is among the top four university spin-off companies in the UK. Now, a new Student Enterprise Centre gives students free access to the training, support and resources they need to turn their business ideas into reality. Based in the Students' Union, the Centre facilities include a suite of five computers, meeting rooms and two dedicated business support professionals as part of the Student Enterprise Team.

STUDENT SCENE

STUDENTS' UNION In Freshers Week there's a different theme every night culminating with the infamous Toga Party, a rare opportunity to go out in public wearing just a bed sheet The Pub Crawl is another highlight – the mission: to visit twenty of Bath's finest drinking establishments and well, get drunk.

'Freshers week was extremely well organised which made settling in easier,' Katie recalls. 'Each kitchen group was assigned a crew to guide them through the first week and to life in Bath. The pub-crawl is legendary, but don't forget your toga. Most fresher events were in the campus sports hall, and drinks were expensive, but with the drinking games with your fresher's crew it soon became less of an issue. You will know at least 40 people before you even start your course.'

Following Freshers Week, first years have the option of socialising at the **Parade Bar**, **Plug** or **Element**, all on campus. The **Parade Bar** is the most upmarket of the three where you can go for a coffee or a cocktail, whichever takes your fancy. The Plug is a small pub style area with pool tables and a big TV for all the sports matches (beware of

---

ACADEMIC EXCELLENCE

TEACHING:
(Rated Excellent or 17+ out of 24)

Mechanical Engineering.	**Excellent**
Architecture, Business & Management Studies, Social Policy & Administration Physics, Maths, Biosciences Politics, Economics Pharmacology.	**24**
Education, Sport	**23**
Civil Engineering	**22**
Materials Technology	**21**
Chemical Engineering, Electric & Electron Eng	**20**
Modern Languages, Sociology	**19**

RESEARCH:
Special 6* status:

Applied Maths, Mech, Aero, Manuf Engineering	**Grade 6***
Top grades 5/5*	
Pharmacy, Applied Maths, Mechanical/Aeronautical/ Manufacturing Eng	**Grade 5***
Biological Sciences, Pure Maths, Statistics, Built Environment, Social Policy, Business/Management, European Studies, Education	**Grade 5**

WHERE BATH GRADUATES END UP

Health & Social Work: 8%; Education: 4%; Wholesale/Retail: 10%; Manufacturing: 18%; Financial Activities: 10%; Public Administration, Civil Service & Defence: 8%; Hotel/Restaurant: 2%; Transport & Communications (including Telecommunications): 4%; Construction:2%; Personnel: 3%; Computer: 4%; Business & Management: 6%; Accountancy: 7%; Media (including Film): 0.5%; Architecture: 2%; Publishing: 2%; Advertising: 0.5%; Sport: 1%.

Approximate 'graduate track' employed **80%**

WHAT IT'S REALLY LIKE

UNIVERSITY:

Social Life	★★★★
Campus scene	**Busy, friendly**
Student Union services	**Professional**
Politics	**Union active**
Sport	**52 clubs**
National team position	**2nd**
Sport facilities	**Excellent**
Arts opportunities	**Good**
Student newspaper	**Impact**
Student radio	**URB**
Student Radio Awards	**4 in last 2 years**
Student TV	**CTV**
Nightclub	**Elements**
Bars	**Plug, Parade, Claverton Rooms**
Union ents	**Score, Funky Guppy, etc**
Union societies	**85**
Parking	**No 1st years**

CITY:

Entertainment	★★★
Scene	**Average clubs, good pubs**
Town/gown relations	**Good**
Risk of violence	**Low**
Cost of living	**High**
Student concessions	**Good**
Survival + 2 nights out	**£75 pw**
Part-time work campus/town	**Excellent/good**

the Welsh contingent out in full force whenever the rugby's on)! **Element** is the university's nightclub. On a Monday night most venture into town.

Writes Katie of campus and city nightlife: 'I came to Bath from a large northern city with a good nightlife, and I must admit it took a while to adjust to all that's worth going to in Bath (two underground nightclubs). They only play cheese here, and I dare say that after four years I will think, if I never hear another cheese song again it will be too soon. But for now I am loving every minute of the social side to my degree. The clubs in town have cheap drinks (£1) and are safe. The main town night for students is on a Monday. Campus has its own nightclub for Wednesdays and Fridays, again playing cheese, and with fancy dress as a must!

'Despite the cheese, and the size of the clubs (on the small side), Bath is a fantastic night out and this I put down to the people. You know almost everyone in the club and have such a laugh that you will not forget a single night out, either on campus or off.

'Two bars on campus host comedy and karaoke events throughout the week, and offer good quality yet affordable food, as well as drinks promotions. Pubs in town also have great food and are good for a quieter night (though not much). The SU also puts on trips beyond the uni to the theatre, ice skating, clothes shows, etc.'

There are 85 societies on offer so it is really easy to get involved. 'We may not have the sort of student traditionally likely to be involved in the arts,' another student told me, 'but that is what actually attracts students here. If we offered a drama course it would be the drama students who would be in all the plays, whereas, here, students have a lot better chance to be involved because there isn't a specific drama course, a specific music course and so on.'

The centre for arts is **The Arts Barn** – drama, dance, music, studio workshop space for visual arts and crafts. BUST is the drama society. There's a musicals society, opera, a choral society – 'not quite so elitist as the chamber choir'. They also have student bands and orchestras.

The University plans to dramatically improve its current arts facilities by developing a centre of excellence for the arts and research on campus. Opening in autumn 2008, a major fundraising campaign is underway to raise £6.25 million.

There is also a direct uni input into extra-curricular culture. Lunchtime and other out-of-hours lectures are the coming thing, generally free but necessarily ticket events, unusual speakers, controversial perhaps, boundary-breaking, and very popular, a good sign that the place is thriving intellectually and culturally.

Media-wise, there's a weekly newspaper, *Impact*, a radio station, URB, and a TV station, CTV, with monitors installed in the Plug Bar. Politics

AT A GLANCE

ACADEMIC FILE:

Subjects assessed	**21**
Excellent	**86%**
Typical entry requirements	**403 points**
Application acceptance rate	**13%**
Students-staff ratio	**17:1**
First/2:1 degree pass rate	**75%**

ACCOMMODATION FILE:

Guarantee to freshers	**Apply early**
Style	**Halls**
Catered	**None**
En-suite	**52%**
Approx price range pw	**£60-£85**
City rent pw	**£60-£70**

brings societies for the three main parties into action, and the popular Debating Soc.

Katie tells of more mundane, but no less vital considerations: 'Cost of living depends on where you buy your food; there are the more expensive supermarkets like Waitrose but also cheaper ones like Iceland. Say £20 for food if you are sensible, £10 for beer, £5 for travel (if that), and £20 for a night out will be adequate. Obviously if you have more to spend then you won't be disappointed.

'The student union has a dedicated careers service, which hosts events to help with recruiting, often with guest speakers. There is also a job service centre that has many part time jobs advertised. I don't have one but my friends do. They love them, not only for the money but also for the different people you get to meet. Bath really is a people place.'

SPORT There are fantastic sports facilities on campus, ranging from an Olympic size swimming pool, 8-lane athletics track, squash, badminton and tennis courts. They attract the sporting elite, but unlike practically any other university, all the sports facilities are free to students. Right on campus there's a generous range of team pitches and no facility is more than a stroll away. The sports village complex, partly built with Lottery money, offers the floodlit running track; 50-metre and 25-metre pools; a 4-court tennis hall; 16 hard tennis courts; 2 synthetic grass pitches; a shooting range; sports hall; squash courts; a performance testing lab; weight training rooms; a physio centre, etc.

Nor does all this professionalism keep the keen amateur away – a statistic, much bandied, is that 80% of students make use of what's on offer (in all, 52 sporting clubs, including American Football).

PILLOW TALK

A new development of 355 en-suite study bedrooms will open in October 2008. At the same time a 2-year refurb. of the rest will be complete, with some having flat screen monitors and upgraded telephone - IP telephony.

Writes Katie: 'Some halls are fantastic, really modern and spacious, but more expensive. My accommodation is very small for its price and I was slightly disappointed, but it is due to be refurbished for next year. In any case, once you have settled it is not an issue. You can literally roll out of bed and go to lectures (I have been in my pyjamas). The weakness has to be the lack of space, but you adapt. Houses in town are cheaper and more spacious, and they have a lounge of course, which is something I definitely miss.'

GETTING THERE

☛ By road: M4/J18, A46.
☛ By rail: London Paddington or Southampton, 1:30; Birmingham, 2:15; Cardiff, 1:50.
☛ By air: Bristol Airport.
☛ By coach: London, Birmingham, 3:15

BATH SPA UNIVERSITY

Bath Spa University
Newton St Loe
Bath BA2 9BN

TEL 01225 875875
FAX 01225 875444
EMAIL enquiries@bathspa.ac.uk
WEB www.bathsap.ac.uk

VAG VIEW

*B*ath Spa, a University College since 1999 and a uni since 2005, came out of Bath Academy of Art, Bath College of Education and Newton Park College, the last two being originally teacher training colleges. There are now four faculties – Applied Sciences, Art and Music, Education and Human Sciences, and Humanities – on two campuses: Sion Hill and Newton Park.

The most extensive building programme in Bath Spa's history, amounting to £11 million, is in progress and includes a

37% — Postgraduates
Female Undergraduates — 43%

STUDENT POPULATION
Total students
6,767

Male Undergraduates — 20%

Students' Union social facility, library and

UNIVERSITY/STUDENT PROFILE

University since	**2005**
Situation/style	**City campus**
Student population	**6767**
Undergraduates	**2501**
- mature	**25%**
- non EU undergraduates	**7%**
- male/female	**31/69**
- non-traditional student intake	**28%**
- state school intake	**94%**
- drop-out rate	**13%**
- undergraduate applications	**Up 26%**

SUBJECT AREAS (%)

Biological Sciences
Education
Combined
Science
Creative Arts — 34
10
31
7
11   5 2
Social Studies
Humanities   Business

ICT suites, a new Performing Arts arena with a 214-seat theatre, rehearsal spaces, associated technical accommodation and changing facilities, a new refectory, and a Creative Writing Centre housed in a 14th-century Gatehouse, renovated in collaboration with English Heritage and equipped with the very latest computers and audio-visual equipment.

In 2006-7 applicants increased by 26%, even though their student-to-staff ratio had in 2005 worsened from 18-to-1 to 24-to-1, and that, while 96.4% graduates found work or further study within 6 months, only 47% undertook 'graduate track' employment. What's winning it for them is the level of teaching. Another National Teaching Fellowship was awarded to a Bath Spa lecturer in 2006. Student satisfaction is high.

FEES, BURSARIES

UK & EU Fees p.a. £3,070 in 2007; 2008 still to be announced. Bursaries for students in receipt of HE Maintenance grant, £100-£1,175 according to income. Scholarships for eligible students on some science-based courses (Biology, Diet and Health, Environmental Science, Food Nutrition and Consumer Protection, Geographic Information Systems, Development Geography).

CAMPUSES

Newton Park is 4 miles west of the city in a landscaped saucer of Duchy of Cornwall countryside, an original Capability Brown design, with a Georgian manor house at its administrative hub and a cash dispenser, recently installed by the Students' Union. There are half hourly and late-

ACADEMIC EXCELLENCE

TEACHING: *(Rated Excellent or 17+ out of 24)*	
English, Environmental Studies	**Excellent**
Theology	**23**
Sociology, Art & Design	**22**
Education	
Environmental Biology,	**21**
Psychology	
Business/Management	**20**
RESEARCH: *Top grades 5/5**	**None**

night buses to and from town.

Sion Hill is within walking distance of the city centre on the north side and is reserved for Art and Design. It comprises a large modern building and the Georgian crescent Somerset Place, set in attractive grounds.

WHERE BATH SPA GRADUATES END UP

Health & Social Work: 4%; Education: 29%; Wholesale/Retail: 15%; Manufacturing: 5%; Financial Activities: 4%; Public Administration, Civil Service & Defence: 8%; Hotel/Restaurant: 7%; Transport & Communications (including Telecommunications): 2%; Personnel: 3%; Media (including Film): 1%; Legal 1%; Architecture: 1%; Publishing: 3%; Advertising: 1%; Artistic/Literary: 4%; Sport: 0.5%

Approximate 'graduate track' employed **52%**

STUDENT PROFILE

It is a small, quiet, supportive community, appealing particularly to females (69% of undergrads) and mature undergraduates (25%) One student told of its 'friendly, warming atmosphere.' She admitted, 'I arrived a timid, not-sure-why-I-was-leaving-home type of person ... if you have a shell to come out of, you'll discard it within weeks of coming here.'

It is far from being some sort of specialist dumping ground for sensitive souls, however. Bath Spa comes out high in any league table of new unis.

ACADEMIA & JOBS

Course design displays individuality and flair. They are known for courses leading to careers in the creative industries (CETL award), and they are a major provider of teacher training. By far the majority of the 30-odd per cent of Bath Spa graduates who find employment in Education do so as primary school teachers, some specialist music teachers among them, for music is another vital string to their bow.

Music technology is one of the fastest growing career opportunities. Graduates are entering the recording industry, new media (web audio, sound design, game audio, VR), the broadcasting industry (composing for TV, film, radio, etc) and the music technology industry (product development, software design). Bath Spa's relevant degree is the BA Creative Music Technology, and now new Foundation Degrees, many run in conjunction with partner FE colleges (eg Broadcast Media, Popular

WHAT IT'S REALLY LIKE	
UNIVERSITY:	
Social Life	★★★
Campus scene	**Quiet/mature teachers, funky artists**
Politics	**Relaxed**
Sport	**10 clubs**
Arts opportunities	**Excellent**
Student news & mag	**H20**
Radio station	**In progress**
Bar/venue	**SU bar and lounge**
Union ents	**Flirt, Friday Flux + live bands, karaoke, etc**
Union societies	**25**
Most active society	**Rugby**
Parking	**None**
CITY:	
Entertainment	★★★
Scene	**Average clubs, good pubs**
Town/gown relations	**Good**
Risk of violence	**Low**
Cost of living	**High**
Student concessions	**Good**
Survival + 2 nights out	**£75 pw**
Part-time work campus/town	**Average/good**

AT A GLANCE	
ACADEMIC FILE:	
Subjects assessed	**12**
Excellent	**75%**
Typical entry requirements	**249 points**
Application acceptance rate	**16%**
Students-staff ratio	**24:1**
First/2:1 degree pass rate	**60%**
Graduate track employment rate	**47%**
ACCOMMODATION FILE:	
Guarantee to freshers	**85-90%**
Style	**Flats in hall**
Catered	**None**
En suite	**44%**
Approx price range pw	**£67-£95**
City rent pw	**£60-£80**

Music, Music Production) are available. There are excellent facilities and well-used industry links. The degree is part of an impressive department,

which includes a Foundation and BA degree in Commercial Music – performance and songwriting are key elements (students played their first live gig in January 2002) – a BA (Hons) Music and a BA Performing Arts.

Specialist facilities have been built for students of creative arts subjects as part of the Artswork project (Bath Spa's Centre for Excellence in Teaching and Learning): MusicLab, DesignLab, BroadcastLab, FashionLab, PerformanceLab and PublishingLab. A new University Theatre has also just been completed. It's a very creative scene at Bath Spa. At Newton Park, an academic interest in music is given a performance dimension at the **Michael Tippett Centre**, recently refurbished and extended to make a 250-seater auditorium.

More than 5% of Bath Spa graduates find their way into jobs as graphic designers, and there's a strong pathway among fine artists, too (painting, sculpture and media).

Again, the excellent BA Creative Studies in English, backed by an MA and taught by practising writers essentially in workshop context, launches many a Bath Spa graduate into print as journalist, editor or author.

See also Environmental Science, Food

Management (this is another strong employment pathway), Human Ecology, Remote Sensing & Geographic Information Systems, and Social Science.

Then there are the regular BA and BSc single awards, for which a second subject must be selected in the first year: arts, humanities, social science, business, religion, health, etc. Finally combined BA/BSc awards give subjects equal weight.

New degree courses in 2007 include Philosophy and Ethics, Human Nutrition ands Film and Screen Studies.

This year a new University Disability Equality Scheme has been launched following a major audit of provision.

SOCIAL SCENE

New student facilities on campus include a refectory, delicatessen, SU bar, lounge, shop and offices, as Bath Spa tools up for life as a university. Say the SU: 'The campus estate is absolutely beautiful and provides a perfect study environment. Bath and Bristol are just a bus ride away. Small numbers creates a real community aspect and a sense of belonging. The new SU is amazing – chill out in the afternoon over coffee and bacon sandwiches or get your groove on in the evening on one of the biggest dance floors and largest capacity clubs in Bath.'

Ents are Monday: Open Mic or Race Night, karaoke or bingo; Tuesday pool or salsa; Wednesday is *Flirt* ('No. 1 National Student Club Night'); Thursday, Band Nite; Friday: *Friday Flux* ('Biggest Night of the Week'); Sunday is Quiz or Film Night.

PILLOW TALK

Accommodation in university halls is not guaranteed to all freshers, but around 85/90% will get in. Private rented houses are reserved for the unlucky few. All self-catering halls, divided into flats. Most on campus, with one new off-site block (located between the university and the town centre).

GETTING THERE

☛ By road Newton Park: from London and east: M4/J18, A46, A4, A39 to Wells, turn left after 200 yards into Newton Park Estate. By road Sion Hill: M4/J18, A46, A420, first left to Hamswell, at second give-way take a right and second right into Landsdown Crescent, over crossroads, first right to Sion Hill on your right.
☛ By rail: London Paddington or Southampton, 1:30; Birmingham, 2:15; Cardiff, 1:50.
☛ By air: Bristol Airport.

UNIVERSITY OF BEDFORDSHIRE

The University of Luton
Park Square
Luton LU1 3JU

TEL   01582 489262
FAX   01582 743400
EMAIL [firstname.surname]@beds.ac.uk
WEB www.beds.ac.uk

Students' Union
Europa House
Luton LU1 3HZ

TEL 01582 743265
FAX 01582 457187
EMAIL [firstname.surname]@beds.ac.uk
WEB www.beds.ac.uk

VAG VIEW

*L*ast August, De Montfort University's Faculty of Education, Bedford campus, became part of Luton University and together they became the University of Bedfordshire. For the first time, the county has a single provider of higher education.

Originally De Montfort's Bedford campus was spread across two sites - Landsdowne (Humanities) and Polehill (Sport and Education - the bit that is now Beds). There was here an exceptional sense of community. It was a thriving, self-sufficient set-up, one we picked out as a model for larger institutions. And they were proud. They'd been BUSA finalists in women's rugby at Twickenham, won the women's football, and were the first men's hockey finalists.

Luton Uni was a different story, beleaguered from the start. After they took university status in 1993, there were associations with Exodus Collective, a free party movement exposed in a Channel 4 documentary for running raves in disused warehouses to which 5,000 party people would flock, and someone joked that all you needed to get in was two Es, but now you needed two Es and a bag of amphetamine. Then a Sunday newspaper tore into them, calling them 'the lowest form of university life'. Quite unjust, we felt, and said so. Since then they have been exemplary in widening access to students beyond traditional socio-economic boundaries. Today, 43% come from the lowest socio-economic classes, 18% from 'low-participation neighbourhoods', and the drop-out rate is inevitably punishing.

But we think this union will work, not least because Luton and Campus Bedford share one important thing in common, a love of sport.

16% — Postgraduates

Female Undergraduates — 56%

STUDENT POPULATION

Total students **11,815**

28% — Male Undergraduates

CAMPUS

PARK SQUARE is the main campus in the centre of Luton. There's a rural mansion a few miles away (Putteridge Bury), a conference centre and home to the Faculty of Management. Then there's a site in Castle Street in town for Humanities.

BEDFORD CAMPUS The Bedford site is 20 miles away. Originally, it was Bedford's Sports College. It is undergoing a £14-million redevelopment, including two new gymnasia, sports science labs, a new Campus Centre with a 300-seat auditorium, and student accommodation.

FEES, BURSARIES

UK & EU Fees, 2007: £3,070. Fees not yet fixed for 2008. If in receipt of full HE Maintenance grant there's a bursary of £1,750; if in receipt of partial grant, between £300-£1,000.

STUDENT PROFILE

At Luton the student body is one of the most diverse – 22% of undergraduates are mature, 30% are from ethnic minority groups, many are from overseas, and there are also plenty of locals. More

than a third of undergrads are part-timers. University may be a bit of a novel thought for many of them, but it is part of their own plan, often after they have been out in the workplace and seen what's missing.

In Bedford, they are largely female, primary school teachers and secondary PE with QTS.

ACADEMIA & JOBS

Luton operates through six faculties: Business, Design & Technology, Health Care & Social Studies, Humanities, Management, Science & Computing, and the Bedford provision, Education.

The new faculty comprises two schools: Education (one of the largest providers of Initial Teacher Training in the UK) and Physical Education & Sport Sciences (with over 100 years teaching experience and a 23 out of 24 teaching ssessment); and two departments: Business & Applied Social Sciences and Performing Arts & English.

In the old days, you thought of Luton, you thought of Vauxhall Motors. Luton has always been heavily into links with commerce and industry, but over a decade it has been expanding in other areas – millions have been spent on an art design studio, a computer centre, and a media centre, including a broadcast television studio, three digital radio studios, a performance studio and editing facilities.

'Media and sport are the big attractions,' one student said. They are indeed Top 10 providers in the radio/TV sector, and film and video operatives and producers come out of such as their Film Studies, Media Production and Photography & Digital Art degrees. Creative Writing is a popular minor in their modular credit scheme, in which combinations may involve two joint subjects or a major subject with a minor. Media scored 22 points on assessment. New is BSc Television Production.

'Besides the broadcasting studio, we've got a massive fitness suite and new scientific body fitness analysis equipment,' our mole continued, and this is surely bound to jive with the Bedford

UNIVERSITY/STUDENT PROFILE	
University since	**1993**
Situation/style	**Town sites**
Student population	**11815**
Undergraduates	**9895**
- mature	**22%**
- non EU undergraduates	**14%**
- male/female	**34/66**
- non-traditional student intake	**43%**
- state school intake	**100%**
- drop-out rate	**25%**
- undergraduate applications	**Up 45%**

provision. It was only a few years ago that the BSc Sports Therapy appeared on the course list, yet sport scores big in the research assessments. BA Sport & Fitness (Management or Studies), Sport Development, Marketing, Tourism, etc, should command an interest, 2-3% becoming physical training instructors (Education), 1% + pro-athletes of one sort or another. Sports Therapy is one of the most sought-after degrees in sport, and Luton is one of only a handful to provide it.

See, too, the nursing provision, which dropped only one point in the teaching assessments. A popular route for non-hospital nurses is BSc Mental Health Nursing, BSc Midwifery, etc, which sit alongside Health Science, Health Psychology, and BSc Psychology.

Graduates of the various Management degrees, Business Decision Mgt, Psychology & Business, tend to become managers in large retail operations, marketing managers and sales managers. Around 5% of graduates go into personnel, their line into the sector via BSc Hons Human Resource Management.

Finally, there are jobs aplenty for graphic artists, designers and Illustrators, who follow their BA Graphic Design and Interior Design, etc.

SOCIAL SCENE

STUDENTS' UNION/LUTON   **Main Bar** is the focal point, replete with all the usual trappings – arcade machines, a juke box, tellies and the like vie for attention. An adjacent, courtyard, beer garden is very popular in the more clement months. The venue for most of the organised hedonism is **Sub Club**, in the basement of the building. Official student nights are *Cheeky Monkey Monday* @ town clubs **Liquid** and **Envy**. *Frenzy* is Wednesday Sports Night @ Sub Club (themed nights once a month). On Saturday, it appears, everyone goes home or to the **Hat Factory** for live bands. The brain-damaging effects of such revelry can be put to the test at the regular Quiz Nights, and students with bright ideas can also put the facilities to their own use if they can convince the powers that be that enough people will attend.

Undisputed highlight of the year is the May

ACADEMIC EXCELLENCE

TEACHING:
(Rated Excellent or 17+ out of 24)

Nursing, Health Science	**23**
Anatomy, Art & Design,	**22**
Pharmacology, Psychology, Organismal Biosciences, Molecular Biosciences, Media Studies, Building Surveying/Construction Mgt	
Linguistics	**21**
Modern Languages, Electrical & Electronic Engineering.	**20**
Sociology	**18**

RESEARCH :
Top grades 5/5* **None**

Ball, which attracts thousands of the Luton faithful. The gowned and tuxedoed masses arrive in such numbers that the event is one of the country's largest. The likes of Prodigy, Tim Westwood, Jeremy Healy, Dodgy, Space and the Bootleg Beatles have rocked their world, while casinos, funfairs and top nosh add to the experience.

Most active societies, of which there are 26 in all, include Islamic, Darts, Christian Union, Creative Writing. Media-wise, there's magazine *Streaker* (student life laid bare) and radio station, Luton FM.

SPORT/LUTON Besides access to pitches, there's the fitness centre, sauna, steam room and solarium. Sport is competitive here, but there was a bit of a dive in form last year.

TOWN/LUTON 'Luton is a brilliant in-between town,' said Becky Hill. 'We have access to London in less than an hour, and Milton Keynes is brilliant for shopping.' If this sounds a bit of a back-handed compliment, it is. Luton is not a place you'd go out of your way to spend time in. But there are pubs galore and a handful of clubs. Most popular club is **Liquid**. Bars - The Park, Riley's for pool, The Galaxy Centre - with arcades, bowling, cinema - **Hat Factory**

WHERE BEDS UNI GRADUATES END UP

Health & Social Work: 9%; Education: 5.5%; Wholesale Retail: 15%; Manufacturing: 7%; Financial Activities: 6%; Public Administration, Civil Service & Defence: 9%; Hotel/Restaurant: 7%; Transport & Communications (including Telecommunications): 8%; Construction: 2%; Personnel: 4%; Computer: 1.5%; Business & Management: 1%;   Media (including Film): 3%; Legal 4%; Architecture: 1%; Publishing: 2%; Advertising: 1%; Artistic/Literary: 1%; Sport: 3%.

Approximate 'graduate track' employed **42%**

(theatre, UBSU Saturday band nights), and **Vauxhall Recreational Centre** for sports and gym access.

STUDENTS' UNION/BEDFORD The £14-million redevelopment brings a new Campus Centre with a 300-seat auditorium, in addition to sport facilities and accommodation. Bedford students spend a lot of their time at the union bar. Town club **Oxygen** and **Bar Soviet** are the official UBSU partners here. Wednesday nights are the stuff of legend. The official student night isMonday at Oxygen. It's Esquires for live bands like Guilly Mots and Electric Soft Parade, and the Corn Exchange for theatre, dance and orchestra. Bedford also traditionally has Freshers, Christmas and Summer balls.

SPORT/BEDFORD features regularly in the BUSA finals. Besides football, rugby and hockey, gongs in BUSA Mountain Biking Championships and White Water Kayak Championships give the spread. The annual Rugby Sevens is as famous as it is notorious.

AT A GLANCE

ACADEMIC FILE:	
Subjects assessed	**26**
Excellent	**54%**
Typical entry requirements	**186 points**
Application acceptance rate	**22%**
Students-staff ratio	**23:1**
First/2:1 degree pass rate	**48%**

ACCOMMODATION FILE:	
Guarantee to freshers	**100%**
Style	**Halls**
Catered	**None**
Approx price range pw	**£60-£72**
Town rent pw	**£45-£65**

WHAT IT'S REALLY LIKE

UNIVERSITY:	
Social Life	**★★★**
Campus scene	**Urban good timers meet primary school teachers**
Student Union services	**Average**
Politics	**Some**
Sport	**33 clubs**
National team position	**130th (Luton) 58th (Bedford)**
Sport facilities	**Good**
Arts opportunities	**Good drama; average art**
Student magazine	**Streaker**
Student radio	**Luton FM**
Nightclub	**Sub Club**
Bars	**Main Bar, Bar Soviet**
Union ents	**Sportsnight, themed nights, town clubnights**
Union societies	**26**
Most popular society	**Islamic (Luton), Dance (Beds)**
Parking	**Adequate**
TOWN:	
Entertainment	**★★★**
Scene	**Pubs, clubs**
Town/gown relations	**Poor**
Risk of violence	**Average**
Cost of living	**Average**
Student concessions	**Good**
Survival + 2 nights out	**£32 pw**
Part-time work campus/town	**Average/good**

TOWN Bedford is home to the international standard Bedford Athletic Stadium and has 3 swimming pools, but is also a place for pubs and bars (more than clubs). **The Forresters** (traditional), **Pilgrims Progress** (excellent value with decent food), the **Bull Nosed Bat**, **The Bedford Lounge** (with dancefloor), the **Litton Tree**, **The Rose** (pop venue with dancefloor), **Venom** for r&b, **New York, New York** (bit cheesy). Late licensing to 2 or 3 a.m. is the thing. There are off-campus club nights at places like **Nexus**, and what was **Limehaus** is now a cool venue called **The Pad** – dance nights, big names, small but intimate. Nightclubs big with students are **Oxygen** (4 floors, masses of rooms, **Bar Soviet** (the student affiliated bar with themed nights), **Time Out** (small & funky, open till 5 a.m.) A bar called **Esquires** is a live music venue with a reputation for hosting new bands – even Cold Play and Oasis – before their time. **Corn Exchange** is a live venue for theatre, music and comedy.

PILLOW TALK

In Luton, the Student Village lies within staggering distance of the Union, town centre and lecture halls, and offers secure accommodation to 1,600 students in eleven separate halls, single-sex and mixed flats, each with shared kitchen, laundry facilities, and bathroom. Several flats are designed for students with disabilities. With around 25% of students living in uni-managed accommodation close by, the town centre feel almost like a campus.

Brand new accommodation at Bedford.

GETTING THERE

- ☞ By road: M1/J10t.
- ☞ By rail: King's Cross, 40 mins; Nottingham, 1:45; Oxford, 2:15; Birmingham New Street, 2:30.
- ☞ By air: London Luton Airport.
- ☞ By coach: London, 1:15; Manchester, 5-6:00.

BIRKBECK COLLEGE

Birkbeck College
University of London
Malet Street
London WC1E 7HX
TEL 020 7631 6000
FAX 020 7631 6351
EMAIL admissions@admin.bbk.ac.uk
WEB www.bbk.ac.uk

Learn as you earn – Birkbeck College, founded in 1823 as the London Mechanics' Institution, became a school of London University in 1920. It provides part-time degrees for adults engaged otherwise during the day.

COLLEGE PROFILE	
College of London Uni since	**1920**
Situation/style	**City site**
Student population	**14905**
Undergraduates: part-time	**11170**
full-time	**5**
Accommodation	**None**

FACULTIES/SCHOOLS:
English & Humanities; History, Classics & Archaeology; History of Art, Film & Visual Media; Languages, Linguistics & Culture, Law, Philosophy, Politics & Sociology

STUDENT BIRMINGHAM - THE CITY

Birmingham has shaken off its grey image to incredible effect in the last decade. Developments right across Britain's second city total hundreds of millions of pounds. Improved social and shopping facilities carry the bonus of better graduate job prospects and mean that whatever you're after from your student career, Birmingham can probably supply.

The most dramatic recent development has to have been Birmingham's **Bull Ring Centre**. There's been a market here at least since 1154, when Peter de Birmingham, a local landowner, obtained a Royal Charter for a cattle and food market. In 1964 a new concrete-smothered mixed market of indoor shops and outdoor stalls was built, a design unintegrated with the city that proved to be locked into its time and of questionable practical form. In 2000 it was reduced to a hole in the ground, and then recently it opened anew in spectacular form to public applause. The big name designers and retailers, like **Selfridges**, have flocked their in droves, and Birmingham Retail has been resurrected, the time the whole operation took to complete giving the rest of Brum's shopping world a chance to flourish, with such as **Mailbox** offering us a chance to drool at **Harvey Nichs**, Armani, DKNY, etc, even if many students will stick to the pedestrianised areas around New Street and the Pallasades, where every high street store you could want is juxtaposed with designer off-cut stores and street markets.

CAFES, PUBS, CLUBS

Aston students report, 'There are so many places to go, and so much to do that you will always be spoilt for choice... Spend an evening in a canal-side café, pub or restaurant, take a trip to the cinema, theatre or ballet or laugh the night away at the **Glee Comedy Club**. The Broad Street, Brindley Place/Mailbox area is particularly popular with our students and has lots of places to eat and drink beside the canals, for example **The Works**, **Flares** (2 floors of cheese), **Hard Rock Café**, **Bar Epernay** (rotating piano), **Fifty Two Degrees North**, the pricier **Zinc** and Aussie-themes **Walkabout** (amongst many others). Rumour has it that there are 100 pubs and bars within a one-mile radius of the Aston University Campus – **The Square Peg** (Wetherspoons), **Bar Med**, **Chambers**, **Sack of Potatoes** (facing Aston Uni), **Gosta Green** (It's A Scream), the stylish **RSVP Bar**...the list is endless. Numerous pre-clubbers like **Poppy Red**, **Ipanema**, **The Living Room**, and **SoBar** are also open late, as you would expect from a real entertainment city like Birmingham. The bars, cafés and clubs at **The Arcadian Centre** (near the Chinese Quarter) are also popular with students.

Birmingham is bursting with clubs playing anything from dance, house, drum 'n' bass and jungle, to hard rock, 70s, 80s, lounge, soul, jazz and garage. **The Que Club** (one of the largest clubs in the UK) alas is no more, but clubs like **The Sanctuary**, **The Medicine Bar**, **Bakers**, new club **Air** (home to Godskitchen), **The Works** and **Bobby Brown's** play host to top DJs and attract clubbing aficionados from across the UK in their coachloads.

LIVE

The recently opened **Birmingham Academy** is the best local venue – it's one of the essential stops on any band's UK tour, its reputation boosted far and wide in 2001 by Radio 1's hosting most of its One Live in Birmingham events there.

The **Wolverhampton Civic**, just a short train ride away, is still seen as a main Midland live venue, and the **NEC** is equally popular with bands of U2 or S Club proportions. In the smaller venues expect massively varying music styles and quality. **Ronnie Scott's** offers more than just jazz, whilst the **Fiddle and Bone** is a pub with a plethora of acts for free – from tribute bands to student musos through to Beethoven. Further into the backstreets you'll find a glut of pubs with fascinating (but sometimes frightening) live acts.

COMEDY, THEATRE, ARTS

Judging by the success of venues like the **Glee Club**, the new rock 'n' roll this may be. The venue attracts the best comic newcomers and the established talents of Eddie Izzard and Harry Hill – all for under a fiver if you go on a student night.

At the newly-revamped **Hippodrome** or **Alexandra Theatre** can be seen an array of Lloydesque and other West End shows, as well as the magnificent Welsh National Opera.

In the **Symphony Hall**, the renowned City of Birmingham Symphony Orchestra resides, playing host also to hundreds of international performers and offering a huge variety of classical music all year round.

For smaller fry the **Midlands Arts Centre**, or **MAC** as it is known, nestles comfortably on the edge of Cannon Hill Park near the University of Birmingham. With its combination of theatre, exhibitions, cinema and a damn fine bar it offers excellent choice and value. **The Electric Cinema**, showing arthouse, world and classic cinema in a charming setting, is the place to go if you want to see something different, although if it's Hollywood blockbusters you're after the **Odeon**, **UGC** and **Starcity** complexes offer about six billion different films, allegedly on twice as many screens.

For theatre **The Rep** in town has come in for a great deal of well-deserved praise lately with their showcase for new work, **The Door**, and also show fantastic productions in their main theatre. Stratford-upon-Avon is but a short train ride away, but watch out for the RSC's value for money student trips to productions there. For community productions (usually) as good as the professionals, check out the **Crescent Theatre**, offering Shakespeare and other productions.

For art you are spoilt in Brum, **The Barber Institute** on the University of Birmingham's campus is astounding. For more modern exhibitions head for **Ikon** or **The Angle** galleries.

Crucially all these places offer heavy discounts for students. Life with a 10% discount is what being a student is all about.

UNIVERSITY OF BIRMINGHAM

The University of Birmingham
Edgbaston
Birmingham B15 2TT

TEL 0121 414 3344
FAX 0121 414 3984
EMAIL admissions@bham.ac.uk
WEB www.bham.ac.uk

Birmingham Guild of Students
Edgbaston Park Road
Birmingham B15 2TU

TEL 0121 251 2300
FAX 0121 251 2301
EMAIL enquiries@guild.bham.ac.uk
WEB www.bugs.bham.co.uk

VAG VIEW

*B*irmingham is the original redbrick uni, with all that that entails beyond its masonry – none of the snobbery attached to Oxbridge and for many a reputation second only to it. The teaching is among the very best in the country and Brum's research record and graduate employment record, particularly in the areas of health, engineering, finance, accountancy and business are equally good. Together with the city and campus scenes, they serve to make this uni an exciting choice. More than 40,000

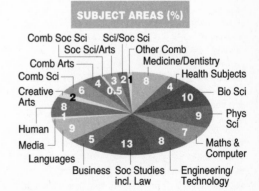

SUBJECT AREAS (%)

apply and around 12% are accepted each year. Birmingham is well-tested, consistent quality.

CAMPUS

The self-contained campus lies a couple of miles south of the city in leafy Edgbaston. Parking is not encouraged.

FEES, BURSARIES

UK & EU Fees, 2007: £3,070 p.a. for first degrees. Bursaries for all students whose family income is £32k or less. University scholarships are available for those who qualify for the HE Maintenance Grant and who have the requisite UCAS tariff points; also subject scholarships in e.g. physics, engineering, computer science.

STUDENT PROFILE

There's a high public school intake, though nothing as large as Oxbridge, Bristol, Durham. Birmingham students come from all over. Southerners think that Brum is north enough for them. Northerners, already bored of Manchester, see it as the next best city without London's expense. Thanks to strong

UNIVERSITY/STUDENT PROFILE	
University since	**1900**
Situation/style	**Campus**
Student population	**30520**
Undergraduates	**18785**
- mature	**16%**
- non EU undergraduates	**6%**
- male/female	**44/56**
- non-traditional student intake	**22%**
- state school intake	**77%**
- drop-out rate	**7%**
- undergraduate applications	**Up 2%**

overseas links there's also a large international community. In fact, be it fashion, music or religion, anything goes. The gist is that there are loads of people with interests sympathetic to yours, and you'll meet them through lectures, accommodation or socialising.

In an effort to ease the plight of disabled students, the uni has recently instigated a five-year action plan to adapt and re-design facilities and access points.

The policy continues with increased disability staffing, expanded equipment pool, better assistive technology in libraries, more specialist software available across computer clusters, more support workers, etc.

For international students, there's now a 'Welcome Week' induction programme before the start of term, and three full-time Student Advisers and free lessons in English during term time.

ACADEMIA & JOBS

Involvement with the world beyond campus is an aspect of a number of courses, and the proximity of important industries and businesses, as well as artistic nuclei, is key. The Arts School non-vocational courses give special attention not just to *what* is studied, but *how*. Skills such as organisation, analysis, presentation, communication and problem-solving are to the fore.

Almost a fifth of Birmingham graduates go to work in the health sector. The degree in Medicine is the 4/5-year MBCgB. There's a 11.5% application acceptance rate (softer than the 10% average), and a Black Country strategy in partnership with hospital trusts in Wolverhampton, Dudley, Sandwell and Walsall. Entry 340-360 points - no BMAT, no UKCAT...yet - including Chemistry and another science (Biology, Physics or Maths). Biology must come at AS level if not at A. For dentists, it's the 5-year BDS; entry ABB-AAB.

Birmingham is one of the few unis offering non-Law graduates a 2-year full-time or 3-year part-time Senior Status Law Degree. They scored an Excellent in a recent inspection, and a Grade 5 in the research assessment. All candidates must sit the National Admissions Test for Law (LNAT).

It is not necessary to take a degree to become a qualified accountant any more than it is to become a solicitor, but at the last annual count nearly 3000 did and more than 850 degree courses are there to ensure the flow continues. Birmingham is the big graduate provider in this sector, with Warwick and Durham not far behind. Dedicated courses at the Birmingham Business School include a 3-year BSc Accounting & Finance and a 4-year Accounting & Finance with French/German (French/German required at A level). A level requirements are high. Maths or Statistics at A level are not required, but

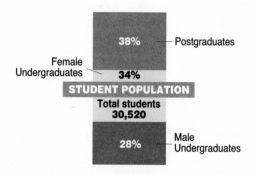

A/B Maths at GCSE is essential. Conceptual, analytical, ICT and problem-solving skill requirements are to the fore, but also communication/discursive skills and the ability to work on one's own (much coursework is outside the lecture hall). Work experience useful, but not essential.

The more accessible route is via the Economics Department – Single, Joint and Combined BSc Hons, including various Language mixes (Japanese among them), Money/Banking/ Finance, Economics and Modern Economic History, and Mathematical Economics and Statistics. Economics dropped only one point at the assessments.

Birmingham also lead in getting graduates jobs as tax experts and consultants, and for a job in banking, look at the BSc Money, Banking & Finance plus one year (well spent) to combine with French, German, Italian, Portuguese or Spanish.

Note the language interest; it's characteristic of all kinds of courses at Birmingham. The department (23 points for Russian at the assessments) keeps it high in the pecking order for graduates wanting jobs as interpreters and leads many into the area of human resource management. Social Sciences contribute 7% of graduates to this last sector:. See also a whole raft of new Public Policy degrees this year.

New Business School degrees include MBA Euro Banking and Finance, MBA Strategy and Procurement Management, MBA Strategy and Procurement Management (Hong Kong), MScCorporate Governance and Corporate Social Responsibility, MSc Human Resource Mgt, MSc Economic Competitiveness and International Business, MSc Economic Policy and International Business.

Would-be electrical, electronic and telecom. engineers note that full marks (24 points at the assessments) and a Grade 5 (international) accolade for research put this uni high on any discerning applicant's list. There are 3/4-year B/MEng options in Electronic & Electrical Eng, and a 4-year MEng option with international study.

There's a Business Management orientation available for most of what's on offer.

Look, too, at B/MEng degrees in Communication Sys-tems (also with possible Computer orientation), Computer Interactive Systems, Computer Science/Software Engineering, Electronic & Computer Eng. Finally, look over the Joint Hons BEng/MEng Electronic & Software Engineering. Again, it's full marks for teaching and a Grade 5 (international) level at research.

Nationwide, some 500 mechanical engineers find employment annually. Birmingham makes a valuable contribution to that figure. There are

B/MEng Mechanical Eng or with Business Management or Automotive possibilities; there's also a Foundation course. See also the joint hons Mechanical & Material Engineering. 20 points at assessment.

In producing working physicists, Birmingham are top of the tree, finding more of them jobs than any other uni last time out. They scored 23 points

---

ACADEMIC EXCELLENCE

TEACHING:
(Rated Excellent or 17+ out of 24)

History, Music, Geography, English, Geology	**Excellent**
Sociology, Elect/Electron Eng, Organismal Biosciences, Maths. Physiotherapy, Classics, Politics/International Studies.	**24**
Russian, Middle Eastern/ African Studies, Biochemistry, Physics, Molecular Biosciences, Psychology, Economics, Theol.	**23**
Dentistry, Italian, Iberian Studies, American Studies, HistoryArt, Dentistry, Nursing, Sport,Tourism Archaeology.	**22**
Chemical Engineering, Civil Engineering, Drama, Business, Education, Philosophy.	**21**
Manufac & Mechanical Eng Materials Technology, Medicine	**20**
German	**19**
French	**18**

RESEARCH:
Special 6 status:*

Clinical Lab Science, Anatomy, Chem. Eng, Metallurgy, Middle East/African Studies, Russian/ Eastern Euro, Sport	**Grade 6***

Top grades 5/5*

Clinical Lab. Sciences, Anatomy, Psychology, Chemical Eng, Metallurgy & Materials, Middle East/African Studies, Russian/E. European Studies, French, German/Dutch/Scand, Italian, Music, Sport.	**Grade 5***
Hospital-based Clinical, Pre-Clinical, Bio-Sciences, Chemistry, Physics, Pure Maths, Applied Maths, Computer, Civil Eng, Elec & Electron Eng, Law, Politics, German, English, Iberian & Latin American, Greek, History, History of Art, Theology, Educ.	**Grade 5**

WHAT IT'S REALLY LIKE

UNIVERSITY:	
Social Life	★★★★★
Campus scene	**Traditional, busy, cosmopolitan**
Student Union services	**Good**
Politics	**Activity high**
Sport	**Key; 43 clubs**
National team position	**3rd**
Sport facilities	**Very good**
Arts opportunities	**Film excellent; drama, dance, music, art good**
Student newspaper	**Redbrick**
Student magazine	**Bugged**
Student radio	**Burn FM**
Student TV	**Guild Television**
TV Awards 2006	**1 commendation**
Nightclub	**The Underground, Deb Hall**
Bars	**Joe's, Beorma**
Union ents	**Theme nights, comedy, drum 'n' bass, old skool, live bands**
Union societies	**150+**
Most active society	**Rock Soc**
Parking	**Poor**
CITY:	
Entertainment	★★★★★
Scene	**Excellent**
Town/gown relations	**Average**
Risk of violence	**High**
Cost of living	**High**
Student concessions	**Excellent**
Survival + 2 nights out	**£75 pw**
Part-time work campus/town	**Average/excellent**

Management/Management Sciences elements in their Physical and Biological Sciences programmes. Would-be zoologists should also be aware of BSc Biological Sciences: Animal Biology.

For media and government research jobs, Birmingham again leads the field. A third come from Social Sciences & Public Policy and Physical Sciences departments. See Media, Culture & Society or Public Policy, Government & Management. Look also at the International Studies combinations (Economics, Greek, German, French, Italian, Japanese, Portuguese, Spanish, Political Science) – same for Economics, Finance, etc. Also Political Science as single hons, Asian Studies with highly relevant combinations, BSc Public Policy, Government & Management, Russian Studies, Social Policy, etc. Also joint hons, such as Economics & Political Science, Planning & Public Policy, Government & Management, etc. It's all here.

Further employment strengths are evident in archaeology, in education (particularly for higher education lecturers), in psychology – BSc Psychology and the BSc Joint Hons Psychology with Artificial Intelligence explain why they are making waves in this sector. That and a world-class Grade 5* for research.

Music is another niche area. There's a world-renowned – Grade 5* – research rating, a Centre for Early Music Performance & Research, excellent rehearsal facilities and a brilliant Electro-Acoustic Music Studio, which is worth exploring in detail on the web. Five different degree routes are offered.

They are one of only three unis with a special Grade 6* research rating in Sport – the others are Liverpool John Moores and Manchester Met. See their Sport & Exercises Sciences and joint honours degrees. There's also an interesting civil engineering degree in Sports & Leisure Facilities Design.

The specialist BA Applied Golf Management Studies assumes a handicap on entry of 4.4 or less (this is a PGA requirement). Coaching is a key element and you'll be expected to take up a summer placement in the community. They also have a golf degree. – not a bad way to spend three years. You might consider their very strong student media as compatible in career terms.

at the assessments and an international Grade 5 for research (as did UCL, Leicester and Nottingham). Physical sciences is also a good route into Defence from here. Birmingham, Nottingham and Warwick universities have founded The Midlands Physics Alliance, a joint School of Physics, with £3.9 million backing from the Higher Education Funding Council, delivering a subject to a new generation of students at a time when other universities are taking it off the curriculum.

Note, too, the Business Studies and Business

> *Birmingham is a big, bustling, happening place and there is that self-same disinterested, confident air that you notice at all our best universities. If you don't enjoy a three-year spell here, it is unlikely to be Birmingham's fault.*

SOCIAL SCENE

GUILD OF STUDENTS The main source of non-academic entertainment on campus is the union,

WHERE BIRMINGHAM GRADUATES END UP

Health & Social Work: 19%; Education: 8%; Wholesale/Retail: 6%; Manufacturing: 10%; Financial Activities: 7%; Public Administration, Civil Service & Defence: 9%; Hotel/Restaurant: 2%; Transport & Communications (including Telecommunications): 3%; Construction: 1%; Personnel: 7%; Computer: 3%; Business & Management: 5%; Accountancy: 7%; Media (including Film): 1%; Legal 1%; Architecture: 1%; Publishing: 1%.

Approximate 'graduate track' employed **68%**

called Birmingham Uni Guild of Students or BUGS for short. This isn't purely to baffle your non-Brummy friends – the Guild was the first union in the country and earned the right to a sophisticated name. By day they offer numerous eateries and bars, from **Joe's**, the typical trendy student bar, to the delicious hot food of **Café Connections**.

There's the chance to join one of over 150 societies, and a huge range of student services (legal advice, local info from the ARC (Advice & Representation Centre – currently in refurb.), part-time job info at the Job Zone, etc).

Media-wise Birmingham is top notch, everything together in the same spot – magazine, newspaper, radio and TV (see *What It's Really Like* box, page 74). You can't do better if this is your interest. Radio & TV broadcasting and broadcast journalism are, like paper journalism, intensely competitive areas. Birmingham does well employment-wise for students, it has a good Media, Culture & Society degree in its Social Sciences faculty (which features, too, in Joint Hons) but the very fine student media set-up is also instrumental.

If there's a catch, it is that these Guild services are part-paid for by bar profits, so, whilst the Guild

AT A GLANCE

ACADEMIC FILE:

Subjects assessed	**48**
Excellent	**85%**
Typical entry requirements	**380 points**
Application acceptance rate	**12%**
Student-staff ratio	**17:1**
First/2:1 degree pass rate	**69%**

ACCOMMODATION FILE:

Fresher guarantee only to	**100%**
Style	**Halls, flats**
Catered	**28%**
En-suite	**37%**
Price range pw	**£68-£95**
Town rent pw	**£55**

still costs less than non-student bars, it's often cheaper to go to student nights in the city centre than to stay on campus. As a result, freshers often go to hall bars before moving on to one of the city-centre clubs and bars. Students living in neighbouring Selly Oak or Harbourne frequent the many local student pubs and balti houses in those areas, as well as the most popular city club nights.

Guild nights are OK, however, and the nightclub, **The Underground** has recently been extended. There's also **Deb Hall**, used for full-building nightclub events, plays, dance shows and formal events, and the bars – **Joes** and **Beorma**, and **Cybercity** – games room, pool, etc.

Typically, there's *Curryoke Thursdays* (karaoke for free curry for 2), theme party nights at Joes on Friday – *Joes Presents...* (*Bad Taste, Tequila Night, 999 Emergency Services*, etc), and *Fab 'n' Fresh* at Joes and The Underground on Saturday.

On campus, artistic input is high. Across drama, dance, music and art, extra-curricular societies are very active. The Film Society is excellent. Musically, there's a chamber orchestra, an orchestra of 100 and a choir of 220. For art there's **The Barber Institute** – founded in 1932 it incorporates both Fine Art and Music departments and has been described as 'one of the finest small picture galleries in the world'. There's also a musical theatre group which nurtures, milks and dispenses talent that abounds among students. If you're into theatre, Birmingham is one of the places to be. There's a Guild group and a Drama Dept group in the uni's **Studio Theatre**; students perform all over the city (often before taking their productions to the Edinburgh Fringe), and there's a student humour night at the **Glee Club** in town.

If you do find yourself dipping into the overdraft it's easy to find a job at the Guild, where students are given decent wages for bar work, security, marketing, and other jobs. Alternatively, businesses around the city always want flexible, enthusiastic part-timers. Most of them advertise in the Guild's Job Zone.

Finally, sports-wise, Birmingham's teams were the third best in the country last year. Only

Loughborough and Bath beat them overall.

SPORT The Munrow Sports Centre's mission statement 'to enhance the sporting experience of the university by providing opportunities at all levels' sums up the sporting situation. For the casual athlete the *Active Lifestyles Programme* offers weekly courses in martial arts, swimming, aerobics and team games.

The Athletic Union is made up of 40+ sports clubs, each with a qualified coach. Last year they had the top one or two national places in athletics and cross country, badminton, gymnastics, hockey, mountain bike and cycling, netball, rowing, squash and triathlon.

Clubs exist also at inter-departmental and inter-hall levels. Interests are more than catered for by the 25m pool, two gyms, a climbing wall and full-size running track, as well as two floodlit, synthetic pitches, physiotherapy and sports science support, and a Fitness Services Unit for all levels.

In addition, there are coaching courses in a variety of sports and activities. And there's a degree in golf.

Off-campus, five miles from home, there are seventy acres of pitches served by coaches and minibuses, and by Lake Coniston in Cumbria, 170 miles away, they have a Centre for Outdoor Pursuits (watersports, mountaineering, mountain biking, etc).

The university supports 30 sports scholarships at international level. This year's scholars compete in skeleton bobsleigh, lacrosse, equestrianism, badminton, hockey, rugby union, cycling, gymnastics, triathlon, netball, athletics, golf and squash.

TOWN See *Birmingham Student City*, page 70. The city does have less desirable areas (name a city that doesn't) but the average student has little contact with them, and if you're sensible about sticking in groups after dark and not flashing your cash around you shouldn't have any problems. As in all student areas there are complaints from disgruntled locals about kick-out time noise and student mess, but the Guild liaises with residents and police to keep the peace.

PILLOW TALK

Most freshers live in university accommodation. The main area is the Vale, a beautiful grassy bit set around a lake which houses catered and self-catered halls, and the Hub Centre (new in 2004) with two bars, eating areas, welfare and committee rooms. It is just 15 mins from the main area of campus. Other self-catered halls are either adjacent to the main campus (the ultra posh Jarratt Hall, boasting 620 en-suite bedrooms) or a bus journey away (The Beeches and Hunter Court). University House, the Oxbridge-style original residence, is ideally situated next to the Guild.

Elgar Court is newish – 236 single en-suite study bedrooms in flats for six. Shackleton Hall was refurbished in 2004, Maple Bank in 2005. A new development is planned to open Sept 2008.

GETTING THERE

☛ By road: A38. Avoid entry through suburbia from the M40; instead use M42/J1, A38.
☛ By rail: London Euston, 1:40; Bristol Parkway or Sheffield, 1:30; Liverpool Lime Street, Manchester Piccadilly,1:40; Leeds, 2:15. Frequent trains from New Street to University Station.
☛ By air: Birmingham Airport.
☛ By coach: London, 2:40; Bristol, 2:00; Manchester, 2:30.

UNIVERSITY OF BOLTON

The University of Bolton
Deane Road
Bolton BL3 5AB

TEL 01204 903903
FAX 01204 903809
EMAIL enquiries@bolton.ac.uk
WEB www.bolton.ac.uk

The old Bolton Institute was formed out of the Bolton Institute of Technology and Bolton College of Education (Technical). Subsequently, Bolton College of Art was incorporated. They have had the distinction

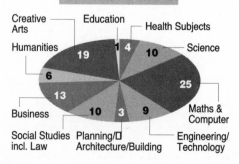

SUBJECT AREAS (%)

Creative Arts — Education

Humanities — Health Subjects

19 — 1 4 10 — Science

6

13

Business — 10 3 9 — 25 Maths & Computer

Social Studies incl. Law — Planning/ Architecture/Building — Engineering/ Technology

Postgraduates 19%

Female Undergraduates 37%

Male Undergraduates 37%

STUDENT POPULATION
Total students 8,050

Other 7%

UNIVERSITY/STUDENT PROFILE	
University since	**1902**
Situation/style	**Campus**
Student population	**8050**
Undergraduates	**5965**
- mature	**65%**
- non EU undergraduates	**8%**
- male/female	**50/50**
- non-traditional student intake	**49%**
- state school intake	**99%**
drop-out rate	**33%**
- undergraduate applications	**Up 5%**

of being able to award their own degrees for some time, but in January 2005 they gained university status, and last year they spent an average of £332 per full-time student on facilities.

CAMPUS

There are two campuses, Deane, on the west side of town, and Chadwick, on the east side. In June 2005 they opened The Design Studio on Deane Campus, a £6-million remodelling of Deane Tower that has completely transformed the face of the uni's main campus. New corporate hospitality facilities adjoin it, including lecture theatre, boardroom and breakout rooms - the Deane Suite. This is part of an extensive, phased landscaping and refurbishment programme which recently completed a one-stop-shop student centre and new labs for their advanced materials research team, an area in which this university is a leader.

FEES, BURSARIES

UK & EU Fees for 2007, £3,070 p.a. Bursary for students on a HE Maintenance Grant. The Bolton Scholarship is also available to those progressing from a partner institution – £700 p.a. There is also help for disabled students.

STUDENT PROFILE

Among undergraduates there is a large mature population (65%) and 44% of undergrads are part-timers. Almost 50% come from families new to the idea of university. Further education students account for around 6%. The diversity is impressive - there is a strong overseas presence - but perhaps not surprisingly there is, at this stage, a very high drop-out rate, indeed the highest in the country, 33%. One heartening statistic, however, is a healthy 18:1 staff:student ratio, maintained at a time when applications increased in successive years by 25%. Oh, and a surprisingly high percentage (51%) of first class and 2:1 degrees are awarded. No word yet on the effect of this upon

their graduate employment record. They claim 93% of their graduates are working or engaged in further study within six months, but graduate track employment figures have yet to be computed.

ACADEMIA & JOBS

Departments are Art & Design, Built Environment, Business Studies, Business Logistics & Info Systems, Computing, Cultural & Creative Studies (from English to Media, from Arts in the Community to stage and screen - based at Chadwick), Education (Chadwick), Engineering & Design, Health & Social Studies, Management, Product Design & Development, Psychology & Life Sciences, Sport, Leisure & Tourism Management.

In addition to the £6m Design Studio, two floors of adjacent state-of-the-art teaching space and a new Product Design Studio, costing £3.5m, opened in September 2006. The next phase in the Deane Campus development will be a £1.6 million Innovation Factory. Due to open in September 2007, the teaching space and workshop areas will

ACADEMIC EXCELLENCE	
TEACHING:	
(Rated Excellent or 17+ out of 24)	
Education, Nursing, Health	**24**
Materials Technology	**23**
Organismal Biosciences	**22**
Art & Design, Leisure, Tourism, Sport	**21**
Civil Eng, Electro & Electronic Eng, Theatre, Film & TV Studies, Communications & Media, Maths	**20**
Modern Langs (French, German, Spanish), Building	**19**
RESEARCH:	
Top grades 5/5*	**None**

WHAT IT'S REALLY LIKE

UNIVERSITY:	
Social Life	★★★
Campus scene	**Largely local, very loyal**
Student Union services	**Galvanising itself**
Politics	**Little interest**
Sport	**13 clubs**
National team position	**83rd**
Sport facilities	**Promising**
Arts opportunities	**Few**
Student newspaper	**Student Direct**
Nightclub/bar	**The Venue**
Union ents	**Live, and light ents progr. + tie-ups outside**
Union clubs/societies	**5**
Parking	**Available**
TOWN:	
Entertainment	★★
Scene	**Student club + pubs, etc**
Town/gown relations	**Good**
Risk of violence	**Average**
Cost of living	**Low**
Student concessions	**Good**
Survival + 2 nights out	**£50 pw**
Part-time work campus/town	**Average**

include glass-fronted 3D art studios leading out into exhibition gardens with full public access.

Bolton has strong links with business and professions, with 79% of students on courses that lead to a vocational or professional qualification.

Keep an eye on their media courses. Bolton are part of a university consortium, headed by Salford University and called Northern Edge, involved with the BBC, now that they have definitely decided to move to Manchester.

Teaching assessments since the mid-1990s have been good and most recently very good, with Art & Design and Leisure, Tourism & Sport dropping only 3 points out of 24 on assessment, and Education and Health subjects (including nursing) scoring full marks, the latter getting a further boost from another expression of confidence in 2006.

It's all a long way from the failures (Mechanical Engineering and Film & TV) in 1993 and 1996 respectively. Both were subsequently approved.

Built Environment is a particular strength, with a 23-point assessment in Material Technology and a Grade 4 (national significance) for research. Computing is also an exciting area, with everything available to the student, from games design, through business computing to computer-aided product design and engineering.

Law (LLB) was introduced this year.

There has been a flexible approach to entry. 'It is what you are capable of doing, rather than what you have already done which interests us,' they used to say. From the start, applications from groups under-represented in higher education were encouraged.

SOCIAL SCENE

STUDENT UNION The Union has shops at both campuses, a café, catering facilities and the **Venue** bar and, well, venue at Deane, with giant TV Screen, pool tables, jukebox and gaming machines. It's safe and grand for all it's meant to be, but it's early days, with little more to shout about than the **Venue Café's**, lighter bites (chip bun, spicy wedges etc), toasties, burgers (beef, chicken or vegetarian), pizza (you can even create your own), hot panini, jacket potatoes, and, wait for it, the Daily Special, 'details of which are written on the board'.

Ents-wise it's quiz on Monday, pool and big screen footie on Tuesday. Mid-week Wednesday is Student Night at **McCauleys** ('Bolton's student friendly nightclub') after drinks warm-up at the **Venue Café Bar**. Thursday is open mic night and Friday live local bands at the **Venue**.

Societies-wise it is again fairly undeveloped as yet, with only five catching the eye of freshers this year: Christian Union, Students with Disabilities, Islamic Soc, Afro Caribbean Soc and Motorsports (Bolton are strong in automobile engineering and product design and offer degrees in Motor Vehicle & Transport.) There's a newspaper, *Student Direct*, and a really quite good student union web site.

SPORT They are BUSA competitive and, positioned 83rd for team sports this year, already ahead of unis with longer histories. Compatible sports rehab., coaching, development and management

AT A GLANCE

ACADEMIC FILE:	
Typical entry requirements	**170 points**
Application acceptance rate	**14%**
Students-staff ratio	**18:1**
First/2:1 degree pass rate	**51%**
ACCOMMODATION FILE:	
Guarantee to freshers	**100%**
Style	**Halls**
Catered	**None**
En-suite	**None**
Price range pw	**£59**
City rent pw	**£35**

degrees that will help. Some niche success stories already are badminton, basketball, hung kuen shoalin, king fu. The annual sports ball and award ceremony is a high point of the social calendar.

TOWN Bolton's proximity to Manchester and to the Pennine Moors makes for a nice balance. A couple of nights of Mancunian debauchery, followed by a soul-searching chill on the wilderness of Tufton moor might be just the thing if you ever manage to tear yourself away from campus. Bolton itself offers a handful of clubs, but **McCauley's** is fave.

There's a cinema complex, the ground-breaking **Octagon Theatre** (modern inter-pretations of Shakespeare and equally at home with Alan Bennett) and live music venue **Albert Halls**, which includes comedy, jazz, classical music. Buit it's nearby Manchester for the high life.

PILLOW TALK

Two modern halls provide 700 single study bedrooms on a self-catering basis. The Hollins (two blocks with flats of 6 to 9) is adjacent to the Chadwick teaching site; the Orlando Village (8 blocks, each with 8 six-bedroom flats, plus a common room) is 10 mins walk from Deane. Both are close to the town centre.

GETTING THERE

☛ By road: M61/J3, A666 for Chadwick; M61/J5, A58 for Deane. Good map on web site.
☛ By coach: London, 5-7:00; Liverpool 2:00.
☛ By rail: Manchester frequent.
☛ By air: Manchester Airport 30 mins.

BOURNEMOUTH UNIVERSITY

Bournemouth University
Talbot Campus
Fern Barrow
Poole
Dorset BH12 5BB

TEL 01202 524111
EMAIL enquiries@bournemouth.ac.uk
WEB www.bournemouth.ac.uk

Bournemouth Students' Union
Talbot Campus
Fern Barrow
Poole
Dorset BH12 5BB

TEL 01202 965774
FAX 01202 535990
EMAIL suvpcomms@bournemouth.ac.uk
WEB www.subu.org.uk

VAG VIEW

*O*ne point about Bournemouth is that it *has found a way in to some seriously good employment niches. The other point is that this premier seaside resort university has some great extra-curricular opportunities.*

Female Undergraduates — **50%**

Postgraduates **13%**

STUDENT POPULATION

Total students 15,300

Male Undergraduates **37%**

CAMPUSES

Talbot (2 miles from the town centre) is the main campus; the other, Bournemouth, or Town Campus, is more of a collection of town sites, with teaching facilities for Business, Health, Design, Engineering, Computing, Conservation. There's a no-parking rule within a mile. Students are also discouraged from bringing cars on to Talbot, though many do. There's a free bus service between campuses and halls.

FEES, BURSARIES

UK & EU Fees, £3,070 p.a. with £1,000 bursary to applicants receiving full HE Maintenance grant and a sliding scale for those receiving partial maintenance grants. Also sporting and academic scholarships. Contact Student Financial support Adviser on 01202 965596.

STUDENT PROFILE

'On first entry to the place you may think you've entered a photo shoot for a *Next* catalogue, owing to arrivistes trying to impress anyone who may be watching,' writes Aidan Goatley. 'Look more closely and you can spot those who've been there longer than a year and for whom ironing is not the most important thing in the world.'

In fact, the main campus is very studenty and unpretentious. This may be a career-orientated student body, but there's an excellent scene both in union and in town, and a relaxed feel.

ACADEMIA & JOBS

A £7.5 million Library & Learning Centre opened in January, 2003, and since 2005 there's been a part-time entrepreneurial course – START – aimed at providing skills and professional support for anyone who wants to turn their ideas into commercial realities.

Around 4% of Bournemouth graduates become advertising account executives with major agencies like TBWA, JWT, WCRS, CIA Medianetwork, New PHD, Mediacom, and Mediapolis, or execs in publishing companies, public relations consultancies, research consultancies or in the marketing departments of other large companies. Bournemouth's Advertising and Marketing Communications needs 300 points (General Studies excluded). The course is 'twinned' with an agency through the Institute of Practitioners in Advertising. Six months work experience is part of it. Some move on to the MA in Marketing Communications. Lecturers here tend to be drawn from the world of work. It's all very practical, job-focused, and the uni overall is very media and business orientated.

They recently merged the Business School and School of Finance and Law. They are specialists in commercial & business law, and the uni has LLB Law & Taxation and BA Accounting & Taxation. You can also take the Common Professional Examination (CPE) here, which you'll need if you want to become a solicitor and don't have a law degree.

Managers and administrators, accountancy staff, marketing and sales managers, advisers, consultants, office and large company general managers proliferate on their graduate employment score card. Their degrees in business, sales and marketing are a main focus. Look at Business Management, a 2-year Foundation followed by 1-year top-up to BA, or the 3-year BA Business Studies (full or part-time, it also comes with Languages). For the more techno-minded, there's a 4-year sandwich BSc Business Information Systems Management – all for just 200 points. Later, there's a Doctorate in Business Administration and MAs in Human Resource Management, Information Systems Mgt and International Business Administration.

Note, too, the Media School Management courses, such as BA International Marketing Management, MAs in Corporate Communication, Marketing Communications and Services Marketing. You can also get as specific management-wise in Retail or Sports or Tourism, etc. Look at the 4-year sandwich International Marketing (Int. Retail Mkting HND top-up available too), 4-year sandwich Marketing or Leisure Marketing. Teaching inspection, 22.

They also have a ground-breaking 3-year, part-time, on-line Foundation Degree in Business and Management, launched by Bournemouth with Leeds Metropolitan and UK eUniversities (UkeU). The Army was the first major corporate client.

Of the many art colleges and universities with Animation degrees, few have as fruitful a line into the film and video world as Bournemouth, hosts to the National Centre for Computer Animation. The recent Grade 5 in research (Art & Design) suggests strength in depth in the area of visual image.

Recently the Media School unveiled a state-of-the-art Motion Capture facility. 'MoCap' tracks and records the movement of a human subject or object as computerised motion data so that three-

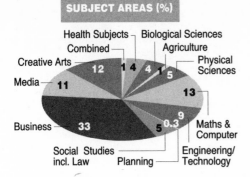

SUBJECT AREAS (%)

Health Subjects
Combined
Creative Arts
Media
Business
Social Studies incl. Law
Planning
Biological Sciences
Agriculture
Physical Sciences
Maths & Computer
Engineering/ Technology

12, 1, 4, 4, 5, 11, 33, 13, 0.3, 9, 5

dimensional images can be animated with realistic motion in real time – animating characters in computer games, film or TV. Look at their animation degrees. There's a range of postgrad courses in Animation, Special Effects and Computer Games Technology & Design, too. The Wallisdown Campus of The Arts Institute at Bournemouth (www.arts-inst-bournemouth.ac.uk) is adjacent, and they have BA (Hons) Film & Animation Production. Students enrolling should have prior film or video experience.

Meanwhile, Bournemouth's BA Hons Television Production (Art & Design Faculty) offers practising TV producers, writers and technicians as your teachers. Great resources and top employment track record. Look also at their BA Hons Multimedia Journalism, Interactive Media Production degrees and Photomedia (Photography, Film & TV) degrees and MA Radio Production (there are also good PG Diplomas).

Activities are backed by good student media. *Nerve Magazine*, Birst Radio (took Best Comedy and Drama in the 2006 national Student Radio Awards). The student-run television station, also Nerve, was runner-up to Warwick in four categories - Documentary, Drama, Open, and Live - at the National Student Television Awards in 2006. The tie-up between extra-curricular and academic activities doesn't stop there. In 2004 student scriptwriter Howard Hunt became the first Briton to receive the Sir Peter Ustinov prize at the International Emmy Awards Ceremony in New York. The relevant degree is Scriptwriting for Film & TV. Media Production and Scriptwriting dropped only 2 points at the assessments. Those not making it straight into scriptwriting find work as script readers, editors, agents, production assistants, researchers, etc, or write for for radio, magazines, corporate videos, even computer games. Recent figures showed that 18 out of 23 traceable graduates were in permanent employment, one was in temporary employment, two were in further study

and one had opted for time out from a career to become a mother. There is also a strong Creative Writing degree.

Computer Science is another strong employment niche. Some 7% + graduates become software engineers or consultants or systems analysts. Look at BSc Software Engineering Management which makes full use of two of their curricular strengths, also BEng Electronic Systems Design, Computer Communications and Applied Computing & Electronics.

Other graduate employment strengths include BSc Archaeology Recently, renowned forensic archaeologist Prof Margaret Cox established the world's first International Forensic Centre of Excellence here.

In sport, golf is a speciality. The third year of their Sport Management (Golf) is spent in industry. The uni's expertise in Business Management and Communications, rather than sport per se, suggests an essentially different approach to the golf course at Birmingham, but no less hopeful employment wise. They're looking to get you employed in golf or health clubs, sports complexes, event management, tourism, local authorities, etc.

Finally, the 22-point teaching assessment scores in nursing and midwifery ensure a steady flow of students into the health sector. Out at Kingston Mauward College, there are also degrees in Animal Management/Health & Nursing Studies.

SOCIAL SCENE

STUDENTS' UNION SU night club, **The Old Fire Station (TOFS** for short) is the envy of many a Student Union up and down the country. It's very cool and has three rooms to play in! The student special is a legendary Friday night out *Lollipop*,

---

AT A GLANCE	
ACADEMIC FILE:	
Subjects assessed	**20**
Excellent	**70%**
Typical entry requirements	**277 points**
Application acceptance rate	**20%**
Students-staff ratio	**18:1**
First/2:1 degree pass rate	**62%**
ACCOMMODATION FILE:	
Guarantee to freshers	**Apply early**
Style	**Halls, flats, houses**
Catered	**None**
En-suite	**1,000+ rooms**
Price range pw	**£65-£88**
City rent pw	**£60-£100**

WHAT IT'S REALLY LIKE

UNIVERSITY:

Social Life	★★★★
Campus scene	**Spin doctors & suits/up-beat ents**
Student Union services	**Good**
Politics	**Little interest**
Sport	**Competitive**
National team position	**36th**
Sport facilities	**Good**
Arts opportunities	**Available**
Student magazine	**Nerve**
Student newspaper	**Student Press**
Student radio	**Birst FM**
National Radio Awards	**Gold, 2006**
Student TV	**Nerve TV**
TV awards	**4 awards, 2006**
Nightclub	**The Old Fire Station**
Bars	**Dylans, D2**
Union ents	**Fancy Dress Mondays, Lollipop, Comedy Factory, RAG, one-off gigs**
Union societies	**40**
Parking	**Poor despite many with cars**

TOWN:

Entertainment	★★★★
Scene	**Beach, shopping, night life vibrant**
Town/gown relations	**Good**
Risk of violence	**Average**
Cost of living	**High**
Student concessions	**Good**
Survival + 2 nights out	**£75 pw**
Part-time work campus/town	**Good**

plenty to chose from - Freshers, Christmas, Valentine's, Sport - and the Summer ball, the crème de le crème of the entertainment calendar. It is held in a large field just outside Bournemouth and is more like a festival than a ball. With three or four tents, thousands of students dressed in the craziest costumes you can imagine, dancing till the early hours of the morning. The survivors photograph is the *piece de resistance*, where all the remaining party people go down to the beach and have their photo taken as the sun comes up to prove their hardcore, all night status!

Talbot Campus is home to **Dylan's Bar**, with very cheap menu - pizza, burgers and healthier options like baked potatoes and omelettes. Evening entertainment includes quizzes, DJ's and live gigs. **D2** is a more relaxed sports bar where football is screened on the large projector screen. Both on campus bars are open seven days a week during term time.

What else is it good for? Well, media of course! *Nerve Magazine*, Radio, TV. These and Nerve Online and Nerve Events are fantastic opportunities to get involved. See Academia, page 81 on their recent award-winning form. Indeed, all elements were commended in national competition last year, and *Student Press*, a paper run independently of the Student's Union won an award at the national Journalism Awards the year before.

There's a vast array of clubs and societies to choose from from diving, computer gaming, poetry to horse riding and music, which is worth a mention: there's a good orchestra and choir.

There are also numerous volunteering opportunities to get involved in throughout the year with MAD days, Community Champions, etc. For more information log on to www.the-hub.org.uk. The Students' Union also provides a free confidential advice service on issues relating to accommodation, course and finances.

Yet, for all this, Bournemouth still doesn't quite have the intense student culture of some other universities. It's not easy to pinpoint why although it may be to do with low participation.

with more r'n'b and cheese than you can shake a stick at. Popular too are the funky fancy dress parties where themes include: *Back to Skool*, *Greece, Dr's and Nurses*, *Chav Party* and *Pyjama Party*. Wednesday's is live band night, Monday nights is also home to *Comedy Factory* where doors open at 8 and Saturday nights sees *Maison* on monthly rotation. The crowning success of the club this year has been the one-off events and the club has been at capacity with artists like Hard Fi, Soulwax and Alan Fletcher aka. Karl Kennedy.

Balls are frequent and memorable. There are

> *Serious, specialist job opportunities are on offer. Though actual graduate track employment is lowish, its students are winning gongs at the national media awards, and enjoying a Brighton-style seaside resort, bursting with hedonistic promise.*

SPORT With the arrival of the course in sports management (see *Academia*), a brand new golf simulator has been installed in the Department of Sport and Recreation. This joins the south coast's premier climbing facility, the Hot Rocks climbing wall. Proximity to the sea encourages windsurfing, sailing, paragliding, jet skiing, etc. The uni provides full-time instructors and facilities for a wide range of other sports, and there has been a huge improvement in their national placings recently (42nd). A sports hall includes squash courts and multigym. Cricketers play at the county-standard ground, Dean Park.

Town Dropped in the middle, where four roads meet, we found wall-to-wall pleasure, whatever your bent. There's no shortage of things to spend money on, and part-time opportunities for work are legion. It is an extraordinary place, a born-again English seaside resort, and if bar and club life proves too much, there's always the beach, and the New Forest is but a short drive away.

PILLOW TALK

Accommodation is guaranteed for first years, but the guarantee includes hotels and guest houses, so get in quick. Places in the student village on Talbot (3 to 7-bed houses; free internet access), and in Hurn House (single study bedroom with sink in central Bournemouth; free internet access), Cranborne House (single en-suite study bedroom 5 mins from Hurn House; no parking; internet access; subsidised uni bus) and brand new Purbeck House (single, en-suite study bedrooms close to Cranborne House; internet with one-off connection charge) are limited to 250, 152, 497 and 518 respectively. Rooms in Talbot are en suite. Abbotsbury House in Pokesdown, close to Bournemouth Hospital is the new residence (4-6 bed flats) for nurses. As in most seaside resorts, town accommodation is plentiful and good.

GETTING THERE

☞ By road: M3/M27/A31/ A338, The Wessex Way; at second r/about follow uni signs to Talbot. From west A35 then A3049 (Wallisdown Road). For Bournemouth campus, leave A338 at St Paul's r/about (Travel Interchange junction) on to St Paul's road and find a car park.
☞ By rail: London Waterloo, 1:45; Bristol, 2:30; Manchester, 5:37.
☞ By coach: London, 2:15; Bristol, 3:10.

UNIVERSITY OF BRADFORD

The University of Bradford
Richmond Road
Bradford BD7 1DP

TEL 0800 073 1225
FAX 01274 236260
EMAIL course-enquiries@bradford.ac.uk
WEB www.bradford.ac.uk

Bradford University Union
Richmond Road
Bradford BD7 1DP

TEL 01274 233300
FAX 01274 235530
EMAIL ubu-communications@bradford.ac.uk
WEB www.ubui.co.uk

VAG VIEW

A university since 1966, it came out of Bradford Technical College, which itself grew out of the textile industry in the 1860s. Today the connection between higher education and the workplace remains key.

Their slogan is 'Making Knowledge Work' and they have erected a 5-metre high, bronze sculpture to celebrate it. There's a first-class Modern Languages Department, which facilitates an international dimension to much else of what's on offer academically, and they ride high in the tables for graduate

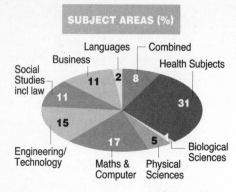

SUBJECT AREAS (%)

Languages — Combined
Business
Health Subjects
Social Studies incl law
11 2 8
11
31
15
17 5
Engineering/ Technology
Maths & Computer
Physical Sciences
Biological Sciences

provision in the health industries, electronic & electrical manufacturing and in the pharmaceutical industry. More than a quarter of intake is now in health/medical sciences and Bradford has the country's largest Optometry Department.

A very healthy student-to-staff ratio of 16-to-1 is reflected in a rising first class and upper second pass rate, currently 60%, and a regular position in the Top 20 nationwide for real (i.e. graduate track) employment.

What's more, students do actually like it here. Bradford is not London, nor is it Milton Keynes (thank God!), nor yet is it Leeds. Bradford may challenge the southern picture of where England is/should be, but what it offers undergraduates is a very studenty, close-knit, pub-based, curry-central experience, uninhibited by issues of wealth and class. To many a Bradford student, the southerner's picture of the acceptable face of the North, namely Leeds, because of its premier-league nightclubs and Harvey Nichs, appears rather expensive and, well, just a tad outré. Bradford students can easily partake of Leeds, as the city is just a few

moments down the road, but few do.

Last year, after much consultation with staff and students, the uni has earmarked £130 million to enhance existing buildings and create more social space for students, bringing facilities onto one campus.

CAMPUS

The main campus, a ten-minute stroll from town, is compact and bounded by roads on all four sides. All teaching, except for Business Studies, is carried out on site, and there are many halls of residence.

It is a relatively small uni and has a reputation for being a particularly close-knit community. There's crime in the city, as in any city, but there's a safety bus at night to truck you anywhere from campus within a seven-mile radius. The union makes student safety an absolute priority.

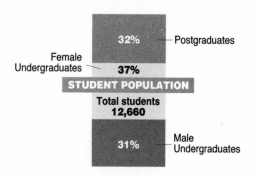

32% — Postgraduates
Female Undergraduates — 37%
STUDENT POPULATION
Total students 12,660
31% — Male Undergraduates

FEES, BURSARIES

UK & EU Fees, £3,070 plus £600 for sandwich year in 4-year course. If in receipt of a Maintenance Grant, regardless of whether partial or full, you get a £500 bursary in the first year, £700 in your second, and £900 in your final year.

STUDENT PROFILE

They have an open access policy, and the intake from the lower socio-economic classes (4-7) is well over their government benchmark (46.3% as against the requirement of Bradford to take 34.8%). The take from the state sector is also generous, at 94.8%, 3% over what is required. Such a policy is often associated with a high drop-out, but theirs is about average, which suggests everyone's happy.

There is a particular welcome to overseas students and careful monitoring of all processes of integration. Most undergrads are scientists and techies, but life doesn't get too predictable.

ACADEMIA & JOBS

Broad study areas at Bradford are Archaeological

UNIVERSITY/STUDENT PROFILE	
University since	**1966**
Situation/style	**City campus**
Student population	**12660**
Undergraduates	**8545**
- mature	**33%**
- non EU undergraduates	**13%**
- male/female	**45/55**
- non-traditional student intake	**46%**
- state school intake	**95%**
- drop-out rate	**19%**
- undergraduate applications	**Up 2%**

Sciences, Chemical and Forensic Sciences, Computing & Informatics, Design & Technology, Engineering, Geography & Environmental Sciences, Health Studies, Humanities, ICT, Law, Life Sciences, Management and Business, Media Studies, Psychology, Social Sciences.

Note the good 'graduate track' employment record (73%). Few did better, and you get it for a relatively light average entry requirement (268 points).

There's a good ratio of PCs to students, and excellent facilities to log into library electronic sources via laptop. A wireless network has been established across the campus so that students can log in free from anywhere. Discounted 'Bradford-ready' student laptops are available

A Disability Office follows a proudly proactive strategy. An organisation called Impact targets ethnic students with a view to enhancing their employment chances.

Bacteriologists and microbiologists work with living organisms, an awareness of human health and environmental issues, food poisoning, drugs, viruses, bacteria and other bugs. It's an important field, and Bradford is a leader, one aspect of the health industry dimension which is indeed their single biggest area of graduate employment, and which includes a pioneering Clinical Science pathway into medicine. Some 30% of graduates do something connected with health, and a quarter of intake is now in health/medical sciences. BSc Hons Biomedical Sciences comes in at 260 points, Medical Microbiology the same. But the uni's expertise is ever wider – biochemists, pharmacists, medical scientists (see their BSc Applied Biomedical Sciences, new this year), physiotherapists (5% of all Bradford graduates), medical radiographers and midwives all look carefully at what is on offer here. A £6-million Institute of Pharmaceutical Innovation has recently been completed.

See their 3-4-tear (sandwich) BSc Chemistry with Pharmaceutical & Forensic Science and a 4-year MChem in this, also the 4-year MSci Forensic and Medical Sciences. Also their pharmaceutical management, pharmacy and pharmacology degrees

Bradford are among the leaders, too, in producing graduate ophthalmic opticians, almost a fifth of them in fact from the country's largest Optometry department. However, they're not giving away places for BSc Hons Optometry. Teaching inspection 23 out of 24 points.

Another fruitful avenue is BSc Archaeology. They earned 22 out of 24 points at the assessments and Grade 5 for research. At least one science will be required. New this year is a BA in it too

The uni's employment map is studded with systems analysts, software engineers, computer/IT

consultants and programmers. Look at the Computing and Cybernetics faculties. There is a fine track record in film through its BSc Computer Animation & Special Effects degree, and the BSc Animatronics is especially interesting in that it teaches technology and skills to create, sculpt and animate motorised puppets – the 'live' monster that you see in movies. New to this field this year are Design for Computer Games and a BA in Computer Animation.

AT A GLANCE

ACADEMIC FILE:

Subjects assessed	**21**
Excellent	**62%**
Typical entry requirements	**268 points**
Application acceptance rate	**21%**
Students-staff ratio	**16:1**
First/2:1 degree pass rate	**60%**

ACCOMMODATION FILE:

Guarantee to freshers	**100%**
Style	**Halls**
Catered	**None**
En suite	**5%**
Approx price range pw	**£54-£79**
City rent pw	**£40-£50**

Among their ICT & Computer Applications degrees is the new ICT with Media, and joining the BSc Media Technology & Production is a raft of six BA Media Studies degrees (cinematics, animation, digital imaging, music techno, TV, web design).

Look, too, at another niche area – their Electrical and Electronic Engineering, Mobile Communications and Telecommunications degrees. Again, the Automotive Design Technology and Integrated Industrial Design (Eco Design, Sports Technology, etc) degrees make them leaders in starting careers for design and development engineers.

Bradford may challenge the southern picture of where England is/should be, but what it offers is a very studenty, close-knit scene, uninhibited by issues of wealth or class, and a graduate track employment record never out of the Top 10 nationally.

Would-be social workers and counsellors note that the Social Work degree is accredited by the General Social Care Council. There's also BA Applied Criminal Justice Studies, and new BA and BSc degrees in Psychology.

Since September 2005, there is also a fully fledged School of Law with an LlB, and BSc Internet, Law & Society.

Other key strands take us further into the ethos of the place, Bradford's famed Department of Peace Studies (studied from the standpoints of ethics, psychology, sociology, history) and such as International Relations & Security Studies and Conflict Resolution.

SOCIAL SCENE

Principal gathering place at the **Richmond** (the uni building) is the **Steve Biko** bar (serves food as well), famous for its appearance in the *CAMRA Good Beer Guide* and distinguished, too, by an L-shaped pool table and jukebox. At the Communal Building there's a small nightclub, **Escape** (100), both with big screen TVs. Also in the Commie are the main venue, **The Basement** (1,300 capacity), home to cheesy/dance Friday night disco, *FND*, and now **Colours** (450), actually part of the Basement, though you can't see the joins, for late-night licence, smaller gigs and club-nights. Other clubnights are currently *Rock Sox* (rock/indie) and *Pop Sox* (cheese/retro), FND (Friday Night Disco) and Allsorts (LGBT night). Live acts too.

There's no arts faculty at Bradford but they have three of the most pulsating arts venues to be found anywhere. **Theatre in the Mill** is home to BUTG (Bradford Uni Theatre Group), which puts on a show (student or pro) every week and has the cheapest bar (**Scaff Bar**) in the uni. **The Tasmin Little Music Centre** does similar stuff for a student jazz ensemble, choral society, chamber choir and three orchestras, and an amazing series of *Music for Lunch* at the **Alhambra Studio** in Great Horton Road. Then there's **Gallery II** for art.

Student cinema, **BSC**, happens three times a week – art movies and the latest blockbusters, many only a few months after general release, all for a couple of quid. Showings are in **Great Hall** (capacity, 1300). Media-wise there's *Scrapie*, the award-winning, fortnightly magazine, RamAir fm for student radio. Among some fifty societies, Twirl Soc and Amnesty are the most popular. Amnesty International is of course the foremost organisation in defence of human rights. Twirl Soc, you may be intrigued to discover is about twirling, throwing, juggling anything that spins in a circle of motion. Politics spins left, activity average – war, racism, recycling.

SPORT There are thirty-five sports clubs – women's volleyball is a particular strength. An on-campus sports centre has a 25m swimming pool, sauna suite, solarium, Nautilus fitness suite, etc. There are squash courts and a dozen or so pitches for cricket, football and rugby, plus 9,000 square metres of artificial turf sand-grass for 5-a-sides, netball, and hockey. One site is behind the halls of residence, the other 4 miles from campus, where the pavilion has a bar.

WHAT IT'S REALLY LIKE

UNIVERSITY:	
Social Life	★★★★
Campus scene	Close-knit, active, studenty
Student Union services	Good
Politics	Left – funding, war, racism, recycling
Sport	35 clubs
National team position	88th
Sport facilities	Good
Arts opportunities	Excellent drama dance, film, music; art avg
Student magazine	Scrapie
Student radio	RamAir
Nightclub	Basement,
Small venue	Escape
Bars	Steve Biko, Courtyard
Union ents	Live plus club-nights Rock Sox, Pop Sox, disco - FND, Allsorts (LGBT)
Union societies	85
Most popular societies	Twirl Soc/Amnesty
Parking	Good
CITY:	
Entertainment	★★★
Scene	Curry central/ rough in parts
Town/gown relations	OK
Risk of violence	Average
Cost of living	Low
Student concessions	Excellent
Survival + 2 nights out	£40 pw
Part-time work campus/town	Good

Town Bradford is curry central and the cheapest university city in the country. You'll be amazed by the cost, the quality and the sheer number of eateries. You eat it with chapatis here, not rice, and a three-year degree is barely enough time to be sure that you have found the best. Prices hover around £3 for a basic chicken dish with chapatis. At **Mumtaz Paan House** on Great Horton Road they charge by weight. Students have curry locals; staff and dishes become firm friends.

Bradford, a city of traditional pubs was shaken a few years ago with the advent of **Hogshead** (aka Bar Ikea), **Varsity**, the **Freestyle & Firkin** – not pubs, but bars where food is part of the deal. **Chicago Rock Café** also came to town – all on Great Horton Road, right by the uni. Still, there's atmosphere in older student haunts, however often they refurbish them – **The Peel** (Richmond Road), **Delius Lived Next Door** (Claremont) and the **Queens Hall**, though this is a bit *ex*-student: replete with MTV during the day, but suits and towny vibes at night.

Gaudi's (was **Tumbler's**) and **Club Rio** – Wednesday night (indie/'80s) are enjoyable venues almost on campus, the first tucked behind the Richmond, Club Rio practically next door to Longside halls. City clubs **Nexus** (was **Underworld**: late night cellar drinking), and **Pickwicks** (now **Bar Margaloof** but still known as Pickwicks: student DJs: pop, dance and indie) are a student institution.

PILLOW TALK

New in 2003 was Wardley House, city centre, en suite flats. Trinity Hall, at the Laisteridge Lane site (5 mins from campus), is also en suite and overshadowed by the two tower blocks, Revis Barber Hall and Dennis Bellamy. Health students occupy Charles Morris Hall here. Halls on campus are cheaper, uncatered, Shearbridge Green, Longside and Kirkstone. Only Bradford and University halls get the thumbs down.

Now, this year an 'ecoversity' project is coming to fruition, boulevards of terraced housing for some 500 students - eight to a house - traditional communities, but with a modern awareness of energy conservation. Design and layout, alternative sources of power (such as wind and solar power), and incentives to householders to minimise use of fuel are all part of the plan - opens, summer 2007.

GETTING THERE

☛ By road: M62 and M606 connect with national motorway network; from north, A629/A650; from northeast, A1 or A19, then A59, A658.
☛ By rail: London King's Cross, Birmingham, 3:00; Edinburgh, 4:00; Manchester, 1:00.
☛ By air: Leeds/Bradford Airport.
☛ By coach: London, 4:30; Manchester, 1-2:30.

STUDENT BRIGHTON – THE CITY

It's often been said there is something a little bit cheeky about Brighton & Hove. Made popular by the flamboyant Prince Regent, Brighton has a

reputation for naughtiness and frivolity. What you will find is a welcoming city full of diversity and tolerance, perhaps the most cosmopolitan place in the UK. It's multitude of clubs, shops, restaurants and vast range of entertainment make Brighton and Hove the 'city by the sea' that really does have everything for everyone, so it's no wonder so many students never leave and settle for good.

NIGHTLIFE

The town has a huge array of clubs and pubs. The place to be for students on a Wednesday is *Ave It!* at **Creation**, where Brighton and Sussex Uni students dance the night away fuelled by the cut price drinks.

Students head for the seafront clubs, including **The Beach** and **Concorde2**, home of the famous *Big Beat Boutique*. If it's drum and bass you're after, lesbian and gay clubs, reggae or salsa, you won't be disappointed; check local listings for info. If trash is your thing go to **Dynamite Boogaloo** and revel in cheesy and camp disco 'toons' and be astounded by the almighty Dolly Rocket and Boogaloo Stu's outrageous live cabaret.

Midweek madness continues with the Latino feel and many participate in the carnival-style nights. You could be forgiven for thinking that no one works in Brighton, as week-night events are often as packed as the big weekend events.

EATS

Brighton boasts cuisine from almost every country in the world. Entire streets, like Preston Street on the Brighton/Hove border are devoted to gastronomic indulgence, there are late-night and 24-hour restaurants, shops and supermarkets for the night owls. There are over 400 restaurants including Cordon Bleu, English, French, Indian, Mexican, freshly caught fish (and chips), Japanese, Thai, tapas, Greek, Spanish, Lebanese, Egyptian, American, Cajun, greasy spoon, vegetarian, places with beautiful views of the sea, sushi and take-away. The numerous Italian eateries situated in the **Lanes** are locked in a price war, each bending over backwards to offer pizzas and pastas at amazingly cheap prices, making it possible to have a filling meal and a pint for under a fiver in a decent restaurant.

It is said that there are nearly as many pubs in Brighton & Hove as there are days in the year, they range from sophisticated late-night-cocktail-bars, high street pub chains to small independent owned drinking dens.

Do head for the student friendly **Ali-Cats** which is good for cocktails and shows free early evening movies. **Mrs Fitzherbert's** offers a cosy drink regular and acoustic nights. For THE student pub experience seek out **The Druid's** where the insatiable landlord Chippy offers students a warm welcome, great food and regular drinks promotions

to make everyone feel at home.

SHOPS

With the best shopping south of the capital, there are more than 700 independently owned shops to browse. For designer clobber and antiques The **Laines** will suit any wannabe David Dickinson, but the prices will not be 'cheap as chips'. The North Laine is the bohemian centre of the town: with feel-good veggie cafés, bars, great second hand emporiums and a mishmash of fabric and clothes shops there is not much you can't get your mitts on in this district. Kemp Town boasts a flea market, a second hand book shop and is home to Brighton's own Lesbian and Gay quarter, with bars, clubs and shops to attract the Pink Pound. Big name stores can be found under one roof at **Churchill Square**, and the **Marina** has designer outlet stores in addition to a gigantic Asda, bowling alley, cinema, casino and other attractions.

STREET/BEACH LIFE

Whether it is the middle of winter and you want to blow away the cobwebs, or top up the tan in the summer you will find the beach is a welcome respite from the hub bub of city life. Boasting two piers, the famous west pier now open again after the huge fire a few years ago, you can visit fortune tellers, play the penny falls, buy more rock than you can shake a stick at and kiss me quick, squeeze me slow to your heart's content.

Highlights of the many events include the month-long **Brighton Festival** held in May, both revellers and locals flock to the beach and streets to enjoy the food, drink, juggling, samba band processions, free film shows on huge screens, firework displays and annual events like the **Pride Parade** and the **Winter Solstice** 'Burning of the Clocks' extravaganzas mean you are never short of something to do. There is also talk of **Fatboy Slim** holding another of his legendary beach parties.

ARTS

All over the city, self-expression is the way. Brighton Uni's **Grand Parade Gallery** and the **Brighton Art Gallery** in Pavilion Gardens feature regular innovative ever changing exhibitions.

Innovative, contemporary art is also displayed in a multitude of cafés, bars and often in the street. There are many live venues, which again cater to all tastes. The **Dome** concert hall has hosted diverse artists including the London Philharmonic, Beverly Knight and Air.

In terms of comedy, theatre and film, Brighton is incredibly spoilt. **The Paramount Comedy Festival** comes to town in October bringing big name talent like Jo Brand, Bill Bailey and Johnny Vegas. The **Komedia Cabaret** bar has two different productions simultaneously each night with deals for students. **The Dome**, **Theatre Royal** and the **Brighton Centre** get the big-name touring artists in addition to the snooker championships. **The Gardner Arts Centre** on the University of Sussex campus plays host to art, film, theatre, comedy and music, and is nationally acclaimed. If it all gets too much you can always nip to the flicks, The **Odeon** is the most student-friendly offering discounts; the **UGC** is part of the **Marina** multiplex, and the **Duke of York's** the only cinema with legs (no it's true they are hanging off the roof!), a Brighton treasure and the oldest purpose-built cinema in Britain shows art-house and classic films.

It is almost as if Brighton was made for students; you cannot ask for a much better place to study.

Harvey Atkinson

UNIVERSITY OF BRIGHTON

The University of Brighton
Mithras House
Lewes Road
Brighton BN2 4AT

TEL 01273 644644
FAX 01273 642607
EMAIL admissions@brighton.ac.uk
WEB www.brighton.ac.uk

Brighton Students' Union
Cockcroft Building
Lewes Road
Brighton BN2 4GJ,

TEL 01273 642870
FAX 01273 600694
EMAIL ubsu@brighton.ac.uk
WEB www.ubsu.net

VAG VIEW

*B*righton *town has been re-born as a city, inevitable consequence of its long-term reputation as London-by-the-sea. Brighton city is an energetic, laid-back, imaginative, vibrant, artistic, commercial, alternative, innovative, refreshing coastal cocktail, and its very own uni evinces some of these elements too.*

The creativity of Brighton students fits them perfectly into the picture. The uni traces its roots back to 1877, when the School of Art opened on Grand Parade, opposite the Royal Pavilion. The Faculty of Arts & Architecture, as it is today, is very much part of the city. The cream of the art world strut their funky stuff around Brighton, while the commercial, innovative and energetic bits find expression beyond its bounds in the Brighton Business School, the School of IT and the Chelsea School of Sport.

All is brought together through CPD, a Continuing Professional Development initiative – the uni works with local councils, health authorities and industry throughout the whole region to educate and re-educate 'the workforce', as they put it like something out of Soylent Green.

And now, in partnership with Sussex University up the road, they have launched

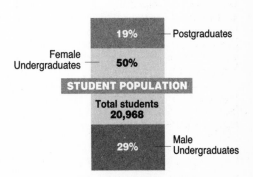

the Brighton & Sussex Medical School, the whole project ensuring ever closer links between the people's University of Brighton and the local community.

CAMPUS

Brighton University spreads through central Brighton and into the surrounding areas of Moulsecoomb, Falmer and Eastbourne. North up the Lewes Road from the self-conscious arts campus on **Grand Parade** – (rail and bus links are good, parking is not) – you get to the **Moulsecoomb Campus**, which houses the Business School, the Faculty of Science & Engineering, which includes pharmacy, maths, engineering, and the Faculty of IT. Further on you find the **Falmer Campus**, actually bang opposite the University of Sussex campus. While Grand Parade is the old art college and Moulsecoomb is the old technical college, the Falmer site was once Brighton's teacher training college and still offers teacher training today, along with health subjects.

Off to the east along the coast from Brighton, is

UNIVERSITY/STUDENT PROFILE	
University since	**1992**
Situation/style	**Seaside campuses**
Student population	**20968**
Undergraduates	**16517**
- mature	**48%**
- non EU undergraduates	**7%**
- male/female	**37/63**
- non-traditional student intake	**30%**
-state school intake	**93%**
- drop-out rate	**20%**
- undergraduate applications	**Up 18%**

the **Eastbourne Campus**, the uni's nationally renowned Chelsea School of Sports Science. They opened a £3-million sports centre there in November 2000. Outdoor pitches and indoor facilities are open to the public – widening access, integrating with the community. It's what this uni is all about, in case you hadn't heard.

Along the coast to the west, the Brighton-backed **University Centre Hastings** is delivering courses in information technology management and business, education, health and social care.

Find out which campus you're bound for and visit it - they are all very different.

FEES, BURSARIES

UK & EU Fees, 2007: £3,070. Sliding-scale bursaries for those in receipt of HE Maintenance Grant. A hundred scholarships of £1,000 each p.a. are awarded on academic merit. There are various sports scholarships too, such as the elite athlete's squad and disabled athletes scholarships. They range from £300 to £1,000. See www.brighton.ac.uk/studentlife/money/scholarships

STUDENT PROFILE

There is no typical Brighton student. It is all very disparate. The cutting-edge artistes may be the most visible in town, but creative arts is not representative of the whole student body.

Most notably, perhaps, students here are mature (48% of undergraduates), which means, not that they are all wrinklies but that they come here after their 21st birthday and may well be more work-orientated than your traditional undergrad freeloader. They are here for a clear-cut purpose.

There is also a big international intake. The 7% figure we give in the *Profile* box above refers only to the full-time first degree undergraduates. Many more from abroad come among the other half of HND undergrads, etc, in the 21,000 total. Brighton has long been known internationally for its language-school history, so those same folk now flock across the Channel to the uni. 'We have a big language school here, do a lot of language work with all kinds of undergraduates.'

ACADEMIA & JOBS

Brighton's strengths in art and design have been recognised in the award of national teaching centres in design and creativity. The uni has a growing reputation in areas such as sport and hospitality, as well as scoring well in teacher education rankings. Health-related subjects have also grown strongly.

WHERE BRIGHTON GRADUATES END UP
Health & Social Work: 15%; Education: 16%; Wholesale/Retail: 11%; Manufacturing: 6%; Financial Activities: 8%; Public Administration, Civil Service & Defence: 4%; Hotel/Restaurant: 5%; Transport & Communications (including Telecommunications): 4%; Construction: 3%; Personnel: 3%; Computer: 2%; Business & Management: 3%; Accountancy: 1%; Media (including Film): 1%; Architecture: 2%; Publishing: 1%; Artistic/Literary: 5%; Sport: 3%.

Approximate 'graduate track' employed **65%**

The uni traces its roots back to 1877 when the School of Art opened on Grand Parade, opposite the Royal Pavilion. Today they have, besides the Fine Art (Painting, Printmaking, Sculpture), BA Fashion with Business. Successes in fashion and textiles have been both local and international and include employment with DKNY, Calvin Klein, Versace, Dolce & Gabbana, Valentino, Givenchy, Alexander McQueen, Hussein Chalayan and Julien MacDonald.

The cream of the art world strut their funky stuff around Brighton, while the commercial, innovative and energetic bits find expression beyond its bounds in the Brighton Business School, the School of IT and the Chelsea School of Sport.

Graphic artists, designers, illustrators, sculptors, ceramists and set designers also fare well, and the faculty leads graduates via Editorial Photography into the print industry via pre-production processes (origination/colour separation work). There's a Grade 5 rating for research, which indicates international status. Teaching inspection 22 out of 24. Clearly a talent and interest in art is essential and generally your portfolio will be crucial.

From Interior Architecture, Product Design (BSc), 3D Design, Music & Visual Art in the Art & Design Faculty to Civil Engineering, Design Engineering, Design Sports Technology in the Engineering Department, and BSc Architectural Technology in Science & Engineering, there is a strand which identifies the symbiotic nature of the uni's academic profile and weaves a colourful thread through the fabric of graduate employment nationally. What's more, entry is not demanding. Further design suggestions are made by BEng Hons Automotive Engineering, a big strength, where would-be racing car designers will be pitted at the Moulsecoomb campus, the old techno college just north of the city. Easy ride by train.

The creeping of skills out of one faculty into another has led to a rationalisation this year. They now have five faculties: Arts and Architecture; Education and Sport; Health; Management & Information Sciences; Science & Engineering.

In the vital health provision, there's a great reputation in Pharmacy, Biomedical Sciences, Biosciences, Nursing and even Acupuncture (BSc Oriental Medicine), and now they've teamed up with Sussex Uni in a new medical school.

The degree is a 5-year BMBS (Bachelor of Medicine, Bachelor of Surgery). A small, personal school, they are looking for commitment and compassion in their applicants, but it's not easy to get in - the application acceptance rate is 5% (10% is avgerage). You'll be based with the teacher trainees and other Health undergrads at Brighton Uni's Falmer Campus, readily accessible by road/train and bang opposite the Sussex University campus. UKCAT is required, along with 320-340 points, including Chemistry at A level and AS biology.

For pharmacists, there's BSc Pharmaceutical & Chemical Sciences (sandwich available) and MPharm. The School has been designated a 'preferred provider' by Boots plc. The new medical school can only raise its profile further. You'll be on the accessible Moulsecoomb Campus. Teaching Inspection 23.

Nationally, over 1,000 graduates become physiotherapists each year. At Brighton, BSc Physiotherapy cuts the mustard in the jobs market, and there's a split tariff – entry is negotiable for mature students. Teaching inspection, 22 points. See, too, the new Occupational Therapy - BSc.

Bacteriologist and microbiologist graduates are similarly popular with employers. The uni is also up there in the Top 10 with its podiatry degrees.

Education is, of course, a major provision here – some 15% of Brighton's graduates will become teachers. Brighton is one of the new unis that outstrips traditionally strong, premier-league secondary school producers, Durham, Glasgow by sheer weight of number. Output: 50% secondary, 31% primary. You'll be at the Falmer site, opposite

ACADEMIC EXCELLENCE

TEACHING
(Rated Excellent or 17+ out of 24)

Philosophy	**24**
Pharmacology & Pharmacy	**23**
Nursing, Maths, Art & Design,	**22**
Subjects Allied to Medicine,	
Organismal, Molecular	
Biosciences, Library/Info Mgt,	
Tourism/Hospitality Mgt	
History of Art, Civil Eng, Educ	**21**
Modern Languages (Dutch,	**20**
French, German, Iberian	
Studies, Italian), Elec/Electron	
Engineering, Building.	

RESEARCH:
Top grades 5/5*

Biomedical Sciences, **Grade 5**
European Studies, Art & Design

Sussex Uni. They gained top marks from Ofsted for Initial Teacher Education in 2002. Primary and Secondary Design and Technology made the highest category. English with QTS (7-14) asks 240 points at entry. Teaching inspection, 21.

For would-be physical training instructors (Education) Brighton leads the way nationally, the self-contained sporting campus is along the coast at Eastbourne, where this year state of the art facilities enabled a simulation by students of the first successful ascent of Mount Everest. Starting at the height of Everest Base Camp (17,600 ft), a relay of students climbed on a Stairmaster to the equivalent height of Everest (29,035ft) while carrying a rucksack and experiencing freezing weather conditions.

See also the new BA (Hons) Sport Journalism degree, which includes teaching for the National Council for the Training of Journalists certificate in magazine journalism. The BBC's director of sport, Peter Salmon, will be helping develop the broadcast aspect. See also the Foundation degree in Broadcasting.

The Faculty of Management and Information Sciences, new in 2003, combines the Business School, School of Service Management and the new school of Computing, Mathematics and Information Sciences, together with the research group CENTRIM. It was created to adapt to changes in the business and management world where the integration of IT and business is key to success.

In computing they offer a B/MEng Digital Electronics, Computing & Communications, BSc Computer Sciences or Computing, Digital Media Development, Informatique, Interactive Computing, Internet Computing or Internet Business Computing, Maths & Computing, Software Engineering, which produce a wealth of IT consultants. Sandwich modes are available. You'll be based at Moulsecoomb.

An interesting niche in the business provision holds a dedicated series of International Travel/Tourism Management degrees, which score well for employment. New this years are Entreprenuership in Hospitality/Ttravel & Tourism, and foundation degrees - Travel & Tourism Marketing and Tourism Enterprise Management.

Note, too, the language provision at this uni, which internationalises the business provision. Brighton has an international Grade 5 for research in European Studies, and a decent 20 points for undergraduate teaching in Modern Languages.

Other new degrees are Management in the Service Industries, Marketing Food & Drink, and Retail Management.

SOCIAL SCENE

STUDENTS' UNION The sad truth is that ents at Brighton have been flattened by a series of mishaps. First they had the **Basement**, a seriously good club/venue that was commandeered by the uni administration. Then they took over **Akademia,** a café bar and theatre on Manchester Street, which again was prised from them. Now all they have is **Falmer Bar, which has been under renovation**. Students make use of Sussex campus, and eat their heart out at The Retreat Café (Falmer) or Cockcroft Café (Moulescoomb), or go into Brighton, which is an amazing scene (see

WHAT IT'S REALLY LIKE	
UNIVERSITY:	
Social Life	★★
Campus scene	**Individual**
Student Union	**Aimless**
Politics	**Average; student issues, anti-war**
Sport	**70 clubs, very competitive out at Eastbourne**
National team position	**28th**
Sport facilities	**Good**
Arts opportunities	**Drama/Dance OK**
Student magzine	**Jon Doe**
National media awards	**2006 nomination**
Nightclub	**None**
Bars	**Falmer Bar**
Union ents	**Ave It! @ Creation**
Union societies	**50+**
Parking	**Not good**
TOWN:	
Entertainment	★★★★★
Scene	**Exceptional**
Town/gown relations	**OK**
Risk of violence	**Low**
Cost of living	**High**
Student concessions	**Good**
Survival + 2 nights out	**£100 pw**
Part-time work campus/town	**Average/excellent**

Student Brighton). The Union promotes the *Ave It!* clubnight on Wednesday nights at **Creation** on West Street. Out on the town can get expensive. Many of the jobs in Brighton are service sector based, so the wages reflect this, but there are opportunities for students to work in call centres and for local businesses where the rates of pay can be well above the minimum wage.

They claim 50 + societies and 70 + sports clubs, and a student magazine called *Jon Doe*. In the 2006 national student media awards, student William

Tidey was nominated in the Sports Journalist category. They used to meddle with Sussex's radio station, but no longer apparently. There seems an aimlessness about the Students' Union, which is not matched by the uni admin, and which the students don't deserve. Perhaps the students couldn't care less what the Union puts on. Perhaps it has become superfluous because there is so much happening in town. See *Student Brighton,* page87.

Perhaps recognising this, over 22,000 separate accounts have been set up to give staff and students their own online space, which includes publicly accessible blogs, newsfeeds and social networking tools. Connecting to friends and colleagues and forming online communities, both for learning and for fun, is now possible.

SPORT Out at the sporty Eastbourne campus there's the new £3 million facility (see *Academia* above). Women's sport is particularly strong, though both sexes do well inter-university.

PILLOW TALK
Accommodation for refreshers is guaranteed only to international students, students under 18, BSMS students, or students with disabilities. It's all self-catered, mainly halls but also uni-leased houses/flats. They claim to be the cheapest in the south of England. New halls of residence on Falmer campus opened in 2003 - 162 en-suite rooms. Last year at Eastbourne came Welkins Halls, the multi-million pound complex accommodating 354, groups of six

AT A GLANCE	
ACADEMIC FILE:	
Subjects assessed	**22**
Excellent	**73%**
Typical entry requirements	**266 points**
Application acceptance rate	**18%**
Med. School acceptance rate	**5%**
Students-staff ratio	**18:1**
First/2:1 degree pass rate	**58%**
ACCOMMODATION FILE:	
Guarantee to freshers	**Very little**
Style	**Halls**
Catered	**None**
En suite	**62%**
Approx price range pw	**£60-£80**
City rent pw	**£70-£75**

rooms, en suite, sharing dining and kitchen areas.

GETTING THERE
☛ By air: Gatwick and Heathrow Airports.
☛ By road: M23 (past Gatwick), A23 to Brighton, A27 eastbound for Falmer, right turn (south on B2123) for Moulsecoomb. From east or west, A27. For Eastbourne, A27 and signs south on to A22.
☛ By rail: London Victoria, 1:10. Change at Brighton for Moulscoomb and Falmer (8 mins).
☛ By coach: London, 1:50.

STUDENT BRISTOL – THE CITY

Billed by many as the London of the South West, Bristol has a distinctly West Country feel and the moment you hear the regional accents you'll know you're a long way from the gold-paved streets of London. Despite this regional feel Bristol itself is a buzzing multicultural city with loads going on and so much to offer that you'll feel as though you're reaping all the benefits of living in a capital city.

ROCK ON
Hills, churches and water are abundant in Bristol and the city has many lush green parks to stroll in. The tastefully-developed Harbourside houses many restaurants and galleries/art centres and is home to much of Bristol's social scene, especially in the summer when the Grolsch musical festivals come to the city (Massive Attack, Basement Jaxx and Kosheen have performed in previous years).

In fact Bristol has a great music scene, born of the days when bands such as Massive Attack and Portishead made their name here. Centres such as **Colston Hall** and the **Carling Academy** host an array of local, national and International bands. Recent acts in the city are Hard-Fi, James Blunt, Babyshambles, The Magic Numbers and K T. Tunstall. The Junction and The Croft at Stokes Croft showcase more alternative or folk music.

The Student Union's **Anson Rooms** have also hosted their own share of great acts; last year saw the Kaiser Chiefs and Franz Ferdinand, while The Rakes are scheduled for the forthcoming term.

Clubs and pubs fill the city, though some are rather expensive. There are plenty of studentier hang-outs though. **Evolution** on the waterfront hosts great nights such as *Wedgies* on Wednesday and

Friday. **Bierkeller** and the **Carling Academy** have good student concessions and put on live alternative/rock music. A fledgling gay scene is to be found at the **Queen's Shilling** or **Vibes** at the bottom of Park Street.

Ninety percent of Bristol's off-licenses and many pubs are located on Whiteladies Road, near the Clifton halls of residence. Ones worth a visit are **Bohemia**, **The Black Boy Inn** and the **Penny Farthing**. However, if you're looking for a stylish joint you should head for **Sloanes** or **Henry J Beans**. And if your parents are in town then a trip to the lovely **Avon Gorge Hotel** is recommended – for a good view of the famous Clifton suspension bridge.

ART

The revamped **Arnolfini** on the Habourside offers a wide range of arty events – from performance poetry to contemporary art. The city of Bristol **Museum** is free entry and currently houses the throne of weapons (installed by artists using de-commissioned weapons from Mozambique) and a rather random collection of pianos and pottery.

Hours can be spent sipping bottomless coffee in cafés around the University areas though particularly good are the **Boston Tea Party** on Park Street and **Toby's Deli Diner** just off Tyndall Avenue. **The York café** in Clifton should also be road-tested for its great fry-up.

THEATRE, FILM

Theatres such as the Old Vic run great deals once a week when students pay a minimum contribution of £3.50 for a ticket. Bristol's **Old Vic** is on a par with London theatres, in terms of variety and standard of drama on offer. Recent plays such as Christopher Marlowe's *Tamburlaine*, starring Greg Hicks, got great reviews from the national press.

For musicals and flashy shows the **Hippodrome** is the place to go though you won't get such cheap tickets. More avant-garde or obscure plays/performances can be found at **The Cube Microplex** (at Dove St South just off King Square). The art centre shows films and art exhibitions but also puts on all sorts of weird and wonderful events such as October's 'Ich bin ein Berliner' festival: a three day celebration of the said city showcasing electronic tunes, films and art.

If film's your thing then the city has a cinema to suit your every taste. **Cineworld**, **Vue**, **Showcase** and **Odeon** cinemas around Bristol show most Blockbusters and mainstream films while the **Watershed** and the Arnolfini on the Harbourside put on art house or International cinema. The **Imax** centre, also on the Harbourside, is worth a visit to see some incredible 3D and special effects. There are also several film festivals on throughout the year, the best being the 'Brief Encounters' short film fest and the self-explanatory 'Animated Encounters'.

OTHER ENTERTAINMENT

Sport is important in Bristol, even though the city lacks a top-flight football club. Bristol City have a large following and have enjoyed success in recent years, unlike local rivals Bristol Rovers.

For rugby, however, though relegated in 2003 from the Zurich Premiership, they are setting new records, finding their way back (and safely so) with extraordinary ease. They can rely too on Gloucestershire County Cricket Club to put a smile on their faces. A visit to all these clubs is well worthwhile.

Laura Cattell

UNIVERSITY OF BRISTOL

The University of Bristol
Senate House
Tyndall Avenue
Bristol BS8 1TH

TEL 0117 928 9000
     0117 925 0177 (prospectus)
FAX 0117 925 1424
EMAIL admissions@bristol.ac.uk
WEB www.bris.ac.uk

Bristol Students' Union
Queens Road
Clifton
Bristol BS8 1LN

TEL 0117 954 5800
FAX 0117 954 5817
EMAIL president-ubu@bristol.ac.uk
WEB www.ubu.org.uk/

VAG VIEW

*S*till considered by many as the 'parent's choice' or the 'home for Oxbridge rejects',

Bristol is managing to break out of this restrictive mould and convince that its exclusivity is simply down to the high entry requirements that admit confident, ambitious

and able students. Its policy to tap the academic potential of a wider range of students is gradually persuading applicants from previously under-represented groups to apply, although, as yet, the uni is still failing to make its Government-set benchmarks in this, and the Independent School intake remains high.

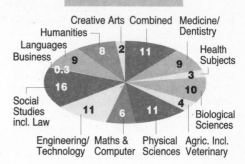

SUBJECT AREAS (%)

Creative Arts — 8
Combined — 2
Medicine/Dentistry — 11
Health Subjects — 9
Humanities — 9
Languages — 0.3
Business — 16
Biological Sciences — 3
— 10
— 4
Social Studies incl. Law — 11
Engineering/Technology — 11
Maths & Computer — 6
Physical Sciences — 11
Agric. Incl. Veterinary

CAMPUS

Set a stone's throw from the city centre and near the trendy Clifton area, Bristol University is a great example of a city campus. It presents a safe but lively environment within a beautiful and vibrant city. University buildings such as the Gothic Wills Memorial Building and the 18th century Royal Fort House fit in well with the historic past of the city. The row of Victorian houses which form the Arts department is also a pretty place to spend your undergraduate days.

UNIVERSITY/STUDENT PROFILE	
University since	**1909**
Situation/style	**Civic**
Student population	**23360**
Full-time undergraduates	**15470**
- mature	**12%**
- non-EU undergraduates	**6%**
- male/female	**44/56**
- non-traditional student intake	**13%**
-state school intake	**64%**
- drop-out rate	**4%**
- undergraduate applications	**Up 16%**

FEES, BURSARIES

UK & EU Fees, 2007: £3,070 p.a. There are bursaries for those in receipt of the full HR Maintenance Grant and for those in need, living in the region, and sport and academic scholarships.

STUDENT PROFILE

Wrote Tony Dunkels ten years ago: 'Bristol University has the reputation, especially among some of its more northerly competitors, as being a bit of a shandy-drinkin', southern poof's university, comprising mostly ex-Oxbridge wannabes and the like.'

Today, if you provoke union bods along these lines they are genuinely hurt: 'The change has occurred. It really isn't actively snooty any more.'

Writes Ruth Naughton Doe, a current Bristol student: 'You will hear the negative "toff" stereotyping, but I have found these to be untrue. Like most other universities, Bristol attracts all

types - although the North is notably under-represented and there are a lot of Londoners and a high proportion of international students.'

ACADEMIA & JOBS

Writes Laura Cattell: 'Cutting edge for Medicine and Veterinary Science, the uni is a mecca for the Science and Technology subjects. However, there are over 34 subjects on offer, and over 20% study Humanities or Languages. The Arts and Social Sciences library is a bit dark and dingy, but there are plenty of good faculty libraries, and excellent access to online journals and resources. The IT provision is good, staff are very helpful and range from the old-fashioned tweedy types to more dynamic younger ones.'

Ruth Naughton Doe draws out Laura's caveats: 'Courses at Bristol vary. Sciences, Medical Sciences, Social Sciences and Law seem to provoke good reviews from the students I talk to, but the Arts Faculty does not. The library is severely lacking in resources (there is a 2-month ban on buying any new books, as I write) There have also been many debates about lack of contact time [with lecturers, tutors], most Arts students having only 6-10 hours a week. Talk to a student before choosing Bristol to do an Arts Degree. Despite all this, they are getting a new Arts and Social Sciences library by 2009.'

A large number of graduates go into the health

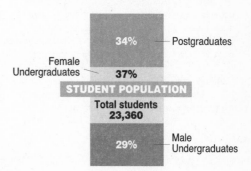

Postgraduates — 34%
Female Undergraduates — 37%

STUDENT POPULATION
Total students 23,360

Male Undergraduates — 29%

industry or into commerce (finance, accounting, business management), but there are alternatives.

Would-be publishers and editors stream out of language, social and physical science, and a strong tradition of student media has helped. Employment figures are for similar reasons sound, too, in the realm of music, backed as that department is by an active student scene.

Popular routes into the Civil Service are social studies, business and language departments, as well as biological and physical sciences.

Social Studies also has a strong line into employment for would-be charity and social workers and counsellors. They are world leaders in research, with a 6* rating. In the same faculty, Law comes with French or German (both 4 years), and non-Law graduates may opt for a 2-year full-time or 3-year part-time Senior Status Law degree here. All candidates must sit the National Admissions Test for Law (LNAT).

Strong extra-curricular activities support careers in the army, the RAF and Royal Navy, and if it's a job in Defence you're after, consider the Engineering route. It's a 3/4/5-year B/MEng programme – the 5-year degree is Engineering Design, which ranks them high in the employment league for engineering design consultants. Aeronautical Eng comes with study in Europe, as does Computer Systems Eng and Mech Eng. There's also Avionic Systems, Electronic & Communications and such as Mathematics Modelling or Mathematics for Intelligent Systems.

Electrical & Electronic took full marks at the assessments and an international Grade 5 for research (as did Mechanical Eng) – many go into telecommunications from here. In Physical Sciences there's a rich BSc/MSci programme, though of course entry requirements are high.

In investment and merchant banking they take the lead nationally by quite a margin. Nearly half come through Economics, which scored 23 out of 24 at the assessments. Look at BSc Economics & Econometrics with Study in Continental Europe, Economics & Finance, etc.

Health is still the strongest area, however, with dentists and doctors, veterinary surgeons and vet nurses finding certain employment. For the 5/6-year MB, ChB, you'll need to be able to tell them what you expect from a career as a doctor, that you are aware of the levels of commitment and challenge, and what you in particular have to offer. It's a 9% acceptance rate, with 344 undergrads joining the course each year. Links are strong with special clinical academies in Bristol, Bath, Cheltenham, Gloucester, Taunton, Swindon, where in years 3-5 you'll spend half your time. Entry typically AAB. 6-year prog: 3 A-levels, one science

ACADEMIC EXCELLENCE

TEACHING:
(Rated Excellent or 17+ out of 24)

Law, Mechanical Engineering, Chemistry, Geography, Applied Social Work, English.	**Excellent**
Electrical & Electronic Eng, Anatomy, Education, Molecular Biosciences, Veterinary	**24**
Drama: Theatre, Film, TV, Maths, Physics, Economics, Pharmacology, Philosophy, Politics, Psychology	**23**
Iberian Studies, Civil Eng, Aerospace Engineering, Organismal Biosciences	**22**
Sociology, Italian, German Classics/Ancient History	**21**
Russian, French, History of Art, Medicine, Theology	**20**
Dentistry	**19**

RESEARCH:
Top grades 5/5*/6*

Clinical Lab Sci, Anatomy, Psychology, Biochemistry, Applied Maths, Statistics, Geography, Social Work, Russian, Drama	**Grade 6***
Community-based Clinical, Clinical Dentistry, Chemistry, Earth Sci, Civil Eng, Education	**Grade 5***
Clinical Laboratory Sciences, Biological Sciences, Veterinary, Physics, Pure Maths, Computer, Electrical/Electronic Eng, Mechanical Eng, Law, Politics, Social Policy, Sociology, Accounting, English, French, German/Dutch/Scandinavian, Italian, Classics, Philosophy, Theology, Music	**Grade 5**

subject accepted; 5-year prog: A level Chemistry + two others (Biology good and can do one 'approved' non-science). Plus 6 Grade A GCSEs. The teaching assessment came in quite low at 20 points, but there's a world-class Grade 5*/6* for research into Community-based Clinical, Anatomy, Psychology, Biochemistry; Grade 5 Clinical Lab Sciences, Biological Sciences.

For dentists, it's the 5/6-year BDS. Entry AAB-ABB including Chemistry – the 6-year course allows entry with 2 non-science subjects. Teaching inspection again low at 19. Grade 5* for research.

For vets, there's the 5-year BVSc. Candidates must sit the Biomedical Admissions Test (BMAT).

Also a 3-year Veterinary Pathogenesis and a 4-year Vet Nursing & Practice Administration. Teaching inspection 24 – better than for humans.

SOCIAL SCENE

STUDENTS' UNION Writes Ruth: 'The Student's Union is housed in one of the ugliest buildings in Bristol and far from where most students spend time, but it is very lively.' Despite persistent rumours about plans to relocate it, there have been recent expensive refurbishments to the interior, including a brand new **Epi** bar, a refurbished Union foyer, Union shop and Chandos Deli (sandwich shop) and **AR2**, the small gig venue, with 900 standing capacity.

The **Epi** is the main student bar. There's also **AR2** (for small gigs and as a bar for larger gigs in the adjacent **Anson Rooms**) and the **Avon Gorge** room (for large society events and awards ceremonies). **Café Zuma** serves hot and cold meals throughout the day.

The Anson Rooms plays host to many up-and-coming bands, and recently, Ash, Jamie T, Kosheen, Hot Chip and Lady Sovereign amongst others. Previously have hosted Prodigy, Coldplay, Franz Ferdinand and Chemical Brothers. Impressive gig listing can be found at www.ansonrooms.co.uk

AR2 have regular *Trash in the Attic* nights with the best unsigned talent, see www.myspace.com/trashintheattic

The Epi has a weekly rota of events including live jazz, screenings of sport, indie to drink to on Thursdays, and on Friday night it turns into a club night called *Spank*, with deals on drinks and cheesy music. On Saturday there's a society takeover night and Sunday is quiz night. There are pool tables, quiz machines and cheap drinks served throughout the week.

Says Laura Cattell: 'The student attitude at Bristol is very much "Work hard, play harder!" and so even if most of the student population do like the Monday 'Vodka' nights they'll still be at lectures on Tuesday morning.

Said a union bod: 'Our Union is notable for its vast amount of student activities: from All You Can

Eat to Yoga. In particular, our RAG (which raises over £100,000 a year) and Student Community Action (which organizes 36 volunteering projects within the local community and co-ordinates over 1,000 volunteers) are so big and popular that they each have individual union officers dedicated to them. Our Debating Society is one of the best in the world, and Ballroom Dancing one of the best in the country. We also have 10 performing arts societies that take 4 arts shows to the Edinburgh Fringe every year.'

Currently, the most active societies are Ballroom Dancing, UBFS (University of Bristol Film-Making Society), Dance soc, BUMS (Bristol University Music Society), STA (Stage Technicians Association), and International Affairs.

The Drama Society utilises two theatres: **the** 200-seater **Winston Theatre**, and the smaller **Lady Windsor Studio Theatre**. *Epigram* is the student newspaper; student radio is BURST; a new creative arts magazine is *Helicon*.

SPORT Says Laura: 'Sports-wise the University really does have something for everyone, from tennis to hang-gliding there are just so many societies. The flashy sports centre on Tyndall Avenue has a large gym and daily fitness classes,

AT A GLANCE	
ACADEMIC FILE:	
Subjects assessed	**37**
Excellent	**89%**
Typical entry requirements	**406 points**
Application acceptance rate	**9%**
Med. School acceptance rate	**9%**
Student:staff ratio	**14:1**
First/2:1 degree pass rate	**81%**
ACCOMMODATION FILE:	
Guarantee to freshers	**90%**
Style	**Halls, houses**
Catered	**40%**
Approx price range pw	**£45-£110**
City rent pw	**£70**

WHERE BRISTOL GRADUATES END UP
Health & Social Work: 20%; Education: 6%; Wholesale/Retail: 5%; Manufacturing: 10%; Financial Activities: 12%; Public Administration, Civil Service & Defence: 6%; Hotel/Restaurant: 2%; Transport & Communications (including Telecommunications): 3%; Construction: 1%; Personnel: 5%; Computer: 3%; Business & Management: 4%; Accountancy: 6%; Media (including Film): 2%; Legal 2%; Architecture: 2%; Publishing: 2%; Advertising: 1%.

Approximate 'graduate track' employed **80%**

and though it's a bit hard to find, there is also a swimming pool on the ground floor of the Union building.' There are 54 sports clubs; the teams came 11th nationally last year.

TOWN Writes Ruth: 'The city is large enough to accommodate everyone's interests yet small enough for it to feel familiar. It is a hip, vibrant hub, catering for all interests and cultures, but also a beautiful city with spectacular views - and prepare to tone your thighs wonderfully from walking up and down its hills. It is also a safe place, bad areas being far away from where you'll be. It is hard to live here cheaply but it can be done. And if it all gets too much, take the Bristol-London 1 pound megabus to London for a clubnight out there.'

PILLOW TALK

Says Laura Cattell: 'Most first year students get allocated a place in halls which means a choice of two locations: Stoke Bishop and Clifton. Stoke Bishop is about 40 mins from the University precinct, while halls based in Clifton are in one of the nicest parts of the city and just a 15 minute walk away.'

Writes Ruth: 'The student link bus from Stoke Bishop to the city campus was recently cancelled and there is currently a war being fought with the Union to encourage them to reinstate it.'

However, says Laura: 'The best choice may seem obvious, but actually Stoke Bishop houses a larger number of students and therefore possesses a vibrant campus atmosphere which halls in Clifton really lack.'

Ruth cannot agree: 'I have visited all the halls of residence and in my opinion Goldney Hall in Clifton is excellent, with a good JCR that organises great events and boasts beautiful gardens.'

The choice is yours. Go and see.

GETTING THERE
☛ By road: M4/J19, M32 or M5/J17 and follow

signs to the zoo (an elephant).
☛ By rail: London Paddington or Birmingham New Street, 1:30; Nottingham, 3:00.
☛ By air: Bristol Airport.
☛ By coach: Birminghan, 2:00; London, 2:20

WHAT IT'S REALLY LIKE	
UNIVERSITY:	
Social Life	★★★★★
Campus scene	**Lively, rich student culture**
Student Union services	**Good**
Politics	**Activity high, mainly student issues**
Sport	**54 clubs**
National team position	**11th**
Sport facilities	**Good**
Arts opportunities	**Excellent**
Student newspaper	**Epigram**
Student magazine	**Helicon**
Student radio	**BURST**
Gig venues	**Anson Rooms, AR2**
Bars	**Epi, Avon Gorge**
Union ents	**Live, disco, etc**
Union societies	**183**
Most active societies	**Ballroom Dancing, Film-Making, BUMS (Music)**
Parking	**Poor**
CITY:	
Entertainment	★★★★★
Scene	**Full on waterfront and fringe**
Town/gown relations	**Clear differences**
Risk of violence	**Average**
Cost of living	**High**
Student concessions	**Good**
Survival + 2 nights out	**£80 pw**
Part-time work campus/town	**Good/Good**

BRISTOL, UNIVERSITY OF THE WEST OF ENGLAND

Bristol, University of the West of England
Frenchay Campus
Coldharbour Lane
Bristol BS16 1QY

TEL 0117 32 83333
FAX 0117 32 82810
EMAIL admissions@uwe.ac.uk
WEB www.uwe.ac.uk

UWE Students' Union
Frenchay Campus
Coldharbour Lane
Bristol BS16 1QY

TEL 0117 32 82577
FAX 0117 32 82986
EMAIL union@uwe.ac.uk
WEB www.uwesu.net

VAG VIEW

*A*t UWE they don't mind being called a 'new' university because they understand that to mean 'positive, forward-looking, a real value university'.

They attract a distinctive breed of student. It is more of a local uni than its neighbour in this vibrant city. Forty per cent of undergraduates come from within a 40-mile radius. Also, nearly a half of them are mature. The result is that already they have a mature outlook on what they want to do. This drives the university's strategy.

Frenchay, the main campus sited in the north of Bristol, is the hub, nestling as it does in Silicon Gorge - Hewlett Packard, Aardman's, the makers of Wallace and Grommit, typifying (with the NHS hard by) two of the university's academic concentrations - health and computer.

There is more. Environment Agency and Airbus are on hand, as is BBC TV's natural history base in Bristol. Producer Mike Salisbury is involved, as is Adam Hart-Davis, and the business guru, Charles Handy, and Sir Digby Jones, ex-head of the CBI, also come in to talk to students.

UWE employs lecturers who are practitioners. The ethos is practical, real-world. Health and social care hopefuls will find themselves in a real hospital, even on Open Day. Their future employment is on the schedule even before Day One. Industry designs the courses, refreshes the curriculum, assesses work - so that student projects in Built Environment are considered locally by real architectural companies. Getting a job at the end is simply another step in a 3-4-year process as inevitable as the one before.

The problem has been that students have been short-dealed on the social side, and the Union is somewhat illusive. There has long been a need for a focus for the huge student body. And now the £80-million development at Frenchay, a brilliantly designed student village with sports hall, has brought 2,000 of them onto campus to that end.

FEES, BURSARIES

UK & EU Fees £3,070 p.a. Bursaries are available for students on the HE Maintenance Grant on a sliding scale according to income. 'Home' students who enter UWE via an Access to HE certificate are entitled to £1,250 bursary regardless of income. Over a third of its students get this. Financial, medical and training support is available to national and international level athletes. There are also subject specific scholarships and a loyalty scholarship of £1,000 if fees are paid in full before study begins. Finally, there are five Music bursaries - up to £600 per year.

STUDENT PROFILE

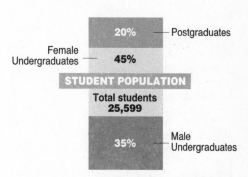

Unlike most other unis established in 1992, there's a high intake from independent schools. UWE actually fails to meet its Government benchmarks for state school intake and for intake from the lower socio-economic classes - just like Oxbridge!

CAMPUS

There are four sites in Bristol itself, mainly around the north of the city, with regional centres in Bath, and Swindon concentrating on nursing. Only Bower Ashton, which houses art, media and design, is in the south. The main campus at Frenchay, close to Bristol Parkway station, but 4 miles out of the city centre, has by far the largest number of students and includes

UNIVERSITY/STUDENT PROFILE	
University since	**1992**
Situation/style	**Campus/ city sites**
Student population	**25599**
Undergraduates	**20436**
- mature	**48%**
- non EU undergraduates	**8%**
- male/female	**40/60**
- non-traditional student intake	**28%**
- state school intake	**87%**
- drop-out rate	**16%**
- undergraduate applications	**Up 6%**

the Centre for Student Affairs, which brings together the various non-academic services. The St Matthias site (social sciences and humanities) and Glenside (health) are more attractive, but less lively. Education now occupies a new, £16-million headquarters at Frenchay.

FRENCHAY (address above) **Location:** north of the city, near Bristol Parkway Station. **Faculties:** Applied Sciences, Business, Built Environment, Computer, Engineering & Maths; Education; Humanities, Languages & Social Sciences; Law. Library has recent £6.5 million extension. Campus security is good. CCTV and this is one of the only campuses to have its own bobby.

BOWER ASHTON Kennel Lodge Road, off Clanage Road, Bower Ashton, Bristol BS3 2JU; Tel: 0117 966 0222. **Location:** south of river, west but in easy reach of city centre. **Faculties:** Art, Media & Design. **£4 million going into a complete redevelopment strategy, the first students to benefit going in this year. Ents facilities:** opening hours short in **Bower's Bar**, but good, buzzy atmosphere.

ST MATTHIAS Oldbury Court Road, Fishponds, Bristol BS16 2JP; Tel: 0117 965 5384. **Location:** sometime monastery, northeast of city centre, near Glenside (see below), good bus service to city action. **Faculty:** Humanities, Languages & Social Science; Applied Science; Psychology. **Accommodation:** two halls. **Learning resources:** library. **Sport facilities:** cricket square, two soccer pitches, gym. **Ents facilities:** St Matt's bar.

GLENSIDE Blackberry Hill, Stapleton, Bristol BS16 1DD. Tel: 0117 958 5655. **Location:** northeast of city centre, nearest to St Matthias, good bus service to city action. **Faculty:** Health & Social Care. **Accommodation:** purpose-built, self-catering. **Learning resources:** library. **Sport facilities:** space for aerobics, etc. **Ents facilities:** student/staff social club, good restaurant, not far from Frenchay.

THE HARTPURY CAMPUS Hartpury House, Gloucester GL19 3BE. Tel: 01452 702132. www.hartpury.ac.uk/. An Associate Faculty since 1997, the college comprises 200 hectares of countryside, with woodlands, farm, lake and equine centre. Animal Science, etc. Students bring their own horses. Oh, and premiere division Gloucester Rugby Club train there.

ACADEMIC EXCELLENCE

TEACHING :	
(Rated Excellent or 17+ out of 24)	
Law, Business & Management, English	**Excellent**
Organismal Biosciences, Pharmacology & Pharmacy, Molecular Biosciences, Education	**24**
Sociology, Town/Country Planning, Business, Economics	**23**
Communication & Media Studies, Land & Property Management., Art/Design, Psychology, Nursing	**22**
Modern Languages (French, German, Spanish, Linguistics), Building, Elec/Electron Eng, Politics, Maths, Subjects Allied to Medicine	**21**
Agriculture	**20**
RESEARCH:	
Top grades 5/5*	
Accounting and Finance	**Grade 5**

ACADEMIA & JOBS

There are pitfalls in the strategy There are 1,200 modules from which to choose. They give you a student adviser to help sort it out, but it can seem daunting to someone straight out of sixthform.

With this in mind they have a Welcome Weekend when you are shown how to use learning resources, to make the most of a tutorial, to orientate yourself to the employability and achievement ethos, which drives this place.

In their strategy to create a seamless provision from university to career they list two dozen skills and traits required by employers over and above knowledge relevant to a particular industry. From 'resilience' to 'logical thinking', from 'team working' to 'time management', UWE sees this as part of the academic brief. There is also an active alumni scheme called 'knowledge exchange', a dialogue between recent graduates actually in jobs that up-coming graduates fancy, so that you really can find out what it is like.

The nine subjects most recently assessed scored between 21 points out of 24 and full marks (for Education), which is exceptional.

In business and finance they do well, and their degrees represent good value, for entry requirements tend not to be high. Accountancy is at the top of the list employment-wise. There's a range of dedicated degrees with interesting add-ons – from business, finance, economics, law, tourism and maths to drama and early childhood studies (some connections looser than others). There's a Grade 5 rating for research; that's international standing.

In the insurance/pension sector, UWE is again a leading force, as they are for would-be investment analysts. It's worth noting that they dropped only one point at the teaching assessments for Business and Economics.

In the field of engineering, their record for employment in aeronautical engineering is second only to Loughborough, and they make it almost impossible not to get on their B/MEng Aerospace Manufacturing/Aerospace Systems programme, with 4- and 5-year extended courses incorporating Foundation years. In electrical/electronic engineering – another successful employment area – there's a healthy 21 points inspection result.

They also make an impact through Architectural Technology & Design and Architecture & Planning, and for jobs in town planning. See the BA Town & Country Planning (also a 1-year HND top-up), Planning with Leisure/Tourism/Transport, and Housing Policy with Management. Also, BSc Built & Natural Environments. Teaching scored 23 out of 24 points.

There's a steady stream, too, into local/regional/central government administration, via Social, Economic & Political Studies departments, Business Administration, and such as BSc Public Health, a one-year top-up programme.

Strong recruitment, too, for the army, defence operatives and equipment engineers. Students often take the biological sciences route. They got full marks at the teaching assessments.

For environmental health and environmental officers there's a host of dedicated courses, and they scored 21 points at the assessments.

Would-be property developers, note the 22-point assessment in Land & Property Management, another employment strength.

Again, nationally, a third of graduates into property development come out of Built Environment and Building & Planning

departments, while 20% graduate from Business departments. UWE accounts for a lot of them.

In Education, they are leaders among the new unis in primary school teacher training, and scored full marks at the assessments.

In Law, they are specialists in European and commercial & business law, and one of the unis to offer a Legal Practice Course (LPC), essential if you want to be a solicitor. They are also one of eight institutions where the BVC (Bar Vocational Course, essential to becoming a barrister) may be undertaken. Bristol University law students take their law practice and bar vocational courses here. There is a mock court on campus. Always this practical, real-world emphasis.

There is also a car crash scene for forensic science students, and participation with the local Bristol police force, and the UWE course is one of only a handful to be accredited by the Institute of Forensic Science.

UWE's top-rated Business School dropped only one point at inspection. There are strengths in human resource management, and the transport industry.

Principal employment strengths in computing include the computer games sector, and systems

AT A GLANCE	
ACADEMIC FILE:	
Subjects assessed	**31**
Excellent	**77%**
Typical entry requirements	**267 points**
Application acceptance rate	**22%**
Students-staff ratio	**20:1**
First/2:1 degree pass rate	**55%**
ACCOMMODATION FILE:	
Guarantee to freshers	**100%**
Style	**Flats, halls, houses**
Catered	**None**
En-suite	**50%**
Price range pw	**£48-£106**
City rent pw	**£70**

WHERE UWE GRADUATES END UP

Health & Social Work: 14%; Education: 9%; Wholesale/Retail: 8%; Manufacturing: 11%; Financial Activities: 11%; Public Administration, Civil Service & Defence: 7%; Hotel/Restaurant: 3%; Transport & Communications (including Telecommunications): 5%; Construction: 2%; Personnel: 5%; Computer: 4%; Business & Management: 5%; Accountancy: 2%; Media (including Film): 2%; Legal 2%; Architecture: 3%; Publishing: 2%; Artistic/Literary: 1%; Sport: 1%.

Approximate 'graduate track' employed **60%**

analysts.

Health-wise, nursing is a big feature and the range of degrees is wide – Health & Community Practice, Learning Disabilities, Adult Nursing, Care of the Older Person, Cancer Care, Emergency Care, Critical Care, Palliative Care, Mental Health, Children's, etc. Check campus situation, many are at Glenside in Bristol, but Adult and Mental are also available at the Gloucestershire site, where there are also Learning Disabilities and Children's Nursing degrees. Teaching inspection, 22

At last, there is a high participation, student representation system, and investment to increase student participation. The new sports facility includes a sports hall with eight badminton courts, aerobics studio, large fitness room and two glass back squash courts.

Also in Health, UWE's BSc in Physiotherapy accounts for roughly 6% of total graduate employment in this sector.

They also have a wide range of animal science degrees (even Equine Dental Science). A popular development has been Veterinary Nursing Science. and this year, Veterinary Practice Management, and Wildlife & Countryside Management Note, you may be ensconced miles away at their Gloucestershire-based campus, Hartpury College.

Millions are being spent on new studios, suites and facilities for art, media and design students at the Bower Ashton campus, widely known for its fashion, and of course the animation courses. Peter Lord, one of the producers of Aardman, teaches there. Sixty UWE students appeared in the list of credits for Chicken Run. It's also good for fine art, the Royal West of England Academy, based in Bristol, has close links and UWE's Dean of Creative Art is a well-known artist in his own right.

SOCIAL SCENE

STUDENTS' UNION **Escape Bar** is the main bar on Frenchay. There's also **Red** (café culture by day, club by night), the main venue for club nights, bands, etc. A number of cafés - **Street Café**, **One Zone**, **Faz**, and another in the sports hall - also attract student custom. There are other bars at St Matthias (friendliest bar at Uni, where everybody knows your name), Glenside (perfect place for a pint before a big night out) and Bower (unique bar that students make their own).

Capacity at Frenchay is about 720. It's *Crunchie* every Friday night in Escape and Venue; *The Great Escape* on Saturday at Escape, and there are regular Friday nights in the campus bars. *Result* is the big Wednesday sports night. Tuesday: *Tiny African Badger* (Indie/live bands night) or Comedy Club.

Recent live acts include Lemar, the Bodyrockers, DJ Spoony and Scott Mills.

The media set-up is good but not this year award-winning. There's *Westworld* (magazine), *Western Eye* (newspaper) and Hub (radio station). 'We also have a very active Drama society, linked with the centre of Performing Arts which the university run, and the standard of our shows is very high. Among societies the Poly Players are a surprise – an 'English drawing room group, comedy': students write and perform their own plays around the sites.

SPORT There is a friendly rivalry with Bristol University, a varsity match (rugby), a boat race (the biggest outside Oxford and Cambridge, they claim), and the new sports centre at Frenchay

WHAT IT'S REALLY LIKE	
UNIVERSITY:	
Social Life	★★★
Campus scene	**Diverse mix**
Politics	**Growing say**
Sport	**43 clubs, new sports hall 2007**
National team position	**65th**
Arts	**Drama very good**
Student magazine	**Westworld**
Student newspaper	**Western Eye**
Student Radio	**Hub**
Nightclub/venue	**Venue**
Central campus bar	**Escape**
Other campus bars	**St Matthias, Glenside, Bower**
Union ents	**Clubnights, good live bands**
Union societies	**40**
Most active societies	**Comets Cheerleaders**
Parking	**Poor**
CITY:	
Entertainment	★★★★★
Scene	**Full on waterfront and fringe**
Town/gown relations	**Good**
Risk of violence	**Average-high**
Cost of living	**High**
Student concessions	**Good**
Survival + 2 nights out	**£70-£100 pw**
Part-time work campus/town	**Good/Excellent**

really is all that it's cracked up to be, with an eight badminton court sports hall, aerobics studio, large fitness room with masses of machinery, and two glass back squash courts. There are 43 clubs - everything from sky diving to American football - and they came 43rd nationally last year.

PILLOW TALK

All the beds at Frenchay (1,932 of them for first years) will have been snapped up by May, so if you want a part of the new student village, get in quick. Security is superb. Besides CCTV, you have to unlock four doors before you get to your en-suite, broad-banded room, six of which make up a flat. With a spacious, sparkling new, multi-purpose kitchen/dining/seating communal area - two

stoves and two monstrous fridge freezers per flat - £90 a week per person 'all in' is a very good deal indeed. Specially designed disabled rooms are also available, of course. The rest of student accommodation is in the city. Very wide range of flats and houses, including harbourside city centre accommodation.

GETTING THERE

☛ By road to Frenchay, Glenside, St Matthias: M4/J19, M32 or M5/J16, A38; Bower Ashton, M5/J19, A369.
☛ By rail: London Paddington, Birmingham New Street, 1:30; Nottingham, 3:00.
☛ By air: Bristol Airport.
☛ By coach: Birmingham, 2:00; London, 2:20.

BRUNEL UNIVERSITY

Brunel University
Uxbridge
Middlesex UB8 3PH

Union of Brunel Students
Uxbridge
Middlesex UB8 3PH

TEL 01895 269790
FAX 01895 203102
EMAIL admissions@brunel.ac.uk
WEB www.brunel.ac.uk

TEL 01895 269269
FAX 01895 462300
EMAIL su.president@brunel.ac.uk
WEB www.ubsonline.net

VAG VIEW

*O*ut of a 19th-century, technical background, Brunel established itself in the late 1960s as a science/technology/ engineering uni, which was 'all well and good if you had long oily hair, wore AC/DC T-shirts and had the personality of a walnut,' recalls Satiyesh Manoharajah. 'But, dammit, it just wasn't sexy. However, things have been a-changing these past few years. The Social Sciences, Arts and Media faculties have greatly expanded, bringing an influx of generally more exciting students and, indeed, women!'

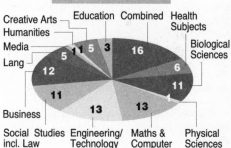

CAMPUSES

Brunel, the University of West London, is based northwest of the city, close to the M25, M40 and M4, Heathrow Airport is also just round the corner - fifty minutes by tube and thirty minutes by overland train to central London.

Uxbridge, always by far the biggest campus in this sometime university of satellite campuses, is this year the uni's *only* campus. Packed with bizarre, grey, concrete buildings, but well laid out,

with all the main facilities (bars, small shop, HSBC bank and cash points, a **Waterstones** and travel agents), it has undergone a huge facelift, the main excitements being a £6.5 million outdoor sports complex, a £7 million indoor athletics facility and a new £9 million Health Services and Social Care Building.

Says undergrad. Olly Wright: 'The library building, called the Bannerman Centre, the refurbished pubs and club, Indoor Athletics Centre and four new halls have made big changes to the landscape.'

FEES, BURSARIES

UK & EU Fees £3,070 p.a. + inflation in 2008. Bursaries on a sliding scale for anyone in receipt of a HE Maintenance grant. Up to 150 scholarships, mostly worth £2,000-£3,000 p.a. awarded to students with exceptional tariff points/entry qualifications Also music awards and 180 scholarships of up to £3,000 for disabled, ethnic or other under-represented groups.

STUDENT PROFILE

Brunel extends its intake more successfully even than the Government demands of into the state school sector and among the four lowest socio-economic classes (4, 5, 6 & 7), exceeding its benchmarks on every count except, interestingly, in the so-called low-participation neighbourhoods. International Pathway Centre facilitates entry of overseas students to provide appropriate orientation and language preparation and support.

Has all this changed Brunel from being a uni for techies and geeks? 'There is more a mix of students doing a whole mix of courses,' writes Olly, 'but there is still the techie element doing the engineering courses. There are a few arty types, but nowhere near as many as at some unis. The general mix is of engineering, computing and sporty types. I was also not surprised to read in the *Guardian* online that there are Islamist groups active at Brunel. Some of them used to meet in a room 3 doors away from mine, although I have no idea what they were discussing. On the other hand the *Guardian* also claims that the BNP is operating in Brunel. I am yet to see any evidence of this.'

SOCIAL SCENE

The Students Union has just completed its biggest ever facelift, with refurbishments of the bars, nightclub and food hall, and new shops balcony cafe and central atrium.

'The nightclub is still the **Academy**,' writes Olly. 'No extra space has been gained, which would have been useful as some nights it does fill up and some people are turned away. The new design is

UNIVERSITY/STUDENT PROFILE	
University since	**1966**
Situation/style	**Suburban campuses**
Student population	**15455**
Undergraduates	**10138**
- mature	**23%**
- non EU undergraduates	**9%**
- male/female	**51/49**
- non-traditional student intake	**36%**
- state school intake	**90%**
- drop-out rate	**14%**
- undergraduate applications	**Up 8%**

better than before, it is a space-age design with lots of stainless steel creating a more light and spacey feel. It is open seven days a week from 9pm or 10 till 2am, apart from Sunday when it shuts at 12.30am. But not to townies, as all entrants are checked against Brunel photographic identification on the door. Students may bring guests as long as they are students and have signed in at the student union reception.

'The best thing I have been to recently is Wednesday night, *Flirt*, who do club nights at other university campuses as well (www.flirt.co.uk). This is the regular night every Wednesday. Most other days are themed nights, with Monday open to societies to put on a night. Tuesdays are sport teams' night. Thursday is generally when any famous names would appear, for example Coolio, The Heartless Crew. Friday is *Elements*, a regular DJ who plays r&b, hip-hop, house, garage, dancehall, trance and drum and bass. Saturday starts off with comedy then moves to a retro disco, and Sunday is rock night. Some examples of themed nights I went to last year are *Pimps & Prostitutes*, *James Bond Night*, *Doctors & Nurses*, and the traditional 1st night for all freshers, *Pyjama Party*. One night the Union hired out a couple of poker tables, a blackjack table, a roulette wheel and some croupiers and put on a Casino night which was free and no real money was gambled, but still fun nonetheless.

'The bar is still **Loco's** and has also been refurbished, like something out of Star Trek, with all new leather sofas, chairs and tables, a no-smoking section, many plasma's covering the walls, three pool tables, a table football table, 2 fruit machines and a couple of monopoly machines. For a uni bar, the drinks are expensive, but compared to London prices they are cheap. At the top end of the scale, a pint of Stella is £2.30, while at the other end a pint of Carling is £1.75. These prices rise about 5% in the **Academy**!

34% — Postgraduates

STUDENT POPULATION
Total students
15,455

Female Undergraduates — 33%

Male Undergraduates — 33%

Again, this is not open to townies and there is security on the doors from 7pm. They also have a typical pub menu and serve food until 7pm.

'There is another pub on campus - **Bishops Bar,** not run by the Union, and generally the drink prices are lower, a pint of Carlsberg Export is £2. This is also the place to go to watch football, while **Loco's** generally shows rugby. **Bishops** has also been newly refurbished and they are still in the process of finishing the balcony. Then there's the **Zest Bar**, located above the gym, a nice place to go to after a workout, smaller and generally quieter than the other two pubs, but still worth checking out if only for the San Miguel bottles. There is also a café which opened recently on the ground floor of the new library, always full of students and lecturers getting their caffeine hit, or a croissant.

'The local London students certainly do desert the uni at weekends, and their exit is noticeable by Friday afternoon when all the car parks empty, apart from one or two lonely cars. But there is still a good amount of students around and the **Academy** is certainly never lacking people on a Friday night.'

The Arts Centre is the platform for musical concerts throughout the year. Student groups include The Brunel Singers, an orchestra, guitar, brass, wind and string groups; all are professionally trained and music bursaries are awarded annually. Classes in photography and various visual art forms are given on a weekly basis by visiting professionals. There are several student drama groups.

SPORT £14 million has been invested in a world-class sports complex, which includes an indoor athletics and netball centre, an outdoor athletics arena and floodlit turf, and all-weather pitches and courts. The gym and free-weights room have also been refurbished. Hurricanes Superleague netball are based here, and UK Athletics use it as a training faculty for elite athletes.

'Many of the students are doing sport science and related subjects,' says Olly. They are indeed one of the top unis for sport, coming 24h overall

ACADEMIC EXCELLENCE	
TEACHING:	
(Rated Excellent or 17+ out of 24)	
Anthropology, Social Policy,	**Excellent**
Social Work	
Drama, Education,	23
Government, Sport Sciences	
Sociology, General Engineering,	22
Economics, Maths, Molecular	
Biosciences, Nursing, Subjects	
Allied to Medicine, Psychology	
Electrical & Electronic Eng	21
American Studies	
Mech, Aero & Manufacturing	20
Eng (Design), Materials	
Technology, Film & TV Studies	
RESEARCH:	
Top grades 5/5*	
Applied Maths, General Eng,	**Grade 5**
Mechanical/Aeronautical/	
Manufacturing Eng, Law,	
Sociology, Library and Info	
Management	

last year and with many championship finals to their credit. You can dabble, satisfy curiosity or take up fanatically more or less what you want to, even become part of a university team.

TOWN 'Mmm...the lovely town of Uxbridge... There are two shopping centres, **The Chimes** and **The Pavilions**, containing all the shops one could ever need. There is even an **Odeon** on the top floor of **Chimes**. Uxbridge also has a few nice student-happy pubs, like **The Hog's Head**, **The Zanzi Bar**, **The Metropolitan**. There's also a nightclub, **Royale's**, not recommended, plays cheesy pop and there is a guaranteed fight at 3am when everyone leaves, the only positive being the cheap drinks.

'Generally, the locals must be used to living with students as there is peace between us. There are many takeaways – if you go a day without a menu coming under your room door in halls then

WHERE BRUNEL GRADUATES END UP
Health & Social Work: 16%; Education: 10%; Wholesale/Retail: 10%; Manufacturing: 9%; Financial Activities: 8%; Public Administration, Civil Service & Defence: 8%; Hotel/Restaurant: 2%; Transport & Communications (including Telecommunications): 4%; Construction: 1%; Personnel: 6%; Computer: 7%; Business & Management: 7%; Accountancy: 1%; Media (including Film): 2%; Legal 2%; Publishing: 2%; Artistic/Literary: 2%; Sport: 1%.

Approximate 'graduate track' employed **64%**

The new Health Services and Social Care Building, library and recently opened Information Technology Lab. point the way - in 2006 all aspects of the quality of learning opportunities in NHS-funded Health programmes were reviewed and rated commendable by the QAA.

Meanwhile, they continues to introduce cutting-edge techno courses such as the BSc in Multimedia Technology & Design - in 2006 Brunel appointed the first UK professor of video games - Tanya Krzywinska leads the uni's new MA in digital games: theory and design; she is also in charge of the uni's MA in cult film and TV (horror, kung fu, etc) - but a few years ago it spread its wings, quadrupled in size and took on a broader academic brief – social work, sociology, politics, law, psychology, health (with a new course in Medical Genetics), sports studies, sciences and arts (from English to Film/TV Studies, from Drama to Creative Writing - the novelist, Fay Weldon, teaches creative writing at Brunel). Overall, teaching assessments have not been as good as some universities that demand less points at A level, but in some of these newer courses (Drama, Film & TV, Sport Sciences), it has performed especially well, as indeed it did in Education (23 points out of 24, see our *Academic Excellence* box, page 105).

Brunel is up among the best for turning out actors, rivalling specialist colleges like The Royal Scottish Academy, The Liverpool Institute (LIPA), The East 15 Acting School, The Central School of Speech & Drama, Rose Bruford College, and The University of Arts, London. Stage Managers come most from RSAMD and then Central and Rose Bruford, followed in a pack by the WCMD, Brunel...

Their Performing Arts Department, which includes the **Rambert School of Ballet & Contemporary Dance**, is a centre for Film & Television Studies (BA as single Hons, or feature of Joint or Major/Minor degrees) as well as drama and music (the latter with a strong practical emphasis and very good employment record).

There's also an interesting media dimension, with Film & TV Studies coupling with Drama or English or Music History - 20 points at the assessments for this.

In the Law Department (Grade 5 for research), they are specialists in Business & Commercial Law. Other social sciences show strong emphasis on politics, sociology (22 points for teaching; Grade 5 for research), psychology (also 22 points) and social

there is something wrong – four pizza houses, a few Indians and Chinese, all of very bad quality. Going out to eat is not much better. I did notice a newly opened restaurant next to the station last time I was there, which looked quite nice. There is also a good Chinese towards West Drayton.

ACADEMIA & JOBS

Brunel provides degree courses in design, systems, electronic, computing and mechanical engineering, education, health and social work and sports science. A large part of their success can be attributed to a long tradition of sandwich placements, incorporated into the majority of subjects offered. There are strong links with industry and business.

> *Out of a 19th-century, technical background, Brunel has become seriously good at Social Sciences and the Arts, bringing an influx of generally more exciting students and, indeed, women!*

anthropology. The American Studies connection that had been prevalent is now out of the window, and the Social Work degree is postgrad entry only, but comes strongly recommended.

In Education, which has a 23-point score at the teaching assessment, there is serious precedent: 51% go to primary, 37% to secondary. There's a long history, too, of producing graduate nurses and health-care professionals, following mergers with the London School of Occupational Therapy, the West Middlesex Hospital School of Physiotherapy and St Mary's Hospital School of Physiotherapy. Look especially at their BSc Occupational Therapy, which accounts for more than 7% of the graduate market Teaching inspection, 22.

They are leaders in finding jobs for graduates in Sport, as well. Players and would-be officials should look closely at the series of Sports Science degrees - coaching, admin. and development, fitness, PE, technology.

In Engineering there's a strong bent for design, for instance Mechanical Eng with B/MEng Automotive Design (4/5-year sandwich).

See also their BA and BSc Industrial Design and Technology degrees, and there's a whole raft of E&E Systems Engineering degrees, including 'Power Systems', 'Control Systems' and 'Communications Systems' degrees. The E & E engineering teaching has a 21-point teaching assessment and there are impressive Grade 5 (international quality) research ratings. See, too, the 3/4-year (thick/thin sandwich) BEng Computer Systems/Systems Engineering courses.

Also, they offer the more tailored Motorsport Engineering with similar promise of work experience. All engineering scored between 20 and 22 points out of 24 at the teaching assessments.

Writes Naveed Mohammed, 'Pressure of work builds gradually in your first year, not too bad unless you go totally wild. It gets more intense after that. Computers are available freely as is the Internet and they have been working hard to get

AT A GLANCE	
ACADEMIC FILE:	
Subjects assessed	**29**
Excellent	**69%**
Typical entry requirements	**303 points**
Application acceptance rate	**14%**
Student-staff ratio	**18:1**
First/2:1 degree pass rate	**66%**
ACCOMMODATION FILE:	
Guarantee to freshers:	**100%**
Style	**Halls, flats**
Catered	**None**
En-suite	**80%**
Approx price range pw	**£75-£92**
Local rent pw	**£75**

network access in all rooms.'

Notably, Brunel welcomes applications from disabled students and those with special needs. They have three disability officers, one of whom is a Dyslexia Co-ordinator.

PILLOW TALK

Halls are self-catering with single rooms. New rents will be set in June 2007. See *At A Glance* box above for current levels. 1,400 en-suite rooms have been made available in the last two years, with 1,400 rooms due to open in autumn 2008.

Says Olly: 'The accommodation is all of good quality, with every room including a connection to the internet, all the most recently built halls are en suite, and the four brand new halls: Bishop, Kilmorey, Lacy and St Margaret's - have the largest rooms on site so far.'

GETTING THERE

☛ By Underground: **Uxbridge** – Metropolitan line and Piccadilly during peak hours. Then bus, U3 or U5.

UNIVERSITY OF BUCKINGHAM

The University of Buckingham
Hunter Street
Buckingham MK18 1EG

TEL 01280 820313
FAX 01280 822245
EMAIL admissions@buckingham.ac.uk
WEB www.buckingham.ac.uk

Students' Union
The University of Buckingham
Hunter Street
Buckingham MK18 1EG

TEL 01280 822522
FAX 01280 812791
EMAIL student.union@buckingham.ac.uk
WEB www.buckingham.ac.uk/life/social/su/

VAG VIEW

*T*his is Britain's only independent
university. Tuition fees were always
thought of as steep, though most degrees have
always been completed within two years.
Now, since September 2006, Buckingham has
reduced its fees for UK and EU students.
With state universities charging top-up fees,
Buckingham's 2-year degrees (which enable
students to start earning a salary in what
would have been their third year) make them
a more competitive option.

In line with its reputation for breaking
new ground, a medical school is planned for
2009 - the first private UK medical school in
over 200 years. It will specialise in offering
fast-track training for prospective doctors.

CAMPUS

The three sites – Hunter Street, 8-acre Verney Park
and the recently developed Chandos Road complex,
are walking distance apart and within the town
boundaries.

FEES, BURSARIES

Fees 2007. For first year UK/EU undergraduates
£7,500 p.a. (2-year degree); (£4,995 p.a. for 3-year
degree). Fees p.a. 2008 same as 2007. There are a
number of scholarships available, some full fee.
See www.buckingham.ac.uk/study/fees/

STUDENT PROFILE

A popular picture of Buckingham is of a place for
rich also-rans, but that isn't a view shared by all
school sixthform advisers to whom we spoke. Many

UNIVERSITY/STUDENT PROFILE	
University since	**1976**
Situation/style	**Town campus**
Student population	**768**
Undergraduate population	**532**
- mature	**30%**
- non EU undergraduates	**61%**
- male/female	**50/50**

undergrads are mature and hie from overseas; as
elsewhere, there are a few more women than men ,
though not apparently among undergraduates.
'Each student mixes with 79 other different
nationalities,' they say, and since there are only 730-
odd students there, that is quite a mix.

ACADEMIA & JOBS

Buckingham has specialised in two-year degrees
since its inception 31 years ago. The degrees
operate on a four-term per year basis (so what
would be a long summer holiday is replaced by a
term of teaching). Their staff:student ratio of 1:9 is
the envy of all but UCL and Imperial.

Departments include Accounting, Business,
Economics, English Language Studies (EFL),
English Literature, Financial Services, History,
History of Art, Information Systems, International
Hotel Management, International Studies, Law,
Marketing, Politics and Psychology. Also available,
and paired with English are degrees in multimedia
journalism and media communications. They say
that for A level candidates they ask for three passes,
but combinations of A and/or AS levels are also
considered.

As this is an independent institution, it is not

obliged to be assessed by the Quality Assurance
Agency for Higher Education (QAA). However, in
November 2003, it submitted itself voluntarily for
an Institutional Audit by the QAA and was awarded
a judgement of Broad Confidence in the quality of
its programmes and the academic standards of its
awards. The new-style QAA Institutional Audit
process introduced in 2002, does not award scores at
subject level but departmental audits (Discipline
Audit Trails) undertaken by the QAA during the
Institutional Audit confirmed that the standard of
student achievement was appropriate to the titles of
the relevant awards in the subjects scrutinised.

Areas of particular strength - Buckingham's Law
and Business Schools are very popular and highly
regarded. 2006 saw the introduction of the Bachelors
in Business Enterprise, which offers students the
chance to set up their own business as part of the
degree. The Aylesbury Vale Enterprise Hub also
opened in 2006 and offers advice and space to start
up businesses in the Vale, incorporating a hatchery
space for entrepreneurs who are at the 'pre-start'
stage of their business plan.

Other new degrees include an MA in Global

Affairs, BA degrees in Business Enterprise, Journalism with English Literature, Journalism with Communication Studies, Journalism with International Studies, and a BSc in Economics with Business Journalism. As said, a new medical school is set to open in 2009.

The international nature of the university (the opportunity to study with students from over 80 different countries) also sets students up well to work abroad after they graduate. There is an excellent alumni network. Graduates' close contact with fellow graduates, offers unique mentoring for their future careers.

There are libraries at each site, a language centre and a networked IT set-up (a computer suite at Verney Park is accessible 24/7). There's a trained teacher of the dyslexic, who works with students from the minute they arrive. Degree courses are very concentrated, however. The intensity of the academic experience leaves little time or desire for the worst excesses of student fun and games.

SOCIAL SCENE

STUDENTS' UNION At one-tenth of the average size of a British university, Buckingham provides a cosy enough environment. The union, located in the **Tanlaw Mill** on the Hunter Street site (refectory and **George's Bar**, pool tables, video games, lounge with Satellite TV), organises discos on Fridays and a Graduation Ball. Then there's the **Franciscan Building** (Verney Park) for private-hire cellar parties. There are currently eleven societies, mainly cultural or departmental, quite a few organised trips and a series of concerts and lectures. The most active student society is Bahamian. There's a magazine called *Cygnet*, and in November 2005, a cinema opened on campus. Films are shown over the weekend, and often one mid-week showing. For escape, there are various restaurants and traditional country pubs in Buckingham, or Milton Keynes (14 miles), Oxford (23 miles), London (58 miles). Bring a car.

SPORT Four all-weather tennis courts, one all-weather five-a-side pitch, a swimming pool, gym complex and sports field; other playing fields a mile away. There are riding schools in the vicinity. The uni teams are mainly locally competitive. Matches played against alumni and staff are also regular features. There is a campus fitness programme – aerobics classes, martial arts – and a well-equipped fitness centre. They are currently raising funds to build a Sports Hall.

PILLOW TALK

Guaranteed first-year, self-catered accommodation in mixed halls of residence at Hunter Street and

WHAT IT'S REALLY LIKE	
UNIVERSITY:	
Social Life	★★
Campus scene	**Small, friendly, multi-cultured, mature**
Politics	**Internal**
Sport	**Local & BUSA**
Arts opportunities	**Few**
Student magazine	**Cygnet**
Union ents	**Functions, films, discos, balls**
Union venue	**Tanlaw Mill**
Union Societies	**11, mainly cultural**
Parking	**Permit required**
TOWN:	
Entertainment	★★
Scene	**Trad pubs**
Risk of violence	**Low**
Student concessions	**Some**
Cost of living	**Average**
Survival + 2 nights out	**£50-£80 pw**
Part-time work campus/town	**Poor/Excellent**

AT A GLANCE	
ACADEMIC FILE:	
Approx. points required	**200**
Student:staff ratio	**9:1**
ACCOMMODATION FILE:	
Guarantee to freshers	**100%**
Style	**Halls, flats, houses**
Catered	**None**
En suite	**10%**
Approx price range pw	**£80-£130**
Town rent pw	**£90+**

Verney Park, or shared flats at Hunter Street. The past few months have seen the introduction of internet access.

GETTING THERE

☛ By road: M40/J9 from the south, then A41, A421. Also A422, A421. A413 from the north.
☛ By rail: Buckingham has no station, the nearest are at Bicester and Milton Keynes. London Euston, 1:00; Birmingham New Street, 1:20.
☛ By air: Heathrow or Gatwick.
☛ By coach: London, 1:20.

BUCKINGHAMSHIRE CHILTERNS UNIVERSITY COLLEGE

Buckinghamshire Chilterns University College
Queen Alexandra Road
High Wycombe HP11 2JZ

TEL 01494 522141
FAX 01494 465432
EMAIL (see website)
WEB www.bcuc.ac.uk

VAG VIEW

*B*CUC can trace its history back to a School of Science and Art founded in 1893 and into Buckinghamshire College of Higher Education, formed in 1975 out of High Wycombe College of Technology and Art and Newland Park College of Education. From 1992 Brunel University validated its degrees.

Then, in 1999, four years after it had been given powers to award its own degrees, the college was confirmed by the Privy Council as a University College.

LOCATION

The college is sited at three locations within a short distance from London. Two – High Wycombe and Wellesbourne campuses – are within the market town of High Wycombe itself, and one – Chalfont Campus – is some 10 miles to the east, centred on an eighteenth-century mansion and set in 200 acres close to the village of Chalfont St Giles. All faculties are located in High Wycombe other than Business (the largest) and Health (nursing), which are on Chalfont Campus.

STUDENT PROFILE

There is a large mature population and many

COLLEGE/STUDENT PROFILE

University College since	**1999**
Situation/style	**Campus sites**
Student population	**9395**
Undergraduates	**8770**
- mature	**30%**
- non EU undergraduates	**9%**
- male/female	**40/60**
- non-traditional student intake	**33%**
- state school intake	**97%**
- drop-out rate	**18%**
- undergraduate applications	**Down 7%**

undergraduates are reading for HNDs and the like. The modern 'non-traditional' student abounds.

ACADEMIA & JOBS

BCUC offer a major portfolio of degrees through six faculties: Applied Social Sciences & Humanities, Business, Art & Design, Health, Leisure & Tourism and Technology.

Advertising degree graduates from Bucks Chilterns are the most popular in the industry. The BA Advertising & Promotions Management and Business Studies and Advertising Strategy degrees have recently been joined by Advertising with Psychology and Business Management with Psychology.

In Art & Design there's a whole raft of excellent BA Graphic Design & Advertising options with specialist illustrative focuses. Other graduates in the faculty find work as graphic artists, designers and illustrators, in media & government research, in textiles (see their BA degrees in Textiles – 3 specialist pathways are available).

There is also a Jewellery degree, which brings graduates into the Fashion industry. HND top-ups are possible. Entry is not too demanding. Teaching inspection, 20.

They are sector leaders, too, by a wide margin, in furniture design. High Wycombe has been associated with the craft for more than a century and BCUC delivers the largest range of furniture design programmes in the world. The sector supports around 400 graduates a year. There is everything here from BA Hons Conservation & Restoration, through Design & Craftsmanship to the HND top-up (2nd/3rd-year entry) Applied Furniture Studies. Then there's the BSc Furniture Manufacture & Design.

Communications & Media earned only 18 points on assessment, but this was some time ago and their media degrees are now difficult to ignore with masses of film studies, journalism, video production and the like combining with such as drama, English or creative writing.

The Technology faculty gets national prominence for its Centre for Rapid Design & Manufacture, while the Business faculty picks up on a college-wide emphasis on language acquisition,

ACADEMIC EXCELLENCE

TEACHING:
(Rated Excellent or 17+ out of 24)

Nursing	**23**
Marketing/Human Resources	**22**
Psychology Tourism/Sport	**21**
Agriculture, Art & Design	**20**
Communications & Media	**18**

RESEARCH:
Top grades 5/5* **None**

featuring European and international courses in collaboration with partners abroad. Jobs come thick and fast in retail, marketing and sales, and there's a niche area in transport planning and distribution. See the range of international, e-commerce, marketing and management degrees – teaching inspection 22 points. There's also a good record in personnel/human resource management, and 5%+ of their graduates go into the hotel and restaurant industry annually, which puts them among the leaders among small unis. When it comes to management there's a specialist line via Music Industry Management, as single subject or applied to Live Production, Marketing, Popular Music or Studio Production.

They are high among the country's suppliers of graduates into sport, too, offering BSc Sports Psychology and BA Sports Stadia Design & Management. Now, up for approval are Sport & Leisure Management and Sports Coaching Management. Teaching inspection, 21.

In the Health faculty, Nursing scored 23 points out of 24 in the teaching assessments. Their two BSc degrees: Nursing (with UKCC Registration) and Nursing Studies put them second to Oxford Brookes in supplying SEN, and they only lost 1 point at the assessments.

Finally, they are specialists in commercial and business law, and have a strong employment track record with BSc Policing See, too, BSc Criminology

degrees, Psychology again playing its part.

SOCIAL SCENE

An active ents scene, profiled in monthly magazine, *The Noise*, is offered at both Chalfont and the main High Wycombe campus, where the bar is **The Lounge** and the nightclub is **The White Room**. 'Bar 1: Bar 2' at Chalfont has recently been refurbished with a fantastic new lighting and sound system. Both have regular club nights and live acts. Event of the year is the May Ball, 'a black-tie, 12-hour blinding party with over 2,000 members of BCSU (the union) attending.

High Wycombe itself has various pubs and nightclubs, a cinema, a theatre and a sports centre.

AT A GLANCE

ACADEMIC FILE:

Subjects assessed	**13**
Excellent	**54%**
Typical entry requirements	**191 points**
Application acceptance rate	**20%**
Students-staff ratio	**21:1**
First/2:1 degree pass rate	**48%**

ACCOMMODATION FILE:

Guarantee to freshers	**90%**
Style	**Self-catered Halls**
Approx cost pw (no food/food)	**£46-£77**
Town rent pw	**£60**

A free minibus to the cinema is available to students, as are lifts home after ents nights.

There is an active sports scene at BUSA and local level. They came 85th nationally last year.

PILLOW TALK

There are two halls at High Wycombe – Brook Street and John North Halls, with self-catering accommodation for 500. At Chalfont a recent development brings the total rooms to 700 (some

WHERE BUCKS CHILTERNS GRADUATES END UP

Health & Social Work: 11%; Education: 3%; Wholesale/Retail: 19%; Manufacturing: 14%; Financial Activities: 6%; Public Administration, Civil Service & Defence: 5%; Hotel/Restaurant: 5%; Transport & Communications (including Telecommunications): 5%; Construction: 1%; Agriculture: 1%; Personnel: 3%; Computer: 2%; Business & Management: 2%; Media (including Film): 2%; Legal 2%; Architecture: 1%; Publishing: 3%; Advertising: 4%; Artistic/Literary: 3%; Sport: 4%.

Approximate 'graduate track' employed **42%**

en suite); there's a choice of self-catering or catered accommodation here.

GETTING THERE
☞ By road to High Wycombe: M40/J4, A4010; to Newland Park, M40/J2, A355, right on to A40, left on to Potkiln Lane.
☞ By rail to High Wycombe: London Marylebone, 35 mins.
☞ By Underground to Chalfont: Chorley Wood (Metropolitan line).

● ●

THE UNIVERSITY OF CAMBRIDGE

Cambridge Admissions Office
The University of Cambridge
Kellet Lodge
Tennis Court Road
Cambridge CB2 1QJ

TEL 01223 333308
FAX 01223 366383
Email admissions@cam.ac.uk
WEB www.cam.ac.uk/admissions

Cambridge University Students' Union
11/12 Trumpington Street
Cambridge CB2 1QA

TEL 01223 356454/333313
FAX 01223 323244
EMAIL info@cusu.cam.ac.uk
WEB cusu.cam.ac.uk

VAG VIEW

*C*ambridge *University began life early in the 13th century, more than 100 years later than Oxford. Its colleges have always been self-governing, with their own property and income, and tradition continues to be an important dimension of the Cambridge experience. With Oxford voting for men to be recruited to their all-female college, St Hilda's, Cambridge's Newham, New Hall and Lucy Cavendish are the last three all-women colleges in the country. Is that part of what we mean by tradition?*

STUDENT PROFILE

First, Cambridge students are bright: 'If you're thinking of applying to Cambridge: congratulations!' writes Caroline Muspratt, a student of Modern & Medieval Languages at Christ's. 'Why do I say that? Because even to consider applying, you must be a straight-A student, from a private school, with a white, middle-class background and parents who earn nearly £100K a year. Right?

'Wrong!. It's a common misconception that state school students, ethnic minorities, poor people, etc, don't get in. None of this matters. It won't affect your application, it won't change the friends you make, the societies you join, or the grades you get. I'm from a state school, I have working-class parents, and I'm the first person in my family ever to go to university. And yes, there are people here who went to Eton and have spent their whole lives being groomed for Cambridge, but students are students and the public-state divide is little more than a media fabrication. The university is extremely welcoming to overseas students and ethnic minorities: CUSU (the students' union) recently won a national award for ethnic diversity and its publication, *The Little Black Book*.'

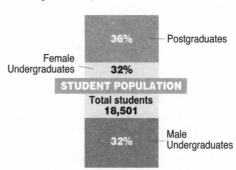

| 36% — Postgraduates |
| Female Undergraduates — 32% |
| **STUDENT POPULATION** |
| **Total students 18,501** |
| 32% — Male Undergraduates |

UNIVERSITY/STUDENT PROFILE	
University since	**1209**
Situation/style	**City collegiate**
Student population	**18501**
Undergraduates	**11903**
- mature	**4%**
- non EU undergraduates	**9%**
- male/female	**50/50**
- non-traditional student intake	**12%**
- state school intake	**57%**
- drop-out rate	**1%**
- undergraduate applications	**Up 0.3%**

Loyalty flies in the face of the facts. Cambridge fails to meet its benchmarks for attracting applicants from the lower classes and families new to the idea of university, but perhaps they have other, more interesting reasons for selecting their students. Perhaps it is exclusive not because it deliberately excludes applicants from state schools or working-class families, but because its dons are looking for young people with whom they can work on a one-to-one basis and push forward a bit, not back into the hopeless class struggle of yesteryear.

Katie Lydon went to school at Bolton Comprehensive and is 'more than fulfilled,' and quite unable to identify the typical Cambridge student or dominant group, only the caricature: 'Cliques grow up around sports, drama and other activities, as well as drinking societies and simple friendship groups. Although there is the odd example of the elitist stereotype, they are in the minority. Some groups, like sports teams and drinking societies, can dominate bar areas and seem intimidating, but this only tends to happen a few times a term, or after sporting victories.'

FEES, BURSARIES

UK & EU Fees 2007 for first year undergraduates £3,070, 2008 not yet known. Bursary for students in receipt of full HE Maintenance Grant, £3,100 per year (£5,150 per year for some mature students). See www.newtontrust.cam.ac.uk/. For sport awards, see www.sport.cam.ac.uk/bursaries/, including their Talented Athlete Scholarship Scheme. Individual colleges offer financial support, which may include scholarships and prizes for academic achievement. For awards to disabled students, see www.cam.ac.uk/cambuniv/disability/support/financial.html. For music awards (choral awards, organ scholarships and instrumental awards) see www.cam.ac.uk/admissions/undergraduate/musicawards/

ACADEMIA & JOBS

Note that all Cambridge undergraduates study for the BA degree, whether they are reading an arts or science subject. Note, too, there are three graduate colleges not profiled below, which do take the odd bod for undergraduate studies if they have already done a degree elsewhere or are over 21 at entry. These are: Hughes Hall, CB1 2EW. Tel 01223 334 897. WEB www.hughes.cam.ac.uk. St Edmund's CB3 0BN. Tel 01223 336 086. WEB www.st-edmunds.cam.ac.uk. Wolfson CB3 9BB. Tel 01223 335 918. WEB www.wolfson.cam.ac.uk.

'The work ethic is very strong throughout the university,' warns Caroline. 'You'll be expected to study hard, and to achieve a lot in a short time... It can initially be intimidating, and I wasn't the only

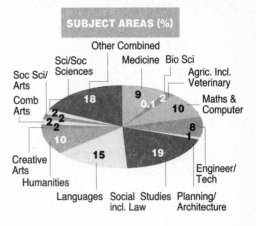

SUBJECT AREAS (%)

one who spent the first few weeks convinced that the interviewers had made a mistake. After a few alcohol-aided evenings out with other freshers, you realise that you are on a level pegging with most of them.

'Teaching is done through supervisions and lectures. Supervisions are given by fellows or research students to one or two students. It's a very intensive way of learning, and the short teaching term (eight weeks) means that there isn't much let up. This can take its toll, especially in the stressful summer exam term. Libraries are excellent, but...it can be difficult to get hold of books when the entire year is doing the same paper.'

The most popular sector for Cambridge graduates is health. The leading Medicine degree is the 5/6-year MB, BChir. Besides scoring AAA, including Chemistry, all candidates applying to read Medicine will in future sit a written test called the Biomedical Admissions Test (BMAT). The test is being used to assess scientific aptitude, not fitness to practise medicine (which will continue to be assessed in interview) and focuses on scientific abilities relevant to the study of medicine.

The MB, BChir involves heavy science-based pre-clinical in first two years, core subject study (Anatomy through to Psychology) the speciality. A number of graduates go into full-time laboratory research. For those who don't there's the chance to do the PRHO at top Addenbrooke's Hospital. Teaching inspection, 21. Research, Grade 5*/6* for Clinical Lab Sciences, Community-based Clinical, Hospital-based Clinical, Psychol, Biochem; Grade 5 for Anatomy. The veterinary degree is a 6-year MB and not available at Peterhouse or King's colleges. Teaching inspection, 23. Research grade 5.

Law is another key Cambridge profession. All candidates must sit the National Admissions Test for Law (LNAT). Non-Law graduates may apply for a 2-year Senior Status Law degree here.

Finance is, though, after health the most popular job sector for graduates from Cambridge. Among routes into investment analysis, banking, merchant banking and share dealing, Economics leads, engineering comes next. In that faculty specialisms such as Information & Computer Engineering and Management Studies are available. Languages are also a well-trammelled route. From Occitan to Hebrew-Biblical, the choice

Humanities is another route to publishing; and journalists and editors come out of Engineering and Social Sciences, and of course student media – the magazines are *Inprint, May Anthologies,* etc; the newspapers *Varsity* and *Cambridge Student* – are regularly award winning, as is *CUR* and *CUTE* (radio and TV). Teaching inspection, 22.

Another effect of cutting-edge student activity is in drama, whence graduate directors, producers and theatre managers proliferate (there being no

AT A GLANCE

ACADEMIC FILE:

Subjects assessed	**35**
Excellent	**97%**
Typical entry points	**525**
Application acceptance rate	**23%**
Med. School acceptance rate	**18%**
Student-staff ratio	**12:1**
First/2:1 degree pass rate	**85%**

ACCOMMODATION FILE

Guarantee to freshers	**100%**
Style	**College rooms**
Catered	**None**
En suite	**Not known**
Price range pw	**£65-£100**
Town rent pw	**£80**

ACADEMIC EXCELLENCE

TEACHING:
(Rated Excellent or 17+ out of 24)

Chemistry, History, Law, Computer Science, Architecture, Music, English, Geography, Geology, Anthropology	**Excellent**
Psychology, Molecular Biosci, Organismal Biosci, Pharmacol, Economics, Classics, Philosophy	**24**
Archaeology, Educ, Celtic, Social/Pol Sciences, Theology, Anatomy, Maths, Chem Eng, Materials Science, General Eng, Oriental Studies, Physics & Astronomy, Vet Science	**23**
Modern Langs, Land Economy, History of Art	**22**
Medicine	**21**

RESEARCH:
Special grade 5/5*6*

Clinical Laboratory Sciences, Community-based Clinical, Hospital-based Clinical, Psychol, Biochem, Zoology, Chemistry, Physics, Earth Sci, Pure Maths, Applied Maths, Statistics, Computer, General Eng, Metallurgy, Law, Celtic, English, French, German/Dutch/Scandinavian, Italian, Iberian, Linguistics, Classics, Archaeol, History, Hist & Philosophy of Science, Philosophy, Music	**Grade 6***
Asian Studies	**Grade 5***
Education, Theology, History of Art, Russian, Middle East & African, Business, Sociol, Economics, Anthropology, Geography, Town & Country Planning, Chemical Eng, Veterinary, Biotechnol, Plant Sciences, Genetics, Pharmacology, Anatomy	**Grade 5**

is wide. Then again, the mind-train of Classics is much sought after in the City of London, and interestingly Cambridge are levelling the playing field socially by introducing a four-year classics degree for students with little knowledge of Latin or Greek from school. Teaching inspection (Economics), 24. Classics scored full marks, too, and took a world-class 5*/6* rating for research.

Software consultants and engineers are popular areas for employment, too. Graduates come to them from Computer Science and Engineering in almost equal proportion, significant numbers (though less) through Mathematics. Specialisms in the 4-year Engineering degree include Information & Computer Engineering, Instrumentation & Control, amongst other subjects sympathetic to this career area. You can opt to study Mathematics with Computer Science.

The Publishing industry takes a shine to Cambridge language graduates in particular. Interestingly, BBC Worldwide is working with Cambridge on a range of new-generation foreign language courses. The agreement will result in the launch of a series of multi-media language courses over the next five years.

vocational drama degree here). Arts administrators and managers are also legion.

The Music Tripos involves history, analysis and compositional technique – intellectual and practical skills with an increasing amount of freedom to develop. There is a world-class Grade 5*/6* research reputation, and a good record in employment for musicians, conductors, composers.

Humanities graduates also become charity officers in quantity. Languages are again to the fore as preparation for lecturers in Adult Education, and in social work. Languages and Social & Political Sciences graduates find ready access to research jobs in media and government.

Re: languages, note that the uni is suspending its degree in Portuguese from October, 2008, although papers in the subject will still be offered to modern and mediaeval language students.

There are two Education routes, one where Education Studies is a complementary but subsidiary focus of Biosciences, English & Drama, English, Geography, History, Maths, Music or Religion; and the other available only at Homerton College, where the emphasis is on Education Studies and the other subjects are add-ons.

SOCIAL SCENE

STUDENTS' UNION 'Fresher's Week is organised by college JCRs (Junior Common Rooms), involving pub crawls and ents,' writes Katie. 'What I found especially encouraging was the willingness of the different year groups to mingle, and the fact that you are assigned "college parents" in different years to help you settle in.'

Societies occupy the free time of a large number, and are a way to create a sympathetic circle of friends, wider than your college might allow. The Cambridge Union boasts more than 400 societies. The most active is LesBiGay. Drama Society is big on tours to America and Europe every year, and a high number of productions go to the Edinburgh Festival. Media-wise, the student papers, Varsty and Cambridge Student, and radio station CUR are award-winning, and positions like May Ball President, Union President and those on the

WHAT IT'S REALLY LIKE

UNIVERSITY:	
Social Life	★★★★
Campus scene	**Bright, exclusive, focused, fun**
Student Union services	**Well organised, but no venue**
Politics	**Active, diverse campaigns**
Sport	**Huge.**
National team position	**9th**
Sport facilities	**Good**
Arts opportunities	**Drama/dance excellent, rest good**
Student magazine	**Inprint, May Anthologies, etc**
Student newspaper	**Varsity, Cambridge Student**
Journalism awards 2006	**1 nomination**
Student radio	**CUR**
Radio awards 2006	**1 Silver, 1 Bronze**
Student TV	**CUTE**
Nightclub	**None**
Union ents	**Town clubs + College JCRs**
Bars	**All colleges**
Union societies	**400+**
Parking	**Buy a bike**
CITY:	
Entertainment	★★★
Scene	**Cheesy clubs, great pubs**
Town/gown relations	**Average-poor**
Risk of violence	**Low**
Cost of living	**Average**
Student concessions	**Good**
Survival + 2 nights out	**£60 pw**
Part-time work campus/town	**Expellable offence**

JCRs are awarded after strenuous public hustings, since they develop the communication, teamwork and leadership skills sought by employers.'

WHERE CAMBRIDGE GRADUATES END UP

Health & Social Work: 16%; Education: 9%; Wholesale/Retail: 4%; Manufacturing: 10%; Financial Activities: 12%; Public Administration, Civil Service & Defence: 6%; Hotel/Restaurant: 1%; Transport & Communications (including Telecommunications): 3%; Personnel: 4%; Computer: 6%; Business & Management: 8%; Accountancy: 5%; Media (including Film): 2%; Legal 2%; Architecture: 2%; Publishing: 4%; Advertising: 1%; Artistic/Literary: 2%.

Approximate 'graduate track' employed **87%**

There is no central nightclub, but CUSU run popular student nights at local clubs and live acts or many and various.

SPORT 'Sports facilities are abundant,' writes Katie, 'but vary between colleges. If sport is your thing, check out the college facilities, where exactly the playing fields and so on are before you apply. All have or share a boathouse and operate a novice rower training programme, which can be a really good way of getting to know people if you can hack the early mornings.

TOWN 'If you're looking for somewhere with 24-hour opportunity, forget Cambridge; take a 45-minute train ride to London.

'Club fare in town ranges from cheesy, sweaty through the slightly nicer smaller, more chilled and alternative. There is a student night every weeknight.

'What the city lacks in clubs, it makes up for in pubs. There are dozens in the town centre, ranging from cosy locals to trendy wine bars. New restaurants are springing up all the time, and Cambridge is,' says Katie, 'a very safe place to live,' but what does it all cost?

'Cambridge is a relatively cheap city,' writes Caroline. 'If you're trying to work out a budget, allow about £60 per week for food, going out two nights a week, and all the other bits and pieces you'll need. I tend to get through about £600 per eight-week term, not including room rent. Books and equipment usually come free of charge: for scientists, all the scary chemicals are provided, and for arts students, the libraries are amazingly well-stocked. Travel costs should be zero: you'll soon find that everything in Cambridge is within walking distance (unless you're at Girton).

PILLOW TALK

'Room rents are subsidised by the colleges and they are increasing, but you can currently expect to pay about £70 a week on average. Every college has a normal canteen and a Formal Hall. You'll pay about £2 per meal. In Formal Hall, you'll pay about £5, but for this you get a three-course meal with coffee, served by waiting staff as you sit on long, candlelit tables. Grace is said in Latin and vast quantities of wine and port are consumed.'

GETTING THERE

☛ By road: M25/J27, M11/J11, A10. From west or east, A45. From northwest, A604.

☛ By rail: London's Liverpool Street, under the hour; Nottingham, 2:30; Birmingham, 3:00.

☛ By air: Stansted Airport, M11.

☛ By coach: London, 1:50; Birmingham, 2:45; Leeds, 5:00; Bristol, 5:30.

COLLEGE CAMEOS
by Katie Lydon

CHRIST'S
Cambridge CB2 3BU
Tel 01223 334 953
WEB www.christs.cam.ac.uk

Founded in 1448, Christ's is a beautiful college situated in its own extensive grounds in the centre of town. It has a strong academic reputation, regularly tops the Tompkins Table, and there's a strong atmosphere of study. Library access is 24-hour access and computer facilities, including room connections, are available. Christ's also makes 'easy offers' to around a third of its intake.

The balance of north/south and state/independent school students is relatively good, with 49% of the 2000/01 intake coming from the state sector. Women are under represented, but not drastically.

Uniquely, there are two bars, though one closes at 8.30pm. The ents committee puts on around four themed nights a term, and there is a formidable biennial May Ball. The JCR publish an alternative prospectus (see web site).

The college sporting reputation has become good and the drama society, CADS, is well known and respected across the university. The college has a squash court and boathouse – sports pitches are twenty minutes away – and use of its own theatre; there is a cinema that puts on both recent releases and classic films.

Writes Christ's Caroline Muspratt of the accommodation: 'The rooms are generally very good apart from the "typewriter", a horrible building at the back of Christ's. You may be lucky enough to get an en-suite bathroom; otherwise you can be sharing with anything from three to twelve people. The kitchens are usually very small and ill-equipped: the college wants to encourage everyone to eat in Hall. Upper Hall opens for breakfast, lunch and dinner, and the food ranges from excellent to mediocre. Formal Hall, which starts later in the evening, is particularly good: you can book in guests, and the three-course meal is served in a medieval dining hall.'

CHURCHILL
Cambridge CB3 0DS
TEL 01223 336 202
WEB www.chu.cam.ac.uk

Churchill was founded in 1960. The distance (five-minute cycle) from town is more than compensated for by the extensive grounds, proximity to sports facilities and the relaxation of being off the tourist trail. Academically it is strong and improving – up six places to ninth in the *Tompkins Table* this year, dominant subjects are computing, natural sciences and engineering

The state school presence is high (around 70%), and men are the dominant sex (around 77%), though Churchill was the first all-male college to admit women (1972). While very different from and less photographed than its older, town centre counterparts, Churchill's modern architecture is Grade I listed and popular for its functionality.

College ents are regular and popular with students throughout the university, as is its huge bar. All rooms have network and phone connections, and there are extensive sports facilities on site.

CLARE
Cambridge CB2 1TL
Tel 01223 333 246
WEB www.clare.cam.ac.uk
Founded in 1326, Clare is the second oldest college. It occupies extensive grounds that begin in a town-centre huddle of other colleges, and stretch to straddle the River Cam across to the University Library and arts faculties. It is friendly and academically successful – rated in the top six of this year's *Tompkins Table* – and is continually over-subscribed. Students are quite evenly divided between the arts and sciences. English and engineering applicants are encouraged to take a gap year.

Clare choir is famed in Cambridge and throughout the country, and Clare is also home to some of the best alternative ents in the university. Its hugely popular cellar based venue hosts regular live band sessions ranging from jazz to drum 'n' bass, attracting names such as the James Taylor Quartet. Its May Ball is renowned and tickets sought after.

The drama and art societies are particularly good, and Clare sports teams, especially rugby and hockey (men's and women's) and boat club are strong.

Accommodation is usually very good, with most first years living together in the same court, many in en-suite bathrooms. In later years there is the opportunity to move out to the large houses that constitute Clare Colony, a short walk along the river.

CORPUS CHRISTI
Cambridge CB2 1RH
Tel 01223 338 056
WEB www.corpus.cam.ac.uk

Founded in 1352, Corpus is situated right in the centre of Cambridge, opposite Kings (popular myth claims that Corpus actually owns Kings' land and that the lease is soon to expire, to the amusement of the inhabitants of the smaller college). Small but friendly, Corpus' architecture is as pretty as that of its bigger neighbours, but the college is better than most at protecting its students from the constant tourist invasion that can be a liability of a central college.

Corpus places a strong emphasis on academic pursuits, and presents an incentive to achievement in the form of its controversial academic room ballot. Strengths are mainly in the arts, especially history and English, but it is also strong in engineering.

Traditionally enthusiasm is the only pre-requisite here for sport, and the college offers a wide range of facilities, including on-site squash and a strong boat club. There's an annual sports 'Challenge' with Corpus Christi, Oxford.

The JCR is active and the bar a central feature, though its opening hours are variable. The film society puts on a regular mix of classic and new titles, and the drama society (*The Fletcher Players*) is well known and has links with the intimate, adjacent venue, **The Playroom**.

DOWNING
Cambridge CB2 1DQ
Tel 01223 334 826
WEB www.dow.cam.ac.uk
Downing is one of the newer town centre colleges, founded in 1800 just off Cambridge's main shopping street, close to the science, architecture and engineering faculties (the Sidgwick arts site is a little further). Once through the gates one finds an array of unusual neo-classical architecture and large, open, green spaces. It's a peaceful retreat, brilliant in summer. The atmosphere is friendly and lively, politically neutral and relaxed.

Academically, Downing is always in the Top 10; all subjects are well represented; law and medicine are particular strengths. The library is well stocked and pleasant, with an especially good law section. The JCR organises a good Freshers' Week; bar, common room and TV room are excellent. Termly events usually attract big name DJs and are popular across the university. They are perennially successful in sports; particular strengths are rowing, rugby and athletics. There are network connections in all rooms.

EMMANUEL (EMMA)
Cambridge CB2 3AP
TEL 01223 334 290
WEB www.emma.cam.ac.uk

Emma is a relaxed, open college founded in 1584 in the centre of town, opposite the arts cinema and the largest pub in the country. Emma students come from a wide range of backgrounds. It offers scholarships and hardship funds; financial status should never be a barrier to entry.

Emma is also outstanding academically, consistently featuring among the top five colleges. Arts are a particular strength, and it is often the most popular choice for English applicants.

The bar runs weekly funk and cheese events and is the best and most popular in Cambridge. Sport is strong, especially women's rowing and football. There's a squash court and an outdoor swimming pool. The municipal (and indoor) pool is close by, as are most of the shops and both cinemas. Drama and film societies are prominent, and a May Ball happens every other year.

Most rooms have network connections; unusually, Emma offers a free, weekly laundry service.

FITZWILLIAM (FITZ)
Cambridge CB3 0DG
TEL 01223 332 057
WEB www.fitz.cam.ac.uk
Founded in 1969, Fitz is one of the newest colleges in the university, occupying modern, spacious, award-winning buildings – the oldest date from 1963, very different from the classical architecture elsewhere but regarded as functional and user-oriented in a way older colleges often aren't.

Being set a five-minute bike ride away from the town centre in open, generally quiet grounds, students have a reputation for being relaxed and sociable. The college is good academically, comes about mid-*Tompkins Table*, but is not as frenzied as some. A high proportion of its intake comes from state schools.

Tradition isn't as prominent as in other colleges, though there is just enough to remind you that you are at Cambridge. The bar is well-loved and is the centre of social activity, and what are widely thought of as some of the best ents in Cambridge are put on twice a term.

Sport, especially football, is strong, and the college has its own squash court and gym.

GIRTON
Cambridge CB3 0JG
TEL 01223 338 972
WEB www.girton.cam.ac.uk
Girton was founded as a women's college in 1869, began to admit men in 1979 and now the latter slightly outnumber the former. It sits on a beautiful 50-acre site a couple of miles out of the city centre and, uniquely, has its own student car park.

Architecturally impressive and undisturbed by tourist invasion, the distance encourages a close-knit community and strong collegiate atmosphere; there's a 24-hour garage across the road for bits and pieces, and Girton village isn't far.

Girton isn't the most academic of colleges, the atmosphere is unpressured and relaxed. The **Cellar Bar** is the social focus and ents venue. Girton formal hall food is famed across the university for its quality, so much that the boat clubs and drinking societies of other colleges strive to get themselves invited for dinner. Sport is popular at Girton, and facilities include an on-site indoor heated swimming pool. The boat club is popular and does well.

Students initially live in college, then move out to nearby houses or Wolfson Court – much more central, near the University Library and Sidgwick site.

GONVILLE & CAIUS
Cambridge CB2 1TA
TEL 01223 332 447
WEB www.cai.cam.ac.uk
Founded as Gonville in 1348, 'Caius' (pronounced 'Keys') was added to the name in 1558. It occupies a convenient city centre site, but tourist traffic is less than might be expected as it sits between Trinity's famous Great court and King's Chapel.

Caius is academically strong, always in the top half of the *Tompkins Table*, and its particular strengths are in economics, law, history and medicine. The always accessible library is excellent, as are the computer rooms, and most student rooms are connected. Drama and music are popular, and *Caius Films* has become a prominent presenter of varied movies, drawing a cross-collegiate audience.

Sport is taken fairly seriously, with the boat club very successful. Squash, netball, football, hockey and racquet facilities are within a few minutes walk of college and served by a licensed pavilion.

Uniquely its students are compelled to buy forty-five dinner tickets per term at around £4 each. While this may seem a little expensive, the result *is* a stronger college atmosphere.

The college can accommodate all undergraduates well, though again, quite expensively.

HOMERTON
Hills Rd, Cambridge CB2 2PH
TEL 01223 507 252
WEB www.homerton.cam.ac.uk
Homerton was founded in 1695 as a college of education and moved to its present site in 1894. It

stills specialises in education, in education, Homerton College now other subjects, including Archaeology and Anthropology, Computing Science, Economics, Engineering, English, Geography, History, History of Art, Land Economy, Music, Natural Sciences, Oriental Studies, Philosophy, Social & Political Sciences, and Theology & Religious Studies.

Situated a bit out of the town centre, close to the railway station, Homerton tends to cultivate a fairly close community. There is a relatively high proportion of mature students, and women outnumber men. They recruit mainly from state schools, though students are drawn from all backgrounds.

Participation in university activities, such as journalism, drama and politics, is strong. Facilities are excellent – Homerton's on-site sound and dance studios are the rehearsal venue for many university productions. It also boasts its own gym, squash court and sports field. Men's rugby and women's rowing are both strong.

Students initially live in college, but there is the opportunity to move out into houses scattered around the town in later years.

JESUS
Cambridge CB5 8BL
TEL 01223 339 495
WEB www.jesus.cam.ac.uk
Jesus was founded in 1496 and, 'greener' and more open than some of its neighbours, overlooks the common and river from its spacious grounds, five minutes from the city centre.

Academically Jesus is relatively strong, and takes its students from a variety of backgrounds. The JCR bar is a popular social hub, but ents are few because of lack of room. Music and drama are strong, and the college offers exhibitions to organ and choral scholars.

Sport is very strong, and the college's location means that all of its facilities, which include pitches for soccer, American football, cricket, rugby and hockey, and squash and tennis courts, are on site. The boat club is a short walk across the common.

Accommodation for all undergraduates is in college or houses across the street – some of the latter have been recently refurbished and a new on-site block of en-suite accommodation opened.

KING'S
Cambridge CB2 1ST
TEL 01223 331 417
WEB www.kings.cam.ac.uk
Founded in 1441, King's and its famous chapel are most popularly representative of Cambridge. Its public perception, however, as the epitome of

prestige and tradition in Cambridge, contrasts sharply with the reality. It takes over 80% of its students from the state sector and is reputedly obsessed with being politically correct. Its students aren't required to wear gowns at formal dinners or elsewhere – in fact, there are *no* formal arrangements for meals.

King's fame attracts more tourists than any other college, but most come only to visit the chapel, and careful controls ensure that this doesn't impinge on study too much.

Academically King's is average, but its students are the most diverse bunch in the university. The atmosphere is relaxed and while students work hard, they make time for other activities – university drama, politics and journalism all feature high numbers of King's students.

Ents, based in their **Cellar**, are among the best in Cambridge, with queues forming long before the tickets for their famous termly *Mingle* events go on sale. The choir is of course world famous, making several recordings a year, and choral and organ scholarships are offered. Sport isn't a King's strength, perhaps something to do with the fact that its rowers wear purple lycra?

LUCY CAVENDISH
Cambridge CB3 0BU
TEL 01223 330 280
WEB www.lucy-cav.cam.ac.uk
Lucy Cavendish was founded in 1965 as a college for mature women. It is placed in a pretty *cul-de-sac* behind St John's, five minutes from the city centre.

Academically, medicine, law and veterinary science are strong. Sport isn't a particular strength, although the first Lucy Cavendish rowing crew hit the river a couple of years ago. Having had to start at the bottom, its reputation has yet to rise to the surface. The college has its own gym and access to squash and badminton courts. There's a summer ball after the festivities of May Week have died down and its own students are still around.

A recently built block of rooms with en-suite facilities has increased the on-site accommodation available to students.

MAGDALENE
Cambridge CB3 0AG
TEL 01223 332 135
WEB www.magd.cam.ac.uk
Magdalene (pronounced 'Maudlin'), founded in 1542, straddles Bridge Street, alongside the river on the north side of the city. Its grounds meet those of St John's and allegedly trespass on its land, which why students of the former refer to Magdalene students as their 'villagers'.

You'll hear that there is an overwhelming public school presence, and that tradition is paramount, with a nightly, formal candlelit dinner. But Magdalene students claim no atmosphere of elitism or arrogance. Most regard the dinner (non-compulsory) as a pleasant social occasion rather than an imposed tradition.

Academically not outstanding, but its students participate widely in university sport, drama and journalism, and have recently had a heavy involvement with the Cambridge Union.

Facilities are good – the college shares playing fields with St John's – and it has its own Eton Fives court. Most impressive facility is its music room, with grand piano, two harpsichords and an organ. The bar and other social facilities are good, and well complemented by the adjacent **Pickerel Inn**.

NEW HALL
Huntingdon Rd, CB3 0DF
TEL 01223 762 229
WEB www.newhall.cam.ac.uk
Ten minutes walk from the city centre, New Hall was founded in the 1950s to increase access to Cambridge for women. It is still a women-only college, but contrary to popular myth is not an introverted, convent-like place.

Indisputably, many New Hall students are pooled here as second choice, but many others chose to be there, and the two 'groups' cohere to form a pleasant and sociable community. In a recent referendum held to decide whether to go co-ed, students voted in favour of remaining single-sex.

Academically New Hall is continually close to the bottom of the *Tompkins Table*. Particular strengths are medicine, physics and economics. The college hosts the largest contemporary exhibition of women's art in permanent residence.

Its futuristic **Dome** houses a famed rising kitchen, applauded when it appears at meal times, and is generally thought of as one of the best ent venues in the university, hosting large events with big-name DJs – including the respected termly *Vibrate* – and yes, men *are* allowed in. No May ball, but a garden party is held.

Sports facilities are good, including tennis, squash and netball courts, and the college is close to playing fields. New Hall rowers are feared by other colleges' women crews.

College accommodation is available to all undergraduates.

NEWNHAM
Cambridge CB3 9DF
TEL 01223 335 783
WEB www.newn.cam.ac.uk

Newnham was founded in 1871 as an all-women college, continues to admit female students only, and, like New Hall, is anything but insular – guests of both sexes are welcome around the clock...as long as they are accompanied.

The college is situated close to the river and Sidgwick arts site, in attractive grounds with extensive gardens (where, uniquely, you may walk on the grass). Students are from a mix of backgrounds, though predominantly state school. Unspectacular academically, Newnham's strengths are in the arts.

Sport facilities include cricket, hockey, lacrosse, football and rugby pitches, a croquet lawn and tennis courts. Newnham's is the oldest women's boat club in England. Newnham students are also heavily involved in life outside college, particularly in drama and journalism.

PEMBROKE
Cambridge CB2 1RF
TEL 01223 338 154
WEB www.pem.cam.ac.uk
Pembroke was founded in 1347 and enjoys the benefits of a central location without the hassles of being on the tourist trail. It has pretty gardens, hidden from the roads by high walls.

Academically strong, computer facilities are good, and student rooms are mostly connected to the network. Pembroke also has busy dramatic, musical and journalistic interests. *The Pembroke Players* and the musical society are known across the university, and the college has its own newspaper, *Pembroke Street*. They also have a popular bar and regular ents, a sports ground and boat club, and enjoy high-level participation and reasonable success in rowing, rugby, football, netball and hockey.

Accommodation is good and either in college or nearby houses; a new block has just been completed.

PETERHOUSE
Cambridge CB2 1RD
TEL 01223 338 223
WEB www.pet.cam.ac.uk
Peterhouse is the oldest and smallest college in Cambridge. Founded in 1284, the buildings are attractive and close to Pembroke and the engineering and science faculties.

Reputed to be more stringent than most in its interviewing and admissions procedures, Peterhouse has particular strengths in classics, English, history, law, engineering, maths, medicine and natural sciences. Its stereotype – oft denied – is that of a staunchly right-wing, public-school environment. Men outnumber women significantly, but allegations of a sexist culture appear unfounded as girls from other colleges choose to join Peterhouse choir and other activities. (the college has its own theatre). Sports are actively pursued, particularly rugby, football and rowing. The college also has its own magazine and many of its students are involved in university newspaper journalism.

QUEENS'

Cambridge CB3 9ET
TEL 01223 335 540
WEB www.quns.cam.ac.uk

Founded in 1448, in pleasant grounds straddling the river, and close to most faculties, Queens' is open, pleasant, and students say the most people-based college in Cambridge. Certainly its students come from staggeringly different backgrounds. Around the top of the academic league tables, strengths are in natural sciences, medicine, engineering, languages and law.

Facilities are fantastic, including a hall that hosts some of the biggest ents in Cambridge (such as the famed cheesy *Jingles*); it doubles as theatre or sporting venue. The entertainment schedule is the envy of the university, and there is a huge May Ball every other year. The drama society puts on some of the most innovative and controversial plays in Cambridge, there's a thriving gossip magazine, the film society provides a college cinema two nights a week, and the sporting ethos, while placing emphasis on enjoyment, embraces success at university level (there are squash courts and playing fields). Yet, Queen's still manages to remain a genuinely friendly, relaxing, unpretentious, but inspiring place to be.

College can accommodate all students, and all rooms are connected to the internet.

ROBINSON

Cambridge CB3 9AN
TEL 01223 339 143
WEB www.robinson.cam.ac.uk

Robinson is the newest Cambridge college, founded in 1979 and based in red-brick buildings behind the University Library and arts faculties, next to the uni rugby ground – slightly out of town (five-minute cycle), but close to sports facilities. Its 'new' status means tradition is kept to a minimum. Here, Cambridge stereotypes are despised and disproved.

Academically average, the emphasis is on personal freedoms and development. Robinson draws the majority of its intake from state schools; the atmosphere between staff and students is very open and respectful, with meetings open to everyone.

Ents are well attended and include karaoke and music nights featuring anything from cheese to jazz. The JCR publishes its own alternative prospectus – check the web site.

Accommodation is comfortable, functional and available to all undergraduates.

ST CATHERINE'S (CATZ)

Cambridge CB2 1RL
TEL 01223 338 319
WEB www.caths.cam.ac.uk

Catz is a small college on the main street, along from King's, almost opposite Corpus Christi, and within ten minutes' walk of the main arts, science and engineering faculties. Founded in 1473, its relatively small size makes for an inclusive community. There's a good social mix, though women are a minority (usually around 40%).

It has a tradition of academic excellence, though it has recently dropped in the *Tompkins Table*. Strengths are in natural sciences, geography and medicine. The library is new and well stocked.

Even though its ents are generally poor, Catz has a good social tradition: Freshers' Week is legendary, recently the bar and common room have been refurbished, and its formal dinners are popular and over-subscribed.

Music and drama are strong, and Catz has its own 150-capacity theatre in the **Octagon** buildings. The literary Shirley society is the best known in Cambridge. Sport is strong, notably rugby and athletics.

The boathouse is a short cycle away, and facilities are generally good – there's an Astroturf pitch, courts for racquet sports, and pitches for field sports. Swimming is a Catz strength, and though it doesn't have its own pool, the excellent, new town facility is close.

Students live initially in college, moving out to the Octagon colony of flats near the Sidgwick site in the second year.

ST JOHN'S

Cambridge CB2 1TP
TEL 01223 338 703
WEB www.joh.cam.ac.uk

St John's was founded in 1511 in the centre of Cambridge, next to its long-standing rival, Trinity. It is the second largest college in Cambridge and so is able to house all its undergraduates. Architecturally impressive, its buildings chart varied and increasingly modern styles, culminating in the listed Cripps Building, seen as ugly by some, but functional and popular accommodation for first years.

Academically, John's is very strong (fourth in the tables for the last couple of years, and generally in the top five) and boasts an impressive and very well-stocked new library. Its beautiful Old Library houses many ancient manuscripts. Computing facilities are excellent, with two main computer rooms and terminals scattered around the library and in the JCR. All student rooms in college have Internet connections. Book grants are automatic; travel grants and hardship loans are generous.

St John's choir is respected globally, the college chapel providing a beautiful setting, and the Jazz Society is famed across the university. Drama – the *Lady Margaret Players* – is a great tradition, the freshers' play a big draw, and they have their own venue in the **School of Pythagoras**, apparently the oldest university building in the country. The film society operates twice a week, and there are disco clubnights three times a term in the underground **Boiler Room**, noted for its drum 'n' bass, hip hop and cabaret. Sport is strong, especially rugby, football and the famous Lady Margaret Boat Club. There are extensive pitches at the back of college and a new boathouse just down the river. There are also squash, badminton, tennis and netball facilities. Finally, John's formal hall is arguably the best (and best value for money), and tickets for their May Ball are among the most sought after.

SELWYN
Cambridge CB3 9DQ
TEL 01223 335 896
WEB www.sel.cam.ac.uk
Selwyn was founded in 1882 and sits in pleasant grounds close to the Sidgwick site of arts faculties. The college's proximity to green fields and 15 mins distance from the bustle of the city centre gives it an atmosphere less claustrophobic than most.

Not noted for its academic reputation, though usually in the top half of the *Tompkins Table*, Selwyn's strengths include engineering, history and natural sciences.

There is an even mix between arts and science students and between men and women, and students come from a wide variety of backgrounds.

Facilities are good – the library is satisfactory. For arts students, faculty libraries are on the doorstep and can be equally accessible. Most student rooms are connected to the internet, and communal computer facilities are good.

Drama (*The Mitre Players*) have their own venue in the **Diamond**, and the music and film societies are also active.

Sport is not a major strength, except rowing, where in recent years Selwyn has become a force. The bar is popular, and there are several student run ents. The impressive May Ball is biennial.

All undergraduates can be accommodated either in college or in nearby houses.

SIDNEY SUSSEX
Cambridge CB2 3HU
TEL 01223 338 872
WEB www.sid.cam.ac.uk
Sidney was founded in 1596 on what is known to today's students as 'Sainsbury's Street'. The modern world beyond the gates may be extremely busy, but once inside you'll find architecture dating back 400 years and a relaxed and unpressured atmosphere.

Accommodating a balance of arts and science students, with an even ratio of women to men, Sidney isn't the most academic of colleges, although it is currently pushing its way up the *Tompkins Table*.

The bar is good and run by students, with a sound system better than that of most other college bars, pool table and table football. The frequent ents are well attended

College food has allegedly improved since it was voted second worst in Cambridge in 1993. Sport isn't strong. A sports ground, a short cycle away, is shared with Christ's; the boathouse is close.

Students are accommodated either in college or in nearby houses.

TRINITY
Cambridge CB2 1TQ
TEL 01223 338 422
WEB www.trin.cam.ac.uk
Founded in 1546, Trinity is the largest college in Cambridge. Situated centrally with beautiful views onto the river and the Backs and next to St John's, Trinity is its (friendly) rival in almost everything.

The college architecture is much admired, notably the Wren Library and Great Court, whose 'run' was made famous in *Chariots of Fire* (though actually filmed at Eton).

There is an impressive academic record – they are rarely out of the top four or five in the *Tompkins Table* (No. 3 this year) – particularly in sciences. Contrary to popular belief, it recruits a significant majority from the state sector; women are, however, poorly represented (around 40%).

As befits the richest college in Cambridge, facilities are excellent, the library well stocked and computer facilities first class. Book grants are available to all students, room rents are among the lowest in the uni (although rooms have varying facilities, due to the age of the buildings, all are comfortable).

Ents aren't particularly notable, but the bar is well used, if a bit small. Extra-curricular activities are fervently pursued, and sport is strong. The boat club has recently listed several impressive victories, facilities are superb and nearby.

TRINITY HALL (Tit Hall)
Cambridge CB2 1TJ
TEL 01223 332 535
WEB www.trinhall.cam.ac.uk

Trinity Hall was founded in 1350 and nestles in pretty riverside grounds next to Trinity, its bigger and richer rival.

There is a popular myth about Trinity porters phoning their Tit Hall counterparts to ask them to turn the music down at some gig – the reply came that Trinity Hall was 'there first' and so would do as it pleased. This anecdote sums up the atmosphere – it's a close, strong community that refuses to be overshadowed by its neighbours simply because of its size. There's a good mix of students and of men and women.

Tit Hall is, according to the *Tompkins Table*, academically average, but its traditional strength is law. The new library, overhanging the river, is well stocked, if a little noisy in the summer, when it's a feature on guided punt tours.

Bar and JCR are lively and ents often referred to as the best. They face tough competition from King's, but are enjoyed for their individual style, the quality that best represents Tit Hall's students.

Sport and sporting facilities are good, and drama and music societies active.

CANTERBURY CHRIST CHURCH UNIVERSITY

Canterbury Christ Church
University
North Holmes Road
Canterbury
Kent CT1 1QU

TEL 01227 782900
STUDENT UNION 01227 782080
FAX 01227 782888
EMAIL admissions@cant.ac.uk
WEB www.canterbury.ac.uk

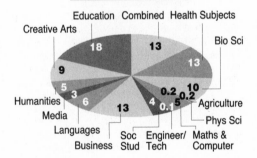

SUBJECT AREAS (%)

VAG VIEW

*B*efore Canterbury Christ Church achieved university status in 2005 it excelled for a decade as a university college, awarding its own degrees. Founded by the Church of England in 1962 (and currently boasting the Archbishop of Canterbury as Chancellor), it is located in modern buildings on part of St Augustine's Abbey (built in AD 597). It began as a teacher training college, but expanded and diversified impressively, with undergraduate applications up 20% this year.

A £40-million development plan underwrites their new status, to include a £30-million learning resource centre at Augustine House in the city and £10 million worth of sport and music facilities.

CAMPUS

Canterbury is a good place to be, small and friendly, if not exactly jumping with action. It is just big enough to hold a cathedral, some run of the mill shops and a fair range of pubs – and on first visit you might wonder that there's room for two degree-awarding institutions. The more widely known of these is the University of Kent (UKC), a traditional campus university situated up what has become known to the thousands of UKC students who trundle up and down it daily as Mount Everest. C4's campus is situated on the east side of the city.

There are also three other campuses: nearby **Broadstairs Campus** (Northwood Road, Broadstairs, Kent CT10 2WA; 01843 609120) - business, computing, digital media, education, health, commercial music, performing arts, policing), **Chatham Campus** (30 Pembroke Copurt, Chatham Maritime, Kent ME4 4UF; 01634 890800) - education, health and policing), and **Salomans Campus** - (David Salomans Estate, Broomhill Road,

Southborough, Tunbridge Wells, Kent TN3 OTG; 01892 515152) - postgraduate study.

And now, there's to be University Centre Folkestone, developed with the University of Greenwich. Folkestone will be offering programmes in Performing Arts, Visual Arts and Entrepreneurship from September 2007.

They are also developing a flagship building in the centre of Canterbury. The £30 million landmark building will provide an integrated library, learning resource centre, with student support facilities, conference and exhibition areas. It will also feature a café, two garden terraces, and an atrium.

FEES, BURSARIES

UK & EU Fees 2007: £3,070 for first year full-time undergraduates (except those on NHS funded bursaries). For 2008, fees will increase in line with inflation. There are means-tested bursaries of £820 for those paying £3,070 tuition fees per year, and sliding-scale bursaries for students in receipt of the HE Maintenance Grant. Also, a £200 scholarship for PGCE Secondary students, plus International (non-EU) student bursaries of £3,000 p.a. (12 available annually).

ACADEMIA & JOBS

The uni is the largest centre of higher education in Kent for the public services - notably teacher education, policing, health and social care, including clinical psychology - and is a significant provider in a wide range of academic and professional areas. There are four faculties, Arts & Humanities, Business & Sciences, Education, and Health.

Education is highly rated and more than a third of C4 graduates find work in this sector, but now the curriculum has expanded to include degrees in English, History, American Studies, International Business, Computing (including Animation), Art, Music, Radio, Film & TV (where there are links with Sky), Religion, Sport Science and social sciences, and since 1987 there has been a major expansion in

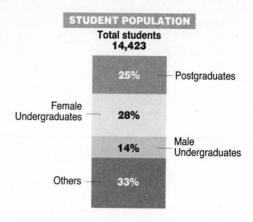

STUDENT POPULATION

**Total students
14,423**

25% — Postgraduates

Female Undergraduates — 28%

14% — Male Undergraduates

Others — 33%

courses for the paramedical and nursing professions., and there are new courses in Speech and Language Therapy.

They claim links with 'some 8,000 businesses managed through academic departments and the Centre for Enterprise and Business Development (CEBD)'. New course in Finance and Accounting. Recent teaching assessments have been uniformly good, but the real acid test was passed when subjects such as music (degrees include Popular Music & Technology), radio/film/TV, art (including Fine Art and Ceramics) and sport began to find popular expression in the extra-curricular life of the university, which is growing fast.

They are among the top suppliers of TV and film camera operators. See the uni's Film/Radio & TV Studies BA/BSc and the MA Media Production.

In the Health field, degrees include Midwifery, Nursing (Adult, Child, Mental Health), Occupational Therapy and Radiography - they account for 5% of the graduate job market with their BSc Medical Imaging (Radiography) – low entry requirements, good assessment results (22 points).

Worth noting, too, is a strong, traditional link with the police – the DIpHE and BSc in Policing, large number of combos with Applied Criminology and Forensic Investigation degrees translate with efficiency into jobs

Business finds sales managers jobs in quantity, and puts 5% or more of their graduates into work in the transport business. Traditionally they are strong, too, in travel – travel and tour agency managers.

Campus Folkestone (see *Campus*, above) will bring new courses in Performing Arts, Visual Arts and Entrepreneurship. Finally, some two dozen Sport & Exercise Science degrees ensures that they are making a mark nationally in this area of graduate employment, too. See *Sport*, below.

There's a good deal of talk about disability support – 'from providing note-takers to sorting out car parking for students with Orange/Blue Badges.'

UNIVERSITY/STUDENT PROFILE	
University since	**2005**
Situation/style	**City campus**
Student population	**14423**
Undergraduates	**6122**
- mature	**27%, high**
- non EU undergraduates	**4%**
- male/female	**35/65**
- non-traditional student intake	**33%**
- state school intake	**96%**
- drop-out rate	**16%**
- undergraduate applications	**Up 20%**

STUDENT SCENE

The Union bar is **CCSUbar**. 'Also we have partnership deals with clubs in town (**Chicago's Nightclub**, a favourite for male students, given C4's 35/65 male/female ratio).' There's something on every weekday night, ranging from *Unplugged* stage, *Pop Factor* to *Flirt* on Fridays. Tuesday nights are either karaoke, live comedy or quiz nights. Wednesdayis Sports Fed night, where all the teams get horrifically drunk in the SU. Thursday is *Frame 25*, the student cinema, which shows recent movies on a weekly basis. There are balls all year round – Freshers', Halloween, Graduation, Christmas – the climax being the huge Summer Ball with fairground and bands.

Student media has been big, but as we went to press there was no newspaper or student magazine. However, C4 Radio has been re-named CSR (Community Student Radio) and has copped a public

---

ACADEMIC EXCELLENCE	
TEACHING:	
(Rated Excellent or 17+ out of 24)	
Geography, History	**Excellent**
Maths, Radio/Film/TV	**22**
Studies, Nursing, Other	
Subjects Allied to Medicine,	
Theology	
American Studies,	**21**
Physics, Chemistry,	
Leisure/Sport, Business/	
Managment, Biosciences	
Psychology, Social Science,	**20**
Media & Cultural Studies	
Art & Design	**19**
RESEARCH:	
Top grades 5/5*	**None**

WHAT IT'S REALLY LIKE	
COLLEGE:	
Social Life	★★★
Campus scene	**Lively, local**
Politics	**Left of Centre**
Sport	**Competitive + sport-for-all**
National team position	**100th; 33 clubs**
Arts opportunities	**Excellent**
Student radio	**CSR**
Student TV	**CCTV**
TV Awards, 2005	**Commendation**
Union ents	**Flirt, Unplugged**
Live venue capacity	**450**
Union societies	**17**
Parking	**Very poor**
CITY:	
Entertainment	★★★
Scene	**Touristy, historic, very studenty; pubs OK**
Town/gown relations	**Good**
Risk of violence	**Average**
Cost of living	**High**
Student concessions	**Adequate**
Survival + 2 nights out	**£80 pw**
Part-time work campus/town	**Average/Good**

---

there are lots of music groups and student bands, which, unfortunately, have been banned by the Council from playing in the union due to excessive noise levels.

TOWN Writes Dominic Conway: 'Nice big cathedral, old cobbled streets, strong whiff of history in the air and a two hour walk to the beach. That is

---

AT A GLANCE	
ACADEMIC FILE:	
Subjects assessed	**23**
Excellent	**74%**
Typical entry requirements	**239 points**
Application acceptance rate	**22%**
Students-staff ratio	**21:1**
First/2:1 degree pass rate	**47%**
Graduate track employment	**63%**
ACCOMMODATION FILE:	
Guarantee to freshers	**100%**
Style	**Halls, flats, houses**
Catered	**13%**
En suite	**38%**
Approx price range pw	**£76-£91**
City rent pw	**£65-£73**

FM licence and is broadcasting across the city. Theirs was the first British student radio station to broadcast all over the world via the Internet. CSR was launched on January 15, 2007. The student TV company has also been re-named - CCTV. Neither appeared among the national awards this year.

There are 17 societies altogether, from Raise & Give to Trampolining, from Pagan to Asian, and

Canterbury. To accommodate the evident wealth of students there are two clubs (plus some secret ones) and plenty of good bars. If you keep your ear to the ground local groups will put on authentic unpretentious rock shows and Whitstable hides a number of world class musicians playing jazz, blues, and Turkish folk music that will content even the most selective muso. There is also a wide variety of shops and supermarkets to take your pick from! The toughest thing is avoiding the temptation to spend money in one of the many restaurants and café bars that line the streets. Apart from that everything is very simple and easy to find. If you come here you will have everything really: countryside and seaside, but still be near to London:; entertainment and nightlife, but still a calm working environment.'

SPORT The uni is developing a much-needed new sports centre including 8 badminton court sports hall, fitness centre and studio scheduled for opening in September 2008. They have 20 acres of sports field with 4 football pitches, 1 rugby pitch and 1 lacrosse pitch. Four tennis courts are located on campus for educational and students casual use.

PILLOW TALK

Style of accommodation includes catered halls (some en suite), self-catered flats (again, some en suite), and self-catered houses. First years are prioritised for halls. On the Canterbury Campus main site, Davidson, Lang and Temple are en suite,

Fynden and Thorne are single rooms with washbasins and catered, but rent quoted does not include meals. Canterbury-based self-catered residences at College Court and Holmes Court are 2 mins from campus. Lanfranc and Oaten Hill are farther, but the latter is a refurbshed oast house and much in demand. Newest is the Parkham Road Student Village (2005), a 10-min walk from campus, with houses and flats for 3 to 7 students. Finally, there's Pin Hill, 15 mins away from campus, a development of 5 halls, Ramsey, Coggan, Runcie and Carey (all very episcopal) and Benson House (which has 40 en-suite rooms). Broadstairs and Chatham cmpuses both have self-catered residences. Opening in September 2007 are various studio, and 2 and 4-bed flats.

GETTING THERE

☞ By road: M2 and A2 connect Canterbury to London and beyond.
☞ By coach: London Victoria, 1 hour 45 mins.
☞ By rail: two or three times an hour from London Victoria, Charing Cross and Waterloo East stations. The fast service takes 1 hour 20 mins.

STUDENT CARDIFF – THE CITY

Cardiff is one of the best places to study in Britain. As well as three universities, it has well-situated, cheap housing, lively nights out, friendly people, great shops and hundreds of miles of countryside just a little to the north. It is all that any right-thinking fresher could desire in a college town.

And, if there's one thing Cardiff has in its bag of tricks that almost all others in the UK haven't, it is its status as a capital. As a result, a medium-sized city with a similar population to Coventry is loaded with amenities, arts venues, stadia, beautiful civic parks, a world-class research university and everything else you, a naive 18-year-old from the backwoods of some distant shire, could want. And cos it's so small, most of it is easily walkable - result.

SHOPPING

If you ignore the Victorian splendour that marks out many of Cardiff's city centre shops and focus on the dull plastic high street facades of Queen Street you could be in Newcastle, Manchester or any city in the UK. But, if you're willing to wander a bit Cardiff has some of the best shops in the UK. From **Spillers** in the Hayes (Britain's oldest record shop don'tcha know), to **Madame Fromage**, a wondrous land of cheeses and continental meats,

in the Castle Arcade, the city has more than enough to entertain, after a few cursory glances at Top Shop and Debenhams anyway.

As any Cardiffian with an ounce of sense will tell you, it's the **Arcades** that house most of Cardiff's best stores. The narrow alleys that splinter various city centre streets are filled with secondhand book shops, vintage and designer clothes stores, cafés and shoe shops. You could live here for years and still discover shops you're sure you've never seen before.

Away from the fun of the arcades, the **Capitol Centre** and **St David's Centre** (and forthcoming **St David's 2** in the Hayes) house most of the dull chemists, opticians and department stores that you can blow your novelty-sized loan cheque on.

FILMS

The best cinema in Cardiff is **Chapter Arts** in deepest, darkest Canton. Canton's actually a lovely part of the city, but it's a good 20-minute walk from the city centre, so 90% of students won't bother with it. You should; this converted school-turned arts complex has one of the best bars in the city and shows films that wouldn't get near a multiplex.

More conventionally there is the huge, and

dependable, **Cineworld** megaplex which has 3 floors of screens, 2 bars, and means to sate any culinary desires you have, as long as they involve hot dogs and gulp-sized colas. Ditto **Vue**, which is lodged in some godawful leisure complex glued onto the **Millennium Stadium**. There's a big **UCI** down in the Bay too. So Cardiff, if you're one for the motion pictures, is super.

ARTS

Cardiff's capital status means it gets more arts money pumped into it than a Tracey Emin cash machine exhibit. With too many art galleries to mention, it's probably best you stop by the **National Museum and Art Gallery** (which is free) and let them point you in the direction of other galleries in the city.

The **New Theatre** is a good stop for standard touring fare and the occasional big budget local show but the city is also home to smaller local theatres like the **Sherman** on Senghennydd Road, which put on shows by local companies as well as small tours and comedy.

Ah, stand-up, a great place for you to show-off that new found campus wit in front of a crowd of literally hundreds with a heckle or too. The Sherman and New Theatre have tonnes of comedy shows throughout the year, but your best bet is **St David's Hall**, which has recently been host to student favourites like Dylan Moran, The Mighty Boosh and Paul Merton. There's also the weekly stand-up show in the students' union as well as **The Glee Club** in the Bay which is host to many a promising chortle merchant.

EATING OUT

Although it has no Michelin stars, Cardiff has many a restaurant for you and your friends to go and have one of those big group meals where one person inevitably doesn't pay and everyone else has to stick an extra quid in. The new Brewery Quarter off St Mary's Street is home to **La Tasca**, **Nando's**, **Hard Rock Café** and many others. It's as safe a bet to take your society chums as it is your parents on a rare visit.

Of course there are plenty of smaller, independent eateries; enough curry houses to smelt you tastebuds (try **Chillis** on Whitchurch Road), enough pub grub to feed a league's worth of hungry rugby players (try the Sunday roast at the **Blackweir** on North Road) and vegetarian options to suit the most hardened carrot muncher (**The Greenhouse** on Woodville Road, for example).

The Bay also offers everything from **Pizza Express** to Turkish to **Harry Ramsden's**. You can stuff yourself before trekking around the fancy new Welsh parliament building or visiting Roald Dahl's old gaff, the **Norwegian Church**.

PUBS

There are, thank goodness, enough pubs to sooth the insistent needs of every kind of student. There are rowdy discount card pubs like the **Woodville** (Cathays Terrace) and the **George** (Macintosh Place), small slightly-traditional, but not quite, pubs like the **Pen & Wig** and **Rummer Tavern**, a smorgasbord of **Wetherspoons**, as well as a few choice, if pricey, city centre watering holes like **Floyds**.

St Mary's Street is the natural home of all the pile 'em high, sell 'em cheap pubs that cause Cardiff to resemble Baghdad on a weekend night. If that's your kind of thing then you'll be thrilled, but if not take the time to explore bars out of the city centre like **Bar En-Route** on Cathays Terrace, the aforementioned Chapter Arts bar and plenty more pubs that aren't full of people dressed for a round of pub golf. Suffice to say, if one of your key aims in exploring higher academia is to consume vault-loads of booze, then Cardiff will service you as well as anywhere.

CLUBS AND LIVE VENUES

Thanks to having venues of almost every size, Cardiff is one of Britain's best cities to catch a gig. Whether it's the noisy and new at **Barfly** and **Clwb Ifor Bach** (or **Welsh Club** as it will quickly become known), the mid-sized rock of the students' union (recent gigs include Bloc Party, Kaiser Chiefs, Panic! At The Disco) or the pomp of the **Cardiff International Arena**, you'll be well catered for. St David's Hall is mainly a classical venue but occasionally hosts the likes of Morrissey. **The Point** at the Bay is a converted church that is probably the city's best small venue, local heroes Super Furry Animals and Stereophonics have played warm-ups there in the not-so-distant past.

If sweaty rock music isn't your thing, and frankly there are better things to do on a Friday night than get your shoes stamped on by Strokes fans in Barfly, you won't struggle to find somewhere to spend your dimes.

All the plastic chain nightclubs are here, **Liquid**, **Jumpin' Jaks**; you name it... But if you check out the likes of super-trendy **Soda**, where Wales's golden couple Charlotte Church and Gavin Henson are regulars, and which is so trendy it doesn't have a sign on the door, you can have a night as good as any in Britain.

Keep an eye out for monthly nights by LAmerica and Cool House which switch residences around the city.

Will Dean

CARDIFF UNIVERSITY

Cardiff University
Cardiff CF10 3AT

TEL 029 2087 4455
FAX 029 2087 4457
EMAIL prospectus@cardiff.ac.uk
WEB www.cardiff.ac.uk

Cardiff Students' Union
Cardiff CF1 3QN

TEL 029 2078 1400
FAX 029 2078 1407
EMAIL studentsunion@cardiff.ac.uk
WEB cardiffstudents.com

VAG VIEW

This is a tip-top uni academically, with as good a student-to-staff ratio as Oxford, yet its entry standards are not nearly as demanding. It is also hugely popular with its students, who run a breathlessly active extra-curricular scene. Yet its number of applicants increased less in 2007 than most of its competitors in the premier league. Is Cardiff the best kept secret among Britain's universities?

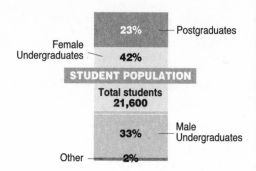

Postgraduates 23%
Female Undergraduates 42%

STUDENT POPULATION
Total students 21,600

Male Undergraduates 33%
Other 2%

CAMPUS

Cardiff is a campus in the city, an academic precinct, separate and yet part of the city. A short walk from the classical lines of the main university buildings brings you to the fastest growing capital in Europe (see *Cardiff City*, above). Yet, when you go there what you notice is its compactness and accessibility, its clean lines and the way they have maintained the airiness of a wide open space. The city is also still a cheap place to live and the crime rate is livable with and minimal on campus since the introduction of CCTV.

FEES, BURSARIES

UK & EU Fees 2007 for first year undergraduates: £3,000 p.a. Students from Wales and non UK EU countries will be eligible for a £1,800 grant. 2008: £3,070 p.a. and £1,845 grant for Welsh residents. There are more than 100 scholarships available to students of Chemistry, Computer Science, Earth Sciences, Engineering, Mathematics, Physics, Archaeology, German, Italian, Music and Welsh, beginning their studies in 2007. Most worth £3,000. Under Access to Learning, a Financial Contingency Fund makes up to £3,500 available per student based on a needs assessment.

STUDENT PROFILE

Writes Lisa Andrews: 'It's all rain, rugby and sheep, right? Wrong. Okay, so if you opt to study at Cardiff, chances are that 9 times out of 10 you'll get soaked on the way to lectures and spend the next hour dripping puddles in your pew. And on match

days, it's hard to avoid the Welsh rugby spirit, if only because your quiet local is heaving with red-shirted fans. But with 16,000 undergraduates of 100 nationalities, Cardiff is nothing if not culturally diverse.' The statistics support Lisa's case. There is also a highish independent school intake balanced by a 22% recruitment from the lower socio-economic groups. It's a well-balanced picture.

ACADEMIA & JOBS

Twenty-one subject areas have been assessed as Excellent, one of the best scores in the UK, and if you may sometimes feel, like Lisa, that 'the

UNIVERSITY/STUDENT PROFILE	
University since	**1883**
Situation/style	**Civic**
Student population	**21600**
Undergraduates	**16300**
- mature	**15%**
- non EU undergraduates	**22%**
- male/female	**44/56**
- non-traditional student intake	**22%**
- state sector intake	**84%**
- drop-out rate	**5%**
- undergraduate applications	**Up 0.4%**

research programmes in which many Cardiff lecturers are involved take a toll on their availability to students outside of lecture times,' you have to derive some confidence from it too.

The international calibre of research can be

gauged by the grades 5 and 5* listed in our *Academic Excellence* box.

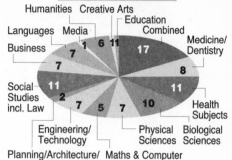

SUBJECT AREAS (%)

Humanities, Creative Arts, Education, Languages, Media, Combined, Business, Medicine/Dentistry, Social Studies incl. Law, Health Subjects, Engineering/Technology, Physical Sciences, Biological Sciences, Planning/Architecture/ Maths & Computer

Recently, Cardiff became home to the UK's first Centre for Astrobiology – it will link the study of biology with astronomy. And millions have been spent on their Chemistry Department, creating a new laboratory and a 500-seater lecture theatre and resource centre, while £12 million has been set aside for a new Life Sciences building.

But when one considers their graduate employment figures, health and finance, if taken together with accountancy and business, they are way to the fore. Health was boosted recently by the merger with The University of Wales College of Medicine. Less obvious is a whole host of international courses in accounting, economics and business administration (human resource managers do well, also – see their BScEcon Sociology & Industrial Relations for something that aims true), and the curriculum makes more than a few tax experts and consultants, too.

The College of Medicine campus has a 920-bed hospital, and the 5/6-year MB BCh degree combines academic study well with clinical and communication skills. There's even a pre-med Foundation for Arts A level candidates or those with one Science and Arts. Entry demands 360 points and UKCAT, the UK Clinical Apptitude Test. They want As in Biology and Chemistry. Teaching inspection, Excellent. Research grade 5. For dentistry, it's the 5/6-year BDS (Foundation year available).

Psychology is strong, too, with an Excellent in the assessments and a world-class Grade 5* for research. With Aston, Cardiff leads nationally for placing psychologists in employment.

Also in the Faculty of Health & Life Sciences, full marks at the assessments and a Grade 5 for research recommend Cardiff's biologists, and BSc Pharmacology, which leads large numbers into

AT A GLANCE

ACADEMIC FILE:

Subjects assessed	**40**
Excellent	**53%**
Typical entry requirements	**371 points**
Application acceptance rate	**14%**
Med. School acceptance rate	**10%**
Students-staff ratio	**13:1**
First/2:1 degree pass rate	**69%**

ACCOMMODATION FILE:

Guarantee to freshers	**100%**
Style	**Halls, flats, houses**
Catered	**5%**
En-suite	**65%**
Price range pw	**£51-£80**
City rent pw	**£54**

employment in pharmaceutical manufacturing and as chemists. There's a Foundation year leading to this and to MPharm (Pharmacy).

There's job certainty too in the Department of Occupational Therapy. Again Cardiff place more ophthalmic opticians than any uni other than Aston and Bradford. A new £16m development is underway to create a new state-of-the-art home for the School of Optometry and Vision Sciences. This will open in 2007. The space formerly occupied by the School of Optometry will provide improved facilities for the expanding School of Pharmacy.

Cardiff graduates find jobs in Defence via their 3/4/5-year B/MEng degrees – Computer Systems, Integrated Engineering, Manufacturing, etc, many with a year in Spain, Germany, France or industry. Physical sciences, which took an international Grade 5 rating in the research assessments, is also a well-trod path to the same end. In physical sciences they have a BSc in Theoretical & Computational Physics; Astrophysics; Chemistry with Bioscience; Maths; Operational Research & Statistics; Maths & its Applications – the Maths degrees are an unusually strong route into Defence at Cardiff. Of course, Politics too makes some good connections in that area.

Becoming an architect is a 6-year commitment, a 3-year BA Hons, a year's practice placement, followed by a 2-year BArch. Cardiff comes out top employment-wise. With its international research rating of Grade 5, and Excellent teaching assessment, as well as a clear lead in the employment table, the Welsh School of Architecture, which is housed as a department within the university, is first choice for many. A 5-year sandwich BSc in Architectural Studies, including a 2-year postgrad BArch, looks after Parts 1 & 2 of the Royal Institute of British Architects (RIBA) exams. There's also facility to take Part 3 for final RIBA recognition. There are 3/4/5-year courses in Architectural Engineering for budding engineering design consultants (many are placed out of Cardiff), some offering a year in France, Germany or Spain.

A BSc degree in City & Regional Planning leads many into government administration (local, regional, central)

Particularly fast-track employment comes for electronic and telecommunications engineers. The 4-year integrated sandwich Electronic BEng (or Electrical & Electronic) sits alongside a 5-year extended MEng sandwich course. There's also a Foundation option.

Cardiff is one of only three unis to be adjudged Excellent for Law by the Legal Practice Association (West of England and Nottingham Trent were the other two). They are also one of eight institutions where the Bar Vocational Course (BVC) may be undertaken (essential for barristers). Non-Law graduates may opt for a 2-year full-time or 3-year part-time Senior Status Law degree here. There's also a strong line into the Police. See their LLB Law & Criminology/ Sociology/Welsh, etc.

For jobs in publishing, Cardiff are again among the big players, and for journalism they have one of the handful of industry-respected postgrad degrees that many careers advisers will recommend you take before you begin the search for full-time employment. The others are to be found at City, Falmouth University College and Central Lancashire. As at City, you get visiting speakers from the media, but there's a 20,000-word dissertation to write.

Cardiff is surely one of the best deals going: tip-top academically, still not the hardest to get into and a fantastic extra-curricular scene.

Meanwhile, Cardiff's BA Journalism, Film & Broadcasting degrees (also with Social Policy or Sociology) are sufficient to get them into the Top 10 for employing journalists. Student media helps, the award-winning newspaper *Gair Rhydd* means Free Word and pulls 14,500 purchasers each week; radio station is Xpress.

Now, Cardiff's International Academy of Voice has just welcomed its first students. Master classes will be delivered by such as Dame Kiri Te Kanawa, Bryn Terfel, Sir Thoms Allen, conductor Zubin Mehta and Antonio Pappano, musical director of the Royal Opera, Covent Garden.

SOCIAL SCENE

STUDENTS' UNION The union is a top-class venue under continual enhancement. **The Taf** bar has recently been extended and changed from 'olde worlde' style to a stylish modern design. Evenings there inevitably lead to nights in **Solus**, the union's 1,800-capacity, custom-built nightclub with an immense dance floor and state-of-the-art sound and lighting systems. With an eclectic music policy crossing the spectrum from big beat to cheese, few would dispute that Solus offers some of Cardiff's best nights out.'

For the discerning, there's **Great Hall**, a major concert hall which has recently seen Kaiser Chiefs, Kook, and Manic Street Preachers. The adjoining all-day café-bar used to transform itself into Seren Las, an intimate club by night. It still has a stage area, but is now called **CF10** and acts much the same after hours - as a chill-out room during club and gig nights, as well as being a popular haunt for club and society ents.

Ents at Solus - on Mondays, 10 pm to 2 am, it's *Fun Factory*, Cardiff's alternative night, featuring bands, a heavy rock room and a generally sweaty, rocked out scene. Plus DJing by Oddsoc. Wednesday is *Rubber Duck*, with a different fancy dress theme each week. On Friday it's *Access all Areas @* **Solus**, a new look Friday that promises the best alternative music and beats to boogie to. Saturday is *Come Play*, party tunes in the main room. Traffic, the students own DJ and Clubbing Soc, plays house music in the other.

Otherwise, get down to favourite superclub **Tiger Tiger** in town (*Vodka Island* on Mondays is a 'must'), or **Jazz Cafe** (Monday's *Jazz Attic* has a 10-year pedigree). Also check out **Barfly** and **Toucan**, and Wednesday's *Popscene @* **Clwb Ifor Bach**, 3 floors of classic funk, motown, indie classics and cheese. See also the films and rootsy music at **Chapter Arts Centre**, comedy, music and other stuff at **St David's Hall** and **Sherman's Theatre**.

The Med School is now part of the uni, of course, but seems to be suffering, losing something of its identity in its new dependence. Their sometime nightclub is being turned into 'a learning/social environment' (sounds something of a yawn) and they will not even keep their own bar. When challenged as to the wisdom of drawing medics in among the student hoi polloi at Solus, a Union bod said, 'Well, a lot of lectures are down here anyway, and a lot of med school sports players play for our sports clubs.' Mmm, let's wait and see.

The union is not just popular for its bargain booze and carefree clubbing. Writes Lisa. 'Besides the regular 6-night ents programme, it is home to 60 sports clubs and 150 societies. High on the list are the Film Society, Act One, for drama, LGB, the lesbian/gay group, SHAG, sexual health awareness group, etc. There's the aforesaid student newspaper, *Gair Rhydd* and Xpress Radio on the fourth floor of the Union. And Act One, the drama soc is especially popular, putting on productions at the Sherman Theatre next door.

Gair Rhydd was runner-up as Best Newspaper and for Best Design, and won the Diversity Award in the 2006 national awards. The SU was runner-up for Best Website and Xpress Radio took Best Interview and was runner-up for Technical Innovation. So, there's no excuse to leave with just a degree on your CV.'

What's more, all of this is about to have an amazing facelift costing some £6 million. 'The building is more than 30 years old and needs a lot doing to it.' Phase 1 of a total refurbishment will see Great Hall turned into 'a more versatile space. Lectures, gigs, ents and society events. It'll be ready this summer. The next three phases will follow on.'

There's the usual Advice Centre and Job Shop, of course, and new this year a Student Union letting agency. No fees and better service for those wanting to live off campus. *Gair Rhydd* has always been littered with complaints of exploitation by

WHAT IT'S REALLY LIKE	
UNIVERSITY:	
Social Life	★★★★★
Campus scene	**Vibrant premier scene**
Student Union services	**Good**
Politics	**Activity high**
Sport	**60 clubs**
National team position	**18th**
Sport facilities	**Good**
Arts opportunities	**Excellent**
Student newspaper	**Gair Rhydd**
Student radio	**XPress Radio**
National Media Awards	**2 wins 2006**
Nightclub	**Solus**
Live venue	**Great Hall**
Bars	**Taf, CF10**
Union ents	**6 nights a week**
Union societies	**150**
Parking	**Adequate**
CITY:	
Entertainment	★★★★
Scene	**Buzzing**
Town/gown relations	**OK**
Risk of violence	**Low**
Cost of living	**Low**
Student concessions	**Excellent**
Survival + 2 nights out	**£80 pw**
Part-time work campus/town	**Excellent**

Cardiff landlords. Now the SU has decided to step in and ensure you get the best that is on offer.

Sport Sporty students at Cardiff, despite the boasts of the university prospectus, have, according to the Union, been badly served. Action works. The Athletic Union President wrote a paper about it and got a £350,000 all-weather pitch. Now they are going for a new swimming pool and other facilities.

All traditional sports are catered for and the uni is a major contender in the BUSA leagues - overall 18th in team sports last year. The Talybont Sports Centre has a £2 million multi-purpose sports hall and there are 33 acres of pitches. The Sophia Gardens Cricket Ground is being redeveloped to stage Test Cricket in 2009. Meanwhile, in Cardiff Bay, an International Sports Village will soon bring first class facilities for swimming, canoeing, white water rafting, skiing, snowboarding and climbing.

PILLOW TALK

The university's biggest hall, Talybont, is student paradise, en suite, own bar and comprehensive sports facilities. It opened in Sept 2005. It's also next to a 24-hour Tesco: perfect for those midnight munchies and obligatory trolley snatches!

The lazy should avoid University Hall. Although recently subject to a £4-million refurbishment, it's a good half-hour away and the free bus service isn't so free – Uni Hall rent is a few hundred pounds extra to subsidise it. All other halls are a walk away.

New to their portfolio is Allensbank, likewise en-suite. A computer network to the student residences has proved to be a huge success.

GETTING THERE

☛ By road: M4/J32, A470 signposted Cardiff or M4/J29, A48(M)/A48 and A470 signposted City Centre. Make for the Cathays area of the city.
☛ By rail: London Paddington, 2:30.
☛ By air: Cardiff airport for USA and inland.
☛ By coach: London, 3:00; Manchester, 5:40.

UNIVERSITY OF WALES INSTITUTE, CARDIFF

University of Wales Institute, Cardiff
PO Box 377 Western Avenue
Cardiff CF5 2SG

TEL 029 2041 6044
FAX 029 2041 6286
EMAIL uwicinfo@uwic.ac.uk
WEB www.uwic.ac.uk

UWIC Students' Union
Cyncoed Road
Cardiff CF23 6XD

TEL 029 2041 6190
FAX 029 2076 5569
EMAIL studentunion@uwic.ac.uk
WEB www.uwicsu.co.uk

VAG VIEW

*U*WIC *is where it's at for sport. They came in 6th place overall among BUSA teams last year. This is a small uni compared to Loughborough, Birmingham, Oxford and Edinburgh, who pipped it, but the college's commitment, demonstrated in its first-class facilities and National Indoor Athletics Centre, is as complete as the students' commitment to the culture that goes with it, 'When a Cyncoed student hits the bar, anything goes,' recalls Rob Blunt, musing on 'one of life's unanswered questions: why the essay that was researched, drafted, redrafted and put in a week early always got a lower mark than the one scribbled at 4 in the morning, assisted*

by six pints of Caffreys?'

Academically, UWIC's assessment results are hardly much to shout about, and 243 points or less will see you in, but they are a unique force in many ways and last year applications increased at a decent rate, where others in Wales fell.

CAMPUS LIFE

An achievement by the union is the purchase of two established venues in Cardiff city centre – **Reds** nightclub and **Stamps Bar** – a deal that makes Wednesday and Thursday student nights at **Chilli's**, as it is now known, on weekends showcases the best of Wales's up-and-coming DJs and plays funky house. Wednesdays is the official UWIC sports night, always sold out in advance.

Keeping the cost down for student living is the Stashcard, a debit card that can be used at all union outlets and at various retailers in the city.

CYNCOED CAMPUS Cyncoed Road, Cardiff CF2 6XD. **Faculties:** Education and Sport. **Ents & Ambience:** Teachers and wannabe sports stars, and the highest concentration of first years. **Taffy's**

INSTITUTE/STUDENT PROFILE	
University College since	**1996**
Situation/style	**Civic**
Student population	**9800**
Undergraduates	**7350**
- mature	**23%**
- non EU undergraduates	**2%**
- male/female	**47/53**
- non-traditional student intake	**27%**
- state school intake	**93%**
- drop-out rate	**17%**
- undergraduate applications	**Up 5%**

Bar (capacity raised to 500 since recent refurb) is is the main campus ents venue. It has a £15,000 sound and light system. Wednesday and Friday are the big nights. There are many other smaller weekly activities such as pool competitions, speed dating, Playstation network, and many live bands perform.

SPORT **Cyncoed** is where the multi-million pound athletics track and Sportlot-funded **National Indoor Athletic Stadium** are to be found alongside rugby, football and cricket pitches, indoor and outdoor tennis courts, gym, indoor cricket nets, swimming pool, volleyball, netball, basketball, badminton and squash courts, and a dance studio.

ACADEMIC EXCELLENCE
TEACHING:
Psychology, Art & Design **Excellent** (Ceramics/Fine Art/Internal Architecture), Biomedical Sciences, Environmental Health, Speech Therapy, Podiatry, Applied Human Nutrition.

As the **Wales Sports Centre for the Disabled** is also here, they've got some of the best resistance-training equipment available anywhere.

COLCHESTER AVENUE CAMPUS Colchester Avenue, Cardiff CF3 7XR. **Faculties:** Business, Leisure and Food. **Ents & Ambience:** Workaday, daytime scene – Sky TV, darts and PlayStation, but no evening ents or bar at Colly Ave, as it's known. So it's off up the hill at Cyncoed, where you're likely to be housed, too, or across the road to the **Three Brewers**.

HOWARD GARDENS Howard Gardens, Cardiff CF2 1SP. **Faculty:** Fine Art. **Ents & Ambience:** Couldn't be more different from, more alternative to, the sporting scene that dominates the personality of UWIC. **Tommy's Bar** is the focus. Eclectic ents on Tuesdays and Fridays.

LLANDAFF CAMPUS Western Avenue, Cardiff CF5 2YB. **Faculties:** Art, Design & Engineering and Community Health Sciences. **Ents & Ambience:** Complete makeover gives us **Union Llandaff** bar. Also – a first for UWIC – an Advice & Representation Centre (**ARC**) with an educational & welfare officer and full-time welfare adviser. Thursday and Saturday are disco nights here.

TOWN See *Cardiff Student City*, page 126.

FEES, BURSARIES

UK & EU Fees p.a. 2007 are: Year 1, £3,070; 2008: £3,070 p.a. Students from Wales and non UK EU countries are eligible for a £1800 fee grant from the

WHERE UWIC GRADUATES END UP
Health & Social Work: 10%; Education: 22%; Wholesale/Retail: 11%; Manufacturing: 8%; Financial Activities: 7%; Public Administration, Civil Service & Defence: 12%; Hotel/Restaurant: 6%; Transport & Communications (including Telecommunications): 5%; Construction: 1%; Personnel: 6%; Legal 1%; Architecture: 1%; Publishing: 1%; Artistic/Literary: 1%; Sport: 5%.
Approximate 'graduate track' employed **57%**

WHAT IT'S REALLY LIKE

COLLEGE:

Social Life	★★★
Campus scene	**Sports crazy**
Politics	**Student issues, interest low**
Sport	**Key**
National team position	**6th**
Sport facilities	**Excellent**
Arts	**Art, dance excellent; drama, music, film good**
Student newspaper	**Retro**
Nightclub	**Chilli's**
Bars	**The Union campus bars**
Union ents	**Cheesy, boozy**
Union clubs/societies	**7**
Most active society	**Christian Union**
Parking	**Just adequate**

CITY:

Entertainment	★★★★★
Scene	**Brilliant**
Town/gown relations	**OK**
Risk of violence	**Average**
Cost of living	**Low**
Student concessions	**Excellent**
Survival + 2 nights out	**£80 pw**
Part-time work campus/town	**Average/excellent**

Welsh Assembly. There are also means-tested bursaries in place and sports and academic scholarships.

ACADEMIA & JOBS

Academic studies are conducted through five schools: Art & Design, Education, Health Sciences, Management, and Sport

UWIC puts some 62% of its Education graduates into primary school teaching, Education accounting for more than a fifth of all graduate jobs. Nevertheless more graduates come off the production line into the job market from Business and Administrative studies than from Education, and Creative Design and Health degrees are also popular springboards into employment.

Business degrees aim at jobs in accountancy, the restaurant and hotel industry, tourism and retail (see appropriate degree courses among the single subject BA Hons), and there's a new BA Marketing. UWIC managers and administrators proliferate in these areas and in leisure and sport, which is a defining mark of the institute. More than 4% of graduates go into sport, nearly half as coaches and trainers. New degrees are available this year in Sport Management, and Sport Conditioning,

Rehabilitation & Massage.

There are, too, some significant career niches. Would-be bacteriologists and microbiologists are especially well served at UWIC. The Biomedical Sciences degrees find graduates jobs in the NHS, public health laboratory service, research institutes and the pharmaceutical, beverage and food industries, and you can come in on it via HND. There's also further study via an MSc in a specialist part of Toxicology of an MSc in Biomedical Sciences. New degrees in this area in 2007 are Public Health Nutrition, Consumer & Nutrition Psychology, Psychology & Human Biology, and Sports Biomedicine & Nutrition.

Another employment niche is for environmental health officers. Environmental Science, Nutrition and Health degrees are to the fore here, and there's a strong HND health course route to this sector with such as Environmental Studies, Food & Consumer Science, Food Science & Technology, etc. They have an 'Excellent' rating for teaching Biomedical Sciences, Environmental Health and Applied Human Nutrition.

Meanwhile, BA Social Work and BA Sociology & Popular Culture, Community Education/Studies ensure some 4% of graduates jobs in social work or community and youth work.

Top flight employment-wise among their health provision are degrees in Podiatry and Speech Therapist/Clinical Language Science and Communication Studies.

They also have BSc Dental Technology, which

AT A GLANCE

ACADEMIC FILE:

Subjects assessed	**18**
Excellent	**39%**
Typical entry requirements	**243 points**
Application acceptance rate	**23%**
Students-staff ratio	**21:1**
First/2:1 degree pass rate	**51%**

ACCOMMODATION FILE:

Guarantee to freshers	**55%**
Style	**Halls, flats**
Catered	**923 places**
En suite	**250**
Approx price range pw	**£67-£97**
City rent pw	**£54**

teaches you how to fabricate restorations, prostheses, appliances – bespoke crowns, bridges and orthodontic appliances. Employment in NHS and private practices is assured. Nearby Cardiff and Bristol dental schools offer employment to one third before they even graduate.

Finally, Product Design and Graphic Communication degrees in the Art & Design school join degrees in Ceramics, Fine Art and Textiles, and now: Illustration, Writing for Media & the Arts, and Media Studies & Visual Cultures.

PILLOW TALK

They have 527 single study-bedrooms on Cyncoed, of which 165 are self-catered and en suite, and 50 are self-catered with shared bathroom facilities. The remaining 312 rooms are catered (meals provided centrally). At Plas Gwyn there are 391 rooms – all self-catered, en suite. The Fairwater

Halls consist of 100 rooms – all catered for centrally. Recently, UWIC have acquired private sector Evelian Court – 250 self-catered, en-suite hall-style rooms, a few are doubles, a few are self-contained flats.

GETTING THERE
☞ By road: M4/J29, A48(M)/A48.
☞ By rail: London Paddington, 2:30.
☞ By air: USA and inland destinations.
☞ By coach: London, 3:00; Manchester, 5:40.

UNIVERSITY OF CENTRAL ENGLAND

UCE Birmingham
Franchise Street
Perry Barr
Birmingham B42 2SU

TEL 0121 3315595
FAX 0121 3317994
EMAIL info@ucechoices.com
WEB www.uce.ac.uk

UCE Students' Union
Franchise Street
Perry Barr
Birmingham B42 2SU

TEL 0121 331 6801
FAX 0121 331 6802
EMAIL union.president@uce.ac.uk
WEB www.unionofstudents.com

VAG VIEW

*U*CE Birmingham, as they like to be known, is a huge, urban conglomeration of sites, incorporating business, engineering & technology, built environment, law & social sciences, computing, health, the Birmingham Institute of Art & Design, an acting school, and two little gems – the Jewellery School, set in the old Jewellery Quarter, and Birmingham Conservatoire.

Incredibly, the uni and the Students Union appear to be bringing this apparently disparate thing together into what one student described as 'a really friendly university, whichever campus you study on and wherever you live.'

They are doing this by means of a big spend, but also with a keen eye as to their essential ethos, which celebrates the bonuses of our multicultural society. Suddenly, UCE is developing an exciting and vibrant social scene, and there's unprecedented energy in the Student Activities department. 'We are now actively building sports clubs, societies and volunteering

opportunities,' we are told. 'SCRatch Radio has taken off, and for the first time there's a lively ents programme at the union bars.'

THE CAMPUS SITES & FACULTIES
A CCTV system covers each site. 150 cameras are constantly monitored and the system is key to supporting the work of a 70-strong security team to ensure a safe environment in which to study.

PERRY BARR
Main UCE campus. **Location:** north of city; approach via M6/M5 Junction 7 and A34 Walsall Road. **Access to city:** 15 minutes by bus plus rail link to Birmingham New Street. **Accommodation:** two halls for 850 students – the Coppice and Oscott Gardens (en suite); both self-catering. **Bars: Bar 42**, pub/food in daytime, nightclub/venue in the evening. **Faculties:** UCE Business School; Education; Law, Humanities, Development & Society; and Health. The Department of Media and Communication, part of the Birmingham Institute of Art & Design (BIAD) is also here.

UCE Business School *www.business.uce.ac.uk Galton Building, Perry Barr Campus* The School provides single and joint programmes to over 4,000 students in such as Accountancy, Advertising,

Business, Business Law, Business Psychology Computing, Economics, Finance, ICT Internet Systems, Human Resources, Management, Marketing, Multimedia, Network Technology, Software Engineering and Public Relations.

Faculty of Education
w w w . e d . u c e . a c . u k *Attwood Building, Perry Barr Campus* The Faculty, both primary and secondary and based at Perry Barr, operates in the multi-ethnic context of the West Midlands. The students who join its initial teacher training courses are also from diverse backgrounds. Teaching inspection 22, special encouragement to mature students.

Faculty of Law, Humanities, Development & Society
www.lhds.uce.ac.uk Perry Barr Campus The Faculty,

> *From being scattered and diverse, suddenly UCE is developing an exciting and vibrant social scene. There's a strongly developing list of student activities, and for the first time a lively ents programme.*

psychology and sociology; there is something for almost everyone.

There is a real practical bent. Law students may spend a summer in America, working on death row cases. The School of Law also boasts a 'highly commended' Legal Practice Course, and all law students can make use of a mock courtroom. Meanwhile, criminal justice students experience real prison visits.

At the National Academy of Writing, published authors, Jim Crace, Melvin Bragg, Jilly Cooper, Ian Rankin, Philip Pullman have been involved.

In the School of Property, Construction and Planning, professional accreditation is available for all would-be surveyors, town planners and construction managers. And so on.

Faculty of Health
www.health.uce.ac.uk Westbourne and Perry Barr Campuses The Faculty of Health attracts over 7,000 full and part-time

UNIVERSITY/STUDENT PROFILE	
University since	**1992**
Situation/style	**Civic**
Student population	**24375**
Undergraduates	**20552**
- mature	**57%**
- non EU undergraduates	**3%**
- male/female	**40/60**
- non-traditional student intake	**40%**
- state school intake	**97%**
- drop-out rate	**18%**
- undergraduate applications	**Up 7%**

which might as well be called the School of Diversity, delivers academic and vocational programmes in construction, criminal justice, English, housing, law, planning, property,

STUDENT POPULATION

Total students 24,375

Postgraduates — 16%
Female Undergraduates — 50%
Male Undergraduates — 30%
Others — 4%

WHAT IT'S REALLY LIKE	
UNIVERSITY:	
Social Life	★★★
Campus scene	**Diverse but friendly & focused**
Student Union services	**Excellent**
Politics	**Practise bent**
Sport	**24 clubs**
National team position	**116th**
Sport facilities	**Extensive**
Arts opportunities	**Good**
Student magazine	**Spaghetti Junction**
Student radio	**SCRatch**
Student TV	**UCEtv**
Venue	**Bar 42**
Bars	**Bar 42, ibar, Village Inn, Lounge, Pavilion, Conservatoire**
Union ents	**Very popular**
Union societies	**30**
Parking	**OK**
CITY:	
Entertainment	★★★★★
Scene	**Excellent**
Town/gown relations	**Average**
Risk of violence	**Average**
Cost of living	**Average**
Student concessions	**Excellent**
Survival + 2 nights out	**£75 pw**
Part-time work campus/town	**Good/excellent**

WHERE CENTRAL ENGLAND GRADUATES END UP

Health & Social Work: 23%; Education: 13%; Wholesale/Retail: 11%; Manufacturing: 7%; Financial Activities: 7%; Public Administration, Civil Service & Defence: 6%; Hotel/Restaurant: 3%; Transport & Communications (including Telecommunications): 3%; Construction: 1%; Mining/Oil Extracting: 1%; Personnel: 5%; Computer: 2%; Business & Management: 5%; Accountancy: 2%; Media (including Film): 2%; Legal 3%; Architecture: 2%; Publishing: 2%; Advertising: 1%; Artistic/Literary: 2%; Sport: 0.5%.

Approximate 'graduate track' employed **62%**

students each year. They have partnerships with NHS Trusts and health and social care providers, and are the largest provider of qualified staff to the NHS and Social Services in the region. All undergraduate courses include practice placements.

In employment terms, UCE accounts for a large number of non-hospital nurses (adult, child, disabilities and mental health) and senior hospital nurses (SRN, RGN), also for 12% of graduate midwives with their 3-year BSc (Hons) Midwifery. Other certainties in this sector are BSc (Hons) Diagnostic Radiography and BSc (Hons) Radiotherapy. Then there's a particular niche – BSc (Hons) Speech & Language Therapy.

MILLENNIUM POINT

Location: on the east side of Birmingham city centre, well served by buses, public car parks and New Street, Snow Hill and Moor Street railway stations. **Faculties:** a £114-million building housing tourist attractions, commercial and retail businesses, and UCE's **Faculties:** Technology Innovation Centre (tic) and Birmingham School of Acting (BSA).

ACADEMIC EXCELLENCE

TEACHING:
(Rated Excellent or 17+ out of 24)

Music	**Excellent**
Art & Design, Education, Radiog/ Podiatry/Health Studies	**22**
Communication & Media Studies, Economics, Politics, Finance/Marketing	**21**
Town & Country Planning, History of Art, Nursing, Information Studies	**20**
Electrical & Electronic Eng, General Engineering, Automative & Manufacturing Engineering	**19**
Sociology, Building & Land & Property Mgt	**18**

Technology Innovation Centre *www.tic.ac.uk Millennium Point* The Technology Innovation Centre (tic) is a key faculty of the University, offering a wide range of interactive media, ICT, design technology and advanced engineering courses.

Birmingham School of Acting *www.bssd.ac.uk The Link Building, Paradise Place* In May 2005 Birmingham School of Acting merged with UCE. Formerly Birmingham School of Speech and Drama, it was founded in 1936. The main focus is acting. There's a BA (Hons) Acting and a one-year Graduate Diploma for postgraduate students. A Musical Theatre course is planned for September 2007. The School's courses are accredited by the National Council for Drama Training.

WESTBOURNE CAMPUS

Location: south city suburb of Edgbaston, on Westbourne Road, accessed via M5/J3, A456 or M5/J4, AA38. **Access to city:** regular, cheap and late-night bus service. **Faculty:** Health. There's been a major £25 million redevelopment of this campus including new classrooms, a suite of clinical skills facilities, lecture theatres, a Students Union complex - including a new shop, a coffee bar, a bar (**The Lounge**), and Student Activities centre. **Accommodation:** one hall – 245 single study-bedrooms and 34 shared (two bedrooms and joint study); self-catering.

GOSTA GREEN

Location: adjacent to Aston Uni campus, edge of city centre; accessed via M6/J6, A38M. Ignoring the signs to Aston Uni, leave the A38M at third exit and take the first exit at Lancaster Circus r/about. **Faculties:** UCE Birmingham Institute of Art & Design (BIAD), but not all the depts. thereof. Here you'll find Fashion, Textiles & 3-Dimensional Design and the Department of Visual Communication. You'll also cop the School of Theoretical and Historical Studies. But look elsewhere (see below) for the rest of BIAD. Big bonus - access to Aston University Student Union facilities (see entry, page 50).

AT A GLANCE

ACADEMIC FILE:

Subjects assessed	**23**
Excellent	**74%**
Typical entry requirements	**242 points**
Application acceptance rate	**18%**
Student-staff ratio	**17:1**
First/2:1 degree pass rate	**60%**

ACCOMMODATION FILE

Guarantee to freshers	**If non-local.**
Style	**Halls, flats, houses**
Catered	**10%**
En-suite	**50%**
Price range pw	**£62-£94.50**
Town rent pw	**£65**

UCE Birmingham Institute of Art & Design (BIAD)
www.biad.uce.ac.uk Gosta Green BIAD dates back to the Birmingham School of Design, founded in 1843. The Faculty is spread across five recently renovated and modernised sites. The main Gosta Green site, close to the city centre, is home to Fashion, Textiles and 3D Design, the School of Architecture, Dept of Visual Communication and School of Theoretical and Historical Studies. Students have access to adjacent Aston Uni union facilities.

BIAD's Dept of Media and Communication is based at Perry Barr, and the School of Jewellery has its own address in Victoria Street, Birmingham's historic Jewellery Quarter. The Department of Art has no less a magnificent home in a Grade I listed Venetian Gothic building in Margaret Street, in the city's museum and gallery district, while the historic Bournville Village Trust is home to the Bournville Centre for Visual Arts.

BOURNVILLE CENTRE FOR VISUAL ARTS
Location: 4 miles to the south of the city on the Bournville Village Trust, an urban village, built by the Cadbury family over a century ago. Two listed buildings, refurbished to the tune of £6 million.

THE ART DEPARTMENT
Grade I listed Venetian Gothic property on Margaret Street, centrally sited.

THE JEWELLERY SCHOOL
Recent refurbishment makes this the smartest, coolest site within UCE; also state-of-the-art workshops and technology. **Location:** Vittoria Street in the city centre – the famous old Jewellery Quarter, a walk from Birmingham New Street.

THE BIRMINGHAM CONSERVATOIRE
Location: This is the purpose-built Conservatoire with small practice rooms and large performance areas. **Location:** Close to the Birimngham Rep Theatre and ICC & Symphony Hall, it is sited on a traffic island (Paradise Circus) a few minutes walk from Birmingham New Street station. It offers more of a challenge by car. From M6 South or North-West leave at J6 and follow the A38(M) and signs to 'City centre, Bromsgrove, (A38)', over a flyover and through Queensway tunnel (signposted 'Bromsgrove and Queen Elizabeth Hospital'). Leave tunnel left but stay in right-hand lane of exit road. No parking for you on Paradise Island. Unload and move on or seek car park close by: after exit for A456 (Broad Street), take left into Cambridge Street.

UCE Birmingham Conservatoire *www. conservatoire.uce.ac.uk Paradise Circus, Birmingham city centre* A little gem, a lively, creative environment, one of our best music colleges, it has been going in one form or another since 1859. Based in the heart of the city centre only a few minutes' walk from Symphony Hall, the Conservatoire has some of the finest performing and teaching facilities of its kind in the country, including the recently refurbished 520-seat Adrian Boult Hall, 150-seat Recital Hall customised for performance with live electronics, four recording studios and a specialised music library, recently rebuilt from the ground up, with around 95,000 individual scores and parts and 10,000 sound recordings. There's both a BMus (Hons) and a specialised BMus (Hons) Jazz. The Conservatoire also works in collaboration with the Technology Innovation Centre (tic) to provide a BSc (Hons) course in Music Technology; with South Birmingham College to provide an HND in Popular Music; and with BIAD to provide a new MA in Digital Arts in Performance.

FEES, BURSARIES
UK & EU Fees for 2007: £3,070 for first degrees. Students in lower income brackets will be eligible for grants for living costs, also bursaries are available to anyone receiving a full or partial maintenance grant.

STUDENT PROFILE
As diverse as its campus sites, but with the emphasis clearly on work-purpose and real-world living. Many are mature, many local and many from overseas, and UCE far exceed their Government benchmarks for recruiting from under-represented groups in higher education. It's an eclectic mix, but it's all beginning to come together.

STUDENT SCENE

Ents-wise, Tuesday is *Mutiny*, an Indie Night, at **Bar 42** on Perry Barr Campus, Wednesday is Sports Night at the **Oceana** nightclub in town, and Friday is Toons at Bar 42 (a cheap drinks disco night). There might be sports & society events on Saturday, and quizzes on Sunday.

ibar is the brand new student bar, located at the prestigious **Millennium Point**. Then there's the **Lounge**, brand new this year at Westbourne Campus and a small bar based at The Conservatoire, the **Village Inn** (friendly, local halls of residence bar at Hamstead halls, see *Pillow Talk*), and **The Pavilion** out at Moor Lane Sports Centre. Parties and events are held every term in the **Village Inn** and **ibar**.

Thirty student societies are now up and running. Student magazine is *Spaghetti Junction*. SCRatch Radio is the student and community radio station, and there's UCEtv too. Student Community Action (SCA), the Union volunteering project, passes on key skills that employers are always asking for, as well as making a real difference to the local community. A so-called LEAP campaign currently promotes sport for local children. Drama, Cheerleading, RAG (Raising and Giving) and ACS (Afro Caribbean Society) are highly active socs. Politically the Union has shown its teeth in campaigns like 'Sentenced to debt', against Top-Up

fees, and in a Housing Accreditation Scheme to improve housing standards in the city.

SPORT The Union runs the massive Moor Lane Sports Centre, with extensive conference and banqueting and partying facilities attached, playing host, too, to the annual Frisbee tournaments.

PILLOW TALK

HAMSTEAD CAMPUS is a 16-acre residential campus 2 miles from the Perry Barr Campus, with good bus services between the two and to city centre. Both self-catering and catered rooms are available, and there's a bar called **The Village Inn**. They guarantee a place in halls for full-time students who hold an unconditional firm or conditional firm offer by 31 May, and live a distance from UCE 'that precludes commuting'. Every room is equipped with a phone line, and all halls have an Ethernet connection to the UCE Birmingham data network.

GETTING THERE

☛ By road: M1, M5, M6 and M40 all give ready access to the city. See also campus notes.
☛ By rail: Bristol Parkway or Sheffield, 1:30; London Euston, 1:40; Liverpool, 2:00; Leeds, 3:00.
☛ By air: Birmingham International Airport.
☛ By coach: London, 2:40; Bristol, 2:00.

UNIVERSITY OF CENTRAL LANCASHIRE

University of Central Lancashire
Preston
Lancs PR1 2HE

TEL 01772 892400
FAX 01772 894539
EMAIL cenquiries@uclan.ac.uk
WEB www.uclan.ac.uk

Central Lancashire Students' Union
Fylde Road
Preston PR1 2TQ

TEL 01772 893000
FAX 01772 894970
EMAIL supresident@uclan.ac.uk
WEB www.yourunion.co.uk

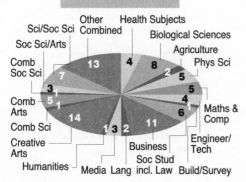

SUBJECT AREAS (%)

Other Combined 13 · Health Subjects 4 · Biological Sciences 8 · Agriculture 2 · Phys Sci 5 · Sci/Soc Sci 7 · Soc Sci/Arts · Comb Soc Sci 3 · Comb Arts 5 · Comb Sci 14 · Creative Arts · Humanities · Media Lang · Soc Stud 11 · Business · Bus/Survey · Engineer/Tech 6 · Maths & Comp 4 · incl. Law 2

VAG VIEW

*U*CLan traces its origins back to 1828, when Preston Institution for the Diffusion of Knowledge was founded. Growth in student numbers makes them one of the largest universities in the country.

Investment remains high: £50 million is being invested in new buildings and facilities, including an award-winning, £6.5 million Student Union building.

UCLan is also known as a caring university. 'The i' is a one-stop-shop (info centre), a first point of contact for such as

14% — Postgraduates

Female Undergraduates — 43%

Male Undergraduates — 43%

STUDENT POPULATION
Total students
30,366

financial support, council tax enquires, international student guidance, to NUS card distribution, accommodation and disabled student advice. A fourth-year health student, confined in a wheelchair since infancy, went out of her way to praise its accessibility to the disabled, the helpfulness of staff, and for the chance they gave her of the 'few wild years' she had enjoyed there. Wild indeed, for its approach to entertainment is legendary.

UNIVERSITY/STUDENT PROFILE	
University since	**1992**
Situation/style	**Civic**
Student population	**30366**
Undergraduates	**17011**
- mature	**35%**
- non EU undergraduates	**9%**
- male/female	**50/50**
- non-traditional student intake	**36%**
- state sector intake	**97%**
drop-out rate	**20%**
- undergraduate applications	**Down 0.5%**

Ultimately, however, the uni is a modern university dedicated to getting graduates jobs, and recruiting from social groups new to the idea of going to university. One result of its open access policy has been a wild drop-out rate, which remains untamed.

CAMPUSES

Besides Preston, they used to have **Penrith Campus** at the head of the Eden Valley, where the Faculty of Land-based Studies was based. Also **Carlisle Campus** for some of the business, computing, travel and tourism degrees. But these are now being subsumed into the new Cumbria University.

FEES, BURSARIES

UK & EU Fees £3,070 p.a., thereafter rising with inflation. £1,000 bursaries available for all full-time undergraduate students who come from homes where the principal earner's salary is less that £60,000 per year. 100 Excellence scholarships, valued in the region of £2,000, will be offered in some specialist subject areas, and in sport. Awards are also made to disabled students, to ethnic students in certain subject areas.

STUDENT PROFILE

UCLan is recruiting a large number of undergraduates from the state sector and students from social groups who haven't traditionally benefited from a university education. More than a third of undergrads are mature at entry, 97% are recruited from the state sector, 36% from SEC classes 4-7 and 21% from 'low-participation neighbourhoods'., figures higher even than the Government's quotas for UCLan.

ACADEMIA & JOBS

Faculties are now: Lancashire Business School; Health; Science & Technology; and Arts, Humanities & Social Sciences. UCLan's Cumbria campuses are now part of Cumbria University.

In 2006 UCLan announced a £10-million investment in areas of research, including an Institute for Advanced Digital Manufacturing technology, a Centre for Creative Digital Industries, a new programme within the Business School to develop international human resource management, corporate social responsibility and other ways forward for the business community.

Maximum QAA scores of 24 out of 24 in areas of American Studies, Psychology, Nursing and Midwifery and Education are impressive. Besides the 4-year BSc Midwifery, there's an 18-month pre-registration course. Look also at their Herbal Medicine and Homeopathy degrees.

They offer a hot executive route into the Civil Service via biological sciences and health (everything from Forensic Science an HND in Public Health and now a BA Public Health). Meanwhile, Civil Service administration takes from Business (good mixes with Psychology, Economics, Info Systems, Management) and creative arts (Design, etc) and the BSc/BA Combined hons programme, which is itself designed with flair.

There is an interesting employment niche in journalism, many of the excellent Journalism courses making a healthy mix with communications and design, and all backed to the hilt by an award-winning student media.

They feature in the Top 10 in various areas. Besides the BA Journalism (also offered with Eng

Lit), there's Photography & Journalism; Fashion, Brand Promotion & Journalism; Audio Visual Media Studies & Journalism; Web & Multimedia with Journalism (the only BSc in the bunch); Film & Media degrees, and a TV production degree. Teaching inspection, 22.

Note, too, their industry-recommended postgraduate degrees – PGDip Newspaper Journalism, MA/PGDip Online Journalism, MA Strategic Communication and PGDip Broadcast Journalism. You will have to be able to show experience of, and commitment to, Journalism, and provide an audio tape for the PGDip.

Another sound area for graduate jobs is the art and design provision. Graduates become graphic artists, designers, illustrators, sculptors. You'll be interviewed with your portfolio to get on the BA Fine Arts, a broad-based introduction, followed by specialist studio work. There's an on-campus **Arts Centre** and a **Centre for Contemporary Art**, as well as a separate **Gallery**. The course has strong links with the **Harris Museum & Art Gallery** in Preston. Teaching inspection, 22.

The 4-year sandwich Fashion Promotion and Design asks 180-200 points (teaching inspection, 21) making it second most demanding at A level nationally, but they do get graduates jobs, and are especially strong on business/creative arts routes into retail management and buying: Retail Management with Fashion/Logistics/Marketing, dovetails with the Art & Design Faculty on Promotion and Marketing – across Fashion, Furniture, Jewellery, etc.

PR and publicity in general are strong graduate destinations. See BA Communication Studies, also BA Marketing & Public Relations, besides the BA Fashion Promotion. Teaching inspection, 22.

A not so dusty niche may be explored in their Antique & Design Studies. It is the only degree to bring a design perspective to theory and practice, ideal for the would-be antique dealer/restorer. You'll need around 180 points to get on it.

UCLan is home to the Cyberspace Research Unit, too, which has a national reputation for its research on children's use of the internet and the

ACADEMIC EXCELLENCE	
TEACHING:	
(Rated Excellent or 17+ out of 24)	
American Studies, Psychology,	**24**
Education, Nursing	
Linguistics, Journalism & PR,	**22**
Subjects Allied to Medicine,	
Art/Design Biological Sciences,	
Business/Accounting, Politics,	
Leisure/Tourism	
Modern Languages	**21**
Building, General Engineering	**20**
History of Art/Architec/Design,	**19**
Physics, Astronomy & Maths	
Sociology, Agric & Forestry	**18**

dangers therein. It acts as a policy advisor, trainer, teacher, and media spokesperson. Findings often contribute to policy-making at Government level.

Recently an assessor for the LPC Board looked at their Law provision and, on a scale of Excellent, Very Good, Good, Satisfactory or Unsatisfactory, UCLan copped a Very Good. There's a strong employment track record for BA Criminology & Criminal Justice and Law & Criminology. Look, too, at the new BSc Police & Criminal Investigation, which breaks new ground by teaching practical as well as academic investigation skills. It is delivered from within the Centre for Forensic Science. On the Newton Rigg campus in Cumbria they have set up Cow Pasture Cottage, a reality crime scene where a catalogue of crimes are recreated to test students of one of Britain's leading forensic science centres.

Note also their Fire Safety and Fire Engineering degrees.

Their sporting provision finds top places in the employment league tables for physical training instructors. There are Sport Science/Psychology/Technology degrees, BA Golf Course Management and now BSc Sports Technology (Golf Operations) for those interested in refining player performance by means of coaching, materials, equipment, ergonomics. Take-up is partly at Myerscough

---

WHERE CENTRAL LANCASHIRE GRADUATES END UP

Health & Social Work: 17%; Education: 6%; Wholesale/Retail: 16%; Manufacturing: 9%; Financial Activities: 9%; Public Administration, Civil Service & Defence: 8%; Hotel/Restaurant: 5%; Transport & Communications (including Telecommunications): 4%; Construction: 1%; Agriculture: 1%; Personnel: 4%; Computer: 2%; Business & Management: 5%; Accountancy: 1%; Media (including Film): 2%; Legal 2%; Architecture: 1%; Publishing: 2%; Artistic/Literary: 2%; Sport: 2%.

Approximate 'graduate track' employed **60%**

College in Preston, where there's a golf course and indeed a Grand Prix track, of interest to putative racing car designers or team managers - see their Motor Sports Eng, BSc Motor Sport and BSc Motor Sport Operations. As at Coventry, they have their own uni racing team. The degrees cover Engineering and Team & Event Management. There's also a separate Event Management degree.

Thanks partly to the international dimension of so many courses, the uni leads the job field in providing lecturers to Further Education. Exchange programmes with Europe and America (American Studies scored full marks at the assessments) are legion and the International Society is very popular among students.

SOCIAL SCENE

STUDENTS' UNION Step into the new, award-winning, £6.5 million Student Union building, and take advantage of all that a new £15.3 media building promises. The latter is still under construction, but in these two areas - hedonism and media - UCLan have for years reigned supreme.

Source is the new Student Union bar in the centre of campus, open Monday to Thursday 10 until 12 midnight; Friday till 2am; Saturday noon till 3am; Sunday noon till midnight. New in a 5-night table of activities is Friday's *Lampshade*. Saturday's still *Flirt*.

FiftyThreeDegrees is the new venue and club, Brook Street, Preston 01772 893000. Was winner of BEDA 'Best Venue" 2005. Combined capacity: 1600; Venue standing: 1200; Club standing: 400. Also, the **Main Room Mezzanine** can be separated as a 600-capacity club. Til 2 a.m. Thurs-Sat and Mon-Tues. All events open to the public. From dance events, to cheesy pop, to world music to hardcore, club nights include the nationally recognised GoodGreef (Manchester Club of the Year, 2004; Best Club in the North - *Mixmag*, 2005) dance events as well as famous DJs such as Radio 1's Tim Westwood.

Live gigs currently Good Shoes, And On The Third Day..., Cradle of Filth, The Levellers, Leeds-based indie group The Sunshine Underground, The Jam - Bruce Foxton & Rick Buckler, Napalm Death. Also Comedy with candle-lit cabaret style seating. The fortnightly sell-out comedy night is *Stand and Deliver*, Lancashire's largest comedy event, opened in 2005 by Peter Kay.

Talking about performance, it is often forgotten that they have a serious crack at the arts too. For the last decade they've taken productions to the Edinburgh Fringe, and this year they've got a performing-arts degree module on offer.

Theatre, music, dance and art all go on in **St Peter's Church** and the **Grenfell Baines Gallery**, the uni's arts centre in town. There's Film and Film

WHAT IT'S REALLY LIKE	
UNIVERSITY:	
Social Life	★★★★
Campus scene	**Local, diffuse, mature but lively**
Student Union services	**Average**
Politics	**Interest low**
Sport	**Competitive**
National team position	**79th**
Sport facilities	**Good**
Arts	**Drama, dance, film, music excellent; art good**
Student newspaper	**Pluto**
Student radio station	**Frequency 1350**
Nightclub	**Award-winning 53Degrees**
Bars	**Source**
Union ents	**Massive club and live events**
Union societies	**33**
Parking	**Adequate**
CITY:	
Entertainment	★★★
Scene	**Good clubs, excellent pubs**
Town/gown relations	**Good**
Risk of violence	**Low**
Cost of living	**Average**
Student concessions	**Good**
Survival + 2 nights out	**£50 pw**
Part-time work campus/town	**Good/average**

production, Creative Arts and Creative Writing societies, Pagan, Wiccan & Earth Rel., People and Planet, and naturally Poker, some 33 societies in all.

Student newspaper *Pluto* regularly picks up student journalism awards (in 2006 they were shortlisted for Travel Journalism), while the student website has won the *Guardian* award. Frequency 1350 is the radio station and they are part of a consotium of universities involved with the BBC, now that they have definitely decided to move to Manchester. *The Bridge* is the SU employment service.

SPORT A £12-million outdoor multisport complex two miles from campus is now open. **The Preston Sports Arena** has 8-lane athletics track, 5 grass pitches, 2 floodlit all-weather, 4 floodlit netball and tennis courts, 1.5 km cycling circuit, 7 floodlit training grids, plus 18-station fitness suite. There's also the on-campus, recently refurbished **Foster Sports Centre** for badminton, tennis, basketball, volleyball, soccer, fencing, martial arts, etc.

AT A GLANCE

ACADEMIC FILE:

Subjects assessed	**31**
Excellent	**65%**
Typical entry requirements	**252 points**
Application acceptance rate	**24%**
Students-staff ratio	**23:1**
First/2:1 degree pass rate	**51%**

ACCOMMODATION FILE:

Guarantee to freshers	**All placed**
Style	**Halls, flats, houses**
Catered	**None**
En-suite	**30%**
Price range pw	**£44-£75.25**
City rent pw	**£45-£75**

Nationally, they are about mid-table in the uni leagues. Good facilities are available at Newton Rigg for rugby, football, hockey, netball, basketball, tennis, badminton, and there's a purpose-built weights room. Cumbrian clubs include Climbing Club, Conservation Volunteers and Clay Pigeon. This year the indoor facilities have been upgraded.

TOWN And Preston? 'With something like 40–50 pubs within 5 mins walk of the university,' writes Neil Doughty, 'there's always somewhere to hide away out of the rain. Some might contest that with so many pubs you'd need to be careful to avoid the "locals only" places where the only use for sawdust is mopping up the blood after a fight. Not so! With 20,000 students making up a sixth of the in-term residents of Preston, the locals are well aware of the benefit of students to the local economy, and are very accommodating – loads of student discounts, tons of shops, a range of restaurants and two large-screen cinemas mean that there's always something to do when the workload lessens. Staff in venues all over town are always friendly. Even the nightclubs are relaxed both in terms of atmosphere and prices. With no dress code in the week, and drinks prices fair, the town is ideally suited to students.'

PILLOW TALK

They guarantee to assist all freshers to find ccommodation either in uni-owned halls and houses or privately owned ones. None of the uni residences are catered, there's a top-up smartcard that students can use to pay for their meals at refectories around campus.

Leighton Hall, a private hall with 350 en-suite rooms and studios, opened in 2006. Get on to it quick.

GETTING THERE

☛ By road: travelling south, M6 (J32/M55), exit 1 (A6); travelling north, M6/J31, A59.
☛ By rail: London, 3:00; Manchester Oxford Road, 50 mins; Lancaster, 23 mins.
☛ By coach: London, 5:15; Liverpool, 1:00.

UNIVERSITY OF CHESTER

The University of Chester
Parkgate Road
Chester CH1 4BJ

TEL 01244 511000
FAX 01244 398470
STUDENT UNION TEL 01244 511574
EMAIL enquiries@chester.ac.uk
WEB www.chester.ac.uk

VAG VIEW

Established by William Gladstone in 1839 as the first teacher-training college in the country with a Church of England foundation, it has just been granted full university status.

Chester is a Roman town with a picturesque centre, a thriving tourism industry and a lowish cost of living.

The university's curriculum has expanded beyond teaching education in recent years into health care, the applied sciences, humanities, social sciences, creative arts &

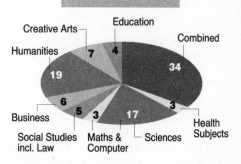

SUBJECT AREAS (%)

Creative Arts
Education
Combined
Humanities
7
4
34
19
6
5
3
17
3
Business
Social Studies incl. Law
Maths & Computer
Sciences
Health Subjects

media, and business and management.

It's a typical story for a new university: massive increases in applications (up 49% last year, 16% this), an increase in entry requirements, and a decrease in application acceptance rate. They can afford to be a bit more choosy. For the time being the number of first class and 2:1 degrees dished out remains low, but the good sign is that the student:staff ratio is coming down, the drop-out rate is steady, and investment is high.

CAMPUS

The uni's Chester campus is a 32-acre site, 5 mins walk from the city centre, and has undergone a variety of developments over the last 18 months. New facilities include a high-tech fitness suite, a modern School of Health and Social Care building, a large state-of-the art multi-purpose building featuring a brasserie, computer suite, conference facilities and high specification teaching areas. Next to campus is a newly built block of self-catered apartments, offering en-suite rooms.

The Warrington campus is set on a 35-acre site a short bus ride away and has benefited from general improvements and refurbishments, including a modern dining area, new facilities within the Department of Media and a brand new Students' Union building, completed January 2006.

By autumn 2007, it will also have a new Lifelong Learning Centre, incorporating new learning resources (libraries etc), learning support services and CITS (computer management/support etc), together with a cafe, lounge area and seminar rooms. A site has also been cleared for a new £2.9 million Business Management and IT Centre.

FEES, BURSARIES

UK & EU Fees: £3,070 p.a. in 2007, likely to rise in 2008 in line with inflation. Two-thirds receive a University of Chester bursary for students in receipt of full HE Maintenance grant. There's also the Chester Sports Scholarship Scheme: £500 p.a., sport being a defining element of student life at Chester. Chester also offers an organ scholarship, currently worth £750, two music scholarships/'Director's Assistant' posts based around the choir, worth £250 each, and two similar positions based around the orchestra, currently worth £150 each. Alto, tenor and bass choral scholarships are available for positions in the Chester Cathedral Choir, worth £1,750 p.a. and tenable for one year in the first instance. Further details from the Cathedral Organist, 12 Abbey Square, Chester CH1 2HU.

STUDENT PROFILE

There is a high number of undergraduates (35%) from backgrounds not traditionally associated with going to university, and many are over 21 at inception. Very few, only 3%, hie from the independent school sector.

It is also a largely (67%) female undergraduate population, once described by the uni as an 'overwhelming majority', but if you're a bloke you

may find you'll be able to cope.

The lean is down to the numbers studying nursing, midwifery and education courses. Finally, very few of Chester's undergraduates come from outside the EU. It is a notably local scene.

When it was a mere college of higher education, this was just as true, and noticeably it was a tight, compact unit, with an overwhelming, friendly and relaxed atmosphere. This is unlikely to change.

ACADEMIA

The uni has been re-organised into 7 schools of study: Applied & Health Sciences; Business, Management & Law, Arts & Media, Education, Health & Social Care, and Social Sciences.

Departments are Biological Sciences, Business, Computer Science, Education, English, Fine Art, Geography and Development Studies, Health & Social Care, History and Archaeology, Law, Leadership & Management, Maths, Media, Modern Languages, Performing Arts, Psychology, Social &

ACADEMIC EXCELLENCE

TEACHING:
(Rated Excellent or 17+ out of 24)

English	**Excellent**
Maths, Sport	23
Theology/Religious Studies,	22
Health & Community	
Business & Tourism, Nursing	21
Health Science/Studies,	20
Psychology	
Modern Languages (French,	19
German, Spanish)	

Communication Studies, Sport and Exercise Sciences, Theology & Religious Studies, Work Related Studies.

Law is new, offered as an LLB and as combined honours. The department has close links with the Chester Centre of the College of Law where LPC and Graduate Diplomas can be studied for - the College of Law is the largest legal training and education establishment in Europe.

Other new or recently added undergraduate courses include Creative Writing, Graphic Design, Photography, Advertising, Marketing, Film Studies, Popular Music and single honours Archaeology.

There are good teaching assessment results, particularly in the most prominent of all its departments, Physical Education/Sports Science, which daily colours the Chester campus lary green with sportswear, and scored 23 points out of 24 at inspection, pipping Theology, the subject truest to its foundation, which managed 22. Also popular are Drama, English and Psychology, which scored 20. Amongst students of science, maths (also 22) and computer, there's a particular attraction in a partnership with some 400 employers involved in course design, work placement, etc – all part of a career-based learning recipe evident in their cross-faculty BA/BSc degree programme and a solid graduate employment rate.

They were rated 'Good' by Ofsted for primary teacher-training and, for secondary – 'Good' in maths and MFL, 'Good to Very Good' in PE and 'Very Good' in Drama, Art and RE.

There are media facilities at Warrington, where an impressive reputation has been built with production courses and links to a range of media organisations including the BBC and Granada Television.

Business, Computer Science, Media, and Sport & Exercise Sciences are all at least part-based at Warrington.

The School of Health and Social Care is the major provider of pre-registration nursing and midwifery education across Cheshire and the Wirral. It also offers a wide range of undergraduate and postgraduate programmes for nurses, midwives and other health care professionals.

They offer nursing courses in Adult/Child Health, Learning Disability, Mental Health, and Midwifery. For DipHE students there are three intakes a year – February, June and September. For degree students, there is an annual intake in September. There is an annual midwifery intake in September (DipHE and BSc). Social work programmes at undergraduate level are offered at the Warrington campus.

New degrees planned for Warrington are Health & Fitness, Muslim Youth Work, and Public Relations. At Chester they are looking at Events Management, Natural Hazard Management and Occupational Psychology.

SOCIAL SCENE

STUDENTS UNION There are two headquarters, one on each of the campuses. The new bar on Warrington Campus (Wazza) is **Fu Bar** (was **Scholars**). It hosts live bands and *T.P.I. Wednesday* (beach party time, grass skirts at the ready, with DJ Paul Webber, 8pm-1am); also games and quiz nights,

WHAT IT'S REALLY LIKE

UNIVERSITY:	
Social Life	★★★
Campus scene	**Active**
Student Union services	**Average**
Politics	**Little interest**
Sport	**Key**
National team position	**80th (Chester)**
	130th (Warrington)
Sport facilities	**Good**
Arts opportunities	**Music, drama excellent**
Student newspaper	**Collegian**
Student Radio	**The Source**
Nightclub	**Max250, Fu-Bar**
Bars	**As above**
Union ents	**Cheesy**
Union clubs/societies	**Mainly sport**
Parking	**Adequate**
CITY:	
Entertainment	★★★
Scene	**Pubs cheesy, clubs OK**
Town/gown relations	**Complaining**
Risk of violence	**No**
Cost of living	**Average to low**
Student concessions	**Good**
Survival + 2 nights out	**£90 pw**
Part-time work campus/town	**Good/excellent**

AT A GLANCE	
ACADEMIC FILE:	
Typical entry requirements	**252 points**
Application acceptance rate	**16%**
Students-staff ratio	**20:1**
First/2:1 degree pass rate	**45%**
Graduate track employment	**49%**
ACCOMMODATION FILE:	
Availability to freshers	**85%**
Style	**Halls, flats, houses**
Catered	**45%**
En suite	**27%**
Approx price range pw	**£72-£107**
Town rent pw	**£40-£55**

and there's a re-launch of classic alternative night, *Deckheadz*. There's also *Padgates* club night on Saturday.

At the Chester campus there is a fractious history attached to the fun and games. Some years ago the so-called **Small Hall** venue had to be closed down. It was so popular that massive queues would form outside, and it fell victim to noise-pollution protestors. These problems still characterise student life on campus, judging by the SU's *Shhh* campaign to highlight problems caused to neighbours.

Still, **Max250**, the Chester student bar, will not be downed. *Freeky Fridays* is the big night out. You get to choose what you want to hear on the SU web site – from Chart to r&b to rap to dance. Fancy dress events occur every few weeks. A new £2m purpose-built Student Union building is under construction and will open in August 2007.

Society activity is as busy as you want to make it, though don't expect radical politics. Arts are well provided for, especially music and drama, with both the Drama Dept and Society putting on frequent productions. Consistent with its C of E foundation, there's an active Christian Union.

SPORT Sport is of obsessive extra-curricular interest on the Chester campus, and there are constantly evolving facilities to support it, including a refurbished all-weather hockey pitch, a 25m pool, a fitness suite and sports hall – all part of a £5-million development. Chester is one of 90 educational establishments across the country delivering sporting services to a variety of Talented Athlete Scholarship Scheme (TASS) athletes.

TOWN Moving away from the campus into Chester itself, you'll find one of the most picturesque, historic city centres in the country. A big plus is that in comparison to most, Chester is relatively cheap. Popular student haunts are the **Odeon** cinema, the **Gateway Theatre**, and over 60 pubs, most in walking distance. There are various students nights at bars and clubs in town.

PILLOW TALK
There is a variety of accommodation available to freshers: halls, flats, houses, on-campus, off-campus, etc, but look in particular at a modern, high-specification, block of self-catered flats for freshers, completed in summer 2006. It's situated directly opposite the Chester campus.

GETTING THERE
☛ By road: the uni is situated at the junction of the A540 and Cheyney Road.
☛ By rail: London Euston, 2:45; Sheffield, 2:25; Birmingham New Street, 1:45; Liverpool Lime Street, 40 mins; Manchester Oxford Road, 1:00.
☛ By coach: London, 6:00; Sheffield, 3:00.

UNIVERSITY OF CHICHESTER

The University of Chichester
Bishop Otter Campus
College Lane
Chichester PO19 4PE

TEL 01243 816002
FAX 01243 816078
EMAIL admissions@chi.ac.uk
WEB www.chi.ac.uk

Chichester University Students' Union
Bishop Otter Campus
College Lane
Chichester PO19 6PE

TEL 01243 816390
FAX 01243 816391
EMAIL student_union@chi.ac.uk
WEB www.chisu.org

VAG VIEW

*S*ituated between the South Downs and the sea at Chichester and at nearby Bognor *Regis, Chichester University was once known as the West Sussex Institute of Higher Education, then as Chichester College of Higher Education, until 1999 when it* *became University College Chichester and gained the power to award its own degrees. Forty-nine per cent of its graduates go into Education, and Sports Science is the popular specialism, but more recently they have built a reputation in the schools of Visual and Performing Arts and Cultural Studies.*

CAMPUSES

The Bishop Otter Campus, in name at least, takes us back to 1839 when Bishop Otter College was founded by the Church of England as a teacher training establishment; there is, today, a striking modern chapel in the grounds of campus, which itself lies within this walled cathedral city, widely known for its annual Festival of Music and Arts.

The less imaginatively named Bognor Regis Campus lies five miles hence. Bognor is, as it sounds, a rather passé seaside resort.

Bishop Otter is the bigger of the two, though Bognor has most of the teacher training. The campuses are far enough apart to cause something of a psychological split, and the Students' Union have been preoccupied with getting the bus service between the two improved.

FEES, BURSARIES

UK & EU Fees, 2007: £3,070 p.a. Bursaries for students receiving the Maintenance Grant - sliding scale according to income. There's also the 'Talented Sports Performer' Bursary Scheme: they offer up to £500 p.a. to outstanding sports persons.

STUDENT PROFILE

Lots of students are local and mature. There is a strong female presence and great sporting prowess.

UNIVERSITY/STUDENT PROFILE	
University since	**2005**
Situation/style	**Coastal sites**
Student population	**5160**
Undergraduates	**3415**
- mature	**37%**
- non EU undergraduates	**6%**
- male/female	**33/67**
- non-traditional student intake	**26%**
- state school intake	**96%**
- drop-out rate	**14%**
- undergraduate applications	**Up 21%**

ACADEMIA & JOBS

There are six schools: Teacher Education; Physical Education; Sport, Exercise & Health Science;

Cultural Studies; Visual & Performing Arts; and Social Studies. Undergraduates may study for single honours, joint or major/minor programmes, or BA (QTS).

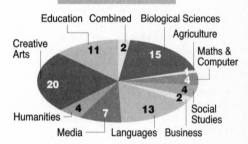

Almost half of graduates become teachers. Of those, 65% go into primary/32% secondary. Physical education with QTS is key.

The religious degrees reflect the college's past, of course, while Sport Science brings to mind the more pervasive modern interest of staff and students, and sustains a well-equipped Sports

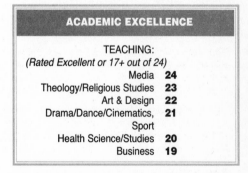

ACADEMIC EXCELLENCE	
TEACHING:	
(Rated Excellent or 17+ out of 24)	
Media	**24**
Theology/Religious Studies	**23**
Art & Design	**22**
Drama/Dance/Cinematics, Sport	**21**
Health Science/Studies	**20**
Business	**19**

Centre, with a new athletics track this year and sports science laboratories. The School of Arts offers modules in Music, Dance, Art, and offers a unique course in Related Arts, which allows specialism in either of the three disciplines, but also looks for useful relationships between them. There is a strong tradition in jazz and classical music and regular student music society performances and workshops (college and cathedral are regular venues). Dance (ballet, jazz and tap) is supported by a Studio, and, like music and art, involves public performance/exhibition at both student and professional level.

There's a Learning Resources Centre at Bishop Otter – a library (200,000 items), a media and computer facility, and art gallery. A similar centre at Bognor Regis has recently been refurbished.

SOCIAL SCENE

STUDENT UNION A new Union building opened at Chichester campus last year, with a 650 capacity ZeeBar. At Bognor, it's The Mack. The majority of students are local, so weekends are not that big, but ents are impressive for so small a clientele. A typical week sees Flirt on Monday, Shagadelic in Bognor on Tuesday. Big Wednesday is Sports Night in Chichester, while down in Bognor it's The Alternative (live music and DJ's). Thursday brings Pre-Club Party to Bognor, and The Alternative to Chichester. Friday is live music in Chichester. Sunday is Quiz Night on both campuses. There were also 10 Paramount Comedy Nights this year (headline acts have included Alan Carr and Brendon Burns), and 4 balls every year – Freshers, Graduation, Christmas and Summer. Recent acts include Brandon Block, EZ Rollers, Jo O'Meara, DJ Spoony, Tim Westwood, El Presidente.

There are alternative music societies, arts societies, a role-playing games, society even an English Literature Appreciation Society. Oh, and an LGB (gay) Society flourishes, regularly holding events on campus and in a gay pub in the town. 'There's been a big growth,' says a bod at the union, which, for a moment, sounded a tad alarming.

Level of political activity has recently been impressively high, with a focus on Drink Awareness, Anti-Bullying, Mental Health Awareness, and a campaign for better inter-site transport and washing facilities.

SPORT Sport is key; last year their teams came 53rd nationally, which is good for so small a uni. There are 13 different sports clubs, all, except netball, having both men's and women's teams.

PILLOW TALK

There is catered accommodation in halls at both sites, and higher capacity and en suite at Bognor. New self-catering halls of residence opened at the Chichester Campus in September 2006, with 124 en-suite rooms with communal kitchens and

WHAT IT'S REALLY LIKE	
UNIVERSITY:	
Social Life	★★★
Campus scene	**Female, sporty, closed weekends**
Student Union services	**Average-high**
Politics	**Active**
Sport	**Key**
National team position	**53rd**
Sport facilities	**Good**
Arts opportunities	**Music, dance, drama excellent**
Student newspaper	**The Clash**
Nightclub	**ZeeBar**
Bars	**ZeeBar, The Mack**
Union ents	**Cheesy. 6 nights, not Saturday**
Union societies	**7**
Most popular society	**Business & Management Soc**
Parking	**Poor**
CITY:	
Entertainment	★★
Scene	**Arts good**
Town/gown relations	**Good**
Risk of violence	**Average**
Cost of living	**Low**
Student concessions	**Average**
Survival + 2 nights out	**£70 pw**
Part-time work campus/town	**Good/**

lounges. They have also acquired 93 extra shared facility rooms close to the university, bringing total accommodation provided to 675 students. This allows them to guarantee accommodation to all freshers. Remaining accommodation is allocated

AT A GLANCE	
ACADEMIC FILE:	
Subjects assessed	**12**
Excellent	**67%**
Typical entry requirements	**239 points**
Application acceptance rate	**19%**
Students-staff ratio	**22:1**
First/2:1 degree pass rate	**46%**
Graduate track employment	**65%**
ACCOMMODATION FILE:	
Availability to UK freshers	**100%**
Style	**Halls**
Catered	**79%**
En suite	**66%**
Approx price range pw	**£70**
Town rent pw	**£65**

on a 'first come, first served' basis.

GETTING THERE

☞ By road: to Bishop Otter campus, A286 from the north. From east and west it's the A27. The road between Chichester Campus and Bognor is the A259.

☞ By rail: London Victoria, 0:45; Birmingham, 4:00.

☞ Frequent trains from Gatwick Airport.

☞ By coach: London, 4:40; Birmingham, 6:00.

CITY UNIVERSITY

City University
Northampton Square
London EC1V OHB

TEL 020 7040 5060/8028/8716
FAX 020 7040 8995
EMAIL ugadmissions@city.ac.uk
WEB www.city.ac.uk

City University Students' Union
Northampton Square
London EC1V 0HB

TEL 020 7040 5600
FAX 020 7040 5601
EMAIL president@city.ac.uk
WEB www.cusuonline.org

VAG VIEW

City University received its Royal Charter granting it full university status in 1966. The university is, as its name suggests, very much at the hub of City life and occupies a singular place in the world of higher education. They have a fine reputation in professional education and pride themselves on close contact with professional institutions, business and industry. Many of the programmes are accredited by

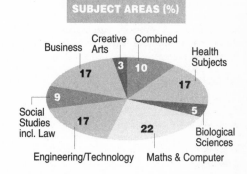

SUBJECT AREAS (%)

Business 17; Creative Arts 3; Combined 10; Health Subjects 17; Social Studies incl. Law 9, 17; Engineering/Technology 22; Maths & Computer; Biological Sciences 5

UNIVERSITY/STUDENT PROFILE	
University since	1966
Situation/style	City sites
Student population	24220
Undergraduates	14958
- mature	30%
- non EU undergraduates	19%
- male/female	43/57
- non-traditional student intake	35%
- state school intake	86%
- drop-out rate	15%
- undergraduate applications	Up 6%

professional bodies, and there is a very healthy graduate employment track record.

CAMPUS

City Uni inhabits the famed City of London, but is only fifteen minutes from the West End, a dawdle from Islington, with its theatres, cinemas, fashionable restaurants, trendy bars, clubs and traditional pubs, and a short way (in the opposite direction) from Clerkenwell, once-artisan London and now a fashionable area for cool, young, City-mile workers.

The main university buildings form part of Northampton Square. Main library, lecture theatres and Students' Union are here. The Department of Arts Policy and Management are nearby in the Barbican Centre. The Dept. of Radiography and halls of residence are also within walking distance. The St Bartholomew School of Nursing is some way

Postgraduates 38%
Female Undergraduates 35%

STUDENT POPULATION
Total students
24,220

Male Undergraduates 27%

away in West Smithfield and Whitechapel in the East End. The Business School now occupies new premises in the heart of the city (see *Academia* below).

'City University is located within walking distance of no less than four tube stations (Barbican, Angel, Farringdon, Old Street), but strangely very few people can ever find it!' writes Catherine Teare. 'Tasteful, grassy Northampton Square, which supports a sizeable bandstand and water trough, has been the site for many an adventure for students – a place to chill in summer and the bandstand a place to shelter when raining. The men's rugby team used to use it for their initiation ceremonies – something about running round it in the buff!'

FEES, BURSARIES

UK & EU Fees 2007: £2,700 p.a. 2008 not yet fixed. £1,000 bursary for students in receipt of full HE Maintenance Grant. Bursaries awarded in shortage subjects. Contact the relevant school directly. www.city.ac.uk/study/money/undergraduate/additionalfunding.html

STUDENT PROFILE

Full-time, first-degree undergraduates, many of whom are mature and from overseas, make up an unusually small percentage of the student body. Many more students are part-timers and there is a large number of postgraduate students. Says Catherine Teare: 'City University is like nowhere else. The mixture of cultures and personalities makes it one of the most diverse university communities in London.'

ACADEMIA & JOBS

Formerly the Northampton Institute, the uni places great emphasis on links with industry and with the professions – journalism, law, banking. A quarter of graduates go into commerce (financial activities, business, etc) and the Business School is now based in the heart of the City, providing, so they say, 'a state-of-the-art resource for management education in the 21st Century'. And then there's the health provision – 15% go into the sector. They have a School of Nursing and Midwifery, and there is a strategic link with University of London Queen Mary's School of Medicine & Dentistry, boosted by a recent £10-million investment. Now there's a new School of Allied Health Professions, which brings together Optometry & Visual Science, Language & Communication Science (speech therapy), Radiography, Health Management and Food Policy (postgrad only). This year there are new state of the art radiography facilities: The Saad Centre for Radiography Clinical Skills Education.

They produce masses of ophthalmic opticians.

The leader in the field is Aston with around 27% of the graduate market. Bradford Uni and City follow. City does a 2-year Foundation in Dispensing Optics, which gives you a Diploma at the end and then the BSc Optometry, if you can hack the high entry requirements. Teaching inspection, 23. Research Grade 5. Two BSc Radiography degrees, Diagnostic and Therapeutic are also well-trod pathways into employment. See, too, the dedicated BSc route into

ACADEMIC EXCELLENCE	
TEACHING: *(Rated Excellent or 17+ out of 24)*	
Music	**Excellent**
Art & Design, Maths, Business & Management, Subjects Allied to Medicine	**23**
Economics	**22**
Electrical & Electronic Eng, Psychology, Library/Info Mgt	**21**
Nursing	**20**
Sociology, Land & Property Mgt, Mechanical & Aeronautical Engineering, Communication & Media Studies, Civil Eng.	**19**
RESEARCH: *Top grades 5/5**	
Music	**Grade 5***
Optometry, Law, Business/ Management, Library/Info Management, Art &Design	**Grade 5**

speech therapy, another cert.

City sends around 10% of its graduates into banking, largely through the Cass Business School. A £50-million building was opened in 2003. The one dedicated course, BSc Banking & International Finance, is what attracts, but doesn't come cheap. Teaching inspection, 23. Research Grade 5. Merchant bankers, sharedealers and investment adviser/analysts also like City. Look at BSc Investment & Financial Risk Management (3 or 4-year sandwich).

60% of 300+ graduates employed nationally as actuaries come via Mathematical Sciences faculties, then it's Business and Economics. City has very big muscle in this area. Half the staff in the Actuarial Science & Statistics Department are Fellows of the Institute of Actuaries. Again there's a high 'ask', but there's also a 4-year version with a first-year Foundation course. There's an appealing study abroad option, too.

City law graduates (who tend to be particularly well schooled in performance skills) have, in City's Inns of Court School of Law, one of a few

WHERE CITY GRADUATES END UP

Health & Social Work: 19%; Education: 5%; Wholesale/Retail: 20%; Manufacturing: 5%; Financial Activities: 16%; Public Administration, Civil Service & Defence: 4%; Hotel/Restaurant: 1%; Transport & Communications (including Telecommunications): 3%; Construction: 1%; Personnel: 1%; Computer: 4%; Business & Management: 3%; Accountancy: 5%; Media (including Film): 5%; Legal 1%; Publishing: 2%; Sport: 0.5%.

Approximate 'graduate track' employed **75%**

institutions validated to run LPCs (Legal Practice Course, essential for solicitors) and came out of a recent LPC assessment with an Excellent rating.

Again, the passage from graduate to barrister is immensely smooth as The Inns of Court School of Law is one of the few places you can study for the Bar Vocational Course (BVC). There's also a LLB Law & Property Valuation, and this year a new English & French Laws LlB.

Location favours City for journalism, too – you are in the very heart of British media, and you will be lectured by practitioners. The portfolio of degrees espouses the idea of combining journalistic skills with knowledge in a particular subject area – in Economics, Psychology, Sociology.

Note, too, City's renowned postgrad journo degrees: International Journalism Diploma/MA is practically orientated with a focus on both print and broadcast – very hands on, very productive. There is also a PhD for mid-career practitioners, who will submit a piece of work and undertake supervised research to produce a thesis.

The department, part of the School of Arts, is internationally respected and has trained the likes of Kirsty Lang (BBC), Dermot Murnaghan (BBC), Gary Younge (Guardian/Observer), Sharon Maguire (Director of Bridget Jones's Diary), Gillian Joseph (Sky News) and Samira Ahmed (Channel 4 News).

City is also traditionally strong in engineering, though teaching inspections were disappointing (variously 19 and 21 points). Racing car enthusiasts should note an interesting niche, the 3-year BEng and BSc Automotive & Motorsport Engineering (4/5-year B/MEng degrees as well).

The BSc Computing Science degrees with AI/Distributed Systems/Games Technology/Music Informatics are gaining a fine reputation. There's also Business Computing Systems, Information Systems or Software Eng. Four-year sandwich courses, all of them, including integrated practical and professional training.

SOCIAL SCENE

STUDENTS' UNION The renowned Journalism course (see above) provides welcome support to the extra-mural media side of life. The monthly glossy

Massive keeps students well informed of forthcoming events and current hot topics, but rather worryingly the radio station (Divercity) and TV station (SUBtv) have gone!

The Students' Union has done well to try to give a stable base for the disparate and scattered student body, but frankly, other than the sound community life in one of the halls, student life at City is London-rather than university-central. Not all do warm to this, and you must be aware that you are not joining a student scene that you'd find at some other London unis.

'Does City have a campus life? Yes and No,' writes Catherine. 'Students use a number of sites dotted around London, which makes it hard for us to feel like we belong.

'Meeting places include the **University**

WHAT IT'S REALLY LIKE

UNIVERSITY:	
Social Life	★★
Campus scene	**Closed weekends**
Student Union services	**Average**
Politics	**Avoided**
Sport	**24 clubs. Striving**
National team position	**127th**
Sport facilities	**Average**
Arts opportunities	**Some**
Student magazine	**Massive**
Nightclub	**Now a study area!**
Bars	**Saddlers**
Union ents	**With London clubs**
Union societies	**50**
Most popular society	**Law, Islamic**
Parking	**Non-existent**
CITY:	
Entertainment	★★★★★
Scene	**Excellent local pubs, clubs, arts**
Town/gown relations	**Good**
Risk of violence	**High**
Cost of living	**High**
Student concessions	**Good**
Survival + 2 nights out	**£100 pw**
Part-time work campus/town	**Excellent**

Refectory (*interesting* food!), the Square and the Students' Union. There is a bar, a shop and an eaterie as well as a Student Advice Centre and clubs and societies.

'Saddler's Bar is open five days a week from 9am, but closes at 11pm. It has a Western theme (check out the saddles!) and offers a few more extras than the usual pub – pool tables, latest arcade titles, quizzes and a chill-out room on major party nights.'

There is, however, no longer a nightclub. The Wonderbar venue, which once masqueraded during the day as Poncho's, a popular Tex Mex-style eaterie, MTV playing in the background to encourage rhythmic chewing., is no more! Instead they have a new study area/common room with widescreen TVs, Internet access and sofas where students can work in groups or just relax.

> *Strong lines into the professions – business, finance, law, health – and very much a London experience. But what have they done to the fun and games at the Student Union?*

With the Union now more or less closed to ents, they organise things with outsiders, like *Quids In* with DJ Tommy A, leading on to Islington's Elbow Room. Monday nights is *Candyfloss* at Islington Carling Academy, with top r&b DJs, like Nicky Smood, Masterstepz and Rampage. They also hold events at Ministry of Sound, Fabric and Turnmills.

As for societies, there is little to shout about, other than that the diverse student population means a huge range of International Societies – from Cypriot to Afro-Caribbean – on offer. There have also been some effective student campaigns on Racism, Women's Safety and Islamophobia.

Town Location is all, as far as City is concerned - 5 mins walk from the attractions of Angel, Old Street, Shoreditch, Hoxton and Farringdon, and just a short bus ride form the West End.

If you walk north towards Angel you come to Upper Street, which must have the most bars and restaurants in one area after the West End. There is something for everyone, cheap and expensive. It has a friendly, safe atmosphere and a 24-hour Sainsbury's on Thursday to Saturday, so you can food-shop at 3am in the morning!

If you walk west down Roseberry Avenue, you come to Exmouth Market and its surrounding area. This offers pretty much the same as Upper Street, but on a smaller scale. Exmouth Market has some of the best sandwich shops in London and, especially in the summer, a really welcoming atmosphere.

Camden is a mere 10-minute tube ride away,

while the West End is twenty minutes on the bus. Many clubs offer discounts to students with an NUS card, but you must make sure you go on the right night. The nearest places to shop are Holloway Road, Oxford Street and Camden.'

See also *Student London*, page 301.

SPORT Interest may be high but levels and facilities are not impressive, and now they no longer have Sports Night at the Wonderbar. There are pitches in Walthamstow; a small rowing club is based, of course, on the Thames; the Saddler's Sports Centre, with badminton, football, netball, tennis, aerobics and yoga and a good martial arts programme, a couple of squash courts; and some Islington facilities are popular nearby.

PILLOW TALK

All applicants over 18 living outside Greater London

AT A GLANCE	
ACADEMIC FILE:	
Subjects assessed	**19**
Excellent	**84%**
Typical entry requirements	**315 points**
Application acceptance rate	**13%**
Students-staff ratio	**22:1**
First/2:1 degree pass rate	**60%**
ACCOMMODATION FILE:	
Guarantee to freshers	**Non-Londoners who apply before May 15**
Style	**Halls, flats**
Catered	**None**
En suite	**1 campus**
Approx price range pw	**£93-£109**
City rent pw	**£85+**

who firmly accept an offer of a place at City and submit an accommodation application form by 15 May are guaranteed a place in halls. There are two , both within walking distance of the main site. The first, Finsbury & Heyworth, are linked by a bar/common room; fees include an evening meal and late breakfast on Saturdays and Sundays. Walter Sickert Hall, which overlooks the Regents Canal, is more plush, with en-suite, single study-bedrooms. Next to Finsbury/Heyworth is a block of purpose-built self-catering flats, 3-6 single study-bedrooms, living room/kitchen and showers. Newly available to first years are self-contained flats (single study-bedrooms with shared facilities) at Francis Rowley Court, about ten minutes' walk from the uni.

'Popular private housing student areas,' reports Catherine, 'include Hackney, Stoke Newington and Shoreditch.'

GETTING THERE
☛ All sites are well served by buses.
☛ Parking is difficult and expensive.
☛ Nearest Underground stations to main sites: Angel (Northern line), Farringdon and Barbican (Hammersmith & City, Metropolitan and Circle).
☛ For the School of Nursing, it's either Whitechapel (District and Metropolitan), Aldgate (Metropolitan), Aldgate East (Metropolitan and District), or Tower Hill (District).

COVENTRY UNIVERSITY

Coventry University
Priory Street
Coventry CV1 5FB

TEL 024 7679 0790
FAX 024 7888 674
EMAIL info.rae@coventry.ac.uk
WEB www.coventry.ac.uk

Coventry University Students' Union
Priory Street
Coventry CV1 5FJ

TEL 024 7679 5200
FAX 024 7655 5239
EMAIL suexec@coventry.ac.uk
WEB www.coventry.ac.uk

VAG VIEW

A fter devastating bombing during the Second World War, Coventry rose from the ashes to become a major industrial force. Elements of what later became the university evolved during this time, and in 1970 the Coventry College of Art merged with Lanchester College of Technology and Rugby College of Engineering Technology to form Lanchester Polytechnic. In 1987 the name was changed to Coventry Polytechnic. Then, in 1992, the poly became a university.

UNIVERSITY/STUDENT PROFILE	
University since	**1992**
Situation/style	**City campus**
Student population	**15676**
Undergraduates	**13757**
- mature	**44%**
- non-EU undergratuates	**6%**
- male/female	**52/48**
- non-traditional student intake	**39%**
state school intake	**96%**
- drop-out rate	**21%**
- undergraduate applications	**Up 9%**

CAMPUS
The modern precinct campus is directly opposite the bombed-out ruins of the original cathedral. Looking around the ecclesiastical shell is a thought-provoking experience. Students from Cov

Postgraduates — 12%
Female Undergraduates — 42%
Male Undergraduates — 46%
STUDENT POPULATION
Total students 15,676

were sketching it at the time I visited. Especially memorable is a sculpture of reconciliation (two figures embrace to express forgiveness for the Luftwaffe's devastation of Coventry) created by Josefina de Vasconcellos and, as it happens, given by Richard Branson. An identical sculpture stands in the Peace Garden at Hiroshima, Japan.

FEES, BURSARIES
UK & EU fees 2007: £3,070 p.a. Bursaries are available on a sliding scale for those in receipt of the Maintenance Grant. Also scholarships of £2,000 p.a. for students who achieve 300 points from 3 full A levels or 31 points from an International Baccalaureate, and for high performing students on new 'STAR' courses. STAR Scholarships are in place to attract students who not only have the potential to achieve high entry qualifications but also can

demonstrate they have the drive and ambition to succeed throughout their studies.' See www.coventry.ac.uk/studentfinance

STUDENT PROFILE

There is a large mature student population, bent on vocational training. Many undergrads come via the state sector from the locality, but also a lot from overseas. A sizeable section of first degree undergrads are part-timers. The uni has been diligent in its open access policy, giving many families their first taste of a university education.

ACADEMIA & JOBS

There are two schools: Lifelong Learning and Art & Design, and three faculties: Health & Life Sciences; Business, Environment & Society; Engineering & Computing.

A school's careers master told us, 'They have deliberately gone for the vocational – that was their background. We have students for whom Coventry is exactly right.' This year they introduce an extensive range of modules, known as 'the Add+vantage scheme' specifically to enable students to gain work-related knowledge and skills, and manage their career development.

The continuing connection with industry helps mould their courses and keeps their employment record good and inward investment healthy, while a programme of expansion continues. Recently, they acquired the Odeon cinema on Jordan Well as home to the Performing Arts and Communications Culture & Media departments (courses in dance, theatre, music and arts practice lend a distinctly different timbre to academic life here), a new £20-million library opened, major investment was made in WebCT (electronic learning environment), and there's a £1.5-million spend for an Advanced Digitisation and Modelling Laboratory to enhance their research into automotive design.

For cars, boats, planes, Coventry is still among the leaders. Would-be aeronautical engineers and manufacturers come bounding out of here. Less well known are low-cost offers for Boat Design (indeed, all sorts of vehicle design) in the developing Art & Design faculty. But this is Coventry, home of car manufacture, and the car industry is central to its uni's calling. There are BA hons degrees in 3D Design Representation, Automotive Design, and Automotive Design & Illustration, as well as the range of BEng hons. Racing car designers and team managers note: the 3-year degree in Motorsports asks is not demanding at entry. There are also Design and Management courses. Six former Coventry Uni design students and a member of staff were identified by an *Autocar* survey as being among the 100 most influential

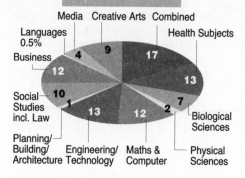

SUBJECT AREAS (%)

Media Creative Arts Combined
Languages 0.5% — Health Subjects
Business — 4 — 9 — 17
12
13
Social — 10
Studies — 1 — 13 — 12 — 2 — 7
incl. Law — Biological Sciences
Planning/ Building/ Architecture — Engineering/ Technology — Maths & Computer — Physical Sciences

Britons in the automotive industry. Note also their Advanced Digitising and Modelling Laboratory, opened in December 2002, formally known as the Bugatti Building. It provides full-sized vehicle design and styling facilities and is the only resource of its kind attached to a university.

Design also favours graphic artists, designers and illustrators (often the advertising industry or journalism as destination). BSc Architectural Design Technology favours the would-be town planner, while jobs in the construction industry are very much available to Cov's Built Environment graduates – see Building Surveying, and Construction Management in particular. Teaching inspection, 19.

In the health arena, BSc Physiotherapy is in a cluster of employer-friendly health science degrees, which includes Nursing, Dietetics,

---

ACADEMIC EXCELLENCE

TEACHING:
(Rated Excellent or 17+ out of 24)

Mechanical Engineering, Geography.	**Excellent**
Subjects Allied to Medicine, Economics, History, Maths Politics	23
Building, Art/Design, Business & Management, Nursing	22
Sociology, Modern Languages, Psychology, Tourism/Leisure/ Sport	21
Town & Country Planning, Civil Eng, Biosciences	19
Communication & Media Studies, General Engineering, Mech/ Aero/Manuf Eng, Electric & Electronic Engineering	18

RESEARCH:
Top grades 5/5* **None**

Midwifery and Occupational Therapy, and dropped only one point at the teaching assessments. Look also at Biological Sciences (BSc Psychology, Applied Psychology, etc – 21 points at inspection).

Would-be solicitors note that Coventry are European, commercial and business law specialists, and non-Law graduates may opt for a 2-year, or 3-year part-time, Senior Status Law degree here.

Finally, if you have an adventurous streak and purposeful outlook, rifle through their Disaster Management courses. This is a genuine niche. Coventry has 10 years experience teaching them.

SOCIAL SCENE

STUDENT UNION The most recent addition to the campus is a new student centre which offers a 'one-stop' service and features all the services students require on enrolment and throughout their time at the University. Students can get help on a range of issues including finance, registry, accommodation, international office, recruitment and admissions and student services.

The campus is a hive of activity revolving around the café/bar **ReUnion** on the top floor of the union building. It serves food from breakfast through to late-night munchies and screens all the top sporting fixtures.

Artie and indie types will be found in the **Golden Cross** and **Fads** cafeteria in the art block. Language and engineering students will be found in the library. Sporting people will be found at the union bar or slumped in the corner somewhere. Overseas students spring up everywhere.

Much of uni social life is dominated by societies, particularly by sports, though the sometime award-winning media, currently *Source* (newspaper) and Source FM, appeal too. Most have their local haunts: the **Hope and Anchor** is frequented by 'The Lanch' Rugby Union team. Sporting societies often organise fund-raising events – Man 'O' Man, The Full Monty, the Slave Trade, etc. – and such events are high on the social calendar.

What was **The Planet** on the corner of Cox Street – a revolution in its day, is now the **Casbar**, **Studio** and **Chiller**. *Phase the Legend* is Friday's cheese in the Studio, there's funk in the Chiller and 'just great music in the Casbar,' they tell me – *Trollied* is on Monday: drink promo and all rooms open. It's but a short walk from campus.

SPORT The uni muscled in at 86th in the overall BUSA ratings for team sports last year. Generally they do much better. It's had its Olympic swimmers and pumped up boxing champions. Central to campus is a new Sports Centre with fitness suite, injury clinic, 4-court and 2-court halls and dance studio. Thirty-seven acres of uni playing fields are at Westward Heath, 4 miles from the city centre, cater for rugby, soccer, hockey and cricket, and there's a 9-hole golf course.

TOWN The compact city centre has a much-loved traditional indoor market. The £33m **Sky Dome** complex houses a multi-screen cinema; bars and café bars, two nightclubs, and restaurants. There is a 4,000-seat arena a popular concert venue that doubles up as an ice rink.

The **Herbert Art Gallery and Museum** and **Belgrade Theatre** provide the cultural dimension. Sport is, however, the thing, with the £60m **Coventry Arena** no longer a dream and a £20m project to include a rugby stadium and a football Academy of Excellence. The **City Sports Centre** has an Olympic-sized swimming pool.

Cost of living is quite low, and there are lots of student discounts. 'Most pubs in Cov are of the Rat, Parrot and Firkin ilk,' says Andrew Losowsky, 'but **The Golden Cross** and **The Hand and Heart** are worth a look for something different.'

PILLOW TALK

'Priory Hall is the largest of the student residences over 600 rooms,' writes Jennifer Johnston. 'It is dominated by lads who haven't yet discovered how to open a tin of beans. Singer Hall is organised into flats and is self-catered. Caradoc Hall is a tower block of self-contained flats and is just out of the city centre. There are lots of suitable student houses in the Stoke, Earlsdon and Radford areas of

---

WHERE COVENTRY GRADUATES END UP

Health & Social Work: 20%; Education: 8%; Wholesale/Retail: 11%; Manufacturing: 13%; Financial Activities: 7%; Public Administration, Civil Service & Defence: 7%; Hotel/Restaurant: 3%; Transport & Communications (including Telecommunications): 6%; Construction: 2%; Personnel: 7%; Computer: 2%; Business & Management: 2%; Media (including Film): 1%; Legal 2%; Architecture: 1%; Publishing: 1%; Advertising: 1%; Sport: 2%.

Approximate 'graduate track' employed **61%**

the city, with good low rents.'

New accommodation includes university-owned Sherbourne House and Lynden House and non-university Liberty Park and Trinity Point. Raglan House is a new development, due to be completed for occupation in September 2007, of

WHAT IT'S REALLY LIKE	
UNIVERSITY:	
Social Life	★★★★
Campus scene	**Culturally mixed, good ents scene**
Student Union services	**Activity high**
Politics	**Internal**
Sport	**Average**
National team position	**86th**
Sport facilities	**Average**
Arts opportunities	**Film, art exc.; dance, music popular; drama improving**
Student newspaper	**Source**
Student radio	**Source FM**
Cox Street Venue	**Casbar, Studio and Chiller**
Priory Street Venue	**ReUnion**
Union ents	**Eclectic**
Union clubs/societies	**50**
Parking	**Poor**
CITY:	
Entertainment	★★
Scene	**Clubs 'n pubs**
Town/gown relations	**Nothing special**
Risk of violence	**Variable**
Cost of living	**Low**
Student concessions	**OK**
Survival + 2 nights out	**£60 pw**
Part-time work campus/town	**Average/Good**

AT A GLANCE	
ACADEMIC FILE:	
Subjects assessed	**28**
Excellent	**79%**
Typical entry requirements	**229 points**
Application acceptance rate	**23%**
Students-staff ratio	**21:1**
First/2:1 degree pass rate	**55%**
ACCOMMODATION FILE:	
Guarantee to freshers	**82%**
Style	**Halls, houses**
Catered	**23%**
En suite	**50%**
Approx price range pw	**£50-£172**
City rent pw	**£65**

self-catered, en-suite cluster flats.

GETTING THERE

☛ By road: from London M1/J17, M45, A45, signs for City Centre. From the south, M40/J15, A46, signs for City Centre. From the southwest, M5, M42/J6, A45. From Northwest, M6/J2, City Centre signs. From north, M1/J21, M69, City Centre.
☛ By rail: London Euston, 80 mins; Manchester Piccadilly, 2:30; Nottingham, 1:45; Bristol, 2:30.
☛ By air: Birmingham Airport.
☛ By coach: London, 1:20; Leeds, 4:00.

UNIVERSITY OF CUMBRIA

The University of Cumbria
Brampton Road
Carlisle
Cumbria CA3 9AY

TEL 0845 6061 144
WEB ENQUIRIES www.cumbria.ac.uk/enquiries
WEB www.cumbria.ac.uk

*T*he birth date of the University of Cumbria is officially August 1, 2007, formed from an amalgamation of St Martin's College, the Cumbria Institute of the Arts, and the Cumbrian campuses of the University of Central Lancashire, all of which have featured in the Guide before. It is a courageous attempt to put higher education on a sound footing in one of our most beautiful, but relatively lightly populated, counties. HQ is in Carlisle.

CAMPUS

These institutions bring with them campuses in Carlisle, Penrith, Ambleside and Lancaster, and a specialist teacher-education centre in London. The uni will also have strong links and close partnership working with 4 FE Colleges in Cumbria (Lakes Colleges, Furness College, Carlisle College and Kendal College).

ST MARTIN'S COLLEGE

St Martin's is a teacher training college with a Church of England foundation (1964), but it is also the base for a number of courses leading to employment in health and the caring professions – nursing, midwifery, occupational therapy, radiography – in the Church, in the worlds of art, design and imaging science, in drama, dance, music, in media, in business and in the sports and leisure industries. Degrees have been awarded by nearby Lancaster Uni since 1967.

The main St Martin's campus is a mile or so from the central shopping area of Lancaster, and offers teacher training, primary and secondary, and degrees in business, sport, arts, humanities, social sciences, health (including nursing). There are also smaller campuses in Ambleside (Lake District) and Carlisle, and Health/ Nursing training centres at Whitehaven and Barrow-in-Furness. Ambleside specialises in Early Years QTS, 3 and 5-11, with drama and PE among the options, and three degrees in Adventure Recreation Mgt and Outdoor Studies. Carlisle is also for Early Years QTS, but with music and religion among the options, and various degrees in social sciences, health (including nursing, radiography, occupational therapy and physiotherapy), and business and info technology. Finally, in Tower Hamlets, London, there's a centre for teacher training, primary years.

CUMBRIA INSTITUTE OF ARTS

Located on 3 sites in Carlisle, the main green-field campus overlooking Rickerby Park and the River Eden – paradise indeed – Cumbria is a cracking college academically, with teaching assessment scores of 21 out of 24 for Art & Design and 19 for Communication & Media. It is also exceptionally well resourced with electronic and media production facilities and a £4.5-million development incorporating a new library, theatre and dance studio, and improved teaching accommodation. Courses focus on creative writing, drama, dance, film, journalism, and fine art and design.

CENTRAL LANCASHIRE UNIVERSITY CAMPUSES

The Cumbrian campuses of Central Lancashire University - UCLan, as it is known, which is head-quartered in Preston - are at Newton Rigg (Penrith) and Carlisle. Newton Rigg has 250 hectares at the head of the Eden Valley, where a faculty of Land-Based Studies had been quietly doing its thing as Newton Rigg Agric College until, in 1998, UCLan took it over. UCLan's Carlisle campus used to be part of Northumbria University, which ran great courses - business, computing, travel, tourism, etc - at generous entry rates, for which many an applicant put his name down before realising to his horror that he wasn't going to be based in Newcastle. It has been well shepherded by UCLan since then and as the Cumbria Business School boasts 'a significant number of international students from a wide variety of countries, including China Nigeria and the USA'.

FEES, BURSARIES

UK & EU Fees, 2007: £3,070 p.a. As yet not fixed for 2008. There are grants, scholarships, teaching bursaries to accompany the Government Maintenance grant (if your parents' earnings are low enough). For students on NHS-funded full-time courses, fees paid are by the strategic health authority. Extra allowances are available for older students and students with dependants. There is also a range of support people studying part-time.

UNIVERSITY/STUDENT PROFILE	
University since	**2007**
Situation/style	**Confederacy**
Student population	**8027**
Undergraduates	**4735**
- mature	**31%**
- non-EU undergratuates	**4%**
- male/female	**76/24**
- non-traditional student intake	**38%**
- state school intake	**97%**
Applications: St Martin's	**Down12%**
Applications: Cumbria Inst.	**Up 12%**

ACADEMIA

The uni has four faculties. Arts, Design & Media will enjoy a £6 million redevelopment programme. Education is delivered across 3 campuses (Lancaster, Ambleside and Carlisle) and at 2 sites in London (Tower Hamlets and Greenwich). Health, Medical Science & Social Care offer training as a nurse (adult, child, learning disabilities or mental health branches), midwife, occupational therapist, physiotherapist, radiographer or social worker. And there's a degree in Child, Young Person and Family Studies.

Meanwhile, Lancaster University is leading the way in a collaboration with UCLan, Cumbria and Liverpool universities, and the University Hospitals of Morecambe Bay Trust in recruiting teaching and research staff to meet the terms of a government decision to allow 50 extra places a year for Liverpool medical students to be based full time at the Lancaster campus.

Finally, there is a Faculty of Science & Natural Resources.

STUDENT UNION

The student scene is even more fragmented at the moment than is academia, but this much we learned. In Carlisle, **The Calva Bar** is open daily from 10.30a.m. to 11 p.m., and stages live bands, hypnotists, comedians and theme nights.

In Ambleside, the **Overdraught Bar** is central to student social life. Regular theme nights and music genre nights make up the programme. There's a 280 capacity and the bar is open seven days a week from 7pm.

The **JCR** is the social heart of Lancaster and offers a programme that dovetails with Liquid, a local club with student nights on Monday and Wednesday. In the JCR, it's 'quality music and pound-a-pint night' on Monday, and *Music Corner* - a live band showcase on Tuesday. *Wild and Wacky Wednesdays* is the pre-Liquid party night. Then there's *Thursday Night Lite* - chilled night - and *Bar FTSE* on a Friday. On Saturday, it's *Chillout* in the JCR, and the *BIG Quiz* on Sunday.

ACCOMMODATION

They offer only 1,200 rooms across the various campuses, so apply early. Internet access is 'planned' but not yet delivered. Some rooms in Ambleside are twins, though many elsewhere are a modern enough conception to be en-suite even.

Town accommodation is plentiful, and the uni office will help you get something. There are 'house hunting help days, where you can meet other students, receive guidance from a buddy (a second or third-year student), view accommodation and question prospective landlords.'

North West England is cheap. Expect to pay around £45-£60 p.p. in Lancaster, Carlisle and Penrith, while for Ambleside, £ 55-£60 p.p.

DE MONTFORT UNIVERSITY

De Montfort University
The Gateway
Leicester LE1 9BH

TEL 08459 45 46 47
FAX 0116 255 0307
EMAIL enquiry@dmu.ac.uk
WEB www.dmu.ac.uk

De Montfort Students' Union
Mill Lane
Leicester LE2 7DR

TEL 0116 255 5576
FAX 0116 257 6309
EMAIL kbutler@dmu.ac.uk
WEB www.mydsu.com

VAG VIEW

*D*MU *has a new Vice Chancellor (its fifth since 1992) and the chance to wipe the slate clean. In the space of a few years, restructuring has lost them eight sites, including campuses at Lincoln, Bedford and Milton Keynes, and forfeited one of the prime live music venues in the country, The Arena.* **Compensation** *was the new £9-million* Campus Centre *building, which opened in September 2003. With restaurants and bar, a Students' Union, a dance theatre and*

16% — Postgraduates

Female Undergraduates — 50%

STUDENT POPULATION

Total students
20,047

34% — Male Undergraduates

performing arts studios, it was an important pointer to the future. For DMU has just been awarded Centre of Excellence status in Performing Arts in recognition of its development of new teaching approaches to dance, drama and music technology. The purpose-built venue will open during 2007.

This and new student accommodation, which gives all first years a place in a hall, are part of a £105-million development, planned to put the uni back on its feet.

Among the partnerships that will enable this to happen is one with the NHS, which is working to create a new professional/education/training centre on the Leicester General Hospital site, to link the Leicester and Warwick Medical School with DMU's health provision – nursing, midwifery, etc – and the NHS staff's own continuous professional development programme.

They have also been given £6 million to launch the Institute Of Creative Technologies, a centre dedicated to innovative research into digital and post-digital technologies for the creative industries, cutting-edge research at the intersection of e-science, the digital arts and the humanities.

Finally, a £35-million building for the Faculty of Business and Law is underway. The 6-storey, 'green', low energy building, with lecture theatres, a new Law Library, mock court room, specialist postgrad and professional suite, and retail units, bookshop and café, will open in September 2009.

FEES, BURSARIES

UK & EU Fees 2007: £3,070 p.a. 2008 not yet fixed. Bursaries for students in receipt of HE Maintenance grant on a sliding scale. Academic scholarships worth £1,000, the Creative Industries Scholarship, worth £1,500, bursaries for students entering DMU from care, and students coming from within a 30-mile radius, all help.

STUDENT PROFILE

There's a large mature undergraduate population and an open-access policy that brings in many who might not have gone to uni a few years ago - 41% from the lowest socio-economic groups, 16% from 'low-participation neighbourhoods' - and such a fun-loving crew that neighbouring Leicester Uni students time and again crash in on their excellent ents.

UNIVERSITY/STUDENT PROFILE	
University since	**1992**
Situation/style	**City campus**
Student population	**20047**
Undergrads	**16886**
- mature	**39%**
- non EU undergraduates	**4%**
- male/female	**41/59**
- non-traditional student intake	**41%**
state sector intake	**96%**
- drop-out rate	**20%**
- undergraduate applications	**Down 15%**

ACADEMIA & JOBS

Faculties are: Art and Design; Business and Law; Computing Sciences and Engineering; Health and Life Sciences; and Humanities.

A feature of many of DMU's programmes is paid work placement. All sandwich courses have placement tutors with extensive employer contacts. The uni runs joint research projects with industry and business, in which students are involved. Employers help plan relevant student projects as well as providing our students with work experience and graduate jobs.

The Business Faculty leads the field for jobs in sales management. Personnel managers also prosper through the Human Resource Management degree. The Marketing degrees have strong relationships with Chartered Institute of Marketing: www.cim.co.uk and IDM: www.theidm.com. Students get exemptions from professional qualifications of both these bodies through study of certain marketing modules.

The BA Accounting and Finance course also offers the maximum exemptions from Association of Chartered Certified Accountants and CIMA qualifications – you can't get more exemptions from an undergraduate degree in the UK.

DMU is also a leader in Public Policy research. Look at the BA Public Policy, Government & Management. The Local Governance Research Centre is internationally recognised.

In Computing Sciences & Engineering, look at BSc Audio & Recording Technology, run in conjunction with Confetti Studios and providing real world industry experience. Also, BSc Forensic Computing, developed in conjunction with electronic crime law enforcement specialists. BSc Broadcast Technology is run in conjunction with BBC Training and Development, and comes with an optional placement year. There's a strong tradition of student radio at DMU. BSc Media Production includes a practical component with the BBC Training and Development unit in Wood

WHERE DE MONTFORT GRADUATES END UP

Health & Social Work: 11%; Education: 18%; Wholesale/Retail: 14%; Manufacturing: 10%; Financial Activities: 7%; Public Administration, Civil Service & Defence: 6%; Hotel/Restaurant: 3%; Transport & Communications (including Telecommunications): 4%; Construction: 1%; Personnel: 5%; Computer: 5%; Business & Management: 1%; Accountancy: 1%; Media (including Film): 1%; Legal 1%; Architecture: 1%; Publishing: 1%; Advertising: 1%; Artistic/Literary: 2%; Sport: 2%.

Approximate 'graduate track' employed **58%**

Norton. BSc Radio Production gives hands-on experience of producing programmes.

Another strong employment destination here is Further Education, via Creative Arts (22 at the assessments, everything from Textiles to Fine Art, Graphics to Photography), Engineering (19 points on assessment), Computer Science (Satisfactory), Social Science and Business (Excellent).

The art and design provision finds all sorts of avenues into employment. BA Contour Fashion is the only degree in the world to specialise in lingerie, bodywear, swimwear, performance sportswear, 'structured' eveningwear and bridalwear, established apparently in 1947 at the request of the corset industry. Students visit underwear manufacturers throughout Europe and Asia, after Hong Kong businessman Andrew Sia set up the Ace Style Institute at the university. Look also at BSc Fashion Technology, as well as all the fashion and textile design and Retail Buying degrees. There is also the expected outpouring of graphic artists, designers and illustrators, and a prized degree in Furniture Design.

In the arts, through BA Arts Management in the Humanities Faculty, DMU turn out as many administrators as Cambridge. Dance is an area of growth and rated 22 out of 24.

Nurses (adult, children's, mental health and learning disabilities nursing, also Dental Technology) and midwives dominate the health provision, but there are 50 places available on the BSc Speech & Language Therapy, and a very good chance of a job. Teaching inspection, 20. Note, there is a new Public Health degree.

ACADEMIC EXCELLENCE

TEACHING:	
(Rated Excellent or 17+ out of 24)	
Business & Management	**Excellent**
Politics	**24**
Land & Property Management,	**23**
Leisure Industry & Sport	
Drama/Dance/Cinematics,	**22**
Art & Design, Nursing, Psychol	
History of Art, Archit & Design,	**21**
Molecular Biosciences,	
Pharmacology	
Communication & Media Studies	**20**
Speech & Language Therapy,	
Maths, Building, Education	
Electric/Electron Engineering,	**19**
Materials Technology,	

RESEARCH:	
Top grades 5/5*	
Politics, English	**Grade 5**

There is also BSc Honours Audiology – all course fees are paid by the NHS. Bursaries of £2500 are available, and a year-long work placement commands a salary. 'Graduates of the course can expect a starting salary in the region of £21,000 per annum,' says the university.

Finally, Biomedical Sciences/Studies, Cell Biology & Genome Studies attract researchers and aspiring pathologists, and there is a sound employment record for chemists, with two degrees feeding the habit: the 4-year Pharmacy and the Pharmaceutical & Cosmetic Science (Drug Delivery or Cosmetic Products) programme.

See also the BSc Human Psychology – there's a history of strong employment in psychotherapy at DMU, and this degree is accredited by the British

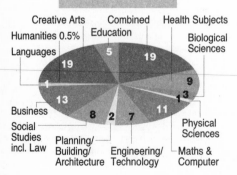

SUBJECT AREAS (%)

Creative Arts — Combined — Health Subjects
Humanities 0.5% — Education
Languages — Biological Sciences
19 — 5 — 19
9
Business — 13 — 3
Social — 8 — 2 — 7 — 11
Studies — Physical Sciences
incl. Law — Planning/ Building/ Architecture — Engineering/ Technology — Maths & Computer

Psychological Society as first step towards becoming a chartered psychologist. There's also a BA Social Work.

SOCIAL SCENE

STUDENTS' UNION The Students' Union has moved into 'a brand spanking new building in the centre of campus, offering the radio station a new studio

> *DMU are pulling in their horns, centring their resources on the Leicester campus in a 10-year, £105-million programme.*

and a venue called **Level 1** – DJ booth, laser lighting, amazing effects. We now have comfy leather sofas and funky chairs, a quadrant of bars – more drinking stations on your nights out.'

Regular ents nights are *Sun Random*, an eclectic mix of activity varying from comedy, to film previews, to karaoke to live gigs, anything Random goes! Monday os *Happy Mondays*, Students and

Societies Night, where any club or society puts on ents and enhances their resources. Tuesday is Quiz Night. Wednesday is *Univibe*, a yea-old night of r&b flava musik, ranging from desi beats, ragga, bangra to hip hop. Thursday is *Kinky*, ar 21st-century disco night. Friday is *Toothpaste*, indie/rock night, with occasional live bands, like so far El Presidente & Imperial Vipers. Saturday is *Flirt*, cheese pop music with promotional acts, entertainment and fancy dress or themed nights. DJ sets that have featured thus far : Kate Lawler, Scott Mills, Fran Cosgrove, Chappers & Dave & more.

There is a real tradition for media. Radio station Demon Fm has won awards for many years and built up a huge reputation within the industry.

Finally, lunchtime and other out-of-hours lectures are the coming thing. Speakers for their *Distinguished Lecture Series 2007* will include Sir Trevor Brooking, Director of Football Development at The FA, George Davies, the *Next* fashion empire guru and driving force behind *Per Una* at M & S, and Louis de Bernieres, author of the incredibly over-written *Captain Corelli's Mandolin*.

TOWN See *Student Leicester*, page 280.

SPORT There's an emphasis on fun rather than serious competition. There's the John Sandford Sports Centre, a fitness studio, solarium, weight training and gym. Basketball team the Leicester Riders have strengthened their ties with DMU and are now known as the De Montfort University Leicester Riders. There's swimming, athletics and

WHAT IT'S REALLY LIKE

UNIVERSITY:

Social Life	★★★★
Campus scene	**Unpretentious, fun-loving, studenty**
Student Union services	**Good**
Politics	**Active**
Sport	**30 clubs**
National team position	**97th**
Sport facilities	**Good**
Arts opportunities	**Theatre, music & film good**
Student newspaper	**Demon**
2005 Journalism Awards	**Winner**
Student radio	**Demon FM**
2006 Radio Awards	**Best Newcomer**
Student TV	**Demon TV**
2006 TV Awards	**Open Award**
Nightclub	**Level 1**
Bars	**Bars 1 to 4**
Union ents	**7 days a week**
Union societies	**30**
Most popular society	**Chinese Soc, Hindu Soc**
Parking	**Poor-adequate**

CITY/TOWN:

Leicester Nightlife	★★★★★
City scene	**Top town - clubs, pubs, curries**
Town/gown relations	**OK**
Risk of violence	**Average**
Cost of living	**Average**
Student concessions	**Good**
Survival + 2 nights out	**£50-£80 pw**
Part-time work campus/town	**Good/Excellent**

AT A GLANCE

ACADEMIC FILE:

Subject assessments	**27**
Excellent	**70%**
Typical entry requirements	**238 points**
Application acceptance rate	**21%**
Students-staff ratio	**21:1**
First Class/2:1 degree pass rate	**39%**

ACCOMMODATION FILE:

Guarantee to freshers	**All full-time**
Style	**Halls, flats**
Catered	**None**
En suite	**61%**
Approx price range pw	**£79-£86**
Average city rent pw	**£60-£85**

cycling close to campus.

PILLOW TALK

The majority of accommodation is made up of cluster flats with 4-6 students sharing. Other units have 7-10 sharing. All accommodation offers internet connection. 1,800 of rooms for freshers

were built in the last 2 years.

GETTING THERE

☛ Leicester by road: M1/J21 or M6 then M69.
☛ By rail: London St Pancras, 75 mins.
☛ By air: Birmingham International Airport or East Midlands International Airport.

• •

UNIVERSITY OF DERBY

University of Derby
Kedleston Road
Derby DE22 1GB

TEL 01332 591167
EMAIL enquiries-admissions@derby.ac.uk
WEB www.derby.ac.uk

Derby University Students' Union
Derby DE22 1GB

TEL 01332 591507
FAX 01332 348846
EMAIL udsu@derby.ac.uk
WEB www.udsu-online.co.uk/

VAG VIEW

*S*ince *it became a university in 1992 Derby has expanded fast and operates now from seven sites. Committed to the ideal of higher education for all, it keeps its entry requirements low and operating an open access plicy which boosts its drop-out rate.*

Now, their spirits boosted by a 5% increase in applications last year, they are moving forward impressively. The £20m Buxton Campus, an historic Grade II* listed building with one of the world's largest unsupported domes, and the creation of a University

STUDENT POPULATION
Total students
24,085

UNIVERSITY/STUDENT PROFILE	
University since	**1992**
Situation/style	**City campus**
Student population	**24085**
Undergraduates	**11475**
- mature	**66%**
- non EU undergraduates	**2%**
- male/female	**42/58**
- non-traditional student intake	**36%**
state school intake	**99%**
- drop-out rate	**27%**
- undergraduate applications	**Up 5%**

Quarter in Derby is underway with additions to the main Kedleston Road Campus – a Clinical Skills Suite with up-to-the-minute digital diagnostic equipment and NHS-specification training wards. This year

students will be faced with a brand new Union bar based on award-winning concepts of their own Architectural Venue Design students. Close by, a new Arts, Design and Technology Campus is taking shape – performance spaces, workshops and studios, as well as facilities for graphic design, film and photography, new media and sound production.

CAMPUS

Derby's campus sites range in size and facilities from the Ritz to B&B. The main site is **Kedleston Road**, 10 minutes walk from the city centre, where all the heavy stuff like law, business and science go on. There are many regular buses to it, it's the home of the Students Union, and the place where most things happen.

The other sites are scattered around, but are also generally well served in terms of transport.

Writes Mario Cacciottolo: **'Green Lane Campus** is a beautiful old Gothic structure near the town centre that is good to look at, but as it's listed there is absolutely no chance of having that much-needed extension.

'**Mickleover Campus** is allegedly made of cardboard, so a dry winter is crucial. It has two drama studios where regular student productions are held. The quality of performance is often high, so a visit is recommended, but the heating is pre-Noah, so bring a coat.

'**Cedars** is where stuff like occupational therapy gets done, though eventually all courses based here will move to the Kingsway Hospital site. Some of the facilities are in need of updating, especially the canteen.

'**Britannia Mill** is another attractive but larger building where art and design students glue and scribble. Not far from Kedleston Road, easily accessible, it's even next to a football pitch. What more do you want?

'**Jackson's Mill** is where the textile people get together to weave, and **High Peak** is the uni's latest site, situated in the north of the county and catering for courses like, well, catering and health and beauty.'

Then there's the new **Devonshire Royal Campus**, Buxton. Grade II listed, it has a dome bigger than St Paul's Cathedral's. Beneath it are an electronic library facility with Internet cafés and coffee bars.

SUBJECT AREAS (%)

Creative Arts
Health Subjects
Humanities | Education | Combined
Media 0.3%
Biological Sciences
19 | 5 | 23
2 | 1
7
14
6
Languages
7 | 1 | 5 | 7 | 3
Physical Sciences
Business
Maths & Computer
Social Studies incl. Law | Building/ Architecture | Engineering/ Technology

> *Derby's operation is about open access and the kind of educational intervention that will translate degrees into careers. The union, meanwhile, provides the anaesthetic. It's a workable collaboration.*

mature and part-time student population and many from so-called 'low-participation neighbourhoods', students from families to whom university is a new experience. Though this has also resulted in a high drop-out rate, it's now apparently under control: many who come here are focused on what they are about. Theirs is a friendly educational community to which mature applicants are particularly welcome. Many undergraduates are over 21 at inception.

FEES, BURSARIES

UK & EU Fees:, 2007 £3,070. A high proportion of Derby students are eligible for bursaries. There's a sliding scale bursary for those eligible for the HE Maintenance Grant, depending on parental income. Also, if you're from Derby, or your immediate family has a DE postcode you'll get an extra bursary of £300. Again, if you come from one of the 53 local schools and colleges in Derby's Compact Scheme, there's another £400.

STUDENT PROFILE

Their open access policy has attracted a large

ACADEMIA & JOBS

Derby's schools are Art, Design & Technology; Business, Computing & Law; Education, Health & Sciences; and University of Derby, Buxton.

The academic bedrock is Education. Education and Health together find nearly a quarter of their graduates jobs. Education-wise, we're talking primary school teachers (around 4% of the total output of Derby graduates) and educational assistants, a handful of higher education lecturers and secondary school teachers.

The single largest sector within Health is

WHERE DERBY GRADUATES END UP

Health & Social Work: 15%; Education: 9%; Wholesale/Retail: 13%; Manufacturing: 11%; Financial Activities: 8%; Public Administration, Civil Service & Defence: 9%; Hotel/Restaurant: 5%; Transport & Communications (including Telecommunications): 5%; Construction: 2%; Personnel: 4%; Computer: 4%; Business & Management: 2%; Accountancy: 0.5%; Media (including Film): 1%; Legal 1%; Publishing: 2%; Advertising: 1%; Artistic/Literary: 1%.

Approximate 'graduate track' employed **60%**

ACADEMIC EXCELLENCE

TEACHING:
(Rated Excellent or 17+ out of 24)

Geology	**Excellent**
Pharmacy	24
Educ, Biology, Subjects Allied to Medicine, Business, Theology	22
American Studies, Tourism, Maths/Computing	21
Art & Design, Psychology	20
Constr Mgt/Architec Tech, History of Art, Electrical & Electronic Eng, Nursing	19
Modern Languages, Sociology, Drama, Dance & Cinematics.	18

RESEARCH:
Top grades 5/5* **None**

Derby's BSc in Occupational Therapy, recognised by the College of Occupational Health and the Health Professions Council, which accounts for 4% of the uni's graduate output into employment, and around 7% of the national market. It scored 22 points at assessment.

Nurses – mainly non-hospital – account for around 3% of the health provision. Then there's a Diagnostic Radiography degree, also a cert for employment, and many a pathologist comes off their biological/forensic science provision. Note, too, they scored full marks (24 points) for Pharmacy at the teaching assessments.

Derby also do their bit in the natural health department. It's is a big growth area, seeding careers in complementary therapy practices, acupuncture, reflexology, aromatherapy, health promotion and jobs in natural health retail outlets with their BA Complementary Therapies and Healing Arts degrees. They also have BA Acupuncture.

Pointing up an approach which is quite Derby's own, an attitude or philosophy that finds expression in the pastoral and mediation aspects of other courses, are Applied Community & Youth Studies, Applied Social Care, Health & Community Studies, and Applied Social Work. The number of graduates into youth welfare, community and social work from Derby suggests the sense of this.

They do well, too, in arts management, with good combinations, such as Business Management & Theatre Studies. Also BA Theatre Arts and a host of other media degrees, Broadcast Media, Film & TV, etc. Figures indicate that their degrees in sound production – BSc Music Technology & Audio Systems Design and BSc Multimedia Technology and Music Production (entry 160-180 points, teaching inspection 19) – are sound value for employment.

The Business Psychology and Creative Writing combinations (the former with such as TV, Marketing, Sociology, etc) score in areas such as advertising. Graphic artists, designers and illustrators proliferate (see also the Architectural Design degrees), and Derby's BA Textile Design and Fashion Studies degrees – yours for 160 points (teaching Inspection 20) – also lead to jobs.

Systems analysts find work out of the computer side. There are new degrees, BSc Computing and BSc Computer Games Programming, and a whole host of Computer Information Systems combinations..

On the business side, employment-wise, sales managers and personnel officers seem to proliferate, the latter recommending the vocational validity of BA Human Resource Management. There are also well-trod pathways into catering and tourism, and transport planning and distribution, retail management and accommodation management.

SOCIAL SCENE

STUDENTS' UNION SUB Bar is the centre of ents at Kedleston Road, but most ents are in town: *Bed @* **Blu Bamboo** on Mondays, *Bombshell @* **Firstfloor** on Tuesdays, *Spank @* **Zanzibar** on Wednesdays, *Jelly Baby @* **Blu Bamboo** on Thursdays. They host 2 balls each year, the *Snowball* in January and the *May Ball* in May, where we take over the University and have a host of acts and entertainment, catering for 1,000s of students.

The SUB bar opened in April 2006, and the Union has just moved to brand new, open plan offices. A retail shop opened at Markeaton Street Campus, also in April 2007.

Currently they have 29 societies, ranging from circus and street performers, break dancing to the radio and LGBT. among the 21 sports clubs football and rugby are most popular, but tae kwon do and basketball compel too.

Dusted is the student magazine, largely put together by students from the Creative Writing Society. There's also D:One, the radio station.

Said a Union wallah: 'We have had a 100% increase in membership to sports clubs and societies for this year as well as having an abundance of involvement in our student media. However, our students continue to slightly non engaging when it comes to NUS and their campaigns, but we are working on that!

SPORT Not a serious contender in the national uni league – they came 111th in the BUSA team sports last year. On-site facilities, a gymnasium and pitches. American Football and martial arts, as well as rugby and cricket, are at the forefront, while support is growing for Ultimate Frisbee.

WHAT IT'S REALLY LIKE

UNIVERSITY:	
Social Life	★★★
Campus scene	**Friendly mix, good ents**
Student Union services	**Good**
Politics	**Interested, but 'non-engaging'**
Sport	**21 clubs.**
National team position	**111th**
Sport facilities	**Poor**
Arts opportunities	**OK drama**
Student magazine	**Dusted**
Newsletter	**The Word**
Student radio	**D:One**
Nightclub	**None: town nights**
Bars	**UDSU Bar, The Lonsdale**
Union ents	**Rock, hiphop, cheese & big balls**
Union societies	**29**
Most active societies	**D:One, LGBT**
Parking	**Poor**
CITY:	
Entertainment	★★★
Scene	**Small, friendly, pub rock/indie**
Town/gown relations	**Good**
Risk of violence	**Low**
Cost of living	**Average**
Student concessions	**Good**
Survival + 2 nights out	**£70 pw**
Part-time work campus/town	**Excellent**

TOWN Derby is nicely poised between 'friendly town' and 'sprawling metropolis'. There are plenty of shops that sell all necessities for the modern undergraduate (HMV, Sainsbury's, Waterstone's, Next, McDonald's), all within a neat and tidy shopping precinct. An increasing number offer student discounts.

Asam Rashid Ali says: "There are many student-friendly bars in Derby that are safe, fun and not so expensive.' There's also a large variety of pubs, all of which are worth at least one visit, plus the **Derby Playhouse** (with which the SU secure good discounts) three cinemas, two of which are multiplexes and require a short trip by taxi. The third is at the Green Lane campus (the **Metro**) and dispenses arthouse fare.

PILLOW TALK

Halls with flats, lodges, and houses are of a good standard at various locations around the city; none is catered; 50% are en suite (all rooms at Peak Court are en suite). All the halls are wired up so

AT A GLANCE

ACADEMIC FILE:	
Subjects assessed	**31**
Excellent	**61%**
Typical entry requirements	**218 points**
Application acceptance rate	**19%**
Student-staff ratio	**23:1**
First/2:1 degree pass rate	**47%**
ACCOMMODATION FILE:	
Guarantee to freshers	**100% in Derby**
Style	**Halls & houses**
Catered	**None**
En-suite	**50%**
Approx price pw	**£67**
Town rent pw	**£39-£69**

you can subscribe to telephone and free internet use. Freshers are guaranteed accommodation if their applications are received by August 31.

GETTING THERE

☞ By road: Kedleston Road campus is just off the A38, the main southwest/northeast thoroughfare which goes south to Exeter and meets the M1 at Junction 28. M1/J25 for access from the east, A6 from the southeast (Loughborough way).
☞ By rail: rail links with Derby are easy. London is two hours away.

UNIVERSITY OF DUNDEE

The University of Dundee
2 Airlie Place
Dundee DD1 4HN

TEL 01382 344160
FAX 01382 348150
EMAIL srs@dundee.ac.uk
WEB www.dundee.ac.uk

Dundee Students' Association
Airlie Place
Dundee DD1 4HP

TEL 01382 386060
FAX 01382 227124
EMAIL dusa@dundee.ac.uk
WEB www.dusa.dundee.ac.uk

VAG VIEW

*F*ounded in 1883 as University College Dundee, seven years later it became part of the St Andrews Uni and remained so until it gained independence in 1967. Today, Dundee is a traditional, premier-league university, but unusually relaxed and friendly. It has a history, but isn't steeped in it. Nor does it feel bound by tradition to repeat itself.

CAMPUS

'Dundee lies on the East Coast of Northern Scotland, a couple of hours away from Glasgow, Edinburgh and Aberdeen,' writes Sameen Farouk. 'Next door is St. Andrews. Dundee is one of a handful of genuine get-away-from-it-all universities. The scenery up here is breathtaking.

'The main campus, with compact teaching facilities, IT centre, the main libraries, the art college, sports facilities, the union, the dental hospital, John Smith Bookshop, Bonar Hall, the famous Wellcome Trust building (all within 5 mins walk of each other), is located on the edge of the town centre. It is safe, clean and increasingly accessible to the disabled community.

'The medical campus is located in the town's main hospital, Ninewells. Other sites, the nursing college (Kirkaldy in Fife, 35 miles from Dundee) and Northern College – the Faculty of Education & Social Work (Gardyne Road) are a little further out.'

FEES, BURSARIES

Fees for students from the rest of the UK: £1,700 p.a. (Medicine: £2,700).

STUDENT PROFILE

'Without being steeped in outmoded tradition,' writes Hannah Hamilton, 'the university retains a strong self-image, and the students form a very real community around the central core of campus.'

UNIVERSITY/STUDENT PROFILE	
University since	**1967**
Situation/style	**City campus**
Student population	**16500**
Undergraduates	**11074**
- mature	**29%**
- non EU undergraduates	**8%**
- male/female	**38/62**
- non-traditional student intake	**25%**
-state sector intake	**91%**
- drop-out rate	**17%**
- undergraduate applications	**Down 3%**

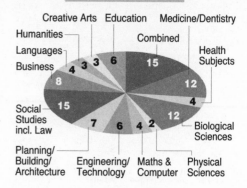

SUBJECT AREAS (%)

Creative Arts, Education, Medicine/Dentistry, Humanities, Combined, Languages, Health Subjects, Business — 4, 3, 3, 6, 15, 8, 12, Social Studies incl. Law — 15, 4, 7, 6, 4, 2, 12, Biological Sciences, Planning/Building/Architecture, Engineering/Technology, Maths & Computer, Physical Sciences

STUDENT POPULATION

Postgraduates 32%
Female Undergraduates 42%
Total students 16,500
Male Undergraduates 25%
Female Undergraduates 1%

Dundee attracts students from all walks of life and from all areas. The inevitable scattering of public school types joins a healthy dose of students from Ireland and a very strong international community.

'Dundee could never be criticised for being a quaint English retreat,' agrees Sameen. 'The university recruits internationally and has strong Arab, Chinese, Malaysian, Korean and Hispanic communities. There is also a substantial South-Asian population. The local communities are also targeted keenly, and there is a growing population of mature students.'

Dundee meets its Government benchmark for student intake from the four lower socio-economic groups and far exceeds the requirement from so-called 'low participation neighbourhoods', making it one of the elite in the context of our Government's aspirations in higher education. What's more, its overall teacher-to-student ratio of 16:1 is healthy and this is no new university bent on teaching pop music; it is a classless university for the professions: medicine, dentistry, nursing, architecture, finance, and law. Dundee sends more graduates into the professions than any other university in Scotland.

ACADEMIA & JOBS

The academic structure changed from seven faculties to four colleges in February 2006: College of Art & Design, Architecture, Engineering & Physical Science; College of Arts & Social Sciences; College of Life Sciences; College of Medicine, Dentistry and Nursing.

'I suppose, if you are a Scot, and you want to study medicine,' said a sixth-form careers mistress, 'Edinburgh would have to be high on the list, but people have had very good experiences of Dundee.'

In fact, in the assessments, Dundee achieved an Excellent rating in Medicine, where Edinburgh achieved only a Highly Satisfactory, and in 1998 they won the prestigious Queen's Anniversary Prize for their pioneering use of keyhole surgery, a success which directs interest to the extraordinary levels of research going on here. Known the world over for cancer research, a radical new approach to cancer treatment has resulted from the merger of the research teams of pioneering keyhole surgeon Professor Sir Alfred Cuschieri and Professor David Lane, who discovered 'the guardian angel of the cell', the p53 gene. The idea is to deliver gene therapy direct to tumours via keyhole surgery, using a specially developed 'poison umbrella' needle.

The degree in Medicine is 5/6-year MBChB. Integrated med school and hospital. Course problem/community-based, i.e. clinical experience from Year 1. Entry AA, 360 points (chem. + 1 science) and UKCAT; AAABB at Highers, plus GCSE (or Standard Grade) Biology. Teaching inspection, Excellent. Research Grade 5*. For dentists it's the 5/6-year BDS. Entry AAA. Teaching inspection, Highly Satisfactory. Research Grade 5.

Dundee also produces psychologists in number. Teaching inspection, Excellent.

What grabs the visitor is the real sense of excitement around here – they leapt eleven places nationally in the research assessments, with medical and biological research achieving the highest accolades. An international survey by *The Scientist* named Dundee as the best UK scientific institution in which to work. Dario Alessi, Professor of Life Sciences, said: 'The advantage of Dundee is that it's very small. Communication in science is so important.' He has access to 500 scientists within two minutes of his lab. 'You can't do these sort of things in London or Oxford.' Said Roland Wolf,

Traditionally a uni for the professions. And now, Dundee-chic! Are we to believe it? From Medicine to Art to pure hedonism, it seems that Dundee has it all.

director of biomedical research: 'You have this underlying feeling that important things are going to happen,' and the feeling is not confined to Medicine.

More recently, Dundee established Scotland's first centre for Interdisciplinary Gender Research at the Mary Ann Baxter Centre.

Art & Design also demands our attention: Textile Design (the city's industrial inheritance) took an Excellent in the undergraduate assessments; companies like Nike and Calvin Kline die for Dundee graduates; the uni is among the leaders for supplying graduates to architecture; and although the faculty fell from Grade 5 to 4 in the research assessments, there is a sense, day-to-day, that the art/design students add vigour and momentum to what is going on in the city.

Besides the reputation of BArch (Architecture), they're in the Top 10 for town planning. On theme, the city of Dundee has reinvented itself, and the uni is, geographically and culturally, at the very heart of its new identity. Bang in the middle of the city's new cultural quarter with its pubs, clubs and gallery shops, the Art/Design College, through its reputation in the fashion and design industries, provides a global dimension to 'Dundee-chic'.

A £9-million, Lottery-funded collaboration

ACADEMIC EXCELLENCE

TEACHING:
(Rated Excellent, Highly Satis. or 17+ out of 24)

Graphic & Textile Design, **Excellent**
Finance & Accounting, Medicine, Cellular & Molecular Biology, Organismal Biology, English, Psychology.

Civil Engineering, Physics, **Highly Satis.**
Environmental Science, Hospitality Studies, Maths & Statistics, History, Law, Politics, Social Work, Fine Art, Dentistry.

Planning & Landscape **21**

RESEARCH:
Clinical Laboratory Sciences, **Grade 5***
Biological Sciences
Hospital-based Clinical Subjects, **Grade 5**
Clinical Dentistry, Applied Maths, Civil Eng, Law, History

WHERE DUNDEE GRADUATES END UP

Health & Social Work: 28%; Education: 7%; Wholesale/Retail: 9%; Manufacturing: 7%; Financial Activities: 6%; Public Administration, Civil Service & Defence: 8%; Hotel/Restaurant: 5%; Transport & Communications (including Telecommunications): 3%; Construction: 3%; Agriculture: 1%; Personnel: 2%; Computer: 1%; Accountancy: 4%; Media (including Film): 1%; Legal 2%; Architecture: 5%; Artistic/Literary: 3%.

Approximate 'graduate track' employed **72%**

between uni and city has resulted in **Dundee Contemporary Arts**, a centre for visual arts with the university's **Visual Research Centre** at its hub, an art laboratory equipped with cutting edge facilities for producing design prototypes, videos, prints, artists' books, etc.

Artists, designers and media types should look closely at the College. Jobs for graduates are diverse, from graphic designers and illustrators to printers, publishing production managers, set designers and jewellery designer-makers. Teaching inspection, Highly Satisfactory.

In Law, they're internationally rated for research, European law specialists and the only uni to offer both Scots and English Law. Non-Law graduates may take a 2-year full-time or 3-year part-time Senior Status Law degree here. Now a new International Water Law Research Institute is to open, it's the first of its kind in the world, and is set to train future leaders to arbitrate water conflicts.

In Education they are traditionally suppliers at primary level, but the first cohort of secondary school teachers graduated in 2005 on a new course which allows distance learning and part-time study.

Generally, teaching is traditional, tutorial-based, but support is also undertaken in an online environment, with 24/7 internet-based access to resources, timetables, lecture enhancements, assessments, assignment submission, discussion boards and collaborative working opportunities.

They claim to have been the first in Scotland to engage with an online Personal Development Planning (PDP) programme which acts to ensure a student's academic education occurs in concert with their personal and career development. Students create portfolios to illustrate their personal development, and these are being utilised for external appraisal such as for job applications.

They also have an excellent 'writing skills' programme, which comes highly recommended and is improving performance both in degree study and in finding jobs. Their graduate track employment record places them in the Top 20.

WHAT IT'S REALLY LIKE

UNIVERSITY:	
Social Life	★★★★
Campus scene	**Diverse culture**
Student Union services	**Good**
Politics	**Society-based**
Sport	**45 clubs**
National team position	**37th**
Sport facilities	**Good**
Arts opportunities	**Music, film, art excellent; drama good; dance avg**
Student magazine	**Magdalen**
Nightclubs	**Mono, Floor 5**
Bars	**Air, The Liar**
Union ents	**Full on**
Union societies	**50**
Most popular	**Lip Theatre, Islamic Society, DARE**
Parking	**Poor**
CITY:	
Entertainment	★★★★
Scene	**Scotland's sexiest**
Town/gown relations	**Average**
Risk of violence	**Low**
Cost of living	**Low**
Student concessions	**Good**
Survival + 2 nights out	**£70 pw**
Part-time work campus/town	**Excellent/Good**

SOCIAL SCENE

STUDENTS' ASSOCIATION There are 2 nightclubs: **Mono** (900 capacity), **Floor 5** (350 capacity) and 2 bars: **Air** (300 capacity) and **The Liar** (650 capacity), plus a huge games room with pool tables, games machines, and a Food on 4 catering outlet.

Ents offer *Dynamite* in Mono on Wednesday: chart anthems and classics; Thursday is *Live Lounge* - acoustic session in Air Bar: open mic and special guests; on Friday it's *Heat* in Mono: mixed chart, rock and pop classics (£2 entry); Saturday: *NOW* in Mono: indie, dance, rock and hip hop mish mash (£3 entry), and *Something for the Weekend* in Floor 5: most wanted pop and chart (free entry); on Sunday, it's *Pub Quiz* in Air (free entry). There's also a monthly *Laughter Lounge* - comedy in Air featuring artists such as Russell Howard, Rhod Gilbert and Steve Hall.

Recent DJ's were Colin Murray, Zane Lowe, Vic Galloway, Fearne Cotton (all Radio 1), Head Kandi, Bloc Party (dj set). Bands have been Cooper Temple Clause, The Kooks, Big Hand plus loads more local ones.

Media-wise, there has been something of a fall from grace, with *Student Times* replaced by a magazine, *Magdalen*, yet to find its way into the national awards or anywhere else. No radio; no TV. Suggest this is an area worth getting into.

There are some 50 societies. 'Most active,' says a union wallah, 'Lip Theatre, Islamic Society, DARE (Development and research expeditions) People and Planet. A large cross section of international students makes for very mixed campus culture. SRC and Many societies push campaigns on global warming, nuclear disarmament, etc.'

SPORT The particularly popular activities are mainstream team sports like hockey, rugby, football (not cricket), boxing and the watersports, but most sports have strong societies. Around Dundee there is also a well-established martial arts scene. The uni sporting facilities are excellent and well managed, as is the on-campus swimming pool.

TOWN Dundee, which already ranks among the world's most intelligent cities for its scientific expertise, has just been voted Scotland's sexiest city by the *Scotland on Sunday* newspaper.

'For many years Dundee has seemed to play second fiddle to Aberdeen, Glasgow and Edinburgh,' writes Michael Sheldon. 'However, if you scratch the surface of the City of the 3 J's (Jute, Jam and Journalism) you will find one of Scotland's most progressive and desirable cities.

'Tired tourist touts will tell you that it is the birthplace of *The Beano* and *The Dandy*, home to the RRS Discovery (made famous by Scott of the Antarctic), and to the **Mills Observatory** (the only full-time public observatory in the UK). And then direct you to the **Verdant Works Museum**, where the history of Dundee's textile industry is documented and non-Dundonians learn what "an ingin ene inna" means!

But this city is not stuck in the past. Recently, it has reinvented itself.

'Two unis - Abertay and Dundee - means two modern centres of entertainment. The new Abertay building (see *Abertay Uni* entry) houses two bars, a night club and a cinema. Across town at Dundee's Student Association, as it likes to be known, there are another two bars, two nightclubs, a huge pool room and regular big name DJ and comedy acts. There are also three cinemas at

AT A GLANCE	
ACADEMIC FILE:	
Subjects assessed	**27**
Excellent/Highly Satisfactory	**70%**
Typical entry requirements	**340 points**
Application acceptance rate	**15%**
Med. School acceptance rate	**10%**
Students-staff ratio	**16:1**
First/2:1 degree pass rate	**62%**
ACCOMMODATION FILE:	
Guarantee to freshers	**100%**
Style	**Halls, flats**
Catered	**None**
En suite	**87%**
Approx price range pw	**£63-£98**
City rent pw	**£40-£60**

Camperdown, Douglas and in the DCA, an Ice rink, loads of Parks and Coffee Shops.

The Perth Road and West Port areas are probably best for pubs, with establishments such as **The Speedwell Bar**, with a huge selection of whiskys, the **Art Bar** and **Tally's**, to name but few. Club-wise, there's **Fat Sams**, open seven days a week, **Underground**, which is not so much a club as a bar open till 2.30 a.m., and for something different, **The Reading Rooms**, host to acts such as Biffy Clyro and Mr. Scruff.

'The new meets the old close to the university in **The Cultural Quarter**, where lie the **Dundee Rep Theatre**, the multi-million-pound **Dundee Contemporary Arts Centre**, **The Sensations Science Centre**, a hands-on science museum for the big kid inside you. All this *and* the city's new multiple-floor shopping centres, **The Wellgate** and **The Overgate**.'

PILLOW TALK

There are five residence sites, each comprising between 30 and 90 self contained flats, all single rooms Four sites offer en-suite facilities. Not all would agree that halls were the best option: 'Personally, I found hall a bit of an expensive option.' says Sameen. However, over 1,000 new en-suite rooms opened in 2006, relatively expensive (see box above), but very nice.

GETTING THERE

☛ By road: M90, M85, A85, A972.
☛ By rail: Newcastle, 3:00; London Euston, 6:00.
☛ By air: Dundee Airport for internal flights; Edinburgh International Airport is an hour away.
☛ By coach: London, 10:05; Birmingham, 10:05; Newcastle, 6:05.

UNIVERSITY OF DURHAM

The University of Durham
Old Shire Hall
Old Elvet
Durham DH1 3HP

TEL 0191 334 6128
FAX 0191 334 6055
EMAIL admissions@durham.ac.uk
WEB www.dur.ac.uk

Durham Students' Union
Dunelm House
New Elvet
Durham DH1 3AN

TEL 0191 334 1777
FAX 0191 334 1778
EMAIL student.uniont@durham.ac.uk
WEB www.durham21.co.uk

VAG VIEW

*F*ounded in 1832, Durham is, like Oxford and Cambridge, a collegiate university, although unlike the Oxbridge colleges, Durham's are purely residential; academically, it is faculty based.

Durham offers all the advantages of the best of British universities and is demanding at entry, shamelessly going after Oxbridge rejects, delaying its selection until after those two more ancient universities have taken their pick. But they combine this policy with another, designed to net applicants from the region, particularly from among what the sector euphemistically calls non-traditional higher education heartlands, 'low participation' neighbourhoods and social classes.

Further south, in an urban regeneration area on Teesside, lies the Stockton campus, with generally lower entry requirements (though not always) to attract the 'new' university population. But the policy extends to the main Durham HQ too, so that sixthformers have got in to Durham with an AS level and a GNVQ, taken at a state school or sixthform college, with the result that the percentage of undergraduates at Durham from these non-traditional backgrounds is far greater than at Oxford or Cambridge, or indeed Bristol, and closer to Nottingham, Bath and Leeds.

CAMPUS

Durham is a small, stunningly beautiful city, 16 miles south of Newcastle. The nucleus of the medieval city, where the five Bailey colleges and the Arts and Social Sciences Departments are located, is formed by a bend of the River Wear around a rocky peninsular, dominated by the 11th-

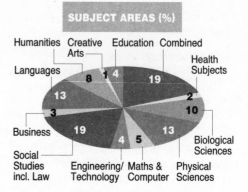

SUBJECT AREAS (%)

Humanities — 8
Creative Arts — 1
Education — 4
Combined — 19
Health Subjects — 2
Biological Sciences — 10
Physical Sciences — 13
Maths & Computer — 5
Engineering/ Technology — 4
Social Studies incl. Law — 19
Business — 19
Languages — 13
— 3

century cathedral and castle.

The other campus, officially known as The University of Durham Queen's Campus, Stockton, lies south down the A1(M), on the outskirts of Middlesbrough. There are two colleges, John Snow and George Stephenson, both self-catering. Infrastructure and resources are good, from en-suite accommodation to library and IT resource centre, lecture rooms, laboratories and student recreational facilities.

FEES, BURSARIES

UK & EU Fees 2007: £3,070 p.a. 2008 fees not yet fixed. One quarter of all home undergraduates will be eligible for a Durham Grant (dependent on parental income), which could provide up to £12,280 in non-repayable support, over and above any grants or loans from the government. Email student.support@durham.ac.uk or access www. durham.ac.uk/student.support

Sport awards (typically £100 and £300) are dependent on students' financial circumstances. In addition 30 small but highly prestigious scholarships are awarded at the end of each academic year, based on academic performance. There are also a few awards for disabled students.

STUDENT PROFILE

'Hi, I'm Alex Pharaoh and I came to Durham from

a grammar school in North Yorkshire, aware that it had a reputation of being a haven for public schoolers and Oxbridge rejects, and, yes, a lot of people here do fall into one of these categories.'

'Hi, my name's Robin Siddle and I come from sixthform college in Scarborough. I thought there'd be a lot of yuppy people there, but there are only two colleges like that – Hatfield and Castle – the other ones are, like, normal...'

Times are changing. 'In what is almost a knee-jerk against Rah-culture,' writes Rik Fisher, 'there is more of an effort made to express personal style and individuality.'

ACADEMIA & JOBS

Physics, psychology, biosciences, maths, philosophy, archaeology, theology, English, history, chemistry, law (candidates must sit the National Admissions Test for Law) – these topped the teaching and research assessments. Up there with the best, 86% of its assessments are Excellent, and in the last research exercise, they leapt from 18th to 12th place nationwide. Languages are an integral part of their graduate profile.

> *'If clubbing is your thing, don't come to Durham. No raves, relatively few drugs; booze is the thing, college bops and black-tie formal dinners. Pick your college carefully. Within a couple of days you'll have learned your college songs and rituals.'*

The medical faculty with neighbours Newcastle is primarily aimed at mature students, with a special Pre-medical programme for applicants without the necessary scientific background for Stage 1 entry. The actual medical course (MBBS) has two years at Stockton before transfer to Newcastle, where in years 3, 4 and 5, students will be assigned a regional clinical unit. Requirements for the degree are AAB + UKCAT, including 2 A levels, and to include chemistry or biology at A level or AS level. They also like one non-science subject at A or AS. Acceptance rates are far higher to get on the Pre-Med than on the degree.

Education is currently the single largest area of graduate employment, primary and secondary – 23 points at the teaching assessments, research assessment Grade 5.

This is a uni with great contacts in the City. In Accountancy, they are one of the three big graduate providers, along with Birmingham and Warwick. They have first-class links with the major firms. Nine per cent of their graduates go into the sector, and overall Durham supplies around 4% of the national quota to it. The dedicated Accountancy

Female Undergraduates — 40%

Postgraduates 16%

STUDENT POPULATION

Total students 15,314

Male Undergraduates 36%

Female Undergraduates 8%

degree is Accounting & Finance at Stockton, with a relatively soft entry requirement of around 280 points. But at Durham, Economics is the most popular route in. There are all kinds of ways you can take it - as BA Hons, as major/minor, as BA Combined Hons or as a component of the BSc Natural Sciences degree. Among the language combinations is Economics with Arabic.

Natural Sciences, with subject combinations (Business, Economics, Maths, etc), is the second most popular way in. Again, there is a whole range of language possibilities which, together with the high-flyer, employer friendly Durham graduate profile, will warm Accountancy firms to the potential in their overseas business. Teaching inspection: Economics 24 points, Maths 21. Research: Applied Maths Grade 5*, Pure Maths Grade 5.

They are big, too, in tax consultancy, banking and merchant banking. Some 60% of graduates who become investment/merchant bankers

UNIVERSITY/STUDENT PROFILE	
University since	**1832**
Situation/style	**City collegiate**
Student population	**15314**
Undergraduates	**11660**
- mature	**7%**
- non-EU undergraduates	**6%**
- male/female	**48/52**
- non-traditional student intake	**16%**
- state school intake	**63%**
- drop-out rate	**5%**
- undergraduate applications	**Up 6%**

nationally each year come into the sector via Economics or Business courses. One third of graduates going into merchant banking from Durham carry a language with them. So you can begin to see the importance of this part of the Durham curriculum.

Defence is another employment strength, through Engineering & Technology, Physical Sciences, Social Sciences, Biological Sciences and Languages again. In engineering, there's BEng General Engineering, the variety coming for some after a 2-year general course in the MEng degrees: Aeronautics, Civil, Electronic (+ Systems Eng), Manufacturing, Mechanical, etc.

Physics, Physics with Astronomy, etc, are very strong. They took full marks in the assessments and an international Grade 5 for research. In the Institute of Computational Cosmology there's now a £1.4-million supercomputer, capable of making ten billion calculations a second and 'recreating the entire evolution of the universe'. Biosciences did similarly well – look at the 4-year BSc Biomedical Sciences at Stockton Campus, too.

Contacts with the military are clearly good, for

graduates come from a range of disciplines. Possibly it isn't a particular course so much as the Durham character that the forces are after.

Politics has an interesting Middle East bias in three degrees, and perhaps we should not be surprised to find the uni in the business of supplying to the British Intelligence Services.

Other social studies and languages (full marks and 22 points at the assessments respectively) find Durham graduates jobs in travel and tourism, as charity officers, market researchers, media and government researchers.

Future environmental officers graduate in physical sciences, biological sciences and in Agriculture. In Durham a steady flow of graduates go into the sector, which suggests a close look, among other courses, at MSci or BSc Geological and Geophysical Sciences, Ecology (optional placement), Environmental Geoscience, Earth Sciences, Geography (optional European Studies). Again, the Natural Sciences BSc combo features Earth Sciences and is very popular. Durham farmers come out of biological sciences, their degrees in Plant Science, Zoology, Ecology, etc.

Editors and other media appointments come out of languages, social sciences (which includes Psychology), physical sciences, maths and humanities. Student media (newspaper and radio) are part of the mix.

Said Alex Pharaoh. 'From what I've heard, and from what I've seen when my friends have left, graduating from this university gives a big head start in the fight for a career.'

DURHAM COLLEGES

The smaller collegiate system promotes involvement, sporting rivalries and the like. Each college has its own distinct identity.

The Durham college stereotype is described in the rivalry between the so-called **Bailey** colleges (John's, Chad's, Cuth's, University and Hatfield), situated in the Bailey area of the medieval city, and the **Hill** colleges (Trev's, Van Mildert, Mary's, Collingwood, Grey's and Aiden's), situated southwest of the Bailey. Sophie Vokes-Dudgeon reports: 'Pick your college carefully. Within a couple of days you'll have learned your college songs and rituals, and feel a strange affiliation with this set of buildings, which will manifest itself loudly on many a river bank or touch line throughout your life as a Durham student. The stereotypical image we have is of Rahs on the Bailey and Plebs on the Hill. And then there's St Hild & St Bede, the biggest college, a minute or two further out, perhaps with a more diverse mix than some of the others. Don't go entirely by the stereotypes though; be sure to visit

'The Hill colleges are more like a campus, all a drunken stagger from one another. Next to the Science site, computers and library too, but what you gain in convenience you lack in history and surroundings. The Bailey colleges are also near enough for a bar crawl, and the cobbled streets and cathedral backdrop make it far more aesthetically pleasing. Chad's and John's bars are barely big enough to swing a cat, however, and you may be more likely to stumble upon Evensong than a pint of lager in St John's. Hild Bede bar resembles an airport lounge, but the tow path leads to nightclub **Klute**?

'Colleges also differ in facilities. Hild Bede has a newish multigym, an abundance of tennis courts, squash courts, gyms, and beautiful if basic accommodation. Castle, on the other hand, offers third years the chance to live in a castle, while Collingwood gives you en-suite shower rooms and kettles. The choice is yours!'

'Trevs is very representative of the whole student body,' writes Eleanor. 'It is also friendly and has strong college spirit. There are loads of social events, two balls a year and one of the larger, and more tasteful bars. We are fairly standard when compared to other colleges. Our accommodation is decent, not as nice as Collingwood, however. Bailey accommodation tends to be the worst, as it is the oldest and they also room some students far from the main building, Cuth's is worst for this. Hill Colleges have purpose built accommodation blocks. John's is very religious, Van Mildert is good for music opportunities, Cuth's is famed for having a bar with proper opening hours!'

Says Alex: 'My college, Collingwood, is known as one of the best. We have the most modern accommodation, more en-suite rooms, more IT networked rooms, less room sharing, better central facilities, such as bar and gym, and allegedly, better food than others. We are one of the newest colleges, and have less tradition than those on the Bailey, which can be seen as a good or bad thing. We have a great social calendar – bar theme nights, "megaformal" dinners, bops, trips, sporting events and the legendary Summer Ball.'

From October, 2006, applicants have been able to opt for a new Durham-based college, the first for more than 30 years, named after the Northumberland-born writer, pioneer of women's education and social reformer, Josephine Butler. The 400 rooms are en suite and self-catering - 6 to a flat - on the southern edge of the city, close to the Science Site and main University Library. Special student rate buses are frequent. There's a bar, a launderette, an IT Suite, a music practice room, a large hall, a variety of smaller rooms available for events, and special provision for the disabled, especially students with special dietary requirements.

Flats are available from October to June, including the Christmas and Easter vacations.

SOCIAL SCENE

STUDENTS' UNION No raves, relatively few drugs; booze is the thing, college bops and black-tie formal dinners. Less formal are the discos and gigs at **Dunelm House**, the Students' Union building. 'The union puts on a range of ents with big name DJs common, but there is a noticeable lack of big bands,' writes Alex. 'Durham can't seem to attract them.'

The SU building and main bar, Kingsgate, have had a facelift, and Pitstop, a shop, has opened at the entrance to the building. **Kingsgate** is the union bar with balcony overlooking the river. Food is served in the nearby **Riverside Café** until 11 pm (waitress service). Venues remain **Vane Tempest Hall** and the **Margot Fonteyn Ballroom**, where they host *Planet of Sound*, the regular Friday club night - a capacity sell-out. Wednesday Night one-offs also highly popular, such as Indie night *I Can't Believe It's Not Cheese* and *Back2School*.

Student media is first class, with *Palatinate* and Purple FM proving to be a worthy claw sharpener for the real thing. The union is active on welfare (Advice Centre, Nightline, etc) and politics extend into high profile – national media – fees campaign.

In student politics, Labour, Conservative and LibDem socs are all active, as well as People &

WHERE DURHAM GRADUATES END UP

Health & Social Work: 6%; Education: 16%; Wholesale/Retail: 6%; Manufacturing: 7%; Financial Activities: 12%; Public Administration, Civil Service & Defence: 11%; Hotel/Restaurant: 3%; Transport & Communications (including Telecommunications): 3%; Construction: 1%; Personnel: 1%; Computer: 4%; Business & Management: 4%; Accountancy: 9%; Media (including Film): 1.5%; Legal 2%; Publishing: 2%; Advertising: 1%; Sport: 1%.

Approximate 'graduate track' employed **72%**

WHAT IT'S REALLY LIKE

UNIVERSITY:

Social Life	★★★★
Campus scene	**Collegiate fun 'n' games; opportunity to do more**
Student Union services	**Good**
Politics	**Active**
Sport	**Key; 46 clubs**
National team position	**8th**
Sport facilities	**Good**
Arts opportunities	**Good**
Student newspaper	**Palatinate**
Student radio	**Purple Radio**
Nightclub	**Fonteyn Ballroom**
Bars	**Kingsgate, Vane Tempest, Riverside Café**
Union ents	**Planet of Sound + dance & cheese**
Union societies	**124**
Most prominent socs.	**Big Band, Durham Revue, Ballads**
Parking	**Poor**

CITY:

Entertainment	★★★
Scene	**Historic city, cheesy clubs, good pubs**
Town/gown relations	**Poor**
Risk of violence	**Low-avg.**
Cost of living	**High**
Student concessions	**Good**
Survival + 2 nights out	**£60-£150 pw**
Part-time work campus/town	**Average**

They have a university security patrol that goes round the city every night. They also have a night-bus which picks up all around town and drops off at all the colleges.

If clubbing is your thing, don't come to Durham. Writes Rick Fisher: 'Some just can't get enough of the dated eighties at **Klute** or the poppy pap at **DH1**, but as my mother is fond of telling me: consuming a generous helping of cheese before bedtime can be the stuff of nightmares.' But as Robin Siddell explains, there are alternatives: 'City nightlife has improved dramatically with the opening of many new bars and bar/clubs. Upstairs at *Cathedrals* (**the Loft**) on a Tuesday a live band plays till late. The beer is cheap and the atmosphere good, not hot and sweaty like other club venues. There's also a new, modern bar/nightclub overlooking the river, called **Chase**.

'Now, too, there's the late licensed bar/club **Walkabout**, one of the Australian sports-bar chain, probably the best thing to hit Durham in my three years here. It's open during the day, serves food such as crocodile and kangaroo, and has hundreds of TVs for worldwide sport. In the evening a dance floor and DJ appear; the beer again is cheap. The only downside is that **Walkabout** replaced an old cinema, leaving us only one very small and busy Imax screen at the **Gala Theatre**.

'The old **DH1** nightclub has been revamped recently and is a little less sweaty, but, as a result, the prices have shot up and seem never to stop shooting up, so fewer students are willing to queue and the feeling is that it's not as good as it once was.

'**Klute** is where all the rugby boys go and it's like sardines in a can, though you can get a pass

Planet and Fight Racism, Fight Imperialism. The Union has an active policy of independence from all political parties. Most debate sadly restricted to issues directly affecting Durham students.

Others of their 124 socieites include Pagan Witches, Bellydancers, Medieval Warmongerers and the Chemistry Society.

Town When term begins, students herd in and outnumber locals. In the past it has proved to be a recipe for disaster. Writes Eleanor: 'Locals are generally friendly, and students are normally safe. Weekends are more dangerous, however, as country locals invade and they are more inclined to indulge in the favourite sport of student bashing.'

Says Alex, 'There is some tension. Trouble is easily avoided if you shun the pink shirt/bodywarmer/scarf, and don't talk in a loud southern accent on your mobile phone at 3 am, drunk, in the middle of the road, wearing a DJ.'

AT A GLANCE

ACADEMIC FILE:

Subjects assessed	**36**
Excellent	**86%**
Typical entry points	**454**
Application acceptance rate	**14%**
Students-staff ratio	**21:1**
First/2:1 degree pass rate	**75%**

ACCOMMODATION FILE:

Guarantee to freshers	**100%**
Style	**Halls, Durham; flats, Stockton**
Catered	**80%**
En suite	**26% Durham; 100% Queen's**
Full board pwx29.3: Durham	**£134**
Self-catered pwx38.3: Durham	**£96**
Self-catered pwx32: Stockton	**£88**
Durham City rent pw	**£65**

and drink cocktails in fish bowls downstairs.

'A Wetherspoons also just opened. **Varsity**, again fairly new, is possibly the best bar in town – high up on the river bank with a large balcony Then there's the boat, a buoyant after-club venue, small dance floor and an even smaller bar, but it's a good laugh.'

SPORT Durham is very sporty, they came 5th last year, and the beautiful river is a temptress to hundreds of novice rowers. Durham finished 5th in the BUSA rankings last year, and has some nationally recognised student societies (for example, Durham University Caving Association).

Academic concessions for sporty types are apparent, though not admitted. High standards are encouraged by inter-college rivalry, Castle vrs Hatfield (rugby), Castle vrs Hild Bede (rowing). College rowing crews are often better than other university crews. Sixty acres of playing fields are maintained to first-class standard.

GETTING THERE
☞ By road: A1/J6. Well served by coaches.
☞ By rail: King's Cross, 3:00; Edinburgh, 1:00.
☞ By air: Newcastle, Teesside Airports (25m).
☞ By coach: London, 5:30; Birmingham, 4:00.

UNIVERSITY OF EAST ANGLIA

The University of East Anglia
Earlham Road
Norwich NR4 7TJ

TEL 01603 591515
FAX 01603 591523
EMAIL admissions@uea.ac.uk
WEB www.uea.ac.uk

Union of University of East Anglia Students
Union House
Norwich NR4 7TJ

TEL 01603 593272
FAX 01603 250144
EMAIL su.comms@uea.ac.uk
WEB www.stu.uea.ac.uk

VAG VIEW

Set apart in rural Norfolk, this excellent university was founded in the 1960s and reaches out to the world with innovation and flair. It is among the best on virtually any grounds you care to mention, and perhaps because they are so cut off from the world, the student body seems more aware, even more wise, than most.

CAMPUS
UEA campus is 15 minutes by road from the centre of Norwich, a city less than fifteen miles away from the Norfolk Broads, an area of outstanding beauty and tranquillity. The campus, built on a 320-acre, sometime golf course, has won awards for its architecture – Denys Lasdun's ziggurats (glass-fronted buildings, tiered upwards like garden terraces after the ancient tiered mounds of Babylonia) continue to amaze, but, as student Daniel Trelfer declares, self-containment isn't to everyone's taste: 'Everything you need is on campus, but while some people are happy to live for twelve weeks inside a square quarter mile, others go insane and have to run to town to feel free again.'

FEES, BURSARIES
UK & EU Fees 2007: £3,070 p.a. Inflationary increase along guidelines is expected in 2008. Sliding-scale bursaries for students in receipt of HE

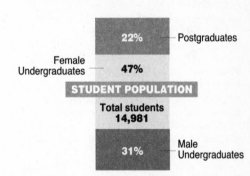

22% — Postgraduates
Female Undergraduates — 47%
STUDENT POPULATION
Total students
14,981
31% — Male Undergraduates

Maintenance Grant, according to parental income. There are awards for sport and music, and a range of scholarships between £500 and £4,000 p.a. for academic performance. See www.uea.ac.uk/ admissions/ueascholarships

STUDENT PROFILE
UEA has a well-balanced student population for a pukka uni, with close on 90% from state schools and a 21% take from non-traditional uni backgrounds. There is a large mature intake (45%)

UNIVERSITY/STUDENT PROFILE	
University since	**1964**
Situation/style	**Edge of city campus**
Student population	**14981**
Undergraduates	**11629**
- mature	**45%**
- non EU undergraduates	**6%**
- male/female	**40/60**
- non-traditional student intake	**23%**
- state school intake	**88%**
- drop-out rate	**13%**
- undergraduate applications	**Up 5%**

nationally, 28% came from Language departments, while 35% studied in Creative Arts or Humanities departments. UEA enjoys particular success in the literary firmament. There are twice-yearly literary festivals, a writer in residence, and it is here that Sir Malcolm Bradbury set the literary firmament alight with his creative writing school, out of which came Ian McEwan and Kazuo Ishiguro, among others. Look at English or American Literature with Creative Writing (also Scriptwriting & Performance). There is also a fine reputation for the 4-year American Studies, which scored full marks in the assessments. Campus is home to the Arthur Miller Centre for American Studies.

Arts graduates are given a ringing endorsement

and a preponderance of females (60%, owing to the nursing degrees). The uni is constantly beset with criticisms about campus isolation and the dire effects of this upon its student clientele, but we see a pretty sharp focus on the business in hand, whether it's academic or extra-curricular, and a happy and fulfilled student body, though its drop-out rate is not as low as some.

ACADEMIA & JOBS

UEA is made up of 23 academic departments known as Schools of Study, these are grouped into the Faculties of Arts & Humanities, Social Sciences, Science and the Institute of Health. New courses introduced this year include a BA Social Work, an academic and professional qualification that will enable graduates to become registered social workers.

Employment-wise there are a few question marks. It's difficult for unis that specialise in humanities and languages to find the ideal job quickly for their graduates. Graduates have to start somewhere, and many who start as clerks no doubt find success in the end, but it has to be said that UEA does turn out a lot of them.

However, a recent survey of UEA's graduates showed that after 3 years (as opposed to 6 months, when these things usually get measured), 81% had not experienced unemployment and 78% were in full-time employment, which must say something.

In point of fact, UEA looks after its humanities graduates well with jobs such as charity officer, museum archivist/curator, and there is a clear, if relatively limited, vocational springboard for Languages graduates via their BA Interpreting & Translating with Double Hons Languages – a 4-year degree. Also, the spread of graduate interest in the publishing industry is wide – it's a regular UEA niche, and a preponderance of those who get into the industry do come from the Languages dept.

Of 36 graduate authors that emerged

ACADEMIC EXCELLENCE	
TEACHING:	
(Rated Excellent or 17+ out of 24)	
Law, Applied Social Work, Environmental Sciences, Developmental Studies.	**Excellent**
Politics, American Studies Philosophy	**24**
Economics, Media Studies	**23**
Maths, Business, Subjects Allied to Medicine	
History of Art, Architecture & Design, Molecular Biosciences, Organismal Biosciences	**22**
Drama, Dance & Cinematics	**21**
Sociology	**20**
Modern Langs & Linguistics, Electric & Electronic Engineering	**19**
Nursing	**18**
RESEARCH:	
Top grades 5/5*/6*	
Environmental Sciences, Media Studies	**Grade 6***
History	**Grade 5***
Biol. Sciences, Chemistry, Pure Maths, Law, Social Work, English, History of Art, Philosophy	**Grade 5**

by UEA's MA in creative entrepreneurship (new this year), which supports artists, writers and musicians in practical business skills.

They have an excellent record of employment in medicine and health-related fields. Its environmental science graduates are also highly prized Many UEA graduates go on to work in law, public sector services and administration, banking and finance, marketing and the media. They have the only School of Social Work consistently top-rated in every Research Assessment Exercise, and teacher training receives glowing OFSTED reports.

In health, Physiotherapy is particularly productive of jobs and directs attention to an expanding aspect of UEA's curriculum – see Midwifery, Nursing (Adult, Children, Learning Disability, Mental Health), Occupational Therapy, and the new programme in Medicine.

MBBS Medicine with a Foundation Year was recently introduced to widen participation in Medicine from under-represented groups.

Theory and practice is integrated throughout in the 5-year MB BS, and clinical experience is yours from the outset, thanks to extensive collaboration with close-to-campus Norfolk & Norwich University Hospital. Entry AAB + UKCAT, including Grade A in Biology. 5 A/Bs in GCSE including Maths and English. Entry from 'approved access courses' is also encouraged, so consult the university.

UEA is also, as it happens, home to the Wellcome Unit for the History of Medicine.

Community youth workers and social workers also come out of this uni in abundance, and UEA are world leaders in research in this area. Naturally they come through social studies (and will come from the new Social Work degree), but also via languages and biological sciences; BSc Psychosocial Studies looks interesting.

They are European and American law specialists. All candidates must sit the National Admissions Test for Law (LNAT).

Key to the uni's identity is its concern for the environment. They are among the top suppliers of graduates to this sector. The feed is mainly through physical sciences. There's a sheaf of Ecology and Environmental Sciences BSc degrees, with options for European and North American experience (the same for Geophysical Sciences). There's also a BA and a BSc Development Studies (one with Overseas Experience). There was an 'Excellent' at the

> *UEA is a top uni with an independent streak and a host of interesting specialisms. Self-containment on the old golf course is choice for some, others feel driven to to run to town to feel free again.*

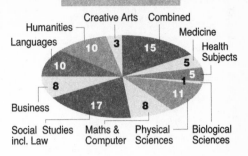

SUBJECT AREAS (%)

Creative Arts: 3; Combined: 15; Medicine: 5; Health Subjects: 5; Biological Sciences: 1; Physical Sciences: 11; Maths & Computer: 8; Social Studies incl. Law: 17; Business: 8; Languages: 10; Humanities: 10

assessments and a world-class Grade 6* for research. The climatic research unit is a world authority, and the uni is home to the Tyndall Centre for Climate Change Research. For undergraduates, UEA marries Meteorology to Maths and Oceanography and offers a honeymoon in North America, Europe or ...industry. The Jackson Institute, with the largest environmental research programme in the UK, has also set up here, and there's a new Institute for Connective Environmental Research – an attempt to bring together science, industry, politics, business to make real steps forward in the area of environmentalism.

Eleven per cent of graduates go into finance, more than 6% into accounts and accountancy. BSc Accounting is available with Finance, Law and Management. Economics and Business both scored 23 out of 24 at the assessments. New this year is BSc Actuarial Science with a Year in Industry and BSc Computing for Business.

Graduates from this degree will be extremely well placed to gain employment in actuarial departments across the finance sector.

Computing is another big area for jobs: graduate IT consultants, software engineers and

WHERE EAST ANGLIA GRADUATES END UP

Health & Social Work: 13%; Education: 7%; Wholesale/Retail: 10%; Manufacturing: 8%; Financial Activities: 11%; Public Administration, Civil Service & Defence: 8%; Hotel/Restaurant: 4%; Transport & Communications (including Telecommunications): 2%; Construction: 1%; Personnel: 9%; Computer: 3%; Business & Management: 4%; Accountancy: 3%; Media (including Film): 3%; Legal 3%; Architecture: 2%; Publishing: 4%; Advertising: 1%; Artistic/Literary: 1%.

Approximate 'graduate track' employed **59%**

WHAT IT'S REALLY LIKE

UNIVERSITY:

Social Life	★★★★★
Campus scene	**Lively**
Student Union services	**Excellent**
Politics	**Active**
Sport	**40 clubs, but not obsessional**
National team position	**54th**
Sport facilities	**Good**
Arts opportunities	**Excellent**
Student newspaper	**Concrete**
Student radio	**Livewire 1350**
Student Radio Awards	**Silver 2006**
Student TV	**Nexus**
Student TV Awards	**2 wins 2005**
Nightclub	**LCR, Waterfront**
Bars	**Union Pub, Blue Bar, Hive, Grads**
Union ents	**Massive**
Union societies	**70**
Most popular society	**Livewire, Concrete, Rock Gospel Choir**
Parking	**Poor**
CITY:	
Entertainment	★★★
Scene	**OK pubs, clubs**
Town/gown relations	**Average**
Risk of violence	**Low**
Cost of living	**Average**
Survival + 2 nights out	**£70 pw**
Part-time work campus/town	**Good/excellent**

AT A GLANCE

ACADEMIC FILE:

Assessments	**24**
Excellent	**83%**
Typical entry requirements	**365 points**
Application acceptance rate	**18%**
Med. School acceptance rate	**8%**
Students-staff ratio	**17:1**
First/2:1 degree pass rate	**67%**

ACCOMMODATION FILE:

Guarantee to freshers	**100% if from 12 miles away**
Style	**Houses, flats**
Catered	**None**
En-suite	**75%**
Price range pw	**£56-£91**
City rent pw	**£56**

systems analysts abound. There's a year in North America with BSc Computing Science and Computer Systems Engineering. New in 2007 is BSc Computing with a Year in Industry.

SOCIAL SCENE

STUDENTS' UNION There's a lively reputation for journalism – their TV station is Nexus TV, their radio station, Livewire 1350. *Concrete* is the newspaper, which incorporates *The Event* entertainment magazine and often wins national awards. Livewire was nominated twice in 2005 and won a Silver Award in 2006. Nexus won twice in its national award category in 2005. There is a track record for graduate careers in radio/TV and publishing, and top ratings for teaching and research in media/communications.

They boast 70 societies and 40 sports clubs. It is a highly developed student culture and has to be because campus is so cut off. Politics is a scene. Currently less on party politics, more on Student Safety, boycotting Coke and Nestlé, and constant student pressure on the uni authorities to become

more environmentally friendly. The 3-weekly Union Council meeting is a passionate event.

Gays get a good deal: LBG is among the most active societies, along with *Concrete*, Livewire, and Rock Gospel Choir which seems to have performed everywhere. **The Studio** is the UEA theatre; drama is another top-scoring course rating. The union also has a reputation for being the biggest ents performer around.

LCR (Lower Common Room) has been voted the best student venue in the country by the music industry's *Live!* magazine. Each year more than 50 live bands grace its stage; gigs are sold out months in advance. 'Too many to give an accurate list,' we're told, 'but recent and scheduled include: Arctic Monkeys, Babyshambles, Dirty Pretty Things, Fat Boy Slim, Motorhead, Jools Holland, De La Soul, Manic Street Preachers.'

Classic student nights like *Skool Daze* and *Club Retro* are also highly popular, as are comedy, poetry and an eclectic list of live acts.

Union Bars feature **The Union Pub** – all-day opening, pool tables, table footie, arcade machines, jukebox and large screen TV. Then there's **The Union Bar (Blue Bar)**, **The Hive** (redeveloped 2 years ago, creating a light, more spacious environment), and **The Grads Bar**. Live in the Hive includes (free) local bands, as well as karaoke, quizzes, games and comedy shows.

Besides the **LCR,** the uni has its own venue in Norwich – **The Waterfront**. There are 3 bars and 2 rooms of music. Every last Friday of the month it's *Rock Club* – bands and rock DJs. Otherwise it's live gigs and clubnights, like *Meltdown* (indie, pop, rock & alternative), *Roobarb* (hard dance all-nighter), *Bounce* (drum 'n' bass).

SPORT Good, though not top notch (halfway up/down the national team table); good facilities. The purpose-built Sportspark continues to attract students to UEA – a £17.6-million, integrated indoor and outdoor facility, including an Olympic-size swimming pool and a human performance laboratory opened recently. Women's hockey is very strong. Other big deals are football, tennis, trampolining, rugby, athletics, kerfball and American footie.

TOWN Apparently, Norwich has a pub for every day of the year. It also has the **Theatre Royal** (touring companies, RSC, National), **The Maddermarket**, a smaller, amateur but vibrant venue. The bohemian **King of Hearts** rules for music, art, jazz, literature readings, and **The Norwich Arts Centre** for live music, from rock and jazz to chamber music, exhibitions, dance workshops and comedy – David Baddiel, Frank Skinner, Lee & Herring and The Fast Show's Simon Day all played here. There are three cinemas – the **ABC** and the **Odeon** (in the heart of the excellent Magdalen Street curry scene – and **Cinema City** for arthouse.

PILLOW TALK
Accommodation is guaranteed to all first year undergraduates who live over 12 miles from UEA and who apply within the deadline. Students live in their own study bedrooms within 8-12 person flats. There is a choice of standard rooms on campus or in the city centre and en suite rooms on campus or in the adjoining university village. A new 200-bedroom en-suite residence recently opened, and a further 150 en-suite rooms will be available in September 2008.

From September 2007, UEA will offer 3,400 rooms, a third of which are less than 3 years old. Refurbishment of all UEAís iconic older rooms will be completed by January 2008.

GETTING THERE
☞ By road: A11(M), A47.
☞ By rail: London Liverpool Street, 2:00; Birmingham New Street, 4:00; Sheffield, 3:50.
☞ By air: Norwich Airport.
☞ By coach: London, 2:50; Birmingham, 6:00; Sheffield, 7:00.

UNIVERSITY OF EAST LONDON

The University of East London
Docklands Campus,
4-6 University Way
London E16 2RD

TEL 020 8223 3333
FAX 020 8223 3333
EMAIL admiss@uel.ac.uk
WEB www.uel.ac.uk
STUDENT UNION TEL 020 8223 7025

VAG VIEW

*I*n UEL we have the former East London Poly. Its stated mission is 'to provide the highest possible quality of education in order to meet' – not the needs of the country or Europe or the world, but – 'the needs of individuals and of the communities and enterprises in our region.' The mission is no less ambitious for its narrower geographical focus, for in many ways UEL has its doors more widely open to the real world than most of its competitors, what with its high intake from beleaguered areas, its Refugee Bursaries, its low entry requirements and determination to hang on to its students for the full term and equip them for a world that many off to Bristol and Durham can barely imagine.*

Following a full-scale institutional audit by the Quality Assurance Agency in 2005, UEL was praised for its culture of equality and diversity, its equitable approach and support for its part-time staff and students, the effectiveness of its staff development, and the integration into

SUBJECT AREAS (%)

Humanities Creative Education
Media — Arts Combined
Languages
9 · 3 · 16 · Health Subjects
2 · 8
7
1
10 · 9
13 · 3 · 8 · 10 · Biological
Business Sciences
Social Studies Planning/ Engineering/ Maths &
incl. Law Architecture Technology Computer

UNIVERSITY/STUDENT PROFILE

University since	**1992**
Situation/style	**City sites**
Student population	**20266**
Undergraduates	**14749**
- mature	**55%**
- non EU undergraduates	**20%**
- male/female	**45/55**
- non-traditional student intake	**40%**
- state school intake	**96%**
drop-out rate	**33%**
- undergraduate applications	**Up 10%**

the curriculum of skills development for students, particularly through the Skillzone, UEL's skills, pre-entry advice and guidance service.

Clearly they are doing something right. There is confidence aplenty, as they concentrate their efforts now on two campuses: Docklands and Stratford.

On Feb 16, 2007, the Queen opened the new Business School and Knowledge Dock Centre on the waterfront of the Royal Albert Dock, in the presence of HRH Prince Turki of Saudi Arabia and Lord Rix - Brian of Whitehall fame, who is UEL's Chancellor. But no farce here. The event followed the successful completion of a £110-million investment and development programme, which also sees an overhaul at Stratford, too.

CAMPUSES

DOCKLANDS CAMPUS 4-6 University Way, London E16 2RD. Located on the waterfront of the Royal Albert Dock and opened in 2000, it is now expanded to serve 7,000 students focused on the new economy, cultural and creative industries. The new Architecture and Visual Arts facility was completed in 2003, and a new Business School and Enterprise Centre opened in 2007. Two new buildings on the waterfront house the Business School, Centre for Entrepreneurship, School of Computing and Technology, Learning Resource Centre and Knowledge Dock. The Business School includes a 650-seat trading floor, and a 400-seat lecture theatre. The design features a dynamic curved roof which forms a wing-shaped protective canopy and a winter garden overlooking the dock and London skyline. There's a restaurant, bar and cafés, and a Student Union development now open too. Also accommodation of course; see *Pillow Talk*.

STRATFORD CAMPUS Romford Road, London E15 4LZ. Tel 020 8223 3000. At Stratford, the historic heart of the university and site of the London 2012 Olympics, they've built a unique Centre for Physiotherapy, Podiatry and Sports Science. The new Centre, which includes clinical facilities run in partnership with Newham Primary Care Trust, builds on our reputation as a centre for physiotherapy, sports science, professional health studies and subjects allied to medicine. As at Docklands, there are brand new Student Union facilities too. This year, work begins on new buildings for our Schools of Law and Education. For accommodation, see *Pillow Talk*.

FEES, BURSARIES

UK & EU Fees, 2007 & 2008: £3,000. Bursary for students in receipt of full HE Maintenance grant: £300 plus £500 Progress Bursary to all who complete first semester and progress to second (there are serious - 33%) non-completion rates at UEL. Also, 200 Achievement scholarships of £1,000 each to first-year students for sport, academic excellence, citizenship, and voluntary work.

STUDENT PROFILE

UEL have large ethnic and overseas populations, a very large mature student population (55%), and a drop-out rate that they have battled to get under control and will conquer when they get their facilities together and teaching as good in every area as it is in some. There is a friendly, laid-back

27% Postgraduates
Female Undergraduates **40%**
STUDENT POPULATION
Total students 20,266
33% Male Undergraduates

feel to the place. Students are getting on, and will do provided they're not bound fast by politically correct red tape, as some seem to be.

ACADEMIA & JOBS

The uni's Skillzone is a learning support and employment service. They are good at raising money for this sort of thing; their mission is in line with Government policy; they are good at speaking the language of the times in which we live, and

WHERE EAST LONDON GRADUATES END UP

Health & Social Work: 23%; Education: 7%; Wholesale/Retail: 16%; Manufacturing: 7%; Financial Activities: 4%; Public Administration, Civil Service & Defence: 12%; Hotel/Restaurant: 2%; Transport & Communications (including Telecommunications): 3%; Construction: 2%; Personnel: 3%; Computer: 2%; Business & Management: 3%; Accountancy: 1%; Media (including Film): 2%; Legal 4%; Architecture: 2%; Publishing: 2%; Artistic/Literary: 1%; Sport: 3%.

Approximate 'graduate track' employed **56%**

they know their way around the forms.

Today, the Knowledge Dock, formerly the Thames Gateway Technology Centre, works with over 2,000 companies and entrepreneurs across the region. It provides a range of business services, training, consultancy, and funded programmes including the DTI flagship Knowledge Transfer Partnerships and the Shell Technology Enterprise Programme (STEP), for which it was named best new agency.'

UEL invests among the highest per student for library and learning resources. It is also a leader in disability and dyslexia support. Facilities include a regional ACCESS centre offering dyslexia screening and tutoring, technology training, exam support and an RNIB Resource Centre for blind and visually impaired students on Physiotherapy programmes.

At UEL, look for degrees in health, psychology, culture, social studies, art, computer and sport, and you will find jobs. In these areas, the uni fulfils its mission to meet 'the needs of individuals and of the communities and enterprises in our region.'

Over 7% of graduates finding employment out of East London Uni do so as social workers, probation officers or community youth workers, and this year there's a new degree in Youth Work. Single honours degrees offer such as Psychosocial Studies, Social Policy, Social Work Studies, Social Work, Third World Development, etc. This year there's a new BA (Hons) Youth and Community Work. Consider the ground carefully, for this is mainstream UEL territory. Their psychologists deal with real issues of the community in which they live and work. UEL's School of Psychology is rated excellent (23/24) for teaching and is now one of the leading schools in Britain for undergraduate and professional diploma programmes. They run a range of postgraduate programmes in partnership with RELATE, the Psychosynthesis and Education Trust, and the Tavistock Clinic, the UK's leading centre for post-graduate training in mental health.

Physiotherapy is a major career field for UEL – some 13% of its graduates become physiotherapists, and they boast a 100%

employment record (as they do in teacher training). The route is straightforward – BSc Physiotherapy provides the single most popular route out of UEL into a job and the lowest entry requirement available anywhere. It is, however, available to mature students only. Teaching Inspection 20. See also the new BSc Podiatric Medicine.

There's also strength in sport academically – coaching, exercise science, etc – and new sports science laboratories, which shows up in the employment figures. Some 3% of graduates from UEL become sports trainers or coaches.

Also, respect their media degrees. They have a research grade which marks their work out as of national significance. Grade 5 does not come easy.

Computer technology is also strong, with IT consultants, computer operators and software engineers making a good show from degrees that include Computer Games Technology, Internet Technologies, Computer Networks with E-Commerce, etc.

Finally, graphic artists and designers and clothing designers proliferate from Fashion Design degrees, some with Marketing, Fine Art (sculpting has been a particular success) and Graphic Design.

ACADEMIC EXCELLENCE

TEACHING:
(Rated Excellent or 17+ out of 24)

Architecture, English	**Excellent**
Psychology	**23**
Art & Design, Civil Eng,	**21**
Economics, Subjects Allied to	**20**
Medicine	
Sociology, Pharmacology,	**19**
Education, Biosciences	
Linguistics & Modern Languages,	**18**
Mechanical, Manufacturing Eng.	

RESEARCH:
Top grades 5/5*

Communication/Cultural/Media	**Grade 5**

WHAT IT'S REALLY LIKE

UNIVERSITY:

Social Life	★★★
Campus scene	**Authentic, urban culture**
Student Union services	**Average**
Politics	**Anti-racism & free education**
Sport	**Relaxed/13 clubs**
National team position	**None**
Sport facilities	**Average**
Arts opportunities	**Some**
Student magazine	**Refuel**
Bars	**Each campus**
Union ents	**Rootsy**
Union societies	**31**
Most popular society	**Islamic**
Parking	**Poor**

CITY:

Entertainment	★★★★★
Scene	**Local clubs 'n uptown flavours**
Town/gown relations	**Poor**
Risk of violence	**Random**
Cost of living	**High**
Student concessions	**OK**
Survival + 2 nights out	**£60 pw**
Part-time work campus/town	**Good, must travel**

In 2003, they brought together the Schools of Architecture and Art and Design to form the School of Architecture and the Visual Arts, located in a new 6,000 sq m purpose-designed studio building at Docklands. UEL is rated Excellent for the teaching of architecture, and there's a strong pathway into the profession. They are one of a few Schools to be awarded unconditional validation by the Royal Institute of British Architects (RIBA) and the Architects Registration Board (ARB).

SOCIAL SCENE

Political awareness is the most notable aspect at student level, and a culturally rich ents programme, including dedicated and *Mixed Flavour* discos – indie, soul, swing, '70s/'80s, jungle, hip hop, ragga, Bhangra, reggae, old school, cheese, pop, rock n roll, triphop, hip hop and dub – comedy nights, cabaret, live bands, video nights and the odd society 'do'. One-offs include Spring Ball, Valentine Bash, Diwali Rave, Hallowe'en Night, Christmas Rave.

They number 31 societies this year (including Respect) and 13 sports clubs (from Rowing to Black Star). A lot of bar activity/events are laid on by students through cultural societies, like Reggae Nite with DJ Freestyle, *Wheel of 4 Tunes* Good

Friday Society Nite, *Calender* (sic) *Club Nite*, DJ's rnb, hiphop, catwalk, samba band.

They say they have 30 societies up and running. Hard to tell which is the most active, but Islamic generally has the largest membership. Student media includes a magazine, *re:fuel*, and that's about it.

At Stratford campus, the new facilities include an internet café and bar in the Passmore Edwards building.

In the political arena, they are one of a handful of universities capable of organising a decent sit-in, getting together with Goldsmiths to do a *Rough Guide to Occupation at one stage.* Currently, they describe the level of activity as 'average, meaning less people compensate with great awareness and enthusiasm!' Campaigns traditionally include Anti-racism/fascism and Free education for all. Speakers recently have been Neville Lawrence, Ken Livingstone and Glenda Jackson.

SPORT Relaxed attitude, twenty teams, not nationally competitive. Teams make use mainly of council pitches and halls that offer student discounts. A swimming pool is used for water polo, sub-aqua and canoeing; there are two gyms, facilities for aerobics, dance, badminton, table

AT A GLANCE

ACADEMIC FILE:

Subjects assessed	**23**
Excellent	**61%**
Typical entry requirements	**192 points**
Application acceptance rate	**23%**
Students-staff ratio	**21:1**
First/2:1 degree pass rate	**40%**

ACCOMMODATION FILE:

Guarantee to freshers	**From afar**
Style	**Halls**
Catering	**None**
En suite	**All**
Approx price range pw	**£89**
City rent pw	**£65-£100**

tennis, karate, circuit training, volleyball, basketball, indoor football, a squash court, four tennis courts, a fitness centre. Playing fields are a few miles away, at Little Heath. Badminton is available near the Stratford campus and there are other recreational activities on offer – golf, sailing, windsurfing, skiing, sub-aqua, riding, and weekend and vacation courses are arranged.

With the Olympics setting up stall around the

corner, it's a good bet sport is going to be a major focus in the future, and they agree that there are plans to develop sports coaching, working with local authority partners to deliver sports programmes for young people, facilities and event management training, engaging and empowering local communities through voluntary action, disability sport in partnership with the National Paralympic Association, and support for elite performers at their new sports science laboratories.

TOWN 'Well it's London, so all bets are off,' said my informant. 'Cost of living is high, general things (food etc) are fairly priced compared to other places. It's the social side of things that costs so much. Start saving now. Risk of violence is, surprisingly random. Arguably, people would say London is prone to greater violence. But really it's all quite random. You'll need about £60 to live on if you want to go out at least two nights. Chance of employment is high. Both within the Students' Union and wider a-field.' See *Student London*, page 301.

PILLOW TALK

Allocation priority is given to students with special needs, and then to students entering their first year at the university from outside the local area. A number of rooms are reserved for applicants whose normal place of residence is outside the UK. What can you expect? At Stratford, university house or flat-share at landscaped Park Village nearby. New accomm. at Cedars Road for this year. At Docklands, self-catering study-bedrooms and flats. The new waterfront Student Village opened spring 2007 with 800 studio flats, café-bar, shops, SU facilities.

GETTING THERE

☛ **Stratford** by Underground, Central Line; closest overland rail station is Maryland (connect London Liverpool Street).

☛ **Barking** by Underground, City & Hammersmith and District lines; Goodmayes overland station.

☛ **Docklands** via the Docklands Light Railway.

EDGE HILL UNIVERSITY

Edge Hill College
St Helens Road
Ormskirk
Lancashire L39 4QP

TEL 0800 1955063
FAX 01695 579997
EMAIL enquiries@edgehill.ac.uk
WEB www.edgehill.ac.uk

VAG VIEW

*E*dge Hill was founded in 1885 as the UK's first non-denominational teacher training college for women. Initially based in the Edge Hill district of Liverpool, the College moved to Ormskirk in 1933. In 1960 it became co-ed, and diversified into health in 1968. In the 1970s it became a partner college of Lancaster University and in time offered a broad range of degree courses.

In 1980 it took into itself Chorley College of Education and in 1993 the Sefton School of Health Studies. In 2006 the college achieved university status. In 2007 its undergraduate applications soared by 40%.

Edge Hill has always been an unusually slick set-up, whose boss used to call himself a Chief Executive and who always had a team of marketing and communications executives

following close behind. It will be interesting to see what they do with their new status.

CAMPUS

The main campus consists of 75 landscaped acres, with lake, theatres and sports centre, 10 minutes walk from the centre of Ormskirk, a thriving market

UNIVERSITY/STUDENT PROFILE	
University since	**2006**
Situation/style	**Town campus**
Student population	**17000**
Undergraduates	**5110**
- mature	**20%**
- non EU undergraduates	**1%**
- male/female	**35/65**
- non-traditional student intake	**39%**
- state school intake	**99%**
drop-out rate	**N/A**
- undergraduate applications	**Up 40%**

town about 30 mins by train from the centre of Liverpool.

In addition to the Ormskirk Campus, they have 2 campuses, at Aintree and Chorley. The Faculty of Health is based at the former, which is known as University Hospital Aintree, and the Faculty of Education's continuing professional development (CPD) work is located at the latter, known as Woodlands Campus.

In addition, there are centres in Liverpool, Silkhouse Court where a part-time BSc (Hons) in Information Systems is studied, and in Manchester, Shrewsbury, Winsford (Cheshire) and the Wirral.

FEES, BURSARIES

UK & EU Fees 2007: £3,070 p.a. Fees for 2008 not yet fixed. There's the usual sliding-scale bursaries for students in receipt of the HE Maintenance Grant and one-off payments of £100 to first year students who complete a student support survey and attend a follow-up meeting with personal tutors - this progression bursary is designed to keep students in study. Also fees for siblings of those studying at Edge Hill and paying the full variable amount, are reduced by £1,000. for sporting and for academic excellence there are scholarships of £2,000 over three years. And one volunteer work, also worth £2,000 over three years. All students, irrespective of means have a £200 uni card to spend on study materials. Nice touch. They won the 2006 Times Higher Education award for Outstanding Student Financial Support.

STUDENT PROFILE

Edge Hill easily surpasses its Government benchmarks for encouraging under-represented socio-economic groups into higher education. Virtually all their undergrads come from state schools, 39% from the four lowest socio-economic classes and a quarter from so-called 'low participation neighbourhoods'.

There is also a large local and mature student population and, mainly on account of the nursing, numbers of women dominate those of men.

None of these stats give a feel of the place, however, which is lively enough. When, a few years ago the college was taken to court by a neighbour for the regular early hours clamour of students enjoying themselves, the judge commented, 'It's like Brideshead Revisited meets St Trinians, isn't it?', as the prosecution itemised the complainants' 5-year 'noise diary'.

ACADEMIA

There are three faculties: Education; Health; and Humanities, Management, Social & Applied Sciences (HMSAS), within which fall the Business

ACADEMIC EXCELLENCE

TEACHING:
(Rated Excellent or 17+ out of 24)

Social Policy & Administration	**Excellent**
Education	**24**
Oragnismal Biosciences	**23**
Nursing, Psychology	**22**
Sport, Maths & Statistics	**20**
Communication & Media	

School, English: Language, Literature, Creative Writing and Film Studies , History, Law and Criminology, Media, Natural, Geographical and Applied Sciences, Performing Arts, Social and Psychological Sciences, Sport and Physical Activity.

Cracking teaching inspection results came for Education (full marks), Biosciences (23/24), Nursing and Psychology (both 22 points), and more recently the QAA has expressed 'Broad confidence in the soundness of the College's current and likely future management of the quality of its academic programmes and the academic standards of its awards.'

Management, marketing tourism, history, nursing, midwifery and other health care have all passed muster recently, as have drama and dance, though learning resources in these areas were simply approved by QAA rather than commended.

Justifiably they boast that they are one of only fourteen institutions to have National Council for the Training of Journalists accreditation for undergraduate journalism programmes, and that their BSc Psychology is accredited by the British Psychological Society. Finally, of course, they are the largest provider of Initial Teacher Training for secondary education in the UK.

Growing student numbers herald a new £14-million building for teaching and learning, due to be completed in 2008, which will house the SOLSTICE e-learning centre and a 900-seat theatre where degree awarding ceremonies will be held.

SOCIAL SCENE

Ten years ago a student described Edge Hill to us as 'a small, friendly community that caters for the basics'. Now, it is less small, but just as friendly, and there is a great deal more on campus than the college bar and dining room.

The Venue is the place for live music, dance nights, themed discos, sports nights, resident and visiting DJs, quizzes, pool, video games, and big screen TV. **Sages** is the original 1930s dining room, but that has now been joined by the **Terraced Café**, **The Diner** (fast food), **Grinders** (coffee bar), and

Water's Edge (restaurant with cyber café).

Still not satisfied students opt for club-loon outings to Manchester, Liverpool and Preston, or slip into Ormskirk, heaven forbid, and sample *The Styles* or **Disraeli** bars.

With some 50 societies on offer, the extra-curricular scene is better here than in many a more mature university. **The Rose Theatre** on campus is used for student theatre and music events, and by visiting companies. Community Action has 150 volunteers. And then there are the 9 sports clubs.

SPORT Which brings us to **Sporting Edge**. There is a sports crazy element at Edge Hill, and the facilities are good, thanks to a £1.9-million Lottery Grant and additional funds made available to afford the £3.9 million it all cost - a 4-court hall, a fitness suite, squash court, 7 floodlit tennis courts, 4 soccer pitches, 2 rugby pitches, 5 netball pitches, a 5-lane athletics track and an 8-lane straight, a cricket square, gymnasium, swimming pool, synthetic hockey pitch and 5-a-side area. On top of this there's the **Wilson Centre** - specialist labs to measure sporting performance.

PILLOW TALK

Halls are based on campus - 19 of them at Ormskirk, satisfying 669 freshers (half of them catered, a fifth en suite). Rooms are allocated on a first come first served basis, although priority will

AT A GLANCE	
ACADEMIC FILE:	
Subjects assessed	**11**
Excellent	**73%**
Average requirements	**170 points**
Application acceptance rate	**22%**
Students-staff ratio	**N/A**
First/2:1 degree pass rate	**N/A**
ACCOMMODATION FILE:	
Guarantee to freshers	**First come, first served**
Style	**Halls, flats**
Catered	**50%**
En suite	**21%**
Approx price range pw	**£46-£75**
City rent pw	**£55-£65**

be given to students with disabilities, care-leavers, and/or to those who live outside a 10-mile radius of the university.

GETTING THERE

☞ By road: M6/J26, M58/J3, A570 to Southport. The uni is 2 miles along on the right.
☞ By rail: Northern Line Merseyrail train connections from Liverpool Central and Preston Stations. Alight at Ormskirk, not Edge Hill.

STUDENT EDINBURGH - THE CITY

Edinburgh has a worldwide reputation for being one of the most interesting and exciting places to live and study. It is a city of contradictions. On the one hand it is an ancient city, with dramatic architecture and a rich cultural history. On the other hand it is a cosmopolitan capital and a critical financial and political centre. It is also a 24-hour city with an eclectic range of bars and clubs to suit any taste. Edinburgh, with consummate ease, combines ancient with modern, and work with play, making it one of the most vibrant and exciting cities in Europe.

CITY SCAPE

Edinburgh is centred round the beautiful castle that heads up the tourist filled Royal Mile complete with ancient cobbled streets and historical landmarks aplenty. The city is compact making it easy to get around simply by walking, although if you do get tired feet, the extensive bus network is ready and waiting. The town is essentially split into two with the ancient

splendour of Old town, which houses the University, and the Georgian New Town separated by the stunning Princes Street gardens. Pay a visit in the festive season and you will find an outdoor ice rink and huge Christmas market. This is also the site of the famed Edinburgh Hogmanay party that leads the world in celebrating the New Year.

COFFEE CULTURE

Edinburgh is typified by its coffee culture. You are never more than 5 minutes away from a good coffee and a comfy seat. Many of the best can be found around George Square, conveniently close to Edinburgh's central campus. **Assembly** and **Negociants** on Teviot place provide good lunches and tasty cocktails. The **Human Be-In** offers chic upmarket surroundings whilst the American style diner, **Favorit**, offers good food at good prices until early in the morning. **Bean Scene** on South Clerk Street offers a comfy haven away from the hustle and bustle. It also boasts its own record label of up and coming talent, and regular live performances from its artists. For those who are star struck, the **Elephant House** is famed as J.K.Rowling's favourite coffee spot. It is where she wrote some of *Harry Potter*. It, and its smaller cousin, **Elephant and Bagels**, offer excellent food and friendly original decor. Those of you with a serious addiction to chocolate won't be disappointed with the range available in Edinburgh. **Plaisir du Chocolat** on the Royal Mile offers the best hot chocolate money can buy, but it will cost you a small fortune. **Chocolate Soup** in Hanover Square offers fabulous hot chocolates in a huge variety of flavours, served in the biggest cups known to man.

SILVER SCREEN

The city excels in cinemas. At the **Cameo** in Tollcross there's thematic music before the credits roll and the pleasure of enjoying a pint in its enticingly comfortable seats. **The Cameo** features a range of unusual films that you won't find at the big chain cinemas. It isn't arthouse cinema, but it is a break from the one-dimensional Hollywood blockbusters. **The Filmhouse** serves the more arty audience, excelling at foreign films. For Hollywood, head to the **UGC Multiplex** at Fountainpark or **Vue** cinema at the top of Leith Walk.

The city also holds an annual International Film Festival in August. The uni's Film Society offers membership at a bargain price of £15 and gets you entry to a massive range of great films throughout the academic year.

SPOTLIGHTS

Due mainly to the Edinburgh festival, the city has an excess of theatres. **The Playhouse** at the top of Leith Walk hosts all the major touring musicals. There are often generous student discounts. **The Lyceum** offers Shakespeare or post-modern avant-garde. The world famous **Traverse**, nestling nearby amongst high-class eateries, dishes up excellent experimental Scottish drama as well as having one of the hippest bars in Edinburgh. If you're into more mainstream theatre or opera, head to the **King's Theatre** or **Festival Theatre**. Then there's the only student-run pro theatre in the UK, **Bedlam** on Bristo Place. Regular favourites are the Improverts, who run a 'whose line it is anyway' style show, and perform every Friday in term time.

Edinburgh is also steeped in comedy grandeur due to the famed festival, but the laughs don't stop there: comedy continues all year round. Edinburgh University Students' Association hold one of the most famous venues, the **Pleasance**, which plays hosts to the Comedy Network every fortnight. Everyone, from Harry Hill to Frank Skinner, has played here on their way to fame. So, there is

plenty of, 'I saw them before they were famous' boasting potential. **The Stand**, in York Place, is the city's only purpose-built comedy venue. It serves up good food and a great ambience in a cosy basement. **Jongleurs** comedy club in the **Omni Centre** is another venue. Although the comedy is average, there are usually good deals on the door.

RETAIL RELIEF

If you fancy some retail therapy, head down to Princes Street, which houses nearly all the major high street brands. If you fancy really splashing out, then George Street has all the fine boutiques, stuffed with luxury goods aplenty.

If retro is the requirement, **Armstrongs** and **The Rusty Zip** deliver the goods, while **Flip** on South Bridge is good for flares, cords and comedy seventies gear. For the ultimate in budget retailing, check out the numerous charity shops on Nicholson Street. Skaterkids are well-serviced in Edinburgh, with both **Cult Clothing** and **Odd One Out** especially popular with the baggy-trousered contingent.

For music, head to Cockburn Street, home to the capital's Number 1 music shops, **Fopp** and **Avalanche**, both of which are infinitely better value than their mainstream Princes Street rivals.

Edinburgh has the largest collection of second-hand book stores in the world. So, for all you book worms, there are plenty of places to spend your days. **Till's** on Buccleuch Street, **Armchair Books** at West Port, **McFeely's** on Buccleuch Street and **MacNaughtons** at Gayfield Place are but a few of the delights in store for you.

PUB IT

Like so much of Edinburgh the key word is variety. Edinburgh's pubs and bars have the benefit of staying open until 1am every night. If a pint in a traditional pub is your aim, head to the **Blind Poet** or the **Pear Tree**. The latter boasts an impressive beer garden and many a late night can be spent clutching a pint in the cold Scottish air. If you are looking for a cheap pint then try one of the Scream pubs such as the **Tron** or **The Crags**, conveniently located next to the main Student Union halls. If you are looking for something a little more fancy then head over to New Town and enjoy the delights of **Prive Council** or **Beluga** on Chambers Street.

Both offer upmarket chic surroundings and not unreasonable prices. The Royal Mile offers a plethora of bars, but often more expensive. Head to the Cowgate where you will find a virtual tunnel of bars. Of particular note is **Bannermans**, which holds live music nights for unsigned bands nearly every night of the week.

IN THE CLUB

Edinburgh has more clubs per head than anywhere else in Britain – fact. This means that you have a massive choice of venues and a huge variety of styles to choose from. For those looking for a traditional chart club night out then **City**, with its excellent lighting and sound, **Faith**, with its impressive décor and **Why Not?**, with its clean crisp image are all favourites. For the more chic amongst you, head to **Opal Lounge** or **Po Na Na** for stylish surroundings and swanky drinks. Beware the price tag that comes with the venue! Goth and Rock are catered for by **Opium** on the Cowgate and **Citrus** on Lothian Road. **Honeycomb** puts on an awesome funk night on Tuesdays, and the unique design of the club, with its literal honeycomb structure, is worth seeing anyway. **Bongo Club** offers the best hip hop and reggae in town. **Liquid Rooms** offers an excellent venue and a huge variety of nights, although it can be pricey. **Ego** on Picardy Place offers nights tailor made for gay clubbers, especially Tuesdays. With two floors of music, dirt cheap drink, and a young crowd this is an excellent night out. **CC Blooms** is the only permanent Gay Club with **Planet Out** and **Habana** providing the best of the bar scene.

Venues chop and change their nights each week, so for complete up-to-date listings pick up a copy of *The List*.

Iain Walters

UNIVERSITY OF EDINBURGH

The University of Edinburgh
57 George Square
Edinburgh EH8 9JU

TEL 0131 650 4360
FAX 0131 651 1236
EMAIL sra.enquiries@ed.ac.uk
WEB www.ed.ac.uk

Edinburgh University Student Association
Student Centre House
5/2 Bristo Square
Edinburgh EH8 9AL

TEL 0131 650 2656
FAX 0131 668 4177
EMAIL president@eusa.ed.ac.uk
WEB www.eusa.ed.ac.uk

VAG VIEW

If you are looking at the employers' surveys or parents' perceptions, it's Oxbridge then Durham and Bristol, and Edinburgh is the Scottish equivalent of these. Edinburgh, they know, is the place to be. An Edinburgh degree is a very good degree to have. It is still considered to be part of a Scottish person's birthright. They do not admit to offering a Scottish quota.

CAMPUS

'The University is primarily divided into two main campuses, two miles apart,' writes James Lumsden. 'George Square (with its central city location) for Arts & Social Science, and KB (King's Buildings) for Science and Engineering. Recently, the university has spent wads of cash reinventing KB into somewhere that you no longer want to leave before you arrive. The result reminds some of a cross-channel ferry. George Square, meanwhile, has its own brand of ugliness, in the shape of Appleton and David Hume towers. For a beautiful city that's known as the "Athens of the North", Edinburgh University seems to have done its damnedest to flout convention.'

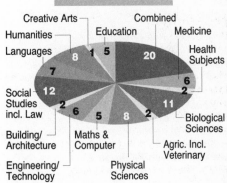

SUBJECT AREAS (%)

Creative Arts, Combined, Humanities, Education, Medicine, Languages, Health Subjects — 8, 1, 5, 20, 7, 6, Social Studies incl. Law — 12, 2, 6, 5, 8, 2, 11, 2, Biological Sciences, Building/Architecture, Maths & Computer, Agric. Incl. Veterinary, Engineering/Technology, Physical Sciences

FEES, BURSARIES

UK students from outside Scotland: £1700 p.a.
The University has a range of bursaries available depending on level of study etc. for more information go to http://www.scholarships.ed.ac.uk/awards/

STUDENT PROFILE

'Often represented by a myopic media as a toffs' university,' James continues, 'the true diversity of

Female Undergraduates — **43%**

25% — Postgraduates

STUDENT POPULATION

Total students 24,468

32% — Male Undergraduates

student and university life at Edinburgh goes misrepresented; there are more than 20,000 students from a wide variety of backgrounds and circumstances.'

Nevertheless, the uni does have its share of

the Crisis Loans are lengthening ... study resources are being stretched to the limit,' said one student. One nice touch at Edinburgh is that students are assigned a Director of Studies, a guardian angel trained to guide you through your course.

Edinburgh responds to needs in a great number of graduate employment areas, but to none more strongly than in Health and Education. The degree in Medicine is the 5/6-year MB ChB. They promise 'early clinical contact' and deliver it in Year 1, together with case-based learning tutorials using problem-based learning methods. Entry AABa + UKCAT, AAAAB at Highers. Grade B GCSE English Maths and a language other than English. It's highly competitive, however; there's only a 9% chance of acceptance; 10% is average. Teaching inspection, Highly Satisfactory. Research Grades 5*. Degrees in Podiatry are also popular and extremely efficient in terms of future employment.

UNIVERSITY/STUDENT PROFILE

University since	**1583**
Situation/style	**Civic**
Student population	**24468**
Undergraduates	**18279**
- mature	**16%**
- non EU undergraduates	**10%**
- male/female	**43/57**
- non-traditional student intake	**17%**
- state school intake	**67%**
drop-out rate	**8%**
- undergraduate applications	**Up 8%**

rahs, and the public school girls come here in their droves. Even if the community is so huge that the young grandees are never really *IT*, we're looking at around 65% only from the state sector, and a very low take (15%) from non-traditional uni-goers.

There is a policy to target state school sixthformers interested in studying law or medicine; they're offering 75 bursaries worth £1000 per year of the degree programme; they are actively involved in LEAPS (the Lothian Equal Access Programme for Schools). Minimum grades for admission to Edinburgh are now 4 B passes at higher level or 3 at A level, but the admission procedure will take into account background and personal qualities.

ACADEMIA & JOBS

Overall, teaching assessments have been top of the range. There is an incredible 2,275,000-vol library, and excellent computer facilities and language laboratories, though there can be a problem in getting to use some of these resources. 'Queues for

ACADEMIC EXCELLENCE

TEACHING:
(Rated Excellent, Highly Satis. or 17+ out of 24)

Computer Studies, Physics, Chemistry, Electrical & Electronic Engineering, Geology, Maths & Statistics, History, Finance & Accounting, Sociology, Social Work, Cellular & Molecular Biology, Organismal Biology, Veterinary Medicine.	**Excellent**
Business & Management, Civil Engineering, Music, Architecture, Geography, History of Art, Law, Philosophy, Politics, Theology, French Studies, Medicine, Nursing, English, Psychology.	**Highly Satis.**
Chemical Engineering	**19**
European Languages	**21**

RESEARCH:
Top grades 5/5*

Hospital-based Clinical, Pure Maths, Computer, Electrical & Electronic Eng, Geography, Middle Eastern & African, English, German/Dutch/Scandinavian, Philosophy	**Grade 5***
Psychology, Bio Sciences, Veterinary, Chemistry, Physics, Earth Sciences, Applied Maths, Civil Eng, Law, Anthropology, Sociology, Asian, Accounting, Celtic, French, Iberian/Latin American, Linguistics, History, Theology	**Grade 5**

Psychotherapists come in a steady stream into the workplace from Edinburgh. There's a BSc and MA Psychology for ABB or ABBB (Highers). Teaching inspection again Highly Satisfactory. Research Grade 5. Interestingly, Languages seed jobs in social work, as at Oxford and Cambridge.

The veterinary provision actually scored better than medicine at the assessments. Edinburgh's 5-year BVM&S has a similar profile to Glasgow's degree. Entry AAB. Teaching inspection, Excellent. Research Grade 5.

The old Moray House Institute of Education is the uni's Faculty of Education. Founded in 1835, there are two campuses, Holyrood in the heart of the Old Town, adjacent to the university's central premises and, 6 miles away on the northwest edge of the city, a campus hitherto known as the Scottish Centre for Physical Education and home to PE, Leisure Studies and Applied Sports Science. The sporting facilities put Edinburgh in the Top 10 for sports trainers and coaches.

For primary or secondary teaching, they ask BCC-BBB: CC for Education Studies. They also provide lecturers for higher education: as at Leeds, it's the joint degrees that are favouring graduates in this area, and again Biological Sciences and Languages. Top-line in the research assessments; 21 points or Excellent in the teaching assessments.

In the financial sector, Edinburgh accountants are in high demand, and their Economics graduates are main runners for jobs in banking. Their MA joint hons programmes draw in Chinese or Arabic with Economics, French or German with Business Studies, Law with either. The 4-year Business Studies & Economics looks the staple.

For merchant bankers Edinburgh is up there with Bristol and Oxford. There's a valuable range of BSc Ordinary and MA Hons combination degrees.

Some 39% entered via a combined course, 28% through Business, 11% through Economics. There are also jobs galore for insurance and pension brokers/underwriters and business management consultants from Edinburgh. Teaching inspections – Finance, Excellent; Business, Highly Satisfactory.

Humanities graduates, and those studying the joint MA hons courses in particular, find work in the advertising, publicity and PR industries, and as archivists, curators, librarians, etc. Language students favour charity organisations and publishing in particular, though sciences, social sciences, law and humanities also provide here, and the extra-curricular student media will have a big effect. Masses of opportunity to hone your publishing skills on such as *Hype* (magazine) and *Student* (newspaper).

Two niche areas worth mentioning are forestry: BSc Ecological Science (Forestry), and BSc Physics with Meteorology.

> *'There's a discernible buzz about the university, a condensed feeling of potential, and energy. This is partly due to the city itself: there's just enough of the "ivory tower" atmosphere to leave you inspired but not oppressed by your impending academia.'*

SOCIAL SCENE

'I know everyone is supposed to fall in love with their university, but Edinburgh just makes it so easy,' writes Holly Crane without a hint of gush. 'It's the ideal advert for higher education: a place where you learn not only facts and formulae from your academic studies, but also about what you can do, what you want to do – and what you don't want to do – with the rest of your life.'

Holly is sensitive to 'a discernible buzz about the university, a condensed feeling of potential, and energy. This is partly due to the city itself: there's just enough of the "ivory tower" atmosphere to leave you inspired but not oppressed by your impending academia. But it's also to do with the type of students. With many doing four-year (or longer) degrees, there is, if not more time, then more reason, to get up off your arse and do

WHERE EDINBURGH GRADUATES END UP

Health & Social Work: 18%; Education: 16%; Wholesale/Retail: 7%; Manufacturing: 6%; Financial Activities: 11%; Public Administration, Civil Service & Defence: 7%; Hotel/Restaurant: 4%; Transport & Communications (including Telecommunications): 2%; Construction: 1%; Agriculture: 1%; Mining/Oil Extracting: 1%; Personnel: 3%; Computer: 2%; Business & Management: 3%; Accountancy: 4%; Media (including Film): 2%; Legal 2%; Architecture: 2%; Publishing: 2%; Advertising: 1%; Artistic/Literary: 0.5%; Sport: 1%.

Approximate 'graduate track' employed **71%**

WHAT IT'S REALLY LIKE

UNIVERSITY:

Social Life	★★★★★
Campus scene	**Diverse, active, self-assured**
Student Union services	**Good**
Politics	**Active**
Sport	**Key**
National team position	**5th**
Sport facilities	**Good**
Arts opportunities	**Good**
Student magazine	**Hype**
Student newspaper	**Student**
National Media Awards	**2 x runner-op**
Student radio	**Fresh Air FM**
National Radio Awards	**Bronze Award**
Nightclub	**Potterow**
Bars	**Sportsman's, Teviot, The Pleasance**
Union ents	**Cheese, comedy, Indie**
Union societies	**200**
Most popular societies	**Amnesty**
Parking	**Poor**

CITY:

Entertainment	★★★★★
Scene	**Seething**
Town/gown relations	**Good**
Risk of violence	**Low**
Cost of living	**High**
Student concessions	**Excellent**
Survival + 2 nights out	**£150+ pw**
Part-time work campus/town	**Good/excellent**

something a bit different.'

There is opportunity aplenty to do just this – loads of clubs and societies, 200 of the latter alone, centred on **The Pleasance**, the most popular being Film Soc, The *Edinburgh Student* (newspaper, there's also a mag called *Hype* and a radio station, Fresh Air fm) and Nightline (welfare). *Edinburgh Student* is Britain's third biggest student newspaper, with a weekly circulation of 12,000 copies distributed to all the universities and higher education colleges around Edinburgh. It is also Britain's oldest student newspaper – Robert Louis Stevenson founded it in 1887. *Hype, Official Magazine of the Students' Association*, is the other student voice box.

Meanwhile the University Theatre Company draws crowds for its many productions at **Bedlam Theatre**, the site of Bristo Bedlam, where 'the mad, manic and mental' were once locked away. Now Bedlam's the UK's only student-run theatre, and every Friday in term time the Improverts do a

'Whose Line is it Anyway' style act here.

All these often win national awards, Fresh Air won Radio 1 Station of the Year award in 2004, and this year radio and magazine won national awards. Then of course there's the politics. Most active student society is Amnesty. All major political parties are represented, and level of union activity this term has been high, issues ranging from removing the honorary degree of Robert Mugabe to equality for all, from age discrimination to religious equality on campus.

For light relief Pleasance has a cabaret bar and 350-seat theatre which plays host to the best comedians from the Comedy Network.

Teviot Union, the oldest purpose-built Students' Union building in the country, has 5 levels of entertainment with 6 bars in operation, a debating hall, recently upgraded **Sportsman's Bar** with big screen and several other bars each with a different identity.

For night-time pleasure it's **The Potterow**, which has been redecorated this year, and decorations used during the Edinburgh festival retained. There's also an extra coffee bar in the Potterow Dome. The venue has 1,200 capacity that regularly reaches capacity on weekends. Highlights include *Big Cheese* on a Saturday, the biggest student night in Edinburgh, and *Different Class* (best of Indie with guest DJs) every Thursday. Bodyrockers, Natasha Hamilton and Belle & Sebastian have all played Potterow this Semester. Richard Herring, Dan Antopolski have all recently done comedy sets.

Down at King's Buildings, there's a £3.4 million student facility for the 7,000 science and engineering campus – catering and bar facilities, a

AT A GLANCE

ACADEMIC FILE:

Subjects assessed	**32**
Excellent/Highly Satisfactory	**94%**
Typical entry requirements	**415 points**
Application acceptance rate	**11%**
Med. School acceptance rate	**9%**
Student-staff ratio	**14:1**
First/2:1 degree pass rate	**78%**

ACCOMMODATION FILE:

Guarantee to freshers	**100% outside Edinburgh**
Style	**Halls, flats, houses**
Catered	**44%**
En-suite	**35%**
Price range pw	**£50-£150**
Approx. city rent pw	**£65-£85**

games room, squash courts, a multi-gym, a sports hall and advisory and welfare services. KB get quizzes, pool comps and film nights by way of ents.

SPORT The university is pre-eminent in sport, came 9th in the UK last year. Besides its twenty-five acres of playing fields and a residential centre on the shore of Loch Tay, there's a sports centre with conditioning gymnasia, a fitness and sports injury centre, and a wide range of team and individual activities. Sports bursaries are offered through the PE Department.

TOWN 'When you do step out, the city offers everything,' writes James Lumsden. 'There are enough bars and pubs to see you from this life into the next, and plenty of theatres, cinemas, clubs, and 'cultural stuff' to stop at, en-route. See *Student Edinburgh* above.

PILLOW TALK

Freshers from outside Edinburgh are guaranteed a place in uni accommodation provided they apply by September 1, and that UCAS has guaranteed their place at Edinburgh by that date. There's a mix of traditional full board halls, student houses, and flats. Main accommodation for first years is Pollock Halls, a complex of houses, together with a bar, shop and dining rooms, which take around 2,000 first years. All rooms are single, but, if you pay extra, you can upgrade to a double bed and en-suite shower. Most people go for full board; breakfast and supper in the week and three meals at the weekend. However, each house has a kitchen area where you can test out your culinary talents (toast). Another residential area is Robertson's Close which consists of self-catering flats. There are also uni-run student houses.

GETTING THERE

☛ By road: M90 or M9 or A1 or M8.
☛ By rail: London King's Cross, 4:30; Glasgow Central, 50 mins; Newcastle, 1:30.
☛ By air: Edinburgh Airport.
☛ By coach: Glasgow, 1:10; London, 9:10; Birmingham, 8:10; Newcastle, 3:10.

EDINBURGH COLLEGE OF ART

Edinburgh College of Art
Lauriston Place
Edinburgh EH3 9DF

TEL 0131 221 6027
FAX 0131 221 6028
EMAIL registration@eca.ac.uk
WEB www.eca.ac.uk

The origins of this college lie in the Drawing Academy, founded by the Trustees of the Edinburgh Board of Manufacturers in 1760. From 1821 an Edinburgh School of Arts was established and thirty years later, as a tribute to the great Scottish engineer James Watt, it changed its title to the Watt Institution and School of Arts, a moment in its history remembered today in the validation of its degrees by Heriot-Watt University. Currently there are talks in progress with the university for a merger by the summer of 2001.

The college today is spread over two campuses within five minutes walk of each other at the very heart of the Old Town. Although there is institutional accommodation for very few, students coming from outside the Edinburgh and Lothian area may apply for college-managed accommodation in the city. There is an active Students' Union, and they have the city's best-loved indie night.

COLLEGE PROFILE	
Founded	**1908**
Status	**Art College**
Degree awarding university	**Heriot-Watt**
Total student population	**1715**
Degree undergraduates	**1295**
ACCOMMODATION:	
Availability	**Limited**
Style	**Edinburgh uni halls**
Cost pw (no food)	**£77**
City rent pw	**£65-£85**

DEGREE SUBJECT AREAS:
Art/Design (Fine Art with Edinburgh Uni), architecture, planning

UNIVERSITY OF ESSEX

The University of Essex
Wivenhoe Park
Colchester
Essex CO4 3SQ

TEL 01206 873666
FAX 01206 873423
admit@essex.ac.uk

Essex Students' Union
Wivenhoe Park
Colchester
Essex CO4 3SQ

TEL 01206 863211
FAX 01206 870915
WEB www.essexstudent.com

VAG VIEW

*E*ssex is considered to be one of the best Social Science universities in the country, especially for law, politics and sociology. There are other good reasons for applying – sport, ents and student media among them. It is also convenient for London.

Applications are up 4% again this year. Investment is keeping pace. They have a new £6 million lecture hall with two new theatres holding 500 people each. They have completely refurbished the Student Union and nightclub, Sub Zero. Now they are launching a new university operation at Southend-on-Sea, and with the University of East Anglia, they're fathering University Campus Suffolk, a new centre on Ipswich waterfront.

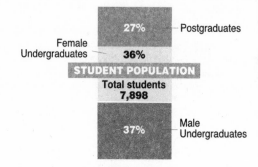

Female Undergraduates **36%**
Postgraduates 27%
Male Undergraduates 37%

STUDENT POPULATION
Total students **7,898**

CAMPUS

Essex will never win any prizes for beauty. It is a grey, drab institution, made almost entirely of concrete. The brick, high-rise towers where students lay their weary heads are a blot on the Colchester skyline, which is not particularly nice anyway.

The campus comprises 200 acres of landscaped parkland, 2 miles from the centre of Colchester, capital of Roman Britain and now commuter and garrison town and a regional centre of commerce, light industry and high technology, an hour away from London by train.

Perhaps a subliminal need for aesthetic redemption has drawn them to the coast. For, as of this year, Essex is up and running with Southend-on-Sea, its address: Elmer Approach, Southend-on-Sea, Essex SS1 1LW. Tel: 01702 328200. The plan has been hatching since further education college South East Essex's move to a new £52 million building there 2 years ago. They're taking over the old Odeon cinema and teaming up with SEEC for everything from library to student sport facilities.

They want to attract 3,000 students and there will be accommodation for them in time for the 2007 academic year.

FEES, BURSARIES

UK & EU Fees 2007: £3,000 p.a. Fees for 2008 not yet fixed. Besides the usual sliding-scale bursaries for those eligible for the HE Maintenance Grant, for students who are engaged on a 4-year degree which involves a foundation or preliminary year, Essex offers a top-up fee waiver, charging only the £1,200 standard fee. Subsequent years will be set at the annual £3,000 fee. They also have two sports bursary schemes for elite athletes, and a sports bursary offered to first year undergraduates in the Department of Biological Sciences.

STUDENT PROFILE

Nick Margerrison notes the mixed student profile as 'one of the best features – it is a small, friendly university; you will enjoy your time here, along with Sharon, Tracey and Wayne. Actually, the

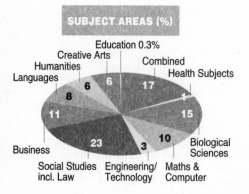

SUBJECT AREAS (%)

Education 0.3%
Creative Arts 6
Humanities 6
Languages 8
Combined 17
Health Subjects 1
Biological Sciences 15
Maths & Computer 10
Engineering/ Technology 3
Social Studies incl. Law 23
Business 11

UNIVERSITY/STUDENT PROFILE	
University since	**1965**
Situation/style	**Town campus**
Student population	**7898**
Undergraduates	**5803**
- mature	**16%**
- non EU undergraduates	**26%**
- male/female	**49/51**
- non-traditional student intake	**30%**
- state school intake	**93%**
- drop-out rate	**14%**
- undergraduate applications	**Up 4%**

ACADEMIC EXCELLENCE	
TEACHING:	
(Rated Excellent or 17+ out of 24)	
Law	**Excellent**
Electronic Systems Eng,	**24**
Sports Science, Philosophy,	
Economics, Politics, Tourism	
Molecular Biosciences	**23**
Sociology, Psychology,	**22**
Art History	
Linguistics	**21**
Maths, Nursing	**20**
RESEARCH:	
Top grades 5/6*	
Economics, Politics, Sociology	**Grade 6***
Psychology, Electrical &	**Grade 5**
Electronic Eng, Law,	
Accounting, Linguistics,	
History, History of Art,	
Philosophy	

university has a large overseas contingent too, especially Greek.' Mixed socially, economically and nationally – almost a third of students come from overseas; people come to Essex University from almost every conceivable part of the known world.

ACADEMIA & JOBS

Degrees out of the new Southend campus will include Project Management, International Enterprise & Business Development, Marketing & Innovation, Business & Service Industry Management, New Technology & Digital Enterprise Management, New Venture Creation & Enterprise Management, Oral Health Sciences, Community Theatre, Physical Theatre, and Popular Culture.

> *Essex is seriously underrated. Tenth best in the country for research, consider it for social sciences – law, politics, economics, sociology; for biosciences; for sport; and much else; but close your eyes to its architecture.*

In Colchester there are five Schools – Comparative Studies (Humanities, but with a cross-cultural, international approach), Social Sciences, Law, Maths & Computer Sciences, Science & Engineering – and consistently good teaching assessments recently – full marks for Electronic Systems Engineering and 22 out of 24 for Psychology, Sociology and Art History. While we're on the subject, a History of Modern Art degree includes a ten-day subsidised visit to New York.

At Essex the first year is thrown open to a study of four or five courses to enable you to investigate your chosen subject from a variety of points of view. This might involve studying Sociology from an Economics point of view, History from a Psychology pov. Then in the second year you move forward to a single or joint honours degree with deeper understanding.

Economics, politics, sociology are world class – special grade 6* at the research assessments. Economics and politics also scored full marks at the teaching inspections, as did other subjects (see Academic Excellence box). What emerges from the

WHERE ESSEX GRADUATES END UP
Health & Social Work: 7%; Education: 11%; Wholesale/Retail: 13%; Manufacturing: 7%; Financial Activities: 11%; Public Administration, Civil Service & Defence: 8%; Hotel/Restaurant: 4%; Transport & Communications (including Telecommunications): 5%; Construction: 3%; Mining/Oil Extracting: 0.5%; Personnel: 4%; Computer: 6%; Business & Management: 2%; Accountancy: 5%; Media (including Film): 2%; Legal 3%; Publishing: 2%; Advertising: 1%; Artistic/Literary: 4%; Sport: 1%.
Approximate 'graduate track' employed **63%**

academic statistics, taken together with the graduate employment info, is that where economics, law, politics, computer, biosciences and sociology are concerned, this uni is without doubt the place to go. The Government certainly knows it. They recruit intelligence officers here, as well as defence operatives and government admin. wallahs.

In civvy street, degrees in Software Engineering, Embedded Systems & Robotics, Internet Technology, Artificial Intelligence, Computer Engineering, Electronic Engineering turn out software engineers, consultants and manufacturers, and computer games designers (there's a dedicated degree for this) by the score. Among smaller unis, Essex is the giant in this sort of thing. Some 6% of their graduates enter the computer industry. This year, Professor Huosheng Hu and the Human Centred Robotics team developed the world's first autonomous robotic fish, which can change direction of its own accord within a pool - part of a public awareness project of the London Aquarium.

Law is another high point. It finds its way into all kinds of courses, and law graduates from Essex are again in demand by Government for defence and admin posts. Essex are European law specialists (and very good at languages too), an interesting joint honours with Human Rights, and a Human Rights Centre on campus. Teaching gets an Excellent rating and research a Grade 5. Last year, human rights lawyers worked with the Centre's Professor Kevin Boyle to win a landmark ruling in the European Court of Human Rights regarding the way conscientious objectors are treated in countries with compulsory military service.

With a world-class Grade 6*, Economics is another subject much in demand. More than 10% of Essex graduates go into financial activities of one sort or another, including accountancy, and some 5% into banking. See in particular, International Economics. There are single honours Accounting and Finance, but also joint honours with Finance, or Management.

Stepping aside from the kind of macho, front-line stuff we find that in the arts they have some specialist employment niches worth noting. In the Autumn of 2000 the famed East 15 Acting School merged with the uni, and so actors, directors, producers and stage managers now abound.

The programme includes a Foundation course and BA Acting and a 1-year Postgrad Diploma. There's also a Postgrad Diploma in Acting for the Media and a new BA in Contemporary Theatre Practice. As of September 2007, the uni's East 15 Acting School, which just won, for the seventh time in eight years, the prestigious Laurence Oliver

Award from the Society of London Theatres, will have a base at the Southend campus. By 2009, 11 programmes of study will be on offer there.

Finally, Essex makes employment waves in sport, too. It is one of the few unis to receive 24 points (full marks) in the teaching assessments, and has led to some very good sporting facilities.

SOCIAL SCENE

STUDENTS' UNION Being close to the metropolis had a negative effect on the uni scene at weekends in the past, but today there's no reason to leave.

The Union nightclub is **Sub Zero**, refurbished and rebuilt last summer for £1.25 million; capacity 1,200, fully DDA compliant, draft products, luxurious seating areas and dancing stage. Two smaller venues are **Level 2** & **Mondo**, used separately and jointly, capacity approx. 250 each.

Mondo was built 4 years ago, Top Bar refurbished in the summer of 2005. Popular with international students, post-grads and staff, there's a large range of draft, including real ales, and a cosy pub atmosphere. Then, of course, there's the SU Bar, the main, pub-type bar, popular with everyone! Regular club/disco nights include the Monday *International Night*, hosted by a different cultural society each week, Tuesday's *Indie Soc* in Mondo and *Urban Groove* (RnB) in Level 2, and, fortnightly, *Comedy Club* in Sub Zero. Wednesday is *Sports Fed*; Thursday, *SU Bar Quiz*, *The Latin Experience* and *SOX* (Societies Guild Night in Mondo); Friday has *TFI Friday* in the Bar, *Flirt!* in Sub Zero, *Global Fusion* in Level 2, and *The Graduate* in Top Bar. On Saturday, it's *Dischord* (rock/indie/ska/metal) in Level 2, live acts/DJs in Sub Zero, karaoke in the SU Bar, and Mondo is available for society nights. On Sunday, it's *Live Lounge* in Mondo.

Live Acts this past term have included (but not

AT A GLANCE	
ACADEMIC FILE:	
Subjects assessed	**18**
Excellent	**78%**
Typical entry requirements	**309 points**
Application acceptance rate	**16%**
Students-staff ratio	**15:1**
First/2:1 degree pass rate	**55%**
ACCOMMODATION FILE:	
Guarantee to freshers	**100%**
Style	**Flats in halls**
Catered	**None**
En-suite	**60%**
Price range pw	**£57-£87**
Town rent pw	**£55-£80**

WHAT IT'S REALLY LIKE

UNIVERSITY:

Social Life	★★★★
Campus scene	**Diverse, fast developing**
Student Union services	**Top notch**
Politics	**Activity high**
Sport	**43 clubs**
National team position	**64th**
Sport facilities	**Excellent**
Arts opportunities	**Good**
Student newspaper	**The Rabbit**
Student radio	**RED AM 1404**
Student TV station	**RTV**
Nightclub	**Sub Zero**
Bars	**SU, Level 2, Mondo**
Union ents	**Full on**
Union clubs/societies	**120**
Parking	**No parking if you live on campus**

CITY:

Entertainment	★★★
Scene	**Clubs 'n pubs**
Town/gown relations	**Average**
Risk of violence	**Low**
Cost of living	**Low**
Student concessions	**Adequate**
Survival + 2 nights out	**£50 pw**
Part-time work campus/town	**Excellent/good**

exclusively) Westwood, Killa Kella, Annie Mac, Hundred Reasons, DJ EZ, Pendulum, Judge Jules, Love Music Hate Racism, Boy Kill Boy, The Young Knives, Dirty Sanchez, Zane Lowe, Dr. Karl Kennedy, Hell is for Heroes.

Proud to be a paperless Union, 'We now have no tickets for events or membership cards for clubs or socs, all is now electronic,' they say.

The investment of time and money is impressive. All SU facilities have been redeveloped and refurbished within the past 5 years, including the Advice Centre, both campus shops, and SU reception, and this year they have opened an International Food Shop, **Go Go Global!**.

They tot up 120 societies and 43 sports clubs, a student newspaper called *The Rabbit*, radio station RED AM 1404, and a TV station: RTV. Winner of last year's Society of the Year Award was the Law Soc, but very popular are Islamic Soc, Indie Soc, RnB Soc, Human Rights Soc, all of which run regular events for their members and the rest of campus.

As for politics, the SU claims one of the highest voter turnouts in the country, and took the second highest number of people to a National Demo this year ('second only to Manchester, who have 38,000

students to their 9,000'). The Union also has a productive relationship with the University and is invited to input to all major decisions.

TOWN 'Colchester suffers from its relative proximity to other major venues in attracting big names in entertainment,' writes Stephen Peters. 'Some occasionally grace us with their presence, but for the real stars get on the train to Cambridge or London. New talent can be seen at the local **Arts Centre**. But if you like a drink, Colchester and its environs can provide. Most tolerate students as long as you don't share your dinner with their toilet floor. The Wivenhoe Run is infamous, and has to be experienced if you reckon you can down a few. Colchester is a garrison town. Students, squaddies and alcohol are a volatile mix. Most of the time, though, you wouldn't know they are there. Find out where not to go in town when you get here (most notably the squaddie pubs).

'The nightclubs are pretty useless. Stick to the university nightclub, and only venture to town clubs for student nights.

'Local transport links are average. Buses are frequent and not too expensive. Have the right change though, or the bus drivers, notoriously miserable, get a bit shirty. Trains to London are quick and reasonably reliable. And if you have a bit of money to spend, **Lakeside** and **Bluewater** are just down the road.'

SPORT The student union website has run a poll as to how many applicants chose Essex for its sport facilities. They are among the best anywhere There's a hall with six badminton courts, fitness room, sauna, sun-bed, squash courts, table tennis, climbing wall, plus a sportsturf pitch, floodlit tennis courts, three cricket pitches (one artificial wicket) plus nets, Squirrel Run circuit, eighteen-hole disc/frisbee-golf, grass and synthetic pitches, and a watersports centre. There are coaching courses in badminton, pilates, squash and tennis, and a relatively new Master's degree in Sports Science (Fitness and Health) is a sign of uni commitment. City clubs offer sailing, windsurfing, canoeing.

PILLOW TALK

More new rooms have recently been built on campus for first years. More than half of students live in uni accommodation, the majority of which is on campus. Tesco is within walking distance of campus, so shopping is easy. Accommodation ranges from flats for 13 to 16 in the famous Towers (tower blocks) to smaller, en-suite flats for six people – South Courts, Houses and University Quays have smaller flats containing 4 to 8 rooms, all of which have en suite facilities. All accommodation is networked so students can use their computer to access the internet and uni network from their rooms free of charge. Each room also has a telephone which provides free use of the internal telephone system.

GETTING THERE

☞ By road: A12. Well served by coach services.
☞ By rail: London Liverpool Street, 1:00, every half-hour; Birmingham New Street, 3:30; Sheffield, 4:00. Ten-minute taxi run to campus.
☞ By coach: London, 2:10; Norwich, 6:15.

UNIVERSITY OF EXETER

The University of Exeter
Northcote House
The Queen's Drive
Exeter EX4 4QJ

TEL 01392 263035
FAX 01392 263857
EMAIL admissions@exeter.ac.uk
WEB www.exeter.ac.uk

The Students' Guild
Exeter University
Devonshire House
Stocker Road
Exeter EX4 4PZ

TEL 01392 263528
FAX 01392 263546
EMAIL enquiries@guild.ex.ac.uk
WEB www.guild.ex.ac.uk

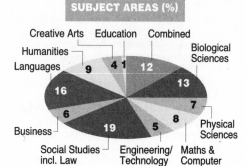

SUBJECT AREAS (%)

Creative Arts 4 — Education 1 — Combined 12
Humanities 9 — Biological Sciences 13
Languages 16 — Physical Sciences 7
Business 6 — 8
Social Studies incl. Law 19 — Engineering/Technology 5 — Maths & Computer 8

VAG VIEW

*E*xeter has experienced one of the highest increases in undergraduate applications this year, which were 23.8% up on January 2006, and has pledged more than £1 million in a range of merit scholarships to attract and support talented students and recognise outstanding ability in science, sports, music, leadership, entrepreneurship or community engagement.

The uni is custodian at the M5 gateway to the West Country, and has, since 2004, celebrated dominion over the region in the new Combined Universities of Cornwall, a collaborative partnership with the University of Plymouth and the Peninsula Medical School, Falmouth College of Arts, The Open University in the South West, The College of St Mark & St John, and with Cornwall's Further Education colleges - Cornwall College, Truro College and Penwith College.

The partnership has attracted massive EU and UK Government funding – £50 million for buildings at the 'Hub' (Falmouth College of Art's

Tremough Campus) and a further £16 million for new buildings at the 'Rim' (the Cornish Further Education colleges). Further funding of £24.5 million has just now been secured, and Phase 2 of the scheme will be launched in 2007.

Exeter has had an interest in Cornwall for some time through its School of Mines in Camborne, and the Institute of Cornish Studies (postgraduate and lifelong learning). Now, they will become a very significant force in the West Country economy right down to Land's End.

There is also a bullish development programme at the Exeter HQ, where over £140 million has recently been invested in new buildings and facilities, ranging from academic facilities to the Students' Guild building and nightclub.

Finally this year, The Peninsula Medical School was the only successful bidder for the creation of a new dental school. The first dental students will start in September 2007.

CAMPUS

THE EXETER CAMPUS 'The university is very easy to

fall in love with,' writes Jo Moorhouse. 'It has one of the most beautiful campuses in the country, in one of the most beautiful counties in Britain.' It is indeed beautifully set on a hill, 15 minutes walk from the centre of the city, which itself lies close to the sea on one side and the moors on the other.

'Students at Exeter have the best of both worlds;' writes Julie Moore, 'a cathedral city with the countryside right on the doorstep.

'Being near the beach makes the surfing society a popular choice, and with Newquay just down the road the summer terms are filled with weekend trips and beach parties.

'Many people, myself included, made Exeter their first choice uni after one tour of the campus. A lush green settlement dotted with ponds and famous sculptures, campus has a relaxed atmosphere with some perfect spots for chilling out with friends in the sun. Everything is within walking distance, which means if you have a lecture at 9am you can get up ten minutes before and still make it. There are no shortage of shops, cafés, and bars and you have no real need to leave.

'The only thing they forget to tell you is that flat roads are a rare luxury in Exeter, and some of the student halls are at the bottom of Cardiac hill, and definitely not advised for anyone with a heart condition! The other side is that you do get used to it, but tend to laugh less at the ongoing joke about "the Exeter thighs".'

St Luke's Campus The schools of Education, Sport and Health Sciences and the Peninsula Medical School are based at St Luke's Campus, about a mile away from the main Streatham Campus. A regular bus service operates between the two.

The Cornwall Campus The £100 million campus at Tremough is on a 70-acre estate deep in Cornwall, overlooking the Fal estuary and offers the very latest in academic, research and residential facilities. The Fal is one of the most beautiful aspects of nature in all England and worth the trip on its own. Tremough is 10 minutes from Falmouth, a seaside town full of trippers in summer, very cheap shopping and access to coves up the Helford River. The new campus is not shared by all the participants in Combined Universities (see *VAG View* above), only by students from the University of Exeter and Falmouth College of Arts. Besides teaching facilities and resources (see *Academia*, below), there's a restaurant and bar, and a fitness studio. Sport is played at local facilities.

FEES, BURSARIES

UK & EU Fees 2007: £3,070 p.a. Not yet fixed for 2008. for all full-time undergraduate programmes,

with the following exceptions: Radiography (tuition fees will be paid by the NHS); Medicine (in year 5 the Department for Health will pay fees). Sliding scale bursary of between £50 and £2,000 p.a. All students with assessed income below £38,330 will be guaranteed financial assistance from the scheme. The University has pledged more than £1 million in a range of merit scholarships to attract and support talented students and recognise outstanding ability in science, sports, music, leadership,

UNIVERSITY/STUDENT PROFILE	
University since	**1955**
Situation/style	**Campus**
Student population	**13827**
Undergraduates	**10269**
- mature	**9%**
- non EU undergraduates	**5%**
- male/female	**46/54**
- non-traditional student intake	**18%**
- state school intake	**73%**
- drop-out rate	**6%**
- undergraduate applications	**Up 24%**

ACADEMIC EXCELLENCE	
TEACHING:	
(Rated Excellent or 17+ out of 24)	
English, Geography	**Excellent**
German, Education,	**24**
Archaeology	
Psychology, Politics, Theology	**23**
Drama, Dance & Cinematics,	**22**
French, Italian, Maths, Physics, Classics, Business/Economics, Biosciences	
Sociology, Materials Technology,	**21**
Sport Sciences	
Russian, Iberian Studies,	**20**
Middle Eastern & African, Studies, General Engineering	
RESEARCH:	
Top grades 5/6*	
German	**Grade 6***
Hospital/Clinical, Applied	**Grade 5**
Maths, Psychology, Physics, Law, Economics, Politics, Sociology, Accounting, Middle Eastern & African Studies, English, Russian/Slavonic/East European, Classics, Archaeology, History, Theology, Education, Sports	

Female Undergraduates — **40%**

26% — Postgraduates

STUDENT POPULATION
Total students
13,827

34% — Male Undergraduates

a concerted effort to widen participation in its degrees in other areas of the socio-economic spectrum. The most recent national statistics show that the proportion of students from state schools/ colleges increased from 71% to 73%; its take from lower socio-economic classes rose from 16% to 18%; and from low participation neighbourhoods, intake is up from 7% to 8%. There was a similar increase a year ago. One result is a growing need to support those students who meet with financial hardship. The non-traditional intake is still not high, but it is increasing and other less Sloaney unis are commenting on it.

entrepreneurship or community engagement. A list of eligible programmes for 2008 entry will be published in Spring 2007 on our Scholarships and Bursaries website at: www.exeter.ac.uk/ scholarships. Vice-Chancellor's Excellence Scholarships offer 10 awards of £5,000 p.a. to students who, in addition to academic excellence (3 A grades at A level or equivalent), are heavily involved in volunteer work, or demonstrate leadership or entrepreneurial skills, or show exceptional talent in music, the arts or sport outside their first field of study. In addition, some 30 scholarships are available in sport, music and for international students.

ACADEMIA & JOBS

Academically, Exeter is one of our premier-league establishments, and teaching assess-ments have been very good. Both Education and Archaeology got full marks, and German took full marks for teaching and world renown (Grade 6*) for research. This year, there are new BA degrees in German, French, Spanish and Russian with Teaching English as a Foreign Language.

'Exeter is known as a university that produces students with a wide range of skills, not merely academically sound,' writes Juliet. They produce a booklet outlining what you will require besides a degree to get a job at a worthwhile level in a competitive industry. There's a team of trainers to enable you to take those skills and training on board, and two recruitment fairs a year in Great Hall, plus a Law Fair because of strength in that area. An Innovation Centre on campus provides start-up homes for small businesses, usually hi-tech. Funding is available in the region. Finally, careers advice is given by alumni through the 'Expert' scheme, on how to get into hard-to-enter sectors like media, and non-profit organisations (charities).

STUDENT PROFILE

The uni has a reputation as a haven

> *The success of Exeter at putting graduates into the City masks other specialities – student cultural activities beyond the curriculum, which are similarly successful in launching graduate careers, especially in the media.*

for the green wellie brigade, hooray Henrys careering down from London by the Golf-full, future City slickers out for a last taste of freedom in the idyllic West Country before being tethered to work stations in the Square Mile. The uni's performance in the accountancy, finance & banking fields seems to support this, and the the Students' Guild's web site address used to be gosh.exeter.ac.uk.

For some time now, however, Exeter has made

WHERE EXETER GRADUATES END UP

Health & Social Work: 4%; Education: 14%; Wholesale/Retail: 8%; Manufacturing: 5%; Financial Activities: 11%; Public Administration, Civil Service & Defence: 6%; Hotel/Restaurant: 3%; Transport & Communications (including Telecommunications): 4%; Construction: 2%; Mining/Oil Extracting: 1%; Personnel: 10%; Computer: 2%; Business & Management: 4%; Accountancy: 7%; Media (including Film): 2%; Legal 2%; Publishing: 1.5%; Advertising: 1%; Artistic/Literary: 1%; Sport: 2%.

Approximate 'graduate track' employed **60%**

School teachers were once the principal educational output, but no more. The University stopped teaching a BEd degree about 5 years ago and now offers BA in Education Studies and Youth & Childhood Studies with a typical offer of BBB-BCC.

Accountancy and finance (investment advisers, analysts) are huge here. They have had an MA in Finance & Investment for nearly 30 years. There are five dedicated courses: Accounting and Finance – 300-340 points required, the same for their Business and Accounting. Both are extended with language options. Mathematics with Accounting is a 3-year degree with at least 25% of the time spent on Accountancy. Just as many graduate accountants come from the Economics department – Economics, & Finance, & Statistics, etc, all with the Euro option of course. Teaching inspection, 22. Research Grade 5.

On the health ticket, increasingly important to the uni, the **Peninsula Medical School** is their new collaboration with Plymouth Uni and the NHS in Devon and Cornwall, the NHS hand ensuring a strong clinical element in the course. Contact: 01752 764439; medadmissions@pms.ac.uk (see also: www.pms.ac.uk).

The BM, BS degree focuses on the biological mechanisms that produce disease and its social impact. It looks very hands-on. First undergraduate intake occurred in 2002, half in Exeter (at St Luke's), half in Plymouth. Both unis already had successful postgraduate medical schools. One of the key points about the new school is that it binds them tighter into the regional community, which will be ever bigger come the CUC. Students work initially with patients in Plymouth and Exeter, then in Truro in Cornwall, finally up with the hillbillies above Dartmoor. Entry 320-340 points + UKCAT, you'll need at least one science subject. There's a 9% application acceptance ratio. There is also a Diagnostic Radiography degree, through which graduates find speedy employ.

The new Peninsula Dental School will train 64 graduates a year and will offer a joint Bachelor of Dental Surgery (BDS) degree through the Universities of Exeter and Plymouth. The undergraduate programme, operating from sites in Plymouth, Truro and Exeter, lasts 4 years and is graduate-level entry only, designed for science graduates or health care professionals. Entry requirements as yet undecided. Probably UKCAT.

A new BSc programme in Human Biosciences this year represents an innovative collaborative teaching response to a broadening demand for graduates with skills in fields relating to medicine, chemistry, biology and physics. The programme builds on Exeter's research strengths and recognises the importance that exercise can play in the prevention and treatment of disease.

There's also a growing reputation at Exeter for getting graduates jobs in the world of sport through the Exercise & Sport Sciences degree.

Another string is a telling modern specialism in things Arabic. 'It has had a lot of inward investment from that direction,' we were told. 'It is very good on Middle Eastern languages, there's a large teaching/library facility on that side.' Arab & Islamic Studies continues to be a growth area at Exeter with rising undergrad and postgrad numbers and an expanding range of courses, including the introduction of Kurdish and Persian options.

'I did politics and there was quite a cross-over with Arab/Islamic, history of the Middle East, Middle East politics, etc,' said a graduate Guild officer, 'and the resource [the Institute of Arabic & Islamic Studies] is really good: letters, firsthand evidence... A lot of people don't realise that you don't have to know Arabic to study there. With the building of the institute – fantastic building! – we have got the largest Arabic Library and Middle East resource outside the Middle East and America. That may seem a bit random, here in Exeter, but the fact is that we are in the forefront on this thing, and it has a knock-on effect.'

In Law, there's an international Grade 5 for research, and they are European law specialists with LLB French Maitrise/German Magister as well as Law with European Study/International Study.

Within the Combined Universities, degrees are offered in Conservation Biology and Ecology, English, Environmental Science and Technology, Geography, Geology, Mining Engineering and Renewable Energy. £3m has been invested in new science laboratories with specialist equipment for

AT A GLANCE	
ACADEMIC FILE:	
Subjects assessed	**32**
Excellent	**78%**
Typical entry requirements	**369 points**
Application acceptance rate	**13%**
Med. School acceptance rate	**9%**
Students-staff ratio	**17:1**
First/2:1 degree pass rate	**70%**
ACCOMMODATION FILE:	
Guarantee to freshers	**100%**
Style	**Halls**
Catered	**50%**
En-suite	**38%**
Price range pw	**£560 - £142**
City rent pw	**£55-£70**

the study of biological and earth sciences and engineering. Geography students benefit from dedicated computer labs with the latest GIS and remote sensing software and a digital map library. The research facilities include a sophisticated computer-controlled electron scanning microscope, QEMSCAN, currently the only one in a European laboratory and the first in any university worldwide.

Phase 2 of Combined Universities, to be delivered in 2007, brings new degrees in Law, History and Politics. As for the Camborne School of Mines, an integral part of the collaboration, despite the decline of British mining there is still high demand overseas for graduates of the BEng Mining Engineering, but the School has been developing its emphasis to environmental science.

STUDENT SCENE

THE STUDENTS' GUILD Union watering holes are The Ram, The Long Lounge, The Lemmy nightclub. Friday and Saturday nights at the Lemmy are hugely popular. Get up to date listings at www.exeterboxoffice.com/diary.aspx. Saturday is the most popular and is student only. Entscard holders get free admission. Friday has a combination of live acts and major DJs and is very popular with both townies and students. Recent and forthcoming acts include Ash, James Lavelle, The Twang, The Maccabees, Hayseed Dixie, Aiden, Embrace, The Delays, Soilwork, The Automatic, Mumm Ra, Hey Molly, The Kooks, Larrikin Love, Cooper Temple Cause, Tim Hughes, Delirious?, Roni Size, DJ Dynamite, Goldblade, Stiff Little Fingers, DJ Format, Salmonella Dub, Graham Coxen, The Switches, DibDub, Stanton Warriors, Pendulum, Ben & Lex, American Headcharge, Mates of State, We Are Scientists, Au Revoir Simone, Alabama3, Paradise Lost, Opeth, Hey Negrita, Less Than Jake, Drunken Monkeys, Goldielookinchain, Dropkick Murphys, The Living End, Spanky Wilson, Quantic Soul Orchestra, Seth Lakeman, Lennon, Dan Donnelly, Soil, Godhead, Brand New Sin, The Days, Paolo Nutini, Newton Faulkner, Hundred Reasons, Mr Scruff, Them Nudes, JamieT, Bloc Party, Metric, DJ Yoda, The Bees, Candy Payne, The View, The Horrors, The Automatic (again).

Then they have the university orchestra and choral society, in the Great Hall. There's also a tradition of musicals in **Northcote**, the part-'pro' campus theatre. Footlights, Exeter Theatre Company and the Gilbert & Sullivan Society perform there, and the Exeter University Symphony Orchestra puts on termly concerts.

There is massive interest in media, too, and although the uni doesn't offer a media course, they have a surprising number of graduates going into the sector. Someone lists, 'Nick Baker, the wildlife presenter, Emma B from Radio 1, Thom Yorke of Radiohead who was a D, Isobel Lang, the weather presenter, people on the production side, like Paul Jackson who produced Red Dwarf - he came back to do a creative writing thing with the students in English, Stewart Purvis, chief exec of ITN.' Some 400 freshers attended a *Welcome to the Media* event in freshers week last year. Those who stuck with it were subjected to a period of training by the *Exeposé* team – the student newspaper is often up for national awards. As well as *Exeposé* they have Xpression fm – radio, and XTV, which was a runner-up in three categories in this year's national competition.

They are proud, too, of their Community Action Group, one of the most active in the country. Student volunteering contributes over

150,000 volunteering hours per year.

SPORT Their £8-million facilities definitely get the thumbs up from students. New indoor tennis facilities to LTA standards opened in 2004. Said Julie: 'This uni is full of sports fanatics, excellent opportunities to join very competitive teams – it's all a very serious business. Also so many surfing, windsurfing and beach bum type societies to join.'

All major team games are well represented, also martial arts, watersports (rowing, canoeing, sailing – six Lark dinghies on the Exe Estuary) and ultimate frisbee. On-campus facilities include sports hall (basketball, netball, volleyball, tennis – there's a new LTA standard indoor/outdoor tennis centre – badminton, indoor cricket net), a climbing wall and traversing wall, rooms for fencing, martial arts, weights, etc. Pitches include 2 all-weather pitches, large grass pitch with nets area, and there are sixty off-campus acres of playing fields nearby.

TOWN 'There are certain pubs that you shouldn't really go into,' warns Juliet Oaks, 'and during Freshers Week the Students' Guild does advise you which to avoid. Also, although Exeter is a city, it is in the West Country: clubbing is not exactly the best. However, there is at least one student night at a club every night of the week. Entry before 10:30 is usually free or very cheap. Some of the clubs distribute tickets beforehand and these are definitely worth getting. A night out can cost around £40 if you push the boat out. For shopping there's enough diversity for anyone, from skaters to Goths.' A £200-million retail centre just opened.'

PILLOW TALK

Wide choice of good catered and self-catered accommodation. The majority of freshers take the catered option, but 250 self-catering rooms are reserved for them too. All the accommodation is either on campus or close by. There are en-suite rooms at ground level in the newer halls and flats suitable for disabled students, as well as some specially adapted rooms in the older residences. With the exception of a small number of rooms in the older residences, study bedrooms have a high-speed connection to the University data network, which can be used for e-mail and Internet access. There is a modest fixed charge for this facility.

GETTING THERE

☞ By road: M5/J30.
☞ By rail: London Paddington, 2:30; Birmingham, 3:00; Plymouth, 1:15.
☞ By air: Exeter Airport for inland, European and some trans-Atlantic flights. Fifteen mins from campus by taxi.
☞ By coach: London, 4:00; Birmingham, 4:30.

UNIVERSITY COLLEGE FALMOUTH

University College Falmouth
Woodlane
Falmouth
Cornwall TR11 4RA

TEL 01326 211077
FAX 01326 212261
EMAIL (via website)
WEB www.falmouth.ac.uk

They were granted University College status in March 2004. Degrees are offered in Broadcasting, English with Creative Writing/Media Studies, Fine Art, Design (audio, graphic, textile, garden, interior/ landscape, ceramics, 3D), Illustration, Journalism, Photography, Film, Media & Business Management. Tthere is a new Media Centre.

Campus is in some of the most lovely scenery that this country has to offer, and is hub of the new Combined Universities of Cornwall (see *Exeter* entry).

Accommodation comprises 450 rooms. Otherwise it's Falmouth student lets.

UNIVERSITY COLLEGE PROFILE

Founded	**1938**
Status	**F/HE College**
Situation/style	**Campus**
Student population	**1990**
Degree undergraduates	**1610**

ACCOMMODATION:

Accommodation guarantee	**42%**
Style	**Flats**
Cost pw (no food)	**£79-£86**
Town rent pw	**£50**

DEGREE SUBJECT AREAS:
Broadcasting, English with Creative Writing/Media Studies, Fine Art, Design (audio, graphic, textile, garden, interior/ landscape, ceramics, 3D), Illustration, Journalism, Photography, Film, Media & Business Management

UNIVERSITY OF GLAMORGAN

The University of Glamorgan
Pontypridd
Mid Glamorgan CF37 1DL

TEL 0800 716925
FAX 01443 480558
EMAIL enquiries@glam.ac.uk
WEB www.glam.ac.uk

Glamorgan Students' Union
Treforest
Pontypridd CF37 1UF

TEL 01443 483500
FAX 01443 483501
EMAIL pres-of-glam@hotmail.com
WEB www.glamsu.com

VAG VIEW

*F*riendly atmosphere, pleasant setting, accessible, sporty, they claim that of all the Welsh universities, Glamorgan has the highest paid new graduates and one of the best graduate employment rates.

The student body is, in higher education speak, 'non-traditional'. Forty per cent are over 21 at inception, and almost 40% from new-to-uni backgrounds, and many do not complete the course.

However, the uni has a bullish investment programme, which has seen new facilities for technology and science, a £5-million refurb. for maths and computing, and a new campus in Cardiff's city centre, with its School of Creative & Cultural Industries.

CAMPUS

Main campus lies at Treforest in the Taff Valley, an ex-coal mining village, so not pretty, but there are stunning views over the valley. It stands a couple of miles from the market town of Pontypridd and a mere quarter of an hour from Cardiff by cheap trains which run every 20 mins from just outside.

'Living up here isn't a drag,' writes Fiona Owen, 'it's nice to belong to a close-knit community, and the college is all on one campus, apart from the Law School, which is across the road. The area is scenic and there are lots of places to go for lovely walks with your friends or your new squeeze. Pontypridd Park is open every day and it's a really nice place to chill on a sunny day.'

ATRiuM, the Universityís brand new campus in the heart of Cardiff city centre opens in September 2007. Home to the Cardiff School of Creative and Cultural Industries, the £35-million development brings together subjects including animation, film, TV and radio, design, drama, music technology and culture and society.

FEES, BURSARIES

UK & EU Fees 2007: £1,200 p.a. for Welsh domiciled; £3,000 for non-Welsh UK. 2008 not yet

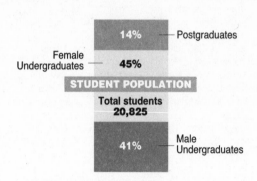

STUDENT POPULATION
Total students
20,825

14% — Postgraduates
Female Undergraduates — **45%**
41% Male Undergraduates

fixed. For 2008, there's an entry scholarship worth £3,000, £1,000 to be paid each year to students who have achieved 300 or more UCAS points. Also, there's a residential allowance worth £1,500, £500 for students from more than 45 miles away.

STUDENT PROFILE

There's a high mature and state school intake and a very high number of students from new-to-uni neighbourhoods. Once on board, there's a friendly atmosphere in a pleasant setting – 'Glamorgan University is small enough to generate real warmth and a sense of close-knit community, but large enough for you to be inconspicuous when that's what you want/need,' writes Beth Smith.

ACADEMIA & JOBS

More than 200 courses are on offer – Arts &

UNIVERSITY/STUDENT PROFILE	
University since.	**1992**
Situation/style	**Rural campus**
Student population	**20825**
Undergraduates	**17898**
- mature	**40%**
- non EU undergraduates	**10%**
- male/female	**48/52**
- non-traditional student intake	**38%**
- state school intake	**97%**
- drop-out rate	**26%**
- undergraduate applications	**Down 0.4%**

WHERE GLAMORGAN GRADUATES END UP

Health & Social Work: 10%; Education: 8%; Wholesale/Retail: 12%; Manufacturing: 8%; Financial Activities: 9%; Public Administration, Civil Service & Defence: 14%; Hotel/Restaurant: 4%; Transport & Communications (including Telecommunications): 4%; Construction: 3%; Personnel: 1%; Computer: 4%; Business & Management: 1%; Accountancy: 2%; Media (including Film): 1%; Legal 4%; Architecture: 2%; Publishing: 0.5%; Advertising: 0.5%; Artistic/Literary: 0.5%; Sport: 2%.

Approximate 'graduate track' employed **58%**

Humanities; Social Sciences; Business; Law; Design; Engineering & Construction; Computing & Technology; Sciences & Maths, Nursing, and a whole raft of joint and combined possibilities. There were 'Excellent' teaching assessments in Business Studies, Mining Surveying, Creative Writing, Theatre & Media Drama, Electrical & Electronic Engineering, Accounting & Finance, Public Sector Schemes, and Welsh, and students will tell you that the teaching is good. Their overall employment record is sound, but not that amazing in terms of 'graduate track' jobs (58%).

There's a clear line into local government administration through to Civil Service executive officer or administrative officer or assistant. The latter comes through biological sciences, business and social, economic & political studies. For executive officers it's much the same, but via law rather than biosciences.

There's a Foundation available for their BA Business Administration, but you might look at Business & Public Services Management, for which there's a Public Sector Management Foundation. Note, too, the BSc Public & Social Policy (with Foundation). There are Foundations, too, in their Law department, where you can study European Law, Criminology & Criminal Justice and Legal Regulation, besides much else. Elements of all these are available in joint, major/minor and combined studies programmes.

Glamorgan are commercial & business and European law specialists. They scored 'Good' in a recent LPC assessment. It's also worth pointing to Glamorgan's BSc Police Sciences (there's also a student society), on offer for around 200 points. See too their BSc Criminology & Criminal Justice degrees (including combos with Psychology, Sociology, Forensic Science), also BSc Forensic Chemistry and BSc Forensic Science. This is a good employment area. There's a Forensic Science Foundation Year.

ACADEMIC EXCELLENCE

TEACHING:
Business Studies **Excellent**
Mining Surveying, Creative
Writing/Theatre & Media Drama,
Electrical & Electronic Eng,
Accounting & Finance,
Public Sector Schemes, Welsh

For local, regional, central government administration, they have a Foundation degree in Public Policy, also Public Sector Management, Leisure & Tourism, and a HND in Public & Emergency Services, as well as the BSc Public & Social Policy, Housing & Environment, International Housing & Society, and other relevant elements in their joint hons programme, such as Environmental Management and Environmental Sustainability. You might also consider the Transport degrees.

Health is a major provision here and dead cert ground for employment. Graduates find their way into jobs as health therapists, psychotherapists, welfare, community and youth workers. Note, too, the BSc Psychology in the Life Sciences faculty, Nursing (mental health, learning disabilities, etc), and BSc Chiropractic (with Foundation).

Glamorgan's Chiropractic course is one of only 2 in the UK. The course has been accredited by both the General Chiropractic Council and the European Council on Chiropractic Education.

For health, sport and science students the

SUBJECT AREAS (%)

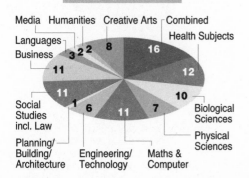

Media Humanities Creative Arts ┌Combined
Languages┐   Health Subjects
Business   3 2 2   8   16
              11   12
              11   10
Social   1 6   11   7   Biological
Studies   Sciences
incl. Law
Planning/   Physical
Building/   Engineering/ Maths &   Sciences
Architecture Technology   Computer

WHAT IT'S REALLY LIKE

UNIVERSITY:	
Social Life	★★★
Campus scene	**Chummy, sporty**
Student Union services	**Good**
Politics	**Some internal**
Sport	**Competitive**
National team position	**65th**
Sport facilities	**Good**
Arts opportunities	**Good**
Student newspaper	**Leek**
Student Media Awards	**R-up for Best Small Budget Publication**
Radio station	**GTFM**
Nightclub	**Shafts**
Bars	**Baa Bar, Smiths**
Union ents	**Chart & party**
Union clubs/societies	**50**
Most popular society	**Chiropractic, LesBiGay**
Parking	**Adequate**
OFF-CAMPUS:	
Entertainment	★★
Scene	**Pubs or Cardiff**
Town/gown relations	**Mostly OK**
Risk of violence	**Average**
Cost of living	**Low**
Student concessions	**Average**
Survival + 2 nights out	**£60 pw**
Part-time work campus/town	**Average/good**

recently opened, £4-million Aneurin Bevan building offers new computer labs, teaching facilities, a restaurant, and clinical practise suites, which include simulated hospital ward environments and the high-tech Clinical Simulation Centre itself, which employs mannequins to simulate human behaviour.

In the Business school, the largest in Wales and 16th largest in the UK, they turn out retail managers and buyers with alacrity. Look at BA Purchasing & Supply Chain Management, and there are a number of management and marketing degrees that support graduates interested in sales and marketing jobs. They have a good record in this area.

For accountancy there's also a good reputation and sound employment figures. You can have International Accounting for 220 points. See also BA Accounting & Finance.

Software engineers and computer programmers abound in a large faculty of Computing, which has dedicated Software Engineering Foundation courses, HNDs and degrees.

For budding construction engineers/managers Glamorgan is up up there with the big suppliers, as are UMIST, Napier and Paisley among the smaller unis. Look at the Built Environment Foundation year (there's also a Building Studies Foundation at Pontypridd College nearby) and consider BSc Hons Architectural Technology or Engineering, or Construction Management. The latter is also part of the Combined Studies route on which you can hold off selecting a main subject for the first year (3 to 5 subjects may be selected). This is a big area for Glamorgan, but you could get in for around 160 points.

Quantity surveyors cost building projects and must have the care for detail of an accountant. Each year nationally more than 300 graduates find employment as quantity surveyors. Glamorgan has a part of that through its dedicated BSc degree.

SOCIAL SCENE

STUDENTS' UNION 'If you're a disco queen and demand that you put your spangly dancing trousers on at least a couple of times a week, the union has a formidable entertainment schedule to tease and tantalise you,' Fiona reassures.

There's **Smiths** bar/café, which serves food, snacks and drinks, accompanied by MTV, pool and arcade machines, and the gorgeously aromatic, freshly baked cookie and baguette bar. Then there's the bar – **Baa Bar**, and **Shafts** nightclub, where there's something on every night of the week, with special participation events, talent nights, etc.

There's an active student media set-up, the student newspaper, Leek, and award-winning radio station, GTFM, offer plenty of challenge and opportunity, and a new society has just been set up to get Glam TV transmitting on campus and on the Internet. Besides other societies, which include the popular Chiropractic and Lesbian, Gay & Bi-sexual, Hellenic, Police Sciences and Christian Encounter – an eclectic mix – there's the uni concert band and big band, and a 40-member mixed choir. Something for everyone, you might say, but students will be students, as Stephen Harley observes: 'There are only three things that dominate every student's life: money, alcohol and sex. But if you come to Glamorgan there is a fourth thing, the mountain on which they built the university. Whenever you go down the hill from the halls of residence you should do as much as possible while you're at the bottom. The first time you go out for the evening and forget your wallet will, I promise you, be the last.

'The second point, important to note, is that the nightlife in Treforest is... well it isn't. There is a handful of good pubs which have the expected student buzz and the ents at **Shafts** make up for the short hours. Generally, life in Treforest is peaceful enough.' (See *Student Cardiff*, page 126.)

SPORT is a major part of university life, in particular rugby, though in recent years, students in karate, football, hockey and basketball have also gone on to gain success at national and international level. Facilities are of a professional standard. There's a Sports Centre with six badminton courts, climbing wall, all indoor sports, but no swimming pool. There's a smaller hall for keep-fit, table tennis, martial arts, fencing, plus four squash courts (one glass-backed), two conditioning rooms, sauna/solarium suite, and 30 acres of floodlit pitches – football, rugby and hockey, plus trim trail, cricket pitch, archery - and one of the UK's only FIFA approved 3 'G' rubber crumb pitches. Coaching and a sports scholarship scheme are available for students at national/international level. Nearby you'll find swimming pools, golf courses, running tracks, and the Brecon Beacons for horse riding, canoeing, mountaineering, hang gliding, walking. Also sailing and windsurfing.

PILLOW TALK

The majority of accommodation on campus (halls) is reserved for first year students (see box, above). They also let houses very near to the University. A meal voucher service is available. New rules allow students to stay over Christmas and Easter vacs at

AT A GLANCE

ACADEMIC FILE:

Subjects assessed	**17**
Excellent	**41%**
Typical entry requirements	**215 points**
Application acceptance rate	**26%**
Students-staff ratio	**19:1**
First/2:1 degree pass rate	**50%**

ACCOMMODATION FILE:

Guarantee to freshers	**75%**
Style	**Halls**
Catered	**None**
En suite	**75%**
Approx price range pw	**£58-£97**
Local rent pw	**£35-£60**

no extra cost. Many students live in private rented accommodation locally; others in Cardiff.

GETTING THERE

☛ By road: M4/J32, A470. Exit Llantrisant, A473.
☛ By rail: London Paddington, 2:45; Birmingham, 2:15; York, 5:00.
☛ By air: Cardiff Airport.
☛ By coach: London, 4:00; Birmingham, 3:40; Bournemouth, 6:00.

STUDENT GLASGOW - THE CITY

'Glasgow - the only place in the world where you can get a free fish supper at 9 in the morning just by picking it out of the hands of a drunk who's passed out in the street the night before.' So said Rab C Nesbitt of his beloved home town, but - while there are still pockets of the city where the claim probably holds true, he neglects to mention the hundreds of other factors that make Glasgow one of the countryís most popular student destinations.

Though not the capital, Glasgow is regarded by many as the only proper city in Scotland. Edinburgh may have the Parliament, Aberdeen has the oil, Dundee... is also a city, apparently, but Glasgow is where the fun is to be had. This is where the clubs, the shopping, the music venues, the theatres, Europe's (formerly the world's) tallest cinema building are. Sure, it may rain more than in any other city in Europe, but Glasgow's famous sense of humour more than makes up for that. Perhaps that's why the city now hosts Europe's largest annual comedy

festival, and is the home of Scottish TV and media.

With relatively cheap rents and centrally located universities and colleges, Glasgow seems purpose-built for student living. Would-be applicants may be put off by perceived crime rates, but according to local police violent incidents are increasingly rare, and students are generally unlikely to fall victim.

In recent years the city has been changing at an incredible pace. Formerly downtrodden areas are undergoing regeneration, in keeping with a city aiming to be at the forefront of the modern Europe, while the historic sites of the old town - including one of the oldest universities in the world - are preserved as a link to the past.

Of course, should you ever find a reason to leave the city - perhaps, after the inevitable excesses of freshersí week, you just want to go and die in a field somewhere - picturesque Loch Lomond is only half an hour away.

Just remember to at least attempt to get a degree while you're here.

CITY SCENE

The Glasgow scene has launched countless stars in recent years, from Franz Ferdinand (not the one who invented World War One) to the outrageously low-camp Shahbaz, who crashed out of TV's *Big Brother* to widespread local amusement. The city boasts clubs for both extremes and all in between, from the achingly hip **Arches** and **Subclub** to student favourites the **Garage** and sticky-floored, pound-a-drink flea-pit **Jumpin' Jaks**. Glasgow is a highlight of many UK music tours, and generally the only stop in Scotland for bigger name acts. The gay scene is just as lively and varied as the rest of the city, with the **Polo Lounge** a staple and nights like **Utter Gutter** catering to the more 'extreme'.

ARTS & ENTERTAINMENT

Glasgow's arts scene is unparalleled outside of London, with a mind-boggling array of theatres, galleries, cinemas and concert halls.

Many of the 14 major theatres offer student tickets for a fiver, bringing a night at the shows within almost any budget. All tastes are catered for - those seeking cutting-edge writing and performance need look no further than the **Arches** or the **Tramway**, more traditional fare is on offer at the **Citizens'** in the Gorbals, and shameless panto-afficionados should check out the **Kings**, or perhaps seek psychiatric advice.

Opera, ballet and classical performances can be found at the **Theatre Royal**, and the **Glasgow Film Theatre** showcases a variety of independent and classic films, complementing the blockbusters at the massive **Cineworld** complex.

The newly refurbished **Kelvingrove Art Gallery and Museum** has a wonderfully eclectic mix of exhibits, and the **Centre for Contemporary Arts** showcases the latest in design and concept art.

SPORT

Home to both of Scotland's football teams, Glasgow affords the unique opportunity to witness the Irish troubles re-enacted weekly on the pitch, though the sectarian clashes which have marred the city's sporting reputation have, receded in recent years. Rugby fans are still within an hour of Murrayfield by train, and those interested in more minority sports should be well served by some excellent university clubs.

PUBS

Glasgow has a thriving pub scene. Some of the lowest drinks prices in the country have cost students many a degree. Central to the life of any West End dwelling student will be Byres Road and the more upmarket Ashton Lane - try **Nude** or **Radio** for £1 cocktails, or **Uisge Beatha** for a proper pint. Those in the city centre may prefer **O'Neills'** mock-Irish charm or the classy appeal of **Royal Exchange Square**, while the **Pot Still's** world-class range of whiskies makes it well worth the trip from any part of town.

Chris Watt

UNIVERSITY OF GLASGOW

The University of Glasgow
University Avenue
Glasgow G12 8QQ

TEL 0141 330 4575
FAX 0141 330 4045
EMAIL admissions@gla.ac.uk
WEB www.gla.ac.uk

Glasgow University SRC
University Avenue
Glasgow G12 8QQ

GUU: 0141 339 8697
QMU: 0141 339 9784
EMAIL enquiries@src.gla.ac.uk
WEB www.src.gla.ac.uk

VAG VIEW

*T*his particular university – one of three in the city – enjoys the rare distinction of having been established by Papal Bull, and began its existence in the Chapter House of Glasgow Cathedral in 1451. Today it still speaks of the city's traditions, but gives an objective sense of its long history. Since 1871 it has been based next to Kelvingrove Park on the Gilmorehill campus, 3 miles west of the city centre in the fashionable West End, with its many listed buildings.

What you get is a twofold opportunity – excellent teaching in a well-respected and traditional university, and, within reach, an *exciting urban culture, which may surprise the unexpected in you.*

CAMPUS GLASGOW

'Glasgow itself has some wonderful sites,' writes Sharon Gaines – 'but the West End, by the university, has its own unique atmosphere. Ashton Lane winds round cobbled paths leading to the trendiest pubs in this friendly part of town, while Byres Road facilitates the most extensive pub crawl – each within spitting distance. If the opulent Merchant City is the heart of the city, Great Western Road is its lungs. An old church looms over small quaint shops while half a mile of animal-like headlights shuffle slowly towards the flyover and three colossal tower blocks stand triumphantly in the distance. An awesome sight.

'If the more tranquil appeals to you, imagine gliding through a collage of a thousand colours of trees winding down a path passing two city heroes, dodging squirrels and birds until you land on a nineteenth-century bridge where the rain crashes down into the River Clyde, gushing downstream. This is the university's Kelvingrove Park – glorious in the autumn, brimming with smiling faces in the summer as everyone collates from across Glasgow on the hills.'

Campus overlooks Kelvingrove Park. Is it always so idyllic? 'Okay, it's not all roses,' Sharon concedes – 'The park is notoriously dangerous at night as are various parts of the city, but this is true of most big cities.'

There are other, less widely-known Glasgow Uni campuses. **St Andrew's College** is the new Faculty of Education, based since summer 2002 on Glasgow Caledonian Uni's old campus on Park Drive, where the West End starts. The Vet school and outdoor sports facilities are located at **Garscube**, with an £8-million development that includes a swimming pool, cardio-vascular suites and a wide range of gym facilities. To the south, in Dumfries, is **Crichton Campus**, which offers innovative study programmes to a mixture of full-time and part-time students, the first of whom are about to graduate.

FEES, BURSARIES

Fees for English: £1,700 p.a. (Medicine: £2,700). The Century 21 Club has enrolled 20 firms to sponsor undergraduates at £1,000 a year, as part of an arrangement to forge closer links with local business. Another ten scholarships for students from poor backgrounds will commemorate the life of Donald Dewar, Scotland's late First Minister and alumnus of the university. The Beaton Scholarship is also part of their widening access scheme. There are also a few bursaries for students tackling a

UNIVERSITY/STUDENT PROFILE	
University since	**1451**
Situation/style	**City Campus**
Student population	**25100**
Undergraduates	**19620**
- mature	**14%**
- non EU undergraduates	**3%**
- male/female	**41/59**
- non-traditional student intake	**23%**
- state school sector intake	**87%**
- drop-out rate	**14%**
- undergraduate applications	**Down 4%**

second undergrad course, a tuition fee waver for self-funding 4th-year undergrads, nine choral scholarships (£300) and one organ (£850), an Italian scholarship (where the language is part of your course), Stevenson Exchange Scholarship for French, Spanish and German study, sports bursaries (www.gla.ac.uk/services/sport). The uni is also considering facilitating access for hard-pressed students with other bursaries - e-mail: L.Hamilton@admin.gla.ac.uk. See also senate.gla.ac.uk/awards/indes.html for other prizes, scholarships and endowments open to students in particular departments.

STUDENT PROFILE

Glasgow has made headway in equal opportunities – more than a fifth of students are from backgrounds new to the idea of uni, and one in six from 'low-participation neighbourhoods. They are actively seeking financial support for these groups.

There are no social divisions on campus, which is almost half made up of students local to the region. As one student commented, 'there's a sense of community – you cannot fail to walk down University Avenue without bumping into someone who wants to nick your lecture notes.'

ACADEMIA & JOBS

Thirty-three assessments and a 91% Excellent or

WHERE GLASGOW GRADUATES END UP

Health & Social Work: 28%; Education: 13%; Wholesale/Retail: 10%; Manufacturing: 5%; Financial Activities: 7%; Public Administration, Civil Service & Defence: 5%; Hotel/Restaurant: 5%; Transport & Communications (including Telecommunications): 3%; Construction: 1%; Mining/Oil Extracting: 1%; Personnel: 2%; Computer: 3%; Business & Management: 2%; Accountancy: 3%; Media (including Film): 2%; Legal 1.5%; Artistic/Literary: 1%; Sport: 1%.

Approximate 'graduate track' employed **66%**

Highly Satisfactory result speaks for itself. One characteristic of the syllabus is a huge programme of joint honours degrees – humanities, arts and social sciences. Research-wise, Glasgow ascended six places overall to 29th in Britain at the last research assessments, quadrupling its Grade 5* ratings (world excellence). Yet, their reputation is for being better focused on teaching their students than most. They make a deliberate effort to get more young staff in, and special needs advisers are on hand for students with disabilities and learning disadvantages.

Applications for science degrees have risen by 25% since the mid-1990s. More than a quarter of all Glasgow graduates get a job in the health industry. The degree in Medicine is a 5-year MB, characterised by clinical scenarios from Year 1, and IT featured instruction (all students are required to qualify for a Cert of Basic IT Competence). Entry AAB + UKCAT (including Chemistry and one of Maths, Physics or Biology; General Studies not acceptable), AAAAB at Highers (including Chemistry and Biology and ether Maths or Physics. Also SG English at Grade 3). Teaching inspection, Excellent. Research Grade 5* Psychology; Grade 5 Clinical Lab Sciences, Hospital-based Clinical, Biological Sciences.

For dentists, it's a 5-year BDS. Entry ABB. Teaching inspection, Highly Satisfactory.

There's a strong call for Glasgow graduates to go into community work/counselling, they come through social studies, languages and BSc Psychology. See, too, their Podiatry degrees, which also have a sure employment basis.

After The Royal Veterinary College, Glasgow's 5-year BVMS Veterinary Medicine captures most of the graduate job market and is slightly lighter on entry, though still AAB. Teaching inspection, Excellent. Research Grade 5. They also have a Veterinary Nursing degree.

For Education, it's CCC or BBBC-BBCCC Highers for primary and secondary. They also turn out more adult education lecturers than anyone else. Languages are far and away the surest route

in, perhaps because shortly after the acquisition of St Andrew's College of Education came the new School of Modern Languages & Cultures, which gives an international dimension to many degrees through six departments – Celtic, French, German, Hispanic, Italian and Slavonic. There's a world-class Grade 5* research rating for the School of English & Scottish Language.

Law, rated Grade 5 for research and coming at undergrad. level with language combos, and biological sciences are the next most certain route to employability. Biological sciences was rated Excellent at the assessments and, together with Law, has an international Grade 5 for research. Also

SUBJECT AREAS (%)

in biosciences is Sport, with a world-class Grade 5* research rating. Glasgow lead in turning out physical training instructors (Education).

They are also big graduate providers of accountants through various dedicated degrees. Note Accountancy with International Accounting in particular, but there are others – Accountancy with Finance looks tempting. The uni is also a proven launch pad for actuaries – look at the Applied Maths degrees.

Engineering and technology degrees lead, in

particular, to jobs in defence. Aeronautical, Audio & Video, Avionics, Electrical Power Engineering, Electronic & Software Engineering, etc, all pull weight in this direction and links are very tight with the Royal Air Force and the Royal Navy.

The faculty has expanded in collaboration with Strathclyde Uni over a series of Naval Architecture degrees. There are also various BEng/MEng Aeronautical, Civil, Electronics & Electrical, Mechanical Design, Mechanical (also joint with E&E, Aeronautics, Music, etc) and Product Design.

A traditionally difficult but successful area for employment is Archaeology, available single hons/joint as part of the Science Group, or as an arts degree in the popular joint hons programme.

> *'Glasgow, the only proper city in Scotland, is where the fun is. This is where the clubs, the shopping, the music venues, the theatres are. Sure, it may rain, but their famous sense of humour makes up for that.'*

There are masses of MA joint hons possibilities, featuring Classical Civilisation, History of Art, Archaeology, Celtic Civilisation, Scottish History, Islamic Studies, etc, and the Language Department excels in its course design, too, adding depth to this joint programme with such as Polish, Czech, Russian, etc.

Teaching inspection was Highly Satisfactory for History of Art, and research Grade 5, and thanks to such as this and the cultural aspect of its many courses, Glasgow leads the field in supplying museum archivists, curators and librarians.

THE CRICHTON CAMPUS Glasgow are offering seven broadly-based MAs, taught through 'virtual' and 'residential' lecturing. Creative & Cultural Studies, Enviro. Studies, Heath & Social Studies, Heritage & Tourism, Liberal Arts, Renewable Energy: Engineering in the Environment, and Scottish Studies. Glasgow-based expertise is on hand through video link-ups, while the benefits of one-to-one small group teaching is also maintained. *Course enquiries:* 01387 702001; Fax: 01387 702005.

SOCIAL SCENE

Glasgow, like UMIST, Imperial College, St Andrews, Edinburgh and Dundee, have cut themselves off from the National Union of Students at a saving of many thousands of pounds each year. Constant political issues this year have been anti students association and anti NUS. It's a moot point, however, whether Glasgow's own bureaucracy is better organised. 'Glasgow Uni is probably the most divided university in Glasgow,' writes Rachel Richardson with reference to the 'different bodies operating different aspects of university life. This leads to certain divisions.'

There are four union-type bodies – the Students Representative Council, Glasgow University Union and Queen Margaret Union. SRC is the political arm and administers the student societies, which are legion, supports volunteers and class representatives and is the official voice of the students on campus. Then there is GUSA, the sports association founded in 1881 that administers the sporting clubs. Adding to the confusion, postgrads have an organisation called the Research Club and there are boat clubs for both men and women, neither of which is affiliated to GUSA.

GUU operate from an impressively scary looking building at the foot of Gilmorehill. They

---

ACADEMIC EXCELLENCE

TEACHING:
(Rated Excellent, Highly Satis. or 17+ out of 24)

Computer Studies, Physics, Chemistry, Geography, Geology, Philosophy, Sociology, Cellular & Molec Biology, Organismal Biology, English, French, Medicine, Veterinary Medicine, Psychology, Social Policy.	**Excellent**
Civil Engineering, Music, Maths & Statistics, Mechanical + Manufacturing, Engineering, History of Art, History, Finance & Accounting, Law, Politics, Social Work, Theology, Dentistry, Nursing, Drama.	**Highly Satis.**
European Languages	**22**

RESEARCH:
Top grades 5/5*

Psychology, European Studies, English, Sports	**Grade 5***
Clinical Laboratory Sciences, Hospital-based Clinical, Biological Sciences, Veterinary, Physics, Pure Maths, Applied Maths, Statistics, Computer, Electrical & Electronic Eng, Mechanical Eng, Town & Country Planning, Law, Politics, Accounting, French, History, History of Art, Theology	**Grade 5**

WHAT IT'S REALLY LIKE	
UNIVERSITY:	
Social Life	★★★★★
Campus scene	**Lively, diverse, fantastic fun**
Student Union services	**Good**
Politics	**Activity average Student issues**
Sport	**45 clubs**
National team position	**32nd**
Sport facilities	**Good**
Arts opportunities	**Drama, music, art exc; dance good; film average**
Student newspaper	**GU Guardian**
Student magazine	**GUM, Qmunicate, GUUi**
Student radio	**SubCity Radio**
Radio Awards	**2005 winner**
Student TV	**G.U.S.T.**
TV Awards	**2006 runner-up**
Nightclubs	**Qudos, Hive**
Bars	**Jim's Bar, Beer Bar, Deep-6, Altitude, Playing Fields**
Union ents	**Cheesy Pop rules + rock & indie, live**
Union societies	**120**
Most active society	**Dialectic or LGBT (lesbian, gay, bi- & transgender)**
Parking	**Poor**
CITY:	
Entertainment	★★★★★
Scene	**Very cool**
Town/gown relations	**Good**
Risk of violence	**High**
Cost of living	**High**
Student concessions	**Poor**
Survival + 2 nights out	**£80 pw**
Part-time work campus/town	**Poor/good**

AT A GLANCE	
ACADEMIC FILE:	
Subjects assessed	**33**
Excellent/Highly Satisfactory	**91%**
Typical entry requirements	**392 points**
Application acceptance rate	**15%**
Med. School acceptance rate	**13%**
Students-staff ratio	**14:1**
First/2:1 degree pass rate	**70%**
ACCOMMODATION FILE:	
Guarantee to freshers	**100%**
Style	**Halls, flats**
Catered	**7%**
En-suite	**23%**
Price range pw	**£69-£115**

the long-running *Cheesy Pop* – Fridays, 10pm - 2pm, £1 members, £2 guests. Says one who knows: 'No two ways about it. Since 1993, when we invented the genre, *Cheesy Pop* has been the biggest and best student night in Scotland. Copied by many, but never equalled, the experience is still unique. Others interpret "cheesy" to mean crass, crap and often just down-right offensive, whereas *Cheesy Pop* is really about music which is fun. Imagine S Club, Rage Against The Machine, Abba, 2 Unlimited, Kylie and Stevie Wonder, all mixed up, then wonder why you ever considered going anywhere else.'

Tuesday is *Revolution* with DJ Muppet – 'rock, metal, hip hop, and a whole lot more', *Chart Attack* - Wednesday, *Style & Substance* - Thursday, and unplugged live acoustic on Sundays

Mention must be made of the lively journalistic scene at the uni: SubCity Radio (they won a Silver Award at the 2005 Student Awards), the *SRC-run Guardian* (newspaper), the *Glasgow University Magazine* (GUM, oldest student magazine in Scotland), the two Union publications, *GUUi* and *Qmunicate*, and GUST (oldest student TV station in the UK and Highly Commended in this year's national student media awards).

SPORT Excellent facilities, including a 25m pool, steam room and sauna, two activity halls with sprung flooring, basketball, volleyball, five-a-side soccer; a fitness and conditioning area, fully equipped. £1,500 pa bursaries offered in squash, athletics, rowing; £1,000 pa, golf: some forty courses in the area.

PILLOW TALK

Catered or self-catered halls of residence and self-catered student apartments are available, 7%

have 6 bars: **The Beer Bar** (traditional, with the names of the campus's fastest drinkers immortalised round the bar), **Altitude, Deep 6** (pseudo-trendy basement music bar – live bands, karaoke, juke box – open till 2am Fridays, half price cocktails, etc.), **The Playing Fields**, **Balcony Bar, The Hive** (the nightclub - *Lollypop* on Thursday; *Brie* (a higher class of cheese) on Friday).

QM's ents programme operates out of **Jim's Bar**, Games Room, the bottle bar and Qudos (their nightclub), 1100 capacity. The QM's main event is catered, 23% en suite. See *At A Glance* box for prices and look out for Queen Margaret Residences – 400 places all new, all en suite.

GETTING THERE
☞ By road: M8/J19 or J18. Good coach services.

☞ By rail: Edinburgh, 50 mins; London King's Cross, 5:00. Main campus Underground Station is Hillhead.
☞ By air: Glasgow Airport.
☞ By coach: London, 8:20; Birmingham, 6:20; Newcastle, 4:20.

GLASGOW CALEDONIAN UNIVERSITY

Glasgow Caledonian University
70 Cowcaddens Road
Glasgow G4 0BA

TEL 0141 331 3000
FAX 0141 331 3005
EMAIL helpline@gcal.ac.uk
WEB www.caledonian.ac.uk

Glasgow Caledonian Students' Association
70 Cowcaddens Road
Glasgow G4 0BA

TEL 0141 331 3886
FAX 0141 353 0029
EMAIL student.association@
glasgow.caledonian.ac.uk
WEB www.caledonianstudent.com

VAG VIEW

They have centralised operations on one site instead of five, opened new accommodation (320 self-catering flats at Caledonian Court), a Sports Centre, a £17-million Health building and a new Learning Centre, The Saltire Centre. Now, their promise of a new Student Union building is about to be fulfilled and perhaps we will see a more concentrated effort to get an extra-curricular, student culture together. It is already looking up, with great success in sport over the past few years.

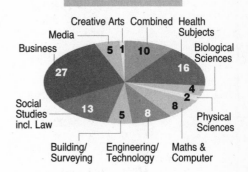

SUBJECT AREAS (%)

Creative Arts 5, Combined Media 1, Health Subjects 10, Business 27, Biological Sciences 16, Social Studies incl. Law 13, Building/Surveying 5, Engineering/Technology 8, Maths & Computer 8, Physical Sciences 2, 4

CAMPUS
City campus is on Cowcaddens Road, opposite Buchanan Bus Station, slap bang in the city centre. There is an amazing concentration of some 50,000 students here – Strathclyde University, the College of Building and Printing, the College of Food & Technology, and the College of Commerce are in the immediate vicinity.

FEES, BURSARIES
Fees for non-Scottish-based UK residents: £1,700 p.a. in 2007. Scholarships in tourism and sport.

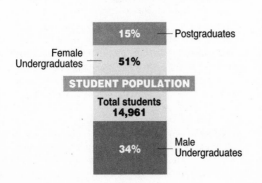

Postgraduates 15%
Female Undergraduates 51%

STUDENT POPULATION
Total students 14,961

Male Undergraduates 34%

UNIVERSITY/STUDENT PROFILE	
University since	**1992**
Situation/style	**City campus**
Student population	**14961**
Undergraduates	**12700**
- mature	**29%**
- non EU undergraduates	**2%**
- male/female	**40/60**
- non-traditional student intake	**37%**
-state school intake	**97%**
- drop-out rate	**18%**
- undergraduate applications	**Down 1%**

ACADEMIC EXCELLENCE

TEACHING:
Chemistry, Physiotherapy **Excellent**
Physics, Consumer Studies, **Highly Satis.**
Maths & Statistics,
Finance & Accounting, Mass
Communications, Sociology,
Social Work, Dietetics &
Nutrition, Occupational Therapy,
Psychology, Radiography,
Biology, Nursing

WHAT IT'S REALLY LIKE

UNIVERSITY:	
Social Life	★★
Campus scene	**Friendly**
Student Union services	**Average**
Politics	**Activity low**
Sport	**Some. Men's Hockey good**
National team position	**93rd**
Sport facilities	**Average**
Arts opportunities	**Slim**
Student magazine	**Re:Union**
Venue	**The Bedsit**
Bars	**Main bar, Lounge, & Games Room**
Union ents	**Quiz, Caleyoke, cheesy disco, some live acts**
Union clubs/societies	**Handful**
Parking	**Poor**
CITY:	
Entertainment	★★★★★
Scene	**Cool**
Town/gown relations	**Good**
Risk of violence	**Average**
Cost of living	**Average**
Student concessions	**Good**
Survival + 2 nights out	**£70 pw**
Part-time work campus/town	**Good.**

STUDENT PROFILE

'Most of Cally's recruits,' writes Rachel Richardson, 'are home-based students looking for a more vocational course.' Statistically, Cally has jumped in at the deep end, exceeding their Government quotas with a 37% take from socio-economic classes 4-7 and 29% from so-called 'low-participation neighbourhoods', and it has not been easy to get a cohesive student culture going. However, there's lots about Cally that's great, not least the ever healthier student-to-staff ratio, which is telling in the decreasing drop-out rate.

ACADEMIA & JOBS

The university's new £20-million learning centre, The Saltire Centre - home to the university library, and offering 1,800 study spaces, 500 computers and every student support service under the one roof - opened last year.

Cally offer courses across six areas – Business, Engineering & the Environment (including Architectural Technology and various building and surveying courses, Music Technology with Electronics, and a host of other engineering and technology courses), Entrepreneurial & Service Sector (all kinds of management/retail/consumer courses), Health (including masses of nursing), Mathematical & Physical Sciences, and Social & Behavioural Sciences (they have recently been accredited by the Law Society of Scotland to run an LlB degree).

A new Learning Centre is planned. Meanwhile there are 350,000 volumes and extensive IT facilities in the library, including the REAL learning café.

Entry-wise, they want students who are motivated with enthusiasm and drive rather than A grades. The 24% health industry provision reveals the most measurable success story in nursing, optometry, podiatry, radiation science, ophthalmic dispensing and the like. They are the only Scottish uni to offer degrees in Optometry, and one of three that offer Occupational Therapy, Podiatry and Physiotherapy. There are also Nutrition degrees and even Medical Illustration, as well as Applied Bioscience courses.

Physiotherapy is a major career field. Over 1,000 graduates become physiotherapists each year. The route is straightforward – dedicated BSc Physiotherapy courses, which scooped the uni's best score at the assessments with an Excellent.

Their Podiatry degrees require only 120 points. the BSc Occupational Therapy is a 3-year sandwich course, undemanding at entry and highly successful in getting graduates jobs. There's a 2-year DipHE Ophtalmic Dispensing (DD at A level, BCC at Highers), and a 4-year BSc Optometry, which is more stretching, requiring BBB (BBBBB Highers, BBB Advanced Highers) to start.

For some time they have been specialists in commercial law. Now, following a new LLB, we can expect to see graduate employment taking off more in that direction. Meanwhile, bedrock Business and Finance courses continue to leave their mark on the graduate employment picture, as do Engineering and Architectural Technology and Built Environment courses.

Nationwide, more than 4,500 graduates find work in the hotel and restaurant industry annually,

WHERE GLASGOW CALEDONIA GRADUATES END UP

Health & Social Work: 24%; Education: 3%; Wholesale/Retail: 14%; Manufacturing: 7%; Financial Activities: 10%; Public Administration, Civil Service & Defence: 7%; Hotel/Restaurant: 6%; Transport & Communications (including Telecommunications): 4%; Construction: 4%; Personnel: 2%; Computer: 1%; Business & Management: 3%; Accountancy: 3%; Media (including Film): 1%; Legal 1%; Architecture: 3%; Publishing: 1%; Sport: 2%.

Approximate 'graduate track' employed **58%**

and Cally are among the giants for the industry. See their Hospitality Management, Tourism Mgt, Entertainment & Events Mgt.

Property Development is another niche. Look at Property Mgt & Development/Property Studies, also such as Construction Mgt, Planning & Sustainable Development, and a good employment opportunity, BSc Quantity Surveying.

In Retail Management Manchester Met leads, followed by Ulster, but then in kicks Cally. Pre-eminent in the Business Faculty are its degrees in Retailing, Consumer & Trading Standards, Fashion Business, etc.

Finally, there is a sound employment track record in Interior Design. Explore their Applied Graphics Technology with Multimedia.

SOCIAL SCENE

STUDENT ASSOCIATION The SA is poised to move lock, stock and barrel to a newish building the other side of campus, previously used by human resources, but as we write, they still have the rather cramped environs of **The Bedsit**.

The **Disco Bar**, also known as the **Front** or **Main Bar** is decorated on a music theme, the wall hung with iconic rock images. Music is a constant feature, and you can even bring along your own CD's for the bar to play. There are 3 plasma screens and a pool table. Sometimes it justifies its name by turning into a club with DJ's playing cheesy pop to rock to r'n'b. Every Friday is *Funky Friday*. Such as Jamelia, Speedway, Ben from Hollyoakes, Scott Anderson, South Beach, Stu from big Brother, Trevor Nelson and Vernon Kay have visited. Then there's the **Lounge Bar**, also known as the **Back Bar** and by day a coffee bar, by night a chill zone, with *Caley Oke* (karaoke talent contest) on Wednesday, with a little help from the Bedsit's own Calley Swalley. There are 2 plasma screens, which show MTV or any large sporting event, and it has recently been refubished. Upstairs is the **Games Room** with a multitude of TV's playing MTV throughout the day, 6 pool tables and food (it's the main place for it in the union).

Then there's the **Hub**, info and resource centre

for sports clubs and societies. Students use it to organise student activities for socs like Alpha for Students, Amnesty International, Chinese Students Association, Christian Union, Music Soc, Muslim Soc, GT Events, Hellenic Society, International Students, Lesbian, Gay, Bisexual Society, SSOS.

Finally, **Arc** gives access to health and fitness services and facilities, including a gym, a place to relax and de-stress at a yoga or t'ai chi class, to work out, play badminton or book in for a therapeutic massage session.

The large mature, local and part-time population is suggested as the reason for the relatively low level of action - Funky Friday is over by 7 pm. The challenge is that after nightfall and at weekends the place is deserted, while in the day, the bars are full to overflowing.

See also *Student Glasgow*, page 205.

SPORT Investment in sport facilities has been rewarded with great success in the British Uni Sport Association (BUSA) league. There are loads of sports clubs: rugby, soccer (male and female), athletics catered for alongside such as snowboarding, hillwalking and table tennis. It's the Bearsden dry ski slopes for GCU Club Ski and the real white stuff for weekends in semester two. The

AT A GLANCE

ACADEMIC FILE:

Subjects assessed	**23**
Excellent/Highly Satisfactory	**65%**
Typical entry requirements	**306 points**
Application acceptance rate	**18%**
Students-staff ratio	**18:1**
First/2:1 degree pass rate	**58%**

ACCOMMODATION FILE:

Guarantee to freshers	**No**
Style	**Halls**
Catered	**None**
En suite	**50%**
Approx price range pw	**£72-£82**
City rent pw	**£60-£80**

Hillwalking and Mountaineering Club is the largest – weekends away in Glen Coe.

PILLOW TALK

For lucky first years, it's Caledonian Court, adjacent to campus, 6-8 bedroom flats.

GETTING THERE

☞ By road: M8/J19 or J18. Good coach services.
☞ By rail: 50 minutes Edinburgh, 5 hours London.
☞ By Underground: Cowcaddens and Buchanan Street Stations are nearby.
☞ By air: Glasgow Airport.

GLASGOW SCHOOL OF ART

Glasgow School of Art
167 Renfrew Street
Glasgow G3 6RQ

TEL 0141 353 4512
FAX 0141 353 4408
EMAIL info@gsa.ac.uk
WEB www.gsa.ac.uk

SCHOOL PROFILE	
Founded	**1845**
Status	**Art School**
Degree awarding university	**Glasgow**
Student population	**1500**
Full-time undergraduates	**1265**
ACCOMMODATION:	
Availability in college	**118 places**
Style	**Flats**
Cost pw (no food)	**£54 to £72**
City rent pw	**£80-£80**
DEGREE SUBJECT AREAS:	
Art, architecture, design & humanities, engineering	

This is one of the oldest and largest independent art schools in the country. It is centred on the Mackintosh Building, generally considered to be the masterwork of former student Charles Rennie Mackintosh.

There are three curricular schools: Design & Craft, Fine Art and Architecture. Teaching assessments have been Excellent for Architecture and Highly Satisfactory for Fine Art and Design & Craft.

Resources include a library, substantial art archives of international significance, two galleries and various other in-house exhibition areas. Becoming a student entails participation in the flourishing artistic community of the city of Glasgow. Tramway, one of the largest and most innovative art spaces in the UK, and The Centre for Contemporary Art (CCA), just next door to the school, provide the platform for this. An active Students' Association promotes educational and cultural activities. Limited accommodation nearby in Margaret Macdonald House (self-catering flats).

UNIVERSITY OF GLOUCESTERSHIRE

The University of Gloucestershire
Park Campus
Cheltenham
Gloucestershire GL50 4BS

TEL 08707 201100
FAX 01242 543334
EMAIL admissions@glos.ac.uk
WEB www.glos.ac.uk

Gloucestershire Uni Students' Union
PO Box 220
The Park
Cheltenham GL50 2RH

TEL 01242 532848
FAX 01242 261381
EMAIL pksu@glos.ac.uk
WEB www.ugsu.org/

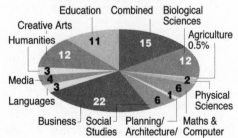

SUBJECT AREAS (%)

Education 15 — Combined — Biological Sciences — Agriculture 0.5% — 12 — 2 — 6 — 1 Physical Sciences — 6 Maths & Computer — Planning/Architecture/ — Social Studies — Business 22 — Languages 3 — Media 4 — 3 — Humanities 12 — Creative Arts 11

VAG VIEW

The sometime Cheltenham & Gloucester College of Higher Education, out of which Gloucester Uni was born in 2001, was established in 1990, following a merger between the College of St Paul and St Mary and the higher education section of Gloucestershire College of Arts and Technology. They also have a campus in Gloucester, initially for the complementary sporting and nursing fraternities.

Female Undergraduates — **46%**

17% — Postgraduates

STUDENT POPULATION

Total students 8,700

37% — Male Undergraduates

CAMPUS

There are three sites in Cheltenham. **Park Campus** is the main site, then there's Francis Close Hall (FCH) and Pittville. When you turn up at Park, don't confuse it with the nearby Gloscat, monstrous further education establishment in crying need of a facelift. No, this is the one up the road that copped the dosh, though there academic asso-

UNIVERSITY/STUDENT PROFILE	
University since	**2001**
Situation/style	**Town sites**
Student population	**8700**
Undergraduates	**7200**
- mature	**30%**
- non EU undergraduates	**5%**
- male/female	**44/56**
- non-traditional student intake	**30%**
- state school intake	**93%**
- drop-out rate	**19%**
- undergraduate applications	**Up 4%**

ciations with their health and teaching foundation degrees. The main campus is leafy, white, everything – halls, bars, lecture theatres – close to hand and spanking new it seems, though many of the buildings must have been here for some time. It was once a botanic garden.

The newer £15-million **Oxstalls Campus** has opened in the nearby city of Gloucester. It was part of their remit that they would open up there. It is being used by the schools of Sport and Nursing, but will be developed and the subject base widened. There's a Student Union building, halls of residence for completion this year, a refectory and astroturf, a sports science building and learning resources centre.

FEES & BURSARIES

UK & EU Fees 2007: £3,070 p.a. Relief on a sliding scale for those meeting the conditions of the Higher Education Maintenance Grant - total support package up to £4,040. There are also sports scholarships - see www.glos.ac.uk/shsc/scholarships

STUDENT PROFILE

Broadly, Pittville attracts interesting/arty-types, Park be-suited-&-booted business management-types, and FCH sporty-types, though presumably they're off to Oxstalls now. Like Oxford Brookes, and unusual in a new-uni demography, there was once a lean to independent school types and a very low drop-out rate. Now the intake of non-traditional uni types has tripled, independent school types are few. Despite big changes, students talk of the 'really great sense of community' – unusual for an institute split into various campuses.

ACADEMIA & JOBS

First degree subjects fall into 3 faculties: Arts & Education (split between Park and Pittville),

WHERE GLOUCESTERSHIRE GRADUATES END UP
Health & Social Work: 5%; Education: 20%; Wholesale/Retail: 13%; Manufacturing: 6%; Financial Activities: 9%; Public Administration, Civil Service & Defence: 7%; Hotel/Restaurant: 7%; Transport & Communications (including Telecommunications): 3%; Construction: 1%; Personnel: 5%; Computer: 4%; Business & Management: 2%; Media (including Film): 2%; Legal 1%; Architecture: 0.5%; Publishing: 2%; Advertising: 1%; Artistic/Literary: 1%; Sport: 3%.

Approximate 'graduate track' employed **55%**

Business & Social Studies (Park), Environment & Leisure (FCH and Oxstalls). The programmes (BA/BSc Hons) are modular and very broad based. There is a choice of single, joint or major/minor courses, each of them composed of more than twenty modules with often less than clear synergy between subjects.

Hundreds of main subject combinations are offered, from which you will build your course. It can be quite daunting.

Sixteen per cent of its graduate output goes into primary education. The courses go from Nursery through Key Stage 2. This is the old Cheltenham & Gloucester College turned uni.

Thereafter, managers and administrators, sales and other miscellaneous occupations proliferate from the modular degree system, with its endless but often tedious-looking combination possibilities. Business and Administrative Studies of one sort or another account for around 20% of the curriculum, even more than Education. The notably vocational interest from applicants who, for one reason or another, do choose to go to Gloucestershire is evident, too, in the recent dropping of Theology from the degree menu. Given that Lord Carey, former Archbishop of Canterbury, is the uni chairman, and that the uni is fathered by two church colleges, and that the department scored 23 out of 24 in the assessments, and Grade 4 for research, this is quite a statement. English also got a Grade 4 incidentally, nationally sound.

One significant interest point in their employment record is the category of sports trainers and coaches, graduates coming from Biological Sciences and Education. The Sport & Exercise Science courses reflect an interest rooted in one of the uni's original constituent parts, a sports college.

There's also a good record in community and youth work – see Community Studies combos, though graduates come from all over the curriculum to this. Also, the Human Resource Management degrees score well in the employment sector, again part of the Business & Admin part of the list.

Among the smaller universities who put 5% plus of their graduates into catering, Gloucester figures strongly with masses of hospitality and hotel/catering degrees on offer. Teaching inspection, 21.

Future events or conference managers should

> *There's a middle-of-the-road feel about this uni, which may be no bad thing. The huge inter-scheme modular programme continues to baffle, but the union is spot on, and the clean white lines of Park promise students the luxury to which many may well already be accustomed.*

also apply. There are dedicated degree courses for this increasingly popular sector, such as Events Management.

Graphic artists and designers also find work and there's a fair reputation here for Film, and an emphasis recently on photojournalism.

New courses this year include interactive games design, media & music management, public relations, criminology, radio production, popular music.

SOCIAL SCENE

'Cheltenham & Gloucester is a fab, mad, lovely place,' I was told and didn't find much to contradict it. There are four bars, one on each campus. A workmanlike ents programme makes good use of the large, airy **Park Bar** with stage and seriously provocative sound and lighting systems.

Fancy dress parties figure, with *Drink Around The World* events, a different country represented at each of the three bars. There's karaoke, fun and games type *Open-the-Box* drink promo nights, **Pittville Bar** *Bingo*, various balls (the Summer Ball sells upwards of 7,000 tickets, then there's Christmas Ball, Freshers Ball, Graduation Ball) and the odd *Doctors & Nurses* night, with *Sub:Mission* the

ACADEMIC EXCELLENCE	
TEACHING:	
(Rated Excellent or 17+ out of 24)	
Geography	**Excellent**
Theology	**23**
Town & City Planning, Art & Design, Psychology, Tourism, Sport	**21**
Sociology, Communication & Media Studies	**20**
RESEARCH:	
Top grades 5/5*	**None**

big Saturday night attraction. Also some local live bands (bigger names at balls). Sports bar, Oxtalls, at Gloucester campus is big on match days, of course.

It is fair to point out, however, that the emphasis is on clubnights in town with the local SU bar providing a kind of pre-club, warm-up session, and at weekends it's quiet.

There is a sense of the society scene maturing. *Space* is the excellent fortnightly newspaper, and

WHAT IT'S REALLY LIKE

UNIVERSITY:	
Social Life	★★★
Campus scene	**Middle of the road, local**
Politics	**Interest low**
Sport	**Very competitive**
National team position	**50th**
Arts opportunities	**OK, film good**
Student newspaper	**Space**
Student Radio	**Tone Radio**
Nightclub	**Sub:Mission @ Park**
Bars	**Park, Pittville, FCH and Oxstalls**
Union ents	**Cheesy + huge Balls**
Union societies	**70**
Parking	**Poor**
TOWN:	
Entertainment	★★★
Scene	**OK clubs, pubs, good shopping**
Risk of violence	**Average**
Cost of living	**High**
Student concessions	**Excellent**
Survival + 2 nights out	**£70-£80 pw**
Part-time work campus/town	**Good**

AT A GLANCE

ACADEMIC FILE:	
Subjects assessed	**17**
Excellent	**53%**
Typical entry requirements	**229points**
Application acceptance rate	**22%**
Students-staff ratio	**18:1**
First/2:1 degree pass rate	**44%**
ACCOMMODATION FILE:	
Guarantee to freshers	**100%**
Style	**Halls, flats, houses**
Catered	**None**
En suite	**80%**
Approx price range pw	**£67-£89**
Town rent pw	**£60**

this year they have a student radio station: Tone Radio. The Film Society is very active. PDS (The Pittville Degree Show Society) puts on charity fund raisers throughout the year. The Art Society puts on fine shows at the end of each year in Pittville. If this is to be but the beginning of something bigger, it will take organisation and investment.

SPORT They do well in the BUSA leagues. It's their big thing. There is a swimming pool, sports hall, pitches (known as *The Folley*), a fitness suite, and at Oxstalls a sports science lab and astro turf pitch.

TOWN Cheltenham itself has fantastic shops (classy, unique and your high street shops too), some good pubs, the **Arts Centre** and a few clubs. 'Gold Cup Week brings the Irish to town and loadsa money,' a student confides, 'a great week for all the girls to go out. You get plied with drink after drink. This week is RAG week, just the best week of the academic calendar!! Tons of fun and misbehaviour, being on a float, driven in front of crowds of people, drunk in charge of a water pistol by 9am, expecting a lot of "cheek" from the rugby boys. And all for charity!' Is it *always* so...baby doll? I venture. 'Well, Christmas carols in FCH chapel are always a laugh...specially with all that *mulled* wine in you.'

PILLOW TALK

Apply early for the luxurious-looking, mixed, self-catered or half-board halls at Park. Priority goes to first years and overseas students. New halls in Gloucester and 100-room Regency Halls in central Cheltenham opened in September 2006.

GETTING THERE

☞ By road: M5/J11 or M40/A40 or M4/J15, A419. Good coach service.
☞ By rail: Bristol Parkway, 45 mins; Birmingham, 1.00; London Paddington, 2:30.
☞ By coach: London, 2:35; Birmingham, 1:10.

GOLDSMITHS COLLEGE, LONDON

University of London Goldsmiths College
New Cross
London SE14 6NW

TEL 020 7919 7766
FAX 020 7919 7509
EMAIL admissions@gold.ac.uk
WEB www.goldsmiths.ac.uk

Goldsmiths Students' Union
Dixon Road
London SE14 6NW

TEL 020 8692 1406
FAX 020 8694 9789
EMAIL gcsu@gold.ac.uk
WEB www.gcsu.org.uk)

VAG VIEW

Goldsmiths is a college of the University of London, famous for its postmodern art department, ents programme, and for the active commitment of its students to fairness and justice. It is located in south-east London, and was listed as "cool brand leader' (with MTV) by the Brand Council in 2004.

'Ours is one of the most exciting colleges in the country,' I was told. 'It's unpretentious [Oh, right], set in London and neatly poised between a bad-ass ents programme and radical action. We have one of the most politically active Students' Unions in the country.'

CAMPUS

'So, you want to know about Goldsmiths?' said Siobhan Daly. 'Well, don't come here looking for the architectural splendours of Oxbridge or the serenity of Durham. This is south-east London: bold, brash and full of embodiments of Delboy Trotter. One of my friends cried when she arrived, saying that it looked more like Grange Hill than a university.'

Writes Laura Cattell: "Oh brave New Cross that has such people in it..." Just a bleak 7-minute train ride from London Bridge will deliver you to New Cross. Although not one of the best parts of London, estate agent rhetoric is beginning to convince some that this is "an up-and-coming urban area". I would-nít go that far, but plans are indeed underway to build a Health and Culture Centre in New Cross.

'Cost of living is cheaper than in many parts of the capital and Campus is open, safe and welcoming. The buildings aren't outstanding, but the students are and this former Arts College has a great, friendly atmosphere. It's one of the most local universities in London, in that it really encourages local people to enrol and also has good links with the community.'

UNIVERSITY/STUDENT PROFILE

College of London Uni since	**1904**
Situation/style	**Campus**
Student population	**8454**
Undergraduates	**3690**
- mature	**36%**
- non EU undergraduates	**13%**
- male/female	**34/66**
- non-traditional student intake	**28%**
state school intake	**88%**
- drop-out rate	**18%**
- undergraduate applications	**Up 20%**

FEES, BURSARIES

UK & EU Fees 2007: 'around £3,000'. Fees for 2008, 'around £3,070'. Bursary of £1,000 if in receipt of full HE Maintenance Grant, £300 if partial. There's a Hardship Bursary to reduce the cost of hall fees by 10-20%, depending on individual need. The Mayorís New Cross Award is an annual award of £20,000 divided equally between one male and one female student with strong academic potential from secondary school or FE college in the Borough of Lewisham. Also four academic achievement scholarship schemes are available.

STUDENT PROFILE

You don't need me to say this. Damian 'pickled-cows' Hirst, Placebo, Julian Clary and Blur all strutted their stuff here. 'This doesn't, however, mean that you have to conform to the general "I'm-finding-myself" principle of dressing,' Siobhan reassures. 'Just do whatever you want; be yourself. If you are a heterosexual man, you'll love it here. If you are a homosexual woman, you'll also love it here. Goldsmiths is 66% women. The competition is hot!

'That said,' writes Laura, 'students here are a diverse crowd - masses of international students, mature students, "non-traditional" students - its widening participation scheme is one of the best in the country.'

STUDENT POPULATION

Total students
8,454

31% — Postgraduates

Female Undergraduates — 29%

14% — Male Undergraduates

ACADEMIA & JOBS

Says the uni: 'Goldsmiths is all about the freedom to experiment, to think differently, to be an individual. That's why our list of former students includes names like Antony Gormley, Julian Clary, Damien Hirst, Mary Quant, Bridget Riley, Vivienne Westwood, Graham Coxon, Malcolm McLaren. We bring creative and unconventional approaches to all of our subjects, but everything we do is based on the highest academic standards of teaching and research.'

Says Laura: 'Teaching couldn't get much better

here. As a Top 20 University, Goldsmiths is no easy arty option and has been rated excellent for a range of subjects: Psychology, Education, Anthropology, Media. Alongside this is its reputation for creative, performance and visual arts. Personal tutors often leave a little to be desired, but this is changing with the creation of a Peer Assisted Learning scheme. The library is fairly new and very well-stocked with excellent provision and lots of study areas. The Education floor is particularly good, as is the language resource centre.'

2005 saw an ambitious new Arts Complex open. The new Centre for Cognition, Computation & Culture houses studios and teaching facilities for the Visual Arts Department.

Fine Arts has the lowest work load. The word

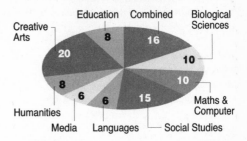

SUBJECT AREAS (%)

Education 8; Combined 16; Biological Sciences 10; Maths & Computer 10; Social Studies 15; Languages 6; Media 6; Humanities 8; Creative Arts 20

London, and that gives you as many choices and opportunities as you are willing to take. A would-be journalist will be in a better position than out of town students when it comes to trying to get a placement on a London-based national paper.

At the end of it all, however, with its cutting-edge, cool appeal, it is all too easy to lose sight of the fact that Goldsmiths, the hip college of London Uni, gives most of its graduates to primary school education, and to the hard reality of life as a clerk, sales assistant, accounts and wages clerks, etc. The glamorous fashionable end of things, it seems, is also highly competitive and will never be open to all. although remember, it takes time to ply your talent as an artist and graduate employment figures are recorded just 6 months after graduation.

A host of employable graduate social workers endorse their BA Applied Social Science, Community Development and Youth Work, BA Social Work, and their excellent BSc Psychology.

See also Computer Science, Computer & Information Systems and Internet Computing (all available as 4-year degree with work experience). These last make IT consultants, software engineers and computer programmers of their students.

ACADEMIC EXCELLENCE

TEACHING:
(Rated Excellent or 17+ out of 24)

Music	**Excellent**
Sociology	**23**
Media & Communications, Drama, Psychology, Art &	**22**
Maths	**21**
Design, Economics, Politics	
History of Art	**19**

RESEARCH:
Top grades 5/5/6**

Sociology	**Grade 6***
Communication/Cultural/Media,	**Grade 5***
Anthropology, English, Art & Design, Music	**Grade 5**

is, never arrange to meet art students in the library, they'll never find it. If they did, they'd discover some 230,000 vols, 9,500 music scores, a computer centre and language facility in the Rutherford Information Services Building. Investment has recently been directed to new music practice rooms for solo and ensemble work.

Also, if you choose to study here you will be in

SOCIAL SCENE

STUDENTS UNION Their building is called **Tiananmen, The Green Room** is the bar, and **The Stretch** is the bar/club venue – recent visitors are Roni Size, Goldie, Athlete. 'Our Students' Union may be a concrete monstrosity, but there's a fab

WHERE GOLDSMITHS GRADUATES END UP

Health & Social Work: 10%; Education: 22%; Wholesale/Retail: 12%; Manufacturing: 5%; Financial Activities: 6%; Public Administration, Civil Service & Defence: 10%; Hotel/Restaurant: 3%; Transport & Communications (including Telecommunications): 2%; Construction: 0.5%; Personnel: 6%; Computer: 3%; Business & Management: 2%; Media (including Film): 3%; Legal 2%; Architecture: 0.5%; Publishing: 3%; Advertising: 1%; Artistic/Literary: 3%; Sport: 0.5%.

Approximate 'graduate track' employed **59%**

WHAT IT'S REALLY LIKE

COLLEGE:

Social Life	★★★
Campus scene	**Trendy, radical**
Student Union services	**Average**
Politics	**Anarchy**
Sport	**Relaxed; 20 clubs**
National team position	**116th**
Sport facilities	**Getting better**
Arts opportunities	**Excellent film, theatre**
Student magazine	**Smiths**
National Media Awards	**Best Design 2006**
Student radio	**Wired**
Club venue + bar	**The Stretch**
Bar & café	**The Green Room**
Union ents	**OK disco**
Union societies	**21**
Most popular societies	**Respect**
Parking	**Non-existent**

CITY:

Entertainment	★★★★★
Scene	**Wild, expensive, but locally not**
Town/gown relations	**OK**
Risk of violence	**Average -high**
Cost of living	**High**
Student concessions	**Good**
Survival + 2 nights out	**£100 pw**
Part-time work campus/town	**Excellent**

well organised and available. They're also a good provider of part-time jobs about campus. A good way of earning is to become a Student Ambassador, assisting in a local school, helping out at a Widening Participation event or a school careers fair.

TOWN 'The local pubs are great - not a pretentious wine bar in sight. **New Cross Inn** is worth a try as is the **Amersham Arms** - particularly on a Monday when you can enjoy top comedy for just £3. Recent acts include Russell Howard and Paul Sinja.

'Cinema is good; nearest is Peckham Multiplex or Greenwich Picturehouse/Odeon Theatre - in general a good arts scene locally, and very close to London's theatreland. Night clubs average/good,

AT A GLANCE

ACADEMIC FILE:

Subjects assessed	**15**
Excellent	**67%**
Typical entry requirements	**296 points**
Application acceptance rate	**17%**
Students-staff ratio	**20:1**
First/2:1 degree pass rate	**61%**

ACCOMMODATION FILE:

Guarantee to freshers	**Priority to non-locals**
Style	**Halls**
Catered	**None**
Ensuite	**87%**
Approx price range pw	**£81-£101**
City rent pw	**£80-£100**

nightlife hidden inside and rather outstanding alcohol prices,' writes Siobhan.

Writes Laura: 'The Student Union shuts down at the weekend, which is a bit of a shocker, but it does make up for it in the week by putting on plenty of cheap nights such as *Club Sandwich* - pop/dance/indie/RnB on Wednesday, *Sidebag* disco on Friday; also bingo, Superquiz and karaoke.'

Student societies range from Respect to Capoeira. In politics generally, anarchy rules! Students love to campaign here, religious awareness and equality being of particular importance. There's also a strong culture of altruism. They piloted a prison visiting scheme, and were nominated for a National Student Volunteering Award.

Student magazine *Smiths* regularly features in the national student media awards, in 2004 took Magazine of the Year and 2005 the Runner-up Award for Best Feature Writer. In 2006 it won Best Publication Design. Student radio is Wired.

'The SU is very active,' concludes Laura. 'There's nearly always a student play on and most days you'll find a free lunchtime recital or musical performance on campus. Welfare is key and support services are accessible, mentoring schemes are

but local **Venue** is pretty awful.

'There are several cheap ethnic restaurants. If you're fed up with New Cross and Deptford then Greenwich is a 10-minute bus ride away - lovely with plenty of great restaurants and trendy bars. Best ones are the **Gipsy Moth** or the **Spaniard**.'

SPORT Not sporty, but there's a new fitness centre (**Club Pulse**. £15 a month gets you use of gym, all exercise classes for free, but no swimming pool. 'They have a good women's football team and their basketball team aren't bad either,' says Laura. 'Playing fields, as on most University of London campuses, are pretty far away, but they do exist.'

PILLOW TALK

They have 1,000 places within walking distance of the campus (most less than 15 mins away) - flats, houses, and purpose-built residences.

'Halls here are quite reasonable for London

[£81-£101 per week]; my flat is £80 before bills so make of that what you will,' reveals Siobhan.

Decent en-suite hall development sees Loring now satisfying 400 students and Dean House 95. 'The on-site Loring Hall is the best on offer in my opinion,' Siobhan confirms, 'every room has an en-suite bathroom, personal telephone (you will be grateful for it!) and you can get cable television. '

Writes Laura: 'Goldsmiths seems to own all the streets around campus, so students pour out of every corner, though they merge pretty well with the locals. Shared private accommodation is a little cheaper than the London average and you can find some decent places in the £75 price mark. Areas such as Brockley, New Cross, Deptford and parts of Peckham are popular with students. Lewisham can be pretty awful in parts, so look carefully. Greenwich and Blackheath are the best and safest parts, but reflect this in the rental prices.'

GETTING THERE

☛ By road: at the junction of A2 and A20.
☛ By rail: New Cross Gate or New Cross Underground and overland.

UNIVERSITY OF GREENWICH

The University of Greenwich
Maritime Greenwich Campus
Old Royal Naval College
Greenwich
London SE10 9LS

TEL 0800 005006
FAX 020 8331 8145
EMAIL courseinfo@greenwich.ac.uk
WEB www.gre.ac.uk
STUDENT UNION 0208 331 7629
SU WEB www.uk250.co.uk

VAG VIEW

*G**reenwich Uni is bit by bit up-rooting from its disparate bases and focusing more keenly on its £50-million headquarters at Greenwich Campus, a setting described by the London Evening Standard as 'one of the grandest of any university in the world'.*

CAMPUSES

GREENWICH CAMPUS has humanities, business, law, computing, maritime studies, maths in the Sir Chris Wren designed, former Royal Naval College, the uni's flagship campus. There's a library, computing facilities of course, some postgrad accommodation, a conference centre and the Greenwich Maritime Institute (a research/postgrad teaching facility). There's also **Bar Latitude**. Excellent party atmosphere, by all accounts, but light on ents. Drinks promos, pool competition nights, karaoke, comedy. Greatly enhanced on-site catering facilities opened on campus in March 2007. Accommodation 10-15 minutes walk away: Binnie Court and Devonport House halls, and new Cutty Sark and McMillan Student Village en-suite residences. Student accommodation is improving greatly, but apply very early for the best.

AVERY HILL Bexley Road, Eltham, London SE9 2PQ, and Every Hill Road, Eltham, London SE9 2HB. Has health & social care, social sciences, education, architecture, landscape and construction. A £14

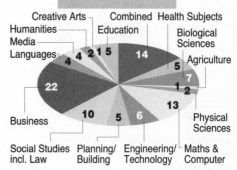

SUBJECT AREAS (%)

Creative Arts, Combined, Health Subjects, Humanities, Education, Biological Sciences, Media, Languages — 4, 4, 2, 1, 5, 14, 5, Agriculture, 22, 7, 1, 2, 13, Business, 10, 5, 6, Physical Sciences, Social Studies incl. Law, Planning/Building, Engineering/Technology, Maths & Computer

million building project features a multi-purpose sports hall, a 220-seat lecture theatre and 4 clinical skills laboratories, which replicate real NHS wards;.

There's a particularly good atmosphere at the Village, on 86 acres of parkland. A short walk away is the **Sparrows Farm Centre**, the sporting facility, situated next door to Charlton Athletic's training ground. It has squash courts, fitness suite, sauna and solarium and the **Sports Bar**. Village accommodation is open to all students from Greenwich Uni (the main campus is 40 mins by bus away – there's a regular peak-time service). Shared flats and maisonettes, some en suite.

MEDWAY Pembroke, Chatham Maritime, Kent ME4 4AW. Has engineering, science, pharmacy, nursing, some business. Incorporates the Natural Resources Institute. Has a sports hall with badminton and bas-

Postgraduates 28%

Female Undergraduates 40%

STUDENT POPULATION

Total students 23,850

Male Undergraduates 32%

UNIVERSITY/STUDENT PROFILE	
University since	**1992**
Situation/style	**City sites**
Student population	**23850**
Undergraduates	**17203**
- mature	**60%**
- non EU undergraduates	**10%**
- male/female	**45/55**
- non-traditional student intake	**43%**
state school intake	**97%**
- drop-out rate	**28%**
- undergraduate applications	**Up 12%**

ketball courts and a weights room. The new Drill Hall Library, shared with the University of Kent, cost £15 million and has 370 PC study spaces, 400 open study spaces and more than 100,000 volumes in what is widely regarded as the longest library in Europe. There's a friendly traditional pub-style bar, **Coopers**, with adjacent **Purple** nightclub – resident DJs and regular ents. There are 3 halls of residence – shared en-suite flats – close to campus.

FEES, BURSARIES

UK & EU Fees 2007/8: £2,560 p.a. Students at the Medway School of Pharmacy, which operates jointly with the University of Kent, will pay £3,070 per year. A separate bursary scheme is available for these students. Cash scholarships of £500 p.a. for UCAS point scores in excess of 300 (excluding AS levels), Mature full-time student bursaries of £500 p.a., but must qualify for means-tested government grants. For sport, there's the £1,000 Gravesend Rugby Football Club Bursary; for music, the David Fussey Choral Exhibition: £1,000 .

STUDENT PROFILE

Many come from overseas and receive sterling support. The university provides immigration info concerning visas, working and health, and academic assistance: English classes, study skills, personal tutors and social events geared to integrate into the British and uni communities. There are also many mature students (60%) (and good childcare facilities) and a number of part-timers. Of full-time undergrads, 97% come from the state sector and 43% from families in the lowest socio-economic groups.

ACADEMIC EXCELLENCE	
TEACHING:	
(Rated Excellent or 17+ out of 24)	
Environmental Studies,	**Excellent**
Architecture.	
Town & Country Planning	**24**
Sociology, Pharmacology,	**23**
Nursing	
Psychology	**22**
Building, Land/Property Mgt,	**21**
Civil Engineering, Politics,	
Philosophy, Theology	
Molecular Biosciences,	**20**
Organismal Biosciences, Educ,	
Economics, Agriculture, Business,	
Sport	
Communication/Media, Maths	**19**
Subjects Allied to Medicine	**18**
RESEARCH:	
Top grades 5/5*	**None**

ACADEMIA & JOBS

The schools, or faculties, are: Architecture &

WHERE GREENWICH GRADUATES END UP

Health & Social Work: 8%; Education: 20%; Wholesale/Retail: 12%; Manufacturing: 5%; Financial Activities: 7%; Public Administration, Civil Service & Defence: 9%; Hotel/Restaurant: 2.5%; Transport & Communications (including Telecommunications): 2%; Construction: 3%; Personnel: 3%; Computer: 3%; Business & Management: 3%; Accountancy: 1%; Media (including Film): 2%; Legal 2%; Architecture: 4%; Publishing: 2%; Advertising: 1%; Sport: 2%.

Approximate 'graduate track' employed **63%**

Construction; Business; Chemical & Life Sciences; Computing & Mathematical Sciences; Education & Training; Engineering; Health; Humanities; NRI (Earth & Environmental Sciences); Social Sciences & Law (Social Science subjects).

Poor students:staff ration of 24.5:1. Best teaching is assessed as being in Pharmacology & Pharmacy, Nursing & Midwifery, Town & Country Planning. Disabled and dyslexic students benefit from a dedicated Resource Centre.

Four per cent of the graduate workforce going into architecture suggests we have a good niche area, and sure enough the department scored full marks at the assessments. There are two BA degrees, one with a landscape focus. BA Architecture with Landscape Architecture finds graduates jobs as landscape designers, plantsmen, etc. There is also a good showing employment-wise in property development. Note their three BSc degrees in this area – Development,

Management and Valuation.

Far and away the biggest area for jobs is Education. Primary and secondary school teachers are trained in a department that scored 20 points at assessment. Would-be lecturers in Further Education come most out of other departments: Business and Architecture & Construction are the two faculties scoring highest in this job sector. There is also a good track record for turning out physical training instructors (Education). Besides HNDs, see degrees in Sports Science and Sports Science with Pro Tennis Coaching.

Property and construction are good areas, too. See the new course in Construction Business Management. Town & Country Planning recently too full marks at the assessments, Building and Land/Property Management scored 21 points.

The nursing (Adult Branch Registration, Children's nursing, Mental Health Registration) and midwifery degrees are responsible for the strong (8%) showing in employment. There is also a big push in the area of natural health therapy here. Degrees in Complementary Therapies, including Aromatherapy and Stress Management, are the focus.

Environmental health is another popular employment area – look at Environmental Sciences, Human Nutrition and a new BSc in Public Health, which may be extended to include industrial placement. There is also Applied Nutrition with European Studies, though this scored just 18 points at assessment.

There is a strong computer provision. Systems analysts come out of Greenwich in number. Look at the BEng Computer Networking and Computer Systems & Software Engineering degrees, which may be 3-4 years depending on industrial placement or Foundation year.

SOCIAL SCENE

The liveliest student venue was The Dome, *which holds 1,000 punters and until this year had big-name music acts, but the Union has had to 'relinquish' all their licences and are reduced to pleading,* '*Give Us Back Our Union!'*

STUDENTS' UNION As there are 3 campuses, the social scene is rather disparate, but there are bars and cafés on each site.

However, Laura Cattell reports that the Greenwich student bar, which once put on some 20 events each week, circulating news of them in a 'what's on' listing called *Get Out*, is currently 'shut by 7pm, so you'll need to explore further for a bit more life. Greenwich is a pricey area to socialise in, but there are some great pubs such as **The Gipsy Moth** and **The Spaniard**, and a

'Give Us Back Our Union!' A sorry tale.

Annual events include the Fresher's Ball, Fresher's Fair, Football Dinner and Dance, Christmas Dizzy and Valentine's Ball. The biggest event of the year is the May Ball. The **Café Royal** in London and **Alexandra Palace** have provided glamorous settings for this black tie evening.

Societies are mainly cultural: Afro-Caribbean, Chinese, Cypriot, Hellenic, Malaysian, Mauritian, Nigerian to name but a few. Rag week brings the disparate strands together in slave auctions, etc.

SPORT Most sporting life goes on at Avery hill (see *Campus* entry above). Football, rugby, hockey, netball, American football, basketball, cricket, and tennis are played at inter-university and inter-southeast club standard, and the boat club trains to a very high standard.

cheesy club, the **North Pole**. Nearby Deptford has a great market on Wednesdays and Fridays with an incredible amount of old bits and pieces.' The liveliest SU venue was **The Dome** at Avery Hill, which holds 1,000 punters and had big-name music acts, but the Union has had to 'relinquish' all their licences on the place and are reduced to pleading,

GETTING THERE

☞ By road from M25, join A2 (J2) and follow signs to Woolwich Ferry, thence Greenwich.

☞ By rail to main Greenwich site: trains to Greenwich or Maze Hill overland stations, or Docklands Light Railway from Bank.

☞ By coach: Bristol, 2:20; Birmingham, 2:40; Newcastle, 6:05; Manchester, 4:35.

HARPER ADAMS UNIVERSITY COLLEGE

Harper Adams University College
Edgmond
Newport
Shropshire TF10 8NB

TEL 01952 820280
FAX 01952 813210
EMAIL admissions@harper-adams.ac.uk
WEB www.harper-adams.ac.uk

Harper Adams is a first-class land-based college on the borders of Shropshire and Staffordshire. They have the distinction of being able to award their own degrees. The college scored 23 out of 24 points for the undergraduate provision. Learning resources include the college's 175-hectare farm, a library (38,000 volumes, 800 journals), a computer centre and the largest covered field demonstration area in the UK. All first-year students are accommodated and catered for in college. This is a very sporty place – rugby, clay pigeon shooting and mountain biking bring them national, even international gongs. Union facilities include a couple of bars.

GETTING THERE

☞ By road: M6 (J 13 or J14), A518, A41, B5062.

☞ By rail to Shrewsbury: Birmingham New Street, 1:10; from London to Stafford, 1:40

HERIOT-WATT UNIVERSITY

Heriot-Watt University
Riccarton Campus
Edinburgh EH14 4AS

TEL 0131 451 3451
FAX 0131 451 3630
EMAIL admissions@hw.ac.uk
WEB www.hw.ac.uk

Heriot-Watt Students' Association
Riccarton Campus
Edinburgh EH14 4AS

TEL 0131 451 5333
FAX 0131 451 5344
EMAIL admissions@hw.ac.uk
WEB www.hwusa.org

VAG VIEW

*H*eriot-Watt is a research-led, technological *university, high on academic, industrial and business collaboration; many of its courses are accredited by professional bodies, and relevant to employers' needs.*

Notable academic centres in the uni include the International Centre for Brewing & Distilling, The Maxwell Institute for Mathematical Sciences, the Centre for Translation and Interpreting Studies, the Logistics Research Centre, and the Institute of Petroleum Engineering - consistently rated one of the top three of its kind in the world.

Sited on the edge of Edinburgh, it is small but achieves big inspection results: 73% of its teaching assessments have scored Excellent or Highly Satisfactory, and it has a sound graduate employment record, a fairly rich student culture and a lot of good sport, yet its acceptance rate is high, and if you're a lass and want to study Engineering and Physical Sciences they'll pay you good money to do so.

Though entry requirements can now be steep, they throw a wide net for applicants, and maintain a dogged policy of targeting 'pupils from schools where applications to university are low, students who have no family background or cultural experience of

higher education and mature students with no formal qualifications who maybe want a second chance to enter university via an access course.'

SUBJECT AREAS (%)

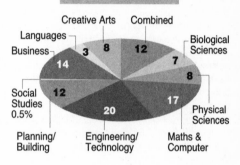

Creative Arts	Combined
Languages	Biological Sciences
Business	
Social Studies	Physical Sciences
Planning/Building	Engineering/Technology	Maths & Computer

Creative Arts 8, Combined 12, Biological Sciences 7, 8, Physical Sciences 17, Maths & Computer 20, Engineering/Technology, Planning/Building, Social Studies 0.5%, 12, Business 14, Languages 3

CAMPUS

The main campus at Riccarton, 6.5 miles south-west of Edinburgh city centre is an attractive 380-acre campus in a huddle with a number of inde-pendent research companies. There's a modern, almost space-age, feel to it: smart, modern build-ings are set in pleasant grounds with trees, playing fields, an attractive artificial loch, squirrels, ducks and swans.

'The sense of seclusion at leafy Riccarton cam-pus definitely aids study,' writes Richard Biggs, 'and

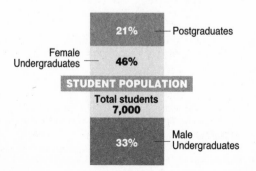

STUDENT POPULATION

Postgraduates 21%
Female Undergraduates 46%
Total students 7,000
Male Undergraduates 33%

UNIVERSITY/STUDENT PROFILE

University since	**1966**
Situation/style	**City campus**
Student population	**7000**
Undergraduates	**5500**
- mature	**30%**
- non EU undergraduates	**9%**
- male/female	**42/58**
- non-traditional student intake	**29%**
- state school intake	**91%**
- drop-out rate	**19%**
- undergraduate applications	**Up 3%**

WHERE HERIOT-WATT GRADUATES END UP

Health & Social Work: 1%; Education: 3%; Wholesale/Retail: 15%; Manufacturing: 14%; Financial Activities: 17%; Public Administration, Civil Service & Defence: 6%; Hotel/Restaurant: 3%; Transport & Communications (including Telecommunications): 4%; Construction: 2%; Mining/Oil Extracting: 3%; Personnel: 2.5%; Computer: 3%; Business & Management: 5%; Accountancy: 5%; Media (including Film): 1%; Legal 1%; Architecture: 7%; Sport: 0.5%.

Approximate 'graduate track' employed **57%**

has given rise to a community spirit that doesn't exist at inner city universities. However, the LRT buses that run to and from campus tend to be erratic – not fun in winter.'

Since the merger with **The Scottish College of Textiles in '99**, H-W also has a Scottish Borders campus. Situated in Galashiels – hence Gala, as the campus is known – a small town in the Scottish Borders, SCoT is only 33 miles/90 minutes by bus from Edinburgh, but unfortunately (if you are in a hurry) some two and a half hours by train, which detours via Berwick-upon-Tweed.

In September 2005, the University opened its Dubai Campus. Initial academic programmes include undergraduate and postgraduate courses in Management and a postgraduate course in Information Technology. It is planned to introduce further courses in the areas of science, engineering and commerce from September 2006.

FEES, BURSARIES

Non-Scottish UK/EU residents pay £1,700 p.a. , but the uni offers UK domiciled students a number of scholarships worth £500 p.a., and keen to attract women into Engineering and Physical Sciences, they have 12 scholarships of £1,000 p.a. are made for female applicants. Again, Schlumberger and MISYS work closely with Heriot-Watt to assist and develop high calibre students through scholarships.

There are also a number of sports scholarships worth between £500 and £1,500 p.a., funded jointly by the University, the Alumni Fund, the Royal & Ancient Golf Club of St. Andrews and the Scottish Physical Recreation Fund.

In addition, there are Alumni Fund, music and pipe band scholarships, and all schools offer overseas applicants for UG programmes the opportunity to apply for a partial reduction in tuition fees. See www.hw.ac.uk/scholarships

STUDENT PROFILE

'The University,' we read, 'is committed to equal opportunities for all, irrespective of age, colour, disability, ethnic origin, gender, marital status, religious or political beliefs, sexual orientation or other irrelevant distinction.' Sounds good, and in H-W's case it *is* good. They go out of their way to pull in a diverse mix of student, being one of the elite universities who show that open access can be made to work by concentrating their efforts on relative merits and on abilities and potential. So, they can gather 29% of the uni's student body from among groups who don't normally think of going to university, hang on to more than most unis for the duration and find almost all of them jobs within six months of graduation.

> *'There is a community spirit that doesn't exist at inner city universities. Modern languages are an outstanding strength. You can walk straight into a job in the EC.'*

The concentration of technical courses accounts for the unusually high male to female ratio – 58% male undergraduates against 42% female. So what does Heriot-Watt do about it? They start up 'Women into Science and Engineering', a scheme offering taster courses, with attendant scholarships, to female pupils. It's a scheme that flows from the university's commitment to equal opportunity. This is a caring university in the best sense, the student is the principal focus.

There is also a big foreign exchange programme – so, you'll find a rich mix of cultures, on campus. All students can choose to study abroad at some point during their course.

ACADEMIA & JOBS

The schools are Engineering and Physical Sciences; Life Sciences; Built Environment; Mathematical & Computer Sciences; Management & Languages; and Textiles & Design.

There are particular niches in photonics, actuarial maths and statistics, languages (translating and interpreting) and petroleum engineering. Recent new subjects in high demand include

Applied Psychology, Chemistry with Forensic Science, Robotics and Cybertronics, Building, Architectural Engineering and Planning & Housing subjects, automotive engineering and sports science.

'Modern languages are an outstanding strength,' one sixthform adviser confirmed, and certainly their employment figures for translators and interpreters is good. 'You can walk straight out of Heriot-Watt into a job in the EC.' Also, for foreign students, the School of Management and Languages now offers a range of language support classes (MA Foreign Languages and TESOL).

School careers staff point to courses aimed at boom areas, such as microelectronics, and the pharmaceutical industry, which is equal to 27% of the UK's manufacturing industry, while their unique BSc in Brewing and Distilling is rarely short of applicants and enjoys a certain symbiosis with extra-curricular activities also popular here.

In actuarial science, three universities are head and shoulders above the rest in equating degree success with employment, namely Heriot-Watt, Warwick and Oxford. Heriot-Watt and Warwick have dedicated Actuarial Maths degrees, and together all three account for more than 20% of jobs in the sector. Nearly 5% of Heriot-Watt's graduates become actuaries. They offer a four-year BSc Actuarial Mathematics and Statistics, for which they only want 280 points. See too the new BSc Mathematical, Statistical and Actuarial Sciences.

Altogether 17% go into the financial sector, 4% into accountancy, 2% as investment advisers and analysts. Finance took a Highly Satisfactory at the assessments; Applied Maths and Statistics were rated international Grade 5 for research. Students interested in working in insurance, pension broking, underwriting should consider this uni, and look at BSc Mathematics with Psychology and BSc General Mathematics with Psychology, new this year.

On the engineering front, the teaching of Electrical & Electronic Engineering was accorded Excellent on inspection, and they have a good employment record. See also the computer and software engineering degrees in the School of Mathematical & Computer Sciences, which take more than 2% of graduates into software engineering, 1% into programming, etc.

Heriot-Watt mechanical engineers also find ready employment, as do design and development engineers, and process and development engineers. Look in particular at Chemical Engineering with Diploma in Industrial Training (Food Processing Technology) – there's a high incidence of graduate employment in this area. Chemical Engineering offers specialist routes into brewing & distilling, oil

& gas production, pharmaceutical and other industries, and BSc Chemistry could take you to Australia or North America for a year.

Their strength is in the close relationship they have with industry, business and national support networks. In cahoots with the Scottish Institute for Enterprise, they deliver an enterprise-training programme, bringing entrepreneurial skills to science and engineering, from the first year of studies.

In the property context, some 6% graduates from here find employment as surveyors. Look at Architectural Engineering, Building Surveying and the two Quantity Surveying degrees in the School of the Built Environment. Note also that Heriot-Watt validates Edinburgh College of Art's degrees and that 29% of their graduates find work in architectural and related consultancies.

As for business, they excel, jobs-wise, in retail and marketing management (see Fashion below), and in business management consultancy. Look at the MA International Management or simply Management , and consider moving onto a postgrad course. If you're interested in retail management, fashion and design, note that this uni is in partnership with George Davies of 'Next', 'George at Asda' and the 'per una' collection for Marks & Spencer, to launch the George Davies Centre for Retail Excellence at Heriot-Watt. There'll be in-company projects and master classes from leading academics and retailers, including George. The first postgrad course in International Fashion Marketing is running from autumn 2005.

ACADEMIC EXCELLENCE

TEACHING:
(Rated Excellent, Highly Satis. or 17+ out of 24)

Electrical & Electronic Eng.	**Excellent**
Civil Engineering, Computer Studies, Physics, Chemistry, Maths & Statistics, Mechanical + Manufacturing Eng, Finance & Accounting, Cellular & Molecular Biology.	**Highly Satis.**
Chemical Engineering	**19**
European Languages	**21**

RESEARCH:
Top grades 5/5*

Mineral & Mining Engineering.	**Grade 5***
Applied Maths, Statistics, Built Environment	**Grade 5**

Graduates of dedicated degrees in Fashion, Textiles and related areas, including Management, Marketing and Promotion are much in demand. Nationally, around 150 graduate textile designers

AT A GLANCE

ACADEMIC FILE:

Subjects assessed	**15**
Excellent/Highly Satisfactory	**73%**
Typical entry requirements	**363 points**
Application acceptance rate	**20%**
Students-staff ratio	**17:1**
First/2:1 degree pass rate	**61%**

ACCOMMODATION FILE:

Guarantee to freshers	**100%**
Style	**Halls**
Catered	**41%**
En suite	**55%**
Price range pw	**£76.44**
City rent pw	**£64**

move straight into the industry, some 260 clothing designers. Heriot-Watt merged with the Scottish College of Textiles in 1999. There's collaboration with industry and business in the design of the courses. They offer the employment-oriented BA Fashion Design for Industry and BSc Clothing Design & Manufacture or Textiles & Fashion Design Management.

Note the Sport and Exercise Science core degree within the School of Life Sciences and combo with psychology. See also *Sport* below.

They engage the support of alumni members in email and face-to-face student mentoring, bringing together graduates from five continents.

SOCIAL SCENE

STUDENTS' ASSOCIATION The Union on Edinburgh campus has three main venues: **Geordies** (bar) – the Heriot-Watt local with hustlers pool area: 3 pool tables and arcades, big screen and plasma screens, and home to the ever-popular and entertaining Monday night pub quiz. Then there's **Liberty's**, a café-bar with free wireless internet access, and **Zero˚** nightclub (capacity 450). Its stage is also used for live music and Comedy Club.

Friday is *JAM* in **Zero˚**: pop, chart, cheese and legendary student anthems; also *Night Train* in **Liberty's**: diverse range of 'quality music'. Every other Tuesday is Comedy Club: 'Well-established laughter session offering a changing line-up of some of the best local comics around. A bargain at only £3,' says *The List*. Saturday is *Lounge* in **Liberty's** – 'chillout to the sound of DJ's playing an eclectic mix of cool tunes" says the Student Association. 'Crayons to play with too!' Thursday in **Zero˚** brings live music and, 'Often attracts Scotland's hottest band talent.' – *The List*. Thursday is *Traffic*, a crossroads of indie and alternative

tunes. Every other Sunday in **Zero˚**, alternating with *Your Turn* (open mic night) in *Liberty's* is *Have you got the S-Factor?*

See also *Student Edinburgh*, page 185.

Down at Gala, they are also getting some sort of scene together. There are newish union premises, a full ents programme, a musician-in-residence and lashings of sponsorship from North Sea oil, which has led to COMA – not a state of unconsciousness due to inebriation, but the name for a network of groups available for gigs.

SPORT The Edinburgh campus boasts the impressive National Squash Centre, but also has a number of large playing fields (five football, two rugby, one cricket), a floodlit training area, jogging track, three tennis courts, three sports halls, climbing wall, two multigyms, golf driving nets, weights and fitness rooms and indoor sports courts. Membership is spilt into Gold, Silver and Bronze tariffs (year, academic year and term), ranging from £18-60. The Heart of Midlothian Football Academy opened recently and includes pro-quality facilities and floodlit and indoor synthetic pitches. The city of

WHAT IT'S REALLY LIKE

UNIVERSITY:

Social Life	★★★
Campus scene	**Like clockwork**
Student Union services	**Good**
Politics	**Low level**
	Student debt
Sport	**30 clubs, hockey strong**
National team position	**38th**
Sport facilities	**Good**
Arts opportunities	**Music, film good; dance, art average, drama poor**
Student newspaper	**Watts On**
Nightclub	**Zero˚**
Bars	**Geordies, Liberty's**
Union ents	**JAM (cheese) heads big ents**
Union Societies	**30**
Most popular societies	**Poker Society**
Parking	**Poor**

CITY:

Entertainment	★★★★★
Scene	**Seething**
Town/gown relations	**Good**
Risk of violence	**Low**
Cost of living	**High**
Student concessions	**Excellent**
Survival + 2 nights out	**£60-£85 pw**
Part-time work campus/city	**Excellent**

Edinburgh has many golf courses, a large swimming pool, ice rink and the Meadowbank Stadium. Half the city is made of parks and open spaces (including Queen's Park and Arthur's Seat).

PILLOW TALK

Catered and self-catered study bedrooms and self-catered flats, all a short stroll away from everything else. Of the 1,800 study bedrooms, more than 1,000 have their own shower and toilet, and there are never more than five sharing a kitchen, which comes with fridge freezer, cooker, kettle etc. Bring your own crockery, cutlery, pots and pans. Catered students have access to a pantry for snacks and hot drinks. For a small subscription, you can have access to a phone, the Internet and the Heriot-Watt Intranet. There is, in any case, free room-to-room and incoming calls, and voicemail.

GETTING THERE

☛ By road: A71 or A70; if the latter, turn off at Currie on to Riccarton Mains Road.
☛ By rail: London King's Cross, 4:30; Glasgow Central, 50 mins; Newcastle, 1:30.
☛ By air: nearby Edinburgh Airport for inland and international flights.
☛ By coach: Glasgow, 1:10; London, 9:10; Birmingham, 8:10; Newcastle, 3:10.
☛ To Gala, A7 south from Edinburgh.

UNIVERSITY OF HERTFORDSHIRE

The University of Hertfordshire
College Lane
Hatfield
Hertfordshire AL10 9AB

TEL 01707 284800
FAX 01707 284870
EMAIL admissions@herts.ac.uk
WEB www.herts.ac.uk

Hertfordshire Students' Union
College Lane
Hatfield
Hertfordshire AL10 9AB

TEL 01707 285000
FAX 01707 286150
EMAIL uhsu@herts.ac.uk
WEB uhsu.herts.ac.uk

VAG VIEW

*H*erts Uni is among the most impressive of the 1992 unis in rate of growth, learning resources and graduate employment. Reason for some of this is the contact with industry and the capital city which their strategically advantageous location gives them on the north-south A1, minutes from the M25 and M1, and within striking distance of four airports – Luton, Stansted, Heathrow and Gatwick.

CAMPUSES

The uni is based at Hatfield and St Albans. The main Hatfield site comprises the original campus and the new de Havilland Campus, half a mile away, the two made one by cycleways, footpaths and shuttle buses.

DE HAVILLAND In September 2003 the new £120-million campus opened, housing the Business School and schools of Education and Humanities. There's a learning resources centre, a £15-million sports centre open to the public – its 3-year membership target met in the first month – an amazing 60-seater auditorium and student residences. It was an incredible undertaking and reports of 350 students having to be placed in hotels at the start of the 2003-4 session give scale to the challenge. Now, there are 1,400 new en-suite rooms on its College Lane campus, so no problems this year.

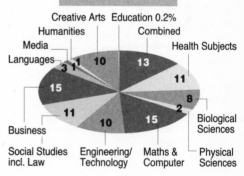

SUBJECT AREAS (%)

Creative Arts Education 0.2%
Humanities Combined
Media Health Subjects
Languages 10 13
3 1 11
15 8
11 2
10 15 Biological Sciences
Business
Social Studies Engineering/ Maths & Physical
incl. Law Technology Computer Sciences

COLLEGE LANE The main campus is College Lane, Hatfield, where the [original] **Learning Resources Centre** is based. With hundreds of computers, your very own e-mail and the facility to look up the George Clooney Web page, a café downstairs serving cheese toasties and banana milkshakes to eager students throughout the day and night, and copies of all the text books you need to research for those lectures you accidentally slept through, you can't complain.

Entertainment facilities include the **Elehouse** pub, which offers a wonderfully healthy food bar during the day, making a change from Pot Noodles and oven chips, and a pleasant pub atmosphere in the evenings. Downstairs there is a shop, open daily

from Monday to Friday, where you can satisfy your cravings for Pringles and cream eggs, as well as allowing you to stock up on paper and pens in preparation for your lectures (you know, those things in between sleep and alcohol).

Across the courtyard is the main venue for big events, the **Font**. Weekly clubnights include *Bonk* – sports night on Wednesday; *Naughty* – main Friday club night; *Swanky* – regular house night; and *360* – alternative night. 'There's a very strong on-campus community,' a student said, 'with venues that people feel safe in. A lot of the social life is based around campus.'

The Summer Ball also offers an interesting combination of food, drink and a selection of fairground rides, only for those with iron stomachs!

Then there's the radio station, CRUSH, which is run by students for students and can be received by the majority of halls, and the *Horizon* newspaper to keep you informed of the good and the bad goings-on. The most active of 17 student societies are Christian Union, Drama and Alternative Music.

There's a 9-screen **UCI** in the **Galleria** centre, and a pub that offers cut-price drinks. The union make merry with a student night at **Pub2Club**, but generally the nightlife is poor. London beckons

ST ALBANS The third campus is in St Albans, a small campus for those studying Law, easily accessible from Hatfield, where most first years are normally housed There is a refectory and a Students' Union area - TV and a pool table. The town has the oldest pub in the UK, **Ye Old Fighting Cocks**.

FEES, BURSARIES

UK & EU Fees 2007: £3,070 p.a. Not yet fixed for 2008. Bursary of £1,350 if in receipt of full HE Maintenance grant; if in receipt of partial grant then it's on a sliding scale down from that figure. Sports (worth up to £3,000 - 01707 281194 or visit www.student.hertssportsvillage.co.uk) and academic scholarships are available.

STUDENT PROFILE

There is a very large student body, mainly drawn from the state sector, 39% from new to uni social groups. Twenty per cent of undergraduates are part-timers and 3% of the total population are further education students. There is also a large very local and overseas population. The mix works well.

ACADEMIA & JOBS

2007 sees a new focus on Creative and Cultural Industries. 3D Games Art, Special Effects, Character Creation and Technical Effects, Media Practices and Management, Digital Film and TV Production (fiction), Digital Film and TV Production, Digital Post Production, Music and Entertainment Industry Management.

The award-winning learning resources centre at College and its twin at adjacent de Havilland are open 24/7. They make use of a computer system, StudyNET, their 'Managed Learning Environment', a personalised academic workspace for students on which appears information relevant to programmes of study, as well as a range of personal information management tools linking students to course data-

UNIVERSITY PROFILE	
University since	**1992**
Situation/style	**Suburban campuses**
Student population	**22000**
Undergraduates	**18188**
- mature	**19%**
- non EU undergraduates	**12%**
- male/female	**44/56**
- non-traditional student intake	**39%**
-state school intake	**97%**
- drop-out rate	**19%**
- undergraduate applications	**Up 7%**

Aerospace Technology with Management.

They also get jobs for their civil engineers, though they come not out of engineering but the Built Environment school, which includes Architectural Engineering, Civil Eng Construction Management and Civil Eng Financial Mgt.

Prospective racing car designers and team managers should explore the BSc Hons Motorsports Technology and BEng Automotive Engineering with Motorsport. They streamline ruthlessly for employment and this is among the most impressive of the new unis, employment-wise. So, they slipped quietly out of subjects like drama, sociology, and invested heavily instead in Pharmacology, benefiting from the location in the most heavily concentrated area of pharmaceutical R&D in the country.

Hertfordshire and Nottingham Trent jostle for top place among those that feed this sector. Look at BSc Pharmaceutical Science (extended with work experience) and BSc Pharmacology, they come with the possibility of a year in Europe or the US, a dimension is a feature of other science courses.

bases.

Recently opened on College Lane is an Innovation Centre to provide incubation resources to spin out new companies, and a new Automotive Centre, dedicated to bring together academia and industry.

Historically, Herts is noted for aero-engineering, computer science, areas into which they still pour graduates. They have progressed rapidly, too, in environmental sciences, in law and in health, and business – Business & Management, Economics, and Tourism picked up 23 points out of 24 in the teaching assessments recently (as indeed did Nursing).

A strong vein in graduate employment is fed by degrees in Aerospace, Automotive and Design Engineering- Airport Operations and Aviation Logistics, Aerospace Technology with Pilot Studies,

> *The new £120-million campus has opened. There's a learning resources centre, a £15-million sports centre open to the public, an amazing 60-seater auditorium and student residences.*

Teaching inspection 22. Health is the most popular area of employment for Herts graduates. In nursing they are big in mental health, adult and children's. Look also at and the Health Management degree in the Business faculty and the sure-fire Paramedic Science, the first degree of its sort, which we may well look back upon as the uni's first step to a degree in medicine.

Herts' BSc Physiotherapy comes expensive BBB-ABB, but this is part of a major drive by this impressive new uni in the Health area. Their employment record speaks for itself, they are always in the Top 10, while their BSc degrees Diagnostic Radiography & Imaging and Radiotherapy & Oncology produce more than 6% of the jobs in this sector nationally. At the teaching

WHAT IT'S REALLY LIKE

UNIVERSITY:

Social Life	★★★
Campus scene	**Lively community, bit spoddy**
Student Union services	**Good**
Politics	**Average: Fees**
Sport	**29 clubs**
National team position	**57th**
Sport facilities	**New/excellent**
Arts opportunities	**Good**
Student newspaper	**Horizon**
Student radio	**Crush 1278 AM**
Nightclub	**Font Bar**
Bars	**Elehouse**
Union ents	**Bonk, Naughty, Swanky**
Union societies	**17**
Parking	**Average**

CITY:

Entertainment	★★ – ★★★
Scene	**London beckons**
Town/gown relations	**Average**
Risk of violence	**Low**
Cost of living	**High**
Student concessions locally	**OK**
Survival + 2 nights out	**£70 pw**
Part-time work campus/town	**Excellent/poor**

AT A GLANCE

ACADEMIC FILE:

Subjects assessed	**32**
Excellent	**56%**
Typical entry requirements	**225 points**
Application acceptance rate	**22%**
Students-staff ratio	**18:1**
First/2:1 degree pass rate	**50%**

ACCOMMODATION FILE:

Guarantee to freshers	**100%**
Style	**Halls, flats**
Catered	**Some**
En-suite	**1,600**
Price range pw	**£57-£99**
Town rent pw	**£50-£65**

The uni has recently launched its own record label offering students a unique opportunity to participate in the creation of a professional production. The label will present non-standard repertoire featuring professional artists and will be produced by an experienced professional producer.

There is also a top-line BA Hons Fine Art, although they stress you will need to be self-motivated, ambitious and want to work as a practising artist to get a place. There's work experience and assessments they scored 22 out of 24.

More than 10% of the nation's biologists come out of Herts Uni, who maintain a dominant position thanks to their excellent contacts with the expanding pharmaceutical, agrochemical and biotechnology industries. There are extended, introductory courses if you don't have the A levels to get in.

They are also in the forefront of providing graduate environment officers, their 3/4-year BSc Hons Environmental Geology/Management/ Studies or Conservation Mgt, all with a year in industry and option for a year in Europe or North America. There's also a range of Geographical Info Science degrees, and plain old Geography itself of course. Environmental Studies also features in the cross-faculty Combine Homs scheme (again with an optional year in Europe or America).

In the arts they have a new dimension in the now highly competitive world of animation. Look at their BA Model Design & Special Effects, itself designed for visual effects designers in advertising, TV and film. Graduates undertake work placements with such as Jim Henson's Creative Workshop, Artme, Asylum and the BBC Visual Effects Department. A new School of Film, Music (there are masses of Electronic Music degrees) and New Media is mooted.

exchanges with various Western and Eastern Euro countries in the second year. Entry via a Foundation Diploma. Teaching inspection, 22.

Business-wise they place a lot of marketing and retail managers. All courses in the Business School modular programme are 3-4 years depending on work experience, or placing in Europe or America. Marketing may be studied as single honours or with languages, Info Systems, Accounting, Human Resources, Management Science, Tourism, etc. Management Science can be taken similarly with or without the other combos. As indeed can Tourism or any of the other combo subjects – tourism is another strong area for jobs for Herts graduates.

There are also Foundation degrees in Business with Marketing, Human Resources or Finance. Then fully-fledged degrees with the same range of employable combinations, or single honours degrees in Business Admin, Business Studies, Management, and Health Management.

The School of Law has launched a Law Clinic, which offers a legal service run by students free of charge under the supervision of experienced solicitors.

The strong education provision is for Education Studies and an Early Years Foundation degree.

SPORT They came 57th in the BUSA inter-university national team league last year. There's the big new, £15-million sports complex, an 8-lane swimming pool, indoor cricket nets, 100-station fitness suite, etc. American Football is key.

PILLOW TALK

Halls are sself-catering: 1,600 en-suite at the de Havilland campus, all with broadband internet access and refrigerator. 1,400 new rooms on the College Lane campus. The union runs a lettings agency for private lets, a professionally run, student-friendly service, a welcome and much needed alternative to using local estate agents.

GETTING THERE
☛ **Hatfield** by road: A1(M)/J3. By rail: London King's Cross, 22 mins. ☛ By coach: London, 1:00.
☛ **St Albans** by road: M25/J22, A1081. By rail: London (Thameslink), 25 mins.

HEYTHROP COLLEGE

Heythrop College
Kensington Square
London W8 5HQ
TEL 020 7795 6600
FAX 020 7795 4200

EMAIL r.bolland@heythrop.ac.uk
WEB www.heythrop.ac.uk

Heythrop is an independent college within the University of London specialising in theology and philosophy and with a refreshingly evolutionary concept of higher education. For their inspiration they turn to the Swiss psychologist Jean Piaget, noted for his revolutionary work on the cognitive functions of children. Piaget wrote that 'the principal goal of education is to create people who are capable of doing new things, not simply of repeating what other generations have done... The second goal of education is to form minds which can be critical, can verify, and not accept everything they are offered.' Trawling through all that the higher educational establishments of this country can offer, such a breathtakingly simple statement seems almost unutterably bold. Their teaching is the traditional university method of tutorials and small-group seminars. They possess one of the finest collections of theological and philosophical literature anywhere to be found, their 250,000 volumes available to every one of their students without queue.

COLLEGE PROFILE	
College of London Uni since	**1971**
Full-time undergraduates	**155**
- mature	**30%**
- overseas	**11%**
- male/female	**70/30**
ACCOMMODATION:	
Availability to freshers	**100%**
Style	**Halls**
Approx cost p.w.	**£100-£130**
City rent pw	**£100+**

UNIVERSITY OF HIGHLANDS & ISLANDS

UHI Millennium Institute
Caledonia House
63 Academy Street
Inverness IV1 1BB

TEL 0845 272 3600
FAX 01463 279001
EMAIL info@uhi.ac.uk
WEB www.uhi.ac.uk

UHI Millennium Institute is a federal network of 15 colleges that makes use of information and communication technologies to overcome geographical distance. Students have a regional reference point of at least one participating college. These are further education colleges. Each UHI academic partner deals with the accommodation for students studying at their campus.

From Sabhal Mor Ostaig in Skye to North Atlantic Fisheries College in Shetland, here's a chance to learn everything from Gaelic to music to environmental studies in the lap of Nature. More than 6,000 full-time undergraduates do, and few, if any, drop out. They have 4 faculties: Arts,

Humanities & Social Sciences; Business and Leisure; Health; and Science and Technology.

Individual colleges within UHI focus on specific subject areas.

UNIVERSITY OF HUDDERSFIELD

University of Huddersfield
Queensgate
Huddersfield HD1 3DH

TEL 0870 901 5555
FAX 01484 516825
EMAIL prospectus@hud.ac.uk
WEB www.hud.ac.uk

Huddersfield Students' Union
Queensgate
Huddersfield HD1 3DH

TEL 01484 4538156
FAX 01484 432 333
EMAIL: su-comms@hud.ac.uk
WEB www.huddersfieldstudent.com

VAG VIEW

*T*he uni traces its history back to the Young Men's Mental Improvement Society, founded in 1841. It was awarded university status in 1992 after two other incarnations, first as a technical college then as a polytechnic. Today it has a city-centre campus (Queensgate), Holly Bank campus, 2 miles to the north, and Storthes Hall, 4 miles to the south-east.

Huddersfield town is an unusual mix. Its roots in the industrial revolution are not in doubt. It is also known far and wide for its annual poetry festival, with famously the Albert pub as artistic font; folk and jazz are equally present. Sometime Heritage minister Stephen Dorrell once famously remarked that Huddersfield was the Paris of the North. One can't pretend this didn't raise a few eyebrows, but he did have a point of sorts.

The uni and the town are of a similar weave. There is this traditional, industrial, people-culture, but the academic spectrum is

wide and its character modern. Major strengths are electronic engineering, IT and

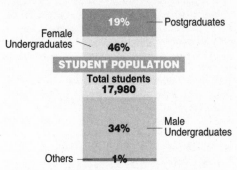

social work, and in health areas such as nursing and midwifery. Then you hear that they have the largest music department of any UK university, and that in the recent research assessment exercise they were awarded a coveted Grade 5 for it. Now, with new drama and media facilities, it is also developing a strong performing arts, broadcast and humanities cluster, aided by the high profile of the University's Chancellor, the film actor Patrick Stewart, who drops by to give drama workshops.

They have recently opened centres in Oldham and Barnsley to encourage participation in Higher Education in both towns.

CAMPUS

The university has given the city-centre Queensgate campus a makeover, replacing some of the 1960s' tower blocks with the new Harold Wilson Building (natch) – HQ for the School of Human & Health Sciences. Holly Bank, two miles north is for teacher training, not a huge element in

UNIVERSITY/STUDENT PROFILE	
University since	1992
Situation/style	Town campus
Student population	17980
Undergraduates	14470
- mature	39%
- non EU undergraduates	3%
- male/female	43/57
- non-traditional student intake	41%
- state school intake	98%
- drop-out rate	22%
- undergraduate applications	Up 0.1%

SUBJECT AREAS (%)

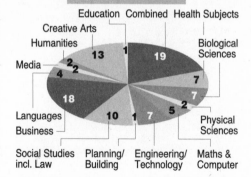

Education Combined Health Subjects
Creative Arts
Humanities — 13 1 19 Biological Sciences
Media — 2 2
4
7
18 7
5 2
Languages — 10 1 7 Physical Sciences
Business
Social Studies Planning/ Engineering/ Maths &
incl. Law Building Technology Computer

ACADEMIC EXCELLENCE

TEACHING:
(Rated Excellent or 17+ out of 24)

Social Work, Music	**Excellent**
Electrical & Electronic Eng	**24**
Politics	**23**
Nursing, Hospitality Management,	**22**
Transport & Logistics, Education, Biosciences, Subjects Allied to Medicine	
Design Technology, Maths	**21**
Food Sciences, Psychology, Sociology	**20**
Communications & Media	**18**

RESEARCH:
Top grades 5/5*
Social Work, History, Music **Grade 5**

the graduate workplace – David Blunkett studied here – (now you're getting warm). Storthes Hall campus is set in 350 acres of parkland 4 miles away from the main campus and connected to it by a subsidised bus service.

The indigenous Yorkshireman is unlikely to shout much about the uni, he doesn't even look at it objectively and certainly won't waste his breath convincing a soft southerner of things he won't understand. Yet, southerners can be the very best ambassadors, should they take time to discover this uni's soul... 'I can't remember a more depressing view,' wrote student Tim Wild, a film-maker who came up from Brighton, possibly the most exciting and sunny blue city in Britain. 'In the forefront, the twin towers of the council blocks, ably supported by the dual carriageway and the gas works. Most people only have the vaguest idea where the bloody place is, so I'll attempt to clear up the confusion. Smack bang in the middle – three hours away from London by car, and about three thousand light years

> *The Huddersfield Business Generator has created over 80 start-up businesses, half of them operated by Huddersfield graduates, with an over 80% success rate, and created two new millionaires.*

away in attitude. That's why this place is special – they really couldn't give a toss whether you're from Taunton or Timbuktu as long as you can hold your ale and laugh at yourself. If it's glamour and sophistication you're after, then stay away, because you'll only spoil it for the rest of us. I won't pretend it's paradise, but that's part of the appeal, in an odd way. Because it's the middle of nowhere, there are no cliques, no élite to try and be part of. It's just cold and grey and everyone here's in it together. Like the blitz, without the Germans.' There are also uni centres at Barnsley and Oldham.

FEES, BURSARIES

UK & EU Fees 2007: £3,070 (£1,225 for foundation years; £2050 for HND/Foundation Degree). Bursary of £1,000 for those in receipt of full

WHERE HUDDERSFIELD GRADUATES END UP

Health & Social Work: 13%; Education: 6%; Wholesale/Retail: 16%; Manufacturing: 13%; Financial Activities: 9%; Public Administration, Civil Service & Defence: 7%; Hotel/Restaurant: 6%; Transport & Communications (including Telecommunications): 5%; Construction: 2%; Agriculture: 1%; Personnel: 2%; Computer: 2.5%; Business & Management: 2.5%; Accountancy: 1%; Media (including Film): 1%; Legal 2%; Architecture: 2%; Publishing: 1%; Advertising: 1%; Artistic/Literary: 1%; Sport: 1%.

Approximate 'graduate track' employed **57%**

Maintenance Grant; £500 for partial grants.

STUDENT PROFILE

39% are mature. Intake from classes and neighborhoods not traditionally represented at university: 41% and 23% respectively, way over Government benchmarks. Huddersfield is real; social climbers need not apply; everyone has a good time.

ACADEMIA & JOBS

A tradition of vocational education dates back to 1841. Many arts and social science courses have a vocational slant. Politics, for example, includes a 6-week work placement, which often takes students to the House of Commons. A third of the students in all subjects take sandwich courses, one of the highest proportions in Britain, and more than 4,000 have some element of work experience.

There's a long-established reputation in textile design and engineering. Electrical and electronic engineering achieved the best score in assessments for teaching quality. Less obvious gems are music and social work, both rated excellent for teaching and Grade 5 for research. Fourteen million pounds will shortly fund the construction of a new building at the entrance to campus for students of music and music technology, fashion, creative imaging, multimedia, and business design.

Most popular courses are in the School of Human and Health Sciences. The other seven schools are: Applied Sciences (Transport & Logistics, Chemical and Biological Sciences, Geographical and Environmental Sciences), Computing and Maths, Design Technology (Textiles, Architecture), Education, Engineering, Business, Music and Humanities. There's 24-hour computer access, and support for disabled students.

The Huddersfield Business Generator has created over 80 start-up businesses, half of them operated by Huddersfield graduates, with an over 80% success rate and created two new millionaires.

They are in the Top 10 for producing architects – see the BA Architecture/Architecture (International). The artistic element is evident, too, in jobs for designers and illustrators, and their fine artists and general artists also do well. Fine Art, Drawing & Painting relates theoretical and practical through evaluation of current practice and then moves the focus of this to student concerns, aims, etc. Perhaps Stephen Dorrell had a point after all. Teaching inspection, 21.

They also make a number of graduates happy as interior designers with a dedicated degree in a department which consistently gets its graduates work. Teaching Inspection 21.

Nursing and midwifery graduates massage the Health figures, and BSc Midwifery Studies comes with an 18-month post-registration course. Teaching inspection 22 and a Grade 5 rating for Social Work. Social workers and counsellors bound out of this uni into employment. Look at BSc Social Work, BSc Social Psychology, Health and Community Studies. Chiropodists also boost the stats in Health with the Podiatry degree. Teaching inspection, 22.

In electronic engineering they are among the top three producers with Loughborough and York.

The music talent come for the BA Music Technology, also with Digital Media or Popular Music, and BSc Music Technology & Audio or Software Systems. The aim is to meld musical knowledge with electronic engineering. You'll be expected to have experience in both areas. As a result, there's a good track record for turning out producers, musicians, composers and sound recordists. 24 points at the assessments.

Fashion, clothing and textile designers should look no further. As befits a uni in the heart of the old woollen/textile industry, Huddersfield delivers more than any other except the London University of the Arts into the textile industry. MText is their Textile Design degree; there's also BA Costume with Textiles, Creative Textile Crafts and a BA/BSc alternative Textile Design. In the Fashion area: BA Hons Fashion with Manufacture, Marketing & Promotion is the main degree on offer. There's also a 1-year HND top-up, BA Fashion Design. 21 points at the assessments (19 for Communications).

Highly employable degrees in Art & Design are also BA Product Design, and BSc Product Innovation, Design & Development for students without specialist mathematical or scientific savvy beyond GSCE. See also their Computer-Aided Design and the BA Smart Design: Architecture ('the poetics of construction'). There's high energy and superb employment results at Huddersfield. Teaching inspection, 21.

AT A GLANCE	
ACADEMIC FILE:	
Subjects assessed	**29**
Excellent	**57%**
Typical entry requirements	**232 points**
Application acceptance rate	**19%**
Students-staff ratio	**20:1**
First/2:1 degree pass rate	**48%**
ACCOMMODATION FILE:	
Guarantee to freshers	**Advice only**
Approved city accommodation	**Halls, flats, houses**
Price range pw	**£54.95-£75.95**

UNIVERSITY:	
Social Life	★★★
Campus scene	**Laid-back, authentic**
Student Union services	**Good**
Politics	**Interest low**
Sport	**Regional force**
National sporting position	**107th**
Sport facilities	**Average**
Arts opportunities	**Music, film; art, drama**
Student newspaper	**Huddersfield Student**
National Media Awards	**Commended**
Student radio	**Ultra FM**
Nightclub & bar	**Venue**
Union ents	**2 club nights and DJ events**
Union societies	**38**
Parking	**Non-existent**
TOWN:	
Entertainment	★★★
Scene	**Pubs, music, poetry, drama**
Town/gown relations	**Good**
Risk of violence	**Low**
Cost of living	**Average**
Student concessions	**Good**
Survival + 2 nights out	**£50 pw**
Part-time work campus/town	**Good**

They are also among the giants for the catering industry with BA Hospitality Management mixed to your taste with Tourism & Leisure/International/Modern Languages/Licensed House Management. Teaching inspection, 22. Said a careers master, 'I have seen more enthusiasm among the staff at Huddersfield – both in the departments of Transport and Logistics and in Hotel & Catering – than at any other university in the land. I had thought, Oh, Huddersfield, can I really afford the time to go? And I was surprised, very surprised. They've looked at the market very carefully and where there's a gap they have gone for it.'

They also find employment for large numbers of IT consultants, through a series of Software Development BSc degrees that come with Artificial Intelligence, Business, Business Computing, Human-Computer Interaction, Management, Maths, Multimedia.

The education provision (primary and secondary) also favours lecturers in Further Education, where the School of Design Technology (Textiles, Architecture) again comes into its own.

But look, too, at their combined BA courses, which open up Creative Writing, Journalism, Advertising, Media (18 at assessment) and much else. Languages also prove popular in this sector.

Finally, they are commercial & business law specialists, scoring 'Good' in a recent assessment by the LPC Board.

SOCIAL SCENE

STUDENTS' UNION There is a new £4-million Student Union building, the current one having been converted to studio space for drama and media. There are both alcoholic and non-alcoholic social areas, space for bands performing and administrative areas for student societies.

The advent of *X-Men* and *Star Trek: The Next Generation* star, Patrick Stewart, as the University's Chancellor has seen him take a keen interest in the Drama and English courses. He will be launching a major literature festival here in the Spring.

The Venue is the multi purpose bar which plays host to a variety of events including club and band nights. UHSU has two regularly scheduled club nights: Friday night is *Grrrr*, an indie, rock and metal night; Saturday night plays host to *Quids In*, with drinks offers and a 'party' DJ playing disco, pop and some dance music. There are also one-off DJ events, this term saw Hed Kandi play.

Student media is consistently good – the newspaper is *Huddersfield Student* (nominated for Best Small Budget Publication in the 2006 National Media Awards), Student radio is Ultra FM. Generally students are pretty apathetic. The SU occasionally attempts to get the student body into a more political frame of mind, this year with a UHSU Campaigns Launch, where students voted on which campaigns they would like to see the Union run, but it didn't run beyond campus student concerns. They also launched a *Give It A Go* programme to galvanise more interest in societies. Islamic Soc remained the preferred choice.

SPORT Facilities are not extensive. There's a sports hall on campus, with a newish fitness centre and playing areas elsewhere, which provide for football, rugby (league and union), hockey, cricket and tennis. There is also a new Astroturf pitch and two new top-quality soccer pitches. Students have a discount at an Olympic standard sports centre with swimming pool in town. Rugby League players enjoy a sponsorship arrangement with Huddersfield Giants

PILLOW TALK

The uni no longer owns any accommodation, but recommends as its preferred and approved accommodation, the Storthes Hall Park Student Village and Ashenhurst Houses. These are privately-owned and operated by Ubrique Investments Limited trading as 'digs'. See www.campusdigs.com for further information.

Other hall-type accommodation and private shared houses are available around the town with rents from around £50 per week.

GETTING THERE
- By road: M62/J24, M1/J38-40.
- By rail: London via Wakefield, 3:30; Liverpool Lime Street, 1:45
- By air: Leeds/Bradford, Manchester Airports.
- By coach: London, 5:00; Leeds, 1:10.

UNIVERSITY OF HULL

The University of Hull
Cottingham Road
Kingston upon Hull HU6 7RX

TEL 0870 126 2000 (prospectus)
    01482 466100 (admissions)
FAX 01482 442290
EMAIL admissions@hull.ac.uk
WEB www.hull.ac.uk

Hull University Union
University House
Cottingham Road
Hull HU6 7RX

TEL 01482 445361
FAX 01482 466280
EMAIL [initial.name]t@hull.ac.uk
WEB www.hullstudent.com

VAG VIEW

*T*he city's most famous literary son, the
late poet and librarian Philip Larkin,
*described the city of Kingston upon Hull as
'in the world, yet sufficiently on the edge of it
to have a different resonance.'*

*For centuries it was cut off from the rest
of the country to the south by the Humber, to
the north by the glorious, wide open
Yorkshire Wolds, and to the west by a large
expanse of nothing. Then all the way from
Liverpool on the opposite coast came the
M62, meeting on its way the A1(M)), and
suddenly Hull became part of the rest of the
world, though as student Adam Ford told me,
'You'd be surprised at the number of people
in Liverpool who still think that the M62
stops in Leeds.'*

The essence of Hull is that it is distinct,

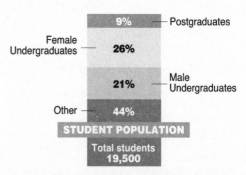

Postgraduates 9%
Female Undergraduates 26%
Male Undergraduates 21%
Other 44%

STUDENT POPULATION
Total students
19,500

*not just because it has its own telephone system
and white phone boxes, 'It is distinct culturally,'
a sixthform careers master said to me in hushed
tones. He teaches just an hour away and still he
can't find his way into it; he sends pupils to
Newcastle (two hours to the north), to York (an
hour to the west), to Sunderland, to Teesside,
but rarely, if ever apparently, to Hull.*

*The point, then, is that in its insularity,
Hull has developed this 'unique resonance.' For
the same reason, it is a cheap place to live,
more than 2% below the national average: you
can buy a three-bedroom house there for what
it costs to send a child to public school for two
years; parents do and sell it when their darling
leaves. But perhaps more important than all
this is that academically the University of Hull
is very strong, with high scores in teaching
assessments, the Queen's Anniversary Prize for
Social Work and Social Policy, a first class reputation for arts & social sciences – politics and*

UNIVERSITY/STUDENT PROFILE	
University since	**1954**
Situation/style	**Campus**
Student population	**19500**
Undergraduates	**9225**
- mature	**24%**
- non EU undergraduates	**12%**
- male/female	**44/56**
- non-traditional student intake	**30%**
- state school intake	**92%**
- drop-out rate	**13%**
- undergraduate applications	**Up 10%**

SUBJECT AREAS (%)

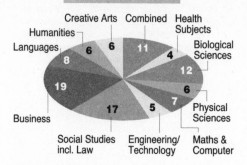

- Creative Arts — 6
- Humanities — 6
- Languages — 8
- Business — 19
- Social Studies incl. Law — 17
- Engineering/ Technology — 5
- Maths & Computer — 7
- Physical Sciences — 6
- Biological Sciences — 12
- Health Subjects — 4
- Combined — 11

ACADEMIC EXCELLENCE

TEACHING:
(Rated Excellent or 17+ out of 24)

Chemistry, History, Social Policy, Social Work	**Excellent**
Hispanic Studies; Drama, Electron Engineering	**24**
Theology, American Studies, Physics, Psychology, Biosciences, Politics, Tourism, Sport, Business Management	**23**
Italian, SE Asian Studies, Maths, Economics, Philosophy	**22**
French, German	**21**
Sociology, Dutch, Education	**20**
Scandinavian Studies	**19**

RESEARCH:
Top grades 5/5*

Geography, Law, Politics , Asian Studies, English, History, Music	**Grade 5**

languages especially – for health, for science and for business. The joint Hull-York medical school is the jewel in the crown.

What's more, the campus is a friendly and creative place to be, and there's a great new Students' Union.

CAMPUS

'The university is situated on Cottingham Road, about half an hour's walk, or a fifteen minute bus ride, from the city centre,' writes Albertina Lloyd. 'Cottingham Road connects Beverly Road and Newland Avenue, and you will come to know these three roads very well – Newland Avenue for shops (one claimed to sell "everything but the girl" and gave the band their name) and cafés, Cottingham Road for take-aways and Beverly Road for pubs. So, all that a student needs is situated within a short distance of the campus itself.'

Writes Laura French: 'It's close enough to the centre of town to satisfy both shopping and partying appetites, whilst being far enough away to provide some peace and quiet when you decide it's actually time to get some work done/sleep.'

'Hull prides itself on being one of the friendliest campuses in the country,' notes Danny Blackburn. 'It is a genuinely warm and welcoming environment, in which everyone feels as if they belong. The bars, corridors and lecture theatres all emanate a tremendous feeling of one-ness; it is apparent from day one. Hull's campus is, on a human scale, large enough always to be fun and exciting, but small enough to be personal, comfortable and unimposing.'

Now, Hull has expanded into the old and neighbouring Lincoln & Humberside Uni campus, locating Health Education there and the new Hull-York Medical School.

There is, too, Hull's **Scarborough Campus**, 40 miles north up the coast, which is known for drama, and is indeed the seat of the NUS Drama Festival, its patron Sir Alan Ayckbourn, whose plays are always premiered in the town's **Stephen Joseph Theatre**, which he runs.

FEES, BURSARIES

UK & EU Fees 2007: £3,070 p.a. Fees for 2008 not yet fixed. If in receipt of HE Maintence grant there's a £1,000 p.a. bursary, and £500-£1,000 on a sliding scale if you are in receipt of a partial grant. For Sir Brynmor Jones/Ferens Scholarships for Academic Excellence (£1,500), see www.hull. ac.uk/money

> *'One of the friendliest campuses in the country. All my lecturers operate an open door policy, and are never too busy to help out. Many of them use the all-important currency of humour in lectures.'*

STUDENT PROFILE

The uni has always been seen as one of this country's 'access elite' in that it enjoys a pukka academic reputation, but has been able to bring in a number of undergrads from poorer areas/classes. While others have more impressive figures for this now, they retain and develop their policy by giving 16-year-olds conditional places and running clubs for 11 and 12-year-olds. Once ensconced on campus, Hull students become stereotypical (beer, beer and more beer) or sign up as members of one of the healthy sub-groups – clubbers, metallers, crusties and skaters. At any rate, all intermingle without any trouble.

ACADEMIA & JOBS

'All of my lecturers operate an open door policy, and are never too busy to help you out,' writes Joe Whinam. 'Many use the all-important currency of humour in lectures.' Who might long for such at university these days.

Resources look good, too: 'The Brynmor Jones Library is absolutely huge, and I have never had problems getting a book from there. Seven floors packed full of books, great views, quiet work places and gorgeous exchange students. The computer network is surprisingly reliable and allows you to access your private account from any computer off campus, as well as course information, lecture notes, e-mail and all the programs you'd even need.

The degree in Medicine at the Hull York Medical School (HYMS) is a 5-year BMBS (Bachelor of Medicine, Bachelor of Surgery). You may be based at either Hull or York Uni campuses (it's a dual effort, both follow the same curriculum). Hull has a decade's experience in Medicine through its Postgrad Medical School, while York's biosciences and health depts are top rated for teaching and research. Small-group clinical contact from Year 1. Equal emphasis on physical, psychological and social aspects. A low student-teacher ratio promised. Entry ABB + UKCAT, including Chemistry and Biology, Caring experience and interpersonal skills will be a significant separator. Tough to get in: there's only a 7% acceptance rate.

In nursing, Hull offer adult, children's, learning disability and mental health degrees, and are the second largest supplier of SRN, RGN and the third of non-hospital nurses. The school did, however, flop at the assessments. Teaching inspection, 17. Assumption is that lessons have been learned and the new broom HYMS attitude will sort it out. The BSc Midwifery suffered at the same assessment and

the entry requirement (240 points) is high, though it hasn't harmed employment rates.

Nationally, more than 3,000 graduates find their way into community work/counselling annually. Over a third come through social studies departments (where you'll find Psychology and Sociology and Social Work degrees, besides a lot else). Lincoln leads the field, then comes Hull. Look at BSc Psychology with Counselling at Hull (there are other interesting Psychology parcels too), also BA Social Work (including professional qualification) and Social Policy.

Next largest graduate provision is in Education. Hull students mostly take the languages route into jobs as lecturers in Adult Education. Spanish took full marks at the assessments, Italian 22, French and German 21, Dutch 20 (you can slip over to Holland for the weekend from here), and Scandinavian Studies got 19. The hub is the Language Institute, incorporating the Open Learning Centre, where you can have a language assessment and teaching programme individually designed for you.

Over at the Scarborough campus, about 40 minutes northwards up the coast, there are masses of primary teachers busy training. But also, the character and environmental problems associated with the Scarborough coastline and seashore have become meat for a host of interesting other degrees – Coastal Marine Biology, Ecology, Environmental Science, and Tourism Management among them.

Back on the main Hull campus a sure line in accountancy jobs should be mentioned. Various degrees (BSc and BA) involving professional experience and international elements make this a very productive area. Another is computing. Programmers and games designers find work comes easy out of Hull. Hull comes within the top three in the employment table for programmers, software consultancy & supply. The 3/4-year BSc Computer Science with Games Development comes with a foundation year.

Finally, there is a good reputation for Law – they are European law specialists (French, German) with a Grade 5 rating for research. There's

---

WHERE HULL GRADUATES END UP

Health & Social Work: 17%; Education: 12%; Wholesale/Retail: 10%; Manufacturing: 9%; Financial Activities: 9%; Public Administration, Civil Service & Defence: 9%; Hotel/Restaurant: 5%; Transport & Communications (including Telecommunications): 3%; Construction: 1%; Personnel: 4%; Computer: 3%; Business & Management: 3%; Accountancy: 4%; Media (including Film): 2.5%; Legal 2.5%; Publishing: 1%; Artistic/Literary: 1%; Sport: 1%.

Approximate 'graduate track' employed **64%**

but the most popular are the Athletic Union nights on a Wednesday. It's wise to buy your tickets in advance. They even sometimes play films up on the big screen, which is cool. Like going to the cinema but cheaper and with a pint. Whilst Hull itself, unfortunately, does not attract a great many live acts, the union is getting increasing numbers of reputable bands to come and play there, The Feeling and We Are Scientists being recent examples. There's always loads going on, including karaoke, open mic nights, a quiz and much more.

The on-campus **Gulbenkian Theatre** is the focus of a drama course which scored full marks in the teaching assessments. There is a newspaper, *Hullfire*, and a student radio station, Jam 1575. The Tech. Comm. is a parallel organisation into sound and lighting systems and gets its performance kicks at the Friday and Saturday discos. They were nominated for the top technical award in the National Radio Awards this year.

Politically the union is averagely active. 'The union council is largely left wing and campaigns are well supported,' says Peter Bainbridge. Campaigns have supported Third World First, Animal Rights and Amnesty International, and there's a particularly active Women's Committee and Lesbian and Gay Society. 'Though the locals aren't the most tolerant of folk,' says Peter, 'there are gay-friendly places.'

TOWN Hull is currently undergoing a major facelift in the form of the St Stephen's Development, a £200 million project that promises to transform the heart of the city. This will include a huge retail centre, a state-of-the-art transport interchange, a hotel, modern residences and a new home for the

also a good line into the police. Note the BA Criminology, Criminology with Psychology, and Criminology with Law. There's also Social Policy & Criminology and now Citizenship & Social Justice, and an intriguing bunch of Chemistry with Forensic Science & Toxicology degrees.

SOCIAL SCENE

STUDENTS' UNION 'Hull Union offers so much that you actually needn't venture off campus for a good night out,' writes Laura French. 'You'll hear third years tell how the newly refurbished bar, **The Sanctuary** is not as good as the **Rezi** (the old bar in the union). Just ignore them, a change is as good as a rest. Another bar, **The John McCarthy**, and a full-sized club, **Asylum**. Asylum is great fun; you will grow to love it, and its predictable soundtrack (mostly 80s/90s cheese and current pop). They have different nights on every night, legendary **Hull Truck Theatre**.

Hull's Old Town is home to some of the city's most traditional pubs and a fine Museum Quarter. The area near the University, Newland Avenue and Princes Avenue has seen a lot of recent investment.

Writes Laura: 'Newland Avenue and Princes Avenue provide everything from greengrocers to convenience stores to café bars. They are slightly bohemian in feel, and, being in Hull, are much cheaper than their equivalents in other cities.

'Whilst Hull may not have the diversity of night life that you would get in other, bigger cities, there is nonetheless something for everyone. There's no shortage of nice pubs around the uni itself - **The Old Grey Mare** directly opposite does good, cheap food, **The Gardener's Arms** is a popular hangout for sports teams (whether you like rugby, or just rugby players) and **The Haworth Arms**, a little further down the road is a good place to hang out with friends.

Beverley Road, one of the main thoroughfares into town has no shortage of bars and pubs either including the obligatory **Wetherspoons**, though some of them it is wisest not to visit unless you want to be confronted by angry, middle-aged locals out for a scrap. **The Old Town** is a popular student haunt on Monday nights when **The Mission** (a nice pub, but watch out for the turbo shandies) is the place to be, followed by **Waterfront**.'

Says Joe Whinam: '**Waterfront** and **Pozition** do fantastic nights for students and both run buses from and to student halls. **Attic** on a Wednesday does a great rock/metal night but it's hard to get back to halls. **Welly** on a Thursday is always popular with indie and punk kids. **Spiders** really needs no introduction - outrageously cheap drinks, friendly staff and great music (ranging from death metal to Sixties soul).

'Hull isn't exactly the safest place in the world, and you are likely to face a chav with a bad attitude at some point. The best thing to do is to stay in the city centre and uni area, and not wander off into the west or north.

'Costs for a decent night out really vary from about £10 - yes, you heard me correctly - in Spiders to about £20-30 in the bigger clubs.'

As for Scarborough, where the satellite campus is, 'The town has been ruined by a Council that can often be seen lampooned in *Private Eye*,' says Peter Coon, noting that the town was the *Eye's* Rotten Borough of the Year, 'but even they can't obliterate the natural beauty of coast and moors. Nightclubs are cheesy and can get violent. Masses of watering holes, some good real ale and some very good 'locals' Old Town hostelries, though they'll never serve you. It's cheap, however, and so long as you've got something to do, you'll survive, unless you get really ill. The hospital keeps the mortuary pretty busy.' Something, perhaps the Hull-York Med School might change.

SPORT Writes Laura: 'Facilities are great. There is a relatively new sports centre with squash courts, halls etc and loads of pitches, both grass and Astroturf across the road from the uni. If, like me, team sports aren't your thing, but you still want to get fit, there is an excellent gym in the fitness centre. A year-long, pay as you go membership (£2.50 per time) is just £15. Oh yeah, and the changing rooms are nice - the showers are better than those in most of the student houses!'

PILLOW TALK

Not before time, the uni is spending £16 million on refurbishments to halls over the next three years. Writes Joe: 'The three halls, Needler, The Lawns and Thwaite are in the village of Cottingham, a couple of miles from campus, great for pubs (karaoke at the **Hallgate** = winner), takeaways and shops. Regular buses run. Lawns is absolutely huge, has its own bar and police station. Thwaite is a posh version of Needler, but it is out of the way of everyone else.'

GETTING THERE

☛ By road: M62, A63, A1079, B1233.
☛ By rail: Leeds, 1:00; Manchester, 2:15; London King's Cross, 4:30; Birmingham New Street, 3:00.
☛ By air: Humberside, Leeds/Bradford Airports.
☛ By coach: London, 5:10; Manchester, 3-4:00.

IMPERIAL COLLEGE, LONDON

Imperial College
South Kensington
London SW7 2AZ

TEL 020 7594 8001
FAX 020 7594 8004
EMAIL admissions@imperial.ac.uk
WEB www.imperial.ac.uk

Imperial College Union
Prince Consort Road
London SW7 2BB

TEL 020 7594 8060
FAX 020 7594 8065
EMAIl (see website)
WEB www.union.ic.ac.uk

VAG VIEW

*P*art of the federal University of London, but enjoying more independence than most, Imperial College is a world beater in the areas of medicine, engineering, technology, maths and science.

Mergers have formed its character since the beginning, where, in 1907, it arose out of the marriage of the prestigious Royal College of Science, the Royal School of Mines and the City & Guilds College.

The RCS gave Imperial pure science, the RSM gave it mining *(and related fields, such as geology)* and the CGC, engineering. Mergers with three London teaching hospitals leave it with a massive medical provision. Now, Imperial have linked up with Thames Valley University to provide an amazing opportunity for students who have the aptitude to study medicine, but not the qualifications. They will study the first year of Human Sciences – Pre-medical Option BSc (Hons) – at TVU, and depending on their first semester exam results they can transfer to the first year of Imperial's 6-year MBBS course.

There are other influences. Wye College in Kent brings the food industry, agriculture, the environment and business management into the equation.

Imperial's research record is amazing, the second best in the entire country. Make no

'This has got to be the best situated college, probably in England, perhaps even in the world. If you come from a small town like I do, you'll be blown away by it. Now, the negative. If daddy doesn't own half the oil fields in Texas you are likely to hit a major financial crisis.'

mistake about it, if you get a place at Imperial and work hard, you will be made. It has one of the lowest drop-out rates in the country (2.9%), which shows that students appreciate the deal on offer.

CAMPUSES

'The main campus is situated in South Kensington, Zone 1, Central London,' writes Saurabh Pandya. 'We are right next to the Victoria & Albert, Science and Natural History museums (and are granted free access to them). Travel is easy, the nearest tube is a ten-minute walk away. Generally, it is a low crime area, well lit and pretty safe for students, especially as the uni, the union and most uni accommodation are all within five minutes of each other.'

Says Sarah Playforth, 'This has got to be the best situated college in London, probably in England and perhaps even in the world. If you come from a small town like I do, you'll be blown away by it. Now, the negative. If daddy doesn't own half the oil fields in Texas you are likely to hit a major financial crisis if you eat out at anywhere other than McDonalds. Yes, central London is an extremely expensive place. By the time you graduate you'll probably have acquired an overdraft equivalent to the annual budget of a small country.'

There is a satellite campus, **Wye College** in Ashford, Kent. Tel 01233 812401, the sometime agricultural arm of London University. Imperial bought it and now it's home to an important Applied Business Management course, taught, it seems rather oddly, by Kent University. You get a Kent degree and an Imperial Associateship.

FEES, BURSARIES

UK & EU Fees, 2007: £3,070 p.a. All students in receipt of a the Government HE Maintenance Grant will receive a student support bursary up to a maximum of four years. Those receiving the maximum award, who have achieved the highest grade in at least three A-Levels and who have firmly accepted an offer of place by the UCAS deadline in May will receive a total bursary of £4,000. If in receipt of partial HE Maintenance Grant, at the midpoint students will receive at least £500, while if in receipt of the minimum Study Support

SUBJECT AREAS (%)

Engineering/Technology — 29
Combined — 5
Medicine — 18
Biological Sciences — 12
Agriculture — 2
Physical Sciences — 16
Maths & Computer — 18

Female Undergraduates — **24%**

36% — Postgraduates

Male Undergraduates — 40%

STUDENT POPULATION

Total students **12,185**

Bursary they'll receive at least £100.

STUDENT PROFILE

There is a sense of privilege in the air. Only Oxbridge take fewer from the state sector than Imperial. Another factor is the gender imbalance, but here things are righting themselves. Only a few years ago an Imperial student wrote: 'The male:female ratio here is about 100:1, but blokes have practically no chance of getting a woman, ever, and consequently Imperial is the sexual frustration capital of Britain!'

Sarah Playforth agreed: 'What you pull is not guaranteed to be human, but the good thing about the student body is that the college's international reputation leads to a large cultural diversity and you can make friends from all over the world.'

Such is the power of the VAG that the male:femal ratio this year is 63:37 – perfectly respectable, and if they tend to be spoddy, well what can you expect?

ACADEMIA & JOBS

'The work is hard, let's get that straight from the outset,' writes Saurabh. 'Most successful applicants have AAB or higher at A-level, and so a high standard will be expected of you. But help is always at hand should you fall behind. There are plenty of tutorials, one-to-one time with the lecturer; lecture

UNIVERSITY/STUDENT PROFILE	
School of London Uni since	**1908**
Situation/style	**City campus**
Student population	**12185**
Undergraduates	**7850**
- mature	**5%**
- non EU undergraduates	**22%**
- male/female	**63/37**
- non-traditional student intake	**19%**
- state school intake	**59%**
- drop-out rate	**4%**
- undergraduate applications	**Up 3%**

ACADEMIC EXCELLENCE	
TEACHING:	
(Rated Excellent or 17+ out of 24)	
Chemistry, Business & Management, Computing, Geology.	**Excellent**
Electrical & Electronic Eng, Materials Technology	**24**
General Engineering	**23**
Chemical Eng, Mech, Aero & Manufacturing Eng, Molecular Biosciences, Organismal Biosciences, Physics	**22**
Civil Engineering, Medicine	**21**
RESEARCH:	
Top grades 5/5*/6*	
Clinical Laboratory Sciences, Hospital-based Clinical, Bio Sciences, Physics, Pure Maths, Applied Maths, Computer, Chemical Eng, Civil Eng, Mechanical/ Aeronautical/ Manufacturing Eng, Mineral/ Mining Engineering	**Grade 6***
Chemistry, General Engineer.	**Grade 5***
Community-based Clinical, Pre-Clinical, Statistics, Electrical/Electronic Eng, Metallurgy, Business, History	**Grade 5**

notes are always on the web, and if you e-mail a particular lecturer they will always meet with you and explain anything that you don't understand. Most subjects have a representative, a student in your year, chosen by your vote, whose responsibility it is to ensure that you know what's going on, that the web notes are of a satisfactory standard, and so on.

'The library occupies five floors and is shared with the Science Museum. It is pretty comprehensive, and as you would expect at a science and technology uni, the computing facilities are also first rate. There are plenty of PCs, and these are upgraded every eighteen months. Staff tend to be leading figures in their field, and regardless of subject you will get a world class education by coming here.'

Ninety-three per cent of Imperial's teaching assessments have been Excellent or scored 21 or more points out of 24. Its research record is second only to Cambridge. Eleven departments were graded 6 (that's the tops), two Grade 5 (world class) and seven scored 5 (mostly world class), and all have either shown improvement or maintained their position, which, as they will tell you, is a unique achievement among the top four universities in the UK.

The Medicine degree in this, the largest med-school in the country, is a 6-year MB BS (including BSc). Application acceptance rate is 12%, which is softer than average, and there's a special route in via a foundation year at Thames Valley Uni (see *VAG View* above). Nearly 30% of Imperial graduates become doctors. All learning is in a clinical context. Traditional, but with special emphasis on commu-nication skills. law, and information technology. Entry AAB + BMAT, including Chemistry, one other science subject or Maths + a third subject. General Studies not accepted. GCSE Biology, Chemistry, English Lang, Maths, Physics essential. At least 3 A grades and 2 B grades. Teaching Inspection 21 Research Grade 5*: Clinical Lab Sciences, Hospital-based Clinical, Bio Sciences; Grade 5: Community-based Clinical, Pre-Clinical.

Since September 2006, there has been a degree programme in Biomedical Sciences – a 3-year BSc or 4-year MSci, a collaboration between the Faculty of Life Sciences and the Faculty of Medicine. Biomedical Sciences encompasses the principles and practice of biology and biochemistry in relation to medicine.

After doctors come financial wallahs in the Imperial job league, many becoming investment advisers and analysts. Graduates of the Faculty of Engineering/Technology lead (Information Systems Engineering, Computing, etc), then those from Physical Sciences (Maths in various guises and including Management. Far and away Imperial's most popular choice for a job in the City is followed by chartered accountancy and business analysts. Average

Around 7% of graduates become software engi-neers, another 4% systems analysts, more than 2% computer programmers. In the Faculty of Physical Sciences, there's a BSc and MSci in Mathematics & Computer Science, and in Engineering, MEng Computing (Software Engineering) as well as a European programme of computer study, and other degrees orientated towards Artificial Intelligence, Computational Management. Research Grade 6*.

Look also at the B/MEng Information Systems Engineering degrees which come with Associateship of the City & Guilds of London Institute. See also Software Engineer.

Defence operatives and equipment engineers come along the Engineering & Technology and Physical Sciences routes.

They have one of the most exciting Physics departments in the country and a world-class Grade 5* for research. For sheer breadth of vision, look at their exciting 4-year BSc (Hons) Physics with Studies in Musical Performance, developed with the neighbouring Royal College of Music, which taps the cerebral contiguity of art and science at its most exquisite – the anatomy and astronomy of the music of the spheres, perhaps.

Graduates find careers in both disciplines and also in broadcasting and recording, where the cross faculty training offers unique, if less immediately obvious, possibilities.

Imperial, in part formed out of The Royal College of Mines in 1907, has a very much more recent world-class Grade 6* for its research facility and a series of BEng/BSc degrees which offer Associateship with the Royal School of Mines; also MEng/MSci degrees with the same Associateship and including, among other degrees, Petroleum Geoscience. Jobs in oil extraction, mining, etc, pro-liferate. Teaching inspection, 22.

Finally, the question of Wye is answered by the college in this way: 'The future of our rural envi-ronment and how we use it to produce safe and healthy food is of critical importance in this new millennium. The Department, already widely known for its interdisciplinary approach (integrat-ing science and management) to new technologies, strategies and policies affecting rural development worldwide, has modern laboratories and facilities, including an award-winning learning resources centre and working farm on a 350-hectare estate.'

SOCIAL SCENE

STUDENTS' UNION The Students' Union, like UMIST, St Andrews, Edinburgh, Glasgow and Dundee, man-age their own affairs. 'Don't worry about your stu-dent discounts,' Ed Sexton assures, 'ICU cards are

---

WHERE IMPERIAL GRADUATES END UP

Health & Social Work: 31%; Education: 3%; Wholesale/Retail: 3%; Manufacturing: 7%; Financial Activities: 15%; Public Administration, Civil Service & Defence: 4%; Hotel/Restaurant: 1%; Transport & Communications (including Telecommunications): 3%; Construction: 1%; Agriculture: 2%; Mining/Oil Extracting: 2%; Personnel: 3%; Computer: 4%; Business & Management: 5%; Accountancy: 4%; Media (including Film): 0.5%; Architecture: 1%; Sport: 1%.

Approximate 'graduate track' employed **84%**

WHAT IT'S REALLY LIKE

UNIVERSITY:

Social Life	★★★★
Campus scene	**Singular**
Student Union services	**Good**
Politics	**Low interest**
Sport	**Good**
National team position	**39th**
Sport facilities	**Good**
Arts opportunities	**Drama, dance, film excellent; art avg; music good**
Student newspaper	**Felix**
Student radio	**IC Radio**
Student TV	**STOIC**
Nat. TV Awards 2003	**3 gongs!**
Nightclub venues	**Da Vinci's**
Bars	**dBs, Union, Beit, Charing Cross, Wye Union**
Union ents	**Pervasive**
Union clubs/Societies	**248**
Parking	**Non-existent**

CITY:

Entertainment	★★★★★
Scene	**Wild, expensive**
Town/gown relations	**Average-good**
Risk of violence	**London v. high**
Cost of living	**High**
Student concessions	**Good**
Survival + 2 nights out	**£100 pw**
Part-time work campus/town	**Good/excellent**

AT A GLANCE

ACADEMIC FILE:

Subjects assessed	**15**
Excellent	**93%**
Typical entry points	**468**
Application acceptance rate	**18%**
Med. School acceptance rate	**12%**
Students-staff ratio	**9:1**
First/2:1 degree pass rate	**75%**

ACCOMMODATION FILE:

Guarantee to freshers	**100%**
Style	**Halls**
Catered	**Almost none**
En-suite	**A few**
Price range pw	**£57-£130**
City rent pw	**£100-£180 Zone 1, £75-£85 Zone 2**

accepted at most places in London, and you can also get a University of London Union (ULU) card, which is widely recognised.'

They have the biggest student venue in London, the cheapest bar prices in the city, the most clubs and societies and an enviable programme of some six clubnights a week and regular top-line live acts and comedy.

Union facilities feature **Da Vinci's**, a modern-style café bar – trivia nights, cocktail nights and live jazz, big screen sport, Wednesday club-nights for the sports crowd (with recent additional barbecue facilities), Saturday pre-club and a non-stop succession of Friday clubnights.

The wood-panelled **Union Bar** is a more typical pub, with reputedly the largest pewter tankard collection in Europe. The **Beit Quad bars** are in the ground floor of the Union building in Beit Quad. Then there's the **Charing Cross (med) Bar**, Fulham, and the **Union Bar,** Wye.

In addition, a **Concert Hall** is used for bigger events and there's a smaller venue, **dBs** (also known by its full name **Decibels**) or **dB's Club Bar**

which is open Wednesday and Friday nights, again with big screen. Another attraction of the union is the cinema – 'the biggest student cinema in the country and the sixth biggest screen in London. It shows films much later than elsewhere but only go if you think the film is worth getting a sore bum for,' says our reporter.

The number of clubs at Imperial is pretty overwhelming – not far short of 250 from which to choose, everything from Chess, to E-commerce, to Rugby to Juggling. And just because they are a techno-based uni, it doesn't mean they don't have any arty clubs – Opera, Drama, Art, Dance, etc are all very active.

Film is rated excellent by students. Media, too, is very active both from a techno and literary pov. There's the award-winning newspaper, *Felix*, and IC Radio and STOIC, the TV arm, which won Best On-Screen Male (Greg Foot) and BO-S Female (Frankie Young), and Best Broadcaster in the 2006 National Media Awards.

Down at rural Wye, your average Wye-guy can be found done up in a penguin suit on his way to a ball, or to one of their eccentric clubs. There are three pubs locally and a Union bar, and a tradition of Thursday nights when peculiar clubs, including the mysterious Druids take over the Union in a whirl of practical jokes, initiation ceremonies and over-consumption of alcohol. Membership is by invitation only.

SPORT Besides national competition in the uni leagues, where Imperial came 47th last year, they excel in the London University league. But in rowing – the big thing at ICS – you're talking international levels. The boathouse is at Putney Bridge.

A new sports centre, Ethos, is opening at the South Kensington campus ithis year – a 70-station fitness gym, 25m deck-level swimming pool, a sauna/steam room and spa, a five-badminton-court sports hall, a state-of-the-art climbing wall, exercise studio, and a sports injury unit. The Sports Centre at Prince's Gardens (Exhibition Road) includes a 25m swimming pool, four squash courts, a gym, a 25m rifle range, a training studio, sauna, steam room and poolside spa bath. Nearby there are tennis and netball courts, and a weights room. The 60-acre pitches are at Harlington, near Heathrow. Facilities include a floodlit multi-purpose surface and a pavilion with bar. There are a further 15 acres at Teddington (four pitches and a cricket square), 22 acres at Cobham, the boathouse at Putney and a sailing club at Welsh Harp Reservoir in North West London. In addition, its site at Charing Cross Hospital has a 25m swimming pool and squash.

PILLOW TALK

You are guaranteed a place in either Imperial College or London University intercollegiate accommodation for the first year of study. Imperial accommodation is self-catering except Linstead Hall on the South Kensington campus and the Wye campus halls. 'If you are lucky,' writes London-based Saurabh, 'you'll get into one of the halls right next to campus, and you can spend all year perfecting your "get up at 8:55 and be in time for 9:00 lecture" technique. These are the Southside, Northside and Beit halls. If you are especially lucky, you will be placed in Beit Hall, which was opened recently and has brand new rooms with Ikea-style kitchens and every amenity you could possibly want. There are other halls in Evelyn Gardens (15 minutes from campus) or Pembridge Gardens (40 minutes, or 20 by tube).'

GETTING THERE

☛ By Underground: South Kensington (Circle, District and Piccadilly lines).

UNIVERSITY OF KEELE

The University of Keele
Keele
Staffordshire ST5 5BG

TEL 01782 621111
   01782 584005/583994
FAX 01782 632343
EMAIL undergraduate@keele.ac.uk
WEB www.keele.ac.uk

Keele Students' Union
Keele
Staffs ST5 5BJ

TEL 01782 711411
FAX 01782 712671
EMAIL sta21@kusu.keele.ac.uk
WEB www.kusu.net

VAG VIEW

Its academic strategy made it unique from the start – the emphasis on a broad education, seen in the dual honours degree, which they pioneered and which offers a rare opportunity to study from both science and arts points of view. Ninety per cent of Keele's students opt for this type of degree. A third of first years are studying a language or a related cultural module. Nearly all undergraduates at Keele, irrespective of the subject combination they are studying have the opportunity to spend a semester of their second year at one of Keele's partner institutions in North America, Australia, South Africa or another part of Europe. Keele is one of 8 unis to have been awarded the European Quality Label for mobility. A certain sort of person thrives there.

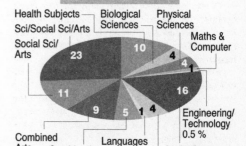

SUBJECT AREAS (%)

Health Subjects — Sci/Social Sci/Arts 23
Biological Sciences 10
Physical Sciences 4
Maths & Computer 4
Engineering/Technology 1
Social Studies incl. Law 16
Business 4
Languages 1
Combined Sciences 5
Combined Arts 9
Social Sci/Arts 11
Engineering/Technology 0.5 %

CAMPUS

It's a 617-acre country estate, with lakes and woodland, 'the centre of England and the middle of nowhere,' write Mark Holtz and Gareth Belfield. 'Keele University's self-contained campus is a stone's throw from Stoke-on-Trent, a constant worry for those students without protective headgear. In theory, the university is set within tiny Keele village, but the campus has grown over such a large area that saying it is part of Keele village is akin to saying that London is part of Westminster. The campus is on a hill top and is so exposed you expect a policeman to come along and arrest it for indecency. Nearby Newcastle-under-Lyme, Hanley (Stoke) and Crewe can be reached by the bus service called (joyfully) PMT. Train-wise, Manchester is only 30 minutes away, as is Birmingham. London direct can be done in around two hours. The M6 is within earshot of the campus, and sounds like the sea if you are drunk enough.'

A 70-acre greenfield site adjacent to the University is about to be developed into a base for new academic buildings and student residences and an expansion of the University's Science Park. Work will begin in July 2007.

FEES, BURSARIES

UK & EU Fees 2007: £3,070 p.a. Not yet fixed for 2008. Undergraduate students in receipt of full or partial maintenance grants can apply for a range of bursaries from £500-£1,000 p.a. There are also 2 scholarships available worth £2,000 p.a. and £1,000 over 3 years. The University's premier award, the Vice-Chancellors Scholarship, is available to all and is worth £4,000 p.a. The Deans Scholarship, worth £2,000 p.a. is awarded to the highest achievers in each faculty. The Mathematics Scholarship (£1,000) is available to students of maths as a single honours course who attain Grade A Maths + 300 points from 3 A-levels. There's £500 p.a. for medicine students and for students coming from Keele's partner schools. There's also an Ethnic Minority bursary of £1,000. See www.keele.ac.uk/undergraduate/bursaries

STUDENT PROFILE

'Take a generous measure of "traditional" students, two heaped tablespoons of mature, nursing, international and local students, heavily season with postgraduates, add a dash of complete weirdoes

UNIVERSITY/STUDENT PROFILE	
University since	**1962**
Situation/style	**Rural campus**
Student population	**10866**
Undergraduates	**8255**
- mature	**20%**
- non EU undergraduates	**8%**
- male/female	**40/60**
- non-traditional student intake	**28%**
- state school intake	**92%**
- drop-out rate	**10%**
- undergraduate applications	**Down 9%**

and you have the recipe for the most diverse and interesting concoction of a university anywhere in the world. It's impossible not to fit in at Keele, with over half the students living together on campus, you're never really in danger of running out of people to borrow sugar from.'

Female students abound (60% of undergrads).

ACADEMIA & JOBS

The dual honours degree is a multi-disciplinary strategy which promises more than a one-plus-one benefit – at best, new, enlightening points of view on a shared subject focus, or the same skills of mind honed simultaneously by different subjects of study. If it is the analytical skills of a top-flight bioscientist that is required in the City, here you can put the theory to the test. Or you can simply look for compatibility, a vocational element that enhances your main subject interest – there are combo degrees in Marketing with Maths, Music Technology, Physics, Psychology, Statistics (as there are with Management).

Half the Keele graduates that become marketing managers (that's 6% of all Keele graduates) ride in on these. The other half look elsewhere in the curriculum for marketing as an addendum to a subject of their choice. Languages are an important entré – e.g. French and Marketing; and sometimes there is a good product-orientated subject given employability by the addition of Marketing, as in Biochemistry and Marketing.

Business Administration makes another highly employable mix with Psychology (or languages, law, media, or Communications & Culture). Such Business Admin combos account for nearly a quarter of jobs at Keele. Another productive multi-disciplinary course is Human Resource Management (with Psychology, Info Systems, etc) – more than 3% of Keele graduates become personnel officers. Finance, Economics and Maths combo degrees lead 10% of all Keele graduates to become accountants or to work in other financial areas.

Computer Science combinations, Education Studies combos, and Social Studies degrees are all major contributors to graduate employment. Law is worth a particular mention. Part of the multi-subject curriculum, but also a single honours subject, there's an international reputation and if you want to work as a solicitor and you already have a degree in another subject, you can take the Common Professional Examination (CPE) here.

Keele now also offer the opportunity to study Medicine (a MBChB degree) to applicants with non-Science A levels. It is a course developed with Manchester University. The new clinical skills lab at the Dept of Nursing & Midwifery, which simulates a ward environment, is a part of this. Since 2003 they have offered a 5-year course at Keele Campus, with the first 2 years in Manchester, or a 6-year course with the pre-med year at Manchester. The 6-year is strictly for pupils taking Arts subjects at A Level (or 2 Arts and 1 Science. GCSEs Chemistry and Maths are 'desirable'). For the 5-year, you'll need AAB + UKCAT, Chemistry and Biology or Physics or Maths + one other. 8-11 GCSEs with a broad spread of subjects.

STUDENT SCENE

STUDENTS' UNION **Sam's Bar** opens up to the Ballroom to take around 1100 on big live act nights. Apparently the KUSU building was originally designed to look like a ship with the **Ballroom** at the heart of the vessel. In the good old days the Rolling Stones used to use it as a rehearsal room and even now, on a still winter's night, faint echoes can be heard of the Eurythmics, UB40, Oasis and a young Jarvis Cocker, who graced the stage. More recent visitors were Fun Lovin' Criminals, Idlewild, Mis-Teeq, Liberty X, Atomic Kitten, Toploader, Reef, The Pet Shop Boys, Levellers, The Proclaimers.

The Lounge is – surprise – a lounge bar. **K2**, formerly **The Club**, is now KUSU's 'premier Entertainment Venue', having undergone a £250k refurbishment three years ago. With a top-specification PA & lighting system, it features a permanent 6m x 4m stage. Here, on a Monday is pop,

ACADEMIC EXCELLENCE	
TEACHING:	
(Rated Excellent or 17+ out of 24)	
Applied Social Work, Music	**Excellent**
American Studies, Politics,	**24**
Philosophy, Education	
Economics, Psychology	**23**
Sociology, Maths, Organismal	**22**
Biosciences, Physics	
Nursing, Molecular Biosciences,	**21**
Management	
French, Russian,	**20**
Subjects Allied to Medicine	
German	**19**
RESEARCH:	
Top grades 5/5*/6*	
Law	**Grade 6***
Applied Maths, General Eng,	**Grade 5**
English, Politics, Social Policy,	
American Studies, History	

chart & dance with resident DJ Chris; alternate Tuesdays is Comedy Club – Mark Lamarr, Peter Kay, Ed Byrne, Paul Tonkinson, Adam Bloom, Richard Morton and more. On other Tuesdays you might have *Stella Screen* – box office smashes before general release. Wednesdays – whole building is *R-wind* (retro - 80s, 90s) and indie/alternative from resident DJ The Rich. They also do monthly fancy dress nights and, in **The Lounge**, Quiz and Cocktail evenings and Sunday karaoke competitions.

There's a variety of restaurants, bars, cafés and retail outlets on campus. **The Comus** offers a Five Day Meal Plan

Keele has a history of political turbulence, but you wouldn't notice now: 'In the '70s,' write Mark and Gareth, 'Keele pre-empted Wales and Scotland by attempting to gain independence from Britain. Passports were issued, border patrols were set up, a national anthem created, and an unsuccessful attempt to enter the Eurovision Song Contest was made. More recently, they were the first university

WHERE KEELE GRADUATES END UP
Health & Social Work: 14%; Education: 8%; Wholesale/Retail: 12%; Manufacturing: 8%; Financial Activities: 10%; Public Administration, Civil Service & Defence: 13%; Hotel/Restaurant: 3%; Transport & Communications (including Telecommunications): 5%; Construction: 2%; Agriculture: 1%; Personnel: 5%; Computer: 3%; Business & Management: 3%; Accountancy: 3%; Media (including Film): 1%; Legal 5%; Publishing: 3%; Sport: 1%.
Approximate 'graduate track' employed **65%**

WHAT IT'S REALLY LIKE

UNIVERSITY:

Social Life	★★★
Campus scene	**Isolated**
Student Union services	**Good**
Politics	**Average**
Sport	**Not impressive**
National teamposition	**61st**
Sport facilities	**Good**
Arts opportunities	**Excellent**
Student newspaper	**Concourse**
Nightclub	**K2**
Bars	**Sam's Bar, Ballroom, Lounge**
Union ents	**Cheesy + live**
Union societies	**80**
Most popular society	**Drama**
Parking	**Good**
TOWN:	
Entertainment	★★
Local (Stoke) scene	**Pubs/clubs**
Town/gown relations	**OK**
Risk of violence	**Average**
Cost of living	**Below average**
Student concessions	**Average**
Survival + 2 nights out	**£50 pw**
Part-time work campus/town	**OK/poor**

to reject the Government's tuition fees proposals.'

SPORT In 2006, the AU won Most Improved University in the annual BUSA Awards, climbing the BUSA Championship ranking by an impressive 49 places - lifting them to 61st place out of 149 competing universities. Facilities include a gym, sports hall, floodlit synthetic pitch, 50 acres of grass pitches, tennis courts, fitness centre, squash courts, etc.

TOWN 'Aaarghh! Keele is in the Potteries, where the main industry is not so much in decline, as plummeting down a precipice of bankruptcy. Locals refer to you as "duck" if they like you. If they don't like you they'll just try to run over you.

PILLOW TALK

'There is something inexplicably nice about campus accommodation,' sigh Mark & Gareth, 'even if the cleaning ladies have mastered the art of knocking, unlocking your door, opening it, coming in, and saying, "Ooh, I'll come back when you've had time to put some clothes on," all in two sec-

AT A GLANCE

ACADEMIC FILE:

Subjects assessed	**28**
Excellent	**68%**
Typical entry requirements	**309 points**
Application acceptance rate	**17%**
Med. School acceptance rate	**21%**
Students-staff ratio	**17:1**
First/2:1 degree pass rate	**53%**

ACCOMMODATION FILE:

Guarantee to freshers	**To firm applicants**
Style	**Halls**
Catered	**None**
En-suite	**25%**
Approx price range pw	**£56-£90**
Town rent pw	**£45**

onds.' Newest accommodation comprises 131 en-suite rooms in 2 blocks, arranged in 6-person flats. The HallsNet Service allows all students direct access to the Internet.

GETTING THERE

☛ By road: from the north M6/J16, A500, A531, right on to A525, right through Keele village; from south, M6/J15, A5182, left on to A53, right at Whitmore following signs.
☛ By rail: good service more or less everywhere, London 1:30 to Stoke-on-Trent station, then taxi.
☛ By coach: London, 4:00

UNIVERSITY OF KENT AT CANTERBURY

The University of Kent at Canterbury
The Registry
Canterbury CT2 7NZ

TEL 01227 827272
FAX 01227 827077
EMAIL recruitment@ukc.ac.uk
WEB www.ukc.ac.uk

Kent University Students' Union
The University
Canterbury CT2 7NW

TEL 01227 824200
FAX 01227 824204
EMAIL union@kent.ac.uk
WEB www.kentunion.co.uk

VAG VIEW

U KC is, in a nutshell, a friendly, politically correct campus, where it is easy to work hard, play hard, or do a little of both.

Writes Dominic Conway: 'If you come to this Uni you will have everything really, countryside and seaside, but still near to London; entertainment and nightlife, but still a calm working environment. For the more hard-core among you it may seem a little too relaxed, but with the facilities and the high teaching standards you should definitely get a good education, and if you don't have enough fun, it's more likely to be your fault than theirs.'

CAMPUS

UKC campus is situated on top of an alarmingly steep hill about a mile out of the main city. You will be assigned a residential college, **Keynes**, **Rutherford**, **Darwin** or **Eliot.** You can be more or less self-sufficient on campus, you could spend your entire first year without visiting the city, and many do.

FEES, BURSARIES

UK & EU Fees: £3,070 p.a. If in receipt of HE Maintenance grant there's a £1,000 p.a. bursary; £500-£750 if on partial grant. There are bursaries for applicants proceeding from less privileged backgrounds, and scholarships for sport and academic achievement.

> *'Nice big cathedral, old cobbled streets, strong whiff of history, a two hour walk to the beach - that's Canterbury. Two clubs, plenty of bars, but one thing that's clearly missing is an exciting music scene.'*

STUDENT PROFILE

UKC is not a place for Oxbridge rejects, but it takes quite a chunk of entrants from independent schools. Intake from the poorer neighbourhoods has, however, risen sharply over the last few years (see *Fees, Bursaries*), and there are strong mature and overseas flavours, too. Indeed, Catherine Robertson goes so far as to maintain that the reason why 'many British people haven't even heard of UKC [is] the uni's dedication to attracting overseas students,' but concludes that multifarious as is its makeup is, 'what you will find is a friendly student body, and lecturers and tutors who pursue their own work as energetically as they do yours.'

ACADEMIA & JOBS

There are some clear strengths in the curriculum.

UNIVERSITY/STUDENT PROFILE

University since	**1965**
Situation/style	**City campus**
Student population	**17060**
Undergraduates	**13190**
- mature	**16%**
- non EU undergraduatess	**8%**
- male/female	**46/54**
- non-traditional student intake	**25%**
- state school intake	**91%**
- drop-out rate	**13%**
- undergraduate applications	**Up 11%**

Drama not only scored full marks at the teaching assessments, but also achieved Grade 5 at the research assessments. Focus for both student and professional theatre companies is the campus-based Gulbenkian Theatre.

In social sciences UKC are pre-eminent, with Social Policy rated world-class Grade 6* for research and Economics dropping only one point at the assessments. Meanwhile, biosciences dropped not a mark at all. Law also enjoys a reputation here, its research assessment international class Grade A. They are European law specialists, and the uni is committed to encouraging the assimilation of European culture far and wide in the curriculum – by study in Europe, by taking a European language, or by combining one of their popular artistic or media packages with advanced work in a foreign language, as in the European Arts course. 'Academically the university has a strong reputation for modern languages,' Catherine acknowledges, 'thanks to it's proximity to Europe and the encouragement to students to study abroad for a year.'

23% — Postgraduates

Female Undergraduates — 41%

STUDENT POPULATION

Total students 17, 060

36% — Male Undergraduates

WHERE KENT GRADUATES END UP

Health & Social Work: 7%; Education: 9%; Wholesale/Retail: 11%; Manufacturing: 12%; Financial Activities: 13%; Public Administration, Civil Service & Defence: 7.5%; Hotel/Restaurant: 4%; Transport & Communications (including Telecommunications): 4%; Construction: 1%; Personnel: 4%; Computer: 5%; Business & Management: 3%; Accountancy: 3%; Media (including Film): 3%; Legal 2%; Advertising: 1%.

Approximate 'graduate track' employed **67%**

A few queries are raised when one sees the sheer number of managers, administrators, sales assistants and clerks that head off Kent's employment return. This appears to be down to their 2-subject combination courses, such as Comparative Literary Studies/Classical & Archaeological Studies, European Culture & Thought/Religious Studies, etc, which certainly don't leap out at one as likely to pay back student investment in the short term.

However, when one looks down the 'graduate track' employment table, which details numbers into real-life graduate jobs, Kent does well, with 67% employed.

The first to give hope are the graduates who become computer programmers, software engineers, IT consultants and the like. This is an area in which Kent is traditionally strong. Look at their department of Electronic Engineering & Computing, BEng and BSc degrees, many of them carved out with industry.

Also crucial to the graduate employment figures is the accountancy package – Accounting & Finance degrees with Business Administration, Management Science, French Business Studies, German, etc. The top-rated Economics provision brings us further into the financial sector, which is well represented, too, by Financial Mathematics, Actuarial Science, Maths and Accounting & Finance, Applied Quantative Finance. High up in the employment graph we find bank managers, financial administrators, actuaries, economists, pension advisers, and so on.

In Social Sciences, the various Industrial Relations and Human Resource Management degrees yield jobs in personnel, and community and youth workers reflect glory on the uni's well-known social studies reputation, while its Social Policy provision (on its own and with Public Management or Computing) turns out local and regional government officers.

The number of graduates who become biological scientists and biochemists attests to the strength of physical and bio-sciences. There are foundation courses, years with industry, and promising medical bioscience aspects, as well as pharmaceutical degrees. At the end of 2006, Kent opened new £1-

SUBJECT AREAS (%)

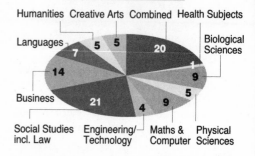

ACADEMIC EXCELLENCE

TEACHING:
(Rated Excellent or 17+ out of 24)

Computing, Anthropology, Social Policy & Administration	**Excellent**
Drama & Theatre Studies, Molecular Biosciences, Organismal Biosciences, Philosophy	**24**
Economics	**23**
History of Art, Classics, Archaeology, Psychology	**22**
Sociology, Electrical/Electron Engineering, American Studies, Subjects Allied to Medicine, Business/Management, Maths, Physics, Politics	**21**
Theology, Film Studies	**20**
Modern Languages (French, German, Italian, Euro Studies, Linguistics)	**19**

RESEARCH :
Top grades 5/5/6**

Social Policy	**Grade 6***
Statistics	**Grade 5***
English, Applied Maths, Law, Anthropology, Drama/Dance/ Performing Arts	**Grade 5**

WHAT IT'S REALLY LIKE

UNIVERSITY:	
Social Life	★★★★
Campus scene	**Friendly, southern but weekday**
Student Union services	**Good**
Politics	**Student issues**
Sport	**50 clubs**
National sporting position	**56th**
Sport facilities	**Good**
Arts opportunities	**Film, drama exc, music art good**
Student newspaper	**KRED**
Student radio	**UKCR**
Nightclub	**The Venue**
Bars	**Lighthouse, Mungo's, Origins, Woodies**
Union ents	**Good but few live bands**
Union societies	**80**
Parking	**Poor**
CITY:	
Entertainment	★★★
Scene	**Touristy, historic, v. good pubs**
Town/gown relations	**Good**
Risk of violence	**Average**
Cost of living	**Average**
Student concessions	**Adequate**
Survival + 2 nights out	**£80 pw**
Part-time work campus/town	**Good**

million teaching facilities for bioscientists.

At the other end of the curriculum spectrum, employment figures for film and video activities, radio and television suggest that the long-term commitment to Film Studies – there are seven degrees (Contemporary Arts, Film, is the new one) – may be paying off, and no doubt the student media nurtures and underwrites the trend. Canterbury and Kent universities have just been awarded the first FM student radio licence.

SOCIAL SCENE

STUDENTS' UNION 'First years tend to remain on campus to socialise,' continues Catherine, 'simply because it is cheaper and more convenient. There are 5 main bars: **Origins** is in Darwin College (trendy-type bar, good fajitas); **Rutherford Bar** – guess where that is (a drinker's bar, good juke box); **Mungo's** is in Eliot (should be better than it is, no atmosphere); and then there's **Keynes Bar** (concrete garden, popular in summer). **Woody's** at Parkwood is more of a pub than a bar and haunted by the more cliquey sports clubs (you'll see what I

mean). For those of you who don't want to spend all your time drinking alcohol, there is also the **Gulbenkian Theatre** coffee bar and 2 new Wicked coffee shops this year.

'Now, what to do with your new-found friends once the bars have thrown you out into the cold, cold, night? Generally, people head onto **The Venue**, the campus club with a capacity of 1200, open six nights a week, and a café bar, **The Lighthouse** (200). Regular nights are Mondays, *Sports Fed Night*, where each sports club takes a turn as host. Thursdays are *Retro* nights Friday is dance, Saturday anything goes, from garage to pop, dance to r&b.'

Writes Dominic Conway: 'The Kent mentality is not a wild one. Although the 5 bars on campus will serve refreshingly cheap drinks nightly (£1.50 cheapest pint, £1 shot promotions) it is more common to see students sharing a few drinks at a comedy night or a salsa party than pushing the boundaries of alcohol consumption. The cultural diversity means that there is no obvious campus consensus, and the ever growing list of societies means that any student will feel well catered for.

'One thing clearly missing is an exciting music scene, the campus bands are sporadic and little talent tours these parts because there aren't any good venues for a live band. If you keep your ear to the ground, however, local groups will put on authentic, unpretentious rock shows and Whitstable (on the coast) hides a number of world class musicians playing jazz, blues, and Turkish folk music that even the most selective muso will be content with.

'Many students however don't make it as far as Whitstable and don't even trouble themselves with town very much, because the campus alone has so much to offer. The shops are a tad over priced but will stock all the essentials and some more exciting ingredients if you have a sudden urge to cook a lavish dinner. The **Gulbenkian Theatre** on campus

AT A GLANCE

ACADEMIC FILE:	
Subjects assessed	**31**
Excellent	**74%**
Typical entry requirements	**316 points**
Application acceptance rate	**21%**
Students-staff ratio	**15:1**
First/2:1 degree pass rate	**60%**
ACCOMMODATION FILE:	
Guarantee to freshers	**90%**
Style	**College halls, student village**
Approx price range pw	**£67-£103**
City rent pw	**£70**

hosts some remarkable shows, the manager is in close communication with the Drama department and is very well informed on the acts that students want to see. Its stage is open to comedy and music, as well as some bright lights in the world of modern theatre. The multitudinous societies keep freshening up the nightlife by hiring out the various venues for evenings for a more specific audience. The hip-hop, drama and rock societies have put in the most effort so far in terms of catering for the uni as a whole. Safety on campus is ensured by Campus Watch, who offer an escort service for anyone walking around late at night on their own. '

The student radio station (UKCR) broadcasts 24/7 on 1350 AM. There are 2 studios. The student monthly magazine is *KRED*, an acronym derived from the initial letter of each of the colleges.

SPORT Sports-wise there are 50 clubs, all the usual stuff plus Choi Kwang Do, Taekwondo and Kendo (one of only five unis to offer this) and American Football (UKC Falcons). It's highly competitive. Various sports offer bursaries, some in cahoots with UKC alumni. UKC does well nationally at all the team sports, coming 44th in the national team league last year.

TOWN Writes Dominic: 'Canterbury is just a 20 minute walk away (or 10 minutes by bus, which comes regularly). Nice big cathedral, old cobbled streets, strong whiff of history in the air and a two hour walk to the beach. Although it is quite a quaint place, it is very lively and friendly – the locals never seem to mind or complain about the amount of students!'

Says Catherine: 'If you're feeling particularly adventurous then go to town for a change of scenery. It is a city because it has a famous cathedral (to which you will no doubt take your parents when they come to visit), but its size is no more than that of a large town, and if you are coming from a large, lively city you may at first be disappointed. However, Canterbury is deceiving in the sense that it appears quieter than it actually is.

'One thing it does not lack is pubs, and many of my friends have spent a happy drunken evening in the enchantingly named **Bishop's Finger** (the nun's delight apparently!). After the pubs shut, things get a bit tricky, as Canterbury is not renowned for it's club scene. **Alberry's** is recommended, but it's pretty cliquey. **The Works** is another favourite!'

PILLOW TALK

Writes Dominic: 'A lot of money has recently gone into accommodation, so the standard is fairly high. The new halls are the most spotless, but can be a little sterile. I would urge new students to brave a shared toilet for the sake of their social life.'

Surely it can't be *that* bad. Most first years opt for halls in one of the 4 colleges or their posher extensions, or in Parkwood student village, made for the purpose. The colleges tend to be the easiest way to make friends as there are usually seven people randomly thrown together in a corridor and you all just mix and match.

The colleges, Eliot, Darwin, Rutherford and Keynes, are where the majority of first years end up, although you can get a place in Tyler Court or Becket Court, both new sets of accommodation.

A problem with the colleges is that they are semi-self-catered, i.e you get breakfast included in the rent, but only until 9.30 am

Parkwood, the student village, is just off the main campus and made up of groups of houses for 4-to-6 students.

The problem here is that it is generally favoured by third years and foreign students, and they seem to get priority. The houses can leave you feeling freer, but a bit detached.

GETTING THERE

☛ By road: from west, M2, A2; south, A28 or A2; east, A257; northeast, the A28; northwest, A290.
☛ By rail: London Victoria, 85 mins; London Charing Cross or Waterloo East, 90 mins.
☛ By air: Heathrow and Gatwick.
☛ By coach: London Victoria, 1 hour 45 mins.

KING'S COLLEGE, LONDON

King's College, London
Waterloo Bridge House
London SE1 8WA

TEL 020 7836 5454
FAX 020 7836 1799
EMAIL enquiries@kcl.ac.uk
WEB www.kcl.ac.uk

King's College Students' Union
Surrey Street
London WC2R 2NS

TEL 020 7836 7132
FAX 020 7379 9833
EMAIL president@kclsu.org
WEB www.kclsu.org/

VAG VIEW

*K*ing's College London is one of London University's oldest and most prestigious colleges, founded by George IV in 1829 and one of the federal university's original colleges in 1836. Undergraduates feel part of this strong tradition, but until recently, when it sold off its Kensington and Chelsea campuses, the scattered nature of the college did little to foster a sense of identity.

In the course of its history it has developed through many mergers, most recently, in the summer of 1998, with United Medical & Dental Schools of Guy's Hospital (where medical teaching began in the 1720s) & St Thomas's (where Medicine has been taught since the 16th century). The correct name for the new merged medical school out of the schools of King's College, Guy's and St Thomas's hospitals, is King's College London Medical School at Guy's, King's College and St Thomas's Hospital. Not the prettiest on the park.

CAMPUSES

There are now five campuses, four of which cluster around the Thames, close to the centre of town. With the Students' Union **Macadam** building at its core is the **Strand Campus**, on the north bank, just south of Covent Garden. Here, too, are the schools of Humanities, Law and Physical Sciences. Just across the river via Waterloo Bridge is the new **Waterloo Campus**, incorporating Education, Management, Health & Life Sciences, Nursing & Midwifery and the Stamford Street apartments with the basement gym, K4, which appeared on TV's *Watchdog* as an exemplary fitness club.

UNIVERSITY/STUDENT PROFILE	
College of London Uni since	**1836**
Situation/style	**Civic**
Student population	**21965**
Undergraduates	**14995**
- mature	**16%**
- non EU undergraduates	**8%**
- male/female	**34/66**
- non-traditional student intake	**21%**
- state school intake	**67%**
- drop-out rate	**7%**
- undergraduate applications	**Up 5%**

Three bridges to the east lies **Guy's Campus**. Students of Medicine and Dentistry entering King's in 1999 were the first to study at this purpose-built centre close to London Bridge. The campus incorporates a new SU building with bar, swimming pool, ballroom, shop and welfare centre, as well as accommodation.

And then there's **St Thomas's Campus** (Continuing Medical & Dental teaching), which overlooks the Houses of Parliament north across the river at Westminster Bridge, and **Denmark Hill Campus**, south of the Oval.

The only site a little out on its own, Denmark Hill is base for clinical teaching at King's College Hospital and the Dental Institute, and home to the Institute of Psychiatry.

All residences – halls (catered or self-catered), apartments or student houses (mainly for mature students) – are within London Travel Zones 1 or 2, and close to one or more of the campuses.

Word on the ground is that KCL succeeds not in spite of, but because of its location: 'Want to live and work smack in the centre of London? You got it,' write Ben Jones and Chris Wilding. 'Want high frequency bus and tube links with a 30% discount? You got it. Clubs? Pubs? Venues? Theatres? Museums? Galleries? Shops? Yeah, got them too.

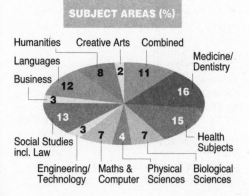

SUBJECT AREAS (%)

Humanities, Creative Arts, Combined, Medicine/Dentistry, Languages, Business, Social Studies incl. Law, Engineering/Technology, Maths & Computer, Physical Sciences, Biological Sciences, Health Subjects

32% — Postgraduates

Female Undergraduates — 45%

STUDENT POPULATION

Total students 21,965

23% — Male Undergraduates

In fact, by nestling snugly and unassumingly within the heart of the capital, King's College London appears to students as a seventh heaven.' But at a price.

FEES, BURSARIES

UK & EU Fees 2007: £3,070 p.a. Bursary of £1350 if in receipt of full HE Maintenance Grant; if in receipt of partial grant there's support up to that figure on a sliding scale.

STUDENT PROFILE

Both King's and University College, London, the mother of all London University colleges, have a high public school intake, UCL's being higher than King's. There is, at King's, what one student described as a 'friendly competitiveness' with UCL. I have heard a KCL student refer to UCL students as 'godless scum', while UCL routinely call KCL the Strand Poly. In apparent contravention of this public school profile, the uni has been digging around and found quite a healthy percentage of applicants from less traditional classes and neighbourhoods - 21% of their freshers came from the lower socio-economic orders last time. They're also encouraging mature students to their medical faculty (see *Academia* below).

ACADEMIA & JOBS

Traditional, small tutorial and seminar teaching methods are one source of the high first and upper second graduation results at KCL (71%, up 4% in 2 years). Extensive and very healthy interdisciplinary course programming (e.g. chemistry and philosophy). Music is as strong as medicine and can be found in harmony with applied computing; war studies combines with theology, and there's an international centre for prison studies within the Law School, which incidentally specialises in English, French and German law. KCL is traditional but smart and always up there with the best in graduate employment, neraly half going into the health industry and large numbers into commerce and, after further training/pupilage, into law (they are European law specialists). There are other interesting scpecialisms, however, notably media.

ACADEMIC EXCELLENCE

TEACHING :
(Rated Excellent or 17+ out of 24)

Law, Geography, History, Music.	**Excellent**
Classics, Dentistry, Philosophy, Politics (War Studies)	**24**
Portuguese, Subjects Allied to Medicine, Education	**23**
Spanish, Pharmacology	**22**
Anatomy, Physics, Environmental, Medicine, Molecular and Organismal Biosciences	
French, Nursing, Maths, Theology	**21**
German, Electronic & Elec Eng	**20**

RESEARCH:
Top grades 5/5*/6*

Community/Clinical (Psychiatry), Clinical Dentistry, War Studies, German/Dutch/ Scandinavian, Portuguese, Spanish, Classics, History, Philosophy	**Grade 6***
Anatomy	**Grade 5***
Clinical Laboratory Sci, Pre-Clinical Studies, Pharmacy, Nutrition & Dietetics, Biophysics, Pure Maths, Applied Maths, Electrical & Electronic Eng, Mechanical/Aeronautical/ Manufacturing Eng, Law, Theology, Music, Education	**Grade 5**

There are no vocational media courses, just film degrees, but the student media is active and good.

The degree in Medicine is the 5-year MBBS - AAB + UKCAT. It's a 9% acceptance rate, which is low, but there's a special Graduate/Professional entry programme for mature students.

There is full integration of medical science and clinical teaching. plus a wide range of special study modules. Fifth year includes opportunity to study

WHERE KCL GRADUATES END UP

Health & Social Work: 47%; Education: 4%; Wholesale/Retail: 9%; Manufacturing: 5%; Financial Activities: 7%; Public Administration, Civil Service & Defence: 5%; Hotel/Restaurant: 1.5%; Transport & Communications (including Telecommunications): 1%; Personnel: 4%; Computer: 3%; Business & Management: 3%; Accountancy: 3%; Media (including Film): 2.5%; Legal 1%; Publishing: 2%; Advertising: 1%.

Approximate 'graduate track' employed **81%**

abroad. Entry 3 A levels (ABB) + 1 AS (B) or 2 A levels (AB + 3 AS (AAA). Chemistry or Biology must be one of A levels, if offered at AS must be B. GCSE to include Grade B English, Maths, Physics or Double Award (if not offered at AS). Teaching Inspection 22. Research Grade 5*: Community/ Clinical (Psychiatry), Anatomy; Grade 5: Clinical Lab Sciences, Pre-Clinical Studies.

They are also well represented in pathology, the branch of Medicine concerned with the cause, origin and nature of disease, biological sciences and subjects allied to Medicine come to the fore – Medical Biochemistry, etc.

With full marks at the assessments, KCL produce most dentists, followed by Manchester, Newcastle, Glasgow, Sheffield and Cardiff. The 5-year BDS plus extra Foundation year is available in Natural Sciences/Dentistry. Entry ABB+b (Chemistry or Biology except in 6-year course. Research Grade 5*. There's also a Diploma in Dental Hygiene.

Another interesting aspect of KCL concerns forensic science. You can find employment in forensic science without a degree. Forensic Scientists who want to make it up the employment ladder will need a degree. There are masses available, but the Forensic Science Society (www.forensic-science-society.org.uk) take most of their graduate members from very few universities – King's is among them.

For a career as musician, composer and conductor, KCL finds success with its 4-year BMus, a collaboration with The Royal Academy of Music. It combines intellectual and practical approaches, the theory being that Academy musicians benefit academically, while KCL academics benefit musically from the tie-up. Both are members of the University of London.

Among the 7% of KCL graduates that hot foot it to the City, quite a number go in as stockbrokers. There are interesting Maths degrees, but no Economics or Finance.

Specials include top-rated Classics, War Studies (10 degrees), Philosophy, and Portuguese (with, uniquely, a department to itself).

> *Music is as strong as medicine and can be found in harmony with applied computing; war studies combines with theology, and there's an international centre for prison studies within the Law School.*

STUDENT SCENE

In keeping with many student unions' apparent assumption that they can educate the masses by naming bars after prominent politicians, the showpiece attraction of King's Strand campus is its airy venue, **Tutu's**. Blessed with a stage, bar, café,

WHAT IT'S REALLY LIKE	
UNIVERSITY:	
Social Life	★★★★
Campus scene	**Cosmopolitan, conservative**
Student Union services	**Average**
Politics	**Average: student issues**
Sport	**44 clubs**
National team position	**52nd**
Sport facilities	**Poor**
Arts opportunities	**Good**
Student mag/news	**Roar**
Nightclub	**Tutu's, Inverse**
Bars	**The Waterfront, Guy's Bar, Tommy's Bar**
Union ents	**Phase, The Hop, Collide-a-Scope, Fuse, Score**
Union societies	**94**
Parking	**None**
CITY:	
Entertainment	★★★★★
Scene	**Wild, expensive**
Town/gown relations	**Average-good**
Risk of violence	**London v. high**
Cost of living	**High**
Student concessions	**Abundant**
Survival + 2 nights out	**£100 pw**
Part-time work campus/town	**Excellent**

dancefloor and spectacular views of the South Bank, this offers an in-house retreat for the college's loose-livered and free of fancy. A bust of the venue's namesake presides with piously disapproving glare over a feast of comedy nights, discos, live acts and all the other student malarkey.

Fave nights are typically *Phase* (cheese/dance), Saturday's indie club night, *Collide-a-scope*, *Score*, which, you may guess, is the sports night, *The Hop* (more cheese), *Fuse* (entertaining and eclectic mix: R&B, house, Bhungra) and *Comedy Basement*, Thursday's comedy night. Recent live acts include Green Day, Beth Orton, Pulp, Linkin Park, Haven, South.

Macadam's third floor contains the traditional student watering hole, just refurbished, **The Waterfront**, which acts as a perfectly pleasant preamble to its big brother, Tutu, upstairs. With beer nearly half the price of the non-student establishments a stumble away, it's not hard to see why it entertains a cheery crowd.

Tommy's Bar and **Guy's Bar** look after the medics at their campuses, the latter apparently especially active on the karaoke and live music menu.

Clubs and societies are legion, with Salsa, Debating and the King's Players (theatre), popular choices. A further popular activity (although one without its own noticeboard) was reported by irreverent and controversial student tabloid, *Roar*. '*Basement Boys Use Bogs for Buggering*' ran the headline. *Roar*, incidentally, is regularly nominated for its reporting. All in all, the union keeps its flock busy – but with the bright lights of the West End topping the list of countless distractions, it will only ever deter a relatively small proportion of its students from finding ways to get deeper in debt.

At Guy's the uni's subterranean nightclub, **Inverse**, rules with its powerful sound system and fully integrated lighting system.

SPORT There are four sports grounds in Surrey and South London, rifle ranges at the Strand, the aforesaid K4 fitness club, a swimming pool and gym at Guy's, and highly successful boat and sub-aqua clubs. Nationally, KCL's teams came 52nd last year in the BUSA (uni) team leagues.

AT A GLANCE	
ACADEMIC FILE:	
Subjects assessed	**30**
Excellent	**83%**
Typical entry requirements	**394 points**
Application acceptance rate	**10%**
Med. School acceptance rate	**9%**
Students-staff ratio	**12:1**
First/2:1 degree pass rate	**71%**
ACCOMMODATION FILE:	
Guarantee to freshers	**100%**
Style	**Hall, flats**
Catered	**18%**
Approx price range pw	**£83-£122**
City rent pw	**£100-£180**

GETTING THERE

☞ **Strand campus**: Temple (District Line, Circle), Aldwych (Piccadilly), Holborn (Piccadilly, Central). **Waterloo campus**: Waterloo/Waterloo East overland; Waterloo Underground (Bakerloo, Northern). **Guy's campus:** (Northern) and overland. **St Thomas's campus**: as Waterloo or Westminster (Circle, District, Northern, Bakerloo). **Denmark Hill campus**: Denmark Hill overland.

KINGSTON UNIVERSITY

Kingston University
Cooper House
40-46 Surbiton Road
Kingston upon Thames KT1 2HX

TEL 020 8547 7053
FAX 020 8547 7080
EMAIL admissions-info@kingston.ac.uk
WEB www.kingston.ac.uk

Kingston Students' Union
Main Site
Penrhyn Road
Kingston upon Thames: KT1 2EE

TEL 020 8547 8868
FAX 020 8547 8862
EMAIL president@kingston.ac.uk
WEB www.kingston.ac.uk/guild

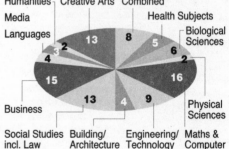

SUBJECT AREAS (%)

Humanities – Creative Arts – Combined – Media – Health Subjects – Languages – Biological Sciences – Physical Sciences – Business – Social Studies incl. Law – Building/ Architecture – Engineering/ Technology – Maths & Computer

2, 13, 8, 5, 6, 2, 4, 3, 15, 16, 13, 4, 9

VAG VIEW

Whatever they tell you about Kingston being the oldest Royal borough, the place where Saxon kings were crowned (the Coronation stone lies in the Guildhall – King's Stone, geddit?), it is, in the cold light of reality, a suburban shopping centre/ housewife's paradise, 25 mins from central London by train.

Shoppers come from miles to the mall, the market and the endless chain-shops, while its pubs and clubs attract streams of youthful revellers and the sometime Kingston Poly delivers higher education to some 19,000 students.

We're talking vocational at Kingston, 'even those courses that don't on the surface appear to be vocational,' says the marketing department. 'The transferable skills that students gain while they're here make them very employable.' Students say that London being only 15 minutes away facilitates the career process further.

UNIVERSITY/STUDENT PROFILE	
University since	**1992**
Situation/style	**London sites**
Student population	**18861**
Undergraduates	**16319**
- mature	**35%**
- non EU undergraduates	**8%**
- male/female	**51/49**
- non-traditional student intake	**37%**
- state school intake	**95%**
- drop-out rate	**19%**
- undergraduate applications	**Up 6%**

CAMPUS SITES

The uni is based at four campuses near the A3, London's south-west outflow – Penrhyn Road, Kingston Hill, Knights Park and Roehampton Vale. Current plans include a £20 million, 6-storey teaching building and land-scaped courtyard at the main Penrhyn Road campus, and extensions to library and teaching facilities at Kingston Hill and Roehampton Vale.

PENRHYN ROAD Kingston upon Thames, KT1 2EE. Tel (all sites): 020 8547 2000. **Faculties:** Science and some Technology.

> *They attract a mix of customer, from engineers to trendy artists, from nurses to would-be lawyers and City types. Entry is not testing. 'Graduate track' employment prospects are good. The problem is not the teaching standard, but the facilities.*

Female Undergraduates — Postgraduates **14%** **42%**

STUDENT POPULATION

Total students 18,861

44% Male Undergraduates

KINGSTON HILL Kingston upon Thames, KT2 7LB. **Faculties:** Business, Education, Music, Law, Social Work, and Healthcare Sciences.

Knights Park Kingston upon Thames, KT1 2QJ. **Faculties:** Art & Design, Architecture, Quantity Surveying, Estate Mgt.

Roehampton Vale Kingston upon Thames, KT1 2EE. **Faculties:** Mechanical, Aeronautical and Production Engineering.

FEES, BURSARIES

UK & EU Fees 2007: £3,070 p.a. Not fixed yet for 2008. Bursaries of between £300 and £1,000 awarded to HE Maintenance grant holders, depending on level of grant.

STUDENT PROFILE

They attract a mix of customer, from engineers to trendy artists, from nurses to would-be lawyers and City types, most notably a mature undergraduate body (35%). A large slice of entrants (37%) come from socio-economic groups traditionally least likely to consider university. Writes Paul Stephen: 'It's an easy place to make friends, and the best time to start is freshers week. Although the events aren't really up to much, due to the limited space, the Students' Union makes a real effort to welcome you. Freshers' Angels work round the clock to show you around, introduce you to others and generally force you to have a good time. Each year it's different, but last year's Freshers Ball featured ice-skating, Laserquest and mechanical surfing. My freshers week was awesome, and I made some friends then that I still hang out with now.'

ACADEMIA & JOBS

'At the moment the problem is not the teaching standard, but the facilities,' writes Paul Stephen. However, they are working on it. Kingston is currently investing more than £20million in three estate projects - a new, six-storey teaching

---

WHERE KINGSTON GRADUATES END UP

Health & Social Work: 7%; Education: 11%; Wholesale/Retail: 13%; Manufacturing: 9%; Financial Activities: 8%; Public Administration, Civil Service & Defence: 5%; Hotel/Restaurant: 3%; Transport & Communications (including Telecommunications): 5%; Construction: 2%; Agriculture: 1%; Personnel: 6%; Computer: 4%; Business & Management: 6%; Accountancy: 3%; Media (including Film): 1%; Legal 2%; Architecture: 3%; Publishing: 1.5%; Artistic/Literary: 1%; Sport: 1%.

Approximate 'graduate track' employed **66%**

---

building and landscaped courtyard at the main Penrhyn Road campus, and extensions to library and teaching facilities at Kingston Hill and Roehampton Vale campuses.

They also have Blackboard, their online learning resource. With it, you can choose when and where you study. Blackboard allows access to course materials, online chatrooms and bulletin boards. There are audio-visual instrument tutorials for music, for example, and students and video tutorials for science students.

Kingston is markedly vocational, into finding jobs for its graduates. Sandwich courses, employment-enhancing language schemes for non-language undergraduate, a Teaching & Learning Support scheme, which supplies individually or group-designed study skills programmes, EFL courses for overseas students and a 'peer assisted' learning scheme for first years with advice sessions from second years.

With full marks in the teaching assessments for building, and property management, town and country planning, you should look hard at Kingston if that's your bent. Property Planning & Development, Real Estate Management degrees, and Building and Quantity Surveying degrees are especially fruitful employment-wise.

There's a number of Applied Economics degrees, Accountancy & Finance, Business Economics, etc, but the high percentage of graduates in employment as accounts and wages clerks suggests that graduates are getting in at ground level.

Education is more of an employment cert. The vast majority come out as primary school teachers, a smattering into secondary teaching.

Kingston excels in getting graduates into software engineering. There's a 3/4-year (with sandwich, industrial placement in year 3) BSc in Software Engineering and a new MComp Software Engineering. Kingston's MComp is a 4-year integrated Master's degree designed to provide high-calibre graduates with an in-depth, research-focused expertise. The third year of the course is split between work in industry and training for professional qualifications.

They produce computer programmers and IT consultants in quantity, and a handful of systems analysts. Look at the BSc(Hons) Cyber Security and Computer Forensics, which explores how computers can be used to prevent and solve crime. Also Games Technology. and Computer Graphics Technology.

Civil Engineers flood out of Kingston, as do aeronautical, mechanical and electronic engineers. There are various automotive, motorcycling and motorsport BEng degrees. New in this area are BSc(Hons) Automotive Design, taught jointly by Kingston's design and engineering departments, and BSc(Hons) Motorsport Engineering, which investigates the underpinning technology and latest innovations in the motor sport industry.

Graphic artists and designers are much in demand from Kingston. Besides Fine Art in Art & Design, they offer Graphic Design, Illustration, Interior Design, Product & Furniture Design, and Fashion. Kingston's BA Hons Fashion produces the second largest number of graduates into the industry. There's a 21-points assessment

---

ACADEMIC EXCELLENCE

TEACHING :
(Rated Excellent or 17+ out of 24)

Business & Management,	**Excellent**
English, Geology.	
Building, Land & Prop Mgt,	**24**
Town & Country Planning,	
Mech, Aeronaut & Manuf Eng.	
Radiography, Maths, Politics	**23**
Civil Engineering, Sport	**22**
Modern Languages, Sociology,	**21**
Electrical & Electronic Eng.,	
Art & Design, Economics	
Hist. Art/Architec./Design	**20**

RESEARCH :
Top grades 5/5* | **None**

WHAT IT'S REALLY LIKE

UNIVERSITY:

Social Life	★★★
Campus scene	**London**
Student Union services	**Average**
Politics	**Student issues**
Sport	**31 clubs**
National team position	**77th**
Sport facilities	**Could do better**
Arts opportunities	**Drama, music, film, art good; dance poor**
Student newspaper	**SUblime**
Student radio	**Stone Radio**
Nightclub	**Bar Zen**
Bars	**Hannafords, Knights Park**
Union ents	**Eclectic**
Union societies	**32**
Most popular society	**Islamic/Afro-Caribbean**
Smoking policy	**Gannets, Hannafords OK**
Parking	**Adequate**

CITY:

Entertainment	★★★★
Local scene	**Club scene OK**
Town/gown relations	**Average**
Risk of violence	**Low**
Cost of living	**Very high**
Student concessions	**Average**
Survival + 2 nights out	**£80 pw**
Part-time work campus/town	**Excellent**

AT A GLANCE

ACADEMIC FILE:

Subjects assessed	**29**
Excellent	**66%**
Typical entry requirements	**207 points**
Application acceptance rate	**19%**
Students-staff ratio	**20:1**
First/2:1 degree pass rate	**50%**

ACCOMMODATION FILE:

Guarantee to freshers	**No guarantee**
Style	**Halls, flats**
Catered	**None**
En suite	**70%**
Approx price range pw	**£84-£105**
Local rent pw	**£75-£90**

tions. Finally, this year 'a super healthcare university' is being launched between St George's, Royal Holloway and Kingston within health, biomedical sciences and business education.

There's a niche for probation officers in the BA Criminal Justice Studies, which includes a diploma in Social Work. There's also BA Social Welfare Studies and various Psychology and Sociology combinations. See, too, Community Care Management, which includes a diploma in Social Work – you must be 20 to apply.

They are European law specialists, and if you do not have a Law degree, but want to become a solicitor, you can take the Common Professional Examination (CPE) here.

There are masses of media, journalism, TV and creative writing degrees here, too.

SOCIAL SCENE

STUDENTS' UNION Writes Paul Stephen: 'The Students' Union runs 3 bars on different campuses. **The Space**, based at the Penrhyn Road, was refurbished last summer, giving it a café bar vibe with the addition of comfy leather sofas, a juice bar and "fair trade" coffee and tea. There is also a **Subway** sandwich counter. It's a good place to chill after lectures or to have a game of pool, but can easily be arranged for pre-club nights or live music.

'Then there's **Hannafords** on the Kingston Hill campus. From the outside it's just an old bomb shelter, but inside it's a fairly modern bar, with Subway again. Seeing as it sits right next to the halls of residence on Kingston Hill, Hannafords has the vibe of a 'local', with regular quiz and pool comp nights.

'Finally, there's **Knights Park Bar** on the artsy Knights Park campus. The bar has a patio, which sits on the side of the Hogsmill River, making it the perfect place for a beer on a sunny day. The small

rating, which is good. Meanwhile, the BA Interior Design scores highly on the employment graph, producing the fifth largest number of graduates into the industry. And a new BSc(Hons) Product Design Engineering combines traditional art and design modules with those offered by engineering-based programmes.

The undergraduate Health provision produces senior hospital nurses, midwives and social workers in quantity, and you can take a degree awarded by Kingston together with the Registered Nurse qualification.. There's also an enterprising Fd Health and Medical Sciences (Paramedic Pathway) - graduates will be eligible for state registration as a paramedic with the Health Professions Council. See also BSc(Hons) Exercise, Nutrition and Health, and FdSc Pharmacy Services, designed for people working as pharmacy technicians, and BSc(Hons) Forensic Biology, which explores the biological subjects and techniques related to biological materials associated with criminal investigabar has a bohemian feel and offers a variety of ents. Three Saturdays a month it is home to *Dickfest* - unsigned bands and artists. The fourth hosts *Preflex*, a straight-friendly gay night - cheesy pop, sparkly house and glam indie. *Non stop erotic dancing* features every other Friday - sleazy electronica, post punk, punk, quality old school indie, dodgy cover versions and Johnny Cash! For the hard-core drinkers among you, ask the bar staff about *Drunk Thursdays*.

'The Afro-Caribbean society and the Islamic society are the busiest on campus, but there are many more, ranging from People and Planet to Circus skills societies. '

TOWN 'In town there is something on offer every night of the week. There are loads of pubs and **Oceana** is Kingston's superclub - 5 bars and 2 nightclubs. Then there's **The Works**, home to RnB, hip hop and garage until the recent arrival of *New Slang* - Thursday's indie and alternative club night, with signed bands and guest DJs. **McCluskey's** is on the river bank and offers cheap drinks and cheesy tunes.

Bacchus is an alternative basement club playing everything from indie and punk to hip hop and house. **Bar Eivissa** is also worth a visit on a Monday or Wednesday, the atmosphere is always good. And gay friendly club **Reflex** was the inspiration for *Preflex* at Knights Park. An average night

out will cost you about £20.'

SPORT From football, rugby and hockey to Gaelic football and snowboarding, some 30 sports clubs fulfil most needs. Much of the activity takes place at the uni's sports facility at nearby Tolworth Court. There are also fitness facilities at Penrhyn Road. Kingston runs an Elite Athlete scheme to encourage students to compete at top levels in their sport. There's rowing on the Thames.

PILLOW TALK

First years have the 'comfort' of halls. If you live in hall at Kingston, you'll have a single room in a flat shared with other students. You'll share the kitchen with between 2 and 9 others. Kingston Hill campus has on-site, en-suite facilities. There are 4 other residential sites including Middle Mill Hall, self-catering flats opposite Knights Park Campus. Most are now en suite.

GETTING THERE

☞ By road: M1/J6a, M25/J13, A30, signs to A308 (Kingston). From London: A3 to Robin Hood Roundabout, then A308.
☞ By rail: frequent trains from London Waterloo to Kingston. No Underground this far out, but well served by buses.
☞ By air: Heathrow.

UNIVERSITY OF WALES, LAMPETER

University of Wales, Lampeter
Lampeter
Ceredigion SA48 7ED

TEL 01570 422351
FAX 01570 423423
EMAIL recruit@lamp.ac.uk
WEB www.lamp.ac.uk

Lampeter Students' Union
Ty Ceredig
Ceredigion SA48 7ED

TEL 01570 422619
FAX 01570 422480
EMAIL president@lampeter.ac.uk
WEB www.lamp.ac.uk/su/

VAG VIEW

L ampeter is a close-knit community with a strong rootstock in higher education. They have been awarding degrees here for longer than any institution in England and Wales other than Oxbridge.

It is a small, cosy uni and the other thing about it is that it is situated in a beautiful place. Rachel Extance recommends opting for it 'if your idea of the perfect university looks

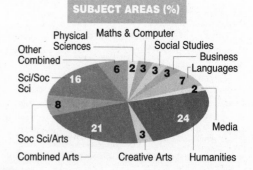

SUBJECT AREAS (%)

Physical Sciences 6
Maths & Computer 2
Social Studies 3
Business 3
Languages 3
Other Combined
Sci/Soc Sci 16
7
2
8
24 Media
21
3
Soc Sci/Arts
Combined Arts
Creative Arts
Humanities

Postgraduates 8%

Female Undergraduates 24%

Male Undergraduates 15%

Other 53%

STUDENT POPULATION

Total students 9,500

The campus is situated in a beautiful and inspirational place, not far from the Preseli Mountains, where the gigantic stones of the innermost sacred circle of Stonehenge, once Britain's national necropolis, are supposed to have been cut. This is mythic Wales, celebrated in the oldest story in *The Mabinogion*, a magical collection of eleven stories sustained orally since earliest times and written down in the fourteenth century. The story which comes from this particular area ('Pwyll, Lord of Dyfed') is probably the oldest, maybe as old as the second millennium BC.

like an Oxbridge college, is peaceful, friendly, tucked away in the country, and is a little bit out of the ordinary.

FEES, BURSARIES

UK & EU Fees - 2007: £3,070. Fees p.a. 2008 c.£3,140. Statutory £1,800 grant for Welsh residents plus various scholarships and bursaries. Approach direct.

CAMPUS

'Don't be surprised if you have only just heard of the place, it is set in the heart of mid-west Wales and its train station was removed by Beeching in the 1960s. Clearly its isolation will be a consideration. Looking at a map, you may note the distance between Lampeter and the nearest towns with more than ten houses, a post office and possibly a branch of Spar, but be advised that it is quite easy to get out of Lampeter if you know exactly when the two-hourly bus service runs.

> *The campus is situated in a beautiful and inspirational place. Look, too, at their niche courses in liberal arts, including Chinese, Islamic, and Medieval Studies; Religion, Ethics and Society; English with Creative Writing; and Media Production.*

ACADEMIA & JOBS

There is much in Lampeter's programme that reflects this backdrop. Its spiritual aspirations for a start. 'Lampeter was founded by Bishop Burgess in 1822 as a theological college for the Church in Wales,' Rachel observes. 'The Theology & Religious Studies Department continues to be strong, with Islamic Studies and Religion, Society & Ethics and Jewish Studies just some of the courses run. A mosque sits at the back of the department.'

'The theoretical advantage of being away from the shops is that your money will last longer. In practice you may spend as much money as your friends in the city because Lampeter contains fourteen pubs within a mile radius, with a cash point next to practically all of them.'

The unique course in Religion, Ethics & Society traces the development of our multi-faith, multi-cultural society and is taught as often by lecturers in English, History and Philosophy as by lecturers in Theology. The Students Union religious societies ('older than the hills') have developed along similar lines. Also relevant to Lampeter's mythic backdrop is the emphasis on Ancient History and Archaeology. The region is littered with burial mounds and cromlechs redolent of civilisations long past.

All courses are modular in scheme and taught in small groups. A fully equipped IT facility joins a library (170,000 vols), developed over 150 years and the Founders' Library (20,000 vols printed between 1470 and 1850).

The graduate employment figures show that a number of graduates find their way into education, mainly as instructors, further education, university and higher education lecturers, and as special school teachers.

UNIVERSITY/STUDENT PROFILE	
University College since	**1971**
Situation/style	**Rural campus**
Student population	**9500**
Undergraduates	**3700**
- mature	**35%**
- non EU undergraduates	**10%**
- male/female	**49/51**
- non-traditional student intake	**29%**
- state school intake	**95%**
- drop-out rate	**24%**
- undergraduate applications	**Down 15%**

WHAT IT'S REALLY LIKE

UNIVERSITY:	
Social Life	★★★
Campus scene	**Small, friendly, relaxed, rural**
Student Union services	**Good**
Politics	**Active**
Sport	**18 clubs**
Sport facilities	**Improving**
National team position	**130th**
Arts opportunities	**Drama, music, film good; art, dance average**
Student news/magazine	**1822**
Nightclub	**The Extension**
Bars	**Old Bar**
Union ents	**Discos + live acts**
Union societies	**29**
Most popular society	**Arts/Crafts, Rock, Underground, Wargames**
Parking	**Good**
TOWN:	
Entertainment	★★
Scene	**Scenic, boozey**
Town/gown relations	**OK**
Risk of violence	**Average**
Cost of living	**Low**
Student concessions	**Average**
Survival + 2 nights out	**£50 pw**
Part-time work campus/town	**Poor**

riculum. Modern languages have disappeared over recent years, but the apparent incursion of Business Management, Information Technology, Film, Media Studies and the like seems somehow now less intrusive, mixing as these subjects do with Greek or Islamic Studies as happily as Archaeology or Anthropology, as if here at Lampeter there is a meeting of worlds – east and west, old and new.

New courses this year are in Archaeology (Forensic) and Media Production.

STUDENT PROFILE
'The student population is incredibly diverse,' writes Rachel. 'A high percentage are mature students; there is also a sizeable band of foreign students (Greeks, Italians, French, Americans, to name just some of many nationalities you will encounter). There's a wide variety of religious groups, too. The place is simply too small for people not to get on with each other. Being in a small community, miles from anywhere is a great way of bonding people.'

STUDENT SCENE
STUDENTS' UNION At the hub, **Old Bar** is the small, warm and friendly watering hole and host to *Band in the Bar* on Tuesdays and occasionally to karaoke nights. **The Extension** is the club venue, holds the latest licence in Ceredigion on a Saturday night, and is scene of discos on Wednesdays, Fridays and Saturdays, also big bands, comedy, games and more. The alcohol is cheap and plentiful, but interestingly the union is looking very seriously at meeting what it detects to be a need for an alcohol-free environment for students in the evenings. 'The union also houses a catering outlet called **Dewi's**,' adds Rachel, 'a TV room, pool tables, a games room, and, all importantly, the pigeon holes for post.'

The summer term President's Ball is a biggie. Live acts, various guest DJs, a 20-piece jazz band and firework spectacular. It's the culmination of a year that has seen such as Annie Mac from Radio 1 and the Queens of Noize from NME, bands like The Hazey Janes, and Kid Carpet, plus student acoustic

There is also a showing of care assistants, welfare, community and youth workers, which one can imagine arises as much out of the culture of the place as any vocational degree.

Otherwise, in the short period of six months post graduation, a great number take work as sales assistants, managers, administrators, clerks, bar staff, local government officers and the like.

It is as if Lampeter has somehow managed to opt out of the commercial pressures that other universities claim they have to deal with. Perhaps there is an optimum size for doing just that.

There is a constant development of the cur-

WHERE LAMPETER GRADUATES END UP

Health & Social Work: 6%; Education: 12%; Wholesale Retail: 25%; Manufacturing: 6%; Financial Activities: 9%; Public Administration, Civil Service & Defence: 13%; Hotel/Restaurant: 11%; Transport & Communications (including Telecommunications): 2%; Personnel: 2%; Computer: 1%; Business & Management: 3%; Media (including Film): 1%; Legal 4%; Architecture: 1%; Publishing: 3%.

Approximate 'graduate track' employed **52%**

AT A GLANCE	
ACADEMIC FILE:	
Subjects assessed	**11**
Excellent	**36%**
Average requirements	**246 points**
Application acceptance rate	**29%**
Students-staff ratio	**25:1**
First/2:1 degree pass rate	**59%**
ACCOMMODATION FILE:	
Guarantee to freshers	**100%**
Style	**Halls, flats**
Catered	**None**
En suite	**46%**
Approx price range pw	**£45-£62**
Town rent pw	**£40-£70**

nights, school disco and cheesy toons.

There are 18 sports clubs and 29 societies, the most popular are Arts & Crafts, Rock, Underground, Wargames. There's also a very active Film Society (commercial and arthouse). They are not overly political, but equal rights is something they take seriously, and this year campaigns have focused on Top-up Fees. SU Disaffiliation. Nestlé. Coca Cola. 24-hour licensing. A satirical student newspaper, *1822*, carries basic union news – 'very popular, always causes a stir,' I am told. Both are always on the look-out for writers, and they are in the process of setting up a radio station. This is the brainchild of an ever-growing Media Department, working closely with the Student union.

With an eye to the sizeable mature student population (47%), the union has set up a nursery. There is even a Welsh language playgroup. All round there's a strong welfare service, including Nightline and two 'pro' counsellors.

For part-time work, the union is the main source. There are jobs available in the bar and Extension, the union shop, security and with Union Entertainments. Working for Ents can mean anything from setting up the Extension for a gig, taking money on the door, or deejaying.

SPORT The 12 clubs range from surfing to Tae Kwon Do. The national uni sports organisation, BUSA, gave it a special 'most improved' award recently. 'Being small, there are brilliant opportunities for everyone to have a go,' said a student, 'and if you're half good at anything, chances are you'll get in a team. Cricket and football are particularly successful.'

TOWN 'Lampeter town itself is compact,' writes Rachel, 'with two supermarkets, a Boots, and a couple of New Age clothing shops. The crime rate is practically non-existent! But unlike in the big cities, entertainment is not handed to you on a plate. Of the fourteen pubs, some are famed for their lock-ins, the **Ram Tavern** is noted for its food, the **Cwmann** for its bar quiz and live music, the **Quarry** for its disco, and the **Kings Head** as the main haunt of the football team.'

PILLOW TALK

Two mainly first-year halls are full board. Most are en suite. All are on campus. Living out in the second year and third year, you can get a nice place for around £40 a week, and you don't have to pay for the summer holidays. The size of the town means you're never living too far away.

GETTING THERE

☛ By road: A485; the M4 is about 45 mins away.
☛ By rail: London Euston, 5:00; Cardiff Central, 1:30; Birmingham New Street, 4:10.
☛ By coach: London, 5:55; Birmingham, 7:25.

UNIVERSITY OF LANCASTER

University of Lancaster
Lancaster LA1 4YW

TEL 01524 65201
FAX 01524 592065
EMAIL ugadmissions@lancaster.ac.uk
WEB www.lancs.ac.uk

Lancaster Students' Union
Slaidburn House
Lancaster LA1 4YA

TEL 01524 593765
FAX 01524 846732
WEB www.lusu.co.uk

VAG VIEW

A *well-thought-out curriculum, a 65% chance of ending up with a first or upper second, consistently good teaching assessments, a recent £50-million capital expenditure on resources (art gallery, libraries, union, music buildings, halls, etc.), a popular college structure, good student ents (they own their own nightclub in town), an active media, drama scene and sporting tradition, and a beautiful 250-acre, landscaped campus within sight of the Lakes – all this contributes to Lancaster remaining a special kind of choice.*

It is a great university in a beautiful part of the world, with excellent extra-curricular life, and there's a strong linkage with America.

Now, they've been ripping it all apart, making a £200-million campus that will increase capacity by 50%. And there is a further key move afoot. Lancaster is leading the way in collaboration with Liverpool, Central Lancashire, Cumbria University and the University Hospitals of Morecambe Bay Trust, recruiting teaching and research staff, following a Government decision to allow 50 extra places a year for Liverpool Uni medical students, which will be based full time at the Lancaster campus. The project may spawn a new medical school.

CAMPUS

The uni is far away from the industrial towns of popular imagination. It sits to the north of the county, sandwiched between the sea and the Forest of Bowland, a huge open fell space giving life to myriad becks. Lancaster itself, which is nearby, is a city, certainly, but it is small and has cobbled streets and well-maintained historic buildings, many are probably protected.

'The university has a beautiful countryside location at Bailrigg, on the outskirts of Lancaster,' writes Lis Maree. 'It is 3 miles from Lancaster city centre and set in acres of landscaped woods and parkland. On a clear day the view can extend as far as the Lakeland fells. Lancaster is just 10 minutes away by bus, a friendly, bustling place which has all the amenities of a larger city, while retaining the unique charm of its antiquity.'

COLLEGE LIFE

The essential element of the Lancaster experience is the collegiate system. Virtually everything is done with or for your college

Writes Lisa: 'The colleges of the university are a very distinctive feature of campus life. Even staff are members, many of them active in collegiate life. The colleges vary considerably in atmosphere and size, but each is a busy centre of social, recreational and educational activity. All on-campus accom-

UNIVERSITY/STUDENT PROFILE	
University since	**1964**
Situation/style	**Rural collegiate campus**
Student population	**11061**
Undergraduates	**8269**
- mature	**9%**
- non EU undergraduate	**13%**
- male/female	**47/53**
- non-traditional student intake	**21%**
- state school intake	**91%**
- drop-out rate	**5%**
- undergraduate applications	**Up 15%**

modation is located within college, which makes it easy to get to know people and quickly to gain a sense of belonging in this kind of supportive community.'

You might think, with campus being a small, all-encompassing 'city' miles from anywhere, it

25% — Postgraduates

Female Undergraduates — 40%

STUDENT POPULATION

Total students 11,061

35% — Male Undergraduates

could get a bit claustrophobic in time, but that is not the experience of students. By your second year you will probably be ready to break out, but the urge is satisfied by leaving your college residence rather than the uni as a whole. For in your second

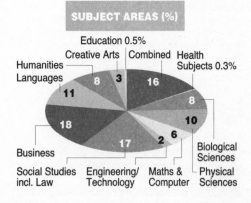

SUBJECT AREAS (%)

Education 0.5%
Creative Arts | Combined | Health Subjects 0.3%
Humanities Languages
8   3   16
11
8
18
10
17   2   6
Business
Biological Sciences
Social Studies incl. Law | Engineering/ Technology | Maths & Computer | Physical Sciences

year renting accommodation in town is actively encouraged, while continuing allegiance to your college is ensured by both sporting and course activities. The result of this very successful organic experiment is that when you ask students what it's like at Lancaster University, the words that crop up time and again are 'friendly', 'relaxed', 'unintimidating'. In fact, I can't imagine that Lancaster's system of 'personal advisers' – a 1:5 staff to student welfare and educational advice service, has much to do.

FEES, BURSARIES

UK & EU Fees 2007: £3,070. Fees not yet fixed for 2008. Sliding-scale bursaries for students in receipt of HE Maintenance Grant. They also operate a Talented Athlete Scholarship, £3,000 p.a., see www.tass.gov.uk. And all courses carry either a subject award or academic scholarship.

All UK students who put Lancaster down as firm choice and who achieve the grades required will automatically receive £1,000 p.a. Subject Awards of £1,000 p.a. for Biological Sciences, Combined Science, Communication Systems, European Languages and Cultures, Engineering, Environmental Science. In 2008, all courses carry an academic scholarship. Many colleges have bursaries, travel grants, scholarships. See www.lancs.ac.uk/ugfunding/

STUDENT PROFILE

'The best thing about the uni is the warm, friendly atmosphere created by the students in their somewhat wind-chilled and rainy environment. The student body comprises a wide cross-section of people, including large percentages of privately educated and overseas students.'

The independent school intake is high relative to most other unis, and although they had been among the UK's 'access elite' in the matter of taking classes of student new to the idea of university, others have now overtaken them.

ACADEMIA & JOBS

Lancaster is among the leaders in the teaching and research assessments, but when your best teaching strengths are in Theatre Studies, Philosophy, Psychology, Theology and Education, you can't be accused of being obsessively vocational. Balance comes with their Careers Service, now the Centre for Employability, Enterprise and Careers (CEEC) better to reflect the extensive range of services delivered: careers education, enterprise skill development for budding entrepreneurs, business support services to increase the number of opportunities available to students and graduates of the university. CEEC hosts one of the largest independent

ACADEMIC EXCELLENCE	
TEACHING:	
(Rated Excellent or 17+ out of 24)	
History, Applied Social Work, Business & Management Studies, English, Environmental Sciences, Geography, Social Policy & Admin, Music.	**Excellent**
Theatre Studies, Psychology, Philosophy, Theology, Education	**24**
Linguistics, Art & Design, Physics, Politics	**23**
Engineering, Maths & Stats	**22**
Sociology, Molecular Sciences, Organismal Biosciences	**21**
French, Italian with Iberian	**20**
German	**19**
RESEARCH:	
Top grades 5/5*/6*	
Statistics,	**Grade 6***
Sociology, Business Physics	**Grade 5***
Psychology, Earth Sciences, Computer, Law, Social Work, European Studies, English, Linguistics, Theology, Education	**Grade 5**

career fairs in the country held every autumn.

There are 3 faculties: Arts & Social Sciences, The Management School, and Science & Technology. There's also a School for Life Long Learning and Widening Participation, and they have recently established the Lancaster Institute for the Contemporary Arts, which brings together the departments of Art, Music and Theatre Studies.

The system is that your first year is a kind of taster year. They've woken up to the fact that a number of students study subjects at degree level that they haven't studied at school. In Part One (your first year) you take three subjects. One of these has to be what you intend to major in, but the other two can be completely off the wall. If you registered to do Politics, but, after a first year studying Politics, Law and Computing (for instance), you decide that you really should have applied to do Law all along, then so long as you get the required marks in your first year exams, transfer between departments is easy. This flexible programme in Part One is very popular.

They also have secret weapons in their educational armoury, like the Active Learning Unit, to which everyone is encouraged to submit. Special modules can be worked into your course-mix which will develop skills that employers want. And there's a first-class exchange scheme with nearly

WHAT IT'S REALLY LIKE

UNIVERSITY:

Social Life	★★★★
Campus scene	**Healthy, lively, college-based**
Student Union services	**Good**
Politics	**Active, not Left: fees, welfare**
Sport	**31 clubs**
National team position	**42nd**
Sport facilities	**Good**
Arts opportunities	**Art, drama, music, film good; dance poor**
Student newspaper	**SCAN**
Student radio	**Bailrigg FM**
National Media Awards	**Best Journalistic radio prog. 2006. Nominated for Best Website**
Nightclub	**Sugar House**
Bars	**College bars**
Union ents	**Indy/Alternative, r&b, hip hop, cheesy pop, live and comedy**
Union societies	**65**
Most popular society	**Theatre group**
Parking	**No first years**

TOWN:

Entertainment	★★★
Scene	**Excellent pubs, main uni club**
Town/gown relations	**Good**
Risk of violence	**Low**
Cost of living	**Average**
Student concessions	**Average**
Survival + 2 nights out	**£60 pw**
Part-time work campus/town	**Poor/average**

AT A GLANCE

ACADEMIC FILE:

Assessments	**29**
Excellent	**86%**
Typical entry requirements	**359 points**
Application acceptance rate	**16%**
Students-staff ratio	**16:1**
First/2:1 degree pass rate	**65%**

ACCOMMODATION FILE:

Guarantee to freshers	**100%**
Style	**College**
Catered	**None**
En suite	**68%**
Approx price range pw	**£57- £77**
Town rent pw	**£45-£60**

Economics & Marketing.

Aspiring environmental officers, cartographers and the like go for Ecology, Environmental Chemistry, Environmental Science: Earth Science with Geography

You could take the BSc Hons Combined Science for a year abroad (Biological & Environmental Sciences, for instance). There's also Physical Geography or Natural Sciences – 3/4 subjects, including one non-science.

Clearly, languages are a strength here and many go into adult education with a language degree from the uni. Humanities and social sciences are also popular routes into the sector (Psychology scored full marks at the assessments, while Politics scored 23).

They are European law specialists with an international Grade 5 rating. Look, too, at their Criminology degrees, where there's a strong line into police work. They also excel in turning out social workers and counsellors. Places on the BA Social Work course are in high demand. They scored full marks at the teaching assessments and there's a Grade 5 rating for research.

No academic run-down would be complete without mention of Lancaster's Physics provision – world-class Grade 5*. They turn out astronomers here. Degrees include such as Physics, Astrophysics & Cosmology, and a peach of a time over four years with Physics/North America, which includes a year at an American university.

SOCIAL SCENE

'Each of the colleges also has its own JCR (Junior Common Room), complete with bar and pool table,' reports Lisa. 'Many universities have only one union bar and the nine we have on campus provide perfect venues for bar crawls that last all night

one tenth of Lancaster students attending European and US institutions during their degree.

Prospective business management consultants and marketing managers should look at BA Management & Organisation/North America-Australasia. Then there's the BBA European Management degrees – French, German, Italian, Spanish, North America/Australasia, and the BSc Marketing Management. They are one of only two UK business schools to be rated a 6* centre of world-class research in business and management. The degrees are very popular with employers.

Accountancy is served by BA and BSc degrees, the latter offering either Computer Science or Maths with Accounting, Finance.

Employers in the advertising industry go for Advertising and Marketing, or Advertising,

WHERE LANCASTER GRADUATES END UP

Health & Social Work: 8%; Education: 9%; Wholesale Retail: 14%; Manufacturing: 9%; Financial Activities: 9%; Public Administration, Civil Service & Defence: 10%; Hotel/Restaurant: 4.5%; Transport & Communications (including Telecommunications): 3%; Construction: 2.5%; Personnel: 5%; Computer: 3%; Business & Management: 4%; Accountancy: 3%; Legal 3%; Publishing: 1.5%; Advertising: 1%; Artistic/Literary: 1%; Sport: 1%.

Approximate 'graduate track' employed **54%**

long. At the end of the academic year each college has its own entertainment event, affectionately named the *Extrav*, which usually results in farcically ridiculous antics and the presence of Chesney Hawkes or Abba and Elvis tribute bands.'

A poll puts **Pendle Bar** in first place in a college league of bars, followed closely by **Grizedale** (*Shite* disco on Friday) and **Lonsdale**. Most colleges organise subsidised fortnightly trips to clubs – Liverpool and Manchester are just over an hour away.

Sugar House is the union nightclub in town. It opens on Thursday, Friday and Saturday for indie, alternative to r&b, hip hop and also cheesy pop, and on other nights for live ents – bands, comedy, etc. – this year the Thrills, Fun Loving Criminals and the Dream Team.

The high-scoring Drama Department (full marks on inspection) empowers a studio theatre and the on-campus **Nuffield Theatre**, used for both student and 'pro' touring companies. The Lancaster Theatre Group is their most active society. Media-wise they are full strength with newspaper *SCAN* nominated for Best Student Critic in the national Journalism Awards 2005, radio station Bailrigg FM (BFM as it is known) winning Best Journalistic Programme 2006. The student web site, meanwhile, copped a nomination for being the Best.

'There is a huge variety of societies,' writes Lisa. 'including alternative music, Taekwando, photography, kickboxing, floorball, debating and juggling. If politics is your passion, the union is one of the most pro-active at the moment, campaigning for just about everything from abortions to AIDS. The Film Society is the largest society, and very popular are Bailrigg fm and *Scan*.'

SPORT Investment has just been approved for the development this year of a new on-campus sports centre.

Inter-college rivalries mean that if you enjoy sport, but aren't good enough to play at inter-university level, you will certainly be good enough to play at college level. A very high proportion of stu-

dents enjoy competitive team sport, even those that aren't that good, but the place really comes alive at Roses – Lancaster vrs York Uni, a huge weekend of sport and socials.

TOWN 'The social life at Lancaster should not be underestimated,' writes Guy McEvoy. 'Lancaster town itself has been transformed over the past five years by massive investment from the major brewers. Trendy pubs are now displacing the traditional Northern watering hole in the centre of town (though these can still be found on the edges if that is your thing). The union-run **Sugar House** remains the most popular club.'

Writes Lisa: 'If you are on a very tight budget I would suggest drinking in the college bars before going out into Lancaster and then clubbing dry.

'Student friendly pubs include **The Merchants**, **The Firkin**, **The Walkabout**, **Paddy Mulligan's**, **The Waterwitch** and **Blob Shop**. Recommended nightclubs are **Sugar House**, of course, and **Liquid**, **The Carleton** (host to Chesney Hawkes in the past), **Elemental**, and **Tokyo Joe's** in Preston.

PILLOW TALK

The majority of the accommodation was built in the 1960's and 1970's and is being demolished and replaced in the £160-million sweep clean. 1,047 new en-suite rooms were opened in October 2006. A further 1,000 are due to be rebuilt or refurbished by October 2008. Rents p.w. in college range from £56.70 to £77.34; studio apartments, £95.20. There is no catered accommodation, but students buy a card useable in the campus catering outlets.

GETTING THERE

☛ By road: M6/J34, A683 or M6/J33, A6.
☛ By rail: London Euston, 3:30; Newcastle, 3:00; Sheffield, 2:30; Leeds, 2:30; Manchester, 1:30.
☛ By coach: London, 5:50; Leeds, 3:55.

STUDENT LEEDS – THE CITY

Leeds is one of the most prosperous cities in Europe, conveniently placed in the middle of the country, where two main motorways, the M1 and the M62, intersect. It has an international airport and the busiest train station outside London, but 'the Jewel of the North' is dominated by its 50-odd thousand students to the extent that it really does seem to die when they go in the vacations.

CULTURE

Leeds is the clubbing capital of the North, but has a fantastic variety on offer, from the **West Yorkshire Playhouse** (Sir Ian McKellan, Ben Elton and Irvine Welsh have all premiered productions here) to **Opera North** to **Back 2 Basics** and **Speed Queen**, with the main nocturnal student activities being based in three areas of the city, Headingley, the Union and the City Centre. The re is, too, a fantastic gay scene, it is home to some of the best urban music nights and altogether it is truly multicultural in nature.

For art truly on the cheap, there are many free galleries, some of which showcase student work. The best of these are **The Henry Moore Institute** and **The Leeds Art Gallery,** which stand next to each other in town. A quick mention must be given to **The Royal Armouries** which was given to Leeds ahead of London and contains 8,000 exhibits for under a fiver.

FILM

In the age of the futuristic multiplex the best thing about film in Leeds is that the cosy independent cinema has survived. Like most places everything is student friendly price-wise, but real value and satisfaction can be found in the cinemas, which are dotted around studentland and cost around £2.50 a pop.

The Hyde Park Picture House is eighty-five years old and the height of cool. Cult and independent films, as well as the occasional blockbuster, can be found here, and its location slap bang in the in the middle of Hyde Park ensures that it's a student favourite. Headingley has two lovely cinemas – **The Cottage Road** and **Lounge** – both quite plush and with a lovely retro feel to them. Finally **ABC** in town plays the latest that Hollywood has to offer for prices that seem to be stuck in 1987.

PUBS

A must in these parts is completing the fabled Otley Run, involving a drink in every establishment from **Boddington Hall**, four miles north of campus, to Leeds Met's **Met Bar** on the outskirts of the city centre – four miles, twenty-odd pubs and a lot of drinking. All these pubs are geared towards students and the best remain the same year in, year out. **The Original Oak** and **The Skyrack** in central Headingley are pretty much the busiest pubs in the world. No space to move, but forever popular – go on your own and you'll soon bump into someone you know. Also cheap and cheerful 24/7 are the union bars: at Leeds Uni, it's **The Old Bar** (rumoured to be the longest in Europe) and now **Stylus** (1000 capacity), and down the road, the aforementioned **Met Bar**, which hosts legendary student events.

CLUBS

A massive explosion. Just down from the uni are **Majestyk** (massive) and **Jumpin' Jaks** (cheap), **Space (mid-week)**, **The Cockpit** (indie), **Tiger Tiger** (wrinklies) Wherever you turn in the city centre there seems to be a new club springing up. Whatever you're looking for is here. Itchy recommends student bars and pubs **Headingley Taps**, **Hyde Park** (both leaving you no doubt where they might be, **Original Oak** and **Skyrack** (both Headingley).

If you're into largin' it at every opportunity then **The Afterdark** in Morley is without doubt the best techno club north of London, with a galaxy of stars playing. Deeply fashionable and just off Leeds University campus is **The Faversham**, a pub in the week but a club on Thursday to Saturday with a crowd that is there to be seen. Situated in Call Lane, the redlight district, **The Fruit Cupboard** hosts the best R&B night in the city and is great for chilling out. Finally, no sampling of Leeds clubland can go by without mentioning the renowned hard house night *Speed Queen*, attracting an up for it gay/straight/TV crowd – was at **The Warehouse**, then at **Strinky's Peephouse** and now rumoured to be on the way back to **The Warehouse**, and *Back 2 Basics* – was at **Rehab**, then at **Peephouse**, a club now re-emerging appropriately enough as **My House** in February 2006. Yet there are many, many gems, many, many facets to explore before you'll find your favourites. Events details can be found in the weekly edition of *Leeds Student*, the newspaper for all students in Leeds.

SHOPPING

Leeds is often called the 'Knightsbridge of the North', but many up here think that Knightsbridge is the 'Briggate of the South'. In fact, from charity shops to **Harvey Nichols** your budget can be catered for. The main areas are in town and the best is **The Victoria Quarter**. Under a stained glass arcade independent and designer labels compete for your loan, but be prepared to spend. **The Corn Exchange** is another big hall much along the same lines, and for value, range and sheer presence the huge, Victorian, covered Kirkgate market is a joy to behold. If strapped for cash go to Hyde Park Corner and Headingley. Both have smaller independents and charity shops at the cheapest prices possible.

Karl Mountsfield

UNIVERSITY OF LEEDS

The University of Leeds
Leeds LS2 9JT

TEL 0113 233 2332 (prospectus)
    0113 233 3999
FAX 0113 233 3877
EMAIL admissions@adm.leeds.ac.uk
WEB www.leeds.ac.uk

Leeds University Union
PO Box 157
Leeds LS1 1UH

TEL 0113 380 1234
FAX 0113 380 1205
EMAIL comms@luu.leeds.ac.uk
WEB www.luuonline.com

VAG VIEW

*T*he *number of applicants to Leeds in 2007 (49,280) was exceeded only by those to Manchester. Graduate employers share their enthusiasm. Not only do they take a keen interest in graduates from here, especially those graduating in two named subjects, they like the independence and width of experience which they associate with the Leeds graduate.*

What's for sure is that Leeds does offer the full thing: academic and extra-curricular - you know that this is what university should be about.

CAMPUS

The campus is a mix of differing architectural styles, ranging from neo-gothic to '70s concrete to modern glass and steel, situated just to the north of the city centre before you get to the bulk of student housing areas.

Everything's within easy walking distance, and 'it's relatively safe,' writes Londoner Amy Shuckburgh. 'On the whole it doesn't have an intimidating feel to it. The same precautions should be taken as in any city: it is inadvisable to walk around late at night on your own; use taxis if possible; union night bus services are provided for girls along all routes, both girls and boys are strongly advised not to walk through Hyde Park at night.'

The union has an arrangement with a taxi service – any student can travel free on production of their union card, which is then presented by the driver to the union for payment. The union settles with the student later.

FEES, BURSARIES

UK & EU Fees: £3,070. If in receipt of the HE Maintenance grant, there's a sliding-scale bursary according to parental income. They also have bursaries to encourage applicants from poorer postcodes and through outreach arrangements with feeder institutions.

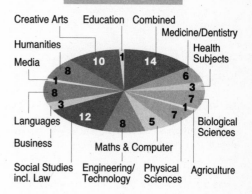

SUBJECT AREAS (%)

Creative Arts   Education   Combined
                            Medicine/Dentistry
Humanities   Health
Media   Subjects
          10   1   14
       8   6
    1   3
    8   7
    3   1
Languages   12   7   Biological
                 8   5   Sciences
Business   Maths & Computer

Social Studies   Engineering/   Physical   Agriculture
incl. Law   Technology   Sciences

STUDENT PROFILE

Do not expect the prevailing atmosphere at Leeds to be like that of any other university. It is on its own. 'What Leeds Uni has to offer, which I doubt anywhere else could match,' observed a recent graduate, 'is the students themselves. There's a real atmosphere about the place. You can do whatever you want without being criticised for it. You can really get involved. And students do. You don't come to a place like Leeds if you're an introvert.'

'The union is never inactive. There is almost something on 24/7,' writes Zoe. They have so many student societies (210) that they split them into 10 groups just so you can absorb what's on offer: Faith & Culture, Departmental, General Interest, Martial Arts & Dance, Media, Outdoor Activities, Performance, Political & Campaigning, Sports, and Volunteering.

But there is a downside. 'On the downside,' writes Zoe, 'student life in Leeds can lack the close-knit community feel of a smaller uni. It can also be a somewhat *overwhelming* experience. Can be over-whelming because there is so much going on you don't know what to get involved in, especially in Fresher's week... People are everywhere... and you have to accept the good with the bad. It can some-times be quite cliquey in societies and halls...'

'There is a left-wing, anti-Capitalist stance at Leeds,' says Jude Corrigan. 'It is very prevalent here.' Nothing wrong with that, except that when you look at the student body, you see anything but true socialist flesh and bones on it. Compare it with neighbouring Leeds Met. Leeds has one of the low-est intakes from the state school sector (73% as

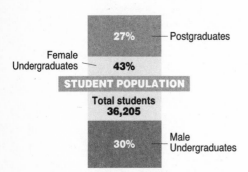

Female Undergraduates — 43%

27% — Postgraduates

STUDENT POPULATION

Total students 36,205

30% — Male Undergraduates

against Met's 93%). Numbers of students from the four lowest socio-economic classes are likewise minimal (19% against Met's 33%). Again, intake from traditionally 'low participation' neighbour-hoods is unusually low (9% against Met's 16%). So, it is anything but a working-class (or indeed partic-ularly socially varied relative to some) student body, and when you look at its student politics closely you have a kind of champagne socialism at Leeds, undergraduates with gusto born of privilege

playing at real life, and leaving the socialist play-ground as soon as they get their well-paid profes-sional jobs. At Met, the truly 'real', socially rootsy university, there is virtually no politics at all and no criticism of being up their rear ends either, while for years a reputation for aching political correct-ness has stuck to the Leeds Union.

So, don't be held in thrall by those in control here; 9 times out of 10 they are not who they think they are (or give you the impression they are). Opt for Leeds, but do your own thing and demand the money from the union to allow you to do it in what-ever type of society you choose to set up, even if it doesn't agree with their politics. Leeds is not a place to follow dumbly behind anyone.

ACADEMIA & JOBS

Said fresher Susan Green last year: 'What's best about this uni is the very approachable lecturers. There's always someone around to help out.' The students-to-staff ratio does not reflect the view. Unlike UCL, where it is 8:1, Imperial (9), Cambridge (12), the ratio at Leeds is 18:1.

Nevertheless, academically, Leeds has a good reputation across the board, and if you are in the top 70% you can expect a First or Upper Second.

The Arts Faculty joint honours courses distin-guish the curriculum. The range of these two-main-subjects programmes is wide and challenging, with Chinese, Japanese and Arabic joining the language provision, while Economics, Accounting, the Law and Politics provide some of the overt vocational elements against a rich worldwide cultural backdrop of Russian, Jewish, Roman and other civilisations. It is a heady mix. Leeds prides itself in offering some 375 of these, involving 58 subjects taught across 32 departments. First-year students divide their time equally between three subjects: the two named subjects and a third or 'elective' subject. Thereafter, they normally concentrate on two of the three. Employers take a keen interest in graduates with two named subjects from Leeds.

There's particular mention by sixthform careers teachers of languages – 'One reason we recommend Leeds is that you can do exotic languages, Arabic,' said one. They are high placed in a league of graduate interpreters and translators (a difficult field), but languages find graduates a whole range of careers, in advertising, market research, media & government research, publicity, PR, government administration and the Civil Service, and it seems more likely than not that a graduate of Leeds will leave with a language or cultural studies course in tow – Asia Pacific Studies and Economics, for instance, seems tailor-made for the new world. The breadth of the academic focus is surely the thing.

Most graduates end up in the health industry or in financial activities, accountancy or business/management. But there are a number of intriguing niche areas. A huge fillip came with the merger with arts/education college, **Bretton Hall** (close to Wakefield), supported by a £9 million investment to rejuvenate the already highly regarded arts college. Directors, producers and theatre managers flow steadily out of what is now Leeds's School of Performance & Cultural Studies. You'll be on an amazing campus – 500 acres of landscaped parkland, supporting an 18th-century Palladian Mansion, lakes, woods, a nature reserve. It's a 30-minute drive down the M1 from Leeds. There is also dance and creative writing and management. The BA Performance Design & Production includes set, costume, light and sound design, learned through practical, performance-based projects.

The Leeds degree in Medicine is a 5-year MB ChB with its 3-phase focus on the fundamentals of clinical practice, clinical practice in context, professional competence. Communication skills, ethics, health & prevention of disease, community-based medicine, medical info & management are recurring themes. Entry AAB + UKCAT, including Chemistry. Teaching inspection, 18. Application acceptance rate is 10%. Research Grade 5. A 5-year BChD allows you to become a dental surgeon. Entry 320 points. Teaching inspection, 23.

They are strong too in producing psychologists. BSc Psychology features in some of the best

BSc/Undergraduate Masters joint hons courses that employers like so much: with Management, Music or Philosophy. There is also a BA Psychology-Sociology in the Arts Joint programme, and an international Grade 5 for research.

There's a nursing provision (child, adult, and midwifery. Teaching inspection, 20. Also BSc Radiography – Diagnostic. Leeds took an international Grade 5 at the research assessments and got full marks for teaching these courses – 6 points better than for its teaching of Medicine.

The city of Leeds is of course the UK's Second City for Finance. Economics holds much appeal

ACADEMIC EXCELLENCE

TEACHING :
(Rated Excellent or 17+ out of 24)

Subject	Rating
Chemistry, English, Geography, Music, Geology.	**Excellent**
Subjects Allied to Medicine, Philosophy, Physics	**24**
East & South Asian Studies, Pharmacology, Dentistry, Fine Art, Electrical & Electronic Eng, Molecular Biosciences, Politics, Psychology, Theology	**23**
Maths, Iberian, French, German, Communication/Media, Anatomy, Organismal Biosciences, Accounting/Finance/Business/Economics	**22**
Arabic	**21**
Sociology, Russian, Agriculture, Nursing, Materials Technology, Food Science	**20**
Italian, Chemical Eng, Classics, Civil Engineering	**19**
Medicine	**18**

RESEARCH :
Top grades 5/5*/6*

Subject	Grade
Food Science, Mechanical/Aeronautical/ Manufacturing Eng, Town & Country Planning, English, Italian	**Grade 6***
Electrical and Electronic Eng,	**Grade 5***
Clinical Laboratory Sciences, Physiology, Other Subjects Allied to Medicine, Psychology, Biological Sciences, Chemistry, Physics, Earth Sciences, Environmental Sciences, Pure Maths, Applied Maths, Statistics, Computer, General Eng, Civil Eng, Geography, Law, Social Policy, Business & Management, Asian Studies, History, Philosophy	**Grade 5**

here, the joint hons programme adding to its allure by mixing it with languages (including Russian) and Management. Investment advisers/analysts, actuaries, tax experts/consultants, stockbrokers, share-dealers and bankers flood out of this uni, as do accountants. BA Accounting comes with Finance or Management, or as joint - both subjects main - with Law. BSc Accounting-Computing or Accounting-Info Systems can be taken as a 4-year course with one year in a European university. Teaching inspection: Economics 22, Business 22. Research Grade 5: Maths (pure and applied) and Business.

There are more barristers in Leeds than any other city outside London, and it is an equally important element of the curriculum. There are 2 and 3-year LLBs and a 4-year French edition. Law was rated international Grade 5 for research, and non-Law graduates may take a 2-year full-time or 3-year part-time Senior Status law degree here.

They are, too, among the leading unis on which the publishing industry draws, indeed they are a contender wherever media is mentioned. Again it's the joint hons programme, with languages to the fore, that appeals, with the award-winning student media providing some of the expertise. Look also at BA Broadcast Journalism or BA Broadcasting, and BA Creative Writing, which covers prose, poetry and scriptwriting, but turns out journalists, too. There was a 22-point score at the assessments.

They are market leaders in Human Resource Management through their BA dedicated degree, though once again languages are an important feed, along with humanities – e,g. BA Management Studies-Psychology. Management Studies is also applied to biological, physical and social sciences.

Physical and biological sciences lead to a whole host of occupations. For chemistry they offer BSc/M (3-year/4-year Undergraduate Masters) and a choice of single or joint hons (various options). There are courses in Medicinal Chemistry, Colour & Polymer Chemistry, Applied Chemistry (general industrial chemistry with special attention to polymer science), etc. Teaching inspection, Excellent. Research, Grade 5.

The 4-year MEng Pharmaceutical Chemical Engineering requires is equally effective job-wise. There are various Pharmacology combinations offered (Biochemistry, Chemistry, Physiology). Teaching inspection, 23. Research, Grade 5.

And they lead the way nationally in turning out environmental officers. The School of Environment tackles conservation, land management, environmental regulation, water resources and sustainable development with its degrees - again, Grade 5 for research, and meteorology is a career niche here.

Mechanical Engineering is another important part of the curriculum, B/MEng and Foundation programmes in Automotive Engineering, Computing in Engineering, Management with Mechanical & Manufacturing Engineering, Mathematical Engineering, Mechatronics and Medical Engineering, in addition to the Mechanical Eng degrees themselves. In the research area they too have a world-class Grade 6* rating.

Software consultants also proliferate, as do civil

AT A GLANCE	
ACADEMIC FILE:	
Subjects assessed	**43**
Excellent	**88%**
Typical entry requirements	**375 points**
Application acceptance rate	**13%**
Med. School acceptance rate	**10%**
Students:staff ratio	**18:1**
First/2:1 degree pass rate	**72%**
ACCOMMODATION FILE:	
Guarantee to freshers	**Apply by 1.6**
Style	**Halls, flats, houses**
Catered	**26%**
En-suite	**15%**
Approx price range pw	**£40-£110**
City rent pw	**£55-£70**

engineers. Teaching inspection, 19. Research, Grade 5.

Ten per cent of graduates go into education – Arts Education and Childhood, Education & Culture, plus a series of named subject Education degrees. Strengths are science and maths, primary education and special needs. There's also a good track record for lecturers into higher education.

SOCIAL SCENE

A recent £4.8m extension has added 40% more shopping and meeting space for students and given the city a new music venue. The nightclub is called **Stylus** (capacity 1,000), which is adjacent to **Pulse** (capacity 290; has been done out really nicely; in general the union doesn't get too shabby before they refurbish). There are then two bars jointly known as **The Terrace** (complete with sun-terrace and disabled access), **Old Bar**, a traditional pub really, down in the basement, and a new food bar called **Mine**. That leaves the **Riley Smith Hall** (capacity 600) to host productions from the students' performing societies and **The Refectory** (capacity 2,000) as the biggest venue in Leeds, which has hosted more of the world's biggest bands that we'd care to mention. There's also a nightclub opened at Bretton campus. In addition, the union now has 6 shops, including Leeds' second largest newsagent, an off-licence, a card and ticket shop, a copy shop, one selling past exam papers and the last union-run bookshop in the country.

Ents can be as cheesy as at any other uni, like Old Bar Idol/Old Bar Karaoke. Friday is *Fill up for Fruity* (urban dance and eclectic dance floor grooves); every first Saturday of the month is *Rock of Ages* (rock and metal madness). Various events on all academic year include New Slang: Live Bands, and Lazy Dayz (Sunday lunch with live acoustic music).

They are good at much more than ents. They pride themselves on their student welfare services. Main political issues in recent years have been tuition fees, Stop The War, participation and diversity, and health, along with perennial ethical, environmental and international issues.

'At Leeds we are very, very strongly two separate institutions, the university and the union,' they tell us. 'Everybody knows that. But there's mutual respect. Community issues, drug and alcohol policy, things like that we work together on, but politically we like to be independent.'

There's an award-winning track record in media. The radio station is LSRfm.com, the weekly student newspaper, *Leeds Student,* a magazine called *Lippy* (women's welfare magazine) and *Leeds Review* (a new interdisciplinary arts society; they publish an arts journal which provides a platform for students to circulate their work), and TV station LSTV. At the 2006 national media awards *Leeds Student* took two runner-up awards; LSR a Silver and a Bronze; and LSTV won 3 awards.

Then there are the arts, and fund-raising, sport and Community Action (over 600 students are involved in this) societies. 'For drama, we've got **The Raven Theatre**. It seats a couple of hundred. The Theatre Group does three or four plays a term. The really big shows, musicals – *Grease, The Whizz, Hair* – are in The Riley Smith Hall.

'There's modern dance (they run jazz, tap, contemporary lessons), there's ballroom and salsa every Wednesday in the **Refectory**, which is packed out. You can barely move in there.

'The Symphony Orchestra and Symphonia and the chorals are all involved in the Leeds concert season, and then there's dance big bands – they've been on tour, had a CD out, played gigs in the city.

'The Film Society is very big, and the Film Making Society has really taken off. For art we've got all the resources in the city – Henry Moore Institute and the galleries and the gallery exhibition in the Parkinson Court.'

Small wonder that, 'Nightline is very high in demand... very heavily subscribed. It isn't any one thing that drives people to use it. You've got financial pressures, academic pressures, and then you've

WHAT IT'S REALLY LIKE	
UNIVERSITY:	
Social Life	★★★★★
Campus scene	**Great but a bit self-conscius**
Student Union services	**Good**
Politics	**18 societies campaigning**
Sport	**34 clubs**
National team position	**14th**
Sport facilities	**Good**
Arts opportunities	**Excellent**
Student magazine	**Lippy**
2005 Awards	**Best magazine**
Student newspaper	**Leeds Student**
2006 Journalism Awards	**2 x runner-up**
Student radio	**LSR FM**
2006 Radio Awards	**Silver, bronze**
Student TV	**LSTV**
2006 National TV Awards	**3 wins**
Nightclubs	**Stylus, Pulse**
Bars	**Terrace, Old Bar**
Union ents	**Funky house & chart, drum n bass/old skool, r&b**
Union societies	**210**
Parking	**Poor**
CITY:	
Entertainment	★★★★★
Scene	**Wild**
Town/gown relations	**Average**
Risk of violence	**Average**
Cost of living	**High**
Student concessions	**Abundant**
Survival + 2 nights out	**£90 pw**
Part-time work campus/town	**Good/average**

got the social pressures – to conform, to party, to pull in the grades, and then you've got other problems like housing. There's pressure from all sides.'

SPORT 'The rivalry between the two unis is friendly and good-humoured,' writes Zoe Perkins. 'Once a year it comes to a head in the Varsity Sports Day where respective teams compete at some 20 different sports for the Varsity Cup. The Met always wins. Leeds are always sore losers.' But overall nationally Leeds came 14th; Met 16th. There are facilities to match attainment – two sports halls, one large enough to take 1,500 spectators. Playing fields are 5 miles from campus; there are also cricket squares, a floodlit synthetic pitch and 6 floodlit tennis courts. There's rowing in Leeds and York, sailing on nearby lakes and reservoirs, hiking, climbing, canoeing and caving in the Yorkshire

Dales. Students use the city's international swimming pool, and golf courses in the area.

PILLOW TALK

There's a variety of halls – standard, type and price very variable, from ridiculously cheap, from traditional to swanky city centre flat. Private city accommodation is reasonable and certainly plentiful. Most people live in shared houses in the Headingley and Hyde Park areas of the city, the ghetto LS6. For people in the private rented sector there is a union and university backed housing standards authority, UNIPOL, for peace of mind. 'Burglary can be a problem,' notes Amy Shuckburgh, 'most student houses have window bars, door grates or alarms as deterrents.'

GETTING THERE

☛ By road: M62/J39, M1; or M62/J27, M621; or A1, A58; or A65, A650.
☛ By rail: Newcastle, 1:45; London Euston, 2:30; Birmingham New Street, 2:20.
☛ By air: Leeds/Bradford Airport.
☛ By coach: London, 4:00; Edinburgh, 6:00.

LEEDS METROPOLITAN UNIVERSITY

Leeds Metropolitan University
Calverley Street
Leeds LS1 3HE

TEL 0113 281 3113
FAX 0113 283 3129
EMAIL course-enquiries@leedsmet.ac.uk
WEB www.leedsmet.ac.uk

Leeds Met Students' Union
Calverley Street
Leeds LS1 3HE

TEL 0113 209 8400
FAX 0113 234 2973
EMAIL [initial.name]@leedsmet.ac.uk
WEB www.lmsu.org.uk

VAG VIEW

*L*eeds Met is the 'low-charging, high impact' university, they say, because they charge only £2,000 p.a. whilst others are charging £3,000 or more.

The uni has full marks or near full marks for teaching vocational subjects like business management, economics, education, health, drama, sport. It is what one student called 'a centre of applied learning', and it reflects the character of the city probably better than its older uni neighbour up the hill. An active union ensures that it is a fun place to be.

CAMPUS

City Campus, close to Leeds Uni campus, has recently undergone a £100-million development. There are teaching facilities both here at Calverley Street and at nearby Queen Square. **Headingley Campus** is 3 miles away in 100 acres of parkland (Beckett Park). The cultures of the two sites differ as to the type of student. Sports, business and computing students colour Headingley, while City has a lot more arts, health sciences and engineering. 'Students who play sport go out there;' said a student. 'Students who want the library and the big ents come down here.'

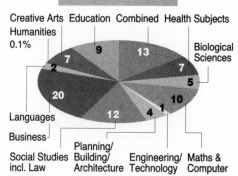

SUBJECT AREAS (%)

Creative Arts Education Combined Health Subjects
Humanities
0.1%
Biological Sciences
Languages
Business
Social Studies incl. Law
Planning/ Building/ Architecture
Engineering/ Technology
Maths & Computer

There is also a new campus in Halifax, a joint venture with Calderdale College

FEES, BURSARIES

UK & EU Fees 2007: Leeds Met has held its fee down to £2,000 for full-time home students in 2007, having seen applications rise by 14%. Plenty of scholarships for sport, academia and overseas students, see www.leedsmet.ac.uk/internat/scholarships_fees.htm

STUDENT PROFILE

'The demographics are quite different to Leeds University,' says student Kate Denby. 'A large proportion of students at our Leeds site are part-time.

They'll come from the Yorkshire area, maybe do evening courses. The full-timers, who come from all over, tend to be more the mature type of student. People who have been out in the world. There are also lots of international students, many of whom come on exchange. It's a more cosmopolitan atmosphere than in Leeds University.'

ACADEMIA & JOBS

There are 6 faculties. The Carnegie Faculty of Sport & Education is self-explanatory. Arts & Society includes Architecture, Landscape & Design; Contemporary Art & Graphic Design; Building & Quantity Surveying, Architectural Technology; Cultural Studies; Film, TV & Performing Arts; Social Sciences; Civil Engineering; Construction; Project Management; Planning, Human Geography & Housing; Youth & Community Studies. Business and Law incorporates all that you might expect, including Accounting & Financial Services. While Innovation North has Creative Technology, Music, Computing & IT. Then, there's the Faculty of Health, and lastly the Leslie Silver International Faculty, including Tourism Management, Hospitality Management & Retailing, Events Management, Applied Global Ethics, and the School of Languages.

The QAA gave the uni an institutional audit in 2004, expressing 'broad confidence' in its provision. In 2003 and 2004, Law, English, History, Computing, Accountancy, all achieved the QAA's highest rating of confidence and were commended.

Both Leeds and LMU want to get their students employed. The difference is that at LMU the approach is direct – degree names point to jobs. 'This is a centre for applied learning,' said Kate. 'I'm doing a degree in Public Relations. It's hands on. What you generally find is a lot of students go on placement. They might have a year's placement or a day each week placement. I have no lectures on a Thursday and go into a company and work one day a week. You can do that sort of thing off your

own bat or you can get placements via the placements office. People who come here have a goal. They know what they want to do. We've got an Events Management course, for example, very popular, been going for about five years. And Tourism Management and people going into leisure studies.

ACADEMIC EXCELLENCE

TEACHING :
(Rated Excellent or 17+ out of 24)

Business/Mgt, Economics	**24**
Education, Subjects Allied to Medicine	**23**
Drama/Dance/Cinematics, Sport, Hospitality Management	**22**
Civil Engineering, Building, Land & Property Mgt, Art & Design, Nursing	**21**
Psychology	**20**
Modern Languages, Communication & Media Studies	**19**

RESEARCH:
Top grades 5/5* **None**

It's across the board – sport, business, computing.'

The language dimension is as significant here as at Leeds, perhaps more obviously as a skill add-on, and students also acquire skills in computing as part of a drive to employability, though sometimes there's a participating European university, which promises more. International Business Finance or European Marketing is run in cahoots with Hochschule Bremen, Germany, or the Groupe ESC Normandie at Caen, France.

Market research is one employment area where both unis, in their different ways, excel, Leeds through its languages and social studies programmes and LMU through social studies, business, and law. LMU's teaching of Psychology scored 20 points at the assessments, Business full marks (24). Note the BSc Applied Psychology.

The Faculty of Health has an extremely high

UNIVERSITY/STUDENT PROFILE

University since	**1992**
Situation/style	**City sites**
Student population	**29136**
Undergraduates	**25132**
- mature	**51%**
- non EU undergraduates	**8%**
- male/female	**47/53**
- non-traditional student intake	**33%**
- state school intake	**93%**
- drop-out rate	**15%**
- undergraduate applications	**Up 14%**

percentage of graduates in full-time paid employment, courses such as Managing in Health and Social Care Organisations, Community Health Care Nursing, Applied Social Work, Health Science boasting a 100% rate. Teaching inspection, 23.

Both unis do well in getting graduates into the Civil Service, but while Leeds does so mainly through biological sciences, law and social science, the Met comes in strongly via computer science.

> *There are completely different cultures in the two universities in Leeds. This is a centre for applied learning and the place with the reputation for nightlife. You'll find no middle-class socialism at Leeds Met.*

In the financial sector, LMU does especially well in banking. Look at BSc Economics for Business, also Accounting & Finance (there's a strong line in tax experts/consultants at LMU too). Note also the Business Computing BSc, and Business Information Systems, a Business & Finance HND + 1-year BA top-up and the BA Economics for Business. The Computer Sciences route is also popular

There is strong graduate employment, too, in architecture and construction.

The education provision looks after around 10% of graduate output – early childhood, primary and BAQ Secondary Physical Education, the latter evincing a strength felt more strongly than at any other uni, in the employment of graduate sports trainers and coaches. Inspection 22.

Students are already enjoying the world-class facilities at the Carnegie Stand at Headingley Carnegie Stadium. The ground floor of the Carnegie Stand is home to a Helpzone and the Carnegie Cafe where students, visitors and guests can rub shoulders with champions. There is also a conference suite, seminar and meeting rooms, a conference and education centre and state-of-the-art coaching facilities, developed by Leeds Met, to allow players and students to use modern technology to analyse team play.

Investment continues apace in other areas.

They acquired the former BBC Headquarters on Woodhouse Lane, which in early 2007 opened as Old Broadcasting House, a meeting place for the arts, enterprise and students, supporting business and finance in the city. New facilities are to be built to complete the new learning environment for the Faculty of Arts & Society surrounding Old Broadcasting House in what they are now calling Broadcasting Place.

Again, The Electric Press in Millennium Square is now home to the uni's School of Film, Television & Performing Arts. Joined to the Carriageworks Theatre on Millennium Square, it features fully-equipped studio spaces, editing rooms, a screening room and production offices.

Web CT is LMU's online learning resource where students can access module information, notes from lectures, the Library catalogue, as well as a wide range of information of activities available in and around the University.

SOCIAL SCENE
'LMU's **Met Bar** hosts legendary student events.' It is a huge area, a whole floor of the building which includes an enormous bar, café and the concert hall itself, which has a stage, decent dressing rooms and a built-in DJ studio block, besides formidable sound and lighting equipment. The whole thing is fully sound proofed, floating in plastic, the Learning Centre next door remains oblivious.

'Anyone who's anyone plays Leeds Met. Leeds Uni are better at things political,' is the considered student opinion. 'Ents is a totally professional area,' Kate Denby says. 'Everyone who works there is a paid professional, although we do have two students who work part-time for us in an events capacity, qualified to do lighting for example. We generally do 9 events a week across all three venues, so there's a lot to organise. Our main venue holds

---

WHERE LEEDS MET GRADUATES END UP

Health & Social Work: 13%; Education: 10%; Wholesale Retail: 12%; Manufacturing: 6%; Financial Activities: 8%; Public Administration, Civil Service & Defence: 9%; Hotel/Restaurant: 6%; Transport & Communications (including Telecommunications): 4%; Construction: 3.5%; Personnel: 3.5%; Computer: 5%; Business & Management:1%; Accountancy: 1%; Media (including Film): 2%; Legal 2.5%; Architecture: 2.5%; Publishing: 1%; Advertising: 1%; Sport: 2.5%.

Approximate 'graduate track' employed **63%**

WHAT IT'S REALLY LIKE

UNIVERSITY:

Social Life	★★★★★
Campus scene	**Sporty, spicy, action focused**
Student Union services	**Good**
Politics	**Student issues**
Sport	**50 clubs. Sport dominates**
National team position	**16th**
Sport facilities	**Excellent**
Arts opportunities	**Very little. Dance good**
Student newspaper	**The Met, Leeds Student**
Student radio	**LSR FM**
Nightclub	**The Met**
Bars	**Sugarwell, Kirstall Brewery, Becketts**
Union ents	**STAR, great live band prog.**
Union societies	**20**
Parking	**Poor**

CITY:

Entertainment	★★★★★
Scene	**Wild**
Town/gown relations	**Average**
Risk of violence	**Average**
Cost of living	**High**
Student concessions	**Abundant**
Survival + 2 nights out	**£90 pw**
Part-time work campus/town	**Good/average**

AT A GLANCE

ACADEMIC FILE:

Subjects assessed	**26**
Excellent	**58%**
Typical entry requirements	**251 points**
Application acceptance rate	**15%**
Students-staff ratio	**24:1**
First/2:1 degree pass rate	**49%**

ACCOMMODATION FILE:

Guarantee to freshers	**Not complete**
Style	**Halls, flats**
Catered	**None**
En suite	**1,688 rooms**
Approx price range pw	**£58-£113**
City rent pw	**£55-£70**

find three sorts centres: the Carnegie Indoor and Outdoor centres and the £multi-million Carnegie Tennis Centre - synthetic turf pitches, gyms, dance studio, swimming pool, sports halls, athletics track, grass pitches, squash courts, indoor and outdoor tennis courts, fitness rooms, climbing wall, strength and conditioning room, gymnastics centre. Competition takes place in all sports, at all levels. 'There's also a students union out at Beckett Park,' informs Kate Denby, 'with a bar (**Becketts**), 450-500 capacity, sports theme, some accommodation.'

TOWN See *Student Leeds*, page 270.

PILLOW TALK

Uni-owned/managed halls or flats, self-catered houses, private lodgings. The £17-million residential development, Kirkstall Brewery, has 2 squash courts, a weight training and fitness centre, a two-floor bar complex (capacity around 1,000), regular weekly and one-off events, laundry and shop.

September 2006 saw the launch Opal One, a pioneering development in the heart of the student community on Burley Road, just outside Leeds City Centre. The flats are en-suite with on-site fitness suite, swimming pool, sauna and jacuzzi. Opal Two, the second development at the Opal complex, is expected to be complete by September 2007.

GETTING THERE

☛ By road: M1, A1 or M62. Good coach services.
☛ By rail: Newcastle, 1:45; London Euston, 2:30; Birmingham New Street, 2:20.
☛ By air: Leeds/Bradford Airport.
☛ By coach: London, 4:00; Edinburgh, 6:00; Bristol, 5:45.

1,500 people; it's the whole of the floor below us.

Regular Friday nights are *STAR* and most nights there are live bands. Recent live acts include Mark Owen, The Darkness, Damien Rice, Funeral for a friend, Athlete, Grandaddy, The Cooper Temple Clause, Electric Six, Shed Seven, New Model Army, Howard Marx.

Then there are the comedy and movie nights, big-screen footie and private parties, all adding up to an ents programme rarely surpassed elsewhere.

Among societies, CALM (Community Action at Leeds Met) is expanding rapidly with over 400 students participating in student-led student projects in the community. Two students are up for National volunteering awards.

They have a presence on the production side of the award-winning Leeds Uni, *Leeds Student* newspaper. They also team up with Leeds for radio – LSR.

SPORT Leeds Met Chancellor is Brendan Foster, so you can expect good sport. At Beckett Park you'll

STUDENT LEICESTER - THE CITY

The city is still sometimes unfairly seen as having little more to it than Walkers Crisps and its most famous son, Gary Linekar, but its profile is always on the up, be it through its football and rugby teams, Comedy Festival (nationally acclaimed comedians attract a 20,000+ audience), curries or nightclubs.

Leicester is compact enough to retain a strong community atmosphere, modern enough to combine this with what you want from a city, and there is always something going on.

Coming to university in a city like Leicester after growing up in a quaint market town could have been daunting, but for me, it was incredibly exciting.

To Londoners coming north perhaps Leicester doesn't sound very glamorous, but you will soon discover behind the grey seventies buildings and run-down knitwear factories that this is a friendly and vibrant city with many hidden gems.

There are of course flaws, the biggest has to be the great big ring road around the city centre that can defeat even the most experienced navigator.

First, being a student in Leicester is great, because there are so many of us about. In term time, students make up a tenth of the population. Consequently there are always offers in bars and shops hungry for their disposable income.

Leicester is also a multicultural city and many different languages are spoken here. 'Diversity' is the buzz word here and on the whole it works very well. It's also the UKís first environmental city, with tons of bike routes and parks dotted about.

My favourite place in Leicester is Bradgate Park. Unfortunately I didn't discover this gem until my final year, so you will be one step ahead. The park is breathtaking and the perfect place to chill out, away from deadlines and other stresses.

Another reason why Leicester is so good for students is its aforesaid compactness. It is easy to cross on foot and both universities are within walking distance of the city centre, train and bus stations, which means you don't spend a fortune on bus fares or petrol. My halls of residence were within stumbling distance of the union bar and I could wake up 10 minutes before a lecture.

My other favourite place is the Narborough Road. This long road near De Montfort University defines being a student. Everything a student could possibly need is all on one road - taxis, kebab shops, a library, convenience stores, charity shops, internet cafés, trendy bars and banks. It's bustling, vibrant and loud, and I love it!

NIGHT LIFE

The nightlife in Leicester is excellent and varied. As well as the big clubs such as **Liquid** and **Zanzibar**, it has a variety of smaller late night clubs like **The Basement** or **Esko** for those who like to party until the early hours. There are also lots of alternative clubs, many with student nights such as **Mosh**, **Fan Club** and **Leicester Square**. The West End, close to De Montfort University, is an up-and-coming area filled with trendy cafés and cool bars. And of course both student unions are popular venues with legendary nights such as *Kinky* at DSU and LUSU's *Red Leicester*. For gigs, **The Charlotte** is the place to go. It's dingy and can get extremely hot, but is the perfect place to see the latest bands and get sweaty in the moshpit.

ART CULTURE

Leicester City Council is investing heavily in the arts and creating a cultural quarter with a new theatre and art-house cinema. Currently, cultural needs are catered for by various galleries, museums and theatres throughout the city. Leicester also hosts one of the UK's largest comedy festivals each February. This hugely successful festival started as a student project at DMU.

There are other festivals throughout the year, including the Summer Sundae - Leicester's answer to Glastonbury, the lively Afro-Caribbean festival and many religious festivals. It also hosts the largest Diwali celebration outside of India and it's really worth heading down to; as well as a whole area lit up with decorations and pretty lights there is also a magnificent fireworks display.

SHOPPING

The city has all the usual high street stores. Most important for students is the recent addition of a huge **Primark**. For those who want something unique, check out the **Leicester Lanes**. They aren't the equal of Brighton's Lanes, but they are filled with boutiques and independent shops, and are perfect for picking up something different.

There are big supermarkets close to both universities, but for bargains there is no better place then the Leicester market, the largest covered market in Europe. Where else can you buy 10 apples for a £1?

Nikki Slawson

UNIVERSITY OF LEICESTER

The University of Leicester
Mayors Walk
University Road
Leicester LE1 7RH

TEL 0116 252 2674
FAX 0116 252 5127
EMAIL study@le.ac.uk
WEB www.le.ac.uk

Leicester Students' Union
Percy Gee Building
University Road
Leicester LE1 7RH

TEL 0116 223 1111
FAX 0116 223 1112
EMAIL [code]@le.ac.uk
WEB www.leicesterstudent.org

VAG VIEW

For successive years, Leicester has been shortlisted for the prize of University of the Year by the Times Higher Education Supplement *- the only university to have been so. Even more significantly, a recent survey by* NME *placed it in the top 5 unis for social life. We say it's a very good deal - small, perfectly formed and only the 30th hardest to get into, with its tip-top medical school operating a 13% acceptance rate, while the national average is 10%.*

The proof of the deal is in its drop-out rate - fifth least embarrassing in the country, and in its soaring undergraduate applications - up 12% this year.

A £300-million development plan is investing in new facilities, including a library, twice the size of the present one, which will be ready in 2008.

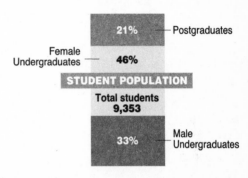

Female Undergraduates — 46%
Postgraduates — 21%
STUDENT POPULATION
Total students 9,353
Male Undergraduates — 33%

CAMPUS

'The main university campus is situated close to the city centre and within walking distance of all university halls of residence,' writes Christina McGear. 'But, unlike many inner city universities, everything you need is situated on campus including banks, restaurants, cafés, shops, the university library and union. This means that you never have far to walk between lectures.'

FEES, BURSARIES

UK & Eu Fees 2007: £3,070. Fees not yet fixed for 2008. Usual sliding-scale bursaries for those eligible for HE Maintenance Grant. See www.le.ac.uk/fees. Sport bursaries are awarded on merit; see su-sportspresident@leicester.ac.uk. A scholarship of £1,000 is available to new students who achieve ABB at A level including AVCE (best 3 A levels, excluding General Studies), 36 points in the IB, if you enter certain specified departments. Free musical tuition is available to first year students with Grade VII -

VIII, and Leicester Cathedral, in association with the University, offers choral scholarships.

STUDENT PROFILE

Student type? They'll tell you many are from the Southeast – which is true, with a number from independent schools, good, white middle-class kids – and then they'll admit that there's a huge contingent from Wales. Why Wales? Because Leicester is far enough from Wales to make you feel like you are away and yet not too far for discomfort. And maybe that's as much of the truth as you are likely to get. For Leicester is the choice of students from more than 100 countries and has always been convenient to a wide cross-section of UK journeymen, including a large number from public schools.

ACADEMIA & JOBS

With 82% of their teaching assessments either Excellent or scoring 18+ out of 24, Leicester's teaching record is first class and backed by an annual £3 million spend in the university library, a Student Learning Centre with workshops and self-learning materials designed to develop study skills and a well-equipped Language Centre supporting the uni's policy of 'languages for all'.

There are five faculties – Arts, Law, Medicine, Science, Social Sciences. Top teaching assessments are in Economics, Sport, Psychology, Physics, Politics, History of Art, Maths, and Biosciences. They are widely targeted by employers. An on-

SUBJECT AREAS (%)

Humanities — Education   Combined   Medicine

Media —

Languages — 9   2   9   1   9   Health Subjects 0.5%

9   7

3   13

29   8

5   6   Biological Sciences

Business

Social Studies   Engineering/   Maths &   Physical
incl. Law   Technology   Computer   Sciences

line database keeps all students up to date with the latest job vacancies

The Faculty of Medicine, which, with Physics and American Studies, clocked 23 out of a maximum 24 points on inspection and has a 13% application acceptance rate (which is soft) would be a jewel in anyone's crown, and was one of three medical schools given the go-ahead to form new joint schools with other universities. Leicester's partner is Warwick. Part of the deal is a fast track medical degree for biological sciences graduates.

The 4/5-year MB ChB is in fact the backbone of Leicester's curriculum in terms of graduate employment. The civil service (chiefly from social studies, languages and humanities), education, finance, accountancy and computing make a showing, but medicine is far and away the most stable element of their employment profile. Entry requirements are four AS levels in first year, including Chemistry and Biology, excluding General Studies. Three A levels at AAB + UKCAT, including Chemistry, excluding General Studies. GCSE English Lang and sciences.

The uni also has a world-class genetics research record – it was here that genetic fingerprinting was first developed. The career pathways of biological science graduates from Leicester are various, but in a given year 15% or so (the biggest proportion of the department) become biochemists, medical scientists, biological scientists or biochemists. Another strength in research is Pharmacology.

There is also a particular reputation in the fields of physics and astronomy, and they claim the largest uni-based space research centre in Europe. The Beagle 2 Mars Probe, the UK's first mission to another planet, had its Operation Control Centre at Leicester. There is a Space Research and Multi-disciplinary Modelling Centre.

Look at the BSc/MPhys degrees like Physics with Space Science & Technology; Physics with Planetary Science; Physics with Astrophysics. They scored 23 points and an international Grade 5 for research

Computer operators, software engineers, IT consultants and systems analysts flow in a steady stream from Leicester, and there is an impressive looking series of Electronic & Software Engineering degrees, again with a year out in USA.

They are an employment leader in Archaeology. BA degrees only are available, though you can take BSc Geography. The department scored full marks in the teaching assessments. Research Grade 5. Geography is also hot at Leicester, BA and Bsc degrees, and links with History or Geology as well as Archaeology. Some graduates become accountants, but theirs are nothing like the bullish figures in this area that you get from Birmingham, Warwick, Durham, Sheffield, Manchester, Leeds, etc, and there are no named accountancy courses. Instead, there are BA and BSc Financial Economics and Business Economics degrees and a range of interesting Maths degrees, such as the 4-year Maths with Computer Science. There are placements in Europe and USA, as well as matches with Management, on the one hand, and Astronomy on the other.

Finally, there's an interesting law provision, for which they have another international Grade 5

> *Student type? They'll tell you many are from the southeast – which is true, with a number from independent schools, good, white middle-class kids – and then they'll admit that there's a huge contingent from Wales. Why Wales?*

UNIVERSITY/STUDENT PROFILE

University since	**1957**
Situation/style	**City campus**
Student population	**9353**
Undergraduates	**7426**
- mature	**14%**
- non EU undergraduates	**15%**
- male/female	**42/58**
- non-traditional student intake	**26%**
- state school intake	**88%**
- drop-out rate	**4%**
- undergraduate applications	**Up 12%**

for research; they are specialists in French law. Explore the difference between English & French Law (LlB/Maitrise) and Law with French Law and Language. The latter lasts four years.

SOCIAL SCENE

When the house scene was in its infancy their *High Spirits* club night travelled to **Es Paradis** in Ibiza, to the **Queen Club** in Paris and the **Venue** in Jersey. There must have been some energy around in the student union those days. Even today, Leicester maintains a full-time, non-student ents manager with two assistants, though, along with student taste, the focus has shifted.

Union ents happen at the **Venue**, at modern, minimalist **Element** and the **Redfearn** pub. As we write, the Arctic Monkeys have just appeared at the Venue, which gives you a level of what goes down.

Element is the premier bar/club for regular ents. Tuesday Nights their *Global* event showcases world music and cultures; Thursday is 60s and 70s night *Shampoo*.

There's a Monday contract with **Zanzibar** in town (*SHAG*). The best way to warm up for itis with a few drinks at the 'fearn, the 'hub' of student life. Then, on Tuesday, after the Pool Competition there's the Clever Fokker Quiz.

The most popular union night they claim they've ever had is Wednesday's night, *Red Leicester*, which takes place in the Venue, '80s classics from Bon-Jovi to Brian Adams. *Madfer-It* is Friday's big deal, which takes over the entire building. Saturday is *Brighton Beach* – mods, rockers, pills and '60s sun, sea and sand...a chance for Leicester's perpetually drunk undergrads to escape the endless hell of '80s cheese and '90s pop. Actually, it's Room one classic soul, '60s, RnB and the newest guitar sounds. Room two has 60s Soul, Northern, Jazz & Freakbeat. There are also many special events.

There are around 100 societies and endless sports clubs (30), the former divided into 'academic, campaigning, performance, recreational, religious and cultural) to join,' writes Christine.'

Leicester University Theatre (LUT) is one of the largest and most active societies, the theatre has

ACADEMIC EXCELLENCE	
TEACHING :	
(Rated Excellent or 17+ out of 24)	
History, Law, Chemistry, English.	**Excellent**
Economics, Leisure & Sport, Psychology, Archaeology, Education	**24**
Physics, Politics, Medicine, American Studies	**23**
History of Art, Maths, Biosciences	**22**
German, Communications/Media	**21**
Italian, General Engineering	**20**
Sociology, French	**19**
RESEARCH:	
Genetics,	**Grade 5***
Pharmacology, Biochemistry, Biology, Physics, Pure Maths, Applied Maths, General Eng, Law, Economics, English, Archaeology, History	**Grade 5**

become recognised throughout the Midlands as a breeding ground for young talent, with many members finding employment after graduation. There's a good campaigning arm and lively media – *Ripple* is the newspaper, Lush FM the radio station. LUST, the TV, took the Light Entertainment Award at the national media awards last year.

SPORT is big, though local competition is with Nottingham rather than international-level Loughborough, and developments are now afoot to lock horns more meaningfully with De Montfort University. There's a sports hall, Greenhouse 1, in the Charles Wilson Building on campus, and new rugby, lacrosse and football pitches at Stoughton Road, east of campus, close to Manor Road Sports Centre (Greenhouse 2) and halls.

TOWN See *Student Leicester*, page 280.

WHERE LEICESTER GRADUATES END UP
Health & Social Work: 20%; Education: 8%; Wholesale Retail: 8%; Manufacturing: 7%; Financial Activities: 12%; Public Administration, Civil Service & Defence: 11%; Hotel/Restaurant: 2.5%; Transport & Communications (including Telecommunications): 4%; Construction: 1%; Personnel: 5%; Computer: 2.5%; Business & Management: 1.5%; Accountancy: 3.5%; Media (including Film): 1%; Legal 2%; Architecture: 0.5%; Publishing: 2%.
Approximate 'graduate track' employed **66%**

PILLOW TALK

'All halls are within walking distance,' writes Christine, 'and are served regularly by the number 80 bus. Beaumont Hall in Oadby is one of the most attractive, set amongst beautiful botanical gardens.'

New Hall opened in 2006, the largest of all halls , with 581 en-suite catered rooms in flats for 4 and 5 students with a lounge/kitchen.

GETTING THERE

☛ By road: M1/J21 or J22. Good coach services.
☛ By rail: London St Pancras, 1:20; Manchester Piccadilly, 1:30; Sheffield, 1:30; Birmingham New Street, 1:00; Nottingham, 0:30.
☛ By air: Bus from Birmingham International and East Midlands International Airports.
☛ By coach: London, 2:30; Leeds, 3:00; Cardiff, 4:10.

AT A GLANCE

ACADEMIC FILE:

Subjects assessed	**28**
Excellent	**82%**
Typical entry requirements	**352 points**
Application acceptance rate	**16%**
Med. School acceptance rate	**13%**
Students-staff ratio	**17:1**
First/2:1 degree pass rate	**64%**

ACCOMMODATION FILE:

Guarantee to freshers	**100%**
Style	**Halls, houses**
Catered	**51%**
En suite	**N/A**
Approx price range	**£64-£128**
City rent pw	**£50+**

WHAT IT'S REALLY LIKE

UNIVERSITY:

Social Life	★★★★★
Campus scene	**Lively, traditional, excellent vibes**
Student Union services	**Good**
Politics	**Involved**
Sport	**30 clubs**
National team position	**76th**
Sport facilities	**Good**
Arts opportunities	**All excellent**
Student newspaper	**Ripple**
Student radio	**LUSH FM**
Student TV	**LUST**
Student Media Awards	**2006 winner**
Nightclub	**Element**
Bars	**Redfearn**
Venue	**Venue**
Union ents	**Red Leicester, Madfer it, Brighton Beach**
Union societies	**100**
Parking	**Poor**

CITY:

Leicester Nightlife	★★★★★
City scene	**Top town - clubs, pubs, curries**
Town/gown relations	**OK**
Risk of violence	**Average**
Cost of living	**Average**
Student concessions	**Good**
Survival + 2 nights out	**£70 pw**
Part-time work campus/town	**Excellent**

UNIVERSITY OF LINCOLN

The University of Lincoln
Brayford Pool
Lincoln LN6 7TS

TEL 01522 882000
FAX 01522 886041
EMAIL enquiries@lincoln.ac.uk
WEB www.lincoln.ac.uk

Lincoln Students' Union
Brayford Pool
Lincoln LN6 7TS

TEL 01522 886006
FAX 01522 882088
EMAIL (see website)
WEB www.lincoln.ac.uk

VAG VIEW

*L*incoln has arrived. No-one can remember Humberside University or the fact that Hull was once its main base; and the bandwaggon still keeps rolling on.

The university has invested over £100 million in its Brayford Pool campus in the heart of Lincoln - new library, performing arts centre, a media and technology enterprise centre - and now they have converted a former railway engine shed into a £6-million stu-

dent union that looks set to make the Lincoln experience complete. The Engine Shed, as it is called, is, with a capacity of 1,500, one of the biggest concert venues in the East Midlands, and all extra-curricular student activities will be focused here too.

The 14% increase in applications suggests that locals in particular like what they see happening. However, the 26:1 students-to-staff ratio is one of the worst in the country and the 45% graduate track employment record suggests that money won't buy everything, or at least has not done so yet.

CAMPUS

Brayford Pool Campus is situated on the riverside in this picturesque cathedral city. It's pretty impressive, although, reports Paula McManus, 'sometimes it feels more like an airport or shopping centre than a university: security guards are constantly on patrol to stop any damage being done to this sparkling new building.' How can they win!

A city-centre **Hull Campus** retains illustration, graphics, social work and community studies degrees, as well as computer games, animation and TV and film design and media technology degrees.

The agriculture and equine provision (once part of De Montfort Uni) is at the 1,000-acre **Riseholme Park Campus**, near Lincoln, while Lincoln's Art & Design is at the old pre-uni college site in the city.

FEES. BURSARIES

UK & EU Fees, 2007: £3,000. Fees for 2008 not yet fixed. There's a £600 p.a. bursary for students in receipt of the full HE Maintenance grant, and a pro-rata bursary for those in receipt of a partial grant.

A £500 scholarship will be available to all enrolling students for each completed year of their course.

STUDENT PROFILE

Recruitment has been successful among social groups that do not traditionally consider university. More than a third of undergraduate entrants come from the middle to lower end of the social spectrum and from new-to-uni social groups. Many are mature; few from the public school sector.

ACADEMIA & JOBS

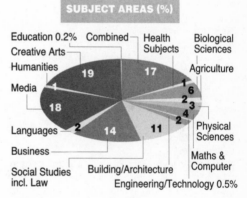

Particular strengths, or niche areas, lie in media production, social policy, animal behaviour, journalism, graphic design, politics, forensic science and architecture.

The Lincoln Business School, the Lincoln School of Architecture and the Institute of Medical Sciences were launched as recently as 2003, yet they are now heavily subscribed, firm fixtures.

They were joined by the Lincoln School of Journalism in 2004, and this year a New School of Performing Arts comes on stream in the new Centre for Performing Arts.

Language and cultural experience is an integral part of the academic recipe. Study abroad arrangements are made in Europe and Australia; formal exchange arrangements are made with sixty-two

UNIVERSITY/STUDENT PROFILE	
University since	**1992**
Situation/style	**City campus**
Student population	**9846**
Undergraduates	**8984**
- mature	**49%**
- non EU undergraduates	**2%**
- male/female	**40/60**
- non-traditional student intake	**37%**
- state school intake	**98%**
- drop-out rate	**19%**
- undergraduate applications	**Up 14%**

ACADEMIC EXCELLENCE

TEACHING :
(Rated Excellent or 17+ out of 24)

Education	**24**
Politics	**22**
Tourism, Health Studies, Psychology	**21**
Food Science, Art & Design	**20**
Agric/Agricultural Sciences	**19**
Engineering (E & E, General, Mechanical, Aeronautical)	**18**

RESEARCH :
Top grades 5/5* **None**

EU universities or colleges; 25% of first degree students take a language as part of their course and 15% spend six months or more abroad.

In the health faculty, Lincoln have teamed up with Nottingham to offer a certificate in health science to students from poor or deprived backgrounds who want to go on to study medicine at Nottingham. This is an amazing opportunity to study at one of the best med. schools in the country. £1,025 p.a. bursary is available to students joining the University of Nottingham through the scheme.

Prospective animal health technicians should also be aware that Lincoln lead in this field, too, followed by Bristol West of England, Aberystwyth and Leeds. Since taking on De Montfort's Lincoln-based agric. operation, they have become a place to watch in this sector.

They also offer a sure track for probation officers through their Criminology degrees, which ties up interestingly with anything from Psychology to Journalism to Forensic Science.

But what's really causing ripples is the art and media provision, the degrees in Animation, Games Design, Architecture, Fine Art, Graphic Design (including design for TV and film), Illustration, Interactive Design, Fashion, Interior Design, Museum/Exhibition Design, Journalism, Media Technology and Media Production (aimed at producing writers and producers), and many others. It really is worth taking the time to look. Phonic Art (a sound-based fine art course), alas, did not stay the distance, but there's a BSc Audio Technology up at Hull, which seems much well placed.

These, and other degrees like them, are responsible for a whole lot of employment niches – such as TV and film industries, radio, architecture, advertising and industrial design.

Look especially at the Lincoln-based Advertising degrees – art direction, fashion, illustration, which will impact heavily on their employment figures. Also, the School of Architecture is going from strength to strength in its £10 million building, designed by Rick Mather for the purpose.

Again, Lincoln's BA Public Relations is clearly adding to its employment success in this artistic area. And the modular degree adjunct Media Culture & Communications leads the way for a host of students in the BA/BSc Joint Honours School. All this may well, with the health provision, be the making of Lincoln. Note, the media, art and design is a split provision, some on the George Street Hull Campus (animation, TV & film, games design, etc).

> *Particular strengths, or niche areas, are Social Work, Journalism, Media and Human Resource Management*

The BA Hons Journalism, now well established in the Top 10 media lists, is worth dwelling on. It covers print, internet, radio and TV and helped capture 4% of the graduate employment market last time. There is also a host of BA/BSc Journalism tie-ups with Politics or Public Relations. See, too, their Media and Multimedia Production courses – would-be printers and publishing production manager are lining up for them.

Finally, a series of sports degrees – one, Sport & Exercise Science, is being developed with nearby Lincoln College. Another is neatly specific, Sports Development & Coaching.

WHERE LINCOLN GRADUATES END UP

Health & Social Work: 11%; Education: 8%; Wholesale Retail: 13%; Manufacturing: 13%; Financial Activities: 7%; Public Administration, Civil Service & Defence: 7%; Hotel/Restaurant: 3%; Transport & Communications (including Telecommunications): 7%; Construction: 1%; Agriculture: 1%; Personnel: 6%; Computer: 3%; Accountancy: 1%; Media (including Film): 5%; Legal 4%; Architecture: 1%; Publishing: 1.5%; Advertising: 1%; Artistic/Literary: 1%; Sport: 0.5%.

Approximate 'graduate track' employed **48%**

WHAT IT'S REALLY LIKE

UNIVERSITY:

Social Life	★★★
Campus scene	**Expanding, diversifying**
Student Union services	**Good**
Politics	**Student issues**
Sport	**Good, 12 clubs**
National team position	**78th**
Sport facilities	**OK**
Arts opportunities	**Film OK**
Student magazine	**Bullet**
Student newspaper	**The Linc**
Student radio	**Siren**
Venue	**Engine Sheds**
Bars	**Tower, Sport, Pod**
Union ents	**Cheese**
Union societies	**62**
Most active society	**International, Equine, Drama**
Parking	**Poor**

CITY:

Entertainment	★★-★★★
Scene	**Good pubs; average clubs**
Town/gown relations	**Average**
Risk of violence	**Low**
Cost of living	**Average**
Student concessions	**Average**
Survival + 2 nights out	**£50 pw**
Part-time work campus/town	**Average/good**

SOCIAL SCENE

STUDENTS' UNION The Engine Shed is the 1,500-capacity night club and live music venue. Within are a main room for live music and club events and 3 bars - **the Tower**, **Sport Bar** and **Pod Bar**. Regular club/disco nights include Wednesday night's *Fever Pitch* (the official Athletic Union club night), featuring a range of DJ's and regular themed events and guest appearances, like Ralf Little, Outhere Brothers and Roy Walker. *Saturday Essential* is the funky weekend club night. Live bands this year have included The Zutons, Ocean Colour Scene, Embrace, The Babyshamles, Dirty Pretty Things and the Kings of Leon.

The building is also home to the SU and a shop, and will soon house a job shop, activities centre and book shop. They claim to have 62 societies up and running, and 12 sports clubs, some with up to 70 members.

The student mag is *Bullet Magazine*, newspaper *The Linc*, student radio station Siren Radio. Among the most active student societies are ACS, International Students, Equine, and Drama.

SPORT There's a Sports Centre with pitches and a gym. Five years ago a student could say, 'We are not major contenders yet against other universities.' Not so now. They have good sports teams for their size, coming 78th out of well over 100 nationally. Golf and football are specialities and badminton, volleyball and rugby made their way commendably in the direction of finals. 'Our Volleyball Team,' they tell us, 'is made up predominantly of International players from Germany and Sweden.'

TOWN Think of the city of Lincoln, doesn't it remind you of Canterbury or York, both highly successful olde worlde cathedral seats of learning? To fresher Caroline Stocks, when she first set eyes on it, the place seemed promising if rather sedate: 'It's easy to see why so many pensioners flock to Lincoln during the summer, or why the annual Derby-and-Joan Christmas outing is to the town's festive market. There's the

AT A GLANCE

ACADEMIC FILE:

Assessments	**20**
Excellent	**45%**
Typical entry requirements	**249 points**
Application acceptance rate	**27%**
Students-staff ratio	**26:1**
First/2:1 degree pass rate	**49%**

ACCOMMODATION FILE:

Guarantee to freshers	**None**
Style	**Halls, flats**
Catered	**12%**
En-suite	**90%**
Price range pw	**£77-£129**
City rent pw	**£60-£75**

majestic cathedral and ancient castle, which sit on a hill overlooking the town, with its tiny old shops on cobbled streets. There are the visitors who stroll along the castle ramparts before taking a look at the 19th-century prison museum. There's the Brayford Pool, where swans paddle lazily, pausing only to let pleasure boats or brightly painted barges pass. And overlooking this pool...there are the university buildings...very modern.

'Basically, Lincoln is a safe, quiet town; perfect if you don't want to be in the centre of the action.'

The campus and all the bars/clubs are right in the middle of the city, based round the Waterfront - you won't use a taxi while in Lincoln, everything is central. The bars do great promotions - Double

Vodka red Bull £1.75; food - £20 - two nights out £25 at the most.

For a cheesy night there are plenty of bars and clubs based around the Brayford Pool, right next to campus, including a **Scream** nightclub. Many find this a great spot to sit outside in the summer, enjoy the atmosphere and watch the boats pass by.

Visiting Nottingham for a night out is possible. Lincoln has no motorways, but you can meander round the country roads to Newark, Sheffield, or indeed Skeggie for a day by the sea.

PILLOW TALK

No guarantee of university accommodation, but they undertake to ensure that all students are found suitable accommodation. There are approximately 3,000 rooms in high-quality purpose-built private student residences just off campus. Private developments near campus include The Junxion (569), Brayford Court (86), Brayford Quays (330), Hayes Wharf (224), The Pavilions (1,022 completed, 1,250 to come in total).

GETTING THERE

☛ By road: from north, A15; northwest, A57, A46 Lincoln by-pass.
☛ By rail: King's Cross, 2:00; Nottingham, 1:00.
☛ By coach: London, 4:10.

STUDENT LIVERPOOL – THE CITY

Visitors to Liverpool are constantly amazed by the rich tapestry of theatres, concert halls, museums, galleries, bars, shops and restaurants which the city centre has to offer. Liverpool also offers an abundance of parks and gardens, including Sefton Park with its beautifully restored Palm House. A short ferry journey across the Mersey will take you to the more rural surroundings of the Wirral.

The city celebrates its 800th Birthday in 2007 and becomes European Capital of Culture in 2008 with the special theme of *Performance* to highlight iys cultural and sporting achievements. As the birthplace of The Beatles, Liverpool is renowned for its musical talents. The *Mathew Street Festival*, *Liverpool Summer Pops* and *Creamfields* are some of the annual music events which take place around the city, with The Royal Liverpool Philharmonic Orchestra providing classical music performances throughout the year.

All three universities will be playing their part in this, as will cultural institutions like the **Playhouse** and **Everyman** theatres, **The Tate** and **Bluecoat** art galleries, the 4th Liverpool Biennial, The Royal Liverpool Philharmonic Society, FACT, the **European Opera Centre** and numerous smaller galleries and theatre companies, several of which are run by Liverpool graduates.

The city's thriving alternative student scene is clustered around three main epicentres: the city centre, Lark Lane and Penny Lane/Smithdown Road. Here's a whistle-stop guide to some of the hidden gems.

STAR PUB

Despite being part of the *It's a Scream* chain of pubs, the **Brookhouse** (Smithdown Road) is one of Liverpool's most popular student pubs, due to its proximity to the centre of student population. **Kelly's**, again on Smithdown, is a regular haunt for second and third years. **The Caledonia** on Catherine Street is always good for a few pints. Most decent nights have a pre-party here. **The Pilgrim** in Pilgrim Street offers cheap beer and passable Sunday lunch fare. It's quiet, safe and pleasant – a good place to chill the morning after the night before. Lark Lane's **Albert Hotel** is a busy, smoky student local with a friendly atmosphere and good draught beers.

STAR BAR

L'agos (or Lago's) is by far the star bar. Trendy decor, wonderfully cheap drinks, soulful music and a good mix of students and locals. **The Magnet** on Hardman Street co-exists with a restaurant, club and a vintage clothing shop. The food not always the best but the atmosphere is always brilliant, and the club is home to some very popular nights. **Hannah's Bar** on Hardman Street has an unpretentious atmosphere, live music or DJs most evenings and good looking bar staff. Fleet Street's **Rocomodo's** (**Modo's**) is suave and modern. It serves posh cocktails at decent prices, is often filled with beautiful people and opens until 2. Also in Fleet Street, is **Baa Bar**, which serves £1 cocktails called 'shooters' and is a common first stop on nights out in the city centre. **The Penny Lane Wine Bar** is friendly and small, with a good summer beer garden.

STAR EATERY

The new **Bluu Bar**, often with big queues (only a good thing?) has really tasty food, with a laid back atmosphere, leather sofas, perfect for a swish lunch.

The **Everyman Bistro** on Hope Street is attached to the famous theatre set up by graduates of the Liverpool Uni in the 1960s. At moderate prices the food is healthy, well presented and often veggie friendly. The adjacent bar was one of the first places in Liverpool to stock the legendary spirit absinthe – scourge of the Romantics and very trendy. **The Tavern Company** on Smithdown Road is a superb Mexican restaurant loved by students and parents alike. **Maranto's** (Lark Lane) is a large restaurant with a huge bar serving good, moderately priced international cuisine. More expensive is nearby **Viva**, but well worth it as a treat (or when the parents are in town). Best take-away in Liverpool is Smithdown Road's little-known **Pizza Parlour** – authentic pizzas at decent prices, with wine or Italian beer to drink at the counter while your order is prepared.

CLUBS

If it's clubbing you want then Liverpool is the place to come. **Cool Seel Street club The Masque was** started by 3 students 6 years ago and is intensely popular, full of beautiful people and attracts the biggest DJs around. It has won *Mixmag's* Club of the Year award.

Cream @ **Nation**? A distant memory... Today, **Nation** hosts *Bugged Out* on a Saturday, and the raucously fabulous student night *Medication* on a Wednesday (probably what it's most well known for now), as well as the drum 'n' bass fest *X*.

But the people behind Cream are back in a lounge bar/restaurant, **Baby Cream**, at Albert Dock.

At the other end of the spectrum is Tuesday night **The Blue Angel** (108 Seel Street) – 'even Johnny Vegas could pull here,' says Itchy. **The Raz,** as it is affectionately known, is Liverpool's cheesiest student dive, but alumni look back with tender memories – 'Best chat up line from a very pissed Welshman:' says Lotty. "I saw you coming down the stairs and I thought you were a vision of loveliness" – I did snog him and my mate snogged him the week after! Happy days...' Others can't imagine why you don't go looking for somethiung finer, like **Le Bateau** on Duke Street, known for its indie.

Look, too, at **L2** (The Lomax) for live and alternative dance nights, **Krazy Horse** for indie and hard rock, **Cavern Club** for Beatles nostalgia. Another outstanding club is the gay friendly **Garlands** (Eberle Street), also a winner of *Mixmag's Club of the Year Award*. Temporarily, **The State** is home to Garland's nights. Meanwhile, Monday's student night is *Double Vision* at **The Guild of Students**, Saturday's is *Time Tunnel* (city centre).

SHOPS

The one shop students couldn't live without is **WRC** (West World Retail Corp.) on Bold Street. For labels and good trainers for boys and girls visit **Open** (city centre) and **Drome** women (sorry lads). Hardman Street's **Bulletproof** is a good retailer of pretty much passé '70s clothing; it sells clothes by weight. Slater Street's **Liverpool Palace** and School Lane's **Quiggins** are *pot pourris* of student goods and services – from tatooists to African art. The University of Liverpool's *Monday Market* taps the same market for books, wall hangings and plants, but some stallholders provide products as diverse as PCs and collector's items.

THEATRE & MOUTH ART

The Everyman, Hope Street, is one of the most student-friendly venues around, is known for giving local writers a break, and has started the careers of several big-name Liverpudlian actors, like Pete Postlethwaite and Julie Walters. The more 'street level' **Unity Theatre** nearby does workshops and alternative theatre experiences. Currently, Hanover Street's **Neptune** is a cosy venue favoured by touring shows and comedy acts. **The Egg Café** (Newington, top floor) has bags of atmosphere and features open floor slots for local poets. **The Everyman Bistro** hosts the Dead Good Poets Society, a collective of performance poets, twice a month.

FILM, MUSIC & COMEDY

The new **FACT** centre – a gateway to the city's **Ropewalks** development, which is regenerating a sadly neglected area of the city – is an arts complex showing a wide range of films from quality blockbusters to the most obscure Eastern European cinema as well as media exhibitions and art installations. There are a few good chain cinemas on London Road, Switch Island and Edge Lane. **The Philharmonic**, Hope Street, shows a series of classic films on its unique raising screen, with its traditional cinema organist.

Probably the two best venues for live music are **Liverpool Academy** at the University and **The Picket** (Hardman Street). The former has three venues with the largest having a 2,000+ capacity and has played host to many big names including Coldplay, Groove Armada, The Hives, Faithless. **The Picket** is famed for showcasing loads of local bands, but at present is under threat of closure.

The Rawhide Comedy Club at **Blue Bar** (the Docks) specialise in the field – essential to book ahead. With the **Everyman** they stage mainly established comedians. Sniggers Comedy at the Guild of Students hosts some decent comedians.

VISUAL ART

The Tate Gallery on Albert Dock has 3 floors featuring major touring exhibitions. **The Walker Gallery** (William Brown Street) offers traditional fare. Liverpool Uni has a small gallery by Abercromby Square. **The Open Eye** (Wood Street) exhibits touring photographic shows. Seek out also a plethora of little-known galleries, like the **Bluecoat Chambers** (School Lane).

Anne Fuell

UNIVERSITY OF LIVERPOOL

The University of Liverpool
Student Services Centre
150 Mount Pleasant
Liverpool L69 3GD

TEL 0151 794 5927
FAX 0151 794 2060
EMAIL ugrecruitment@liv.ac.uk
WEB www.liv.ac.uk

Liverpool Guild of Students
PO Box 187
160 Mount Pleasant
Liverpool L69 7BR

TEL 0151 794 6868
FAX 0151 794 4174
EMAIL guildcomms@liv.ac.uk
WEB www.guildofstudents.com

VAG VIEW

*E*stablished *in 1881, this is the original redbrick university, a great big bustling traditional university, which far from feeling a need to keep up with the times seems somehow to absorb modern exigencies and move at its own pace.*

Liverpool is a well-balanced university. They meet their Government benchmarks for widening participation in higher ed. with ease (and oddly they are not too testing), there are rising applications year on year, lowish average points requirement for a top uni, a healthy staff to student ratio (1:17), a low drop-out rate, and a good chance of a graduate track job at the end. That you'll have an excellent time here goes without saying, but don't expect all mod cons.

SUBJECT AREAS (%)

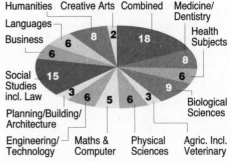

UNIVERSITY/STUDENT PROFILE	
University since	**1881**
Situation/style	**Civic**
Student population	**21210**
Undergraduates	**16905**
- mature	**16%**
- non EU undergraduates	**7%**
- male/female	**47/53**
- non-traditional student intake	**24%**
- state school intake	**85%**
- drop-out rate	**7%**
- undergraduate applications	**Up 11%**

CAMPUS

The campus **Precinct** is a few mins walk from the centre of this city, famous for football, the Beatles and the Mersey ferry. With Liverpool Uni, John Moores, and Liverpool Hope, this same city is now, also, one of the major centres of higher education in Britain - home to three universities.

FEES, BURSARIES

UK & EU Fees, 2007: £3,070 p.a. Bursaries of £1,350 if in receipt of full HE Maintenance grant; £1,000 if in receipt of partial grant. The University is committing £6 million each year to support significant numbers of students through substantial bursaries and scholarships. Up to 10 Alumni Scholarships of £2,000 are available on the basis of academic excellence. Attainment scholarships are available if studying: Aerospace Eng, Avionic Systems, Biomaterials Eng, Materials Science Eng, Mechanical & Manufacturing Eng, Medical

Female Undergraduates — 44%

Postgraduates — 20%

STUDENT POPULATION
Total students 21,210

Male Undergraduates — 36%

Electronics, Mechatronics, Civil Eng, Electrical Eng & Electronics, Chemistry, Physics, Computer Science, Earth & Ocean Sciences. See www.liv.ac.uk/study/undergraduate/attainment_scholarships.htm

There's an Access to Learning Fund for those in financial need, of between £100 and £3,500, which may change. See www.liv.ac.uk/studentsupport/finance/access_to_learning

STUDENT PROFILE

Liverpool Uni is popular with state and public school kids and students from a whole range of backgrounds. The perennially low drop-out rate (7%) shows that everyone's having a good time.

ACADEMIA & JOBS

Medicine, Philosophy, Physics, Veterinary, Town/Country Planning, Maths, Anatomy, Politics & Media, and Management are the top scorers, and for research, it's Physiology, and Engineering.

Faculties include Arts, Engineering, Law, Medicine & Dentistry, Science, Social & Environmental Studies, and Veterinary Science. There are some interesting inter-faculty combos, such as Maths & Philosophy.

Within Social & Environmental faculty lie accounting and economics (BA and BSc) degrees. Liverpool is highly productive career-wise in this area Around 9% of their graduates go into the financial sector, most popular avenue after Health and Manufacturing. Economics scored 22 points at the assessments.

Health soaks up not far short of 30% graduates. Liverpool is one of four med-schools awarded 24 points (full marks) for its teaching. The others are Manchester, Newcastle and Southampton (Cardiff was Excellent on the Welsh criteria). The degree is a 4/5-year MC ChB. Clinical skills are introduced in Year 1. Entry 340-390 points - no admissions test: Chemistry + one other science + one other. There is a 11% acceptance rate, which is average.

Graduates with a 2:1 in an approved biomedical discipline or health/social care profession may apply. The course focuses particularly on the abili-

ty to use and apply information in the clinical setting. Research Grade 6*: Physiology; Grade 5: Clinical Lab Sciences and Biological Sciences.

Dentists go for the 5-year BDS – entry 360 points; teaching inspection, 21 points. Vets meanwhile opt for the 5-year BVSc, which requires relevant work experience. There's a 6-year BSc Intercalated Honours Year. Look also at the BSc degrees: Bioveterinary Science and Veterinary Conservation Medicine. Teaching inspection, 24. Research Grade 5.

Liverpool has been allowed to recruit an extra 50 medical students and 32 dentistry students each year to enhance medical and dental provision in Lancashire and Cumbria. The dental students will be based at Central Lancashire University and the medical students at Lancaster University.

The uni also places quantities of educational

ACADEMIC EXCELLENCE

TEACHING:
(Rated Excellent or 17+ out of 24)

History, Law, English, Geology & Environmental Sciences.	**Excellent**
Medicine, Philosophy, Physics, Veterinary	**24**
Town/Country Planning, Maths Anatomy, Politics & Media, Management	**23**
French, Civil Eng, Psychology, Economics, Pharmacol, Nursing, Arachaeology, Classics	**22**
Iberian Studies, Sociology Materials Technology, Dentistry, Electron & Electric Eng	**21**
General, Manufacturing & Aerospace Eng, Subjects Allied to Medicine	**20**
German, Organismal Biosciences, Molecular Biosciences	**19**

RESEARCH:
Top grades 5/5/6**

Physiology	**Grade 6***
Mech/Aero/Manufacturing and Civil Engineering	**Grade 5***
Clinical Laboratory Sciences, Pharmacology, Biological Sciences, Veterinary, Chemistry, Physics, Earth Sciences, Pure Maths, Applied Maths, Computer, Electrical & Electronic Eng, Metallurgy, American Studies, English, French, German/Dutch/Scandinavian, Archaeology, History	**Grade 5**

psychologists in work – there are four BSc degrees with a 22 out of 24 points rating. There are healthy employment stats, too, for the degrees in Diagnostic Radiography, Radiotherapy, Physiotherapy and Occupational Therapy. Nursing struggled on its first teaching assessment, but came through with 22 points in the end.

Architecture leads to Top 10 graduate employment figures, and the planning theme continues into BA Urban Regeneration & Planning and MPlanning Town & Regional Planning – all of which make their graduate would-be town planners irresistible, it seems. There's also a combined hons Environment and Planning. Entry 320 points. Teaching scored 23.

Liverpool graduates find quality jobs in the Civil Service. Law is a reliable pathway into the former, as are languages. They are European specialists in law See, too, their BA Legal & Business Studies.

Biological sciences find graduates jobs in higher education (only 19 at teaching assessment, but Grade 5 at research), also in Defence. Liverpool turns out more than most defence operatives and equipment engineers. For a career in the Royal Navy or RAF (a popular choice here), look at their Engineering Group of degree programmes, from Aerospace Engineering to Digital Signal Processing & Communications to Civil & Maritime Engineering. Teaching assessments range from 20 to 22 and there's a Grade 5* for research into Mechanical, Aeronautical and Manufacturing Engineering.

Also out of the Engineering Faculty comes a host of furniture designers to help make them the sixth biggest supplier in the country. Look at the BSc Product Design with Multimedia, and Design & Technology with Multimedia. Consider, too, the BEng Materials, Design & Manufacture. 21 points at assessment.

> *The Students' Guild has four live music venues which go by the name of* Liverpool Academy. *This is the biggest capacity venue in the city. Annually, they run in excess of 180 live music events.*

They also have a reputation for producing chemists. BSc/MChem Chemical Sciences comes with numerous combinations, such as Pharmacology, Industrial Chemistry, Industrial Management, Management, Materials Science, Oceanography or a European language. Research Grade 5.

SOCIAL SCENE

STUDENTS' GUILD The Guild has four live music venues which go by the name of **Liverpool Academy**, the biggest capacity venue in the city. Annually, they run in excess of 180 live music events. BLOC Party, Rooster, Subways, Motorhead, Texas, The Kills have all played here, as have Goldfrapp, The Coral and KT Tunstall within memory of those who tell us. They have two weekly club nights, called *Time Tunnel* (Saturday) and *Double Vision* (Monday) and the capacity for these is 2,600. In total, the Guild has nine bars, of which, **The Gilmore**, **The Liver Bar** and the **Saro Wiwa** are open throughout the day.

The student newspaper, *Liverpool Student*, like other top student city newspapers, *Leeds Student*, Manchester's *Student Direct* and *London Student*, has become a virtual passage into the media. If that's your thing, get involved. ICON is the radio station.

As elsewhere, there are all kinds of societies with which to get involved – 90 at the last count and 45 sports clubs. Among the former, the most popular are Islamic Soc, Drama, RockSoc, and LUST – that's Liverpool Uni Show Troupe.

The Guild runs LUSTI (Liverpool Uni Student Training Initiative) to train students in communication, assertiveness, time and stress management, meeting skills etc.

PULSE is a new job-centre service to help students find part-time jobs with local employers during term and more full-time during the vacations.

WHERE LIVERPOOL GRADUATES END UP

Health & Social Work: 28%; Education: 7%; Wholesale Retail: 7%; Manufacturing: 10%; Financial Activities: 9%; Public Administration, Civil Service & Defence: 8%; Hotel/Restaurant: 3%; Transport & Communications (including Telecommunications): 2%; Construction: 2%; Personnel: 4%; Computer: 2%; Business & Management: 2%; Accountancy: 3%; Media (including Film): 2%; Legal 2%; Architecture: 2%; Publishing: 2%.

Approximate 'graduate track' employed **73%**

SPORT The Sports Centre – extended in 2004 – includes swimming pool, squash courts, weight training, indoor cricket nets, climbing wall, sunbeds, facilities for aerobics, dance, trampolining. There's a hall at the gym for judo, fencing, archery, four additional squash courts, rifle and pistol range and a weights room. The main sports ground, near the halls, includes two floodlit artificial turf pitches for hockey, field sports, five rugby and six soccer pitches, four tennis courts, a lacrosse pitch, two cricket squares and two artificial wickets, bar and cafeteria. Two other grounds add a further six soccer pitches, and there's a base for climbing, walking, canoeing and field studies in Snowdonia, which accommodates eighteen.

TOWN See *Student Liverpool* page 288.

PILLOW TALK

Most first years dwell in massive catered halls (Greenbank or Carnatic) 3 miles out. All freshers who apply by August 31 are guaranteed a place. See *At A Glance* box for prices. If you're expecting luxury accommodation you'll be sorely disappointed, though the community spirit which grows up in halls like Rankin on the Carnatic site stand you in

great stead. They have bars and ents, and are linked to uni and city centre by a regular bus service.

GETTING THERE

☛ By road: M6/J21a, M62, A5080, A5047. Well served by National Express coaches.
☛ By rail: Manchester, 40 mins; Sheffield, 1:45; Leeds, Birmingham, 2:00; London King's Cross, 3:00.
☛ Liverpool airports for inland/Ireland flights.
☛ By coach: London, 5:00; Manchester, 50 mins.

WHAT IT'S REALLY LIKE	
UNIVERSITY:	
Social Life	★★★★★
Campus scene	**Great time, unpretentious, rich opportunity**
Student Union services	**Good**
Politics	**Activity high: student issues**
Sport	**45 clubs**
National team position	**41st**
Sport facilities	**Good**
Arts opportunities	**Excellent**
Student newspaper	**Liverpool Student**
Student radio	**ICON**
Nightclub venue	**Academy**
Bars	**9 bars, Gilmore, Liver Bar, Saro Wiwa...**
Union ents	**Time Tunnel, Double Vision, major live gigs**
Union societies	**90**
Most popular societies	**Islamic**
Parking	**Adequate**
CITY:	
Entertainment	★★★★★
City scene	**Fab**
Town/gown relations	**Good**
Risk of violence	**Average**
Cost of living	**Low**
Student concessions	**Excellent**
Survival + 2 nights out	**£70 pw**
Part-time work campus/town	**Good/Excellent**

AT A GLANCE	
ACADEMIC FILE:	
Subjects assessed	**37**
Excellent	**84%**
Typical entry requirements	**352 points**
Application acceptance rate	**14%**
Med. School acceptance rate	**11%**
Students-staff ratio	**16:1**
First/2:1 degree pass rate	**64%**
ACCOMMODATION FILE:	
Guarantee to freshers	**For firm acceptances**
Style	**Halls**
Catered	**60%**
En-suite	**3%**
Approx price range pw	**£69-£108**
City rent pw	**£50-£70**

LIVERPOOL HOPE UNIVERSITY

Liverpool Hope University
Hope Park
Liverpool L16 9JD

TEL 0151 291 3295
FAX 0151 291 2050
STUDENT UNION TEL 0151 291 3651
EMAIL admissions@hope.ac.uk
WEB www.hope.ac.uk

*L*iverpool Hope University has a reputation as a major provider in the field of Education, although this is anything but the whole story. For years they offered degrees in a variety of subjects, all of them awarded by Liverpool University. In those days, the Pro-rector's introduction – 'Hope is a great virtue with both sacred and secular connotations,' - sounded a bit like a sermon, and we should not be surprised, for Liverpool Hope, once the Liverpool Institute, has its roots in an ecumenical amalgamation of two colleges with religious foundations – St Katherine's, an Anglican foundation, and Notre Dame, its Roman Catholic neighbour – a union championed years ago by the then Bishop of Liverpool – the cricketing David Sheppard. In 2005, when Hope became a university, its first Vice-Chancellor, Professor Gerald John Pillay, was fittingly a theologian.

Liverpool Hope offered Liverpool University course elements, such as Theology and Religious Studies, which the it lacked. At the same time, Liverpool offered Hope top-notch facilities for its Sport, Recreation & Physical Education courses, which are still part of the syllabus today. It was a good marriage – made in heaven you might say.

But Hope was always bound to come good in its own right in these days of 'widening participation' because at the heart of its mission is a determination to make higher education more widely available, not for political correctness, but because it is an essential part of its ethos, and always has been. It was doing it already – for real.

Springing from its religious roots is a determination to provide for 'those who have hitherto not had the most distinguished or easy path to academic honours.' Foundation courses prepare students without the required grades to study a degree course. Lecturers go out into the community and preach, sorry teach, those who for one reason or another can't take up a place at Hope. They called it their 'Reach Out' degree route long before Blair's Labour called it 'out-reach'. At Everton, a £15.5-million development was set up to house Hope's community-education strategy. More recently, they developed what they call a Network of Hope, a partnership with communities further afield that would otherwise not have had such a provision. It is now possible for students to undertake full- and part-time degree level study in Hope courses at colleges within the bounds of their local communities.

Characteristic of the Hope community ethos is Urban Hope, a uni company dedicat-

UNIVERSITY/STUDENT PROFILE	
University since	**2005**
Situation/style	**Civic**
Student population	**7705**
Undergraduates	**5810**
- mature	**28%**
- non EU undergraduates	**5%**
- male/female	**30/70**
- non-traditional student intake	**39%**
- state sector intake	**97%**
- drop-out rate	**24%**
- undergraduate applications	**Up 14%**

ed to widening participation in the grandest sense. It raised £3.6 million and in 2005, in the deprived Kensington area of the city, built the award-winning Life Bank building, which accommodates a 62-place nursery, the local Sure Start project and a primary care trust, as well as accommodating courses for the local community college. Urban Hope is now building a 'community campus' nearby. It already includes a £1.6-million Sports Centre.

CAMPUS

With such an eternally optimistic agenda, how disappointing that its name comes from its situation in Hope Park, Childwall, some 3 miles from the centre of Liverpool, the original buildings of the two constituent colleges forming the basis of a campus none too exhilarating architecturally.

24% — Postgraduates

Female Undergraduates — 54%

STUDENT POPULATION

Total students 7,705

21% — Male Undergraduates

Others — 1%

This is the centre of operations, however, and where you'll find the student union HQ. Hope at Everton, a few miles away, has two Grade II Listed buildings, a hall of residence offering self-catering en-suite accommodation for 180 students and the refurbished St Francis Xavier's Church. It is well-established as one of the most important arts venues on Merseyside.

Here, students study Creative & Performing Arts subjects, Fine Art & Design, Film Studies, Dance, Drama & Theatre Studies and Music. Wholly appropriately, they share with the European Opera Centre, the Music Space Trust and The Cornerstone Gallery, with its continuous exhibition of professional art. Playwrights, artists and musicians, including Visiting Professors Willy

SUBJECT AREAS (%)

- Creative Arts
- Education
- Combined
- Humanities 16
- 7
- 5 1
- 3
- 6
- 62
- Business
- Social Studies incl. Law
- Science

Russell and John Godber, Alan Bleasdale, Julian Lloyd Webber, Joanna McGregor and ex-Beatle Stuart Sutcliffe complete the scene.

The Reach Out Community Forum ties up with such as the Everton Development Trust, the Rotunda Community Arts Centre, local churches and secondary schools. The Hope Community Youth Theatre is based here, and The Royal Liverpool Philharmonic Orchestra, the 10:10 Ensemble and youth and community choirs all practise here.

Hope is running with a strong current in this vibrant, ever evolving city, and it was rewarded first with university college status and then university status because it is running with it rather well. Numbers of applicants are leaping (up 19%), but the drop-out rate in the transformational process is also running high (16%).

FEES, BURSARIES

UK & EU Fees, 2007: £3,070 p.a. Fees not yet fixed for 2008. Bursaries of between £400 and £1,000 p.a. are available on a sliding scale accoring to parental income. Academic scholarships worth £2,000 and

£1,000 p.a. are available depending on UCAS points and £500 for applicants from partner schools and colleges are also available. See www.hope.ac.uk/studentfunds/pages/2007-08/eng/scholarship.htm

STUDENT PROFILE

Around a third of undergraduates are mature, 70% of them are female, which is apt, because its constituent colleges were both women's colleges; 25% are part time, 97% are from the state sector and 39% from the lower socio-economic classes. Many, of course, are also local. Beyond statistics, there is a spirit about the place – a relaxed, focused, community spirit – which is Hope's own, although campus can be a bit lonely at weekends.

ACADEMIA

Subjects at Liverpool Hope are grouped into four *Deaneries*: Arts & Humanities, Education, Business & Computing, and Sciences & Social Sciences. All of the undergraduate programmes are modular. There are BA and BSc single honours, BSc combined honours (major/minor), BA combined honours (major/minor), and equal weight combined honours for both BA and BSc subjects. There are also a load of 1-year Certificates in HE, the BA with

ACADEMIC EXCELLENCE	
TEACHING: *(Rated Excellent or 17+ out of 24)*	
Geography & Environmental Studies.	**Excellent**
Business	24
Theology	23
Psychology, Sociology	22
Maths, Biosciences	21
Art & Design	20
Modern Languages, American Studies, Drama & Theatre, Leisure and Sport degrees	19
RESEARCH: *Top grades 5/5**	**None**

QTS teacher training degrees, and a BDes (Design), the first year of which can be studied on the Isle of Man. Students are stimulated by the content and sympathetic delivery of the programme, and produce some imaginative work in response.

Theology is, of course, still on offer and scored 23 points at the teaching assessments and a Grade 4 at the research assessments. Business, however, scored full marks at the assessments and features in the BA single honours and widely throughout the 450 combination courses offered. There is also an

LIVERPOOL HOPE UNIVERSITY

apparently improbable course called Gaming Technology, which has in fact nothing to do with gambling, but computer games technology.

Art and Design, and performing arts – Dance, Drama & Theatre Studies, music, are a core provision at Everton, and were rewarded with a 20-point teaching assessment. From this year, staff in the music department providing tuition, recording and venue management, are to be drawn in future from the Royal Liverpool Philharmonic Orchestra.

Teacher Training focuses on primary teaching (English lang/lit, art/design, geography, history, information technology, maths, music, special needs, sport studies, religion, and a series of Advanced Study of Early Years is part of the BA Hons combined course strategy.

Among social sciences, Psychology is recommended and Sociology (both with a 22-point assessment), and clearly their Childhood & Youth Studies, Social Work, Special Needs and Pastoral Leadership programmes are central to the Hope's ethos. Note, too, the BSc Health & Fitness, Sports Psychology, Sport Studies and Sustainable Sports Management (19 points at the assessments). There is a new air-conditioned fitness suite, equipped with state-of-the-art cardiovascular and resistance equipment.

The £5.3 million Sheppard-Worlock Library houses 250,000 books, many PCs and 500 study places. There is an on-site nursery that even provides for children younger than two years, and the future prospects of both its many mature and more youthful students are encouraged by elective modules in languages and IT, and by modules which take students out into the workplace and community, both in the UK and overseas.

SOCIAL SCENE

STUDENT UNION The two student bars are **D2** (with video wall) on the ground floor of the Union, and the lounge-style **Derwent Bar** upstairs.

There is also a Union presence (and bar) at Everton. Ents are traditional fare - bands (of the

WHAT IT'S REALLY LIKE	
UNIVERSITY:	
Social Life	★★★
Campus scene	**Friendly, focused**
Student Union services	**Good**
Politics	**Caring**
Sport	**Competitive**
National team position	**73rd**
Sport facilities	**Good**
Arts opportunities	**Excellent**
Student newspaper	**Liverpool Student**
Bars	**D2, Derwent**
Union ents	**DJs, cheese, karaoke, quiz**
Union societies	**45**
Parking	**Adequate**
CITY:	
Entertainment	★★★★★
City scene	**Fab**
Town/gown relations	**Good**
Risk of violence	**Average**
Cost of living	**Low**
Student concessions	**Excellent**
Survival + 2 nights out	**£70 pw**
Part-time work campus/town	**Good/Excellent**

tribute variety), comedians (Jack Dee and Lee Evans have played here), karaoke, jazz nights, and a multitude of society thrashes. Tuesday takes students out to **The Blue Angel** in town (108 Seel Street) – 'even Johnny Vegas could pull here,' says Itchy. **The Raz,** as it is affectionately known, is Liverpool's cheesiest student dive, but alumni look back with tender memories – 'Best chat up line from a very pissed Welshman:' says Lotty. '"I saw you coming down the stairs and I thought you were a vision of loveliness" - I did snog him and my mate snogged him the week after! Happy days...'

Regular DJ Welsh Dave of the **Derwent** grooms Hope students for such antics. Wednesday is sports or societies night. 'It's always a popular night in **D2** with each team coming up with a weekly theme to get ya involved.' On Friday comes 'The WORLD Famous all day party. Music and fun throughout the day in the **Derwent** bar from 12 with Karaoke and DJ's starting at 6. Getting you warmed up and in the mood for our Flagship night *Reload*, starting at 9.' It's DJ Welsh Dave again plus up and coming DJ's eager to fill his shoes. Saturday most people have gone home and it's live football and rugby on the screens. Then it's the *Sunday Night Social* – quiz, bingo, sing-a-long, 'with great acts every week'.

There are plenty of societies and an opportunity to be part of the team that produces the award-

AT A GLANCE	
ACADEMIC FILE:	
Typical entry requirements	**208 points**
Application acceptance rate	**21%**
Students-staff ratio	**26:1**
First/2:1 degree pass rate	**49%**
ACCOMMODATION FILE:	
Guarantee to freshers	**100%**
Style	**Halls**
Price range pw	**£56-£85**
City rent pw	**£50-£70**

winning *Liverpool Student* newspaper that serves all 3 Liverpool universities.

SPORT They have recently installed a floodlit, all-weather astroturf pitch for hockey, tennis, football; there's a gym, and the Athletics Union is involved in all the usual inter-Uni competitions, with not at all a bad record, given the size of the student population. They came 82nd nationally last year.

Hope Park Sports is managed by Healthworks, an outside firm. Facilities include a multi-purpose sports hall for 5-a-side football, badminton, basketball and tennis, volleyball, netball and hockey. There's access to football and rugby pitches and squash courts and the new fitness suite mentioned under *Academia* above. There are exercise classes and coaching courses for all abilities and levels of fitness,.

Among a handful of unusual clubs is Kick Boxing, and the Mountaineering club is worth a mention not least because of **Plas Caerdeon**, Hope's Outdoor Education Centre. This old manor house in 18 acres of woodland overlooking the glorious Mawddach Estuary (Snowdonia) hosts field and study trips, but it's also a bolt hole for music students on Composition weekend, Drama students for rehearsals and anybody for simpler regenerative pleasures. There is good accommodation.

CITY See *Student Liverpool*, page 288.

GETTING THERE
☛ By road: easy access M62 (east/west), which connects with M6 (north/south) at Junction 21a.
☛ Well served by National Express coaches.
☛ By rail: Manchester, 0:40; Sheffield, 1:45; Leeds or Birmingham, 2:00; London Kings Cross, 3:00.
☛ Speke Airport 5 miles away.

LIVERPOOL JOHN MOORES UNIVERSITY

Liverpool John Moores University
Roscoe Court
4 Rodney Street
Liverpool L1 2TZ

TEL 0151 231 5090
FAX 0151 231 3462
EMAIL recruitment@ljmu.ac.uk
WEB www.ljmu.ac.uk

Liverpool John Moores Students' Union
The Haigh Building
Maryland Street
Liverpool L1 9DE

TEL 0151 231 4900
FAX 0151 231 4931
EMAIL lsujmill@livjm.ac.uk
WEB www.l-s-u.com

VAG VIEW

*L*iverpool John Moores (JMU) is Liverpool's metropolitan university, more part of the city than the older campus-based university.

JMU's many buildings are strewn all over the city, and the 3-bar Students' Union building, The Haigh, is an integral part of the Liverpool scene. Through the uni's affiliation with Sir Paul McCartney's Liverpool Institute for Performing Arts, JMU has a proud association with the city's most influential artists of all time. Also, they draw many students from the region, and the university's roots run deep into the city's industrial history.

Origins go back to 1823 as the Liverpool Mechanics' and Apprentices' Library. As poly, the institution brought together the City Colleges of Art and Design and Building, Commerce, and the Regional College of

Technology, the City of Liverpool College of Higher Education, the IM Marsh College of Physical Education, the FL Calder College of Home Economics and the Liverpool College of Nursing and Midwifery – all of which give a good clue to the uni's academic profile today.

Finally, JMU owes its name and ethos to one of the city's most famous entrepreneurs. Sir

Postgraduates 17%
Female Undergraduates 45%
STUDENT POPULATION
Total students 22,955
Male Undergraduates 38%

John Moores CBE (1896-1993) built Littlewoods – the football pools organisation – from scratch. 'Sir John's business success was built upon his philosophy of the equality of opportunity for all,' the uni says. 'This fundamental belief... is a reflection of the university's commitment to higher education, to access, to flexibility and to participation.' Most of all, perhaps, it gives the clue to the underlying ethos – applied learning – they are very hot, across the board, on how what is learned and imbued here can be applied on graduation in the world of work.

Students are requested to identify any disabilities including Dyslexia as early as possible, so as to take advantage of JMU's rigorous support programme.

CAMPUS

JMU is roughly three main sites: Mount Pleasant, Byrom Street/Henry Cotton campus and IM Marsh. Each has lecture theatres, seminar rooms, laboratories, editing suites, individual study and computer rooms, as well as union bars, shops and sports facilities. Everything is in and around the city, accessible to public transport and in easy reach of the city centre and halls of residence.

Writes Emma Hardy: 'JMU buildings are scattered across the city, many are impressive. The School of Media, Critical and Creative Arts, where I study, is one of the most impressive buildings in Liverpool. Located next to the Anglican Cathedral, the views from it are spectacular and the facilities are exemplary. The main library is a great glass structure of imposing stature and, like much of the rest of the university, likely to take your breath away when you first see it. But there are some grim high rise blocks too. Prospective students do well to bear in mind that what they see on Open Day are the best bits.'

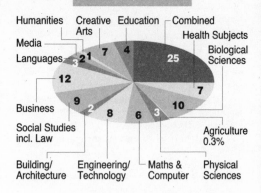

SUBJECT AREAS (%)

Humanities · Creative Arts · Education · Combined · Health Subjects · Biological Sciences 25 · Media · Languages · Business · Social Studies incl. Law · Building/Architecture · Engineering/Technology · Maths & Computer · Physical Sciences · Agriculture 0.3%

UNIVERSITY/STUDENT PROFILE	
University since	**1992**
Situation/style	**Civic**
Student population	**22955**
Undergraduates	**19105**
- mature	**35%**
- non EU undergraduates	**6%**
- male/female	**46/54**
- non-traditional student intake	**37%**
- state school intake	**95%**
- drop-out rate	**24%**
- undergraduate applications	**Up 10%**

FEES, BURSARIES

UK & EU Fees, 2007: £3,070. If in receipt of full HE Maintenance grant there's a bursary of £1,000; if in receipt of partial grant, it's £400. There are sports scholarships - contact Sports Scholarship Manager (David McDermott); also Dream Plan Achievers for those getting three As at A level – £1,000 per year. Achievers award, connected to 'link' schools are £1000 p.a.

STUDENT PROFILE

Asked to give us a profile, Emma concluded, 'Despite the huge diversity in matters of taste and style, your JMU student is a mellow person, out to enjoy their time at university. The general atmosphere is far from snobbish, and with such a wide range of people studying here, friends are not hard to find, no matter what your age, or what your interests.'

The statistics show that 95% of applicants come from the state sector and 37% from the lower socio-economic groups, and that 24% - nearly a quarter - come from so-called 'low participation neighbourhoods'. This is interesting because Liverpool Hope, who always reckon to be the university of the 'low participation neighbourhood', take far fewer. There is also a large mature population and a significant overseas presence.

As a result, JMU's problem has not been getting students so much as hanging on to them: their drop-out rate tends to run quite high.

ACADEMIA & JOBS

Writes Emma: 'JMU are big on student feedback. Tutors are approachable and changes do get made. Questionnaires regarding each and every module taught are distributed to students and the uni does listen to complaints. The emphasis is on making

ACADEMIC EXCELLENCE

TEACHING :
(Rated Excellent or 17+ out of 24)

Health Studies, Food & Nutrition, Sport, Tourism	24
Pharmacology, Organismal Biosciences	23
Communication & Media, Building, Land & Property Management, Nursing, Politics, Molecular Biosciences, Business & Management, Economics	22
Drama & Dance, American Studies, Maths, Education	21
Civil Engineering	20
Modern Languages (French, German, Russian, Spanish), Psychology, Art & Design	19
Sociology, Town & Country Planning, Electric & Electron Eng, General Eng	18

RESEARCH :
Top grades 5/6/6*

Sport	**Grade 6***
General Engineering	**Grade 5**

the experience as enjoyable as possible.'

Vocational bias, strong on sandwich courses, good contacts with industry – professional associations offer direct employment routes, for example, in pharmacy, surveying and engineering. And now they've established a business club for graduates called NEXUS, through which you'll be able to network and tap into uni-based expertise and resources.

Faculties include: Business & Law; Education, Community & Leisure; Health & Applied Social Sciences; Media, Arts & Social Science; Technology & Environment.

Education is a defining provision – 59% from the faculty go into secondary teaching; 32% into primary. There are also ESOL and TESOL courses – English for non-English speakers and courses for

teachers of same. Teaching inspection, 21 points.

Among engineering graduates in a department that won a Grade 5 listing for research (international level), civil engineers proliferate, then it's design & development engineers, computer programmers and systems analysts, sound recordists, IT consultants, software engineers, process and production engineers and construction engineers. Radio & TV broadcasters and sound recordists love JMU, in particular their BSc Broadcast Technology. There's Granada TV partnership status and great tie-ups with Sky TV.

Look, too, at BA Hons Journalism, which includes practical TV Journalism (there's also International Journalism) and Media Professional Studies for TV production, business and management enterprise, info technology and media theory. The latter is run in partnership with Mersey Television (*Brookside* and *Hollyoaks* producer, Phil Redmond, is their Honorary Professor). Teaching inspection, 22.

Prospective social worker/counsellors also treat JMU with respect. They are in the top echelon of graduate providers in this sector through a series of Applied Community Studies/Social Work/ Youth & Community Work Studies BA degrees.

Nursing and midwifery students now benefit from 'SimMan' – a high-tech 'universal patient simulator' mannequin, which is part of the new Clinical Practice Suite, developed in partnership with the Cheshire and Merseyside Strategic Health Authority: 6 rooms designed to function like real hospital wards.

There are good career figures too for animal health technicians, carers, nurses. They leave the vet degrees to their neighbour and position themselves instead with the likes of .BSc Animal Behaviour and Zoology.

Another key area can be gleaned from the *Academic Excellence* box, above. Full-mark scores (24 points) were had for Food & Nutrition, and 23 points for Biosciences. A 4-year sandwich BSc Hons Applied Microbiology is one of a range of similar courses, from Applied Biochemistry to Nutrition, all with foundation years. Many go on to become bacteriologists or microbiologists, who work with living

WHERE LIVERPOOL JOHN MOORES GRADUATES END UP

Health & Social Work: 10%; Education: 17%; Wholesale Retail: 12%; Manufacturing: 8%; Financial Activities: 7%; Public Administration, Civil Service & Defence: 8%; Hotel/Restaurant: 4%; Transport & Communications (including Telecommunications): 4.5%; Construction: 2%; Personnel: 4.5%; Computer: 3%; Business & Management: 2%; Accountancy: 0.5%; Media (including Film): 3%; Legal 2%; Architecture: 2%; Publishing: 1%; Advertising: 0.5%; Artistic/Literary: 1.5%; Sport: 1%.

Approximate 'graduate track' employed **61%**

organisms, focused on human health and environmental issues, food poisoning, drugs, viruses, bacteria, etc. See also BSc Nutrition.

There's a good employment track record, too, for prospective chemists and those planning a career in Pharmaceutical Manufacture. There are degrees in Industrial Pharmaceutical Science, Pharmaceutical Science or Analysis, as well as an MPharm. JMU take 3% + of the graduate employment market. Teaching inspection – 23 out of 24 points.

In computing, the degree that opens doors is BSc Computer Games Technology degree. Computer programmers (also highly in demand from here) should look at their BSc Computer Aided Design or simply BSc Computer Studies.

The BA Architecture attracts employers, and JMU is in the Top 10, too, with its Property Management degree (see also the Real Estate Management degrees and BSc Quantity Surveying).

Work continues on The Design Academy, the new £23.5million home for Art and Design Academy due to open in time for the 2008 Academic year.

In Law, JMU was assessed 'Good' on a scale of Excellent, Very Good, Good, Satisfactory or Unsatisfactory by a reporting assessor for the LPC Board – the Legal Practice Course is essential for becoming a solicitor. Moot Court is or 'mock' courtroom to give law degree and legal practice students the chance to gain intensive trial practice There is no dedicated policing degree – you'd have to go to Central Lancashire, Glamorgan, Central England in Birmingham or Buckinghamshire Chilterns University College for one of those, but as is so often the case in a city uni with good Criminology, Forensic Science and Youth & Community degrees and a strong sporting provision, jobs come easy with the police.

JMU have the only Sport & Exercise Science department in the UK with a maximum teaching assessment rating of 24, and a maximum research assessment rating of Grade 6*. Prospective pro players and officials should look at BSc Sport Science, Sport Technology, Applied Psychology and BA Sport Development & Physical Education. JMU will be awarded around £4.5 million over the next five years in recognition of its teaching excellence in the fields of PE, Dance, Sport and Exercise Sciences, to create a new Centre of Excellence in Teaching and Learning.

Finally, drama students and local community

> *Students are requested to identify any disabilities including Dyslexia as early as possible, so as to take advantage of JMU's rigorous support programme.*

groups Black Box Theatre Company, Momentum Theatre Company, Liverpool Youth Service and Unity Theatre will benefit from a £200,000 refurbishment of the uni's Joe H Makin Drama Centre.

SOCIAL SCENE

STUDENTS' UNION As a prospective student, bear in mind that it is up to you to make the most of your time at JMU. This means finding out about what is going on and getting involved in what interests you. Radio stations, newspapers, clubs, societies and events need student support.

The union building, the Haigh, has a bar – **Scholars**, the newest venue, designed trad. pub-style with pool tables, jukeboxes and three televisions – and a club, **The Cooler** – a 500-capacity nightclub with new air-conditioning system, hence its name, and late bar, disco, stage facilities, Playstation and a giant television screen for sport and films. Entry is free. Every night of the week there is a different music theme in **The Cooler – from Doctors & Nurses to Ann**

AT A GLANCE	
ACADEMIC FILE:	
Subjects assessed	**37**
Excellent	**68%**
Typical entry requirements	**207 points**
Application acceptance rate	**20%**
Students-staff ratio	**18:1**
First/2:1 degree pass rate	**48%**
ACCOMMODATION FILE:	
Availability to freshers	**100%**
Style	**Halls**
Catered	**None**
En suite	**80%**
Approx price range pw	**£58-£90**
City rent pw	**£50-£95**

Summers, and there are screenings of recent movies and big screen football.' Saturday's *Loveshack* ('60s, '70s, '80s, '90s) has long been rated the best retro night in town. Now, too, there's Lush (funky dance) and drinks promos like *Vodipop*.

Another popular meeting place is **Sanctuary**, a café bar, chill-out zone with sofas, speciality coffees, etc. There are also bars at the IM Marsh (Education) and Byron Street sites.

Among the most successful student societies is

the radio station, Shout fm, and now there's a student magazine, *Re:load*, which in its previous incarnation as *Shout* figured in many a national awards ceremony.

Situated in the Haigh is UNITEMP, JMU's own employment agency. It does offer some exclusive Unitemp related jobs, but doesn't beat getting the local newspaper, visiting the job centre, or simply asking around for vacancies.

SPORT Good facilities for uni team sports, most are 3 miles from the city centre at the Education & Community base – gym, dance studios, sports halls, indoor swimming pool, pitches, all-weather athletics track – and at the St Nicholas Centre by the cathedral – sports hall, gym, weight training room. JMU's proudest boast is its Base Fitness Centre, well equipped and professionally staffed. There's a student sports pass for free/reduced price access to facilities – badminton courts, swimming pools, squash courts, athletics tracks.

TOWN See *Student Liverpool*, page 288.

PILLOW TALK

'Pretty much all university halls and JMU residences are fine except Crete and Candia Towers, which should be avoided at all costs,' said a student. 'You have been warned.'

All freshers are now guaranteed university owned or private specialist student accommodation - modern halls of residence (shared flats).

GETTING THERE

☞ By road: M62, M6/J21a. Well served by coach.
☞ By rail: Manchester, 40 mins; Sheffield, 1:45; Leeds, Birmingham, 2:00; London King's Cross, 3:00.
☞ Liverpool airports for inland/Ireland flights.

☞ By coach: London, 5:00; Manchester, 50 mins.

WHAT IT'S REALLY LIKE	
UNIVERSITY:	
Social Life	★★★★
Campus scene	**Local, top scene**
Student Union services	**Good**
Politics	**Active: safety, sex, housing**
Sport	**19 clubs**
National team position	**45th**
Sport facilities	**Good**
Arts opportunities	**Music excellent; drama, dance, film, art good**
Student magazine	**Re:Load**
Student radio	**Shout fm**
Nightclub	**The Cooler**
Bars	**Scholars, Sanctuary, IM Marsh, Byron Street**
Union ents	**Pop, retro, funky dance**
Union societies	**72**
Most popular societies	**Ski/Snowboard, Afro-Carribean, Christian Union**
Parking	**Poor**
CITY:	
Entertainment	★★★★★
City scene	**Fab**
Town/gown relations	**Good**
Risk of violence	**Average**
Cost of living	**Low**
Student concessions	**Excellent**
Survival + 2 nights out	**£70 pw**
Part-time work campus/town	**Good/Excellent**

STUDENT LONDON – THE CITY

London is an expensive place to live. Everything from shopping to travel can bite huge chunks out of your student loan. Sometimes it can feel like the only thing you've achieved during your course is a hefty debt. That is unless you learn to flash your student card at every opportunity. Although you may face ridicule for being a 'bake bean loving, beer-swilling creature of the night', you will be the envy of every non-student when you get offered a rather nice discount just about everywhere you go.

With a population of over seven million, London is one of the most diverse cities in the world – 30% of residents were born outside England. Greater London not only covers a lot of multicultural ground, but also physical, as it spans 1584 square kilometres. That space is filled with so many interests and attractions that you could not visit them all in one lifetime; London plays host to more than 200 carnivals and festivals annually. With its mixture of historical landmarks and modern masterpieces, London is a great place to learn, and not just in the lecture theatre.

THEATRE

On an average day in London you will be able to watch one of 76 plays, 33 musicals, 19 operas or 16 dance performances. If you were to go to one a day starting on the first of January, you wouldn't be finished until the end of May. The West End is one of the UK's biggest attractions: the choice of plays and shows is superb, but you often end up paying more up there. **The National Theatre** (Southbank, Embankment tube, +44 (0)20 7452 3000) and **The Globe Theatre** (21 New Globe Walk, Mansion House tube, +44 (0)20 7902 1400) are two of the most popular repertory companies. Playing less commercial performances, they often have the best offerings. The NT is subsidised. Otherwise there are countless fringe theatres showing allsorts for allsorts.

TKTS is the place to go for theatre on a budget. As the only official half price and discounted theatre ticket operation in London, they offer tickets on the day of the performance only, and have no phone number, so you have to visit. They are based in both Leicester Square and Canary Wharf DLR Station. Many theatres offer student tickets with proof of ID, otherwise it can be worth waiting at the venue box office for returns or standby tickets before the performance.

DANCE

Whether you're up for a class or just sitting back and watching somebody else shake their thang, London is a great place for dance.

The Barbican Centre (Silk Street, +44 (0)20 7638 4141, Barbican tube) is Europe's largest arts venue and a key member of the dance scene, especially the unconventional. Students get half price tickets in advance for all Wednesday evenings. **The London Coliseum** (St Martin's Lane, +44 (0)20 7836 0111, Leicester Square tube) is home to the English National Opera and is the London base of the English National Ballet. Standby tickets are available to students. There are many more major venues including **The Place**, Riverside Studios, Royal Opera House and Sadler's Wells.

To get involved yourself, there are classes of many different styles held in many venues. **Dance Attic** (Old Fulham Baths, 368 North End Road, +44 (0)20 7610 2055, Fulham Broadway tube) costs £50 a year for students to join, you then just pay per class. **Pineapple Dance Studios** (7 Langley Street, +44 (0)20 7836 4004, Covent Garden Tube) costs £70 a year, that's half price for students. For full Dance listings visit www.londondance.com.

COMEDY

A comedy club is a great choice for an evening out in London. There are dozens of great venues scattered around, but here are a few of the more student friendly offerings.

Backyard Comedy Club, 231 Cambridge Heath Road, +44 (0)20 7739 3122, Bethnal Green tube. This converted factory is now a club owned by comedian Lee Hurst, who quite often acts as host. There is also a restaurant and disco after the show for anyone wanting a full night out.

Chuckle Club, London School of Economics, Houghton Street, +44 (0)20 7476 1672, Holborn tube. For less than a tenner you can see a host of comedians, including household names. Being a student union bar the drinks are all fairly cheap.

The Cosmic Comedy Club, 177 Fulham Palace Road, Hammersmith tube. This club is free to get in. You just have to pay what you think it was worth afterwards. Also, every week the BBC makes comedy programmes for radio. It's free, so anyone can go along. Call BBC Radio Theatre +44 (0)20 8576 1227.

CLUBS AND VENUES

London has around 15% of all the clubs in Britain. That means that you are never lost for a place to go for a spot of late night drinking. The biggest clubbing nights are still Friday and Saturday, but any day is a good day. Some of the bigger names include **Fabric**, **Ministry of Sound** and **The Cross**, but there are hundreds of other venues catering for every taste. www.londonnet.co.uk has a great clubs section where you can select which day of the week you want to go out, or which style of music, and see complete listings. For free entrance into 25 London nightclubs, including **Café de Paris** and **Elysium**, become a Circle Club member, for just a £5 admin fee. It gives you free admission during the week and half price at weekends, and you can also purchase 2-4-1 drinks vouchers in advance. Visit www.circleclubcard.com for full details.

CINEMA

London has almost 500 cinema screens and a choice of over 100 films showing at any time. Leicester Square is the centre for cinema in London. Every year it hosts numerous star-studded premieres on the many huge screens. But it isn't particularly student friendly with rather expensive ticket prices, making London's independent cinemas the better option. The **Prince Charles Cinema** (7 Leicester Place, Leicester Square tube) is one such place. *Feel-good Fridays* cost just £1 and the most non-members have to pay for a regular performance is £4. Annual Membership is just £7.50. For a search that allows you to find a cinema by a particular postcode, tube location or where a certain film is showing visit www.viewlondon. co.uk. Alternatively most of the chain cinemas in Greater London offer student prices. **UGC** offers an unlimited monthly card for £13.99. Orange mobile customers can text FILM to 241 on Wednesdays and receive a code allowing them two tickets for the price of one.

ART

In London there are around 50 exhibitions open to the public each day. 17 national museums and galleries, as well as many other smaller, local galleries, allow free entrance. These include the **British Museum**, **National Gallery**, **Tate Modern** and **V&A Museum**. London exhibits countless works or all kinds, both permanent and temporary collections. For a list of all the contemporary exhibitions London has to offer at any time, visit www.newexhibitions.com. For more details about all the major London galleries go to www.londontourist.org/art.

MUSIC

There are 9 major concert halls in London – **Barbican** (where they often hold free events), **Purcell Room**, **Royal Albert Hall**, **Royal Festival Hall**, **Royal Opera House**, **Queen Elizabeth Hall**, **St John's Smith Square**, **Wembley Arena** and **Wigmore Hall** - as well as 47 major rock and pop venues, including **Astoria**, **Barfly**, **Brixton Academy**, **Forum and Garage**. From ultra-trendy to cheesy and trashy, international superstars to local legends, you will find whatever type of music you are after in London, and all of your favourite musicians will have played here, or will play here at some time. www.bbc.co.uk/music/whatson has regularly updated information covering all kinds of music. For the cheapest tickets go direct to the venue box office and avoid those booking fees, but for the best tickets visit www.gigsandtours.com or www.ticketmaster.co.uk

SHOPPING

Camden is a great place to shop. The cheap goods and cosmopolitan atmosphere make it a unique experience. You can find just about anything there and can easily spend a day wandering the many shops and stalls. The market is open seven days a week and the nearest tube station is Camden Town. Covent Garden market offers more specialist goods with many arts and crafts. This historic setting is full of street entertainers and is easily accessed from a number of tube stations including Covent Garden and Leicester Square. **Portobello Road**, in the trendy Notting Hill area , is also worth a mention (open on Saturdays). Then there' **Oxford Street (Selfridges)**, Knightsbridge **(Harrods)**, Regents Street. Most High Street stores offer a student discount, just remember, always flash your student ID, and don't be afraid to ask.

Paul Stephen

LONDON METROPOLITAN UNIVERSITY

London Metropolitan University
31 Jewry Street
London EC3N 2EY

TEL 020 133 4200
    020 7753 3272 (Campus North)
EMAIL admissions@londonmet.ac.uk
WEB www.londonmet.ac.uk

London Metropolitan Students' Union
2 Goulston Street
London E1 7TP

TEL 020 7320 2233
FAX 020 7320 2244
EMAIL president.su@londonmet.ac.uk
WEB www.londonmetsu.org.uk

VAG VIEW

*N*orth London and London Guildhall unis have become one. 'The new university is one of the biggest in the UK,' writes John Shaw, who was on the future strategy task group. 'With 13 main sites, grouped into two campuses (London North and London City),' it was Mr Shaw's job to identify the 2 unis' very different histories and cultures and direct the way forward.

They are a new amalgamation, and so, as our info boxes show, some facts and fig-

STUDENT POPULATION

Total students 36,000

15% — Postgraduates
Female Undergraduates — 26%
31% — Male Undergraduates
Others — 28%

ures have yet to come on line, but in niche areas, such as art, architecture, business, science, education, psychology, sport, there is much to shout about. At inspection, the Business School was awarded full marks by the QAA, placing it in the top 5% of business schools in the UK. Results published by the Chartered Institute of Marketing show London Met pass rates are 15-20% above the national average. The uni has recently invested more than £30 million in a new Science Centre. Sixteen students from the Sir John Cass department of art, media and design received awards at the annual Goldsmiths Craftsmanship and Design Awards. Two London Met students scooped the prizes in the Formica Student Design Competition last year. In sport, London Met leads the nation's unis in hockey and tennis, and its sports teams were, overall, more successful than any other in London last year.

CAMPUS SCENE

CITY CAMPUS It is an unusual set-up for a uni, with its sites strewn around London's Square Mile financial district – 8 sites: Calcutta and Central Houses, Jewry Street, Moorgate, Goulston Street, Whitechapel, Tower Hill and Commercial Road.

The East End is a racially diverse area with, in particular, a thriving Bangladeshi community giving the cultural flavour to the eating and shopping delights of Brick Lane.

The campus's main Moorgate site is built on what used to be one of the most (in)famous insane asylums in England. The Bethlem Royal Hospital (originally based at nearby Liverpool Street Station) moved to the site in the late 1670s.

CAMPUS NORTH comprises a collection of sites around the Holloway Road. Writes Maureen Okolo: 'We is in the right place for a great, big, delicious slice of London's night life. Step outside and find yourself in the infamous Holloway Road. Packed with takeaways, cafés, restaurants and shops. Totally student friendly in prices. At one end [south] is Highbury and Islington; at the other, Archway (very long road, this, but with day and night bus routes galore, tube and train stations close to uni and halls, you'll be able to get around)...'

Campus North doesn't just preach wider access to higher education, it ensures it. It is as far away from the punts and gowns of Oxbridge as you can get. It is a people's university, as much a part of the local scene as the Arsenal up the road. 'Uni life is great, if you like that sort of thing. You get everyone

who's into everything,' promises Maureen. 'Just expect constant rounds of socialising with chic, retro, funky, cool, funny individuals from all walks of life.'

So there we have it. Chapel Market and Camden Lock meet Aldgate, Petticoat Lane and Spitalfields.

FEES, BURSARIES

UK & EU Fees, 2007: £3,070. Fees not yet fixed for 2008. If in receipt of full HE Maintenance grant there's a bursary of £1,000; if in receipt of partial grant, bursaries are on a sliding scale up to £975 as to parental income. They also have scholarships. See www.londonmet.ac.uk/scholarships

STUDENT PROFILE

A century and a half after London Guildhall started out by offering 'evening classes for young men', there is still a significant student population on part-time courses. The uni is one of the largest providers of part-time business courses in the country. It's this part-time population that boosts the mature student percentage, and you will in fact meet many youthful full-time undergrads, as well as many students studying subjects other than business.

Besides Barings broker and breaker, Nick Leeson, and multi-millionaire Mark Thatcher, the former Tory PM's son, both of whom did time at City, the mass of its students are very interesting. 'A high proportion originate from London and the surrounding Southeast, but the melting pot,' confides Stuart Harkness, 'is fuelled by those from farther afield, to the tune of 110 countries. The cosmopolitan flavour makes LGU a truly multi-cultural university. Multiple faiths are therefore evident and

SUBJECT AREAS (%)

Other Combined Sci/So Sci — 7
Soc Sci/Arts — 14
Biological Sciences — 2
Maths & Computer — 10
Engineering/Technology — 4
— 20
Combined Arts — 6, 7
Combined Sci — 3, 6
Creative Arts — 20
Social Studies incl. Law
Business
Humanities 0.5%
Media 0.3%
Languages 0.5%

well catered for with prayer rooms at various university sites, a chaplaincy and numerous students' union-funded cultural societies, including Christian, Islamic, Muslim, Afro-Caribbean, to

UNIVERSITY/STUDENT PROFILE

University since	**1992**
Situation/style	**Civic**
Student population	**36000**
Undergraduates	**20400**
- mature	**55%**
- non EU undergraduates	**25%**
- male/female	**55/45**
- non-traditional student intake	**40%**
- state schhol intake	**97%**
- drop-out rate	**N/A**
- undergraduate applications	**Up 3%**

ACADEMIC EXCELLENCE

TEACHING - CAMPUS NORTH:
(Rated Excellent or 17+ out of 24)

English	**Excellent**
Business/Management	**24**
Film Studies, Art & Design, Electric /Electron Eng, Philosophy	**22**
Modern Langs (Dutch, French, German, Iberian Studies), Education	**20**
Maths, Nursing, Other subjects Allied to Medicine	**21**
Materials Technology, Food Sciences, Psychology	**19**
Library/Info, Biosciences,	**18**

TEACHING - CITY CAMPUS:
(Rated Excellent or 17+ out of 24)

Social Policy & Admin	**Excellent**
Art & Design, Economics	**23**
Business/Management, Politics, Psychology	**22**
Materials Technology	**20**
Modern Languages (French, German, Spanish)	**19**
Maths	**18**

name but a few. All seem to respect each others' practices under the umbrella of LGU brotherhood.'

It is true. They have more international students than any other new university in the UK and they run their own offices in China, India, Pakistan and Bangladesh. They provide a three-day orientation course for international students each September. There is also a successful peer support scheme, involving language support, a buddy system and subject area support. But all that aside, what we have is a cultural recipe with flavour, which is also what we have at Campus North, whose undergraduate body is to a large extent drawn from the local, notably ethnic population.

SOCIAL SCENE

STUDENTS UNION London Met's **Rocket** has a fascinating history, worth a book of its own. It has been around since the inception of the North London Poly itself. It began as the Great Hall when the first students arrived in 1896. Some of the concerts there were actually conducted by Proms inventor Sir Henry Wood. Since then it became a proscenium arch theatre, the arch picked up for a song from the old **Marlborough Theatre** down the road opposite the **Nag's Head**, after which it was used as a cinema, whose organ was played by William Lloyd Webber, father of millionaire musical maestro Andrew... And so the tale goes on. Today, the **Rocket Complex**, as it is known, is a meeting place of some style, cool enough for like-minded City students, used to their ground-floor **Sub Bar** in Goulston Street (where one of Jack the Ripper's victims was found) to get up and out, and go along. Certainly the **Rocket's** entertainment list looks suitably enticing.

However, and this may need to be addressed, neither this nor the facilities at City campus are run by the Student Union; they are run by the university. The union has no venues of its own.

'The award-winning venue the **Rocket Complex** comprises a nightclub, live music venue

(with the latest turbo sound floodlight system), 2 licensed bars, external courtyard, pool and games room, coffee bar and shop,' chirps a union wallah only barely hiding his true revolutionary mission from our star-struck eyes. 'The weekly events programme includes *The Big Fish* ("the best student night in London" - *Time Out*), *Pint Sized Comedy Club* and regular events showcasing music and culture from around the globe. Recent headliners... Trevor Nelson, Jools Holland, Punjabi Hit Squad, Asian Dub Foundation, Kele le Roc, Ms Dynamite, Artful Dodger, Timmi Magic, DJ Hanif, DJ Luck + MC Neat, Jah Shaka, Latina Max + London's largest Brazilian Carnival.'

Sounds even more enterprising than the ents down in City campus's **Sub Bar** – *Cheese and Teese*, *Funk da House* and *Silver Tonic*, and the latest pool and games machines in the bar. Student night specials include *S*M*A*S*H*E*D*, *Funkin' Fridays*, *Time of the Month*, and recent headliners... Kele le Roc, Terri Walker, DJ Fidgit (Missy Elliott UK Tour DJ), DJ X Ray.

There's a student mag: *Independent Student Metro*, and a radio station is scheduled for this year, Ear Fm. There are internal media and arts awards aplenty and excellent departments in these areas. There is also political activity (and a tradition of that). This term there was a campaign about the enforced closure of the Islamic Students Library. Apparently Islamic Soc is the most active society.

SPORT The sports teams do very well (22nd nationally last year) on account of the excellence of the sports department, and good players are given scholarships. In 2006 they were the UK's top uni for men's tennis and hockey and the top London University for sports.

Sports facilities are shared with Arsenal FC and Essex CC. The new Arsenal stadium is right behind one of the university buildings. Pitches, courts, sports halls, all the usual requirements are to a high standard.

ACADEMIA & JOBS

Around a third of Campus North students graduate in business subjects (they scored full marks at the teaching assessments for Business Management), and there is a dominant but well thought-out joint degree series, which accounts for just less than a quarter of graduates and explores, amongst much else, particular possibilities in employment for business-minded students. Down at City around a third of students graduate in a very similar joint vocational degree system and more than a quarter graduate in business subjects. From both campuses, many go into retail.

Some joint courses require travel to both campuses – Economics & International Business and International Relations and Peace & Conflict Studies among them. Check out where you'll be.

Meanwhile, aspiring accountants should consider the flagship Accounting & Finance (City and North), which leads to complete exemptions from professional examination, but also the joint degree extrapolations of that – such as Accounting & Business Economics (City and North), Accounting & International Business or Accounting & Banking (North), Accounting & Investment (City) – and most important Professional Accounting (City), a degree that incorporates examinations of the Institute of Chartered Accountants of England and Wales.

Another strength is in computing, with such as Computer Science, Computer Visualisation & Games, and Computer Animation. There is also a mass of Music Management and Technology/Audio Systems/Audio Electronics, a retail management dimension, and a niche area in radio and TV broadcasting, City campus popping up in the Top 10 nationally for employment in this.

Then we have another important area – health, with degrees such as Herbal Herbal Medicine Science alongside Pharmaceutical Science and Pharmacology, and Biomedical Sciences, a programme that scores particularly strongly in the employment table. There is also a notable lean at North towards the therapeutic care side, with degrees in Social Work and BSc

WHAT IT'S REALLY LIKE	
UNIVERSITY:	
Social Life	★★★
Campus scene	**Mature, local, urban, easy going**
Student Union services	**Average**
Politics	**Internal**
Sport	**Very competitive**
National team position	**22nd**
Sport facilities	**Professional**
Arts	**Available**
Student magazine	**Independent Student Metro**
Student radio	**Ear Fm**
Nightclub venues/bars	**Sub Bar, Sub Club (Aldgate), Rocket (Holloway Road)**
Union ents	**Big Fish (Rocket), Time of the Month (Sub)**
Union societies	**44**
Most active	**Islamic Soc**
Parking	**Non-existent**
CITY:	
Entertainment	★★★★★
Scene	**Wild, expensive**
Town/gown relations	**Average-good**
Risk of violence	**'Average'**
Cost of living	**Very high**
Student concessions	**Locally adequate**
Survival + 2 nights out	**£100 pw**
Part-time work campus/town	**Good/excellent**

Psychology (Applied) & Health Studies.

Still on the professional front, look to either campus for LlB Law. While City are commercial & business law specialists, North have LlB (Social Justice).

Another string to North's bow is sport – BSc Sports Nutrition, Psychology & Performance, Science, Science & Coaching, Therapy, as well as Management and Technology modules in the joint course series.

Another defining niche at City, for which they scored a near perfect score at the assessments, is Fine Art, Design, and Silversmithing, Jewellery & Allied Crafts), appropriate to the traditional strength of this area of London in the art and craft movement. Writes Sam Hall: 'The university is gaining a reputation for artistic excellence, with well-respected jewellery-making and furniture departments, and many student-led initiatives leading to national awards.'

Jewellery design/making may be a small, specialist field, but City hits the spot employment-wise. The Art Foundation course is the required entry point for the BA Hons Silversmithing, Jewellery & Allied Crafts.

Furniture design and manufacture is another

AT A GLANCE

ACADEMIC FILE:

Subjects assessed	**44**
Excellent	**61%**
Typical entry requirements	**N/A**
Application acceptance rate	**15%**
Students-staff ratio	**N/A**
First/2:1 degree pass rate	**N/A**

ACCOMMODATION FILE:

Guarantee to freshers	**OK if from 25 miles away**
Style	**Halls, flats**
Catered	**16%**
En suite	**None**
Approx price range pw	**£82-£103**
City rent pw	**£85 Zone 2**

Design & Realisation and Restoration HND routes.

North's response in this area is the BA Interior Architecture & Design, and a very sound employment record in architectural consultancy and construction with BA Architecture.

PILLOW TALK

Students have access to over 1300 rooms in halls, each situated close to either the London City or London North campuses. Accommodation is guaranteed for all first years who live more than 25 miles away and who accept a conditional or unconditional offer of a course and return their halls application by the 8th August. For more detail go via the web address (www.londonmet.ac.uk/accommodation) or email accommodation@londonmet.ac.uk

GETTING THERE

☛ By Underground to City Campus: Aldgate (Metropolitan and Circle lines), Aldgate East (District and Hammersmith & City).
☛ By Underground to Campus North: Holloway Road (Piccadilly Line).

area of supreme confidence here. There's the 3D Design (Furniture & Product), but also a huge number of combinations with Textile Furnishing Design – elements as diverse as Art & Design History, Computer-Aided Design, European Studies, etc. There are also

LONDON SCHOOL OF ECONOMICS & POLITICAL SCIENCE

The London School of Economics & Political Science
Houghton Street
London WC2A 2AE

TEL 020 7955 6613
FAX 020 7955 6001
Email stu.rec@lse.ac.uk
WEB www.lse.ac.uk

LSE Students' Union
East Building
Houghton Street
London WC2A 2AE

TEL 020 7955 7158
FAX 020 7955 6789
EMAIL su.gensec@lse.ac.uk
WEB www.lse.ac.uk/union

VAG VIEW

*L*SE is part of the federal University of London. It is famous the world over for research. It may have been pipped into fourth place after Oxbridge and Imperial in the research assessments, but by any standards that is good, particularly when you consider that the proportion of staff selected for assessment was higher than at any other establishment. Teaching inspection results have been high, and the LSE is as secure as the British Establishment, with which, despite the school's history of '60s student revolt – Mick Jagger, Grosvenor Square and the Vietnam War and all

– it is, indeed, synonymous.

LSE goes hand in hand with Westminster, with Whitehall, with the City and with the legal and the media sub-strata too. In fact, its geographical position ensures it closer contact with all departments of the Establishment than either Oxford or Cambridge, and its specialist areas – Economics, International Relations, Government, Law, Finance – are what you might call the active ingredients of life in the Establishment. That is why many of its academic gurus are recognisable faces or by-lines in the media. If analysis is required, it's the LSE they call up.

It is difficult to see what better finishing

school you could find than that. Concludes our student mole: 'The LSE is no Utopia, but it is definitely one-up with its individual culture, school of thought, and world of opportunities.'

Now, they plan to grow 4.6% to 9,000 students by 2012. To that end, they are about to invest £63 million in an academic building on Kingsway, with 4 lecture halls, and 16 seminar rooms and study spaces.

CAMPUS

'The LSE is the filling in a sandwich,' writes Dominique Fyfe, a student from America. 'On one side (the capital's financial and legal district) the air is serious and the suits Armani, and the *FT*-reading societal stress-set is on the go until long after the sun is down. On the other, west of Kingsway (hitherto the dividing line, a road where all those who cannot drive test their inabilities), lie the expensive, funky, multi-purpose Covent Garden and London's theatreland and Soho, haven for sex addicts and non-traditionalists, and the book lovers' paradise of Charing Cross Road.'

In translation, LSE is situated between Kingsway and the Strand, at the heart of London culture and the legal establishment, and not far from the City or Westminster either. It is a campus crowded with buildings, the so-called Old Building being on the site of the small hall, where it all began and from which it has steadily expanded into buildings close by – the East Building, Clare Market, St Clement, St Philips, Clement House, all built on land which is among the most expensive per square foot in the world.

FEES, BURSARIES

UK & EU Fees, 2007: £3,075. Fees not yet fixed for 2008. If in receipt of full HE Maintenance grant, there's a bursary of £2,500; if in receipt of partial grant, there's a sliding scale according to parental

income up to that figure. For changing bursary and scholarship info, see www.lse.ac.uk/collections/studentServicesCentre/financialSupportOffice/

STUDENT PROFILE

They come from all over the world. This is the cream of students anxious to acquire the LSE cachet, and there is a snobbery attached. Last year it took fewer from the state sector in the UK than all but Oxbridge, Imperial and University College London, oh and the Courtauld Institute of Art. But interestingly, their take from the lower socio-economic classes is half decent, around 20%, and they keep their students - only 4% drop out.

'Interesting conversation is one thing you will not find a lack of at the LSE,' writes Dominique. 'The students here think critically in the classroom but also have a point of view in friendly discussion outside. Many are highly driven, always ready for an intellectual challenge and very competitive. However, not all are so intense; some don't even find the library until summer exams!

'Naturally, most of the students you will meet here are reading for a degree in Economics, but what makes the school a fascinating place is that there are so many studying other subjects, like

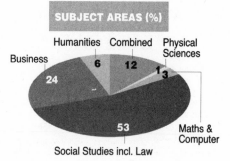

SUBJECT AREAS (%)

Humanities 6, Combined 12, Physical Sciences 1 3, Business 24, Maths & Computer 53, Social Studies incl. Law

anthropology, finance, social psychology and philosophy, and you learn from everybody.

'The LSE is a breeding ground for global nomads. In between lectures, the Houghton Street hub of LSE activity overflows with student representatives of all races of our world. Languages you will begin to learn in this global microcosm are Indian, French, Italian, Spanish, Russian, German, not to mention English of course. Not only do these students of all cultures bring their traditions but they also bring the trendy, money-sucking, modern fashions, but don't worry if your wardrobe didn't appear in the latest issue of *Cosmo* or *GQ*; nobody really cares whether its Oxfam or Armani.'

ACADEMIA & JOBS

Writes Dominique, 'Lectures and classes are well

UNIVERSITY/SCHOOL PROFILE	
School of London Uni since	**1900**
Situation/style	**City campus**
Student population	**8600**
Undergraduates	**4300**
- mature	**1%**
- non EU undergraduates	**38%**
- male/female	**50/50**
- non-traditional student intake	**20%**
- state school intake	**62%**
- drop-out rate	**4%**
- undergraduate applications	**Up 15%**

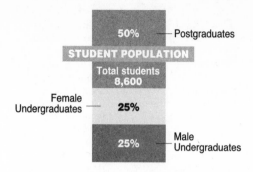

STUDENT POPULATION
- 50% — Postgraduates
- Total students 8,600
- Female Undergraduates — 25%
- 25% — Male Undergraduates

ics), 10.3%. A few recalcitrants – about 1% – become social workers.

Last year a new Department of Management was created. It is developing a range of new programmes and initiatives.

LSE has been teaching accountancy since 1896. It is one of only two provisions nationally that received a top Grade 6* in the research inspection exercise (the other is Manchester). Many come from the Accountancy & Finance degree, but some 30% become accountants via the economics route – BSc Economics or with Economic History or Econometrics & Mathematical Economics (there's a host of other possible combos).

enough taught. In fact I find myself wanting to go to them – a truly novel experience for me! Don't be surprised if the reading list for a class is more like a library's inventory record! The lectures are monologues, but the classes are interactive and "cosy" in size (maximum fifteen students). Essays are written for classes but not always formally assessed or given a definitive deadline, which can make procrastination seem dangerously attractive.'

The LSE library, the British Library of Political and Economic Science, contains one million volumes, 28,000 journals (10,000 on current sub.), numerous specialist manuscripts – all totalling some three million items. Founded in 1896, it recently enjoyed a multi-million pound overhaul by architects Foster and Partners. Even so, it is not immune to student criticism: 'LSE's library is overwhelming and quite frankly I would not go there if I didn't have to. The process is as follows: when you reach the library half of the books you are looking for are not there and if they are, there is only one copy of the main text for about twenty to forty-plus students and are titled as set texts, which means that they can only be borrowed for twenty-four hours. Return it twenty-four hours too late and the librarians grow the devil's tail and horns and collect a large amount of your own precious money! If that seems a tough sentence, it is and is meant to be.'

The Top 10 sectors of employment for LSE graduates, six months after graduation are: banking, financial services and accountancy, 33%; education, 11.4%; central and local governments 11.3%; and management consultancy (including econom-

ACADEMIC EXCELLENCE

TEACHING:
(Rated Excellent or 17+ out of 24)

History, Anthropology, Applied Social Work, Business, Law, Social Policy & Admin.	**Excellent**
Industrial Relations	24
Psychology, Economics	23
Politics, Philosophy, Maths, Media	22
Sociology	20

RESEARCH:
*Top grades 5/6**

Economics, Law, Anthropology, Social Policy, Accounting, International History, Philosophy	**Grade 6***
Politics, Sociology, Geography, Management, Economic History	**Grade 5**

More than a quarter of graduates go into banking. Some 50% choose Economics, which dropped only one point at the teaching assessment and has a world-class Grade 6* research rating. Thirty per cent opt for the Business route, Management, Management Sciences, etc. These degrees produce many business management consultants as well – see in particular Human Resources Management & Employment. Teaching inspection: Economics 23,

WHERE LSE GRADUATES END UP

Health & Social Work: 5%; Education: 5%; Wholesale Retail: 5%; Manufacturing: 2%; Financial Activities: 32%; Public Administration, Civil Service & Defence: 7%; Hotel/Restaurant: 2%; Transport & Communications (including Telecommunications): 2.5%; Personnel: 3%; Computer: 2%; Business & Management: 5%; Accountancy: 18%; Media (including Film): 2%; Legal 2%; Publishing: 1%; Advertising: 1%; Sport: 1%.

Approximate 'graduate track' employed **82%**

Business 24. Research Grade 6*: Economics. Grade 5: Management.

More than 3% of graduates end up in merchant banking via business degrees such as Business Mathematics & Statistics, and via economics and maths – see Business Mathematics & Statistics, Econometrics & Mathematical Economics, Mathematics & Economics. Maths scored 22 out of 24 points at assessment.

Then there is the core of graduates who become investment advisers and analysts. More than 16% choose this sector; it is in fact the single most popular LSE graduate occupation, many choosing from the range of economics degrees, about a third preferring the business route.

Sharedealers come via business, stockbrokers via economics. There is no dedicated degree for computer/IT consultants, who come via business and social studies, mainly the latter.

A dedicated Actuarial Science degree finds some 2% of LSE graduates jobs with insurance companies, their function of course to calculate risk.

Law is rated world-class Grade 6*, and there is a specialist French Law degree. There is no social work degree as such. Besides Sociology, they offer Social Policy and four combinations – with Economics, Sociology, Government, and Criminal Justice & Psychology. Ther's also an interesting BA Anthropology & Law.

A language Centre specialises in creating courses targeted to the particular needs of students and offers EAP, French, German, Italian, Japanese, Russian, Spanish, Arabic, Chinese, Portuguese, Norwegian, Basque, Turkish.

SOCIAL SCENE

STUDENTS' UNION **The Three Tuns**, **Underground Bar**, **Quad** and shop are all newly refurbished. 'Many students drift in the direction of the pub, **The Three Tuns**,' says Dominque, 'which has a "cool" atmosphere. The drinks are cheap, the company is friendly and the music plays at a level that doesn't reach eardrum-damaging decibels.

'The Students Union offers a wide range of societies at the Freshers' Fair! The Socialism Society and other political groups will attack in a desperate attempt to sway you, but other societies adopt a less obtrusive approach. There are plenty of opportunities to get involved, be it through the arts, politics, radio, religion (most religions and denominations are observed), business, or cultural groups. Sports teams exist, but I can give you little information about them, as I am motivationally challenged as regards any kind of physical activity.'

LSE claims the only weekly Students Union General Meeting in the country. More than 200 students regularly attend to hold union officers to account and to debate campus level, national and international issues. 'Those who get involved in the SU are usually left-wing,' says one who does; 'those who focus on careers are right-wing. Occasionally there are clashes.'

Excellent media: magazine *Script*, newspaper *Beaver*, radio station PuLSE FM, and TV LooSE TV.

LSE also has its own dedicated ents manager and the Friday night clubnight, *Crush*, is one of the

> *The LSE is a breeding ground for global nomads. The Houghton Street hub of LSE activity overflows with student representatives of all races of our world.*

WHAT IT'S REALLY LIKE

UNIVERSITY:

Social Life	★★★★★
Campus scene	**Small: driven, global nomads**
Student Union services	**Good**
Politics	**Active: weekly debates, local, national & internat. issues**
Sport	**30+ clubs**
National team position	**51st**
Sport facilities	**Average**
Arts opportunities	**Limited**
Student magazine	**The Script**
Student newspaper	**The Beaver**
Student radio	**PuLSEfm**
Student TV	**LSETV**
Venue/bars	**Three Tuns, Underground Bar, Quad bars**
Union ents	**CRUSH, Comedy, live events**
Union societies	**150+**
Parking	**Non-existent**

CITY:

Entertainment	★★★★★
Scene	**Wild, expensive**
Town/gown relations	**Average-good**
Risk of violence	**'Average'**
Cost of living	**Very high**
Student concessions	**Good**
Survival + 2 nights out	**£100 pw**
Part-time work campus/town	**Excellent**

most popular student nights in London every Friday. TOther regular ents are *Mind the Gap*, and for LGBT students - gays - there;s a gay salsa night, *Exilo*; *Afta Skool* (indie) is a Saturday clubnight at **Quad**. They can get 1000 bodies in to the 3-room club, made up of the **Tuns**, the **Quad**, with its sofa-strewn mezzanine, and the smaller venue, the **Underground**. There are also students nights at selected sites in London's clubland.

Town Top tip from Dominique: 'On arrival in London, buy the *London A-Z* (to avoid looking like a tourist only whip it out in times of emergency) and the student's bible, *Time Out*, essential to any-body's social survival kit. Manage limited finances by drinking your fill at the cheapest union bar before a night out.'

Sport In the basement of the Old Building there's a training room and multigym. The school also has its own sports grounds in South London. There are also netball, tennis courts and four large swim-ming pools within two miles of Houghton Street. The University of London Union has facilities for squash, basketball, rowing and swimming. LSE cricketers may use the indoor facilities at Lords. LSE sports teams came 89th nationally last year in the national team league.

PILLOW TALK

All first year students are guaranteed a place in LSE or London University accommodation – basically halls and one block of self-catering flats. 'Residence halls are cheap and easy,' writes Dominique, 'but in my opinion the London University intercollegiate option is preferable. You will find the quality of

AT A GLANCE	
ACADEMIC FILE:	
Subjects assessed	**15**
Excellent	**93%**
Typical entry requirements	**467 points**
Application acceptance rate	**8%**
Students-staff ratio	**13:1**
First/2:1 degree pass rate	**74%**
ACCOMMODATION FILE:	
Guarantee to freshers	**100%**
Style	**Halls, flats**
Catered	**75%**
En-suite	**N/A**
Price range pw	**£90-£173**
City rent pw	**£100-£180**
	Zone 1; £75-£85 Zone 2

food to be not much better than that of pig slop, but living next door to two vets, across the hall from a nurse, next door to a musician, down the hall from an opera singer, and one floor above a physiothera-pist could only happen in an intercollegiate hall (see *Introduction*). This option definitely widens your social circle. Rooms are basic with a small sin-gle bed (not much room for two if you have big plans), a desk and a wardrobe. Your room is your home and you make it your own.'

GETTING THERE

☛ Holborn (Piccadilly, Central lines), Temple (District, Circle lines), Charing Cross (Jubilee, Northern, Bakerloo lines).

LONDON SOUTH BANK UNIVERSITY

London South Bank University
103 Borough Road
London SE1 0AA

London South Bank Students' Union
Keyworth Street
London SE1 6NG

TEL 020 7815 7815
FAX 020 7815 8273
EMAIL enquiry@lsbu.ac.uk
WEB www.lsbu.ac.uk

TEL 020 7815 7815
FAX 020 7815 6061
EMAIL vpcomms@lsbu.ac.uk
WEB www.lsbu.org

VAG VIEW

*L*ondon South Bank projects you into the *big city, where the streets are paved with whatever you want them to be paved with. You come to South Bank University, you come to London... for a bit of gritty realism.*

CAMPUS

Much of it is clustered around a triangle formed by Borough Road, London Road and Southwark Bridge Road, just south of the Thames at Elephant and Castle. 'LSBU is on London's cultural doorstep - The National Theatre, The Globe, and the British Film Institute are a walk away from the main campus.

The City of London lies just over the river with the Houses of Parliament and Westminster Abbey close by,' writes Laura Cattell.

'Location – prime,' agrees Lola Brown. 'Situated in Zones 1/2, the main campus is indeed ideally located on the uber trendy South Bank, but Elephant & Castle itself is a bit of a hole, though it is improving rapidly with some major urban regeneration happening. It has its own tube station (Bakerloo & Northern lines).'

The learning resources (including a library) and the students union is currently on Keyworth Street, where two years ago the brand new 9-storey Keyworth Centre opened. There are two other sites further away – the Faculty of Health & Social Care at Harold Wood Hospital (Romford) and Whipps Cross Hospital (Leytonstone) – a situation rather optimistically 'solved' by calling these two distinct sites the Redwood Campus.

There are now big plans afoot for bringing everything together at the Southwark campus, and there will be major changes over the coming years. Two buildings are scheduled for completion by the end of 2008. The first - known less than imaginatively as Keyworth II - will house the Faculty of Health and Social Care, the departments of Education and facilities for Sports and Exercise Science. There'll be simulated hospital wards and specialist rooms for training, teaching and health promotion activities. The second is a development of the sometime Presbyterian St George's Chapel, now to be the Student Centre, and home for a Southwark Primary Care Practice.

FEES, BURSARIES
UK & EU Fees, 2007: not known at going to press - see www.lsbu.ac.uk/fees for the latest info. Last year there were bursaries, but no means testing - all full-time Home and EU undergraduate students were entitled to an annual bursary worth £2,250 over three years. The uni expects a similar level of support this year. There are scholarships for sport and academic prowess, and support for ethnics.

STUDENT PROFILE
63% undergrads are mature, almost a third come from the London Borough of Southwark, over half from ethnic minorities, and nearly 40% are from overseas (from more than 120 different countries). In socio-economic terms, 98% come from the state school sector, 38% from SEC classes 4-7, and 15% from 'low-participation neighbourhoods'. A very large section drop out before completing their courses. 'A real cross section,' says Lola, though it is no more representative than Oxford, of course. 'Freshers here are not generally middle-class white kids, though there are a fair few of those too.'

ACADEMIA & JOBS
The portfolio of degrees is markedly vocational. There's a feel of Salford Uni about it – the health – nursing (child, adult, mental care), the nutrition, occupational health & safety, sociology, engineering, media, computing, business, sport, built environment – South Bank is No 5 and Salford is at No 6 nationally in our Employment Top 10 for the construction industry. Again, as at Salford, many undergraduates are on sandwich courses. There's a

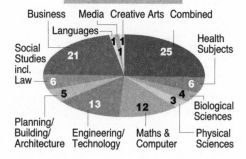

taste of the workplace about much on offer, though the course list is not as well developed as Salford's: there's not such a priority language pro-vision, for example – Salford's is first class and all-pervasive – and the media is more general and bland. There are some good BA/BSc combinations of the subjects that are on offer, and our advice is to pick subjects where skills content is high.

Besides Built Environment, faculties include Business & Management (by far the largest), Engineering, Computing, Design & Technology, Science, Humanities & Social Science and Health & Social Care.

The course programme is modular in structure. There are decent learning resources, a centre has

UNIVERSITY/STUDENT PROFILE	
University since	**1992**
Situation/style	**City sites**
Student population	**22300**
Full-time undergraduates	**15471**
- mature	**63%**
- non EU undergraduates	**8%**
- male/female	**41/59**
- state sector intake	**98%**
- non-traditional student intake	**38%**
- drop-out rate	**28%**
- undergraduate applications	**Up 6%**

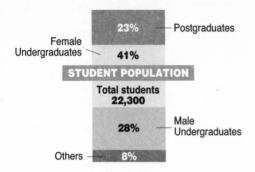

STUDENT POPULATION

23% — Postgraduates

Female Undergraduates — 41%

Total students 22,300

28% — Male Undergraduates

Others — 8%

400 Pentium PCs with Internet facility and allows access to a CD-ROM network.

In addition, there are four libraries, one at each of the four sites, with a total of 300,000 books. The teaching picture is very good., while asking grades are low.

Health steals the scene career-wise – 17% of LSB graduates go for it. Hospital staff nurses, non-hospital nurses, medical radiographers, medical practitioners dominate the employment figures. Look at BSc Nursing (Adult Health, Mental Health, Learning Difficulties, Child Care), various psychology BSc degrees, including Psychology with Sexuality.

There are, however, far more business graduates emanating from LSB each year, and a less than certain employment pathway. A large number enter employment as general administrators, sales assistants, and accounts and wages clerks. Accountancy, market research, personnel and travel/tour agency business are probably the brightest opportunity areas. Look at Accounting & Finance and the BA/BSC combined hons programme (another seven degrees there). Similarly there's Tourism & Hospitality Management and various Human Resources or Tourism tie-ups (perhaps the best with Marketing) in the list of combined BA/BSc degrees. Marketing comes with Tourism, Sociology, Social Policy, but not Psychology, which is a pity.

There's also Management & Marketing. 20 points at assessment. Average entry requirements 160-180 points.

For aspiring property developers the fount is BSc Building Surveying & Property, Commercial Management (Quantity Surveying) and similar. There's a traditional focus on Built Environment, Planning and Property Management here. Look also at Architectural Engineering, also Technology, Building Services Eng, Commercial Management (Quantity Surveying), Construction Management, etc. Teaching Inspection 18-22.

A smattering of computer graduates find employment as IT consultants, computer engi-neers, software engineers and computer programmers, and it's a useful line into the civil service and local government.

Law. Recently a Reporting Assessor for the LPC Board (a Legal Practice Course is essential to becoming a solicitor) rated them as *Good* on a scale of Excellent, Very Good, Good, Satisfactory or Unsatisfactory.

Finally, there are the sports courses – Sport & Exercise Science and Sports Product Design. It is very likely that this will be an expanding area, considering the incredible success the uni Athletic Union has enjoyed this year. See *Sport*, below.

SOCIAL LIFE

'It's London, innit,' exclaims Lola. 'Anything, anytime, whatever you like to do. The South Bank itself has a buzzing vibe every night and there are some fantastic restaurants in the Elephant – **Pizza Castella**, Ivory Arch (Indian cuisine) and Tai Won Mein (super cheap scrummy noodle bar). We're close to both the **Old Vic**, Shakespeare's **Globe** theatres and the famous South Bank arts complex, **National Theatre** and **Royal Festival Hall**, which'll inject you with culture. There's the **IMAX** cinema and it takes only about five minutes on the tube to get to Oxford Circus so the whole of London is your oyster.

'Elephant is not, however, the nicest of areas, but keep your wits about you and everything's cool.

'On campus the **Isobar** is used for clubnights and parties – Oblivion, Wednesdays; once-a-month *Raise the Roof* (garage) whilst the **Arc** (huge) hosts bigger do's. Several big name acts have played.

ACADEMIC EXCELLENCE

TEACHING:
(Rated Excellent or 17+ out of 24)

Education	**23**
Modern Languages, Town & Country Planning	**22**
Subjects Allied to Medicine, Politics	**21**
Communication & Media, Civil Eng, Anatomy, Biosciences, Business/Management, Economics, Nursing, Psychology	**20**
Sociology, Electrical & Electronic Engineering.	**19**
Chemical Engineering, Land & Property Mgt, Mechanical & Manufacturing Engineering, Building, Food Sciences.	**18**

RESEARCH:
Top grades 5/5* **None**

WHAT IT'S REALLY LIKE

UNIVERSITY:	
Social Life	★★★
Campus scene	**More of a London than a uni scene**
Student Union services	**OK**
Politics	**Student issues, activity low**
Sport	**10 clubs**
National team position	**49th**
Sport facilities	**Improving**
Arts opportunities	**Music excellent, drama, dance, film good; art poor**
Student newspaper	**Scratch**
Nightclub	**Isobar**
Bars	**Tavern**
Union ents	**Oblivion**
Union societies	**7**
Most popular societies	**Afrikan, Islamic, Forensic Science**
Smoking policy	**Union, halls OK**
Parking	**Poor**
CITY:	
Entertainment	★★★★★
Scene	**Excellent**
Town/gown relations	**Average**
Risk of violence	**'Average'**
Cost of living	**Very high**
Student concessions	**Excellent**
Survival + 2 nights out	**£90-100 pw**
Part-time work campus/town	**Average/excellent**

'Just around the back of the students' union is the **Ministry of Sound**, an experience everyone has to try once so they can see London's entire tourist population crammed into one small space. Ministry are starting a student night soon, though if past experience is anything to go by the drinks will still cost a high percentage of your student loan.

'In the main Students' Union building there are three bars, the **Tavern** (traditional pub type, TV screens for sport, pool table), the **Snug** (a cosy no smoking zone) and the **Isobar**, with a café area and pool tables by day then turning into a club by night. These are always fairly busy and there is usually plenty of free entertainment. Alcohol is relatively cheap compared to drinking in the rest of London.

'Generally, coming to study at South Bank will not be cheap, but it depends how you want to spend your time. There is plenty of opportunity to find a job however, so you can earn to support whatever habits you acquire living in the city.'

A social life can also be lived through one of the sports clubs & societies – not a great number, 20 of the former and only 7, they say, of societies this year, yet they claim the range is 'vast, from Friends of Spartacus to Socialist Resistance'. The most active student society is tabled as Arts & Media, but there is a grand tradition here of very successful cultural societies, such as the Afrikaan society with its hugely successful club night, *Black Pepper*. Islamic is also big – there are prayer rooms for Islamic students. There is also plenty of scope for students to get involved with the student magazine, *Scratch*, or indeed to organise your own thing – as elsewhere, if you get a quorum, the union will fund it.

'Politically,' writes Lola, 'we're verging on the left wing, but the most political thing to happen is an occasional guest speaker or a meeting.'

SPORT There has been a spectacular enhancement of the fortunes of LSB's Athletic union. Last year they finished above half way (49th) in the national leagues. The union was awarded the H G Messer Trophy for 'most improved university in 2003' from BUSA. Now the uni has created an Academy of Sport, Physical Activity & Wellbeing. The indoor sports facilities on the main campus include a 40 + station fitness suite, weights room, sports hall and injury clinic.

The sports ground is a 21-acre site at Turney Road, Dulwich, with pavilion and bar. There are coaching courses and sports scholarships.

PILLOW TALK

They say: 'At least 95% of all first years who want accommodation, meet the selection criteria and complete relevant paperwork by the required deadline are offered places. It is usually only those sliving very locally who applications will be held back until the main intake has been catered for then, if rooms are available, they will be offered accommo-

AT A GLANCE

ACADEMIC FILE:	
Subjects assessed	**28**
Excellent	**75%**
Average requirements	**192 points**
Application Acceptance	**20%**
Students-staff ratio	**20:1**
First/2:1 degree pass rate	**53%**
Graduate track employment	**66%**
ACCOMMODATION FILE:	
Guarantee to freshers	**95%**
Style	**Halls**
En suite	**65%**
Approx price range pw	**£83-£101**
City rent pw	**£100**

dation. We have 495 rooms at £82-84 per week (all shared bathing facilities inclusive of utilities, internet access and basic insurance cover), and 900 rooms at £101 per week (all en-suite facilities, all inclusive of utilities, internet access and basic insurance cover).' These are 2007/08 rates.

GETTING THERE
☛ By Underground: Elephant and Castle (Bakerloo and Northern Lines) or mainline Waterloo station.

LOUGHBOROUGH UNIVERSITY

Loughborough University
Ashby Road
Loughborough
Leicestershire LE11 3TU

TEL 01509 223522
FAX 01509 223905
EMAIL admissions@lboro.ac.uk
WEB www.lboro.ac.uk

Loughborough Students' Union
Ashby Road
Loughborough
Leicestershire LE11 3TT

TEL 01509 635000
FAX 01509 635003
EMAIL president@lborosu.org.uk
WEB www.lufbra.net

VAG VIEW

*W*hen people think of Loughborough, which has been a university since 1966, they think of its engineering capability – it came out of Loughborough Technical Institute – and they think of sport, for today it is the best UK university at sport by such a long way that some of its teams can't find decent opposition on the university circuit and turn to professional clubs to sharpen their teeth on.

Surprise then that the weekly student magazine, Label, received a letter from a reader complaining that coverage favoured the arts at the expense of sport. Surprise that the official uni line is: 'Contrary to popular belief, sport does not pervade everything at Loughborough – couch potatoes are also welcome, and there are plenty of non-sporting activities for students to get involved in.' Surprise, too, that alongside aeronautical and electronic and electrical manufacturing, and sport, and defence, and the construction industry, we find artistic/literary, film/video and publishing as categories of graduate employment in which Lboro students excel.

The uni is now pre-eminent in social science, in English, in library & information management – these have been adjudged research areas of renown. Meanwhile, Psychology, Drama and Art & Design are among its top teaching subjects at inspection, and the student media is making waves in national competitions.

Having said all that, it is good for sport. In fact, it is the very best. They did better in last year's Commonwealth Games than 32 countries, including Malaysia, Singapore and Kenya, and almost equalled New Zealand's performance.

CAMPUS

Loughborough is a campus university situated just off the M1. 'It is one of the largest campuses in Europe,' writes Vicky Cook, 'and conforms to the stereotype of a leafy, green, self-contained campus. This has its advantages, everything is located within walking distance from halls (though the free campus bus is worth remembering on rainy days). There are bars, restaurants (although nothing gourmet) and three food shops to buy overpriced

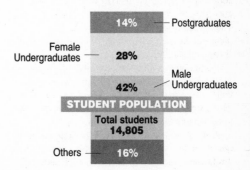

14% — Postgraduates
Female Undergraduates — 28%
Male Undergraduates — 42%
STUDENT POPULATION
Total students
14,805
Others — 16%

essentials when a walk into town is too great an effort. And, should campus and small market town become too claustrophobic, Leicester and Nottingham are mercifully close.

The uni recently acquired the Holywell Technology Park on the edge of the campus, making it one of the biggest campus universities in the UK, with a total area of 410 acres. The new space is used to enhance its research portfolio and links with industry.

Campus has been beset with would-be rapists and murderers of late, but no doubt that has meant tighter security and a closed door policy to hip hop and gangsta freaks from off the M1.

FEES, BURSARIES

UK & EU Fees, 2007: £3,070. Fees for 2008 will rise according to inflation. Bursaries for students aged under 21 on entry and in receipt of full HE Maintenance Grant are £1,300 p.a.; for others on the grant, it's £2,600 p.a. For students in receipt of partial HE Maintenance Grant there's a sliding scale. There are scholarships available for top sports performers, and £1,000 merit-based scholarships for top achieving students on certain science and engineering courses. Also, 2 music awards of £500, plus 880 music tuition bursaries of £150 each. Mature students bursaries of £400-£2,600, depending on household income.

STUDENT PROFILE

Mostly male (60/40), many from independent schools. 'A typical Lboro student,' Vicky writes, 'is one who enthuses about sport and thrives on competition, and appears to be a walking advert for sportswear companies. There are students who are not like this, but they make less noise and therefore attract less attention. Sport at Lboro is impossible to ignore. This enthusiasm is not a bad thing, but if you don't share a love of sport it can become a tad irritating.'

Writes Jennie Byass: 'The only problem that comes with such a high standard of facilities is the limited times non-elite athletes can use them. The focus here is undoubtedly on the elite athlete, and I've found it quite hard coming here after being towards the top standard of sports back home to being right at the bottom of the pile here. That's not to say there aren't opportunities, and if you don't get into the university team for your sport there are intramural games which are good fun. Matches take place on an evening and with the support of your

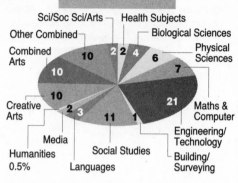

SUBJECT AREAS (%)

Sci/Soc Sci/Arts — 2
Health Subjects — 2
Other Combined — 4
Biological Sciences — 6
Combined Arts — 10
Physical Sciences — 7
Maths & Computer — 21
Engineering/Technology — 1
Building/Surveying — 11
Social Studies — 3
Languages — 2
Humanities — 0.5%
Media
Creative Arts — 10
10

whole hall the games are thoroughly enjoyable and very competitive.'

Students like it here, the drop-out rate is very low.

ACADEMIA & JOBS

Though known for engineering, business and built environment, the uni is pre-eminent in art & design, in social sciences (notably Bsc Social Psychology, Sociology, Psychology, Psychology with Ergonomics), and in drama (also publishing/English). These faculties or departments achieving either full marks or 23 out of 24 points in recent inspections by the QAA or featuring at world class level in the recent research assessments, which put the uni up in the top third of the national league table. More than a fifth of graduates go into some sort of manufacturing. Sport is obviously a niche area, but they do not enjoy the dominance in the work place that they do in the undergraduate sports ratings.

> *'The focus here is undoubtedly on the elite athlete... I've found it quite hard coming here after being towards the top standard of sports back home to being right at the bottom of the pile here.'*

UNIVERSITY/STUDENT PROFILE	
University since	**1966**
Situation/style	**Town campus**
Student population	**14805**
Undergraduates	**10413**
- mature	**6%**
- non EU undergraduates	**8%**
- male/female	**60/40**
- non-traditional student intake	**23%**
- state school intake	**82%**
- drop-out rate	**7%**
- undergraduate applications	**Up 11%**

'How much help is given to find a career and key skills taught appears to depend greatly on the department you are in,' says Vicky. 'The university does run seminars on such issues, though they are few and far between and take some tracking down.'

In 2005 the University was awarded over £4 million in recognition of its excellent practice in linking industry and employers with engineering teaching and learning. This funding was used to set up a Centre for Excellence to enhance teaching facilities.

For prospective aeronautical engineers, the big four players are Loughborough, Bristol West of England, Hertfordshire and Sheffield Hallam. At Loughborough they'll ask you for around 340 points, but that's less than at Cambridge and Southampton.

Look for Aeronautical Engineering, the 4-year Aeronautical Engineering or 4-year sandwich MEng Aeronautical Engineering, or the 5-year Aeronautical Engineering. Teaching inspection 23. Research Grade 5.

Automobile engineers are similarly well placed careers-wise – look at BE/MEng Hons 3-5-year (sandwich) Automotive Engineer-ing and a range of Automotive Materials degrees. Entry 280 points.

Again would-be civil, mechanical and con-struction engineering graduates are served well here, Loughborough enjoy a Top 10 position in the employment league table for all these core areas.

The BEng Hons Mechanical Engineering is 3-4 years depending on the extra sandwich year; MEng is 4-5 years. It's a balanced theoretical/practical course. There are also Materials Eng degrees, the latter with a Management Studies component. Note, too, the 4-year sandwich BSc Construction Engineering Management. Again teaching worth 22 points at the assessments and world-class Grade 5* rate research.

Prospective electrical and telecommunications engineers can spend up to 5 years on an MEng and combine with French or German, or there's a 4-year sandwich BEng & Diploma in Industrial

Studies, or the 3-year BEng. Teaching inspection, 22. Research Grade 5.

Look also at Computer Systems and Software Engineering orientations: Many graduates become software engineers and consultants – they are up there with Brunel as the largest suppliers to the sector. They come not only off the computer cours-es but also through maths.

IT consultants also boost their graduate employment figures. There are 4-year BSc sand-wich degrees in Computer Science, CS & E-Business, Computing & Management, and new - Computer Science & Artificial Intelligence. The first two can also be taken as 4/5-year MComp degrees – on the 5-year placement course you get a Diploma in professional studies as well.

ACADEMIC EXCELLENCE

TEACHING:
(Rated Excellent or 17+ out of 24)

Business & Management	**Excellent**
Anatomy & Physiology, Other Subjects Allied to Medicine, Psychology	**24**
Art & Design, Sociology, Drama, Mechanical, Aeronautical, Manufacturing Eng, Politics, Economics, Tourism, Physics	**23**
Maths, Chemical Eng, Electron/Electric Eng, Civil Eng, Business & Management, Building	**22**
Materials Technology	**21**

RESEARCH:
Top grades 5/5/6**

Sociology	**Grade 6***
Built Environment, Sports	**Grade 5***
Electrical and Electronic Eng, Mechanical/Aeronautical/ Manufacturing Eng, Geography, European Studies, English, Library & Info Management	**Grade 5**

WHERE LOUGHBOROUGH GRADUATES END UP

Health & Social Work: 3%; Education: 4%; Wholesale Retail: 8%; Manufacturing: 21%; Financial Activities: 12%; Public Administration, Civil Service & Defence: 5%; Hotel/Restaurant: 2%; Transport & Communications (including Telecommunications): 4%; Construction: 5%; Mining/Oil Extracting: 1%; Personnel: 3%; Computer: 6%; Business & Management: 4%; Accountancy: 6%; Media (including Film): 1%; Legal 1%; Architecture: 1.5%; Publishing: 1%; Advertising: 1%; Artistic/Literary: 1%; Sport: 3%.

Approximate 'graduate track' employed **71%**

Many of these engineering and technological strengths forge pathways into Defence, either as operative or equipment engineer. They lead with the likes of Southampton, Bristol, Nottingham, Bath, Durham, Imperial and Glasgow in this regard. Look, too, at their BA/BSc Industrial Design & Technology.

Meanwhile, their Visual Communication: Illustration degree makes graphic artists, designers, illustrators in quantity, and textile design is a particular speciality. For a few years now the old Art College down the road has been making a welcome impact on the engineering/techno-based population, both socially and academically. The strength in textiles was awarded full marks at the teaching assessments: Multi-Media Textiles, Printed Textiles, Woven Textiles are the three BA degrees on offer.

Aspiring bankers/ merchant bankers should look at BSc Business Economics & Finance and, at BSc Management Sciences and the economics, languages and computer sciences areas, each of which contributes some 10% of the graduate feed into this area.

Accountants (see Economics with Accounting) and stockbrokers also graduate in quantity from here. In fact, the 6% of graduates who become accountants make up the single largest group by destination. Economics dropped only one point at the assessments.

Loughborough's Business School has the cornerstone 4-year sandwich degree, International Business, but the choice of degrees suggests an eye for business in every aspect of the curriculum, from engineering to fashion. Look at Retail Management in this regard.

In Built Environment, Loughborough are Top-10 rated for the deployment of quantity surveyors. The 3-year BSc Commercial Management & Quantity Surveying has a good teaching assessment, a world-class rating for research. In both Management and Construction industries Loughborough is a classy product. Entry 280 points. Teaching inspection, 22. Research Grade 5*.

Unis with a Grade 5*/6* research rating for sport are Loughborough, Manchester Met, Glasgow, Liverpool John Moores and Birmingham. For pro athletes, sportsmen, players and sport officials it's Surrey Roehampton then Loughborough. For sports trainers and coaches, it's Leeds Met, Abertay Dundee, Sheffield Hallam, De Montfort, Gloucestershire, St Mary's, Manchester Met, then Loughborough. But overall they lead: BSc Sport & Exercise Science. Sports Science mixes with Management, Physics, Social Science, Chemistry, Humanities, also BSc Sports Technology and Sports Science & Physics. Teaching inspection, 23.

SOCIAL SCENE

STUDENTS' UNION Writes Jennie: 'The union club has much to offer, primarily *Friday Night Disco (FND)* and *Envy* (r&b) on a Saturday night; both are wicked nights out. By far the best night, however, is *Hey Ewe* on a Wednesday Night after all the sports matches have been played (and usually won!) during the afternoon. We all meet up with our sports or social clubs for an hour or so for some social drinking, and then proceed onto **Fusion**, where the key theme to the night is 'cheesy music' and lots of dancing. Midnight Madness happens between half 11 and half 12 at which time all drinks are only one pound!

'**JC's** is the sports bar, where everyone goes to celebrate victories. **Cognito** – bar – flashing dance floor, what more can I say? Recent live acts include Girls Aloud for the Freshers Ball, DJ Spoony, and Navi, a Michael Jackson impersonator, amazing!'

We asked an anonymous student about that hour's drinking on match night. 'There are certain rituals and traditions which we here in Loughborough have developed and institutionalised over the years,' I was told: 'The rugby shirt worn with jeans, AV's, collars up, *Hey Ewe* mayhem on a Wednesday evening, drinking games and of course Nasty...the Lufbra drink...' This latter, though increasingly at risk to the almighty Red Bull/voddie alternative (decried by purists as expensive and injurious to health), remains the people's choice.

There are 40 societies, the more traditional such as the International Students' Association and the LGBT Association, while quirkier ones, like the Hot Air Balloon club, the Breakdancing club and the circus society, Fever, show the possibilities.

Recent expansion reveals a **Media Centre**, var-

AT A GLANCE	
ACADEMIC FILE:	
Subjects assessed	**20**
Excellent	**85%**
Typical entry requirements	**363 points**
Application acceptance rate	**16%**
Students-staff ratio	**19:1**
First/2:1 degree pass rate	**65%**
ACCOMMODATION FILE:	
Guarantee to freshers	**If first choice**
Style	**Halls, flats, houses**
Catered	**60%**
En suite	**10%**
Cost pw (no food/food)	**£54-£128**
Town rent pw	**£50-£75**

ious franchise shops, banks, etc. The venue itself is open for event nights every night of the week, with 9 bars and the newly refurbished **Room 1**.

The **Media Centre** houses the 24/7 student radio station (LCR), the student magazine offices (*Label*) and a TV/video editing suite. LSUTV won the Light Entertainment award in the 2005 national judgings and were runners-up for News & Current Affairs. The 'talk' studio and production studio (drum booth, guitar booth) beyond leave you in no doubt that these students have not been overcharged at £1.4 million. Sound, vision, print, web, all of it together on a single floor and serviced by student engineers who know their stuff.

While a rapist stalker patrolled outside, miserable members of the uni and National Student Union came out against student magazine sponsored Totty TV contests. The awful NUS, which puts its foot in its mouth at every opportunity, objected to 'top three' pictures of a semi-naked Kate, studying for a degree in primary teaching at Derby University. 'The truth is that these shows and contests on campus and on websites show that sexism is as alive today as it ever was,' said NUS women's officer Kat Stark[ers]. Lboro then got its own back by taking 2 gongs at the national student TV Awards (News & Current Affairs and Music), and being highly commended for their factual progs and broadcasting skills.

The SU also has a student advice centre and employment exchange, and adjacent nursery with subsidised places for students' children.

SPORT Lboro teams beat everyone every year. Supportive of the effort is a huge investment in facilities on campus, including a 'supergym' strength and conditioning centre, high-performance indoor and outdoor athletics centres and an Olympic-size swimming pool.

TOWN Writes Jennie: 'Loughborough is quite a small market town, with 12,500 students dominating a 60,000 population. The town itself is pleasant, with all the basic shops you need, and plenty to offer. Also, Loughborough offers a greater sense of security when compared to the majority of the big cities. But it is quite a different proposition to the other cities of sport, such as Manchester or Sheffield...

PILLOW TALK

'All freshers are guaranteed hall accommodation and it is usually possible to remain in hall throughout your time at Lboro, although a lot of people choose to spend a year in town. The halls are very varied. Don't set your heart on a particular one, the allocation process appears random.'

WHAT IT'S REALLY LIKE	
UNIVERSITY:	
Social Life	★★★★★
Campus scene	**Well resourced, sports crazy**
Student Union services	**Good**
Politics	**Light**
Sport	**Simply the best**
National team position	**Always 1st 53 clubs**
Sport facilities	**Excellent**
Arts opportunities	**Very good**
Student magazine	**Label**
Student radio	**LCR**
Student TV	**LSUTV**
2005 TV Awards	**1 win, 1 highly commended**
Nightclub	**Fusion + bar upstairs**
Bars	**JC's, Cognito**
Union ents	**FND (disco), Hey Ewe (cheese), Envy (r&b) + live**
Union societies	**40**
Most popular society	**International**
Parking	**No 1st years**
TOWN:	
Entertainment	★★
Scene	**Market town, good pubs**
Town/gown relations	**Good**
Risk of violence	**Average**
Cost of living	**Average**
Student concessions	**Excellent**
Survival + 2 nights out	**£70pw**
Part-time work campus/town	**Good/average**

Says Jennie: 'I am in catered accommodation and my hall is situated in the heart of the student village, with food, washing rooms and leisure facilities all within in about a minute's walk. Some people are not so fortunate and I have seen some of the halls which could certainly do with some attention.'

Accommodation in town is more expensive, because of the utility bills, but it is quieter, less claustrophobic and less intrusive as you choose who you live with. All hall rooms are computer networked and carry phone sockets. There's something to suit every pocket, 'and the sense of loyalty and community spirit in these halls is of an intensity usually reserved for centuries-old universities.'

For 2008, three new on-campus halls for 1,000 students are planned in a courtyard development with mixed self- catering facilities and flexible dining packages from the nearby restaurant and social centre.

GETTING THERE
☞ By road: M1/J23, A512.
☞ By rail: London St Pancras, 1:45; Birmingham New Street, 1:30; Sheffield, 1:30; Nottingham, 0:20;
Leicester, 0:15.
☞ By air: East Midlands Airport close by.
☞ By coach: London, 2:45; Exeter, 6:50; Newcastle, 8:10; Manchester, 4:30.

STUDENT MANCHESTER – THE CITY

Writes fun-loving Alexandra Negri Not unlike London, Manchester is a city that never sleeps. Whatever day of the week or time of night, there is always somewhere to go, whether it is in the centre of town or the 'fields of fallow' - Fallowfield is the area of student residences at the furthest end of the Oxford Road corridor.

Oxford Road is of course student central. It sees tens of thousands of students pacing up and down it each day, whether it's to go to the various libraries, the lecture theatres, eateries, the infamous **Academy** (where the supremely tacky, yet unmissable *Torremolinos* is held every year), or the ridiculously cheap student bars (favourites including **Kro 1 & 2**, **The Footage**, **Sku Bar** and the Student Union of course.

The social scene in Manchester is endless and there is definitely something for everyone's taste and these are just a few suggestions and popular attractions.

Fallowfield is the perfect place to start for student nightlife. If you find yourself so far-flung and are not looking to venture far from your squalor, it's a passable destination for cheesy nights, stick-to-the-floor dance halls and cheap drinks. **Robo's** (popular on a Tuesday night), **Queen of Hearts** and the **Orange Grove** are a few of the famous haunts for students, all of which have their particular qualities; Robo's is a *Scream* bar, so with a yellow card you can gain even cheaper cheap drinks, and Queen of Hearts and Orange Grove are both pub-based, showing sports, serving pub grub and furnished with the odd pool table.

For first years, or those still clinging on to their youth, there is the infamous *Bop* held at **Owen's Park** every Friday. Don't be put off by the thousands that turn up hoping to be one of the lucky ones to enter the youth club come school gym. Turn up early, 10pm-ish, and either drink your wait away, or get legless inside for a tenner on Kermit's spunk, cheeky vimto's, snakebites or whatever other exotic tipple takes your fancy.

If you're feeling like breaking free of Fallowfield, then all the way down Oxford Road, right into the centre of town are places worthy of a visit. First hit the aptly named Curry Mile, either to start the night, or to satisfy the after-hours munchies - most curry house, kebab shops and pizzerias are open until the early hours.

If it is just a cheap meal you are after, then Rusholme is the place, as many restaurants here do BYOB (bring your own booze). Be careful though, because of the Muslim culture some restaurants do not allow alcohol at *All!!*

Through Rusholme and onto Oxford Road takes us past **Revolution**, **Space**, **Dry** and **Font**, a few other watering holes worth a visit.

Before you know it, you're in town and across the border between 'night out on a tenner', and tenner a drink'!! For the more hard-up students do not fear, there are still many establishments that cater for the tightest wallet.

If it's the clean cut, well chiselled, cologne-smelling ladies man that takes your fancy then **42's** is definitely NOT the place for you. Long haired, scruffy t-shirt, skinny jeaned Indie boys fly the flag for 42's. Probably my, along with another 50% of the student population's, favourite place to be on a Thursday night. It's hot, it's sweaty, it's smoky, it's cheap, it's indie rock and roll, to quote one of the more frequently played artist there. Other Indie nights include **5th Avenue**, and **The Venue**.

The famous **Sankies** is host to some, if not all, the world's most famous DJ's, and after a recent re-vamp, promises to be worthwhile to those of you who do not fight shy of a good rave. Be sure to check the listings, as nights do vary, and in the summer, be prepared to stay til the break of dawn. Their boat parties, the 'Smugglers Run', down the Irwell (yes the Irwell!) are a real summer treat!

Or for the more elite who prefer to spend your student loan sipping Champers and gazing at footballers, try the bars on Deansgate, **Panacea** and **Coco Rooms**.

Northern Quarter has an eclectic mix of bars from live jazz and open mic nights at **Matt and Phredís** to soul and funk at **Bluu** bar and burlesque nights at **Mint Lounge** and the newly opened **Birdcage**. It is also home to the highly acclaimed **Affleck's Palace**, an eccentric shop where one can find anything from vintage classic to the best fancy dress.

Like most cities Manchester does have areas with a bad reputation, but in general, it's a safe city if you find yourself having to walk home, kebab in hand with not a penny to your name. For those in 4-inch stilettos I recommend a taxi. There are always black cabs around, and it will cost you around £7 to get back to Fallowfield, depending.

After a night out in the **Printworks** which holds **Tiger Tiger**, **Pure** and **Opus**, as well as one of the only 24 bars, a **Weatherspoons**, which I don't recommend, there is a late night bus service that stops right outside. An eventful ride home is usually guaranteed for those who prefer this mode of transport in the early hours.

Canal St., the home of 'pride' is defiantly worth a visit for some fantastic restaurants, happy hour deals, varied bars, and overall friendly fun, and sometimes bizarre service!

For the more refined there are two main theatres in Manchester, **The Palace Theatre** and **The Opera House**, which see many major productions. There are also a number of art galleries and exhibitions around town, a favourite of mine being in the **URBIS**, which recently displayed an exhibition on Graffiti Art and hosted the infamous 'Little Black Dress' design competition. **G-mex** is one of the larger exhibition centres which holds events like the ideal home show and career fairs.

THEATRE

Writes Elka Malhotra **The Royal Exchange Theatre** offers 2 stages (one in the round) and a combination of modern and traditional plays (all at student discounts). Situated in a rather nice area right in the city centre, it's also a good place to pop in for a cuppa during the day. **The Palace Theatre** in Oxford Road is designed for more family-friendly showings, they offer a good mix of shows and fairly big names. **The Contact Theatre** caters more to the student market and has occasional art exhibits as well as writing, DJ and drama workshops. **The Contact** also features the **Café Deluxe**, which makes hearty sandwiches and a mean cup of coffee. **The Green Room** is another avant-garde venue which, like **The Contact**, boasts its own nightclub nights, a small theatre and a small café-bar. **The Lowry** is also worth a mention here. Although a little more out-of-the-way than its rivals, it offers the largest stage outside of London, with Ferrari-designed seating! On a more low-key note, **The Library Theatre** offers a range of events from jazz to comedy, and traditional plays.

CINEMAS

Going to the cinema in Manchester costs about £4 pretty much everywhere. **The Filmworks** is by far the most popular, and despite seeming a little like an airport, boasts a ridiculous number of screens, some of which show IMAX 3D movies as well as arthouse and mainstream films. **The Odeon** is the city centre's only mainstream cinema, a quieter venue. In his days as Manchester United's captain,

Eric Cantona used to get his French film 'fix' at the **Cornerhouse**, the best place for arthouse, foreign and small budget films. It also features a small but interesting art gallery and what is arguably the first modern-style bar in Manchester. Opened in 1985 it has an arty clientele and Belgium beers.

There is also the **AMC** situated in the Great Northern building on Deansgate, which usually shows all the latest releases. Although quite a way to travel out of the city and relatively expensive, **The UCI** at The Trafford Centre is also a nice little cinema complex (the outer facia has Islamic pillars beside the centre's themed food court).

COMEDY

Manchester knows how to have a laugh and **The Comedy Store**, situated on Deansgate Locks is definitely the best for doing that. *The Best In Stand-Up* on Friday and Saturday provide a fantastic night out and offer great student concessions, just make sure you buy tickets in advance the night is known to sell out. **The Frog and Bucket** is another popular comedy venue, although different in style, less slick and more traditional in its humour. They offer open mic nights on Mondays. **The Buzz** is possibly the longest running venue and has featured many a great, such as Jack Dee. **The Dancehouse Theatre** is also known to host occasional comedy nights, as is **The Contact**, known for its up-and-coming, very modern acts). Other popular comedy venues include **Bar Risa** and **Jongleurs**.

SHOPPING ON A LOAN

Affleck's Palace alone features more interesting little stalls than you can shake an oversized stick at, and is quite a Manc institution. A maze of a place it offers piercings, tattoos, t-shirts, CDs, vintage clothing, condoms, fancy dress, fetish wear and the ever popular rainbow-coloured hair extensions. **The Coliseum** is similar, situated behind **Affleck's**, on a smaller scale and with more of a gothic twist. **The Arndale Market** is handy for picking up cheap, fresh food as well as clothes, shoes and practical jokes – all fairly cheap.

The Student Market in the Academy sells bikes, clothes, hippie items, discount CDs and a variety of other stuff and is a favourite haunt on a Tuesday lunchtime. **The Trafford Centre** is the second biggest shopping centre in England and has literally miles of shops, but it's so big that your funky new purchases will probably have gone out of fashion by the time you leave.

Most chain shops can be found in the city centre. Student discounts are ubiquitous. A little more up market are **Harvey Nichols** and **Selfridges**, as well as the King Street area of the city centre which also features **DKNY**, **Max Mara** and **Hermes**.

UNIVERSITY OF MANCHESTER

The University of Manchester
Oxford Road
Manchester M13 9PL

TEL 0161 275 2077
FAX 0161 275 2106
EMAIL ug.admissions@manchester.ac.uk
WEB www.manchester.ac.uk

Manchester Students' Union
Oxford Road
Manchester M13 9PR

TEL 0161 275 2930
FAX 0161 275 2936
E: communications@umsu.manchester.ac.uk
WEB www.umsu.manchester.ac.uk

VAG VIEW

*B*y 2015 The University of Manchester aims to be among the top 25 universities in the world. £630 million is currently being invested on campus in new buildings and facilities.

They are now one unit with UMIST, the world-famous Institute of Science and Technology up the road, and the Manchester Business School, and are joined in this feverishly studenty neck of the woods by another university, Manchester Met, and Salford University is only a 15-minute bus ride away.

So it is that whole areas of this elegant, busy city are, to all intents and purposes, campus, and particularly, Oxford Road. With the Royal Northern School of Music, this must be the largest conglomeration of students anywhere in the world.

CAMPUS

Manchester Uni has grown up with the city. The Wilmslow/Oxford Road runs right through the centre of campus, linking it at the top end with Manchester Met, Whitfield Street (gateway to the city's legendary Gay Village) and the old UMIST, and at the bottom end with the most populous areas of student residences – Rusholme, Fallowfield, etc. See *Student Manchester*, page 320.

The whole street is campus, but it is also city. Manchester University has a theatre (**Contact**) and a premier gig venue (**The Academy**) and a museum (**Manchester Museum**, currently undergoing a £20-million facelift) and an art gallery (**Whitworth**) which are all key sites of this city.

City and university are absolutely inseparable, not least because they share the same vibe. It is an active, buzzing scene, a place some parents dread their children choosing.

26% — Postgraduates

Female Undergraduates — 40%

STUDENT POPULATION

Total students
35,665

34% — Male Undergraduates

FEES, BURSARIES

UK & EU Fees, 2007: £3,070. If in receipt of full HE Maintenance grant there's a bursary of £1000;. They say: 'The Manchester Guarantee Bursary is available to all students with a household income of around £26,500 or less.' Scholarship-wise, there's the Talented Athlete Scholarship Scheme, The Manchester Advantage Scholarship (£5,000 for UK students with 3 A grades or equivalent a family income of £17,910 or less), The Manchester Success Scholarship (£1,000 on same basis but for certain areas of study), The President's Award (£10,000 p.a. to 10 outstanding students), and there are music scholarships, and 30 accommodation bursaries, according to area of residence and financial circs.

UNIVERSITY/STUDENT/PROFILE	
University since	**1903**
Situation/style	**Civic**
Student population	**35655**
Undergraduate	**26460**
- mature	**10%**
- non EU undergraduates	**10%**
- male/female	**46/54**
- non-traditional student intake	**21%**
- state school intake	**78%**
- drop-out rate	**8%**
- undergraduate applications	**Up 3%**

STUDENT PROFILE

In general, Manchester is a university for kids who like to make things happen – they're an intelligent, resourceful, lively crew, not afraid or too lazy to lay themselves on the line and apply themselves, and not averse to letting their hair down either. Here's the advice of one of them, Alexandra Negri: 'For anyone going to a) a city as big as Manchester, b) leaving the tlc of your family, and c) being thrown into a world of slightly smelly, converse wearing, hard-up students, can be a bit daunting. However, the first days if not weeks could be the best you will ever imagine. I was in halls with 7 other fun and friendly students, all of whom were as nervous as me. The messy yet slightly constructive 'freshers' week' enables you to make one too many drunken friends and attend events and socialize with people on your course. I met my now best friend sat in one of those induction meetings. No one will dare to speak in these first meetings, but try to break the ice because it is definitely worth it.

'Uni really opens your eyes to different social groups, cultures and religions and this is especially the case in Manchester, where they have one of the biggest international student bases in the UK. Do not be put off by this, because you get to met even more weird, wacky and wonderful people than you ever hoped.'

ACADEMIA & JOBS

There is no limit to the number of top-rated course assessments – 96% make our criteria of Academic Excellence, and research here has a pedigree of its own – this is where Ernest, First Baron Rutherford did the work which led to the splitting of the atom, and where the computer was invented. They are still pre-eminent (with the likes of Birmingham, Bath and Imperial College) in the provision of graduate physicists. Overall, the uni came 9th in the research assessments and claims the top grade 5, 5*or 6* ratings in 37 out of 46 subjects.

On-campus resources include the John Rylands Library, the third largest uni library in the country with more than 3.5 million books. There is no shortage of computer technology – there are now 6000 PCs in public clusters on campus.

There are 4 Faculties: Engineering & Physical Sciences; Humanities; Life Sciences; Medical & Human Sciences.

With more than half graduates entering the Health sector, and Manchester creating Europe's premier biomedical campus, a series of linked scientific and hospital facilities on Oxford Road, it is right to open with the 5/6-year MB ChB: AAB + BMAT rquired. It scored full marks at the teaching assessments. There has long been a medical faculty at Manchester Uni. Now, 50 students can also

study an identical programme at Keele University (see entry). Critical faculties and communication skills are to the fore, as is constructing a methodology of self-education. There is also MBChB with European Studies – six months at a partner institution in France (Rennes), Switzerland (Lausanne) or Germany (Homberg). Entry AAB including Chemistry, one of Maths/Physics/Biology + one other, not necessarily Science, not General Studies, Media, Theatre or Home Economics. Grade A GCSE Chemistry, Physics, Biology, Maths. Grade B English Language.

Biological Sciences are of course key elements in the same faculty and attracted the highest listing – Grade 6* – in the research assessment.

Manchester also scored full marks at the teaching assessment of its 5/6-year dental degree. Entry ABB. Prospective dental hygienists and nurses note the BSc Oral Health Science (BBC to get in).

Finally, Manchester is one of only three unis to be awarded Grade 5 for research in nursing, Pharmacy took full marks at the teaching assessments and is a Top 10 job provider, and there is a

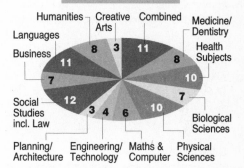

SUBJECT AREAS (%)

Humanities — 8
Creative Arts — 3
Combined — 11
Medicine/Dentistry — 8
Health Subjects — 10
Languages
Business — 11
Social Studies incl. Law — 12
7
Biological Sciences — 7
Planning/Architecture — 3
Engineering/Technology — 4
Maths & Computer — 6
Physical Sciences — 10

BSc Physiotherapy taught at the Manchester Royal Infirmary.

For psychology there's a 22-point teaching assessment and international Grade 5 for research, and they are among a few unis whose postgrad provision is approved by the British Psychological Society for career psychologists.

Equally impressive is the Manchester Business School, currently rated third in the country. Writes Alexandra: 'The teaching standard at Manchester Business School is high,' writes Alexandra. 'You will get the grades you deserve as long as you take courses you are interested in and are prepared to put the work in. Saying that a few slip-ups may be kindly overlooked in the haze of first year, and in general teachers are helpful and approachable if you are struggling. Personal mentors are allocated to small groups of students and deal with any queries, problems or just general discussions. The workload is substantial but not great. You may find you have more lecture hours than fellow students on other courses. However, there will be less reading or coursework as a result. The Business School has its own library and computer clusters on hand, but you are still free to use any of the other resources around campus. The usual rush in the first weeks to secure text books from the library always occurs and it always seems to be the exchange students who get there first. Do not fear, either the books will be available at other libraries or you can purchase all set textbooks at Blackwell's located in the Precinct. Manchester Business School has a real sense of community because it is set aside from the rest of campus.'

For would-be accountants, there's a flexible option. Accounting or Accounting & Economics/ Finance/Law (4 years), or Accounting with Business Information Systems are among the degrees on offer. See also the Management degrees, one of which focuses on accountancy & Finance. Teaching inspection: Economics 24, Business 24. Research: Grade 6*. Research Grade 5 for Management.

IT consultants also proliferate, see BEng, MEng and BSc degrees.

The defence industry plunders many a Manchester graduate from the School of Biological Sciences, while the Royal Air Force Officer concentrates on Aerospace Engineering (B/MEng), the MEng Avionics degrees and the Computer Science and Engineering degrees: international Grade 5 for research. Manchester are perennially among the Top 10 providers of aeronautical engineers, and offer enticing combinations involving Business and/or European industrial experience.

Within the education provision, both adult and higher education sectors are particularly well served. By far the most popular route is via the joint hons Languages, from which there's also a Top 10 provision of translators and interpreters. At the teaching assessments they scored 19 for French, Italian; 20 for Spanish; 21 for Linguistics and German. French and German were awarded a world-class Grade 5* rating at the research assessments; Iberian Grade 6*. Look, too, at the series of Middle Eastern studies degrees, including Arabic, Hebrew (& Jewish Studies), Persian, Turkish, Islamic. There's an international Grade 5 for research.

Manchester send many languages graduates into personnel. Sciences and Social Studies are also strong in this employment area. Note an excellent series of Social Policy (international Grade 5 for research), Sociology and Social Anthropology

ACADEMIC EXCELLENCE

TEACHING:
(Rated Excellent or 17+ out of 24)

Chemistry, Law, Mechanical Engineering, Anthropology, Business & Management, Computer Studies, Music, Geography, Social Policy & Administration, Earth Sciences	**Excellent**
Physics, Management, Politics, Economics, Philosophy, Dentistry, Medicine, Pharmacology, Classics, Theology	**24**
Anatomy, Archaeology, Biosciences, Nursing, Education	**23**
Psychology, Maths, Leisure, Subjects Allied to Medicine	**22**
German, Linguistics, Sociology, Materials Technology, Drama, History of Art	**21**
Iberian Studies, Electrical & Electronic Eng, Aerospace Eng, Town & Country Planning, Middle Eastern Studies	**20**
French, Italian	**19**
Civil Engineering	**18**

RESEARCH:
Top grades 5/5/6**

Pharmacy, Biological Sciences, Computer, Metallurgy , Sociology, Accounting, Iberian/ Latin American, Theology, Music	**Grade 6***
Pre-Clinical Studies, French, German, Dutch/Scandinavian	**Grade 5***
Community & hospital-based Clinical Subjects, Nursing, Subjects Allied to Medicine, Psychology, Chemistry, Physics, Earth Sciences, Pure Maths, Applied Maths, Civil Eng, Mechanical/Aeronautical, Manufacturing Eng, Law, Anthropology, Politics, Social Policy, Management, Middle Eastern and African Studies, English, Italian, Linguistics, Classics, History, History of Art, Drama/Dance/Performing Arts	**Grade 5**

degrees and combinations, also the BA and BSc Psychology degrees (22 at assessment).

Architecture, town planning and property

development are all rich employment seams out of Manchester. There's BA Architecture, but also an interesting series of MEng Structural Engineering & Architecture. See, too, the 4-year MTCP Town & Country Planning and BA City & Regional Development. Teaching inspection 20.

There is a sterling reputation for both English and Drama. The enfant terrible of the '70s and '80s, miniature Martin Amis, author of *The Rachel Papers* (or *Dead Babies*, as it was first entitled), *Money* and the like, has at length found sanctuary in Manchester University, where he has the title of Professor of Creative Writing. Students will no doubt queue up in the hope that they might feature in the novel that comes out his experiences.

> *City and university are absolutely inseparable, not least because they share the same vibe. It is an active, buzzing scene, a place some parents dread their children choosing.*

Finally, Man Uni are European law specialists and were awarded an international Grade 5 for research in this area.

SOCIAL SCENE

STUDENTS' UNION It is an unadventurous soul who appears at the foot of MUSU's steps any day in term time and resists propulsion inside – bodies hurry purposefully like ants, while as alien visitors we were drawn irredeemably by the sights and sounds of the new **Solem Bar**. The sound inside is the city and has the power during the day to reconfigure the cranium back into last night's form. The bar's design – 'Swedish sauna meets trendy metal,' sourpussed someone in earshot – actually makes for a cosy place to hang out, and perhaps shoot some pool on the new tables. It's a vast improvement on the old Serpent Bar.

'Next door to the union is the **Academy**, a 1,200-capacity live band venue,' Leonie Kenyon tells us, 'and, on the top floor of the union, is the **Hop & Grape**, not actually a pub despite it's name, but a small bar and occasional venue for live bands. The Academy pulls itself round in time for the Student Market during the day. It's a prime spot for

posters, bikes, CDs, clothes and hippy items, a favourite haunt of students especially at lunchtime when the homemade chocolate cakes are rather popular! Another union nightclub is the **Cellar**, which features *Horny* on Friday, and plays a mixture of pop and cheese. On weekday afternoons it is also used as a café.'

Meanwhile, students galvanise themselves into national prominence with their media. Manchester's *Student Direct* is the city's No. 1 student newspaper. Fuse FM (radio) and MSTV complete the picture. No surprise the uni is high in the employment league for editors, publishing and the like. Last year in the national student awards *Student Direct* had 2 nominations, for Best Travel Journalist and Best Photographer, and at Fuse they won Best Male Presenter.

In the area of drama, the uni is a major force, the annual springtime student festival still reigns supreme. And politically, the union's campaigning reputation still goes unquestioned.

NORTH CAMPUS The old UMIST SU, the Barnes Wallis Building on the North Campus off Sackville Street still has ground floor **Harry's Bar** and **Paddy's Lounge**, U-Print, a Union Shop, the North Campus Advice Centre, and the RAG and Student Action Office. Meanwhile, **Club Underground** still attracts a faithful few in the basement.

SPORT The teams came 10th in the national uni team ratings last year. Facilities include a boat house on the Bridgewater Canal, Yacht Club at Pennington Flash, Leigh, 18 miles west of the city. Pitches (31 acres) for rugby, soccer, hockey, lacrosse, cricket, netball, are close to the student village at Fallowfield, also tennis courts, all-weather, artificial grass areas and pavilion. In Fallowfield, too, is the **Armitage Centre** with sports hall and squash courts close by. A further 90 acres lie ten miles south, below the M63, at Wythenshawe sports

---

WHERE MANCHESTER GRADUATES END UP

Health & Social Work: 26%; Education: 6%; Wholesale Retail: 8%; Manufacturing: 7%; Financial Activities: 9%; Public Administration, Civil Service & Defence: 6%; Hotel/Restaurant: 3%; Transport & Communications (including Telecommunications): 3%; Construction: 1%; Mining/Oil Extracting: 1%; Personnel: 5%; Computer: 4%; Business & Management: 5%; Accountancy: 5%; Media (including Film): 1%; Legal 2%; Architecture: 1%; Publishing: 2%; Artistic/Literary: 0.5%; Sport: 0.5%.

Approximate 'graduate track' employed **67%**

WHAT IT'S REALLY LIKE

UNIVERSITY:

Social Life	★★★★★
Campus scene	**Big, busy, self-assured**
Student Union services	**Good**
Politics	**Active & widely representative: fees, war, housing, racism**
Sport	**Key**
National team position	**10th**
Sport facilities	**Good**
Arts opportunities	**Excellent; high profile drama, dance, film**
Student newspaper	**Student Direct**
2006 National Awards	**2 nominations**
Student radio	**Fuse FM**
2006 National Awards	**1 win**
Student TV	**MUSTV**
Nightclub and venues	**Cellar, Academy 1,2 & 3**
Bars	**Solem, Hop & Grape, Lunar**
Union ents	**Club Tropicana, Horny and much much more live**
Union societies	**200**
Parking	**£80 p.a. permit**

CITY:

Entertainment	★★★★★
City scene	**Legendary**
Town/gown relations	**Average-poor**
Risk of violence	**High**
Cost of living	**Average**
Student concessions	**Good**
Survival + 2 nights out	**£90 pw**
Part-time work campus/town	**Average/good**

ground. On campus itself is the **McDougal Centre**, which has a swimming pool, indoor games hall, gym, squash and fives courts, an outside five-a-side court, rifle range, climbing wall, bowls carpets, sauna and solarium. The new Commonwealth Games swimming pool is open to students. There are bursaries, two offered by the exclusive XXI, an elite sports club founded in 1932.

TOWN See *Student Manchester*, page 320.

PILLOW TALK

All freshers are guaranteed a place in halls and flats. The most populous areas of student residences – Rusholme, Fallowfield, etc – are at the bottom end of the Oxford Road corridor. Writes

Leonie: 'Under the railway line and through Rusholme's Curry Mile – which, as the name would suggest, is full of curry houses and interesting Eastern-style shops. Although located next to the infamous Moss Side, it's quite safe.

'Fallowfield is the ideal place to live as it is secure, lively, and features some very nice little houses. The student halls range from very nice to eyesore (The Oak House Tower - eek!), and are backed by the university-owned Armitage Sports Centre, which offers student discounts on a range of sporty activities.'

Writes Alexandra of 'the tower': 'Prepare yourself for TV's falling from a great height, trolley races round each floor and cows in the lift (just a few things that happened when I was in my first year)! Apart from that all other residences are fairly similar, the slightly newer and nicer are Richmond Park with Willow Court and Poplar, built for residents when the Commonwealth Games were held in Manchester.'

Withington is a little quieter, a little more expensive, and that little bit further away from uni and the town centre, but has a good variety of pubs, shops and coffee shops. Similarly Didsbury (home of the 'Didsbury Dozen' series of pubs – a pub crawl classic) has a good deal to offer, but is more expensive than the wholly studenty Fallowfield area.

Victoria Park is seen as the posh alternative, probably because most of its halls are large, leafy, Victorian buildings. It's an area between Fallowfield and the main campus – approximately 15 minutes walk from the main university buildings. The Students' Union is located at the top of the Victoria Park area, as is Whitworth Park Hall, affectionately known as the Toblerone building and the perfect choice for Arts students, since you can stagger out

AT A GLANCE

ACADEMIC FILE:

Subjects assessed	**47**
Excellent	**96%**
Typical entry requirements	**396 points**
Application acceptance rate	**12%**
Med. School acceptance rate	**9%**
Students-staff ratio	**14:1**
First/2:1 degree pass rate	**70%**

ACCOMMODATION FILE:

Guarantee to freshers	**100%**
Style	**Halls, flats**
Catered	**26%**
En-suite	**27%**
Price range pw	**£57-£104**
City rent pw	**£50-£65**

of bed and be right outside the Faculty of Arts. These halls tend to be a tad more expensive because the rooms are nicer and most are catered.

There are also private halls of residence in the city centre Student Village, popular with students at Manchester Met since it is right on their doorstep. Victoria Hall is another privately owned student residence near the city centre.'

'Safety-wise, all the residence are patrolled 24 hours and there is secure parking in some of the residences,' concludes Alexandra. 'Taking a car to uni is not really necessary, as public transport is so good and you just end up being the local taxi ser-vice. It also costs extra for a parking permit - approx £80 a year. A weekly guideline to expenses: £150; £75 (self-catered halls), £30 (food shop), £2 (weekly bus-pass) and £40 (two nights out).'

GETTING THERE
☛ By road: M63/J10, A34.
☛ By rail: London Euston, 2:30; Leeds, 1:45; Liverpool Lime Street, 0:50.
☛ By air: Manchester Airport for international and inland flights.
☛ By coach: London, 4:35; Bristol, 5:00; Newcastle, 5:00.

MANCHESTER METROPOLITAN UNIVERSITY

The Manchester Metropolitan University
All Saints
Manchester M15 6BH

TEL 0161 247 2000
FAX 0171 247 6871
EMAIL prospectus@mmu.ac.uk
WEB www.mmu.ac.uk

Manchester Met Students' Union
99 Oxford Road
Manchester M1 7EL

TEL 0161 247 1162
FAX 0161 247 6314
EMAIL mmsu@mmu.ac.uk
WEB www.mmsu.com

VAG VIEW

*M*anchester Met, formerly Manchester Poly, is situated on various sites in Manchester and in Crewe and Alsager, two towns either side of the M6 between junctions 16 and 17.

People pick MMU for its reputation as a party-till-you-die university. When you visit, they do not disappoint: 'Everyone gets very focused on what's going here, which is massive,' confessed a student.

CAMPUS
The Manchester base is centred at the All Saints site on Oxford Road, very close to Manchester Uni, making, with UMIST and a couple of other colleges in the vicinity, a quite extraordinary concentration of students (around 100,000) within the square mile.

Crewe & Alsager are towns about 6 miles apart, some 35 miles south of Manchester, their semi-rural campus environments a million miles away in spirit from heaving Oxford Road. 'There's not a lot of contact with Crewe & Alsager,' my guide admitted. 'They always say there is, but in practice there's not. They have their own set-up down there. They're very sports and drama orientated. I think you still get some who enrol for C&A and are quite surprised that it's not just down the road and you can't always get up here on a Saturday night! I understand quite a few drop out over that.'

FEES, BURSARIES
UK & EU Fees, 2007: £3,070. If in receipt of full HE Maintenance grant there's a bursary of £1,000; if in receipt of partial grant, there's a slidong scale of awards.

STUDENT PROFILE
At MMU there is a high percentage of mature and part-time students, more from state school and far more the lower socio-economic reaches. Bruce McVean sees only advantage in this. 'MMU is perceived to be the younger more dynamic university because it is not as staid as Manchester University.' Bruce was an engineering student at Manchester Uni and, seeking a course change to Geography, was turned down and then accepted by MMU. 'But I now know people doing Geography at Manchester and there's not a lot of difference between the two departments. When students are actually here, I don't think they perceive much difference between the two establishments.'

ACADEMIA & JOBS
The modular courses have a practical emphasis,

tracing a clear vocational line to jobs in industry, where their employment rate is good.

More than 400 courses are offered from within Art & Design; Community Studies, Law & Education; Food, Clothing & Hospitality Management; Humanities & Social Science; Management & Business; Science & Engineering.

At Alsager there's a range of sports science subjects available, plus the departments of Humanities & Applied Social Studies (Sociology scored an excellent 21 on inspection) and the Modular Office, which looks after all inter-departmental modular mixes. At Crewe, the Business & Management Department sits alongside the Department of Environmental & Leisure Studies with its own stream, woodland and conservation habitats. Other than that, there is the School of Education (PGCEs and Primary and Secondary degrees)

For jobs in retail management Manchester Met leads. There's a retail marketing Foundation and application in a variety of areas. For example, Fashion Buying For Retail (HND and BSc) is a major contribution to employment figures in the fashion sector, even though in textile design the designers themselves make waves almost as big as the London Uni of the Arts and Huddersfield.

BA degrees: Fashion, Fashion Design Technology and Embroidery degrees are joined by BA Clothing Design & Technology and Textiles for around 180 points. There's a 22-point assessment.

Meanwhile, in furniture design, Manchester Met's involvement is more markedly on the non-artistic side, through business courses and Marketing and Retail Management, only lightly through the Art & Design facility. These also turn out numbers of graduates into market research, where again they are among the sector leaders. See also Food Marketing (with Foundation).

In advertising, their Art & Design Faculty *is* to the fore, with such as Design & Art Direction. Graphic artists, designers, illustrators (including Illustration with Animation) also proliferate. Set design is another niche.

STUDENT POPULATION	
Postgraduates	19%
Female Undergraduates	46%
Total students	32,475
Male Undergraduates	34%
Others	1%

In their Department of Contemporary Arts, positive employment figures in a difficult area point up Dance, which may be studied in combination with another Arts subject or as a single subject. There's also an interdisciplinary BA Contemporary Arts degree or a joint hons with a subject available in the Joint Hons faculty. No formal academic qualifications required. Teaching inspection 23.

There is a sound track record, too, in architecture. BA Hons Architecture cane be combined with

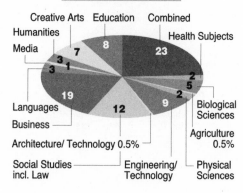

SUBJECT AREAS (%)

Creative Arts 7 · Education 8 · Combined 23 · Humanities 3 · Media 3 · Health Subjects 2 · 5 · 2 · Biological Sciences 9 · Languages 19 · Business 12 · Architecture/ Technology 0.5% · Agriculture 0.5% · Social Studies incl. Law · Engineering/ Technology · Physical Sciences

Structures, Construction, Environmental Studies, or with humanities (History, Social, Cultural, Urbanism, etc), and is required to move onto the postgrad BArch, a 2-year degree, unless you have ARB/RIBA Part 1. Teaching inspection 20.

MMU is also up there with a top league of landscape architects led by the likes of Sheffield, Leeds Met and Greenwich. BA Landscape Architecture is the degree. Teaching inspection 22.

In Law only 8 institutions undertake the BVC (Bar Vocational Course), and MMU is one. They were rated 'Good' recently by the LPC Board.

They are, too, major providers of health sector

graduates, though on a different wicket to the uni up the road. MMU supplied more than half the dental technicians registered as finding employment last time. See their BSc Dental Technology and BSc Dental Technology with Study in Industry. There are Foundation courses; otherwise, it's 160-220 points at A level. Speech therapy is another proven slot. It's BSc Speech Pathology & Therapy or BSc Psychology & Speech Pathology. Teaching inspection 22.

BSc Environmental Health sits with various Enviro Management and Protection degrees and Enviro Science or Studies programmes, which have the possibility of time in North America – perfect for budding environmental health officers. Look, too, at the Food Technology/Nutrition degrees.

There's a Foundation, too, for their list of Hospitality Management degrees and a sterling record in employment in the catering industry. Courses include Culinary Arts, Tourism, International and Licensed Retail Management by way of orientation. Teaching Inspection 22.

Their Human Resource Management programmes are also to the fore (200-260 points required at entry). There's a host of possible combinations, Psychology and Sociology being two most

'It's true, we still have a really strong gay scene. Gays won't need to be told about Manchester's Mardi Gras... but the hub – day in, day out – is the Village: late licensing, all-night cafés and a huge choice of venues.'

clearly relevant.

Finally, sports trainers and coaches, and physical training instructors (Education) need look no further than MMU's Alsager Campus. There's a world-class Grade 5* research rating and a very strong graduate track record in employment.

SOCIAL SCENE

STUDENTS' UNION There are of course many collaborations between Manchester Uni and Manchester Met, the unions being but a walk apart on Oxford Road, the most visible of which is *Student Direct*, the paper which won 2 national awards last year. *Student Direct* and Manchester Met's *Pulp* magazine now get distributed to all three unis (Salford included). There are, nevertheless, marked differences between the two unis. There is great activity within student societies at Manchester Met – 70 all told, but, as one student said to me, 'Politics is a dirty word... We don't have a very political union. We have political groups – Socialist Workers and so on, but that whole scene is more active at Manchester University. It's a lot more that our union here provides a service, it's more of a social and representational thing.

'It's true, we still have a really strong gay scene within the union.' Gays won't need to be told about Manchester's *Mardi Gras*, an unforgettable weekend of parades and parties. But the hub – day in, day out – is the Village: late licensing, all-night cafés and a huge choice of venues, all within walking distance of one another and MU and MMU.

Watering holes at union headquarters on Oxford Road include **Blue Café**, open from 8.30 am Monday to Friday for breakfast, lunch. Then, there's **MancUnion Bar** with big screen TV and bar promotions. **K2** is the nightclub. They say that when **K2** is open till 2, **MancUnion** is also open till 2, but then MancUnion has a licence till 2 every day except Sunday. Almost every major DJ has graced the K2 decks.

The MancUnion is a 450-capacity bar open 7 nights a week on the 2nd floor of the Student Union building on All Saints Campus, Oxford Road. **K2's** the 900-capacity nightclub downstairs, where after-match joys and blues are danced away on a Wednesday. Friday is *Double Vision* (party toons) – 2 floors of 'utter madness' – in the main room, commercial dance and chart stompers from past to present, plus r&b, soul and jazz upstairs and hip hop treats and laid back beats in the back room. On

ACADEMIC EXCELLENCE	
TEACHING:	
(Rated Excellent or 17+ out of 24)	
Mechanical Engineering	**Excellent**
Drama, Business & Mgt, Philosophy	**23**
History of Art & Design,	**22**
Materials Technol, Psychology, Subjects Allied to Medicine, Anatomy, Art & Design, Tourism, Molecular & Organismal Biosciences, Politics, Sport	
Sociology, Modern Languages, Electron & Elect Eng, Dental Technol, Nursing, Information Library Management	**21**
Maths, Town/Country Planning, Education, Economics	**20**
Food Science	**19**
RESEARCH:	
Top grades 5/5/6*	
Sports-related Subjects	**Grade 6***

WHERE MANCHESTER MET GRADUATES END UP

Health & Social Work: 9%; Education: 18%; Wholesale Retail: 13%; Manufacturing: 8%; Financial Activities: 9%; Public Administration, Civil Service & Defence: 7%; Hotel/Restaurant: 5%; Transport & Communications (including Telecommunications): 4%; Construction: 1%; Personnel: 5%; Computer: 3%; Business & Management: 1%; Accountancy: 1%; Media (including Film): 1%; Architecture: 3%; Publishing: 0.5%; Advertising: 1%; Artistic/Literary: 1%; Sport: 1%.

Approximate 'graduate track' employed **57%**

Saturday, it's *Rock Kitchen* and 'rock music played loud' through 2 rooms, 'hosted by DJs Stevie B, Adam, the Rock-It-Crew, and Boxer.' Plus specials like *Sex Lies and R&B*, and *Skool Disco* – 'free sweets, soggy school dinners and prizes for the best fancy dress', and live acts like Timmy Mallett and Pat Sharp. All of which culminates in the Summer Ball at the Palace Hotel, Manchester.

Down in Crewe + Alsager there is a union presence, and bars, shops, clubs and societies at both campuses, and even a nightclub at Crewe. Currently they're running a competition to name their bars, and advertising for students to come help run ents. It is not Manchester, so don't come here if that's

AT A GLANCE

ACADEMIC FILE:

Subjects assessed	**35**
Excellent	**74%**
Typical entry requirements	**262 points**
Application acceptance rate	**19%**
Students-staff ratio	**23:1**
First/2:1 degree pass rate	**47%**

ACCOMMODATION FILE:

Guarantee to freshers	**70%**
Style	**Halls, houses**
Catered	**4%**
Approx price range pw	**£50-£90**
City rent pw	**£50-£65**

what you're after, but there are bus nights to city clubs and among a handful of societies may be found four – Live Music, Alternative Music, Music and Film – which suggest a commendable do-it-yourself artistry to life.

Alsager has an **Arts Centre** with a resident theatre company and a packed programme of performance and literary arts. There are two theatres (the **Axis Theatre** seating 500), a dance studio and an art gallery, and it is here that is run a Drama course so good that it was awarded 23 points out of 24 after a recent inspection. The mind/body balance is made at Alsager by one of the best sports outfits in the country. There are 32 acres of playing fields, an athletics track, swimming pool, indoor facilities galore and a 1,000 square metre laboratory complex, which features a 33 x 6m track for performance data collection, regularly visited by top athletes.

PILLOW TALK

The university halls are good for first years wanting to meet people, but are not cheap and it is fairly difficult to get your first choice. The halls at All Saints have the best location; those at Didsbury require a considerable bus journey. See *Manchester Uni* entry, Pillow Talk, for city accommodation.

WHAT IT'S REALLY LIKE

UNIVERSITY:

Social Life	★★★★
Campus scene	**Huge, diverse happening place**
Student Union services	**Average**
Politics	**Low interest**
Sport	**Competitive**
National team position	**70th**
Sport facilities	**Good**
Arts opportunities	**Music, film excellent; rest good**
Student newspaper	**Student Direct**
Student magazine	**Pulp**
Nightclub	**K2**
Bars	**MancUnion**
Union ents	**Double Vision**
Union societies	**70**
Parking	**Poor**
CITY:	
Entertainment	★★★★★
City scene	**Legendary**
Town/gown relations	**Average-poor**
Risk of violence	**High**
Cost of living	**Average**
Student concessions	**Good**
Survival + 2 nights out	**£90 pw**
Part-time work campus/town	**Average/good**

GETTING THERE

☞ By road: Manchester, M63/J10, A34. Coach services good. Crewe/Alsager, M6/J16.
☞ By rail to Manchester: London Euston, 2:30; Leeds, 1:45; Liverpool Lime Street, 0:50. Crewe, connections from Manchester Piccadilly.
☞ By air: Manchester Airport for international and inland flights.
☞ By coach: London, 4:35; Bristol, 5:00; Newcastle, 5:00.

● ●

MIDDLESEX UNIVERSITY

Middlesex University
Trent Park
London N14 4YZ

TEL 020 8411 5000
FAX 020 8362 5649
EMAIL admissions@mdx.ac.uk
WEB www.mdx.ac.uk

Middlesex University Students' Union
Trent Park
London N14 4YZ

TEL 020 8411 6450
FAX 020 8440 5944
EMAIL [[initial.name]@mdx.ac.uk
WEB www.musu.mdx.ac.uk

VAG VIEW

*L*ondon's strength derives from its unique mix of cultures, as does Middlesex's, so they say. The capital's 9 million residents speak some 300 languages. Middlesex's student body includes students from all over the world.

There are many impressive elements in Middlesex's strategy, not least their Able Centre, *a disability support centre with recording studios turning out audio texts for blind students, a dyslexia support co-ordinator and a sign language bureau, which has appealed to thousands beyond campus too. But there is a huge locally based and mature student population and it would be a mistake to believe that this uni picks you up and takes you out of life in quite the same way as a traditional campus university like Nottingham, Kent or Sussex.*

Most people who come to Middlesex are not that bothered that the extra-curricular scene at the Students' Union is second rate, or that much of what is on offer has been taken out of the hands of the students, but it may be that this aspect of a traditional university education is precisely what will be seen to be important to the applicant. The drop-out rate is certainly high.

CAMPUS

Getting to grips with this university has been like wrestling with a family of octopuses, so many tentacles are there reaching out across North London and beyond. At one time there were some 18 sites and campuses, but today they are based at 2 or 3 main campus sites, and offer 4 schools of study.

The School of Arts & Education is based at the Trent Park/Cat Hill campus. they concentrating their energies on 2 or 3 main-campus sites, pulling the whole operation together in a £100-million strategy. Trent Park Bramley Road, London N14 4YZ, is set in 900 acres of woodlands and meadows. Cockfosters or Oakwood tubes (Piccadilly line). Performing Arts, IT, Cultural Studies, Education Product Design & Engineering, Biological Science. For Cat Hill, Barnet, Herts EN4 8H, go to Cockfosters (Piccadilly line).

The Business School, the School of Health and Social Sciences and the School of Computing Science are based at the Hendon campus in North West London. Students in some health areas also study at the Archway campus, well placed for local hospitals and health care providers.

For Hendon, The Burroughs, London NW4 4BT, go to Hendon Central (Northern line). A new £17-million learning resource centre opened here recently.

FEES, BURSARIES

UK & EU Fees, 2007: £3,070. There are 3 Middlesex First Scholarships, worth £30,000 for full time undergraduate putting Middlesex first choice, the Chancellor's Scholarship for academic excellence, sporting achievement or community involvement (£2,000), Achievement Scholarships for academic excellence(£1,000 p.a. if 360 or more UCAS points), 10 North London Scholarships (£2,000 for students getting involved in the North London community), 2 Future Gold Scholarships (£30,000 to undergrads with 2012 London Olympics potential), and the Middlesex Bursary (£305 p.a. to all who qualify for the Government's HE Maintenance Grant).

STUDENT PROFILE

Middlesex is a large university and has anything but a traditional university clientele. Many undergraduates are mature, many come from new-to-uni social groups. There is also a large number of part-timers among non-degree (HND) undergraduates. Where numbers have escalated since 1995 is in overseas recruitment. They have won awards for attracting students in from Europe and further afield. Language support is an essential require-ment – there's a series of courses incorporating a Foundation year for non-EU international stu-dents. Coping with the high drop-out rate that their open-doors policy has helped create is clearly the thought behind the £1000 bursaries for applicants with 300 points at entry, mentioned in *Fees, Bursaries* above.

ACADEMIA & JOBS

Full-time courses are made up of 4 year-long mod-ules, each worth 30 credits. A student needs to amass 120 credits in each year before progressing onto the next, and 360 in total to be awarded an honours degree. Examinations for each module take place at the end of the year. There is contin-ual assessment, and coursework also contributes to the overall assessment result.

The 4 academic schools are Arts & Education, Computing Science, Health & Social Sciences, and Business.

Jobs for graduates in Art & Design proliferate for graphic artists, designers and illustrators, and elsewhere there's a dedicated BSc Computing Science Graphics & Games which puts them up there in the Top 10 for computer game design. Back in the arts area, BA Interior Design is a fast track to employment, while among Fine Art, Fashion (also Knitwear and Textiles), Product Design, and Jewellery, the latter stands out as a good niche.

Musicians, composers, music industry man-agers are all well served here, too, and Dance,

STUDENT POPULATION

Total students
25,515

Female Undergraduates — 35%
Postgraduates — 23%
Male Undergraduates — 23%
Others — 19%

Drama, Music & Performing Arts are a thoroughly practical niche area, with a good (22-point) teaching rating. Be aware, also, of the Jazz specialism at Middlesex.

For actors, directors, producers there are two BA degrees: Drama & Theatre Studies and Technical Theatre Arts.

They also make arts administrator/managers in quantity – they've cornered 5% of the employ-ment market in this area. Look at the BA Music &

SUBJECT AREAS (%)

Combined — 4
Health Subjects — 4
Education — 3
Biological Sciences — 5
Creative Arts — 2
Agriculture — 2
Humanities 0.3% — 22
Physical Sciences 0.2%
— 20
Media — 7
— 2
— 1
Languages — 2
Social Studies incl. Law — 22
— 10
Business
Engineering/Technology
Maths & Computer

Arts Management degree. And Journalism, Publishing and TV Production have dedicated degrees.

Health is another strong area jobs-wise (again a 22-point assessment). They do brisk business with their top-up diploma and foundation course pro-grammes – Nursing, Pre-Registration Midwifery, and Veterinary Nursing, a joint course with the Royal Veterinary College (the best in the field). See, too, the Herbal Medicine and Traditional Chinese Medicine degrees, where Middlesex was a pioneer. The BSc Vet Nursing also leads to the RCVS Vet Nursing Certificate.

There's also a strong line in psychotherapists at the graduate job bank. Look at the Social Sciences

UNIVERSITY/STUDENT PROFILE	
University since	**1992**
Situation/style	**Campus/ city sites**
Student population	**25515**
Undergraduates	**14923**
- mature	**43%**
- non EU undergraduates	**14%**
- male/female	**44/56**
- non-traditional student intake	**42%**
state school intake	**N/A**
- drop-out rate	**27%**
- undergraduate applications	**Down 0.2%**

ACADEMIC EXCELLENCE

TEACHING:
(Rated Excellent or 17+ out of 24)

Philosophy	**23**
Drama, Dance, Cinematics,	**22**
History of Art, Architec & Design, American Studies, Education, Nursing, Subjects Allied to Medicine, Politics, Sport, Marketing/Management, Tourism	
Art & Design, Economics,	**21**
Psychology	
Maths	**20**
Sociology, Modern Langs, Electric & Electron Eng	**19**

RESEARCH:
Top grades 5/5*

History of Art, Architecture & Design, Philosophy	**Grade 5**

WHAT IT'S REALLY LIKE

UNIVERSITY:

Social Life	★★
Campus scene	**Friendly, mature, colourful, not campus focused**
Student Union services	**Average**
Politics	**Active**
Sport	**Competitive**
National team position	**55th**
Sport facilities	**Good**
Arts opportunities	**Excellent**
Student magazine	**MUD: Middlesex Union Direct**
Nightclub	**Enfield forum**
Bars	**1 on each campus**
Union ents	**Not a lot**
Union societies	**30**
Most active society 2005	**Stop The War**
Parking	**Poor**

CITY:

Entertainment	★★★★★
City scene	**Wild, expensive**
Town/gown relations	**Average-good**
Risk of violence	**Average**
Cost of living	**Very high**
Student concessions	**Good**
Survival + 2 nights out	**£100 pw**
Part-time work locally	**Fair**

with Communication & Language Studies and the BSc Psychology, which carries British Psychological Society accreditation.

Finally, there is a discernable pattern of careers in environmental health and a whole range of Health & Policy Studies degrees in the BSc joint degree series, also Occupational Health & Safety and BSc Environmental Health. The latter is a joint course with the College of North East London – 22 points at the assessments.

Middlesex have plenty of Management degrees with such as Marketing, Business, Info Systems, and International-style biases, and their joint hons programme allows Management combinations in a whole host of areas.

Sales managers proliferate, most of them with an Art & Design bias – textiles, knitwear, jewellery, fashion providing the focus.

They are also commercial and business law specialists incidentally, a subject that carries some useful management and other tie-ups.

SOCIAL SCENE

STUDENTS' UNION Shame, the bars and ents are now run by a private contractor (Scolarest) and competitive sport is run directly by the University. This is no way to encourage a strong student culture. The four bars – Enfield, Tottenham, Trent Park and Cat Hill – provide drinks promos and ents during the week, but they close at weekends. There's a Freshers' Ball, of course, and some tell of a Middlesex extravaganza, a 36-hour festival in the summer at Trent Park, and there's a student magazine called *MUD – Middlesex Union Direct.*

SPORT Gym facilities exist on all campuses. Sport is

WHERE MIDDLESEX GRADUATES END UP

Health & Social Work: 12%; Education: 11%; Wholesale Retail: 16%; Manufacturing: 6%; Financial Activities: 8%; Public Administration, Civil Service & Defence: 8%; Hotel/Restaurant: 2%; Transport & Communications (including Telecommunications): 3%; Personnel: 3%; Computer: 4%; Business & Management: 1%; Accountancy: 1%; Media (including Film): 1.5%; Legal 2%; Publishing: 1%; Advertising: 1%; Artistic/Literary: 1%; Sport: 0.5%.

Approximate 'graduate track' employed **56%**

an area of continual investment, and students are good at it (came 55th nationally in 2006). Recent large projects include a £2.5m state-of-the-art gym, the Real Tennis Centre at Hendon, and two artificial hockey pitches at Trent Park. Students have access to uni swimming pools, indoor and outdoor, football and rugby pitches and a golf club.

PILLOW TALK

There are 2,400 places in halls, all of which are self-catering. Student union facilities and local supermarkets suffice. All students have a shared kitchen too. Most halls have been built over the past 6 years; all are within easy reach of their respective campuses. A security officer is on sight from 5pm to 9am Monday to Friday and all weekend. There's also an interactive website (studentpad) with details of private houses/flats to rent and also rooms within family homes.

AT A GLANCE	
ACADEMIC FILE:	
Subjects assessed	**29**
Excellent	**62%**
Typical entry requirements	**200 points**
Application acceptance rate	**15%**
Students-staff ratio	**23:1**
First/2:1 degree pass rate	**51%**
ACCOMMODATION FILE:	
Guarantee to freshers	**All get it**
Style	**Halls, flats, houses, rooms**
Catered	**None**
En suite	**65%**
Approx price range pw	**£80-£95**
City rent pw	**£75-£85 Zone 2**

NAPIER UNIVERSITY

Napier University
Craiglockhart Campus
10 Colinton Road
Edinburgh EH10 5DT

TEL 08452 60 60 40
    0131 455 2801
FAX 0131 455 2588
EMAIL info@napier.ac.uk
WEB www.napier.ac.uk

Napier Students' Association
12 Merchiston Place
Edinburgh EH10 4NR

TEL 0131 229 8791
FAX 0131 228 3462
EMAIL nsa@napier.ac.uk
WEB www.napierstudents.com

VAG VIEW

*N*apier *has a fair reputation for getting its graduates jobs. Its difficulty has always been that it is a bit split up with no central focus, and very little going on outside the lecture theatre to amuse or interest its students. Whether this has caused the huge 81% mature student population is not clear, but it must have encouraged the whopping dropout rate. Now, however, they have set about putting this right, by rationalising the split-campus format, and there is a healthier student-to-staff ratio (17:1), and applications were up 14% this year.*

CAMPUS

'Napier is not a campus university,' writes Gareth L Mackie. 'Instead it has 4 major sites [whose faculties are currently in flux] – **Merchiston**, **Sighthill**, **Craiglockhart** and **Craighouse** – and 5 minor ones, spread out mostly through the south and west of Edinburgh. Each site has an atmosphere of its own: Merchiston is probably the busiest and liveliest, as it is the nearest to the city centre. Craighouse only received a student bar in November 1998. There is no one place where Napierites congregate.'

The long-term policy is to have one campus per faculty with state-of-the-art facilities, student accommodation and hopefully a proper Student Association presence (though they don't mention that). The first step was completed in August 2004 with the opening of the Craiglockhart Campus, now home to the Business School. Their sights are now set on redeveloping Sighthill over the next 5 years 'to create a new purpose-built campus for the Faculty of Health, Life & Social Sciences'. They also plan to refurbish the campus at Merchiston where the Faculty of Engineering, Computing & Creative Industries is based, to include 'a social learning space'.

FEES, BURSARIES

Fees for non-Scottish UK & EU: £1,745 p.a. See

www.napier.ac.uk/studentfunding

STUDENT PROFILE

The student profile shows a 95% state school intake, 37% of the undergraduate population coming from the lowest socio-economic groups, 23% from 'low-participation neighbourhoods'. But the most noticeable statistic is that of the mature student population (81%).

ACADEMIA & JOBS

There are 3 faculties: Business; Engineering, Computing & Creative Industries; and Health, Life & Social Science.

Their roots are in science and engineering – the broad-based BEng in Energy and Environmental Engineering is one of many courses typically well conceived for a job in industry. The uni is known for business, too, and this year they have got together with Paris-based French business school IPAG to offer an MSc in international marketing and tourism.

Their graduate placement record in engineering and industrial design, in manufacturing (particularly in electronic & electrical manufacturing), in finance and in the construction industry, is good.

Also, in Civil Engineering, given that it's a

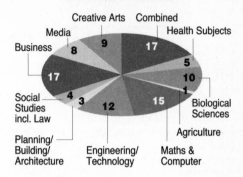

small uni, Napier has done well to find employment for sufficient graduates in this area (some 3% of its annual output) to make the national Top 10. There are some specialist niches, as you might expect from a uni focused on getting its graduates jobs: Civil & Transport Engineering, Civil Eng. & Computing, Civil & Timber Eng (there's a spin-off here into forestry as a career path) – you can bet they know exactly where to place you. Note also BSc Architectural Design & Civil Eng. Teaching inspection, Highly Satisfactory.

There is a range of architectural design and technology degrees, of construction industry and surveying degrees, bringing it Top 10 status in the area of Construction Engineer/Manager. A quantity

surveyor costs the building of our constructed environment and must have the care for detail of an accountant. This is a very effective niche area too (around 2% of graduates find jobs in it), and an accessible opportunity at point of entry. They have the BSc Single Hons and BSc Quantity Surveying with Computing. Teaching inspection, Highly Satisfactory. Jobs are also plentiful in Electronic or Telecommunications Engineering for Napier graduates, most come from dedicated Engineering degrees, a handful via Computer Science and Physical Sciences.

The uni is also big on the engineering design consultant job front. Napier's BEng and BSc degree courses range from Computing Networks & Distributed Systems to Polymer Engineering, Architectural Design & Information Systems, Computer-Aided Design & Business Studies and Product Design Engineering. Average

The uni is pre-eminent, too (more than 2% of graduates), in software engineering via its BEng and BSc software degrees.

Next, cut to the uni's extraordinary success in journalism – more than 2% of its graduates are find-

UNIVERSITY/STUDENT PROFILE	
University since	**1992**
Situation/style	**Civic**
Student population	**13570**
Undergraduates	**11322**
- mature	**81%**
- non EU undergraduates	**15%**
- male/female	**47/53**
- non-traditional student intake	**37%**
-state school intake	**93%**
- drop-out rate	**30%**
- undergraduate applications	**Up 14%**

ACADEMIC EXCELLENCE

TEACHING:
(Rated Excellent, Highly Satis. or 17+ out of 24)

Civil Engineering, **Highly Satis.**
Building & Surveying,
Chemistry, Hospitality Studies,
Mass Communications, Maths
& Statistics.
European Languages **19**

RESEARCH :
Top grades 5/5* **None**

---

ing jobs in the sector. There is a dedicated degree, and one in publishing, too, Napier now mount an amazingly strong challenge in these areas, being right up there in employment terms with unis that have double their number of undergraduates. And this year, they have a new course in creative advertising, tutored by Susie Henry of Saatchi and Saatchi, a company with a past in politics, notably during Margaret Thatcher's term. A project at the uni is already part of one Scottish MP's campaign.

Look, too, at their Art & Design courses, with Photography and Film. These are very popular areas for applicants, and you will likely be interviewed. There is also a new £22-million Scottish Centre for Creative Industries, which pulls together all the faculty elements and brings a studio and recording space into the picture. On the music front, there's a BMus and BA Pop Music.

Prospective investment advisers and analysts in the insurance and pension fields should be interested that 27% of Napier's applicants are taken into the Business Faculty and 18% of all their graduates get a job in the financial sector (more than any other single sector), a third of these into the insurance and pensions fields. Note also in the Business

School the marketing degrees, which are bringing 2% of their graduates work as marketing managers or in related occupations. Business Studies links also with Finance, Entrepreneurship, Languages, Psychology, Operations Management. Accounting comes with Finance or Economics. Nearly 2% of their graduates find jobs in the hotel and restaurant management sector – look in particular at the Tourism Management with Entrepreneurship and similar degrees.

Nearly 2% of their graduates find work as bacteriologists and microbiologists. There is a BSc Microbiology & Biotechnology.

Meanwhile, there is a School of Nursing, Midwifery & Social Care, and word is spreading about the degrees in natural health therapies – Aromatherapy, Reflexology and Herbal Medicine. Recently, another popular niche development has been the introduction of Veterinary Nursing.

SOCIAL SCENE

The **Union Bar**, 12 Merchiston Place, is round the corner from Merchiston Campus. Sports night is on Wednesday, sponsored by *Cool It Events*. Open Mic nights feature every other Thursday.

> *So great has been their employment muscle that a few years ago the* Financial Times *named Napier Scottish Uni of the Year.*

Friday is *Cocktails Night*. And that's about it. There are 11 student societies on offer and 21 sports clubs. Their teams came 92nd nationally last year. There is a student newspaper, *Veritas*, and the most active student society is the Drama Club. Recent political campaigns of interest have included Student Retention, Access to Top Quality Sports Facilities and the Student Experience - which shows just how overdue it is for the authorities to give Napier students a decent deal.

There is pride in the student body yet, however: 'We have many of our sports team who are regularly involved in BUSA Championship Finals such as Gaelic football, hurling, volleyball, football,

---

WHERE NAPIER GRADUATES END UP

Health & Social Work: 7%; Education: 3%; Wholesale Retail: 10%; Manufacturing: 10%; Financial Activities: 18%; Public Administration, Civil Service & Defence: 6%; Hotel/Restaurant: 8%; Transport & Communications (including Telecommunications): 4%; Construction: 5%; Agriculture: 1%; Mining/Oil Extracting: 9%; Personnel: 1%; Computer: 2%; Business & Management: 4%; Accountancy: 1%; Media (including Film): 3%; Legal 2%; Architecture: 4%; Publishing: 4%; Advertising: 2%; Sport: 1%.

Approximate 'graduate track' employed **58%**

WHAT IT'S REALLY LIKE

COLLEGE:

Social Life	★★
Campus scene	**Suffering**
Student Union services	**Average**
Politics	**Interest low**
Sport	**21 clubs**
National team position	**90th**
Sport facilities	**Improving**
Arts opportunities	**Average**
Student mag/news	**Veritas**
Bars	**Union Bar**
Union ents	**DJs**
Union societies	**11**
Most popular society	**Drama**
Parking	**Poor**

CITY:

Entertainment	★★★★★
Scene	**Seething**
Town/gown relations	**Good**
Risk of violence	**Average**
Cost of living	**High**
Student concessions	**Excellent**
Survival + 2 nights out	**£50+ pw**
Part-time work campus/town	**Poor/excellent**

shared bathroom; five-person flats have two shared bathrooms. Developments are all centrally located, modern, purpose built student accommodation, all within easy access of Napier's campuses.

Says Gareth: 'Napier provides housing for over 1,000 students, it's quite expensive but is quickly snapped up. Edinburgh has an abundance of reasonably priced flats, so it should be easy to find one

AT A GLANCE

ACADEMIC FILE:

Subjects assessed	**18**
Excellent	**50%**
Typical entry requirements	**264 points**
Application acceptance rate	**30%**
Students-staff ratio	**17:1**
First/2:1 degree pass rate	**59%**

ACCOMMODATION FILE:

Guarantee to freshers	**Non-locals OK**
Style	**Flats**
Catered	**None**
Approx. price range pw	**£72**
Approx. city rent pw	**£65-£85**

rugby league, snow sports. We also have a lot of members of these sports clubs who regularly gain representative honours for Scotland.'

TOWN See *Student Edinburgh*, page 185.

PILLOW TALK

Uni accommodation in apartment developments in the city centre is guaranteed to freshers coming 'outwith a 30-mile radius of Edinburgh'. There is no catered accommodation. Four-person flats have one

in an area that suits you and your pocket. Areas to consider include Tollcross, Gorgie/Dalry, Marchmont and Bruntsfield. You may see cheaper areas, but they may not be student-friendly.'

GETTING THERE

☛ By road: from north, M90; from Stirling, M9; from Newcastle, A1; from Glasgow, M8.
☛ By rail: London King's Cross, 4:30. Glasgow Central, 50 mins; Newcastle, 1:30.
☛ By coach: Glasgow, 1:10; London, 9:10.

STUDENT NEWCASTLE – THE CITY

The Toon is at the cutting edge of student life. Offering the very best in entertainment, its lively and vibrant atmosphere, progressive and diverse character make it an essential stop for any fun lovin' student. Ranked as the 7th best party city in the world, Newcastle is also heading up the field in all things cultural. Along with Gateshead, its neighbour on the Tyne, recent years have witnessed a massive boom for Newcastle Arts - the **Baltic Centre for Contemporary Art**, a 4- storey converted flour mill which houses numerous temporary exhibitions, and the **Sage Music Centre** on Newcastle's very own south bank.

NIGHTLIFE

Geordie attitude turns on the old adage, 'work hard, play hard', and be it the legendary **Bigg Market**, the swanky watering holes of the Quayside or the cosmopolitan bars of Jesmond's Osborne Road and the area around Central Station, there is opportunity for everyone to play as hard as they like, often at a price most students can afford.

When it comes to clubbing and live acts, both universities are up there with the best in live entertainment. The Darkness, Coldplay, Kosheen, Shed 7, Elbow, Starsailor, Mark Owen and Jools Holland are just a few of the big name acts to have played

. **The Telewest Arena** attracts all the major national tours, from Justin Timberlake, Beyonce and Blue to Stereophonics and Craig David, while the **City Hall** has it's own share of the stars, the likes of Norah Jones and Travis The only downside is that our location means a lot of small tours do not visit. Don't expect to see everyone.

If you want to sample musical delights a little closer to home there are also smaller more intimate live venues such as **The Cluny** and **The Head of Steam** which showcase the cream of Newcastle's homegrown musical talent.

The city's club scene has rocketed to success in recent years with the launch of numerous highly acclaimed club events. Writes Katie Ashworth: 'When it comes to clubs, I generally go to alternative clubs and pubs, as opposed to ones that would play dance music. For indie buffs, I would recommend: **The Cooperidge** on a Monday, **The Cluny**, *Stone Love @* **Digital** on Thursdays, **The Forth** generally every night, **The Global** on gig nights, **The Head of Steam**, **The Hancock** pub any night, *Bulletproof @* **Carling Academy**... there's a lot more if you search around!

'For the rock/metal crowd: *Krash @* **Venue** on Thursdays, *Stone Love @* **Digital** on Thursdays, **Trillians** any night, **Legends**, *Red Room @* Northumbria, Uni. **The Hancock** pub upstairs any night, *Where Angels Play @* **Carling Academy**.. . Again, look around, keep your eyes and ears open for gigs and nights.

'For general drinking nights out: **Tiger Tiger**. **Sam Jacks** is always a laugh too, anywhere in **The Gate**, **Liquid**, **Flares** (a disco theme club), **The Goose**, *Solution @* Newcastle Uni on Fridays, *Wiggle @* Northumbria. **Blu Bambu** is ok, too.

'What does it cost? Night out anywhere from £10 to £50! I personally never spend more than about £15, but that's because I go to cheaper places and don't drink expensive things. Proper night out to "real clubs", anything around £30 or more. But I'd rather go to a pub, bar or gig, which are always cheaper. Entrance to clubs, anything from £3 to £12, although on average £4 is normal for the places I go to.'

SPORT

The whole city revolves around the fortunes of Newcastle United, so get informed. St James's Park is the most imposing landmark on the city skyline and the second largest stadium in the Premiership. Getting tickets can be a problem, however, despite the 52,000 capacity, but well worth trying for.

Elsewhere, Johnny Wilkinson (occasionally) and the rest of the Newcastle Falcons offer a student friendly environment for rugby fans, while the Newcastle Eagles do the same for basketball followers. Wherever you go, don't mention any allegiance to Northeast rivals Sunderland or Manchester United or you are liable to end up in a bit of bother.

CINEMA

The Odeon is the most central cinema and with its brand new multiplex having recently opened in **The Gate** on Newgate Street, you can enjoy all the top films at student prices right on your doorstep. Also in the city centre is a 12-screen **Warner Village**, while a short drive will take you to **UCI Silverlink** or **Metro Centre**. For the more artistic, the **Tyneside Cinema** on Pilgrim Street is one of the best independent cinemas in the country.

THEATRE AND COMEDY

Newcastle is one of the Royal Shakespeare Company's second homes. In the autumn, it doth take over most of the city's stages for a month of highbrow entertainment. The major venue is the **Theatre Royal**, the poshest of Newcastle's theatres. For a smaller, cheaper alternative, try the **Live Theatre**.

If it's a more relaxed, studenty atmosphere you're after you can't beat the **Playhouse** and **Gulbenkian Studio** to get the best in up and coming talent. Both theatres are housed in the same building at the edge of Newcastle University's campus, and are home to the more cutting-edge Northern Stage company.

For comedy look no further than the fantastic **Hyena Café**, open 12 months of the year, and the annual Newcastle Comedy Festival, which plays a number of venues across the city for a two-week spell. **Newcastle Student Union** also puts on a comedy night every Monday during term-time, in it's **Global Café** venue.

SHOPPING

The only major studenty shop is **Period Clothing**, with some fantastic stuff in store. Otherwise Newcastle blends high street stores with smaller designer boutiques well. On Northumberland Street you can check out all the high-street brands such as **H&M**, **Zara** and **Warehouse**, whilst **Eldon Square Shopping Centre**, just off Northumberland Street is home to **Top Shop**, **USC**, **Oasis** and all the major department stores. Grainger Town is where you'll find the 'trendier' and more expensive shops as well as some quality boutiques.

Check out **Mint**, just off Grey Street, it's a truly awesome shopping experience. A short journey will take you to the Gateshead **MetroCentre** and the major stores/labels. For music, **Steel Wheels**, **RPM** and **Flying Records** offer good independent options.

UNIVERSITY OF NEWCASTLE

The University of Newcastle upon Tyne
Kensington Terrace
Newcastle upon Tyne NE1 7RU

TEL 0191 222 5594
FAX 0191 222 8685
EMAIL enquiries@ncl.ac.uk
WEB www.ncl.ac.uk

The Newcastle University Union Society
Kings Walk
Newcastle upon Tyne NE1 8QB

TEL 0191 239 3916
FAX 0191 222 1876
EMAIL comm.union@ncl.ac.uk
WEB www.unionsociety.co.uk

VAG VIEW

*A*cademically, Newcastle is good right across the board. 'Those who live in the north perhaps understand how good it is better than those from the south,' said one Yorkshire-based school careers teacher, adding with weight, 'It is very popular among students who go there.'

Good across the board, certainly, but at the very height of academic excellence sit Medicine, Physiological Sciences, Psychology, Molecular Biosciences, Pharmacology and subjects allied to Medicine. These are the departments that scored full marks in the assessments. True, nothing has scored less than 20 points out of 24, but these did not drop a point. The subjects allied to Medicine are speech language sciences. All the top ratings are sciences with a medical tinge. In the national research assessments, high among the departments adjudged world class are Clinical Laboratory Sciences, Psychology, Biological Sciences... and Music, the latter reminding us that there are dimensions to the Newcastle experience beyond clinical laboratories.

Where Newcastle scores over London and, yes, over Manchester, is in its packing an incredible array of cultural, artistic and hedonistic power centres into a very small space (and at relatively low cost). So much is going on, and all of it so concentrated, that the buzz on the street at night is ten times what you will feel in the greater, but more dispersed metropolis.

Newcastle's undergraduates have a real and vibrant city to discover, but the loyalty of its students is down to what goes on in the Students' Union.

Go there and see. What you notice on campus is people doing, things happening, students in control... of themselves and what they are about. 'We actually own the whole set-up,' they say. They do – union building and all.

CAMPUS

Newcastle is a campus university situated right in the heart of this compact and compelling city, within walking distance of theatres, cinemas, shops, bars, pubs, restaurants, but equally only a short way from the eye-catching north-east coast.

FEES, BURSARIES

UK & EU Fees, 2007: £3,070 p.a., with bursaries on sliding scale if on the Government HE Maintenance Grant.

STUDENT PROFILE

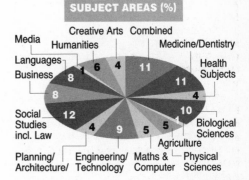

SUBJECT AREAS (%)

Media — Creative Arts — Combined — Medicine/Dentistry — Humanities — Languages — Business — Health Subjects — Social Studies incl. Law — Biological Sciences — Planning/Architecture/ — Engineering/Technology — Maths & Computer — Physical Sciences — Agriculture

1, 6, 4, 11, 8, 11, 8, 4, 12, 10, 4, 9, 5, 5

The student profile reveals a low proportion of state school entrants: 'The pink pashmina and boat shoe brigade do seem to claim the majority,' as a student put it, 'but people tend to separate into their own different groups according to individual taste. There is enough to do to keep all parties happy. Freshers Week tends to be the only time when you have to put up with people who aren't necessarily "your kind of people", to quote Michael Barymore.'

Writes Katie Ashworth: 'There is something that we call 'Rahs' in the halls where I live... they wear tracksuit bottoms and UGG boots, fake tans and all shout at each other in the halls. "Chavs with too much money" is a good description. They're all from down south. Apparently some duke's daughter came here a few years ago, so there's been an influx of the more posh crowd. However, in the rest of the accommodations, there has been more "normal people"; it's just the big self-catering hall that I'm in tends to attract the more sheltered types! I'm in the rock and indie societies, as well as music; there'a a lot of music-obsessed people here, and also some people who would be "alternative". Apart from a few exceptions, I've got on with pretty much everyone I've met here. No one cares about what kind of person you are, as long as you're easy to talk to and friendly, everyone gets on.'

ACADEMIA & JOBS

'The general ethos seems to be work hard, play hard,' writes Geraldine England. 'The standard of teaching is generally high, some lecturers being able to communicate with their students better than others. Workloads differ, but as a rule, students doing a science degree have a whole lot more lectures than do arts students. However, when it

23% — Postgraduates

Female Undergraduates — 39%

STUDENT POPULATION

Total students
18,412

38% — Male Undergraduates

comes to coursework and exams, the pressure seems to equalise, as all courses are based on a similar modular system.'

Katie Ashworth is doing language and literature (Q300): 'The second semester is better it terms of content for me, as the first was full of fundamental language concepts that were pretty hard to grasp. Syntax could have been taught better, and my seminar leader assumed that we all were at the same starting level. Not true, as some people had done A-level Eng Lan, but I hadn't!

'Tutorials are vital. They give you a chance to ask questions and share ideas. I always go to my seminars, even ones that I don't really have to go to. I think it's important that we all meet as a group every week. Seminars for me have a social side. A few of my tutors are postgraduates, so we sometimes have general chats before we start the academic side. I have met some of my best friends through my tutor groups!

Geraldine continues: 'There are two main libraries, the Robinson library and Medical library, both are well resourced, well staffed and fully computerised, but be prepared for a massive demand on books when it comes to exam time. Don't think that you will be able to pop into the library a day before the holidays and find all the books you need, because you won't. The geeks will have got there first.

'Computing facilities at Newcastle are excellent, each department having a number of its own computer clusters, all linked to the net, in addition to those available in the libraries. There is even a large 24-hour access cluster, a godsend because, though you might find it difficult to imagine now, you may well have to work through the night.'

An Enterprise Centre turns ideas into action by creating new business, using public and private sector experts as mentors for students, brokering industry expertise in curriculum development and inviting entrepreneurs and other professionals to lecture to students. The culture enabled student companies from Newcastle to win four awards in the national final of the Graduate Enterprise Programme in Leicester this year.

In 2006, the University sought the views of hundreds of organisations to determine what skills they required of graduates. From this feedback, a skills framework was developed which will be used to embed skills development within the curriculum and throughout extra-curricular activities.

Besides the usual contact with employers and milk round, etc, 'Graduate Connections' is an online database of over 600 Newcastle graduates now employed in a wide range of jobs and professions. They give individual advice, information and insight about the work they do and how to get into a profession.

Almost one fifth of undergraduates go into the health sector, and the medical school took full marks at assessment and is regarded by many as the best in the country. There's a 10% chance of

UNIVERSITY/STUDENT PROFILE	
Independent university since	**1963**
Situation/style	**City campus**
Student population	**18412**
Undergraduates	**14163**
- mature	**11%**
- non EU undergraduates	**6%**
- male/female	**50/50**
- non-traditional student intake	**20%**
- state school intake	**70%**
- drop-out rate	**7%**
- undergraduate applications	**Down 0.2%**

getting in, but that's about average. Besides the 6-year MB BS (with pre-med year for students without the necessary science background), there's a 4-year accelerated MB BS designed for graduates and a 5-year MB BS, Phase 1 of which can be undertaken here or at Durham Uni's Stockton Campus (south down the A1 on the outskirts of Middlesbrough); 245 places at Newcastle, 95 at Stockton – all come together at Newcastle for Phase II training in cahoots with the NHS. Clinical relevance is emphasised throughout. Entry The 6-year course requires AAB (chem., biol.) + UKCAT excluding General Studies + 5 passes at GCSE including English, Maths and a science subject. For the 5-year Stockton/Newcastle degree, it's AAB including Chemistry or Biology but not General Studies (2 AS levels are accepted in place of 1 A). GCSE Biology, Chemistry, Physics, Maths, English. Teaching inspection 24. Research Grade 5*: Clinical Lab Sciences, Psychology, Biological Sciences; Grade 5: Community-based Clinical, physiology. The dental degree is a 5-year BDS. Entry ABB-AAB. Teaching inspection 23. Research Grade 5.

The 10% provision of graduates to public admin, the civil service and defence points us in other directions. Look especially at the 4-year Government & European Union Studies degree. The Law is a recognised pathway for defence executives from Newcastle, while defence operatives and equipment engineers often come the biological sciences route, look at Biological Sciences, Biomedical Sciences, Medical Microbiology & Immunology, Biochemistry with Immunology, etc. There's full marks at the assessments for biosciences and subjects allied to medicine, and world class, Grade 5* ratings for Clinical Laboratory Sciences and Biological Sciences, too. The army and Royal navy are popular among Newcastle graduates, and there's a good track record for government researchers.

The 3% provision into accountancy points up BA Accounting & Finance and Business Accounting & Finance with a business placement (4 years). There are also BSc joint hons degrees in Accounting with Computer, Info Systems, Maths, or Statistics – a department where you'll also find Economics & Maths or Statistics. Graduate stockbrokers proliferate at Newcastle.

ACADEMIC EXCELLENCE

TEACHING:
(Rated Excellent or 17+ out of 24)

Architecture, English, Geology, Social Policy & Administration	**Excellent**
Medicine, Physiological Sciences, Psychology, Molecular Biosciences & Pharmacology, Subjects Allied to Medicine	**24**
Dentistry, Maths, Economics, Politics	**23**
Modern Languages, Linguistics	**22**
Agric, Forest & Agric Sciences, Organismal Biosciences, Classics, Education, Theology	
Chemical Engineering, Electrical & Electronic Eng, Town & Country Planning, Physics, Archaeology	**21**
Civil Engineering/Geomatics, Marine Technol, Art & Design	**20**

RESEARCH :
Top grades 5/5*/6*

Clinical Laboratory Sciences,. Psychology, Biological Sciences, Music,	**Grade 6***
Community-based Clinical, Hospital-based Clinical, Clinical Dentistry, Physiology, Nursing, Earth Sciences, Pure Maths, Statistics, Computer, Chemical Eng, Civil Eng, Electrical/Electronic Eng, Town /Country Planning, Geography, Law, Politics, Accounting, English, Iberian and Latin American, Linguistics, Theology	**Grade 5**

WHERE NEWCASTLE GRADUATES END UP

Health & Social Work: 19%; Education: 5%; Wholesale Retail: 8%; Manufacturing: 9%; Financial Activities: 7%; Public Administration, Civil Service & Defence: 10%; Hotel/Restaurant: 3%; Transport & Communications (including Telecommunications): 3.5%; Construction: 1%; Agriculture: 2%; Mining/Oil Extracting: 1%; Personnel: 4%; Computer: 2.5%; Business & Management: 2%; Accountancy: 3%; Media (including Film): 1%; Legal 1.5%; Architecture: 2%; Publishing: 1%; Advertising: 1%; Artistic/Literary: 0.5%; Sport: 1%.

Approximate 'graduate track' employed **75%**

Architecture is a strength that converts into jobs on a big scale. There's BA Architectural Studies (recognised by RIBA) and a raft of interesting nautical developments in the Newcastle and Strathclyde University Engineering faculties, both names traditionally associated with shipbuilding. Engineering design consultants proliferate. Cartographers should look to the Geomatics Department and its Surveying & Mapping Science degree.

> *Where Newcastle scores over London and, yes, over Manchester, is in its packing an incredible array of cultural, artistic and hedonistic power centres into a very small space (and at relatively low cost).*

Electrical and telecommunications engineers at Newcastle find careers come easy, and entry is no problem thanks to Foundation courses available for both the BEng and MEng routes. Teaching inspection 21. Research Grade 5.

IT consultants pour out of Newcastle. Look in particular at the B/MEng Computer Systems Engineering and the BSc Computing Science, and Software Engineering.

The language provision at Newcastle is first class, and very often they lead the way in finding employment for graduate translators, and many also find jobs in advertising. Newcastle offer Chinese, Japanese, European and Modern Languages with all sorts of orientations. There's a teaching assessment of 22 points out of 24.

In farming there's the top employment-rated Agri-Business Management and other Management courses – Farm Business, Rural Resource, also mainstream Agriculture, Applied Biology and the non-practical Agronomy, plus a host of animal science degrees. There's also a tie-up with Tesco on the organic food production wicket. Teaching inspection, 22.

Finally, two courses command serious attention. Newcastle and Nottingham Trent lead in what is not (unfortunately for the consumer) a crowded field. Their MEng Mechanical & Railway Engineering is, as far as we can tell, one of only two degrees in this field. It has been developed with a whole lot of operators and equipment manufacturers, including Virgin Trains, Bombardier Transportation, The Engineering Link & Arriva Trains Northern. Get on it as quickly as you can and pray it arrives on time.

SOCIAL SCENE

STUDENTS' UNION It's the central point of social life here, with 6 bars and 3 clubs, **Global**, **Bassment**, and **Beats**. It plays host regularly to big name bands and DJs.

Every Friday there's *Solution*: cheesy main room, indie side room, lots of drinks offers. Recent guests include: Futureheads, Goldie lookin chain, elbow, Hard fi, 2manydjs.

Writes Katie: 'Newcastle SU is MASSIVE! Although the SU night, *Solution*, is alright, but I'm very into music, so I'd prefer to go to a gig or something. I go to about 2/3 a week. Me and my friends went to a play last semester at the theatre, which is gorgeous, and directly opposite the Union. Nice restaurant, too.'

There are monthly music events, *Turbulence*, which has been rated the best drum 'n' bass night in the North, *Brighton Beach* (indie), *Substance* (eclectic breaks and beats), and *Universal* – chart 'n'

WHAT IT'S REALLY LIKE

UNIVERSITY:	
Social Life	★★★★★
Campus scene	**Lively, aware, middle-class**
Student Union services	**Good**
Politics	**Active, mainly student issues**
Sport	**57 clubs**
National team position	**15th**
Sport facilities	**Good**
Arts opportunities	**Drama excellent; rest good**
Student magazine	**Pulp**
Student newspaper	**The Courier**
Student radio	**NSR**
Nightclubs	**Global, Beats, Bassment**
Bars	**Mens Bar, Green Room, Cochrane**
Union ents	**Chart, dance, Indie, drum 'n bass, live**
Union societies	**100**
Most popular societies	**NUTS (theatre), Cheerleading, Jazz**
Parking	**Adequate**
CITY:	
Entertainment	★★★★★
Scene	**Vibrant, fun**
Town/gown relations	**OK**
Risk of violence	**Low**
Cost of living	**Low**
Student concessions	**Good**
Survival + 2 nights out	**£70 pw**
Part-time work campus/town	**Average/excellent**

cheese.

The Bassment takes about 1,000 and then they've got the 300-capacity **Global Café**. Once a term they have *Arcane* – all the proceeds fund a student from some underprivileged area of the dark continent. *Arcane* lasts from about 8pm until 6am. As well as the two main dancefloors (**Bassment, Global**), there are specialist drum 'n' bass areas and chill out rooms.

There's a comedy night every Monday during term-time in the **Global Café** venue, and monthly local band showcases – student and local bands do gigs, and there's an annual battle of the bands when they invite A&R men to seed record deals. Then there's also a weekly quiz night.

Whatever's on, they open all the bars in the building (total capacity 2,200), and with a new lift installed they have open access to all floors, which makes for a climactic scene. When one bar shuts down – the **Men's Bar** and the smoke-free **Cochrane Lounge** seem first to go, everyone goes on to wherever the action is. Other bars are **Subterranean**, **Subversions**, **Beats** and **The Irish Bar**. **Beats** has recently been renovated – meals during the day, venue at night.

'With all these great nights out, some extra cash is bound to come in handy,' writes Geraldine in practical mode. 'The SU provides a job shop, advertising all kinds of part-time vacancies with accredited employers. It also offers welfare and advisory services in addition to supporting over 100 different societies and more than sixty sports clubs.'

Ents are, indeed, but the beginning. Much is done in the context of the real world outside. Student drama producers, for example, have to survive in real terms, are dependent on public audiences, arrange sponsorship and all the rest. Two or three student-produced plays appear each year at **The Gulbenkian**, a small, vigorously experimental studio-type place. There might be a production at **Live**, the theatre on the Quayside.

The *Courier* office (student newspaper) is a crammed galley of a room, space enough for the award-winning weekly (nominated for Best Reporter this year) to be committed to Quark. There's the award-winning radio station, NSR, too.

Writes Katie: 'There's a MASSIVE range of student societies. I fully recommend joining a few! I'm in English society, indie soc, rock soc and radio society. I participate mostly in radio society, as I interview bands, review gigs and cd's and go to meetings every Tuesday. I go to rock soc socials a lot, some indie and barely any English socs, as I see the English crowd every day anyway! My social life generally revolves around my course, and music. I've pretty much met all of my friends through English lectures and seminars, and gigs, and radio,

AT A GLANCE	
ACADEMIC FILE:	
Subjects assessed	**36**
Excellent	**78%**
Typical entry| requirements	**385 points**
Application acceptance rate	**17%**
Med. School acceptance rate	**10%**
Students-staff ratio	**17:1**
First/2:1 degree pass rate	**66%**
ACCOMMODATION FILE:	
Guarantee to freshers	**100%**
Style	**Halls, flats**
Catered	**38%**
En-suite	**14%**
Price range pw	**£54-£105**
City rent pw	**£35-£70**

and stuff like that. I like the girls in my corridor, but I don't have a lot in common with them. The people who I'm moving in with next year are actually from the corridor next to mine: 3 people who I've met here, and my best friend, who I sort of knew from home. I'm good friends with her brother, and he introduced us at a party in the summer holidays. Outside of lectures, I enjoy going to gigs, sleeping and wandering around Newcastle with my friends.'

SPORT There's a Talented Athlete Sports Scholarship (TASS) scheme and a new £5.5m indoor sports facility, opened in August 2005. There are 57 sports clubs on offer and the uni came 15th nationally last year out of all universities (observe: 2 places below Northumbria). The much-respected American Football team is called Newcastle Mariners or Crazy Blue.

On-campus **sports centres** provide for aerobics, badminton, basketball, indoor hockey, soccer, netball, squash, tennis, trampolining, volleyball, fitness training, martial arts, dance, gymnastics.

Track and field athletes use the **Gateshead International Stadium**. There are pitches and courts at Cochrane Park, Heaton (Medicals), Longbenton (with its new all-weather pitch), and at Close House, the uni estate - note - is 10 miles to the west! Rowing is also popular and successful.

TOWN See *Student Newcastle*, page 337.

PILLOW TALK

Newcastle have a torturously worded test for uni accommodation, but as it allows first year undergraduates 'who will be coming alone to the University for the full academic year', the policy is effectively pretty inclusive. Local students will have more of a problem than those from afar, and be sure to get the application form in by 30 June.

Castle Leazes Halls and Henderson Hall are catered. Self-catered flats include: Richardson Road, Marris House, St Mary's College, Windsor Terrace, Leazes Parade, and Bowsden Court Shared Flats. There's also couple and family accommodation, and places adapted for students with disabilities.

Opening this year is Magnet Court, 3 and 4-bed-roomed flats with en-suite shower rooms, situated in city-centre, just 5 min. walk from campus.

GETTING THERE
☞ By road: A1, A167/A696; A167 exit.
☞ By rail: Edinburgh, 1:30; Leeds, 1:45; London King's Cross, 3:00; Manchester Piccadilly, 3:00; Birmingham New Street, 4:00.
☞ By air: Newcastle International Airport.
☞ By coach: London, 6:05; Birmingham, 4:25.

UNIVERSITY OF WALES, NEWPORT

University of Wales, Newport
Caerleon Campus
PO Box 101
Newport NP18 1YH

TEL 01633 432030, 432432
FAX 01633 432850
EMAIL admissions@newport.ac.uk
WEB www.newport.ac.uk

Newport Students' Union
College Crescent
Caerleon
Newport NP18 3YG

TEL 01633 432076
FAX 01633 432688
WEB www.newportunion.com

VAG VIEW

University of Wales, Newport, comes out of Gwent College of Higher Education. It became a University College in 1996 and a fully fledged university in 2003. During this period we watched it achieve huge success in a particular area, oblivious to Government assessment that most of its courses were merely Satisfactory. While the wheels of bureaucracy ground it down, Hollywood beckoned, and its students were being nominated for Oscars and winning BAFTA awards. Finally, in 2001, the Establishment had to take notice, and awarded its Art, Media & Design provision a Grade 5 rating for research, recognising its international importance. In the 2008 assessment exercise, we can expect it to do even better. Meanwhile, applicants are flooding in. A figure up 41% for 2005 was reported, and even in 2007, it's up 4%. But it's a question of cherry-picking, because clearly not everyone is happy. Many don't complete their courses.

CAMPUS

Newport, Gwent, lies half way between Bristol and Cardiff; it is the first town of any size you come to travelling west along the M4 from England. Activities are split between two campus sites: Newport itself and, 10 mins to the north, **Caerleon** – 'City of Legions and Court of King Arthur,' according to Geoffrey of Monmouth. Caerleon is where all the real stuff goes on.

The village of Caerleon, supposed site of Camelot, takes us back into the mists of time. There are still Roman baths and a fortress to be seen, but the area is a tourist draw as much for its beauty. To the east lies the Wye Valley and the Usk, on whose banks lie the ruins of Tintern Abbey, which inspired Wordsworth to write one of his most important poems. To the west are the Welsh valleys, industrial heartland of South Wales.

It is a safe and friendly campus, and typically a guy from Gloucestershire reading documentary photography said he had been won over by the green fields as much as the course.

The second campus, **Allt-yr-yn**, is home to the Newport Business School, to computing, engi-

UNIVERSITY/STUDENT PROFILE	
University since	**2003**
Situation/style	**Campus**
Student population	**9315**
Full-time undergraduates	**7240**
- mature	**41%**
- non EU undergraduates	**1%**
- male/female	**42/58**
- state sector intake	**99%**
- non-traditional student intake	**39%**
state sector intake	**98%**
drop-out rate	**24%**
- undergraduate applications	**Up 4%**

neering and the School of Health and Social Sciences. It has none of the mystery of Caerleon, but seems to be enjoying Newport's rise just as much. There's an hourly shuttle between the two.

All is soon to change, however, for Newport has been given the go-ahead to build a new campus, first phase in a £50-million expansion. Due to be built down in the valley, by the river, opposite the **Riverfront Arts Theatre**, which one hears so much about and which has its own bar and independent film club and art gallery, the new campus will be ready by 2009 and will house the School of Art, Media and Design. With it, the uni is looking to double its population within a year.

FEES, BURSARIES

UK & EU Fees for 2007, £3,000. Welsh entrants are eligible for a grant of £1,800. There are £8,000 scholarships available to students who have represented their country or region in sport. An assault on the BUSA league – the national UK students sports league – is Newport's next move.

STUDENT PROFILE

The Caerleon profile is not easy to run to ground. You've got arty types and rugger buggers and mysterious geeks with hobbit-style goatees left to run wild. They are broadly a new-university crew, and there's a markedly local 'take' overall. With the huge recent hike in numbers, however, some of the statistics may speak more of the past than the present. More than a fifth of the undergraduate population is mature. The gender balance is pretty healthy (42% male).

ACADEMIA

The faculty or school that is causing all the fuss is the Newport School of Art Media and Design. It offers courses under the banners, Art & Photography, Film and Animation, Performing Arts, and Design.

Film is a big deal here. There are some of the best art and design facilities in Europe, whose students are taking the world of film animation by storm, with one film, *Famous Fred*, being nominated for a Hollywood Oscar, others, such as *Human Traffic* and *Waking Ned* enjoying great commercial success, and *The Gogs* winning its student makers a clutch of BAFTA awards. Not only could the uni boast 60 of its graduates no less on the credit list of the massive hit, *Chicken Run*, but also *Women in Love* director Ken Russell (he late of *Big Brother*) is this year working closely with the department of film and video.

Camelot has become the International Film School, Wales, with BA (Hons) Animation, Cinema Studies & Scriptwriting, Computer Games Design,

Documentary Film & Television, Film & Video, Performing Arts, MA Animation, and MA Film, BA Creative Sound & Music, Documentary Photography (BA and MA), Fine Art, Photographic Art, Photography for Advertising & Fashion, New Media Publishing, and MA Art.

If this is your bent, go for it, not least because they are among the top graduate providers to the film industry. Eight years ago, we wrote: 'What comes across is that Newport provides an imaginative environment. Subtlety, humour and creative thinking are to the fore.' We can find no reason to change that view.

Meanwhile, there's the Newport Business School, the School of Health & Social Sciences, the Centre for Community and Lifelong Learning, and Education – Primary Initial teacher training at the uni was designated as 'Excellent' by the Higher Education Funding Council for Wales in 2000.

Foundation courses leading to direct entry into the uni are available in Science, Technology, Info Technology (Computing, Business Studies, Statistics), Humanities (English, History, Media Studies), Labour Studies, Business Studies, Social Studies, Youth & Community Work and Politics.

SOCIAL SCENE

STUDENTS' UNION For ents, Caerleon is the centre of

WHAT IT'S REALLY LIKE

UNIVERSITY:	
Social Life	★★★
Campus scene	**Lively**
Student Union services	**Fair**
Politics	**Active**
Sport	**Relaxed**
National team position	**102nd**
Sport facilities	**Good**
Arts opportunities	**Good**
Student newsletter	**Grapevine**
Venue	**Main Hall**
Bar	**The Clarence**
Union ents	**Chees and live; good May Ball**
Union societies	**23**
Most popular society	**Rugby**
Parking	**Adequate**
TOWN:	
Entertainment	★★
Scene	**Pubs, clubs**
Town/gown relations	**OK**
Risk of violence	**Low**
Cost of living	**Average**
Student concessions	**Good**
Survival + 2 nights out	**£60 pw**
Part-time work campus/town	**Good**

things, and students from Allt-r-yn flock to it. Halloween Ball in Main Hall (now 1,000 capacity) is the big deal. Meanwhile, the Rathwell building is student central, with its **Clarence Bar**, refectory and café bar. I tried the vegetable curry, £2.30, at the café. The refectory meals looked better, but the rice was a well-advised solid base for a night's drinking at the Clarence, still smoky with cigarettes in the Spring of 2006 and equipped outside front with one of those cash machines that charges you for use, a dirty touch, I thought, targeting those with weak wills like me at their weakest moment.

The most popular society is Rugby, so Wednesday's post-match disco is one big focus, as are Sky big screen nights. Drawing big audiences currently among the student throng, however, is live music in the **Clarence**, which also hosts karaoke, Chris Tarrant-inspired 'Who wants to win a crate of beer?' and other quizzes. Also figuring large in students' lives is Newport's own **TJ's** – bar, disco and music venue. Others stagger down the road into Cardiff (see *Student Cardiff*, page 126).

The union is active on student and awareness campaigns, which have included breast cancer, access & equality, anonymous marking, sexual health and drug awareness. There is, of course, a good focus on theatre, dance, etc, through the Performing Arts department, and Newport's

Riverfront Arts Theatre figures strongly.

It is all a surprisingly eclectic and energetic mix, with regular art exhibitions vying with sporting nights, e-culture (cyber café) and student concern (a student development officer is in place).

Societies are, however, so far fairly thin on the ground: Lesbian, Gay, Bisexual, Trans-gender (LGBT), Socialist Workers, Circus Skills, Students Against Anti Social Behaviour, Literate Soup, Christian Union, Photographic Society, and Film Makers Soc. is the mix.

SPORT There are 15 clubs, from Surf to Skiiing, Rugby to Mountain Sports, boosted on Caerleon with a Sports Centre, hall, gym, fitness suite; also a rugby pitch and 2 floodlit tennis (there's a popular Tennis Academy) and netball courts. There is a need for more sports fields, and the athletic union eye one particular car park with degrees of envy and bitterness, as it was once a hockey pitch. There's no squash or swimming. For these it's off to public facilities in Newport, a centre where some champion Norwegian cyclist, who I should have heard of, does his stuff. This is the place, too, for live gigs - Arctic Monkeys have visited. They get involved with the Welsh Rugby Union and Cricket Association, and run courses to enable students to pick up nationally recognised coaching qualifications. Within easy reach are facilities for sailing and windsurfing, dry-slope skiing, caving, canoeing, mountain biking, rock climbing, orienteering and hill walking.

PILLOW TALK

They have 650 self-catered single study bedrooms on Caerleon. Every first year student who applies

AT A GLANCE

ACADEMIC FILE:	
Subjects assessed	**8**
Excellent	**Education**
Art and Design	**Grade 5 Research**
Typical A level requirements	**217 points**
Application acceptance rate	**28%**
Students-staff ratio	**20:1**
First/2:1 degree pass rate	**54%**
Graduate track employment	**55%**

ACCOMMODATION FILE:	
Guarantee to freshers	**100%**
Style	**Halls, student village**
Cost pw (no food)	**£51-£60**
Town rent	**£45**

before September 1 will be satisfied. 447 en-suite rooms cost £60 p.w.; traditional halls Abergavenny, Blaenavon, Camelot cost £51, while Dolaucothi, more bog standard than most, comes in at £49.

GETTING THERE

☞ By road: M4/J25. If approaching Caerleon from Cardiff, there is no direct exit from the J25.

Either exit at J26, or take J24 and U-turn at r/about to approach Junction 25 from the East.
☞ By rail: London Paddington, 1:50; Birmingham New Street, 2:00; Cardiff, 40 mins; Bristol Parkway, 25 mins.
☞ By coach: London, 2:45; Manchester, 5:15.
☞ By air: Heathrow, 2 hours; Cardiff and Bristol, 1. Direct coach service, Heathrow and Gatwick.

UNIVERSITY OF NORTHAMPTON

The University of Northampton
Boughton Green Road
Moulton Park
Northampton NN2 7AL

TEL 0800 358 2232; 01604 735 500
FAX 01604 713083
EMAIL admissions@northampton.ac.uk
WEB www.northampton.ac.uk

Northampton Students' Union
Boughton Green Road
Moulton Park
Northampton NN2 7AL

TEL 01604 734567 X2818
FAX 01604 719454
EMAIL [firstname.surname]@ucnu.org
WEB www.ucnu.org

VAG VIEW

University College Northampton became Northampton University in October 2005. But it nearly didn't happen. Apparently, Henry III dissolved the original Northampton University in 1265, for no other reason than that it posed a direct threat to the University of Oxford – he had been advised by his bishops that many students from Oxford had migrated to it. A Royal command is law, but UCN put their legal beavers onto it, and the way was made clear. Oxford must be quaking in anticipation of the application backlash.

CAMPUS

The main Park campus, an 80-acre estate on the edge of town, has been well designed. What strikes the visitor immediately is the careful architectural integration of facilities and services, none of which limit or indeed offend the eye. Halls are in among lecture theatres, sports centre by the nightclub, eaterie and bar; a rugby pitch in the centre of things gives a welcome sense of space and a reminder that rugby is a religion both here and in town, which has one of the best teams in the Premier League.

UNIVERSITY/STUDENT PROFILE	
University College since	**1999**
Situation/style	**Town campus**
Student population	**10455**
Undergraduates	**9025**
- mature	**29%**
- non EU undergraduates	**4%**
- male/female	**36/64**
- non-traditional student intake	**36%**
- state sector intake	**97%**
- drop-out rate	**19%**
- undergraduate applications	**Up 22%**

Close by is the intriguing Leather Conservation Centre – (Northampton is the centre of the shoe industry; the football ground is called **The Cobblers**). Some buildings are named after villages in the county, the halls after notable people of the area, including the tragic Northamptonshire poet John Clare, whose parents were illiterate, but who achieved national renown in his day by imbibing the spirit of this place before going insane.

Artistically, the focus is at UCN's Avenue campus in town, however. This 24-acre site – 20 mins.

Postgraduates 14%
Female Undergraduates 56%

STUDENT POPULATION
Total students
10,455

Male Undergraduates 30%

ACADEMIC EXCELLENCE

TEACHING:
(Rated Excellent or 17+ out of 24)

Art & Design	**23**
Anatomy, Nursing & Other Subjects Related to Medicine, Materials Technology	**22**
Communication & Media Drama, Dance, Cinematics, Education	**21**
Psychology, Sociology	**20**
Building & Civil Engineering	**19**
American Studies, General Eng & Electric/Electron Eng	**18**

away from Park and linked by a free bus service – houses Art, Design, Technology and Performance Arts. In particular there's quite a theatre tradition. A few years ago they won the Playwright Bursary at the NUS Drama Festival.

ACADEMIA

There are three faculties. **The Faculty of Applied Sciences** includes schools of Leather Technology, Built Environment, Engineering & Technology, Environmental Science, Health & Life Sciences, and Nursing & Midwifery. Medical sciences have links with the General Hospital in Northampton and with Milton Keynes, 'Nursing courses are always over-subscribed,' I was told.

The Faculty of Arts & Social Sciences includes Art & Design, Behavioural Studies (including a BSc in Psychology), Cultural Studies (such as a cross-cultural degree in Performance Studies – Drama, Dance, Music), Education (BA Hons QTS Primary), and Social Studies (American Studies, History, Sociology).

The Faculty of Management & Business includes the schools of Business, Information Systems, Law & International Business, Professional Studies (Finance and Accounting) and Management (MMB, MSc Management Studies).

A first this year is a degree in accounting, a foundation degree developed with the NHS and directed specifically at the Service's perennial problem in balancing its budgets.

Career strength in the health sector comes out of the occupational therapy and podiatry degrees. Countrywide, Salford and Northampton probably offer the best value – entry requirements to job satisfaction. There are strong links with the General Hospital in Northampton and Milton Keynes, a top notch teaching assessment result and a low entry requirement as well as the strong employment reputation that puts them in the Top Ten. Teaching inspection 22

Furniture design and manufacture is another niche employment strength. Northampton is in the heart of the leather industry, and furniture was probably always on the agenda for Product Design students. There is also a fast employment flow into these industries out of the Management & Business faculty up at Park (design being at Avenue Campus).

Graphic artists are particularly employable through BA Graphic Communication, and designers and sculptors also register with relatively strong prospects in the employment league.

In the business sector personnel officers/managers are particularly well served, the rush of graduates into the sector coming from a range of courses featuring Human Resource Management, like the 4-year sandwich BA Human Resource Management.

92% of the education provision finds expression in primary school teaching. You'll be at Park. Teaching inspection 21.

AT A GLANCE

ACADEMIC FILE:

Subjects assessed	**21**
Excellent	**48%**
Typical entry requirements	**219 points**
Application acceptance rate	**20%**
Students-staff ratio	**22:1**
First/2:1 degree pass rate	**54%**
Graduate track employment	**52%**

ACCOMMODATION FILE:

Guarantee to freshers	**95%**
Style	**Halls, flats**
Catered	**None**
En-suite	**67%**
Approx price range pw	**£41-£66**
Town rent pw	**£45**

SOCIAL SCENE

STUDENTS' UNION All the chat was of the opening of the new £1.65m 'Student Centre' on Park Campus in 2006, as yet unveiled when going to press.

Pleasure-seeking students have moulded town and uni alike. 'In the last two years no end of new pubs have opened,' a student told me. Lots of clubs offer student nights. There are free buses from Park into town.

There are two bars on Park, **Pavilion**, with views over games pitches and Sky TV, and the main union bar with drinks promos, etc – **nn2**. By night, the newly refurbished bar becomes a nightclub, with a storming new lighting and sound rig and a 12 foot big screen. By day, **nn2 is a** stylish diner.

Thursday night's *Shots in the City* is the main ents fare. Saturdays you get discos, live bands, theme nights and foam parties.

Then there's **Laidback** on the ground floor, relaxed café-bar, Sky TV, pool, games machines and music of course. **Laidback** also does events, such as 'open mic', quiz and karaoke.

At **George's**, the hub of Avenue Union, a bar is open till 2 am Fridays for the regular clubnight, variously known as *Club Friday* and *Friday the 13th*. While we were there they had a hypnotist and comedian and *Bar Footsie* (Stock Exchange drinks promo).

The student newspaper is *Wave*, the newsletter *Xpress*, and altogether 20 societies, the most active being Christian Union, kickboxing and Islam, and there are 20 sports clubs and some 50 teams. Music is prolific and student led. There is a choir, chamber orchestra and other ensembles. Students play in the Northampton Symphony Orchestra, and sing in the acclaimed Central Festival Opera.

PILLOW TALK
Uni accommodation is guaranteed to 'first and firm choices' in halls or flats (some 67% are en suite. Price per week ranges from £41 to £70, while average town rent is £45 per week.

GETTING THERE
☛ By road: M1/J15/15a/16; easy access to M5/6/25/40, A1 and A45.
☛ By rail: London and Birmingham, 1:00.
☛ By coach: London, 2:00; Birmingham, 1:35; Leicester, 1:00.

UNIVERSITY OF NORTHUMBRIA

University of Northumbria
Northumberland Road
Newcastle upon Tyne NE1 8ST

TEL 0191 243 7420
FAX 0191 227 4561
EMAIL ca.marketing@northumbria.ac.uk
WEB www.northumbria.ac.uk

Northumbria Students' Union
2 Sandyford Road
Newcastle Upon Tyne NE1 8SB

TEL 0191 227 4757
FAX 0191 227 3760
EMAIL su.president@unn.ac.uk
WEB www.mynsu.co.uk

VAG VIEW

*T*he two universities in the city of Newcastle are situated within walking distance of one another. Health is now a crucial provision of both, having overtaken Business as Northumbria's defining interest. While Newcastle Uni has medicine, Northumbria has nursing (which achieved full marks at the teaching assessments), midwifery, physiotherapy, occupational therapy.

There are also some excellent social science courses, including a key Law degree, a 4-year 'fast-track' Exempting degree. Another defining mark of Northumbria is its fashion department.

But that is not all. Some 1992 unis have not taken on board the significance of the student culture in student development. Northumbria has, and took big strides. Then it seemed to lose steam. Now it's back on top again with more than 50 student societies, a refurbished Students' Union, and sports teams that came 13th nationally last year, that's 2 places ahead of Newcastle Uni.

CAMPUSES
CITY CAMPUS (address above) Student Union, library, sports centre, language laboratories, art gallery. A wireless computing network, providing internet access for laptops has been instituted across the uni.

COACH LANE CAMPUS Coach Lane, Benton, Newcastle upon Tyne NE7 7XA. Tel: 0191 215 6000. Recent beneficiary of a £40-million development. Health, Social Work & Education are here. Coach Lane also has a union, library and computing facilities, a sports hall, fitness suite, activity studio and

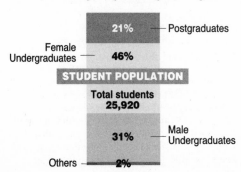

Postgraduates 21%
Female Undergraduates 46%
STUDENT POPULATION
Total students 25,920
Male Undergraduates 31%
Others 2%

UNIVERSITY/STUDENT PROFILE

University since	**1992**
Situation/style	**Civic**
Student population	**25920**
Undergraduates	**20070**
- mature	**35%**
- non EU undergraduates	**7%**
- male/female	**41/59**
- non-traditional student intake	**29%**
- state school intake	**91%**
- drop-out rate	**18%**
- undergraduate applications	**Up 3%**

all-weather hockey pitch.

FEES, BURSARIES

UK & EU Fees, 2007: £3,070 p.a. except for nursing, midwifery, social work, physio. and occupational therapy, where they are picked up elsewhere. Law students on the Exemption course pay an extra £900. On a year out in a sandwich course, you pay only £750. Built Environment Foundation year is £1,500. There's a Northumberland Scholarship, worth between £250 and £1,000 in first year, not dependent on household earnings, but on course studied (see web site for listing). In subsequent years it's dependent on your exam results.

STUDENT PROFILE

Relative to many other unis, there's a sound balance between applicants from state and private sector (considerably fewer public school boys than Newcastle Uni, but more than many a newish uni) and an average sort of take from socio-economic classes new to the idea of university. More notable are the figures for mature undergraduates (35%) and part-timers (24%), part of their Lifelong Learning policy. Basically, the mix works; everyone has a cool time in a very cool place. 'Best thing,' said Jack Ford when he alighted there for the first time, 'was the relaxed atmosphere that enables students to bond and make lots of new friends.'

ACADEMIA & JOBS

Seriously good reputation on graduate employment and less demanding at entry than many. Contact with firms in the North East region is facilitated by all sorts of strategies, not least Northumbria's e.Business Centre, which dispenses advice and support to small and medium sized businesses, utilising uni expertise in law, technology, marketing and business.

Property developers, architects, construction managers, quantity surveyors and estate agents pour out of Northumbria. The big four for property development nationwide are Sheffield Hallam, Northumbria, Nottingham Trent and Manchester Met. At Northumbria there's a mix of Business and Building/Engineering graduates boosting employment figures in Property Development. The uni's Business & Management expertise is second to none – see the new 3-year Corporate Management degree, broken down into one year intensive learning, then two years on a work placement followed by a final six months to complete a dissertation. Also BA Business Management, Business Admin top-up ('Excellent' in the assessments), qand various Joint Business degrees.

In building, BA Architectural Design & Management sits alongside BEng Building Services Engineering, and BSc Architectural Technology, Building Design Mgt, Building Project Mgt, Commercial Quantity Surveying, Building Surveying, Construction Management, Estate Management, etc (foundation degrees available in many of these). Teaching inspection 22.

Meanwhile, prospective engineer design con-

> *Northumbria's School of Law is authorised by both the Law Society and the Bar Council to run the only 4-year Exempting LLB degree, in the UK*

WHERE NORTHUMBRIA GRADUATES END UP

Health & Social Work: 13%; Education: 11%; Wholesale Retail: 10%; Manufacturing: 9%; Financial Activities: 6%; Public Administration, Civil Service & Defence: 9%; Hotel/Restaurant: 4%; Transport & Communications (including Telecommunications): 5%; Construction: 2%; Agriculture: 1%; Personnel: 5%; Computer: 3%; Business & Management: 5%; Accountancy: 2%; Media (including Film): 0.5%; Legal 4%; Architecture: 2%; Advertising: 0.5%; Artistic/Literary: 1%; Sport: 1%.

Approximate 'graduate track' employed **63%**

ACADEMIC EXCELLENCE

TEACHING:
(Rated Excellent or 17+ out of 24)

Business & Management, English, Law.	**Excellent**
Nursing, Education	**24**
Languages (French, German, Russian, Spanish), Physics, Subjects Allied to Medicine	**23**
Drama/Dance /Cinematics, Built Environment, Electrical & Electronic Eng, Art, Economics, Library/Info Mgt, Politics & Design, Business, Psychology	**22**
History Art/Design & Film, Town/Country Planning, Maths, Sport, Molecular Biosciences	**21**
Sociology	**20**

RESEARCH :
Top grades 5/5*	**None**

sultants leap at their computer-aided design degrees, such as BEng Computer Aided Engineering and Manufacturing Systems Engineering, as well as BSc Computer & Network technology.

Electrical, electronic and telecommunications engineers are especially well served by a strong 22 points out of 24 at the assessments, and

AT A GLANCE

ACADEMIC FILE:
Subjects assessed	**30**
Excellent	**77%**
Typical entry requirements	**272 points**
Application acceptance rate	**24%**
Students-staff ratio	**20:1**
First/2:1 degree pass rate	**53%**

ACCOMMODATION FILE:
Guarantee to freshers	**100%**
Style	**Halls, flats, houses**
Catered	**18%**
En-suite	**13%**
Price range pw	**£65-£105**
City rent pw	**£35-£70**

Northumbria came top among those unis that offer games degrees for getting programmer graduates employment. Have a close look at their 4-year sandwich BSc Computer Games Software

Engineering. See also Computer for Business and Computer Studies degrees: it's a very strong employment area.

The School of Law is authorised by both the Law Society and the Bar Council to run the only 4-year Exempting LLB degree, in the UK, which gives students the opportunity to work on real client cases through the Student Law Office. This exempts from the need for further professional vocational training, namely the Legal Practice Course and the Bar Vocational Course, both of which are also offered as stand alone programmes.

Showing the department's practical bent, recently, Kevin Kerrigan, principal lecturer in Law, and his final-year students helped quash the sentence of a man, Alex Alan, who had already served 6 years in jail after being wrongly convicted of robbery. They then secured £170,000 compensation.

SUBJECT AREAS (%)

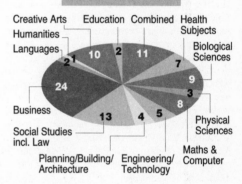

Government administration (local, regional, central) is another sector served well by Northumbria – various Politics degrees, BSc Social Work, and Social & Public Policy. Probation officers proliferate, and most graduates into government admin come from the Social Studies area. Look closely at the Professional Practice Studies & Advice Guidance & Counselling, Childhood Studies, Disability Studies, etc. While on the social studies ticket, note, too, Drama scored 22 out of 24 at the assessments – it's a performance-related course with a community focus,

One fifth of intake goes into business and employability is high, but one interesting scoop in the transport business is a design pathway. You'll need to go through the Foundation Art course (portfolio required) to join the BA Transportation Design, which builds on a tradition of supplying Design graduates into the automotive, marine, rail and aviation industries. Teaching inspection 22.

Another excellent career niche degree is their

4-year sandwich BA Human Resource Management, which looks after a third of their large contingent going into the sector. Sciences and Social Sciences are also popular routes (all 22 points at assessment). Psychologists find the BSc degree (and another with Sports Science) very efficient career-wise, both accredited by the British Psychological Society.

There's also a dedicated Physiotherapy degree. The nursing, midwifery, physiotherapy, occupational therapy side helps to find some 13% of its graduates jobs, and Northumbria is one of only four institutions to attain full marks in the teaching assessments for nursing. They cover adult, children's nursing, learning disabilities and mental health. Most graduates are SEN and half as many, non-hospital nurses.

The Pharmacology and Pharmacy degrees spawn pharmaceutical manufacturers and chemists in number. Passport to success here is BSc Pharmaceutical Chemistry. Teaching inspection 23.

The fashion department excels. They have two degrees, Fashion and Fashion Marketing, a 4-year sandwich. Excellent careers track record here, as there is for graphic artists and designers and set designers.

SOCIAL SCENE

At City Campus the **Venue Bar**, on the first floor, is the place for live music (capacity now 3000), while **Reds** (circular bar, 550 capacity), on the second floor, is for discos. There's also **Bar One,** on the ground floor. Coach Lane campus has a big hall, one bar and one major clubnight on a Thursday.

Reds has new night *Hype* on a Friday – indie, electro, rock, r&b, soul – at **Reds**. On Saturday, *Wiggle* survives: it's a tradition, it's the biggest night of the week – 'pulling not posing' – both upstairs in **Reds** and downstairs in the **Venue**. 'Last year we had it upstairs only and we'd sell out in the first fifteen minutes,' we were told. It's chart, cheese and party + £1.50 VK flavours all night.

They boast live gigs this term from Junco Partners, Julian Cope, Death Cab for Cutie, and the usual run of hypnotists and ceilidhs. 'We promote our own DJs in Reds.' There are also good opportunities for DJs to make the transition to city clubs. 'One of our DJs, who does Saturday night *Wiggle*, was a student here, and now he's working six nights a week in bars and nightclubs in town.'

There's also a decent drama society – 3 or 4 productions a year, a monthly newspaper (*Northumbria Student*) looking for contributors, and they're part of Newcastle Uni's LSR radio station.

Probably the most active of the 30 societies is Community Student Action. GLOBE – Gay, Lesbian & Bisexual – get involved in national campaigns. Three years ago they invested £1 million in the Student Services department – the counselling, careers and study skills services.

SPORT Lots to offer, well-equipped sports hall, gym and indoor tennis courts, options to do anything from scuba diving to rugby, which has some very high-class teams and regularly trounces Newcastle Uni, good hockey, football and tennis. They run an Elite Athlete Programme – Team Northumbria – which offers practical and financial support to students with particular potential. Maybe too high class, one student complained that there's only 3 uni football teams and it's hard to get a trial date.

WHAT IT'S REALLY LIKE	
UNIVERSITY:	
Social Life	★★★★
Campus scene	**The lively, less self-conscious one**
Student Union services	**Average**
Politics	**Average**
Sport	**Key**
National team position	**10th**
Sport facilities	**Good**
Arts opportunities	**Drama, music, film good; dance, art average**
Student newspaper	**Northumbria Student**
Nightclubs	**Venue**
Bars	**Reds, Bar One, Coach Lane**
Union ents	**Big club nights and live**
Union societies	**53**
Parking	**Poor**
CITY:	
Entertainment	★★★★★
Scene	**Vibrant, fun**
Town/gown relations	**OK**
Risk of violence	**Low**
Cost of living	**Low**
Student concessions	**Good**
Survival + 2 nights out	**£70 pw**
Part-time work campus/town	**Average/excellent**

PILLOW TALK

They guarantee 100% freshers uni accommodation, with priority given to non-local first-years. First-year accommodation consists of halls and flats. Claude Gibb is the most popular hall, being in crawling distance of town and lectures – 'more of a public school crowd here,' said one. The Larches is the one to avoid (rough area). Lovaine, also on campus, is handy but poky. Of flats a student said that Glenamara and Stevenson both have the advantage of a very central location. Only 18% of accommodation is catered and 13% en suite. Last new residences with en-suite and internet sockets have opened adjacent to City Campus in September 2002, before the opening in autumn 2005 of two large residential developments, which will boost the en-suite complement considerably.

GETTING THERE

☛ By road to Newcastle: A1(M) from the south and north; A19 from York; A69 from the west; M6 from the southwest.

☛ By road to Carlisle: A7 from the north; M6 from the south; A69 from Newcastle (the east).

☛ By rail to Newcastle: Edinburgh, 1:30; Leeds, 1:45; London King's Cross, 3:00; Manchester Piccadilly, 3:00; Birmingham New Street, 4:00.

☛ By air: Newcastle International airport.

☛ By coach: London, 6:05; Birmingham, 4:25.

STUDENT NOTTINGHAM – THE CITY

Nottingham is without doubt, the best city in the country for a student. Situated in the Midlands, it's never too far UK students to get home, and being in the middle of the country, you get a really good mix of both southern and northern students along with the grounded Nottingham locals themselves.

There are two universities and eight further education colleges in Nottingham, a bustling city that has come into its own, it almost seems, in the very process of catering for the huge number of students it attracts.

LIVE MUSIC

For its sheer size and the big names it attracts, the best venue for live music has to be the **Ice Centre**, situated in the **Lace Market**. The Strokes, Kelly Clarkson and the Little Britain Tour have all been there recently. The drinks are extortionately priced, but if you want to see the big names it generally does mean big bucks.

A venue for live music acts with more *cred.* is the less-commercial **Rock City**. City centre situated, and a lot more edgy, **Rock City** has hosted such as The Killers and Oasis in this small but very atmospheric club. With student club nights throughout the week, this is a *must* if you want to dodge the cheese and get heavily into eyeliner.

If its un-discovered talent you're after, then look no further than the **Rescue Rooms**, which is just round the corner and almost a pint-sized version of **Rock City**.

Live music is really taking off in Nottingham and even Trent's Student Union is jumping on the bandwagon, hosting its very own live music night with some great up-coming bands every second Friday.

CLUBBING

Nottingham is now seen as a bar city, not first and foremost club orientated. Yet, with the mix of clubs it has, catering for all wants and tastes, you will be hard pushed to find better elsewhere. The newlish **Oceana** is very popular with students – 5 rooms filled with different atmospheres and music – but again be prepared to spend a penny or two. The city also has **Mode** nightclub and **Lost Weekend**, both with great student nights, cheap drinks and cheesy tunes.

But the clubs of all clubs remains the mighty **Ocean** nightclub. Not to be confused with **Oceana**, it has just become solely a student nightclub every day of the week, with both universities holding nights. You're guaranteed a good night out, if drunken sportsmen, scantily clad ladies and cheap drinks and cheese is your cup of tea.

For an alternative night, try **Stealth**, **The Cookie Club** and **The Bomb**. The venues are slightly more intimate, a lot smaller, but by no less lively.

DRINKING

Nottingham Trent Students Union offers a fantastic place to drink with its **Glo** bar being well equipped for both chilling out and dancing, and its **Sub** bar to kick back and play some pool. **The Ark** at Nottingham Uni's Students Union is no way near as big, but still offers the usual guarantee of cheap drinks and cheese.

In the city centre, **The Horn in Hand**, **Varsity**, **Templars**, **Up and Down Under** and **Walkabout** are very student populated, give student discounts and offer a relaxed atmosphere. Each has a new deal each week.

For more sophistication, try Hockley and the Lace Market, where most of the following are situated – **Revolution** (over 100 different vodka shots can be tried and consumed), **Tantra** (you can hire out beds for the evening), **Quilted Lama** (with its enormous fish bowls), and the sometime church come bar, **Pitcher and Piano**. But be warned, it won't come cheap.

The **Waterfront** takes it home at the other side of town, and has 7 bars spread across 7 floors. In summer time, the canal-side terrace is packed.

SHOPPING

Prepare to spend, spend, spend when you come to Nottingham and hit the shops. It is worryingly easy to blow your student loan on the incredible shopping experience that Nottingham offers. There are all the chain stores, many cool trendy shops and it's rife with factory shops. Go to the **Victoria Centre** for day-to-day student favourites, the brand new **Topshop**, **La Senza**, **Republic**, and such as HMV, Boots... Along with its market, department store and supermarket, it caters for everyone. **The Broadmarsh** is at the other end of town and is again a shopping complex, but offers fair-priced **H&M**, **TK Max** and **New Look**. **The Broadmarsh** is very handy for fancy dress outfits at a cut rate, too.

If you want to spend that bit more, then walk down Bridlesmith Gate to **Flannels**, **Diesel** and **Kurt Geiger**. You really can get your heart desire,

from retro gear at **Ice Nine** and **Wild Clothing** to everyday fashions at **Warehouse** and Zara.

EATING

Whether you are looking for quality (somewhere to drag your parents), quantity (eat all you want), or somewhere to bring your own wine, Nottingham does not disappoint. The **Corner House** in the city centre offers an array of different cuisine from Flaming Dragon, the Chinese buffet, to Bella Italia, a very fair priced and tasty Italian. American style diners proliferate around the city centre, including **Hard Rock Café** and **Frankie and Benny's**, while Hockley has **Fresh**, a great place to eat and very healthy, and some great bars that offer good, extravagant bar meals, like **Browns** and the **Hog's Head**.

For daytime snacking, it's **Subways**, the individual outlets scattered across the city, and you'll find a favourite dive among a whole host of small, reasonably priced city café's.

Whatever you're in the mood for, whatever your needs and requirements, Nottingham really does have something for everyone.

Annabel Woollen

UNIVERSITY OF NOTTINGHAM

The University of Nottingham
University Park
Nottingham NG7 2RD

TEL 0115 951 4749
FAX 0115 951 4668
EMAIL ugadmissions@nottingham.ac.uk
WEB www.nottingham.ac.uk

Nottingham Students' Union
University Park
Nottingham NG7 2RD

TEL 0115 846 8800
EMAIL studentsunion@nottingham.ac.uk
WEB www.students-union.nottingham.ac.uk

VAG VIEW

*N*ottingham *is a top university with a 91% Excellence rating, and students enjoy a 75% chance of graduating with a first or upper second class degree.*

More than this, it is one of the most employer-friendly universities in the world, and students are happy here. After Manchester and Leeds, more apply than anywhere else, and its drop-out rate, at 5%, is very low.

Known, among much else, for its medical provision, the uni launched a School of Veterinary Science last year, a landmark – it was the UK's first new Vet School since the

1950s. Students will study ten miles out, at Sutton Bonington. Go there, see it, do the trip to main campus on Open Day.

This year there's a whole raft of new Chinese courses, as the uni has set up shop there, though there are as many new Russian and Spanish courses, and some interesting film and TV degrees, too. Nottingham students are hot on media. They win nearly everything at the nationals.

CAMPUSES

The 300-acre **University Park**, home to 3,000 students, workplace to a further 26,000 students and staff, and located just a short bus or bike ride from Nottingham city centre, is the main campus – huge lake, views over Trent valley, rolling Downs that sweep away into the distance, all a neat ten minutes by bus from town.

There is a 16-hectare satellite campus at **Sutton Bonington**, 10 miles distant, for the School of Biological Sciences, and now the new Vet School. Besides teaching and research facilities, the James Cameron-Gifford Library and student residences, there's a sports centre, bank and bookshop. A free shuttle-bus service runs between it and University Park during the day.

The **Jubilee Campus**, on a site close to University Park, houses the Schools of Education, Computer Science and Information Technology, as well as The Business School. The site is also the home of The National College for School Leadership. Green in concept and design, an important feature is the series of lakes which, as well as being home to wildlife, provide cooling for the buildings in the summer and receive all surface water. Less visible – but equally important to this model of a sustainable campus – are the roofs which are, quite literally, green. A carpet of low-growing alpine plants helps maintain steady temperatures within the buildings throughout the year and is more effective than traditional insulation. Buildings also feature a super-efficient mechanical ventilation system, lighting sensors to reduce energy consumption, and photovoltaic cells integrated into the atrium roofs. The environmentally-friendly nature of the campus and its buildings have been a big factor in the awards that it has received, including the Millennium Marque Award for Environmental Excellence, the British Construction Industry Building Project of the Year, the RIBA Journal Sustainability Award and the Civic Trust Award for Sustainability.

'When I first visited the university, all fresh-faced and eager,' recalls Mark Tew, 'I couldn't help but be struck by the sheer size of the place. It's BIG.' Writes Phil Barnett: 'Walking through, with the river on one side and incredible architecture on the other, is an experience never to grow tired of. But, when the need arises, living away from main campus does mean a 20-minute walk or a free bus, which is supposed to leave every 15 minutes but always seems to be leaving as the bus stop is approached. The facilities are fantastic and all day to day necessities are available. It has its own shop and a sports centre with good facilities, but no gym (one occasion when a visit to main campus is necessary).

'Accommodation is all en-suite, fully catered, and the food is more than satisfactory, with a choice of 2 cafés or the main hall.

'A lot of Jubilee students study business, of course, and can leave hall less than a minute before lectures begin. If you are one of these, living at Jubilee does means that a lot of your course friends are also the people you live with. However, a fair few Jubilee students do in fact study on the main campus, so there must be advantages in this. If you are visiting Nottingham, I'd advise you take a look around. New work to enhance the campus further began in February this year.'

FEES, BURSARIES

UK & EU Fees, 2007: £3,070 p.a. Fees p.a. 2008 are available on website from February next year. There are bursaries for those receiving the full Government Maintence Grant and, on a sliding scale, according to parental income, for those on a partial grant. If you are a local student and on a low income you can apply for the First-in-the-Family (£1,000 p.a.) or the Ethel and Kevin B. Malone (£1,000 p.a.). There are also subject specific scholarships - see www.nottingham.ac.uk/financialestimator. A sports bursary is available for students at regional or international level, or, in some instances, county level in any sport.

UNIVERSITY/STUDENT PROFILE	
University since	**1948**
Situation/style	**Edge of city campuses**
Student population	**32770**
Undergraduates	**24565**
- mature	**9%**
- non EU undergraduates	**15%**
- male/female	**49/51**
- non-traditional student intake	**16%**
- state school intake	**68%**
drop-out rate	**5%**
- undergraduate applications	**Up 6%**

STUDENT PROFILE

The uni has one of the lowest intakes from the state sector and from so-called non-traditional uni

20% — Postgraduates

Female Undergraduates — 37%

38% — Male Undergraduates

STUDENT POPULATION

Total students 32,770

Other — 5%

heartlands (lower socio-economic groups and neighbourhoods). However, they want to change this. To encourage applicants from poor areas of the local community with potential, they have an outreach programme offering summer schools, drama workshops, campus tours, coaching in study skills and interview techniques.

'I was told to expect a lot of bitter and twisted Oxbridge rejects with a big fat chip on the shoulder, but this hasn't been the case,' Mark recalls. 'The "rah-rah, sooo drunk!" toff brigade, however, is definitely out in full force! Being from up t' North, it was a culture shock to say the least. But it's well worth being here if just to take the piss. "Another bottle of champers Roger?"'

ACADEMIA & JOBS

The medical degree, BMBS, is rigorous – 3 years to BMedSci, then 2 increasingly clinical years. They want AAB + UKCAT. There's an 11% chance of getting in. Must have Chemistry and Biology (A).

There's also a fast-track graduate entry version based at Derby, a £12 million Medical School and Clinical Sciences building opened on a site at Derby City General Hospital. GEM – Graduate Entry Medicine is for graduates of any discipline with a 1st or 2:1 (no fixed upper age limit). Typical offer for the traditional degree is ABB: Chemistry + one other science + one other. Teaching inspection, 21.

The Nottingham Law degree was recently assessed by the LPC Board, and it was among the very few to be rated Excellent. International Grade 5 for research. All candidates must sit the National Admissions Test for Law (LNAT).

Some 11% of Nottingham graduates go into Finance. Most become chartered accountants, investment analysts and actuaries. They offer BA Finance, Accounting & Management, while the Social Sciences Faculty has such as BSc Economics & Econometrics, and the joint hons. programmes have BSc Maths & Economics, Maths & Management Studies, and BC Economics and Philosophy. Teaching inspection: Economics 24, Maths 23, Philosophy 22. Research Grade 5: Maths, Economics and Philosophy.

There's a BA Industrial Economics with Insurance degree, also productive of jobs in the investment analyst sector, in which this uni seems particularly to excel.

Would-be business management consultants look at BA Management Studies and a range of joint degrees with French, German, Spanish, Asian or Chinese Studies. There's a research Grade 6* for some of these. There are interesting language and management tie-ups, too, with engineering.

Industrial relations are good. Blue-chip companies that maintain ongoing research relationships include Powergen, The Boots Company and GlaxoSmithKline. The Ford Motor Company and AstraZeneca have both been involved with the University for over 30 years. The University's relationship with Rolls-Royce includes hosting two Technology Centres in the areas of gas turbine transmission systems and manufacturing technology. They are also working together on a research programme aimed at improving the performance of aerospace engines for which the uni will receive £2.2 million.

Look closely at BA Industrial Economics. This is Jessie Boot territory, so expect jobs, too, for chemists. Nottingham's eco-friendly philosophy, a main principle behind the Jubilee campus is evident in their Green Chemistry & Process Engineering, their aim to produce graduates with a blend of knowledge and skills that will enable chemical industry to move in harmony with the environmental sustainability that is on everyone's long term strategy.

Aspiring Pharmacists read Pharmacy, and the uni's 23 points out of 24 in the assessments for the 4-year MPharm, and Grade 5 for research, confirm its status at the top.

Aspiring biologists and physicists also find their needs met here. There's a 23-point assessment score in these areas and strong bio-medical-agri links within the wider curriculum, as well as a Grade 5 for Genetics.

Engineering is a big strength for Nottingham, 15% graduate in it. It's a route into Defence, among many other areas, but there's an interesting employment strength in design here. They have long had a lean towards interesting eco-friendly structural design through such as the Institute of Environmental Science and the Institute of Building Technology, and now strong prospects for all sorts of design-orientated courses, from the arts group BArch degree through B/MEng

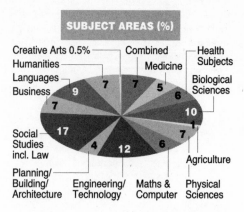

SUBJECT AREAS (%)

Architectural Environment Engineering and Architecture & Environment Design. Note also MEng Mechanical, Design, Materials & Manufacture. They're similarly productive of civil engineers. Full marks in the teaching assessments, 22 points for Civil Eng. International Grade 5 for research.

Again, they are among the leaders in the field for finding jobs in computer programming. BSc degrees include Computer Science, e-Commerce & Digital Business and Computer Science & Management Studies. Research Grade 5.

Jobs also abound in forestry and agriculture through their degrees in Plant/Animal Science, Food Science/Microbiology, Zoology, Ecology, Botany, etc. Note, too, the new Veterinary Medicine/Science degree and 1-year Pre-Vet Science Certificate.

Finally, Nottingham's top-rated BSc Psychology leads graduates into all sorts of areas, including market research, publicity and PR, choice too of many of Nottingham's sought-after graduates in languages, social studies, business and humanities.

SOCIAL SCENE

STUDENTS' UNION This is housed in the newly extended Portland Building, which overlooks the lake and which at long last has undergone a multi-million pound makeover, with a new SU shop, banks, Blackwells and Boots outlets, and a type of revolving door that spews students with armfuls of books out onto the steps. The renamed **Buttery** bar, **The Ark,** has also had a makeover, but, according to one student 'with little discernible difference other than a coat of paint and a cashpoint, although the hatch serving food – healthy sandwiches by day, greasy chips by night – is very welcome.' In addition, the **D H Lawrence** bar can be found in the Lakeside **D H Pavilion**, where exhibitions and stage productions run as prolifically as in the **New Theatre**, which is elsewhere, tucked up behind Portland and as old as the hills.

There are also bars in the 14 halls of residence, and no difficulty in seeing how the drinking binge known as "Campus 14" became so popular. First-year social life spins off halls, off societies, off departments and off sport, rather more than off the Union: 'It still amazes me how such fine, upstanding, intelligent people, who clearly had the "right stuff" to get into Nottingham University, all seem mystically drawn to the Union on a Friday night,' writes Mark. 'Why? It's a *dive*! Maybe that's harsh. It's actually really nice during the day, its only real crime may be overcrowding on the weekend.'

Lurve Machine @ **The Ark** has been a perenni-

al fave. They've also had Blues Brothers Experience and Chesney Hawkes, Feeder and Queens of the Stone Age, and the Comedy Society does a regular stand-up open mic session there and plays host to such as Ross Nobel and Johnny Vegas.

The Ark was also home to Radio 1's Live in Nottingham gig – both Emma B and Jo Whiley in attendance. Nottingham radio is huge. The students have won more national awards than any other university. Last year, they took 5 Gold Awards, including Station of the Year, 1 Silver and 2 Bronze. *Impact* was runner-up nationally for Best Magazine.

Nottingham has also long had an enterprising drama society. **The New Theatre**, which

ACADEMIC EXCELLENCE	
TEACHING:	
(Rated Excellent or 17+ out of 24)	
Chemistry, Law,	**Excellent**
Mechanical Engineering,	
Architecture, Business &	
Management, English,	
Geography, Music. German,	
Manufacturing Engineering &	**24**
Operations Mgt, Classics,	
Psychology, Economics, Politics	
Agriculture & Food Sciences,	**23**
Art History, Urban Planning,	
Pharmacology, Biosciences,	
Physics, Maths, Theology	
Civil Eng, Nursing, Anatomy	**22**
Electrical & Electronic Eng,	
American Studies, Philosophy,	
Education	
Sociology, Chemica Eng,	**21**
Materials Technology,	
Subjects Allied to Medicine,	
Archaeology, Medicine	
Russian & East Euro Langs	**19**
.RESEARCH:	
Top grades 5/5*/6*	
American Studies, German/	**Grade 6***
Dutch/Scandinavian, Iberian/	
Latin American, Theology,	
Music	
Pharmacy, Psychology,	**Grade 5**
Genetics, Agriculture, Food	
Science, Chemistry, Physics,	
Pure Math, Applied Math,	
Statistics, Computer, Civil Eng,	
Mechanical/Aeronautical/	
Manufacturing Eng, Geography,	
Law, Economics, Management,	
English, French, Russian/Slavonic/	
East European, Philosophy	

once exuded all the spit-and-sawdust appeal of true fringe theatre, now more suits its name.

UNIVERSITY:	
Social Life	★★★★★
Campus scene	Well-heeled, bright, sporty, creative
Student Union services	Good
Politics	Activity high
Sport	Key nationally & v. active inter-hall. 67 clubs.
National team position	7th
Sport facilities	Good
Arts opportunities	Drama excellent; music, art good; dance, film great
Student magazine	Impact
2006 National Awards	R-up Best Mag.
Newspaper	Grapevine
Student radio	URN
2006 National Awards	5 Golds, 1 Silver, 2 Bronze
Venue	The Ark
Bars	D H Lawrence + all halls
Union ents	College & town club based
Union societies	207
Most popular society	Christian Union, Cock Soc, Dance Soc
Parking	Adequate
CITY:	
Entertainment	★★★★★
Scene	Serious nightlife, good arts
Town/gown relations	OK
Risk of violence	High
Cost of living	Average
Student concessions	Good
Survival + 2 nights out	£90 pw
Part-time work campus/town	Good/excellent

They write, produce and direct up to twenty plays a year and invariably take a production or two to Edinburgh. Theatre has always been big in this city, the **Playhouse**'s deep-rooted reputation to the fore, and **Malt Cross Music Hall** offers an eerie alternative with drama, music hall, comedy, jazz and folk, with poltergeists in attendance and spooky goings-on that no one seems able to explain. Then there's the **Theatre Royal** of course (Gilbert & Sulivan, *Rocky Horror*, Arthur Miller, *My Fair Lady*, etc.), and music and dance at the **Palace Theatre**, Mansfield.

On campus, music societies proliferate, such as Blow Soc (wind, to be sure), and for music and art there's the **Arts Centre** – a superb art gallery (with artist in residence) and recital hall next door.

Students may come from comfortable backgrounds and rarely set the firmament alight with radical political action, but they apparently have a caring nature, expressed in the extraordinary agenda of Community Action, some 2000 student volunteers getting involved in arts projects (drama, music), welfare projects (including prison visiting), health, education, housing, sport, environmental projects.

SPORT Notttingham teams came 7th nationally for the last 2 years, but they also claim the largest and most comprehensive inter-hall league. There is opportunity at all levels to participate in as many as 67 clubs. Facilities include two sports halls, rooms for martial arts, aerobics, etc., climbing wall, fitness/weights room, **Champions** bar and restaurant, six squash courts, and at long last they have their own swimming pool (25 x 18m). Outside, there's a floodlit, artificial turf hockey pitch and athletics track. Boating (with boathouse) on the tidal Trent. Sutton Bonington has its own sports centre, squash and tennis courts, rugby, football and cricket pitches. Bursaries are available.

PILLOW TALK

Freshers are guaranteed a place in halls if they receive your Preference Form by August 1. You're

Health & Social Work: 22%; Education: 5%; Wholesale Retail: 7%; Manufacturing: 9%; Financial Activities: 11%; Public Administration, Civil Service & Defence: 7%; Hotel/Restaurant: 2%; Transport & Communications (including Telecommunications): 4%; Construction: 1%; Agriculture: 1%; Personnel: 3.5%; Computer: 5%; Business & Management: 4%; Accountancy: 5%; Media (including Film): 1%; Legal 2%; Architecture: 0.5%; Publishing: 1%; Advertising: 1%

Approximate 'graduate track' employed **71%**

AT A GLANCE

ACADEMIC FILE:

Subjects assessed	**43**
Excellent	**91%**
Typical entry requirements	**429 points**
Application acceptance rate	**13%**
Med. School acceptance rate	**11%**
Students-staff ratio	**16:1**
First/2:1 degree pass rate	**75%**

ACCOMMODATION FILE:

Guarantee to freshers	**100%**
Style	**Halls, flats**
Catered halls	**40%**
En suite	**29%**
Approx. price range p.w.	**£71-£118**
City rent pw	**£60**

sharing a bedroom to your own bathroom. Each hall offers great amenities – coin-operated laundry facilities, pantries to make snacks, chill-out areas like a bar, Junior Common Room, TV and games room, plus a mini library and computer suite.

Writes Mark: 'To be fair, all the halls are pretty nice. Being a former Lincolnite, my totally unbiased opinion is that it is by far the best hall in the world. Small, yet cosy bar, good food, big rooms, our very own library and even cheese and wine nights in the SCR! What more could you want? OK, so Hugh Stu has the best bar, Derby has the best women and Sherwood has a slide shaped as a dragon. So what!'

Check web site for the latest on the new Veterinary Medicine and Science school's purpose-built accommodation.

If you have a disability and need accessible accommodation, you'll be guaranteed a suitable room. Email: disabilityadviser@nottingham.ac.uk

talking fully catered halls & self- catering flats. about a third are en suite. There's lots of other accommodation in flats, but catered halls it probably will be, unless you're at Sutton Bonington. There are 14 halls in total, home to approximately 4,000 students, across two sites – Jubilee Campus and University Park. All of the halls provide three meals a day, every day during term time, as part of the accommodation fee. There are 5 different room-types, ranging from

> *The New Theatre, which once exuded all the spit-and-sawdust appeal of true fringe theatre, now more suits its name. They write, produce and direct up to 20 plays a year.*

GETTING THERE

☞ By road: Nottingham, M1/J 25, A52. Sutton Bonington, M1/J24, A6, then left turn.

☞ By rail: London St Pancras, 1:50; Edinburgh, 4:30; Exeter, 4:00; Birmingham New Street, 1:30.

☞ By air: East Midlands Airport.

☞ By coach: London, 2:55; Birmingham, 1:30; Newcastle, 5:00; Exeter, 6:30.

NOTTINGHAM TRENT UNIVERSITY

The Nottingham Trent University
Burton Street
Nottingham NG1 4BU

TEL 0115 848 2814
FAX 0115 848 6063
EMAIL admissions@ntu.ac.uk
STUDENT UNION TEL 0115 848 6200
WEB www.ntu.ac.uk

VAG VIEW

*C*entred on the building in Shakespeare Street where, in 1887, the foundation stone was laid by Gladstone for University College Nottingham, the institution later to become Nottingham University, this, the second uni in town began life as Trent Poly in 1970.

Writes Thomas Bell: 'As you may know, Trent is a former poly, now referred to as a

"Moderní Uni". We are often compared to the older, and by repute, better universities. This is not true across the board. For instance, my Law school runs some of the best courses around, and even Oxbridge postgrads are drawn to the department. Again, fashion and textiles courses are considered to be very good at Trent.

'We have a charity Varsity sports series with Nottingham University each year, which attracts large crowds from both universities, *and whatever happens nationally [Nottingham 7th; Trent 33rd last year], we usually prevail, if not so regularly in rowing, where, for a number of reasons, we get our bums paddled. Despite this, in true "Trent" style, we still go out and celebrate like good underdogs should!*

CAMPUS SITES

CITY CAMPUS Burton Street is the location of the central admin building, 'front' for a whole load of buildings in neighbouring streets, 2 mins from the action. Writes Thomas: 'The city site is by far the most exciting campus, as its right in the centre of Nottingham. A brand new tram line runs through 'Studentville', past the uni and into the town centre, terminating at the train station.'

The Students' Union HQ, with Byron Sports Hall, are here, along with the £13-million Boots Library, student residences and five of the uni's academic schools: Art & Design, Business, Law, Built Environment, and Social Sciences.

A £70 million regeneration of two buildings at City campus will be completed in 2009.

CLIFTON CAMPUS Clifton Lane, Nottingham NG11 8NS. This is a spacious, green field campus some 4 miles southwest of the city centre along the A453. It is wholly self-contained with its own SU, sports grounds and student village, and is home to Arts & Humanities, Education, Biomedical & Natural Sciences, and Computing & Informatics.

'Clifton is the smaller of the two campuses with around 5,000 students,' writes Daniel Ashley, 'and still thrives on the community atmosphere. Probably not a bad thing, as the Clifton locals are not famed for their tolerance of us.'

The Student Village has a bar and diner, supermarket, bank, refectory and bookshop. The Student Union has an active programme here and as Clifton is home to Trent's sports department, there's a pro sports hall, all-weather floodlit sports pitch, a cricket pitch, and well-equipped gym

Clifton Hall, Clifton Village, is a Georgian manor house a few minutes walk from Clifton campus and includes lecture halls for use by the faculty of Education, a resource centre, dance studio and refectory.

Brackenhurst College is Trent's Department of Land-based Studies near the historic town of Southwell, 10 miles north east of Nottingham, which for years has offered Trent degrees and comes with a 200-hectare farm. There's a whole Student Union set-up here, bar, sports, ents, etc and special things with clubs in town.

FEES, BURSARIES

UK & EU Fees, 2007: £3,070 p.a. £1000 for all full-time undergraduate home students in receipt of the full statutory maintenance grant. £200-£800 for all full-time undergraduate home students in receipt of a partial statutory maintenance grant. There are 25 competitive scholarships of £2,000 p.a. for students eligible for the full maintenance grant, and small bursaries for locals to Notts in need.

STUDENT PROFILE

The student body is better balanced class-wise than at Nottingham Uni. State school intake is 91%, as against 68% at Nottingham; the take from the lower socio-economic brackets is 31%, as against 16% at Nottingham. There's also a much larger mature undergraduate population at Trent.

At the city site there is enthusiasm and a high focus. We had the impression that students make the most of their time here.

Writes Thomas: 'Trent is a very diverse university, with a large Asian community. There is currently a banner outside our Student Union, which reads: 'Proud to be diverse'. The socio-economic backgrounds of a large amount of our students differs from that of a university like

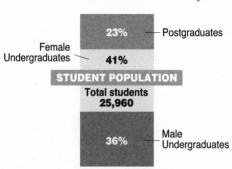

Postgraduates **23%**

Female Undergraduates **41%**

STUDENT POPULATION
Total students **25,960**

Male Undergraduates **36%**

UNIVERSITY/STUDENT PROFILE	
University since	**1992**
Situation/style	**Campus & city site**
Student population	**25960**
Undergraduates	**20057**
- mature	**31%**
- non EU undergraduates	**3%**
- male/female	**47/53**
- non-traditional student intake	**31%**
- state school intake	**91%**
- drop-out rate	**16%**
- undergraduate applications	**Up 10%**

Nottingham. If you don't achieve your full potential at A-Level, coming to Trent may well be the best thing that's happened to you. Here you will meet and mix with many students from different walks of life, form a well-shaped outlook on the world, and develop skills and an understanding of people you would not get elsewhere.

'The one downside in my opinion is the lack of tradition and formality. Our annual Sports Excellence Ball, for example, seems to be simply an expensive lash-up, without any sort of real occasion - we gather at a hotel to eat and watch the award ceremony, perhaps throw some food about, then go on to the student union to do something you can do any other Saturday.'

ACADEMIA & JOBS

As rivals Nottingham gets into Veterinary Medicine, so a new Veterinary Nursing centre is completed by Trent in 2006 on the university's Brackenhurst campus, where their land-based courses are studied. The unit will offer a Integrated Veterinary Nursing Foundation Degree course.

At Trent they claim more students on sandwich courses than any other unis, students experiencing the real world of work as part of their courses. This and the uni's strong links with employers, is the basis of their strength in graduate employment.

Trent University and industry scratch each other's backs in a way that gets right to the spot. In particular, graduates from the School of Property and Construction attract some of the highest starting salaries in the country. With their Architectural Technology BSc they have the edge. It sits comfortably among their Building, Design and BSc Construction Management degrees. The architectural input brings social, political, economic, environmental features to the fore in an otherwise out-and-out technological degree. It can get you a job with an architectural practice, a building contractor, a local authority or a large property developer. There's now also BA Architecture. Teaching inspection 22.

Big in property developing are Sheffield Hallam, Northumbria, Manchester Met and Trent. Look at BSc Planning & Property Development, Property & Management, Building Surveying, Quantity Surveying (two degrees, the Single BSc Hons and Quantity Surveying & Construction, which suggests an even more hands-on approach), and Real Estate Management. Teaching inspection 23.

Prospective construction engineers look at BEng Civil & Structural Engineering.

For numbers of graduates, government administration, Trent lead the way nationally. Look at their Euro Studies, Global Politics, Politics, Political Economy, International Studies. A high level of public administration jobs comes down to Social Studies and Education (which dropped only one point at inspection) in the end.

In teaching, there's a primary specialism, also advanced early years, and Design & Technology (secondary), while graduates to further education tend to come (in quantity) mostly from biological sciences (full marks in the assessments) and creative arts (22 points at assessment – from Fashion to Furniture to Photography). Then it's Social Sciences (there's a very good Euro Law degree), Education (23 points at the assessments), and animal and horsey things out at the land-based department, Brackenhurst College, north east of the city.

For aspiring environmental health officers, BSc Environmental Health hits the spot in a cluster of BSc degrees, which tie in Biology, Chemistry, Physics, and Enviro Science.

For prospective environmental officers there's BSc Environmental Conservation & Countryside Management at Brackenhurst, where a new £3-million teaching and laboratory facility has been completed. Other Brackenhurst degrees are Physical Geography, Landscape & Heritage, Equine Sports Science (one including Equestrian Psychology), Wildlife Conservation - and there are foundation degrees to see you in.

Meanwhile, back in the city, chemical company BASF has donated a research and development facility, probably the largest known corporate gift to a new university. It's the base for BioCity Nottingham, purported to be the UK's largest bio-

ACADEMIC EXCELLENCE	
TEACHING:	
(Rated Excellent or 17+ out of 24)	
Chemistry, Business & Management	**Excellent**
Physics, Molecular Biosciences, Organismal Biosciences	24
Subjects Allied to Medicine Education, Politics, Sport	23
Building, Psychology, Art & Design, Economics	22
Communication/Media, Maths	21
Electric/Electron Engineering, Civil Eng, Land & Property Mgt Materials Technology	20
Sociology	19
RESEARCH :	
Top grades 5/5*	
Subjects Allied to Medicine , English, Media Studies, Drama/ Dance/Performing Arts	**Grade 5**

SUBJECT AREAS (%)

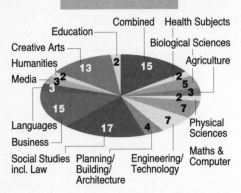

science and healthcare innovation centre – 12,000 square metres of labs, equipment and office space for bioscience start-ups and established ventures.

In the heady realm of pharmaceuticals, Hertfordshire and Trent jostle for top place as biggest graduate provider, followed by Leeds and Nottingham. Trent has a 3/4-year BSc/MSci Pharmaceutical & Medicinal Science, BSc Pharmacology & Neuroscience, BSc Physiology & Pharmacology. Teaching inspection 23. Research Grade 5.

For banking, Trent is again among the leaders, their degrees far more accessible than many others. This year Barclays is sponsoring the country's first retail banking degree here The BA (Hons) Business Management (Retail Banking) places employability and workplace performance at the centre of its course design. The bank and the Business School also run a BA (Hons) in Leadership. Also new this year is a BA Hons Business Management.

Computer Sciences is also a popular route into banking. The BA Business Info Systems asks 260 points, BSc Business & Info Communications Technology, 240. Jobs also go in quantity to invest-ment adviser/analysts.

Showing faith in Trent's business provision, in 2002, auto-giant Toyota joined forces with them on Clifton campus to build a £3-million training centre, the only one of its kind in Europe. The uni's so-called Nottingham Business School will work with the company on a portfolio of formal qualifications and professional programmes.

In Law, there is a choice of eight institutions where the Bar Vocational Course may be undertaken, Trent's Nottingham Law School is one of them. The BVC course lasts for a year and is followed by a year's pupillage – practical training under the supervision of an experienced barrister.

Their Art & Design Faculty is renowned for its fashion and textile courses. It also leads many into advertising, Design for Television is a particular niche in dedicated design/IT studios. Look, too, at the BA Communications and the Media & Cultural Studies.

In the same faculty, Theatre Design put students to work in set design, and you could get to study Fashion, Knitwear or Textile design. No surprise that such a construction-intensive uni should come up with the highly vocational 4-year sandwich BA Furniture & Product Design (engineering design students have a hand in it too). Always there is this lean towards a job, even in difficult art and design. Teaching inspection 20.

> '*In the first week freshers rapidly form social groups. Key to survival is eating well and sleeping, neither of which I did. My most memorable times were with the rowing team.*'

For radio and TV broadcasting, it's Leeds, Bournemouth and Nottingham Trent. Their Centre for Broadcasting & Journalism is housed in the old BBC studios in Nottingham, making it the only training centre in the UK to have access to authentic broadcasting facilities, so we should not be surprised to find an international There's a new course in Print Journalism this year. Grade 5 rating for research in this area. Teaching inspection 21.

Finally, their sports provision (BSc Sport Science & Management, Sport & Exercise, etc) produces more physical training instructors than any uni outside of Brighton.

SOCIAL SCENE

The Students' Union bar at City has undergone a £300,000 facelift, giving a new continental café bar and late-night (2 am at weekends) drinking spot, **Glo** bar, in addition to **Sub** bar, itself refurnished this year. At Clifton campus there's the **Point** bar and at Brackenhurst, the **Museum** bar.

'In the first week freshers rapidly form social groups. Freshers week is very well organised and provides an action-packed induction course in how to exploit the vibrant nightlife of Nottingham. The key to surviving the first term is eating well and sleeping, neither of which I did much of. My most memorable times were with the rowing team. Our weekly socials were well structured and action packed, if occasionally dangerous (beware "the post-box challenge" - bones have been broken!). These socials end up at **Ocean** nightclub with all the other sports clubs. Ocean itself is pretty nondescript, but what really matters is who you're with.'

WHAT IT'S REALLY LIKE

UNIVERSITY:	
Social Life	★★★★
Campus scene	**Streetwise, fun**
Student Union services	**Average**
Politics	**Interest low**
Sport	**42 clubs**
National team position	**33rd**
Sport facilities	**Average**
Arts opportunities	**Drama,art, music, good; dance avg; film poor**
Student newspaper	**Platform**
National awards 2005	**1 nomination**
Student radio	**Fly FM**
Venue/bars	**Glo, Sub, Point, Museum**
Union ents	**Wild**
Union societies	**76**
Parking	**Clifton good, City campus poor**
CITY:	
Entertainment	★★★★★
Scene	**Clubby, pubby, good arts**
Town/gown relations	**OK**
Risk of violence	**High**
Cost of living	**Average**
Student concessions	**Good**
Survival + 2 nights out	**£90 pw**
Part-time work campus/town	**Good/excellent**

AT A GLANCE

ACADEMIC FILE:	
Assessments	**25**
Excellent	**68%**
Typical entry requirements	**276 points**
Application acceptance rate	**18%**
Students-staff ratio	**21:1**
First/2:1 degree pass rate	**56%**
ACCOMMODATION FILE:	
Guarantee to freshers	**70%, apply early**
Style	**Halls + flats**
Catered	**None**
En-suite	**65%**
Price range pw	**£60-£102**
City rent pw	**£60**

Explains Annabel Wollen: 'Once a month we have a legendary fancy dress night called *Kinki* at **Ocean** nightclub in town, each month with a different theme. It is somewhat infamous (a bit of a religion at Trent). Also at **Ocean** we have a Wednesday sports and societies night called *Campus*. Then there's a Thursday night called *DV8* at **Walkabout**. Both these mid-week nights play mainly commercial music and a big dollop of cheese is always on offer. On Fridays we hold *Flirt* at Clifton campus and alternate between *Assault* (a rock night) and *The Tone* club (live) at City, **Sub** bar being transformed into a late bar, chilled out and relaxed. Finishing the week is Saturday night – *Climax* – where our City site venue is transformed into a nightclub holding 2500 people. Music policy is cheese and golden oldies downstairs with a mix of r&b and garage upstairs. All our nights are NUS only, and packed to the rafters, but on a Saturday we do allow our members to sign townies in as guests.

Platform is the weekly paper, which the *Nottingham Evening Post* prints for them. 'They have nothing to do with editorial, well ... they sort of peruse it, nick some of our stories.' It has won many awards. The Trent student radio station isFly FM.

The Students' Union is also proving that what it has long been doing for student entertainment it can do equally well for more serious pursuits: a Community Action Group was set up, an Employment Store has grown from one small office to two massive departments that together will deal with upwards of 9,000 placements in part-time employment this year, and the SU employment skills training programme, Stride, has broken all expectations, with every programme either full or over-subscribed.

TOWN The city is very popular with students – see *Student Nottingham* (page 353). Writes Thomas: 'Nottingham is regarded as a dangerous and unfriendly place to live. This, you will find, is not entirely fair. Every city can be dangerous, and part of being 'street aware' is learning to avoid the dodgy places, read and avoid potential situations when you're out. If you don't feel so sure, there's a number of bars and clubs that only let students in during the week.'

SPORT Their teams came overall 33rd in the nation last year, but won the annual Varsity series against arch rivals Beeston Tec, as Nottingham University is known. They have many TASS athletes and also a handful who represent the country – in hockey, archery and canoe. A £2 million sports hall plus all-weather pitch opened in 2001 at Clifton. There are 42 clubs, offering everything from circus skills to rugby league, traditionally the most successful club in the university.

PILLOW TALK

They accommodate 70% of first years; 25% live in flats and shared houses in the private sector. Not sure where the residual 5% end up. All halls are self-catered, approximately 65% of rooms are en suite. New residence of approximately 440 en-suite rooms were made available in 2005.

'City site freshers are likely to find themselves in one of the many halls scattered within a mile or so,' writes Daniel, 'so it is possible to get to college both on foot or by bike. Early enthusiasm for this does tend to wane as it gets a bit colder. However, the parking facilities in City are not brilliant, and a permit must be applied for. Do this as soon as you arrive.' At Clifton, the student village has 720 en-suite bedrooms with broadband access.

GETTING THERE

☞ By road: M1/J25/6. Good coach service.
☞ By rail: London St Pancras, 1:50; Edinburgh, 4:30; Exeter, 4:00; Birmingham New Street, 1:30.
☞ By air: East Midlands Airport 12 miles away.
☞ By coach: London, 2:55; Birmingham, 1:30.

UNIVERSITY OF OXFORD

The University of Oxford
Undergraduate Admissions Office,
Wellington Square
Oxford OX1 2JD

TEL 01865 288000
FAX 01865 270708
EMAIL undergraduate.admissions@admin.ox.ac.uk
WEB www.admissions.ox.ac.uk

OUSU
28 Little Clarendon Street
Oxford OX1 2HU

TEL 01865 270777
FAX 01865 270776
EMAIL info@ousu.org.uk
WEB www.ousu.org

VAG VIEW

*A*s a sixthformer, the great thing is not to be fazed by the clichéd reputation. If you fancy the trademark one-to-one tutor system (and who wouldn't?), simply apply. So few do apply that there's straightway a one-in-four chance you'll get in, which is way better than any other university but Cambridge.

FEES, BURSARIES

UK & EU Fees, 2007: £3,070 p.a. 2008 fees not yet available. For full financial information see the Finance Guide at www.admissions.ox.ac.uk. For students in receipt of the full HE Maintenance Grant, there's an Oxford Opportunity Bursary of £4,000 in year 1, £3,000 p.a. thereafter. Students on a partial grant benefit from a bursary on a sliding scale. In addition, Oxford colleges offer various financial awards and funds to their students, including scholarships and exhibitions, awarded after the first year for excellent academic achieve-ment, etc.

STUDENT PROFILE

'Oxford as a vanguard of elitism and discrimina-tion has made the headlines countless times in the past few years. Personally, I haven't experienced any discrimination,' writes history undergraduate Rachel Cocker, 'but as a white, middle-class girl from an independent school in the North West I am not exactly a member of a minority group here.'

Rachel will tell us more, but perhaps Christabel Ashby, from a different background, may have a different story: 'I'm Christabel Ashby, I'm from

London. I went to a state school, and I'm a final-year student at Keble, studying Theology. I'm not going to lie; my first few days in Oxford were terrifying. In Freshers Week we were inundated with information and events. There were both the university and the college fresher fairs [presentations to freshers by sports clubs and societies], and we were forced into going out and getting drunk by well meaning second-year students. Despite this it was really easy to make friends, and after two weeks I felt as at-home and confident as if I'd been there for years.

'The nice thing about the Oxford student scene is that it is so *inclusive*. Whatever you're into, you are bound to find people to hang out with. You will probably meet a few people who are a bit elitist or arrogant, but I suspect that is true of any university.'

ACADEMIA & JOBS

'The myth that Oxford students have no time for a social life is false, but that we have a very heavy workload is, however, perfectly true,' continues Rachel. 'Eight weeks is a short period for a term and a lot of work is packed into it. Scientists, medics and lawyers have by far the most to do. Historians get off relatively lightly. Still, it's hard when you hear your mates at other unis talk of two-month deadlines when you're going through the weekly essay grind. It *is* stressful, but none of my friends have, as yet, launched themselves off Magdalen Bridge. Tutors are generally willing to give more guidance and leeway than you might imagine. At the end of every term you will be given a feedback form, and although for some this may be simply a faculty-proscribed exercise, for others students' comments have shifted the focus and structure of the course they teach.

'All colleges have computer facilities where you can type up your work or check your e-mail, an Oxford e-mail address is provided for everyone upon arrival.

Oxford has some of the best libraries in the world, the state of your college library depends on its personal wealth but as the Bodleian has a copy of every book ever written, or something like it, you don't have much of an excuse for not reading that "essential" item on the reading list.'

The uni is developing a rich diversity of online resources and course materials – full details can be found at http://www.online.ox.ac.uk/. There are also little known welfare resources – a disability service, for example, even grants available from such as the Dyslexia Fund. Again, the Oxford University Resources for the Blind provide tape recordings for students with a print impairment, including dyslexia sufferers. Note-takers or readers are also available.

To become a doctor at Oxford you will need the 4 or 6-year BM BCh. Oxford now stipulate that all candidates applying to read Medicine will sit athe Biomedical Admissions Test (BMAT). The test is being used to assess scientific aptitude, not fitness to practise medicine (which will continue to be assessed in other ways, including interview) and focuses on scientific abilities relevant to the study of medicine. AAA (chem. + 1 from sci/maths). A 13% chance of getting in, a better application acceptance rate than most.

For the degree they have retained a 3-year pre-clinical course with small group tutorial teaching (often pairs). There are regular GP visits, too, and clinical experience. Nearly 20% of those who apply get in. Entry AAA: Chemistry with either Maths or Biology or Physics. Humanities subject welcomed. Teaching inspection 21.

The Law Faculty has a world-class Grade 5* for research. They are European Law specialists. Non-Law graduates may opt for a 2-year Senior Status Law Degree. All candidates must sit the National Admissions Test for Law (LNAT).

The appearance of Oxford University among the Top 10 providers to accountancy gives the lie to the proposition that vocational courses are what is needed in this area (in fact a degree is not needed at all). What they have is a small number of very high-powered courses in physical and biological sciences, which dispense skills of analysis so commanding as to question the wisdom of too early a specialisation. These, together with abilities honed in departments of Modern Languages, Mathematics and even Humanities, provide 90% of Oxford's graduate accountants.

Likewise, analysing and understanding how people think, how communities respond, is what is required at the sharp end of market research, which is why 25% of Oxford graduates into this area

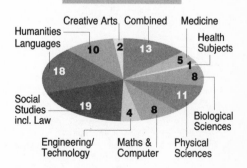

SUBJECT AREAS (%)

Creative Arts 2, Combined 13, Medicine 5, Health Subjects 1, Biological Sciences 8, Physical Sciences 11, Maths & Computer 8, Engineering/Technology 4, Social Studies incl. Law 19, Humanities Languages 18, 10 have analytical minds honed in the study of biological sciences.

For anyone wanting to become an actuary three universities are head and shoulders above the rest in equating degree success with employment, namely Heriot-Watt, Warwick and Oxford. Again, there are no dedicated degrees, but look at maths, of course, and also the Physics Department, which is also where Oxford's actuaries come from.

It may seem strange to choose Oxford particularly if you want to be a management consultant, there being many more vocational courses elsewhere, but they are way out front in the stats for graduates into this sector. The degree that causes all the fuss is BA Economics & Management. There are also combinations with Engineering or Materials.

Bankers, merchant bankers, stockbrokers, sharedealers, investment advisers and analysts all proliferate out of Oxford. The Arts & Social Studies BA hons programme accounts for more than a third of them. This includes Economics & Management, but also a number of Classics combinations, and Oxford Classics graduates have always been much in demand in the City. Then it's Physics and Languages and Mathematics. Employers are after analytical and flexible thinking.

Plenty of their language graduates make it into translating/interpreting, but how interesting, too, that Oxford language graduates get jobs as social worker/counsellors in number, and probably at levels higher than those reading Social Work degrees elsewhere.

At the same time, many of their language graduates are sought by advertising agencies – any European Language adjunct goes down well in this sector from Oxford. Languages are to the fore again in jobs for government and media research. As at Durham, there is an interesting focus here on European and Middle/Far Eastern Languages.

For jobs in publishing, Oxford is No. 1, and languages are again the most popular route, followed by the Arts & Social Studies combos (everything from English Language & Literature or Classics & English to Archaeology & Anthropology), followed by humanities.

They also turn out more graduate editors than most – nearly half are languages graduates again, then come students of humanities, biological sciences and law. Similar areas train a good number of those that take up journalism after Oxford – another powerful graduate employment area.

Languages and humanities graduates also find work in charities, and dominate the civil service and adult education sectors, and, as elsewhere, it's the arts & social studies joint degrees, languages, biological sciences and humanities that lead the

UNIVERSITY/STUDENT PROFILE	
University since	**1096**
Situation/style	**City collegiate**
Student population	**18431**
Undergraduates	**11185**
- mature	**5%**
- non EU undergraduates	**12%**
- male/female	**52/48**
- non-traditional student intake	**12%**
- state school intake	**53%**
- drop-out rate	**2%**
- undergraduate applications	**Up 8%**

way for lecturers into higher education .

Finally, Oxford is one of the top graduate providers to automobile engineering, with Loughborough, Oxford Brookes, Bath, Swansea Institute and Coventry University. Good to think of them hand in glove with the Swansea Institute. All engineering students here follow a general course for the first year before naming a MEng specialism.

SOCIAL SCENE

STUDENTS' UNION Once you've made your new-

found friends, there is a reasonable social life to be had with them. A lot of it is college based; most have weekly bops. One thing Oxford seriously lacks is a central student venue, but once you venture outside the walls of your cosy college environment there are plenty of university-wide activities in which to get involved. Theatre, journalism, music, student politics and Anglo Saxon re-enactment (apparently) are all strong. *Cherwell* and *ISIS*, famous Oxford student magazines are not in fact published by the Union. *The Oxford Student* is the student newspaper, and Oxide, the student radio station, which won a Bronze award at the national media awards last year. Every year the Oxford University drama festival, 'Cuppers', sees around 30 productions performed, directed and often written by freshers. Hacks tend to gravitate towards the famed Oxford Union, where they can fine tune their debating and back-stabbing skills, and it is possible to infiltrate or avoid their number at will.

SPORT... 'is a big deal from football to ultimate frisbee. There are college leagues for every sport you can think of; even pool. Most colleges have their own sports ground and of course there are the university facilities down Iffley Road, the 25-metre, eight-lane Rosenblatt swimming pool has now opened. The pool is part of the training facilities for the OU Swimming and Water Polo Clubs, but it's available for recreational use too. Most people try their hand at rowing at some point during their university career and many, many join the ranks of "boaties", consigning themselves to years of early morning outings and gruelling weights sessions. All very rewarding, especially for all who get to cheer them to victory during Eights Week, while getting pissed on Pimms.

TOWN 'There are some great pubs; the most studenty of which are the **Kings Arms** and **The Turf**, both rammed to the rafters after exams. The city is also a haven for cocktail bars, and the **Duke of Cambridge** is immensely popular for its very happy "happy hour", which lasts from 5 till 8.30pm every single day of the week. Oxford also boasts some fantastic restaurants, although some of these are so fantastically priced you might have to wait until your real Mummy and Daddy come to take you home before sampling them.

'Oxford Brookes' Union hosts live touring bands and probably the best student nights to be had in the city on Fridays and Saturdays. College balls also feature largely in Oxford life and for an average non-dining ticket you are looking at around £50. The larger balls, such as Merton in the winter and Magdalen, New, Trinity and Worcester in the summer can set you back up to £110 per person. Luckily, these only take place once every three years so a lot of people attend but one during their time here. Once you get in there, of course, everything is free.

'*Cost of living*: if you take into account that the average student here goes out at least twice a week (most people's workloads make it hard to manage more) then I would say someone with stronger self-discipline than myself might survive on £70.'

If you're a home/EU publicly-funded first-yea, you may be eligible for a bursary. Go to www.admissions.ox.ac.uk/finance/bursaries/index.shtml

'*Safety*: everything being just down the road encourages a feeling of safety, but there have been several attacks on students since I've been here.

ACADEMIC EXCELLENCE

TEACHING :	
(Rated Excellent or 17+ out of 24)	
Chemistry, History, Law, Anthropology, Social Work, Computing Science, English, Geography, Geology.	**Excellent**
Organismal Biosciences, Forestry & Agric Sciences, Classics, Philosophy, Politics, Psychology, Biochemistry, Fine Art	**24**
Engineering, Materials Tech., Economics, Physics, Theology	**23**
Asian/Mid-East/African Studies, Archaeology, Oriental Studies, Maths	**22**
Modern Languages, Medicine, Anatomy	**21**

RESEARCH :	
Top grades 5/5*/6*	
Pharmacology, Pathology, Community & hospital-based Clinical Subjects, Psychology, Chemistry, Physics, Earth Sciences, Pure Math, Statistics, General Eng, Metallurgy, Law, Politics, Asian Studies, English, French, Italian, Russian/Slavonic/ East European, Linguistics, Classics, Archaeology, Philosophy, Theology, Music	**Grade 6***
Clinical Lab. Sciences, Anatomy, Physiology, Zoology, Biochemistry, Applied Math, Computer, Anthropology, Economics, Sociology, Management, Middle Eastern/ African Studies, Celtic Studies, German/Dutch/Scandinavian, Iberian/Latin American, History, Education	**Grade 5**

You do still need to be on your guard. Town/gown relations don't seem to be anywhere near as bad as in Durham, but there are a few unofficially designated townie pubs and clubs, which students avoid, though not through fear for their lives.'

PILLOW TALK

All freshers are guaranteed college accommodation for their first and at least one additional year. Facilities offered by the college include a library, bar, common room, laundry facilities, computer room, sports ground and dining room, where three meals are offered every day. Costs vary from college to college – as a rough guide, £700 per term usually to include rent, cleaning, heating, water and electricity. If you were to take three meals a day in college, it might cost you an additional £350-£425 a term.

COLLEGE CAMEOS
by Caroline Rowe & Sacha Delmotte

BALLIOL
Broad Street, Oxford OX1 3BJ
TEL 01865 277777
WEB www.balliol.ac.uk
Founded in 1263, Balliol has a claim to be the oldest Oxford college and is situated right in the centre of town, so access and convenience are optimum. Balliol has very high academic standards, and is proud to boast its 'effortless superiority'. Today its main strengths lie in Classics, PPE, Physics and Philosophy. The college used to be very left-wing, which is still evident today in one of the most active JCRs in the university, and the bar being entirely student-run (only Hertford does this as well). There is also a notable absence of Balls or even formal hall.

Balliol has, however, always been very liberal, and was the first college to admit international students (today it has the highest percentage of overseas students of all colleges), and the first to allow women into Oxford academia. There is a fairly high proportion of state-school students, and social elitism is not rife, despite the existence of the Annandale Society (a pretentious, all public school gentlemen's club of sorts).

Balliol provides a JCR Pantry, which is open all day, serving breakfast until 11:30, and provides colossal portions. College ents are of high standard, rent is second lowest in Oxford and the bar is small but relaxed. There is a long-standing feud between Balliol and Trinity, orchestrated by a (rather rude) song, the 'Gordouli'. College gossip is assured instantaneous propagation via the *John de Balliol* bogsheet.

BRASENOSE
Radcliff Square, Oxford OX1 4AJ
TEL 01865 277510
WEB www.bnc.ox.ac.uk
Founded in 1509, BNC, as it is known, is renowned for its tourist-friendly location and its sporting exploits rather than for academic excellence. Rugby is very big and indeed sports in general tend to be edified, though to be fair it does have a good reputation for PPE and Law. The main social focus of the college is the infamous Gertie's Tea Bar, and it has a medium-size May Ball every summer term. BNC has a fairly low profile within the university, but is interestingly named after the brass door-knocker in hall.

CHRIST CHURCH ('The House')
St Allgates, Oxford OX1 1DP
TEL 01865 276150
WEB www.chch.ox.ac.uk
Founded in 1546, Christ Church is the biggest college (both in number of undergrads and in area), and still to this day has an (entirely undeserved) reputation of being a haven for rich Etonians and other public-school types. Typically, Christ Church students are fairly good at sport, and have the best kept and most central sports ground. The college does well academically and has a strong reputation for law with a specially dedicated library. Christ Church is also the second richest college after St John's and thus welfare and accommodation provisions are excellent, with rooms available for all your time in Oxford. The college is extremely beautiful, with extensive meadows, Oxford's mediaeval cathedral and an art gallery containing works by Leonardo da Vinci and Michelangelo. It holds a yearly impressive ball. Pembroke as its rival, not surprising as it technically owns the college. Film wise, while Magdalen has *Shadowlands*, Ch Ch can boast being the location for much of the new Harry Potter film!

CORPUS CHRISTI

Merton Street, Oxford OX1 4JF

TEL 01865 276693

WEB www.ccc.ox.ac.uk

Founded 1517, Corpus is tiny, really tiny, both in land area and in student number. This feature gives it a sense of intimacy that other colleges cannot claim, and accommodation is guaranteed for all students. Corpus excels academically and is quiet as a result of all the hard work. Recently it has introduced a new tradition, the Tortoise Race, where the Corpus reptile races against the demon speed-machine from Balliol. Corpus puts on a small-scale Summer Event (advertised as the cheapest Oxford Ball) at the beginning of every Trinity term, but on the whole it has a low profile in the university.

EXETER

Turl Street, Oxford OX1 3DP

TEL 01865 279660

WEB www.exeter.ox.ac.uk

Founded 1314, Exeter is a compact college and is so close to the Bodleian Library it may as well be part of it. Public perception is that it contains rowdy, sport-playing types. This certainly appears to be the case as the bar is very active, with lots of cool, outgoing people, and intimate ents – the JCR is famously apathetic, and one rarely hears of political activism from within Exeter's walls. The college has a long-standing rivalry with its neighbour, Jesus, also on Turl Street.

HARRIS-MANCHESTER

Mansfield Road, Oxford OX1 3TD

TEL 01865 271009

WEB www.hmc.ox.ac.uk

Founded in 1786, there is very little to be said about this college since it only admits mature students, mostly to read an Arts degree. The college was founded in Manchester to provide education for non-Anglican students, who at the time were not allowed into Oxbridge. Following a move to Oxford, it was granted Permanent Private Hall status, and only recently (1996) become a full college. Currently the college faces long-term financial and governance problems. In 2003 they asked Derek Wood QC to review resources, particularly for history, PPE and related subjects. The upshot was to ditch history. Pleasant Gothic Revival buildings.

HERTFORD

Catte Street, Oxford OX1 3BW

TEL 01865 279400

WEB www.bertford.ox.ac.uk

Founded in 1740, Hertford has had a tumultuous past with various changes of name, owner and status over its 250-year history; it used to be a subdivision of Magdalen. Hertford is very central and opposite the ever-popular **King's Arms** pub. Hertford students really know how to party (their bar is rumoured to have the highest fiscal turnover in the university). Whether this is explained by its large population of state-school students, and the distinct Northern flavour of the undergrad body in particular, would not be PC to enquire. Altogether it is a progressive establishment and was one of the first all-male colleges to admit women and the first to make the entrance exam optional. Students enjoy full accommodation, an excellent atmospheric JCR bar, which is entirely student run and concocts brilliant, toxic cocktails.

JESUS

Turl Street, Oxford OX1 3DW

TEL 01865 279720

WEB www.jesus.ox.ac.uk

Founded in 1571, Jesus is small, beautiful and wealthy, and has a reputation for being the 'Welsh College', which is perfectly fair since a not insignificant proportion of students come from Wales. The college bogsheet is *The Sheepshagger*. The college is quite insular and politically unmotivated. Jesubites have it easy: accommodation is excellent and hall food is cheap. Recently Jesus is feared in rugby circles, and does well in other sports too. It has a feud with Exeter.

KEBLE

Parks Road, Oxford OX1 3PG

TEL 01865 272711

WEB www.keble.ox.ac.uk

Founded 1870. Writes Christabel Ashby: 'Keble College is notable for being the only redbrick,

AT A GLANCE	
ACADEMIC FILE:	
Subjects assessed	**30**
Excellent	**97%**
Typical entry requirements	**512 points**
Application acceptance rate	**24%**
Med. School acceptance rate	**13%**
Students-staff ratio	**13:1**
First/2:1 degree pass rate	**88%**
ACCOMMODATION FILE:	
Availability to freshers	**100%**
Style	**College rooms**
Catered	**100%**
En-suite	**Some**
Average price pw	**£103-£118**
Average city rent pw	**£70-£80**

Victorian college. It is ideally placed for town and most university facilities, and is right opposite the University parks. College facilities are good; we have phone and internet lines in every room, and all the rooms are nicely furnished. The college guarantees you two years accommodation.

'Keble is also rather traditional, there is formal hall every night, which means you wear your gown to dinner, which has waiter service. On the social side, there's a mixed bag. It has one of the largest undergraduate populations of Oxford colleges, which means there are lots of people with whom to make friends, but also means you will never know everyone, and seeing people you don't recognise all over the place can be a little disconcerting.

'Keble is sporty, there are lots of teams and clubs, and the bar is also fairly popular. Ents are predictable however, usually consisting of a live band or karaoke nights. These events happen once or twice a term. The JCR is well stocked with electronic games, pinball, table-footy and pool, and also has sky TV. Unlike some of the other colleges, however, there is no JCR shop.

'There is a strong sense of equality at Keble, both in terms of women's and men's rights and in gay/lesbian rights. The environment is welcoming and friendly to anyone and everyone, but at the same time its size means you are able to retain a degree of anonymity not possible in many of the other colleges.'

LADY MARGARET HALL
Norham Gdns, Oxford OX2 6QA
TEL 01865 274300
WEB www.lmh.ox.ac.uk
Founded 1878. LMH was the first college founded solely for women in the university. Since there was no vacant land in the centre of town, LMH is fairly far out of town, but this has resulted in the luxury of extensive gardens. The college began admitting men in the '70s, and since that day and age LMH has achieved an unparalleled male/female ratio of 1:1 at levels of college hierarchy. LMH is socially self-sufficient and has a low profile in the university. It is neither renowned for scholastic or sporting brilliance, and has no great political aspirations. Its sole reputation is for producing Thespians, who tend to hang out in cliques with other college actors (read 'actoars'). Otherwise unpretentious and not intimidating.

LINCOLN
Turl Street, Oxford OX1 3DR
TEL 01865 279800
WEB www.linc.ox.ac.uk
Founded in 1427, Lincoln is the smallest of the three colleges on Turl Street, but beautiful. The col-

lege is a rather wealthy one, which is evident from the extensive facilities provided to students: good accommodation, excellent sporting facilities, and allegedly the best hall food in the university. This comfort of college life means that very few Lincolnites emerge from their cushy environment to participate in university-wide activities, and thus charges of insularity are fair and merited. Overall, the college is a rather 'shy' one on the university scene, and is not really noted for spectacular achievement in any academic, political or sporting field. Tradition has it that on Ascension Day, Lincoln undergrads stroll around town in subfusc (formal wear) with the vicar of St Michael's in the Northgate and a gang of choristers 'beating the bounds', or thrashing at the town limits with canes. Then the students drink lots of ivy beer and toss hot pennies at the choirboys.

MAGDALEN
High Street, Oxford OX1 4AU
TEL 01865 276063
WEB www.magd.ox.ac.uk
Founded in 1458, Magdalen (read 'Maudlin') is a gorgeous college in every respect. It is one of the oldest, richest and most beautiful. Its buildings, extensive grounds (including the famous Deer Park), beautiful cloisters, and Magdalen Tower, and location on the banks of the River Cherwell are stunning, breathtaking. On May Day the choir sings from the top of Magdalen Tower and the tradition is to jump off the bridge into the river, although the police keep deciding to cordon it off. The film *Shadowlands* was shot there, and the money earned was spent on renovating certain college rooms. Accommodation facilities are second to none (everyone can live in throughout their whole student career), and some of the sets offered are simply amazing (bedroom, living room, and bathroom!). The college has a huge and lively bar, and puts on very good ents events, but is pretty insular (the **Lower Oscar Wilde Room** is often the site of debauched and drunken student carnage). Magdalen, like Christ Church, owns its own punt. It is academically successful and socially intense, but rather uninterested in political and JCR issues.

MANSFIELD
Mansfield Road, Oxford OX1 3TF
TEL 01865 270970
WEB www.mansfield.ox.ac.uk
Founded in 1886, Mansfield only obtained its college status in 1995; prior to that it was a Permanent Private Hall. It is among the smallest of colleges, only admitting about sixty undergrads every year. This leads to a very close-knit yet appreciably claustrophobic community. Due to the small size

of the college many students explore extra-curricular opportunities in the university, and the college is famous for drama. The college is very poor and thus room rents are relatively high. Mansfield has a reputation for tolerance and is sometimes known as the LGB (Lesbian Gay Bisexual) college. Ents are diverse, with bops, karaokes, trips to the theatre, Laserquesting, and there is a triennial Venetian Masked Ball held in the seventh week of Michaelmas term.

MERTON

Merton Street, Oxford OX1 4JD
TEL 01865 276329
WEB www.merton.ox.ac.uk
Founded in 1264, Merton, along with Balliol and University, has a claim to be the oldest Oxford college, and is very rich and beautiful, containing the oldest surviving Oxford quad (Mob quad). The college has an undisputed reputation for being a centre of academic excellence, fuelled by SCR encouragement and a competitive spirit among the student population. Socially Merton appears to be fairly insular, and one rarely meets Mertonites around the university; in fact it would seem that Mertonites are quite dull. Nonetheless every year Merton puts on the only Christmas Ball in Oxford, on the last day of Michaelmas term, which is usually a roaring success. It is particularly popular with Freshers who are able to finish their first term at Oxford with style and panache (and a random snog perhaps!). Merton's tradition, the Time Ceremony, has existed for barely fifteen years, but is now firmly implanted in the college calendar, and for a day lifts the veil of seriousness which rests upon the college. It involves students walking backwards around Merton's Mob Quad while continuously downing port, on a particular day of each year.

NEW COLLEGE

Holywell Street, Oxford OX1 3BN
TEL 01865 279590
WEB www.new.ox.ac.uk
Founded in 1379, here's another beautiful college, and very inappropriately named too! New is one of the oldest, largest and most impressive colleges in Oxford and takes in part of the city walls, as well as a few ancient plague-heaps. Widely accepted as having the best and most beautiful student bar, New puts on great ents: the bops are legendary, and the Long Room is as much a site of drunken mayhem as the Lower Oscar Wilde Room at Magdalen, with many different societies hiring the room to throw crazy parties. New also puts on a gargantuan Commemoration Ball every three summers, described by many as the best ball in Oxford.

Scenes from the Bond film *Tomorrow Never Dies* were filmed at New College, and the college has a fair share of Bond-girl lookalikes. New is particularly accomplished in musical matters: the college choir is one of the best in Oxford. New has been described as 'one of Oxford's least stressful places to live'.

ORIEL

Oriel Square, Oxford OX1 4EW
TEL 01865 276555
WEB www.oriel.ox.ac.uk
Founded in 1326, Oriel is mostly famous for its monotonous and undeniable domination of the river: it's a boatie's college. Apparently Oriel brings in students from America especially for their rowing prowess, regardless of their academic (in)abilities, and provides them with the best en-suite rooms in college and lavish free meals. Every extra year that sees Oriel come out victorious of the Summer Eights rowing race, another of its old boats is religiously burnt in the middle of their quad (that's Oxford tradition for you!). Architecturally the college is something of a rabbit warren. The distinctive front quad sees a Shakespeare production every summer, and the college is strong musically, with its own orchestra and choir. Academically very relaxed, the college reveres sport: those who can participate, do, and those who can't, support from one of the best boat houses on the river.

PEMBROKE

St Aldates, Oxford OX1 1DW
TEL 01865 276412
WEB www.pmb.ox.ac.uk
Founded in 1624, Pembroke is one of the poorest colleges in Oxford, and allegedly the college Boat Club Trust Fund is richer than the rest of the college put together! This astonishing fact holds its currency in donations from rich alumni rowers. Thus Pembroke is very strong at rowing, and the only plausible pretender to Oriel's rowing crown. In fact in the fifteen or so years of Oriel dominance on the river, Pembroke has been the only college capable of beating them once, several years ago; now the college is regularly second behind Oriel. Socially Pembroke is rather insular, has a low profile in the university, and academically it is laid back. A college rivalry exists with Christ Church.

QUEEN'S

High Street, Oxford OX1 4AW
TEL 01865 279167
WEB www.queens.ox.ac.uk
Founded 1624. Despite having a very high-profile location, right in the middle of the High, the col-

lege has a very low profile in the University; one rarely meets students from Queen's. It has some of the most obviously dramatic architecture in Oxford, ranging from the classical cupola to the UFO-like Florey building off St Clement's. Queen's is very rich and is one of the cheapest colleges to attend, offering full accommodation for all your Oxford years. There is also a particularly good library. Excluded are undergrads wanting to read Single Hons English, however, a fact unconnected with the college being a home from home to Northerners. Quirkily, Queen's has an annual dinner to celebrate the survival of an undergraduate who in 1935 was viciously attacked by a boar and defended himself by driving a tome of Aristotle into the boar's mouth.

ST ANNE'S
Woodstock Rd, Oxford OX2 6HS
TEL 01865 274825
WEB www.stannes.ox.ac.uk
Founded 1879. St Anne's, very far away from the city centre, is atypical – laid back and unpretentious and lacking in the pomp and archaic traditions of older colleges. Isolation breeds self-sufficiency, and the college has a low profile in the university. A large proportion of the undergraduate community come from a state-school background, and the college is now one of the largest in terms of undergraduate numbers. Despite being a poor college, the library has around 100,000 volumes for current use, and is one of the two largest undergraduate college libraries in Oxford. The architecture is modern and unusual for Oxford, and the gardens are pleasant in the summer.

ST CATHERINE'S (St Catz)
Manor Road, Oxford OX1 3UJ
TEL 01865 271703
WEB www.stcatz.ox.ac.uk
Founded in 1963, St Catz possesses some breathtaking architecture, much of which is Grade 1 listed. Designed by Arne Jacobsen, the famous Danish architect, a spirit of openness infuses the place, with quads having no enclosing ends. It is located just outside the tourist-infested city centre, lending it some peace and tranquillity, but is still within a convenient distance of all central facilities. St Catz has exceptional resources, including the largest student theatre in Oxford, an extensive JCR building, and a moat. It is the youngest college, and, though obviously lacking traditions, has a very friendly atmosphere. Every summer St Catz has a Summer Ball which is a big success, and good bops are laid on regularly.

ST EDMUND HALL (Teddy Hall)

Queen's Lane, Oxford OX1 4AR
TEL 01865 279008
WEB www.seh.ox.ac.uk
Founded 1278. Teddy Hall, as it is informally known, is a very poor college, and rumours abound that it has been financially helped by its close neighbour Queen's. Its main reputation across the university is for being very good at sports: men excel at rugby in particular. Despite not being one of the highest profile colleges, Teddy Hall students still manage to get involved at most levels of university life, and are particularly good at drama and music. Teddy Hall is known for being the party college, where academia is not taken too seriously, and it puts on good ents.

ST HILDA'S
Cowley Place, Oxford OX4 1DY
TEL 01865 276816
WEB www.sthildas.ox.ac.uk
St Hilda's, all-female since its foundation in 1893, voted in June 2006 to accept male students. Up until then, the college was home to the notorious, roaming 'Hildabeasts', among the most active members of the university, getting involved in many sports, societies and other extra-curricular pursuits. College buildings are bland but pleasant, and the site is on the banks of the Cherwell, with beautiful gardens adding a colourful touch to the landscape. The college is fairly poor, and facilities are limited. St Hilda's is strong at rowing. Lots of ents are put on, with something to keep the lasses happy every weekend. The bar is unexciting, despite being the cheapest in Oxford. Being next to the river, the college owns its own punts, which are free for use by St Hilda's students and their guests. The college is seldom visited by tourists, which is a good thing.

ST HUGH'S
St Margaret's Rd, Oxford OX2 6LE
TEL 01865 274910
WEB www.st-hughs.ox.ac.uk
Founded in 1886 St Hugh's is so far out (geographically) it may as well be part of another university, and the walk into the centre of town can be long and laborious, although buses are very frequent. This is both an affliction and an attraction: St Hugh's has huge grounds (including croquet lawns and tennis courts) and there is (unfortunately small and ugly) on-site space to accommodate all students. College facilities are good and social life is tumultuous and intense. Ents are good, with a large-scale bop including a bouncy castle and barbecue organised during the summer. Despite being so far out of town, St Hugh's students are reasonably involved across the university activities, espe-

cially in art and drama.

ST JOHN'S

St Giles, Oxford OX1 3JP
TEL 01865 277317
WEB www.sjc.ox.ac.uk

Founded 1555. This is the richest college in Oxford. St John's provides excellent facilities: there are financial rewards for the academically strong (1st, Norrington Table 1999): on-site accommodation (including luxurious sets and the strange honeycomb structures for Freshers) is guaranteed for everyone, there is a modern conference centre, and beautiful gardens adorn the quads. St John's is academically very strong and there is considerable pressure on students to work hard.

The college performs well in sports as well, at rugby and rowing in particular. On the social front St John's doesn't deliver quite as well: students tend to be quite dull, a fact reflected by the college bar which is very nice and spacious, but rarely alive and kickin'.

ST PETER'S

New Inn Hall Street, OX1 2DL
TEL 01865 278892
WEB www.spc.ox.ac.uk

Founded in 1929, St Peter's is a relatively new college in Oxford history, and covers very small grounds in the centre of town. Priorities here are much higher on social issues than on academic matters, and St Peter's doesn't excel at sports either. Nevertheless students seem fairly involved around the university, and the JCR is very active. St Peter's is very poor, which is obvious from the blatant lack or inadequacy of certain facilities. The college has a reasonable bar and puts on good ents events. Every year a middle-size Summer Ball is organised.

SOMERVILLE

Woodstock Road, Oxford OX2 6HD
TEL 01865 270629
WEB www.some.ox.ac.uk

Founded in 1929, Somerville is the most recent of colleges to have gone mixed (1994) and is located just beyond the reach of annoying tourists, yet close enough to the city centre for convenience. The generally left-wing college [with some notable exceptions – this was Margaret Thatcher's college] has always been politically very active and JCR members voice their opinions loudly. Indeed, Somervillians are active in every respect of university life, and the college has a fairly high profile amongst university students. College atmosphere is easygoing though the number of political hacks and activists can sometimes be distressing.

WHAT IT'S REALLY LIKE	
UNIVERSITY:	
Social Life	★★★★
Campus scene	**Intense, challenging, satisfying**
Student Union services	**Well organised, but no venue**
Politics	**Active**
Sport	**Key**
National team position	**4th**
Sport facilities	**Good**
Arts opportunities	**Excellent**
Student mag/news	**Oxford Student**
2006 National awards	**Nominated for design**
Student radio	**Oxide**
2006 National awards	**Bronze award**
Nightclub	**None**
Bars	**College bars**
Union ents	**College-based**
Union clubs/societies	**200+**
Parking	**Buy a bike**
CITY:	
Entertainment	★★★
Scene	**Small, good pubs, OK clubs**
Town/gown relations	**Average**
Risk of violence	**Average**
Cost of living	**High**
Student concessions	**Good**
Survival + 2 nights out	**£70 pw**
Part-time work campus/town	**Good**

Somerville has good ents although the college bar is dull and bare.

TRINITY

Broad Street, Oxford OX1 3BH
Tel 01865 279910
web www.trinity.ox.ac.uk

Founded in 1554, Trinity is centrally located, next door to its arch-rival Balliol. The college has spacious and attractive grounds (which it leases from Balliol!) and elegant buildings. The undergraduate body is fairly small which lends to an intimate college atmosphere. Trinity used to be dominated by public-school types, but this has now changed. Accommodation provisions are good, and the college flats on Woodstock Road are regarded as among the best and poshest in Oxford. Trinity students have a high profile in the university, and are popular and involved in many activities. A Commemoration Ball is organised every three years in the summer and, on a more day-to-day basis, ents is good with fun bops, and Trinity men and women enjoy a lively and atmospheric bar.

UNIVERSITY

High Street, Oxford OX1 4BH
TEL 01865 276602
WEB www.univ.ox.ac.uk
Founded 1249. University is one of the colleges Oxford students hear the least about: it has an extremely low profile and is very quiet. This is despite the fact it is one of the oldest colleges (holding a claim, with Balliol and Merton, to being the oldest, although there is evidence that the college forged some deeds in 1381 to prove that it was founded in advance of Merton). The college is undeniably ancient, however, and very beautiful. Like St John's, it has a reputation for being full of bookworms who take life far too seriously and are unaware of the existence of the words 'fun' and 'enjoyment'. College life is said to be a little slow, although the alleged existence of bops and a good bar do redeem it a little.

WADHAM

Parks Road, Oxford OX1 3PN
TEL 01865 277946
WEB www.wadham.ox.ac.uk
Founded in 1610, Wadham is a bastion of the left, with an even greater lefty image than Balliol. Getting involved in JCR and student affairs is a great springboard into the political limelight. It has always been liberal, and is very involved in LGB affairs: it hosts Queer Week, which culminates in an S&M and Fetishes Bop (where you get to see some quite outlandish costumes...). The college is also strong in music and drama (helped by the fact that Wadham has one of the university's only reasonably sized theatres), and the Saturday night bops are legendary.

WORCESTER

Worcester Street, Oxford OX1 2HB
TEL 01865 278391
WEB www.worcester.ox.ac.uk
Founded 1714. Worcester possesses huge and beautiful grounds, including tennis courts, sports grounds and a lake. Beautiful gardens decorate the college and provide a suitable backdrop to the medieval cottages and classic colonnade. All students are accommodated on the main college site. The college is presently enjoying some success at rowing and rugby, but is not known for any academic excellence. Lord Sainsbury was a Worcester student, thus hall food is very cheap and also very good. Every three years the college hosts a huge Commemoration Ball in the summer. Worcester is lively, fairly rich and somewhat self-contained.

OXFORD BROOKES UNIVERSITY

Oxford Brookes University
Gipsy Lane Campus
Headington
Oxford OX3 0BP

TEL 01865 483040
FAX 01865 483983
EMAIL admissions@brookes.ac.uk
WEB www.brookes.ac.uk

Oxford Brookes Students' Union
Helena Kennedy Student Centre
London Road
Headington
Oxford OX3 0BP

TEL 01865 484715
FAX 01865 484799
EMAIL obsu.president@brookes.ac.uk
WEB www.theSU.com

VAG VIEW

If you are looking for a university not too demanding at entry, which offers a host of well-conceived modular courses in some interesting niche areas, and which enjoys the atmosphere of one of the world's true student cities, then Brookes might well be for you.

Adding to its lustre this year is a move by Spanish Formula One racing driver Fernando Alonso to sponsor a course in motor sport engineering, a field in which Brookes is already a well-known force.

CAMPUS

Brookes is based over three main campuses; two in Headington (approx. 1.5 miles from city centre) and one at Wheatley (5 miles away). A free inter-site bus service runs every half hour during the day. The Helena Kennedy Student Centre (HKSC), the main Students' Union, is housed with teaching facilities and accommodation across the road from Gypsy Lane on the Headington Hill site, formerly the house of beleaguered tycoon Robert Maxwell, who called it the largest council house in England, which indeed it was. He never owned it.

FEES, BURSARIES

UK & EU Fees, 2007: £3,070 p.a. 2006 not yet set. If in receipt of full HE Maintenance grant there's a bursary of £1,500; if in receipt of partial grant, the bursary is on a sliding scale from £300 to £1,500, according to household earnings. They offer £2,000 p.a. for students passing in who achieve top grades (3As or the equivalent). There is also a system of £1,000 p.a. community scholarships for applicants from schools or colleges in Oxfordshire, designed to recognise and reward non-academic achievement and commitment.

STUDENT PROFILE

Oxford Brookes is uncharacteristic of most recently founded universities because of its high independent school intake (30% of undergraduates). There's a statistical lurch towards the middle class, which serves to prompt the stereotypical image of the uni as a hang-out for air-head Sloanes who couldn't get a place at Durham. However, there is, too, a large overseas body of students, and Giles Balleny insists that whatever the statistics indicate, on the ground the perception is of a rich tapestry of life.

'Brookes has an unusually varied cross section of students, which gives it a cosmopolitan outlook in everything it does,' writes Giles. 'Among the more prominent groups, public-school student types are not as dominant as people suggest, although there probably is a larger public school contingent than at any other of the 1992 universities [Bristol West of England comes nearest]. Most ignore their fraternising and get on with doing their own thing. Whether you are from an independent school or from a state school you will undoubtedly find "your type".

'There is also a large proportion of foreign students from a huge range of countries. Ethnic minorities from the UK are also very well represented and play a large part in the overall feel of the place.'

There are also quite a few part-timers (approx. a quarter of undergraduates), further education students and mature students in the mix.

ACADEMIA & JOBS

There are 8 academic schools: Arts & Humanities, Built Environment, Biological & Molecular Sciences, the Business School, the Westminster Institute of Education, the School of Technology, Health & Social Care, Social Sciences & Law.

Modular joint hons degrees characterise the curriculum, and an academic year-structure made up not of terms but semesters. Ground-breaking when first launched more than a quarter of a century ago, the modular system can be made to work to your advantage, but individuals are left pretty much to design their own courses, and, so student Emily Waller says: 'All the rules and regulations can be confusing, so get help if you need it.

'The work load is manageable, but depends on the course that you are taking. Work placements both abroad and in Britain are common. Teaching staff are generally very helpful (if you can find them). Each student is assigned a personal tutor for their years of study.

'There are 3 libraries, well stocked with up-to-date and ancient texts and an easy-to-use computerised catalogue; friendly individual subject librarians are always willing to help. The main library has over 1,000 private study desks and some group study rooms (great for catching up on gossip, if not for study!). It is open until 10.00 pm weekdays. Every student has free Internet and e-mail access, and com-puters are accessible 24/7. Computer Services – in particular the help desk – are invaluable, as the network has an annoying habit of crashing (normally about five minutes before an assignment is due in!).'

The Disability team includes a Dyslexia Support Tutor. Her work encourages dyslexic students to develop 'their innate, non-language intelligences and explore how to use them as study skills'; there's also extra time for exams, etc.

More than a quarter of graduates go into the health field. They educate by far the largest number of graduate nurses, the majority SEN. There are BA degrees in midwifery, learning disability, mental health, specialist interest community practitioner (district nursing, school, etc), and BSc also in midwifery (post-experience), adult, children's. cancer

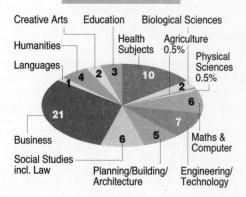

SUBJECT AREAS (%)

UNIVERSITY/STUDENT PROFILE	
University since	**1992**
Situation/style	**Campus**
Student population	**18727**
Undergraduates	**13711**
- mature	**27%**
- non EU undergraduates	**13%**
- male/female	**40/60**
- non-traditional student intake	**26%**
- state school intake	**70%**
- drop-out rate	**20%**
- undergraduate applications	**Up 6%**

care, palliative care, rehabilitation. 'Post Experience' means an 18-month programme for Registered Nurses. Teaching Inspection 20. Entry BB.

Aspiring occupational therapists note, they take nearly 6% of the annual graduate employment market.

Brookes also has a large primary teaching provision: BA Primary (Work-based) and BA Initial Teacher Training – 13% of their graduates go into teaching.

Their engineering graduates are among the most popular in the automobile industry. The B/MEng 3/4-year Hons degrees in Automative Engineering take 16% of the jobs in the sector. There's also a BSc Motorsports Technology and an HND in Motorsports Engineering. Civil engineers also find ready employment.

Environmental Biology, WEnvironmental Science, and Public Health Nutrition also find graduates certain jobs in the public sector.

They are of course renowned for their Publishing degrees, having produced the prototype. Some, like Accounting/Publishing in the Joint Hons programme have obvious relevance, others less so, but the single hons BA Publishing is undoubtedly the industry's favoured vocational entré. It illuminates the entire process: editorial, production and marketing. Teaching inspection 21.

Estate agent/managers also proliferate. look at BSc Real Estate Management, also BA Business of Real Estate. Real Estate Management only dropped one point at the teaching assessments; Business and Economics took full marks. So, you are in good hands. Planning is big here, too, and also scored full marks: see BA Cities - Environment, Design & Development or BA City & Regional Planning. There are jobs in the construction industry too for students of such as BSc Construction Management or Foundation Built Environment.

They are also management leaders in the catering and hotel trade. The choice degrees here are the 4-year sandwich BSc Hotel & Restaurant Management and the two International Hospitality/Tourism Management, again 4-year sandwich BSc.

Graduates of Marketing and Languages find employment in market research, and aspiring marketing managers finding ready work armed with their Marketing Management Communication and Business & Marketing Management BA degrees, available in combination with a host of interesting focuses – Publishing, Psychology, Performing Arts, Retail, Sociology, Tourism look like good synergy.

SOCIAL SCENE

STUDENTS' UNION There's an active ents programme with regular clubnights, film nights, comedy nights and termly balls. Wednesday is *Playground* (new themes and promos each week); Friday is *Pleasuredome* (9 pm-2 am) – 'the best sound system, lighting and dance tunes in Oxford', a mixture of styles at the main SU **Venue**, which has a capacity of over 1,200.

The main union bars based around the university are the **Harts** lounge bar, **Morals Bar** and the **Mezzanine**. **Morals Bar** is the home of *Blitz* (9 till 2 pop tunes), *Chalk & Cheese* (from live jazz to comedy) and the SU's rock and indie night *Feedback* – the best grunge, rock, metal, punk, alternative with resident DJs Sht Chaos and Hell. High above **The Venue**, the **Mez Bar** is the home of the Sunday Session.

'A free and confidential advice and counselling service is on offer, as is representation for all stu-

ACADEMIC EXCELLENCE	
TEACHING:	
(Rated Excellent or 17+ out of 24)	
Law, Anthropology, English, Geography.	**Excellent**
Planning, Business, Economics	**24**
History of Art, Real Estate Mgt,	**23**
Building, Psychology, Biology & Enviro Science, Art & Design, Theology	
Italian & Spanish, French,	**22**
Maths, Politics, Tourism	
Sociology, Publishing, Civil Eng, Education	**21**
Food Science, Nursing, Subjects Allied to Medicine	**20**
German, Electronic Eng	**19**
RESEARCH:	
Top grades 5/5/6**	
History	**Grade 6***
English, French	**Grade 5**

dents on academic, personal and financial issues. Over sixty clubs and societies ensure that there really is something for everyone. Currently the most popular society is Cocktail.'

There's a monthly student paper called *OBScene*.

SPORT Facilities are excellent and include Astroturf, squash courts, health suite, heavy weights gym, tennis courts, rugby, football, cricket and hockey pitches, fitness trails, two boat houses and a multi-purpose sports hall for aerobics, martial arts, women's boxing, circuit training, etc. The Centre for Sport is open from 7.30 am to 11.00 pm. The university teams came 41st overall last year.

TOWN 'The night life in Oxford, always busy and full of tourists and students, is varied but expensive, even with the student discount that most clubs, pubs, bars and restaurants offer.

There is a great music and theatre scene with lots of theatres, gig venues and cinemas, but the clubbing scene is definitely mediocre (unless you are a big cheesy '60s to '80s fan). Travel around the city is regular and simple, and for women the Students' Union runs a special Safety Bus from campus to doorstep. As long as 'home' is within the Oxford Ring Road, this is a free service. Coaches run every ten minutes to London, Gatwick, Heathrow and Cambridge. Student discounts are available.

PILLOW TALK

There are nine halls of residence, all with easy access to the university, and many, but not all, with an internet facility available in each room. Clive Booth Hall was opened last autumn, and Cheney Student Village in the spring. Although in practice most freshers live in halls, priority is given

WHAT IT'S REALLY LIKE

UNIVERSITY:
Social Life	★★★★
Campus scene	**Cross section**
Student Union services	**Good**
Politics	**Average**
Sport	**Competitive**
National team position	**47th**
Sport facilities	**Good**
Arts opportunities	**Drama, music, art excellent; film good; dance avg**
Student newspaper	**OBScene**
Nightclub	**The Venue**
Bars	**Morals, Harts, Mez**
Union ents	**Pleasuredome, pop, jazz, comedy**
Union societies	**60**
Most popular society	**Cocktail**
Parking	**Poor**

CITY:
Entertainment	★★★
Scene	**Small, good pubs, OK clubs**
Town/gown relations	**Average**
Risk of violence	**Average**
Cost of living	**High**
Student concessions	**Good**
Survival + 2 nights out	**£70 pw**
Part-time work campus/town	**Good**

AT A GLANCE

ACADEMIC FILE:
Subjects assessed	**37**
Excellent	**76%**
Typical entry requirements	**283 points**
Application acceptance rate	**16%**
Students-staff ratio	**16:1**
First/2:1 degree pass rate	**55%**

ACCOMMODATION FILE:
Guarantee to freshers	**95%**
Style	**Halls**
Catered	**20%**
En suite	**48%**
Approx price range pw	**£79-£113**
City rent pw	**£70-£80**

to those living farthest distant from Oxford. Facilities generally accommodate both sexes, although single sex accommodation is available on request. With the exception of two halls, it's a condition of residency not to keep a car.

GETTING THERE
☛ By road: from north, A423 or A34 or A43; London, M40; south, M4/J13, A34. Wheatley campus, M40/J8, A418. Good coach service.
☛ By rail: London Paddington, 1:00; Birmingham, 1:30; Bristol, 1:45; Sheffield, 3:30.
☛ By air: Heathrow/Gatwick; coaches/buses will stop outside Gypsy Lane campus on request.
☛ By coach: London, 1:40; Birmingham, 1:30; Leeds, 5:30; Bristol, 4:30.

UNIVERSITY OF PAISLEY

The University of Paisley
Paisley PA1 2BE

TEL 0141 848 3727
    0800 027 1000 (prospectus request)
FAX 0141 848 3623
EMAIL alison.copland@paisley.ac.uk
WEB www.paisley.ac.uk

Paisley Uni Students' Association
Storie Street
Paisley PA1 1DN

TEL 0141 849 4169
FAX 0141 849 4158
EMAIL theunion@upsa.org.uk
WEB www.upsa.org.uk

VAG VIEW

*P*aisley University came out of Paisley Technical College, founded in 1897. In the same year as it became a fully fledged university (1995) it began its development into nursing and midwifery, a faculty largely to be found at its campus to the south, in Ayr – Robbie Burns country. The main university campus is in Paisley itself, the largest town in Scotland and just a mile or so from Glasgow Airport. Only a few years old is a third campus, a joint venture with Glasgow Uni and Dumfries & Galloway College, on an 80-acre parkland site half a mile from the centre of Dumfries, which is many miles to the south, close to the Solway Firth.

While most unis are struggling to meet government targets to diversify their student body by delving into sections of the public that haven't traditionally gone to university, Paisley has plenty of those and there's a very high drop-out rate.

Recently, the uni began the process of seeking permission to re-name itself University of the West of Scotland, pointing to its satellite campuses in Ayr and Dumfries, and in the hope that a proposed merger with Bell College in Hamilton, 11 miles south east of Glasgow, would go through. As we went to press, the merger with Bell got the green light. The result is a 4-campus uni, opening its doors to more than 17,000 students in Autumn 2007. It will be backed by an investment of £21 million.

CAMPUS
PAISLEY CAMPUS takes getting to know: 'It would be really easy for a fresher, such as yourself, to mistake the main campus for a hospital wing in need of a cosmetic facelift,' writes Nausheen Rai. 'The "traditional" building has a blend of lino-type tiled floors, a supposed up-to-date glass "hamster" tunnel walkway (for fashion purposes *darling*), a surgical hospital smell that leaves one feeling oddly confused, and a brand new, £6-million, out-of-sync library with glass lift, plush pink carpets, novelty chairs and lots of space.'

AYR CAMPUS (known as 'Craigie') Tel 01292 886000. Opines Nausheen: 'This is definitely the more friendly campus (if that were to make the choice). Being smaller, it's more cosy. Males may count themselves fortunate to study in this sister campus tucked away on the west coast. There's an

11% — Postgraduates
Female Undergraduates — 59%
STUDENT POPULATION
Total students 12,760
30% — Male Undergraduates

estimated ten women to every one of them.'

DUMFRIES CAMPUS Tel 01387 702060. It is situated beside the Crichton Business Park in eighty-five acres of parkland and gardens. A £1.8-million grant from the Scottish Funding Council is underwriting the development, which builds on franchise links which Paisley has had with Dumfries & Galloway College since 1994. The campus is an element in their open-access strategy, an attempt 'to widen the provision of higher education in the south west of Scotland.' It's worked.

HAMILTON CAMPUS Tel 01698 283100. This is the old Bell College, its higher education portfolio including business, accounting, law, journalism, sport (management, coaching, etc), social sciences, environmental sciences, engineering, product design, biosciences and computing. There is also a thriving further education provision.

FEES, BURSARIES
Fees for English students: £1700 p.a. Contact uni direct for bursaries, etc.

ACADEMIC EXCELLENCE	
TEACHING :	
(Rated Excellent, Highly Satis. or 17+ out of 24)	
Civil Engineering,	**Highly Satis.**
Chemistry, Maths & Statistics,	
Mechanical (incl Manufacturing)	
Engineering, Teacher Education	
Sociology, Social Work, Cellular	
& Molecular Biology,	
Organismal Biol, Psychology.	
European Languages	**19**
RESEARCH:	
Top grades 5/5*	
Accounting & Finance,	**Grade 5**

STUDENT PROFILE
Many students are local, mature and/or part-timers (35%) and almost exclusively come to Paisley from the state sector, flooding in from neighbourhoods which haven't traditionally supplied universities.

ACADEMIA & JOBS
Faculties at Paisley include Engineering, Information Sciences, Science & Technology, Social and Management Sciences (and some midwifery and nursing). Faculties at Ayr are Education, Media Studies, Business, Nursing &

UNIVERSITY/STUDENT PROFILE	
University since	**1995**
Situation/style	**Town campuses**
Student population	**12760**
Undergraduates	**11295**
- mature	**43%**
- non EU undergraduates	**2%**
- male/female	**34/66**
- non-traditional student intake	**40%**
- state school intake	**99%**
- drop-out rate	**31%**
- undergraduate applications	**Up 5%**

Midwifery (apply through CATCH: 0131 220 8660). Subjects at Dumfries include Computing, Business & IT, along with Childhood Studies.

The big swell here is the increase in degrees in media, computing and technology. There has been a transformation at Ayr, where the largely female body of primary school teachers (Education is the most popular employment sector, 11% of graduates) and nurses have been getting cosy with the largely male students of BA Digital Art, BA Commercial Music, and BA degrees in Cinema, Media and Screen Practice. There are great media and broadcasting facilities at Ayr. They even run their own digital radio station.

Nevertheless, the real powerful computer and technology courses are still at Paisley, such as BSc Computer Games Technology, BA Computer Animation & Digital Art, BSc degrees in Computer-Aided Design, Digital Modelling,

WHERE PAISLEY GRADUATES END UP
Health & Social Work: 8%; Education: 11%; Wholesale Retail: 17%; Manufacturing: 10%; Financial Activities: 7%; Public Administration, Civil Service & Defence: 9%; Hotel/Restaurant: 5%; Transport & Communications (including Telecommunications): 4%; Construction: 4%; Personnel: 2%; Computer: 4%; Business & Management: 1%; Accountancy: 1%; Media (including Film): 1.5%; Legal 0.5%; Architecture: 3.5%; Publishing: 1%; Sport: 1%.
Approximate 'graduate track' employed **52%**

Computer Animation, Multimedia with Interactive Entertainment Technology, etc, and BEng degrees in Design and Product Design & Development, as well as BSc Music Technology.

Civil engineering is still a major focus, too, and they make as good a showing as Manchester Uni in the employment league. You get a BSc/BEng option in the single hons and three additional orientations for the BEng – Project Management, Environmental Mgt, Architectural Studies. Teaching inspection, Highly Satisfactory.

See also the Business IT & e-Commerce Department – BA Business Info Technology with either Accounting (there's an international Grade 5 in Accounting & Finance for research), Human Resource Management, Management or Marketing; or BSc with Multimedia or e-Business.

Note also an employment strength in social work, community and youth work – around 5% of graduates. See their Social Sciences faculty, which has a common first year before specialisation: Social Work, Sociology, Social Policy, Psychology, etc.

Paisley degree courses are designed with input from industry and commerce. Languages, IT training and work placements are key. IBM, M&S, BBC, Volkswagen, Standard Life and BAe all take Paisley undergrads on annual placements.

Another boost recently has been the offer of a

AT A GLANCE	
ACADEMIC FILE:	
Subjects assessed	**17**
Excellent/Highly Satisfactory	**65%**
Typical entryl requirements	**265 points**
Application acceptance rate	**26%**
Students-staff ratio	**20:1**
First/2:1 degree pass rate	**46%**
ACCOMMODATION FILE:	
Guarantee to freshers	**90%**
Style	**Halls, flats**
Cost pw (no food)	**£48**
Town	**£40**

BSc Sports Studies, with its dedicated option routes. It's designed for students building on HNDs to degree level. Special focus areas are sports therapy, exercise, health and fitness, sports development, outdoor recreation administration.

SOCIAL SCENE

STUDENTS' ASSOCIATION UPSA have been campaigning for a proper union building since 1971. Now, following a new SU at Ayr – café-style, chrome tables, Chesterfield sofas, very slick – they have one, a £5-million town centre HQ.

Hitherto they have held comedy and home-grown theme nights, karaoke, quizzes and talent contests.

Now they do much the same. but with **Big Bar** the venue – a massive hanger of a place – and *Salamander* returns with resident DJs Brad and Anthony as the official Friday night extravaganza. Monday is pub quiz, *Universally Challenged;* Tuesday is Karaoke; Wednesday is Games Nights. A trip the six miles into the centre of Glasgow is a regular alternative.

At Craigie there are two or three discos, a Saturday party, quizzes, karaoke, etc, and a popular live act Acoustic Night. In town there's the **Wulf & Whistle** and **O'Briens**, virtually union property by adoption, and three cheesy nightclubs with weekly student nights.

SPORT The Robertson Trust Sports Centre is located in the student village in Paisley and has had a £1.5-million facelift. Some 1,500 students are members. Recent improvements include turf pitches for rugby and soccer and floodlit synthetic pitches. There are also facilities for squash, multi-gym workouts, badminton, hockey, netball, tennis, basketball, volleyball and table tennis.

There's not much sport in Ayr.

WHAT IT'S REALLY LIKE	
UNIVERSITY:	
Social Life	★★★
Campus scene	**Friendly, local, urban cowboys**
Student Union services	**OK.**
Politics	**NUS issues**
Sport	**Relaxed**
National team position	**119th**
Sport facilities	**Average**
Arts opportunities	**Few**
Student newspaper	**Banter**
Student radio	**UCA Radio**
Venue bar	**Big Bar**
Union ents	**Games, karaoke, clubnights**
Union societies	**12**
Parking	**Poor**
TOWN:	
Glasgow	★★★★★
Local scene	★★
Town/gown relations	**Poor**
Risk of violence	**Average**
Student concessions	**Adequate**
Survival + 2 nights out	**£60 pw**
Part-time work campus/town	**Fair/good**

PILLOW TALK

Apply early for accommodation; it's in short supply, though at Paisley unbelievably cheap. Most students bed down in flats or 'villas' in the student village at Thornly Park, two miles from campus, hard by the uni's sports facilities. Other residences are more central; all are self-catering.

Accommodation at Craigie comprises catered single or shared study-bedrooms. No accommodation at Dumfries.

GETTING THERE

☞ By road to Paisley: M8 – M74, A726, A737. For Ayr, M77/A77. For Dumfries, A76 or A701 from the north; A75 from the south.
☞ By coach to Glasgow: London, 8:20; Birmingham, 6:20; Newcastle, 4:20.
☞ By rail to Paisley: Ayr, 45 mins; Glasgow Central, 15 mins. Glasgow to London, 6:00; For Dumfries: Glasgow, 2:00; Ayr, 1:50.
☞ By air: Glasgow International Airport.

UNIVERSITY OF PLYMOUTH

The University of Plymouth
Drake Circus
Plymouth
Devon PL4 8AA

TEL 01752 232 232
FAX 01752 232 141
EMAIL prospectus@plymouth.ac.uk
WEB www.plymouth.ac.uk

Plymouth Students' Union
Drake Circus
Plymouth PL4 8AA

TEL 01752 238500
FAX 01752 251669
EMAIL
presplymouth@su.plymouth.ac.uk
WEB www.upsu.com

VAG VIEW

*P*lymouth has made a vigorous rise since gaining university status – teaching assessments, if not amazing, are consistently good.

The uni majors in marine and maritime courses, water sports and Australians – there's even a Surf Science & Technology degree – believe it, dudes, this really does exist. Last year they won their 5th consecutive national surfing championship held at Newquay's Fistral Beech, and celebrated by attempting to seduce potential undergraduate recruits with branded sun block handed out from a beach buggy.

Meanwhile they have been developing a more serious strategy to serve the region. They began by galvanising local colleges in partnership schemes, and then nearby Exeter Uni and the regional NHS in the Peninsula Medical School at Derriford, Plymouth, which has been an unqualified success. They followed this with a £4-million Allied Health Centre for dietetics, physiotherapy, podiatry, midwifery and speech & language therapy. And now, this year they have launched, with Exeter University, a new dental school, operating from sites in Plymouth, Truro and Exeter.

Besides all this, there's a new £8-million library extension, with a café, 24/7 access computing and media area, extended stock to cater for students moving to Plymouth from other campuses. For, millions of pounds have been and are being spent on a centralisation project that will bring their scattered satellite campuses home. In 2005, their famous Agric arm (Agriculture, Tourism, Hospitality, Food Science, etc) moved from Seale-Hayne, Newton Abbot, to the Plymouth campus. Now, Education is moving from Exmouth to the heart of the Plymouth campus, from Autumn 2008. The new £40-million Education building will include purpose-built teaching space and living accommodation for students.

And this year, a £27-million Faculty of Arts building will open, for arts, architecture and humanities. No doubt students can't wait for the dust to settle.

FEES, BURSARIES

UK & EU Fees, 2007: £3,070 p.a. If you qualify for the HE Maintenace grant, you might get anything from £305 to £512 p.a. - not much in comparison with others. There are sports scholarships, and academic ones up to £3,000, and automatic £500 p.a. scholarships for students reading chemistry, civil engineering, theatre and performance, and modern languages degree courses.

There are also mature student bursaries (including relocation support of up to £1,535); field-work bursaries available; bursaries for students from university 'compact' schools/colleges and those from the South West Peninsula region.

STUDENT PROFILE

There's a huge mature and international student draw from 100 countries and an active international office and International Students' Society. Applicants from the UK tend to be drawn from below a line drawn south of the Midlands through Wales, Bristol and London, and from the surf cities of the world. Is that why there is a preponderance of female undergraduates (62%)? Whatever, it's easier on the eye, and no one's complaining.

CAMPUSES

PLYMOUTH CAMPUS Faculties: Science, Technology, Human Sciences, Business. But now the agrics, and goodness who else is going to pour in any day. See *Social Scene*, below.

EXMOUTH Douglas Avenue, Exmouth EX8 2AT. Tel: 01395 25509. There's an ´in principle´ decision to relocate the Faculty of Education from Exmouth to the Plymouth campus, from autumn 2008. A final decision will be made in October, 2006. What will become of the new £2.1 million centre with performance space, lecture theatre and seminar rooms? **Ents, campus & city:** second biggest campus (approx 1,000 students). Ents facilities exist: **S.U.B. Station** – two bars, but if you're expecting the bright lights and big sailors of Plymouth, you'll be disappointed. Exmouth is the relaxed, seaside campus. The **S.U.B. Station** bars provide theme nights, discos, live bands, hypnotists, club trips to Plymouth, etc.; LGB to **Boxes** or **The Loft** in Exeter. Popular local nightclub is **Samantha's**; there's a strong local live music culture. **Sport:** playing fields with pavilion close to campus. Rolle Rovers

(soccer), men's and women's rugby teams, netball, basketball and cricket all perform well within their respective leagues. Diving, sailing and windsurfing facilities locally. **Media:** *Rolle-Up* is the student magazine 'because our full title is University of Plymouth: Rolle College Faculty of Arts & Education.'

EXETER Earl Richards Road North, Exeter EX2 6AS. Tel: 01392 475004/9. Faculties of Arts (art, design, media, photography, humanities), and Health & Social (nursing, midwifery, occupational therapy).

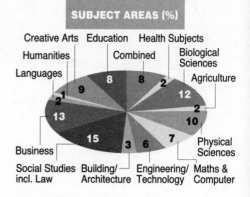

SUBJECT AREAS (%)

Creative Arts, Education, Health Subjects, Humanities, Combined, Biological Sciences, Languages, Agriculture, Business, Social Studies incl. Law, Building/Architecture, Engineering/Technology, Physical Sciences, Maths & Computer

8, 8, 2, 9, 2, 1, 12, 2, 13, 10, 15, 3, 6, 7

Ents facilities: bar, 266 ents capacity. Ents, campus & city: regular ents – Wednesday Film Club, Thursday pool competition, Friday theme nights – *Tarts & Trannies*, '70s, etc. A busy arts schedule includes trips to London, Birmingham, Cardiff and Cornwall art galleries and theatres. See *Exeter Uni* entry for lively student city nightlife. **Media:** *Illuminate* magazine. **Sport:** local sports facilities only; uni teams include football, hockey, rugby.

ACADEMIA & JOBS

The new faculty structure is as follows: Arts (arts, architecture and humanities), Education, Health & Social Work, Science, Social Science & Business, Technology. Plymouth is also a partner in the Peninsula Medical School (see below). The final faculty, formed last year, is a network of partner colleges in Cornwall, Devon and Somerset, known as the University of Plymouth Colleges (UPC). Plymouth is also part of the Combined Universities of Cornwall project (see separate entry).

They are hot on study skills support programmes. There are disability services, support for dyslexia, specialist assessment for students applying for the Disabled Student Allowance, and training in the use of specialist technical equipment. They boast a higher percentage of disabled students than any other university.

UNIVERSITY/STUDENT PROFILE	
University since	**1992**
Situation/style	**City/town campuses**
Student population	**30676**
Undergraduates	**25092**
- mature	**63%**
- non EU undergraduates	**3%**
- male/female	**38/62**
- non-traditional student intake	**31%**
- state school intake	**92%**
- drop-out rate	**16%**
- undergraduate applications	**Up 9%**

So, what was that about a degree in surfing? 'This is the first academically rigorous surf science course in the world,' boasts Dr Malcolm Findlay of the Institute of Marine Studies. The first year dwells on oceanography, surfing materials and business studies. The second moves uncontroversially into areas like human biology and human performance, but in the third year you develop your own specialism. Head for the beach presumably.

There is all sorts of marine interest (the Nautical School, the original fount of this uni, was established in 1862, and marine courses account for almost a quarter of Plymouth's undergraduate programme) – Aquaculture, Marine Biology, Marine Navigation, Applied Marine Sport Science, Nautical Studies and Ocean Science, Civil & Coastal Engineering, Geography or Geology with Ocean Science, Ocean Exploration. This year, degrees in Marine Studies appear with options to specialise in Ocean Yachting, Merchant Shipping or Navigation.

There's also a trio of Maritime Business degrees, and, they have a BSc in Cruise Operations Management, with support from Princes Cruises (hospitality, marine studies, business plus a year on a cruise liner!), directing our interest into their hospitality and tourism programme: Business & Tourism, Hospitality & Tourism, International Tourism Mgt, etc. Plymouth takes up the challenge from the Devon Riviera, excellent International and Euro Business degrees, plenty of sea air and extra-curricular encouragement.

But most especially, the marine bias takes the uni deep into biological sciences. Biologists are made aplenty here in courses with a 23 out of 24-point success rate at the assessments. There are interesting medical, agricultural and computer applications, as well as marine. And now, the new Peninsula Medical School, a partnership with Exeter Uni and the NHS in Devon and Cornwall, is a wholly compatible development. Plymouth's Institute of Neuroscience opened as the new £30-million Portland Square building opened to student doctors, nurses and all the other health care professionals.

Tying up with the NHS ensures a strong clinical element. The medical course focuses on the biological mechanisms that produce disease and its social impact. It looks very hands-on. Entry ABB-AAB, at least one science subject. There are various sites, Exeter, Plymouth, Truro, Barnstaple, Torbay, and you will move around during the course. Applications have soared, but there's still a 10% application acceptance rate.

Well over 2500 graduate nurses pour out of our universities each year, many off the Plymouth degrees in Adult Nursing, Community Health Care, Mental Health, Midwifery, Physiotherapy and Podiatry, Dietetics, and Occupational Therapy.

Again, clinical psychologists abound from their BSc Psychology, which also comes with a host of adjuncts. The psychology and mental health provisions lead to an employment track record in psychotherapy.

Meanwhile, graduates in BSc combinations with their Criminal Justice Studies, Psychology, Social Policy, Social Research, Law, Sociology, Statistics, etc, find a variety of jobs, often probation officers. Plymouth accounts for 13% of the total nationwide.

The Faculty of Agriculture, like Harper Adams, covers the whole gamut of courses, from Management to Nutrition, from Agriculture to Estate Management, and there's a Wildlife Conservation option too. Teaching inspection 22. A recent popular development has been the Veterinary Nursing & Management degree.

Foresters also find jobs in quantity from Plymouth, and aspiring environmental officers

enjoy a strong niche (see their Enviro. Science degrees).

Besides the BSc Civil & Coastal Engineering, in the same faculty you'll find BSc Civil Eng & Computer-aided Design, Construction Mgt and the Environment and Environmental Construction Surveying, all of which put Plymouth into the Top 10 for supplying construction engineer/managers. 23 points at the assessments. An international Grade 5 for research covers their Architecture degrees, too, which include BA Architectural Design with Digital Media, one source probably for their strong employment line int town planning.

Cartography is another niche – they are leaders in the field at Plymouth. See degrees like Design: Graphic Communication & Typography (or Illustration or Photography). Others in 3D Design, with 'Designer-Maker' or 'Furniture & Interior Design' or 'Product Design' are especially produc-

ACADEMIC EXCELLENCE

TEACHING:
(Rated Excellent or 17+ out of 24)

Environmental Science, Geography, Geology, Oceanography.	**Excellent**
Psychology, Civil Eng, Building, Nursing	**23**
Food/Agriculture, Biosciences, Politics, Sport, Tourism, Education	**22**
Art & Design, Media, Drama, History of Art	**21**
Sociology, Subjects Allied to Medicine, Maths	**20**
Materials Technology	**19**
Electronic & Electrical Eng	**18**

RESEARCH :
Top grades 5/5*

Psychology, Computer, History Art/Architecture/Design	**Grade 5**

tive of careers – 21 points at assessment. But there are as many graduates finding their way into the furniture manufacturing business through Plymouth's excellent International Business faculty. Aspiring market researchers and marketing managers build careers out of the BA Marketing (260 points), which comes with a 2-year Foundation at Plymouth College of Further Education.

Meanwhile, computer science finds Plymouth graduates jobs in media and government research. Look , for example, at their Computing Informatics and Statistics (Applied) & Management Science with Computing BSc degrees.

More than 10% of graduates go into education: 86% of them become primary teachers. Teaching inspection, 22.

SOCIAL SCENE

STUDENTS' UNION The Plymouth Students' Union has undergone a refurbishment and now boasts leather sofas, Sky TV and new games machines. A new **DJ** bar has met expectations.

They have a dynamic ents manager, digging out new local bands, and as a result Plymouth is featured in many a uni tour. The May Ball, we are told, 'attracted 3,500 to a field', actually Newnham Park, the classical Georgian manor between the outskirts of Plymouth and the foothills of Dartmoor National Park.

Friday night's *Burn* sets the scene for the week-end on the main campus – two dance rooms, 1,450 capacity – cheese and party in **Ignition**; indie to rock, ska to punk in **Illusion**. Saturday is regulation SU fare: *Flirt* in Ignition. Comedy nights (*Laughing Goldfish*) are especially popular, as are *Spin What You Bring* and *Open Mic Night*. *S.I.N.* is the official sports & societies DJ night, then it's on to **C103** in town for more, where Wednesday is *Boogie Nights* (chart & cheese; Friday is *Total Rock* (Room 1: rock; Room 2: heavy metal).

They say the superclubs are closing down in Plymouth and students are going more for the pub music scene. The union still team up with clubs for student nights – **C103** in Union Street is the present choice, and the Plymouth **Walkabout** does good business with them.

When not clubbing and surfing, there are society activities, notably *Fly* magazine and SCAP, Community Action, which has BIG ideas, last year an international project in Thika, a small town in Kenya no less.

Now, in line with Plymouth's bid to become a 'European City of the Sea', they are planning to develop a 'cultural quarter'. The idea came simultaneously to Newcastle, and it's a good one – a conglomeration of galleries, cinemas, exhibition areas theatre space, and a café. The first building, due to open in 2007, will be a base for the Faculty of Arts and a new home for the Plymouth **Arts Centre**.

SPORT £850,000 has been invested in a new fitness complex with squash courts and resistance and cardiovascular training equipment, and over £70,000 has gone into new boats and dinghies for the University's own Diving & Sailing Centre. There's

WHERE PLYMOUTH GRADUATES END UP

Health & Social Work: 8%; Education: 11%; Wholesale Retail: 9%; Manufacturing: 11.5%; Financial Activities: 6%; Public Administration, Civil Service & Defence: 12%; Hotel/Restaurant: 4%; Transport & Communications (including Telecommunications): 6%; Construction: 3%; Agriculture: 2%; Mining/Oil Extracting: 0.5%; Personnel: 3%; Computer: 3%; Business & Management: 3%; Accountancy: 1%; Media (including Film): 0.5%; Legal 1.5%; Publishing: 1%; Advertising: 0.5%; Artistic/Literary: 0.5%.

Approximate 'graduate track' employed **56%**

WHAT IT'S REALLY LIKE

UNIVERSITY:

Social Life	★★★★
Campus scene	**Lively ents, water sporty**
Student Union services	**OK**
Politics	**Interest low**
Sport	**47 clubs**
National team position	**31st**
Sport facilities	**Average**
Arts opportunities	**Drama, dance, music, art avg; film poor**
Student magazine	**Fly!**
Nightclub/bars	**Ignition, Illusion**
Union ents	**Party, cheese, indie**
Union societies	**78**
Most popular society	**Football**
Parking	**Non-existent**

CITY:

Entertainment	★★★★
Scene	**Clubs, pubs OK**
Town/gown relations	**Poor**
Risk of violence	**Average**
Cost of living	**Below average**
Student concessions	**Average**
Survival + 2 nights out	**£70 pw**
Part-time work campus/town	**OK**

Like nearby Exeter, Plymouth has recently become more cosmopolitan. Think huge shopping centre and **Barbican**. **The Barbican** is, of course, waterside, the olde worlde bit of town – boats, fish and tourists, but more to the point, pubs, clubs and restaurants. Arts-wise, there's the **Theatre Royal**, which had the Royal Shakespeare Company in residence when we were there, and the alternative **Drum Theatre** for more progressive fare. If you're seriously into painting, why not cross the border into Cornwall – many do so as to chase the surf in Newquay (current international surf and clubland Mecca) – but continue west, down to St Ives, the 'Tate of the South West,' as it is known.

PILLOW TALK

Freshers are guaranteed a room in halls if they live more than 25 miles from the campus at which they will be studying, if Plymouth is your first choice uni, if the academic criteria of your original offer are met, and if your application for a halls place is received before July 9. So they don't ask much then! In fact, there are even more ifs and buts, so you'd better speak to them, or their lawyers, personally...and get in quick! Note, all medical students are guaranteed an offer of a place in halls for their first year of study. There are mixed-sex halls, flats and houses, all self-catering.

national/world-class water-sport – sailing, diving, surfing, windsurfing, power-boating, wakeboarding, canoeing and waterski. A fleet of dinghies and yachts provide sailing opportunities. Plymouth is the only UK uni to have its own diving and sailing centre. Students can learn to dive pro-fessionally as part of their course (selected disciplines only) or take a recreational diving course, which is open to all students.

There's also the usual land-based team stuff. They came 56th nationally last year – most popular club is soccer, though it was their American football squad that was named 'Team of the Year' by the British Collegiate American Football League last year.

Town Plymouth – destroyed during the war and rebuilt at a low point in British architecture – has been designated second poorest ward in Europe, but you wouldn't know it since it has won huge EU investment. There's a surfeit of accommodation which costs upwards of £40 per week, you can walk anywhere, it is a safe, friendly, smiley place. When the sun shines it is unbeatable, the beach is 10 minutes away, and when it doesn't shine, maybe the snow on the nearby moors is not so bad an option.

AT A GLANCE

ACADEMIC FILE:

Subjects assessed	**24**
Excellent	**75%**
Typical entry requirements	**263 points**
Application acceptance rate	**22%**
Med. School acceptance rate	**9%**
Students-staff ratio	**18:1**
First/2:1 degree pass rate	**56%**

ACCOMMODATION FILE:

Guarantee to freshers	**Medics & overseas**
Style	**Halls, flats, houses**
Catered	**None**
En-suite	**64%**
Approx price range pw	**£68-£96**
City rent pw	**£50-£100**

Mary Newman hall, with 157 en-suite rooms, opens in September 2007. In addition, 350 en-suite rooms will be available on campus in the new Faculty of Education development, due to open in September 2008 (see *VAG View*, above)..

GETTING THERE

☛ By road: M5, A38 Exeter, Plymouth; Newton Abbot, A38, A383; Exmouth M5/J30, A376. Good coach services to Exeter and Plymouth.
☛ By coach to Plymouth: London, 4:40; Bristol, 2:30; Exeter, 1:05. Exeter: London, 4:00.

☛ By rail to Plymouth: London Paddington, 3:30; Bristol Parkway, 3:00; Southampton, 4:00; Birmingham New Street, 4:00. Exeter from London Paddington, 2:30; Bristol Parkway, 1:30; Birmingham New Street, 3:00.
☛ By air: Exeter or Plymouth City Airports.

UNIVERSITY OF PORTSMOUTH

The University of Portsmouth
University House
Winston Churchill Avenue
Portsmouth PO1 2UP

TEL 02392 848484
FAX 02392 843082
EMAIL admissions@port.ac.uk
WEB www.port.ac.uk

Portsmouth Students' Union
Cambridge Road
Portsmouth PO1 2ET

TEL 02392 843640
FAX 02392843667
EMAIL student-union@port.ac.uk
WEB www.upsu.net

VAG VIEW

*P*ortsea behaves like an island, it has its own microclimate, slightly warmer than nearby Brighton or Bournemouth, as it sits snugly behind the Isle of Wight. For centuries, because of its strategic position, it was an important naval base, but now the focus is moving away from the military, the old naval dockyard giving itself to a pleasure zone of shops, nightclubs, bars, called Gun Wharf.

What once we detected as a military ethic in the university's 'Code of Student Discipline' seems also to have slipped away – though there remains an active OTC (Officer Training Corps), and a high input of graduates into the defence arena from a variety of departments. Today, however, military-style disciplines seem to have been sublimated in a caring ethos, modern, civilian, and maybe a slip laden with PR. They describe themselves as 'a hands-on student university: we care that our students turn up at lectures.' There is no clock-watching, but they want to find out why a student's interest is dropping away, if it is.

The uni serves up business, engineering, science, and media, art & design – vocational fare, true to its roots that lead us back to 1869, foundation year of Portsmouth & Gosport School of Science & Art. It was 100 years later that the college became Portsmouth Polytechnic, before receiving its

Royal Charter as a university in 1992.

CAMPUS

Guildhall Campus is the name they give to the collection of sites in the centre of town, which has a European, café-style feel to it, and there are so many students marauding about that it seems not so much town as university precinct. Indeed, it is now known as the University Quarter.

Within it there is now an almost entirely wireless campus, allowing students to communicate, research and work wherever they choose. The transition from desktop computer use to wireless has quadrupled usage to more than 6,000. All rooms in halls of residence have free, very high-speed broadband (10Mbps).

Two other campuses, Milton and Langstone, 2 and 3 miles away, are less and less significant.

FEES, BURSARIES

UK & EU Fees, 2007: £2,070 p.a. 2008 will rise only slightly, in line with, inflation. If in receipt of the HE Maintenance grant there's a bursary of £820. An additional non-income assessed £300 annual bursary is available to students who apply from an eligible local college. Further details are available at www.port.ac.uk/money .

The uni has set aside an additional £750,000 over 3 years (£500,000 in 2007/08) for students with genuine financial difficulties.

STUDENT PROFILE

It is a predominantly male student body. A lot of mature students come here too. They tend to recruit from the south of England. For many, Portsmouth is the local university. There is a high state-school intake, and 29% of the undergraduate population come from sections of societry new to university. Given the unpractised element, their drop-out rate of 9% should suggest there's something to stay for.

Support for the new uni intake is as good as they claim. 'There's a full-time counselling service,' a student tells me. Why? 'Students find it hard at this...at university, money problems, pressures. People think being at university is easy. It is not. I am the only child of five in my family to have gone to university. It wasn't part of the culture of my family. I have struggled here, had to get jobs. People have this concept of university, students getting drunk all the time, having a good time...I have heard about that, but never experienced it.'

ACADEMIA & JOBS

Faculties are Humanities and Social Sciences; Science; Technology; Environment; and Business.

Top recruiters from Portsmouth are the NHS, central and local government, National Probation Service, IBM. Now, too, the uni has Purple Door Recruitment, an agency working in collaboration with local and national business, which offers work experience and career opportunities.

The Grade 5 for research in European Studies and Russian/Slavonic/East European languages describes one special dimension of Portsmouth's portfolio. One student in five takes a language course and around 1,000 go abroad for part of their course. French achieved a near perfect teaching score. There are sound degrees in Applied Languages, Combined Modern languages, Euro Studies with various combination subjects, international dimensions to Business or International Trade, language add-ons to everything from American Studies to Creative Writing to Film Studies. And there is a strong contingent (5%) among undergraduates from elsewhere in Europe.

The Business School has moved into a new £12-million building on the main campus. Accountants

do well here. There's a range of BA degrees with Business, e-Business, and Business Law. Then there's Accountancy Studies or Accountancy & Financial Management for students with sufficient experience or qualifications to miss out on Year 1 of a regular accountancy degree.

The Portsmouth Business School accounts for around 18% of students at undergraduate level. International and European options are legion. There's also BA Marketing, Marketing & Psychology or Leisure Management & Marketing.

Female Undergraduates — 39%
Postgraduates — 17%
STUDENT POPULATION
Total students 18,390
Male Undergraduates — 44%

Sales managers pour out of this faculty, but also out of biological sciences, where there is that in-depth strength and opportunity for sales focus in the pharmaceutical/biotech industry, medical sales, etc, mentioned below. Finally, they are commercial & business law specialists.

There is, too, an ever-increasing focus on health. The new School of Professionals Complementary to Dentistry delivers dental nursing, hygiene and therapy. Housed in a purpose-built £4-million building, the school is the first new dental education facility in England for 50 years.

The School of Pharmacy & Biomedical Sciences is recommended by both teaching assessments and employment data. Look at the 4-year MPharm, also Pharmaceutical Science and Pharmacology degrees (full marks at the assessments).

Now a new £4.5million ExPERT Centre is manned by computerised mannequins, which breathe oxygen, drool, secrete fluids, blink, bleed and even react to drugs injected into their bodies. The centre trains students in biomedical sciences and healthcare professionals and has two simulation suites (operating theatre and hospital ward). Teaching inspection 22 for biosciences.

The Faculty of Humanities & Social Sciences has a tie-up with Southampton University to train health care professionals to work together: trainee nurses alongside trainee pharmacists and trainee radiographers, and so on. Health subjects, such as nursing, radiography were also top scoring at the teaching and research assessments.

SUBJECT AREAS (%)

Humanities — Creative Arts — Health Subjects
Media — Combined
Languages — 12 — 12 — Biological Sciences
4 — 1 — 6
4 — 11
16 — 6
Business
Social Studies incl. Law — 10 — 2 — 7 — 9 — Physical Sciences
Building/ Architecture — Engineering/ Technology — Maths & Computer

Clinical and educational psychologists find jobs in number from here. Their BSc Psychology is accredited by the British Psychological Soc., and if you get at least a second class degree you've taken the first step to becoming a chartered psychologist.

There's also BSc Psychol. with Criminology. Many graduates find careers with the police and the probation service. One little gem is the Institute of Criminal Justice Studies, whose work on counter-fraud, benefits fraud and so on, has brought it links with TV's *Crimewatch*. Crime author PD James opened a library extension in January 2007. Teaching inspection, 23.

Additions to the degree portfolio this year also include a new faculty of Creative and Cultural Industries, working out of refurbished facilities for media studies and art and design. There's even a facsimile newsroom to service a new journalism course.

Graduates get jobs as designers, illustrators, set-designers and film/video producers. There' are Photography, Video Production and various Film Studies degrees, and facilities include broadcast TV studios and a digital development laboratory.

They produce a big share of architects, too.

> *Portsmouth is massive in software engineering and systems analysis, coming third nationally for producing software engineers and fourth for software consultants.*

Causing a stir is the BA Hons Architecture which comprises 50% design projects and 50% taught courses. It earns exemption from Part 1 RIBA. Likewise, property and construction employment markets like stocking up from this uni. Portsmouth has been No. 1 in the field of quantity surveying. The dedicated degree has been replaced by BSc Property Development with Quantity Surveying. There's also a good employment record (Top 10) for civil engineers and construction engineer/managers – the B/MEng Civil Engineering is accredited by the appropriate Institute. Teaching inspection 20.

There's a traditional tie-up with the navy, excellent career prospects with the army and a good number of jobs, too, for defence operatives and equipment engineers. The Institute of Maritime Heritage Studies preserves the tradition, it's based in an old boathouse in the naval dockyards area. Portsmouth is of course famous for being the site where the Mary Rose is docked.

Portsmouth lead the field in supplying to the Electrical and Electronic manufacturing industry. Computing degrees are very strong, information and internet systems and much else besides, a particular strength in the employment sector being computer games technology.

Portsmouth is also massive in software engineering and systems analysis, coming third nationally for producing software engineers and fourth for consultants. There's a BSc Software Engineering (and an HND if you need it). Look, too, at their BSc Computer Science(s), Systems Eng, Management & design. On the BEng route there's Computer Eng or Technology (the former also an MEng).

Finally, there are BSc degrees in Sports Development, Sports Science, Water Sports Science. A £2.5 million sports science building houses labs, a swimming flume and two British Olympic

ACADEMIC EXCELLENCE

TEACHING :

(Rated Excellent or 17+ out of 24)

Geography	**Excellent**
Pharmacology	**24**
French, Psychology, Politics,	**23**
Subjects Allied to Medicine, Education	
Maths, Biosciences, Nursing	**22**
German, Economics, Leisure/Sport	**21**
Sociology, Italian, Civil Eng, Electric & Electron Eng, Building, Land & Property Mgt, Physics, Art & Design	**20**
Russian, Iberian Studies	**18**

RESEARCH:
Top grades 5/5*

Studies/Professions Allied to Medicine, Applied Maths, European Studies, Russian/Slavonic/East European	**Grade 5**

Medical Centre accredited climatic chambers.

STUDENT SCENE

STUDENTS' UNION The new SU building gives them a 2,500 capacity. The investment is £8 million. The nightclub, **LUX**, alone can take in 1,100. This year it's getting a new lighting and sound system. Then there's the sportsbar **Waterhole** (500), chill-out bar **CO2** (500) and international bar **Embassy** (400). Regular ents are *Purple Wednesdays*, *Forbidden Fruit* (Fridays), *Flirt* (Saturdays)

Top of the ents menu are their mammoth balls – a new Presentation Ball for Purples (full/half colour awards: sport is big here), various societies' balls, Graduation Ball (Republica played last year) and so on.

Media-wise, students are active with monthly magazine, *Pugwash*, one of four nominated last year for the Best Magazine Award in the national media awards. Pure Radio has been enjoying its most popular year with daily Internet broadcasts.

SPORT Men's sports teams are consistently high in the BUSA league. Geographical position gives them special potential – sailing (larks and lasers), wind-surfing and canoeing. Applications for scholarships in hockey, rugby, swimming, water sports, gymnastics and netball are encouraged.

TOWN The new 170m Spinnaker Tower is already a major British landmark, looming over the buzzing

Gunwharf Quays designer shopping area with its numerous restaurants, bars and nightclubs. The Historic Dockyard is one of the top 10 heritage attractions in Britain, while the city centre will soon be transformed by a £350m project to confirm its position as the south coast shopping and leisure choice.

Student and singer Genna Hellier says the nightlife was part of the reason she opted for Portsmouth: 'Also, it was a really nice summer's day and I saw the cafés lining the streets. It looked beautiful. I love it here. I came here shy and now I am going into PR! I never did any sport and now I work out every day. This union here provides amazing sporting opportunities.

'**Gun Wharf** is really nice,' Genna went on, 'all the London-based clubs are here. There is no rivalry between locals and students. It is a very safe place to live. Music is especially good here. More locally we have the **Wedgwood Rooms** and **The Pyramid**. There's a place called **Havana** for student bands, and we organise open mic nights at the

WHAT IT'S REALLY LIKE

UNIVERSITY:

Social Life	★★★★
Campus scene	**Good mix**
Student Union services	**Good**
Politics	**Average**
Sport	**50 clubs**
National team position	**59th**
Sport facilities	**Good**
Arts opportunities	**Plenty dance, music, film**
Student magazine	**Pugwash**
2006 Media Awards	**Runner-up Best Magazine**
Student radio	**PURE FM**
Nightclub	**LUX**
Bars	**Waterhole, CO2, Embassy**
Union ents	**Rock, cheese, r&b, comedy**
Union societies	**40**
Most active societies	**People & planet, Breakdance**
Parking	**Poor**

TOWN:

Entertainment	★★★
Scene	**Good: pubs, clubs**
Town/gown relations	**Good**
Risk of violence	**Low**
Cost of living	**Average**
Student concessions	**Excellent**
Survival + 2 nights out	**£70 pw**
Part-time work campus/town	**Average**

There's a bountiful supply of clubs, cafés and wine bars in the Guildhall area. Other student hang-outs, such as the Havana Café Bar and the **Frog on the Front**, are within walking distance. The club scene ranges from cheesy handbag to razor-tuned, techno beats. Then, of course, there's Premiership Football.

PILLOW TALK

Around 3,000 places are available. 710 en-suite, self-catered beds are now up for grabs at James Watson Hall, which opened recently. Every first year who makes the uni their first choice by end April will qualify for a place in hall. If you don't get a place with them, then the uni will sort you out: 'It is our philosophy to care all the way through.'

GETTING THERE

☛ By road: A3(M), 2 hours from London.
☛ By rail: London Waterloo, 1:30; Bristol Parkway, 2:15; Birmingham New Street, 3:30; Sheffield, 4:45.
☛ By coach: London, 2:30; Exeter, 6:45.
☛ By air: Southampton Airport.

union and so on. The local theatre is the **Theatre Royal**, nice little theatre in the **Guildhall**, often used for student productions. The uni also built **Wiltshire Studios**, where a lot of student productions are done.'

QUEEN MARGARET UNIVERSITY COLLEGE

Queen Margaret University College
Clerwood Terrace
Edinburgh EH12 8TS

TEL 0131 317 3247
FAX 0131 317 3248
EMAIL admissions@qmuc.ac.uk
WEB www.qmuc.ac.uk

Queen Margaret's began in 1875 as the Edinburgh School of Cookery and was re-named in 1930 The Edinburgh College of Domestic Science. Today there are four faculties: Arts, Business & Consumer Affairs, Social Sciences & Health Care, and Health Sciences, and they have become a university college with direct line into a number of career opportunities. They are located at three sites in Edinburgh. At the main Corstorphine campus near Edinburgh Airport, in the grounds of a former stately home, are the departments of Business & Consumer Studies, Communication & Information Studies, Hospitality & Tourism Management, Management & Social Sciences, Dietetics & Nutrition, Health & Nursing and Speech & Language Sciences. Leith Campus in old Edinburgh is home to the departments of Occupational Therapy, Physiotherapy, Podiatry and Radiography, while The Gateway Theatre in nearby Elm Row is the base for Drama.

5% plus of their graduates go into the hotel and restaurant trade. In the Health Sciences faculty, they produce 17% of all graduate physiotherapists nationwide; also from here come 6% of the entire provision of speech therapists. BSc Speech Pathology & Therapy is the course.

Accommodation at Corstorphine is in 3 halls. They have a swimming pool, gym, squash courts and all-weather surface for tennis, football, hockey and netball. The Students' Association has a bar.

QUEEN MARY, UNIVERSITY OF LONDON

Queen Mary, University of London
Mile End Road
London E1 4NS

TEL 020 7882 5511
Freephone: +44 (0)800 376 1800
EMAIL admissions@qmul.ac.uk
WEB www.qmul.ac.uk

Queen Mary College
Students' Union
432 Bancroft Road
London E1 8031

TEL 020 7882 5390
EMAIL president@qmsu.org
WEB www.qmsu.org

VAG VIEW

A constituent college of the federal University of London, QM, once known as Queen Mary & Wesyfield, arose out of the merger (in 1989) of two colleges: Westfield College, a 19th-century pioneer in higher education for women, and Queen Mary College, founded in 1885 and located at the People's Palace in Mile End Road, ideally situated for its essential purpose, namely to educate the East End poor. This is the uni's base in Mile End Road today. A later, medical foundation arose out of a merger in 1995 between the Royal London School of Medicine & Dentistry and St Bartholomew's Hospital Medical School, now QMW's Medical School. Medical students undergo their clinical training at the Royal London in Whitechapel and Barts in West Smithfield.

QMW's location thus keeps it true to its roots, while its large overseas student contingent – they draw from some 100 countries worldwide – reflects the multi-cultural character of the area as it is today. Central to this strategy is a Study Abroad programme. Languages are to the fore throughout the curriculum, and have scored highly in both teaching inspections and research assessments.

FEES, BURSARIES

UK & EU Fees, 2007: £3,070 p.a. Fees for 2008 N/A. If in receipt of a full HE Maintenance grant there's a bursary of £1,024 p.a.; if in receipt of partial grant, £819. QM also offer £4,000 p.a. to students who who qualify for the full HE Maintenance Grant and who achieve three 'A' grades in A-Levels taken in the same year. See www.qmul.ac.uk/undergraduate/feesfinance/#homebursaries

STUDENT PROFILE

'Integration between medical students and the rest of the college leaves a lot to be desired,' writes Kieran Alger, 'the two groups preferring to indulge in separate activities, the medical students enjoying their own bar, for example, and playing for separate sports teams while the main body of students mixes well, regardless of subject.'

As at other medical schools, the medical students sharply increase the public school quota and give QMW a state/public school ratio akin to Reading's or Southampton's, Warwick's or York's. The Mile End Road student population is another story. 'Queen Mary proper is a cultural melting pot,' agrees Kieran – 'a fascinating blend of overseas students, a large ethnic contingent and UK residents,' and a 31% draw last year from the new-to-uni social groups. There are also larger than average local and mature populations (they even have 'mature student socials' at the student union), which serve to distinguish the clientele from what Kieran describes as 'the stereotypical beer and beans, lazy student'.

CAMPUS

'QM, with its modern architecture, is one of the few universities to combine the class of the well established with the youth, vigour and dynamism of an ex-polytechnic,' continues Kieran. 'Set in the heart of the multi-cultural hotch-potch which forms the East End, the student population reflects its intriguing surroundings. The East End, home of imports, the cloth trade, Phil, Grant and the Kray twins, has an illustrious history of intermingling races. From jellied eels at Spitalfield's Market to chicken balti in one of Brick Lane's curry houses, this area caters for a huge range of tastes. It is also asserting its own brand of sophistication in the stunning Docklands development. The combination of Canary Wharf Tower dominating on one side and the trendification of the E1, E2, and E3 postal areas is causing a surge in social and cultural activity. The East End, with its fashionable gangster land history and eerie Jack the Ripper connections, is the place London's affluent young professionals want to live. Neighbouring areas, such as Bow and Aldgate, are being inundated with new eateries, coffee houses, galleries and nightclubs.'

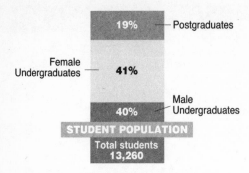

Female
Undergraduates — **41%**

19% — Postgraduates

40%

Male
Undergraduates

STUDENT POPULATION

Total students
13,260

Clinical students head the new award-winning Medical School Building, a landmark building providing innovative research and laboratory facilities. Its Centre of the Cell for Bioscience Education Centre launched in March 2007 and is dedicated to inspiring curiosity and learning by connecting science to everyday life.

ACADEMIA & JOBS

First, note the excellent 12: 1 students-to-staff ratio, the low drop-out rate (expressing student satisfaction) and a genuine desire to help with dyslexic and other disability.

Forty per cent of QM graduates are destined for the health sector. The medicine degree, a 5-year BM BS (Medicine, Surgery), stresses clinical method and communication skills and the experience of the patient in the community, and there's a significant element of problem-based learning (small-group explorations of particular scenarios). First 2 years at the Mile End campus, final three at the the Royal London Hospital, Whitechapel Campus. There's a 4-year graduate entry, too. Entry ABB-AAB + UKCAT, including Biology and Chemistry.

Of interest to future dentists, the dental schools with full marks at the assessments are King's College London, Manchester University, Queen's Belfast and Queen Mary College London. It's a 5-

year BDS plus a B/MEng Dental Materials. Entry AAB including a science subject + Chemistry/ Biology. Research Grade 5.

Safe ground, too, is Law. QM are world-class European law specialists, and non-Law graduates may opt for a 2-year full-time or 3-year part-time Senior Status Law degree here. Last year QM law students launched a Legal Advice Centre - unique in London as it is the first university-run centre to offer free legal advice to members of the public.

Investment advisers/analysts, accountants are also to the fore, and there's a bunch of good Economics and Finance degrees. So, too, IT consultants, software engineers, programmers, who attest to the sound Computer Science, IT Science and Computer Engineering degrees. There is a foundation programme attached to all BEng, BSc and BSc (Eng) degrees.

Languages feature strong. Graduate jobs for language students vary widely, some find a use in

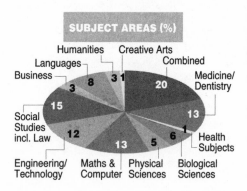

SUBJECT AREAS (%)

Humanities Creative Arts
Languages Combined
Business Medicine/
  3 **8** **3** **1** **20** Dentistry
  15 **13**
Social
Studies
incl. Law **12** **5** **6** **1** Health
  13 Subjects
Engineering/ Maths & Physical Biological
Technology Computer Sciences Sciences

community and youth work, others take a vocational direction from a subject studied in combination, as in chartered accountancy, investment, management, etc. Others become teachers (5%), but there is a great mass of language graduates here who become sales assistants, clerks, etc, and one cannot help but advise applicants to stick to QM's mainstay areas if, that is, paying back fees and loans are uppermost in mind.

An interesting novelty is a degree in Journalism & Contemporary History, run jointly with City University, a world leader in journalism.

SOCIAL SCENE

The medics have their own union – SoMaD Students' Association. There are two bars: the **Clubs Union Bar** at the Royal London Hospital (Whitechapel), and **Bart's Bar**, close to Bart's Hospital in Charterhouse Square (where there is also a swimming pool, squash, tennis and badminton courts). There's also a glass-fronted bistro

UNIVERSITY/STUDENT PROFILE	
School of London Uni since	**1915**
Situation/style	**Campus**
Student population	**13260**
Undergraduates	**10691**
- mature	**20%**
- non EU undergraduates	**23%**
- male/female	**50/50**
- non-traditional student intake	**32%**
- state school intake	**85%**
drop-out rate	**10%**
- undergraduate applications	**Up 5%**

bar, **BarMed**, in the Medical Science building looking out on to Library Square. Regular high jinks are the Association Dinner, the Christmas Show, Burn's Night and the sporting cup finals. There's a flourishing drama society – plays, a Christmas Show, a production for the Edinburgh Fringe – a Gilbert & Sulivan Society, a choir and orchestra, and of course Rag. Otherwise, they bounce around at *Toga Nights, Star Wars Night, Austin Powers Night,* and *Mummies and Daddies Night.* I guess *Doctors & Nurses Night* is simply 'too day-time' to compete.

In Mile End Road, the more dissipated wind up rather than down at looking for 'the best student nightclub in London' (the Union's boast) at **Club e1**. Complete with 12K JBL sound system and state of the art computer-controlled lighting rig it is open till 2 am from Thursday through Saturday. Then, there's **The Drapers Arms**. The **e1** nightclub has a 750-capacity, top sound and lighting systems and a reputation built on the sometime, much-vaunted, *Time Out*-supported *Time Tunnel* ('60s to '90s) on Saturdays, a once regular Saturday pop ('70s to the present day) extravaganza, *ROAR*, and more recently, *FIZZ*, on Saturday night, *Gagging for it* on Tuesday, *Hail Mary* on Wednesday, *Now Music* on Thursday, *Take a Ride* on Friday... However, this year there's a more basic menu of *Flirt! Toga & Tequila Party, Ann Summers Night* followed by *Flirt, Saints + Sinners Flirt, Flirt! Halloween, Mary's Cheese, Hail Mary. Flirt* is a national SU package, and the cheesy home-bred stuff suggests QM may have lost its way a bit. Mind you, they had a long way to fall, and they're feeling very defensive this year, what with Ismail Malik's article in *London Student* suggesting that 'a whole host of students who fail to get into other University of London institutions go to Queen Mary'. The pages of QMSU's newspaper, *CUB*, have been putting Ismail right.

No stranger to student media awards, *CUB*, founded in 1947, is one of the oldest student papers in London. There's a clubs and societies resource centre.

SPORT Sports fields are at Chislehurst. 'Sports are abundant,' Kieran writes, 'from rock climbing, netball and fencing, to the somewhat more comfort-

ACADEMIC EXCELLENCE	
TEACHING:	
(Rated Excellent or 17+ out of 24)	
English, Geography	**Excellent**
Dentistry	**24**
Politics, Modern Languages	**23**
Biosciences, Subjects Allied to Medicine	**22**
Medicine, Electric/Electron Eng, Maths, Physics, Drama	**21**
Materials Technology	**20**
General Engineering	**19**
RESEARCH:	
Top grades 5/5*/6*	
Law, Linguistics, Iberian/LatinAmerican	**Grade 6***
Clinical Dentistry, Physics, Pure Maths, Statistics, Mechanical/Aeronautical/ Manufacturing Eng, Metallurgy, Geography, Law, English, French, German/Dutch/ Scandinavian, Russian/ Slavonic & E. European Languages., History	**Grade 5**

able pastimes of rowing and rugby. The football club is of a particularly high standard, as is the women's football team. Collegiate London Uni delivers many an opportunity for battle.'

PILLOW TALK

For first years it's London University 'intercollegiate halls' (catered), where you could be with anyone, or QM's own (self-catered) at the Mile End campus (2,109 places), where since last year there's a new Student Village – 995 rooms (15 for wheelchair users), all with computer connections, village shop, café bar... Mile End Park has single rooms, en-suite facilities, arranged in flats – lawns, woodland courtyards. The older (pre-Village) accommodation at Mile End is the cheaper.

50 rooms available at Dawson Hall, Charterhouse Square, close to Barts, and at

---

WHERE QUEEN MARY GRADUATES END UP

Health & Social Work: 39%; Education: 5%; Wholesale Retail: 9%; Manufacturing: 5%; Financial Activities: 10%; Public Administration, Civil Service & Defence: 7%; Hotel/Restaurant: 2%; Transport & Communications (including Telecommunications): 2%; Construction: 0.5%; Personnel: 3%; Computer: 2%; Business & Management: 1%; Accountancy: 3%; Media (including Film): 1.5%; Legal 1.5%; Publishing: 1%; Advertising: 0.5%; Artistic/Literary: 1%; Sport: 1%.

Approximate 'graduate track' employed **72%**

WHAT IT'S REALLY LIKE

UNIVERSITY:

Social Life	★★★★
Campus scene	**Lively**
Student Union services	**Average**
Politics	**Apolitical**
Sport	**19 clubs**
National team position	**90th**
Sport facilities	**Average**
Arts opportunities	**Drama excellent**
Student newspaper	**Cub**
Nightclub	**Club e1**
Bars	**The Drapers Arms, Barts, Union Bar**
Union ents	**Flirt**
Union societies	**52**
Most active siocieties	**Islamic Soc, Friends of Palastine**
Parking	**Poor**

CITY:

Entertainment	★★★★★
Scene	**Wild, expensive**
Town/gown relations	**Average-good**
Risk of violence	**London**
Cost of living	**High**
Student concessions	**Good**
Survival + 2 nights out	**£100 pw**
Part-time work campus/town	**Excellent**

AT A GLANCE

ACADEMIC FILE:

Subjects assessed	**21**
Excellent	**71%**
Typical entry requirements	**314 points**
Application acceptance rate	**15%**
Med. School acceptance rate	**9%**
Students-staff ratio	**12:1**
First/2:1 degree pass rate	**58%**

ACCOMMODATION FILE:

Guarantee to freshers	**Non-locals OK**
Style	**Halls, flats**
Catered	**None**
En suite	**50%**
Approx price range pw	**£80-£110**
City rent pw	**£100-£180 Zone 1; £75-£85 Zone 2**

Floyer House on the Whitechapel campus.

GETTING THERE
☞ By Underground: QMW, Stepney Green (District, Hammersmith & City) or Mile End (+ Central line). The Royal London, Whitechapel tube (East London, District, Hammersmith & City lines); nearest Bart's is Barbican. St Paul's (Central).

THE QUEEN'S UNIVERSITY, BELFAST

The Queen's University of Belfast
University Road
Belfast BT7 1NN

TEL 028 9097 5081
FAX 028 9097 5131
EMAIL admissions@qub.ac.uk
WEB www.qub.ac.uk

Queen's University Students' Union
University Road
Belfast BT7 1PE

TEL 028 9097 3106
FAX 028 9023 6900
EMAIL su.president@qubsu.org
WEB www.qubsu.org

VAG VIEW

*N*orthern Ireland's leading educational institution has its origins in the Queen's College, Belfast, founded in 1845. There is a traditional Oxbridge-style reputation, with good lines into the professions, medicine, dentistry, the City and law.

Now, under the leadership of Vice-Chancellor Professor Peter Gregson, who took up office in August 2004, Queen's is implementing an ambitious Vision for the Future, beginning with a new academic framework (see Academia below), a £200 million investment in staff, students and facilities, including a £44-million library project, a £45-million student village, replacing the present high-rise catered tower blocks with self-catered three-storey villas in a village setting by 2009/10, and an extensive refurbishment to the Students' Union and the Physical Education Centre.

CAMPUS
Set a few kilometres from the city centre in a so-called 'safe' area of Belfast, the campus encompasses the Botanic Gardens and Ulster Museum.

Areas around Queen's University, Stranmillis and Botanic Avenue are now busier than ever and spilling over into the once isolated city centre.

Writes Laura Cattell: 'The big red buses that pass by Queen's every few minutes are packed with camera-happy tourists snapping a shot of the redbrick Lanyon hall. The impressive building (apparently modelled on Oxford University's Magdalen College), is at the heart of the city campus and though few actual lectures take place in the building it's the focus for academic and ceremonial life at Queen's. Set in the southern and leafier part of Belfast, most of the departmental buildings are housed in the Georgian terraces along University Square, opposite Lanyon hall or in the larger more modern Ashby Hall further along Stranmillis Road. As a student, most of your social life will be based in this area – from Eglantine to Botanic Avenue. The Student Union is located opposite the Lanyon buildings and as with most 1960s university structures it's not architecturally stunning, but it has everything you need – from banks, second-hand bookshops, convenience stores and a laundry, to cafes, bars, toilets and a nightclub. Although much of Belfast has been affected by the troubles in recent years this part of the city remains largely untouched by sectarianism.'

FEES, BURSARIES

UK & EU Fees, 2007: £3,070 p.a. 2008 will rise in line with inflation. There's a generous system of means-tested support, i.e. if in receipt of the HE Maintenance grant, also sports awards and entrance scholarships.

STUDENT PROFILE

Queen's claim to be 'one of the most socially inclusive universities in the United Kingdom. It consistently out-performs national benchmarks in attracting students from poorer backgrounds.' Perhaps they should do more for the beleaguered English public school boy and girl who, for example, find themselves victims of discrimination too. Certainly there are some opportunities for them here. For example, Queen's Uni's medical school is one of the best in the world, and the application acceptance rate is three times what you'll find in most English med schools.

The fact is that most of the student population is local, and 31% of undergraduates are part-timers. There is, however, a very low (8%) take from underprivileged so-called 'low participation neighbourhoods', but a high take (34%) from the four lowest socio-economic classes. Almost all that come here had a state school education, but this is not the land of the English public school after all.

ACADEMIA & JOBS

'Academically,' Laura continues, 'Queen's is Northern Ireland's best University and lies in the top three of Ireland's higher education institutions. It is still overlooked by many students in mainland Britain not only because of its location, but also because of its lowly ranking alongside U.K institutions. It is let down by a few weak departments, but this is counteracted by other world-class departments: Medicine, Engineering, English and Politics.

'There is a thriving literary scene, enlivened by the excellent teaching and research record of the English department. The School of English has

UNIVERSITY/STUDENT PROFILE	
University since	**1908**
Situation/style	**Civic**
Student population	**17300**
Undergraduates	**14400**
- mature	**18%**
- non EU undergraduates	**5%**
- male/female	**42/58**
- non-traditional student intake	**34%**
state school intake	**100%**
- drop-out rate	**13%**
- undergraduate applications	**Up 8%**

SUBJECT AREAS (%)

Humanities, Creative Combined Arts 2, Medicine/Dentistry 15, Languages 5, Health Subjects 7, Business 5, Social Studies 13, 5, 9, Planning/Building/Architecture 10, Engineering/Technology 9, Maths & Computer 8, 1, Biological Sciences, Agriculture, Physical Sciences, Social Studies incl. Law 4

some of the best academics in their field and is of course well-known for being the alma mater of Northern Ireland's most celebrated poets: Seamus Heaney and Paul Muldoon.'

Queen's is an artistic hub, home to Belfast's International Festival and to Northern Ireland's sole arthouse cinema in the Queen's Film Theatre, and to the region's newest museum, the Naughton Gallery. The University runs a host of musical events, including an annual international festival of Contemporary Music. Courses in drama and film studies underpin its cultural contribution and the Seamus Heaney Centre for Poetry reinforces the university's reputation as a world literary force.

'Famous-Seamus has also given his name to several buildings around campus and is an occasional visitor at the university,' writes Laura. 'The Heaney Centre, found at the back of the School of English, organises regular literary events - most of which are free and usually boast free wine as an incentive (if you need one!). Recent guests to the

Female Undergraduates — **47%**

STUDENT POPULATION

Total students 17,300

17% — Postgraduates

36% — Male Undergraduates

centre have been Jackie Kaye, Nick Laird, Ali Smith, Paul Durcan and Terry Eagleton. There's also a lively English Society and several reading and writing groups. Last year's poet-in-residence was Sinead Morrisey, who ran the writing group, while this year sees young poet Leontia Flynn as chair.'

The new academic framework consists of 21 large schools within 3 faculties: Arts, Humanities & Social Sciences; Engineering & Physical Sciences; and Medicine, Health & Life Sciences. It is too early to say how successful the reorganisation will be, though there have been criticisms about the organisational sense of the reshuffling of some schools into super-schools. The new library is due for completion in 2009 and will accommodate 2000 reader places and house 1.5 million volumes. There will also be an exhibition space, café, language laboratory, information points and multimedia resources.

A quarter of graduates enter the health sector. The 5-year MB has a pre-med year for applicants with broader based qualifications than A levels, but only 5 places on it. Nevertheless, there's a 39% of reading medicine here if you apply, which makes it the easiest med. school to get into by far (the average application acceptance rate is 10%), even if the A level requirement is the highest. Scientific and Clinical Medicine is taught for each system of the body – system by system, rather than Physiology, Anatomy, etc. Strong emphasis on clinical skills. Average Entry Requirements AAA including Chemistry A + Physics ir Biology or Maths, or AAB including Chemistry A + A at AS level. Teaching Inspection 22. Research Grade 5 for Community-based Clinical subjects. The Dental School scored full marks at the assessments, the 5-year BDS requires AAB at entry. For midwifer Queen's look all round the best bet. They produce around 7% of graduate midwives, not with a dedicated Midwifery degree, but through BSc Hons/Higher Diploma in Nursing Science. The entry requirements in this instance are surprisingly low. Take advantage! The reputation in engineering is world class: Mechanical, Aeronautical and Manufacturing Engscored Grade 5* at the assessments. Jobs are legion in aeronautical, and note the Mechanical with Food Engineering speciality. Electrical and telecommunications engineers proliferate and benefit from Electrical & Electronic Engineering taking full marks for teaching, and a Grade 5 (international reputation) for research. There are good sandwich/professional experience opportunities.

Architecture, Environmental Planning, Structural Engineering with Architecture, Civil Engineering, Environmental & Civil Engineering are B/MEng sandwich courses speak of their employment strengths in built environment. There are decent teaching assessments and an international track record in research. Teaching inspection, 22. Research Grade 5.

Accountants are legion in the Management & Economics School, the named degree coming also with French, German or Spanish – 7.5% of all Queen's graduates become accountants. The

Management degree also comes with three language options and Information Systems. They put very high numbers into retail management.

They are also high up among unis producing actuaries. Look at the Economics and Finance degrees, but especially the Maths (Pure/Applied) and extended for a year in Europe.

Note also Law & Accounting, one of an interesting bunch of degrees, which includes Common & Civil Law with French/Spanish (4 years). There's also a Law with Politics, and non-Law graduates may opt for a 2-year full-time or 3-year part-time Senior Status Law Degree here.

Computer programmers pour off a 4-year sandwich Business Information Technology BSc, there are BEng and BSc Computer Science, both 4-year sandwich, and a 4/5-year MEng Computer Science (the extra year in industry).

For teaching, it's largely St Mary's University College, Belfast. Output: 23% Secondary, 77% Primary. Roman Catholic teacher training college recently given UC status with a broader, less vocational syllabus including such as BA Liberal Arts. Degrees awarded by Queen's. Stranmillis University College is another Belfast university college closely involved with training Queen's Uni students to become teachers. Output: 20% Secondary, 80% Primary.

SOCIAL SCENE

STUDENTS' UNION There are various SU pleasure zones – the plush **Speakeasy Bar** with big screen sport, pub quizzes, Playstation challenge and hedonistic nights on the pull, the subterranean **Bunatee Bar** and intimate venue, **Bar Sub**, **Mandela Hall** (capacity: 1000, one of the best live venues in Belfast, home to the **Underground** and the Comedy Network) and **Varsity** (just round the corner from the Union buidings).

Writes Laura: 'The Union is a hub of activity during term time and the long opening hours mean you can always pop in to grab something to eat or drink or even to buy some paper to print those essays on... Every night there is something going on - usually in the dingy **Speakeasy**, or there are cheap comedy nights in **Mandela Hall**. Although the **Mandela Hall** supports local talent by showcasing local acts on Thursday's, the best music venues are to be found in the city. Northern Ireland's Ash as headlining act meant that last year's Fresher's ball was a big success. Every department within the university seems to have its own social events so there's no shortage of pub crawls/balls to attend.

'A typical week's ents is Monday: *Student Anthems* in **Speakeasy**; Tues: *Motherfunk*, free before 11pm and very cheap spirits; Society's Quiz Night; Wed: hip hop and r&r; Comedy Night in **Mandela Hall**; Thurs: *Radar Live* (showcase of local bands); Fri: *Good Friday* (all drinks £1.50 from 4pm till close); Sat: *Shine* – infamous house night (non-Union run). Recent live acts were Babyshambles and Fun Lovin' Criminals. Altogether the union building can take 2500 for entertainments.'

Naturally students are highly politicised, with a strong focus on Northern Ireland politics, but also on student issues. The union is generally characterised as nationalist and left of centre.

Student media is generally rather poor. Newspaper is *The Gown* (Laura gives it 4/10). More independent publications are such as the polemic, *The Vacuum* ('had many run-ins with Belfast City council resulting in a 'Sorry' day about the city earlier this year...)'. A radio station is just

---

ACADEMIC EXCELLENCE

TEACHING:
(Rated Excellent or 17+ out of 24)

Applied Social Work, History, Law, English, Geology, Music.	**Excellent**
Elec & Electron Engineering, Dentistry, Psychology, Economics/Accountancy	24
Management , Archaeology, Education, Physics, Politics, Classics, Celtic Studies	23
Civil Eng, Enviro Planning, Medicine, Anatomy, Maths, Nursing, Theology	22
Iberian Studies; Chemical Engineering; Mechanical, Aeronautical & Manufacturing Engineering, Food Sci, Agric, Podiatry, Biosciences, Philosophy	21
French	20
Sociology, Modern Languages (German, Italian, Russian & E. Euro languages).	19

RESEARCH:
Top grades 5/5*

Mechanical/Aeronautical/ Manufacturing Engineering.	**Grade 5***
Community-based Clinical Subjects, Physics, Civil Eng, Electrica & Electronic Eng , Law, Anthropology, Politics, Sociology, European Studies, Irish Studies, Celtic Studies, English, Archaeology, History, Music	**Grade 5**

setting up and going on air.

Queen's clubs and societies are legion, but most of the Irish students at Queen's clear off home at the weekend to get their washing done and to raid the family fridge. There's a very good cinema on campus – called Queen's Film Theatre – which runs a film club, a short films festival, and lots of arthouse films every day of the week. £2.50 on Monday, as it's student night. Its also £2.50 on Tuesdays (*Crazy Tuesday* it's called) at the Moviehouse on Dublin Road – for all films.

SPORT They have two swimming pools (diving, subaqua, water polo and canoeing facilities), conditioning rooms, squash courts, badminton, basketball, tennis courts, volleyball, handball, hockey, netball courts, two judo squares, cricket nets, a

AT A GLANCE

ACADEMIC FILE:

Subjects assessed	**44**
Excellent	**84%**
Typical entry requirements	**350 points**
Application acceptance rate	**19%**
Med. School acceptance rate	**39%**
Subjects assessed	**17:1**
First/2:1 degree pass rate	**63%**

ACCOMMODATION FILE:

Guarantee to freshers	**100%**
Style	**Flats, houses**
Catered	**None**
En suite	**50%**
Approx price range pw	**£56-£79**
City rent pw	**£45**

WHAT IT'S REALLY LIKE

UNIVERSITY:

Social Life	★★★★
Campus scene	**Craic is good**
Student Union services	**Good**
Politics	**Yes**
Sport	**Competitive**
National team position	**74th**
Sport facilities	**Improving**
Arts opportunities	**Cinema excellent; theatre poor**
Student newspaper	**The Gown**
Venue/bars	**Speakeasy, Bunatee, Bar Sub, Mandela Hall, Varsity**
Union ents	**Shine (infamous house), Good Friday + live acts**
Live venue capacity	**1,000**
Union societies	**100**
Parking	**Adequate**

CITY:

Entertainment	★★★
City scene	**Clubs, pubs, arts**
Town/gown relations	**Generally OK**
Risk of violence	**Average-high**
Cost of living	**Low**
Student concessions	**Good**
Survival + 2 nights out	**£65 pw**
Part-time work campus/town	**Average**

purpose-built mountain wall and facilities for gymnastics, athletics, fencing, golf, karate, bowls, yoga and archery, seventeen pitches for rugby, soccer, gaelic, hockey, hurling, camogie and cricket, netball and tennis courts, a floodlit training area and an athletics arena where the Mary Peters Track is situated. Opportunities for golf at Malone Golf Club (3 miles away), sailing at Belfast Lough and Lough Neagh, waterskiing at Craigavon, gliding and parachuting at Magilligan, mount-aineering in the Mourne mountains, caving in Fermanagh and rowing on the nearby River Lagan. Fifteen sports bursaries are available, sponsored by Guinness. Use of the pool or gym costs a mere £1 and is located a 5-minute walk from campus. When renovations to the P.E.C are complete, they'll have Northern Ireland's largest sports facility on the doorstep.

PILLOW TALK

Five additional en-suite apartments opened in September 2006, one in January 2007, and three open in September 2007. Each apartment accommodates 33 students.

'Most freshers are allocated rooms in the Queen's Elms halls of residence,' writes Laura. 'These 60s monstrosities are a 20-minute walk from campus and although the tower blocks can seem rather bleak there are new cafés and bars being built on the site, which will create a better atmosphere. All the room facilities such as internet connections and en-suite bathrooms are excellent. If you're lucky enough to get a place in any of the university-owned houses then Mount Charles just off Botanic Avenue or Guthrie house on Fitzwilliam Street are the best of the bunch.

'In general, though, living in privately-owned accommodation is much cheaper so most students move out once they finish the first year. Most students live in South Belfast, along or off the Lisburn or Ormeau Road and rent per month varies from as little as £130 to £200 a month. Stranmillis, just a ten minute walk from the campus, is the most sought-after area, though naturally as a result it's a bit pricier – all to be expected if you want a BT9 postcode.'

GETTING THERE

☞ An hour by air from London, with at least 24 flights a day each way.

STUDENT BELFAST – THE CITY

TENSIONS

Town/gown relations are good and local businesses tend to recruit heavily from the university. Recent tension in the Holylands between students and residents has meant that the university comes down very hard on any students thought to be displaying 'anti-social behaviour'. Good community relations are very important and as such there are many local volunteering and work experience opportunities on offer at the uni careers service.

Belfast is one of those places that is stereotyped over and over again – descriptions such as 'divided', 'troubled', 'industrial' and 'the wettest place on earth' all come to mind. There are re-occurring sets of binaries that fracture the city: politically, socially and religiously. And whether you are from Northern Ireland or not, these fractures cannot be ignored, but this doesn't mean the city can't overcome such problems and enjoy itself.

Despite the tensions and occasional setbacks (the riots and fires of last October caused blockades and chaos around the city for several days), Belfast is a lively and great place to live. It's a small and compact city so you'll soon find your way around. The new bus system is cheap and efficient and as such you'll rarely find it necessary to get a train anywhere – they're far too pricey anyway. Unless you have a car already, don't get one to live in Belfast – driving around the city can be a nightmare.

Central and South Belfast is the focus for most of student life. Botanic gardens are a haven away from the busy city; the green is packed in the summer and there's often a brass band playing on the bandstand by the rose garden. Inside the gardens you'll find the pretty **Palm House** and also the **Ulster Museum**, which tends to show interesting contemporary art and houses the permanent 'Ireland in Conflict' exhibition. Botanic Avenue and Dublin Road lead the way from the city to the University area – a mere 15-minute walk.

Apart from the stunning white marble **City Hall** and several redbrick Victorian buildings (**The Linen Hall** and **Marks & Spencer**), the rest of the centre is fairly unspectacular. The waterside is still being developed although the **Waterfront Hall** and the **Odyssey Complex** are already good music and entertainment venues, and along and near Royal Avenue there are the usual High Street stores, lots of secondhand bookshops, plus, off Queen's Street, some pricier boutiques. But if you want to do any serious shopping, take the 2-hour train journey to Dublin. It is well worth it.

CRAIC

As a newcomer to Belfast you'll soon learn the true meaning of the famous 'craic'. People really know how to go out and have a great time here. Bars and pubs are plentiful (though very smoky!) – from trendy 'sit-in-and-be-seen' cocktail bars, such as **The Apartment**, to traditional taverns such as **Whites**. In the city centre the Cathedral quarter contains the lovely **John Hewitt** pub (with an excellent choice of ales & beers) and **The Spaniard** – a great bar with quirky décor and fantastic music – serves tapas and light meals. **The Kitchen Bar** in the nearby **Cornmarket** is very classy and holds a jazz night every Monday. Going away from the city centre and leading towards the uni area, **Katie Daly's** and the **Limelight** are well known for their student-orientated theme nights. Closer to Queen's there's always a good atmosphere in **Auntie Annies** while **The Bot** and **The Egg** (off Eglantine Avenue) are convenient and cheap student dives (**The Egg** does a £5 Sunday roast). Though the variety of nightclubs doesn't really rival that of pubs, there are a couple worth checking out – **Milk** and **The Pothouse** being the best of the bunch. Although there isn't much of a gay/lesbian scene in Belfast there are a couple of sympathetic clubs in the cathedral quarter: **The Cremlin** and **The Nest**.

ART

Belfast is full of poets and musicians and as such there's always a poetry reading or a band playing in a pub nearby. All music events are listed in the free pamphlet – *The List*, or you can find full entertainment listings in the *Belfast Telegraph* on a Friday. Traditional music sessions can usually be heard at **Whites**, **The John Hewitt** or **Kelly's Tavern**, while folk or rock bands often play in **Katie Daly's**, **The Empire** or **Auntie Annies**. **The Limelight**, **The Ulster Hall** and **The King's Hall** all host bigger bands – such as The Magic Numbers, K.T. Tunstall and Gabriel y Rodrigo.

Spring and autumn see lots of festivals in Belfast – such as the big Belfast Festival (all over the city), Between the Lines (literature & music – at **The Crescent Arts Centre**), Belfast Film Festival, the Cathedral Quarter Arts Festival and the new Holylands Arts Festival. Throughout the summer there are Irish festivals or fleadh held in West Belfast, and the **An Cultural Ann** (Culture Centre) on the Falls road has a lovely café and an Irish language book shop, where you can often hear local musicians.

Laura Cattell

UNIVERSITY OF READING

The University of Reading
Whiteknights
Reading RG6 6AH

TEL 0118 378 5439
FAX 0118 378 8924
EMAIL student.recruitment@reading.ac.uk
WEB www.reading.ac.uk

Reading University Students' Union
PO Box 230
Reading RG6 2AZ

TEL 0118 378 4100
EMAIL (see website)
WEB www.rusu.co.uk

VAG VIEW

*T*he *student body is far from being limited to the marauding agrics of popular legend. Reading's areas of academic strength cover a wider spectrum than many imagine – cybernetics, classics, environmental sciences, agriculture, meteorology, film & theatre.*

We know, too, that investment remains high - a Student Services Building opens in Summer 2007, which will provide a one-stop-shop for student support and welfare; the sports facilities have recently been extended; and a new-look Student Union development was unveiled in February 2007.

Oddly, however, their performance in the graduate-track employment league table has been erratic of late, and they showed one of the smallest increases in applications this year, which was a bumper one nationally.

Finally, it has just been announced that Physics, which has been a big thing at Reading, one of 5 departments that scored full marks at the assessments, is to close by 2010. No more applications are sought.

CAMPUS

Writes Laura Cattell: 'Set in the leafy Whiteknights grounds on the outskirts of the town Reading maintains a close campus atmosphere while being only a stone's throw from the bright lights of London. One and a half miles from the town centre the University actually has two campuses – the larger Whiteknights where most undergraduates study and live and then the smaller Bulmershe, a further mile out of the city (home of Education faculty and unlucky Erasmus students who didn't get a place in halls on the main campus).'

FEES, BURSARIES

UK & EU Fees, 2007: £3,070 p.a. If eligible for full HE Maintenance grant there's a bursary of £1300; if in receipt of partial grant, bursaries are on a sliding scale from £330 to £1,320, according to household earnings. There are £2,000 entrance scholarships for firm-choice applicants with requisite points in departments of Agriculture, Biology, Chemistry, Classics, Film, Theatre & Television, Food Biosciences, History of Art, ICMA, Management, Mathematics, Modern Languages, Natural Sciences, Pharmacy, Politics, Systems Engineering; and Typography. Music scholarships yield £800 p.a. Sports scholarships for successful applicants of county or national standard are worth £1,500-£500 plus free use of a selected facility. UK undergraduates from a Berkshire state school may be awarded £1,000, and £500 p.a thereafter.

STUDENT PROFILE

Life is relaxed and sport-orientated at Reading and the majority of students are southern and well-heeled, many of them from public schools. However, there is also a large take from overseas, and an increasing take (22%) from among families new to the idea of university. 'Nevertheless,' says Laura, 'despite the government's widening participation scheme and a huge influx of international students, the uni still retains an upper to middle class/middle England feel.'

ACADEMIA & JOBS

Reading's reputation may be for agriculture, land management, cybernetics, food and soil sciences, but there's a huge range of arts, humanities, education, languages, and social studies courses, and Education is the single biggest graduate job market at Reading. Still, the sparkling exterior of the ISMA building (Investment Banking, International Security, and Finance) and the hi-tech Agri Department dominate one's image of the place.

All undergraduates are matched with a personal tutor, a constant for the duration. This can work well as long as you attend some lectures and meet with him/her when you're meant to. Within your undergraduate degree it's possible to take courses in other departments and taking on a free language class (part of the IWLP - Institution-wide Language Programme) is also a good way to supplement your studies and gain a further qualification. You can also take more free courses in the Library if you feel the need to update your computer skills or learn to use electronic databases more effectively.

They are big providers in accountancy – three degrees, two with Economics (one BSc), the other with Management, and there is great employment strength in both finance and business management.

Five per cent of Reading graduates go into architecture, and more into the construction business. We are talking here about a BSc in Building Construction & Management and one in Construction Management & Surveying that gives you the entire construction process, from brief to architect through design, planning and project completion. The Chartered Institute of Building (CIOB) grants membership after two years experience. Teaching inspection Excellent. Research Grade 5. See also BSc Building Surveying

Electronic Engineering – B/MEng – with Computer Science, Cybernetics, etc ensures a fast flow of graduates into electronics and telecommunications engineering, and if you fancy tinkering with control systems in electronic devices, look at their Cybernetics & Control Engineering (also 4-year MEng) – there's been a lot in the press about this. This year there's a new BSc Systems Engineering and BSc Robotics. Cybernetics also

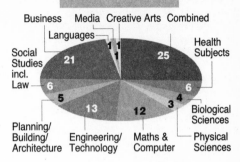

SUBJECT AREAS (%)

mixes with Computer Science (BSc or MEng). Reading scores highly with employers for software consultancy & supply and in IT consultancy.

Farmers know this as the top-rated research establishment, and very strong on Agricultural Business Management, but also other sorts of management - Rural Resource, Landscape, Habitat & Soil. Also very big in Food Science, with Business, or Food Technology.

Aspiring curators study Zoology, Botany &

UNIVERSITY/STUDENT PROFILE	
University since	**1926**
Situation/style	**Campus**
Student population	**16160**
Undergraduates	**10786**
- mature	**13%**
- non EU undergraduates	**5%**
- male/female	**45/55**
- non-traditional student intake	**22%**
-state school sector	**83%**
- drop-out rate	**10%**
- undergraduate applications	**Down 0.7%**

Zoology for certain careers, and aspiring animal health technicians/nurses take Animal Science. Reading is also among the country's leaders for finding employment for landscape designers, plantsmen, gardeners. BSc Horticulture joins one of the best agric departments in the country with a Grade 5 international rating for research in Agriculture and Plant Sciences. See also the 4-year sandwich BSc Landscape Management. Teaching inspection 21. Research Grade 5.

Geography, Rural Environmental Science, Rural Resource Mgt, Land Mgt – this is all mainstream Reading. This year there's a new BSc Applied Ecology & Conservation. Other useful niches for jobs include cartography – Physical

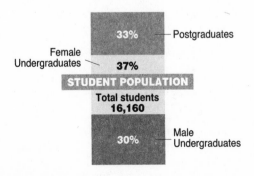

STUDENT POPULATION

Total students
16,160

Postgraduates 33%
Female Undergraduates 37%
Male Undergraduates 30%

ACADEMIC EXCELLENCE

TEACHING:
(Rated Excellent or 17+ out of 24)

Geography, Mechanical Engineering, Environmental Sciences, Geology.	**Excellent**
Drama, Dance & Cinematics, Physics, Philosophy, Nursing, Psychology	**24**
History of Art, Typography, Archaeology	**23**
Sociology, Land & Property Mgt, Town/Country Planning, Food Science, Maths, Politics, Classics	**22**
Economcs, French, Building, Forestry & Agric Sciences, Anatomy, American Studies, Business, Biosciences, Elec/Electron Eng.	**21**
Italian, German	**20**
Linguistics, Art & Design	**19**

RESEARCH:
Top grades 5/5*/6*

Psychology, Environmental Sciences, English, Italian, Archaeology	**Grade 6***
Agriculture, Plant Sciences, Food Science, Applied Maths, Electrical and Electronic Eng, Built Environment, Town/Country Planning, Law, Politics, Business, French, Philosophy, Typography, Drama/Dance/Performing Arts	**Grade 5**

Physical Health. Also Drama, which finds its place among Film & Theatre degrees and BA Theatre Arts Education & Deaf Studies, and with English, of course, which has a world class Grade 6* for research.

Educational Studies with Art/Music/English to primary level is only part of the story for teachers. Language graduates find jobs as lecturers in further education (French 21 points at assessment, Italian and German 20, Linguistics 19), as do many graduates from the famous Faculty of Letters & Social Sciences with its unique set of arts and social science mixes.

Humanities pack them into libraries and museums as curators, librarians, archivists; archaeologists abound (the dedicated degree leaving few hungry), and publishing is a very popular recourse from Reading. There's also a good track record for musicians. Music comes with languages and with History of Art – practical attainment important.

Library and computer resources are brilliant and there are 200 networked PCs in the main library and several other computer suites, some offering 24-hour access.

There are three main libraries – the main library on Whiteknight's campus, the music library, and Bulmershe library. The first is the largest with longest opening hours although Bulmershe can be a quieter choice to study in if you need to get away from any distractions.

That said there are plenty of big tables and study booths to be found on three floors of the main library. The demand for set texts is served by a short loan system and popular books are loaned out for 4hr/7day loans.

Geography and Meteorology. Reading's BSc Meteorology sits alongside one with a year in Oklahoma, and there's a Foundation year opportunity.

Top scoring assessments include Psychology. There are BA and BSc degrees, pairing with such as Biology, Philosophy, Childhood & Ageing, Mental &

Life is relaxed and sport-orientated at Reading and the majority of students are southern, many of them from public schools.

SOCIAL SCENE

STUDENTS' UNION
'The RUSU houses a student advice centre, large shop, off-licence, insurance outlet, student travel agency and three entertainment venues,' writes Laura. 'By day there are plenty of eateries and cafes

WHERE READING GRADUATES END UP

Health & Social Work: 8%; Education: 14%; Wholesale Retail: 8%; Manufacturing: 11%; Financial Activities: 9%; Public Administration, Civil Service & Defence: 8%; Hotel/Restaurant: 3%; Transport & Communications (including Telecommunications): 3%; Construction: 1.5%; Agriculture: 2%; Personnel:3.5%; Computer: 5.5%; Business & Management: 4%; Accountancy: 5%; Media (including Film): 1.5%; Legal 1%; Architecture: 5%; Publishing: 2%; Advertising: 1%.

Approximate employed **59%**

WHAT IT'S REALLY LIKE

UNIVERSITY:

Social Life	★★★★
Campus scene	**Middle class, southern, sporty.**
Student Union services	**Average**
Politics	**Strong internal**
Sport	**52 clubs**
National team position	**29th**
Sport facilities	**Good**
Arts opportunities	**Good, esp. drama**
Student newspaper	**Spark**
Student radio station	**Junction 11**
Nightclub	**3sixty**
Bars	**Mojo's, Breeze, Café Mondial, Bully's**
Union ents	**6 nights eclectic**
Union societies	**48**
Most active societies	**Campaigns Forum**
Parking	**Adequate**

TOWN:

Entertainment	★★★
Scene	**Pubs, clubs OK**
Town/gown relations	**Average**
Risk of violence	**Average**
Cost of living	**High**
Student concessions	**Good**
Survival + 2 nights out	**£90 pw**
Part-time work campus/town	**Excellent**

open to grab a cheap lunch while by night the impressive Union offers up **Mojos**, **Café Mondial** and **3sixty** as watering holes/dance floors. Wednesday and Saturday are the biggest nights at the Union - and the most expensive too. For a majestic £4 the Union offers up cheesy chart music, r&b, retro '70/'80s hits - and all with a few rugby/hockey players covered in snake bite&black thrown in for good measure. A cheaper alternative is Friday night at the refurbished **Breeze Bar** on Bulmershe campus. Before 11pm it's free and vodka shots cost just £1.

'The Union also occasionally attracts big bands such as Kosheen, Goldie Lookin' Chain and Travis, but regularly gets local bands to perform as well.

'The lively music department organises regular choir recitals and concerts. RUMS (Reading University Music Society) has a Choral Society, Gospel Choir and the also the more relaxed University Singers. There's also an orchestra, concert and jazz band, and it's home to the infamous Reading Rock Festival and the WOMAD world music festival, which liven up the town in the summer and offer up volunteer opportunities if you want a chance to see your favourite band for free.'

The HUB, within the Students Union is the central resource for students seeking any kind of advice or information, or backing/facilities for sports clubs and societies, the most active of which is Campaigns Forum. They also support around 1,500 volunteer groups of students working on projects within the local community. Despite Reading being a university focused on elite sportsmen and women at the expense of participation, students from around the campus have gained notable success in a wide range of activities from arts and music to firmly being at the heart of the student movement nationally. Reading is now a very active student community, demanding more from the student experience, though it's been a while since student media cut the mustard in the national awards.

'There is a student newspaper – *The Spark* – and the Union claims a 3,000 weekly run, but the quality has slipped over the years,' writes Laura. 'Nevertheless, it is a good opportunity to improve your writing skills and to learn how to use some of the computer software important for journalism today. Junction 11, the student radio station is accessible on campus and in halls. If you are interested in media, the way is open at Reading for a bit of ingenuity.

SPORT 'Sport is an integral part of life on campus. The sports facilities are excellent and most of the playing fields are on campus so whenever there's a big match there's a great atmosphere and everyone goes along to watch. The Wolfenden Sports Centre has a flashy gym and there are squash courts and several halls where most of the fitness classes and clubs/societies take place. £120 for six months may seem a bit steep at the beginning of term, but it does entitle you to use all facilities in the centre at

AT A GLANCE

ACADEMIC FILE:

Subjects assessed	**41**
Excellent	**81%**
Typical entry requirements	**342 points**
Application acceptance rate	**13%**
Students-staff ratio	**16:1**
First/2:1 degree pass rate	**65%**

ACCOMMODATION FILE:

Guarantee to freshers	**96%**
Style	**Halls, flats**
Catered	**50%**
En-suite	**40%**
Price range pw	**£61-£145**
City rent pw	**£70**

any time you like and you don't have to pay another penny after that.

Generally, team standards are pretty high, especially for women's netball and hockey.

Town 'Reading is set in picturesque countryside and pretty villages such as Sonning or Pangbourne are never far away if you fancy a walk along the river. Reading has bowed to the fashion for making every British town centre look exactly the same. There is the standard riverside development, known as the **Oracle**, full of chain restaurants and High Street stores. Look beyond the main High Street – to places like the Chinese supermarket or the **Global Café**. There are lots of good restaurants, especially Indian ones, but the best ones in town are **La Tasca** (Spanish/tapas style) and **Ninos**. Pubs and clubs-wise there's plenty of choice – **Café Iguana**, **Purple Turtle**, **Mangos** and the **Vodka Revolution** bar being among the best. And of course London and Oxford are only a 30-minute train ride away.'

PILLOW TALK

60–70% of first years are allocated catered hall accommodation, and if you want to make lectures in your first year, it's no bad idea. The best has to be Whiteknights, but equally fun and popular halls are Wantage, an Oxbridge-style building just off campus, but very close, St Patricks, and, for friendliness, Bridges. A redevelopment of St Georges Hall recently opened - 426 bedrooms, majority en-suite. If you're studying Education or Film & Drama you may be placed in modern Bulmershe halls, where there's a closer, friendlier, if quieter, atmosphere.

GETTING THERE

☛ By road: M4/J11, A33. An express bus service to London leaves from outside the university.
☛ By rail: London Paddington, 0:30; Birmingham, 2:15; Oxford, 0:40; Bristol Parkway, 1:00.
☛ By air: Heathrow and Gatwick.
☛ By coach: London, 1:20; Brighton, 3:45; Exeter, 3-5:00; Leicester, 5:00.

THE ROBERT GORDON UNIVERSITY

The Robert Gordon University
Aberdeen AB10 1FR
TEL 01224 262105
FAX 01224 262185
EMAIL admissions@rgu.ac.uk
WEB www.rgu.ac.uk

Robert Gordon Students' Association
Aberdeen AB10 1JQ
TEL 01224 262294
FAX 01224 262268
EMAIL rgusa@rgu.ac.uk
WEB www.rgunion.co.uk/

VAG VIEW

*R*obert Gordon is consistently in the UK Top 20 for getting its graduates real, 'graduate track' jobs. It owes its foundation to philanthropist Robert Gordon, from whose estate the Robert Gordon's Hospital was created in 1750, and which developed into a college half a century later. It is also the beneficiary of another Aberdeen entrepreneur, an architect by name of Tom Scott Sutherland, who presented them with the grounds and mansion at which the Scott Sutherland School of Architecture is based, a beautiful site overlooking the River Dee. Another of RGU's constituent parts is the Gray's School of Art, named after Aberdeen engineer John Gray; it was founded in 1885.

Now, they are investing £115 million over ten years to create four 'academic precincts' for art, business, health and technology - what they call 'the best riverside campus in Europe'.

CAMPUS

While the Students' Association and uni are based at the Schoolhill site in Aberdeen, 75% of RGU students are now taught at the Garthdee Campus on the south side of the city on the banks of the Dee. Over £60 million has been invested in the development of this campus in the last four years.

FEES

Non-Scottish-based UK residents pay £1,700 p.a. for all courses at Scottish universities, except Medicine, for which they will be charged £2,700 p.a. These will rise with inflation.

STUDENT PROFILE

There is a large state sector intake, many local (though a rapidly growing overseas contingent), many part-timers, a large (37%) intake from socio-economic classes 4-7, and a relatively high proportion of students (17%) from so-called low participation neighbourhoods. There are also a number of participants in RGU's Virtual Campus courses (for info, visit www.campus. rgu.com).

ACADEMIA & JOBS

The university has three faculties: The Aberdeen Business School, The Faculty of Health & Social Care and The Faculty of Design & Technology.

They make their traditional contribution to oil extraction and mining consultancy through Mechanical & Offshore Engineering, Mechanical & Environmental Engineering, etc, but that is no longer their defining area. There's now a major career focus in the area of health – nursing (adult, children, mental) radiography, nutrition, occupational therapy, physiotherapy are among the best from an employment point of view. There is a new, purpose-built Faculty of Health & Social Care building. See also their Biomedical Sciences degrees and the new MPharm Pharmacy; also Forensic Science (there's a traditional fast track into police work); and the BA and MSc (postgrad) Social Work.

In the Aberdeen Business School, they have great strength in the tourism and hospitality area – they are regularly No. 1 in Britain as graduate suppliers to the catering industry through dedicated degrees. Also, there's BA Retail Management, which accounts for a strong showing in retail (15% of graduates) and BA Accounting & Finance.

Look, too, at their in-depth strength in Computing – Artificial Intelligence, Electronic Engineering, Robotics, Computing for Graphics & Animation, Computer for Internet, for Mobile Applications, for Business.

And then there's the traditional good showing employment-wise in Built Environment – BSc Architectural Technology, Construction Design, Surveying (Quantity Surveying, a dedicated degree, is a particular strength). Three degrees: BSc Architecture, Architec. (European Practice) and Interior Architecture are recognised by RIBA. See, too, their Design for Industry programme – Digital Media, Graphic, Product Design degrees.

A longterm specialism in Law & Management has now been joined by a fully fledged LLB, recog-

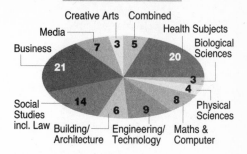

nised by the Law Society of Scotland.

Finally, there is now, too, a Sports Science degree, backed up by a multi-million pound sports and leisure centre at its new Garthdee Campus.

SOCIAL SCENE

STUDENTS' ASSOCIATION RGUnion has two bars in the Union building at Schoolhill which provide a wide range of entertainment 7 nights a week. Regular nights include: open mic, *Karaoke Idol*, r&b

UNIVERSITY/STUDENT PROFILE	
University since	**1992**
Situation/style	**Civic**
Student population	**12715**
Undergraduates	**8915**
- mature	**18%**
- non EU undergraduates	**3%**
- male/female	**34/66**
- non-traditional student intake	**37%**
state sector intake	**94%**
- drop-out rate	**19%**
- undergraduate applications	**Up 2%**

hip hop, *The Master Chill*, and everyone's disco favourite, *Thursday Night Fever*. The downstairs bar is available for private functions on Tuesdays and Sundays; students have recently used these nights for events such as speed dating and games like *Play Your Cards Right*.

The whole building is currently being refurbished and now provides a Volunteering Centre to help students gain recognition for unpaid work. The Union actively encourages students to get involved in university life by awarding recognised certificates for their volunteering efforts. A new Marketing and Communications Centre opened in January 2006, with up to date software that'll be used to develop the re-vamped student magazine, which goes by the name of *Cogno*.

AT A GLANCE

ACADEMIC FILE:

Subjects assessed	**21**
Excellent	**57%**
Typical entryl requirements	**306 points**
Application acceptance rate	**24%**
Students-staff ratio	**19:1**
First/2:1 degree pass rate	**54%**

ACCOMMODATION FILE:

Guarantee to freshers	**100%**
Style	**Flats**
Catered	**None**
En-suite	**20%**
Price range pw	**£65-£80**
City rent pw	**£35-£100**

SPORT The new Sports Centre will revolutionise things. There's hockey, athletics, rugby, rowing, football, archery, badminton, basketball, and of course all those outward bound activities – skiing, hill walking, etc, naturally available in this area.

ACADEMIC EXCELLENCE

TEACHING:
(Rated Excellent, Highly Satis. or 17+ out of 24)

Chemistry, Dietetics & Nutrition	**Excellent**
Physics, Business & Management, Graphic/Textile Design, Maths & Statistics, Mechanical & Manufacturing Eng, Architecture, Social Work, Pharmacy, Physiotherapy	**Highly Satis.**
European Languages	**19**

RESEARCH:
Top grades 5/5* **None**

PILLOW TALK

Accommodation is thin on the ground, and students' advice is to get in quick. There is a commendable lack of fuss, however, at the uni:

'Everyone who applies for accommodation,' they say, 'is usually allocated accommodation.' It consists of self contained, self-catering flats, six to eight sharing, all with own bedroom, 20% en suite. Price per week ranges from £65 to £80.

GETTING THERE

☞ By road: from south, A92, thence ring road for signs; from north, A96 or A92.
☞ By coach: London, 11.30; Newcastle, 7.35.

WHAT IT'S REALLY LIKE

UNIVERSITY:

Social Life	★★★
Campus scene	**Part-time, local but increasingly cosmopolitan**
Student Union services	**Poor**
Politics	**Interest low**
Sport	**9 clubs**
National team position	**87th**
Sport facilities	**New centre**
Arts opportunities	**Drama, dance, music good; film, art average**
Student magazine	**Cogno**
Nightclub/bars	**U-bar, Blue Iguana**
Union ents	**7 nights a week**
Union societies	**30**
Most active society	**Cogno**
Parking	**Adequate**

CITY:

Entertainment	★★★★
Scene	**Intoxicating**
Town/gown relations	**Good**
Risk of violence	**Low**
Cost of living	**Average**
Student concessions	**Average**
Survival + 2 nights out	**£60 pw**
Part-time work campus/town	**Good/excellent**

☞ By rail: London King's Cross, 7:00; Glasgow, 2:45; Edinburgh, 2:30; Newcastle, 4:30.
☞ By air: Aberdeen International Airport.

WHERE ROBERT GORDON GRADUATES END UP

Health & Social Work: 16%; Education: 3.5%; Wholesale Retail: 15%; Manufacturing: 6%; Financial Activities: 4%; Public Administration, Civil Service & Defence: 7%; Hotel/Restaurant: 4%; Transport & Communications (including Telecommunications): 3.5%; Construction: 2%; Mining/Oil Extracting: 18%; Personnel: 1%; Computer: 3%; Business & Management: 1.5%; Accountancy: 4%; Legal 1%; Architecture: 2%; Sport: 1%.

Approximate 'graduate track' employed **76%**

ROEHAMPTON UNIVERSITY

Roehampton University
Erasmus House
Roehampton Lane
London SW15 5PU

TEL 020 8392 3232
EMAIL enquiries@roehampton.ac.uk
WEB www.roehampton.ac.uk

Roehampton Students' Union
Froebel College
Roehampton Lane
London SW15 5PJ

TEL 020 8392 3221
EMAIL info@roehamptonstudent.com
WEB www.roehamptonstudent.com

VAG VIEW

*R*oehampton University offers vocational courses in the arts, education, social sciences, sciences and sports areas, but with a rather attractive, artistic and caring ethos, which is part and parcel of the place.

Of its four constituent colleges, Digby Stuart College (Arts & Humanities) has a Roman Catholic foundation; Froebel College (Education) follows the teachings of Friedrich Froebel, the caring chappie who invented kindergartens; Southlands College (Social Sciences) has a Methodist base; and Whitelands College (Science) has a Church of England base.

They are not, however, in the business of shoving this down your throat. Now, with university status, they have fathered their sometime scattered colleges into one campus in south west London, and things are look-ing very bright indeed.

CAMPUS

The uni's four colleges are cosily set together on the edge of Richmond deer park. Writes Becky Neaum: 'Roehampton University is situated in an affluent area of south west London, and within a 20-minute train ride of the central of the capital city. It is set within lush green grounds and only a fe minutes from Richmond Park; a 9-mile deer park. So, if you are torn between choosing country and city, and if you love the bright lights of the city, but also the peaceful landscape of the coun-try, then this University really is ideally located.'

'Roehampton combines the best aspects of liv-ing in London,' agrees Gina Wright. 'I cannot imag-ine a more perfect site – a peaceful green campus set in landscaped grounds with lakes and trees, yet near enough to buses and tubes to make the jour-ney into central London in about half an hour.'

Digby College has the **Belfry Bar**, a **Learning Resource Centre**, self-catering flats and a warm, welcoming atmosphere. Froebel College is domi-nated by the imposing, **Georgian Grove House**, its

period feel making it popular with students and TV productions such as *Inspector Morse*. It also has the music venue, Montefiore Hall.

Southlands, relocated from Wimbledon in 1997, is clean, modern and the musical pulse of the uni, with studios, a Steinway concert grand and a double-manual French harpsichord.

Whitelands founds its way here in 2004, and occupies an 18th-century Palladian mansion, Parkstead House, at the heart of campus.

FEES, BURSARIES

UK & EU Fees, 2007: £3,070 p.a. If in receipt of the Higher Education Maintenance grant, there's a £300 p.a. bursary. There are also academic achievement scholarships worth £1,000.

STUDENT PROFILE

A third of undergraduates come from the lowest four socio-economic classes, and 13% from so-called 'low participation' neighbourhoods, for whom university is a new experience. Only about

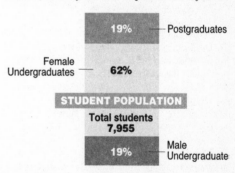

Postgraduates 19%

Female Undergraduates 62%

STUDENT POPULATION
Total students
7,955

Male Undergraduate 19%

7% come from the independent school sector. The application acceptance rate is high - more than a quarter who apply get in.

ACADEMIA

Continues Becky: 'It being a small university, the lecturers have time for the students, and it's true that you feel a name, not a number here. Lecture and seminar groups are relatively small, which allows for more interaction and discussion. Workloads are not immense. Pressure does build up towards the deadlines, but you are given plenty of time to do the work in. There is 24/7 Internet access in the library and in most halls.'

Faculties include Arts & Humanities, Education, Sciences, Social Sciences.

When it comes to graduate supply to primary teaching, Roehampton mounts a very strong case. Output: 93% Primary. They are renowned for their Drama and QTS courses and dropped only two points at their assessment (22 out of 24).

The teaching for biosciences is even better – 23 points at the assessments: BSc Biological Sciences, Biological Anthropology, Biomedical Sciences, Biology, Conservation Biology.

The religious background to the constituent colleges comes through in courses for the caring professions, such as healthcare and therapeutic work (and teaching too, under their particular educational regime). Look at the foundation course, Childcare and Early Years Education, and BSc Integrative Counselling, Counselling, Psychology & Counselling, Psychology, Psychology & Health, BA Early Childhood Studies, BSc Health & Social Care, Health Studies, and BA Human Rights.

Dance is outstanding. Their reputation is rated international Grade 5. Besides BA Dance Studies, BA Drama, Theatre & Performance Studies is also rated high, and their music and film courses are very popular. New to media, and much vaunted, is BA Journalism and News Media.

They are also among the leaders in getting jobs for graduates in sport – as players or sport officials. The BSc Sport & Exercise Science is the prototype, a good balance of Physiology, Biomechanics and Psychology.

SOCIAL SCENE

'Unlike other universities in the London area, Roehampton has its own, very beautiful campus, and campus life is brilliant,' writes Becky. 'It is a small uni, but sizeable enough for footy games, summer sports day and an amazing annual summer ball. It is friendly as well, with a huge mix of people from all walks of life and of all ages. This is one of the first things that attracted me to Roehampton. Freshers Week was a fantastic experience here. The first week, although daunting at times, was packed with things to do, day and night, and by the end of it I felt truly settled in. Now in my second year, I live no longer in hall, but in a house off campus with friends I made in halls. The social life is still abundant, if not better than the first year. The social scene off campus is rich and varied; with many student nights at nightclubs just a bus ride away, such as **Oceana**, **Cheapskates** and the **Hammersmith Palais**. Putney is our local pub haunt, where you can get a reasonably priced pint; it is not too expensive considering this is London. I'd say £20 would be average for a big night.'

Each of the four campuses has its own bar. Ents are OK. In the week this is being written, Thursday is Bands Night, featuring, for example, Last Gang In Town, Blue Mojo, Dancing Bears at **Belfry Bar**, Digby. Friday, at Froebel, is invariably *The Bop: Heaven or Hell*, or *Vicars and Tarts*, or some other theme. Monday might be comedy at the **Lounge**. Wednesday, Sports Night, is held at **Fez Club**, in nearby Putney. They have things with **Hammersmith Palais**, too. Events, such as fashion shows or the long-running *Roehampton Idol* might be held at **Monte Hall**. There are also balls, the year culminating in the infamous, extravagant Summer Ball. Froebel boasts the second largest ball after Oxford and Cambridge.

Societies tend to be transient. Large and long-standing socs are RIACAS, which promotes Afro-Caribbean and Asian culture, and top soc. Open Mic. There's a monthly newspaper, *Fresh*, and other societies spin off undergraduate courses.

Writes Gina: 'I enjoy the many reasonably priced concerts promoted by the active Dance

WHAT IT'S REALLY LIKE

UNIVERSITY:

Social Life	★★★
Campus scene	**Diverse, friendly**
Student Union services	**Good**
Politics	**Apathetic**
Sport	**Keen**
National team position	**119th**
Sport facilities	**Poor**
Arts opportunities	**Very good**
Student newspaper	**Fresh**
Venue	**Monte Hall, RSU Lounge, Belfry Bar**
Bars	**College bars**
Union ents	**Chav Night, Heaven or Hell + live bands**
Union societies	**25**
Parking	**Poor (permit)**

CITY:

Entertainment	★★★★★
Scene	**Wild, expensive**
Town/gown relations	**Average-good**
Risk of violence	**High**
Cost of living	**Very high**
Student concessions	**Abundant**
Survival + 2 nights out	**£80 pw**
Part-time work campus/town	**Excellent**

AT A GLANCE

ACADEMIC FILE:

Subjects assessed	**16**
Excellent	**69%**
Typical entry requirements	**229 points**
Application acceptance rate	**26%**
Students-staff ratio	**21:1**
First/2:1 degree pass rate	**50%**
Graduate track employment	**50%**

ACCOMMODATION FILE:

Guarantee to freshers	**60%**
Style	**Halls, houses**
Catered	**13%**
Price range p.w.	**£85-£114**
City rent pw	**£100-£180 Zone 1; £75-£85 Zone 2**

library too. Off campus, there are plenty of shops and cafes nearby where students often find part time work. The university's career centre advertises all sorts of part time work all year round.'

SPORT Roehampton competes in the BUSA leagues, and a local rivalry with Kingston Uni adds spice to the rugby especially. Also popular are tennis, football and rowing on the Thames. Each college has its own teams, and the football battles between the Digby Lions and their 'natural prey', the Froebel Zebras, are legendary.

PILLOW TALK

'Accommodation at Roehampton ranges from typical halls, with up to 25 or so people sharing a floor, and all facilities, to flats of 6 to 10 with private facilities,' Becky writes.

Two new student residences opened in 2004. All Colleges cater for vegetarians. There are some en-suite ground floor rooms for students with disabilities. They allocate rooms on a 'first come, first served basis', so get onto it fast.

GETTING THERE
☛ US Roehampton, Barnes British Rail station or No. 72 bus from Hammersmith Underground; No. 265 runs from Putney Bridge.

Department. A series of open events in the outstanding **Michaelis Theatre** attracts audiences from both inside and outside the university. Students are given every opportunity to perform their own works, view professional companies and share the results of collaborating with well known dance companies.'

COST OF LIVING Says Becky: 'I spend £85 a week on accommodation, £25 a month on bills, and £40 a month on food. Going out money ranges from £5-£20 a week, depending on what I do. This is my personal budget, and in this way I have managed to avoid taking out an overdraft. Part time jobs are readily available for students who can be bothered to search for one; I have a part time job at the university. I work in the enquiries office, and in the packing room and on campus tours on Open Days. There are jobs available in the bars and in the

ROYAL ACADEMY OF MUSIC

The Royal Academy of Music
Marylebone Road
London NW1 5HT

TEL 020 7873 7373
FAX 020 7873 7374
EMAIL registry@ram.ac.uk
WEB www.ram.ac.uk

A collaboration between the Royal Academy and King's College, both of London University, is what distinguishes the BMus degree. Academy musicians benefit academically by attending lectures at KCL, King's undergraduates from the performance culture at the Royal Academy. There is a diverse student mix, with 40+ countries represented. London University halls of residence are available.

ROYAL AGRICULTURAL COLLEGE

The Royal Agricultural College
Cirencester
Gloucestershire GL7 6JS

TEL 01285 652912
FAX 01285 650219
EMAIL admissions@rac.ac.uk
WEB www.rac.ac.uk

The college runs the largest agri-student European exchange programme in the country, and it's the principal's boast that there's 'hardly a major farming/business or land-management employer in the UK and beyond that who doesn't have a former RAC student in a decision-making position.'

Accommodation is guaranteed for first years. There is a bar, a union, and sport is big news.

ROYAL COLLEGE OF MUSIC

The Royal College of Music
Prince Consort Road
London SW7 2BS

TEL 020 7589 3643
FAX 020 7589 7740
EMAIL info@rcm.ac.uk
WEB www.rcm.ac.uk

The famed 4-year BMus is joined by BSc Hons Physics with Studies in Musical Performance, an exciting cross-faculty joint venture with world-class Imperial College nearby. Halls accommodation is available. A Student Association promotes ents. Students use Imperial's local Sports Centre.

ROYAL HOLLOWAY, LONDON UNIVERSITY

Royal Holloway College
Egham
Surrey TW20 0EX

TEL 01784 434455
FAX 01784 473662
EMAIL liaison-office@rhul.ac.uk
WEB www.rhul.ac.uk

Royal Holloway Students' Union
Egham
Egham TW20 0EX

TEL 01784 486300
FAX 01784 486312
EMAIL reception@su.rhul.ac.uk
WEB www.surhul.org.uk

VAG VIEW

Royal Holloway, a college of London University, is situated on a 120-acre campus at Egham in Surrey, far enough to the south west of London's bright lights to favour a well-focused regime. Students almost uniformly mention the workload, although there is a lively campus social scene too. The regime is very productive: there's a 14:1 student: staff ratio and 67% of students obtain firsts or upper second class degrees.

CAMPUS

'Holloway, isn't that a women's prison?' iterates Sarah Toms with a sigh which suggests she has heard the jibe many times before. 'It is of course, but not here, it's in South London! You'll get used to that question. This is *Royal* Holloway, University of London – yes, the one with THAT building (Founders Hall). Located a train ride from central London – forty minutes on a good day, barring leaves on the line or the wrong kind of snow.'

It has been called 'London's Country Campus', and it is certainly a beautiful spot, made distinctive by Founder's Building, a copy of the Chateau de

Chambourd in the Loire built by Thomas Holloway, who in 1886 founded a college for women there. Nearly a century later it merged with another all-female foundation, Bedford College, creating Royal Holloway and Bedford New College. You may be interested to know that there is still a preponderance of females here today.

FEES, BURSARIES

UK & EU Fees, 2007: £3,000 p.a. If eligible for a HE Maintenance Grant, there's a bursary of £500 p.a. There are also the Founder's Scholarship - £3,500 p.a., and Bedford Scholarships - up £1,000 p.a. Other awards are made through the Talented Athlete Recognition Scheme - up to £750 p.a., and the Lyell Bursaries in Geology - up to £500 p.a., the Bioscience Entrance Scholarships and Physics Bursaries - both up to £1,000 for the first year of undergraduate study. There are also choral and organ scholarships - up to the value of £500 p.a. and £1,000 p.a. respectively, and instrumental scholarships/RCM exhibitions - £300 tenable for one year (renewable) and £200. Finally, they offer computer science scholarships - up to £1,000 during the first year of study, renewable at the rate of £500 for years two and three.

STUDENT PROFILE

The student body is small, little more than a third the size of King's College or University College, London. Public school intake is high, as it is from overseas (the relatively new African-Caribbean society is among the strongest in the Union). They're a very happy crew: only 6% don't finish.

ACADEMIA & JOBS

University of London degrees are offered in biological and physical sciences, maths, computer science, humanities, languages, arts, social sciences and management. Their success in the teaching assessments include full marks for Psychology and Biosciences, 23 points out of 24 for Drama, Physics and Classics, 22 for Maths, and 21 for languages,

UNIVERSITY/STUDENT PROFILE	
School of London Uni since	**1800**
Situation/style	**Campus**
Total student population	**7736**
Undergraduates	**5470**
- mature	**12%**
- non EU undergraduates	**19%**
- male/female	**44/56**
- non-traditional student intake	**24%**
- state school intake	**77%**
- drop-out rate	**6%**
- undergraduate applications	**Up 14%**

Sociology, and Business.

It's a well balanced mix, more so when you see that they have developed a course unit method study that allows groupings of subjects across an often imaginative spectrum. For example, Latin is offered as a BA single hons, but also with English (a tantalising prospect for students of syntax and etymology). The English department has a national reputation for research. The Creative Writing course has benefited from the attentions of poet

laureate Andrew Motion, Holloway's Professor of Creative Writing, and some of his students have achieved publication. Meanwhile, this year Creative Writing Fellow, Giles Foden, has seen the film adaptation of his first novel *The Last King of Scotland*, directed by Kevin Macdonald, win The Alexander Korda Award for the Outstanding British Film of the Year and the Best Adapted Screenplay at the BAFTA Awards. Clearly, there is a markedly practical shift to creative writing at Holloway.

Languages are clearly another strength. French and German were rated world class at the research assessments. The International Building incorporates the English, French, German, Hispanic and Italian departments, a dedicated Japanese Studies section (including the Noh theatre – donated by the Japanese government), and

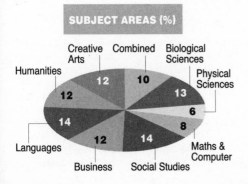

TEACHING:
(Rated Excellent or 17+ out of 24)

History, Geology,	**Excellent**
Psychology, Organismal	**24**
Biosciences	
Drama, Theatre & Media Arts,	**23**
Physics, Classics	
Maths	**22**
French, Italian, Sociology,	**21**
Molecular Biosciences, Business	
German	**19**

RESEARCH:
Top grades 5/5*/6*

Geography, French, Music	**Grade 6***
German/Dutch/Scandinavian	**Grade 5***
Drama/Dance/Performing Arts,	**Grade 5**
History, Classics, English,	
Computer, Pure Maths, Earth	
Sciences, Biology, Physics,	
Psychology	

a stylish café. Languages and European Studies, Literature, Culture are frequent course elements.

The Drama & Media Arts provision (which took an international Grade 5 for research) lands graduates real jobs in such as publishing, radio, TV, film, advertising and market research. Music also has a world-class reputation (Grade 6* for research; there's a link with the Royal College of Music) and can be studied as a single hons or with Maths or BA Psychology, or taken with a year abroad, a language thrown in.

Accountants proliferate. The number of independent school applicants and strength of Maths, Management (note BSc Management with Accounting) and Economics help to ensure this.

Management also hooks up with Marketing, with Human Resources (another strong take-up for jobs), and with Information Systems and Technology & Operations. While the Computer Science facility produces numbers of software engineers, computer analysts/programmers, systems analysts, IT consultants, etc.

Science looks to be the new way forward here, with interesting developments in biological science – a degree in Molecular Biology & Genetics recently. And the 23/24 teaching rating (and Grade 5 for research) for Physics is leading to a new BSc degree in Astrophysics and another in Physics with

Particle Physics, which already figures in a fine list of MSci degrees.

Geography is another science with a world class reputation here (Grade 6* for research).

That science is now a main current of academic policy here is confirmed by their offering a science foundation course to partner colleges in the region, and by the more recent collaboration in 'a super healthcare university' with St George's Hospital and Kingston universities within the disciplines of health, biomedical sciences and business education, following a £4 million grant.

SOCIAL SCENE

STUDENTS' UNION The college is largely self-sufficient and most students spend their social hours on site, rather than succumbing to the distant twinkling lights of London. Frankly, the hour-long hike to the capital is seen as a hassle by most, as the last train back is at 11:30 pm, with no more links until 6 am the next day.

In contrast to the friendly, welcoming campus, the nearest town, Egham, remains aloof, a cultural and social pit of suburban blandness.

To compensate for the paucity of local entertainment, the SU serves up a social calendar of unprecedented fullness for an establishment of this size.

Every night is an ents night of some description, ranging from the usual pub quizzes on quiet Sundays to the late bars and DJs which dominate weekends and have a significant foothold in the working week as well.

There's a late licence five nights a week, main hall functions two to three times a week, bar ents every other night. How many unions boast two resident DJs poached from the brighter lights of London? Both Brandon Block and DJ Swing are employed to keep the body student moving, and the latter has been known to hurl the crispest of currency into the crowd too, enhancing popularity and drinks consumption in equal measure. Imported additions include Ministry of Sound, A1, Trevor Nelson, Apollo 440.

Tommy's is the newest bar in the union, and the most popular haunt of the socialites. Only Tuesday and Sunday see it shut before midnight, so the quiet beer with a friend at nine has a sneaky habit of turning into eight loud beers with a roomful of pissheads by kicking out time.

The **Dive Bar**, attached to Tommy's, isn't as seedy as it sounds, and offers a cosier venue. The

> *The student body is small; public school intake is high, as it is from overseas. They're a happy crew: only 6% don't finish.*

WHERE ROYAL HOLLOWAY GRADUATES END UP
Health & Social Work: 7%; Education: 8%; Wholesale Retail: 14%; Manufacturing: 9%; Financial Activities: 12%; Public Administration, Civil Service & Defence: 8%; Hotel/Restaurant: 3%; Transport & Communications (including Telecommunications): 4%; Personnel: 6%; Computer: 4%; Business & Management: 5%; Accountancy: 4%; Media (including Film): 3%; Legal 2%; Publishing: 3%; Advertising: 1%.

Approximate 'graduate track' employed **67%**

Union Bar is a pretty standard affair, and it is these three which combine to hold 1200 for the big function nights – it has its own in-house technical crew.

Also on campus is the strangely named **Stumble Inn** ('Stumble Out' would surely have been more appropriate), a pub to all intents and a popular one at that, ideal for those nights when aggravating your tinnitus shies you from Tommy's.

Holloway's Bar houses sixteen pool tables, dart boards and a host of ever-changing video games, a free Playstation for the deprived, and live sports courtesy of the ubiquitous Sky TV.

There is also the coffee bar, **TW20's**, a food and caffeine establishment that, according to some, is lamentable, but being dirt cheap and on campus attracts students like flies around the proverbial.

Every June they run a Summer Ball in the quads of Founders: 2000 tickets are sold in exchange for big name acts, cocktail bar, Champagne bar, Glastonbury stage, dance tent, fairground rides, hog roast – it runs from 7 until 7 all through the night.

Media, drama and entertainments in general, are of a high standard. The Musical Theatre Society goes to the Edinburgh Fringe. The radio station, 1287 Insanity, took Silver at last year's national media awards (Best Male Presenter), and the student mag, *Orbital*, was nominated for three awards and won Best Magazine. Politics, on the other hand, are less of a preoccupation.

SPORT The college has a reputation as the best sporting college in London University, and it does well in inter-LU leagues, though it languished at 70th position nationally last year.

A new sports complex has lifted it above its neighbours. Cricket, women's football have bossed the London indoor leagues for a few years, and men's rugby supplies players to senior sides, such as Harlequins and London Welsh.

TOWN 'Sadly, the surrounding area, quaint little Egham, with as many useful shops as you are likely to see students at a nine o'clock lecture, fails to happen,' Sarah Toms reports, 'though it does have three supermarkets, a covey of takeaways, a bevy

of student-friendly pubs, and **The Staines Massive**, which boasts not only a cinema, but wait for it... a *nightclub*! Those for whom the excitement proves too much, worry not. Royal Holloway is positioned a train ride away from the capital – deliberately, strategically even, to enable you to

WHAT IT'S REALLY LIKE	
UNIVERSITY:	
Social Life	★★★
Campus scene	**Active, friendly, artistic, female**
Student Union services	**Good**
Politics	**Big right now**
Sport	**36 clubs**
National team position	**60th**
Sport facilities	**Good**
Arts opportunities	**Drama excellent; music, film good; dance, art avg**
Student magazine	**The Orbital**
2006 National Awards	**3 nominations and Best Magazine**
Student radio	**1287 Insanity**
2006 National Awards	**Silver award**
Nightclub	**Union +Tommy's**
Bars	**Union, Tommy's, Stumble Inn, Holloway's, Dive**
Union ents	**Cheese, Spaced, Orgasmatron, etc**
Union societies	**99**
Most popular society	**James Bond Appreciation Soc**
Smoking policy	**No smoking**
Parking	**Adequate**
CITY:	
London	★★★★★
Local scene	**Good pubs, but London beckons**
Town/gown relations	**Good**
Risk of violence	**Low**
Cost of living	**High**
Student concessions	**Average**
Survival + 2 nights out	**£40 pw**
Part-time work campus/town	**Good/poor**

enjoy London life without paying a high price.

'Sure, the prices locally are higher than average, but not too damaging, and there is the advantage of the London loan rate and that both campus and surrounding area are fairly safe.

PILLOW TALK

'On the one hand, there is Founders Hall,' writes Sarah. 'Its rooms are fairly large and filled with an odd assortment of furniture from across the centuries. On the other, we have New Halls, built in the 1950s by an architect who won a prize for designing a Swedish prison! Affectionately known as 'Cell Block H', the rooms are, let us say, cosy...'

New Halls – Athlone, Cameron and Williamson – are catered and come with common rooms, bar, snack bar (**Times Square**), and a good community spirit. Founder's comes with common rooms, TV rooms, bar/snack bar (**Crossland Suite**); it's hard to get a room here. Reid Hall, near New Halls, is catered with en-suite rooms. Runnymede is self-catered, flat-style around a central kitchen/social area, en-suite.

Three halls – Beeches, Chestnuts, Elm Lodge – are converted Victorian houses, catered but with small kitchen/pantries and laundries. Kingswood is catered, off campus (but less than a mile away and with a free bus service to campus during the day)

AT A GLANCE	
ACADEMIC FILE:	
Subjects assessed	**19**
Excellent	**74%**
Typical entry requirements	**229 points**
Application acceptance rate	**15%**
Students-staff ratio	**14:1**
First/2:1 degree pass rate	**67%**
ACCOMMODATION FILE:	
Guarantee to freshers	**100%**
Style	**Halls, flats, houses**
Catered	**46%**
Approx price range pw	**£56-£104**
Average local rent pw	**£80**

and has rooms and flatlets on a hillside overlooking the Thames at Runnymede with squash and tennis courts, TV/common room, tapas bar and dining room.

GETTING THERE
☞ By road: M25/J13, A30.
☞ By rail: London Waterloo, 35 mins; Reading, 40.

ROYAL SCOTTISH ACADEMY OF MUSIC & DRAMA

Royal Scottish Academy of Music & Drama
100 Renfrew Street
Glasgow G2 3DB

TEL 0141 332 4101
FAX 0141 332 8901
EMAIL registry@rsamd.ac.uk
WEB www.rsamd.ac.uk

RSAMD is the only school for music and drama in Scotland. The curriculum explores Scottish music, in particular piping, as well as opera, composition and conducting. In theatre, there are degrees in

Technical & Production Arts, Digital Film & TV, and a Master of Performance in Musical Theatre.

Accommodation is available in halls. See Glasgow universities and Student City entries.

ROYAL WELSH COLLEGE OF MUSIC & DRAMA

The Royal Welsh College of Music & Drama
Cathays Park
Cardiff CF1 3ER

TEL 029 2034 2854
FAX 029 2039 1304
EMAIL info@rwcmd.ac.uk
WEB www.rwcmd.ac.uk

Music teaching involves the Welsh National Opera and the BBC National Orchestra of Wales. Performance is central; every student has a personal tutor. The Grade 2 listed Castle Mews next to the

Welsh conservatoire opened as the Anthony Hopkins Centre a year ago, providing new teaching, rehearsal and performance facilities.

No college accommodation available.

ROYAL VETERINARY COLLEGE

The Royal Veterinary College
Royal College Street
London NW1 0TU

TEL 020 7468 5148/9
FAX 020 7468 2342
EMAIL registry@rvc.ac.uk
WEB www.rvc.ac.uk

The RVC is a specialist college of London University that achieved full marks in the teaching assessments. All candidates must sit the Biomedical Admissions Test (BMAT) to assess scientific aptitude. The undergraduate programme includes Batchelor of Veterinary Medicine, BSc (Hons) Veterinary Pathology, BSc (Hons) Veterinary Sciences, BSc (Hons) Veterinary Nursing, BSc Intercalated courses, BSc (Hons)/BVet Med Combined Degree Programme. They excel, too, at extra-curricular activities, especially in Women's Rugby.

Your first two years are based in Camden, a fun place with its outdoor market, some very good pubs and well placed for city nightlife. Accommodation is in London University intercollegiate halls (£95-£115). In Year 3 it's off to 230-hectare Hawkshead campus, Potters Baaa, with its new Learning Resource Centre and Diagnostic Imaging Unit with the first uni-based CT scanner.

UNIVERSITY OF ST ANDREWS

The University of St Andrews
Old Union Building
St Andrews
Fife KY16 9AJ

TEL 01334 463324
FAX 01334 463330
EMAIL student.recruitment@st-andrews.ac.uk
WEB st-andrews.ac.uk

St Andrews Students' Association
St Mary's Place
St Andrews
Fife KY16 9UZ

TEL 01334 462700/1
FAX 01334 462740
EMAIL pres@st-andrews.ac.uk
WEB www.yourunion.net

VAG VIEW

St Andrews has a very old foundation (1410) and appeals almost as much to English students as to Scots as an alternative to Oxbridge. It is a small, very traditional university, set in an out-of-the-way seaside place known for its golf.

Jargon is as prevalent here as in the great Imperial days of the public school system, whence many of its students come. Some of its practices earmarked as traditions are in fact only a few years old, so the tradition of being traditional is not about to change.

The recent appearance of a future King of England on the list of undergraduates underlined that, as firmly as it may yet the statistic that more undergraduates of St Andrews get married to boy/girlfiends they meet there, than at any other university. There's also a good (75%) chance of a first or a 2:1, but they are way down on Oxford and Cambridge when it comes to getting graduate-track jobs.

CAMPUS
St Andrews is a long way away from a lot of places, a small, ancient seaside town in north-east Scotland - beautiful, but you would not have to be an urban warrior to find it a bit soft, or maybe a bit too rah?

FEES, BURSARIES
Non-Scottish-based UK residents pay £1,700 p.a. for all courses at Scottish universities, except Medicine, for which they will be charged £2,700 p.a. These will rise with inflation. Subject-based scholarships worth from £250-£1,000 are awarded

Postgraduates 16%
Female Undergraduates 47%
STUDENT POPULATION
Total students 6,799
Male Undergraduates 37%

on academic merit and made in the year of entry only. You might also merit a scholarship awarded on the basis of financial need - £500-£7,000 p.a. Also, St Andrews receives a grant annually from the Royal & Ancient Golf Club; no academic dispensations are given to bursars.

STUDENT PROFILE

The student body is dominated by public school types, and for a Scottish university there is a surprisingly large percentage of English students. Most students are from the middle and upper classes. They fail hopelessly to make their quota for socioeconomic classes 4-7, managing only a 13% take from them. As for intake from the so-called new-to-university, 'low-participation neighbourhoods', there's barely a sign (6%). Indeed, it would be a hopelessly one-dimensional scene if it did not have an unexpectedly high intake from countries beyond the EU.

It is a friendly community. 'You can almost guarantee that every time you leave your front

ACADEMIC EXCELLENCE

TEACHING:
(Rated Excellent, Highly Satis. or 17+ out of 24)

Physics, Chemistry, Economics, Geography, Maths & Statistics, History, Cellular & Molecular Biology, Organismal Biology Psychology.	**Excellent**
Computer Studies, Business & Management, Geology, History of Art, Philosophy, Theology, English, Medicine.	**Highly Satis.**
European Languages	**22**

RESEARCH :
Top grades 5/5*

Psychology, English	**Grade 5***
Chemistry. Biological Sciences, Physics, Pure Maths, Applied Maths, Statistics, Computer, Anthropology, Politics, Iberian/ Latin American, Classics, History, History of Art, Philosophy, Theology	**Grade 5**

UNIVERSITY/STUDENT PROFILE

University since	**1410**
Situation/style	**Town campus & sites**
Student population	**6799**
Undergraduates	**5746**
- mature	**6%**
- non EU undergraduate	**18%**
- male/female	**44/56**
- non-traditional student intake	**13%**
- state school intake	**65%**
- drop-out rate	**2%**
- undergraduate applications	**Down 6%**

door, you'll see someone you know,' writes Melanie Hartley, though that has to be said to be true of most small universities. 'When you've just crawled out of bed for a 9 am tutorial and you've only had four hours sleep, it's debatable whether that's a good thing or not! But St Andrews is a pretty close-knit society. Indeed, once people get here they don't tend to leave. They'll even tell you that one in three graduates end up marrying other St Andrews graduates!'

ACADEMIA & JOBS

When we look at graduate careers, we find an emphasis on analysis, management science and interpersonal skills, which St Andrew's clearly teaches well in whatever subject form.

But this is a small uni, with nearly a fifth of graduates on humanities degrees and another fifth

on combined subject degrees, many of them involving languages and humanities, and one fears that job hunting, for some at least, might be a lottery.

Do subjects like Mediaeval History, Hebrew, Biblical Studies, Classical Studies, Art History and the like find their graduates jobs, however well taught? After six months a tidy number of St Andrews graduates appear in the statistics as secretaries, sales assistants, clerks, bar staff and receptionists. However, their showing in the 'graduate track' employment chart (26th) shows that in time graduates find their feet.

Originally, the more vocational degrees were based in Dundee and became the curriculum of Dundee University, when the split came in the 1960s. Recently, the two have moved closer again with the launch of a joint degree in engineering – Microelectronics & Photonics (there had already been a parlay through their pairing of Art History with Dundee's excellent school of Art & Design). But there is evidence, too, that this very traditional university somehow gets behind the new-uni 'how-to' ethos into a kind of 'can-do', that in their hands the business of university is, as it was originally meant to be, a training of the mind per se, that far from being out-of-date, they are moving forward with insight. They show this not least in their inspired cross-faculty strategy.

Besides an increasing range of sciences with language degrees, there are some tantalising com-

WHERE ST ANDREWS GRADUATES END UP

Health & Social Work: 8%; Education: 14%; Wholesale Retail: 8%; Manufacturing: 7%; Financial Activities: 16%; Public Administration, Civil Service & Defence: 9%; Hotel/Restaurant: 4%; Transport & Communications (including Telecommunications): 2.5%; Computer: 2%; Business & Management: 6%; Accountancy: 6%; Media (including Film): 2%; Legal 2%; Artistic/Literary: 2%; Sport: 1%.

Approximate 'graduate track' employed **66%**

binations such as Arabic-International Relations, Classics-Integrated Information Technology, Hebrew-Mathematics, and Economics-Social Anthropology. There is even the ultimate cross-faculty mesh – Integrated Information Technology and Theological Studies, which if not exactly offering a fast-track to the meaning of life, suggests a challenging examination of the traditional tensions between science and humanities.

> *The most famous St Andrews tradition is on Raisin Monday when first years are dressed in costumes, dragged to St Saviour's Quad in the centre of town and pelted with eggs and covered in shaving foam.*

End result is a sound training for whatever you do, and a good record for jobs that do not require specific training at degree level – journalists and editors abound, for instance.

Elsewhere on the list, education and financial activities are to the fore. Instructors and secondary school teachers come from here in great number, the languages and humanities provision serving them well. For finance, Financial Economics MA Hons points the way. MA Management is also a popular route. Economics, Financial Economics, Economics in combination with Russian (and including a year there), International Relations, Euro languages, Management, Mathematics, etc, sustain a reputation in the job market for chartered, certified and management accountants, investment advisers/ analysts, merchant bankers and business analysts. There's a top – Excellent – rating for Economics.

The medical degree asks ABB + UKCAT: Chem. + Phys. or Maths; GCSE grades A*, A or B.. There's a 12% chance of getting in, which is just about average, and a better one if you happen to attend Perth College, with which a new Pathway to Medicine initiative allows mature students from non-traditional backgrounds achieving an HNC in Applied Sciences to graduate to Medicine at the uni.

Clinical training for medical students now no longer takes place at Manchester, but at Glasgow, Edinburgh, Aberdeen and Dundee universities.

There's a good employment reputation for psy-chologists and care assistants, BSc Psychology providing the harder edge to what is offered in the MA joint hons system, where a good combo may be had with, say, Social Anthropology. Look also at Physiology, Neuroscience, Medicinal Science, Medicinal Chemistry.

There is also a fair number of graduates getting jobs as software engineers, IT consultants, computer programmers, which shows that where they do go for a vocational dimension they can get it right. Computer Science comes with languages, Maths, Linguistics, Philosophy, Management, Physics, or Statistics. A new computer building opened in 2004.

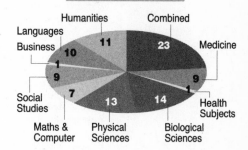

SUBJECT AREAS (%)

Finally there's traditionally a close relationship with the army, and a big take-up in the civil service and defence.

A Learning and Teaching Support Unit (LTSU) works closely with the academic schools to co-ordinate and advise.

SOCIAL SCENE

STUDENTS' ASSOCIATION The student population makes up a large proportion of the town and the social life is created by students. Location denies them any big bands at the union.

Reports Melanie: 'There is no club as such; the union doubles up as a venue (**Venue 1** and **Venue 2**: 1,000 capacity), hosting events all through the week. Every Friday is the *bop* – a cheesy night [*Red Not Bed*], very reminiscent of your old school discos, but a particularly revered part of student life. **Venue 2** hosts a range of different nights; *Rock-soc*, *Bulletproof* (alternative music) and *Jazz-soc* are regulars.' Saturday clubnights include *Squeeze* ('80s), *Explosion* (R&B), *Ebenezer* ('90s) or *Retro*.

'Pre-Sessional week – known as Freshers Week everywhere else – is non-stop events, including some biggish acts: recent weeks have hosted Space, Toploader and Euphoria. There are lots of 2nd, 3rd and 4th years willing to make friends – (some a bit too willing!) – and to show you around. Some will become your academic parents, a tradition that

involves a weekend of parties with them, some time in November, before you get dressed up – many wittily/ridiculously as as bottles of wine, Care Bears or condoms – and are frogmarched to the Quad on the Monday morning for a huge shaving foam fight. So fondly do many look back on their *Raisin* experience that they try to recreate it every year. [It can in fact degenerate into a mass piss-up and/or an excuse to pull: "Remember not to be forced into anything ..." warns the SA's *Alternative Prospectus*.]

'Student life is very much centred around the pubs. There are reputed to be more pubs per square mile than in any other university town, which means you're never stuck for choice: **Broons** or **Bridges** if you want to hang with the yahs, **Ogstons** or **The Raisin** if you want large and loud, **Drouthy Neebors** or **The Cellar** if you're into Real Ale. Such is the pace of life that by the time you've been here a fortnight, you should have an encyclopaedic knowledge of what's available, and your weekly "happy hour'" schedule will be sorted!

'There are lots of ways in which this is a relatively cheap place to live, not least because it's small, though in fact taxis do a healthy business with flat fares anywhere in the town.

'For entertainment other than pubs, most students look to student societies. Everybody is a member of at least one, and most people more. Options range from academic to music to political. The International Politics society recently had Michael Douglas to talk on behalf of the United Nations. You might prefer the Tunnocks Caramel Wafer Appreciation society or Quaich (whisky appreciation). You could also get involved with *The Saint* (student newspaper), which often wins awards, or the new radio station: Star FM.'

The Union also has one of the oldest debating societies in the world, and drama is an active aspect of student life. Each year Mermaids, a sub-committee of the Students' Association, gives financial assistance to several productions, some of which go to the Edinburgh Festival.

Part-time work opportunities are poor, but, 'if you're looking for a bit of extra cash, the Dunhill Cup creates the possibility of a job washing up or directing traffic for the weekend,' Melanie reports. 'The attitude of most students is that term time isn't for working, but there are occasional jobs behind bars. Most of the shops, however, seem to favour 16-year-old Madras College kids over us students when it comes to weekend work.'

SPORT Golfers' paradise – the student team is one of the best in Britain. 'If this isn't your thing,' says Melanie, 'you still get to see the likes of Hugh Grant and Samuel L. Jackson strutting their stuff

WHAT'S ITS REALLY LIKE	
UNIVERSITY:	
Social Life	★★★
Campus scene	**Conservative, traditional, uni by the sea**
Student Union services	**Good**
Politics	**Student issues; activity high**
Sport	**50 clubs**
National team position	**27th**
Sport facilities	**Excellent**
Arts opportunities	**Drama excellent; performing arts all very popular**
Student magazine	**The Vine**
Student newspaper	**The Saint**
Student radio	**Star FM**
Nightclub	**Venue 1**
Bars	**Main Bar, Venue 2**
Union ents	**Disco dance, retro, live acts massive & refined**
Union societies	**130**
Most popular society	**Breakaway (outdoor pursuits), Debating**
Parking	**Adequate**
TOWN:	
Entertainment	★★
Scene	**Pubs, coffee houses**
Town/gown relations	**Average**
Risk of violence	**Low**
Cost of living	**High**
Student concessions	**Average**
Survival + 2 nights out	**£100 pw**
Part-time work campus/town	**Poor**

around town at the Dunhill Cup every October.'

In the national team championships they came 33rd last year. There's a sports centre with sports hall, gym, activities room, weight training room, squash courts, solarium. Extensive playing fields, jogging and trim tracks. Golf bursaries are funded by the Royal and Ancient Golf Club.

PILLOW TALK

Final phase of £35-million David Russell Apartments opened in September 2006. Environmentally-friendly (a grass and Sedum roof), award-winning en-suite single/twin rooms for 887 students in flats with shared living room/kitchen, grouped around man-made lake and central facilities.

'Most of the halls are in the centre of town, and are steeped in traditions,' writes Melanie. 'Most first years procure an undergraduate gown soon after arrival – a tasteful red fleece type-thing and a bit pricey. Although it varies from hall to hall, there will be occasions throughout the year when you can wear these – hall dinners, photographs, chapel. Most of the halls are catered, and the food is pretty reasonable, although you'd be well advised to avoid the universally acclaimed lemon "toilet duck" mousse. Self-catering accommodation can be found in Albany Park and in Fife Park, which provide some of the most economical student accommodation in the country. "Simplistic" isn't the word for these flats, but they're cheap.'

Around half St Andrews students live in halls or other uni-owned accommodation Freshers are almost automatically given a place, but you must apply for it by May 31 in the year of entry. From then on there is no guarantee and the hunt for flats,

AT A GLANCE

ACADEMIC FILE:

Subjects assessed	**18**
Excellent	**100%**
Typical entry requirements	**431 points**
Application acceptance rate	**12%**
Med. School acceptance rate	**12%**
Students-staff ratio	**14:1**
First/2:1 degree pass rate	**75%**

ACCOMMODATION FILE:

Guarantee to freshers	**Single non-locals who apply in time**
Style	**Halls**
Catered	**42%**
En-suite	**42%**
Price range pw	**£53-£147**
City rent pw	**£80**

particularly near the centre of town, can begin around the middle of January. Accommodation is quite expensive for such a small town – £80 per week – largely because students make up a high proportion of the population.

GETTING THERE

☛ By road: Forth Road Bridge, M90/J3, A92 to Kirkcaldy, A915 to St Andrews; or M90/J8, A91.
☛ By rail: Nearest station on main line London (King's Cross) – Edinburgh – Aberdeen line is Leuchars (5 miles). Then bus or taxi.
☛ By air: Edinburgh Airport, airport bus to Edinburgh, thence by rail.

ST GEORGE'S, UNIVERSITY OF LONDON

MEDICAL SCHOOL PROFILE

Founded	**1751**
Status	**Associate of London Uni**
Situation/style	**City site**
Student population	**3510**
Full-time undergraduates	**2930**

ACCOMMODATION:

Availability to freshers	**100%**
Style	**Halls**
Cost pw (no food/food)	**£63**
City rent pw	**£80-£100**

St George's, University of London
Cranmer Terrace
Tooting
London SW17 0RE

TEL 020 8725 5201
FAX 020 8725 5419
EMAIL adm-med@sghms.ac.uk
WEB www.sgms.ac.uk

St George's entry policy is AAB + BMAT, Chemistry or Biology; if Biology then AS Chemistry is required; but if Chemistry the other two A levels can be a modern Euro language and a Social Science. BBC if your school averages 245 points at A. There's also a Foundation for mature students. Ten years ago, they were ahead of the game, wanting to bring clinical training in earlier, looking for problem solvers, allowing an Arts subject A level in.

Leisure-wise there's a Friday disco at the **Med School Bar** (650 capacity) and 42 clubs and societies, Rowing and Film being the most popular. Rootin' Tootin' itself has a colourful culture, plenty of curry houses, and - incomprehensibly to anyone not born of the London property boom - is now classed as a gentrified area.

The sports grounds are in Cobham, Surrey - 9 winter pitches and 2 cricket squares, grass and hard tennis courts. They also keep an eight and a four in the London Uni boathouse and have facilities for sailing. Back at the hospital there's the Lowe Sports Centre, 6 squash courts, gym and areas for badminton, basketball, etc.

GETTING THERE
☛ Tooting Broadway Underground station (Northern Line), Tooting overland.

ST MARY'S UNIVERSITY COLLEGE

St Mary's University College
Waldegrave Road
Strawberry Hill
Twickenham TW1 4SX

TEL 020 8240 4029
FAX 020 8240 2361
EMAIL admit@smuc.ac.uk
WEB www.smuc.ac.uk

St Mary's is a self-contained campus situated south of the England rugby ground at Twickenham, between Richmond and Kingston. Many undergraduates are destined to become teachers, but there is a wide range of subjects on offer - drama, English, theology, Irish culture, sport, biology, health, environment, sociology, classical studies, media, geography, history. It is a Roman Catholic foundation and they are good at sport - they came 30th in the national uni team ratings last year, a fantastic result for the college's size.

Two halls (Cashin and Cronin) offer en-suite facilities. Students' Union bars include **SU Bar** (600-800 capacity) and **Tartan Bar** (100-150) - 2 weekly discos, theme nights or live gigs.

COLLEGE PROFILE	
Founded	**1850**
Status	**HE College**
Degree awarding university	**Surrey**
Situation/style	**City campus**
Total student population	**3500**
Full-time undergraduates	**2720**
ACCOMMODATION FILE:	
Availability to freshers	**100%**
Style	**Halls**
Cost pw (no food/food)	**£73-£123**
City rent pw	**£80-£100**

UNIVERSITY OF SALFORD

TheUniversity of Salford
Greater Manchester M5 4WT

TEL 0161 295 2892
FAX 0161 295 4705
EMAIL ugadmissions-exrel@salford.ac.uk
WEB www.salford.ac.uk

Salford Students' Union
The Crescent
Salford M5 4WT

TEL 0161 736 7811
FAX 0161 737 1633
EMAIL students-union@salford.ac.uk
WEB www.salfordstudents.com

VAG VIEW

*E*veryone knows that Salford is good at built environment, at science, engineering, computer and business, but a closer look reveals a developing picture - in particular into the arts, languages (also feted in the research assessments) and media - now eminently worth considering.

CAMPUS
'The main campus, Peel Park, is 2 miles from Manchester City Centre,' reports Shauna Corr.

'There are 3 main campuses: Adelphi, Frederick Road and the main campus: which is known as Peel Park.'

'So what do you know about Salford? Well, have you ever seen the opening credits of *Coronation Street*? That's Salford,' informs Lindsay Oakes. 'It's where *Corrie* is set and filmed. You may also have heard that it's a rough area with a high car crime rate. Sadly, Salford is known more by its bad reputation than for any of its good points. Of course I'd be lying if I told you that there aren't any negative aspects to living here; it's like any suburban city area: if you're not sensible then it could be dangerous. But where better to spend three or four years of your student life than in the student capital of Britain – Manchester? Salford University actually lies closer to the centre of Manchester than Manchester University itself. It is only a fifteen-minute bus ride away, or five minutes in a taxi, the way they drive round here!

FEES, BURSARIES

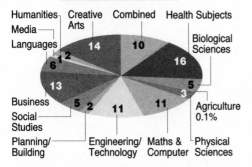

UK & EU Fees, 2007: £3,070 p.a. If in receipt of full HE Maintenance grant there's a bursary of £300. Scholarships worth £3,000 are available for undergraduate study, two reserved for local students.

STUDENT PROFILE

'There are students from all walks of life here, and from practically every continent. There is a real international feel to Salford because of all the links we have with universities abroad [see *Academia*, below]. And it may be true of many universities, but there is a real community among Salford students,' notes Lindsay, in particular among freshers in the student village. There is also a high percentage of mature students.

ACADEMIA & JOBS

They are a pioneer of sandwich courses, work

placement schemes, and their links with local firms are legendary. 'There are certainly strong links with industry,' says Shauna, 'and opportunity on many courses for industrial sandwich years, home and abroad.' The culture is fostered by Academic Enterprise their 'integrated third strand alongside teaching and research. Many students experience a work placement as part of their course and 50% of programmes offer the chance to work or study abroad. Our Business Enterprise Support Team (BEST) encourages staff and students to build upon their ideas for self-employment,' they say.

Graduates pour out of Salford to be lecturers in higher education, and interest is directed at their School of Languages and its contemporary Euro culture degrees with a language, Linguistics with a language, three language mixes, languages with Marketing, Translation and Interpreting Studies. A new £1-million, campus-based Language Resource Centre offers advanced multimedia and language facilities. Biosciences is another popular route into higher education teaching - full marks at the assessments.

Meanwhile the faculty's School of Media, Music & Performance has employment success with dedicated degrees in radio/TV, journalism, music & recording. The 23/24 assessment for Drama/Dance/Cinematics shows that they, too,

ACADEMIC EXCELLENCE	
University since	**1967**
Situation/style	**Campus**
Student population	**18469**
Undergraduates	**15366**
- mature	**36%**
- non EU undergraduates	**5%**
- male/female	**44/56**
- non-traditional student intake	**37%**
- state school intake	**95%**
- drop-out rate	**21%**
- undergraduate applications	**Up 8%**

ACADEMIC EXCELLENCE

TEACHING:
(Rated Excellent or 17+ out of 24)

Music	**Excellent**
Organismal Biosciences,	**24**
Politics, Molecular Biosciences	
Drama/Dance/Cinematics,	**23**
Physics	
Housing, Subjects Allied	**22**
to Medicine, Nursing	
Art & Design, Maths	**21**
Economics, Sociology, Media,	**20**
Modern Languages & Arabic	
Civil Engineering, Tourism	**19**
Building & Land/Property Mgt	**18**

RESEARCH:
Top grades 5/5/6**

Built Environment, Library &	**Grade 6***
Information Management	
Statistics, European Studies	**Grade 5**

are performing well.

Aspiring music producers should look at the Faculty of Science, Engineering & Environment – the BA Acoustics, which prepares students for jobs with such as Philips (Holland) and Bang & Olufson (Denmark). Sound recordists and technicians look to the BSc Audio, Video & Broadcast Technology. Strong emphasis on practical work. BSc Audio Technology includes industrial placement. Meanwhile, in Media, Music & performance BA Popular Music & Recording is the business.

A BA Journalism & Broadcast joins BA Hons Television & Radio (theoretical elements married to practical modules, such as editing, producing, directing). There are 5 other Journalism combinations. Look, too, at their BA Media & Performance and BSc Media Technology, the latter aimed at technical operators and operational engineers. Great student media – Shock FM and Channel M (TV). Teaching inspection, 20.

In the bedrock subjects, aspiring property developers still flock to Salford's world-class School of Construction & Property Management. Look at BSc Property Management & Investment. There's a world class Grade 6* rating for research. Teaching inspection, 18. Construction engineers/managers should consider the 4-year BSc Construction Mgt, or Construction Project Mgt. There's a dedicated degree in Quntity Surveying.

Salford's civil engineers also get jobs in number. There's a BSc or B/MEng route plus an option to mix with Environmental Engineering. Teaching assessment for Civil Eng (19 points) is less overpowering however.

Other sure-fire career hits are for aeronautical engineers. Salford places more graduates than most in the industry with its Aerospace courses, including the interesting e-design/Aerospace.

Health care professionals are equally well served by courses in Radiography, Midwifery, Occupational Therapy, Physiotherapy, Podiatry, Prosthetics/Orthotics, Sport Rehab – all 22 points at assessment; they also offer one of the few Traditional Chinese Medicine/Acupuncture degrees.

Their Faculty of Business & Informatics is a leading edge into employment, with Business Decision Analysis (study in North America a possibility), Business Economics (with Gambling Studies – yes, you read right!), and a raft of Management Science degrees, with study in North America.

Serious employment strengths in the business sector include retail management and buying. Look at the School of Leisure, Hospitality & Food

They are No. 1 countrywide for jobs in sales management. The Art Department, Product Design, Sports Equipment Design and Fashion provide the focus for this. Engineering/business is another popular route into sales management.

They score well, too, with jobs in government administration (local, regional and central) – degrees such as BSc Environmental Health helping graduates in. See also the environment and conservation

Many courses have an international dimen-

WHERE SALFORD GRADUATES END UP

Health & Social Work: 13%; Education: 5%; Wholesale Retail: 10%; Manufacturing: 11%; Financial Activities: 7%; Public Administration, Civil Service & Defence: 9%; Hotel/Restaurant: 6%; Transport & Communications (including Telecommunications): 5%; Construction: 4%; Mining/Oil Extracting: 1%; Personnel: 2%; Computer: 5%; Business & Management: 2%; Accountancy: 2%; Media (including Film): 2%; Legal 1%; Architecture: 1%; Publishing: 0.5%; Advertising: 0.5%; Artistic/Literary: 0.5%; Sport: 1%.

Approximate 'graduate track' employed **56%**

sion, most offer the chance to study abroad. Excellent relationships with Europe and farther afield have produced interesting curriculum groupings

Not surprisingly translators and interpreters come in number from Salford, though it is not a crowded profession. Look at their Translation and Interpreting degrees – Arabic/English, Italian/ Portuguese, German/Spanish require Teaching inspection, 20. Research Grade 5.

> *Salford has all the advantages of a small town – cheap rent, everything close by, a friendly atmosphere – yet with the facilities of a city nearby. But don't expect cheap beer – unlike most unis, it is not subsidised.*

SOCIAL SCENE

STUDENTS' UNION 'The union runs 4 bars (one being a nightclub-come-bar),' writes Shauna. '**The Pav** (at Castle Irwell student village) has two main nights: Tuesday and Friday. Tuesday's *Flair*, '60s, '70s and '80's music, is a constant, and whatever they call Friday night when you get there, it won't be retro. **The Lowry Bar** on Peel Park is situated in University House, it's a good day-bar. So far this year we have had a Ministry of Sound night, at which Youseff played, and we've had Jason Donovon, Timmy Mallet and Tymes Four as well as student bands and DJs. We also have the **Wallness Tavern**, recently refurbished, open all day. **The Sub Club**, Frederick Road, is a good day bar for students on site. All bars have games' machines and pool tables. Local pubs are a bit rough and not always safe for students.

'One thing I should point out,' writes Lindsay, 'is that unlike most unis, beer and food at Salford are *not* subsidised.'

Especially active among numerous sports clubs and societies is the LGB group – lesbian/gay. '*Student Direct* is our weekly publication,' Shauna continues, 'shared with both Bolton Uni and Manchester University.' The union rates most active societies as Plastic Surgery/Shock fm, both music societies: 'Plastic Surgery is the DJ soc, and Shock fm deals with the student radio station.' The campus-based (TV) Channel M broadcasts to half a million people in the Manchester region with programmes developed and made at Salford's media facilities. Channel M recently beat BBC and Sky One to a Royal Television Award.

Reflecting the growth in arts degrees – note the 23 points out of 24 for Drama at the teaching assessments – students describe extra-curricular arts opportunities as excellent too. The **Robert Powell Theatre** was opened by namesake Salfordian actor, Robert Powell.

The central, Peel Park Campus contains the Lowry Museum and Art Gallery. L S Lowry was born in the town.

Salford Community Action Project (SCAP) is a student project involved with children in the locality, and senior citizens, the disabled, ex-offenders, and in giving English lessons to overseas students and others.

SPORT 'The union runs a very cheap Leisure Centre which provides a swimming pool, climbing wall, weights room, badminton, tennis and squash courts, five-a-side football pitches, sun beds, sauna and jacuzzi. There is a large sports hall with just about every indoor pitch marked down, facilities for trampoline, and sports pitches at Castle Irwell for rugby, football, hockey and cricket.'

WHAT IT'S REALLY LIKE	
UNIVERSITY:	
Social Life	★★★
Campus scene	**Friendly, boozy**
Student Union services	**Good**
Politics	**Interest low, but SWSS & Anti-Nazi League**
Sport	**19 clubs**
National team position	**91st**
Sport facilities	**Good**
Arts opportunities	**Excellent**
Student newspaper	**Student Direct**
Student radio	**Shock fm**
Student TV	**Channel M**
Nightclub	**The Pav**
Bars	**Lowry, Sub Club, Wallness Tavern**
Union ents	**Themed, requests, tours**
Union societies	**19**
Most popular societies	**Plastic Surgery**
Parking	**Adequate**
CITY:	
Entertainment	★★★★★
City scene	**Legendary**
Town/gown relations	**Average-poor**
Risk of violence	**High**
Cost of living	**Average**
Student concessions	**Good**
Survival + 2 nights out	**£90 pw**
Part-time work campus/town	**Average/excellent**

TOWN Cost-wise, as Suzanne Ashton points out, 'Salford has all the advantages of a town – cheap rent, everything close by, a friendly atmosphere – and yet still with the facilities of a city nearby.' See *Manchester City* article. 'There's part-time work in union bars, in ents, in the library and in Manchester,' notes Shauna, 'and a Job Shop to help you find reliable and safe, part-time or holiday work. There are loads of part-time jobs to be had.

PILLOW TALK

They guarantee a place in one of the 4,000 study bedrooms to all freshers who have an unconditional offer and whose accommodation application form has been received by 12 noon on the September 1 in the year of admission.

The 3 main campuses (Peel Park, Frederick Road, Adelphi) are within walking distance of the residences. 'There is a good selection of accommodation ranging from Castle Irwell Student Village to blocks of flats and on-campus catered accommodation,' Shauna reports. 'Castle Irwell has 1,612 rooms and is 25 minutes walk from Peel Park campus. It boasts numerous playing fields, an astro-turf pitch, and **The Pav**. There is also a laundrette, taxi rank and a house with disabled access.'

Writes Lindsay: 'In the summer, the entire village turns out on to the playing fields to play sports, sunbathe or even have barbecues. In the winter, you'll find yourself having a snowball fight

AT A GLANCE	
ACADEMIC FILE:	
Subjects assessed	**26**
Excellent	**69%**
Typical entry requirements	**249 points**
Application acceptance rate	**21%**
Students-staff ratio	**18:1**
First/2:1 degree pass rate	**53%**
ACCOMMODATION FILE:	
Guarantee to freshers	**100%**
Style	**Halls**
Catered	**7%**
Price range pw	**£51-£95**
City rent pw	**£70**

with someone you've never met before.'

GETTING THERE

☛ By road: M62 (which connects with the M6, M63)/M602. Coach services good.
☛ By rail: Salford Crescent station is on-campus; Manchester Oxford Road is a few minutes away; Liverpool, 1:20; Sheffield, 1:30; Birmingham New Street, 2:30; London Euston, 3:30.
☛ By air: Manchester Airport,.
☛ By coach: London, 4:35; Bristol, 5:00.

SCHOOL OF ORIENTAL & AFRICAN STUDIES, LONDON UNIVERSITY

School of Oriental & African Studies
Thornhaugh Street
Russell Square
London WC1H 0XG

TEL 020 7898 4034
FAX 020 7898 4039
STUDENT UNION TEL 020 7898 4997
EMAIL study@soas.ac.uk
WEB www.soas.ac.uk

STUDENT POPULATION
Total students 4,300
48% Postgraduates
Female Undergraduates 30%
Male Undergraduates 22%

SOAS, part of the University of London, is situated in Bloomsbury and has a close working relationship with branches of the Civil Service, especially the Foreign Office (SOAS actually teach their staff). This year, plans are being developed for the expansion of the central London campus.

Teaching assessments are first class. Connections with overseas governments, industry and commerce facilitate, among other things, the college's study-abroad programmes.

There are more then 300 degree combinations available in the social sciences, humanities and arts, languages & Cultures. More than 24% of degree programmes include spending a year abroad while the staff:student ration (12:1) is one of the best in the UK. In the last Research

Assessment Exercise, 10 SOAS departments were awarded top ratings of 5 and 5*.

Another way of looking at it is that SOAS does most of the usual disciplines, but with reference to Asia, Africa and the Middle East. This means that in Geography you're more likely to be looking at the 'Bio-geography of Savannahs in Sub-Saharan Africa' than the spatial planning of Birmingham town centre. It's strong on languages, from Chinese and Japanese to a whole lot you may not have heard of. Colloquial Cambodian, for example, looks great on your CV.

The bar, capacity 200, is renowned the world over (by a discerning few). Accommodation is provided as single, en-suite study-bedrooms in cluster flats 15 minutes' walk away on the Pentonville Road. Alternatively, London Uni's intercollegiate halls. There are two squash courts on site and a sports ground at Greenford. London Uni Students' Union sport and fitness facilities are nearby.

SCHOOL/STUDENT PROFILE	
School of London Uni since	**1916**
Student population	**4300**
Undergraduates	**2250**
ACCOMMODATION:	
Guarantee to freshers	**100%**
Style	**Halls**
Cost pw SOAS halls	**£108.01**
Cost pw London Uni halls	**£105-121**

GETTING THERE
☞ Underground: Russell Square (Piccadilly line).

SCHOOL OF PHARMACY, LONDON UNIVERSITY

School of Pharmacy
29-39 Brunswick Square
London WC1N 1AX

TEL 020 7753 5831
FAX 020 7753 5829
EMAIL registry @ulsop.ac.uk
WEB www.ulsop.ac.uk

The School of Pharmacy is a specialist school of the University of London. A Grade 5 in the research assessments confirms its national and international reputation. Situated within walking distance of the British Museum, it has a small amount of its own accommodation, otherwise it's London Uni's intercollegiate halls, or living out. For sport, the school shares grounds out at Enfield with the Royal Free Hospital Medical School (now part of University College, London); closer to home are facilities for squash, badminton, swimming, etc., and the London University Union is close at hand. There is a union bar, a theme night on Friday, and facilities for table tennis, pool, etc.

GETTING THERE
☞ By tube: Russell Square (Piccadilly line); overland stations (King's Cross, St Pancras and Euston) are all within a short walk.

SCOTTISH AGRICULTURAL COLLEGE

Scottish Agricultural College
Ayr Campus
Ayr KA6 5HW

TEL 0800 269453
FAX 01292 525357
EMAIL recruitment@sac.ac.uk
WEB www.sac.ac.uk

SAC is a small college based at three sites, in Aberdeen, Edinburgh and Ayr. Halls accommodation is available. Technical and management skills required to manage livestock or crop enterprise are to the fore; it's a three-year course, four for an honours degree. Degrees in related specialisms are also available. *Aberdeen* has BTechnol Agriculture, BTechnol Countryside Management and BTechnol Business Management; *Ayr* BTechnol Agriculture, BSc Horticulture or Horticulture with Horticulture Mgt (first 2 years at Strathclyde Uni), BSc Landscape Management, BTechnol Environmental Protection & Management (years 3 & 4 in Edinburgh), BTechnol Countryside Management, BTechnol Leisure & Recreation Management, BSc Applied Plant & Animal Science, and BTechnol Food Technology; *Edinburgh* has BTechnol Agriculture, BTechnol Rural Resources Management, and BTechnol Environment Protection & Mgt (first 2 years at Ayr).

STUDENT SHEFFIELD - THE CITY

Steely Sheffield is a born-again cosmopolitan city offering pretty much anything you desire. For some it may never rival Leeds, Manchester or Nottingham, but come here and you will soon discover that it has its own inimitable charm. People are friendly to all, even if you are a student! And many students choose to stay after graduation, which proves that it is a place to live and work in, not just somewhere to pass through.

CLUBS
Sheffield placed itself in the vanguard of the club revolution with several big names – Gatecrasher: 'Gatecrasher One has taken over *Skool Disco* duties, providing salivating perverts a new location to drool over girls in pigtails and pleated skirts,' writes Itchy, 'while *Blessed @* **Republic** on a monday night is absolute quality, if you like r&b and hip hop.' With major acts and DJ's plying their trade, there are no end of nights to check out and something to suit everyone's taste. Sheffield Hallam's **NMB** also provides, and sells out its *Stardust* and *Sheff 1* clubnights on a weekly basis.

The alternative scene is not to be missed though, with Sheffield University's Student Union offering a great live venue in the **Octagon** (yes, it has 8 sides) for touring bands. They are even kind enough to put on indie clubnights to fill the gaps between gigs. Look in particular for the *Fuzz Club* on a Thursday night.

Other venues include the popular indie haunt **Leadmill** (voted best venue outside of London a while back) and **City Hall** for the more 'cultured' acts. While Hallam's **Arena** and the **Don Valley Stadium** provide the capacity required by the really big bands, like recent Paul McCartney and Eric Clapton.

GALLERIES AND THEATRES
The Crucible and **Lyceum** are Sheffield's 2 major playhouse venues, they have shows running all year round, ranging from pantomime, to ballet to Shakespeare. Both offer discounts for students, who also have their own productions at the **Drama Studio** on Glossop Road.

Among major arthouses, the star attraction is the **Millennium Galleries**. **Graves Art Gallery** has smaller, but still great, exhibitions, a recent highlight the William Blake show from the Tate in London.

SCREENS
Film buffs love the **Showroom** on Paternoster Row, an arty cinema with bar attached; it even does a 'film and meal deal'. Cheap and cheerful in-town cinema is the 10-screen **Odeon**, while out at **Meadowhall** there's a 15-screen multiplex, where a film can be incorporated into a day out shopping. The **UGC, also** outside the city centre, boasts a huge 'Full Monty' screen, perfect for watching the latest blockbuster.

SPORT
Sheffield is home to 2 football teams – Sheffield Wednesday, who play at **Hillsborough**, and Sheffield United at **Bramall Lane**. Whatever you do, don't confuse the two. We also have ice hockey team and basketball teams. The Sheffield Steelers glide across the ice at **The Arena,** and the Westfield Sharks shoot the hoop there on non-ice days. Look, too, for the world-class swimming pool at **Ponds Forge**. And, of course, the **Crucible** is transformed once a year into a sporting venue, when it hosts the Embassy World Snooker Championship. Alternatively, many like a flutter at **Owlerton Greyhound Stadium** on Penistone Road.

STUDENT GHETTOES
As with most cities, students have monopolised a couple of areas. Broomhill, a paradise of pubs, takeaways, a supermarket and the ever popular **Record Collector** – whatever your taste in music, they'll stock it. Convenient for the Sheffield Uni campus – 10 minutes away on foot – it's reasonably cheap and pretty safe. Hallam students, meanwhile, tend to congregate around the Ecclesall Road area, or roads just off the city centre, being just a stone's throw away form their 3 campuses. Again, these areas have everything a student needs – supermarket, pubs and the odd bookshop or two.

There are endless pubs and bars, in particular in the student areas of Broomhill, Crooks and Ecclesall Road. Division Street also has a good dozen, while outside the city centre there are loads of vast watering holes.

CONSUMERISM
The debt-riddled student gets a lifeline from Broomhill's array of charity shops, also from **Castle Market** – brilliant for cheap veg, fish and meat. Those past caring visit Division Street, where all the latest trendy and alternative gear purveyed in chic boutiques and the **Forum Shopping Centre**. Chapel Walk is full of small shops with large price tags, and although Ecclesall Road is a student area, it, too, has shops generally far too expensive for a student's pocket.

Then there is the experience of **Meadowhall**

(Meadow 'hell' on a Saturday) – shop after shop selling its wares, all under one roof, again some- times at high prices.

Ellen Grundy

UNIVERSITY OF SHEFFIELD

The University of Sheffield
Western Bank
Sheffield S10 2TN

TEL 0114 222 1255
FAX 0114 222 1234
EMAIL www.sheffield.ac.uk/asksheffield
WEB www.sheffield.ac.uk

Sheffield University Students Union
Western Bank
Sheffield S10 2TG

TEL 0114 222 2000
FAX 0114 275 2506
EMAIL [firstname.surname]@sheffield.ac.uk
WEB www.sheffieldunion.com

VAG VIEW

Sheffield is a top university across the board. Whichever one of our statistical boxes you care to consult – 'Where Sheffield Graduates End Up', 'Academic Excellence', 'What It's Really Like' – they excel.

As student Rose Wild wrote: 'In today's cut-throat world, where new students have to pay just to enter this carnival of hedonistic abandon, and thereafter graduate to a future in which security is not guaranteed, it is probably worth choosing a university which gives you best value for your dosh and which has a reputation that will outshine the competition. That university is Sheffield.'

As we went to press work was due to be completed on the £23 million Information Commons - a new undergraduate learning, study and IT facility with 1,300 study places, 100,000 textbooks in areas of heavy demand, and 550 computers.

CAMPUS

The city of Sheffield is roughly in the centre of England. The uni and student ghettoes are all on one side of it and there's a friendly community-feel, although Sheffield is most definitely not a campus university.

One word describes Sheffield, and that's 'hilly'. Most students walk everywhere, but public transport is reliable and cheap, and there's also Supertram, which runs from the centre to numerous places, including Meadowhall, the famous, out-of-town shopping centre. Having your own transport enables you to enjoy weekends, though. When you come here you'll be on the edge of the Peak District, one of the last great, beautiful wilderness areas of England.

FEES, BURSARIES

UK & EU Fees, 2007: £3,070. If in receipt of full HE Maintenance grant there's a bursary of £3,070 p.a. There are 3 types of bursary, and students can qualify for more than one type, to the maximum of £3,070: £665 for household incomes under £16,000; £410 for incomes between £16,000 and £33,000. Awards also (£255 to £1,585) for pre-uni academic achievement and if a Graduate Priority Subject is chosen. Support, too, if applying from partnership colleges or schools. There are also sports bursaries and several funds available for students who face unforeseeable costs associated with study or who fall into the following categories, mature students, lone parents, students with dependants, and students with a disability.

STUDENT PROFILE

There are plenty of bright undergraduates, most of them capable of 400 points at A level. There's a high proportion of public school type, but there is a growing number, too, of new-to-uni social groups (20%). The mature population at 41% (includes both full-time and part-time undergraduates) is unusually large. So, students come from a variety of backgrounds and together they are happy enough

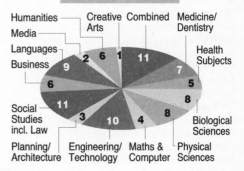

SUBJECT AREAS (%)

Humanities — Creative Combined Medicine/ Arts Dentistry
Media
Languages — Health Subjects
Business — 9 2 6 1 11 7
6 5
Social — 11 8
Studies 3 10 4 8
incl. Law Biological Sciences
Planning/ Engineering/ Maths & Physical
Architecture Technology Computer Sciences

to achieve a 10% drop-out rate, not big these days. Writes Rose: 'One of the most striking and pleasing things about the cosy little cocoon of life, which makes this university a very pleasant place to be, is that you will rarely – if ever – come across prejudice of any sort. The union's absolute tolerance of the sizeable gay community is but one reflection of this. Another striking feature is the high visibility of the university's religious community. A small but significant proportion of Sheffield's students, embarking upon their journey of self-discovery, stray off more well-trod paths and instead find God.'

ACADEMIA & JOBS

A new £16-million Learning Resource Centre was completed in late 2006, with provision for nearly 1,000 study places, state-of-the-art IT facilities and 100,000 undergraduate textbooks.

Almost a fifth of graduates go into health. A new £3.1-million Health Centre opened in September 2004. £26 million was spent on the refurbishment of teaching and research facilities in the Medical School. However, there is no longer undergraduate intake for Nursing and Midwifery, which has moved to Sheffield Hallam University.

In the 5/6-year MB ChB there's an emphasis on self-learning and computer-aided learning packages. Wide clinical experience offered. The

6-year course includes a pre-med year for students with non-scientific backgrounds. Entry requirements AAB + UKCAT in 2 science subjects, one of which must be Chemistry. Grade B in any other subject. A 7% application acceptance rate marks out Sheffield as one of the more popular schools among applicants.

A new £5.5 million extension has been built to the School of Clinical Dentistry, which offers the BDS/Dent for AAB.

Another noticeable career strength within the sector is BSc Psychology, fully accredited and first step to becoming a Chartered Psychologist. And speech therapists also thrive on the BMedSci Speech Science.

Accountancy is also very big at Sheffield. BA Accounting & Financial Mgt degrees combine with Business Mgt, Economics, Info Mgt, or Maths. Tax consultants also thrive, and aspiring actuaries get happy with their Maths degrees especially BSc Financial Mathematics.

UNIVERSITY/STUDENT PROFILE	
University since	**1905**
Situation/style	**Civic**
Student population	**24075**
Undergraduates	**18656**
- mature	**15%**
- non EU undergraduates	**7%**
- male/female	**46/54**
- non-traditional student intake	**20%**
- state school intake	**83%**
- drop-out rate	**10%**
- undergraduate applications	**Up 3%**

Sheffield claim to attract more undergraduates in their School of Architecture than any other. There are 7 courses, a single hons – BA Architectural Studies, and landscape and urban environment degrees. Also, in Engineering, MEng Structural Engineering & Architecture. Teaching inspection, Excellent. Research, Grade 5. As for landscape architecture they find more graduates employment than any other uni. Teaching inspection, 23.

A new £25 million multidisciplinary science and engineering campus is being developed, the first stage of which opened in June 2005.

Engineering design consultants find their way from all over the Engineering faculty. Look at their 3 to 5-year B/MEng Civil Engineering degrees, but also a range of design engineering degrees, such as B/MEng Medical Systems Engineering, Computer Systems Engineering, Systems & Control Engineering. There's also Biomedical Engineering, which gets into design for prosthetics.

The Faculty of Engineering, which took full marks at teaching inspection and world class Grade 6* for research, has established the Advanced Research Manufacturing Centre with Boeing and opened its third Rolls-Royce Technology centre in Advanced Electrical Machines and Drives. They are also collaborating with British Aerospace.

The Sports Engineering degree (introduced in 2004) has now been joined by a degree in Motor Sports Engineering Management, and a new degree course in Aerospace Engineering with Private Pilot Instruction is proving popular.

Electronic and telecommunications engineers abound. A number of army officers come out of this department, as they do from physical sciences, where in civvy street chemists (research grade 5) and archaeologists (teaching assessment 22, research grade 5) flow in greatest number, then software engineers and computer operators.

Sheffield's Faculty of Pure Science offers a whole range of 3/4-years BSc and Masters degrees, Chemistry, for example, coupling with Chemical Engineering, Maths, study in Europe or Australia or Japan or the US or in industry.

Computer Science (with Foundation year if you want it) has various language possibilities and Physics might come with Medical Physics, Maths, Study in Europe, or there's a 4-year MPhys in Theoretical Physics. There's also a BSc Science Foundation (4/5 years).

The Faculty of Social Sciences mixes social and political studies and reaches into China, Korea and Japan, and this is also where you'll find a raft of Economics degrees and Accountancy & Finance. Researchers for media & government come out of here, and out of language degrees. Aspiring translator/interpreters note the 4-year BA Modern Languages with Interpreting. A new Confucius Institute offers a valuable resource for Chinese-related studies, in partnership with Beijing Language and Culture University (BLCU) and Nanjing University.

Languages and Sciences produce editors, too, and look out for BA Journalism Studies (backed by superb student media). Sheffield is also good for publishing.

Instructors by the dozen come out of Sheffield and would-be adult education lecturers find a certain route via languages, where Russian is a particular strength, with full marks at the teaching assessments as well as Grade 6* (world class) for research. Also popular ways into adult education are biological sciences (full marks at the assessments) and social sciences (Politics full marks, Psychology 22. Law is Excellent).

SOCIAL SCENE

STUDENTS' UNION If you arrive by train or bus you'll be met by Student Reception; volunteer students will beard you in the bars, in halls – every fresher will get a visit, even those in private accommodation.

Fulcrum of the ents scene is **Bar One**, which recently had a £500,000 makeover. It serves over 30 varieties of beer and takes more in a night than most pubs do in a week. Bar One gives way to the **Raynor Lounge** - a venue for gigs and small club nights. Every Sunday it hosts *The LastLaugh Comedy Club,* and through the week isbooked by students for parties and club nights.

Interval (600 capacity) is the continental

ACADEMIC EXCELLENCE

TEACHING:
(Rated Excellent or 17+ out of 24)

History, Mechanical Engineering, Law, Sociology, Social Work, Architecture, English, Geography, Music, Social Policy, Initial Teacher Training.	**Excellent**
Russian, Automatic Control & Systems Engineering, Electron/Electric Eng, Mechanical Eng, Theology, Education, Anatomy, Biosciences, Philosophy, Politics	**24**
Landscape/Town & Regional Planning	**23**
Linguistics, East Asian Studies, Materials Technology, Physics, Archaeology, Library/Info, Psychology	**22**
Hispanic Studies, Chemical Engineering, Civil Eng, French, Maths, Pharmacology, Other Subjects Allied to Medicine, Nursing, Economics	**21**
German	**20**
Medicine	**19**

RESEARCH:
Top grades 5/5/6**

Pre-Clinical Studies, Electronic/Electrical Eng, Metallurgy, Politics, Russian/ Library/Info Mgt.	**Grade 6***
Animal & Plant Sciences, Molecular & Cellular Biology, Automatic Control/Systems Eng,	**Grade 5***
Hospital-based Clinical Subjects, Clinical Dentistry, Nursing, Psychology, Chemistry, Physics, Medical Physics & Clinical Eng, Pure Maths, Statistics, Computer, Civil Eng, Mechanical/Aeronautical/ Manufacturing Eng, Built Environment, Town/Country Planning, Geography, Law, Social Policy, English, French, Iberian/Latin American, Archaeology, History, Philosophy, Theology, Music, Education	**Grade 5**

style café bar – pasta, baguettes, pastries and cabaret acts. **Fusion** (600 capacity) is the intimate venue for live bands and clubnights. Then there's **The Foundry** (1,000), which, with Fusion, is host to an amazing series of clubnights. *Tuesday Club* is drum 'n' bass/hip hop, Wednesday's *Juice,* with top line DJs, Thursday's *Fuzz Club* (indie/metal in two rooms). Then there's *Frouk*'s traditional roof-raising eclectic mix on Friday, and *Pop Tarts, Saturday,* the ultimate '60s/'70s retro party – which now employs two dancefloors. The monthly *Climax* is LGB night, now a widely known favourite on the gay scene. Other mega nights are *Cuba Libre* (monthly), *Urban Gorilla* (one per term), and *End Of Year Carnival* (annually). The **Octagon Centre** is the major, national-circuit venue (1,600 capacity), feted as *Club Mirror's* 'Venue of the Year'. Recent gigs at the uni include: Arctic Monkeys, Little Man Tate, the View, Automatic, Amy Winehouse, Ash, Brakes, Bat For Lashes, Rakes, Bloc Party, Milburn, Dirty Pretty Things, Charlatans, DJ Shadow, Beverley Knight, Paul Weller, Long Blondes, We Are Scientists, Orson, Russel Brand, Kooks, Maximo Park.

There's also **Coffee Revolution**, the Union's own eco-friendly 'Fair Trade' coffee shop.

Not all is ents, however. At the top of the Union building, you'll find the **Gallery**. Heart of sports clubs and societies, it consists of meeting rooms and work areas with telephones and computing facilities that members can use to contact each other, meet and organise events. One floor down is **Source**, information bank on the Union's 200 societies and sports clubs, and events across Sheffield. Currently the most popular societies are: Street & Breakdance, People & Planet, and Gospel Choir.

Here, you'll also find a multimedia computer

> *'In today's cut-throat world, where new students have to payto enter this carnival of hedonistic abandon, and thereafter graduate to a future in which security is not guaranteed, it is probably worth choosing a university which gives you best value for your dosh. That university is Sheffield.'*

suite, with digital cameras and camcorders available for hire. A recent initiative is the *Give It A Go* programme. The idea is to encourage you to dip in to a whole host of activities – suck it and see before making a long-term commitment to one society or another. In 2005/06 around 12,000 tickets were sold for *Give it a Go* activities.

Behind Source is Sheffield Volunteering, gateway to community projects in and around Sheffield. They won the Outstanding Project Award in the 2006 Volunteering Awards, and with students raising around £100,000 each year for charity, they also copped the Royal Mail Community Impact Award.

Societies cover almost everything, as Rose discovered: 'Whether you're one of the rare few who actually come here to learn, or you're one of the many who come to play rugby, edit a newspaper, watch bands, worship God, fight injustice, walk up big hills, practise politics, become an actor or do any number of diverse and often bizarre activities, you can not only do them here, but you can meet a load of people who'll do them with you.'

Sheffield is politically very active, with strong representation from across the political spectrum. Union Elections receive the highest turnout of any Union in the country and are hotly contested attracting a large number of high quality candidates for the eight positions. Below this there are a number of Committees and a strong Union Council, and numerous student political interest groups from the classic Socialist Students, through People and Planet to Conservative Future.

The Radio Society, SURE fm, started as an individual's idea and they're now broadcasting around the union from their own studio. *Sheffield Base took Best Website at last year's national media awards,* and the student newspaper, *Steel Press,* won Newspaper of the Year more times than one cares to remember

---

WHERE SHEFFIELD GRADUATES END UP

Health & Social Work: 19%; Education: 8%; Wholesale Retail: 7%; Manufacturing: 9%; Financial Activities: 9%; Public Administration, Civil Service & Defence: 8%; Hotel/Restaurant: 3%; Transport & Communications (including Tele communications): 4%; Construction: 1%; Personnel: 3%; Computer: 2%; Business & Management: 3%; Accountancy: 5%; Media (including Film): 1%; Legal 2%; Architecture: 5%; Publishing: 1%.

Approximate 'graduate track' employed **69%**

WHAT IT'S REALLY LIKE

UNIVERSITY:

Social Life	★★★★★
Campus scene	**Diverse, lively, sporty, happening and safe**
Student Union services	**Excellent**
Politics	**High level: fees, war, abortion, fair trade**
Sport	**Key, 48 clubs**
National team position	**19th**
Sport facilities	**Good**
Arts opportunities	**Film excellent, drama, dance music, art good**
Student magazine	**Stainless**
Student newspaper	**The Steel Press**
2006 National Awards	**Newspaper of the Year**
Student radio	**SURE FM**
Nightclub	**Fusion & Foundry, Octagon**
Bars	**Bar One, Interval + SU pubs in town**
Union ents	**Drum 'n bass, hip hop, dance, pop, Indie, rock&roll electro punk, retro + live**
, Union clubs/societies	**188**
Parking	**Poor**
CITY:	
Entertainment	★★★★★
Scene	**Seriously good**
Town/gown relations	**Good**
Risk of violence	**Low**
Cost of living	**Low-average**
Student concessions	**Good**
Survival + 2 nights out pw	**£80**
Part-time work campus/town	**Good**

(including last year, indeed).

The Union is one of only a few to boast its own 400-seat cinema, run by students, who picked up a Distinction at the 2006 British Federation of Film Societies Awards.

The Theatre Company uses the **Drama Studio** for productions ranging from Shakespearean tragedy to student-written plays on pornography to musicals.

A 400-seat auditorium, extension to the union, is used by the Film Unit as a cinema four times a week, showing films prior to release on video.

SPORT The Goodwin Sports Centre, which includes a first-class (but cold) swimming pool, gym and numerous astro-turf pitches, has had major improvements to its facilities recently at a cost of £14 million. There are currently some 40 sports clubs with the policy 'sport for all', covering traditional sports like rugby, hockey and cricket and newer sports like frisbee, step and skiing. You can be as involved as you like, many aerobics classes work a 'pay as you go' system for example.

TOWN 'Roughly a third of all Sheffield University students stay in the city after they graduate,' notes Rose, 'which indicates either a staggering lack of imagination or a real affection for the place.' See *Student Sheffield*, page 426.

PILLOW TALK

Ranmoor is the biggest hall and has a bar to rival no other, although smaller halls like Stevenson or Halifax are friendlier. Self-catering flats are popular with those who appreciate their independence and enjoy cooking. Some, like Crewe Flats, offer entertainment like a hall, others like Riverdale Flats are cheaper and quieter. But there is about to be a revolution in what is available.

New accommodation - all en-suite and on the north side of campus, on the old site of its student residences (many of which were 40 years old), at a cost of £160 million. The first phase opened in September 2006, and the project - 38 new blocks of residences for up to 4,200 students - will complete in 2009. Two whole villages are to be created in the next two years: Endcliffe will provide catered and self-catered accommodation - some of which will be available from September 2007- focused around the innovative social facilities of **The Edge**. Ranmoor Village will begin in 2008 and follow a similar pat-

AT A GLANCE

ACADEMIC FILE:

Subjects assessed	**47**
Excellent	**89%**
Typical entry requirements	**405 points**
Application acceptance rate	**14%**
Med. School acceptance rate	**7%**
Students-staff ratio	**16:1**
First/2:1 degree pass rate	**72%**

ACCOMMODATION FILE:

Guarantee to freshers	**100%**
Style	**Halls, flats, houses**
Catered	**42%**
En suite	**41%**
Approx price range pw	**£75-£130**
City rent pw	**£52-£78**

tern, focused around the social hub, **The Ridge**. The aim is to create thriving communities. The accommodation is set in the heart of one of Sheffield's most attractive leafy suburbs, just to the south of campus.

GETTING THERE

☞ By road: M1/J33, A630, A57.
☞ By rail: London, 2:30; Liverpool Lime Street, 1:45; Manchester Piccadilly, 1:00; Nottingham 1:00; Leeds, 30 mins.
☞ By air: Manchester Airport.
☞ By coach: London, 3:45; Newcastle, 4:45;.

SHEFFIELD HALLAM UNIVERSITY

Sheffield Hallam University
City Campus
Sheffield S1 1WB

TEL 0114 225 5555
FAX 0114 225 4023
EMAIL admissions@shu.ac.uk
WEB www.shu.ac.uk

Sheffield Hallam Union of Students
The HUBS
Paternoster Row
Sheffield, S1 2QQ

TEL 0114 225 4111
FAX 0114 225 4140
EMAIL [initial.name]@shu.ac.uk
WEB www.hallamunion.com

VAG VIEW

*H*allam is big business. With around 28,000 students, 4,000 staff, they turn over some £150 million a year, have invested £81 million on teaching and learning facilities in the last 10 years and plan to invest a further £80 million up to 2010.

the uni took over Sheffield University's nursing and midwifery provision. Then, last year, the Faculty of Arts, Computing, Engineering and Sciences moved from depressing Psalter Lane to the Students' Union building on City Campus. Worry not, however, the SU has itself moved to the former National Centre for Popular Music, which couldn't be more

UNIVERSITY/STUDENT PROFILE	
University since	**1992**
Situation/style	**City campus**
Student population	**28350**
Undergraduates	**20660**
- mature	**12%**
- overseas	**5%**
- male/female	**50/50**
- non-traditional student intake	**30%**
-state school intake	**95%**
- drop-out rate	**14%**
- undergraduate applications	**Up 12%**

Female Undergraduates 37%
Postgraduates 26%
STUDENT POPULATION
Total students **28,350**
Male Undergraduates 36%
Others 1%

Its work-orientated courses suggest that it is bent on stoking the nation's economy.

Recently they have made a huge investment in reorganisation, shedding one campus site and boosting two others, one in the city centre, the other in the suburbs. Last year, following the opening of the Adsetts Centre, a multimedia Learning Resources Centre, their new 'beacon for health and social care education', the £15-million Health and Wellbeing building opened on Collegiate Campus, and

appropriate. It was back up and running over a year ago.

CAMPUSES

SHU is based around 3 sites, City, Collegiate Crescent, and Psalter Lane. The latter, the runt of the litter, with it's school-like corridors and grim exterior, will close on completion of a new city-centre site adjacent to Sheffield's Cultural Industries Quarter, when the Students Union will also move into the former National Centre for Popular Music. Now – this year – an £8-million School of Health and Social Care will open on the Collegiate

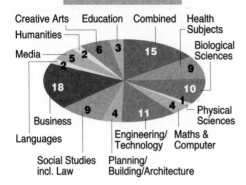

SUBJECT AREAS (%)

Creative Arts — Education — Combined — Health Subjects
Humanities
Media
Biological Sciences
Business
Languages
Social Studies incl. Law
Engineering/ Technology
Planning/ Building/Architecture
Maths & Computer
Physical Sciences

(pie chart values: 5, 2, 6, 3, 15, 2, 9, 10, 18, 1, 4, 9, 4, 11, 4)

Crescent site.

'Collegiate campus is really quite good,' writes Chris Gissing. 'It's a traditional, leafy campus, ideally placed on the *revelation* that is Ecclesall Road. Sheffield's Eccy Road is the hub of student ents, with about 830 bars and 6,000 coffee houses (well, maybe not as many as that, but after the first 5 pubs, who cares?).

'City Campus is excellent too, centrally located and based around 4 or 5 disparate buildings, connected by the stunningly designed **Atrium**. This glass/steel construction has masses of open space, and is like a cosmopolitan street café with tables and chairs and...well...a café. The Adsetts Centre is based here and offers 24-hour access to computers, Internet, books, photocopying etc. Fortunately, the library staff who seemed to fine me on a weekly basis don't work twenty-four hours.'

FEES, BURSARIES

UK & EU Fees, 2007: £3,000. Fees for 2008 not yet known. If in receipt of full HE Maintenance grant there's a bursary of £700. Support, too, if applying from partnership colleges or schools. A limited number of scholarships of £1,000 and based on academic achievement are also available for first years.

STUDENT PROFILE

'We have the whole range,' Chris continues, 'from working-class-kid-scraped-through-on-a-BTEC/ through-Clearing sort, to Mummy-and-Daddy-paid-for-my-flat-and-course-fees-darling sort. They're all here in this city – 12% of the city's population are students. Sheffield Hallam has more working-class students than Sheffield University does.' In fact, the 30% figure is now no longer a big deal in the context of UK unis, and, as Chris says, 'we all seem to get along fairly well, and we are of course allowed to use each others' union bars/women/ blokes (delete as appropriate).'

ACADEMIA & JOBS

Tom Bilton writes: 'Your degree will find you a job, but 'you will need to be self-motivated. If you're after close-knit tutorials with tutors that take a thorough interest in you, you'd be better off at Sheffield University.' At Hallam the student:staff ratio is 25 to 1; at Sheffield it's 16:1.

Back-up resources are increasingly good, however, and Chris Gissing concludes: 'The teaching within my school (Computing & Management Science) was on the whole very good. I cannot fault the department for what they offer in terms of specialist knowledge and resources. On the IT courses there is a strong bias towards industrial placements and business skills, invaluable when going into the real world of work.'

More than 10% of graduates go into education – secondary and primary. Top scoring at the teaching assessments, it's not too difficult to get in, and Education is one of three subjects to score 23 points out of 24 for teaching. The others were maths and health.

Graduates of Computer Science, Health, Business, Social Science, and Creative Arts also march confidently into the higher education sector as lecturers. Art & Design and Social Science scored 22 points at the teaching assessments and Art an international, Grade 5 rating for research.

Hallam is among the leaders for sheer numbers of graduates into banking, a 3/4-year sandwich BA in Banking & Finance requires 240 points only. A BSc Business & Finance is a top-up alternative.

ACADEMIC EXCELLENCE

TEACHING:
(Rated Excellent or 17+ out of 24)

English	**Excellent**
Psychology, Physics, Tourism	**24**
Maths, Education, Subjects Allied to Medicine	**23**
Sociology, Materials Technology Art & Design, Molecular Biosci., Business/Finance	**22**
General Engineering; Mech, Aeronautical & Manufacturing Engineering, Nursing, Building	**21**
History of Art, Design & Film	**20**
Modern Languages (French, German, Italian, Spanish) Communication Studies.	**19**
Civil Eng, Elec & Electron Eng.	**18**

RESEARCH:
Top grades 5/5*

Metallurgy, History, Art & Design	**Grade 5**

Hallam is again the place for insurance/pension brokers/underwriters. These sectors account for between 2% and 3% of all graduates from here.

Business scored 22 out of 24 points at the assessments. They have recently launched an Enterprise Centre to imbue the whole uni with an enterprise culture. There are Finance, Human Resources Mgt, Marketing or Financial Services adjuncts and a series of International Business Studies (French, German, Italian, Spanish) and languages with e-Commerce degrees.

Employment figures show success in personnel in particular through the 4-year sandwich BA Hons Business & Human Resource Management. Look, too, at transport, where Hallam is out in front for graduate employment. BA Planning & Transport or Geography with Transport are the degrees. For the catering trade (another key graduate employment area) there's BSc Hons Hospitality Business Management with Conference/Events or Culinary Arts possibilities, or Leisure Events Management with Arts & Entertainments, Outdoor Recreation, or Tourism. They scored full marks at the assessments.

Marketing is also a strength and there is a steady flow of graduates into advertising. See the BA Communication and Information degrees – Communication Studies, and in the Art & Design Faculty, Information Design & Multimedia.

Engineering has always been a strength. For mechanical engineers they ask least at entry among the employment leaders. BEng Hons include Mechanical & Computer-Aided Eng and Mechatronics, and there's a major/minor route for Mechanical Engineering with minor options being Automotive, Control, Environmental Management, Business Management or Electrical Eng. 21 points at the assessments.

Again, like Bath Uni, they lead the way in guiding Electrical Engineering graduates into telecommunications. Look at the E & E and Computer

Aided Engineering & Design degrees. There may be a low teaching assessment, but employers still love them. Teaching inspection 18.

Computer programmers come thick and fast off the Hallam production line with BSc Computing and its applications – Networks, Software Eng, Visualisation, Web Info. Systems & Services, or with Management Science.

BSc Pharmaceutical Sciences puts the uni into the Top 10 for finding graduates work in the pharmaceutical manufacturing industry. Meanwhile, health subjects make a huge impact on their employment figures – degrees in Physiotherapy, Occupational Therapy, Radiotherapy, Oncology, Nursing… They have opted for areas where the other Sheffield university doesn't tread, and they dropped only one point at the assessments. The Diagnostic Radiography and Radiography & Oncology BSc degrees corner well over 4% of the national employment market in this sector at a low asking rate. Teaching inspection, 23.

They're among the leading providers, too, for social workers/counsellors. The BA Social Work Studies hits the spot, but see, too, Social Policy, Social, Cultural and Psychology mixes.

See also the BSc Psychology, fully accredited by the British Psychological Society and first step to becoming a Chartered Psychologist.

Stats show, too, that BSc Architectural Technology or Architecture & Environmental Design are both solid lines into a career. Look also at Construction Management, Construction Commercial Management and Building Surveying. There is employment strength in-depth at Hallam for jobs in the construction industry and BSc Quantity Surveying is no exception. Teaching inspection, 21. There's a track record, too, in property – look at BSc Property Studies.

Law also has a good reputation. Note the LLB

> *'In recent years, Sheffield has undergone a renaissance. You come to Hallam, you come to the city. It may never rival Leeds, Manchester or Nottingham, but you will soon discover why so many students choose to stay after graduation.'*

WHERE SHEFFIELD HALLAM GRADUATES END UP

Health & Social Work: 12%; Education: 11%; Wholesale Retail: 9%; Manufacturing: 10%; Financial Activities: 9%; Public Administration, Civil Service & Defence: 10%; Hotel/Restaurant: 6%; Transport & Communications (including Telecommunications): 2%; Construction: 3%; Personnel: 4.5%; Computer: 4%; Business & Management: 2%; Accountancy: 1%; Media (including Film): 1%; Legal 4%; Architecture: 1.5%; Publishing: 1%; Advertising: 1%; Artistic/Literary: 0.5%; Sport: 1%.

Approximate 'graduate track' employed **61%**

/Maitrise En Droit (Francaise) – 2 years in Paris – and the joint degrees with Criminology, Business, Psychology. It is not difficult to see why more probation officers come out of Hallam than anywhere. You can study BA Criminology and Psychology/Sociology, Social Work Studies, Society & Cities, Social Policy, Social Policy & Sociology.

The Law is also a recognised pathway into Civil Service administration from here, while local and regional government administration call on Hallam graduates in such as Social Policy, Society & Cities, Urban Regeneration, Education, Architecture, Building & Planning, and Business & Administration. BA Business & Public Policy is clearly useful. Note also their BSc Public Health Nutrition, and the Planning & Transport BA.

Finally, they are employment leaders in sport, a fact which knits academia together with student leisure – they came 18th in the national sporting league last year. The department was among the few nationwide to score 24 points (full marks) in the teaching assessments.

SOCIAL SCENE

STUDENTS' UNION The stunning silver drums of the new Union Building (known as HUBs) beat a fanfare to what the uni describes as 'a unique and unrivalled welfare and social facility for 28,000 stu-

AT A GLANCE	
ACADEMIC FILE:	
Subjects assessed	**27**
Excellent	**78%**
Typical entry requirements	**264points**
Application acceptance rate	**21%**
Students-staff ratio	**25:1**
First/2:1 degree pass rate	**53%**
ACCOMMODATION FILE:	
Guarantee to freshers	**100%**
Style	**Halls**
Catered	**10%**
En-suite	**50%**
Approx. price range per annum	**£50-£90**
City rent pw	**£52-£78**

dents'. It cost them £5 million, so we should allow them that.

There's a student advice centre and volunteering team, a shop, social space and activities area, plus 3 multi-functional entertainment rooms and a café/bar. **Bar Phoenix** is the focal point, downstairs from the club nights. Ents come on weekday nights in the shape of *Souled* – 6ts guitar, Motown and northern soul, and *You Bring We Spin*, pub quiz etc. On Fridays, it's *Stardust* (6ts/7ts - geddit?), back from its intergalactic break, while Saturday is, and always has been, *Sheff 1* (chart and dance favourite choice of the city).

Stardust and Sheff1 have been so popular that battles have been known with ticket touts re-selling tickets bought at cheaper advance prices.

Meanwhile, if the thought of another night of cheesy chart music 'sends a chill down your spine,' says the increasingly sassy union, 'you'll be glad to know that every Tuesday the HUBs become home to the weekly indie rock'n'roll ruckus that is *Plan B*!'There's also Feliz: Sheffield's newest Gay friendly night, Feliz (fi-leeth), Spanish for 'happy and gay'.

There are 30 student societies, Media = the weekly *HUGE - Hallam Union Guide to Events*, also *SHU-Print* their monthly paper, and RUSH radio, 'with a brand new look and a brand new attitude!'.

War, fees housing and 'Free Wednesdays from lectures' have been the substance of highly active campaigning. Amazing to think that they have to free Wednesdays, given that it's sports day and they are one of the most competitive in the country – there are 35 sports societies and thoroughly professional facilities are available.

SPORT The new fitness suite spans 600 square metres and has more than 70 fitness stations, an

WHAT IT'S REALLY LIKE	
UNIVERSITY:	
Social Life	★★★★
Campus scene	**Massive, diverse**
Student Union services	**Good**
Politics	**Activity high**
Sport	**35 clubs**
National team position	**19th**
Sport facilities	**Good**
Arts opportunities	**Few**
Student magazine	**SHU-Print**
Student radio	**RUSH**
Nightclub/bars	**Bar Phoenix**
Union ents	**Cheese, indie**
Union societies	**65**
Most popular society	**RUSH fm**
Parking	**Poor**
CITY:	
Entertainment	★★★★★
Scene	**Seriously good**
Town/gown relations	**Good**
Risk of violence	**Average**
Cost of living	**Average**
Student concessions	**Good**
Survival + 2 nights out	**£80 pw**
Part-time work campus/town	**Good/excellent**

array of the latest equipment, and an advanced weights and training area. The changing facilities are fully equipped for the disabled, and there's also 'a sunbed, assessment rooms and full audio and satellite TV system' – they call that exercise? There's another suite on Collegiate Campus.

TOWN See *Student Sheffield*, page 426.

PILLOW TALK

Catered halls and self-catered purpose-built complexes are available. Some catered – about 10%. The Trigon - A newly developed site offering 361

en-suite rooms will include all utility bills, 24 hour emergency repairs service, CCTV, security patrols, on site office, laundry facilities. Besides halls, there are partnership schemes in the private sector.

GETTING THERE

☛ By road: M1 (J33), A630, A57.
☛ By coach: London, 3:45; Newcastle, 4:45; Exeter, 6:30-7:30; Manchester, 3:00.
☛ By rail: London, 2:30; Liverpool Lime Street, 1:45; Manchester Piccadilly, 1:00; Nottingham, 1:00; Leeds, 0:30.
☛ By air: Manchester Airport.

UNIVERSITY OF SOUTHAMPTON

The University of Southampton
Highfield
Southampton SO17 1BH

TEL 023 8059 5000
FAX 023 8059 3037
EMAIL admissions@soton.ac.uk
WEB www.soton.ac.uk

Southampton Students' Union
Highfield
Southampton SO17 1BJ

TEL 023 8059 5201
FAX 023 8059 5252
EMAIL susu@soton.ac.uk
WEB www.soton.ac.uk/~susu/

VAG VIEW

Southampton has one of the best academic records in the country, but has suffered a poor reputation for student satisfaction beyond academia – historically the social side of things has been a bit limp. Now it has been revitalised by a huge investment in the Student Union, so that this year they have had to call upon 20 or so members of the uni rugby teams to act as marshalls for students returning home from the nightclub on Highfield Campus, not to protect them, but to keep down the noise.

CAMPUS

HIGHFIELD CAMPUS From east or west you rattle along the M27 until you hit Junction 5, whereupon you dive down south, following the uni signs, and suddenly, 2 miles from the centre of the city, there you are in it. You don't *enter* the main Highfield campus as you might Sussex campus or Nottingham. It is a campus split by University Road, a public road with uni buildings off to the left and right, so that you're not sure whether the city has wandered onto the campus or the campus has not yet quite commandeered its piece of the city (there is nothing of the excitement of Manchester's Oxford Road, where such questions would never occur).

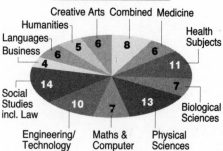

SUBJECT AREAS (%)

Creative Arts 5, Combined 6, Medicine 8, Health Subjects 6, Biological Sciences 11, Physical Sciences 7, Maths & Computer 13, Engineering/Technology 7, Social Studies incl. Law 10, 14, Business 4, Languages 6, Humanities 5

There's a chemically, sciency feel to it. It's all rather laboratorial, claustrophobic, bursting at the seams, for such an eminent university. And then

Postgraduates 31%
Female Undergraduates 41%

STUDENT POPULATION
Total students
23,595

Male Undergraduates 28%

you are transported into some carefully landscaped botanical gardens with stream, and on, across The Avenue, eventually to be released onto the huge open acreage of Southampton Common, where you can...breathe!

Arts are at The Avenue Campus nearby. Finally, you arrive at their internationally renowned **Waterside Campus**/Oceanography Centre.

FEES, BURSARIES
UK & EU Fees, 2007: £3,070 p.a. If in receipt of the HE Maintenance grant there are sliding-scale bursaries according to household earnings. There are also bursaries to encourage applications from a wider section of the population and scholarships for academic achievement.

STUDENT PROFILE
The tradition is that, apart from a small scattering of minority groups and locals, Southampton students are middle-class, although the public school kid intake is in fact similar to that of Reading or Warwick, and less than at Bristol, Durham or Exeter. In a survey of student drug-taking habits by the Adam Smith Institute, they came out 'most abstemious'. The survey was undertaken before the opening of the new on-campus pleasure dome (see *Social Scene* below). It is as yet unclear whether students' habits have changed, only that everyone is having the time of their lives at Highfield.

What's more, against any charges of social elitism they can point to an impressive campaign last year, which saw Southampton students spend a week living rough on the streets of the city, with no access to money. The project was in aid of Student Action for Refugees, a campaign supported by two dozen other universities.

ACADEMIA & JOBS
The 5-floor Hartley Library on the main Highfield campus has recently undergone a massive refit, making it one of the most advanced university libraries in Britain. Access to resources has been improved and personal study areas have been restyled to allow more privacy.

The Medical Faculty was rated full marks in the teaching assessments. It's a 5-year BM with integrated course structure and clinical contact from first year. A 4th-year 8-week period of clinical experience may be had in subject and place of your choice (many opt to go abroad). There's a 6% application acceptance rate, makig it more competitive than most (the average is 10%). Entry AAB, 340 points + UKCAT, including Chemistry A. 7A/B at GCSE to include Maths, English and Double Award Science. Teaching inspection 24 (full marks). Research Grade 5: Clinical Lab Sciences, Hospital-based Clinical, Psychology, Biological Sciences. They are looking for the committed, well-rounded applicant capable of approaching problems with a certain flair, not confined by specialism. Coursework is geared towards problem-solving; patient contact is made in the first term in order to develop communication skills.

Other departments that scored full marks for teaching are: Education, Philosophy, Economics, Electrical & Electronic Engineering, Archaeology and Politics.

If you look at another area in which the uni is renowned – Geography – you see a similar sort of picture. Analytical skills, problem-solving and written and oral expression are to the fore – it's an approach to which employers relate.

Physiotherapy, Occupational Therapy and Podiatry degrees further boost the health sector. There's also Nursing (Adult, Child, Learning Disability, Mental) and Midwifery. Psychotherapists also bound out of here. Look at their Applied Social Science degrees (Anthropology, Criminology), as well as the BSc Psychology and BSc Social Work.

After health, the City claims most of Southampton's graduates. Accounting & Economics or Finance ensure good employment figures, and there's a leaning to careers for tax expert/consultants and actuaries. For the latter, look especially at Economics with Actuarial Studies and Mathematics with Actuarial Studies. Teaching inspection 20. Research Grade 5.

Economics, Maths and Business are the main routes for aspiring bankers, financiers and investment advisers/ analysts. Economics took full marks at the assessments and an international Grade 5 for research; Management scored 23. Maths 20 and again a Grade 5 for research.

Southampton are hot on student enterprise. 'Spin out' companies have raised more than £20 million of private funds. More than 60 students enrolled with the Student Entrepreneurs Club.

UNIVERSITY/STUDENT PROFILE	
University since	**1952**
Situation/style	**Campus**
Student population	**23595**
Undergraduates	**16185**
- mature	**14%**
- non EU undergraduates	**6%**
- male/female	**40/60**
- non-traditional student intake	**19%**
- state school intake	**80%**
- drop-out rate	**8%**
- undergraduate applications	**Up 9%**

SETsquared is a dedicated support and mentoring facility for entrepreneurs and fledgling enterprises.

In the Oceanography Centre at Southampton's Dockside, Marine Science students again have access to exceptional analytical and research facilities. The faculty produces partnership degrees with Biology, Geology, Geography, Maths, Physics, which have led to Excellent ratings in the assessments. Ellen MacArthur's stunning performance in Kingfisher, in the Vendee Global Challenge, carried with it tank and wind-tunnel research work done by the university. The yachtswoman was closely involved in the design and testing processes.

Defence is clearly a priority. Like Portsmouth along the coast, Southampton has an active OTC. There's a University Air Squadron and Royal Naval Unit. Many Southampton graduates bound for the Defence industry come from the Faculty of Engineering & Applied Science, which gained world-class ratings in the research assessments, and Electronics scored full marks in the teaching assessments: Acousitical, Aerospace, Civil, Electrical & Electronic, Electromechanical and a number of Engineering Management degrees, also Computing Engineering.

The uni has more than a 27% share nationally of RN officers. See in particular the B/MEng Ship Science, the MEng comes in various orientations: Yacht & Small Craft, Naval Architecture, Inter-Disciplinary, and the 4-year Advanced Materials. There's a 23-point assessment for Ship Science and an international Grade 5 level for Operational Research. For RAF officers, there's a BEng Foundation year and everything from Computer Science/Engineering through MEng Aerospace Engineering with European Studies. Army officers' interest tips in favour of Physical Sciences, where there are 4-year Masters degrees and 3-year BSc Hons from which to choose. There are good joint Chemistry or Physics courses with specialisms such as Laser Science, Maths and Theoretical Physics (5* world-class research rating).

No mention of Southampton ever goes without a nod to Medicine, and in this context, some 8% of graduates going into Defence do so with some

medical science background – Medicinal Chemistry, Biomedical Sciences, etc.

Computer programmers and software engineers also proliferate. They offer BSc Computer Science and various orientations – with AI, Distributed Systems & Network, Image &

ACADEMIC EXCELLENCE

TEACHING:
(Rated Excellent or 17+ out of 24)

Chemistry, Applied Social Work, Computer Studies, Geography, English, Oceanography, Geology, Music.	**Excellent**
Philosophy, Electric/Electron Eng Economics, Education, Medicine, Archaeology, Politics	24
General Eng, Management Ships Science, Biosciences	23
Art & Design, Nursing, Physics	22
Psychology, Sociology, Civil Eng, Mech, Aeronaut & Manuf Eng	21
History of Art, Maths, Subjects Allied to Medicine	20
Modern Languages (French, German, Iberian Studies).	18

RESEARCH:
Top grades 5/5/6**

Computer, Electrical/Electronic Eng, Mechanical/Aeronautical/ Manufacturing Eng, Law, European Studies, Music	**Grade 6***
Physics, Civil Eng,	**Grade 5***
Clinical Laboratory Sciences, Hospital-based Clinical, Psychology, Biological Sciences, Chemistry, Environmental Sciences, Pure Maths, Applied Maths, Statistics, Operational Research, Geography, Economics, Social Policy, English, Archaeology, History	**Grade 5**

WHERE SOUTHAMPTON GRADUATES END UP

Health & Social Work: 21%; Education: 4%; Wholesale Retail: 7%; Manufacturing: 9%; Financial Activities: 11%; Public Administration, Civil Service & Defence: 9%; Hotel/Restaurant: 4%; Transport & Communications (including Telecommunications): 4%; Construction: 1%; Personnel: 5%; Computer: 3.5%; Business & Management: 3%; Accountancy: 4%; Media (including Film): 1%; Legal 2%; Publishing: 1.5%; Advertising: 0.5%; Sport: 1.5%.

Approximate 'graduate track' employed **70%**

Multimedia Systems, Software Eng. There are also two MEng degrees: Software Engineering and the 4-year Computer Engineering, and a facility, too, to study Computer Science for a BEng with Foundation year.

For would-be sound recordists Southampton leads the employment field with B/MEng Acoustical Engineering. Look at course links between their Institute of Sound & Vibration and the Dept of Music: BSc Acoustics and/with Music and the Acoustical Engineering Foundation course. Full marks and a world class reputation for Electronic Engineering and an 'Excellent' for teaching Music and Grade 6* for research give one confidence.

> '*Southampton have called up members of the uni rugby teams to act as marshalls for students returning home from the nightclub on Highfield Campus, not to protect them, but to keep down the noise.*'

Boat/ship designers/surveyors/brokers are all served well. Southampton satisfies through design, construction and operation in its Department of Engineering. Maths and a science (preferably Physics) or a techno subject are essential for the various Ship Science courses. Among the Masters and Bachelor degrees on offer is Ship Science/Yacht & Small Craft and SS/Naval Architecture asking the same; 350 points will get you the main BEng, Ship Science, and there's a 4-year version with Foundation if you need it. Teaching inspection 23.

For aspiring environmental officers the 4-year MEnvSci Environmental Sciences does the trick. Similar Masters degrees are available in Geology, Geophysics, and Oceanography, and then a whole range of BSc degrees variously offering French or German options, and there's an Environmental Sciences Foundation year too.

Humanities spawn their fair share of librarians and museum curators from here, while in the business sector a number become sales or travel agency managers.

Their Sports Management & Leadership and Sport Studies degrees put them in the Top 10 for athletes, sportsmen, players and officials, and ensure a very healthy spin-off in performance levels in the BUSA league (13th this year).

Finally, Law is also a big draw, they have a world-class Grade 6* rating for research.

WINCHESTER SCHOOL OF ART Park Avenue, Winchester SO23 8DL. Tel 01962 842500 is Southampton's Art & Design faculty, 12 miles distant. Recently, £3 million bought new studios, a library, a lecture theatre, photo and digital workshops, seminar rooms and a Students' Union. Degrees are offered in Fine Art, Practice & Theory and Textiles, Fashion & Fibre. Teaching inspection 22.

SOCIAL SCENE

STUDENTS' UNION A new Student Services Centre, site for SUSU's Advice & Information Centre opened in October 2005.

For the past few years SUSU has been a bit of a building site, but now boasts a new cinema and nightclub with three bars collectively known as **The Cube**, increasing capacity to 1700. At the Friday night *Kinki* event – low drinks prices and music across three floors (from cheese, to dance, to indie) – it's heaving.

The Cube is open until 2 am, three nights a week. **The Stag's Head** is a pub-style bar with

WHAT IT'S REALLY LIKE	
UNIVERSITY:	
Social Life	★★★★★
Campus scene	**Active, impressive**
Student Union services	**Good**
Politics	**Tory heartland**
Sport	**70 clubs**
National team position	**20th**
Sport facilities	**Excellent**
Arts opportunities	**Drama, film excellent**
Student newspaper	**Wessex Scene**
Student radio	**Surge**
2006 national awards	**1 Gold; 2 Bronze**
Nightclub	**The Cube**
Bars	**Bridge Bar, Stag's Head**
Union ents	**Kinki, Generator, Fat Poppadaddys**
Union societies	**160+**
Most active society	**Theatre Group**
Parking	**No first years**
CITY:	
Entertainment	★★★
Scene	**Pubs, clubs, water**
Town/gown relations	**Average-poor**
Risk of violence	**Average**
Cost of living	**Average**
Student concessions	**OK**
Survival + 2 nights out	**£80 pw**
Part-time work campus/town	**Good/excellent**

license until midnight, and runs events such as Karaoke and the Sunday Quiz.

There is also the **Bridge** bar, located at the top of the Union building and with a view of campus and stream below. **The Bridge** hosts the *Jazz Lounge*, the *Laughter Lounge*, and the chill-out *Living Room* events.

Fat Poppadaddys comes to town on Saturday (funk, 60s, hip hop, reggae, drum 'n' bass). Thursdays hosts *Generator* – their indie and rock night, which feature live bands, like Arab Strap.

Over the past couple of years, SUSU has also hosted big name DJs such as Dave Pearce, Carl Cox and Judge Jules. The Cut Up Boys kept the Grab Ball pumping, and Colin Murray took to the decks in Freshers' Week last year. Radio 1 Zane Low's *In New Music We Trust* tour came to the Union as well and Razorlight played live. More recently, Zane hijacked the student radio station, Surge, and took over the Saturday night show.

Societies have always been strong at Southampton. *Wessex Scene*, the student paper, and Surge Radio remain a feature, as does *The Edge*, the ents paper. *Wessex Scene* won the 2004 *Guardian* Media Award for Website of the Year and has been nominated in that category for 4 successive years. Surge, which has recently benefited from a new £20k studio, scooped 2 gold awards at the National Student Radio Awards in 2005 – for best newcomer and best news and talk. They also received nominations for best technical achievement, best male and best off air marketing and publicity. Then last year they took a Gold for Best Entertainment Show, and Bronze awards for Outside Broadcast and Journalistic Programme.

For Drama, there's the highly rated **Nuffield Theatre,** and there's a thriving Film Society. They have a 400-seat cinema showing second-release films through Dolby surround sound. There's also a tradition of student bands.

SPORT Sport is huge at Southampton. Last year saw the opening of a brand new sports centre on the campus, complete with swimming pool, gym, 8-badminton court sports hall and 140-station fitness suite. And in Autumn 2005 the new Wide Lane Sports Complex was opened by John Inverdale. This £4.3m complex boasts 76 acres of pitches (including 2 floodlit synthetic pitches), 24 changing rooms, meeting rooms and a fully-licensed bar. There's also a boatyard for watersporters. The sailors have won the BUSA championship more times than Portsmouth care to recall.

TOWN While Southampton itself has neither the size nor vigour of Manchester or its football team, nor yet the groovy cuts of Brighton or even

AT A GLANCE	
ACADEMIC FILE:	
Subjects assessed	**34**
Excellent	**91%**
Typical entry requirements	**387 points**
Application acceptance rate	**13%**
Med. School acceptance rate	**6%**
Students-staff ratio	**16:1**
First/2:1 degree pass rate	**69%**
ACCOMMODATION FILE:	
Guarantee to freshers	**If uni first firm choice**
Style	**Halls, flats**
Catered	**25%**
En-suite	**45%**
Price range pw	**£65-£128**
City rent pw	**£48-£70**

Bournemouth, it's a lively enough place to live. Having been a Regency holiday resort, the city centre has a large number of spacious parks and waterfront attractions.

'If Southampton were a person, it would be a dedicated alcoholic,' said a student. 'The city centre and waterfront have a network of colossal alcohol palaces (including Britain's largest pub, the **Square Balloon**), yet the city lacks a twilight zone, for, owing to a local statute, even nightclubs are not allowed to open later than 2.'

There are three cinemas and the **Mayflower Theatre**, which plays host to several major West End shows. Musically, Southampton lacks a major venue and is often ignored by the larger acts: consult your Bournemouth train timetable.

PILLOW TALK

University accommodation (halls and flats) is guaranteed to all first year undergraduates who meet the terms of their offers, and name Southampton as their firm choice.

There are new and notably enlightened residences now for couples, too: Shaftesbury Avenue and Edwina House. Facilities may include a library and music room, and computer, TV and games rooms. Some halls have sports facilities, all have launderettes and many have shops and bars. Every room has a phone. Avoid Bencraft and Stoneham halls. Bencraft is miles from anywhere and Stoneham is Southampton's answer to the walled city of Kowloon apparently.

GETTING THERE
☛ By road to Southampton: M3/J 14, A33. To Winchester: M3/J10 or A34.

☛ By coach to Southampton: London, 2:30; Bristol, 2:45; Birmingham, 3:40. To Winchester: London, 2:00; Birmingham, 5:30.

☛ By rail to Southampton: London Waterloo, 1:40; Bristol Parkway, 2:15; Birmingham, 3:30; Sheffield, 4:45; Winchester, 20 mins.

☛ By air: Southampton International Airport

• •

SOUTHAMPTON SOLENT UNIVERSITY

Southampton Solent University
East Park Terrace
Southampton
Hampshire SO14 ORT

TEL 023 8031 9039
FAX 023 8022 2259
EMAIL enquiries@solent.ac.uk
STUDENT UNION TEL 023 8023 2154
WEB www.solent.ac.uk/

VAG VIEW

Southampton Institute, out of Southampton's College of Art and College of Higher Education, and the College of Nautical Studies at Warwash, looks an attractive thoroughbred in its own right. There is an innovative vocational portfolio, an enviable record of excellence in teaching assessments, a lively student scene, and it is not too demanding at entry. What's more, its investment in student residences (they tell us they can meet 'all demand') even three years ago indicated an appeal not restricted to a local clientele. As we said at the time: 'We should not be surprised that the institute has on its longterm plans the desire for University status.'

Well, now they have it, and this year applications rose by 28%. They say: 'We have no intention of changing our mission or ethos. Our focus will remain on accessibility and teaching strongly underpinned by research and community engagement. We will continue to offer and develop innovative courses with an

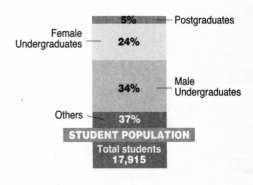

emphasis on preparing students for work.'

FEES, BURSARIES

UK & EU Fees, 2007: £3,070 p.a. There are bursaries for students in receipt of the HE Maintenance Grant on a sliding scale, according to parental income. Sports scholarships are available, as are the Lisa Wilson scholarship and Toft Scholarship for students 'who have overcome adversity or can demonstrate why he/she needs extra financial help with his/her studies' (£1,000).

UNIVERSITY/STUDENT PROFILE	
University since	**2005**
Situation/style	**Civic**
Student population	**17915**
Undergraduates	**10415**
- mature	**40%**
- non EU undergraduates	**6%**
- male/female	**59/41**
- non-traditional student intake	**27%**
- state sector intake	**95%**
- drop-out rate	**21%**
- undergraduate applications	**Up 28%**

STUDENT PROFILE

Writes Tanver Hussain. 'The blokes all look like fugitives from just about any boy band and the girls could form All Saints 100 times over. This excludes Art students and the rugby team, as you will find that they are in worlds of their own! Don't be frightened! You'll find a group of people you will naturally slot into and pretty soon you will go drinking with them every night until you run out of money or are barred from every club, pub or bar in the city.'

Tanver's judgement may have been swayed by the thousands of FE students that inhabit Solent. Among undergraduates there is the expected majority from the state school sector, but for a new university, there's a relatively small number from new-to-uni groups. They are way down on their Government benchmark for recruiting from the lowest four socio-economic groups, and taking in nearly half of what is expected of them from the so-called 'low participation neighbourhoods'.

ACADEMIA & JOBS

The faculties are: Business; Media, Arts and Society; and Technology. Besides Maritime (including yacht and powercraft design), departments include Design (Fashion, Fine Art, Graphic Design, Interior, etc); Built Environment (big strength in Architectural Technology degrees, Construction Management, etc); Business (Tourism Management is new with options like Cruise and Travel Operations); Law (Commercial Law degrees); Media Arts (Film, Fiction, Journalism, Advertising); Social Science (Community Studies, Psychology, Criminology, Politics); Systems Engineering (masses of computer courses and a tasty specialist degree in Media Technology for the broadcast, film & entertainment industries). The curriculum is exciting, innovative, expanding fast.

This year, Solent has a raft of new music, media and broadcasting courses, including TV and video production, screenwriting, print journalism, popular music and cultural theory and fashion. This follows investment of £500,000 to upgrade studios, create digital radio facilities and set up a new centre for professional development in broadcasting and multimedia production in collaboration with ITV Meridian. Film cameramen/women (TV & Film) look to their BSc Film & Video Technology, BA Television & Video Production. BSc Media Technology & Music, and BSc Studio Technology find graduates jobs in the music business. Now comes BA Popular Music Studies & Record Production.

Creative writing is a developing area. New last year was BA Popular Fiction, Screenwriting, Magazine Journalism & Feature Writing, Comedy -

ACADEMIC EXCELLENCE	
TEACHING :	
(Rated Excellent or 17+ out of 24)	
Civil Eng, Building, Land &	**22**
Property Mgt, Business	
Drama, Dance & Cinematics,	**21**
Leisure/Sport	
Psychology, Sociology,	**19**
Electric & Electron Engineering,	
General Eng, Mechanical	
& Manuf Eng, Aero Eng,	
Materials Tech.	
Town & Country Planning,	**18**
Communication & Media	
Art & Design	**17**

Writing & Performance, Sport Writing.

Among the smaller student populations Solent and Napier (Edinburgh) mount an amazingly strong challenge to the big boys in getting graduates into publishing, being right up there with universities that have double their number of undergraduates. Solent mounts its strategy through Media with Cultural Studies, Media Writing, Advertising, Journalism, Marketing with Media & Design, and through its Graphics, Design Studies, Product Design with Marketing, etc degrees. Its general Marketing, Management and Communications degrees are also a gateway.

It also claims to have a world first in its Comedy Writing and Performance BA, devised and run by academic and stand-up comic Chris Ritchie. Other institutions do run modules in comedy, often as part of drama courses. Kent is one.

To be an advertising account executive, you can hardly do better than this university. They place more graduates into the sector than virtually any other. Look at the Design courses and the 3-year Advertising BA or the 1-year Creative Industries top-up for their 2-year HND, Advertising and Media Communication.

Emphasis is on developing the creative faculties by means of idea generation exercises and creative thinking workshops. Budding art directors or copywriters will also get genned up on campaign planning, media buying, targeting and brand positioning. Conversely, if you want to play a strategic role as account planner, handler, media buyer or brand manager, you get a chance to produce campaign concepts for a creative portfolio of work. There's a twinning with a London ad agency, and terrific hands-on experience available from tutors.

Meanwhile, trainee antique dealer/restorers revel in BA Antiques (History & Collecting) – fine arts valuation and appraisal with sharp focus on collecting and the history of collecting from an aesthetic, cultural and financial viewpoint. That's how vocational the set-up is. If you're interested, look at their BA Fine Arts Valuation, too. Both courses are linked to national auction houses.

There's constantly new things going on in art and design – a whole host of new fashion, fashion photography, interiors degrees last year – and recently Muti-media Design and Digital Imaging degrees have led to a big increase in jobs. BA Illustration with Animation also scores high in the world of computer games design.

BSc Mobile Web Technology was new last year, and Electronic Engineering is another big strength. Many come through the HND or Foundation years, their destination almost exclusively telecommunications. Employment figures are good.

Finally, boat/ship designer/surveyor/brokers find their way to courses dedicated to their interests – such as Merchant Ship Operations, Maritime Business, Shipping Operations BSc, Yacht Manufacturing & Surveying and Yacht & Powercraft Design. Foundation years are invariably available, if necessary.

SOCIAL SCENE

STUDENTS' UNION The union has two bars, renovated

AT A GLANCE	
ACADEMIC FILE:	
Subjects assessed	**20**
Excellent	**70%**
Typical entry requirements	**225 points**
Application acceptance rate	**28%**
Students-staff ratio	**30:1**
First/2:1 degree pass rate	**42%**
Graduate track employment	**48%**
ACCOMMODATION FILE:	
Guarantee to freshers	**95%**
Style	**Halls**
Catered	**None**
En suite	**45%**
Approx price pw (no food)	**£83-£94**
City rent pw	**£48-£70**

WHAT IT'S REALLY LIKE	
UNIVERSITY:	
Social Life	**★★★**
Campus scene	**Active, diverse**
Student Union services	**Good**
Politics	**Not much**
Sport	**Competitive**
National team position	**43rd, 31 clubs**
Sport facilities	**Good**
Arts opportunities	**Available**
Student magazine	**Re:SUS**
Student radio station	**SIN Radio**
Nightclub	**In-town clubs**
Bars	**Top Bar, Bottom Bar**
Union ents	**Fat Poppadaddys, city student nights**
Union societies	**28**
Parking	**Poor, permiy**
CITY:	
Entertainment	**★★★**
Scene	**Pubs, clubs, water**
Town/gown relations	**Average-poor**
Risk of violence	**Average**
Cost of living	**Average**
Student concessions	**OK**
Survival + 2 nights out	**£80 pw**
Part-time work campus/town	**Good/excellent**

within the not so distant past, the imaginatively named **Bottom Bar** (downstairs) opens during the week, 11am-5pm, and on Saturday 7pm-11pm in concert with **Top Bar** (11am-11pm in week, 7pm-11pm Saturday). Saturday is the same here as it is at the other uni in Southampton – *Fat Poppadaddys* (funk, 60s, hip hop, reggae, drum 'n' bass). *Fridays @ Solent* are £1-a-shot funky house nights. Thursdays are *Paper Scissors Rock* (alternative). Wednesdays, there's *Loaded*, 9-10pm @ Top Bar, pre-club for *Cheeky Monkey* @ **Ikon Diva** or **Kaos** in town (with an Express Pass which beats the inevitable queue at these the biggest nightclubs).

This union/town tie-up is typical of the weekly ents menu. Tuesday is *Funkie Junkie* (mainstream r&b, house & party anthems) at newest club, **Junk**, on the London Road, again after a **Top Bar** warm-up. Monday, meanwhile, is *Acoustic Night* at Top Bar, a 'bring mates, bring a guitar' affair.

Media-wise there's SIN Radio and Re:SUS magazine. There are 28 societies in operation, not counting course-related efforts.

SPORT There were 31 sports clubs up and running this year, from Capoeira to roller hockey, and triathlon to taekwon do, as well as the more usual – rugby, rowing, American Football and, as expected in a college dedicated to maritime subjects, water plays a key part.

Solent is improving rapidly in its strength in sports and is now 43rd in the national BUSA leagues. Sailing is the strongest sport – they've been national champions three times in the past four years (came second the other time) and three times in the top three in the world. Students come to the university because of its reputation in this sport. Sports scholarships were introduced to attract top performers in all sports. Ground-based sports facilities include a sports hall and fitness suite, sauna and solarium. Playing fields are 4 miles from the city. There's a licensed pavilion, the **Budweiser Sports Bar**.

PILLOW TALK

Cream of the halls crop would have to be Lucia Foster Welch, not only is it the biggest, but it has the advantage of having Ocean Village on its doorstep. The downside is that you are 15 minutes away from the main campus and there is no common room. The other halls all have their plus points, Kimber and its spangly new kitchens or Deanery, one of the newest. All have their own laundry, and all have recently been wired for intranet and intranet access, giving students 24-hour on-line access to the university's managed learning environment and email and internet. You can't choose where you live, but you can choose to have an en-suite bathroom or not.

GETTING THERE

☞ By road: M3/J 14, A33. Warsash: M27/J8, A27.
☞ By coach to Southampton: London, 2:30; Bristol, 2:45; Birmingham, 3:40.
☞ By rail: London Waterloo, 1:40; Bristol Parkway, 2:15; Birmingham, 3:30; Sheffield, 4:45.
☞ By air: Southampton International Airport.

STAFFORDSHIRE UNIVERSITY

Staffordshire University
College Road
Stoke-on-Trent ST4 2DE

TEL 01782 292753
    01782 292752 (prospectus)
FAX 01782 292740
EMAIL admissions@staffs.ac.uk
WEB www.staffs.ac.uk

Staffordshire Students' Union
College Road
Stoke-on-Trent
Staffs ST4 2DE

TEL 01782 294629
FAX 01782 295736
EMAIL theunion@staffs.ac.uk
WEB www.staffsunion.com

VAG VIEW

*T*he sometime Staffordshire Polytechnic has expanded enormously and has the necessary contacts with industry to sustain a strong vocational curriculum. There's also good sport, a strong local ents scene and plenty of student activities to widen your perspective on life. But be aware, Staffordshire is very different from neighbouring Keele

CAMPUSES

There are sites in Stoke and Stafford, 12 miles to the south, opposite the railway station. This is an area known as the Potteries, a borough incorporated in 1907 to include Stoke-on-Trent, Hanley,

UNIVERSITY/STUDENT PROFILE	
University since	**1992**
Situation/style	**Campus/ town sites**
Student population	**14181**
Undergraduates	**12085**
- mature	**30%**
- non EU undergraduates	**4%**
- male/female	**49/51**
- non-traditional student intake	**36%**
- state sector intake	**97%**
- drop-out rate	**23%**
- undergraduate applications	**Down 1%**

Burslem, Tinstall, Longton and Fenton. Its most famous son, Arnold Bennett (author of *Clayhanger, Anne of the Five Towns* – he preferred the sound of five, so left out Fenton) couldn't get away fast enough, but that had nothing to do with the university, which only gained its status in 1992.

FEES, BURSARIES

UK & EU Fees, 2007: £3,070 p.a. If eligible for a HE Maintenance Grant, there are bursaries on a sliding scale according to household earnings.

STUDENT PROFILE

The student profile is as you would expect. There's

Postgraduates 24%
Female Undergraduates 39%
STUDENT POPULATION
Total students 14,181
Male Undergraduates 37%

WHERE STAFFORDSHIRE GRADUATES END UP

Health & Social Work: 7%; Education: 7%; Wholesale Retail: 15%; Manufacturing: 11%; Financial Activities: 6%; Public Administration, Civil Service & Defence: 10%; Hotel/Restaurant: 4%; Transport & Communications (including Telecommunications): 5%; Construction: 1%; Mining/Oil Extracting: 0.5%; Personnel: 5%; Computer: 6.5%; Business & Management: 6.5%; Accountancy: 1%; Media (including Film): 2.5%; Legal 2.5%; Architecture: 1%; Publishing: 1%; Advertising: 0.5%; Sport: 0.5%.

Approximate 'graduate track' employed **54%**

---

a sizable mature population and a sizable local intake. Most entrants are from state schools, and a third of non-mature entrants from social groups 4 to 7, while some 23% come from 'low participation neighbourhoods', i.e. new to the idea of university. The uni appeals to the region with a priority application scheme for locals.

ACADEMIA & JOBS

The faculties are Arts, Media & Design; Business & Law; Computing, Engineering & Technology; Health & Sciences; the Staffordshire University Business School; and the Staffordshire Law School. At Stoke there's Art & Design, Business, Law, Humanities & Social Sciences and Sciences. At Stafford, Computing, Engineering & Advanced Technology and Health. But what's novel is the HE-FE federation being developed with Tamworth & Lichfield College and other further education colleges. There is a Lichfield Campus for the purpose and a whole range of courses, degrees and HNDs with links to what's going on at the mother house.

There are top teaching assessments in Economics (full marks), Psychology, Philosophy, Art & Design, Physics, Sport, Biosciences, Nursing and other subjects allied to Medicine – the latter

ACADEMIC EXCELLENCE

TEACHING:
(Rated Excellent or 17+ out of 24)

Economics	**24**
Psychology, Philosophy	**23**
Art & Design, Physics,	**22**
Leisure/Sport, Biosciences,	
Nursing, Other Subjects Allied	
to Medicine	
Modern Languages (French,	**21**
German, Iberian Studies),	
History of Art.	
Electronic & Electrical Eng.	**20**

RESEARCH :
Top grades 5/5* **None**

featuring midwifery and the nursing (adult, child and mental health). A new healthcare facility opened in 2004 at the Stafford campus to provide NHS care to students, staff and the community. There are doctors' consulting rooms, a practice nurse physiotherapy service and a retail pharmacy.

SUBJECT AREAS (%)

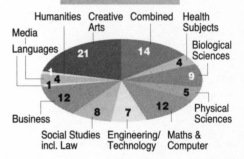

Meanwhile, Staffs' IT & Computing faculty is brimming with opportunity: Graphics/Imaging /Visualisation, Science, Systems, Applicable Maths, Internet Technology, Intelligent Systems, Software Engineering, Forensic, Mobile, computer Design, Games Design, Network Engineering... Aspiring computer programmers and IT consultants (they lead the employment field nationally) should go through it with a toothcomb, Staffordshire Uni is the top graduate supplier to this sector. Entry 240 points. Resources in computing are especially good – two IT centres, the £5-million Octagon centre being a central focus with 800+ workstations.

Graduates acquire accounting knowledge with computer-based analytical, management and design skills. The single honsBA Accounting is joined by combos with Business, Economics and Law.

There's a £1.25-million incubation business project at the Stafford Business Village, with 'high specification incubation' for 40 businesses. Marketing is one highly successful employment area at the Business School, which also explores management and entrepreneurship in areas such as personnel, travel and tourism, as well as having a clutch of degrees in business, computing and IT.

A large number of graduates go into welfare, community and youth work. Look at the Applied Social Studies top-ups, the Sport degrees and high-flying BSc Social Psychology, or the Psychology degrees, which can be done alone or with Criminology or Sport & Excercise. Also, BA Social Work.

The Sport & Leisure Department, which is up there employment-wise with the big boys at Brighton and Nottingham Trent.

The Law Society has awarded the University's LPC course an 'Excellent' rating, the highest accolade it can bestow. Staffordshire is one of only five to share this status. See their recent additions to the curriculum: LLB Sports Law/Human Resources Management/Human Rights/Business Law. A Crime Scene House provides simulated scenes for forensic students to develop detection skills. BSc Forensic Science can be studied alone or with Criminology or Psychology.

For niche employment areas, media is also to the fore. The BA degrees come in Journalism, Film, TV, Broadcast Journalism, Music Broadcasting, Sports Journalism, TV & Radio Documentary. While in Media & Entertainment Technology are the BSc degrees in technology in areas such as film, music, computer games design, 3D animation,, simulation, etc, etc.

Art & Design melds media with art – Animation, Media Production, Photography, for example, and BA CGI Animation & Special Effects.

SOCIAL SCENE

STUDENTS' UNION There are three bars – two at the Stoke campus, **Leek Road Venue** (**LRV** – 1800 capacity) and College Road's newly refurbished **Ember Lounge** (500) and one at Stafford, **Legends**, which goes forth as **Sleepers** during the day.

LRV stages some of the biggest student nights in the Midlands. There are two resident DJs and guest appearances by the famous (DJs and bands). There's also *Comedy Club* on Saturday. It's a busy, well-worked scene. 'We're not on the main gig circuit,' they admit, 'but the DJs and their agents now ring us!' There are also three balls a year, May in March, Summer in June and Graduation in November. May Ball's the biggest.

It isn't all music. There are in fact twenty-three societies at Stoke, and the most active is Drama – there's a good Drama & Theatre Arts degree; at Stafford there are a further ten. The uni newspaper is *GK* (*Get Knotted*) and the student radio station, GK Radio. The paper has received awards from the *Guardian* and the *Daily Telegraph*. Politics are low

on the agenda, though they joined the national march on the tuition fees issue.

SPORT Academic influence brings good facilities for all and fame for some. They have 41 clubs and came 99th nationally in the team ratings. Hockey is their sport. Cross country and badminton teams are also strong, and they have had their top-ranked swimmers, too.

Facilities include a sports centre, sports halls, squash courts, floodlit synthetic and grass pitches for football or rugby, fitness suites, gym with multi-gym, weights and fitness machines. There's also a dance and aerobics studio at the Sir Stanley Matthews Sports Centre in Leek Road.

TOWN Contrary to expectation Hanley, not Stoke, is the main man down among the potteries. There are pubs and clubs in both, however, to which you will soon feel like is home. Just outside Hanley is **Festival Park** – multi-screen cinema, Quasar, Water World, Super Bowl, etc. Stoke has a dry ski slope.

Theatres include the **New Victoria** at nearby Newcastle-under-Lyme, the **Rep Theatre** (Stoke)

WHAT IT'S REALLY LIKE	
UNIVERSITY:	
Social Life	★★★
Campus scene	**Unpretentious fun**
Student Union services	**Good**
Politics	**Activity low: fees**
Sport	**Busy**
National team position	**96th**
Sport facilities	**Good**
Arts opportunities	**Drama, music excellent; dance, film, art good**
Student newspaper	**Get Knotted**
Student radio	**GK Radio**
Nightclub	**Legends**
Bars	**LRV, Ember Lounge**
Union ents	**Serious clubnights & live**
Union societies	**23**
Most active society	**Drama**
Parking	**Adequate**
TOWN:	
Entertainment	★★★
Town scene	**Pubs, clubs**
Town/gown relations	**Average**
Risk of violence	**Average**
Cost of living	**Average**
Student concessions	**Good**
Survival + 2 nights out	**£60 pw**
Part-time work campus/town	**Good**

AT A GLANCE

ACADEMIC FILE:

Subjects assessed	**27**
Excellent	**48%**
Typical entry requirements	**236 points**
Application acceptance rate	**21%**
Students-staff ratio	**18:1**
First/2:1 degree pass rate	**48%**

ACCOMMODATION FILE:

Guarantee to freshers	**85%**
Style	**Halls**
Catered	**None**
En suite	**25%**
Cost pw (no food/food)	**£57-£75**
Town rent pw	**£45**

Wednesdays are film nights at Legends in Stafford; the Drama Soc. is forty strong and puts on four plays a year, including panto.

PILLOW TALK

Stoke: 6 on-campus halls of residence, 8 off campus. Student houses: 36-bedroom houses on Leek Road. Student Flats: blocks of flats, two thirds sharing, within two miles of Leek Road. **Stafford:** Stafford Court includes 249 en-suite rooms; an additional 307 rooms will be open by the time you get there and Yarlet House with fifty-one.

GETTING THERE

* By road: Stafford – M6/J14, A513. Stoke – M6 (J15 from south; J16 from north), A500.
* By coach: London, 4:00.
* By rail: Birmingham New Street, 40 mins; Manchester Piccadilly, 1:20; London Euston, 1:45; Nottingham, 2:00; Sheffield, 2:15.

and **Theatre Royal** (Hanley). Sundays and

UNIVERSITY OF STIRLING

The University of Stirling
Stirling FK9 4LA

TEL 01786 467044
FAX 01786 466800
EMAIL admission@stir.ac.uk
WEB www.stir.ac.uk

Stirling Students' Association
University of Stirling
Stirling FK9 4LA

TEL 01786 467166
FAX 01786 467190
EMAIL susa-president@stir.ac.uk
WEB www.susaonline.co.uk

VAG VIEW

Stirling is a premier-league university with a reputation for leading the way. It was the first traditional uni to grasp the nettle of modularisation and reap the benefits of doing it in proper semesters – two blocks of fifteen weeks.

Its 15-to-1 student-staff ratio is appealing and puts it in the Top 20. The whole campus, including accommodation, is undergoing an extensive programme of refurbishment.

CAMPUS

Gateway to the Highlands, the 360-acre campus is set in beautiful surroundings – a loch, Airthrey Castle, even a golf course – well away from big city life.

The student community is small, relaxed and very friendly. Chances are that you will already know from this description whether you are the kind of student that will suit Stirling. It has suited various writers (Iain Banks among them) and

many golfers too. Some find it pleasantly secure, others slightly claustrophobic, but the spirit of the place espouses a student-centred ethos.

One told me that he felt that Stirling had given him the kind of individual teaching and personal treatment that he imagined he might have enjoyed as a sixthformer had he gone to a public school. He didn't and many don't – 92% entrants are from the state sector and many represent social groups which haven't traditionally gone to university.

22%	Postgraduates
Female Undergraduates — 51%	
STUDENT POPULATION	
Total students 9,000	
27%	Male Undergraduates

FEES, BURSARIES

Non-Scottish-based UK residents pay £1,700 p.a. for all courses at Scottish universities, except Medicine. Sports bursaries are worth between £900 and £2,000, and the have just launched an international sports scholarship with legendary Kenyan runner and humanitarian Kip Keino, which will give talented Kenyan sportsmen and women access to Stirling's sport science expertise. Stirling students will also travel to Kenya on athletics and development projects.

Applicants for academic scholarships should contact the relevant department. There are access bursaries and adult returning students bursaries.

STUDENT PROFILE

The uni has been ranked first in the UK for widening access to Higher Education. Currently 28% of the undergraduate student body are from new-to-uni social groups and 21% from so-called 'low-participation' neighbourhoods. There are also many foreign students, mature students, sporty types and stereotypical broke studenty types. Around half are Scottish, and Stirling attracts a lot from

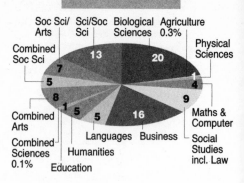

SUBJECT AREAS (%)

Soc Sci/Arts 7 — Sci/Soc Sci 13 — Biological Sciences 20 — Agriculture 0.3% — Physical Sciences — Combined Soc Sci 5 — Physical Sciences 1 — 4 — 8 — 1 — 5 — 5 — 16 — 9 — Maths & Computer — Combined Arts — Combined Sciences 0.1% — Humanities — Languages — Business — Social Studies incl. Law — Education

UNIVERSITY/STUDENT PROFILE	
University since	**1967**
Situation/style	**Rural campus**
Student population	**9000**
Undergraduates	**7000**
- mature	**16%**
- non EU undergraduates	**3%**
- male/female	**35/65**
- non-traditional student intake	**28%**
- state sector intake	**92%**
- drop-out rate	**14%**
- undergraduate applications	**Up 0.2%**

Ireland and from Greece for some reason. A nursing and midwifery course accounts for the 35/65 gender balance in favour of girls.

ACADEMIA & JOBS

They were the first to introduce a semester system of modular degree programmes, which has been taken up by many other unis.

Building a degree with subject modules across faculties can make for an invigorating course. A subject, whatever it may be, is given application. And even if the application doesn't draw you into a career in that area, you will have applied your knowledge-base, rehearsed it for real.

Continuous assessment inherent in the semester system (as opposed to the traditional end-of-year system) minimises the stress of 'all or nothing' final exams.

The first semester in the year is fitted in before Christmas. Then follows a 7-week Christmas holiday before the second 15-week semester, which finishes at the end of May.

Students study three courses per semester and for most of these the coursework content is high. Grades are awarded for each course and these determine whether you may study honours, and later what degree you get.

Sensitivity to the particular abilities of a student, where his or her strengths lie, and to the fact that an idea of these emerges in the process of a course is endemic to the modular ideal and seems to flow from sensibilities at the heart of the ethos at Stirling, set as it is in the lap of such beauty

Nevertheless, it is a wholly practical ethos, too. A quarter of graduates come out of the business end of the curriculum, another quarter out of social sciences and biological sciences.

The picture, six months after graduation, is of clerks, sales assistants/managers, personnel and marketing managers, chartered accountants, bank managers, retail managers, general administrators, business analysts, investment advisers and financial administrators.

Social science graduates add a scattering of social workers to the mix, more clerks and sales managers, assistants, etc. Biological scientists supply natural scientists, teaching professionals, and the health provision gives hospital staff nurses (SEN), midwives, care assistants.

One area in which huge sums of money have been spent recently is Sport. Stirling is the home of the Scottish Institute of Sport; there are national tennis and swimming centres; a centre for golf opened in 2004. There are sports bursaries, and sports trainers and coaches make their mark on graduate employment figures.

Media is another area in which the uni has been making waves. There's a series of film and

WHERE STIRLING GRADUATES END UP

Health & Social Work: 13%; Education: 6%; Wholesale Retail: 12%; Manufacturing: 4%; Financial Activities: 5%; Public Administration, Civil Service & Defence: 7%; Hotel/Restaurant: 8%; Transport & Communications (including Telecommunications): 3%; Agriculture: 0.5%; Personnel: 4%; Computer: 3%; Business & Management: 2%; Accountancy: 3.5%; Media (including Film): 3%; Legal 1.5%; Sport: 2%.

Approximate 'graduate track' employed **56%**

media degrees, and some convincing sounding BA Journalism tie-ups, perhaps Politics or Sport being more cutting edge than Religious Studies. Two years ago a news room became part of the teaching resources.

Interesting development on the nursing front is a return-to-practice scheme after a period of absence – online learning, a dissertation and clinical practice. Stirling's Dementia Services Development Centre has the Iris Murdoch Building for the cognitively impaired.

Stirling has scored high in the teaching assess-

Look at Stirling for social sciences, languages, media, biological sciences, accounting, marketing, management, as well as subjects like religious studies (the combo with politics suddenly looks very modern), psychology (both as social science and as science), tourism and environmental/conservation.

SOCIAL SCENE

STUDENTS' ASSOCIATION To sustain life far from the city, SUSA puts on a fairly uninspired show from its base in the **Robbins Centre**, but no-one seems

ACADEMIC EXCELLENCE

TEACHING::

(Rated Excellent, Highly Satis. or 17+ out of 24)

Economics, Environmental Science, Theology, Sociology, English, Psychology.	**Excellent**
Business & Mgt	**Highly Satis.**
Teacher Education, Maths & Stats, Finance & Accounting, Mass Communics, Philosophy, Politics, Social Work, History, Cellular & Molecular Biology, Organismal Biology, French.	
European Languages	**20**

RESEARCH:
Top grades 5/5*

Psychology, Agriculture, Social Work, Accounting, English, French, History, Philosophy, Theology, Media	**Grade 5**

WHAT IT'S REALLY LIKE

UNIVERSITY:

Social Life	★★★
Campus scene	**Small, friendly, beautiful scene**
Student Union services	**Average**
Politics	**Student issues**
Sport	**Very competitive, 38 clubs**
National team position	**23rd**
Sport facilities	**Top notch**
Arts opportunities	**Excellent**
Student newspaper	**BRIG**
Student radio	**Air 3**
Student TV	**Air TV**
Nightclub	**Glow**
Bars	**Studio, Glow, Cocktail Bar, Sports Bar**
Union ents	**Hip hop, cheese, retro**
Union societies	**37**
Parking	**Expensive permits**
CITY:	
Entertainment	★★
Scene	**Pubs, 3 clubs**
Town/gown relations	**Average**
Risk of violence	**Low**
Cost of living	**Low**
Student concessions	**Some**
Survival + 2 nights out	**£60**
Part-time work campus/town	**Fair**

ments, partly due to their student-centred ethos which touches all faculties. Top of the tree are Economics, Environmental Science, Theology, Sociology, Psychology, English, Business & Management. See, too, the results of the most recent research assessment – ten subjects at Grade 5, in which national and world-class excellence is implicit.

to mind. In fact, the SA won the title of Best Student Union in Scotland (Bar Entertainment & Dance Association) in 2003, and Best Bar None in both 2005 and 2006 (for excellence in 'corporate social responsibility').

There are 5 bars: **Studio**, with its breathtaking views, is open from 9.30am for breakfast, and on into the small hours. Although it has its own programme of ents (pub quizzes, NFL Sundays, *Studio Downloaded* – live gigs online), its main function in the evening is as pre-club for **Glow**, the nightclub downstairs, with 3 bars and massive dancefloor. Thursday is *Rock Night*; Friday, *Alter Ego* (indie), Saturday is *Flirt!* (cheese). There isn't a large enough venue to attract many big name groups, but they've had Radio 1's Trevor Nelson recently, and Edith Bowman, and there are live nights and comedy nights too. They won *Student Union of the Year* in the BEDA Scotland Awards (2003).

'Besides SUSA's ents, the halls of residence hold parties each semester, an excellent opportunity to get pissed and finally profess your undying love to the guy/girl across the corridor, whom you've fancied all semester,' writes Suzanne Bush. 'Some academic departments also have parties at the end of the year. But the best ones are those put on by assorted sports clubs every Thursday night in the meatmarkets, sorry, clubs in town.'

There are the usual clubs and societies – 'SUDS, the Drama Society, aims to put on at least a couple of productions each semester,' Suzanne continues, 'and there's a ready supply of theatre, cinema and music in the form of the **MacRobert Arts Centre** in the middle of the campus.'

> *Stirling is one of only 16 universities in the UK with 5-star sports facilities. This is a small uni, yet their teams came 23rd in the national league tables last year.*

The MacRobert Arts Centre underwent a £6.3-million refurbishment programme in autumn 2002, creating the only professional space for children's theatre in Scotland. In addition to the main theatre, the Centre now houses a full-time dedicated cinema, café bar, crèche, children's room, children's gallery, workshop and rehearsal space.

'The student Musical Society works towards one big production every year. The University Choir brings together students and people from the community and puts on a big concert every semester in Dunblane Cathedral. Also, the university has an orchestra and there's a thriving Live Music Society with student performances on a Sunday night.

'Also, Stirling has a thriving media, a student newspaper, *BRIG*, a campus radio station, Radio Airthrey, offering music, and news programmes, and now Air TV.' Politics is not a big issues until a big issue finds its way into this far-off campus, namely Car Parking!! Some time ago the barriers went up and parking permits were required.

SPORT They call themselves 'Scotland's premier University for Sport', although Edinburgh Uni teams beat them. Anyway, on the strength of their reputation they are greatly enhancing the sports facilities and have just secured funding for a football academy to add to their sports portfolio.

There are excellent sports facilities – one of only 16 Universities in the UK with 5-star sports facilities (*Sunday Times*, 2003), and the teams came 23rd overall last year. Particular strengths are tennis, swimming and of course golf. They have a particular strength in the BUSA championship for golf, coming 1st in the UK in 2005. Campus is home to the Scottish Institute for Sport, the Commonwealth Games Council for Scotland, Scottish Swimming, and is now a preferred training site for the Scottish men's rugby team, but Stirling have established a national reputation for its 'sport for all' programmes.

Every week, hundreds of students participate in a range of activities.. The sports hall is the size of 8 badminton courts or 2 basketball courts and can be divided into 2 or 4 activity areas. The Robertson Trust swimming pool within the National Swimming Academy is a 6- lane, 50-

AT A GLANCE	
ACADEMIC FILE:	
Subjects assessed	**20**
Excellent	**95%**
Typical entry requirements	**342 points**
Application acceptance rate	**15%**
Students-staff ratio	**15:1**
First/2:1 degree pass rate	**67%**
ACCOMMODATION FILE:	
Guarantee to freshers	**100%**
Style	**Halls, chalets**
Catered	**None**
En-suite	**10%**
Price range pw	**£58-£73**
Town rent pw	**£55-£70**

metre pool, which can be split into two 25 metre pools by a moveable boom. One of the 25 metre pools has a moveable floor, changing the water depth from 0 metres to 2 metres. There's a conditioning room next to the pool, as well as an Omega timing system and a full range of water polo fittings and equipment. Four indoor tennis courts form the heart of the National Tennis Centre, and there are three squash courts and viewing gallery. The MP Jackson Fitness Centre houses 3 sports science laboratories: athlete assessment laboratory, research laboratory, analytical laboratory, a fitness suite with 50+ pieces of cardiovascular and resistance equipment, and there's a strength and conditioning "super centre" with 5 lifting platforms. By the sports centre there are 3 football pitches, a 6-lane running track with an 8-lane straight with a terracotta blaes surface, and a grass cricket square with artificial wicket. There are also 2 floodlit terracota blaes pitches for hockey, 6-a-side football and training by football and hockey squads. By Airthrey Castle there are 2 rugby pitches, a putting green and a sports pavilion overlooking the 9-hole, par-3 parkland course, which provides breathtaking views of the Ochil Hills and the Wallace Monument. Airthrey Loch forms the beautiful centre piece of the campus, but is also for angling and canoeing: at the northern end there's a practice area for slalom canoeists.

PILLOW TALK

All freshers are guaranteed uni accommodation and will normally be allocated a single study bedroom in an on-campus hall. But, if demand is high, you may have to share a twin room, or they'll find you alternative accommodation. In addition to halls, there are 33 on-campus chalet bungalows and flats in Stirling. In halls you may be as many as eighteen to a kitchen, in the uni-owned Bridgehaugh flats in town you can enjoy en-suite facilities. The Swiss-style chalets are on the less than enticing-sounding Spittal Hill, but in any case they're reckoned to be for fourth years.

There's no catered accommodation but cafés and restaurants are plentiful, just a few minutes' walk away from the Halls. Meals Package and Flexi Meal Cards make a big saving on till prices, and may be purchased at the start of semester.

GETTING THERE

☛ By road: M9/J11, A9 or A91, A907, A9.
☛ By coach: London, 9:00; Edinburgh, 2:20.
☛ By rail: Glasgow/Edinburgh, 55 mins ;Aberdeen, 2:30; London King's Cross, 6:00.

UNIVERSITY OF STRATHCLYDE

The University of Strathclyde
Graham Hills Building
50 George Street
Glasgow G1 1XQ

TEL 0141 548 2814
FAX 0141 552 5860
EMAIL scls@mis.strath.ac.uk
WEB www.strath.ac.uk

Strathclyde Students' Association
90 John Street
Glasgow G1 1JH

TEL 0141 567 5000
FAX 0141 567 5050
EMAIL theunion@strath.ac.uk
WEB www.theunion.strath.ac.uk

VAG VIEW

Strathclyde's niche strengths are business and engineering. It had its beginnings in 1796 with Anderson's Institution, an equal-opportunity, science and technology college. John Anderson had been Professor of Natural Philosophy at Glasgow University and the institution that bore his name was founded under the terms of his will. University status came in 1964 following the merger of the Royal College of Science and the Scottish College of Commerce, which fact alerts us to Strathclyde's second largest faculty after Engineering, the Strathclyde Business School. In 1993, Glasgow's Jordanhill College joined the fold and became Strath's third largest faculty, Education.

CAMPUS

Today Strathclyde University occupies the same site as Anderson's Institution in the heart of Glasgow, though the original buildings have long gone. The concentration of students in the immediate vicinity is extraordinary: Strathclyde and Caledonian universities, the College of Building and Printing, the College of Food & Technology, and the College of Commerce. The Jordanhill campus is in the West End of the city, close to Glasgow

University. Jordanhill will close in 2010 and the Education Faculty move to a new building in the city centre.

FEES, BURSARIES

UK & EU Fees, 2007: Non-Scottish-based UK residents pay £1,700 p.a. for all courses at Scottish universities, except Medicine. For scholarships, see www.strath .ac.uk/scholarship.htm. There is a University Golf Programme and a Sports Bursary Programme. See www.strath.ac.uk/sport/sports-bursaries/

STUDENT PROFILE

Strathclyde is one of three unis in the city. 'Vibe wise, it has a more relaxed atmosphere in comparison with Glasgow University, which tends to have a more academic outlook,' said a student of Glasgow Uni. Peter Mann, a student at Strathclyde, suggested differences run deeper: 'Caledonian and Strathclyde have a similar kind of population. Glasgow is quite different and generally disliked because it is full of English people. There is not a tremendous amount of mixing.' A student of Caledonian offered this Pythonesque picture of the pecking order: 'Glasgow University looks down on Strathclyde as being John Street Poly, although it's been a university since 1964. And Strathclyde looks down on us as being the old Glasgow Technical College, the lowest of the low.'

There's a 93% state school population and a 27% take from non-traditional uni goers. It's not that different from the Cally profile, but Strathclyde carries none of the poly cultural baggage. It was the *Royal* College; Cally was the Poly. Nevertheless, a lot of the students are local. 'There's one guy in SUR [student radio],' said Peter, 'who's from Surrey, and he sticks out like a sore thumb.'

ACADEMIA & JOBS

There is a fine academic reputation. Strathclyde's 92% Excellent and Highly Satisfactory rating in the teaching assessments actually puts it a nose ahead of Glasgow University. The uni came 44th in the last research assessments – with Queens Belfast, Stirling, London Goldsmiths, Kent and Leicester for close company – and the edge which returned them a Grade 5* (that's world class) was neither engineering nor business, the two subjects to which one's mind turns when talking of Strathclyde, but Biomolecular & Medicinal Chemistry. The key thing is the way they teach: audio-visual, video, visual materials, computer-assisted learning programmes are all to the fore. Very close links with industry and commerce ensure a real-world, highly practical emphasis. They have a Learning Resources Base which,

among other things, is there to help you in adjusting to study methods, curriculum design etc. Every student is assigned a personal tutor, and there's a built-in early-warning system to prevent any first year getting lost along the way.

The uni's Careers Service has twice received the National Charter Mark for excellence in customer service.

Strath's biggest single graduate employment successes are in the Education Faculty, especially in relation to teaching, social work and speech & language therapy. Key to the social and community work are degrees in such as Community Arts, Community Education, Outdoor Education in the Community, Social Work, Sport in the Community, etc. Also, in Science, the Pharmacy course almost always has 100% employment. Strathclyde's MPharm brings it 8% of the career market. The next largest professional class of graduate jobs goes to accountants – the course is BSc Mathematics,

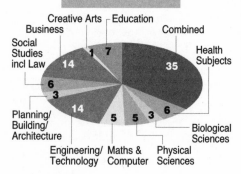

SUBJECT AREAS (%)

Statistics & Accounting.

Next, in number, are software engineers, and mechanical, process and production engineers, with jobs aplenty in manufacturing, as well as defence, telecommunications, etc – BEng Mechanical, Aero-Mechanical, Electrical & Mechanical, plus a series of MEng Mechanical with Aeronautics, Automotive, Biomedical or Material Engineering orientations, and one combo with Financial Management.

In Mechanical Engineering they lead in the employment table. This is a major focus for Strathclyde, they have an Excellent rating for teaching and an international Grade 5 for research.

The faculty is expanding in a collaboration with Glasgow Uni over Naval Architecture degrees. Oil/mining consultants already benefit from Naval Architecture & Offshore Engineering, which is top rated for teaching and research.

They come second only to Queen's Belfast in

STUDENT POPULATION
Total students
24,305

38% — Postgraduates
Female Undergraduates — 35%
27% — Male Undergraduates

the matter of finding employment for electrical engineers into telecommunications, and second to Portsmouth for getting graduates into electrical/electronic manufacturing. Teaching inspection, Excellent. Research Grade 5.

Architecture also shows up as a strong area. Besides the naval architecture degrees, there's the traditional 4-year BSc Architectural Studies (with European Studies); also BEng Architectural Engineering. Teaching inspection, Excellent.

Finally, there's a strong reputation for law – they're commercial & business and European law specialists, and have LLB (based on Scots Law) too.

They are also leaders in forensic science. UCAS list 298 courses, but the Forensic Science Society (www.forensic-science-society.org.uk) take most of their members from Strathclyde and King's College London. Both offer MSc degrees in Forensic Science (KCL's is called Chemistry with Analytical Chemistry). The University of Strathclyde has MSc Forensic & Analytical Chemistry.

A new Centre for Forensic Science – the first of its kind in the UK – will build on the University's international reputation and provide a comprehensive range of educational, research and consultancy services to laboratories, police forces and other agencies.

UNIVERSITY/STUDENT PROFILE

University since	**1964**
Situation/style	**City campus**
Student population	**24305**
Full-time undergraduates	**10831**
- mature	**16%**
- oon EU undergraduates	**8%**
- male/female	**49/51**
- non-traditional student intake	**27%**
- state sector intake	**93%**
- drop-out rate	**17%**
- undergraduate applications	**Up 6%**

SOCIAL SCENE

Strathclyde is Glaswegian not only because of the number of Glaswegians who attend, but in the very Glaswegian way students here go about having a good time. 'Their ents are marvelled at by other unions for their ability to bring in droves of students from rival unis, and give them just what they want – an excellent hangover for those on a budget!' reports Rachel Richardson. In fact, it is hard to assimilate the energy that is devoted to exciting pleasure in the students at Strathclyde. Whatever the legal capacity for the big night, it is not uncommon to find between 2,000 and 2,500 students here totally out of their heads. The legendary pleasure zone itself is 10 floors high, yet it is not the skyscraper you expect because in some extraordinary Alice-in-Wonderland fashion they have conspired to fit its ten floors, mezzanine-style, into the space of six or seven, leading this first-time visitor into utter confusion.

Last summer one of their bars was refurbished and rebranded into a Miller's sponsored bar. It's the ideal venue for small gigs, comedians and DJs, due to its intimate atmosphere. So, now the fun elements of the world-famous 10-floored Union are –

ACADEMIC EXCELLENCE

TEACHING:
(points out of 24)

Physics, Business & Management, Architecture, Electrical & Electronic Engineering, Geography, Mechanical (incl Manufacturing) Engineering, Pharmacy, Chemistry, Politics.	**Excellent**
Civil Engineering, Computer, Psychol, Hospitality Studies, Maths & Statistics, Teacher Education, History, Law, Sociology, Social Work, Cellular & Molecular Biology, English.	**Highly Satis.**
Chemical Engineering	**19**
Planning & Landscape	**20**
European Languages	**22**

RESEARCH:
Top grades 5/5*

Subjects Allied to Medicine.	**Grade 5***
Pharmacy,Studies/ Professions Allied to Medicine, Applied Maths, General Eng, Electrical/ Electronic Eng, Mechanical Eng, Law, Politics, Accounting/ Finance, English	**Grade 5**

Level 2: **Barony Bar** (main bar/club which is home to most of our regular nights); Level 3: **Gameszone** (Scotland's largest pool hall with 26 tables); Level 4: **Darkroom** (second room); Level 5: **Miller's**; Level 6: **The Priory** (relaxed non-smoking café bar); Level 8: **Vertigo** (the larger gig space).

Ents include *12-hour Tuesdays*: 3pm-3am, all drinks 99p (**Barony** & **Darkroom**) and comedy in **Miller's**; *TFI Friday* is hosted by legendary DJ Phil, this night has been running for 9 years and is the most successful student night in Glasgow. Cheap drinks and crazy antics, *TFI* is not for the faint hearted; Wednesday is touted as 'the only university gay night in Glasgow', every Wednesday comes with cocktails, and tunes from DJ Ricci.

Recent live acts include El Presidente – Glasgow's hottest new band, Trevor Nelson, Complete Stone Roses (tribute), Colin Murray – a favourite at Strathclyde, Sara Cox (played a 2-hour set to a packed and jumping crowd; Alabama 3 (band behind the Soprano's theme tune), My Latest Novel (supported the Pixies on their recent tour). Up-coming at point of writing is the Smirnoff Tour - Rodney P, Skitz & Nextmen DJs; Xmas Allnighter – Edith Bowman, Rachel Stevens.

Nor is it all booze and sweat at Strath. There are 70 or more clubs and societies. Sport is excellent (see below) and media-wise they have a cracking set-up. 'Three year ago radio station SUR had its first restricted licence,' Peter Mann told me. 'It was funded from our *alumni* fund but we couldn't afford to buy our own equipment at that stage. Nor could we broadcast the following semester due to licensing conflicts with other stations. In that time we have been working to get funding for our own equipment and sorting out webcasting – broadcasting on the Internet. Now we have got the necessaries for the basic studio equipment and an Internet deal with Yahoo., and broadcast full-time. We have more DJ talent than we could possibly use.

We get DJs from all over, we don't restrict ourselves to students.

'Then we've got the *Strathclyde Telegraph*. There's a real professionalism around and that shows. There's no TV yet, but there will be. Basically, I started up Fusion last year and then took this sabbatical year to get it off the ground. TV will come later. I did a degree in marketing. I've learned the bits and pieces as I've gone along, electrocuted myself a few times. When I leave here I am going for a job connected with the Internet.'

You'd better believe it.

For drama, they have two theatres – the **Ramshorn** at John Anderson, the **Crawfurd** at Jordanhill; both offer courses in all aspects of theatre and there's plenty of opportunity, too, just to be involved in student productions. The Strathclyde Theatre Group puts on ten major productions a year. The **Collins Gallery**, also on campus, runs year-round exhibitions and workshops, and there's also a concert hall for the many musical productions. Choirs, bands, a symphony orchestra, ensembles, etc go to make up the Music Society, which presents weekly lunchtime recitals by visiting artists as well as by students in the National Trust for Scotland's **Hutchesons' Hall**.

> *Strathclyde is Glaswegian not only because of the number of Glaswegians who attend, but in the very Glaswegian way students here go about having a good time.*

See also *Student Glasgow*, page 205.

Sport They came 34th in the national BUSA team league. Successes: Rugby Men won British Unis' Plate; Football Men won British Unis' Vase. Badminton, Volleyball, Rugby, Hockey and Football all won their respective Scottish Leagues.

At John Anderson campus there are indoor facilities for basketball, netball, archery, volleyball, tennis, badminton, handball, martial arts, fencing, table tennis, gymnastics, circuit training, yoga, indoor training facilities for track & field, cricket, golf and hockey, a weight training & con-

---

WHERE STRATHCLYDE GRADUATES END UP

Health & Social Work: 10%; Education: 13%; Wholesale Retail: 13.5%; Manufacturing: 12%; Financial Activities: 9%; Public Administration, Civil Service & Defence: 5%; Hotel/Restaurant: 4%; Transport & Communications (including Telecommunications): 3%; Construction: 1%; Agriculture: 1%; Mining/Oil Extracting: 2%; Personnel: 2%; Computer: 2%; Business & Management: 2%; Accountancy: 4%; Media (including Film): 0.5%; Legal 1%; Architecture: 3%; Sport: 1%.

Approximate 'graduate track' employed **69%**

WHAT IT'S REALLY LIKE

UNIVERSITY:

Social Life	★★★★★
Campus scene	**City centre**
Student Union services	**Good**
Politics	**Student issues**
Sport	**38 clubs**
National team position	**33rd**
Sport facilities	**Good**
Arts opportunities	**Drama, music, film, art good; dance poor**
Student newspaper	**Strathclyde Telegraph**
Student radio	**SUR**
Nightclub	**Vertigo**
Bars	**Barony, Darkroom, Miller's Lounge, Priory**
Union ents	**Club nights, cheese, live bands**
Union societies	**35-40**
Most active society	**SUPSA, SUDS**
Parking	**Poor/non-existent**

CITY:

Entertainment	★★★★★
Scene	**Very cool**
Town/gown relations	**Good**
Risk of violence	**Average**
Cost of living	**Average**
Student concessions	**Poor**
Survival + 2 nights out	**£70 pw**
Part-time work campus/town	**Good/excellent**

sports – from mountaineering to sailing, from rowing to skiing. There are eight bursaries available for low handicap golfers from The Royal and Ancient.

PILLOW TALK

In the city, most uni accommodation is single or shared rooms in self-catering flats, some of it at a student village on JA campus, some of it a walk away. At Jordanhill it's on-campus, catered halls.

GETTING THERE

☛ By road: The John Anderson campus – M74, M8/J15 or A82, M8/J15 or M8/J15. Jordanhill –

AT A GLANCE

ACADEMIC FILE:

Subjects assessed	**26**
Excellent/Highly Satisfactory	**92%**
Typical entry requirements	**382 points**
Application acceptance rate	**18%**
Students-staff ratio	**18:1**
First/2:1 degree pass rate	**69%**

ACCOMMODATION FILE:

Availability to freshers	**100%**
Style	**Halls, flats**
Catered	**7%**
En suite	**19%**
Approx price range pw	**£61-£82**
City rent pw	**£60-£80**

ditioning room, squash courts and swimming pool. Beyond campus there are grass pitches, artificial floodlit pitches, and a pavilion – team games include hockey, rugby, American football and soccer. Jordanhill has a similar range of indoor and outdoor facilities on campus. Proximity to river, sea and mountains enables a whole range of other

M74, M8/J19 or A82, M8/J19 or M8/J19.
☛ By rail: Edinburgh, 0:50; Newcastle, 2:30; Aberdeen, 2:45; Birmingham New Street, 5:30; London King's Cross, 6:00.
☛ By air: Glasgow Airport, 15-20 minutes' drive.
☛ By coach: Edinburgh, 1:10; London, 8:20; Birmingham, 6:20; Newcastle, 4:20.

UNIVERSITY OF SUNDERLAND

The University of Sunderland
Student Recruitment & Admissions
Edinburgh Building
Chester Road
Sunderland SR1 3SD

TEL 0191 515 3000
FAX 0191 515 3805
EMAIL student-helpline@sunderland.ac.uk
WEB www.sunderland.ac.uk

Sunderland Students' Union
Wearmouth Hall
Chester Road
Sunderland SR1 3SD

TEL 0191 514 5512
FAX 0191 515 2441
EMAIL su.president@sunderland.ac.uk
WEB www.sunderland.ac.uk

VAG VIEW

Sunderland was an area robbed of its core industries a few decades ago, but has since been reborn and its uni with it. The poly became a university in 1992, the very year that Sunderland became a city. Since then they have been engaged in expansion.

Their niche areas are media, design, law, education, business, psychology, pharmacy, computing and social work.

CAMPUS SITES

The uni's Chester Road campus is in easy reach of

UNIVERSITY/STUDENT PROFILE	
University since	**1892**
Situation/style	**City campus**
Student population	**18635**
Undergraduates	**15975**
- mature	**34%**
- non EU undergraduates	**16%**
- male/female	**45/55**
- non-traditional student intake	**40%**
-state school intake	**97%**
- drop-out rate	**32%**
- undergraduate applications	**Up 0.6%**

the town centre and the newer, award-winning St Peter's campus is but a stone's throw out at the mouth of the River Wear. The plan is to get everything over to St Peter's before too long.

Glass was one of the 19th-century industries on which the wealth of Sunderland was created (along with shipbuilding, coal mining and pottery), and in partnership with the National Glass Company, Sunderland's School of Computing levied £6 million from the National Lottery. The school is housed with the Business School at St Peter's, where they also opened a £15-million National Glass Centre. In September 2003 a new £9m Media Centre opened there, part of a centre of excellence for the arts, comprising 4600 square metres of studios, workshops and edit suites, along with facilities for TV & radio production and journalism (note the new MA Journalism). There are also specialist research centres – the Industry Centre, the Ecology Centre, and the Centre for Japanese Studies. Japanese? Well, the mighty Nissan's in town!

The uni's whole strategy is focused on student employability, entrepreneurship and creativity. Work has begun on the first phase of a £7-million Science Park, which will provide incubator units for

fledgling entrepreneurs and accommodation for established knowledge-based businesses at St Peter's Riverside, but it will also offer a first step for businesses set up by Sunderland students.

You can see why the awards were won. St Peter's fits unobtrusively into the landscape, obediently following nature's contours as they fall down to the river. Wearmouth's iron bridge arches splendidly across the water like a young relation of Stephenson's famous iron bridge at nearby Newcastle; cranes complete the backdrop of the area's industrial past, against which the campus is heralded as an expression of the re-born character of the area. The Informatics building and Business School acquiesce in that, and there are clear practical benefits in their design, too. The jutting roofs and walkways (a modern version of Oxbridge cloisters) keep students dry as they criss-cross University Square, to and from the Prospect Building, or stand outside this no-smoking, catering and library resource while pulling on a fag (often in defiance of horizontal rain and a biting North Sea easterly). Rainwater plunges dramatically down huge chrome pipes from roofs topped with strange deckchair-shaped receivers, scanning the northern skies (for light?). Impressive, though the design never quite recovers from the creams and browns that threaten to make St Peter's old before its time.

Postgraduates 14%
Female Undergraduates 49%

STUDENT POPULATION
Total students
18,635

Male Undergraduates 37%

FEES, BURSARIES

UK & EU Fees, 2007: £3,070 p.a. 2008 fees to be confirmed. If in receipt of all students receiving a HE Maintenance grant there's a bursary of £525 p.a. There are also academic achievement scholarships - up to £965 over 3 years subject to progress.

STUDENT PROFILE

Sunderland are leaders for widening participation in higher education – attracting young people (36% of undergraduates) from 'low participation' neighbourhoods, and 40% from the lowest four socio-economic groups.

Sunderland is also one of the few campuses on which our senior reporter, who is of a certain age, can pass unnoticed in the SU bar. Besides a large local intake, international students are also attracted in increasing number.

ACADEMIA & JOBS

The university has a strong Disability Support Team, offering a range of advice, including an outstanding learning support programme for dyslexic students.

Education accounts for some 17% of graduate jobs, 75% of school-teacher output is into secondary, which is the largest single graduate employment provision. The primary provision is also strong and there's a well-trod path into Further Education lecturing via the media and communications degrees and biological sciences, which scored full marks at the assessments.

Next most popular occupation is in pharmacy, which accounts for around 8% of graduates. There are foundation courses for both Chemical & Pharmaceutical Science and Pharmacology. These

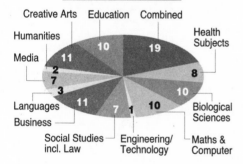

in addition to the flagship MPharm degree. Teaching inspection, 22.

Computing is another popular and successful employment pathway – AI, Business Computing, Forensic Computing, Intelligent Robotics, Network Computing and a strong Computer Studies presence on the joint honours scheme (a defining factor of the curriculum at Sunderland; most subjects figure). Graduates get jobs as IT consultants and software engineers in particular, as well as programmers and computer operators.

Graphic artists and designers also proliferate and a look into the art and design provision brings us unerringly to another defining aspect, the Glass, Architectural Glass & Ceramics degree. See also, here, the Photography, Video & Digital Imaging

<table>
<tr><td colspan="2">**ACADEMIC EXCELLENCE**</td></tr>
<tr><td colspan="2">TEACHING:
(Rated Excellent or 17+ out of 24)</td></tr>
<tr><td>Organismal Biosciences,
Molecular Biosciences</td><td>**24**</td></tr>
<tr><td>Physiology, Nursing</td><td>**23**</td></tr>
<tr><td>Media, Pharmacy</td><td>**22**</td></tr>
<tr><td>Sociology, Art & Design, History
of Art, Music, Education</td><td>**21**</td></tr>
<tr><td>Sport, Politics, Psychology</td><td>**20**</td></tr>
<tr><td>Electric & Electron Engineering,
Mechanical & Manuf Eng</td><td>**19**</td></tr>
<tr><td>Iberian Studies</td><td>**18**</td></tr>
<tr><td colspan="2">RESEARCH EXCELLENCE:
Top grades 5/5* **None**</td></tr>
</table>

degree and those in Animation and Advertising & Design.

Among other notably strong employment niches are sport, journalism and film/TV production, broadcast, etc, and drama, a difficult employment sector but one where they figure relatively strongly.

A new £5-million Sony Media centre lifts Sunderland into the forefront of UK teaching and research in TV, radio, video and new media production, journalism, public relations, film and culture studies, with the provision of studios and editing suites for TV and radio, workshops, newsrooms and a 207-seat cinema.

A new sports centre suite is kitted out with a range of high tech equipment, providing sports injury treatment, tests and analysis for athletes as well as students and members of the public. Students on the sport and exercise courses benefit from working with equipment normally only used by sports science professionals.

Business is always quoted as a big strength here, and around 16% of Sunderland students do graduate with business degrees. Accounts clerks, retail managers, marketing managers, sales consultants are among the most likely jobs in the first six months, however.

There's Business & Administration/Human resource Mgt/Marketing/Enterprise/etc They are commercial and business law specialists and have a LLB with Business Studies.

There's a very strong showing in welfare and community care, and in nursing, where they dropped only one point at the assessments.

SOCIAL SCENE

STUDENTS' UNION The 3 main student haunts are the **Wearmouth Bar** at Chester Road campus, **Manor**

WHERE SUNDERLAND GRADUATES END UP

Health & Social Work: 9.5%; Education: 17%; Wholesale Retail: 17%; Manufacturing: 9%; Financial Activities: 9%; Public Administration, Civil Service & Defence: 7%; Hotel/Restaurant: 4%; Transport & Communications (including Telecommunications): 3%; Construction: 1%; Personnel: 3.5%; Computer: 3%; Business & Management: 4%; Media (including Film): 2%; Legal 2%; Publishing: 1.5%; Advertising: 0.5%; Artistic/Literary: 1%; Sport: 2%.

Approximate 'graduate track' employed **62%**

Quay nightclub at St Peter's and the **Bonded Warehouse** across the river from St Peter's at Panns Bank.

An early 19th-century marine store and smithy, the **Bonded Warehouse** has a shop and bar downstairs and right across the first floor is this large, beamed bar with snooker table and big screen. Initial custom was 'a slow but steady stream,' then they started a series of comedy nights, which won them a decent audience.

The main nightspot remains **Manor Quay**, however. The club incorporates **Roker Bar** and operates daily as watering hole, food bar, pool and games room. For footie nights *et al* it boasts 'the biggest screen in Sunderland'. With no residents in the near neighbourhood the 3 am chuck-out time on Mondays, Tuesdays and Thursdays causes no grief. The club is cool, with good size stage, balcony and bar. It's a major town venue and they sort it so that whatever's on at Manor Quay is not duplicated elsewhere.

Tuesday is *Rock Night*; Wednesday, 80's/90's; Friday, *Commercial* (dance and r&b); Saturday, *Volume* indie or *Bands Night*. Recent acts include Dead 60's, Arctic Monkeys, Golden Virgins, The Stranglers, The Subways. There's a Sunday Quiz in **Wearmouth Bar**, and a Karaoke Night on Friday in the **Bonded Warehouse**.

Besides all this, throughout the year, poets and musicians (roots, jazz, classical) perform on campus.

The Royal Shakespeare Company, Northern Playwrights and Ballet Rambert have done workshops with the drama and dance elements of the Faculty of Arts, Design & Communication. Also on campus is the uni's **Screen on the River**, based in the 400-seater **Tom Cowie Theatre**, a focus for weekend film festivals, and sister cinema to Newcastle's little **Tyneside Cinema**, renowned for its arthouse fare.

There are 19 societies and as many as 32 sports clubs, the most popular being Football, Netball, Rugby and CCSA. The student radio station, nominated 3 times in the national awards in 2005, won the Silver Award for Live Outside Broadcast last year. The magazine is *Degrees North*.

SPORT Sports Centre has a 2-storey fitness and cardiovascular suite, a 25-metre swimming pool with canoeing facilities, and a sports hall for badminton, football and basketball.

Otherwise it's the city, which 'has a number of fitness clubs and sports centres – the Puma Tennis Centre, Nissan Sports Centre (brilliant football and basketball pitches), and Silksworth

WHAT IT'S REALLY LIKE

UNIVERSITY:	
Social Life	★★★★
Campus scene	**Friendly, local**
Student Union services	**Good**
Politics	**Student issues Activity low**
Sport	**32 clubs. Skid Snowbound, Gaelic Footie strong**
National sporting position	**72nd**
Sport facilities	**Improving**
Arts opportunities	**Film good; rest 'average'**
Student magazine	**Degrees North**
Student radio	**Utopia fm**
2006 National Awards	**Silver award**
Nightclub	**Manor Quay**
Bars	**Wearmouth, Roker, Bonded Warehouse**
Union ents	**Commercial, Volume, Live**
Union societies	**51**
Parking	**Adequate**
CITY	
Entertainment	★★★
Scene	**Cheap fun**
Town/gown relations	**Poor**
Risk of violence	**Average**
Cost of living	**Low**
Student concessions	**Average**
Survival + 2 nights out	**£65 pw**
Part-time work campus/town	**Excellent**

Sports Complex, with dry slope ski centre.

Town Masses of pubs around Chester Road and city clubs keep students happy. Cost of living is low. Every university wants to play down hassle in town, but Sunderland cannot be classed as the safest of the cities we visit, though uni properties seem to be well protected.

PILLOW TALK
They guarantee all first-years accommodation, whether or not you apply through Clearing. There are self-contained flats, a small number of family houses, and flats in halls. A Domestic Services Manager and a team of domestic staff manage the halls, all of which have 24-hour security. A team of resident tutors is on call during the evenings, throughout the night and at weekends to offer advice and support. 80% of the accommodation is designed and built post 1994. They also manage a range of private properties throughout the city, available to let. Halls are situated on both sides of the river, with the newest, Panns Bank and Scotia Quay, being close to the Bonded Warehouse.

GETTING THERE
☛ By road: A1(M), A690 or A19, A690.

AT A GLANCE	
ACADEMIC FILE:	
Subjects assessed	**28**
Excellent	**61%**
Typical entry requirements	**234 points**
Application acceptance rate	**21%**
Students-staff ratio	**18:1**
First/2:1 degree pass rate	**52%**
ACCOMMODATION FILE:	
Guarantee to freshers	**100%**
Style	**Halls, flats, houses**
Catered	**None**
En-suite	**20%**
Approx price range pw	**£52-£67**
City rent pw	**£60**

☛ By rail: Newcastle, 0:25; Leeds, 2:15; Edinburgh, 2:30, Manchester, 3:30, London King's Cross, 3:45.
☛ By air: Newcastle International Airport.
☛ By coach: London, 6:20; Bristol, 6:25.

UNIVERSITY OF SURREY

The University of Surrey
Guildford GU2 7XH

TEL 01483 689305
FAX 01483 689388
EMAIL admissions@surrey.ac.uk
WEB www.surrey.ac.uk

Surrey Students' Union
Guildford GU2 7XH

TEL 01483 689223
FAX 01483 534749
EMAIL ussu.president@surrey.ac.uk
WEB www.ussu.co.uk

VAG VIEW

*S*urrey, or UniS as it likes to be called, has roots in Battersea Poly. The rise of Surrey is a triumph of the career orientation of its courses and its teaching. It is many students' first choice.

Since receiving a Royal Charter in 1966, they have gone their own way, done their own thing, and with a great deal of success, making the business of higher education seem almost clinically straightforward.

They have the 7th best graduate-track employment rate in the country and an average points entry 200 less than Cambridge. This year they had a massive 39% increase in undergraduate applications.

There is no apparent link between this statistic and rumours of their cutting their ties with the State, and going private.

CAMPUS
UniS's self-contained, concrete, in-fill, landscaped campus lies just off the A3 in the ancient city of Guildford, adjacent to the cathedral, 15 minutes walk from the city centre. Writes Madeleine Merchant: 'The campus contains most first-year residences, all the teaching buildings, lecture theatres, library, computer labs, a sports centre, a shop, a health centre, a counselling service, a post office, a NatWest bank, many cafés, restaurants, and bars, the Students' Union building, picnic areas and a lake. It is in an attractive setting with many trees and shrubs, on a hill in the shadow of Guildford Cathedral. Many students complain of

being woken up on Sunday mornings by the cathedral bells! A train line runs around a third of the perimeter, and the trains can also be heard in some of the residences.'

Much of the area is covered by CCTV cameras, and it is generally well-lit and perfectly safe, but three years ago, the Student Council debated whether more cameras should be put in for greater safety in off-campus paths nearby, which were deemed not so safe, even if the cameras might overlook some student residences. The Students' Union reported that the university had assumed responsibility of up-keep and maintenance from the council for some of these paths, and improved safety.

FEES, BURSARIES

UK & EU Fees, 2007: £3,070 p.a. 2008 not yet known. If in receipt of full HE Maintenance grant there's a bursary of £1,020; if in receipt of partial grant, bursaries are on a sliding scale up to £1,000, according to household earnings.

Scholarships are available for sporting performance and for academic achievement.

STUDENT PROFILE

'The University of Surrey may be a depressing collection of ugly concrete monstrosities,' writes Alistair Gerard, 'but it's not the buildings that make a university, it's the people, and I wouldn't have chosen to be anywhere else. Campus is a cosmopolitan enclave in the whole middle-class Caucasian experiment that is Guildford. Besides the obvious lean towards science and engineering bods at UniS, around a fifth of undergraduates are from overseas, nearly a quarter are mature students, and the state/independent ratio is well balanced. Students are saved from the male dominance that can affect science unis by the nursing provision and Human Studies. Everyone is happy.'

ACADEMIA & JOBS

Characteristically, Surrey graduates get jobs for

which they have been educated – they enter employment not only at graduate level but in occupations directly related to their degrees. This is not typical through the length and breadth of the graduate nation.

'In the third year, most students work for companies in placements, and earn lots of money,' Madeleine reports, 'and from what I've heard, most of these come back in the fourth year with clear

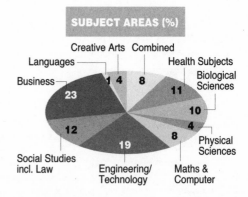

ideas about whether they really want to continue working in that field, and many have definite job offers for when they graduate.'

UniS lead the nation in producing computer programmers. See BSc Computer Modelling & Simulation and various alternative applications – Engineering, Communications, Info Technology. All are 4-5 years, depending on whether you take one of these professional years out, after which you are eligible to Associate Membership of the Uni. Look, too, at their BEng Electronics & Computer Eng, and the BSc/MPhys Physics with Computer Modelling.

Most students at Surrey graduate in business and engineering subjects, and the manufacturing industry benefits by taking around a fifth of all those graduating from the uni.

Computer Science, Engineering and Business

UNIVERSITY/STUDENT PROFILE	
University since	**1966**
Situation/style	**Town campus**
Student population	**11646**
Undergraduates	**6273**
- mature	**18%**
- overseas	**18%**
- male/female	**45/55**
- non-traditional student intake	**24%**
- state sector intake	**88%**
- drop-out rate	**11%**
- undergraduate applications	**Up 39%**

TEACHING:

(Rated Excellent or 17+ out of 24)

Business & Management, Music	**Excellent**
Physics, Electronic Eng,	**23**
Education, Economics	
Psychology, Civil Engineering,	**22**
Materials Science & Eng	
Organismal Biosciences,	**21**
Subjects Allied to Medicine,	
Food Science, Sociology,	
Molecular Biosciences, Maths	
Dance	**20**
Nursing	**19**
Chemical Eng, Modern Langs	**18**

RESEARCH :

Top grades 5/5*/6*

Subjects Allied to Medicine,	**Grade 6***
Electrical & Electronic Eng,	
Sociology	
Psychology, Physics,	**Grade 5**
Applied Maths, Statistics,	
Chemical Eng/Environmental	
Strategy, European Studies,	
Russian/Slavonic/East European	

Civil engineers are the next most in demand in the engineering sector. They mix with Computing in the 3/4/5-year B/MEng programmes, or you can of course take the single hons. Again, there's an Associateship of the University in the offing.

Then there's mechanical, process & production, electronic and software engineers, all well serviced with dedicated degrees and interesting combo options relevant to these job sectors.

Note also the B/MEng Space Technology & Planetary Exploration degrees, remembering that both Physics and engineering achieved near full marks in the assessments.

The health provision is next most productive, and is served by the European Institute of Health & Medical Sciences (nursing, midwifery, etc), which scored a world-class Grade 6* for research.

In the business sector the Retail Management degree is singly the most productive at point of employment, and the International Hospitality degrees lead unerringly to careers in the field of hotel management. Throughout the faculty, sales managers, marketing managers and management consultants are produced in quantity.

Graduates of Financial Mathematics and Business Economics degrees find their way, in number, into accountancy, and economists also proliferate.

are the main routes into electrical and electronic manufacturing, with the occasional input from Surrey's sound recording courses. For electronic and aspiring telecommunications engineers, you're talking a world class (Grade 6*) department, with dedicated 4-5-year degrees like B/MEng Telecommunication Systems.

Aaspiring sound recordists and technicians take note, there's also the 4-year BMus Music & Sound Recording (Tonmeister) for the performance spin. Teaching inspection 23 out of 24.

'Surrey may be a depressing collection of ugly concrete monstrosities, but it's not the buildings that make a university, it's the people… Students are saved from the male dominance that can affect science unis by the nursing provision and Human Studies. Everyone is happy.'

Again, the biomedical and life sciences provision translates just as successfully into healthy employment figures, especially Surrey's Counselling degrees and their much sought-after BSc Psychology.

SOCIAL SCENE

STUDENTS' UNION **Chancellors** bar, one of 5, can be found under Union House and opens as restaurant from 8.30am, transforming itself into a venue in the evening for Cocktail Nights, Chancellors Comedy, Pre *Citrus* and *Flirt* Drinks, Open Mic Night and Live Sky Footy on Saturdays.

WHERE SURREY GRADUATES END UP

Health & Social Work: 6%; Education: 6%; Wholesale Retail: 8%; Manufacturing: 20%; Financial Activities: 7%; Public Administration, Civil Service & Defence: 6%; Hotel/Restaurant: 7%; Transport & Communications (including Telecommunications): 1%; Construction: 2.5%; Personnel: 2.5%; Computer: 4%; Business & Management: 4%; Accountancy: 4%; Media (including Film): 1%; Legal 1.5%; Publishing: 1%; Artistic/Literary: 2%.

Approximate 'graduate track' employed **80%**

WHAT IT'S REALLY LIKE

UNIVERSITY:

Social Life	★★★★
Campus scene	**Efficient, techy**
Student Union services	**Good**
Politics	**Low interest**
Sport	**45 clubs**
National team position	**74th**
Sport facilities	**Good**
Arts opportunities	**Dance, music good; drama avg, film, art poor**
Student newspaper	**Barefacts**
Student radio	**GU2**
Nightclub	**Rubix**
Bars	**Chancellors + 4**
Union ents	**Cheese, r&b, dance**
Union societies	**120**
Parking	**Non-existent**

TOWN:

Entertainment	★★
Scene	**Rich man's clubs/pubs**
Town/gown relations	**OK-good**
Risk of violence	**Low**
Cost of living	**Very high**
Student concessions	**Good**
Survival + 2 nights out	**£70+ pw**
Part-time work campus/town	**Excellent/good**

AT A GLANCE

ACADEMIC FILE:

Assessments	**22**
Excellent	**86%**
Typical entry requirements	**326 points**
Application acceptance rate	**21%**
Students-staff ratio	**17:1**
First/2:1 degree pass rate	**59%**

ACCOMMODATION FILE:

Guarantee to freshers	**100%**
Style	**Flats**
Catered	**None**
En-suite	**45%**
Price range pw	**£52-£111**
Town rent pw	**£65+**

Nightclub is **Rubix**, with a capacity of 1600. Regular ents are *Flirt!* with Duncan Wilson – 'the cult of chav is with us, homage to world of Burberry, Elizabeth Duke & the Citroen Saxo' – and *Citrus* with Leroy Wilson. Then there are sell-out specials, which go under the name of *UNIFIED*, with such as 'Nicholas from X Factor, Master Stepz, Da Jump Off Ent, to mention a few', across 2 rooms.

Music and dance departments evolve their own series of concerts and the uni choir, orchestra, chamber orchestra and student Drama Society regularly perform.

UniS also has a special relationship with Guildford School of Acting, validating its degrees in Acting and Stage Management. See web: www.gsa.drama.ac.uk. Tel: 01483 560 701; e-mail: enquiries@gsa.drama.co.uk.

There is an award-winning student radio station, GU2 (nominated in 2005), newspaper *Barefacts* (award-winning in both 2002 and 2003). There is also a film unit and many other societies in a Student Activities Centre, cultural, religious, political, course/interest-based. Lesbian/Gay is active, but generally, due to student apathy in this direction, political activity is low.

SPORT The Campusport Centre is the sports hall. The Varsity Centre is for field, squash and tennis, and pitches. Guildford's Spectrum Leisure Centre, home to ice hockey team, the Guildford Flames, provides facilities for swimming, ice skating and athletics, and the uni provides a bus linking Spectrum with other pick-ups in the city and the uni campus. Uni teams came 60th nationally last year, they have a world-class trampolinist apparently, and the gymnastic team was sent to the world championships in China. Sports bursaries are available.

Writes Madeleine: 'There are many clubs, both competitive – e.g. hockey, waterpolo – and non-competitive: mountain climbing, hiking, etc. Everyone gets Wednesday afternoons free of lectures as these are set aside for BUSA matches. If you aren't interested in sports, the university offers free language courses. As in sport, all levels are catered for.'

TOWN Writes Alistair. 'London is only 35 minutes away by train. Ergo, Guildford is very expensive. With the introduction of tuition fees, this must now be a consideration. There are sociological implications, too. It's a notoriously blue pocket of middle-class conservatism. Guildford shuts at 11 pm, with the exception of its nightclubs, where prices reflect this. The people who live in Guildford have done their partying; they have moved to a gilt-edged ghetto to live in peace and tranquillity.'

Writes Madeleine: 'There is a mixture of the usual high street shops with student discounts, and the more expensive variety such as French Connection, Gap, House of Fraser etc, two theatres and a large Odeon, two or three nightclubs and many pubs and bars.

'For temporary ways to earn money, Guildford

shops and businesses usually have positions available, and the university runs a Job Shop. The union also employs many casual staff. Many student nurses supplement their income by working at the local hospital as "bank" health care assistants, and for agencies.'

PILLOW TALK

All freshers are guaranteed accommodation in the uni's courts of residence flats. None is catered, 30% are en suite, the price per week ranges from £49.00 (duplex) to £85 (en suite). Millennium House is the newest court, the 3-storey building opened in 2001. It has 200 en-suite rooms arranged into flats of six rooms with a shared kitchen. All student rooms have telephones. Calls

across campus and modem links to the academic network are free; all 3,000 phones have voice mailboxes. Rent in town is anything from £65.00.

PILLOW TALK

Accommodation in flats arranged in residential courts on campus. Many en-suit roooms are available. For 2006-07 students, the p.w. rent ranged from £51.45 to £110.25. A new student village, Manor Park, opened in September 2006.

GETTING THERE

☛ Surrey Uni by road: A3, signs to University.
☛ By coach: London, 1:00; Birmingham, 4:30.
☛ By rail: London Waterloo, 30 mins.
☛ By air: Gatwick and Heathrow.

UNIVERSITY OF SUSSEX

University of Sussex
Sussex House
Falmer
Brighton BN1 9RH

TEL 01273 678416
FAX 01273 678545
EMAIL ug.admissions@sussex.ac.uk
WEB www.sussex.ac.uk

Sussex Students' Union
Falmer House
Falmer
Brighton BN1 9QF

TEL 01273 678555
FAX 01273 678875
EMAIL info@ussu.sussex.ac.uk
WEB www.ussu.co.uk

VAG VIEW

*S*ussex University first admitted students in October 1961. In its first decade or more it was the place to be – home of '60s radicalism, fighter of causes, defender of the student realm. Then all went quiet. Financial problems and a mouldering of relations between the uni and its students meant that 'any student triumphs occurred despite rather than because of the powers that be,' as a student put it.

Now, they are back on top, and it is all happening once again. A 12-to-1 student-to-staff ratio (7th best) and a 75%-pass rate for first-class and upper-second degrees in the last released figures, give an additional endorsement to student satisfaction.

CAMPUS

The Sussex campus, its award-winning design by Sir Basil Spence, is an 18th-century park designated as an area of outstanding beauty, on the South Downs, 5 miles north east of Brighton.

'At times being on campus can feel a bit isolated and claustrophobic,' writes Keren Rosen, 'but it is fifteen minutes to Brighton by bus and you are never more than ten minutes walk from the fields of the South Downs. Escape is always possible.

FEES, BURSARIES

UK & EU Fees, 2007: £3,070 p.a. If in receipt of full HE Maintenance grant there's a bursary of £1,000. Scholarships are available for applicants living in certain postcodes, and for ethnic minorities.

STUDENT PROFILE

'Owing to its strong international links, roughly a third of the student population comes from foreign

27% — Postgraduates

Female Undergraduates — **46%**

STUDENT POPULATION

Total students
12,205

27% — Male Undergraduates

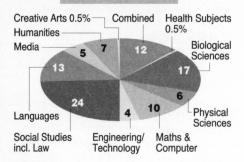

SUBJECT AREAS (%)

Creative Arts 0.5% — Combined — Health Subjects 0.5%
Humanities
Media
Biological Sciences 17
5 7 12
13
24
10
4 6
Physical Sciences
Languages
Social Studies incl. Law — Engineering/ Technology — Maths & Computer

and are articulate and confident, that they think on their feet, are analytical.'

Two-thirds of Sussex students graduate in social studies, languages, humanities and biological sciences – 20%, 18%, 12% and 17% respectively. More than a third of graduates enter health, education, finance and business management fields. There are strong pockets of jobs in computing, media, publishing, drama and music, and there is something about this liberal, free-thinking campus that favours the generation and development of artistic ideas. They produce writers and Sussex's student media is

parts and although the rest tend to come from London and the south of England, in general there is quite a nice mix of backgrounds,' continues Keren. 'There is also a large number of mature students studying at Sussex and although socially it is quite divided they definitely add a different perspective to study.' The ratio of state to independent entrants is roughly 4 to 1. There is likely to be an increase in local students as a deal has been struck whereby Sussex, Brighton and the new University of Chichester guarantee to offer places to applicants from local sixthforms and further education colleges as part of a widening participation policy.

ACADEMIA & JOBS

Sussex don't have the industrial links-ups of Surrey. They are more tied up with what they refer to as 'the knowledge economy' than with industry, so to produce articulate, adaptable adults, capable of finding fulfilment in their own way, not slotting in to someone else's production line. This, they believe, is where the cross-faculty potential inherent in the original academic strategy of this very individual university takes Sussex students. 'Also, we get the feedback from employers that they like the fact that our students are taught in seminars and are used to getting up and giving presentations

ACADEMIC EXCELLENCE

TEACHING :
(Rated Excellent or 17+ out of 24)

English, Music, Anthropology	**Excellent**
Philosophy, Sociology	**24**
Politics, American Studies,	**23**
Maths & Statistics	
Linguistics, French,	**22**
Physics, Biosciences	
Education	
Electric & Electron Engineering,	**21**
Economics, Psychology,	
Media	
History of Art	**20**

RESEARCH:
Top grades 5/5*

Psychology, Chemistry,	**Grade 5**

Biological Sciences, Physics,
Applied Maths, Computer,
General Eng, Anthropology,
Science/Technology Policy
Research, American Studies,
English, History of Art/
Architecture/Design,
Philosophy, Music

very active – newspaper *Badger*, magazine *Pulse*, radio station URF, all frequently award winning. Average entry requirements are high, but not unreachable for many.

But at the end of the day, social studies and humanities have less vocational relevance than other areas of study, and it is interesting to see where graduates of these actually do end up.

First, however, it is not true that Sussex has no vocational nous. 'We have an Innovation Centre, where a number of outfits up there were student-started. It is an incubation centre rather than a money-making business park.'

The more obvious vocational academic/job tie-ups produce software engineers, IT Consultants and computer programmers, who come out of com-

UNIVERSITY/STUDENT PROFILE

University since	**1961**
Situation/style	**Campus**
Student population	**12205**
Undergraduates	**8935**
- mature	**23%**
- non EU undergraduates	**3%**
- male/female	**48/62**
- non-traditional student intake	**18%**
- state sector intake	**85%**
- drop-out rate	**11%**
- undergraduate applications	**Up 1%**

puter sciences and engineering. There is a fine reputation for Computer Systems Engineering, AI, Robotics, Cybernetics & Process Automation, etc.

For biosciences they have a similarly fine track record for degrees and jobs. The BSc Psychology (with American Studies, Cognitive Science or Neuroscience) looks particularly attractive, and the new Brighton & Sussex Medical School has lift-off: 5-year BMBS (Bachelor of Medicine, Bachelor of Surgery). Small, personal med school, they are looking for personal qualities, commitment, compassion as well as... Entry GCSE Grade B Maths and English, ABB or 320 points at A level. There was a 10% application acceptance rate in 2004, which is average.

Computing, Psychology and Biological Sciences have international Grade 5 ratings for research, and Electrical & Electronic Engineering and Biosciences scored 21 and 22 points at the teaching assessments respectively.

In social studies, humanities and languages we get a less focused picture, although it is precisely in these areas that they have done well in the teaching assessments: Philosophy and Sociology scored full marks, and Politics and American Studies 23 points, Linguistics and French 21. These are the six best results the uni achieved, and their strategy here is to provide subject combinations that are more than the sum of their parts. The curriculum is indeed planned with flair.

Civil Service administration is one significant pathway into employment for Sussex law graduates. In fact, Sussex leads the way countrywide into Civil Service administration through Social, Economic & Political Studies, languages and biological sciences (computer science is important too), and there's a significant flow from these areas of the curriculum into adult education.

Again, with social and biological sciences (including psychology) they have a significant rep-

utation, relative to other unis, in finding graduates jobs in social work and counselling.

But it is also true that a significant number of graduates from these parts of the curriculum are registered as clerks six months after graduation. The same is true of physical sciences, where again they enjoy a strong reputation for teaching and research.

What is interesting is that graduates entering the niche areas of employment at which Sussex excel, such as publishing, radio/TV, journalism come not from departments dedicated to turning out media types – Media Studies and the like – but from across the scholastic board, out of a combination of application encouraged through the cross-faculty curriculum and extra-curricular interest, which is exactly what you want from a university.

Sussex is a small university, but it has more extra-curricular clubs and societies (200) than many. There is a vigorous student culture, and employers like to pick the fruits of that.

> *There are strong pockets of jobs in computing, media, publishing, drama and music, and there is something about this liberal, free-thinking campus that favours the generation and development of artistic ideas.*

STUDENT SCENE

STUDENTS' UNION The focus is **East Slope Bar**: 'Live music, football, barbeques, but above all a great place to meet friends any night of the week,' says Tom Harle, 'and a great place to watch out for your next bus into town if the weather's not so good. Then there's **Park Village Lounge**: sea, sun, sand, well no, but a huge range of well-priced cocktails, wines and beers and a great place for a quiet evening chill-out. Get a free cocktail if it's your birthday! **Falmer Bar** is the place for a lunch time coffee, or your usual tipple on the way home, a (veggie) burger or nachos to share. Meanwhile, **The Hothouse** is packed out every weekend, a great place to hide from over-priced central Brighton clubs.'

Every Friday at the **Hothouse** is *EASY*: hip-hop, r&b, garage, urban, 10pm till 2am, £3 entry.

WHERE SUSSEX GRADUATES END UP

Health & Social Work: 11%; Education: 12%; Wholesale Retail: 8%; Manufacturing: 9%; Financial Activities: 10%; Public Administration, Civil Service & Defence: 7%; Hotel/Restaurant: 4%; Transport & Communications (including Telecommunications): 4%; Construction: 0.5%; Personnel: 8%; Computer: 5%; Business & Management: 4%; Accountancy: 1%; Media (including Film): 2.5%; Legal 2%; Publishing: 3%; Advertising: 1%; Artistic/Literary: 1%; Sport: 1%.

Approximate 'graduate track' employed **59%**

Saturday is *YOOF CLUB*: all the songs you love to hear', also till 2am.

What of student politics in the midst of all this middle-class reverie? I ask. Isn't Sussex all yesterday's '60s-student glory? Apparently not. 'Politics are as important today as they were in the late '60s.' Student politics at Sussex is 'doing the right thing', removing Coca-Cola from all Union outlets, presenting a motion of no-confidence in the University Council, campaigning on housing issues for first year students, campaigning about the Falmer (football) stadium project, on widening participation, encouraging a wider social mix among Sussex's privileged student clientele.

Student media is great: *The Pulse* (magazine), *The Badger* (newspaper) and URF, Unversity Radio Falmer. They received 2 nominations (*Pulse* and URF) in the national awards this year and a bronze award for URF's Mara Webster in the Female Presenter of the Year section.

SPORT It's sport-for-all at Sussex, not too keenly competitive – they came 48th in the national team ratings last year. There are two large sports halls, a fitness room with multigym and training facilities, four glass-backed squash courts, sauna, solarium, café and bar. Elsewhere on campus are the pitches, tennis courts, and five more squash courts.

TOWN 'The town centre is small enough to be covered in its entirety on foot, but it manages to squeeze in a huge amount of clubs, pubs, bars and shops to suit every taste,' writes Keren. 'The theatre and art scene has a real emphasis on individuality. As the gay capital of England, Brighton has a laid back, party atmosphere and students and locals live in peaceful harmony. Brightonians do have a

WHAT IT'S REALLY LIKE

UNIVERSITY:	
Social Life	★★★★
Campus scene	**A freshers-only holiday camp**
Student Union services	**Average**
Politics	**Aware**
Sport	**Lightweight**
National team position	**66th**
Sport facilities	**Good**
Arts opportunities	**Drama, film excellent; dance, art, music good**
Student newspaper	**Badger**
Student magazine	**Pulse**
Student radio	**URF**
Nightclub	**The Hot House**
Bars	**Falmer Bar, Grape Vine, East Slope, Park Village**
Union ents	**Cheese**
Union societies	**200**
Parking	**Poor**
CITY:	
Entertainment	★★★★★
Scene	**Exceptional**
Town/gown relations	**OK**
Risk of violence	**Low**
Cost of living	**High**
Student concessions	**Good**
Survival + 2 nights out	**£80 pw**
Part-time work campus/town	**Average**

tendency to be a little self-consciously cool, verging at times on the pretentious, but there are enough different types of people that it is possible to avoid that world completely if its not your thing.'

It's a great city, lots of free festivals. Right now, Sussex students tend to frequent **Paradox**, the **Event** and **Club Barcelona**.

See *Student Brighton*, page 87, for more.

PILLOW TALK

The majority of first years get housed on campus, but get in quick or you'll have to share. This works on a first come, first served basis. Standard of accommodation is pretty high, all self-catering and varies between flats and rooms on corridors.

GETTING THERE

☛ By road: M23, A23, A27.
☛ By coach: London, 1:50.
☛ By rail: London Bridge/Victoria, 1:10; Portsmouth, 1:30; Birmingham New Street, 3:45; Leeds, 4:15; Manchester Piccadilly, 5:00.
☛ By air: Gatwick and Heathrow Airports.

AT A GLANCE

ACADEMIC FILE:	
Subjects assessed	**29**
Excellent	**66%**
Typical entry requirements	**366 points**
Application acceptance rate	**15%**
Students-staff ratio	**12:1**
First/2:1 degree pass rate	**72%**
ACCOMMODATION FILE:	
Guarantee to freshers	**95%**
Style	**Halls, houses, flats**
Catered	**None**
En suite	**9%**
Approx price range pw	**£45=£87**
City rent pw	**£65-£90**

UNIVERSITY OF WALES, SWANSEA

University of Wales, Swansea
Swansea SA2 8PP

TEL 01792 295111
FAX 01792 295110
EMAIL admissions@swansea.ac.uk
WEB www.swansea.ac.uk

Swansea Students' Union
Swansea SA2 8PP

TEL 01792 295466
FAX 01792 206029
EMAIL president@swansea-union.co.uk
WEB www.swansea-union.co.uk

VAG VIEW

If Swansea isn't a university that you would immediately consider, despite the evidence of the teaching assessments that the academic provision is excellent, do yourself a favour, go and see it – submit to the evidence of your senses.

'You can come here and never leave it,' a student said to us when first we asked. 'It's a bit like a black hole', a place of exquisite beauty and distinctly laid-back vibes.

The uni is also home to the National Assessment and Training Centre for Students with Disabilities, and politically it has shown itself capable of standing on its own two feet. Like Cardiff, but unlike Bangor and Aberystwyth at time of writing, Swansea has its own degree-awarding powers, but chooses to continue to award University of Wales degrees.

CAMPUS

The campus is set in a glorious position with wide open Swansea Bay stretched out in front and parkland behind, just a couple of miles west of the town. Further west along the coast you come to the old fishing village of Mumbles (birthplace of Catherine Zeta Jones), its pubs, fish & chip and Indian restaurants a favourite trawl for students, and the Gower Peninsula, described by Dylan Thomas as 'one of the loveliest sea-coast stretches in the whole of Britain.' On a sunny day I didn't disagree, nor do Swansea's surfer dudes. 'It's all so easy, see; everything's in walking distance,' the same student opined. 'Students come to Swansea for that alone.' He was pointing at the surf.

Writes Maxine French: 'The Gower is a stretch of coastline incorporating bays such as Caswell, Port Eynon and Langland, the last a favourite spot for surfers and host recently to the Welsh leg of some mad, never-ending surf competition. During the summer term its almost compulsory to go to Caswell when the Geography Society holds its annual beach party. For those whose lives are not ruled by tide tables, the coast means the Mumbles, renowned for the "Mile", strictly non-athletic, a pub crawl to end all pub crawls, something Dylan Thomas might have liked too.'

He did. In 'Who Do You Wish Was With Us?' he wrote – 'Why don't we live here always? Always and always. Build a bloody house and live like bloody kings!'

FEES, BURSARIES

UK & EU Fees, 2007: £3,075 p.a. This will affect students whose studies commenced in 2006 (who will be entering their 2nd year), as well as new students starting in 2007. Students who normally live in Wales (and EU students) will be entitled to a 'Fee Grant' of £1,800. Ten sports scholarships of £1,000 are available from the uni, and academic scholarships from some departments. The awards range in size from £400 to £3,000. From 2007/08 a national bursary scheme will be introduced for students attending HE institutions in Wales. See www.swansea.ac.uk/international/money/Scholar shipsandFees/Scholarships

STUDENT PROFILE

Swansea was quoted as one of the government's favoured 'elite access' universities, but now many others have caught up, and their figures of 28% intake from social classes new to the idea of uni, and 18% from 'low partiticpation' neighbourhoods, are less than unique. 93% of students come from the state sector, but that is not unusual either. The high mature-student intake is more so, and there's 15% more students in receipt of Disabled Students' Allowance than the sector average. There's also a healthy intake from overseas, and yet a more noticeably Welsh student body than at Cardiff.

Statistics aside, the real point is that Swansea campus, with its healthy population mix, is a very friendly sort of place. People are chatty, the scene a good deal less pressured than in some more cosmopolitan, civic universities. 'There's a fantastic, multi-cultural community feeling at Swansea,' said one student. It does strike one that it would be an easy place to settle, and not simply for the duration

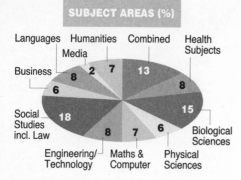

SUBJECT AREAS (%)

Languages 8, Humanities/Media 2, Combined 7, Health Subjects 13, Biological Sciences 8, Physical Sciences 15, Maths & Computer 6, Engineering/Technology 7, Social Studies incl. Law 8, Business 18, 6

of a 3-year degree course.

Last year the uni received a national award for the 'Best Mosque Provision' from the Federation of Islamic Student Societies in the UK and Ireland. The award recognised their support of the Islamic Society over the past decade, and the quality of facilities available to Muslim students.

ACADEMIA & JOBS

Academia is structured into 10 schools, Arts, Business & Economics, Engineering, Technology, Environment & Society, Health Science, Human Sciences, Humanities, Law, Medicine, and Physical Sciences.

Entry requirements are not overly taxing, and there's a good chance of getting in anyway – a 26% application acceptance rate – possibly because Swansea is thought of as a bit off the beaten track. 'Once they are here, people do well,' a student said, adding rather languidly as he nursed a Sunday morning hangover, 'but I guess it comes down to nothing else to do but work.'

Besides the definitive strength of engineering, languages are an important element; both teaching and research assessments show the department as especially strong, and every area of the curriculum benefits from it. New this year are BA Cymraeg

UNIVERSITY/STUDENT PROFILE	
University since	**1920**
Situation/style	**Campus-by-the-sea**
Student population	**15780**
Undergraduate	**12080**
- mature	**20%**
- non EU undergraduates	**5%**
- male/female	**44/56**
- non-traditional student intake	**29%**
- state sector intake	**93%**
- drop-out rate	**11%**
- undergraduate applications	**Up 0.3%**

gyda Ffrangeg (4 blynedd)/Welsh with French, gyda Almaeneg (German), gyda Sbaeneg (Spanish).

Engineering is indeed an enduring strength. Following the introduction of BEng Aerospace Engineering and BEng Aerospace Communications, this year they have BEng Aerospace Engineering with Power Electronics. Civil engineering is a particularly strong employment sector out of this faculty, and achieved a world-class 5* rating in the research assessment. Employment figures lead us next into the electronic area, well served in the faculty with degrees such as the 3/4-year BEng Electronics with Computer Science or BEng Communications Systems (the extra year in Europe, America, Australia or industry). The uni is highly productive of software engineers and programmers, and there's a fast track into telecommunications and defence from Swansea. Almost as many mechanical and chemical engineers follow in their wake.

Now, a £4.3-million Digital Technium building has opened housing a new Department of Media

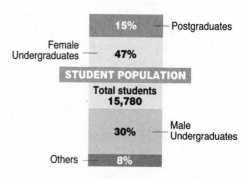

STUDENT POPULATION

Postgraduates 15%
Female Undergraduates 47%
Total students 15,780
Male Undergraduates 30%
Others 8%

and Communication Studies – research labs for digital science, incubator units for enterprise, space for partners from the private sector, but linked with the School of Engineering and Department of Computer Science. See degrees like BSc Multimedia Technology, Internet Technology, etc.

There are also BA media and screen studies degrees, and this year BA Screen Studies and a language (French, German, Spanish, Italian, Welsh); also BA Public & Media Relations, Language & Communication, English & Creative Writing. News of the opening of a Richard Burton Centre for Film and Popular Culture follows the handing over of the first of screen legend's diaries to the university by the actor's widow, Sally Burton. The diaries will form part of an archive of her late husband's papers

But look, too, at Swansea's ever sharper and increasingly defining focus on medicine and health sciences. Nursing degrees, Clinical Physiology, Audiology, Midwifery, and BSc Psychology (recognised by the British Psychological Society and the first step to becoming a Chartered Psychologist), all perform well in the employment market. And now, of course, Swansea has launched a MBBCH/Med degree – graduate entry only. The fast-track programme will take students to graduation in 4 years. The Medical School is adjacent to Swansea's Singleton Hospital, but students will enter the University of Wales College of Medicine and the All-Wales Clinical Training Scheme for the final two years of their studies.

In December 2006, the uni's £50m Institute of Life Science will become home to the School of Medicine's research arm, housing hundreds of interdisciplinary specialists, scientists and researchers.

Aspiring social workers and counsellors should look at the new BScEcon Social Work. They are Grade 5 in research in this area, and supply large numbers of graduates into the sector. There's also a BScEcon joint honours programme, incorporating American Studies, Economic History, Politics, Psychology, Social Policy, etc.

Look, too, at the sporting prowess of this uni. Extra-curricular interest is enormous, and employ-ment stats are good. There is both an HND and BSc Sports Science. See *Sport* below.

Finance is another significant employment area. The record shows some 8% of graduates going into accountancy jobs (3% as chartered accoun-tants). There is also a BSc Actuarial Studies, with the option of an additional year abroad, and a new BSc Actuarial Studies with Accounting. Business admin. degrees yield jobs – some 4% go into this area and a rash of new BA Business Administration/BSc Management/Management Science degrees with a specialization in Accounting is expected this year.

Look, too, at the Economics degrees. There's a foundation course for applicants from outside the EU who want to get on the BSc/MSEs Integrated Management Science/Economics degree (with deferred choice of specialisation).

Education is a major field here – more than 10% of graduates choose it, 5% become instructors in some capacity, there's a well-trod pathway into primary and secondary, and 2% find jobs as educa-tional assistants.

The Law is another good option, with a series of language add-ons and an intercalary year in the US with Law & American Studies.

SOCIAL SCENE

STUDENTS' UNION There are 2 bars: **Idols** at Hendrefoelan student village – cosy atmosphere with karaoke every Tuesday, and **JC's**, on campus – great pub with big screen for all sporting events, friendly and popular venue. **Divas** is the union nightclub – extremely popular, with a wide range of nights to cater for all tastes.

Time and Envy in the city centre hand over their club to the Union on Mondays and Wednesdays – Monday is *Student Night*, and Wednesday is *AU Night* (Athletic Union). Besides karaoke at **Idols** every Tuesday, there's a pub quiz at **JC's** each Sunday, and in Divas *Flirt!* on a Friday and *Live and Wired* (basically like an open Mike night) on Sunday.

There are 70+ sports clubs and 50+ societies up and running, RAG and Dance being the most active right now, though politics is a perennial interest, 'all parties represented, Lib Dem and Socialist and Respect,' they say. And the Tories? main issues this year have been about changes to the university, campaign against the arms trade, and student safety. *Waterfront* is the newspaper; X-treme Radio rules the airwaves.

> *As Dylan Thomas wrote about this place in* Who Do You Wish Was With Us? *– 'Why don't we live here always? Always and always. Build a bloody house and live like bloody kings!'*

There's an international Swansea Arts Festival every autumn. **The Glynn Vivian Gallery** in town, **The Swansea Arts Workshop** in the Maritime Quarter (the former docklands) and **The Taliesin Arts Centre** on campus, deliver year-round exhibitions and events. Taliesin was and is the poetic spirit of Wales, his story among the oldest of Welsh myths. Here is a constantly unfolding programme (for and by students and outsiders) of drama, dance, film and concerts from classical through jazz and rock. The building has a bar and a bookshop. For Swansea-based opera and comedy there's the **Pontardawe Arts Centre**; for comedy,

rock, classical and musicals there's the **Penyrheol Theatre**, while **The Grand** delivers Welsh National Opera, Lily Savage, *The Pirates of Penzance*, Paul Merton and the *South Wales Evening Post Fashion Show* in quick succession (classify that!).

SPORT Interest in sport is huge. They held the British University games here in Spring 2006. Rugby is bigger than huge; Robert Howley and Dafydd James are alumni. Football and netball teams have been Welsh champions. Sports facilities were boosted last year with the opening of the Olympic-size Wales National Pool Swansea and the development of a new athletics track, two outdoor all-weather pitches and an indoor training centre for athletes at the University's sports centre site adjacent to campus.

There's a sports centre with hall, squash courts, weight training room, climbing wall and indoor swimming pool (a new Olympic-size pool was

WHAT IT'S REALLY LIKE

UNIVERSITY:	
Social Life	★★★★
Campus scene	**Laid-back surfers**
Student Union services	**Good**
Politics	**NUS and national issues**
Sport	**70+ clubs**
National team position	**35th**
Sport facilities	**Good**
Arts opportunities	**Drama, dance excellent, music, film, art good**
Student newspaper	**Waterfront**
Student radio	**X-Treme**
Nightclubs/bars	**Divas, Idols, JC's**
Union ents	**Flirt!, Live & Wired; Time & Envy in town**
Union societies	**50+**
Parking	**Adequate**
TOWN:	
Entertainment	★★★
Scene	**Clubs, pubs, sea**
Town/gown relations	**Good**
Risk of violence	**Low**
Cost of living	**Low**
Student concessions	**Good**
Survival + 2 nights out	**£60 pw**
Part-time work campus/town	**Good**

AT A GLANCE

ACADEMIC FILE:	
Subjects assessed	**26**
Excellent	**46%**
Typical entry requirements	**288 points**
Application acceptance rate	**22%**
Med. School acceptance rate	**14%**
Students-staff ratio	**17:1**
First/2:1 degree pass rate	**57%**
ACCOMMODATION FILE:	
Guarantee to freshers	**98%-100%**
Style	**Halls, houses**
Catered	**25%**
En suite	**18%**
Approx price range pw	**£45-£91**
City rent pw	**£40-£48**

recently completed). There are two sets of playing fields, field sport areas, six tennis courts, two netball courts, a rifle range and fishing lake.

There's also sailing, rowing (on the River Tawe), surfing and canoeing, and annual sports scholarships, for which you should apply before you join up.

PILLOW TALK

A place is guaranteed to all new full-time undergraduate students holding a firm offer who accepted their confirmed university place by 31st August. Where possible, this guarantee is extended to insurance offer students. A range of options is available: en-suite, self-catering rooms arranged in flats of 8, en-suite part catering rooms 200 semi en suite, part-catering rooms (bathrooms shared by 2 rooms), standard rooms with shared kitchen and bathroom facilities. The Hendrefoelan student village (approx 2 miles from the campus) provides accommodation for 1,600 students in flats and houses for 4 to 11 students. Shared kitchen, dining and bathroom facilities.

'Swansea is small. Wherever you choose to live you'll find a community of really good friends,' writes Maxine. 'The same is true even in private accommodation at Brynmill, an area close by but considered by many (though probably not by its long-term residents) as a second student village. There is this sense that everyone is linked in some way, friends, friend of a friend and so on. Students here are generally very laid back, and not just the surfers.'

GETTING THERE
- By road: M4/J42B.
- By coach: Cardiff, 1:10.
- By rail: London Paddington, 2:50; Bristol, 2:00; Cardiff, 0:50; Birmingham, 3:15; Manchester, 4:30.
- By air: Cardiff Airport.

UNIVERSITY OF TEESSIDE

The University of Teesside
Middlesbrough
Tees Valley TS1 3BA

Teesside Students' Union
Borough Road
Middlesbrough TS1 3BA

TEL 01642 218121
FAX 01642 342067
EMAIL registry@tees.ac.uk
WEB www.tees.ac.uk

TEL 07977 508025
EMAIL st.union@usu.org.uk
WEB www.utu.org.uk

VAG VIEW

Teesside call themselves the opportunity university and sit high in the league table of those that have widened access to higher education. What this means in their case is that entry requirements are not demanding, may well not include A levels, and that the undergraduate population, many of whom are mature, is largely drawn from the region.

Out-of-towners will cloud these facts with their own preconceptions, just as surely as one's first time view of the town is clouded by the Satanic vision of sulphurous chimneys off the A1. But they would be wrong, for when it comes to 'graduate track' employment, they sit comfortably higher than mid-table nationally.

Teesside is particularly strong in computer games design and animation, design, digital media, sport and exercise, forensic science and health-related courses such as physiotherapy and radiography.

Over £22m is being invested this year in two new developments on campus - the £12m Institute of Digital Innovation and the £10m Centre for Creative Technologies. Both will open in 2007 and enhance Teesside's reputation as a leading university for digital innovation and design.

CAMPUS
The campus is located within a few minutes walk of the centre of Middlesbrough, on the south bank of the River Tees, a short hop from the North Yorks Moors and Redcar and Saltburn beaches.

Students using the union building must run a gauntlet of pubs on Southfield Road: **The Dickens' Inn**, licensed till midnight, **The Star & Garter**, offering '£1-a-pint, £2-for-2' (to whom in their cups does that seem like an increasingly good deal?) and **The Fly & Firkin.** The architecture of the union and adjacent, £11-million, 5-storey Learning Resources Centre stuns – these delicately ribbed, green-tinted glass buildings glistening with seductive appeal.

FEES, BURSARIES
UK & EU Fees, 2007: £3,070 p.a. If in receipt of full HE Maintenance grant there's a bursary of £1,300;

if in receipt of partial grant, it's £500. All new undergraduate students (home and EU) receive a £500 Welcome grant. There's also a £2,000 Elite Athlete bursary scheme, and £1,000 p.a. for applicants with 300 points from 3 A' levels, including two grade B.

STUDENT PROFILE

There's a large mature student intake and many come from non-traditional uni heartlands close by. They have a job-seeker's attitude to academia, i.e. serious, and a similar appetite for the hedonistic pleasures that Students' Union and town afford.

ACADEMIA & JOBS

Teesside's two largest academic schools are Health & Social Care and Computing. Both have increased dramatically in size over the last five years. Together they account for half the student population.

Extensive use is made of the Universityís Virtual Learning Environment - E@T (Elearning@ Tees). Each subject has its own support site for students and this contains a range of online learning tools, resources and links. The sites are accessible both on and off campus 24/7.

Significantly more than a quarter of Teesside students enter the health sector on graduation – by far the most becoming senior hospital nurses (SRN, RGN), then it's physiotherapists, community & youth workers, non-hospital nurses, occupational therapists, medical radiographers, social workers and midwives.

Teesside dropped only 1 point at the assessments and offer Adult, Child, Learning Disabilities and Mental Health nursing. Note also BSc (Hons) Youth Studies and Youth Work, and the various Youth Studies combinations with Sociology, Criminology or Psychology. Most social worker/ counsellors come through biological sciences – BSc degrees in Social Work, and BSc Psychology (accredited by the British Psychological Society and

the first step to becoming a chartered psychologist), which comes on its own or with Counselling or Criminology. They turn out a number of probation officers. See also the new BSc (Hons) Psychology and Education Studies.

A significant niche area lies in computer games

Female Undergraduates — **54%**

10% — Postgraduates

STUDENT POPULATION

Total students 21,354

36% Male Undergraduates

design. See their 3/4-year dedicated degrees (Animation, Games Art, Games Design, Games Programming, Games Science, Graphics Science). The first subject to be assessed Excellent was Computer Science and this has been a crucial focus of investment. The Innovation Centre incorporates the unique Virtual Reality Centre, with large-scale VR development and viewing facilities, including a purpose-built Hemispherium (immersive VR experience) and VR cinema, as well as labs for the development of VR environments. Look at BScs in Digital Forensics, Digital Music, Digital Music Creation, BA(Hons) Post-Production and Visual Effects, BSc (Hons) Technical Direction in Computer Animation. The uni is part of a plan to create a digital city in Middlesbrough. There'll be new teaching, learning and commercial facilities as well as opportunities for graduate start up-businesses. Opening in 2007, as part of the Digital City project, is an £11m Institute of Digital Innovation, which will incorporate business accommodation, commercialisation space, concept testing and shared development facilities for research between business and academia.

Business-wise there's a strong lean towards information management and marketing, with BA e-Business, Business Information Systems, Accounting with Information technology, etc. See also vocational lines such as BA Marketing, and combinations with Retail Mgt, Advertising Mgt, Public Relations. Also the new BA (Hons) Corporate Leadership and Management.

Their own business start-up scheme - Upgrade2 has assisted over 40 fledgling student companies. Collaboration with local and regional industry is the nub of their strategy in business and industry, which is why the Northern Region Film &

UNIVERSITY/STUDENT PROFILE	
University since	**1970**
Situation/style	**Town campus**
Student population	**21354**
Undergraduates	**19331**
- mature	**68%**
- non EU undergraduates	**3%**
- male/female	**40/60**
- non-traditional student intake	**44%**
- state sector intake	**98%**
-drop-out rate	**25%**
- undergraduate applications	**Down 8%**

ACADEMIC EXCELLENCE

TEACHING:

(Rated Excellent or 17+ out of 24)

Computer Science	**Excellent**
Nursing	**23**
Art & Design Subjects Allied to Medicine	**22**
Electric & Electron Eng, Sport	**21**
Psychology	**20**
Civil Eng, Sociol & Criminology	**19**
Civil Engineering	**18**

RESEARCH :
Top grades 5/5*

History	**Grade 5**

Television Archive is housed on campus in a temperature controlled environment, with it's own screening facilities and archive, providing a resource for students of history and media.

Note, too, that they are specialists in European and commercial law. Again, there's a tie-up with Criminology, and a Senior Status LLB for graduates

SUBJECT AREAS (%)

Humanities — Education 0.2%
Creative Arts — Combined
Media — Health Subjects
Languages — 3 3 1 6 — 13
12 — 10
11 — 12
Business — 8 — 20 — Biological Sciences
Social Studies incl. Law — Engineering/ Technology — Maths & Computer — Physical Sciences

holding a non-Law degree. Links with Cleveland and Durham constabularies underwrite the pioneering BSc in Criminology. See also Crime Scene Science, Applied Science & Forensic Investigation, etc, and Fraud Management. They claim their

Crime House Lab, where forensic science students put their investigative skills into practice, is the most elaborate facility of its kind in any UK university, and have just opened a Vehicle Examination Centre for forensic and crime scene science students to practise their skills. See the new BSc Digital Forensics, BSc (Hons) Forensic Investigation and Consumer Law, and BSc (Hons) Medico-Legal Death Investigation.

A significant graduate population find work as graphic designers, set and interior designers, and there are interesting interior design and advertising specialisms Interior Architecture & Design, Creative Advertising & Promotion, Advertising Management & Public Relations. The Art & Design provision has spawned a useful local project, plans for a new showpiece centre for Art and Design education in collaboration with **Cleveland College of Art and Design**, which has three campuses, two in Middlesbrough, one in Hartlepool. Cleveland is hand in glove with Teesside. They are a large art college with 2000 students, about 10% of whom study for Teesside degrees in Design Crafts for the Entertainment Industries, Fine Art, Photography, and Textiles. There's synergy, too, with Cleveland's TV & Film production degree. Web: www.ccad. ac.uk

They also run various media degrees - Digital Media, Radio Production, and a Journalism foundation degree with specialist Darlington College, and this year are launching a BA (Hons)Multimedia Journalism Professional Practice accredited by NCTJ.

Teesside are also among the top unis for turning out sports players and officials through their Coaching and Applied Sports Science/Exercise Science degrees. See also the new BA Sport and Leisure Management, BA Sport Management and BSc Sport and Exercise Psychology. See *Sport* below.

SOCIAL SCENE

There's **The Terrace Bar**, and **Club One** is the 1000-capacity nightclub, a huge space with specially treated dancefloor, 8000 watt sound system, DJ control bridge, raised seating areas and no-smoke chill-out room. There's a clubnight every Friday

WHERE TEESSIDE GRADUATES END UP

Health & Social Work: 27%; Education: 5%; Wholesale Retail: 13%; Manufacturing: 9%; Financial Activities: 4%; Public Administration, Civil Service & Defence: 11%; Hotel/Restaurant: 5%; Transport & Communications (including Telecommunications): 5%; Construction: 1%; Personnel: 3%; Computer: 5%; Business & Management: 1%; Accountancy: 0.5%; Media (including Film): 1%; Legal 4%; Advertising: 0.5%; Sport: 1.5%.

Approximate 'graduate track' employed **62%**

and Saturday, the first being current chart and r&b, and Saturday rotates with indie, retro, school disco and current chart.

On a Friday evening in **Club One** the buzz is tangible. 'I've lived down south,' said Michelle, 'and I am not being biased, but the scene up here is great, one of the best in the North East. We've got far too many bars, people are just competing with each other, so it's great for students. We have the **Empire** [renowned for *Sugar Shack* – Jeremy Healy, Boy George, Paul Oakenfold and Sasha and Digweed hit the decks]; it's one of the best known nightclubs in the country, if you look in dance mags. We've got **Tall Trees** in Yarm, which is internationally recognised [a huge club set in fantastic grounds with inimitable nights]. We have our balls there. There are plenty of others, and the **Arena** is nationally known.'

Nor is it all night-time reverie. There are 20 societies and 40 sports clubs. Student media includes a monthly magazine, *Cup of Tees*. Most popular is the

> *On a Friday evening in Club One the buzz is tangible. 'I've lived down south,' said Michelle, 'and I am not being biased, but the scene up here is great, one of the best in the North East.'*

International Students Society with about 100 members. Then there are things like the Dilated Pupil Society, the dance music society which is very active now. Drama is doing a series of satirical sketches this Christmas; they do plays regularly. There's a singing society and they're doing a Christmas concert. There's a Cultural Studies society that organises exchange trips and so on, a film sci fi society. Our Law society is very successful in the courtroom battles with high profile universities in the North East, Durham, Newcastle, etc. Art comes via Cleveland College of Art & Design [see above]. They set up the Burlam Road Society.'

SPORT In 2004 they opened the £6.5 million Olympia Building with squash courts, floodlit artificial pitch and large sports hall, plus a range of up to the minute teaching facilities and the latest climate simulation facility – designed to test sporting performance in a range of temperatures. But they are languishing 40 places further down the BUSA national team league (at 95th) than they were 2 years ago. No wonder they are offering such generous sports scholarships.

PILLOW TALK

Campus residences are exclusively for first years. Allocations are made on a first come first served basis. Apply early for any accommodation as there isn't enough to go round. There are houses, halls, flats and managed housing off campus. Five mixed halls of residence all have self-catering facilities; 34% of campus accommodation is en suite.

WHAT IT'S REALLY LIKE

UNIVERSITY:

Social Life	★★★★
Campus scene	**Lively, local scene**
Student Union services	**Good**
Politics	**Activity low: fees, safety, health**
Sport	**Competitive**
National team position	**106th**
Sport facilities	**Poor**
Arts opportunities	**Dance, music excellent, rest OK**
Student magazine	**Cup of Tees**
Student newsletter	**Teesguide**
Nightclub	**Club One**
Bars	**Terrace Bar**
Union ents	**Chart, r&b, indie, retro, disco**
Union societies	**60 (40 sport)**
Parking	**Poor**

TOWN:

Entertainment	★★★★
Scene	**Pubs, big-time clubs**
Town/gown relations	**Average**
Risk of violence	**Average**
Cost of living	**Low**
Student concessions	**Good**
Survival + 2 nights out	**£50-£60 pw**
Part-time work campus/town	**Excellent/good**

AT A GLANCE

ACADEMIC FILE:

Assessments	**20**
Excellent	**50%**
Typical entry requirements	**224 points**
Application acceptance rate	**25%**
Students-staff ratio	**21:1**
First/2:1 degree pass rate	**46%**

ACCOMMODATION FILE:

Guarantee to freshers	**Most**
Style	**Halls, flats, houses**
Catered	**None**
En-suite	**21%**
Price range pw	**£34-£59**
City rent pw	**£50**

GETTING THERE

☛ By road: A19, or A1/M, A66.
☛ By rail: Newcastle, 1:15; Leeds, 1:45; Manchester Piccadilly, 2:45; Liverpool Lime Street, 3:45; London King's Cross, 3:30.
☛ By air: Teesside International Airport.
☛ By coach: Birmingham, 3:15; York, 1:15.

THAMES VALLEY UNIVERSITY

Thames Valley University
St Mary's Road
London W5 5RF

Thames Valley Students' Union
St Mary's Road
London W5 5RF

TEL 0800 036 8888
FAX 020 8231 1353
EMAIL learning.advice@tvu.ac.uk
WEB www.tvu.ac.uk

TEL 020 8231 2276
FAX 020 8231 2589
EMAIL [firstname.surname]@tvu.ac.uk
WEB www.tvu.ac.uk

VAG VIEW

*F*ormerly West London Poly and incorporating the Ealing School of Art, where Pete Townshend (the Who), Ronnie Wood (the Stones) and Freddie Mercury (Queen)... erm...studied, TVU works with local colleges on access programmes, allowing successful completion of an access course as an alternative to usual entry requirements.

On the face of it, TVU is a model of the government's policy to facilitate access for social groups without a tradition in higher education.

They have had a time of it making that work, after a slamming from the Quality Assurance Agency in 1998, and their non-completion rate is still among the highest in the land.

However, there is much optimism following their merger with Reading College and School of Arts & Design, from the new Brentford Campus, home to their enormous Faculty of Health, and perhaps most promising of all, a tie-up with the mighty Imperial College London over a degree in Medicine.

CAMPUS

TVU is based on sites in Ealing (West London, where the Student Union is based) and Slough, and now at Reading and Brentford. Shuttle buses run between the campuses until late each night. There is no university-owned residential campus accommodation at Ealing or Slough, but they will sort you out.

The Reading Campus, Crescent Road, Reading RG1 5RQ (0800 371 434), previously known as Reading College and School of Arts & Design, had been in TVU's sights for some time. After some to-ing and fro-ing, and a serious blip in negotiations when the college's computer provision failed a re-inspection by the Quality Assurance Agency, in January 2004 they merged with the uni and became the Reading campus.

For years TVU had awarded degrees here. The special deals at the college were then HNDs which convert with an extra year into degrees, including

Female Undergraduates — 22%
Postgraduates — 4%
Male Undergraduates — 12%
Others — 62%

STUDENT POPULATION
Total students
52,885

engineering, multimedia systems & design, business, fine art, fashion & textiles, design, photography. TVU is now offering business, music (technology and performance), computing, applied law, arts in the community, design, film, graphics, fine art, photography.

There is a Student Union presence, accommodation, an activities centre and football pitch. Nearby there are leisure centres with multi-sports tracks, gymnasiums, dance studios, swimming pools and tennis, squash and badminton courts. See *Reading University* entry for more details about the city.

Brentford Campus is still in the making, off Boston Manor Road. It will be home to TVU's

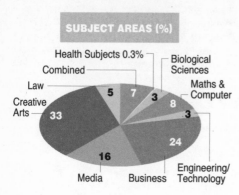

SUBJECT AREAS (%)

- Health Subjects 0.3%
- Combined
- Law
- Creative Arts — 33
- 5
- 7
- 3
- Biological Sciences
- Maths & Computer — 8
- 3
- 24
- 16
- Media
- Business
- Engineering/ Technology

Faculty of Health and Human Sciences – with its many nursing and midwifery students, this is the largest healthcare faculty in the UK. The first phase of the development is completed, and the campus is due to be fully operational by September 2006. It includes 849 study bedrooms, 221 key worker flats and 12,000 sq.m of teaching/office accommodation.

FEES, BURSARIES

UK & EU Fees, 2007: £3,070 p.a. If in receipt of a Government Maintenance Grant, there's a bursary.

STUDENT PROFILE

'The most positive point to be made about TVU concerns the diversity,' writes student Ian Draysey. 'Students of all ages come from all over the world, and studying there has given me the opportunity to meet people I never would have otherwise. The majority of universities make similar claims, but in this case it's true, honest!'

Today, with most students from the locality, high ethnicity, many from overseas and many mature students, its boast of a diverse mix is valid, but only up to a point – they barely take 2% from outside the state school sector.

ACADEMIA & JOBS

More than 40% of their students graduate in business and administration, and many find jobs in marketing and market research. There are BA Marketing degrees with Business or Advertising. See also the Public Relations provision. There's also a particular slant towards the catering industry (see their Hospitality Management degrees and International Hotel degrees). See, too, their BA Business Travel & Tourism, Aviation & Business Tourism; Travel & Tourism Mgt, Resort & Event Mgt, which carve out careers.

Advertising is itself a sound niche graduate employment area for TVU. There are well targeted degrees, such as Advertising Specialist and Advertising with options ranging from Design through Radio Broadcasting, Video Production, Photography & Digital Imaging to Marketing. There is indeed a strong (5%) career claim on the media sector. See also BA New Media Journalism.

Smart music producers choose their 3-year Music Technology BA, which gives this uni one of its strongest employment records. Again there is the Specialist degree or one with options.

Statistics also show there's a track record for composers and musicians at TVU. See the BMus (Performance/Composition) and Popular Music Performance degrees.

The big news is that Imperial College London and Thames Valley University (TVU) have cleared a way for people not up to following the usual route to studying medicine at Imperial to do so. TVU's BSc (Hons) Human Sciences (Pre-medical Option) is a way of widening participation in medicine for students who otherwise wouldn't have the opportunity to study at Imperial, which has one of the best medical schools in the world and is normally extremely testing to get into. But don't think you'll just sail in from TVU. Students planning on applying must first apply via UCAS to TVU for the for the BSc (Hons) Human Sciences (B9C1). Those who

UNIVERSITY/STUDENT PROFILE	
University since	**1992**
Situation/style	**City/suburban campuses**
Student population	**52885**
Undergraduates	**18010**
- mature	**77%**
- non EU undergraduates	**7%**
- male/female	**35/65**
- non-traditional student intake	**36%**
- state sector intake	**98%**
- drop-out rate	**31%**
- undergraduate applications	**Up 2%**

ACADEMIC EXCELLENCE	
TEACHING:	
(Rated Excellent or 17+ out of 24)	
Sociology, Linguistics, Tourism	**22**
Psychology, Nursing, Health	**20**
Business/Marketing	**19**
Modern Languages	**18**

meet the entry requirements for the Pre-medical Option will be invited to TVU for interview and a written exercise. Only Home/EU students who do not already hold a degree need apply, and they must have Grade C AS Level in Chemistry, plus A

WHERE THAMES VALLEY GRADUATES END UP

Health & Social Work: 12%; Education: 7%; Wholesale Retail: 18%; Manufacturing: 5%; Financial Activities: 8%; Public Administration, Civil Service & Defence: 7%; Hotel/Restaurant: 6%; Transport & Communications (including Telecommunications): 9%; Construction: 0.5%; Personnel: 3%; Computer: 6%; Business & Management: 1%; Accountancy: 1%; Media (including Film): 5%; Legal 3%; Publishing: 0.5%; Artistic/Literary: 1.5%; Sport: 0.5%.

Approximate 'graduate track' employed **60%**

Level Grades C and D in 2 further subjects, plus GCSE Grade C in English and Maths. A Level equivalents are not accepted. Assuming all that, the following November they must sit the the BioMedical Admissions Test (BMAT) (see our Introduction) and will be invited to interview at Imperial if they obtain a 60% aggregate result in their first semester modules. Still, it's easier than getting on the Imperial medical course by the noraml route. Much easier. Be interesting to see who manages it, and what they go on to do.

Otherwise, TVU's health provision, which will be moving to the new Brentford campus, focuses on Nursing and midwifery and accounts for a hug proportion of jobs for graduates from TVU. There's also Health & Exercise Science, Health Studies, Sports Science & Medicine, a top-up Complementary Approaches to Health degree, and BSc Psychology with Counselling Theory, as well as the single hons accredited by the British Psychological Society, first step to becoming a chartered psychologist. The BSc has an OK assessment, 20.

The law degree recently got a fillip from the LPC Board (a Legal Practice Course is essential to becoming a solicitor) who pronounced it 'Good'.

Finally, there's a strong showing in financial administration. See their Accounting and Finance degrees and foundation year.

It is in line with their academic strategy to have help at hand for literacy, numeracy and IT skills.

SOCIAL SCENE

STUDENTS' UNION **The Studio** opens Monday to Friday, 11 am to 11 pm, the **Coffee Stop**, 8 am - 6 pm, Monday to Thursday, 8 am - 4 pm on Fridays. At the Ealing campus, traditional pool table and jukebox scenario is supplemented by Bhangra music and Hindi films. Ents include live bands, karaoke, DJs and drinking competitions. The uni's degrees in music (including Popular Music Performance) and its association with the London College of Music and Media provide input, and the fledgling Tube Radio, ambitiously aimed not just at students but at the wider community around Ealing, benefits from LCM's hardware.

AT A GLANCE

ACADEMIC FILE:

Subjects assessed	**19**
Excellent	**42%**
Typical entryl requirements	**203 points**
Application acceptance rate	**23%**
Students-staff ratio	**24:1**
First/2:1 degree pass rate	**49%**

ACCOMMODATION FILE:

Availability in college	**None**
Town/city rent pw	**£85-£127**

WHAT IT'S REALLY LIKE

UNIVERSITY:

Social Life	★★
Campus scene	**London diversity, closed weekends**
Student Union services	**Average-poor**
Politics	**No interest**
Sport	**Local**
National team position	**119th**
Sport facilities	**Poor**
Arts opportunities	**Music, film, art**
Student magazine	**Undergrad**
Student newspaper	**The Voice**
Student radio	**Tube**
Nightclub	**The Studio**
Bars	**The Studio Bar**
Union ents	**Some**
Union societies	**11**
Most popular society	**Tube Radio**
Smoking policy	**None**
Parking	**Adequate**

CITY:

Entertainment	★★★★★
Scene	**London**
Town/gown relations	**Average**
Risk of violence	**Average**
Cost of living	**Very high**
Student concessions	**Good**
Survival + 2 nights out	**£80 pw**
Part-time work campus/town	**Average/excellent**

The largest venue at TVU is **Artwood's**, with a capacity of 1,200. It has attempted to overcome its school hall demeanour with the installation of a bar to complement its livestock-bothering sound system, and has a good atmosphere when crowded.

Over at the Slough campus, the **Moon and Cucumber** bar, buffet bar, **Hamlyn Hall** and the smokeless **Studio Bar** offer alternative recreational facilities. Slough also houses a gym for those who'd rather build up their muscles than their beer guts.

They say that societies range from the Radio Society to the Asian Society and come under four categories, Cultural (Asian, Chinese), Religious (Christian Union, Islamic), Social (Radio, Music Industry), and Academic (Law, Psychology). Sport at TVU has swung away from the more team-oriented stance of many universities, with activities such as badminton, fencing and aerobics gaining more members than football. There was no team placement in last year's national uni leagues.

GETTING THERE
☛ Ealing: Ealing Broadway Underground (Central and District Lines).
☛ Slough: By road: M4/J6, A4. By rail: London Paddington, 25 mins.

UNIVERSITY OF ULSTER

University of Ulster
University House
Cromore Road
Coleraine
Co. Londonderry BT52 1SA

TEL 028 7032 4221
FAX 028 7032 4908
EMAIL online@ulster.ac.uk
STUDENT UNION TEL 028 7032 4319
WEB www.ulst.ac.uk

VAG VIEW

*U*lster is the largest of the 9 universities in Ireland. Spread across four sites (between seven and eighty miles apart) it is an enormous place in terms of students, 80% of whom are local.

The uni came out of a merger in 1984 between Ulster Poly (now the Jordanstown campus) and the New University of Ulster (which was the old university, if you follow). Sites are at Belfast (art college), at Newtownabbey, in the hills above Belfast (the Jordanstown campus), at Coleraine (this is HQ, far northwest of Belfast, near the Giant's Causeway), and in Londonderry (Magee College campus, founded in 1865), yet further west.

To solve communications problems they have formed a wireless microwave network capable of transmitting data of Encyclopedia Britannica *proportions in a second. The Centre for Communications Engineering links them to Queen's Uni and Nortel Networks, and is a feature of their strategy for close working with industry.*

There are plans afoot for massive improvements and expansion.

STUDENT PROFILE
There's a high mature undergrad percentage and an

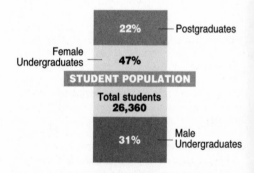

unusually high number of part-timers among the predominantly local student body; university strategy ensures that many, too, come from social groups with no great tradition of higher education. Together with all this socio-educational progress comes a high drop-out rate – 13% of non-mature entrants.

CAMPUS
BELFAST York Street, Belfast BT15 1ED. **Location:** close to city centre, part of the city's up and coming Cathedral Quarter, is traditionally considered the home of the School of Art and Design, though other disciplines are increasingly being taught there. **Faculty HQs:** Art & Design (including Interior Design and Textile & Fashion Design). Also American Studies, Architecture, Irish Literature, Chinese, English. **Accommodation:** none, but small number of Belfast students may use Jordanstown. **Ents facilities: Conor Hall** (400-

SUBJECT AREAS (%)

Humanities 3, Media 3, Languages 3, Creative Arts 7, Combined 16, Health Subjects 16, Biological Sciences 5, Physical Sciences 2, Engineering/Technology 10, Maths & Computer 4, Planning/Building/Architecture 6, Social Studies incl. Law 8, Business 17

capacity venue). **Sports facilities:** 'What's sport?' said a student when asked. Arts facilities: foyer exhibition area, art shop, artist (writer, artist or musician) in residence. **Arts opportunities:** 'Second to none, vibrant, innovative, love it!' said our student contact. **Media:** monthly magazine, *Ufouria.* See *Student Belfast*, page 399.

JORDANSTOWN Newtownabbey BT37 OQB. **Location:** seven miles north of Belfast on the shore of Belfast Lough; largest site. **Faculty HQs:** Business & Management (including Government, Law, Marketing), Engineering (including Biomedical Eng), Informatics, Social (economics, accounting, politics, social policy, sociology, counselling) & Health Sciences (nursing, physiotherapy, podiatry, speech & language therapy). Also architecture and construction, languages library management, sport. **Accommodation:** res. blocks, six-bedroom houses, flats & study-bedrooms in halls; self-catering.

Ents facilities: Students' Union Bar (700 capacity), split level, two stages, tiered seating/standing; regular disco night is Monday. **Sports facilities:** two large sports halls, gym, fitness suite, six squash courts, eight-lane swimming pool and hydrotherapy pool, playing fields, synthetic training pitch, local water sports facility and River Lagan. **Arts facilities:** recital rooms, concert hall. Low key. **Media:** *Naked* is student newspaper.

COLERAINE (address with entry title) **Location:** market town close to north coast, 35 miles from Derry. The original uni, admin HQ and home to the Centre for Molecular Sciences. **Biosciences, health (nursing, optometry), pharmacology, environmental science, dietetics, social sciences (psychology,), humanities (history, geography) languages and Euro studies, media (film, journalism, publishing), business, computer.** **Accommodation:** residential blocks and student houses. Most students prefer to live out in coastal resort towns Portrush and Portstewart. **Ents facilities:** Biko Hall (venue) and recently rebuilt **Uni-Bar**; 550 capacity. Regular disco night is Monday. **Sports facilities:** Biko Hall is sports hall by day, five squash courts, fitness suite, solarium and steam room, playing fields, floodlit football pitch, pavilion, tennis courts, water sports centre on River Bann. **Arts facilities:** the **Octagon** (500-

UNIVERSITY/STUDENT PROFILE

University since	**1984**
Situation/style	**4 urban/rural campus sites**
Student population	**26360**
Undergraduates	**20490**
- mature	**20%**
- non EU undergraduates	**0.5%**
- male/female	**39/61**
- non-traditional student intake	**47%**
- state sector intake	**100%**
drop-out rate	**17%**
- undergraduate applications	**Down 9%**

seat recital room), the **Diamond** (1,200-seat concert hall, prestigious **Riverside Theatre**, third largest pro theatre in Ireland, venue for drama, rock and classical concerts, ballet, opera, etc.

MAGEE COLLEGE Northland Road, Londonderry BT48 7JL. **Location:** residential quarter of Derry, Ireland's second largest city. A mixture of historical and new buildings and modern and traditional facilities, a small and tightly knit student population. New moves bring drama, music, dance and com-

WHERE ULSTER GRADUATES END UP

Health & Social Work: 20%; Education: 4.5%; Wholesale Retail: 14%; Manufacturing: 8%; Financial Activities: 7%; Public Administration, Civil Service & Defence: 10%; Hotel/Restaurant: 4%; Transport & Communications (including Telecommunications): 2%; Construction: 4%; Agriculture: 0.5%; Personnel: 1.5%; Computer: 5%; Business & Management: 2.5%; Accountancy: 4%; Media (including Film): 0.5%; Legal 1%; Architecture: 2%; Sport: 0.5%.

Approximate 'graduate track' employed **63%**

puting to the bedrock business, humanities, social sciences (psychology, law, politics, social policy, community youth work, sociology) & nursing. Languages are also to the fore, and Irish Studies. It is home to the Institute for Legal & Professional Studies. **Accommodation:** three halls of residence and student village (modern houses). **Ents facilities:** two bars, **The Terrapin** (known as 'the wee bar') and **The Bunker** (bar/nightclub, 400 capacity). **Ents:** bands and discos (Thursday); Derry wild with pubs. **Sports facilities:** sports hall, fitness suite and solarium; recent additions include sports pavilion, sand-carpet soccer pitch, synthetic training pitch; sailing at Fahan, rowing and canoeing on the Foyle. **Arts facilities:** the **Great Hall**.

ACADEMIA & JOBS

Here the emphasis is on jobs in the health sector, in retail, in public administration, civil service, etc.

In the former, where there's a good 22-point score in the teaching assessments, most jobs go to nurses (including mental health), to occupational therapists, to ophthalmic opticians – they have between 6% and 10% of the graduate employment market. There's a world-class Grade 5* for research.

Then it's physiotherapists, radiographers (diagnostic and therapeutic), chiropodists (the Podiatry degrees, and speech therapists. The BSc Speech & Language Therapy asks BBB.

Social workers/counsellors spring into the work sector via BSc Social Work. See also BSc Social Psychology. Other Psychology combinations include languages, marketing, international politics and human resource management.

In retail management, for sheer bulk of graduate output, Manchester Met leads, followed by Ulster with their Business Studies programmes and Retail Management, Consumer Studies and Marketing degrees. Note Business & Management scored full marks at the teaching assessments, and there's a sure path to hotel, restaurant manager through their international hospitality management and hotel and tourism management degrees.

For civil service admin and local/regional government admin, Ulster's BSc Economics & Government, Law & Government, Housing Management, Community Development, Social Administration & Policy, Health & Social Care Policy, Social Policy & Governance, etc are clearly relevant, but in fact the majority of their graduates into the sector come on the Health ticket - subjects allied to Medicine: besides the many keenly focused degrees alluded to above, there are courses in Human Nutrition, Food & Nutrition, Dietetics, Clinical Physiology, etc and a Postgrad Diploma/MSc in Health Promotion. See also their Psychology with International Politics out at Magee Campus. Biological Sciences is also a popular route and part of the same Faculty of Life & Health Sciences.

The Faculty of Engineering & Built Environment is also productive through various degrees: Environment Engineering, Architectural Technology/Construction Eng & Management, Building Surveying, Transport & Supply Chain Management and BSc Environmental Health.

Construction engineers/managers also proliferate. BSc Hons Construction Engineering & Management, Architectural Technology & Management, or Building Surveying are the key focus courses, 21 points at assessment, international Grade 5 for research. Property developers, quantity surveyors and estate agents also come out of Ulster in quantity. There's BSc

Property Development & Investment, which puts their employment record out of sight of most of their competitors and they are responsible for 9% of all graduate quantity surveyors, even though the dedicated degree is new. Land & Property Mgt took full marks at the assessments and you won't have to punt as high as the asking grades for their flagship Architectural Technology & Management degree, which helps to make them clear market leaders in engineering design consultancy.

Civil engineers also make a strong showing in the employment figures.

There's a strong showing in accountancy, too –

WHAT IT'S REALLY LIKE

UNIVERSITY:	
Social Life	★★★
Campus scenes	**Local, lively, diverse**
Student Union services	**Average**
Politics	**High activity: Irish politics, student funding**
Sport	**Big at Coleraine & Jordanstown**
Sport facilities	**Good**
National team position	**81st** (Coleraine) **130th** (Jordanstown)
Arts opportunities	**Art excellent; drama, dance, film, music good**
Student magazine	**Ufouria**
Union ents	**13 pw**
Live venues	**Conor Hall** (Belfast), **Biko Hall** (Coleraine), **The Bunker** (Magee), **Arthur's** (Jordanstown)
Union clubs/societies	**100+**
Most popular society	**Irish Society**
Smoking policy	**Union OK**
Parking	**Adequate**

AT A GLANCE

ACADEMIC FILE:	
Subjects assessed	**42**
Excellent	**67%**
Typical entry requirements	**263 points**
Application acceptance rate	**15%**
Students-staff ratio	**20:1**
First/2:1 class degree pass rate	**62%**

ACCOMMODATION FILE:	
Guarantee to freshers	**100%**
Style	**Halls, flats, houses; not Belfast**
Approx price range pw	**£48-£90**
Approx off-campus rent pw	**£40**

a dedicated degree and one with Business Studies. Another field where acute powers of analysis are to the fore is in biosciences and Ulster was awarded a world-class Grade 5* for research into Biomedical Science. One result is a niche employment area for bacteriologists and microbiologists. The BSc Environmental degrees may be 3 or 4 years with a Diploma in Industrial Studies or Area Studies (that means a year in Europe or USA). There are also Food & Nutrition and Food Production degrees. There's an Excellent for teaching Environmental Studies and more recently a 22-point tick for Health Sciences.

Many Ulster graduates go into computing as programmers, software engineers/consultants or telecommunications engineers. Besides the BEng Electronics & Software and MEng Software Engineering, there's BSc Computer Science and Computing with orientations like E-Business, Entrepreneurship, Marketing, Psychology or Mathematics.

Check campus location foe course you want to study.

GETTING THERE

☞ An hour by air from London, with at least 24 flights a day each way.
☞ Ulsterbus operates a fast and frequent service across Northern Ireland.

UNIVERSITY COLLEGE, LONDON

University College, London
Gower Street
London WC1E 6BT

TEL 020 7679 3000
FAX 020 7679 3001
EMAIL degree-info@ucl.ac.uk
WEB www.ucl.ac.uk/prospective-students

UCL Students' Union
25 Gordon Street
London WC1H 0AH

TEL 020 7387 3611
EMAIL mc.officer@ucl.ac.uk
WEB www.uclu.org

VAG VIEW

*T*he college was the original University of London, the first in England after Oxford and Cambridge, inspired by the first principle of Utilitarianism, 'the greatest happiness of the greatest number'. It was a pioneering move by a group of thinkers, John Stuart Mill among them, for an alternative

STUDENT POPULATION
Total students
19,365

38% — Postgraduates

Female Undergraduates — 32%

30% — Male Undergraduates

approach to higher education, which, in 1826, meant the privileged education dished out by Oxford and Cambridge.

The idea was to open the doors of education to the rising middle-classes and to free the educational establishment from the doctrinal prejudices of the Anglican Church. Roman Catholics, Jews and Nonconformists were barred from an Oxbridge education in those days. To ensure freedom from dogma, it was decided not to have subjects appertaining to religion taught at UCL.

UCL remains one of our foremost seats of learning, its research record formidable and its Slade School of Fine Art reckoned to be the best in its area. UCL's merger with the School of Slavonic & East European Studies and the foundation of the Wolfson Institute for Biomedical Research would seem to shore up the academic infrastructure yet further.

CAMPUS

The location of UCL's main sites, just to the north of London's West End and hard by the University of London Students' Union building, provides students with amazing resource opportunity. What's

more, most halls of residence are within walking distance.

SATELLITE CAMPUSES

ROYAL FREE HOSPITAL MEDICAL SCHOOL merged with UCL to form the Royal Free & University College Medical School. It is situated in Hampstead, one of the safest, most aesthetically pleasing areas of London.

SCHOOL OF SLAVONIC & EAST EUROPEAN STUDIES – SSEES (pronounced Cease) is an enigmatic institution specialising in the study of Eastern Europe, 'It holds the academically acknowledged best lecturers in their fields,' says Gideon Dewhurst, 'and the largest East European library in Britain. They have new purpose-built premises in Taviton Street.

FEES, BURSARIES

UK & EU Fees, 2007: £3,070 p.a. 2008 fees not yet known. If in receipt of the HE Maintenance Grant, bursaries up to £2,600 are available, depending on household income. There are bursaries for students studying particular courses. for Chinese national, for students in financial hardship who plans to get involved in the Students' Union. Check all info. at www.ucl.ac. uk/scholarships.

STUDENT PROFILE

The heavy imbalance in favour of public school wallahs is quite ironic in the light of its history. Today, they hardly fill the bill as 'Cockney College', the name given in the 19th century by those who feared the consequences of UCL's open-access stance. Few universities take a smaller percentage of state sector pupils. However, judging by the recent concentration of activity in the areas of special needs and academic counselling, UCL just might be tooling up to make a big change.

ACADEMIA & JOBS

UCL places great importance on its tutorial system, and their overall student-to-staff ratio of 8-to-1 is the best in the country. All students are allocated a personal tutor for consultation on academic or personal matters. Further support is offered by departmental and faculty tutors and two advisers specialising in women students. There's also a professional counselling service and a Students' Union Rights & Advice Centre to see you through any problems academic, financial or emotional. Also, a special educational needs IT suite was opened in December 2001, offering computers and related software and equipment. An IT trainer and a disabilities co-ordinator are at your disposal.

To become a doctor here, you'll need to be accepted onto the 4/5-year MB BS. UCL stipulate

UNIVERSITY/STUDENT PROFILE	
College of London Uni since	1826
Situation/style	Civic
Student population	19365
Undergraduates	11930
- mature	16%
- non EU undergraduates	18%
- male/female	47/53
- non-traditional student intake	18%
- state sector intake	61%
drop-out rate	7%
- undergraduate applications	Up 9%

ACADEMIC EXCELLENCE

TEACHING :
(Rated Excellent or 17+ out of 24)

History, Law, Anthropology, Architecture, English, Geography, Geological Sciences	**Excellent**
Economics, History of Art, Organismal Biosciences, Subjects Allied to Medicine	**24**
German, Scandinavian Studies, Dentistry, Maths, Physics, Archaeology, Philosophy, Classics, Art & Design	**23**
Linguistics, Dutch, Electrical & Electronic Eng, Psychology, Molecular Biosciences, Anatomy, Library/Info, Politics, Psychology	**22**
Medicine, French	**21**
Italian, Chem & Biochem Eng Pharmacology	**20**
Iberian Studies, Civil Eng	**19**

RESEARCH
Top grades 5/5*/6*

Hospital-based Clinical - Child Health/Neurology/ Ophthalmology, Pharmacology, Psychology, Chemistry, Chemical Eng, Geography, Law, Anthropology, Economics, English, German, Italian, Classics	**Grade 6***
Linguistics	**Grade 5***
Hospital-based Clinical - Royal Free, Clinical Dentistry, Anatomy, Other Subjects Allied to Medicine, Biochemistry, Biology, Physics, Earth Sciences, Pure Maths, Applied Maths, Statistics, Computer, Civi/ Environmental Eng, Electrical/ Electronic Eng, Mechanical, Aeronautical/Manufacturing Eng, European Studies, French, Dutch, Scandinavian, Archaeol, History, History of Art, Philosophy, Art and Design	**Grade 5**

that all candidates applying to read Medicine sit the Biomedical Admissions Test (BMAT). The test is being used to assess scientific aptitude, not fitness to practise medicine (which will continue to be assessed in other ways, including interview) and focuses on scientific abilities relevant to the study of medicine.

The approach of the MB BS is lectures, tutorial and lab classes in Phase 1, with a lot of computer-assisted learning and problem-solving exercises. Only in Phase 2 do you go out in small teams of consultants and doctors. Phase 3 offers intensive clinical experience. Entry AAB to include Chemistry + one AS level. Biology must be offered at A or AS. English and Maths at Grade b, GCSE. Teaching inspection, 21.

The application acceptance rate was 16% last time, 6% more promising than average. Research Grade 6*: Hospital-based Clinical, Child Health/Neurology/Ophthalmology, psychology; Grade 5: Hospital-based Clinical.

Chiropodists and speech therapists are part of the picture too. Teaching inspection, 23. BSc Speech

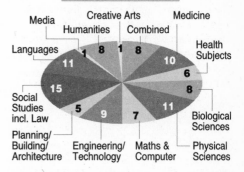

SUBJECT AREAS (%)

Science has an international-standard Grade 5 rating for research. and full marks at inspection.

After medicine, languages (21 are offered), and physical and social sciences degrees are popular. A language GCSE, or similar, is now a compulsory qualification for acceptance at UCL. New state-of-the-art language teaching facilities were opened in February 2007 as part of the Centre for Excellence in Teaching and Learning - Languages of the Wider World. This is run in cahoots with the School of Oriental and African Studies (see entry).

With the takeover of the School of Slavonic & Eastern European Studies in 1999, the Language options increased dramatically. This is a premier route into Adult Education for would-be lecturers. On inspection, German and Scandinavian Studies were awarded 23 out of 24, Linguistics and Dutch 22, French 21, Italian 20, Spanish 19. There were both Grade 6* and Grade 5 accolades at the Languages research assessments.

The BA degree in Language and Culture combines study of one foreign language to degree level, plus one or two other languages, with a particular focus in a chosen area of cultural studies – comparative literature, film studies, linguistics, history of art or cultural history – giving students the opportunity to apply their language skills in deepening their knowledge of different cultural fields from a broader and comparative perspective.

UCL have recently teamed up with the famous School of Oriental & African Studies (also part of London University) in a Centre of Excellence in Teaching and Learning: Languages of the Wider World, which 'recognizes, promotes and develops the excellent teaching and learning in less commonly taught languages'.

Physical sciences, humanities and language graduates put UCL among the leaders at point of employment for museum archivists, curators and the like.

Geology, Geophysics, Earth & Space Science are cheek by jowl with History & Philosophy of Science and Information Management, and what about Palaeobiology to set you up in a museum career?

UCL's BSc/MSci degrees in Natural Sciences combine science subjects into a structured and coherent degree, exploiting the increasing overlap of traditional science disciplines such as Biology, Chemistry and Physics which has created new and existing areas of scientific study.

See, too, the Faculty of Social & Historical Sciences, where you'll find Ancient History, Anthropology, Archaeology (Egyptian, General, Mediaeval), History of Art, and what about Archaeology, Classics & Classical Art?

Archaeology is an especially popular degree here. Besides the BA and BSc single hons, there's Mediaeval Archaeology, joint degrees with History of Art and a 4-year Classics & Classical Art. Teaching inspection, 23. Research, Grade 5.

Physics scored 23 points at the assessments and was rated international Grade 5 for research. It's a top flight department. Courses in Astronomy, Astrophysics, Chemical Physics, Theoretical Physics, Earth & Space Science seem to take one a million miles away from investment analysis – and they make their share of physicists and astronomers here – but Maths shares the faculty, and investment advisers and analysts are in fact drawn from here in equal quantity with those from economics.

In the context of Economics, note the single honours BSc degree and BSc Economics & Statistics, etc, as well as BA Economics & Business with East European Studies (in the School of Slavonic & East Euro Studies). They took full marks at the assessments and have a world-class Grade 6* rating for research. It's a launch pad for merchant bankers too, while others again came through maths and the largest group (28%) through Information Science.

As we have seen, they actively encourage you to add an international dimension to your degree programme. A growing number of courses now include a year abroad, and many more can provide an opportunity for students to spend some time abroad, for example as part of a Socrates exchange. A newly established Study Abroad Office advises students on the opportunities open to them, ensures that students going abroad are fully briefed, and also works to expand further UCL's links with overseas organisations.

UCL is of course renowned for Law – they took a world-class Grade 6* for research, and their drive to promote the internationalisation of study now has German Law sitting alongside English and French Law. UCL in partnership with a consortium of 11 UK universities has agreed that all candidates applying to read Law will be required to sit a written test called the Law National Admissions Test (LNAT). The test is designed to provide an assessment of a candidate's potential for law degree programmes but

> *Academically the college is strong, its reputation world class. Aware that some might be left feeling slightly daunted, there's a surprise new focus on special needs and academic counselling.*

WHERE UNIVERSITY COLLEGE GRADUATES END UP

Health & Social Work: 30%; Education: 7%; Wholesale Retail: 7%; Manufacturing: 7%; Financial Activities: 9%; Public Administration, Civil Service & Defence: 6%; Hotel/Restaurant: 2%; Transport & Communications (including Telecommunications): 3%; Construction: 1%; Mining/Oil Extracting: 0.5%; Personnel: 3.5%; Computer: 2%; Business & Management: 4%; Accountancy: 4%; Media (including Film): 3%; Legal 1%; Architecture: 2%; Publishing: 2.5%; Advertising: 0.5%; Artistic/Literary: 0.5%; Sport: 0.5%.

Approximate 'graduate track' employed **78%**

is not a replacement for A levels.

SOCIAL SCENE

STUDENTS' UNION UCL obviously lacks the feel of a campus university, but not to its detriment. **Phineas** is the hub. The largest venue is the comfortable **Windeyer**, with a capacity of 550, large dance floor and a variety of catering. Wednesday attracts *SportsNite* to the **2econd Floor** bar. Thursday's *2Phat* runs across **Phineas** and **Windeyer**.

The union oversees more than 144 clubs and societies, based, for the most part, in a specially created, open plan area with computers, phones, photocopy and TV/video facilities. The union's many arts societies fill a gap in UCL's academic curriculum. Drama Soc performs to professional level at UCL's **Bloomsbury Theatre** and there's a smaller experimental **Garage Theatre** and a stage in Huntley Street. Student media is active with *Pi*

WHAT IT'S REALLY LIKE	
UNIVERSITY:	
Social Life	★★★★★
Campus scene	**Affluent south-east dominates**
Student Union services	**Good**
Politics	**Activity average: ethical, anti-war & internal**
Sport	**54 clubs**
National team position	**44th**
Sport facilities	**Good**
Arts opportunities	**Excellent**
Student magazine	**Pi Magazine**
2006 Media Awards	**Pi took Silver**
Student radio	**Rare FM**
Student TV	**BTV**
Nightclub	**Windeyer**
Bars	**Easy J's. Gordons, 2econd Floor, Huntley, Phineas, SSEES**
Union ents	**SportsNite, 2Phat**
Union societies	**90**
Most active society	**Indian Society**
Parking	**None**
CITY:	
Entertainment	★★★★★
Scene	**Wild, expensive**
Town/gown relations	**Average-good**
Risk of violence	**Average**
Cost of living	**High**
Student concessions	**Abundant**
Survival + 2 nights out	**£100 pw**
Part-time work campus/town	**Good/excellent**

Magazine (which took a Silver Award at the national media awards last year), the student radio station, Rare fm, and student TV – Bloomsbury Television (BTV). The college has also just signed up the New London Orchestra to boost its musical culture. It will become a kind of orchestra-in-residence at the Bloomsbury Theatre.

Lunchtime and other out-of-hours lectures are the coming thing at UCL. They are generally free but necessarily ticket events. Unusual speakers, controversial perhaps, boundary-breaking, are very popular. When you go to Open Days, ask about extra-curriciular lectures. They are as popular with lecturers as they are with students, and a sign that the place is thriving intellectually and cutlurally.

SPORT There are 54 active sports clubs, but there's been a massive drop in performance in 3 years from 17th to 44th place in the national BUSA team league. Facilities include two large grounds (with bars), a gym, fitness centre (with multigyms, squash courts, Dojo, aerobics/dance hall, sunbeds & sauna) and a large sports hall. For those who want to swim, there is access to the University of London Union pool, next door to UCL.

TOWN See *Student London*, page 302.

PILLOW TALK

Accommodation is guaranteed to freshers if they firmly hold an offer of a place on a degree programme, apply for accommodation by the deadline (currently May 31 of year of entry), and have not previously been a degree student living in London.

There are two types of accommodation on offer: halls of residence (catered/breakfast and evening meal) and student houses (self-catering accommodation, some purpose built, others converted private houses). UCL has a rolling programme of upgrading its accommodation; a 100 bed extension at Ramsay Hall is due to be completed in 2008. Newer residences have en-suite facilities and computer points networked to the UCL system. Frances Gardner House is newly built – 215 single

en-suite rooms, just 20 mins' walk from campus.

GETTING THERE
☛ UCL: Euston Square (Metropolitan, Circle, Hammersmith & City lines), Warren Street (Victoria, Northern), Euston (Victoria, Northern). Royal Free: Belsize Park Underground (Northern line) or overland railway, Hampstead Heath.

UNIVERSITY OF THE ARTS, LONDON

University of the Arts
65 Davies Street
London W1Y 5DA

TEL 020 7514 6000
FAX 020 7514 8179
EMAIL info@arts.ac.uk
WEB www.arts.ac.uk

VAG VIEW

*G*ranted University title in 2003 and re-named the following year, this is the old London Institute, Europe's largest university for art, design, fashion, communication and the performing arts, and one of the biggest arts institutions in the world.

Described by Newsweek as 'the epicentre of London style', their glittering alumni include some of the most celebrated artists and designers of the past century, including Gilbert and George (artists); Alexander McQueen (fashion designer); Chris Ofili (artist); Rebekah Wade (newspaper editor); Mike Leigh OBE (director); Simon Callow (actor), Rankin (photographer); Sir Terence Conran (design entrepreneur), Stella Mcartney and John Galliano (fashion designers), and Alan Fletcher (designer).Offering a comprehensive range of courses in art, design, communication and performance, the University of the Arts represents 6 distinguished colleges with roots that run as deep as 1842.

COLLEGE SITES
CAMBERWELL COLLEGE OF ARTS
TEL:† +44 (0)20 7514 6302
FAX: +44 (0)20 7514 6310
EMAIL: enquiries@camberwell.arts.ac.uk†
WEB: www.camberwell.arts.ac.uk/
Camberwell College of Arts has an international reputation in the field of art and heritage conservation, with graduates working in some of the most important museums and galleries in the world. The undergraduate and postgraduate courses pro-

vide exceptional teaching in conservation practice, science, history and museology.

Each College has its own gallery space and this year Camberwell gets a new one, the Peckham Pier.

CENTRAL SAINT MARTINS COLLEGE OF ART AND DESIGN
TEL: +44 (0)20 7514 7022
FAX: +44 (0)20 7514 7254
EMAIL: info@csm.arts.ac.uk†
WEB: www.csm.arts.ac.uk/
Courses range from foundation to PhD. Fashion and Textiles, Media Arts, Fine Art, Graphic Design, Theatre and Performance, 3D Design, Interdisciplinary.

Drama Centre, part of Central Saint Martins, is one of only two drama schools to operate in Central London.

CHELSEA COLLEGE OF ART AND DESIGN
TEL: +44 (0)20 7514 7751
FAX: +44 (0)20 7514 7778
EMAIL: enquiries@chelsea.arts.ac.uk
WEB: www.chelsea.arts.ac.uk/
In 2004, Chelsea moved to a single campus on Millbank by the River Thames, next to Tate Britain. Courses: Art and Design, Communication, Digital Arts and Media, Drawing, Film and Video,F i n e Art, Furniture, Graphic Design, Interactive Multimedia, Interior Design, Knitwear, Model Making, New Media, Painting, Photography, Printmaking, Printed Textiles, Screenprinting, Sculpture, Stitch/embroidery, Textile Design, Visual Design and Display.

LONDON COLLEGE OF FASHION
TEL: +44 (0)20 7514 7407
FAX: +44 (0)20 7514 7484
EMAIL: enquiries@fashion.arts.ac.uk
WEB: www.fashion.arts.ac.uk/
Courses: Accessories, Beauty Science and Beauty

Therapy, Business and Management, Buying and Merchandising, Culture and Communication, Cosmetic Science, Costume, Curation, Design and Technology, Fashion Design, Footwear, Journalism, Make up and Hair Styling, Marketing, Media, Menswear, Millinery, Photography, Promotion, Styling, Tailoring and Garment Production, Technical Effects, Textiles for Fashion, Womenswear.

When Cordwainers College, a name in footwear, saddler and leathercraft since 1887, joined the University in 2000, it brought with it an expertise in footwear and accessories, two of the fastest growing areas in the fashion industry, and contact with the very roots of footwear craft skills.

LONDON COLLEGE OF COMMUNICATION
TEL: +44 (0)20 7514 6569
FAX: +44 (0)20 7514 6535
EMAIL: info@lcc.arts.ac.uk
WEB: www.lcc.arts.ac.uk/
Courses: Book Arts & Crafts, Film & Video, Interior Design, Photography, Print Media, Sound Arts, Surface Design, Graphic & Media Design, Advertising, Digital Media Production, Journalism, Magazine Publishing, Marketing & Advertising, Public Relations, etc, and foundation degrees in some of these and such as sports journalism and print and production.

Their specialist Printing and Publishing School is founded on 100 years of expertise and recently launched a unique MA course in Print Media Management, run in partnership with Heidelberg Print Media Academy in Germany. Students spend two intensive weeks at the Print Media Academy - the training centre for Heidelberg Druckmaschinen AG, in Heidelberg, Germany.

Finally, the college is soon to be home to the extensive Archive of the late acclaimed filmmaker Stanley Kubrick.

WIMBLEDON COLLEGE OF ART
TEL: +44 (0)20 7514 9641
FAX: +44 (0)20 7514 9642
EMAIL: info@wimbledon.ac.uk
WEB: www.wimbledon.arts.ac.uk
Wimbledon School of Art joined the uni as its sixth college in August 2006. The merger saw it renamed Wimbledon College of Art. It enjoys a reputation for excellence in theatre design, boasting the UK's largest School of Theatre, home to the largest theatre centre in the UK offering undergraduate and postgraduate degrees in design and related studies for stage, screen, costume and special effects.

Drawing is also a key focus - the distinguished Jerwood Drawing Prize is offered here. The College has produced many of the greatest names in theatre design and the arts, including triple Oscar winning

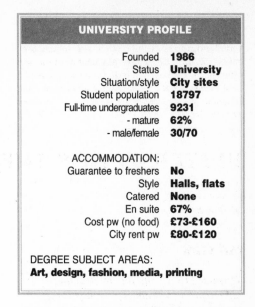

UNIVERSITY PROFILE	
Founded	**1986**
Status	**University**
Situation/style	**City sites**
Student population	**18797**
Full-time undergraduates	**9231**
- mature	**62%**
- male/female	**30/70**
ACCOMMODATION:	
Guarantee to freshers	**No**
Style	**Halls, flats**
Catered	**None**
En suite	**67%**
Cost pw (no food)	**£73-£160**
City rent pw	**£80-£120**

DEGREE SUBJECT AREAS:
Art, design, fashion, media, printing

costume designer James Acheson, production designer Sarah Greenwood, fashion designers Georgina Chapman and Phoebe Philo, guitarist Jeff Beck, and Turner Prize winner Tony Cragg.

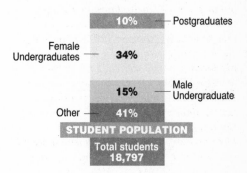

10% — Postgraduates
Female Undergraduates — 34%
15% — Male Undergraduate
Other — 41%

STUDENT POPULATION
Total students
18,797

FEES, BURSARIES
UK & EU fees p.a. 2007 for first year undergraduates. Home students pay up to £3,070 p.a. for first degrees. 2007/08 students in receipt of the full government Maintenance Grant are automatically entitled to a £305 bursary. First generation HE students may apply for £1,000 Access Bursaries. There's also a range of privately funded scholarships.

ACADEMIA
UA offers a distinctive education in art, design, communication and performance in a range of distinct and distinguished Colleges across London..

Learning is characterised by being practice-based, creative and strongly linked with industry.

Half the teaching is undertaken by Associate Lecturers, who combine teaching with their own practice and up to the minute industry experience.

Specialist facilities include a 3D body scanner at London College of Fashion; radio, TV and film broadcast studios, sonic arts studios, and a real-life facsimile of a newsroom at the London College of Communication, and a professional theatre at Wimbledon College of Art.

University of the Arts London also owns The Cochrane Theatre, a professional theatre open to the public and based in Holborn.

The uni's dyslexia support service was used as an example of best practice in an article in the Times Higher Education Supplement in 2000. They provide dyslexia screens in five languages including Japanese, and formally assess (PATOSS registered) for Disabled Student Allowance. All tutors are dyslexia trained.

SOCIAL SCENE

There are student bars at the various colleges, of course, and quite frankly you are as much a part of London as you are of a college. Still, last year saw the uni trying to centralise things a bit, by opening the Student Hub at their headquarters in Davies Street, Mayfair, the heart of the West End of London.

It's a focus for student services and the idea is that it provides a central place for students to come together to work, learn, exchange ideas, be inspired, relax and socialise as part of a community. Besides the offices, there's an Arts Gallery which shows work by graduates and is open to the public, a cafe bar, an activities studio, computing facilities and the Learning Zone, with 'key library texts', PCs and Macs, laptops for use in the area, WIFI interactive and standard whiteboards, projectors, photocopiers and printers, spray mount booth, cutting tables and mats, trimmers, and light-box facilities.

PILLOW TALK

They provide 1,754 beds. Students with a disability or who are under 18 years at the start of their course and live outside of London are guaranteed accommodation. Accommodation is self- catering halls and flats, with an average of six people sharing a kitchen, along with traditional halls of residence. Limited accommodation in studio flats is also available to couples. A new hall of residence opened in Camberwell in September 2006 providing modern en-suite accommodation to 126 residents within 5 minutes walk of Camberwell College of Arts.

UNIVERSITY OF WARWICK

The University of Warwick
Senate House
Coventry CV4 7AL

TEL 02476 523723
FAX 02476 524649
EMAIL ugadmissions@warwick.ac.uk
WEB www.warwick.ac.uk

University of Warwick Students' Union
Gibbet Hill Road
Coventry CV4 7AL

TEL 02476 572777
FAX 02476 572759
EMAIL enquiries@sunion.warwick.ac.uk
WEB www.sunion.warwick.ac.uk

VAG VIEW

*W*arwick has exploded upon the university scene and there can be few who wouldn't want to have it on their UCAS list. 'I knew from the first time that I visited that it was the place for me,' writes Emma Burhouse. 'As far as I could see, it had the ideal balance of a good reputation, a sound education and excellent social life.'

But the social life is not the only dimension of life outside the lecture hall here. Is it because Warwick is a campus bubble in the midst of the dreadful city of Coventry and that the alternative of actually going off it concentrates the minds wonderfully on more worthwhile pursuits? We can't tell, but sportswise last time their teams rose 7 places in the national leagues, and student media ran riot at the national media awards, the radio station picking up a Gold, 3 Silver awards and 2 Bronze; the TV station taking 2 wins and 2 highly commendeds, the website being nominated among the 4 best in the country, and the student newspaper, Warwick Boar, clearing the likes of Manchester and Leeds off the student media map and winning no less than 8 nominations, 1 runner-up and 4 wins.

When you come away from Warwick, there's a 78% chance that you will graduate with a First or Upper Second degree, but you will take away with you much more than that, which is why applications were up 12% this year.

CAMPUS

Warwick, lovely little market town, big castle... And not a university within ten miles of the place. Don't be fooled, the University of Warwick is not in Warwick, it's in Coventry. The reason it's called Warwick is that it was part-funded by Warwickshire County Council.

'Campus architecture is entirely uninspiring,' reports Simon McGee, 'but the greyness of the endless car parks and square buildings is fortunately balanced by hundreds of acres of surrounding grassland and forest.'

A second campus, ten minutes' walk away, houses the university's Education Institute and Westwood Halls of Residence. The point about Warwick is that like UEA, it is a campus apart from the town, and may seem to some a bit like living in a box.

'If you' re not paying attention, campus can feel a Doctor Seuss cartoon – you are surrounded by pointy concrete and sculptures straight off the set of *Blake Seven*. Some people take to campus life, and others quite frankly don't,' writes Andrew Losowsky.

'If your first priority is the ability to step straight from your lectures into a bustling shopping centre, then Warwick probably isn't for you. Students here have to get a bus in order to clap eyes on old people, babies, dogs. If, however, you enjoy a friendly community, like spending time with lots of students, then maybe you'll fit right in.'

FEES, BURSARIES

UK & EU Fees, 2007: £3,070 p.a. If in receipt of the HE Maintenance Grant there's a sliding-scale bursary dependent on household earnings.

STUDENT PROFILE

'You get the usual independent school boys and girls, for whom going to a university is the first time they haven't had to wear a uniform,' and, as Andrew points out, 'an unusually high mix of international students, meaning that, although most of the British students are from a middle-class background, there is still plenty of variety propping up the bar with you. The English – there are few Scots and Welsh – generally have the bland accentless tone of the home counties. Regional individuality may be gently mocked, but is in fact both envied

and welcomed. Students on the whole are genuinely friendly here, and if you can't make any friends then you probably don't deserve to.'

ACADEMIA & JOBS

It is a top-rated uni academically – 92% Excellence ratings or 20+ out of 24; and latterly seven perfect scores – full marks for Politics and International Studies, Philosophy, Economics, Sociology,

UNIVERSITY/STUDENT PROFILE	
University since	**1964**
Situation/style	**Campus**
Student population	**29795**
Undergraduates	**19910**
- mature	**8%**
- non EU undergraduates	**12%**
- male/female	**43/57**
- non-traditional student intake	**18%**
- state sector intake	**76%**
drop-out rate	**5%**
- undergraduate applications	**Up 12%**

Theatre Studies, Physics and Warwick's Education Departments (Institute of Education and Continuing Education).

With Birmingham and Nottingham they have just founded The Midlands Physics Alliance, a joint School of Physics, with £3.9 million backing from the Government, delivering a subject to a new generation of students at a time when other universities are taking it off the curriculum.

There's a fine research record, too – the uni came 6th in the last assessments, only Oxbridge, Imperial, LSE and the Institute of Cancer Research were ahead of them. Small wonder, perhaps, that 75% of graduates attain a first class degree or upper second. Many choose Warwick over Oxbridge and few look at it as second choice. Nottingham may at one time have had the edge with their Faculty of Medicine, but the new Warwick/Leicester graduate medical school

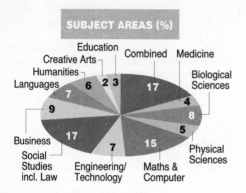

SUBJECT AREAS (%)

Education, Creative Arts, Humanities, Languages, Combined, Medicine, Biological Sciences, Physical Sciences, Maths & Computer, Engineering/Technology, Social Studies incl. Law, Business

opened recently, albeit a graduate not an undergraduate school.

The Leicester Warwick Medical School is a new accelerated 4-year MB ChB for graduates of biological and health sciences, and there's a very good chance of getting in. At the last count the application acceptance rate was 21%. The national average is 10.

They are heavily targeted by employers. Over 100 visit campus each autumn to give presentations and skills training sessions; many conduct first interviews with undergraduates on site. There are also five major recruitment fairs here each year.

In the matter of accountancy, there is nothing between Birmingham, Durham and Warwick. Together they are responsible for around 12% of the total number of graduates into the sector. Accounting and Finance, a 3-year BSc, is the dedicated course. Also of interest is Warwick's Mathematics Institute, from which more graduates find their way into Accountancy than at any other university. Various joint courses are available, with, for example, Philosophy, Politics or Economics, all of which scored full marks at the teaching assessments.

It's definitely worth a trawl through their web site, not least because they have a PYDC (Plan Your Degree Course) strategy, which will give serious mathematicians hours of fun.

Education and finance dominate the graduate employment picture. After accountants it's invest-

ment analysts. Warwick's programmes stress business skills and enterprise 'working in interdisciplinary terms, just as they would in a corporate setting.' Tax experts and consultants also proliferate, as do actuaries. Three universities are head and shoulders above the rest in equating degree success with employment in actuarial science, namely Heriot-Watt, Warwick and Oxford.

Heriot-Watt and Warwick have dedicated Actuarial Maths degrees (Warwick's is BSc Maths-Operational Research-Statistics-Economics (Actuarial and Financial Mathematics), and together the big three account for more than 20% of jobs in the sector.

Of the 5,000+ graduate teachers that spill onto the scene each year those destined for primary schools generally come through specialist colleges. Warwick is one very important exception, much to be recommended – as usual, they earned full marks in the assessments.

They are European law specialists, too – four years, including a year abroad. There are also Law degrees combined with Business and with Sociology.

They are high up in the employment league, too, for electrical, electronic manufacturing and electronic/telecommunications engineering, and some 5% of software engineers come out of Warwick Uni. – engineers and consultants. There's a BEng/MEng Electronic Eng and Systems Eng, and MEng Computer Science and Computer Systems. There are five BSc Hons - Computational Biology, Computer Systems, Computer Science, single or with Business Studies or Management Sciences. Research Grade 5.

Warwick's Business School certificate in Apllied Management is designed to develop the management skills of professional footballers who are in, or who want to take on, football management roles. Students include England players Les Ferdinand, Paul Ince and Steve Hodge.

There's also a strong English/creative writing scene – a whole raft of fascinating degrees that combine English with Theatre Studies, languages, American, even Latin, literature. And a useful employment niche in theatre. They have the

WHERE WARWICK GRADUATES END UP

Health & Social Work: 4%; Education: 15%; Wholesale Retail: 7%; Manufacturing: 10%; Financial Activities: 14%; Public Administration, Civil Service & Defence: 6%; Hotel/Restaurant: 2%; Transport & Communications (including Telecommunications): 3%; Construction: 1%; Personnel: 5.5%; Computer: 5%; Business & Management: 4%; Accountancy: 12%; Media (including Film): 2%; Legal 2%; Publishing: 1%; Artistic/Literary: 0.5%; Sport: 1%.

Approximate 'graduate track' employed **70%**

ACADEMIC EXCELLENCE

TEACHING:

(Rated Excellent or 17+ out of 24)

History, Business & Management, Computer Science, English, Law.	**Excellent**
Sociology, Theatre Studies, Politics, Philosophy, Economics, Physics, Education	**24**
Classics, German, Film & TV, Organismal Biosciences, Molecular Biosciences	**23**
Maths	**22**
Italian, French, Engineering, History of Art, Psychology	**21**

RESEARCH:

Top grades 5/5*/6*

Applied Maths, Statistics, Drama/Dance/Performing Arts.	**Grade 6***
Economics, Business, English	**Grade 5***
Psychology, Biological Sciences, Chemistry, Physics, Pure Maths, Applied Maths, Computer, General Eng, Law, Politics, Social Work, Sociology, French, German/Dutch/Scandinavian, Italian, Classics, History, History of Art, Philosophy, Media Studies	**Grade 5**

national teaching centre with the Royal Shakespeare Company – again, full marks for teaching and world-class Grade 6* for research.

STUDENTS' UNION

STUDENTS' UNION There is one all-purpose venue containing 3 nightclubs: the **Market Place**, the **Cooler** and the **Graduate Club**, plus **Cholo** bar and the **Graduate** pub. The venue can operate as up to 4 different events, if required. Regular club-nights include *Top Banana*, party music; *Score*, Wednesday's after sports entertainment; *Coalition*, hip hop; *Pressure*, drum 'n' bass; *Heat*, international music; *Latin Night*, salsa rhythms; *School Dayz*, relive the best days of your life; *Vapour*, our very own house night; *Crash*, one of the biggest alternative nights in the Midlands; *Pure*, r&b; *Time Tunnel*, 60s, 70s and 80s music; *Metropolis*, the union gets turned into a major city for the night; and live music. Recent acts include: The Go Team, the Skalatities, Jo O'Meara, Chaka Deamus and the Pliers, 911, Grandmaster Flash, Lee 'Scratch' Perry, the Ratpack, The Departure, Bowling for Soup, American Hi-fi, Layo and Bushwaka, etc.

Strong in the student scene are not only ents but clubs & societies – there's an amazing 249 (74-

odd sport), which must be a record, and they don't sustain them if interest flags. Encouraging them each year are their own society awards.

Media is especially strong – magazine (*The Word*), newspaper (*The Boar*), student radio (RaW), and WTV, the new student television station. They are always in the national awards. The media website, www.warwickboar.co.uk, won in 2004, was runner-up in 2005, and, in 2006, oh so nearly became the first university to challenge Nottingham's supremacy in this area, winning Gold for Technical Innovation, 3 Silvers and 2 Bronzes. While WTV won Best Documentary and Best Live

WHAT IT'S REALLY LIKE

UNIVERSITY:	
Social Life	★★★★★
Campus scene	**Good mix, non-elitist, vibrant**
Student Union services	**Good-excellent**
Politics	**Activity high, whole spectrum**
Sport	**74 clubs**
National team position	**17th**
Sport facilities	**Good**
Arts opportunities	**Drama, music, film, art excellent; dance good**
Student magazine	**The Word**
Student newspaper	**Warwick Boar**
2006 media awards	**8 nominations, 1 runner-up, 4 wins**
Student radio	**RaW**
2006 media awards	**1 Gold, 3 Silver, 2 Bronze**
Student TV	**WTV**
2006 media awards	**2 wins, 2 highly commended**
Nightclub	**3: Market Place, Cooler , Graduate Club**
Bars	**Cholo bar, Graduate pub**
Union ents	**Top Banana, Score, etc, etc**
Union societies	**175**
Most popular society	**Cinema**
Parking	**None**
TOWN/CITY:	
Entertainment	★★★
Scene	**Local homely**
Town/gown relations	**Average**
Risk of violence	**Average**
Cost of living	**Average**
Student concessions	**Average**
Survival + 2 nights out	**£60 pw**
Part-time work campus/town	**Excellent/good**

Show and took 2 highly commended awards, and *Warwick Boar* took Best Reporter, Best Feature Writer, Best Sports Journalist and Best Photographer.

Strong, too, are arts activities – the **Warwick Arts Centre** is the second largest in the country, has recently been refurbished thanks to a £33 million lottery grant. There is a concert hall, theatre, cinema, and art gallery. Student theatrical societies do well in the Edinburgh Festival and regular get gongs at the NUS Drama Festival. RAG and Community Action (13 projects in Coventry and Leamington Spa) are popular and the non-party political union works hard on ethical, human rights and environmental campaigns, though recently effort has been focused on anti-war and education funding.

SPORT Facilities are excellent – athletics track, games fields, artificial pitch and recently completed, £1-million sports pavilion. The Sports Centre is free for students, and also hosts Bear Rock, a rather vicious looking climbing wall for eager lemmings to try and scale. Teams came 24th last year in the national BUSA league. They have an Olympic trampolinist, but perhaps the general tenor is more accurately given by Ultimate Frisbee being Sports Club of the Year for two years in succession.

TOWN 'Cov has a reputation for being dangerous,' writes Andrew, 'though in fact it's just like any other city. But even cities can be a shock after a year on campus, and few people spend time in Coventry. Which is a shame, as underneath the concrete nightmare is a friendly enough place, if you give it half a chance. Reasons to "brave" Cov practically quadrupled with the recent opening of **Skydome**, a huge multiplex with a sizeable gig venue, nine screen cinema, bars, restaurants and two outstanding clubs. It'll never quite beat the **NEC**, but a valiant effort nonetheless, and much closer to home. Most pubs in Cov are of the Rat, Parrot and Firkin ilk, but **The Golden Cross** and **The Hand and Heart** are worth a look for something different.

AT A GLANCE	
ACADEMIC FILE:	
Subjects assessed	**25**
Excellent	**92%**
Typical entry requirements	**448 points**
Application acceptance rate	**11%**
Med. Scool acceptance rate	**21%**
Students-staff ratio	**16:1**
First/2:1 degree pass rate	**78%**
ACCOMMODATION FILE:	
Guarantee to freshers	**100%**
Style	**Halls, flats**
Catered	**8%**
En suite	**20%**
Price range pw	**£60-£97**
City rent pw	**£60-£75**

'As for Leam, it's a haven for trendy bars and homely pubs – don't miss **The Sozzled Sausage**, **Ocean** and **The Jug and Jester**.'

PILLOW TALK

From top quality en-suite halls to basic single rooms in shared accommodation with a lower rent, all study bedrooms have unmetered high-band-width connection to ISP services. Everyone gets thrown out in their second year to live in Coventry or Leamington. The university owns plenty of houses, but most people end up going private. Leam is cheap, Cov even more so. If you can't handle a twenty-minute bus ride each day, then Leam is not an option.

GETTING THERE

☛ By road: M1/J21, M69, A46; or M1/J17, M45, A45, or M40/J15, A46; or M5/J4a, M42/J6, A45.
☛ By rail: Birmingham New Street, 30 mins; Manchester Piccadilly, 2:30; Nottingham, 1:45; Bristol, 2:30; London Euston, 1:20.
☛ By air: Birmingham International Airport.
☛ By coach: London, 1:20; Leeds, 4:00.

UNIVERSITY OF WESTMINSTER

The University of Westminster
309 Regent Street
London W1B 2UW

TEL 020 7911 5000
FAX 020 7911 5858
EMAIL admissions@wmin.ac.uk
WEB www.wmin.ac.uk

Westminster Students' Union
32-38 Wells Street
London W1T 3UW

TEL 020 7911 5000 x 5454
FAX 020 7911 5793
EMAIL gensec@wmin.ac.uk
WEB www.uwsu.com

VAG VIEW

*T*he uni comes out of The Royal Polytechnic Institution, established in 1838 by (among others) Sir George Cayley, the North Yorkshire squire who invented the first man-powered flying machine, inveigling his unwilling butler to fly it solo down Brompton Dale.

On the surface, Westminster might appear to suffer all sorts of drawbacks characteristic of a new university in the metropolis – split sites, low entry requirements/high non-traditional student intake/high drop-out rate. Drop-out rate aside, because of its challenging commitment to an impressive curriculum, Westminster, in point of fact, flies higher than ever Cayley could have dreamt it would.

And right now they are giving their London campuses quite a shake-up, mainly to increase space for ex-curricular student activities.

CAMPUSES

REGENT CAMPUS (address above). **Faculties** on four neighbouring sites: *Regent Street* (Social & Behavioural Sciences, including Psychology, some Business courses), *Little Titchfield Street, Euston Centre* and *Wells Street* (Law and Languages). **Academic resources:** Self-Access Language Centre, libraries, IT suites. **Leisure facilities:** Sport and Fitness Centre with cardiovascular and resistance equipment, saunas, solaria and indoor games hall; **Deep End Café** (Regent Street). The gym is on the way out and a bigger social space is in the making.

CAVENDISH CAMPUS 115 New Cavendish Street, London W1M 6UW (use main phone number above). The campus is undergoing a £25-million development, the first phase of which is due for completion this summer. **Courses:** Biosciences, Computing, Health. **Academic resources:** computer suites, science labs, library. **Leisure facilities:** bar and refectory. Soon to be the home of The Hub, see *Social Scene*, below.

MARYLEBONE CAMPUS 35 Marylebone Road, London NW1 5LS (use main tel. above). **Faculties:** Westminster Business School, School of Architecture and the Built Environment. **Academic resources:** library and laboratory. **Leisure facilities:** bar and **Café West**. A new venue is the big new gift to students. See *Social Scene* below.

UNIVERSITY/STUDENT PROFILE	
University since	**1992**
Situation/style	**City sites & campus**
Student population	**26775**
Undergraduates	**18345**
- mature	**43%**
- non EU undergraduates	**9%**
- male/female	**44/56**
- non-traditional student intake	**44%**
- state sector intake	**96%**
- drop-out rate	**26%**
- undergraduate applications	**Up 10%**

HARROW CAMPUS Watford Road, Northwick Park, Harrow HA1 3TP. Tel: 020 7911 5936; Fax: 020 7911 5943. **Style:** well-designed, self-contained campus, close to horrendous looking hospital. **Faculties:** Harrow Business School, Computer Science, Media, Arts & Design. **Academic resources:** Information Resources Centre, including library, computers (1,000+ campus-wide), AV aids for presentations; also TV, radio, photography and music studios. **Leisure facilities:** venue (**Area 51**), open-air performance court, **The Undercroft Bar**, sports hall, fitness suite and playing fields close by.

FEES, BURSARIES

UK & EU Fees, 2007: £3,070 p.a. If in receipt of a HE Maintenance Grant there's a bursary, and academic scholarships are also available.

STUDENT PROFILE

In its student clientele, Westminster mirrors many other ex-polys. There's a sizeable mature, part-time, local and overseas population – they received a Queen's Award for Enterprise for their success in International Markets, and were the first post-1992 uni to have been so rewarded.

There's also a significant non-degree student

Postgraduates 31%

Female Undergraduates 38%

STUDENT POPULATION
Total students
26,775

Male Undergraduates 31%

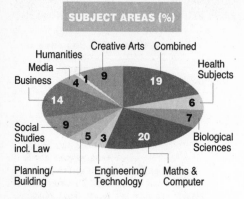

SUBJECT AREAS (%)

Humanities — Creative Arts — Combined
Media
Business — 4 1 9 — 19 — Health Subjects
14 — 6
Social — 9 — 7
Studies — 5 3 20 — Biological Sciences
incl. Law
Planning/ — Engineering/ — Maths &
Building — Technology — Computer

population, and many students are the first in their families to experience university – 44% are from new-to-uni social groups.

ACADEMIA & JOBS

In their vocational, modular course planning they have taken advice from the professions and industry, and translated it into a strategy underpinned by an expert language provision. Their School of Professional Language Studies lays claim to one of the widest range of language teaching in the UK – they are particularly strong on Asian Studies: 23 points out of 24 for teaching and an international Grade 5 for research. Russian, Arabic and Chinese also feature.

There's a reputation for finding students work in those most difficult areas of art, design and media. Though it would be wrong to suggest that these jobs come in a flood, relative to most other unis they are areas in which Westminster enjoy success and have some very good courses.

In Art & Design they have graphic design, illustration, photography, animation, mixed media fine art and ceramics. In Communication/Design & Media they cover digital and photographic imaging, film and TV production, journalism, public relations, radio production, music informatics, and commercial music. The latter, for aspiring music industry managers, concerns music production, but also the business side, including the law. Strong

industry links, good reputation in business management. You'll be based at the Harrow Campus. They have an international Grade 5 rating for research in media and dropped only one point at the teaching assessments.

The majority of undergraduates read for degrees in business, many of them destined for jobs as accounts and wages clerks – at least in the first instance. Retail is a strength, as is marketing; there are dedicated degrees. See also their human resource business degrees, e-business, commercial law, etc, and the International degrees, making use of their excellent language provision. There are degrees in business at both central London and Harrow campuses, so be sure you know where you are destined.

In Law, they are commercial, business and European specialists, but with an interesting range

---

ACADEMIC EXCELLENCE

TEACHING :
(Rated Excellent or 17+ out of 24)

Tourism, Psychology	**24**
French, Asian Studies, Media,	**23**
Subjects Allied to Medicine	
Building, International Relations	**22**
Electric/Electron Eng, Anatomy,	**21**
Art & Design, Biosciences	
Linguistics, German, Civil	**20**
Eng, Business/Finance, Maths	
Italian	**19**
Russian, Sociology, Iberian	**18**

RESEARCH :
Top grades 5/5*

Law, Asian Studies, Linguistics,	**Grade 5**
Communication, Cultural &	
Media Studies	

---

of courses. They are one of a very few unis to receive 24 points (full marks) in the teaching assessments for this.

The computing provision is also strong and directs graduates along the clearest employment

---

WHERE WESTMINSTER GRADUATES END UP

Health & Social Work: 9%; Education: 8%; Wholesale Retail: 16%; Manufacturing: 8%; Financial Activities: 9%; Public Administration, Civil Service & Defence: 6%; Hotel/Restaurant: 3.5%; Transport & Communications (including Tele- communications): 3%; Construction: 2%; Personnel: 3%; Computer: 5%; Business & Management: 1.5%; Accountancy: 2%; Media (including Film): 5%; Legal 3%; Architecture: 2%; Publishing: 2%; Advertising: 2%; Artistic/Literary: 3%.

Approximate 'graduate track' employed **51%**

pathways. IT consultants, systems analysts, software engineers, analyst/programmers, etc. Westminster's central London Cavendish campus offers BSc degrees in Computing, Computational Mathematics and Software Engineering, each with the possibility of a Foundation or International Foundation (4 years). In Harrow they offer BSc Computer Science (with/without Foundation), Systems Technology, E-Business, Multimedia Computing, AI, etc. There's an international Grade 5 for research.

There's enormous strength in architecture and the building industry. The Architecture degrees are mostly technology, engineering, and there are BA degrees in Interior Design and Urban Design. See, too, the Construction, Surveying and Property degrees, Urban Estate Management. Architects proliferate out of Westminster, as do property/estate managers and developers, town planners and surveyors. Of particular note are their BA Tourism & Planning degrees (and Tourism with Business). They scored full marks at the teaching assessments for these.

Then there is the health provision, with a full-marks assessment score for BSc Psychology with Neuroscience, which comes with accreditation from the British Psychological Society and is the first step to becoming a chartered psychologist. Note there is a foundation course into this, and a sound reputation for employment.

There are nutrition and health degrees, physiology and pharmacology, sport and exercise, and a whole raft of complementary medicine degrees – they were one of the first to offer these and have made them a success. Traditional Chinese Medicine: Acupuncture, Homeopathy, Nurtritional Therapy, Therapeutic Bodywork – there is a consistently good record of employment in 'human health activities', as well as an impressive 23 points out of 24 in the teaching assessment. The degrees are developed with The London School of Acupuncture & Traditional Chinese Medicine and The London College of Classical Homeopathy. You'll be based at the Cavendish Campus in central London. Westminster also award the degrees of The British College of Osteopathic Medicine.

There's a hands-on approach that sets students up for the real world. Bookworms need not apply.

SOCIAL SCENE

The Uni has revamped their central London campuses, so it's a pretty exciting time to be a student here. They've opened up a new venue at the Marylebone campus (that's the one opposite Madame Tussauds) which is going to be, well, 'the best student venue in London'. It's costing a bomb, it's got alcoholic and alcohol-free sections, giant movable plasma screens and little TVs in every table.

They are also moving the gym from Regent Street elsewhere and creating a big new social space there too. Meanwhile, at New Cavendish Street, they are creating **The Hub**, a kind of central social space for West End students. They are also working on plans to improve the central London halls.

Out at Harrow, the self-contained campus close to the station, students already have their infamous nightclub, **Area 51**, and a cosy little bar, **The Undercroft**, as well as their typical Student Union

WHAT IT'S REALLY LIKE	
UNIVERSITY:	
Social Life	★★★
Campus scene	**Diverse, non-traditional**
Student Union services	**Average**
Politics	**Interest low**
Sport	**15 clubs**
National sporting position	**130th**
Sport facilities	**Improving**
Arts opportunities	**Drama excellent; film, music good; dance, art poor**
Student magazine	**The Smoke**
2006 media awards	**Nom. Best Mag.**
Radio Station	**Smoke Radio**
2006 media awards	**1 Gold, 2 Bronze**
TV station	**Smokescreen TV**
Nightclub	**Area 51**
Bars	**Dragon Bar, Undercroft Bar**
Union ents	**R&B and Bhangra, Indie**
Union societies	**20**
Most popular society	**Law Soc, Dram Soc**
Parking	**Adequate**
CITY:	
Entertainment	★★★★★
City scene	**Wild, expensive**
Town/gown relations	**Average-good**
Risk of violence	**Average**
Cost of living	**Very high**
Student concessions	**Good**
Survival + 2 nights out	**£120 pw**
Part-time work campus/town	**Poor/excellent**

dive-in central, the **Dragon Bar**.

Says Rob: 'We've got a pretty full schedule of events at all these bars and clubs, including club nights and live music nights. We cater for most tastes, with the hugely successful *BLUSH* playing r&b and Bhangra, and *FONO* playing indie. The Freshers and May Balls bring in some of the best performers in the country. This year we had Raghav and the quite brilliant Mitchell Brothers, along with Queens of Noize. But because we cater for so many international and non-drinking students, we also provide activities around London.

'We're battling against student apathy, because many students in our central campuses live at home and don't get involved. We've a huge number of different nationalities and races here, and we have to try and cater for so many different interests, its a big job.'

Some of the best society activity comes out of course disciplines (media, music), and you can't help wondering whether, if they really got this aspect of student life together, they might whittle down the drop-out rate. Clearly, with all these new social spaces in the West End, already showing in the autumn of 2006, that's what's in the mind of the uni, too.

The student media is excellent. Magazine *The Smoke* has been nominated in the Best Magazine category at the national media awards for the last two years, which means it is among the 4 best in the country, and the brand new radio station, Smoke Radio has just won a Gold for Best Journalistic Programme and 2 Bronze awards. There is now, too, a student television station: Smokescreen TV.

SPORT The uni is not known nationally for its sporting prowess; there is no position recorded in the

AT A GLANCE	
ACADEMIC FILE:	
Subjects assessed	**30**
Excellent	**73%**
Typical entry requirements	**218 points**
Application acceptance rate	**20%**
Students-staff ratio	**18:1**
First/2:1 degree pass rate	**56%**
ACCOMMODATION FILE:	
Guarantee to freshers	**65%**
Style	**Halls**
Catered	**None**
En-suite	**Harrow Hall**
Price range pw	**£87-£95**

BUSA leagues, although their football and cricket teams are amongst the best in their leagues, and the Ju-Jitsu team win tournaments up and down the country.

PILLOW TALK

There are halls, rooms or flats in Marylebone Road, Highgate Village and Victoria. The accommodation at Harrow is all en suite.

GETTING THERE

☛ To Regent Campus: Oxford Circus Underground (Bakerloo, Central and Victoria).
☛ To Cavendish Campus: Warren Street Underground (Northern and Victoria lines).
☛ To Marylebone Campus: Baker Street Underground (Bakerloo, Metropolitan, Hammersmith & City, Circle, Jubilee lines).
☛ By road to Harrow Campus: A404 accessible via M25, M1 or M40/A40; by Underground – Northwick Park (Metropolitan line).

UNIVERSITY OF WINCHESTER

The University of Winchester
Winchester
Hampshire SO22 4NR

TEL 01962 827234

FAX 01962 827288
EMAIL course.enquiries@winchester.ac.uk
WEB www.winchester.ac.uk
SU TEL 01962 827415
SU WEB www.winchesterstudents.co.uk/

VAG VIEW

*F*ounded as a Diocesan teacher training establishment, and until recently King Alfred's College, a university sector college with a range of Southampton University degrees and a speciality in producing primary school teachers, they are now, since 2005, a university.

They always had ambitions to be something other than what they were, and tried various things to hasten the process. In 1994, for example, they took over, or merged with, The Basingstoke and Winchester School of Nursing and Midwifery and began developing all sorts of multi-disciplinary courses in Health Care. But you'll not find a student nurse or midwife closer than

Southampton today. Then, in September 2003, a 'new' Basingstoke campus opened with 'new earn-while-you-learn Foundation Degrees', a feeder site for a future university, the perfect thing to satisfy the widening participation requirement of all universities.

Meanwhile, one or two unusual specialities were emerging, a course in Biopsychology, another in Archaeology (taught by people actively involved on site work), an East Asian Studies course with Business Studies and BA hons combos with Japanese. All but Archaeology disappeared as magically as the nursing provision, but teaching assessments, after years of scoring 18-21 points at best, suddenly returned results of full marks for Archaeology and Education, and 23 out of 24 for bedrock Theology, and 22 points for Business and Sport.

After all, that was the way to go, and, following a swift baptism as University College Winchester, Alfie moved with all speed to achieve university status.

Today, there are three BSc undergraduate courses only, Horticulture, Social Care Studies and Sports Science. The rest are BA (and QTS) or DipHE. There are genuine strengths in arts (particularly performing arts) and in humanities, and a push towards media.

STUDENT PROFILE

There is a high proportion of mature students, and the student body is overwhelmingly female (77%), as you would expect from a uni where many are still studying to be primary school teachers. There are also many part-timers (25% of undergraduates) and locals. There is a kind of

UNIVERSITY/STUDENT PROFILE	
University since	**2005**
Situation/style	**Campus**
Student population	**4940**
Undergraduates	**4170**
- mature	**37%**
- non EU undergraduates	**2%**
- male/female	**23/77**
- non-traditional student intake	**32%**
- state school intake	**96%**
- drop-out rate	**13%**
- undergraduate applications	**Up 19%**

innocent cheery fun about the place, modernity, in the shape of such as the Lesbian, Gay and Bisexual Society, managing a pally epiphytic hold on an institution rooted in Christian Fellowship.

Big fish will find it something of a small pond. Indeed, they call their student magazine, *Big Fish Little Pond*. So, perhaps the big fish are already arriving and have wisely begun by taking over the media, and perhaps soon Winchester University will not seem so much like the college of education, which only yesterday it was.

FEES, BURSARIES

UK & EU Fees, 2007: £3,070 p.a. There are bursaries for those eligible for the Government Maintenance Grant, and ll UK domicile students are eligible to receive the Winchester Scholarship, a package of financial support specially designed to put money in your pocket during your study here at Winchester. This can be as much as £1,300 over a 4-year course, £900 on a 3-year programme. All 4th-year BA Education undergraduates get a scholarship of £1,800, in recognition of the extra costs compared with the three year and PGCE qualified teacher status routes. There are also Winchester Partner Colleges Scholarships, and the King Alfred Scholarship of £2000 (one-off payment) for students under 25 at entry who have been 'looked after' for at least 13 weeks since the age of 14 and who have left care (as defined by the Children (Leaving Care) Act 2000).

CAMPUS

This is a campus uni overlooking the historic cathedral city of Winchester in Hampshire, 15 miles north of Southampton. It has its own theatre and dance studio, Student Union and accommodation.

ACADEMIA

Winchester offers undergraduate courses in

16% — Postgraduates

Female Undergraduates — 65%

STUDENT POPULATION
Total students 4,940

19% — Male Undergraduates

American studies, archaeology, English, creative writing, dance, drama, education, film, heritage, history, horticulture, journalism, leisure, management, marketing, media, performing arts, psychology, religious studies, social care, sports, teaching tourism.

There is a feeder site in Basingstoke, where a variety of programmes is offered, including earn-while-you-learn foundation degrees in subject areas taught within the three faculties at the Winchester campus: Community and Performing Arts, Cultural Studies, Education & Social Sciences.

The teaching assessments suggest their strengths lie in Education, Archaeology, Theology,

SUBJECT AREAS (%)

- Education 28
- Combined 28
- Business 5
- Humanities 22
- Creative Arts 17

ACADEMIC EXCELLENCE

TEACHING :
(Rated Excellent or 17+ out of 24)

Archaeology, Education	**24**
Theology	**23**
Business	**22**
Psychology, Sport	**21**
Asian Studies, Japanese	**20**
Drama, Dance & Cinematics	**19**
American Studies, Media & Film	**18**

RESEARCH:
Top grades 5/5* **None**

Business, Psychology, Sport, while the research assessments – 16% of the student population is postgraduate – show no national or global strengths, but Grade 4 in History and Theology. Archaeology, Media, Performing Arts and Education all scored Grade 3; Psychology Grade 2.

Media and film courses at Winchester are about to benefit from a link-up with the Asian Academy of Film and TV in the Bollywood city of Noida, near Delhi.

SOCIAL SCENE

STUDENT UNION The Union provides three bars - **Bar 22**, **The Lounge** and **C2H** (Close to Home), recently refurbished at a cost of £100,000. Ents include club nights (*Timewarp* or *Club Tropicana*), bar quizzes, comedy evenings, live music, promotions, multi-venue events and theme nights, plus society nights, like *Indie Three Sixty* recently from *BFLP* Magazine. Bigger occasions are the Winton Reunion Weekend (sporty), and the Freshers, Christmas, Summer and Graduation Balls which traditionally play host to top name acts in the **Guildhall**, 'a great venue, with a main hall and lots of smaller rooms with jazz, karaoke, live music and a casino.'

The Stripe Theatre is the performing arts space and film studio on campus, hosting live productions by students and visiting professionals. In town, it's the **Town Arts Centre** and **Theatre Royal** for everything from stand-up comedy to children's theatre, music and dance to plays.

There's a year-round welfare-themed campaign called Play Mates, various societies, from Alternative Music to Ultimate Frisbee, and a media group that is causing something of a stir with *Big Fish Little Pond* magazine and Voice Radio.

WHAT IT'S REALLY LIKE

UNIVERSITY:

Social Life	★★★
Campus scene	**Emerging**
Student Union services	**Embryonic**
Politics	**Dormant**
Sport	**Regional**
National team position	**112th**
Sport facilities	**Poor, but new Club House bar**
Arts opportunities	**Good dance, theatre, media**
Student magazine	**Big Fish Little Pond**
Student radio	**Voice Radio**
Nightclub/bars	**Bar 22, The Lounge, C2H**
Union ents	**Cheese, comedy, studenty**
Union clubs/societies	**Approx. 20**
Parking	**Permit**
CITY:	
Entertainment	★★
Scene	**Quiet, expensive**
Town/gown relations	**Average**
Risk of violence	**Low**
Cost of living	**High**
Student concessions	**Fair**
Survival + 2 nights out	**£80 pw**
Part-time work campus/town	**Excellent**

SPORT They play in BUSA – 5 football teams (1 women's), 2 netball teams, men's rugby and men's basketball – at regional level, against the likes of Plymouth, Bristol, Bath, Bournemouth and Southampton. Other sports teams participate in the Southern England Student Sports Association (SESSA) all over the South East as far as East Anglia, and in SUSC, a collection of local universities. There is currently 1 rugby pitch and 2 football pitches a mile from campus; also a New Club House with bar. A sports hall hosts 5-a-side football, badminton, netball, hockey, volleyball, cricket, and is the home of the Knights and Angels Basketball teams. There are also 2 tennis courts on campus, next to Alwyn Halls, a squash court next to the sports hall, and the uni has recently invested in a new fitness suite – treadmills, bikes, cross trainers, rowing and step machines, and any number of ratchets to stretch, curl, extend and crunch the various parts of you.

CITY There are nightclubs in nearby Eastleigh and Woodmancote, and 15 miles away in Southampton there's **Ocean + Collins** in Vincent Walk, with 1000 capacity, late bar, and a *Big Cheese* Student Night on Thursdays, but Winchester itself is fairly barren. Do not expect the *Brooks Experience* in the Shopping Centre to have anything to do with Jimi Hendrix. Pubs like **The Mash Tun**, the **King's Arms**, the **Forester** have music, and **O'Neills** has a big screen in the High Street, but watch out for squaddies from the nearby barracks. In general, they don't appreciate students, 'unless served on a plate with chips,' writes Stephanie Kirk, who in fact always feels safe here.

'If you have lived in a small town and feel threatened in a large city, Winchester may be the place for you. It is a city, not because of size, but because of its cathedral. It is quiet, picturesque and may prove to be a bit dull for some people.

'Winchester is steeped in history, not only due to King Alfred, but also to King Arthur. Allegedly his famous round table is housed in the city's Great Hall. the cathedral, where our graduation ceremo-

ny takes place, is the main focal point, along with Winchester boys' school, second only to Eton.'

There is also another side to the city, however. 'I follow Drama, Theatre and Television Studies, and a small group of us worked with a day centre. Most of the people were homeless, or on a very low budget, some are ex-offenders, some drug addicts. None of them wanted anything to do with drama! It took us ten weeks to get a workshop up and running, but the course was so satisfying in the end.'

PILLOW TALK

There are fewer than 1000 study bedrooms available to students, self-catered at West Downs

AT A GLANCE	
ACADEMIC FILE:	
Subjects assessed	**15**
Excellent	**73%**
Typical entry requirements	**264 points**
Application acceptance rate	**26%**
Students-staff ratio	**22:1**
First/2:1 degree pass rate	**59%**
Graduate track employment	**48%**
ACCOMMODATION FILE:	
Guarantee to freshers	**100%**
Style	**Hall, flats**
Approx price range pw	**£70-£82**
City rent pw	**£60**

Student Village, catered on the main campus. Some specially adapted rooms are available for disabled students.

GETTING THERE
☞ By road: M3/J10; northwest, A272, B3041; southwest, A3090.
☞ By rail: London, 1:00; Bristol Parkway, 2:15; Birmingham, 3:15; Southampton, 20 mins.
☞ By air: Gatwick, Heathrow, Southampton.
☞ By coach: London, 2:00; Birmingham, 5:30.

UNIVERSITY OF WOLVERHAMPTON

The University of Wolverhampton
Compton Road West
Wolverhampton WV3 9DX

TEL 01902 323730
FAX 01902 323744
EMAIL enquiries@wlv.ac.uk
WEB www.wlv.ac.uk

Wolverhampton Students' Union
Wulfruna Street
Wolverhampton WV1 1LY

TEL 01902 322021
FAX 01902 322020
EMAIL president@wlv.ac.uk
WEB www.wolvesunion.org

VAG VIEW

*T*he university was spawned by the Wolverhampton Poly following a merger with three teacher training colleges and West Midlands College of Higher Education. Operating on campus sites in and around Wolverhampton and in Shropshire, they have recruiting associations with dozens of colleges, and were the first to attract entrants via a High Street shop. As many as 25,000 people a year visit the shop and more than 7% sign up.

CAMPUSES

CITY CAMPUS **Location:** a few minutes walk from Wolverhampton rail and bus stations. **Campus scene:** the busy centre of it all. **Courses:** Applied Sciences, Art & Design, Computing, Construction, Engineering, Health Sciences, Languages, Humanities and Social Sciences, including Law.

COMPTON PARK CAMPUS Compton Road West, Wolverhampton WV3 9DY. **Location:** mile or so west of main campus. **Courses:** Business Admin, Info Management, some Human Resourcing, Marketing, some Computing.

WALSALL CAMPUS Gorway Road, Walsall WS1 3BD. **Location:** six miles east of town centre. **Campus scene: known as** 'the concrete jungle', but strong community spirit. **Courses:** Education (incl. Sports Studies). New this year 350 study bedrooms, all en-suite. A £7.1 million Sports and Judo Centre includes a full fitness suite, coffee bar and crÊche, new tracks and all-weather pitches and the surrounding community will also have access to the facilities.

SHROPSHIRE (TELFORD) CAMPUS Priorslee Hall, Shifnal Road Telford TF2 9NT. **Location:** 12 miles northwest of town. **Campus scene:** the International Students' Association thrives. **Courses:** Business, Computer-aided Product Design.

FEES, BURSARIES

UK & EU Fees, 2007: £3,070 p.a. Fees p.a. 2008 not yet known. £500 - £1,000 'startright' bursary if eligible for HE Maintenance Grant. There's the Sports Excellence Scholarship, worth £3,000 over a 3-year full-time undergraduate degree, and the Excellence in Science and Technology Scholarship, worth £2,000. Then, there's a £1,000 regional 'cashback' bursary for local students, and a Euro social fund bursary worth up to £1,000 in 2007 (dependent on domicile and course attended full or part time).

STUDENT PROFILE

As many as 50% are from the lowest 4 social groups and 26% from 'low-participation neighbourhoods', families who have previously not considered uni an option. Perhaps that explains the persistently cheerful student scene at Wolverhampton, which was voted the friendliest university in the

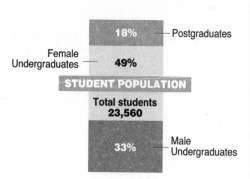

18%	— Postgraduates
Female Undergraduates — 49%	
STUDENT POPULATION	
Total students 23,560	
33%	Male Undergraduates

West Midlands via the Friends Reunited website.

More than 70% of its undergraduate intake is mature, a great number are part-timers, and the SU tells us that there is a high percentage of disabled students, too. There are certainly a number of very good special needs degree courses.

They are in that sense a modern university, playing an ambitious game. 'If there is any university with ambition, giving clear signs that it wants to play with academia's big boys, then Wolverhampton surely is the one,' said Mark Wilson. 'It may take a few years, but there is no doubt that it will get there. We are fortunate to have a 23,000-strong melting pot of cultures, skills, talents – sectors, like Lesbian, Gay & Bisexual (LGB), mature students or ethnic minorities, get people

UNIVERSITY/STUDENT PROFILE	
University since	**1992**
Situation/style	**City campus, town sites**
Student population	**23560**
Undergraduates	**19390**
- mature	**71%**
- non EU undergraduates	**9%**
- male/female	**40/60**
- non-traditional student intake	**50%**
- state sector intake	**99%**
drop-out rate	**27%**
- undergraduate applications	**Up 11%**

together and entertain them. It may take time to shake the wally poly stereotype, but the future is looking blinding from where I stand.'

ACADEMIA & JOBS

'The teaching is particularly good for the vocational courses on which we focus,' says Mark. 'Lectures and seminars, but also film screenings, guest speakers, hands-on activities and group work with assessments. The best thing may be that they teach subjects which lead to jobs, engineering, film, computer programming and many more.'

Wolverhampton is taking the relationship between academia and industry to a new level by insisting that its teaching staff take part-time jobs in local industry under the aegis of 'staff development'. The deputy vice-chancellor said: 'Our staff already work in partner organisations. We have people working one day a week in the health service or people on secondments. We are now looking at joint appointments as well.'

Many courses are devised in consultation with businesses and the uni is committed to increasing the number of courses which offer accreditation or a licence to practice alongside a degree. However, the subject that attracted the highest mark – full marks, in fact – at the teaching assessments was Philosophy.

They have a newish £4.5-million Learning Centre – 967 study spaces, 130 IT spaces, 200,000 volumes – following the opening of a similar centre in Shropshire.

A close association with industry in this high density industrial area, as well as commerce and the professions, gives confidence, and their employment record is good not only locally. A particular emphasis is on languages – students of all disciplines may study a language and the teaching assessments have been good: Russian scored 22 points out of 24, Spanish 20, French 19, German 17. There's a particular niche in British Sign Language Interpreting, the 3-year degree being pretty much a dead cert for getting a job. A foundation year is available.

Around a fifth of Wolverhampton students graduate in business subjects. The next most popular degrees may be found in Art & Design, although

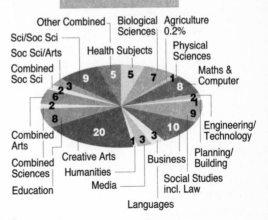

SUBJECT AREAS (%)

Other Combined · Biological Sciences · Agriculture 0.2% · Sci/Soc Sci · Soc Sci/Arts · Health Subjects · Physical Sciences · Combined Soc Sci · Maths & Computer · Engineering/Technology · Combined Arts · Planning/Building · Creative Arts · Business · Combined Sciences · Humanities · Social Studies incl. Law · Education · Media · Languages

the employment picture for the latter is less sure in the first six months following graduation. Plenty of work for the graphic designers, artists and photographers, with some others finding jobs in further education as teachers, and in galleries.

The business/finance ticket is more certain. Accountancy, for instance go for the 3 or 4-year sandwich Accounting & Finance, or joint hons with Computing, Law or Marketing. Personnel – look at the Business & Human Resource Management combination. Sales and marketing, look for their dedicated degrees Marketing, Retail Marketing, Entrepreneurship, etc. Or explore the joint honours scheme for tie-ups between Marketing and such as Tourism or Media & Communication. Look also at their series of nine Tourism Management degrees.

There's are strong employment lines at Wolverhampton into the Civil Service through business and through the computer provision. And besides the expected computer engineers, analysts and programmers (4-year sandwich Computer Science/Software Engineering), there's a niche for games design – see the 4-year sandwich Computer Science (Games Development). There's a Virtual Reality Centre in the School of Engineering. Look also for up-and-coming courses in Automative Systems Engineering, Computer-Aided Engineering/Product Designs.

WHERE WOLVERHAMPTON GRADUATES END UP

Health & Social Work: 12.5%; Education: 15,5%; Wholesale Retail: 16%; Manufacturing: 6%; Financial Activities: 7.5%; Public Administration, Civil Service & Defence: 7%; Hotel/Restaurant: 4%; Transport & Communications (including Telecommunications): 4%; Construction: 3%; Agriculture: 0.5%; Personnel: 3%; Computer: 6%; Accountancy: 1%; Media (including Film): 1%; Legal 3%; Artistic/Literary: 3%; Sport: 0.5%. Approximate 'graduate track' employed **51%**

ACADEMIC EXCELLENCE

TEACHING :
(Rated Excellent or 17+ out of 24)

Philosophy	**24**
Education, Molecular &	**23**
Organismal Biosciences,	
Politics	
Russian, Subjects Allied to	**22**
Medicine, Economics,	
Hospitality Mgt, Sport, Dance	
Linguistics, American Studies,	**21**
Nursing, Art & Design,	
Psychology, Theology	
Iberian Studies, Sociology,	**20**
Building, General Eng, Maths,	
Civil Engineering, Mathematics	
French, Drama, Dance &	**19**
Cinematics, Media	

Certain, too, are the educational and health provisions. They are one of the best teacher training providers in the country, rising from 39th place to fifth last year - as a result of dramatically improved Ofsted inspection grades. They produce primary and secondary teachers, educational assistants – there are some good specialisms in the joint hons degree programme, like Special Needs & Inclusion Studies and Deaf Studies – physical education instructors, and further education lecturers.

In health, non-hospital nurses, nurses and midwives proliferate. There's also a Cancer Care top-up. There are also BSc degrees in Complementary Therapies and Health Sciences, and BSc Psychology and BSc Counselling Psychology – 21 out of 24 at the assessments.

Biochemists, biomedical scientists and pharmacists also come out of here in number – this department dropped only one point at the teaching assessments.

The 3% graduates joining the construction industry come out of BA Architecture or BSc Architectural Technology, Building or Quantity Surveying, Civil Engineering, Construction Management, Computer Aided Design (Construction), Interior Architectural Design, Project Management, etc.

Success in the creative arts/design and radio/TV industries directs us to their performance arts and media degrees, to the £2-million, Lottery-funded redevelopment of their **Arena Theatre**, and to the School of Art & Design's **Gallery** space, home to a range of courses, from Animation to Journalism & Editorial Design, from Computer-Aided Design to Sculpture, from Floorcoverings & Interior Textile Design to Painting.

New Sound Production and Music Industry

Practice foundation degrees are believed to be the first of their kind in the UK. See also new degrees in Music Technology, and Entertainment & Industries Management. Just how switched on they are to the power of entertainment media was shown last year when they produced a multimedia CD-i with local rock radio station Kerrang!, which included 16 tracks interspersed with promotional messages about Clearing and was distributed free from HMV stores throughout the West Midlands.

Finally, there's a good reputation for Law. Non-Law graduates may opt for a 2-year full-time or 3-year part-time Senior Status Law Degree, and recently the LPC Board assessed the department 'Good' on a scale of Excellent, Very Good, Good, Satisfactory or Unsatisfactory.

SOCIAL SCENE

STUDENTS' UNION At City Campus, it's **Fat Micks** (dance floor, food, pool tables, widescreen TV, 1,200 capacity, licensed till midnight and till 2 am Wednesday, Friday and Saturday), the **Poly Bar** (a pre-club comedy or light entertainment venue) and

WHAT IT'S REALLY LIKE

UNIVERSITY:	
Social Life	★★★
Campus scene	**Local, lively**
Student Union services	**Average**
Politics	**Student issues**
Sport	**20+**
National team position	**69th**
Sport facilities	**Good**
Arts opportunities	**Music, art excellent; drama, dance good; film average**
Student magazine	**Cry Wolf**
Nightclub	**Zone 34**
Bars	**Fat Mick's, Poly Bar, Bertie's, Auntie Rita's**
Union ents	**Chart and cheese**
Union societies	**50**
Most popular societies	**Qur'an & Sunnah, Christian Union**
Parking	**Poor**
TOWN:	
Entertainment	★★★
Scene	**Pubs, diverse studenty clubs**
Town/gown relations	**OK-ish**
Risk of violence	**Average**
Cost of living	**Low**
Student concessions	**Good**
Survival + 2 nights out	**£50 pw**
Part-time work campus/town	**Good**

now they also have **Zone 34** (**The Zone**, as it's known), replacement for the JL nightclub, which is now the Student Activities Hub. Yet, Tuesdays is student night in **Walkabout**, the new club in town - indie classics and alternative in main room, old skool in surfers paradise upstairs. Not until Wednesday does it warm up in the SU, when in parallel, at Fat Mick's and The Zone respectively, there's *Cut Loose* - indie, alternative, hip hop, soul, funk, and *BassSick* - RnB, hip hop, soul. Then Friday it's good old *Flirt!* - the student cliché that wows a nation - and Saturday, *FHUK* funky house.

There's much else besides, both in and out of the bars and clubs. Wolves has a strategy for developing an on-going programme of these to help students develop the skills they'll need. If you flip onto their web site you'll see the kind of helpful community this union is striving to create, whether it's revision classes, welfare or just plain fun.

At Telford, it's **Auntie Rita's** (capacity 250), licensed to 11 pm – 12 on Wednesday and Friday. **Berties Bar** (capacity 300) is on the third floor of Walsall Campus. Ents are theme nights, quizzes, movie nights, barbecues.

SPORT There are sports hall, squash courts, fitness centre at Wolverhampton; sports hall, playing fields, running track, swimming pool, dance studio, tennis courts at Walsall, where judo hopefuls for the 2012 Olympic Games are using the uni's National Judo Centre of Excellence. This is also home to the town's basketball national league team, and at Telford, there's a new sports centre.

TOWN Wolverhampton can be unnerving, but the SU supplies advice, information, attack alarms. Clubland is good for house, garage, rock, indie,

AT A GLANCE
ACADEMIC FILE:
Subjects assessed **38**
Excellent **71%**
Typical entry requirements **200 points**
Application acceptance rate **24%**
Students-staff ratio **23:1**
First/2:1 degree pass rate **50%**
ACCOMMODATION FILE:
Guarantee to freshers **90%**
Style **Halls, houses**
Catered **None**
En suite **50%**
Approx price range pw **£52-£75**
Town rent pw **£55**

bhangra, jungle techno, acid jazz, folk. Cinemas include **The Light House** (mainstream/foreign); **Wolverhampton Art Gallery** for British and American Pop Art; the uni's own **Arena Theatre** for alternative, touring, student drama and music; the city's **Grand Theatre** for London shows.

PILLOW TALK
Walsall Student Village opened in 2005. All its rooms are fully furnished, with en-suite shower and wireless internet access. There is a safe courtyard with 24-hour security, CCTV and free parking. There are also specially-designed rooms for students with disabilities.

GETTING THERE
☛ By train: London Euston less than two hours;
☛ By road: M6/J10, M54/J2, M5/J2
☛ By coach: London, 4:00.

UNIVERSITY OF WORCESTER

The University of Worcester
Henwick Grove
Worcester WR2 6AJ

TEL 01905 855111
01905 855141 (prospectus request)

FAX 01905 855377
EMAIL admissions@worc.ac.uk
WEB www.worcester.ac.uk
SU TEL 01905 855188

VAG VIEW

Worcester began as a teacher training college in 1946. In the '70s it became a college of higher education. In 1995 it merged with a college of nursing and midwifery, and in 2002 it was granted university college status, platform for their bid for full university status, which was secured last year.

Worcester University is the only Higher Education Institution in Herefordshire and Worcestershire, and has a largely female

UNIVERSITY/STUDENT PROFILE	
University College since	**1999**
Situation/style	**City campus**
Total student population	**7595**
Undergraduates	**6095**
- mature	**60%**
- non EU undergraduates	**1%**
- male/female	**24/76**
- non-traditional student intake	**36%**
- state sector intake	**96%**
- drop-out rate	**18%**
- undergraduate applications	**Up 41%**

student body (76%), owing to the primary teacher training and nursing courses. It is not a place for the faint hearted. University of Worcester graduates, Joanne Yapp and Mel Berry, were rival rugby captains last year in the England and Wales Women's Six Nations clash. Sport is another of this uni's major preoccupations.

CAMPUS

Headquarters is a parkland campus within walking distance of the centre of this Cathedral city. On campus there's a new Digital Arts Centre, a Drama Studio, Sports Centre and Students' Union. Now, flush with a £10-million grant from the Government they are creating an additional campus on a 5-acre site in the city, which will include a new library and Learning Centre, teaching and residential accommodation. It is due for completion in 2008.

FEES, BURSARIES

UK & EU Fees, 2007: £3,070 p.a. Eligibility for the HE Maintenance Grant confers a bursary. Up to 50 academic achievement scholarships of £1,000 are available after the first year of study. The uni also works in partnership with Worcestershire County Cricket Club and the Worcester Wolves Basketball

Club to award sports scholarships to talented players.

STUDENT PROFILE

Many of the mainly female undergraduates are local and 60% are mature; a fair proportion (36%) are from the lowest 4 socio-economic groups, new to the idea of going to university, and 15% from 'low-participation neighbourhoods'. They have partnerships with colleges in the region, in order, they say, to widen participation further, though widening into the upper socio-economic and overseas groups might seem to be more of a challenge.

ACADEMIA & JOBS

There's a modular course structure and 6 academic departments: Applied Sciences, Geography & Archaeology; Arts, Humanities & Social Sciences; the Worcester Business School; Education; Health & Social Care; Sport & Exercise Science.

A strong educational, nursing and sporting

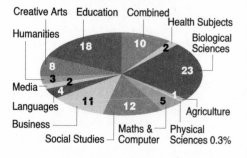

provision (their teams came 38th in the national BUSA league last year, which is amazing for so small a university), together with degrees in drama and social welfare, make for a strong employment record of great use to the health and welfare of the community they serve.

Teaching inspections results have been fair. Out of 24 points, Education did best with 23; then Sport and Nursing scored 22; Sociology, Art & Design; and Business 21; Biosciences and Psychology, 20 (there is a BSc Psychology accredited by the British Psychological Society, first step to becoming a chartered psychologist); and Health 19. In the 2001 research assessment no subject reached higher than Grade 2 (out of 5).

Primary school teachers account for almost a quarter of graduates; then there are educational assistants, welfare, community and youth workers, nursery nurses, physical training instructors, police, secondary school teachers, etc. There are also strengths in business, especially personnel,

TEACHING:
(Rated Excellent or 17+ out of 24)

Education	**23**
Nursing, Sport	**22**
Sociology, Art & Design, Business	**21**
Psychology, Biosciences	**20**
Health Sciences	**19**

accounting and marketing. There are strong links with firms and organisations in business, creative, education and health.

Among their regional network of partner colleges, the following feed the uni with students on foundation degrees and HNDs: Evesham & Malvern Hills College, Halesowen College, Herefordshire College of Technology, Josiah Mason College, Kidderminster College, Pershore Group of Colleges, Stourbridge College, and Worcester College of Technology. Foundation degrees include Business in the Electronic Age, Commercial Web Development, Food Safety & Quality Management, Learning Support, and Adventure Tourism.

Writes Emma Aves. 'UCW gains greatly from the sense of intimacy which its size brings, you feel truly part of the institution, one that supports you throughout your course. The onus is on you to balance your interests and ensure academic requirements are fulfilled, but a personal tutor system is available to all and helps to compensate for the formal nature of lectures.' They also have a Student Advice Bureau and Employment Bureau, and are active in work-related skills training of undergrads.

SOCIAL SCENE

STUDENTS' UNION There are decent ents in the **Dive Bar**, which celebrated its 40th birthday in February 2006 with a party – 2 Bands, DJ, free cake, bar promos. Besides this sort of cheesy fare, they have a Battle of the Bands event and an active Alternative Music Society, which keeps people on their toes into the small hours. Birmingham is 45 mins to an hour away by train, with all its nighttime distractions; a return fare without rail card costs £6.40 to £10.70. See *Student Birmingham*, page 70.

'Activities such as RAG and Student Community Action are enthusiastically attended in order to establish that we are here for more than personal gain,' Emma continues. Indeed, English Student Sophie Nixon runs Kids Club in Dines Green, a local estate, and was recently presented

with the Millennium Volunteer of the Year award for the West Midlands. With 15 other student volunteers, Sophie raises drama productions, discos, music lessons, arts & craft sessions, and organises trips out.

There are 33 clubs and societies at Worcester this year, from mountain boarding to the new dance soc. and Loco Show Co., the tried and tested musical theatre society. *The Voice* is the student newspaper, issued twice a semester.

SPORT There is a multi-million pound Sports Centre on campus and huge interest in sport, both through the sports courses and competitively across the board. They have all the traditional sports, and on, right through to Y'ai Chi. Worcester County Cricket Ground overlooks the River Severn – they list a Men's Cricket club only, odd that the women aren't interested. Worcester Rugby offers some of the the best premiership rugby you can see anywhere in England, its ground at Sixways a true Centre of Excellence. The uni's close association with the club – both Men's and Ladies Rugby (always 'ladies' at Worcester, never 'women's'; but never 'gentlemen's', always 'men's') provides exceptional facilities/expertise.

TOWN Pubs and cheesy clubs predominate, but

WHAT IT'S REALLY LIKE

COLLEGE:
Social Life	★★
Campus scene	**Local, lively, largely female**
Politics	**Controlled**
Sport	**Competitive**
National team position	**47th**
Arts opportunities	**Excellent across the board**
Student magazine	**The Voice**
Nightclub/bar	**The Dive**
Union ents	**Cheese, live + 4 big balls**
Union clubs/societies	**33**
Parking	**Adequate**

CITY:
Entertainment	★★
Scene	**Cathedral, arts, cricket, rugby, pubs**
Risk of violence	**Low**
Cost of living	**Average**
Student concessions	**Excellent**
Survival + 2 nights out	**£560 pw**
Part-time work campus/town	**Excellent**

AT A GLANCE

ACADEMIC FILE:

Subjects assessed	**14**
Excellent	**64%**
Typical entry requirements	**233 points**
Application acceptance rate	**25%**
Students-staff ratio	**21:1**
First/2:1 degree pass rate	**42%**

ACCOMMODATION FILE:

Guarantee to freshers	**90%**
Style	**Halls**
Approx price range pw	**£45-£65**
City rent pw	**£45**

within a 30-mile radius there's Shakespeare country to the east, the Malverns Welsh borders and Wye Valley to the west, the Cotswolds to the southeast, and big city Birmingham an hour to the north.

Royal Worcester (porcelain) is their heritage, but the **Edward Elgar Birthplace Museum** points to another distinguishing mark, England's greatest composer. **The Swan Theatre** (for drama, comedy, dance) and **Huntingdon Hall** (seriously lively venue for jazz, folk, blues and classical), the **Odeon Film Centre**, the **Vue Cinema** complex, the **Worcester Arts Workshop**, and the recently reconstructed **Festival Theatre** at nearby Malvern complete the arts picture.

PILLOW TALK

Accommodation on campus ranges from ancient room-only halls to comfy, modern flats, but there are enough only for 90% of first years and international students.

GETTING THERE

☞ By road: M5/J7.
☞ By rail: Birmingham, 60 mins; Cheltenham, 24 mins; Hereford, 40 mins.

UNIVERSITY OF YORK

The University of York
Heslington
York YO10 5DD

TEL 01904 433533
FAX 01904 433538
EMAIL admissions@york.ac.uk
WEB www.york.ac.uk

Student Union
University of York
Heslington
York YO10 5DD

TEL 01904 433724
EMAIL president@yusu.org
WEB www.yusu.org

VAG VIEW

*F*ounded in 1963, York is a small uni with a huge reputation for its teaching. Students are drawn fairly evenly from the Southeast, from the North and elsewhere.

Their academic strengths span a wide disciplinary range within the arts, social sciences and sciences and attract students with high career ambitions. Whilst York offers perhaps fewer vocationally orientated programmes of study than some other universities, its graduates are highly sought after by employers. What's more, it is very popular with its students, who are bright, fun-loving and notably unpretentious.

CAMPUS

It's a purpose-built campus at Heslington, on the south-east edge of the city: 'Very suburban, not at all monumental. It could get on the garden register,' mused Elaine Harwood of English Heritage. Student Gemma Thomas disagrees, 'Overall, the campus is a very pleasant place to live and along with York itself, one of the safest places. Heslington Hall, a gorgeous manor house on the edge of campus, provides an antidote to some of

24% — Postgraduates

Female Undergraduates — 43%

STUDENT POPULATION
Total students
11,820

33% — Male Undergraduates

the bleaker aspects. It possesses extensive gardens, part of which, the Quiet Place, a collection of gigantic topiary knobs, is perfect for late-night games of hide-and-seek, or whatever else springs to mind.' The York Quakers, who were among those responsible for raising £70,000 for the Georgian gazebo and garden known as the Quiet Place will no doubt be pleased it is being put to such imaginative use. But, warns Gemma, 'Do NOT come here if you are anything less than tolerant of ducks. They are everywhere. On the lake, crossing paths, dive-bombing students wending their way to early morning lectures (or not).'

FEES, BURSARIES

UK & EU fees, 2007: £3,070 p.a. Bursary for those in receipt of HE Maintenance Grant, from £614 to £1,434, according to parental income.

STUDENT PROFILE

'After ducks, students form the most numerous campus species,' Gemma continues. 'No one type dominates, the balance between state and private sectors a surprise bonus in a university with this much prestige. York is a small, friendly, unpreten-

UNIVERSITY/STUDENT PROFILE	
University since	**1962**
Situation/style	**City campus**
Student population	**11820**
Undergraduates	**8958**
- mature	**23%**
- non EU undergraduates	**8%**
- male/female	**43/57**
- non-traditional student intake	**16%**
- state sector intake	**77%**
- drop-out rate	**5%**
- undergraduate applications	**Down 2%**

tious university, which makes it incredibly easy to settle in. Also, student welfare is taken very seriously. Nightline, chaplains, a range of counselling services and equal opportunities are promoted heavily.'

ACADEMIA & JOBS

York is known for social sciences, technology, and science. The top 10 subjects at the teaching assessments lost only one point between them.

Computer Science & Engineering is top-rated for teaching and has a world-class Grade 6* reputation for research. There are BSc, BEng, MEng and MMath degrees, regular 3 or 4-year sandwich. Computing is a significant graduate employment area; jobs in electrical and electronic manufactur-

ACADEMIC EXCELLENCE	
TEACHING:	
(Rated Excellent or 17+ out of 24)	
History, Applied Social Work, Architecture (MA), Computing, English, Music, Social Policy	**Excellent**
Electric & Electron Engineering, Archaeology, Economics, Education, Philosophy, Politics, Biosciences, Physics, Psychology	**24**
Sociology	**23**
Management, Languages, Maths	**22**
History of Art, Nursing	**21**
RESEARCH:	
Top grades 5/5*	
Psychology, Computer, English	**Grade 5***
Community-based Clinical, Nursing, Biological Sciences, Chemistry, Pure Maths, Applied Math, Economics, Politics, Social Policy, Social Work, Sociology, Linguistics, History, Philosophy, Music	**Grade 5**

ing are also legion, and for electronic and telecommunications engineers they are leaders.

Social Sciences are also pre-eminent Applied Social Work, Social Policy, Economics, Politics were all top-rated for teaching; Sociology scored 23 points out of 24; and they achieved Grade 5 for research. The £4.2 million Alcuin Research Resource Centre (ARRC) now further enhances its research capacity in this area.

The single most popular employment pathway out of the faculty is accountancy, though accountants also come strongly through mathematics and some through physical sciences. Actuaries also proliferate in these disciplines too. This Economics bias and a Management and Industry axis in physical sciences (also full marks at the teaching assessments) encourage placements in business analysis, finance and investment consultancy, marketing management and management consultancy work. Note that York Management School has replaced the Department of Management Studies.

Jobs also flow in welfare and youth work and care work in the community, from the Applied Social Science – with its Crime, Health, Children & Young People specialities. See also the BA/MA Social Work, and the newer Nursing degree programme: BSc Evidence-based Nursing Practice – Adult, Child, Learning Disability, Mental Health. York is one of a few unis to be awarded Grade 5 for

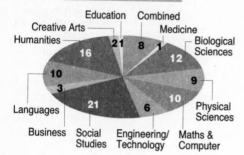

SUBJECT AREAS (%)

Education — Combined
Creative Arts
Humanities — 21 — 8 — 1 — Medicine
16 — Biological Sciences
12
10
9
3
21 — 6 — 10
Languages — Physical Sciences
Business — Social Studies — Engineering/Technology — Maths & Computer

research in Nursing.

In Applied & Natural Science, biosciences (a new BSc Bioarchaeology joins this year) scored full marks at the assessments and Grade 5 for research, and courses such as Chemistry: Biological & Medicinal Chemistry, Chemistry: Management & Industry, Chemistry: Resources & the Environment show the way, and, as in the Social Sciences, illustrate the widely varying ambitions of York's students. Look, too, at BSc Psychology, with its maximum teaching score and world-class reputation for research. Accredited by the British Psychological Society, it's the first step to becoming a chartered psychologist.

The launch of the Hull York Medical School in 2003 has been a great success, as evinced in the low application acceptance rate (7%). They offer a 5-year BMBS (Bachelor of Medicine, Bachelor of Surgery). You may be based at either Hull University campus (see entry) or York; all follow the same curriculum. Hull has a decade's experience in Medicine through its Postgrad Medical School, while York's Biosciences and Health depts are top rated for teaching and research. There is a new Mother and Infant Research Unit (MIRU) at York.

There's an international class Grade 5 rating for research: Community-based clinical subjects, and for medical students, small-group clinical contact from Year 1. Equal emphasis on physical, psy-

chological and social aspects. Entry ABB, including Chemistry at A level and Biology at A or AS. Caring experience and interpersonal skills significant.

Well-trod pathways for humanities and language graduates include education and marketing, museum and gallery work, library and archival work. Note that Spanish has now been added to the Language and Linguistics degree. Here go some of the graduates from the BA Archaeology degrees (full marks in the assessments and a strong employment picture; available too as BSc/Arch), Linguistics (there's an international, Grade 5 for research), Philosophy (again, full marks for teaching), History of Art (21 points), and History – the new £6.5 million, climatically-controlled building housing the Borthwick Institute is the new home for more than seven centuries of North of England history.

Like History Music was top-graded in the assessments and there's a good track record both for musician/composers and music producers. Look at their first class Music Technology Systems B/Meng for the latter. Jazz musicians Jonathan Eato and John Taylor are now part of the department, signalling new initiatives in undergraduate education and a new Master's degree in Improvised Music and Jazz.

Their English/Writing & Performance is another arts niche, a practical, contemporary course pulling directly on the experience of current actors, writers and directors. When the Heslington campus is extended this is one of the areas likely to benefit.

SOCIAL SCENE

Each college has its own Junior Common Room (JCR) Committee, who run about two events per week per college and two or three big events per year. The Students' Union organises up to five large-scale clubnights or other events per 10-week term.

The point about York is the interest and activity levels beyond mere ents. 'Students get involved,' said Helen Woolnough. 'The university has an excellent academic reputation, but its students

---

WHERE YORK GRADUATES END UP

Health & Social Work: 8%; Education: 10%; Wholesale Retail: 9.5%; Manufacturing: 12%; Financial Activities: 11%; Public Administration, Civil Service & Defence: 8.5%; Hotel/Restaurant: 3%; Transport & Communications (including Telecommunications): 3%; Construction: 1%; Personnel: 7%; Computer: 5%; Business & Management: 4%; Accountancy: 4%; Media (including Film): 2%; Legal 1%; Publishing: 1.5%; Artistic/Literary: 0.5%; Sport: 0.5%.

Approximate 'graduate track' employed **66%**

don't work themselves into the ground twenty-four hours a day and they certainly don't take themselves too seriously.'

Student media: University Radio York (URY), launched by John Peel thirty years ago and now with fm licence, York Television (YSTV), and two fortnightly newspapers, *Nouse* (pronounced 'Nooze' after the River Ouse, which flows through York, and of course 'news', which is what it dispenses) and *York Vision*. In the 2006 national student awards *Nouse* took Best Small Budget Publication and was nominated for Best Newspaper and Best Feature Writer. YSTV won a gong for Best Station Identity and was runner-up for Best Broadcaster. All this after sweeping the board the previous year.

Other publications appear occasionally – *Point Shirley*, a literary arts magazine; *PS...*, an arts review; *Havoc*, a miscellany of creative writing; *Matrix*, a women's issue paper; *Christis*, a Christian magazine, and *Mad Alice*, an on-line features magazine.

There is a tradition of political activity and a left-wing slant. Campus-based issues and wider student issues find a place (tuition fees, differential rents, campaign for a venue, security on campus, etc), but national and international issues are also very much on the agenda.

Among some 90 societies there are 8 active drama societies with three venues, the intimate **Drama Barn**, the large and versatile **Wentworth College Audio Visual Studio** and the aforementioned Central Hall, which is huge.

SPORT For such a small uni they do well at sport, and recently have leapt up the BUSA league table to 39th position. The Boat Club goes to Henley Royal Regatta, the Lacrosse team to the world championships, basketball is a bit a speciality and they have the best parachutists in the country apparently. There are forty acres of playing fields – rugby, football, hockey, cricket – floodlit artificial hockey pitch, all-weather (three floodlit) tennis courts, squash courts, a sports centre for archery, badminton (seven courts), basketball, climbing, cricket (five nets), fencing, five-a-side soccer, judo, karate, netball, sauna, table-tennis, tennis, trampoline, volleyball, a 400-metre, seven-lane athletics track. Rowing and sailing are on the Ouse about a mile from the University, golf at Fulford Golf Club, swimming at the Barbican Centre half a mile from campus. Gliding, hang-gliding, riding and other facilities also found locally.

Highlight of the year - both socially and sportswise is The Rose, when the white rose of York meets the red rose of Lancaster in sporting competition and two days of wild socialising that takes over the entire campus in May.

TOWN York itself is one of our most beautiful cathedral cities, a magnet for tourists from all over the world owing to the wealth of Viking and Roman remains, as well as its mediaeval resonances in the Minster, in streets like the Shambles (where buildings lean inwards and over you as if out of a fairytale), in street names like Whip-Ma-Whop-Ma-Gate, and in the snickleways which offer those in the know an alternative way to scuttle about. Then there are the waters of the Ouse, lapping over green-field banks or warehouse walls, redolent of the city's merchant past.

WHAT IT'S REALLY LIKE

UNIVERSITY:	
Social Life	★★★★
Campus scene	**Bright, friendly, small and unpretentious**
Student Union services	**Good**
Politics	**Activity high**
	Student issues
Sport	**50 clubs**
National team position	**39th**
Sport facilities	**Good**
Arts opportunities	**Drama, film excellent; dance, music, art avg**
National drama awards	**Craft/Imagination**
Student newspapers	**Nouse, York Vision**
National Awards 2006	**1 Gong & 2 runner-ups**
Student radio station	**URY**
Student TV	**YSTV**
National Awards 2006	**1 Gong , 1 runner-up**
Nightclub	**College-based only**
Bars	**1 in every college**
Union ents	**Club D, House Trained, Cooker, Dust**
Union societies	**140**
Most popular societies	**Media, Drama**
Smoking policy	**Bars, halls OK**
Parking	**Non-existent**
CITY:	
Entertainment	★★★
City scene	**Tourist haven**
Town/gown relations	**Good**
Risk of violence	**Low**
Cost of living	**Average**
Student concessions	**Good**
Survival + 2 nights out	**£50 pw**
Part-time work campus/town	**Excellent/good**

It is, however, far from being the clubbing capital of the North. 'From the relaxed atmosphere of the Deramore in Heslington,' notes the union's excellent *Alternative Prospectus* (phone for one), 'to the vibrancy of O'Neill's, ideal as a starting place for a night of fun and frolics in the clubs...' If you are a hardened clubber, take a ride to Leeds.

For theatre, there's the **Arts Centre** and the **Theatre Royal** (good rep), and the **Grand Opera** has a full programme of touring companies and performances, both theatre and music. There's a multi-screen **Warner's** cinema out at Clifton Moor Estate (on the north side of the city), **Odeon** and independent **City Screen** in York, as well as **York Student Cinema** on campus.

PILLOW TALK

All freshers are guaranteed a place in uni accommodation – halls, flats and houses. None is catered – all pay-as-you-eat. Around 40% are en suite.

GETTING THERE

☛ By road: A1237 ring road; Heslington is on the southeast side, 10 miles from A1/M1; 20 from M62.

☛ By coach: London, 4:30; Edinburgh, 5:15.
☛ By rail: Leeds, 20 mins; Sheffield, 1:15; Manchester, 1:30; London King's Cross, 2:00.
☛ By air: Nearest airport is Leeds.

AT A GLANCE

ACADEMIC FILE:

Subjects assessed	**23**
Excellent	**96%**
Typical entry requirements	**436 points**
Application acceptance rate	**11%**
Med. School acceptance rate	**7%**
Students-staff ratio	**16:1**
First/2:1 degree pass rate	**70%**

ACCOMMODATION FILE:

Guarantee to freshers	**100%**
Style	**Halls, flats, houses**
Catered	**None**
En-suite	**40%**
Approx price range pw	**£67-£81**
City rent pw	**£67-£81**

YORK ST JOHN UNIVERSITY

York St John University College
Lord Mayor's Walk
York YO31 7EX

TEL 01904 876598
FAX 01904 716940
EMAIL admissions@yorksj.ac.uk
WEB www.yorksj.ac.uk

VAG VIEW

*F*ounded by the Anglican Church in 1841 as a teacher training college, York St John now offers very much more.

In February, 2006, it was granted University College status and the power to award its own degrees, and on October 1 that year, full university status.

It is lucky to have Dr John Sentamu, Archbishop of York and the most acute mind in the Church of England, as its first Vice Chancellor.

It is appropriate that a university that has risen to prominence partly on a reputation for pastoral care should have made the invitation.

All that notwithstanding, applications are up 11% and York St John have grasped their new status with both hands. Campus is a hive of activity and there is a freshness

and a buzz about the place. This is a new university, and you get the feeling it is going to lead the way in some interesting areas.

CAMPUS

The college is situated close to York Minster on a very attractive, newly re-vamped campus on this ancient site. The only worry is that there is